THE SCHIZOPHRENIC DISORDERS

The Schizophrenic Disorders

Long-term Patient and Family Studies

Manfred Bleuler

Translated by Siegfried M. Clemens

New Haven and London, Yale University Press

1978

Originally published in West Germany as *Die schizophrenen Geistesstörungen im Lichte langjähriger Kranken- und Familiengeschichten* by Georg Thieme Verlag, Stuttgart, 1972.

Published with assistance from the Scottish Rite Schizophrenia Research Program, Northern Masonic Jurisdiction, U.S.A., and from the foundation established in memory of Calvin Chapin of the Class of 1788, Yale College.

Designed by John O. C. McCrillis
and set in Baskerville type by Asco Trade Typesetting Ltd., Hong Kong.
Printed in the United States of America by
The Murray Printing Co., Westford, Massachusetts.

Published in Great Britain, Europe, Africa, and Asia (except Japan) by Yale University Press, Ltd., London. Distributed in Australia and New Zealand by Book & Film Services, Artarmon, N.S.W., Australia; and in Japan by Harper & Row, Publishers, Tokyo Office.

Library of Congress Cataloging in Publication Data

Bleuler, Manfred.
   The schizophrenic disorders.

   Translation of Die schizophrenen Geistesstörungen im Lichte langjähriger Kranken- und Familiengeschichten.
   Includes bibliographies and index.
   1. Schizophrenia. I. Title. [DNLM: 1. Schizophrenia.
WM203 B649s]
RC514.B5813   616.8'982   75-43303
ISBN 0-300-01663-8

Contents

Tables

Figures

Charts

Translator's Note

When the first copies of Professor Bleuler's original work began to circulate among the staff of the National Institute of Mental Health, the spontaneous—and virtually unanimous—reaction was: "This kind of research could never be done again." and "This book must be translated into English to enjoy the broadest possible readership."

I am proud and deeply honored to have been instrumental in propagating a work of such enduring merit among the English-reading public. The most recent acclaim this book has received in the way of reviews and awards is the first prize in psychiatry, awarded to the author in Munich in September 1976: the Kraepelin Medal in gold.

The labor of my translation is respectfully dedicated to the memory of Professor Susan Emolyn Harman, who taught me English.

I owe a full measure of gratitude to the author himself, whose guiding words and friendly counsel extended through the translation and the final revision of the manuscript. I am deeply grateful to Yale University Press for their meticulous care in editing out my errors and polishing the syntax of my translation. I shall always be thankful to Dr. Loren Mosher, Chief of the Center for Studies on Schizophrenia, National Institute of Mental Health, who was among the first to appreciate the value of this work, to suggest its translation, and to establish contact between me and the publisher.

A special word of thanks is extended to the many friends and professional colleagues who gave generously of their time and talents to help me along the way, among them: Mrs. Sylvaine L. Kenyon of the Institute for her help with the passages in French; Mr. Howard S. Alenier, statistician with the US Postal Service, for his help with mathematical and statistical terminology and formulae; Miss Bette L. Runck of the Institute, formerly managing editor of the *Schizophrenia Bulletin*, for her suggestions in technical and other esoteric terminology; and to Professor Norman Garmezy of the University of Minnesota, for his continuous moral support and encouragement throughout the project. A very personal word of gratitude is reserved for Margaret, my dear and faithful wife, who suffered the privations of my companionship for nearly a year—in stoic silence and saintly understanding.

Silver Spring, Maryland, 1977   Siegfried M. Clemens

Author's Preface to the English Edition

The efforts of psychiatrists from all nations to work together and to compare their experiences and ideas is indeed great. In particular, the psychiatrists from the European continent follow with keen interest the developments in the field of psychiatry in English-speaking countries. Despite all good intentions, however, the existing language barriers are formidable obstacles to mutual understanding. Even some of the important works from some language areas are ignored in other language areas, and it still happens that observations or hypotheses are published as new material in one language when, in fact, they have been well known for a long time in another. It was this need for a better mutual understanding across language barriers that gave me the courage to consider an English edition of my book.

In preparing and organizing reports of his lifelong experiences with schizophrenics, my father found especially valuable the teachings of Emil Kraepelin and those of Sigmund Freud. When I began my own professional career with schizophrenics, I was influenced by the ideas of Adolf Meyer of Baltimore and Eugen Bleuler of Zürich, between whom existed a cordial relationship of mutual professional cooperation. My own work with schizophrenics was influenced by psychiatric concepts in America and Switzerland; therefore, I am particularly happy to see them presented in both English and German. Since I had pursued a large portion of my postgraduate training in the United States, I was able to incorporate in my book my experiences with patients from Switzerland and those with patients from the Boston Psychopathic Hospital (now the Massachusetts Center for Mental Health) and the Bloomingdale Hospital in White Plains, New York (now the Westchester Division of the New York Hospital).

To all those who have made the English edition of my book possible I should like to express my deeply felt gratitude. These include most especially the editors of Yale University Press, the administrators of the Schizophrenia Research Program of the Supreme Council of 33° Scottish Rite Masons, Northern Masonic Jurisdiction, U.S.A., and to the translator, Siegfried Clemens. Without great sacrifices on part of the publisher and without the financial support of the "Schizophrenia Project," the English translation would have been impossible. Mr. Clemens has worked with tireless dedication not only to reproduce the text verbatim, but to make its content and spirit his own as well.

I have already expressed my thanks in the preface to the original German edition to the many who helped me process my research. I should like to reiterate, however, that even then I received support from the United States, specifically from the Foundations' Fund for Research in Psychiatry in New Haven. I should like to acknowledge also the valuable cooperation I received from Ambros Uchtenhagen, whose Rorschach studies with my proband families unfortunately could not be included in the translation because of publication problems.

Zollikon, April 1977   MANFRED BLEULER

Preface to the Original German Edition

In the book that follows I intended mainly to depict the life vicissitudes of 208 schizophrenics and their families as I had personally observed and experienced these, together with them, over a period of more than 20 years. For comparative purposes, and to round out my own material, additional material from investigations of other patients was required, and for the same reasons, I reached back for some notes from my own previously published papers. In evaluating the findings, I was able to support my theories on the basis of the experience of having treated schizophrenics over several decades. For decades, too, I had made the effort to work up significant aspects of the international literature on schizophrenia.

In Chapters 2–5 individual findings are discussed, and their results are compared with existing theories. In Chapter 1, the selection and the backgrounds of the schizophrenic probands are described, in order to provide a means for judging whether, and to what degree, my findings may be considered as generally applicable (compared to other patients selected by other methods, from other locales, and at different times). For Chapter 7, I selected those aspects of schizophrenia that are related to my investigations. They are intended to outline how individual problems show up in the context of my investigations. Chapter 8 summarizes the theories about the nature of schizophrenic illnesses that I have arrived at over the years. It is labeled "Theories," for the results of the investigations that make up the principal portion of the book can be evaluated and applied independently of my theoretical concepts.

The reader who may be interested in only one or another problem area discussed should not be constrained to read the entire book. Each chapter is intended to be readable and understandable separately, and for this reason some repetitions occur. But let me not make a virtue of necessity. Some repetitions resulted in part from the fact that I was not able to work without interruption on the book, the writing of which extended over more than five years, since my principal activity at the clinic—and particularly my personal association with the schizophrenics—occupied the greatest portion of my working time. It is impossible to continue weaving the same lines of thought over many years, interspersed with lengthy interruptions, without losing the thread from time to time, and having to pick it up again later. Still, the book is by no means merely a collection of individual papers.

In general, lengthy statistics concerning the courses of disease and the occurrences of illness in families are reported by investigators whose "subjects" represent mere research tools to them. My reports are not about "subjects" in this sense; my probands are my patients. As a result, apparent inconsistencies may be found in my presentation which—I fear—may on occasion seem strange or peculiar. Reports of clinical experiences that were emotional experiences personally shared with the patient may appear next to empirical statistics. But I have sought consistently to identify clearly what was objective and what was not. Personal relations with a patient certainly can at times jeopardize this objectivity, but, on the other hand, they do frequently transmit more penetrating and more reliable information. A necessary attribute of a good physician is to be at one and the same time a critical observer and a good friend and helpmate to his patient.

Without the assistance of many, I could not have accomplished my investigations. First, I owe a debt of gratitude to all the many patients and their families who participated. I owe sincere thanks to my colleagues at Burghölzli, all of whom assisted me in one way or another, by their encouragement, stimulation, and criticism, and by their participation in caring for our joint patients. And I owe thanks especially to those men and women who became directly involved in my investigations: Dr. Ambros Uchtenhagen (whose studies appear in Chapter I of the German edition), those colleagues who carried through supplemental investigations for comparison purposes, namely, Dr. Eberhard Gabriel (on stepparents), Dr. Alois Hicklin and Dr. Siegfried Rotach (on early loss of parents of military conscripts), Dr. Rosmarie Nagel (on the children of seniles); Dr. Christian Scharfetter (on symbionic psychoses). The last-named critically examined the entire manuscript.

I needed a great deal of help on the sections involving mathematical statistics. I had made use of calculations in my 1941 paper that were still mathematically correct, but no longer valid. Since I was familiar with them and since they made comparisons with previous studies considerably easier, I have retained some of them. Dr. Thomas Marthaler (of the Biostatistical Center of the University of Zürich) gave unstintingly and indefatigably of his expertise in counseling me in the preparation of the new calculations. Similarly I received continuous advice and valuable guidance from Professor Jules Angst and from Adolf Dittrich, practicing psychologist at the Psychiatric University Clinic of Zürich, and both of them did many of the probability calculations for me. Dr. Erwin Hansert of the Max Planck Institute of Psychiatry in Munich, who had been recruited through the kind efforts of Dr. Edith Zerbin-Rüdin, proofread the meticulous calculations from Chapter 5. His critique is included in that chapter. In the application of the Haldane formula, Professors Friedrich Vogel and Johannes Röhrborn and Jens Krüger from the Institute for Anthropology and Human Genetics of Heidelberg University, a professional mathematician, advised me, and on the latter's method of calculation of disease occurrence probabilities, Professor Erik Strömgren and Dr. Niels Engkilde (Psychiatric

Clinik in Risskov, Denmark) rendered valuable assistance. I was privileged to be able to discuss the biohereditary aspects with Professor Ernst Hadorn of the Zoological Institute of the University of Zürich.

The exacting secretarial tasks—and even more than just these!—have been supervised since 1946 by Miss Thilde Dinkelkamp. Among other duties, she handled the volumes of correspondence, procured and arranged for the necessary literature and bibliographies, compiled bibliographic references, made calls to obtain information, collected extracts from probands' histories, and spot-checked the manuscript for minor errors, even in the final typing. Without her dedicated care and competence I might never have completed my work. A number of other secretaries participated successfully in clerical duties, among them, in an outstanding capacity during 1942–1946, Miss Annemarie von Bidder, and since 1965 Mrs. Ruth Frey-von Aesch, who with astounding skill compiled the numerous tables.

Many colleagues and members of advisory and administrative agencies made their files, patient histories, and a wealth of other information available to me, and gave freely of their time, expertise and meticulous care in support of the project.

The means at my disposal at the clinic during the period in question would never have been sufficient to cover the high costs involved in performing the investigations. For years secretarial help had to be paid out of private funds, since the secretarial staff at the Clinic was fully occupied with routine work. Doctors who assisted me from time to time had to have substitutes to cover their routine duties, and these had to be compensated. Patients and their families who had to travel long distances for conferences were paid for travel expenses and compensated for time lost on their jobs, if their incomes were small. Most of these expenses (and a number of others as well) were covered by the generous contributions of two sponsoring organizations: the "Foundations' Fund for Research in Psychiatry" in New Haven, Connecticut, through the good offices of Dr. Fredrick C. Redlich, Professor of Psychiatry at Yale University, and the Gertrud Rüegg Foundation in Zürich, through the good offices of Dr. Armin Haemmerli-Steiner of Zürich. For all this great moral, scientific, and financial support I should like here to express my deepest, most sincere gratitude. But for the expression of my thanks to my wife, who helped and supported me indefatigably in every phase of this study, this preface is not the proper place.

Zollikon/Zürich, October 1971   MANFRED BLEULER

**Explanations of Some
Frequently Used Concepts**

The place names of small localities may be unfamiliar to readers who are
strangers to Switzerland, and it is possible that the mathematical terms are not
known to psychiatrists of those generations that did not have the benefit of
schooling in statistics.

**Place names of localities and terms used in the
clinical material described in this book**

The principal probands of this study (see Chapter 1): 208 schizophrenic probands of the investigation, who were admitted to the Psychiatric University
Clinic of Burghölzli between 1942 and 1943, and whose histories were followed
until their death or until more than 22 years of observation had elapsed.
Additional schizophrenic probands: Other patients who were used for specific
studies described in individual sections of the book. They include, among
others, groups of "additional schizophrenics," "young schizophrenics,"
"middle-aged schizophrenics," and "private schizophrenic patients," whose
histories were checked for incidents of early loss of parents (see Chapter 2).
American Schizophrenics (or Schizophrenics from New York): Patients from
the Bloomingdale Hospital in White Plains, N.Y. whom I studied for purposes
of comparison with the principal probands.
Basel Schizophrenics: Patients from the Psychiatric University Clinic at Basel
in Switzerland, whom I studied for purposes of comparison with the principal
probands.
Pfäfers (or St. Gallen) Schizophrenics: Patients from the St. Pirminsberg
Psychiatric Clinic at Pfäfers, whom I studied for purposes of comparison with
the principal probands.
Rural-Basel: Swiss semicanton in the Jura area, principally rural in character
at the time of my investigations.
Bloomingdale Hospital: Today this is the Westchester Division of the New
York Hospital in White Plains, New York.
Burghölzli: Psychiatric University Clinic of Zürich.
New York Hospital, Westchester Division: see Bloomingdale Hospital, above.
Pfäfers: Mountain village in the Swiss Canton of St. Gallen.
St. Pirminsberg: Former monastery in Pfäfers, for over 100 years the canton's
psychiatric clinic for St. Gallen.
Zürich: Name of the university city in which Burghölzli is situated as well as
that of an entire Swiss canton.

Statistical Terms

p = probability of an observed difference in frequency. For instance, we find in one sample a given percentage (x) of people with a certain characteristic, and in another sample a different percentage (y) of people with that same characteristic. We should like to know how likely it is that the difference between x percent and y percent may be based purely on chance $(= p)$ or how likely it is in reverse $(= 1\text{-}p)$, that is, that the difference is based on the chance that samples were taken from different basic groups or populations. If, from the outset, different populations are involved $(=$ basic groups$)$, p tells us the degree of probability with which the relative frequency of the characteristic in the two samples may be ascribed to pure chance.

If, for example, calculations show that p represents a difference less than 0.05 $(p < 0.05)$, it means that the probability that the calculated difference reflects only an accidental chance amounts to less than $\frac{1}{20}$.

Significance of a numerical difference increases uniformly as p decreases; it operates as $1\text{-}p$. Summarily and arbitrarily—although in conformity with most investigators—I label a difference as significant whenever p is smaller than 0.05; that is, I assume that a difference in figures is generally meaningful if it is 95 percent certain that such a difference (in the figures in question) was not due to mere chance.

Confidence Interval of 95 percent: If from a large population a sample N (for example, 100 individuals) was selected, and a number of them (say 50) had a certain characteristic, it is naturally not correct to conclude that, with certainty, exactly half the total population had that characteristic and the other half did not. Of course, this proportion is closer to the real proportion than any other given ratio; however, it is possible that the true proportion may be closer to 1 or to 0 than the indicated 1 to 2. (It would be closest to 1 if, by chance, exactly all of the individuals with that characteristic in the entire population had been counted in, and closest to 0 if, by chance in the opposite direction, all nonpossessors of the characteristic had been counted in.) Slight deviations between the number found and the number sought (the true proportion) are possible; however on the other hand, the possibility of larger deviations is less likely as the difference increases in size. The confidence interval of the proportions counted in at 95 percent (in the sample at 50 percent) indicate between what limits the true (sought) proportion may be assumed to range with a probability greater than 19/20. (For the 50 percent figure from the sample, the confidence interval ranges between 39.8 percent and 60.2 percent.) Only with a probability of less than 1 in 20 does the interval between 39.8 percent and 60.2 percent not include the true proportion of the population in that sample. (I used the confidence intervals from the Geigy tables.)

Standard Deviation: The notation of a standard deviation (or the median error) of a given number has the same connotation as the notation of a confidence interval. If on occasions I indicate in my statistics a standard deviation (or a median error) instead of a confidence interval, it may be for one of two reasons: In my original investigations I had no Geigy tables to use as reference, so I calculated the standard deviations and possible errors myself. When indicating results in tables, less space is required to show the standard deviation by a single figure than to show confidence intervals, which requires two entries.

The standard deviation is a measure of what deviations of a given number upward or downward might be expected through chance at a certain expected probability.

Example: Among 100 siblings of schizophrenics, 10 schizophrenics are to be expected. The standard deviation of this figure is then calculated by the formula $\sqrt{\dfrac{(10)\ (90)}{100}} = 3$. If now I were to add to—or subtract from—10 percent a single standard deviation, my results would be 13 and 7 percent, respectively. In that case the true proportion of schizophrenics among the siblings of schizophrenics could be expected to range between 7 percent and 13 percent, at a probability of 67 percent. But if I add to—or subtract from—10 percent three times the standard deviation, I get 1 percent or 19 percent, and I may assume with a probability of approximately 99.7 percent that the interval between these limits is the true proportion of schizophrenics among the siblings of schizophrenics. The multiple of 1.96 of the standard deviation corresponds to a confidence level of 0.95. The confidence intervals of the above example amount to 10 percent $\pm$ 1.96 $\times$ 3 percent, that is, 4.12 percent and 15.88 percent. These intervals are approximations of the extremely accurate approximations 4.90 and 17.62, which appear in the Geigy tables.

1 Establishment of Goals, Fundamental and Supplemental Data, Methods of Research

Planning the Investigations

The planning of the investigations whose results I am presenting here began in 1942. At that time I had just assumed the directorship of the Zürich Psychiatric University Clinic at Burghölzli. This gave me the rare opportunity of beginning a long-term study that might extend over two to three decades and of selecting my own staff for the project. Since schizophrenics were by far the largest group of mental patients entrusted to my care, the problems concerning the schizophrenias became the focal point of my interest.

I wanted to approach an understanding of the nature of the schizophrenias by two different methods.

One set of investigations at the clinic was to address the long-standing question of whether there were tangible, comprehensible, physical determinants that favored the development of the schizophrenias. Up to that time, the problem had been approached principally by examining schizophrenics physically, using all methods available at the time. I wanted to approach the same problem from the opposite angle, by asking whether schizophrenic or schizophrenia-like mental disorders occurred in conjunction with any physical illnesses. Since at the time various opinions were expressed about endocrine disorders being the cause of schizophrenias, and since little was yet known about mental disorders among patients with endocrine diseases, I first narrowed the question down to whether there were endocrine disorders that were accompanied by schizophrenic psychoses.[1] Later we expanded the investigations to inquire whether schizophrenias occur in conjunction with brain tumors,[2] with chronic alcohol poisoning,[3] and whether, in general, the disorders resulting from acute exogenous reactive disorders could be distinguished from the

schizophrenias.[4] The most important result of all these investigations supports the view that mental disorders that have identifiable and definite relationships to pathological physical processes are basically and clearly distinguishable from the schizophrenias. Most especially, the psychic disorders of mental patients with endocrine dysfunctions are never in any sense schizophrenias. Only in isolated phases and among a small minority of patients does the psychopathology of schizophrenics overlap with that of patients with identifiable physiological disorders.

But all of this is not the subject for discussion in the study presented here. It is based rather on a completely different investigation of the problems inherent in schizophrenia, which I began to plan in 1942 and have since continued to pursue without interruption: I wanted personally to investigate and to study anamnestically some 200 nonselected schizophrenics from our clinic and to follow their development along with that of their relatives for at least 20 years. I wanted particularly also to pursue long-term studies on the interweaving relationships of the patients' life vicissitudes and those of their immediate relatives. Simultaneously our therapeutic activity was to be critically evaluated in the light of longterm catamneses.

This plan of procedure developed out of the state of knowledge of schizophrenia at the time, out of the limited investigative facilities at our clinic, and out of my own need to check and expand the results of my previous investigations with schizophrenics.

In previous investigations of schizophrenia, the long-term course of the illness was not accorded as much attention as were its other facets. It was especially unusual to have longterm courses investigated continuously. Most of the former investigations are related only to the conditions existing at certain points in time after hospitalization and disregard in its entirety the course of the disease. A great deal more is known about the successes from shortterm treatments than long-term ones. Also,

1. I summarized these results in a monograph (1954) titled "Endokrinologische Psychiatrie (Endocrinological Psychiatry)" and in a handbook (1964) titled "Psychiatrie der Gegenwart (Psychiatry Today)."

2. Walther Büel et al. 1951.

3. G. Benedetti, 1952.

4. M. Bleuler, J. Willi, H. R. Bühler, 1966.

the family relationships of schizophrenics were heretofore studied principally in cross section with emphasis on a certain point in time, whereas longitudinal studies depicting the development over longer time spans are still too little known. Furthermore, the relationships between family histories and long-term courses of mental illness had not yet been investigated using a large sampling of patients. The planned investigations were designed to help close such gaps in the knowledge about the schizophrenias. On the other hand, the psychopathology, the phenomenology, the psychodynamics, the pathological anatomy, and the physiology of the schizophrenias have in recent times been so thoroughly and frequently investigated from so many different aspects, that new developments of any importance about them are hardly to be expected in the near future without some basically new techniques, methodologies, or new hypotheses on investigative procedures being developed.

My research, however, could not be directed solely toward scientific needs; it had to be adapted also to the limitations of the locale in which it was performed. In 1942, our clinic had no access whatever to any experimental laboratories or investigative personnel, and had to operate within the extremely limited funds allotted to these investigations. Thus, the schizophrenia research project was to cost as little as possible, and the time devoted to it could be used only when the investigative activity and routine clinical work with patients could be combined with it. On the other hand, some perfectly ideal conditions were present that were favorable specifically to long-term research on the courses of mental illness and to family studies. In 1942 Switzerland was surrounded by powers at war with one another, and travel was difficult. During those times the population of Zürich remained far more stationary than that of many other locales and during other times. Thanks to this relative stability, it was possible to observe uninterruptedly the development of the 208 schizophrenics selected for catamnestic research from the 212 originally admitted to Burghölzli between 1942/1943, together with their immediate families, for a period of more than 20 years or until they died. It seems unlikely that, with the increasing population shifts and the constantly weakening bonds to hearth and home of modern man, such a degree of completeness of long-term catamnestic data can ever again be achieved. The

period 1942/43 was furthermore favorable for the selection of probands for research in our canton, since there were still relatively few refugees and almost no foreign laborers living within the jurisdictional area of the clinic, and most of the troops assigned to Zürich that had been mobilized for border defense were stationed near their homes and almost always went to clinics in Zürich for treatment of the more serious illnesses.

Local conditions, however, were favorable for the planned investigations not only because of the exceptional stability of the population residing within the jurisdictional area of the clinic at that time, but also because the traditional methods of operation of the Zürich clinic were particularly well suited to this type of investigation. Human and scientific interests, as well as practical necessity, had brought about a condition by which Burghölzli had virtually become specialized for the task of collecting precise data on life and family histories, as well as on the social conditions of its patients. The clinic is responsible for important social decisions, of which psychiatric university clinics in other locales are usually relieved. Once a patient is accepted, the clinic must decide not only the amount of time, medical care, and hospitalization that are indicated, but also whether the retention of the patient against his will or that of his family is legal, necessary, and justified. In only very few isolated instances have administrative authorities heretofore been helpful in bearing this responsibility. (Not until a new set of health laws was enacted in 1962 have any changes taken place in this respect.) A large number of our patients was also in serious need of involuntary commitment, guardianship, and court detention. The clinic's decisions on release, retention, need for guardianship, involuntary detention, and legal representation were frequently subjected to bitter, malicious, and hostile criticism by the public. Yet, all these issues could be decided only on the basis of thorough investigation of the health, the family, and the social history of the patient. The smallest error in assembling these data could lead to time-consuming arguments and vicious attacks. The very precision demanded of the medical and scientific disciplines was in itself the best possible protective measure against such direct threats. All of this affected every colleague at the clinic, immediately and profoundly, even the youngest among them, and bore fruit in the exactitude with which the medical histories of patients were compiled. While no research based on laboratory experiments could be planned, the routine clinical procedures did lay an excellent foundation for the long-term studies of the life and family histories of our patients.

In addition, I was planning my 1942 investigations as extensions of my 1929 investigations, which had already been established as valid life- and family-histories of schizophrenics. The schizophrenics I had previously studied came from a number of widely separated localities, including the Westchester Division of the New York Hospital, the St. Gallen Sanitarium of St. Pirminsberg in Pfäfers, and the Basel Psychiatric University Clinic of Friedmatt; that is, from American, and Swiss rural and urban population groups. Many of the conclusions reached at that time remained in doubt, because they were based on samples that were too small in number to be considered valid. I felt constrained to prove or refute these findings in the light of the new, more extensive, and more precise medical and family histories. Besides, even long before 1942 I had studied representative population samples from the Basel and Zürich areas, which I found useful for comparison with the wealth of material gathered from the schizophrenic patients. One principal goal for the scientific evaluation of these findings had occurred to me from the outset, and that was to become much better acquainted with the conditions that influence the origin, the symptomatology, and the course of schizophrenic disorders. To be sure, I was getting into such a difficult set of problems that had already been studied by so many for such a long time, that from the very beginning I could expect no more than the most modest contributions toward their clarification. But especially because these problems were of such magnitude and importance, even the promise of the tiniest vestiges of progress was ample encouragement to work on the project for many years.

Specifically, I had the following concepts about the evaluation of long-term patient and family histories: Primarily, the investigative results were to document what familial and personal backgrounds may be common to schizophrenic disorders of a particular population and at a particular period of time, how they run their course under the given cultural conditions, and how the lives of close relatives and families develop under those same conditions. However, what is valid for the schizophrenics of a given population group

at a given time does not necessarily hold for all schizophrenics. It is instructive to compare conditions in one limited locale and during a limited time span with those in a different locale and at a different time. In this way it is possible to search for indicators as to which conditions may cause or favor illnesses under certain cultural postulates, and which do not. It does seem that the significance of "geographic" and "historic" medicine is gaining increasing attention in recent years.

The *family relationships*— whether good or bad—of schizophrenics were to be compared with those of other schizophrenics, with those of the normal population, and with those of other patients. Corresponding comparisons were to be made in respect to the prepsychotic personalities of the schizophrenics themselves and to the mental health status and the social position of their relatives.

The *long-term studies* on the course of illness were to concentrate primarily on what previous research had neglected, that is, on the condition of the patients, not merely years, but decades after the first onset of the disease, and then on the entire course of the disease over periods of years, and not only on spot checks of the patient's condition at certain intervals after his hospitalization. The medical report of the patient was not to be evaluated as it had been in most investigations, merely as to whether the patient's condition warranted hospitalization, but on the basis of his actual condition, regardless of the arrangements or disposition as to his care.

The reported findings on the mental health conditions of relatives differ from those of other investigators, in that they have been followed up and checked periodically over more than 20 years.

The offspring of the probands were to receive special attention. What was the fertility rate of the schizophrenics we studied, and did it correspond to that of other schizophrenics and to that of the normal population? This in itself suggests the question as to how frequently schizophrenias would "originate," be it by mutation of biological hereditary matrices that may predispose them, or by a process of "learning irrationality" from latently or manifestly schizophrenic parents, as some recent schools consider significant.[5] Are

5. G. Bateson et al. (1956), L. C. Wynne et al. (1958, 1963), D. D. Jackson and J. H. Weakland (1959, 1961), M. Bowen et al. (1960, 1961), and Y. O. Alanen (1966).

there as many cases of mental disorders among the children of my schizophrenic probands as in other investigations? What are the reasons for the differences? How is the development of children influenced, subjectively and objectively, who are exposed to schizophrenia in one of their parents? Does it make a difference in the children's state of health whether they lived together with schizophrenic parents in a close relationship and for long periods of time, or not? Does schizophrenia in one generation imply a social decline in the following one?

A particular task consists of properly interrelating the various courses of illness with varying family backgrounds and varying states of health of close relatives. Do the schizophrenias run a different long-term course when patients have lived under chaotic conditions in the home rather than under well-adjusted, orderly ones, and whether the close relatives are or are not frequently schizophrenics or psychopaths? Can subtypes of schizophrenia be identified in which family conditions (inherited or experienced) are of greater or lesser significance than for others? Can the large group of schizophrenias now be better subdivided according to ancillary causes than formerly? Such questions begin to approach solution when inquiry is made into what aspects of schizophrenic psychoses are similar and which are dissimilar in the schizophrenic relatives of schizophrenics. Comparisons of the courses of illness among the relatives of schizophrenics will therefore have to receive special attention.

In reporting my investigations, it seemed important to me always to distinguish clearly which findings, and in what form, may be considered objective, and which, subjective. Beyond that, a distinction of the following stages in reporting seemed important:

1. Reporting the basic data collected from the 208 probands and their families. They include childhood conditions, backgrounds, premorbid personality traits, course of the disease, its outcome, mental disorders, and the styles of coping with life on the part of members of the family.

2. Correlation studies of the various data yielded by these investigations

3. Comparisons of findings and correlations of conditions in the proband group with those found in the normal population and among other schizophrenics from my own previous investigations and from investigations by colleagues working at Burghölzli

4. Comparisons of these findings and these correlations with those of other investigators

5. Evaluation of the significance of the various findings and correlations

6. Incorporation of the results into a total concept of the nature of the schizophrenic illnesses, their causes, and possible methods of therapy and prophylaxis.

The distinctions listed in 1 through 5 above are discussed in the individual chapters. A summary of the theorizing (or shall we say speculation?) on the nature of schizophrenic illnesses, on the other hand, is limited to the two final chapters. The essence of this work is a factual report of findings and not an interpretation of facts. Still, it is hardly possible for anyone who has pondered the nature of the schizophrenias for decades, as I have, to suppress his thoughts about it when he presents investigative data that are so closely allied to his topic. My hypothetical concepts about the nature of the schizophrenias will be shared by very few, for most modern schools will regard them either as too little psychodynamic or, on the contrary, as too little somatically oriented. I hope, however, that the main part of the work, the factual portion of it, will benefit all readers, regardless of whether they share my views on the nature of the schizophrenias, and regardless of what conflicting or opposing views they may hold.

During the many years in which the investigations presented here were in progress, our principal mission at Burghölzli was the treatment of schizophrenics, and not research. My investigations were closely interrelated with the problems inherent in treatment. They were particularly well suited for establishing and maintaining a closer relationship with the patients and their families, and for counseling them better and prescribing appropriate treatments.

Concurrently with the investigations on the relationships between physical and mental disorders, on the long-term courses of diseases, and on the relationships between our patients and their families, we continued to follow up the successes and the failures in our treatment methods. That topic will be discussed just briefly in this book. I have already described investigations on insulin and shock therapy in 1942. Since 1946, Baer (1946), Büel (1954), Ernst (1954), Weber (1954), Avenarius (1956), Benedetti (1956), Mielke (1956), Vogt (1956), Angst (1960), von Brauchitsch (1961), von Brauchitsch and Bukowczyk (1962), Angst and Pöldinger (1963), Kirchgraber

(1963), Kind (1964), Hicklin and Angst (1967), Corboz (1968), and Stoll (1969) have investigated the implications of psychopharmacotherapy at our clinic. Benedetti (1954) and Müller (1958) described their experiences in psychoanalysis at the clinic. I personally was primarily concerned to see that the schizophrenic patients were receiving continuous care, that we were establishing and maintaining close relations with them in every way possible, and that they were being integrated into active communities.

Selection of the 208 Schizophrenic Probands (the "Principal Probands")

Two hundred and eight schizophrenic patients admitted to the Psychiatric University Clinic of Burghölzli in Zürich during 1942 and 1943 became probands for this project, 100 men and 108 women. The *only acceptance criteria* for inclusion in the project, as mentioned, were: hospitalization at Burghölzli during a particular time span and a diagnosis of schizophrenic psychosis.

How was the figure 208 determined? Early in 1942 I had decided to use 100 men and 100 women as probands. From the outset, I had hoped that the majority of these patients with their families could be studied catamnestically for several decades. Still, I could not assume that this goal would be met in every instance. I expected that in later years more women than men would drop out of the investigation, since they are more difficult to trace. Finding the whereabouts of women becomes difficult when they are married to foreign nationals, and when they relocate and change their names because of marriage or divorce. I estimated that about 100 male and 100 female probands with long-term catamneses would remain with me if I accepted 103 men and 109 women. By pure chance, the estimate for the males worked out exactly: of the 103 men selected as probands, 100 were studied for over 20 years, or until they expired. But even after a patient died, we were able to follow the lives of members of his family many years beyond his demise. However, the women exceeded our expectations: Of the 109 women originally selected as probands for the project, only one was disqualified for our long-term catamneses, which left 108 female probands for the investigation.[6] If out of 212 originally

selected probands only 1.9 percent were lost for reasons other than death in over 20 years, the statistical difference could hardly be significant. It would be a rare coincidence indeed if patients and their families could ever again be assembled for such a complete study over so long a time span. These exceptionally favorable conditions are attributed to the exceptional stability of our population in 1942, in part a by-product of the war, as previously explained.

The limitation to about 200 probands seemed necessary, since I could not expect to find enough time and resources over a span of 20 years to perform any more extensive research.

The periods during which I made probands out of hospitalized schizophrenics ranged, for the women, from April 18, 1942, through June 27, 1943, and for the men from April 15, 1942, through December 15, 1943. The longer recruitment period for men became necessary, since more female than male patients were being hospitalized. In order to obtain as many male as female probands, the selection time for males had to be longer than that for females. Between April 15, 1942 and December 15, 1943, the only interruptions in the recruitment of probands occurred during my vacations and during periods of extremely heavy work loads at the clinic. I wanted to become personally acquainted with all the probands from the very beginning. Any adverse effect in the selection due to these interruptions during the recruitment period is quite out of the question.

All schizophrenics selected as probands during the recruitment phases (except the four cases mentioned in n. 6, above) became probands. One might ask whether it would not have been better to select only initial

---

6. Reasons why 4 of the selected patients dropped out of the project
—One proband could not be located after 1948. He was

single, an only child, and both his parents had died many years before. A distant female relative who visited him sporadically during the time of his hospitalization had also died. Neighbors from his hometown did not know his whereabouts.
—Another proband was a refugee from an internment camp, who later emigrated to the United States and failed to reply to correspondence.
—One proband had his attorney inform us that he was withdrawing authorization for any further inquiries about him. His family refused any further cooperation.
—One female proband moved back to Germany, her home, before the war was over, and all efforts to locate her failed.

hospitalization cases as probands. Among other requirements, we wanted to find out how schizophrenics hospitalized at least once would develop, and only those hospitalized for the first time are suitable for providing a meaningful answer to this question. But among the total number accepted for the project, two types of patients are under-represented: those who, once hospitalized, remained hospitalized, and those who, after once being released, remained socially adapted or even recovered completely. The majority of the entire group, however, compared to first timers, were patients in whom the disease oscillated in cycles. If, in spite of these facts, I decided to use all selected schizophrenics for the investigation (rather than only those hospitalized for the first time), the following four reasons influenced that decision: First, experience had proved that it was not as simple as it may seem to determine whether a patient was being hospitalized for the first time. Surely there was no problem in determining whether or not a patient was coming to Burghölzli for the first time, but we had to consider also whether the patients had previously been hospitalized in some other psychiatric clinic. This issue is not always clear, particularly when patients have spent much time in foreign countries.

Often the question whether certain institutions can be regarded as psychiatric clinics remains ambiguous, which is true also of homes for the infirm operated by religious organizations or of the neurology sections of military hospitals. Furthermore, patients may have been hospitalized not with the diagnosis of a schizophrenia, but with the diagnosis of a depression, a neurosis, or a puberty crisis. Should such a patient be registered as first-time hospitalized when he arrives at Burghölzli? Nor could this decision be made without some arbitrary guesswork. Second, the repeated interviews of readmitted patients were valuable, and each time new acquaintance was made with previously unknown relatives of the patient. By comparing the interview data from several different meetings at various times and from a larger number of people, greater objectivity and supporting information for the basic factual data of the investigation were realized. It would have been too bad to exclude those with multiple admissions, through which a wealth of important, objective, and valuable data became available to us. Third, the number of first-time admissions at Burghölzli is smaller than that of patients who had previously been

hospitalized for psychiatric illness elsewhere and at other times, and it would have taken several years more to study initially and in person 200 initial admission cases. Besides, with that much extra time, the necessary cohesiveness of a catamnestic study might have been sacrificed. Fourth, a selection based on first-time admissions would have been essentially meaningful only to a portion of the planned investigations, namely for the statistics on the long-term courses of the disease. On the other hand, for many other facets of these investigations, all admitted schizophrenic patients served just as well as probands, for example, in investigations of the "broken home" and of schizophrenic relatives.

Among the 208 probands admitted to Burghölzli during the critical period, 68 were first-time admissions to a psychiatric hospital for schizophrenias (and for reasons explained above, that figure may be inaccurate). In all conclusions where a distinction between first-time and multiple hospitalization is important, this distinction will be indicated.

Characterization of the 208 Principal Schizophrenic Probands

The sex ratio (100 men to 108 women) was arbitrarily established, as outlined above. It does not correspond exactly to the sex ratio of all schizophrenics admitted to Burghölzli, for that ratio is certainly subject to considerable shifts, which are partly due to external conditions (for instance, a fully occupied women's ward may be the cause for refusal to admit more women). In 1942, 126 men and 182 women, and in 1943, 141 men and 204 women were admitted and diagnosed as schizophrenic. For 100 schizophrenic men among my probands, there were 108 women, and for 100 schizophrenic men admitted to Burghölzli, 144 women were admitted.

Burghölzli can accept only patients for which the Canton of Zürich is responsible, that is, principally patients whose permanent home is in the Canton of Zürich, and a small minority of patients who have citizenship rights in a Zürich community but who become ill in a different canton, from which they are transferred to a hospital in the area of their homes, usually because of poverty. A still smaller minority comprises patients who happened to be in our canton when they were beset with sudden attacks of mental disorder and had to be hospitalized immediately. In principle, Burghölzli may also accept patients from anywhere else in Switzerland or from foreign countries. Usually this is impossible, however, because beds must always be kept available for patients from the canton. In keeping with these admission criteria of the clinic, all probands were patients for whom the Canton of Zürich was "responsible"; that is, the great majority of them actually were living in the Canton of Zürich when they were hospitalized. A small minority lived outside its limits but held citizenship rights in the Canton of Zürich, and only eight probands were hospitalized during a temporary sojourn in the canton.

The residences of the probands when they were hospitalized and selected as probands, that is, during 1942 or 1943, were as follows:

	Men	Women	Total
City of Zürich	54	59	113
City of Winterthur	3	1	4
Remainder of Canton of Zürich from rural or suburban communities	23	39	62
Cantons adjacent to the Canton of Zürich: (Schaffhausen, Thurgau, St. Gallen, Schwyz, Zug, and Aargau)	10	2	12
Remaining cantons of Switzerland	8	7	15
Migratory	2	0	2
	100	108	208

Because of certain peculiarities in the citizenship laws in Switzerland, our population can also be characterized according to citizenship rights. A Swiss citizen is not a citizen of Switzerland, but a citizen of a certain community. Until a few decades ago, a large portion of the population resided in the community of which they were citizens by having been born there. The institution of this citizenship right in a certain community is in keeping with the exceptional stability of the population throughout the centuries. On the other hand, this stability has the effect of making one a true citizen of his community. Residence in one's own community was (and still is, though to a lesser degree today) advantageous in certain respects, for instance: better welfare assistance in case of need, illness, or old age, better recognition of one's opinions in political discussions, and partly also more substantial gains and benefits from community goods and projects. For carrying out my investigations, the institution of citizenship in a community was immeasurably helpful. Inquiries to community administrative offices

were answered promptly, reliably, and accurately with respect to names, number of relatives, dates of their births, marriages and deaths, and often even forwarding addresses were furnished. To anyone who understands the Swiss system, specifying the communities of origin of the probands is both informative and important. The cultural and social background differs appreciably according to the citizenship standards of a particular community. Such differences are valid even within the same canton, and not only between, say, Zürich-City and Zürich Rural—, but also between rural communities in the foothills along the Töss or in the Jura countryside of the Wehn valley. Any Swiss psychiatrist knows also that in the different local psychiatric hospitals, marked differences exist in the entire treatment atmosphere of a department, and therefore also in nuances in the symptomatology of schizophrenics. Among others, Rorschach (1921) in his monograph on the interpretation of forms indicated that he was aware of such distinctions, and cited as an

Table 1.1. Home districts of the 208 principal schizophrenic probands

Locale of citizenship	Male probands	Unmarried female and married, widowed, and divorced female probands before marriage	Married, widowed, and divorced females[1]
City of Zürich	23	19	9
City of Winterthur	5	3	0
Other communities of the Canton of Zürich	29	36	23
Communities in cantons adjacent to Zürich Canton	23	10	5
Communities from remainder of Swiss cantons	16	22	17
In foreign countries	4[2]	18[3]	2[4]
	100	108	

1. Identical with citizenship of husband.
2. Of these, 2 in Italy, 1 in Austria, and 1 in France.
3. Of these, 8 in Germany, 4 in Austria, 2 in Hungary, 1 in France, 1 in Czechoslovakia, 1 in Russia, and 1 in Italy.
4. Both in Germany.

example the distinctions existing between patients from Appenzell and from Bern.

The locales of the citizenship of our probands are listed in Table 1.1. It shows that 24 percent of our 208 probands originated from the two cities of Zürich and Winterthur, that 31 percent came from other communities of the canton (mainly from the suburban communities of Zürich), 16 percent from communities in neighboring cantons, and 18 percent from communities of other cantons. Ten percent were foreigners.

No age limits were set in selecting the probands. All patients of any age admitted to the clinic were considered as probands if they were definitely schizophrenics. If children and youths are poorly represented, a partial reason is that, based on the experience of our child psychiatry service (directed by Prof. Dr. J. Lutz), we are extremely careful with a diagnosis of schizophrenia in children, and another, that very young schizophrenics are often hospitalized in private clinics. The upper age limit results simply from the fact that diagnoses for schizophrenia-like psychoses are virtually impossible with senile patients.

Birth dates of probands ranged as follows:

	Men	Women
1874–1889	10	25
1890–1899	25	21
1900–1909	33	35
1910–1919	21	24
1920–1929	11	3

The youngest patient selected during the 1942/43 recruitment period was 16, the oldest $67\frac{1}{2}$ years old. The average age of all probands at that time was 40.

Marital status of the probands in 1942/43 was as follows:

	Men	Women
Single	63	56
Married	27	31
Widowed	0	5
Divorced	10	16

Religious affiliation among the probands were as follows: 159 affiliated with the National Reformed Church, 45 with the Catholic, 1 with the Greek Orthodox, 1 with the Adventists, 1 Jewish, and 1 was unaffiliated.

Table 1.2 gives a summary of all 208 probands, arranged according to ages and marital status at the beginning and at the end of the investigation, their sex, and their

deaths (Table 1.3 is a similar summary of probands from other investigations). The principal *occupations* of probands, which they held at the conclusion of the project, subdivide as follows:

Occupations of the 52 unmarried female probands

Maidservant on a farm	4
Factory worker	7
Housekeeping help in parents' home	6
Maid, domestics	18
Waitress, chambermaid	4
Dressmaker, seamstress	5
Salesclerk	2
Clerical, office, and secretarial employee	5
Changed jobs	1
	52

Occupations of 100 male probands

Farmer (landowner)	2
Farm laborer (employed)	5
Handyman, helper, and odd-job worker	17
Factory laborer	6
Solicitor, peddler, door-to-door salesman	5
Cook, innkeeper, hotel porter	4
Hairdresser, barber	2
Postal or railroad employee, chauffeur	5
Clerical or administrative employee	9
Businessman	3
Engineering, architectual draftsman	2
Mechanic, artisan, construction worker	26
Heraldry specialist, glass painter, music teacher	3
Teacher	2
Academic professional	2
Student	1
Unemployed and unemployable	6
	100

Occupations of the 56 married, widowed, and divorced female probands (before marriage)

Maidservant on a farm	1
Farmer's daughter	1
Factory employee	13
Peddler, door-to-door saleswoman	2
Household employee	17
Waitress, chambermaid	2
Dressmaker, seamstress, milliner	12
Free-lance artist	1
Rooming house proprietress	1
Office, clerical, and secretarial employee	1
Teacher	2
Jobless, never employed	3
	56

Table 1.2. Vital statistics of the 208 principal probands

Columns 2–6 are *At outset of the investigation (1942/43)*. Columns 7–16 are *At end of the investigation (1965/65)*.

100 Male probands

	Single	Married	Widowed	Divorced	Total	Single Alive	Single Dead	Married Alive	Married Dead	Widowed Alive	Widowed Dead	Divorced Alive	Divorced Dead	Total Alive	Total Dead
10–19 years old	3	0	0	0	3	0	0	0	0	0	0	0	0	0	0
20–29	18	2	0	1	21	0	3	0	0	0	0	0	1	0	4
30–39	19	6	0	3	28	1	3	1	0	0	0	0	1	2	4
40–49	16	10	0	4	30	7	3	5	1	0	0	0	0	12	4
50–59	5	8	0	1	14	12	6	5	2	0	0	4	1	21	9
60–69	2	1	0	1	4	10	0	4	3	0	1	6	2	20	6
70–79	0	0	0	0	0	5	2	4	1	3	0	1	1	13	4
80 and over	0	0	0	0	0	0	0	0	1	0	0	0	0	0	1
Totals for males	63	27	0	10	100	35	17	19	8	3	1	11	6	68	32

108 Female probands

	Single	Married	Widowed	Divorced	Total	Single Alive	Single Dead	Married Alive	Married Dead	Widowed Alive	Widowed Dead	Divorced Alive	Divorced Dead	Total Alive	Total Dead
10–19 years old	1	0	0	0	1	0	0	0	0	0	0	0	0	0	0
20–29	14	2	0	2	18	0	0	0	0	0	0	0	0	0	0
30–39	19	8	1	4	32	1	1	0	1	0	0	0	0	1	2
40–49	11	8	0	3	22	9	4	2	2	0	0	0	0	11	6
50–59	9	8	1	5	23	12	3	6	2	3	1	6	2	27	8
60–69	2	5	3	2	12	10	3	3	0	1	1	5	2	19	6
70–79	0	0	0	0	0	4	5	1	2	2	5	4	2	11	14
80 and over	0	0	0	0	0	0	0	0	0	1	2	0	0	1	2
Totals for females	56	31	5	16	108	36	16	12	7	7	9	15	6	70	38

Table 1.3. Overview of probands from this and my earlier investigations

Research groups	Years of recruit-ment	Latest & earliest birth dates	Probands			No. studied of:		Locale of original residence	General social status of probands	Duration of catamneses
			No.	Men	Women	Parents	Siblings			
Schizophrenics										
New York Group	1929/30	1866/1913	100	68	32	200	351	Major cities in USA	Wealthy and intellectuals	8 years
Pfäfers Group	1933/36	1863/1919	100	92	8	200	492	Canton of St. Gallen	Crisis-ridden country and mountain people	1–3 years
Basel Group I (Insulin-treated)	1936/40	1881/1920	89	45	44	175	368	Basel-City	Mildly economically depressed population from commercial and industrial center	1–5 years
Basel Group II (Late-onset schizophrenics)	1941	approx. 1875/1900	130[1]	32	62	130[2]	264	Basel-City		(none)
Our present 208 probands	1942/43	1874/1926	208	100	108	412	933	Canton of Zürich	Prosperous city, suburban, and rural population	20–23 years
Normal Population										
Basel area	1930/31	1853/1918	200	86	114	400	1111	Upper Rural-Basel	Rural population, economically depressed	(none)
Canton of Zürich	1933/34	1870/1908	100	44	56	199	479	Canton of Zürich	(Same as for our present probands)	(none)
Alcoholics										
New York Probands	1949/50	1879/1930	50	34	16	100	114	Major cities in USA	Wealthy and intellectuals	(none)
Zürich Probands	1950	1880/1920	50	38	12	98	173	Canton of Zürich	(Same as for our present probands)	(none)

1. Sixty-one of these are identical with schizophrenic probands of previous investigations. In the original study, the sexes were differentiated in just 94 cases. Sexes were not differentiated in the subsequent printing of an additional 36 cases that had been selected for a special study.

2. The families of only half these probands were studied completely.

*Occupations of husbands of the married, widowed,
and divorced female probands*

Farmer (landowner)	6
Farm laborer (employed)	1
Handyman, helper, part-time laborer, factory worker	16
Newspaper seller	1
Cook, hotel porter	2
Postal and railroad employee, chauffeur	3
Business and clerical employee	6
Businessman	3
Prison guard	1
Engineering employee, chief engineer	2
Mechanic, artisan, construction worker	19
Hotel keeper	1
Teacher	1
Academic professional	3
Unknown	1
	66[1]

1. Six female probands had married twice; 3 of them three times.

The distribution of occupations was influenced by the war and the conditions at Burghölzli at that time. For instance, the lack of motor fuel meant there were almost no professional truck drivers—and we had none among our probands. On the other hand, there were plenty of maids and domestics. Shortly after I had assumed directorship of the clinic, very few private patients were being admitted; as a consequence, there were very few academic professionals among its patients. It does seem that the farming occupations were rather poorly represented, since the Canton Psychiatric Clinic of Rheinau was located in that part of the canton where agriculture is the dominant activity. Joblessness or menial occupations requiring no education or apprenticeship were frequently consequences of slowly developing psychoses or prepsychotic personality disorders.

Are the Principal Probands Representative of a Local and Contemporary Population of Schizophrenics?

To render a scientifically valid judgment from the present investigations, a further question is important: To what extent do the 208 probands represent all schizophrenics hospitalized in the Canton of Zürich in 1942–43? To what extent are these probands merely a group of schizophrenics selected by other than random criteria from among all schizophrenics hospitalized in the canton during that time? In what respects do they differ from other schizophrenics hospitalized in the Canton of Zürich?

To answer these questions a brief explanation of the nature of psychiatric hospitals in our canton will be helpful. In addition to our own University Clinic, the canton also supports the Psychiatric Clinic of Rheinau, which is geared primarily to treating chronic cases, but also admits acute cases, particularly from its immediate vicinity. Besides, there are four rather large private psychiatric hospitals, operated in part by community or religious organizations, and all are at least at times government-supported, directly or indirectly. One of these is not considered in our comparisons because it accepts principally epileptics. The vast majority of schizophrenic patients needing hospitalization from the Canton of Zürich are therefore admitted either to Burghölzli, to the Rheinau Clinic, or to one of the three large private psychiatric hospitals. Schizophrenics referred to smaller private sanatoria in the canton or to hospitals outside the canton comprise a small minority that is not statistically significant.

The relation of schizophrenics hospitalized at Burghölzli in 1942–43 to all schizophrenics hospitalized throughout the Canton of Zürich can be fairly accurately derived from the following data:

Admissions of Schizophrenics	*1942*	*1943*
At Burghölzli	308	345
At Rheinau	35	39
At the three large private psychiatric hospitals in the Canton of Zürich[1]	370	380

1. Actual admission figures from two, and estimated figures from one of these hospitals.

The three private psychiatric hospitals admit patients not only from the home canton, but also those from other cantons and foreign countries in large numbers (much larger than we do at Burghölzli). The proportion of hospitalized patients from Zürich admitted to private hospitals was accurately determined by Dr. H. Büchel in 1963 at 65 percent. Of the 750 schizophrenics admitted to the three private hospitals in question during 1942 and 1943, only 487 were from the Canton of Zürich, as compared to 653 schizophrenics admitted to Burghölzli and 824 to Rheinau and the three private psychiatric clinics.

These data show that our 208 probands represent 653 nonselected schizophrenics who were admitted to Burghölzli during 1942–43. The latter figure makes up about 45 percent of all schizophrenics hospitalized from the

Canton of Zürich during 1942–43. To what extent do the 824 schizophrenics from the Canton of Zürich, who were admitted to hospitals other than Burghölzli differ from those admitted to Burghölzli with respect to their backgrounds?

Based on the knowledge of conditions at local hospitals, we can safely reply that there are some differences, but they are unimportant.

This statement is based on the following facts: The Rheinau Clinic has no section for private patients. It admits very few patients who have adequate financial means, and caters more to the chronic than to the acute cases. Its acute patients come mainly from the neighboring communities in the "Unterland" of Zürich. The Rheinau schizophrenics therefore do differ markedly from those of Burghölzli, but the difference is of little statistical significance because of their small number. It is statistically more important for our investigation to consider the conditions for admission to the private clinics. They differ in reverse from the distinction between admission policies of Rheinau and of Burghölzli. On the average, the private clinics admit more acute schizophrenics and more patients from economically well-to-do families. This does not by any means imply that Burghölzli admits only the financially depressed, and that private hospitals admit only the financially independent patient. On the contrary, at Burghölzli patients are also treated privately or semiprivately; in fact, we have a number of well-do-to patients among our probands. The three private clinics under discussion are not equipped to cater exclusively to the "private" or wealthy patient either, rather, all of them operate large general-admissions wards. However, since the costs of care on their general-admissions wards are higher than those at Burghölzli, the average financial conditions of patients in the general-admissions wards of private hospitals are somewhat—but not appreciably—better than of those at Burghölzli. One of these private clinics during the period of this study, accepted only women, which led to a rather insignificant shift in favor of male admissions to the other clinics. A preference prevails among the population for sending children and adolescents who need psychiatric hospitalization to private institutions rather than to the Burghölzli or Rheinau clincis, for fear that the canton clinics would be more inclined to "brand them insane for the rest of their lives"—as it is popularly phrased. Some sections of the population prefer to send their patients to a predominately religious, church-supported private clinic, whereas others want specifically to avoid any such influence and prefer the canton-supported clinics because of their religious neutrality.

The financial, emotional, and religious reasons outlined above, however, are by no means the only determinants that indicate whether a schizophrenic patient from the Canton of Zürich is to be admitted to Burghölzli or to any other particular psychiatric clinic in the canton for hospitalization. It is far more important that these extremely variable conditions and attitudes do not exert any direct or consistent influence on admission policies, and especially not the kind that would have a bearing on the scientific evaluation of investigative results to be presented. Primarily, a patient's hospitalization at one clinic or another depends mainly on such unpredictable factors as: Whether the patient himself, members of his family, or others counseling them happened to have heard something good or bad about one clinic or another, or whether they have any sort of personal acquaintance with one of the doctors or administrators of the clinic. Frequently one clinic or another is filled to capacity, and admission takes place quite by chance at the one that first responds affirmatively to an inquiry by telephone. Often admission depends on whether the referring doctors studied under the particular professor in psychiatry presently in charge at Burghölzli, or whether they were trained at other universities and may be better acquainted with colleagues at the private clinics. In some cases a member of the administration's health insurance office will advise the client, basing his counsel on any personal whim or prejudice, etc.

In general, we have found that essentially our probands come from about the same sectors of the population as do all schizophrenics hospitalized in the Canton of Zürich during the period in question. Some minor differences occur in that, on the average, the probands came from a slightly lower socioeconomic class than the corresponding population of their communities, and that the juvenile patients and those from families closely associated with religious organizations are somewhat underrepresented.

Sociological Factors of the Canton of Zürich

After it was determined that the 208 probands were representative of all the schizophrenia admissions to Burghölzli for the period covered by the report, and that they are—if not completely—generally representative of all admissions for schizophrenics in the Canton of Zürich, the question still needing an answer was: To what extent are the schizophrenics from Zürich representative of schizophrenics from other cantons and other countries? I should like to present the following data, so that colleagues who are not familiar with Switzerland can form a concept on the subject.

The Canton of Zürich encompasses an area of 1729.1 square-km. and in 1941 had a resident population of 674,505.[7] Fifty-one and a half percent of these held citizenship rights in the Canton of Zürich, 42.9 percent in the rest of Switzerland, and 5.6 percent were foreigners. The mother tongue of most of the population is the Zürich dialect of German, or the Swiss-German dialect spoken in the neighboring cantons. Seventy-five percent of the 1941 population were members of the National Reformed Church, 22 percent were Catholics, barely 1 percent were Christian-Catholic, somewhat over 1 percent Jewish, and about 1 percent either belonged to other confessions or were freethinkers.

Zürich, the capital of the canton, had 336,395 inhabitants in 1941; the second largest city, Winterthur, had 58,883. Over half the rest of the inhabitants lived in suburbs or in larger, heavily industrialized towns in which the life-style approached that of major cities. Still, in those times there were some purely farming and mountain communities, in which a small minority of our probands had made their homes. The canton had even then been largely industrialized. The following figures show the general occupational activities of the population at the time:

In the original German edition of this volume, Figures 1.2–1.15 show the types of multiple dwellings occupied by the majority of the 208 principal probands, as well as by their parents and siblings. They depict typical housing of the Zürich residents who were living under middle-income to lower-class-income conditions. At that time slum dwellings did not exist in the Canton of Zürich, and very few probands came from families who could afford expensive mansions or one-family houses.

Some of the figures show residential structures in the Old Section of Zürich, some are suburban houses, large numbers of which were built in the nineteenth century, and some are city and suburban multiple dwellings from the turn of the century. Included are old houses around Lake Zürich belonging to farmers engaged in such cottage industry as silk processing as an added source of income, as well as simple houses in the Zürich highlands where the inhabitants were chiefly small farmers and workers in the textile industry. One figure attests to the fact that none of the probands came from the high alpine regions, although some of them did come from the foothills. Also shown are the ancestral home of Adolph Meyer and that of the author. In a later chapter of the German edition of this book, there are photographs of the three main clinics from which the probands here discussed were recruited. They are: 1. The Psychiatric University Clinic of Burghölzli, just outside the City of Zürich, as it looked in 1870. Here all 208 of the principal probands were at one time hospitalized. 2. Bloomingdale Hospital in White Plains, New York State, now Westchester Division of the New York Hospital.

7. According to census figures compiled at the time.

General fields of occupation	No. employed	No. employed and their families[1]
Farming and Forestry	34,188	74,627
Mining and Quarrying	513	1,225
Industry and Skilled Trades	153,648	297,933
Business, Banking, and Insurance	51,586	94,595
Hotel and Tourist Industry	17,292	21,690
Traffic and Transportation	13,099	30,966
Public and Private Services	28,007	54,420
Housework and Personal Services	20,507	21,538
Day-Labor and Odd Jobs	340	478
Unemployed	6,152	10,293
Institutions	8,130	10,221
	333,462	617,986

1. Data from 1941 census, taken from *Zürcher Wirtschaftsbilder* 10:½, September 1954 (Office of Statistics for the Canton of Zürich).

3. The Psychiatric Clinic of St. Pirminsberg in Pfäfers, situated in the mountains of the Canton of St. Gallen. This building, originally an old monastery, was adapted and equipped in 1848 for its new function. From both these last-named institutions, probands for earlier investigations had been recruited.

In the period between the two World Wars there was a serious unemployment problem throughout the population of Zürich. It imposed considerable restraints on the life-styles of many families and forced many to work in occupations at lower standards than those for which they had been trained. Still, enough jobs existed for providing a living, and unemployment compensation and other social assistance sources were sufficient to provide necessary food, shelter, and other material necessities. In the years just before 1942, however, unemployment had decreased significantly.

The World War spared Switzerland, although it did have an enormous impact on the lives of the people of Zürich. A possible military invasion was a constant threat, particularly in 1939 and 1940. A large portion of the male population was in uniform. Privations suffered by Swiss troops, of course, cannot in any way be compared to those of troops in the actual field of combat, even though duty to provide military border security did impose some harsh and unaccustomed restrictions on their style of living. The constant need for readiness to enter defensive combat, with its ceaseless, strenuous military preparations and maneuvers, without actually being at war, yet without any end in sight to the exceptional conditions imposed by its threat, implied stresses of a peculiar kind. In addition to the threat of armed aggression, the population lived under the constant threat of famine, since it was never sure when food imports might be stopped. But the famine never occurred. Rationing of life's necessities restricted the accustomed life-style, but the allowances were always sufficient to ward off hunger. Avitaminosis and other manifestations of undernourishment occurred, when they did, mainly among some of the feebleminded or the mentally ill, who had difficulty adjusting to the more restrictive conditions. But the war years also generated conditions that were favorable from the standpoint of mental hygiene. The population was conscious of a unity of will and spirit to render armed resistance to any invasion, and to exploit every last plot of arable land to prevent a possible famine. Military service created a bond of comradeship that deeply and beneficially affected the personal development of many a citizen. The so-called "battle of cultivation"; that is, the efforts toward the productive utilization of every last scrap of earth for growing food, gave entire families a worthwhile common project to which they often dedicated themselves with total devotion and which contributed a great deal toward healthy family relationships. Alcoholism reached a new low during those years. All these circumstances became manifest in the premorbid histories of many of the probands.

The educational level of the population was good and relatively uniform. The majority of children went to the same public schools for 6 years. All children had access to 3 years of further education and good vocational training, if they were capable and wanted it. Advanced education was even then available to young people of limited means, even if it was harder for them than for children with good financial backing.

In over twenty-odd years since the recruitment of the probands, Switzerland underwent a development similar to that of many other countries. This has been characterized especially by an enormous increase in population (in the Canton of Zürich, from 674,505 inhabitants in 1941 to 1,032,000 in 1965); by the elimination of unemployment and a great demand for labor, which favored importation of labor from foreign countries (133,000 in the Canton of Zürich in 1965); by rapidly increasing industrialization along with a marked reduction in farming, particularly of smaller farming operations; by severe inflation, by which, on the whole, the income of most population groups increased by more than their expenses for the necessities of life; by a marked expansion in motorization and all technological means of recreation and entertainment; by a surfeit of foods and the opportunity for vacations and pleasure travel for all elements of the population; by a housing shortage and an acutely perceptible price increase in housing; by an increase in alcoholism, and a craving for soporifics and for pain-killers containing phenacetin. As in many other places, the internal human values that make for security and stably became threatened in that many of the old religious, philosophical, social, and political guideposts and ideals were ignored or given up, without being replaced by new ones. Many contemporaries believe to have detected a loosening of family ties; a view, however, based on my clinical experiences, with which I am not in agreement. The family lives of my probands are especially clear indications that the binding forces and the character-building relationships among the next of kin have remained sound and strong.

Criteria in the Diagnosis of Schizophrenia

More important for the characterization of our probands than all the aspects described in the preceding section is the manner of delimiting the concept of the schizophrenias. The diagnosis of a schizophrenia is by no means determined according to the same criteria in all schools or at all times. The question as to what in this study may be regarded as schizophrenia, therefore, deserves a thorough, detailed commentary.

The concept of the "schizophrenic psychoses," as it was applied in the selection of probands and in the diagnosis of psychoses in their families, has been set forth in detail by Eugen Bleuler in his book, *Dementia praecox oder die Gruppe der Schizophrenien* (Dementia Praecox or the Group of Schizophrenias), 1911. It was summarized more briefly in Eugen Bleuler's *Lehrbuch der Psychiatrie* (Textbook of Psychiatry). Eugen Bleuler, who was the first chief of the Rheinau Clinic (1886–1927), subsequently headed the Burghölzli Clinic and died in 1939, was personally acquainted with a number of probands who had been ill long before 1942, and a good number of their schizophrenic parents, whom he himself had diagnosed as schizophrenic.

It is important to establish that we regard schizophrenia as a mental illness, a psychosis, a form of "insanity." Only mental disorders that were popularly and forensically regarded as mental illnesses were considered by us in a diagnosis of schizophrenia. The mental disorder had to have developed proportions of a magnitude that would cause any normal, healthy person, whose judgment was based on experience with himself and with his normal fellowmen, to regard the personality of the patient as totally strange, puzzling, inconceivable, uncanny, and incapable of empathy, even to the point of being sinister and frightening. This is the context in which the term mental illness is used in the popular sense, and simultaneously in the sense of Swiss forensic psychiatry. It has been masterfully described by H. Binder a number of times (1952, 1955, 1964). And actually, the numerous probands on whom expert opinions were expressed by administrative authorites were consistently declared as "mentally ill" in the context of civil or criminal law, and based on this qualification, serious decisions had to be rendered as to their mental competence, court commitment, right to marry, or even decisions involving divorce and the custody of children. Those probands who had not been officially adjudicated as mentally ill, would also have been declared mentally ill in the legal sense, if the occasion had arisen.

An expanded diagnosis of schizophrenia was not permitted in the selection of probands or in the diagnosing of their relatives. I emphatically refuse to permit a diagnosis of "latent schizophrenia," for example, in neurasthenic complaints or in somewhat uncharacteristic mood disorders. Any doctor has the liberty of assuming in such cases that a schizophrenia is beginning to develop or that the case is one of the more benign disorders, similar to the nature of schizophrenic psychoses. For my part, I prefer the attitude that a brief, clearly formulated diagnosis of schizophrenia should be used only when schizophrenia is determined to be the actual psychosis, and not when it is merely suspected as a latent or developing psychosis or as a "schizophrenia manifesting as a neurosis." I also most especially refuse to accept a diagnosis of schizophrenia based solely on a projection test.

But it is sufficient to permit the diagnosis if a patient has at any time suffered a schizophrenic psychosis. Before or after that, the psychopathological symptoms (judged by the patient's capability for human contact and social efficacy) need never again be so severe as to warrant designating a patient as "mentally ill." Actually, the great majority of our patients had suffered conditions with milder psychotic disturbances before or after schizophrenic phases of psychotic dimension that would under no circumstance be regarded as mental illness under the popular and the forensic definition. In many of these patients, who had previously been assigned a guardian because of mental illness, the legal commitment was officially cancelled by the authorities of the local administration, because such authority had determined that in these cases the schizophrenic illness had been cured, while mild residual symptoms persisted.

In view of this, clear general characteristics of mental illness had to be identified before a diagnosis of schizophrenia could be considered. At least three of these applied to all probands.

—Confusion to a degree where the patient's train of thought would be incomprehensible to a normal person, or at least difficult to understand, and this not only in relation to topics of severe emotional impact;

—A total incapacity for emotional empathy that had no relation to the patient's actual condition on any normal psychological basis;

—A state of abnormal excitement or stupor of intense magnitude that could not be explained psychologically and might last more than just a few days;

—Illusions and hallucinations of long duration;

—Delusions;

—Total and abrupt changes in activities, commonly either by total neglect of matter-of-course obligations or by senseless, unprovoked acts of brutality against others;

—The firm conviction on the part of normal family members and intimates that the patient had suddenly become completely different, and that he could no longer be understood.

As in identifying a psychosis per se, the same principles recognized in modern psychiatry applied in formulating a diagnosis on the type of psychosis. These were strictly observed.

Naturally, all psychoses that occurred in connection with a proven brain disease, an endocrine disorder, a poisoning or any other severe physical illness were *excluded*. As soon as an anamnestic psychosyndrome or a definite psycho-organic thought disorder was determined, the diagnosis of a schizophrenia was no longer considered.

Of the generally accepted, positive criteria for suspecting a type of schizophrenia, the following seemed to be particularly significant:

—Keeping a double set of books, in the sense that a normal degree of intellectual accomplishment potential was evident along with severe psychotic manifestations;

—Definite schizophrenic distractedness in thinking, that is clearly distinguished from other kinds of confusion such as: loss of train of thought; disjointed thinking of the acute exogenous reactive type: results of labile attentiveness; results of failure to comprehend a situation; organic disorder with perseverations; confabulations and verbose rambling; dream-like thinking in exceptional hysteria manifestations, monoideistic thinking in times of dejection

—severe inner strife reflected in all affective expression (voice, gesture, movement, direct verbal reports about the emotions), so that the customary capability for affective contact was lost;

—severe manifestiations of depersonalization, such as transitivism, obedience automatism, identity loss, thought hearing, the feeling of complete personality change (not being a person any more); but only when several of the same manifestations are identifiable in the same patient, not when only one of them was in evidence, as sometimes happens without schizophrenic disorders;

—severe catatonic muscular symptoms while the body is healthy and the mind alert;

—delusions of the type frequently found in the schizophrenias but rarely in other illnesses, for example, constant, manifold and disordered relationship delusions without any corresponding mood change;

—hallucinations as they are frequently found among schizophrenics but rarely in other patients, for example, grotesque sensations of irradiation, hearing everything the patient plans to do, etc.

—secondary, severe memory illusions and hallucinations, while primary memory function remains intact.

All our probands had several of these characteristics, and yet the diagnosis was much more oriented toward the entire syndrome than toward the sum of individual symptoms.

Under no circumstances, however, was it permitted to consider the *course* of a psychosis in the diagnosis of a schizophrenia. This demand is an obvious necessity in a study intended specifically to investigate the course of the illness. If I had discovered that a quick cure was a definite indicator for the absence of schizophrenia, it would have been nonsense to plan a set of statistics for the prognosis. It would have been a touchy question, whether very brief conditions of schizophrenic symptomatology, that heal in just a few days, should be included under the schizophrenias (they were described by Rohr [1961, 1964] from our clinic). At the time the probands were recruited, however, no such cases were being admitted to the clinic, so that I did not have to deal with this question.

Difficulties in rendering diagnoses occurred mainly from just two areas. That is, in relation to psychoses of schizophrenia-like symptomatology, which do not become manifest until late in life, and in relation to a clear distinction between the schizophrenias and manic-depressive states.

The nature of the schizophrenia-like psychoses in senility is still one of the least investigated areas in the field of psychiatry. When its symptomatology indicates a schizophrenia, it is still rare that it is entirely characteristic. In addition, because of the advanced age of the patient one must suspect a brain involution, and based on that assumption alone, some misgivings would be felt in the diagnosis of a schizophrenia. The schizophrenia-like psychoses in seniles are furthermore usually associated with loss of memory, and to date no valid standards have been developed for determining in the aged what is physiological and what may indicate a cerebral process that may be the cause of other psychopathological symptoms. No psychiatrist will hesitate to render a diagnosis of a schizophrenia when a psychosis with purely schizophrenic symptomatology breaks out in a person in his forties, without the presence of any indicators of a brain disease; but no psychiatrist would dare any longer to diagnose a schizophrenia in a 90-year-old man under the same conditions. It would appear to him that the specification "no brain disease" would be impossible because of the advanced age. But where are the limits within these extremes for patients between 50 and 90 years old? In this study I excluded the diagnosis of a schizophrenia whenever clear amnestic symptoms were scattered through a schizophrenia-like psychosis. The oldest patient in whom I still suspected a schizophrenia, and who was the last to become psychotic, was 66 years old at the time she was hospitalized.

In respect to distinguishing the limits of manic-depressive states, I accepted the following principles. I always diagnosed a schizophrenia whenever a patient had suffered a phase of schizophrenic symptomatology, in fact, even when purely manic or purely depressive phases had preceded or followed it. Stupor and depressive illusions during depression, excitement, aggressiveness, and delusions of grandeur in mania never troubled me in the diagnosis of a manic-depressive state, and they never appeared to me in any way to be indicators of a schizophrenia. But I did suspect schizophrenia when I found stuporous symptoms with euphoria, ideas of persecution without guilt feelings in depressions, a clear transition from mere memory loss to total absent-mindedness or hallucinations that did not match the mood of the

occasion. These criteria are in fairly common use throughout the field of psychiatry, and hardly deserve any further commentary.

Based on all these (and all other commonly known) criteria, I consider the diagnosis of a schizophrenic psychosis definite for all 208 probands. I am convinced that nearly all Swiss psychiatrists would confirm this opinion. Actually, the diagnosis of schizophrenia for the probands was not only in common and regular agreement with the opinions of many doctors of our clinic, but was further confirmed for all probands by doctors from outside the clinic, and often by large numbers of them after clinical observation in other hospitals. If it was possible to attain such a degree of diagnostic certainty, it was partly due to the fact that Burghölzli was known as a clinic for severe mental cases among referring physicians and the population as well, and that we regarded it as a special and distinct privilege to treat the most severe of them. For these reasons, diagnostic borderline cases were more rarely referred to us for admission than to other university clinics or to private sanatoria, which were popularly regarded as hospitals for cases of nervous disorders, for rest cures, for fatigue cases, or for curing "cases of nerves."

The diagnostic aspects in regard to the schizophrenias are relatively uniform in Switzerland, a tiny country. But among the psychiatrists in Switzerland I belong to that group who adhere to the concept in the strictest sense. It is well known, however, that diagnostic practices in the schools of other countries differ considerably from ours. I must therefore check whether the diagnosis of a schizophrenia of the 208 probands would be the same under the diagnostic criteria of schools in other countries. Obviously I did not accept a large number of patients in my recruitment of probands that would have been diagnosed as schizophrenics by other schools. This holds particularly for suspected schizophrenic neurotics and psychasthenics, for "pseudoneurasthenic" developments. On the other hand, I believe to have determined that the greatest majority of the probands selected would have been diagnosed as schizophrenic by all or certainly most schools of psychiatry. Exceptions were as follows:

1. Psychoses in which the symptomatology of schizophrenic types intermingles with that of manic-depressives may be designated as "mixed psychoses." Some apply the same expression also to psychoses with a totally

schizophrenic symptomatology that run in phases, as do the manic-depressive states. If one extends the concept of such a mixed psychosis, one could assume a mixed psychosis in nine (7 male and 2 female) of the probands. But I do want to reemphasize, all 9 probands had suffered through phases that unequivocally revealed a symptomatology of schizophrenia, and that could not simply be passed off as "manic" or "depressive." Most especially the phase of illness that made them probands was a schizophrenic one, although a number of them had suffered depressive or manic episodes before or after that.

2. In 3 patients (all females) many schools might have contested a diagnosis of schizophrenia because of the late onset of the disease (after age 60). However, from the standpoint of symptomatology, these too were typically schizophrenic.

3. In 3 male probands the first indications were alcoholic hallucinoses, but these gradually developed into chronic psychoses that corresponded fully in symptomatology to a serious schizophrenia. It is conceivable that in these cases some few schools might have considered them as "chronic, schizophrenia-like alcoholic hallucinoses" rather than as schizophrenias.

4. Short-term psychoses with a schizophrenic symptomatology that occur in conjunction with severe psychic traumas are diagnosed by many schools as "schizophrenic reactions" or by others as "psychogenic psychoses." There were 6 (3 male and 3 female) patients among my probands who might have been diagnosed that way.

5. Borderline cases of nonschizophrenic hallucinatory psychoses appeared twice (1 man, 1 woman). They could not be regarded as paranoic in Kraepelin's interpretation of the term, because, in addition to the characteristic systematic delusionary development, there were clearly other symptoms dominating the syndrome (bewilderment, numerous illusions, etc.) It would still be possible that some few schools would regard these as paranoid developments rather than paranoid schizophrenias.

Other schools might possibly have doubted a diagnosis of schizophrenia in at most 23 of my 208 probands. For the remaining 185 probands we may assume complete international concurrence with the diagnosis of a schizophrenia.

In further support, the long-term courses of illness did not reveal any diagnostic errors

either. None of the probands became ill or died of a brain disease (such as brain tumor, a postencephalic morbus Parkinson, or a Huntington's chorea), that would have called for a revision of the original diagnosis during the period of more than 20 years since that initial diagnosis.

Representative Patient Histories

In the following section I shall attempt to illustrate briefly by means of a few examples, for which probands I might assume international concurrence with a diagnosis of schizophrenic psychosis and for which ones a different diagnosis might be preferred by other schools.

Examples of my diagnoses of two cases of definite schizophrenic psychoses that I assume would enjoy general concurrence

Proband 34, born in 1906, is alive at the end of the study at the age of 58. His father (1876–1942), a railroad employee, was a severe alcoholic of dipsomanic proportions who brutally abused his family. His mother (1873–1949) was a capable woman who took good care of her two children (the proband and a sister 4 years older). To outward appearances, the family relationship was normal, and there was no material want. The proband was brought up at home, where he remained until he was hospitalized, except for job-related sojourns abroad. He had been an average student. After high school he completed business school with little difficulty and worked as a clerk until he was hospitalized.

From his childhood on, he had been rather sensitive and difficult to get along with. He seemed moody, secretive and withdrawn. He did not make friends. He seemed to "study" a great deal. Beginning at puberty he maintained an intimate friendship with a girl 6 years his senior that lasted 10 years, without ever deciding to become engaged. He had never had relationships with other girls and hardly ever went out during his free time, but pored over his books. He dressed very carefully and spent a lot of money for clothes. He had to be dismissed from military basic training because of anxiety and fear, and was mustered out as a psychopath.

His psychosis began to creep up on him about 1936, when he was 30 years old. Slowly and with increasing frequency the stereotypic-behavior manifestation began to appear. For instance, sealed letters, ready for mailing, he would open and reseal repeatedly, without any apparent reason; during meals he would suddenly get up without reason or provocation and then sit down again. At first he seemed to remain in control of his senses during such spells, and seemed quite unchanged in other respects. Then he gave up his regular employment without any reason and worked only sporadically as a travelling salesman. At the same time he began the practice of suddenly, out of total silence or in the midst of sensible conversation, to speak or sing a few words totally out of context with the situation as, for instance, "Emperor Napoleon." Further, it was now noticed that he would stand before a mirror grimacing for minutes at a time. From 1938 on he expressed ideas of persecution such as that everybody was laughing at him, and that he heard threatening voices. His thoughts were being "repeated in public" and he was being "tortured by rays." He would scream at passersby from his balcony, or he would threaten to break everybody's windows if they didn't "put a stop to all this chicanery." On one occasion he rang the doorbell of a woman unknown to him, and warned her that something dreadful would happen "if she didn't stop soon." When he began to disturb the sleep of family and neighbors by pounding on the walls, he was first hospitalized at our clinic on October 6, 1938 at age 32. During the interview at the clinic he reported his ideas of persecution with piercing, paranoid glances and stiffly posed attitude. He claimed "an all-out conspiracy of harrassment" had developed against him, and that people on other floors of the building had transmitted to him via the central heating system messages that were at first harmless, but then became abusive. Passersby on the street would make remarks about him, and that was why he could not think straight any more. He believed people wanted to take away his thoughts. He often grimaced or laughed boisterously. He was difficult to approach, but he was able to discuss normally topics that had no personal connotation.

Since that time, this proband never recovered, in fact his condition never even indicated any improvement in spite of intensive personal efforts on his behalf, an insulin cure, and later attempts with neuroleptics. Between 1938 and 1943 three attempts were made to send him home, but soon after each release the same old conditions re-emerged.

During this period of alternating between hospital care and care at home is when the admission occurred at our clinic that made him a proband (October 13, 1942). Before that he had been able to live at home for nearly 2 years, but during this time, he had changed jobs constantly because he continued to feel persecuted and harrassed wherever he went, and finally ended up without employment of any sort. He had never stopped hearing voices. Rehospitalization had become necessary, since he had become inconsiderate and cruel toward his mother (his father had died of stomach cancer in the meantime); in fact, she had sensed his presence as downright sinister and threatening. Compared to his previous stays at the hospital, he seemed "more deteriorated" and even less communicative than before. He was violently irritable, spoke of his mother as "that lousy slut." He claimed that at every place where he was employed people would bore him and "applied indirect and cowardly methods against him." He claimed to be learning through "lipreading and hearing voices" that others were continually talking about everything that he was experiencing. He wanted to renounce his Swiss citizenship and to escape the persecutions in Spain. He complained about sensations in his hair and scalp "as if they were congealed," and that when this was happening he became unable to think. At this point, a perceptible though mild degree of confusion began to emerge, even in conversations about impersonal topics. In the weeks that followed he became somewhat calmer. In January 1943 an attempt was again made to have him remain at home for a few days. He then attempted to escape his pursuers over the border, but, since there was a war, the border was patrolled by the military. He was stopped at the border and hospitalized again on January 27, 1943.

Since that time he has been hospitalized without interruption until the end of 1965. He spent only a little more time at our clinic and has been at another hospital for the past 21 years. In all those years only minor fluctuations in his condition occurred (sometimes he was more irritable than usual, sometimes he expressed his illusionary idea even more crassly than usual, or he would occasionally refuse to work temporarily). He was continually obsessed with his notions of persecution and prejudicial acts against him, and with the voices he heard. He appears eccentric and affected and often grimaces. He affects various stereotypies, for instance, when he washes himself he executes all sorts of strange movements as if he were under a shower. He retreats as much as possible from his surroundings and exists with a bare minimum of human contact. Generally he performs work assigned to him willingly, in the yard or the office, and occasionally he also does translations. Occasionally one can still converse with him adequately on impersonal topics, even though a degree of flightiness becomes evident.

Basis for statistical evaluation

Prepsychotic personality: Schizoid psychopath

Intelligence: Average

Onset of illness: Chronic at age 26

Course of illness: Chronic to chronically residual state

Outcome: Chronic, severe "end-state"

Duration of "end-state": 22 years.

Female proband No. 71, died at age 70.

The patient, born in 1878, comes from a normal, orderly home. Her father (1845–1918) simultaneously operated a shoe store and a restaurant that did not serve alcoholic drinks. In his youth he had been a male nurse in a church-operated, private home for the mentally ill; his strong religious convictions remained with him throughout life. He had poor control over his temper and was given to fits of anger. Her mother (1851–1901) suffered through a mild case of depression

during her menopause, but was otherwise healthy, a good mother, and an efficient housekeeper. The family lived in modest circumstances and maintained close contact with religious and humanitarian endeavors, partly because of contacts of some close relatives (an uncle of hers was superintendent of an orphanage and her maternal grandfather a high-ranking army officer), and partly because of personal inclination.

As a child she was easy to raise, and was one of the best pupils in school. After completing basic schooling, she worked in her father's restaurant, and for one year as a child's nurse in Holland. As a young girl, some clashes occurred between her and her irascible father, who once even ordered her out of the house. But she came back, and then worked in several good jobs as a waitress.

In 1907 she married a man 3 years her junior, to whom she remained married until her death in 1948. The husband was first a warehouse man and then a blue-collar worker. He was fanatically and rigidly religious; in other respects he was a good provider and a good father to his family.

Five children resulted from this marriage, with whom the proband had numerous problems. One died at an early age, one son was a deaf-mute from birth, one became a dissatisfied, taciturn lone wolf, one was justifiably dubbed a "pedantic, religious hypocrite," and one became a case of severe intermittent schizophrenic psychosis.

The unanimous premorbid evaluation of the patient reads: loyal, diligent, and efficient

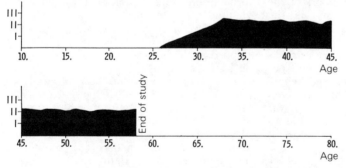

Fig. 1.1. Summary of the course of illness of Proband 34. The horizontal scale represents the age, and the vertical the approximate seriousness of the disease. Mere character changes without psychotic symptoms or clear indications of disturbances in work performance have not been entered, either when they precede a psychosis or when they follow an episode.

Degree I: No special care required, capable of working, psychosis not immediately discernible in association with the patient.

Degree III: Severe need of special care, incapability of performing useful tasks, relations to outer world severely distorted, even in the simplest situations.

housekeeper, warmhearted mother, tender but also strong-willed when the occasion demanded it, happy disposition, receptive to anything that is good, full of idealism. She was pyknic of stature and generally in good health before the onset of her serious age-related illnesses, which will be discussed later.

The illness began during her fourth pregnancy in 1912 with her jealousy-ridden imaginings about her husband, which were totally out of context with her previous nature. During and just after childbirth she seemed normal again.

Five weeks after the birth of her child, however, a peracute, severe catatonic psychosis erupted in August of 1912, after an insignificant argument with a subtenant. One night the proband suddenly cried out, "What's coming over me?" and fell into a rage, flailing about with arms and legs. She kept saying that the spirit of her subtenant "had come over her," and that she was being tormented by Satan. While this condition persisted, she passed water. During the days that followed, periods of calm alternated with periods of illusionary, hallucinatory agitation. During such periods she would shout such expressions as: "There are legions of devils, but they're leaving now. Jesus is the victor." She imagined time and again that Satan had come over her or that one or the other of her relatives had arisen from the dead. There was no evidence of any depression; on the contrary, she often gave in to laughter during her spells of excitement. Intermittently and for brief periods she would appear rational and quite clear. For a month and a half her condition kept fluctuating constantly. During this time she received some care in religiously administered homes, partly in a private psychiatric hospital, and partly, on an experimental basis, in her own home.

From October 6 through November 4, 1912 she was at our hospital for the first time. Her condition before this time was described as follows: The patient had suddenly seized upon the idea that a neighboring pastor had to be summoned, because she wanted to marry him. Despite this, she also wanted to remain with her husband. Without any provocation, she then broke a window and hurt herself in doing so. She spoke disjointedly about a missionary and his hypnotic skills, through which she claimed to have seen snakes. She equated the man with the devil, and saw him with horns.

During her admission on October 6, 1912,

she alternately screamed and laughed, and made unrelated, confusing and unintelligible statements. She claimed her name was Sarah and that she did not know her family name. She said she had had sparrows at the theatre; but in spite of all that, she knew where she was. She would hear women's voices, but also the voice of God and of the Savior. A day later, her patient history records among other notations: "Patient has an exaggerated, histrionic, inadequate manner of expressing her emotions, she weeps while she says she's happy that her husband is at home; her laughter and weeping appear forced, with a rapturous, pathetically exuberant manner of expression."

On October 8, E. Bleuler, director of the clinic at the time, noted in this patient's history: "She slept until 2:30, wept for 5 minutes, and was intermittently noisy from 4 o'clock on, ejaculating: 'Everybody is avoiding me, no, thanks, no, no, I'd sure like to have a beer. Eli, Eli, you darling child, quick as the wind, bally-bally-hoo, sure it isn't true, yeah, it's death'" (spoken in Swiss dialect). E. Bleuler performed a complete examination on the proband on October 12 and summarized: "Highly emotional, erotic, sudden mood changes, stiff, exaggerated expressions, grotesquely theatrical, associations disjointed, minimal intellectual rapport, no information on hallucinations, barriers." He diagnosed a catatonia.

On October 18 the notes include: "Today she lay on her back most of the time, kicked her legs and was totally uncommunicative. . . . more communicative during the visit, she said: 'Now's the time for the Last Judgment, every second one will come to grief. Are you innocent? Where are the spell-weavers? . . .'"

On November 4, 1912 she was transferred to a private institution run by a religious sect. For weeks she remained there in a highly excited state, lying naked in her cell with legs spread wide and demanding sexual satisfaction, and finally beating the door loose from its frame. Without any special attempts at treatment, she began to recover during January 1913 and was allowed to go home. Disregarding the early symptoms during her pregnancy, the entire illness had lasted scarcely 6 months.

Most surprisingly, her condition remained normal for the next 27 years. The proband attended to her household and children in an exemplary way, although these latter were the cause of a great deal of concern. On

November 24, 1918 she gave birth to her fifth child, which turned out to be a deaf-mute; but she bore this misfortune bravely. In December 1939, at age 60, a severe peracute psychosis erupted with the same intensity as that of 1912, without any discernible provocation. The proband would scream for nights on end in the most piercing tones, would yodel and sing in spurts of confused disorder. For instance, once she called out, with false pathos, "Holland, I'm putting the torch to you, Hitler, Mussolini, Jerusalem, Jerusalem! My God, I thank you, you are the hero." (Then turning toward the nurse:) "Nitwit that you are, good God!" and so on.

During the period immediately following, that is, from 1939 through 1942, her condition varied; however, the patient was never fully normal again during this period. She transferred to various psychiatric hospitals, and was at home a few times in between on an experimental basis. Periods of severe catatonic agitation were usually of short duration. During interim periods she was often manic and distracted. It was during this period that she was admitted to our clinic, becoming a proband for this study on July 14, 1942. Once again she exhibited undue excitement, confusion, and vivacious hallucinations during the interview, although she was fully coherent and, interspersed with some confusing expressions, asked pertinent and sensible questions about her former acquaintances at the clinic. Her emotional state seemed "devastated." On the ward she was filthy and required a great deal of attention. But within a few days she appeared improved. As early as July 22, 1942 I recorded in her patient history: "Still distracted, but with good emotional rapport. Troublesome because of her noisy, unruly nature, otherwise good-natured and harmless. Chronic manic schizophrenia." On October 3, 1942, her condition had improved further. She was still hypomanic, but schizophrenic symptoms were no longer in evidence.

The next and final phase of her life lasted from the last release from our clinic on October 3, 1942 to her death on November 7, 1948. Again, it was remarkable that during this time there were no indications whatever of a psychosis, and particularly no signs any longer of a schizophrenia. The proband was mentally completely well, in fact she bore up under her severe physical illness with astounding equanimity and again became the focal point of her family. She suffered from a slowly progressive, extremely severe chronic polyarthritis that rendered her bedridden and finally completely helpless. There then followed a clouding of the corpus vitreum and a detachment of the retina until she became totally blind in one eye and retained a minimum of vision in the other. During a hospital visit for a periodic checkup she was confined to bed, but submitted to her suffering with religious stoicism. She reported convincingly how she managed her household from her bed and was able to think of everything, thanks to her naturally good memory. Her husband and a hired housekeeper did the actual housework according to her instructions. She was vitally interested in the activities of her family and in events outside her home. She had even written a letter to the Commander in Chief of our army, General Guisan, at the time of demobilization when the war had ended, thanking him for having saved the country from war. (There was nothing unusual in such an act at that time; others of rather modest social standing did similar things since they had followed the events of the war with interest and understanding.) She was justifiably proud of his handwritten letter of thanks.

In a letter of May 4, 1946, she replied to an inquiry of ours as follows:

> I have just received your kind letter, for which I thank you very much. Since I have been confined to bed with the gout for the past 38 months and have plenty of time for writing, I am happy to comply with your wishes and let you have some information about my present state of health.—I can neither stand nor walk. —My fingers are partly stiff.—My right eye is totally blind, and the left one has a detached retina and an opaque glass-body (corpus vitreum). My bed is right by a window, which is why I am able to write to you, especially with this bright spring sunshine and all this beauty of springtime that makes me feel so good and refreshed, and that fills my heart— in spite of all the suffering—with ardent thanks to God.—I should be happy to have you visit me, so that you might tell me how those persons I've grown so fond of at Burghölzli are getting along. . . .

Then there followed a clear, precise and accurate description of how to get to her house. Her family confirmed her excellent mental condition from 1942 until her death. After her death, her husband wrote us: "In reply to your kind inquiry of the 27th, I wish to inform you that my beloved wife peacefully passed away November 7, 1948. She had suffered from rheumatic pains for the past 6 years and had been confined to bed for many years. In all that time there wasn't a trace of any sort of mental disturbance. Those who wanted to comfort her always left her bedside comforted themselves. She spent her time writing, reading, and writing poetry. During the last half year, as her strength began to ebb, she gradually stopped doing these things and just waited day after day for the hour of returning home to her Heavenly Father...."

self was to suffer later. In other respects, he was brought up by both parents in good internal and external circumstances. As a child he was quiet and peace-loving, and presented no problem at home or in school. He got along well with his playmates and went along with the crowd. He was exceptionally tall (190 cm) and husky. After 9 years of elementary and secondary schooling he served an apprenticeship in a machine shop.

The first psychotic phase began acutely, as early as age 17, during his apprenticeship. While retaining orientation, perception, and memory, he became totally bewildered. He

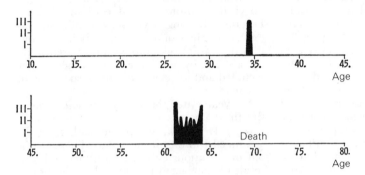

Fig. 1.2. Summary of the course of illness of Proband 71. The horizontal scale represents the age, and the vertical the approximate seriousness of the disease. Mere character changes without psychotic symptoms or clear indications of disturbances in work performance have not been entered, either when they precede a psychosis or when they follow an episode.

Degree I: No special care required, capable of working, psychosis not immediately discernible in association with the patient.

Degree III: Severe need of special care, incapability of performing useful tasks, relations to outer world severely distorted, even in the simplest situations.

Basis for statistical evaluation

Prepsychotic personality: Normal, healthy
Intelligence: Above average
Onset of illness: Acute at age 34
Course of illness: Acute intermittent
Outcome: Recovery
Duration of final residual condition: 6 years.

Example of a schizophrenia diagnosis considered certain by me which might be considered by others a schizophrenic- manic- (depressive) mixed psychosis

Proband 72, born 1922, is alive at the end of the study at age 43. Proband is the son of a master painter and the youngest of three children. Between ages 10 and 12, his father had spent most of the time hospitalized for a psychosis similar to the one the proband him-

hallucinated severely but did not react to it very much. Externally he became conspicuous by inappropriate, stereotyped laughter. From a conversation with him, in reply to the question what he was planning to do, he said, "I've got plenty of work here, I've got postcards." Then he claimed to hear voices; they were saying, "Johnnie and Captain Meier." "They're not following me, I myself know how to shoot. I'll ride in a police car with the police so they can't do anything to me. The police won't do anything to me anyhow, because I know how to shoot. I went riding with the police last night, because I know how to shoot...." The voices, he said, were men's and women's, and he said he heard them saying, "Young Men's Christian Association, I'm supposed to go to the vacation camp at Greifensee."

Two days after this bewildered state had

begun he was hospitalized, but within a few weeks the condition abated under a work-therapy program, and after one month and 9 days he was released and pronounced "recovered." He then continued his apprenticeship, completed it successfully, and worked at his trade in a machine shop. As a recruit in basic military training he had no difficulties, passed the course, and served a tour of active duty as a rifleman with the border patrol.

The second psychotic phase began 3 years later, at age 20, and again acutely. As a result he was admitted to our clinic, and became a proband. The psychosis began after a quarrel at his place of employment, after which he threatened arson, summarily ran away, donned his military uniform without authorization to do so, slung his carbine over his shoulder and rode away on his bicycle in partial military garb. This led to his arrest by the police. (He had been released from active military duty, was supposed to keep his uniform and weapons at home, and had no authority to be in uniform.) When he was questioned about this discrepancy, he answered incoherently that he was "just simply a patriot and a militarist," and that he was on his way to take part in military maneuvers (which was not the case). Once he was hospitalized, he feigned an absurd attitude of indifference. He became vacuously euphoric. Although severely bewildered, at times he seemed merely scatterbrained or slightly distracted rather than bewildered. During this phase he reported about his hallucinations only superficially and imprecisely. They seemed to be less the center of this psychosis than of the first one. He claimed he had been electrified, "but only for a little while"; he heard voices, "but only very softly." Or else: The voices had left him soon after he had come to the hospital. Once he claimed to be in contact with a girl by way of voices. This second phase of his illness lasted longer than the first, that is, 5 months. After that time he had become completely calmed down under a work-therapy program. When he left the clinic he was still in a mildly maniform state, but from the moment of his release, at home, all visible symptoms of illness had left him. For the following 6 years his condition was excellent. He worked at his job and maintained pleasant relations with his parents and friends. But by and large he remained rather secluded and in general did not associate with women.

Six years after the second phase of illness, the third phase set in acutely. This time it was in Denmark, where he had gone for advanced training in his trade. There, without provocation, he attacked a girl and as a result of that act was confined to the Sindssygehospitalet in Nykøbing. I am grateful to the attending physician there, Dr. O. Jacobsen, for the following report:

"Upon admission, patient was hallucinating severely, excited, restless, and threatening. He calmed down gradually, but retained

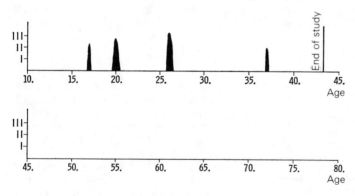

Fig. 1.3. Summary of the course of illness of Proband 72. The horizontal scale represents the age, and the vertical the approximate seriousness of the disease. Mere character changes without psychotic symptoms or clear indications of disturbances in work performance have not been entered, either when they precede a psychosis or when they follow an episode.

Degree I: No special care required, capable of working, psychosis not immediately discernible in association with the patient.

Degree III: Severe need of special care, incapability of performing useful tasks, relations to outer world severely distorted, even in the simplest situations.

many of his illusionary notions; for instance, he claimed to be a member of the secret police, wanted to have a policeman's uniform, and claimed he had to ferret out 'political parasites' to bring them before an 'SS Court'." After a lapse of 2 months, he suffered a period of illness with exaltation, during which his hallucinations increased, he became excessively talkative, but at the same time more autistic and less communicative. Actual contact with him was virtually impossible because he was so completely absorbed in his hallucinations. At the same time he was very restless, this restless phase lasting about 14 days. While being processed for release he hallucinated only mildly, but was calmer, emotionally indifferent, less autistic, with good communication, but did not realize at all that he had been ill."

The diagnosis at the hospital in Denmark read: "Schizophrenia (catatonic?)".

After a 3-month sojourn at the hospital in Denmark, proband was returned to Switzerland. He came back to us at Burghölzli voluntarily for further treatment. At the time I summarized the findings as follows: "Scatterbrained loquaciousness and excitement accompanied by expressionless, vacuous emotional state. Fussy, inclined to argument and minor disturbances, but by and large adaptable and harmless. No further evidence of hallucinations or delusions." Proband remained with us for 3 months without any apparent improvement in his general condition. In spite of that, his parents took him back home on probation, and again, from the very first day, exceptional improvement was noted. The third phase of the illness had lasted $7\frac{1}{2}$ months.

During the next 17 years, until the study ended in 1965, the proband remained completely normal, with the exception of a fourth and final phase of illness.

This fourth phase emerged 11 years after the third, at age 37, and lasted for 2 months. It was milder than the former ones. This time the patient was not treated at our clinic. In his patient history he is described similarly to the way he appeared to us during his preceding hospitalization. The diagnosis read: "Manic excitability with hebephrenia." This mild disturbance soon receded completely.

In the 6 years since his last phase of illness, as well as in the previous intervals of normalcy, absolutely no indications of illness were observed, neither subjectively, nor by members of his family, nor in subsequent medical checkups. The proband worked at his trade in a quite suitable, though modest shop. Frequently he attended courses to improve his skills and to advance his general education, and he maintained a warm and cordial relationship with his parents as long as they lived. He lived with both parents until his father died; then alone with his mother. Since his mother died, he lived in rooms he usually rented from landlords who were family connections. He keeps up regular contact with his sisters. He also has friends and comrades, but relations with them are not very active. Occasionally he had brief acquaintanceships with women, but he remained unmarried. His attitude toward the possibility of a marriage is somewhat resigned, and he indicates that he no longer feels adequately qualified for marriage after his experiences with his phases of psychoses. This large and rather plump man has an air about him that is somewhat sad and rather pensive, and a naiveté that is attractive, rather touching, and childlike. His mother's last letter about his condition reads, in part: "... He prefers to spend his free time in reading the newspapers, listening to the radio, and just taking walks. He is gentle and kind to us, his parents, and his fellowmen. I noticed just one thing, that he is somewhat withdrawn since his sojourn at the institution, and then he once said to me: 'Since I've been sick, I've sort of lost my courage.' Let us hope that he may find a way to get it back."

Discussion of Diagnosis

According to the above, we are dealing with a patient who has suffered a total of 4 psychotic phases. In the first, the symptomatology was purely schizophrenic, in the sense of schizophrenic confusion and hallucinosis. At the peak of the third and most severe phase, exacerbations emerged in which the patient hallucinated intensely, was totally distracted, and inaccessible—in short, he exhibited the classic syndrome of an extremely severe schizophrenia. This was my reason for accepting him as a schizophrenic among my probands. Of course, it is also accurate to say that the psychosis revealed tendencies that bring to mind a manic-depressive state and that, for this reason, it would not have been incorrect to have classified him as a case of "mixed psychoses." These tendencies were: During the second phase (the one that qualified him as a proband) the hebephrenic syndrome was clearly interspersed with maniform manifestations. Near the termination of the third phase, and in the fourth and last, the syndrome was even more clearly manic while the schizophrenic symptoms remained in the background. The illness progressed in phases, not unlike a manic-depressive psychosis, and left no discernible traces on the patient's personality, except, possibly a certain resignation and dejection.

(Psychoses similar to the one this proband suffered developed also in his father and one of his sisters. His father's was manic-depressive, but in his sister's case, the schizophrenia emerged closer to the surface than it did in the proband's. The other sister had intermittent depressions without any schizophrenic coloring.)

Basis for statistical evaluation

Premorbid personality: Normal
Intelligence: Average
Onset of illness: At age 17
Course of illness: In acute phases
Outcome: Recovery
Duration of normalcy: 6 years.

Example of a diagnosis of schizophrenia that appeared positive to me, that might be considered doubtful by others because of its onset late in life

Proband 58: female, died at age 77. (Proband was born in South Tirol, and in order to obtain vital data on her own and her family's histories, a trip abroad had to be undertaken.)

Her father was a truckfarmer and small-scale livestock dealer. He was industrious, sober, and honest, but oppressed by his poverty. The children remember their mother as an industrious, careworn and overworked woman. As long as both parents were alive, family relations were good. In 1890, when proband was 11, her father was killed by a steer. In spite of her hard work, the mother had to place her 10 children in foster care, where they were usually not very well treated. One little brother died of starvation. From age 11, proband was a servant on a farm and received almost no schooling. She was about 30 years old before she finally learned to read and write, but she had been trained as a seamstress. After becoming pregnant, in 1904 she married a man 3 years younger than she was. This man—a tailor by profession—was a distinctly strange individual who cared little about his family, was a flagrant, confirmed philanderer, and often went off on hikes to pick mushrooms or to climb mountains instead of pursuing his trade. Two children resulted from this marriage (1904 and 1908). In 1911 the family moved to Switzerland. The husband, who had previously been accustomed to living with his various mistresses, became a frontline soldier during World War I, and after this absence, deserted the family for good in 1922.

The proband earned the family's living by waiting on tables and sewing, and often had to take the children along to her place of work. In spite of such circumstances, both children (a son and a daughter) developed splendidly. The son finished a trade apprenticeship brilliantly, worked his way through college for a teaching degree and is still teaching today. His marriage is a happy one. The daughter became a saleswoman and was also happily married, until she died of breast cancer at age 45.

The personality of the proband is, of course, marked by her constant, tireless efforts to earn her living and her employment under extremely difficult circumstances. Although she was illiterate until maturity, she was a skilled seamstress and did excellent work. In other respects, however, even as a child, among her siblings she was regarded as odd, difficult, "nervous," and irritable. She complained regularly about her relatives and was —they said—"a tightwad" (which, to be sure, is understandable in view of her poverty). She used to justify her stinginess by some peculiar rationalization, for instance, she would refuse to give her husband a spare shirt for his hikes "because he talked only disparagingly about me anyway." The children also reported the way she would become uncontrollably angry about trivial things, so that members of the family "never felt quite at ease with her at home." Yet, she had a number of diversified interests, attended lectures and was an enthusiastic supporter of one of the political parties.

She was mentally sound until age 60. In her 61st year, her husband, who had not cohabited with her for the preceding 18 years, asked for a divorce, which he was granted. One might have assumed that this divorce, which actually did not change any facet of her accustomed life-style, would no longer have held any importance for her; yet, her psychosis set in immediately after this divorce. At first, she phantasied a love relationship with the attorney representing her in the divorce suit. After the divorce, she developed fits of yelling and screaming. A few months after the divorce a serious psychosis set in acutely. Her daughter reports the following about its onset: "She began talking confusedly and said that everybody had it in for her; they were gathering in the yard. She felt people were stealing from her, persecuting her, attempting to poison her, that she heard voices and shots. She thought that her son was dead, even when he was at home with her. She felt she was being observed and even mentioned that 'secret openings' were concealed in the ceiling from which she was being watched. For nights on end she would poke noisily about the house."

When she was first admitted to the clinic on July 20, 1940 she was mutistic, in that she moved her lips slightly in a peculiarly affected way, without uttering a sound. Instead of extending her hand for a greeting, she executed peculiar trembling, wobbling motions. Only later did she begin to talk. She expressed confused delusions and complained of vivid illusions: that her lips were burnt, she heard voices in the walls, her lips had swollen and then contracted again. The condition alternated between stupor and excited, hallucinatory bewilderment.

Beginning on July 20, 1940, the psychosis lasted another 2 years and 2 months. During this period her condition varied. Part of the time the proband was hospitalized for conditions similar to those already described, part of the time, in better condition, she stayed with her son or, after she had run away from there, in rented rooms. Temporarily she herself rented an apartment and sublet rooms from it. Even in her better moments, "It was just barely feasible to keep her outside the institution." And even then she was restless, often confused and delusional.

Her last hospitalization occurred on April 19, 1942, and this was when she was selected as a proband for this study. She was being hospitalized, because she had screamed in confusion and had yelled abusive language, had lain down on the floor of the balcony and stayed there until she was picked up. She arrived at the clinic as though collapsed into herself, her eyes tightly closed and refusing to answer when spoken to. Her nose had to be wiped for her; she did not do it herself, although she had asked for a handkerchief. Then she began to speak for a time, but in total confusion. Her gestures were rigid and wooden and her whole behavior was manneristic, in typically catatonic form. Often she assumed stereotyped poses, by extending her arms over her head. Without any con-

nection or prompting she would begin frequently to talk of her early home. In the course of several months her condition improved slowly and gradually. On September 22, 1942 she was released to her daughter's home since at the time no more psychotic symptoms were in evidence.

During the period of clinical observation her memory and observation faculties remained intact. The proband had no trouble finding her way around the wards, and was physically in good health. What was most noticeable was that there were no pathological neurological symptoms in evidence. Blood pressure remained within normal limits.

After the last discharge from our clinic on September 22, 1942, the patient lived another 14 years. Never again did she have to be referred to a psychiatric hospital, and she passed as mentally healthy among all those with whom she associated. She supported herself by taking an apartment, renting out rooms which she kept clean and in order. In addition, she dealt in vegetables and maintained diversified interests. Out of purely humanitarian motives she took an interest and became active in refugee aid programs, and also took active part in a political party. A slight estrangement took place between her and the two children, because she disagreed with both her son-in-law and her daughter-in-law; she took exception to the fact that her daughter-in-law principally spoke French.

In 1954–55 the patient was treated for lumbago, sciatica, and arthritis. Her family doctor records her mental condition during treatment as follows: "During this entire time she was quite talkative, and I still remember well how she discussed her childhood, her home at that time and all her relatives, but without being in the least confused. She was very strong-willed." This strong will of hers became manifest, among other incidents, when she quickly returned to her home after her family physician had referred her to a nursing home for her rheumatic condition. She always felt a bit "too independent" to move in with her son or daughter, although either would gladly have taken her in.

Until she died, she fulfilled all her own needs without assistance from any quarter, and she was particularly adept at handling money.

Shortly before she died, she occasionally expressed the idea that people were stealing from her, and at one time claimed that someone was hiding under her bed at night. On

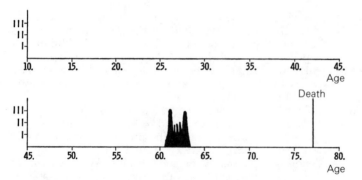

Fig. 1.4. Summary of the course of illness of Proband 58. The horizontal scale represents the age, and the vertical the approximate seriousness of the disease. Mere character changes without psychotic symptoms or clear indications of disturbances in work performance have not been entered, either when they precede a psychosis or when they follow an episode.

Degree I: No special care required, capable of working, psychosis not immediately discernible in association with the patient.

Degree III: Severe need of special care, incapability of performing useful tasks, relations to outer world severely distorted, even in the simplest situations.

June 14, 1956, the venerable, 77-year-old woman was found dead in her bed. There was no autopsy.

Discussion of Diagnosis: The symptomatology of the severe psychosis of the patient, that had lasted, with interruptions, from 1940 to 1942, was without a doubt schizophrenic. There were no psychopathologic symptoms in evidence that would have contradicted this diagnosis, and especially, there were no amnestic disturbances. No neuropathological indications were found, nor was there any evidence that arteriosclerosis or any other physical illness might have had any connection with the psychosis. The only objection that might be voiced against assumption of a schizophrenia is the advanced age of the patient at the onset of the psychosis (61 years). In my judgment, such a late onset is a good reason for being extremely careful with a diagnosis of schizophrenia, but no reason for excluding it entirely. The fact that the patient remained mentally sound for 14 years after the psychosis had run its course, and that there was no evidence of brain damage during this period, are also indications against the assumption of an arteriosclerosis- or otherwise brain-induced psychosis. Her memory, particularly, remained excellent until just before her death.

I believe, therefore, that it was correct for me not to refuse this patient as a proband. It would have been a most arbitrary restriction in the process of selecting probands, if I had set an upper age limit for accepting a diagnosis of schizophrenia. Certainly I, too, am disturbed at having to set a diagnosis of schizophrenia at such an advanced age, but I consider it scientifically more responsible to regard the patient as schizophrenic, than to eliminate her from consideration because of her age; after all, our intent was to gain an insight into all forms of schizophrenia by means of these investigations.

Basis for statistical evaluation

Prepsychotic personality: Strange, exceptionally excitable, (but not typically schizoid)

Intelligence: Within average limits, but low

Onset of the psychosis: Subacute at age 61

Course of the psychosis: In acute phases approaching recovery

Outcome: Recovery

Duration of recovery state: 14 years.

Example of a schizophrenia diagnosis appearing certain to me which others might considered a chronic alcoholic hallucinosis

Proband 71, living today at age 59.

Proband comes from the mountains in the French section of Switzerland. His father and most of his male relatives work in various jobs with the local mountain railways. There is considerable addiction to alcohol among his relatives, including his father, who often mistreated his family brutally. The mother became bitter and irritable. Relations at home, where proband grew up, were unfavorable for that reason. He did well in school, finished a business course, but scarcely ever worked at the profession for which he had trained. He preferred to do odd jobs until at age 24, in keeping with the family tradition, he took a job with the mountain railway as a conductor. He worked at this job for 13 years, until he became ill. He was gregarious, well liked and indeed, was generally regarded as a man more of the heart than of the mind. But he was passive, rather unenterprising, and independent.

He married at age 32, about which event his uncle reported: "The fact is, that his mother shackled him to his wife-to-be. His mother kept nagging him into marrying this girl." The uncle reported further that the woman was "an impressionable, excitable waitress with little capacity for real love." The marriage remained childless.

For years before his marriage, the proband had been a heavy drinker, particularly of beer. When he was intoxicated he was quiet and withdrawn, so that for a long time his problem remained unnoticed. At the time of his hospitalization, his expenses for alcoholic drinks amounted to $\frac{1}{5}$ of his income, that is, about 100 francs a month. From beer he changed over to wine, drinking up to 2 liters a day. At age 37, after having been repeatedly warned about his drinking habit, he lost his job because of his alcoholism. At the same time, his wife succeeded in obtaining a divorce for that reason.

Having lost his wife and his job, the patient deteriorated rapidly. At times he stayed with relatives, but no longer accepted any regular employment. Sometimes while intoxicated he would disturb the peace at night until the police was summoned, from whom he would promptly take flight.

During this period he was drafted for military service, from which he had been exempt because of his railway job. In the service, he would become drunk, lose his way during an inebriation, and was referred to a psychiatric outpatient clinic for a thorough medical examination and evaluation of possible curative measures. To be sure, this intoxication was not the only reason for having him committed; the military physician had also noticed that the patient had been rambling incoherently about "the struggle of the laboring classes and a new world order," and had given indications of some suicidal preoccupation.

When admitted to our clinic he was 38 years old. He was at the time taciturn and difficult to approach, but at first still displayed no psychotic symptoms. Three weeks after admission an entry in his patient history notes that, in spite of his history as an alcoholic, he did not give the impression of being the typical alcoholic, but that he was "emotionally monotonous" and behaved like a schizophrenic. Shortly after that, in the course of a longer examination, he revealed hallucinations, which, however, he did not want to describe more accurately. He claimed constantly to have heard "voices out of the air" for about the past 9 months, during the day as well as at night. They would come "though the air, like electricity." He claimed he had been afraid to talk about this before; that he had heard some talk of having to face a firing squad, and at times he had had the impression that he was being persecuted. He felt that someone was out to kill him, and at that moment he claimed to hear "something like a buzzing or humming sound coming from the bushes nearby."

Shortly after that the patient was referred to a nonmedical institution for the cure of alcoholics, but once there, he soon showed signs of confusion and began again to complain of hearing voices. As a result, he was readmitted to our clinic and became a proband for this project, shortly before his 38th birthday.

At our clinic the proband displayed a gloomy and excitable nature, while apparently remaining in control of his senses. He was still difficult to approach. His orientation was normal, and there were no indications of mnestic disturbances. In his sullen, laconic manner he revealed in response to questioning a number of hallucinatory and delusionary experiences, such as: All this electrical stuff had completely demolished his brain. The "electrical force" has been acting on him for the past year and a half. There was "heavy traffic and a buzzing," and he did not know whether to call this medical technology or medical achievement, and whether it was a new weapon for modern warfare or not (he was admitted to the clinic during the last World War). Day and night he claimed to hear men's and women's voices, saying that this was "the political element." The voices were saying that the country was at war, and that the war was being waged electronically. Whatever else they had to say, he claimed, he would not tell the doctor, that it was personal and besides, the doctor could hear it himself. "The fact that my thoughts are being disturbed is an achievement of this electrical force." He heard roaring noises in his head, and "could hear" the electrical rays coming up from below. Further, he had the feeling that he had become a different person in the past year and a half. Because of the electricity, everybody knew all about him, and he had been "examined via the radio by the divisional court." After one month's stay at our clinic the proband was transferred to the psychiatric clinic of his home canton. His condition was unchanged.

Since then 22 years have passed, and except for a brief interruption, during which home care was attempted, but without success, the proband remained hospitalized in his canton's psychiatric clinic. He is now 59 years old and still there. In the beginning he reported about the same kind of hallucinations as he had at our clinic, claiming to hear voices through electricity, in fact, they were "voices characteristic of the police." He reported that if he moved, his head would begin to buzz, that the doctor must certainly be able to hear the buzzing too. Furthermore, that "the electric pressure from the electrotelephony was set too high," and that since then everything he did was jammed by electrical interference. Voices of a political nature were coming from certain persons, whom he named. Members of the Federal Congress were also addressing him by means of electrical voices. He was never able to rid himself of these hallucinations, but his mood did undergo changes. At one time he would scold and remonstrate, next, he would appear to be freer and more approachable.

One year after admission to the clinic near his home, his father died. The subject was then 38 years old, and did not believe the news of his father's death; yet, he issued instructions for interment, insisting on burial rather than cremation, because this method would help the gravediggers and flower vendors. He seemed incapable of any rational emotional reaction.

In the following period, his pathological experiences exceeded even the previous ones, going beyond merely hearing voices. He felt "transmissions from a young lady by aero-electrical means" and complained about "electricity with flatulence" and "secret telegraphy."

At age 40, phases of the illness emerged in which he became exceedingly noisy and vociferous. Running excitedly about the garden he would scream that he was being treated by electrical rays, and he asked that a certain person should turn them off. Often he became unruly at night, as well. Except for these periods of excitement, however, he still appeared as courteous, gentle, and well-mannered. At this time the impression still persisted that, in spite of his delusional experiences, his personality had remained intact. He still worked frequently in the garden and in the carpenter shop. In the years that followed, however, onsets of excitability increased in frequency, during which he felt himself persecuted by electric currents and the radio, which he attempted to elude. An insulin treatment yielded only temporary improvement. He was in almost constant need of treatment with a number of different neuroleptic agents.

At this time, that is, after his 50th birthday, he began gradually to become more distracted even in conversations of impersonal content. His politeness emerged merely as an external facade, and any meaningful communication became impossible. Influenced by his hallucinations, he often became vociferous.

During the final years (he was 59 at the end of the study) he had to be moved to an intensive-care ward. He became slovenly and filthy, and his principal activity was to write mysterious-looking figures on small scraps of paper. He claimed they were "a kind of stock market quotations," but refused to explain them in any more detail. In conversation with the doctors, he is not hostile, but often distracted, and rather conspicuous by his grimacing and hasty, abrupt demeanor. His fellow patients, however, did not notice anything unusual in his speech, if his personal delusional experiences were not discussed. But the conversations he carried on with himself were totally confusing. He was constantly plagued by illusions, feeling currents running through him and claiming that his bed was electrified, etc. The only feasible work assignments had to be simple mechanical tasks, carefully explained, (for example, folding papers), and to reduce his states of agitation he was given neuroleptics.

Discussion of Diagnosis: Without a doubt, this patient was a serious alcoholic before the onset of his illness. At the beginning, certain symptoms were in evidence that would have suggested the diagnosis of an alcoholic hallucinosis. He was hearing all sorts of voices,

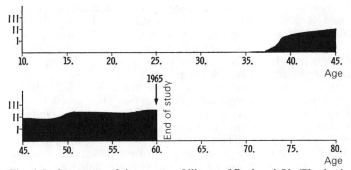

Fig. 1.5. Summary of the course of illness of Proband 71. The horizontal scale represents the age, and the vertical the approximate seriousness of the disease. Mere character changes without psychotic symptoms or clear indications of disturbances in work performance have not been entered, either when they precede a psychosis or when they follow an episode.

Degree I: No special care required, capable of working, psychosis not immediately discernible in association with the patient.

Degree III: Severe need of special care, incapability of performing useful tasks, relations to outer world severely distorted, even in the simplest situations.

including some of a threatening nature. But from the very outset, the syndrome was suggestive of schizophrenia to such a degree that during the first psychiatric examination in another clinic, the diagnosis of an alcoholic hallucinosis had not even been considered. Admittedly, there were hallucinations and delusions in evidence at the time of his admission to our clinic that resembled an alcoholic hallucinosis, but they were only a part of the whole psychopathological syndrome. The emotional incapacity for communication dominated the foreground. The pathological world of the proband revolved more around abstract and abstruse concepts with prejudicial connotations of all sorts and around manifestations of depersonalization than with merely imaginary voices with their implications of persecution. During the years that followed, his condition completely approximated that of a full-blown chronic schizophrenic dementia, in spite of years of abstinence that his life in hospitals had forced on him. I therefore feel that the diagnosis of a schizophrenia is valid.

Basis for statistical evaluation

Prepsychotic personality: Alcoholism
Intelligence: Average
Onset of illness: At age 37
Course of illness: Chronic to the most severe residual condition (atypical in that the hallucinosis was subacute)
Outcome: Severe residual state
Duration of residual state: Almost 10 years.

Example of a schizophrenia diagnosis that appeared certain to me which might be diagnosed by others as a schizophrenic reaction or psychogenic psychosis

Female proband 23, living at age 59 at termination of study.

When this patient was referred to us 25 years ago, at age 37, she had come from exceptionally favorable circumstances. Her husband was a minor civil service employee, there were no children, and she managed a branch of a grocery business that employed several apprentice clerks. The referral documents read, laconically, that "Some time ago she had allegedly begun to suffer from a depressive state. Today an acute schizophrenia erupted which makes her continued presence in the home an impossibility."

The psychosis had developed dramatically: The patient had set out to go out into the street undressed. One reason she gave on one occasion was that she could not help it, that she was acting without volition, and on another occasion, that the Savior was commanding her to do it. During and after her admission to the clinic in 1942, she spoke confusedly about delusional impressions, hallucinations, and manifestations of depersonalization: She told how an acquaintance had given her something to read about superstitions, from which she recognized that she was superstitious. She claimed that she had tried to put up a struggle against it. The Savior had almost always helped her before, so she had begged Him to give her ears so that she might hear. Then she had heard in church, (actually in her hallucination) an entire sermon. Suddenly she had had the ability to sing, but only as long as she had believed she could. She had always prayed fervently, but she was able to produce only moanings. She had listened to herself praying in a foreign language that she was unable to understand. And she had heard voices— evil voices—"... and when I prayed, and I prayed a lot, then the voices would come, a lot of them, and all at once in pell-mell confusion—I could hear them, but I couldn't understand all of them. I listened to the evil voices instead of the good ones." She claimed that the pastor had said something that was meant especially for her, about the living death of Jesus. A voice had told her that she now had to see the pastor to tell him that He had not died for the Lord. "The voices commanded me to go to the pastor and to tell him that. I could not do otherwise or hear anything but those voices." She felt that she had been bewitched and transfigured.

Soon after admission to the clinic the excitation from the beginning of the psychosis subsided quickly, and the patient became friendly, rational, and communicative, although her hallucinations continued. In the weeks that followed she insisted that the voices had ceased. Both she and her husband pressed us for her release, which was granted after a $2\frac{1}{2}$-month hospitalization. As later checkups revealed, however, this early release was a poor decision that might have cost her her life. According to her own admissions later, she had purposely dissimulated her hallucinatory experiences in order to gain her release. During later checkups she admitted hearing raucous mocking laughter in the halls of the clinic while she was being released, although to all external appearances she was communicative, friendly, and contented. At home she continued to experience the sounds of voices, automatized actions and suggestions while performing her work. Among other experiences, she had noticed repeatedly that, though rationally conscious, she would take a sudden notion to dive into the street from her balcony. Hallucinations that followed this urge, however finally dissuaded her. In spite of her seriously pathological mental condition, at home obvious external symptoms of mental disorders were no longer apparent, except that she would at times seem depressed and become unapproachable. She continued to do her work willingly and correctly.

Her pathological inner disturbances ceased 3 years after her first hospitalization ($3\frac{1}{4}$ years after the first changes), and this happened when the patient became aware that, shortly before her menopause, she had become pregnant for the first time.

Physically she had remained healthy during her entire hospitalization. The psychotic syndrome at the clinic had corresponded in every detail to a paranoid schizophrenia.

The precise study of her life history, which was made as part of a checkup for research purposes after her cure, revealed a dramatic development that suggested considering the psychosis as the high point in the tragic marital history of the proband. Superficially her life history was normal and unnoteworthy. Her father operated a bakery that had been in the family for generations. The patient grew up in normal, well-regulated family circumstances with her parents, although 4 of her 8 siblings had died young. She herself presented no problems at home or in school, and then took a training course to become a saleswoman. She was proficient enough to be put in charge of a branch of a large grocery chain, where she employed several apprentices. She married at age 26 a man in a minor civil service position, and since there were no children, she continued to operate the business until she was 40. Both she and her husband were absorbed in their jobs. At the time her illness began, her husband was called into military service, where he served during the war as a border guard.

In contrast to this apparently happy, normal development, however, there were developments in her intimate existence. Her father had been irascible, moody, and quick-tempered with his family, while her mother was tender-hearted, kind, and sensitive. The proband found that "the blood of both parents had blended within me," that she, too, had been short-tempered and mean as well as tender and somewhat frightened. As a child she also suffered from an inferiority complex when she compared herself to her younger, more attractive sister. As a baby she had cried more than most infants. Later she was regarded as hypersensitive and excessively precise in her work. In school and in her job she was ambitious and excessively industrious, and she also exhibited tendencies toward hypochondria. As a business woman she felt that she resembled her father; yet, at the same time, she believed she was too tender, too delicate, and too vulnerable for her profession and longed to be more womanly. A turn for the worse began with her marriage, in that she had hoped for understanding and tender loving-care, but had married a man whose disposition resembled that of her father. He was grumpy and uncommunicative toward her. She felt herself misunderstood and more firmly than ever forced back toward her business interests, while he pursued his occupation and his own interests outside the home. In addition, sexual problems emerged. The husband had had syphilis before his marriage and was suffering from a hypospadias. Because of it he felt sexually inadequate, feared and avoided sexual intercourse, and could not rid himself of the thought that he might infect his wife. He got into the habit of masturbating, which caused his wife additional acute suffering, to the point where she often considered divorcing him. In one of her letters on the subject she writes: " . . . actually I was disappointed from the very beginning of this marriage. . . . He never did satisfy me sexually. Only God knows how often I buried my face and bit into my pillow to keep from screaming out loud. . . . If I took him to task he only laughed at me, or if I threatened him with divorce he would be better for a little while. . . . In the beginning my parents were still living, and I did not want to saddle them with this trouble . . . later I could not break away from my own home, so I stayed on. But inwardly I had effectively separated from my husband. I sought satisfaction in my work and was successful. . . . My husband begrudged me any sort of praise of credit, in fact, he became jealous of the success I enjoyed in my work. He began to rage and scold and then would not speak a word to me for weeks on end. . . . I would cook his favorite dishes, which he bolted down gluttonously and coarsely, like a greedy animal. . . ."

During military service this man became ill with a serious polyarthritis. During the examination a positive Wassermann result was discovered. The family physician informed our proband and asked her to submit to blood tests. Very shortly thereafter anxiety attacks set in; she was afraid of syphilis. She reported a number of times in succession for blood tests, and the doctor was never able to allay her fears. After more than a year she began to consult ministers and quacks for help. Then she became afraid that relations with one of the latter might take an erotic turn. On her way home from a visit to such a quack, a woman remarked to her that it was a sin to consult such charlatans, and immediately thereafter she began to hear confusing voices, and the manifestations of the psychosis followed shortly thereafter.

It is interesting to note how the proband recovered from this psychosis. Immediately after her 40th birthday the patient became pregnant by her husband. When she became aware of her pregnancy, the psychosis disappeared. Since that time she has never again had any more hallucinations nor any other psychopathological manifestations. She was suddenly faced with the multiple problems of raising a son, simultaneously caring for a husband who was rapidly becoming an invalid, and earning a living for her family by operating her business as efficiently as she could. She displayed a remarkable capability for this combination of tasks during these last 24 years. Her son developed exceptionally well and is successfully completing his education. It appeared that the proband's character grew and improved along with the magnitude of her problems. Her bad temper receded and the temptation to masturbate disappeared. Her relationship with her invalid husband improved also, and she felt fulfilled, useful, and happy. She is the focal point of her family and in every sense a true mother.

Discussion of Diagnosis: Life had failed the patient in her efforts to attain marital fulfillment. The psychosis emerged at the time when her matrimonial misfortune had reached its height. The psychosis ended when she became a mother and assumed a maternal role and maternal responsibilities. This much is fact. Whether there is a cause-and-effect relationship between this life history and the course of the psychosis cannot be asserted. It cannot be determined on the basis of a single case. The possibility of it will be discussed later. At this point I merely want to justify why it appeared scientifically worthwhile to me to take on this patient as a proband: The psychopathology of her illness was purely schizophrenic. There was no physiological basis for her illness. The only possible objection to the diagnosis of a schizophrenia may be based on the fact that the psychogenic influences were more obvious and more readily discernible than one would commonly expect in schizophrenias. To reject this case as schizophrenic for this reason seems erroneous to me, since we have specifically set out to investigate whether and which psychological manifestations play a role in schizophrenias.

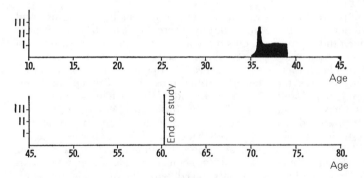

Fig. 1.6. Summary of the course of illness of Proband 23. The horizontal scale represents the age, and the vertical the approximate seriousness of the disease. Mere character changes without psychotic symptoms or clear indications of disturbances in work performance have not been entered, either when they precede a psychosis or when they follow an episode.

Degree I: No special care required, capable of working, psychosis not immediately discernible in association with the patient.

Degree III: Severe need of special care, incapability of performing useful tasks, relations to outer world severely distorted, even in the simplest situations.

Basis for statistical evaluation

Prepsychotic personality: Schizoid-aberrant

Intelligence: Average

Onset of psychosis: At age 37

Course of psychosis: Single, acute-onset episode

Outcome: Recovery

Duration of residual state: 21 years.

Example of a schizophrenia diagnosis appearing certain to me which might be diagnosed by others as paranoia

Female Proband 2, alive today at age 79

Proband comes from a family in which some members quickly attained substantial wealth, while others remained poor. The wealthy ones had achieved riches easily (by advantageous marriages or some peculiar but lucrative business ventures), and some then quickly lost their acquired wealth again. The poorer members of the family attempted to live in the style of the wealthy, or at least wanted to give the impression of affluence. As a result of devious pretentiousness and falsifications on the part of some of proband's relatives, it was difficult to compile a valid anamnesis, some details of which remained somewhat uncertain at best. One of the proband's sisters suffered an acute schizophrenic episode and has been hospitalized for a long time for a severe schizophrenic residual state.

Proband's father is said to have squandered a handsome fortune, according to some sources, on an alcoholic spree, and according to others on poor business ventures. At age 16 or 17 the proband left home. She went into training as a hairdresser and worked partly in this job, and partly in various jobs in hotels. At age 20 she gave birth to an illegitimate daughter. This daughter stayed alternately with her grandparents and with her mother; she died at age 26 of an undiagnosed fever. According to divorce records, the proband was married twice and had no children in either marriage. The first marriage lasted from age 25 through age 28. The court granted the divorce on the grounds that her criminally inclined father-in-law had come to live with the family and had there caused arguments and quarrels. At the time she was declared free of blame for the separation. Her second marriage lasted from age 32 through 42. The second husband had been an innkeeper. This marriage was dissolved because the proband neglected her household, spent too much time visiting cafes and committed acts of financial irresponsibility by making expensive purchases without her husband's knowledge. In this divorce case she was judged to be the guilty party, and the decree stipulated a 2-year abstention from future marriages. Even before the onset of her psychosis the patient made some untruthful, rather fantastic allegations about both her marriages that were easily refuted by the divorce records.

From age 21 on, court records showed that she had been convicted a number of times for a number of offenses both at home and abroad. Most of these were for fraud; others for theft, slander, and verbal abuse. Her acts of fraud invariably revealed her passionate need for personal aggrandizement. She strove ceaselessly to play the role of the wealthy grande dame, and many of her acts of fraud or embezzlement resulted from her inability to pay extravagant bar and restaurant checks, or else she had goods sent on credit that were beyond her means. She had an exceptional flair for concealing her financial embarrassment and for feigning wealth In court she usually pleaded innocence, claiming that she had expected to defray her debts from expected contributions by wealthy members of her family or from forthcoming windfall profits from lucrative business ventures. Until her second divorce, that is, until age 42, her punishments had amounted to a number of small fines or short jail sentences.

By the time she was 50, Swiss criminal investigative agencies had discovered a whole series of offenses involving financial fraud, which amounted to a total of 5327 Swiss francs. And some undetected or uninvestigated delinquencies of similar nature might possibly be added to this from foreign quarters. Hereafter the patient was committed temporarily in lieu of bond to a psychiatric hospital for evaluation. Psychiatrist consultants concluded that the proband was a fully responsible, morally defective swindler. An intelligence test administered at the time indicated an average intelligence level or rather slightly below average.

From that time on, until her permanent psychiatric hospitalization 6 years later (at age 56) she was almost continually in punitive custody.

Her psychosis became apparent during her period of punitive confinement, at age 57, although it seemed at the time that it might have begun some time before that. The patient's last criminal acts seemed in retrospect to be ascribable rather to her belief that she was a wealthy duchess than to selfish, intentional deception merely for the sake of financial gain. But it is certain that, during her punitive confinement, at age 56, she developed a paranoid psychosis which continued to emerge with increasing clarity over the months that followed. As a result, she was hospitalized at our clinic at age 56, and became a proband at that time. After a lapse of 9 months, she was transferred to another psychiatric hospital, where she is still under care today—22 years later; she is now 79 years old.

The psychosis, as it revealed itself before and after admission to our clinic, when the patient was transferred to us from a punitive institution, consisted principally of an absurd, poorly systematized, and not at all logically supported case of megalomania, intermingled with delusions of persecution. Sparse hallucinatory experiences followed. The psychopathological syndrome approximated that of a classic, expansive paralysis. Repeated examinations of her cerebrospinal fluid showed complete normalcy, Wassermann reactions in her blood were consistently negative, there were no neurological indications of paralysis in evidence; and besides, the 25-year course since then proves that there was no paralysis. There was no antisyphilitic treatment; but despite that, her condition developed neither in the direction of an organic dementia nor were there later any discernible physical symptoms of a paralysis.

From the time the patient was hospitalized, she insisted consistently that she was a duchess, a queen, or an empress. Her explanations about the nature and origins of her titles varied constantly and without any prompting. Once she was of French nobility or royalty; another time the "Countess of X," in which X represented a small Swiss town; and again, she was the Duchess of Geneva; as a queen she held court in X; or she was the "proprietress of a castle in Kyburg." On one occasion her "ducal palace" had been in existence for a long time; on another, she had just engaged the services of an "adjutant" or "commander" or "an armed guard" who would have to "get things organized." She would still have to go to France to fetch her crown. She would place her military forces at the disposal of the Swiss Confederation—with the exception of her personal body guard or the palace guard, of course.

Although during the time immediately following her hospitalization she was friendly and talkative, she made no particular effort to make her stories credible. Questioned as to how she had got the idea she was a duchess or a queen, she answered, for instance, that she had simply heard what the keepers at the prison were saying. When she had insisted that certain castles had been the property of her family for many years, she was asked how she could prove ownership. Her answer was: "Of course, of course, I personally heard about it, back about the time they were talking about that colonel who was murdered. . . . " She further claimed that she was being anesthetized with "dirty anesthesia," which was the reason behind her peculiar way of walking about the institution "as if I were intoxicated"; the other women there were "being prepared" the same way. That then the director of the institution came in with friends to mistreat sexually the women who had been "prepared" and "narcotized" this way. She plugged up the keyholes of doors to keep the poisonous gases from entering. Often her speech took on eccentric and peculiar twists, as for instance: "They're saying that in X another throne is going up." The director of the institution was a poor "show-off," who had always run after her before. She was able to recognize his brand of anesthetic by its sharp, pungent odor; it smelled as if rubber was being burned.

During the early period of the psychiatric hospitalization the proband was still candid and communicative. She was able to carry on a reasonably rational discussion about impersonal topics without undue excitement. But soon her attitude changed, and she became excited or refused to cooperate. She became haughty in an exaggerated, affected way and began to use abusive language vociferously if anyone tried to help her. Her excitement rose to such a pitch and she became so tense that physical violence seemed on the brink of eruption.

In the second clinic, in which she has now been cared for for the past 22 years, her megalomania became even more absurd. Among other ideas, she has been insisting for years that she was empress of all the Russians, that she controlled large armies that she would commit if any little thing happened to displease her (for example, if flowers had to be taken from her room because she kept so many that space was becoming a problem). In general she is difficult to approach and lives autistically for herself alone. Her memory has remained intact; there are no indications of senile dementia. She is remarkably well preserved for her age, and splendidly overcame the effects of surgery for an impacted hernia at age 76.

Disscussion of Diagnosis: In my judgment, the delusions in this case are so poorly systematized and are expressed without the slightest trace of logical structure or sensible foundation so that the diagnosis of a paranoia is not justified. In spite of the long-term observation of the proband, neither physical nor psychopathological findings have turned up that might suggest a cerebropathological basis for the psychosis. In my judgment this was a case of late-onset paranoid schizophrenia.

Basis for statistical evaluation

Prepsychotic personality: Self-aggrandizing psychopath, emotionally cold
Intelligence: Average
Onset of illness: At the latest at age 55, possibly a few years earlier
Course of illness: Chronic to severe residual state
Outcome: Severe chronic residual state
Duration of residual state: 22 years.

Diagnosis of the Subgroups of Schizophrenias in the 208 Principal Probands

Subdividing the 208 probands into schizophrenic subgroupings of catatonia, paranoia, hebephrenia, and schizophrenia simplex proves to be largely an arbitrary task, when disease courses in excess of 20 years are being considered. The longer and the better one knows his patients, the more one detects delusions and hallucinations, and the more likely it becomes to indentify catatonic episodes of the type that are marked by either stupor or hyperexcitement, or individual catatonic symptoms in old age. In the majority of cases a distinction between catatonia and paranoia is hardly feasible. Dependent on the phase that is being observed, either a paranoid or a catatonic symptomatology may be closer to the surface and more readily discernible. In long-term observations hebephrenia and schizophrenia simplex are becoming increasingly rare. The silly, infantile elements of hebephrenia begin to recede with advancing age, and if the evaluator knows his patients well, he will find that well-systematized illusions and delusionary structures still emerge in those patients who might have been labelled as hebephenia or schizophrenia simplex by someone with more superficial experience. Certainly there are conditions that correspond precisely and unequivocally, and for decades on end, to the syndrome of pure catatonias, pure hebephrenias, pure paranoid schizophrenias (especially late-onset paranoids) or to pure cases of schizophrenia simplex. But these occur in a small minority among my 208 probands. The great majority reveals a mixed symptomatology and phases of illness of diversified syndromes.

Janzarik (1968), among others, arrived at

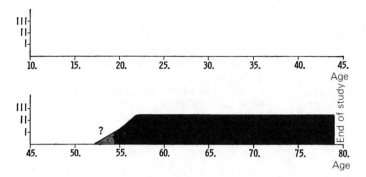

Fig. 1.7. Summary of the course of illness of Proband 2. The horizontal scale represents the age, and the vertical the approximate seriousness of the disease. Mere character changes without psychotic symptoms or clear indications of disturbances in work performance have not been entered, either when they precede a psychosis or when they follow an episode.
Degree I: No special care required, capable of working, psychosis not immediately discernible in association with the patient.
Degree III: Severe need of special care, incapability of performing useful tasks, relations to outer world severely distorted, even in the simplest situations.

similar interpretations. In his descriptions of long-term schizophrenic courses he mentions:

Profiled types ... are not the rule in a given average group of experimental subjects, but rather the exceptions. The characteristic of changeability of the disease courses, not that of consistency, predominates. The statistical typologies that have become current since Kraepelin and Wernicke have fulfilled their mission of establishing order. In the process of studying disease courses running into decades, for the purpose of establishing a form of order in the mass of material on noncharacteristic observations, the types no longer emerge as relatively constant, readily distinguishable entities, but rather as significantly suggestive variations of extremes or as combined forms at the terminals and the intersection points of transitional series.

To be sure, certain other schools have retained the customary subdivisions according to schizophrenic subgroupings with considerably greater conviction than we have. One of the reasons why, in contrast to them, I was not as successful as they in attempting such rigid typification was probably due to the frequent change of environment of my probands. They were often released experimentally, even when they had not fully recovered. Occasional transfers were made from one hospital to another. A number of probands

were treated, at intervals of several years, first with insulin, then with cardiazole or electroshock, and later with neuroleptics, each of which treatments brought about a change in the external syndrome. Contrary to this, patients of other investigators, who were for years able to devote all their efforts to a certain subgroup, without restrictions, were treated and cared for under steadier, more regular, and less changeable conditions. Changes in their immediate environments and changes in treatment methods produced fewer changes in their symptomatology.

But probably another reason was operative as well, and it concerns the method of observation. The probands were not examined minutely for catatonic or hebephrenic symptoms or the formally defined thought disturbances; instead, our full attention was focused on finding out and experiencing jointly with them their needs and desires, their inner experiences, their attitudes toward their families and toward their own past. Through this manner of living an existence in common with the patients, the emergence of interrelated delusions is more readily discernible than that of many other individual symptoms. There are two reasons for this phenomenon. Such individual symptoms escape the observer rather easily if he directs his attention principally toward the conversation, and in an absorbing conversation many of the catatonic and hebephrenic symptoms of a patient are simply lost.

If I attempt to categorize the 208 probands according to symptoms of the most distinctive typology and those of longest duration, I arrive at the following groupings:

	Men	Women
Catatonias	31	39
Paranoid schizophrenias	45	56
Hebephrenias	6	4
Schizophrenias simplex	4	0
	86	99

—to these should be added:

	Men	Women
Schizophrenias with serious manic-depressive manifestations	7	2
Schizophrenias emerging after age 60	0	3
Schizophrenias resembling chronic alcoholic hallucinations	3	0
Schizophrenias that could in time be regarded as schizophrenic reactions	3	3
Schizophrenias that could in time be regarded as paranoias	1	1
	100	108

Collection and Processing of Data Assembled from the 208 Principal Probands

Here are the sources from which the presented investigative results were gathered
—My personal knowledge of the probands as their physician, and that of many of their relatives as their medical advisor
—The patient histories at our clinic about the probands and about a portion of their relatives who had become ill
—The supplementation of our routine patient histories, the compilation of catamneses, and the follow-up of life histories of family members of the probands, by checkups of the probands themselves, by interviews with the relatives, and by written inquiries. These types of supplemental data were gathered continually during the 23 years of the study.

All 208 probands were personally known to me in 1942 or 1943. I had taken an active part in their examination and their treatment. Insofar as the patients remained hospitalized at Burghölzli, or were readmitted after a dismissal, I also directed their examinations, their treatment, and their care. In the process I became personally acquainted with a number of their immediate families, whom I could question about the patient's past or with whom I could discuss their care, important therapeutic interventions, transfers to other clinics, and the like. The fact that I was not only working at Burghölzli, but was also in residence there, contributed to the fact that I kept meeting with patients or their visiting relatives again and again outside the examination or consultation rooms.

The patient histories of our clinic are particularly well adapted to those facets of information that I needed for my investigations; that is, to the exact life histories in regard to origin, schooling, professional training, and social, vocational and familial development. The course of illness is usually described in them with utmost accuracy. Almost never did the data come from a single source, but corroborating facts were assembled from a number of sources. Even family histories were usually well documented. The reasons why and how such a high degree of specialization in the medical work at the clinic was feasible at the time the probands were being recruited have already been outlined.

The routine patient histories of the clinic usually also contain excellent descriptions of the psychopathological findings and their development during treatment at the clinic. Notations on patients' physical conditions, as they were revealed after admission of the patient according to methods in common practice, were entered in every instance. As a matter of routine the results of simple blood tests, urinalyses, and Wassermann tests were entered in the patient histories. When data on physical conditions was difficult to obtain at the clinic, the reports of consulting physicians at somatic university clinics were included.

The completeness of anamneses, however, is somewhat overshadowed by the scarcity of investigative data from other areas, in particular, by the paucity of routine neurological laboratory data. Air-encephalography, electroencephalography, and spinal fluid tests were undertaken only when individual conditions indicated their necessity (the clinic lacked the amount of equipment needed for routine series examinations of all patients). Similarly, routine psychodiagnostic test examinations were not regularly given. Usually only simple intelligence tests were administered, in which education and academic knowledge were compared, a few simple problems were presented whose solution indicated an understanding of relationships (the clinic with considerable success for many years used the reproduction of Aesop's fable of the donkey loaded down with salt), and questions were asked on the comprehension of facts that would have been assimilated by a rational person in his practical life, such as the system of weights and measures. The intelligence quotient itself, however, was determined only in borderline cases. Jung's Association Test and Rorschach's Form Interpretation Test were usually available as projection tests, but by no means always.

The investigations that supplemented my own observations and the routine patient histories of the clinic comprise the major portion of the findings in this exposition, for they were by far the most lengthy and the most time consuming. During the course of 23 years—from the summer of 1942 until the summer of 1965—work on the project was continuous. Naturally, the time allotted to the study varied considerably, depending on my personal work-load, routine duties at the clinic, and other scientific investigations.

These supplemental investigations were always carried through to the point where the previously determined goal was attained. This process of goal setting is outlined below, involving
—Supplementation of the anamnestic data of patient histories from 1942/43, insofar as such supplementation was necessary
—The catamneses of the patients up to 1963, 1964, or 1965,
—Inquiries about relatives
Each of these three sets of data divides into two parts, which must be independently evaluated. For a first part of the inquiries, completeness was attempted and achieved for all probands. The data compiled from them were extensive and objective. The accuracy of information could be checked against other additional information; accordingly, the data are reliable. I refer to them below as the objective and complete data.

But the case is different in a second part of the inquiries. These concern evidence, the determination, categorization, and interpretation of which depend on the subjective evaluation by the informants as well as by the investigator. In part this category involves the reporting of emotions and emotional attitudes, which are by their very nature unsuited to objective evaluation, in part involving reports from foreign countries or out of the remote past (the last century), which are often affected by faulty memory or the possibly dubious reliability of the informant. In many of the data concerning psychological facts, the perception, the ability to report accurately, and the willingness of informants to cooperate were of major importance. We cannot assume any degree of completeness in this area. I shall refer to these data briefly below as nonobjective and incomplete data.

For the supplemental investigations the following goals were established and achieved.

In order to fill in the gaps in anamnestic data of the routine patient histories of 1942/43, the following objective and complete inquiries were processed for all probands:

The living conditions of the probands in childhood, that is, whether they had lost either mother or father through death before age 20, or whether the family was broken up for other reasons before age 20; the progress of their schooling and vocational training and the type of jobs they held, and with what results; how family relationships were changed by deaths, marriages, divorces, and births; how the premorbid personality of the proband was to be characterized in broad terms and whether it had developed pathologically.

The history of a proband's schizophrenic psychosis had to consist without exception of at least the following entries before inquiries were ended: Date and description of the initial onset; living conditions and state of health at the beginning of the illness; course of the illness, so that in every instance a graphic representation could be drawn of its course, that is, accurate information was needed as to time span, in what manner, and to what degree the illness stabilized, when the condition remained stable, deteriorated, or improved; the patient histories from psychiatric and other hospitals to which the probands had been admitted had to be collected, and from them a picture of the type of schizophrenic disturbance had to be constructed; valid testimonies from several relatives, acquaintances, or employers had to be assembled as to the behavior of the patient during periods of his life when he was not under medical observation.

The following types of inquiries for closing the gaps in routine patient histories were nonobjective and incomplete:

Covering the time before onset of the illness: the proband's attitude toward his parents, siblings, spouse, and children; whether the environment in which the proband had lived as a child was rated as favorable, average, or unfavorable; facts about his sex life.

Covering the time after the schizophrenic onset: facts on the development of relations toward members of the proband's immediate family; about their reactions toward deaths, marriages, or births, in that family, toward divorces or other such significant events.

The catamneses of the probands for the periods 1942/43 and 1963/65 encompassed the following objective and complete inquiries:

Precise data on additional hospitalizations and study of the patient histories that were compiled during all such hospitalizations; data that yielded the most reliable information concerning periods of nonhospitalization after 1942/43, as to where probands were living (with what relatives? alone in rented rooms or apartments? in nursing homes? etc.), whether they were gainfully employed (in what jobs? and with what degree of success?), whether they got married, were widowed or divorced during that period? or whether any children were born to them? How did informants close to the patient judge his mental condition? Periodic personal checkups were made on the patients insofar as it was feasible.

The following inquiries for the catamnesis were nonobjective and incomplete:

Relationships of the patients to their next-of-kin after onset of their illness, and especially also how such relationships were affected by the patient's illness (whether they dissolved, remained close, and were such relationships an aid or a burden either to the patient or to the relative?); information about the influence of deaths, divorces, marriages, births and other such significant events on the patients; about their sex lives.

Inquiries about patients' families had to be strictly delimited from the outset, or we should have been swamped with work. I subdivided relatives into three categories, according to the degree of completeness of facts that we were to collect on them. Those relatives, all of whom had to be located and about whom every vital detail was to be acquired included:
—Legitimate fathers, legitimate or unwed mothers
—Siblings, spouses, all children of female probands
—Legitimate children of male probands

Relatives that should have been investigated as thoroughly as the category above, but about whom complete statistics were not available, comprised the second category.

Although I had to be satisfied with less detailed information on these, the majority of them became known, and data at least on their ages, social status, and the presence or absence of a psychosis were noted. They include: stepparents, half-siblings (a few of these were omitted since the proband and his immediate family had lost all contact with them), nephews and nieces (time was too short to gather precise data on every one of their unusually large number), illegitimate children of the male probands and unwed fathers (the latter two were, understandably, frequently hard to locate or to determine with reasonable accuracy).

The remaining relatives made up the third category, but it became impossible to include still further groups, even in a majority of cases. By neglecting them, of course, the possibility of expanding and exploiting other data statistically was lost. Nevertheless, when it was feasible, information on the mental conditions and circumstances of more distant relatives was collected and processed. Such data served two purposes: to make comparisons between the courses of schizophrenic illnesses of more distant relatives, and to gain a more intimate knowledge of the subject's extraction in every instance.

The following objective data are complete for family members of the first category (legitimate fathers, etc.), nearly complete for those of the second (stepparents, etc.), and extremely spotty for those of the third (remaining relatives).

The first step was to locate and identify these family relatives by name, birth date (or date of death), and marital status. When this was not possible from mere statements of informants to any degree of reliability, local administrative agencies without fail supplied the data fully. Then information had to be collected on life histories, which yielded at least the occupations and social standing. The state of mental health was investigated at least to the point where it could be determined whether a psychosis existed or whether the individual had ever been admitted to a psychiatric hospital. If this was the case, patient histories and other related information were procured, until in cases of schizophrenic psychoses, (as with the probands themselves) the type of disturbances had been ascertained, and an exact graph of the course of illness could be constructed.

The following types of information on relatives were nonobjective and incomplete:

Data on schooling and vocational training, occupation and success in it, matrimonial status, character and intelligence, etc. (In part, this type of information on the probands is objective, because information on the probands could be checked and corroborated by several sources, while we had to stop at a single source—or at best a few sources—for this kind of information on some of the relatives.)

As far as the sequence of all these supplemental inquiries is concerned between 1942/43 until 1963/65, only the following seems worthwhile mentioning: A portion of the probands was continuously hospitalized during this period, and a larger portion was repeatedly or intermittently hospitalized. All the rest who were still living in 1963/65 were either personally reexamined, or again so much information was collected during that period that I was satisfied to incorporate such information in the appropriate statistics of the probands, fully confident of its reliability. For patients who had died, I used the data available immediately preceding their expiration. The catamneses up to the time of death or to 1963/64/65 are, therefore, complete for all 208 probands. But inquiries for catamneses were made repeatedly, at least three times for every proband in the course of the 23 years of catamnestic studies. Similarly, inquiries about relatives continued almost constantly during that period, and all members of families were investigated as completely as possible at least three times. A final set of data were procured between 1963 and 1965 on the majority of the relatives observed in the investigation at the same time that the last catamnestic inquiries were made on the corresponding proband. Nonetheless, a number of relatives had already dropped from the investigation in the early period of the study. In the statistics about such relatives, their age refers to the time I last had information about their condition.

How were the informants recruited? Based on routine patient histories, we checked which relatives could most easily be contacted as informants, and from whom the most reliable information could be expected. According to the results of the initial interviews, other relatives were contacted and questioned, until the investigative goals described in the planning phase had been attained. The relatives were interviewed principally for catamnestic data on the probands and their other relatives; then followed a talk with them about their own health and their own life situations.

Former patients and their informants were summoned to the clinic for these discussions. Those among them with limited means were paid travel expenses and compensation for time lost from work, if applicable. If the informants summoned could not or did not want to come to the clinic, an attempt was made to obtain information from them at least by letter or telephone. In some isolated cases, prearranged personal calls were made at the homes of prospective informants.

Many of the relatives did not reply to the first letter sent them. As was learned later, this was usually due to a busy work schedule, or to their being unaccustomed to or inexperienced in writing. Most relatives summoned for interviews did come, if not after the first invitation, at least after a follow-up letter or telephone call. Many made efforts to cooperate and assist in the investigation to a point where their eagerness was touching. With many, a rather close contact was established, especially because they used the interview for medical consultations, for instance, on mental hygiene matters concerning the children of probands. Few of them refused out of hand to give information of any kind, and only two reacted with threats and abuse.

Summoning former patients to come in for checkups proved to be a more delicate and difficult problem than persuading relatives to come for interviews. To be sure, a major portion of released patients were in a regular aftercare program of our polyclinic, our family-care program, or one of my own, and these did not have to be specially invited. But again with others, the possibility of unfavorable consequences resulting from invitations to visit the clinic had to be taken into consideration. Aftercare programs were not a regular service for all mental patients released from our clinic. It is considered most valuable to point out the way toward the organization of suitable aftertreatment and aftercare to those patients and their relatives who want it, but it is equally important that the patient and his family should have the freedom of choice of accepting or rejecting any such advice. I maintain that for some individual patients it is advantageous to sever every contact with everything that—as they sometimes express it—"smells of psychiatry" once they have been released from the hospital. Some patients express precisely that wish. We have also had numerous urgent requests from relatives to cease asking questions about their patients. Before asking released probands who were not in regular contact with us to make appointments for checkups, I always considered whether they might not be sensitive or react with undue excitement with respect to such a meeting, and also frequently discussed this possibility with their families. In order to spare those patients who wanted a complete break from their "psychiatric past," and also to spare the families who might fear unfavorable reactions to such meetings on the probands, I did not insist on personal post-release examinations for all probands. Nevertheless, it was always possible to get reliable and current data on the health of all the released probands who lived outside psychiatric hospitals from other doctors, local agencies, or family members. For probands who were hospitalized elsewhere after release from our clinic, the patient histories were consulted and then supplemented by specific inquiries from those clinics that were treating the patient at the time.

Insofar as it was at all possible, I personally did the questioning and investigations of relatives or families. But in those 20 families that Dr. Uchtenhagen undertook to investigate, he simultaneously obtained data and performed interviews that I required for my investigations. It did happen that I would be suddenly called away for emergencies while in the midst of an interview with some patient's family and in such cases my highly capable and psychiatrically dedicated secretary, Miss Thilde Dinkelkamp, continued the interviews. I could not always make housecalls to families in person because of the great loss of time involved. When they were essential to the investigation, Dr. Uchtenhagen and Miss Dinkelkamp made the visits.

For a realistic evaluation of the facts, it is desirable to have as precise an idea about the scope and depth of the interviews as possible. The figures that follow relate exclusively to investigations for supplementing the routine patient histories of the probands and my personal knowledge about them. For purposes of clinical examination, treatment, rendering expert opinion and care of the probands, as previously mentioned, many pertinent data were recorded in the routine patient histories that make up the foundation of this study. Such data as were collected in the course of routine patient treatment are not included in the figures that follow, nor are the numerous copies of patient histories from other clinics and protocols on conferences with probands' families contained in the dossiers.

The supplemental investigations include 2913 letters written by clinic staff members (mainly invitations to come for conferences and requests for information), 1019 written reports received (usually replies to questions sent in by members of families, doctors, or official agencies), 902 patient histories from other clinics and detailed official records about the probands and their families, 418 family members interviewed in person, whose state of health and personality were simultaneously revealed during such interviews (many of these family members were seen several times), 244 of these were personally interviewed by me, and 104 of them were visited in their homes, 36 previously released probands were reexamined by me for research purposes (omitting those I personally saw in the course of medical practice), and 44 released probands who were seen by other doctors of the clinic for post-hospitalization examinations.

The time spent on the investigations cannot be accurately determined. To a great extent the basic information for this book came from the daily routine work with the probands, while I also reserved a considerable portion of time each day for over 28 years exclusively for this project. During several extended vacations, each ranging from 1 to 4 months, I was able to devote full time to the study. Altogether the time spent on these investigations and the preparation of the manuscript amounted to full working time well in excess of 4 years.

Chief physician Dr. A. Uchtenhagen utilized a 12-month vacation period for the supplemental tests and investigations and for his assistance in gathering data for catamneses. Drs. S. Rotach and A. Hicklin were given leaves of 3–4-week duration for the procuring of data to be used for comparisons. Chief physician Dr. Christian Scharfetter critically examined and edited the entire manuscript, which required considerable (but not measured) time. Primarily Prof. Dr. T. Marthaler of Zürich and Dr. E. Hansert of Munich worked over the intricate mathematical problems in great detail, and many of the difficult calculations were made by Prof. Dr. J. Angst and Mr. A. Dittrich, professional psychologists.

A psychiatrically experienced and dedicated secretary spent about a quarter of her full working time over the past 28 years independently handling the clerical problems, gathering personal data, procuring needed literature, compiling the bibliography, etc. From 1942 to 1946 it was Miss Annemarie von Bidder, and from 1946 to 1970 Miss Thilde Dinkelkamp. From April 1, 1965 to the end of 1969 Mrs. Ruth Frey worked with us half time. She mainly did the work in compiling the statistics and preparing them in their final form. On a number of occasions additional secretaries had to be called in to help out.

The costs of the labor could be defrayed in small part only from the research funds of the clinic. These costs consisted mainly of the salaries of secretaries, the financing of vacation pay for the doctors, and the mathematical and statistical services required. Among many other incidentals, there were compensatory payments for travel and time-losses from jobs to released patients and their families for interviews and post-hospitalization checkups at the clinic.

The Foundations Fund for Research in Psychiatry in New Haven, Conn., through contacts established by Prof. Dr. F. C. Redlich, and the Gertrude-Rüegg Foundation in Zürich, arranged through Dr. A. Haemmerli-Steiner, have assumed by far the largest portion of these expenses. An anniversary grant from the University of Zürich made credits available to cover the costs of the mathematical-statistical services.

Collection of Supplemental Research Material for Comparison with Data on the 208 Principal Probands

The investigations reported here are principally concerned with manifest schizophrenias. The frequency of these among family members of schizophrenics is compared with their frequency among the normal population. It may be assumed, however, that there are latent schizophrenias as well. Whether such latent schizophrenias, which cannot be readily identified by the behavior of, or in conversation with the patient, can be diagnosed with the aid of projection tests is open to debate. Therefore, the investigator faces the task of examining the family members of schizophrenics as well by means of projection tests. But it is not enough to determine how often findings suggestive of schizophrenia may show up in projection tests administered to relatives of schizophrenics. Rather, the frequency of such findings in the relatives of schizophrenics must be compared with that among the normal population.

Dr. Uchtenhagen, chief physician of our clinic, chose to deal with this specific problem. He tested 122 family members of 17 of my probands with Rorschach's Form Identification series. For comparison purposes he used 98 family members of geriatric patients from our clinic. His investigations are contained in the German original of this volume as a separately authored chapter.

In performing my own investigations I did not make use of any of the systematized methods of serial investigations that employed psychodiagnostic tests, although a number of the probands and many members of their families were examined by such tests. I used the results of these only for cross-checking the clinical evaluations of individually tested patients, and did not include them in statistical evaluations. When I did apply them, I used principally Jung's Association Test, developed at our clinic, and the Form Interpretation Test which Rorschach himself had introduced at our clinic. Hamburg–Wechsler style intelligence evaluations were more rarely used, and other types of tests were used only in exceptional cases.

According to my scientific judgment, schizophrenic psychoses (and many other personality disorders) must be studied primarily by clinical means, and not through examinations using tests. I maintain that such disorders are most readily and reliably recognized and understood in their uniqueness, from examinations based on the medical interview, a record of the patient's ability to deal with life, and clinical observations. Some schools have, to be sure, attempted to evaluate schizophrenic life by means of psychodiagnostic tests, expecting that tests could objectively perform that task, could size it up in precise figures and thereby elevate schizophrenic investigation to an "exact science." I am not of the opinion that any such attempts have as yet succeeded, nor that they may have a chance of succeeding in the future. On the other hand, it is true that projection tests (and they alone are what I am discussing) always reflect something personal, and with schizophrenics often something pathological. What they really do yield are some indications that there is an inner existence, but not necesarily that which is actually being experienced. Every personality is multifaceted, and its own ways of functioning, of thinking, and of feeling are multifarious. Some of these are revealed in a projection test, but most frequently others are operative that actually determine the true course of the person's life. In my opinion (I shall discuss this at the end) a schizophrenic existence is not alien to healthy individuals and is not brought on by a pathological process. Instead, it is a manner of living that can surreptitiously impose itself on any healthy individual. The schizophrenic is not ill because he lives and experiences life in a new and different way, but because his inner thoughts find expression in his daily life, while those of the nonschizophrenic remain hidden. Schizophrenia could be detected only by a test that reveals which life potentials are actually being lived out, and that is precisely what projection tests cannot fully accomplish; they merely show what facets could possibly be influencing a person's external existence. Whether these theories are true or false, one fact is certain. Neither diagnoses nor treatment procedures of schizophrenics can be determined on the basis of examinations by tests, but only on the basis of clinical examinations. A goodly number of normal, healthy people would appear as schizophrenics in projection tests, and vice versa.

For all these reasons the close studies of the disease courses and the family histories seem far more important than those of projection tests. In spite of this, however, I regard the projection test as interesting for the study of schizophrenia—if its meaning is properly understood. It seems to me to be improperly understood when attempts are made to convert immeasurable quantities into measurable ones, when it is presumed that a personality in its entirety can be regarded simply as the sum of its individual parts, or when the attempt is even made to draw significant conclusions about the course of a life from the solution of a test question. But among many others, one important question in conjunction with testing methods seemed to deserve study, and it was precisely the one involving the correlation between schizophrenia-like interpretations from tests and being schizophrenic in real life, where the family members of schizophrenics were concerned. How often do they, in fact, correspond, and how often do they differ? What is the significance when they differ? Is there a preponderance of schizophrenia-like indications from projective tests among the relatives of schizophrenics? Can something generally applicable be inferred with respect to the natural tendencies or life experiences from the consistency of schizophrenia-like test results as between schizophrenics and their mentally normal relatives? Or are schizophrenia-like test results among the relatives of nonschizophrenic patients as frequent as they are among the

relatives of schizophrenics?

For statistics with regard to the frequency of parent loss in childhood or premature disruption of the family, no comparative material was available concerning similar conditions among the normal population. Drs. S. Rotach and A. Hicklin gathered suitable data from interviews of 1508 draftees; reports of the investigations appear in the chapter on broken homes.

In processing statistics on premature loss of parents, new, time-consuming, large-scale investigations became necessary for two reasons: (1) Comparability of our representatives of the normal population with the schizophrenic probands was inadequate. By adding more experimental groups of schizophrenics that could be better equated with the representatives of the normal population, we hoped to gain new insights. (2) It had been noticed that schizophrenic women had more often lost their parents prematurely than schizophrenic men. This difference between the sexes that had turned up among the principal probands was at first statistically insignificant. Proof had to be secured as to whether these differences were actual or dependent on chance. This was the reason for wanting larger experimental samplings, and as a result, additional groups of schizophrenics were investigated for their childhood circumstances. Mrs. Ruth Frey went over the patient histories for relevant information, and Dr. A. Hicklin and I, with her cooperation, worked on the additional data and on the processing and formal incorporation of the findings. These additional data were assembled from the dossiers of 744 schizophrenics. Most of these were at Burghölzli, and a small portion of them were under treatment at other clinics.

In the family-histories of my 208 probands, their like-sexed relatives were more often schizophrenic than their opposite-sexed relatives, but this finding, too, lacked statistical significance. To achieve a better ratio for comparison, 895 patient histories of schizophrenics other than the principal probands were examined with regard to this same question. To a large extent they were the same patient histories mentioned above, as well as information on 239 schizophrenics who were hospitalized at Burghölzli on the key-dates May 31 and June 11, 1965. Mrs. Frey and I did the processing.

Current knowledge about the stepparents of schizophrenics is still sparse. The principal schizophrenic probands had very few stepparents, and information on these was to be cross-checked with additional stepparents, a task which Dr. H. E. Gabriel undertook. In the process of looking over 267 patient histories of schizophrenics, he found 48 stepparents. He investigated the mental health conditions and life-styles of these 48 additional stepparents and, in turn, that of their parents and siblings. Mrs. Frey did the supporting secretarial work for him.

Little is presently known about the half-siblings of schizophrenics that can be regarded as certain, although the data on half-siblings would be valuable for theoretical studies. Therefore, the findings concerning half-siblings of the 208 principal probands were supplemented by taking two samplings, 10 years apart, of all half-siblings of schizophrenics at Burghölzli (a total of 100) for the investigation. These investigations were done by Dr. K. Vogt and Miss Dinkelkamp.

There are many more unmarried probands than there are unmarried people in a corresponding group among the normal population. A check was attempted to determine whether the same thing held true among other groups of schizophrenics being admitted to Burghölzli. To accomplish this, a set of statistics was procured concerning the marital status of all schizophrenics admitted to Burghölzli in 1962 and 1963 (there were 660, all of Swiss nationality).

Certain data discovered about the schizophrenic probands gave rise to the supposition that there were more psychotic seniles among their parents and siblings than there were among the normal population. To check this hypothesis, Dr. Rosmarie Nagel of our clinic in 1969 investigated the state of mental health of 169 children of 73 patients with senile psychoses.

Previously Published Papers of the Clinic Suitable for Comparison with the Findings of This Project (see Table 1.3)

The best possibilities for comparison between the long-term-course-of-illness information and that concerning the families of the 208 schizophrenics of this study are offered by my 1941 monograph "Krankheitsverlauf, Persönlichkeit und Verwandtschaft und ihre gegenseitige Beziehungen" (Disease Course, Personality and Kinship of Schizophrenics and their Mutual Relationships). I refer to the experimental subjects used for such comparisons briefly as the "Pfäfers Untersuchungsgut" (Pfäfers probands). The pro-

bands of this investigative material are 100 schizophrenic patients that were being treated at the St. Gallen Sanatorium of St. Pirminsberg in Pfäfers between 1933 and 1936. They were selected from among a number of new admissions and hospitalized cases by pure chance and at random (57 of them were admitted during the planning phase of the study, and 43 had already been hospitalized). Since at the time I was Chief Physician and in charge of the men's ward, most of the group were men (92, and 8 women). Most of the probands (75) lived in the Swiss canton of St. Gallen, and the rest (except for 1 alien) in the neighboring cantons (14), in other cantons, and in the adjacent principality of Liechtenstein (10). By far the largest representation within the Canton of St. Gallen was from the highlands and the Rhine Valley, with relatively few from the City of St. Gallen.

The population from which the Pfäfers probands had been recruited was accordingly quite different in origin from that of the 208 probands of this study. The major part of it came from the rural and mountainous regions nearby. The proportion of Catholics was much larger than among my present probands. Their economic circumstances were considerably lower. During the decades preceding my investigations a large portion of this population had enjoyed an excellent source of income in addition to their farming occupations by doing embroidery, in which both men and women engaged with considerable diligence and astounding artistic skill. Then the embroidery business completely collapsed. Large portions of the populations became impoverished and had to revert to small-scale farming, mining, or odd jobs to eke out their existence. The people were embittered about their undeserved catastophe. Still, most of the probands were not entirely without means; they were simply not affluent. The circumstances from which they came were not those of abject poverty.

The diagnosis of a schizophrenia was determined according to criteria similar to those of this study.

Processing the findings differed in the fact that investigative data for the Pfäfers probands included not only next-of-kin, but also a number of more distant relatives, so that information on over 8,776 relatives was collected in Pfäfers. Of these, 200 were parents, 492 siblings, and 62 children and grandchildren (all those in these categories were thoroughly investigated). In addition, at that time absolutely all of the 464 unselected nephews and nieces were completely covered. Furthermore, the Pfäfers studies included also material on the siblings of the parents, their offspring (4,061 persons), grandparents, and the siblings of grandparents and, in turn, their offspring (2,460 persons), as well as several other categories of relatives, none of whom had been investigated in the present study. On the other hand, the findings from Pfäfers contained only brief catamneses covering the few years during which they were being compiled. The anamneses of the Pfäfers probands in respect to premorbid personality, onset, and course of the schizophrenia, were again treated and recorded in the same way as they were in the present investigations. The premature loss of parents was not considered in the Pfäfers investigations.

Some remarkable correlations emerged in the comparisons between courses of illness among the interrelated schizophrenics of the Pfäfers probands. In an effort to augment the data on this phenomenon, the schizophrenics who had schizophrenic relatives and who were hospitalized at the Basel University Clinic of Friedmatt were added to the study. These schizophrenic patients and their schizophrenic relatives constituted a total of 116. Their disease courses were categorized and compared.

Furthermore, I was able to procure additional material for comparison from American sources, which I had been permitted to collect at the former Bloomingdale Hospital in White Plains, New York (presently the Westchester Division of the New York Hospital) during 1929/30. Henceforth I shall refer to it briefly as the New York material; it was published in 1930 and 1931. The probands were schizophrenics admitted to Bloomingdale Hospital in 1929/30. In this group also males predominated (68 men and 32 women), and again because I was working at the time on the men's ward. Principally they were American citizens, and for the most part from urban communities. As a private institution, Bloomingdale Hospital dealt principally with patients of financial means and intellectual backgrounds. I determined the diagnosis of a schizophrenia at that time, too, according to the same standards that I do today.

Included in that study were 2,634 relatives, of whom 200 were parents, 351 siblings, 31 children and grandchildren, 128 nephews and nieces, 1,310 siblings of parents and their offspring, 467 grandparents and their off-spring, and 147 other relatives. The anamneses and the family investigations in cross section were processed in the way as they are now. In 1938 Dr. Cheney, then director of the clinic, made available to me the catamneses of these 100 patients that could be applied to that data in the monograph on the Pfäfers probands. These catamneses were 8 years old, and had been collected by different doctors and from different viewpoints than those of the present investigation.

In 1941 I published investigations on all 89 schizophrenics who had been subjected to an insulin cure at the Basel Psychiatric University Clinic of Friedmatt between 1936 and 1941. Most of these patients had come from the population of Basel-City, that is, from a medium-size city whose population was principally engaged in industry and trade and, at the outset of the investigations, was suffering from an economic crisis, yet was not starving. The principal criteria determining admission for treatment were an acute onset, brief duration of the phase of illness at the time while intensive care was indicated, and a good state of physical health.

In a paper on syndromes involving late-onset schizophrenia (which comprehensively covered the existing literature), I reported in 1943 about 130 late-schizophrenics and their relatives. Of these, 61 had already been included in the previously mentioned investigative groups. Added as new material were 69 late-onset schizophrenics from the Basel University Clinic of Friedmatt. These represented approximately the late-onset schizophrenics of the entire population of Basel that was hospitalized in 1941. Of 65 of these late-onset schizophrenics, all 264 siblings and 130 parents were investigated.

In 1932 I published a compilation on psychiatric diseases among the average population of the rural area around Basel. As probands 200 non-selected cases of physical disorders were studied, who had been in a hospital geared mainly to surgical and some internal cases. In addition to the probands themselves, all their 1,111 siblings and 400 parents were included in the study. They belonged to a rural population that made its meager but adequate living mainly in small-scale farming supplemented by some cottage industry and partly also in industry itself. At the time, this population was suffering severely from the economic crisis.

In 1935 I published an investigation, together with Rapoport, on the mental disorders of 100 tubercular patients and all of their 479 siblings and 199 parents (one unwed father remained unknown). The patients were selected in 1933/34 from inmates of the Wald Sanatorium in Zürich. They were principally tubercular patients of average severity from the entire Canton of Zürich. The tubercular patients themselves, and to a lesser degree their relatives, for various reasons did not necessarily represent the average population in relation to psychiatric illness. Still, there are reasons for assuming that these tubercular patients, and particularly their relatives, were mentally disturbed as frequently as were members of the average population. At any rate, it was the only investigation in the Canton of Zürich that would permit some careful estimates on the expectations of psychiatric illness among the average population. The relative ages of the tubercular patients of that investigation did not vary appreciably from those of the schizophrenic probands of this investigation.

In 1955 I published findings on 50 alcoholics each at Burghölzli and from the Payne Whitney Clinic in New York. They are likewise suitable for certain comparisons with existing data.

Table 1.3 compares the essential characteristics of my various investigations of different groups of schizophrenic probands and of representatives of corresponding average populations, with one another. It aims to make clear in what respects the data lend themselves to comparisons. In addition, the problems inherent in these methods of comparison will be discussed in subsequent chapters.

Individual sections have incorporated the results of investigations from our clinic, processed according to the same clinical aspects, on the long-term disease courses of other than schizophrenic illnesses. They include papers by Ernst (1959, 1964), K. and C. Ernst (1965), Ernst, Kind and Rotach-Fuchs (1968) on neurotics, by Angst (1966) on depressives, and by Willi (1966) on patients with organic deliria and states of semi-consciousness.

In addition I suggested topics for four dissertations that aided in procuring figures for comparison with the investigations presented here. To be sure, only three of these were carried out under my continuous supervision, while material for the fourth came, in the main, from other clinics, the details of which concerning methods of assembling materials for this paper were not sufficiently familiar to me. All four of these dissertations

concerned mainly problems of early parent loss and premature separations from families of late-onset schizophrenics. The section on the broken home deals with this problem in detail; therefore, it is mentioned only in brief summary form here:

Huber (1954) selected for his investigation 100 schizophrenics (60 male, 40 female), who were on the general ward of our clinic during the winter of 1953/54. He eliminated those about whose past no reliable informants could be located, such as the aged and aliens. His investigations were concerned with premature loss of parents, premature dissolution of the home, and a summary descriptive statement of the general environment during childhood.

Doris Morf (1962) began with 300 copies of expert opinions from our clinic that had been issued to official agencies in the years 1942/44. Most of these opinions had been requested for determining the need for court commitment of the patient; a smaller portion concerning mental competence, and divorce cases citing mental illness as causes, and only very few others for other reasons. Those expert opinions of ours are well suited to family and anamnestic studies, since they contain essentially facts about close family members, and cover rather carefully the patient's previous history. Sixty-five of Morf's (1962) probands were schizophrenics (35 men and 30 women); the rest suffered from a variety of other mental disorders. Her method of inquiry was the same as that of Huber (1954), except that in addition she attempted to find indications of the subjective attitudes of the adult probands toward their parents.

Illberg (1961) selected 100 patients who had been hospitalized in each of three clinics in the USA and ours, without distinguishing between the sexes. He checked for the frequency among them of broken homes, using the same method of inquiry as Huber.

Rubeli (1959) chose 102 schizophrenics (59 women, 43 men) as probands, who had in part been admitted to the Breitenau Psychiatric Clinic at Schaffhausen between 1930 and 1945, and in part had already been hospitalized there when he began his study. In selecting his probands the decisive factor was an assured diagnosis and easy access to precise anamneses. Rubeli (1959) not only studied the frequency of the broken home, but especially also the catamneses up to 1957. She made comparison studies involving the broken home, family data, and the course of illness.

Papers of Other Investigators

The exposition here presented is intended to contain mainly the reports of my own investigations and—incidentally—the incorporation of these results of investigations into a theory on the nature of schizophrenia. A systematic listing of pertinent literature is not intended. Purposely, only such literature as was specifically needed to compare these investigative results with those of other authors was selected.

Yet, as a matter of course, the plan of the investigation, the line of questioning, the interpretation of findings and their incorporation into a unified concept are all based upon a thorough, multifaceted study of the existing schizophrenia literature over a period of decades. On a portion of these extensive papers my colleagues and I have reported in summary articles, which include:

(a) The papers published between 1933 and 1941 on the incidence of mental disorders among the relatives of schizophrenics, other mental patients, and the general population, I have summarized and discussed in *Fortschritte der Neurologie, Psychiatrie und ihrer Grenzgebiete* (Progress in Neurology, Psychiatry, and allied Fields) and, in the process, consulted 198 other studies.

(b) In the monograph "Krankheitsvertauf, Persönlichkeit und Verwandschaft Schizophrener" (Course of Illness, Personality and Kinships of Schizophrenics) (1941) I consulted a portion of the available literature (107 papers) concerning the subject in greater detail.

(c) In 1951 I attempted to make a survey of all the literature published on schizophrenia between 1941 and 1950. But even then the literature was so vast that it was impossible even to approach any degree of completeness. Nevertheless, I discussed some 1,101 papers on schizophrenia from that period in *Fortschritte der Neurologie, Psychiatrie und ihrer Grenzgebiete* in 1951.

(d) The problem of reporting on large and significant parts of the total international field of schizophrenia research was undertaken by Benedetti, Kind, and Mielke from our clinic. Their reports covered periods from 1951–1955, 1956–1961, and 1961–1965, and were published in *Fortschritte der Neurologie, Psychiatrie und ihrer Grenzgebiete* in 1957, 1962 and 1967.[8] In connection with the published material of 1962 and 1967, Angst (1969) discussed in summary form what was available on "Die somatische Therapie der Schizophrenie," (Somatic Therapy of Schizophrenia). This paper, refuting a journal article on the topic, appeared in *Sammlung psychiatrischer und neurologischer Einzeldarstellungen* (Collection of Psychiatric and Neurological Presentations) published by Georg Thieme in Stuttgart. I had consulted all this literature in detail, insofar as it pertained to the inquiries of the present study.

(e) I paid special attention to the literature on questions involving endocrinology, as well as to that which dealt with the endocrine functions of schizophrenics, and that which discussed the psychopathology of endocrine disorders (the latter subject is important for problems involving schizophrenia in that it inquires into the possibility of endocrine disorders being the cause of schizophrenias). In a summary discussion in the *Zentralblatt für die gesamte Neurologie und Psychiatrie*, in my monograph *Endokrinologische Psychiatrie* (Endocrine Psychiatry) in 1954 and my article bearing that title in *Psychiatrie der Gegenwart* (Psychiatry Today) in 1964, a total of 3,377 papers are discussed of which about one tenth deal with problems of schizophrenia.

In spite of the great effort I put forth attempting to cover this immense volume of multifaceted literature, I must still point out some gaps and one-sided partiality in my own knowledge of the existing literature. It is, for example, one-sided in that it is oriented, from the standpoint of the clinic, on psychopathology, on the course of illness, on the family histories and on the physiological findings, which means, toward the medical and biological aspects of the problem. The philosophical literature is insufficiently covered. Schizophrenia research by sociologists and nonmedical psychologists that is not published in medical journals received very little attention. Contributions on the problems of psychoanalysis are well represented, insofar as they were published in journals devoted to psychiatry or psychosomatics; on the other hand, they are poorly represented if they appeared exclusively in psychoanalytic journals.

I experienced some regrettable limitations in my studies of the literature because I did

---

8. In the last of these summary reports colleagues from the Psychiatric University Clinic at Basel also made significant contributions: G. Benedetti, formerly of Burghölzli in Zürich, Johannson, presently in Helsinki, Verena Wenger, and Galli from Milan.

not have adequate knowledge of foreign languages. I was able to read efficiently only those papers that were originally written in German, English, or French, and with some considerable effort the Italian ones as well. But for a large number of very important papers in other languages I had to depend on summaries, reports, or reviews, as was the case with papers in Dutch, Japanese, Yugoslavian, Polish, Portuguese, Russian, the Scandinavian languages, Spanish, Turkish, and Czechoslovakian. Some of these that were particularly vital to my work, of course, I had translated for my use.

2 The Childhood Backgrounds of Schizophrenics

Mental Disorders among the Parents of Schizophrenics

Four unwed fathers of female probands remained unknown; accordingly, all tabulations in this chapter refer to 412 instead of the actual 416 parents of the 208 probands.

Schizophrenias

The same criteria as those used for the diagnoses of the probands themselves were applied for the diagnoses of schizophrenias in the parents of the probands.

Among the 412 parents, 19 positively and 9 very probably suffered schizophrenic psychoses (see Tables 2.1 and 2.2). In 26 cases the schizophrenic parent was married to a nonschizophrenic. One father was a probable schizophrenic and his wife a positive schizophrenic. In another set of parents, the father was a positive schizophrenic while his wife at times shared his delusions of having been poisoned, although this woman was not counted among the schizophrenic parents. Her psychosis appears in Table 2.2 under "Induced delirium."

The reasons for uncertainty as to the diagnosis in 9 of the parents are as follows: Eight of these parents had already expired in 1942 at the time the investigations got under way, without ever having been hospitalized in a psychiatric clinic; but we had obtained such vividly accurate descriptions of their behavior from relatives that this diagnosis is highly probable. These descriptions are briefly summarized in the footnotes to Tables 2.1 and 2.2. The ninth of the parents with probable schizophrenia was a father who was treated at our clinic shortly before he died; but at the time he was such a severe case of senile dementia, that an examination for schizophrenia was no longer possible. In his case also we were dependent on statements by relatives.

In accordance with the customarily acceptable views on the rapid decline of the probability of schizophrenic symptoms after age 40, one can hardly expect that, at the conclusion of the studies (1964/65), new onsets of schizophrenia would still occur among these parents, and certainly not among many of them. At the time, 399 of the 412 parents had

passed their 40th birthdays (among the 13 parents that died before age 40, the youngest death was at age 28). Most of the parents, however, (323) were over 60 years old at the conclusion of the study without ever having suffered a schizophrenia, and 84 of them even survived their 80th birthday without any indications of it. Under these circumstances it is hardly possible that the percentage of schizophrenics found among all parents should differ appreciably from that percentage of all parents which would result if and when the fate of all parents with respect to the onset of schizophrenia had been fulfilled, that is, if one were to add to the existing cases of schizophrenia before 1964 those rare eruptions of the disease which might break out in old age. In the calculations on the frequency of schizophrenia among the parents of our probands, therefore, no corrections for age have to be undertaken. The so-called raw percentage figure (the percentage of schizophrenics among all parents) will agree almost exactly with the onset-probability figure for schizophrenia (percentage of the diagnosed and still-to-be-expected cases of schizophrenias among all parents). Although there is no significant difference between the two figures, I list below not only the raw percentage figures, but also the onset-probability statistics calculated according to the old Weinberg method.[1] This is advantageous because the

---

1. The percentage figure, corrected for age, was obtained in the customary way, according to Weinberg's method: The number of schizophrenic parents was compared with the number of all parents over age 40, plus half the number of all parents between ages 18 and 40. This method presupposes the following summary assumptions: Schizophrenias seldom occur before one's 17th birthday; among people whose age is evenly distributed between ages 20 and 40, approximately half the schizophrenias that occur at all have become manifest; and after age 40, new onsets of schizophrenia are very rare. It is true, however, according to our recent experience, that a number of schizophrenia onsets do occur after age 40, indicating that this traditional assumption ought to be corrected. On the other hand, such a correction would cause considerable difficulties in making comparisons between existing experimental probands and those of future investigations, and it could not materially influence any of the conclusions I am attempting to draw.

comparison figures from other studies were determined according to differently structured parent groups, and adjustments as to age had to be made in them in order for the comparisons to be meaningful.

Figures among parents	Uncorrected calculated percentage	Percentage adjusted according to Weinberg's abbreviated method
For definite schizophrenia only:	4.6 ± 1.0[2]	4.7 ± 1.0
For definite and probable schizophrenia together:	6.8 ± 1.2[3]	6.9 ± 1.3

The onset expectancy of schizophrenia among parents of probands in this study corresponds (within probable chance fluctuations) to that of the parents of my schizophrenic probands from Pfäfers. In this latter group it amounted to 5.6 percent ± 1.6 for the positive schizophrenics, and 6.1 percent ± 1.7 for the positive and probable schizophrenics together (as compared to 4.7 percent ± 1.0 and 6.9 percent ± 1.3).

Luxenburger (1940) counts on 5–6 percent schizophrenics among the parents of schizophrenics. The number of schizophrenic probands of Kallmann's studies (1938, 1946) is considerably greater at 1,087 than that of any other investigator studying psychiatric disorders among families of schizophrenics. If the unknown, unwed fathers are omitted, Kallmann's schizophrenics (1938, 1946) had 1,963 parents. The uncorrected percentage figure of schizophrenics among them was not mentioned by the author, but it can be calculated since he reports the percentages on how many legitimate and illegitimate probands had schizophrenic parents. The result yields a percentage of 3.3 for the positive, and 8.4 for the positive and "doubtful" schizophrenics together (as compared to 4.6 percent and 6.8 percent, respectively, in the present investigative material). According to that, Kallmann (1938, 1946) had more doubtful cases of schizophrenia in comparison to his definite schizophrenics than I did. The reason

2. Confidence interval at 95 percent: 3 percent–7 percent.

3. Confidence interval at 95 percent: 5 percent–10 percent.

for this is that the average age of his probands was considerably higher than that of mine. The parents of his probands had, on the average, been born about the middle of the last century, so that their mental illnesses were categorized almost 100 years ago in terms that would be unintelligible today, and they were described according to characteristics different from those in current use. He therefore could not be as certain about his diagnosis as often as I could. For the same reason also, there would be more "other psychoses" than schizophrenias among the parents of his probands whom he designated as "doubtful" than there were among my very probable schizophrenics. Furthermore, among Kallmann's parents there would also have to be more early deaths than among mine, so that his corrected percentage figures for schizophrenia are higher than the uncorrected ones. The difference between his two percentage figures must be greater than it is for my probands. Taking all this into consideration, we can be assured that Kallmann's figures do not contradict mine.

Among 55 parents of schizophrenics studied by Alanen (1966), there were 4 schizophrenics = 7.3 percent ± 3.5, a figure that likewise approximates my own calculation.

While she takes into account the statistics of Erlässer (1952), Kallmann (1938, 1946), Schulz (1933, 1949/50), Sjögren (1957), Slater (1953, 1958) and mine, Edith Zerbin-Rüdin (1963) finds that the onset probability of schizophrenia among parents of schizophrenics ranges between 5 and 10 percent. My own calculations of between 5 and 7 percent occur within these extremes.

The percentage of schizophrenic parents among my New York probands was smaller (2 percent definite, and 3.5 percent definite and probable schizophrenias combined). This was caused by the method of selecting probands. The New York schizophrenics came from a private clinic. Schizophrenic psychoses in one of the parents can so seriously deplete the financial resources of a family, that the schizophrenic offspring can no longer be adequately hospitalized under optimum, high-cost care facilities.

It is evident, therefore, that the frequency of schizophrenic psychoses among the parents of schizophrenics (so long as obvious selection criteria do not disturb the comparisons), at different times, in different places, and determined by different authors, is always nearly the same, and fluctuates only minimally

Table 2.1 Parents of the 100 male principal probands, arranged according to whether they were living or dead at end of study, according to sex, and according to age at death or end of study

Age	Living or dead	Sex	All parents of probands	Cases of mental disturbances No. and types of disorders in all parents of male schizophrenic probands							
				Schizophrenia	Probable schizophrenia	Manic-depressive states	Senile psychoses	Other psychoses	Feeblemindedness	Alcoholism	Suicides
28–39	Dead	m	6		1[1]					1	
		f	2								
40–49	Dead	m	7							2	2
		f	1								
50–59	Dead	m	17		1[2]	1				6[9]	1
		f	6		1[3]					1	
60–69	Living	m	2	1							
	Living	f	6								
	Dead	m	24	1			1			10	1
	Dead	f	24	1		1		1[7]	1	1	
70–79	Living	m	3							1[10]	
	Living	f	5				1				
	Dead	m	25	2		1	2			4	
	Dead	f	32	2	1[4]	3[5]	6[6]	1[8]			
80 +	Living	m	2								
	Living	f	8	1							
	Dead	m	14	1			7		1	3	
	Dead	f	16			1	7		1	1	
Totals:			200	9	4	7	24	2	3	30	4

1. Father died at age 31 in 1918 and was never hospitalized for his psychosis. However, his behavior was not only peculiar, but on long-term observation he developed the most diversified delusions of persecution. The peculiarity of his nature became manifest in an unusual and terrible coldness, a rejection of human contact and withdrawal into himself. He was so shy and frightened of people that he only went out with his wife after dark. He had the feeling that he should not be seen with her during the day. He felt certain that co-workers were shutting off his alarm clock in some mysterious way so that he would arrive late for work. He regarded harmless drunks on the street as dangerous potential burglars intending to rob him, etc. He told his wife, among other things, without any sensible reason, she would have to take her newborn child to France and turn it over to the French Army (Case No. 35).

2. Father expired in 1933 at age 59, exhibited peculiar behavior all his life and deserted his family on numerous occasions. The following is what records show about his psychosis: as an adult he was mentally ill for one month. He exhibited confusion, refused to eat, locked himself into his room, and slept with a knife under his pillow (Case No. 90).

3. This mother was murdered by her son, our proband, at age 56 in 1906. He gave her mental illness as a reason for her murder. Actually, from testimony of people who knew him, the mother had been almost constantly confined to bed during the immediate past, had been extremely irritable, had scolded and nagged him incessantly, had hurled away the food she had been given, and had complained about hearing voices (Case No. 78).

4. This mother, deceased at age 74, developed a chronic delusional psychosis in her 60s. She felt herself persecuted by her deceased husband, claiming he stood behind her, that she could hear his voice, but she continued working despite persistent hallucinations, and without being hospitalized (Case No. 47).

5. One of these had indications of schizophrenia.

6. One of these, a former psychopath; his condition was induced by the delusions of the proband, his son.

7. Senile epilepsy.

8. Neurasthenic-hysteric psychopath with delusions induced by her schizophrenic husband.

9. One of these, after meningitis.

10. Also criminal tendencies, required court commitment.

Table 2.2. Parents of the 108 female principal probands, arranged according to whether they were living or dead at end of study, according to sex, and according to age at death or end of study

Cases of mental disturbances
No. and types of disorders in all parents of female schizophrenic probands

Age	Living or dead	Sex	All parents of probands	Schizophrenia	Probable schizophrenia	Manic-depressive states	Senile psychoses	Other psychoses	Feeblemindedness	Alcoholism	Suicides
30–39	Dead	f	5								
40–49	Dead	m	9							1	1
		f	8[1]	2	1[2]				1		2
50–59	Dead	m	16							5	
		f	12	1					1		
60–69	Living	m	1								
	Living	f	3								
	Dead	m	30	1	1[3]		2		1	8	2
	Dead	f	29	1	2[4,5]		1		1		1
70–79	Living	m	5			1	1			1	
	Living	f	6				1	1[7]			
	Dead	m	21				1		1	5	1
	Dead	f	23	5			5		1	1	
80 +	Living	m	4							1[8]	
	Living	f	2				1				
	Dead	m	18		1[6]		4			1	
	Dead	f	20				6				
Totals:			212	10	5	2	22	1	6	23	7

(Four of the mothers were unmarried.)

1. One of these missing at age 48, fate unknown.

2. This mother committed suicide in 1894 by cutting open her abdomen with scissors. She had been ill since early in life and is reported to have suffered continually from delusions of persecution; had never been a patient in a psychiatric hospital (Case No. 57).

3. The father died at age 69 in 1929; had never been hospitalized. Still, in the course of many years it was determined by various doctors who associated with him that he suffered repeatedly from delusions of persecution, and that he led the life of a mild schizophrenic in other respects as well (Case No. 38).

4. The mother died in 1941 at age 63, an exceedingly peculiar personality. Various doctors who came in contact with her through illness of her children, described her as confused and distracted. One of them, who had met her once, diagnosed her as a hebephrenic, but she was never hospitalized (Case No. 3).

5. Mother committed suicide in 1918 at age 63. Years before, she had suffered a depression which appeared in many aspects like schizophrenia. Information about her emphasized how she had felt "mixed up," how she used

to make peculiar, eccentric remarks: " . . . it constricted the tones in my heart" and other similar ones (Case No. 48).

6. Father expired at age 81. At age 38 he suffered a severe psychotic episode in which he mistook the identity of people, spoke confusedly, and attempted to jump from a window. For a long time (exact time-span unknown) he had to be under guard continuously at his home. Since then, sporadic stuporous states and depressive moods. In his 70s a massive senile dementia set in during which he was hospitalized at our clinic. An examination for schizophrenia was no longer feasible (Case No. 78).

7. Mother never was in Switzerland but lived in a distant East European country; nevertheless, we received the following definite notes: She had become acutely mentally ill at age 30 and remained mentally ill until today, 44 years later. She often wandered aimlessly about and had also attempted suicide. She had been treated at a psychiatric clinic once and had since then been placed with a foster family as a mental patient (Case No. 4).

8. A schizoid eccentric.

around the figure of 5–7 percent as calculated for the probands of this study.

Only very few American authors arrive at different, higher ratios, and their assumption even goes so far as to consider virtually all parents of schizophrenics as schizophrenic. Such assumptions are explained by the fact that these authors expand the basic concept of schizophrenia very considerably. They apply it also to parents who are in no sense psychotic, as the term is usually applied, who in current terminology would more readily be classified, for example, as schizoid psychopaths or eccentrics and cranks. If the mere suspicion of schizophrenia derived from a Rorschach test is diagnosed as a schizophrenia without the presence of supporting clinical symptoms, the number of such "Rorschach schizophrenics," of course, should not be compared with the number of actual schizophrenics.

The findings of this study confirm again that schizophrenias among the parents of schizophrenics occur much more frequently than among parents of the normal population. While among the 612 parents of my schizophrenics (the ones from this and the Pfäfers studies combined) there were 40 definite and probable schizophrenias combined, there were only 4 schizophrenias among 599 parents of representative subjects from the average Swiss population.[4] In considering the age structure of the parents from the 4 investigative groups in question, these values result for the onset probability of schizophrenia

Among 612 parents of Swiss schizophrenics	6.7% ± 1.0%[5]
Among 599 parents of representative subjects from the Swiss general population	0.7% ± 0.3%[6]

In studies of the representatives of a different average population by other authors, the schizophrenia-frequency among parents turned out to be even smaller than in my own investigations.

Ten of the 28 certain or probable schizophrenic parents of my probands are fathers and 18 mothers (if only the definite cases are counted, the ratio is 6:13). The Pfäfers schizophrenic probands had 4 fathers and 8 mothers with definite or probable schizophrenias. From both studies—this one and the Pfäfers study—combined, and considering the definite as well as the probable schizophrenias, the resultant proportion is 14 schizophrenic fathers to 26 schizophrenic mothers.

It has long been accepted as a fact that mothers of schizophrenics become schizophrenic at approximately twice the rate that fathers of schizophrenics do. Essen-Moeller (1963) assembled the findings of ten authors on the subject, in which there are 63 definite schizophrenias among the mothers of schizophrenics as compared with 28 among such fathers. Some time ago this difference was explained on the theory that schizophrenic mothers are more likely to cause schizophrenias in the children than do schizophrenic fathers. But Essen-Moeller (1963) showed convincingly that the effects of pure chance in selection caused the preponderance of schizophrenias in mothers of schizophrenics, for mothers are, on the average, younger than fathers when they marry and have children. If they become schizophrenic, then, in comparison with the fathers, it is usually after they have married and after the children are born. The men, on the other hand, who become schizophrenic at the same age as the women, are usually still unmarried and have no offspring, and the probability that they marry and propagate after onset of their psychosis is minimal.

Except for possible chance fluctuations, the schizophrenic parents of my male and female probands occur at about the same ratio (6.5 percent and 7.1 percent). If I add to this the

---

4. Two hundred patients, principally surgical cases from a general hospital in the Basel area and 100 tubercular patients from a sanatorium in Zürich were used as probands representing the average population. There may be some valid argument against the assumption that parents of general patients are representative of parents from the general population in comparisons that concern schizophrenic illnesses. But experiences from the 20's and 30's, gathered from representatives of the general population by a number of different selection criteria, do show that the frequency of schizophrenic disorders among relatives of general patients does not deviate appreciably from that of schizophrenias among representatives of the general population that were selected by other methods. Insofar as deviations do occur, they cannot be so significant as to alter the above conclusions in any way. This topic on the frequency of mental disorders among general populations has been regularly discussed in the literature for the past decades, and such discussions need not be repeated here.

5. Critical limit at 5 percent = 5 percent–9 percent.
6. Critical limit at 5 percent = 0.2 percent–2 percent.

figures from the Pfäfers probands, the rather insignificant difference increases slightly, but reaches no statistical significance.

By inspecting only the figures of this study, one might suppose that among the parents of male schizophrenics more of the fathers, and among the parents of female schizophrenics, more of the mothers were also schizophrenic. The relationship between schizophrenic fathers to schizophrenic mothers among the male schizophrenic probands is, indeed, 7:6, and the same relationship among the female schizophrenic probands is 3:12. The figures, however, are too small to be significant, and besides, the figures on the Pfäfers probands, which are not significant either, indicate precisely the opposite trend. Therefore, from my own investigative material, no significant difference is indicated between male and female schizophrenics in respect to the frequency between the sexes of schizophrenia among their parents. The same holds true in findings reported in the previous literature on the subject. They likewise contradict each other, and in no investigative material attain any statistic significance.

One peculiarity about schizophrenic psychoses in the parents is, that from the outset it can be expected that, on the average, they began later and are milder than the schizophrenias of the probands and of schizophrenias in general. It is, of course, almost impossible for early-onset and serious schizophrenias to occur among the parents, since they virtually preclude marriage and propagation. The following presumption is also borne out by facts:

In the following comparisons the parents of the male and the female probands are examined together. The figures are much too small to indicate definite trends in sex differences for the courses of psychoses among the 28 schizophrenic parents. Furthermore, the definite and the probable schizophrenias are reckoned together. For conversion of the concepts: age at onset, type of course of illness, "end state," and prepsychotic personality, see pp. 189–92.

Age at onset of schizophrenia lay

between 20 and 29 years	in 5 parents,
between 30 and 39 years	in 11 parents,
between 40 and 49 years	in 2 parents,
between 50 and 59 years	in 3 parents,
over 60 years	in 2 parents,
not determined	in 5 parents.

The course types of schizophrenias of probands' parents may be subdivided as follows:

Acute onset, then long-term, extremely severe "end state"	1
Chronic development of extremely severe "end state"	2
Acute onset, then long-term milder "end state"	0
Chronic development, milder "end state" (particularly late-paranoid schizophrenias)	7
Cyclic course, severe "end state"	1
Cyclic course, milder "end state"	4
Cyclic course, outcome in recovery	10
Other atypical course	2
Undetermined course	1

The "end states" could be determined for 26 of the 28 parental schizophrenias. They were characterized as follows:

Severe "end state" (dementia)	4
Moderate "end state" (severe personality defects)	2
Mild "end state" (mild personality defects)	10
Outcome in recovery	9
Expired during acute psychotic episode	1

The condition labelled "end state" lasted between 1 and 5 years in 2 cases, between 5 and 10 years in 3 cases, and over 10 years in 17 cases. Duration of the "end state" was determined for only 22 of the schizophrenic parents, it was unknown for 5, and 1 parent died during an acute episode.

Prepsychotic conditions of probands' parents

Nonaberrant and healthy	8
Schizoid behavior within norms	3
Other than schizoid behavior, within norms	3
Schizoid psychopathic	6
Other than schizoid psychopathic	2
Prepsychotic condition unknown	6

In summary, the schizophrenias of the parents of probands may be characterized in general as follows: The illness begins for the most part, after age 30. Intensity of the illness is predominantly mild; frequently the course runs in acute phases that subside or lead quickly to recovery, or there are chronic developments of a rather benign late-paranoia. The prepsychotic personality of the schizophrenic parents is not significantly distinguished from that of the schizophrenic probands; the figures alone seem to indicate that these parents were more often normal before their illness than other schizophrenics were.

These findings were predictable; for schizophrenics who experience an onset late in life and whose illness runs a benign course, more often have children than do the early and more severely schizophrenic patients. Almost no descriptions of schizophrenias among parents of schizophrenics exist by which these conclusions could be verified.

Manic-Depressive States

Among the 412 known parents of my 208 probands there were 9 typical cases of manic-depressive states, of which 7 were depressions and 2 were manias. (There were no cases of psychotic phases including both manic and depressive manifestations). The uncorrected percentage figure for manic-depressive states is therefore 2.2 percent $\pm$ 0.7, and the figure adjusted according to age grouping is 2.3 percent $\pm$ 0.7.[7]

Among the 200 parents of my Pfäfers probands there were 4 depressions in the manic-depressive category, but no manias, that is, 2 percent uncorrected and 2.2 percent after adjustment according to age. The frequency of manic-depressive states, therefore, corresponds almost exactly in the two parent groups. Nor is there any significant difference in the frequency of depressions alone. And certainly it is obvious that the incidence of 2 cases of mania in the larger sample compared to none in the smaller one, is of no statistical significance.

Among the families examined by me for physical illnesses in Switzerland (tubercular patients in the Canton of Zürich and surgical cases in the Canton of Rural-Basel), as representatives of the general population, there were 2 definite and 1 doubtful cases of endogenous depression among the 599 parents. According to whether the doubtful case is included or excluded, the adjusted percentage figures are 0.6 percent $\pm$ 0.3 and 0.4 percent $\pm$ 0.28, respectively.

Accordingly, the probability may be assumed as valid that endogenous depressions among the parents of schizophrenics are more frequent than those among the general population; but they are still much less frequent among the parents of schizophrenics than they are among parents of manic-depressives.

The clinical impression of many psychiatrists is that there are more manic-depressives among parents of schizophrenics than there are among parents of the general population. The same theory agrees also with the investigative results of Edith Zerbin-Rüdin (1963) and several other authors. Kallmann (1938, 1946), however, finds that among the relatives of schizophrenics only schizophrenias and schizoid eccentricities were frequent, and he suspects that the other investigators mistook disguised schizophrenias for endogenous depressions. But today the supposition is that Kallmann overestimated schizophrenia-like symptoms among manic-depressives as to their diagnostic significance, and therefore much more rarely recorded the endogenous depressions as compared to the schizophrenias, than is customary in diagnostic practice. (This problem will be discussed below [see pp. 315–20]. There also the incidence of manic-depressives among siblings of schizophrenics will be mentioned).

Among the depressive parents of my schizophrenic probands there are 2 fathers and 5 mothers. General experience, according to which endogenous depressions are more frequent among women, is reflected in these figures (among the Pfäfers probands the relationship is 1:3). Manic states among the probands' parents of this study occurred in 1 father and 1 mother. Among the 200 parents of the male probands of this study there were 6 cases of depression and 1 of mania, and among the 212 parents of the female probands, 1 of depression and 1 of mania. Among the 200 parents of the almost exclusively male Pfäfers probands, there were 4 endogenous depressives. But even these figures must not be regarded as a valid indication that there are more depressives among the parents of male schizophrenics than among the parents of female schizophrenics.

---

7. It used to be the custom to calculate the percentage figures corrected for age, that is, the expected onset frequency, under the assumption that the most vulnerable age span for onset of manic-depressive states lay between 20 and 50 years, and that such onsets were evenly distributed over that age span. In accordance with this theory, the number of parents between the ages of 20 and 50 was halved, and only parents over 50 years old were fully counted in order to provide a figure with which to compare the number of manic-depressive parents. This theory hardly corresponds to the actual conditions existing, as Slater (1953, 1958), among others, has demonstrated. But for the problems under discussion here, the summary expectancy of onset according to the abbreviated Weinberg method is sufficient.

All 9 manic-depressive parents had been hospitalized in psychiatric clinics during at least one phase of illness, and all are definite and serious cases. According to typologies they can be characterized as follows: 6 depressives passed through several severe depressive phases, and 1 depressive through a single phase. Between the phases, 3 probands practically recovered, 3 were subdepressive and hypersensitive, and 1 hypomanic. The manic father was a schizoid psychopath who went through several typical severe manic phases with hospitalization. During the transition periods he also exhibited mildly depressive moods. The manic mother suffered from frequent, long-term, serious manic phases from age 26 until her death at age 72, so that she spent most of the time during all these years in the hospital. In between phases she almost never fully recovered; instead, she was usually submanic or subdepressive.

Indications in the literature about the frequency of psychoses of the manic-depressive typology among the parents of manic-depressives are sparse and varied. Nevertheless, it has been established that manic-depressive psychoses among the parents of manic-depressives occur more frequently than among the parents of schizophrenics.

Senile Psychoses

The senile psychoses involved principally parents who had expired before the investigations began, or who expired during these investigations. At the end of the investigations only 4 parents with senile psychoses were still alive, and 42 had died. In very few was I able personally to confirm the senile psychosis, and for only very few were patient histories accurate and complete. Most of the senile psychotics were receiving care at home, in nursing homes, foster homes, or in hospitals for various physically illnesses. Their patient histories contain insufficient entries about the mental condition of the aged.

The counting of senile psychoses, however, is fraught with some additional difficulties. Chronic senile psychoses are difficult to distinguish from other manifestations of aging within the norms. It is virtually impossible to distinguish psychoses in the presence of sclerosis of the blood vessels of the brain from an extended terminal state.

Notations concerning merely a decline of memory never were enough to assume a senile psychosis. However, notations that a patient was no longer able to leave the house

for fear that he would lose his way, or that he no longer recognized members of the family, that he spoke so confusedly that he could no longer be understood when vital matters were being discussed, and the like were accepted. Organic confusion before impending death was regarded as senile psychosis only when it had lasted for several weeks. A real distinction between simple senile dementia and psychoses with cerebral arteriosclerosis was possible for the most part only when patient histories had indicated cerebral damage. In what follows I treat both under the collective term "senile psychoses."

Among the parents of male and female probands the incidence of senile psychoses is equal (24 among the 100 parents of male, and 22 among the parents of female principal probands); hence, senile psychoses among all the 412 parents can be considered together.

No senile psychoses were considered before age 60. Among the 239 parents of probands who dropped out of the investigation between age 60 and 80 (dead or alive), 21—or 9 percent—were senile psychotics, and among the 84 over-80-year-old parents, 25—or 29.8 percent.

Table 2.3 shows a comparison of the frequency of senile psychoses among the parents of the principal schizophrenic probands of this study with that among the parents of my schizophrenics from the Pfäfers study and the parents of general patients I examined as representatives of the general population of Switzerland.

No statistically valid differences show up in the table. The fact that senile psychoses increase markedly after the seventh decade in life is self-evident. But it is of more interest to note, as the figures of Table 2.3 indicate, that senile psychoses among the parents of schizophrenics might occur more frequently than they do among parents of the general population.

One can only speculate as to the reasons. I personally like to pose the question whether there might not exist concealed among the "senile" psychoses of the parents of schizophrenics, some latent schizophrenic psychoses that become manifest in old age. It is certainly possible, or perhaps even probable, that schizophrenic psychoses do break out in old age, but that they are no longer recognized as such. In the same context (but with even less significant probability) the findings from siblings of probands indicate a similar phenomenon. The supposition that the presence of

Table 2.3. Senile psychoses in probands' parents compared to senile psychoses of parents of other schizophrenics and of patients with physical disorders

Parents of:	Parents between ages 60–70	Senile psychotics among them	Parents over age 70	Senile psychotics among them
The schizophrenics in this study	119	4 = 3.3% (1–8%)	204	42 = 20.6% (16–27%)
The Pfäfers group of schizophrenics	55	1 = 1.8% (0.05–10%)	66	9 = 13.6% (6–24%)
American schizophrenics	41	2 = 4.9% (0.6–17%)	49	3 = 6.1% (1–17%)
General patients from my 1932 and 1935 studies	186	1 = 0.5% (0.01–3%)	117	7 = 6.0% (2–12%)

The confidence intervals to 95% of the percentage figures have been adjusted upward or downward according to the Geigy table.

a schizophrenic psychosis in a child may weigh so heavily on the parents that it would favor the onset of a senile psychosis in the parent is quite improbable.

In Chapter 5 on siblings of probands, and in a special section in Chapter 6 on the frequency of schizophrenias among children of senile psychotics, I shall return to the question of the relationship between senile and schizophrenic psychoses.

Alcoholism

I classify as alcoholics only those male and female consumers of alcohol on whom proof was available that their mental or physical health or their social well-being had been damaged by the consumption of alcoholic beverages. In most of such cases, damage to health and social well-being were jointly supportive of the diagnosis. The most frequent type of physical damage among my probands was alcoholic cirrhosis of the liver. Mentally the most frequent manifestation is a severe change in personality. The customary social consequences are divorce, poverty, loss of capacity to earn a living, and need for personal care and looking after because of intoxication. Patients categorized as alcoholics always revealed the unmistakable und usually severe characteristics associated with alcoholism.

As shown in Tables 2.1 and 2.2, there were a number of alcoholics among the 412 parents of my principal schizophrenic probands, specifically 53 (49 fathers and 4 mothers). The fact that alcoholism occurred more than 10 times as frequently among fathers as among mothers corresponds approximately to the

experience of the period in which these parents lived. The alcoholics were distributed about evenly between parents of male and of female schizophrenic probands (30 of the 200 parents of male and 23 of the 212 parents of the female schizophrenic probands).

Three of the 4 alcoholic mothers are married to alcoholic fathers. Of course, this might be a coincidence, but the relationship agrees with the results of previous investigations of alcoholics, which show that frequently one alcoholic spouse will either entice the other to become an alcoholic or will support and further the other's alcoholism. On the other hand, it is rare that both spouses suffer from schizophrenia (although both parents of 1 of my principal schizophrenic probands are schizophrenic).

Among all the fathers, 24 percent were alcoholics. This percentage does not change appreciably if one counts only the alcoholics among fathers over age 40; these amount to 24.2 percent. Table 2.4 shows comparative figures from my investigations of Pfäfers and American schizophrenics, of two groups of general patients from Switzerland, and of American and Zürich alcoholics. Corresponding figures from collective statistics by Brugger (1929, 1934), representing the general populations of Munich and Basel, are added for comparison.

In studying Table 2.4, it is to be noted that the error coefficient for such small numbers is great, and that most of the differences in percentages are statistically not significant. Still one trend shown in the table is clear: The preponderance of alcoholics among the fathers of my principal schizophrenic probands can-

Table 2.4. Alcoholism in probands' fathers compared to alcoholism among fathers of other schizophrenic investigative groups and fathers of alcoholics and of general patients

Fathers of:	No. of fathers over age 40	Figures	No. of alcoholics among them: Percentages
208 schizophrenic probands of the present study	198	48	24.2 ± 3.0
100 schizophrenic probands of the Pfäfers study	98	12	12.2 ± 3.3
100 schizophrenic probands of the New York study	95	3	3.2 ± 1.8
50 alcoholics from Zürich	45	16	35.5 ± 7.1
50 alcoholics from New York	49	11	22.4 ± 5.9
Alcoholics from Basel and Munich by C. Brugger (1929, 1934)	61	16	26.2 ± 5.6
General patients from the Basel area	192	25	13.0 ± 2.4
Tubercular patients from Zürich	88	16	18.2 ± 4.1

not be regarded as typical for fathers of schizophrenics. It is conditioned by the fact that my probands came from a certain region during a certain period in history. Actually there were considerably fewer alcoholics among the Pfäfers and the New York schizophrenics. Among the New York probands the reason is obvious: These were patients from private clinics who in general came from upper-class and high-income circumstances—that is to say, circumstances that are jeopardized when the head of family becomes a severe alcoholic. The smaller number of alcoholic fathers among the parents of the Pfäfers probands can still be explained as a lessening through chance. But it is more probable that this difference is related to the fact that the Pfäfers probands came from the mountain areas in which habitual alcoholism was not very common at the time. In considering the great error of the smaller number, it is noteworthy that the frequency of alcoholism among the parents of Zürich schizophrenics is hardly any different from that of parents of the Zürich tubercular patients. But alcoholism among the fathers of alcoholics is more frequent than alcoholism among the fathers of schizophrenics or the fathers of general patients.

These conclusions from Table 2.4 will, in turn, later be compared to the findings about alcoholism among the siblings of various types of patients. They agree remarkably with the general impressions from medical experience on alcoholism.

Other Mental Disorders

Among the mothers there was one case of an undetermined psychosis. This mother lived in

a distant country, and no data suitable for diagnosis could be obtained. This mother was obviously suffering from an induced delusional illness, in this case induced by her husband. Except for the schizophrenias, senile psychoses, this induced delusional psychosis and one psychosis that could not be diagnosed, there were no psychoses among the parents.

Eleven of the 364 parents who had died (= 3 percent) had committed suicide. Among the deceased parents of the Pfäfers schizophrenics, 0.9 percent (1 out of 107), and among the American schizophrenics 4.3 percent (3 out of 71) died by committing suicide. The suicide figures on the parents of general patients lay within these figures, among the parents of various schizophrenic groups: 2.6 percent (5 out of 189) of the parents from the Basel area's general patients and 1.7 percent (2 out of 117) of the parents from the Zürich tubercular patients committed suicide. From statistics on the causes of death of the entire population, the suicide rate of parents cannot be determined. They indicate only how many suicides occurred among all those who died: Between 1890 and 1925, at most 8,095 and at least 5,971 died per year in the Canton of Zürich.[8] The suicide rate for individual years varies between 1.3 percent and 2.3 percent. In all probability it would be somewhat lower among those of the dead who had been parents.

A survey of these figures does not reveal whether the suicide rate among parents of schizophrenics was higher or lower than among parents who had no schizophrenic

8. Only the years divisible by 5 are included in these figures, that is, 1890, 1895, etc., through 1925.

children.

In my investigations on the relatives of the Pfäfers schizophrenics I included also the schizoid psychopaths among the parents. The finding that schizoid psychopaths under Kretschmer's definition among the parents of schizophrenics were considerably more frequent than among parents of the general population was unequivocal: 16.5 percent of schizoid psychopaths (33 out of 200) among the parents of schizophrenics compared to 1.2 percent (7 out of 599) among the parents of general patients. Kretschmer (1944) accepted these figures in the 17th and successive editions of his book *Körperbau und Charakter* (Body Build and Character), and determined that in essence they agree with the findings of other authors. Since then it has become established that schizoid psychopaths among the parents (and other relatives) of schizophrenics occur with remarkable frequency. It is no longer necessary to document this fact anew.

But if I seem in this study to neglect schizoid psychopathy in parents, there is still another reason operative. It is a fairly easy and unarbitrary process to decide whether a father or a mother of a schizophrenic is to be categorized as a schizoid psychopath when one has investigated his or her life history and has become personally acquainted with him or her even for a short period. These conditions certainly existed for the probands of my Pfäfers investigations. But when one spends a great deal of time, as I did, during this study for a number of years, on the relationships of parents to their children, the same problem increases rather than decreases in difficulty. One begins now to gain an insight into these relationships from another angle. As a result of years of friction and chafing among the members of a family, one notices the emergence of autistic, tyrannical, rigid, hypersensitive, and other "schizoid" characteristics, sees them become prominent, change, and sometimes also recede again. One is led to believe then that such attitudes develop from the interactions of human relationships, rather than to regard them as something concrete, rooted in the patient's constitution. But Kretschmer and most of his contemporaries have consistently regarded schizoid psychopathy as a constitutional characteristic.

In one case like the following, I doubt in retrospect that a "schizoid psychopathy" should have been assumed: The mother of a proband led an uneventful life as a girl; she was quiet, shy, and retiring, but did learn a simple trade and worked at it. She got along well with other girls, and even joined some clubs; she was no problem to raise and did well in school. In her marriage to a coarse, quick-tempered, alcoholic man she withdrew more and more, gradually ceased to participate in human intercourse, and spent days during which she wept without apparent provocation. In disciplining her children she became obstinate, strict, pedantic, and mean. This attitude increased in intensity as the children became increasingly difficult to manage, until finally she had to be denied parental custody of them. If this mother were to be observed at this particular time "cross-sectionally," the category "schizoid psychopath" would have been applied justifiably. If she had been one of my Pfäfers probands, I would have applied the same characterization. But when one knows the history of this mother longitudinally, doubts arise as to the validity of this qualification, and one begins to ask the obvious question, "Would this woman have been the same in a different marriage? Or would she have become a tender, warm-hearted mother, had she been married to someone else?" Such doubts do spoil one's pleasure at the neat counting up of "schizoid psychopaths."

Obviously other authors have had similar problems, consciously or unconsciously. The mere counting up of schizoids among relatives of schizophrenics is rapidly losing in popularity; nevertheless, the concept of the "schizoid" remains a valid and meaningful concept. It remains to be checked to what degree a person is constitutionally schizoid, to what degree he is forced into a schizoid set of attitudes only by the events and circumstances of his life, and to what degree the schizoid aspects of his being have resulted from the intertwined and complex development of his personality and his environment arising from his relationships with others. These facets will be discussed later.

Among the 412 parents 9 (2.2 percent) are clearly feebleminded; of these 3 are parents of male and 6 parents of female probands. Two of the feebleminded parents are fathers and 7 are mothers. Of course, these differences are statistically insignificant.

Among the parents of the schizophrenic probands from Pfäfers, 5 (2.5 percent) were feebleminded; while there were no feebleminded among the parents of the American schizophrenics, who had come from affluent families.

Among the 599 parents of the tubercular patients from Zürich and the general patients from the Basel area there were only 2 feebleminded (0.3 percent).

The difference in the frequency of feeblemindedness among the parents of schizophrenics and those representing the normal population seems considerable, but is actually not significant.

The degree of feeblemindedness among the 9 parents of the schizophrenic probands was mild. Within the concept of debility it varied between the limit of the norm and debility to the limit between debility and imbecility. The 2 mentally debilitated fathers later also became schizophrenic; 1 such mother also became schizophrenic; 2 others became senile and another depressive.

Premature Loss of Father or Mother (Broken Home)

Introduction

When one becomes more closely acquainted with schizophrenic patients it soon becomes evident how many of them during their childhood lacked normal, orderly family relationships. This fact gives rise to two questions:

(1) Don't other patients or normal, healthy people come from family circumstances just as—or even more—disrupted than these patients?

(2) Do disrupted family circumstances have a causal influence on the later onset of the psychosis?

Almost all doctors from ages past who studied schizophrenics eventually arrived at this line of questioning, but to this day none has succeeded in supplying a clear-cut answer.

At the beginning and near the middle of the last century a patient's unfavorable family background was uncritically regarded as a contributory cause for all subsequent mental disorders, just as it was assumed that anything that hurts, torments the body and depresses the mood would cause not only immediate distress, but also every kind of mental illness as well.

Towards the end of the last century, after today's schizophrenias had been labelled as "endogenous" mental disturbances, and after they had been dogmatically represented as being of "hereditary" and cerebropathological origin, the judgment based on family circumstances in the patient histories of schizophrenics lost meaningful impact. When it was revealed that a patient's parents were divorced, that his father had abandoned the family, that his mother had callously turned over her child to foster care, such circumstances served as definite indications of a psychopathic constitution of the progenitors and of an inherited background favorable to schizophrenia in the patient. There was little inclination to consider the miseries of childhood as possible contributory cause or partial cause of mental stresses responsible for the psychosis in the person who becomes a patient. After the last World War a number of schools of thought changed their opinions to the contrary. Now, all at once, a number of investigators held the dogmatic conviction that the long sought-after etiology of schizophrenias could be found in the severe chaotic childhood experiences. Bias and prejudice led even serious investigators astray in the past decades in supplying "proof" that cannot be sustained by honest criticism. By the employment of statistics that do not adequately satisfy the simplest demands, it was "established" that disruption of family relationships in the patient histories of schizophrenics was greater than it was when compared to the normal population. The erroneously derived higher frequency in unfavorable family relationships was then even designated as being the principal cause of schizophrenia, without even considering how varied the possibilities of their origins might be. The likelihood that disrupted family relationships in the patient histories of schizophrenics might also be the consequence of schizophrenic or psychopathological developments among the family members of these later schizophrenics was overlooked. It is discouraging that the very same circumstance—the frequency of the broken home—(in some cases not even proved) should indicate to one investigator proof of hereditary factors at work and to another proof of the psychogenesis of schizophrenias.

Although an earlier investigation had presented as valid doctrine the fictitious proof that had been dragged in by the hair, leaving behind a scrap heap of loose ends, we must admit that it did create adequate incentive for attacking the question impartially today. And precisely such adequate, impartial investigations of the facts have gotten under way in recent years.

Statistical proof is obviously not the only, nor necessarily the best method for clarifying family circumstances in which schizophrenics grew up, in all their etiological ramifications. Statistically determined data on disturbances in the family community cannot be equated with all the agonizing, sickness-inducing influences in a family. And statistically determined data, such as the loss of a parent by death or divorce, can (perhaps) be compensated for in their psychological impact by the exceptionally favorable circumstances of a good foster family, or a good home. Again, the most horrible, potentially sickness-inducing internal chaos may prevail in a family that to outward appearances conveys an impression of togetherness. Far more essential than the bare statistics is a complete understanding of childhood experiences in all their psychological refinements and in each individual case. But despite that, it was always tempting by means of data that could be mathematically determined, at least to seek out some points of reference for psychodynamic investigation. If it were certain that numerical calculations of family disturbances in the patient histories of schizophrenics occurred with greater or less frequency, or in a different manner than they do in the histories of other patients or normal people, then, to be sure, it would be possible to glean certain indications from them that would help in the planning of future studies. The real significance of psychological experiences with individual patients could be more accurately evaluated.

The death or long-term absence of a parent, the divorce or separation of parents, illegitimate births, or the placement of children in forster care, can indeed be counted and statistically recorded. If the bond between father or mother and child has been severed by one of these portentous acts of destiny, it is reasonable to speak of a "disturbed family relationship among the parents," a parental loss, or the premature dissolution of the home. It has become customary, however, to apply the English term *broken home*, which cannot really be expressed in German with equal brevity and which would be understood just as well internationally.

Statistical Investigations by Other Authors

It took a number of years before the realization was accepted that the statistical reckoning of early parental loss was a difficult and laborious task. Many pitfalls lie in the path to a set of data that retains validity, and many investigators have been trapped in them. Most of the statistical investigations up to now have been laid out in such a way that only the extreme frequencies of early parent loss by schizophrenics would have been detectable.

But there simply have not been parent losses of such magnitude compared to those among the general population, as we know with certainty today.

By today it has been demonstrated that none of the early statistics on premature parent loss in the childhood histories of schizophrenics is reliable or would permit definitive generalizations. The reasons for this insufficiency are many, among others the following:

1. In former times the errors in smaller figures received too little attention. Whether the purported "results" might have been due to a mere caprice of chance was often not sufficiently considered. It occurred at times that percentages were calculated on the basis of 50 or less cases, which were regarded seriously as being generally valid.

2. Often the background of patients was judged only on the basis of the data contained in the routine patient histories. But no clinic is really capable of achieving an equally complete, equally reliable compilation in every single patient history, nor the guarantee that it was compiled from exactly the same viewpoints as all the others. Differences between the patient histories of different groups of patients will develop simply from the fact that different doctors record their patient histories differently. Many patient histories contain only imprecise notes on patients' families; these must then be omitted from statistical calculations. But by such elminations a factor of selection is created that makes the statistical results useless. The physician may probably be inclined to describe dramatic childhood histories in greater detail than the more colorless ones; and for this reason alone it is possible that unusually many of those patient histories concerning patients without parental loss are the ones that are eliminated.

3. There are only very few statistics so selective as to record the relationships only among schizophrenics. Justifiably, most investigators want to compare their findings in schizophrenics with those of a normal, average population. The difficulties in finding a comparable average population, however, have so far proved insurmountable. To date no one has ever succeeded in finding a representative "average population" group that could be considered truly comparable in every respect with the schizophrenics being studied. In order to ensure the comparability of the representatives of the average population with the schizophrenics, both would have to be

similar in many differents respects, as for instance, in respect to birth years, since the probabilities of death and divorce rates change in the course of years. If the parent losses of schizophrenics that were born at the beginning of this century are compared with those of the general population who were born twenty years later, a lowering in mortality rates and an increase in divorce rates would be reflected in the normal population, and those differences with respect to the schizophrenias of the other group would be hidden. It must further be borne in mind that mortality and divorce rates vary in different areas and among different social classes. In the United States the great differences between early parent losses of whites and Negroes have long been evident (Gardner and Saaron, 1946). It is impossible to arrive at valid results, if one compares the childhood backgrounds of hospitalized schizophrenics of any ordinary psychiatric clinic with, for instance, that of the hospital's personnel, of recruits who have volunteered for a specific arm of the military service, or of medical students.

4. One great, almost insurmountable difficulty with statistics lies in the fact that it is not possible to interview schizophrenics and representatives of the general population with comparable methods in regard to their childhood histories. The motives of schizophrenic patients, of their families, and of the general population in revealing or concealing the truth are totally different. Representatives of the general population probably give more reliable information than do schizophrenics, whose testimony would be distorted by delusionary ideas and prejudicial attitudes. But it is possible that the representatives of the general population might find it a bit dull to provide the annoying interrogator with the correct answer, or they might fear disadvantages if they were to report the tragedies of their own childhoods (for instance, recruits would fear being passed over for officer-candidate selection). Very few among the investigators have fully confronted such sources of errors in the statistics.

5. It has further been forgotten that general conclusions drawn from any arbitrarily selected group of schizophrenics cannot be valid for schizophrenics in general. The childhood of schizophrenics is not the samce for all, according to whether they come from a clinic that admits all schizophrenics from a certain area, or one that preferentially admits only the affluent or only the poor, or only acute and curable cases, or prefers only chronic patients. The frequency of early parent loss even depends surprisingly also on how the two sexes are distributed within a group, and also on the ratio of severe to mild cases of illness.

6. The true evaluation of many investigative findings becomes impossible not only because of such vast and basic difficulties, but it collapses just as often because of tiny, insidious trivialities. All too often one receives no replies from publications and the like to questions such as: How are those cases recorded in which parents are lost by a combination of death and divorce? What does the concept "separation of parents" involve—only legal separation or separation without a court decree as well? Are those separations included that do not actually involve any loss of parents, as, for instance, those brought about by military service or by extensive travel on his job on the part of the father? Is it a matter of the separation of the child from the parents when the child lives outside the family for a number of years while attending school?

There are no statistics on the frequency of early parent loss in the childhood histories of schizophrenics, the interpretation of which would be free from one or a number of such sources of error. No statistic so far has been capable of answering satisfactorily the apparently simple question whether loss of parents (and the loss of which parent) is more frequently found in the childhood history of schizophrenics than among the general population. But then a number of the most varied conclusions were drawn from the existing statistics, for instance, that older schizophrenics more often suffered early parent loss in childhood than nonschizophrenics, or else it was asserted that this was not the case; loss of mothers occurred more frequently than loss of fathers, or the reverse was claimed; loss of parents was more frequent among schizophrenics, particularly in early childhood, or that there was no apparent frequency in evidence during those years, etc. It is disturbing that all too often conclusions were drawn from such unreliable statistical data, that would not have been justifiable even if the statistics had supplied incontestable data. For instance, from an alleged frequency of premature parent loss the assumption for an etiological significance was derived, as though it could not possibly have been based on other reasons, such as, for example, because of hereditary tendencies for schizophrenia in the parents that might have favored a marital crisis, or because of premature death caused by poor hygienic standards in the home. It is just as unlikely that the frequency of premature parent loss proves a psychogenesis of schizophrenias, as that the absence of such losses would constitute proof against such a psychogenesis. There certainly are many and more weighty psychotraumatic situations, other than externally assessable parent losses, that should be taken into account for determining a psychogenesis; among others, for instance, the loss of emotional ties to parents who are still living together.

The following paragraphs list the most important findings on the childhood parent losses of older schizophrenics and include brief discussions. They include work done in the United States, Canada, England, and the Scandinavian countries. I emphasize only those portions of this material that are meaningful for the evaluation of my own investigative material. The papers are listed according to dates of the first publication by an author on the topic in question.

In 1939 Pollock [et al.] compared parent losses that schizophrenics suffered in childhood with those of depressives. They discovered a much greater frequency of parent loss in the childhood histories of schizophrenics than in those of manic-depressives (38 percent to 17 percent, respectively). Their subjects were patients who had been admitted to state hospitals in New York.

In 1949 Ruth and T. Lidz compared the early parent losses among schizophrenics and among medical students. Such losses proved to occur much more frequently among their schizophrenics (40 percent to 17 percent)—but their study included only 50 schizophrenics.

In 1952 and 1965 Oltman and Friedman published two extensive sets of statistics (in 1952 together with McGarry) that compared parent losses of schizophrenics in state hospitals with those of hospital personnel. They arrived at the conclusion that loss of parents occurred with equal frequency in both groups (loss of parents before age 19 in the first set of investigations was 34 percent, 35 percent in the second; and for those among the hospital personnel, 32 percent and 34 percent, respectively). But parent losses by divorces or separations of the parents (sometimes in connection with a psychosis in one of the parents) were more frequent among schizophrenics than among the hospital personnel, in contrast to parental losses by death. Early-onset schizophrenics more often suffered the loss of a parent before age 19 than did the late-onset patients. Loss of parents in early childhood among the examined schizophrenics was somewhat greater than such loss later in life in the same group, but not significantly so. Among both schizophrenics and the normal population, loss of fathers was more frequent than loss of mothers.

Neurotic and psychopathic investigative subjects showed considerably higher parent-loss figures in childhood than did the schizophrenics or the hospital personnel.

The authors themselves noticed that hospital employees do not necessarily represent the average population in all respects. Their average family backgrounds may be somehow unique and different from popular norms. Many of the hospital employees never filled out their questionnaires, so that from this fact, too, some doubt arises as to the validity of statistics concerning their parent losses. These and other shortcomings in the comparison material selected by the authors had to be tolerated, since at the time there were no better statistics available on the frequencies of parent loss among an average population group that would adequately compare with the patients. The authors were able to find no more than four studies in the literature up to 1949 (and two more by 1965) that had dealt with statistical data on frequencies of parent loss among the general population. But none of these statistics would have been more suitable for comparisons with the authors' findings among schizophrenics than their own findings among hospital employees. A number of other, much more serious objections than the selection of hospital employees as representatives of the general population could be raised against all these earlier attempts to determine the frequency of parent loss among the general population. Still, most of these statistics yielded similar figures for parent losses, which is rather surprising, since they originated from totally different investigative groups, of which none could adequately represent the average population. For example, Ingham (1949) found a 35 percent parent loss among college students before their 22nd. birthdays, Gardner and Goldman (1945) a 32 percent parent loss among personnel of the American Navy before age 17, Wahl (1956) a 30 percent loss among American draftees (as compared to 32 percent and 34 percent among the hospital employees reported by the authors).

In 1954 and 1956 Wahl published statistics on parent losses among schizophrenics. In the first paper he compares the parent losses among schizophrenics from a state hospital with parental deaths from statistics on an average population group by Fisher (1950), and in the second paper schizophrenic members of the Navy are compared to Navy recruits. Wahl (1954, 1956) reaches the conclusion that loss of parents is more frequent among schizophrenics than among members of the comparison groups. Among his schizophrenics loss of father occurs more frequently than loss of mother. Schizophrenics had lost a parent between ages 1–5 and 10–15 more frequently than between ages 5 and 10, according to these statistics. In the first set of statistics by this author, loss of parents among the schizophrenic males is more frequent than among the schizophrenic females.

In the evaluation of figures by Wahl (1954, 1956), consideration must be given to the fact that the childhood histories of schizophrenics were evaluated on the basis of information contained in the routine patient histories, and that for this reason, those patient histories containing insufficient data on childhood conditions had to be eliminated. The median errors and the statistical significance of the differences were not calculated in this paper, nor can they be determined from these publications, partly because they include no indication as to how many samples were taken from among 100,000 recruits. The comparability of schizophrenics with the representatives of the average population, for instance, in relation to birth years, cannot be checked either. The loss of parents is circumscribed in a way that was not applied in any other papers, so that the application of the figures from it is not entirely relevant.

The great achievement of Gregory is that he demonstrated in several publications since 1958 that the preceding publications about the frequencies of parent losses did not measure up to the demands of accurate statistics. He clearly outlined the statistical methods that favor the compilation of reliable data. Among several examples he showed how the frequency of early parent loss by death could be calculated for a certain age group of an average population by starting with the major statistics on average life-spans of the general population. In so doing, a number of circumstances must be carefully considered, such as the age of the parents at the time the

child is born, the year of birth of the child, the longer life-spans of married as opposed to unmarried people, the losses of fathers caused by wars and, in America, the proportions between white and black people.

Based on the death-rate statistics of the population, Gregory determined parent losses by death among children born in Minnesota between 1939 and 1954. Of the 15-year-old children among these, 5.6 percent had lost their fathers, 2.5 percent their mothers and 0.2 percent both parents, according to his calculations. (The individual percentages for loss of only father or only mother include the children who lost both parents. The figures, therefore, amount to a total of parents lost of 5.6 percent + 2.5 percent, and not to 5.6 percent + 2.5 percent + 0.2 percent.) Gregory (1965) now compared these percentages rendered from the mortality statistics with the direct calculations by Hathaway and Monachesi (1963) for 11,329 15-year-old children from Minnesota. In respect to the losses of fathers, the two percentages obtained by such totally different methods are in remarkable agreement. On the other hand, somewhat fewer losses of mothers were discovered by direct questioning of the children than might have been expected according to the calculations. One possible reason why all losses of mothers were not reported by the children questioned may be that widowers usually remarry sooner than widows do, and that children with stepmothers, either are not aware of having lost their real mothers or are more reluctant about discussing it than are those children who live alone with their mother, do know about the death of their father, and feel free to talk about it. Another reason for the lower figures for losses of mothers, while the count of lost fathers remains complete, as it appeared when children were being questioned, might also lie in the fact that the mortality rate among children who have lost their mothers is greater than that of children who have lost their fathers. However that may be—for this discussion of ours it is important to remember what possible unexpected sources of errors threaten an accurate, reliable set of statistics on parent losses among the general population.

Gregory (1965) reworked the investigative material of Oltman et al. (1952, 1965), that has already been mentioned, for its statistical reliability. Based on this study, he concludes that the only fact statistically certain that this investigation revealed was that psychopaths and neurotics lost more of their parents before their 19th birthday than schizophrenics or the general population did. While an increase in all parent losses together among schizophrenics cannot be proved, there is an increase in the case of the schizophrenics as compared to the general population only among those whose parents die as a result of psychoses. For all examined mental disturbances taken together (including schizophrenias) an increase in parent losses during the child's first 5 years of life can be determined in comparison to the average population. This increase is brought about mainly by early losses of the parents of neurotics. Among the calculated and mathematically checked results by Oltman et al. (1952, 1965), which have but minimal statistical significance, the following is worth mentioning in our evaluation: Schizophrenics reaching their 19th birthday lost their parents more often by divorce or separation of the parents than did children under corresponding conditions among the normal population.

Nielsen in 1954 compared the childhood histories of 55 schizophrenic women in Sweden with those of a carefully selected group from the general population. He detected no appreciable differences worth mentioning in respect to early parent losses in the two groups.

Eva Johanson published studies in 1958 of 138 male schizophrenics in Göteborg, Sweden. For her comparisons she uses investigations by Ramer (1941) of normal subjects from Stockholm, whose value as comparison subjects, however, she does not rate very highly. The comparison reveals no difference of any statistical significance, yet the number of broken homes among families of schizophrenics appears rather to be greater than it is among normal groups, although the schizophrenics were less frequently illegitimate children than the normals were. Schizophrenics who came from broken homes suffered earlier onsets of illness, on the average, than did others. But Eva Johanson (1958) did not find any relationship between childhood conditions in the home and the prognosis or symptomatology of schizophrenias.

A paper by Petursson (1961), recording parent losses among 225 patients, has no value for studies of schizophrenics, since it considers only 13 of them. I mention it anyway, because it is one of the few studies on parent losses prepared outside North America. Among the subject patients of this Icelandic author there were fewer parent losses among schizophrenics than among neurotics, alcoholics, or depressives.

Josefine Hilgard and Newman (1963) investigated loss of parents by death among 1,561 schizophrenics, 929 alcoholics, and 1,096 representatives of the general population selected according to the modern principles of opinion surveys. The loss of parents among schizophrenics and alcoholics was determined from patient histories. Statistically reliable differences in the frequency of parent losses among schizophrenics and alcoholics as compared to those of the average population were not evident. Losses of parents before age 19 among the schizophrenics as well as the alcoholics, amounted to 26 percent for each group, and among the general population to 21 percent. The increase in loss of parents among schizophrenics referred only to hospitalized patients between the ages of 20 and 40, and not to very early-onset or very late-onset cases. Among those patients becoming ill between ages 20 and 30, losses of mothers exceeded losses of fathers, in comparison to the average population. Pitts et al. (1965) found no increase in parent losses during childhood among schizophrenics in comparison to the general population, in losses either through death or divorce or separation. As representatives of the normal population they used patients hospitalized for physical illnesses. The study included 101 schizophrenics and the same number of patients for a control group. (Among manic-depressives, alcoholics, and neurotics, also, no differences in premature parent losses emerged from this investigation.)

Brill and Liston (1966) investigated the loss of parents in 5,479 psychiatric patients of a polyclinic. They did not specifically identify schizophrenics, but compared just groups of "psychotics," of organic patients, of psychoneurotics, and of patients with personality disorders. It is possible, however, that schizophrenics made up the majority of the "psychotic" group. In connection with our inquiry, their findings yield the following: Differences in frequency of parent losses among the various groups did not exist that had any statistical significance, and particularly not among the psychotics, the neurotics, and the cases of personality disorders. The total figure for parent losses among the patients of the polyclinic was no different from that of the normal population. On the other hand, the patients (including the schizophrenics) had suffered more parent losses by divorce or separation than had the general population. Furthermore, the statistics indicated—but with no statistical validity—that female patients showed more parent losses in their childhood histories than male patients did.

In 1966, Brown criticized the older broken-home statistics the same way that Gregory and I had done. His own investigations do not relate to schizophrenics, but from having surveyed the literature he infers that premature parent loss in the childhood histories of "various types of mental patients" occurs more frequently than it does among the general population. But he records an even greater frequency of premature parent losses in his own investigations from among the childhood histories of delinquents. Brown (1966) also mentions that Gregory in retrospect reported on his own statistical findings, according to which schizophrenics more frequently came from broken homes, as being no longer valid. Brown (1966) mentions also that parental loss has a much lower impact on child development than the way in which such children are treated and cared for later as half orphans.

Constance Dennehy succeeded brilliantly in 1966 in handling with unparalleled reliability the concept of premature parent loss in a general population group. She uses as a basis the census figures of 1921 in England, also population estimates from the Social Security Administration in the United States, and the "Chester Beattie Serial Abridged Life Tables," and adds to these, further representatives of the general population, by persuading some of the personnel of a large department store in London to participate. Her figures on parental loss by death were derived from a study of 336 schizophrenics from three different London hospitals. Working carefully, she achieved a basis for comparison of data from the general population and the schizophrenics by, among other things, considering the birth years of her probands.

The comparison showed that schizophrenics of both sexes more frequently suffer the loss of their mothers by death in the first 5 years of their lives than do representatives of the general population (three times as frequently!). In addition, male schizophrenics more often experience also the death of their fathers, particularly between the ages of 5 and 10. The author assumes that these findings confirm the theory that premature loss of mothers favors the emergence of schizophrenia.

But at the same time, Granville-Grossman (1966) arrives at the opposite conclusion. He studies the broken-home problem from a new and illuminating angle. Beginning with 82 sets of siblings in England, among whom at least one member is schizophrenic and another set has lost a parent prematurely, he tests whether those siblings who lost their parent early become schizophrenic sooner than those who lost their parent later in life. He finds no difference, and with that, no causal relationship either, between premature parent loss and the onset of schizophrenia.

The broken-home statistics on schizophrenics should not only be compared with those of the general population, but comparisons between them and patients with other mental illness are also of interest.

The results of investigations of depressives are contradictory, but those findings predominate that oppose the theory that many come from broken homes. More frequent childhoods involving broken homes among depressives than among the normal population were recorded, among others, by Stenstedt (1952, 1959), Forrest et al. (1965) and Brown (1966). Oltman et al. (1952), Pitts et al. (1964/65), Angst (1966), Munro (1966), Perris (1966), and Angst and Perris (1968), on the other hand, found no differences. The contradictions in the investigative findings are partly explained by the fact that the authors were studying various types of depressions. The frequency of premature parent loss is greatest among the neurotic and reactive depressives treated at hospitals, but hardly any were found among the phasic depressives.

There is considerable agreement in the broken-home statistics developed by many investigators in respect to neurotic and psychopathologic personalities, particularly to criminal types and alcoholics. All these types of patients more frequently come from broken homes than do representatives of the general population or schizophrenics (Madow and Hardy 1947, Ingham 1949, Glueck and Glueck 1950, Jane Oltmann et al. 1952, M. Bleuler 1955, Petursson 1961, Andry 1962, Hegg 1962, Borowitz 1963, Baxter 1966, and Brown and Epps 1966). Of course, there are some contradictory findings, as well, as indicated by Josefine Hilgard and Martha Newman (1963), Pitts et al. (1964/65), Brill and Liston (1966).

The literature to date therefore yields the following information:

(1) Early parent loss is not notably frequent among schizophrenics in comparison to its frequency among the general population.

(2) It is still uncertain whether early parent loss among schizophrenics compares even slightly in frequency with that among the normal population.

(3) Early parent loss among patients with neurotic, psychopathic, and addictive personality developments occurs more frequently than it does among schizophrenics.

(4) Nothing certain, or even probable, is known about whether various groups of schizophrenics are distinguishable in any way as to the frequency of early parent loss.

Survey of My Own Investigations

In view of the great interest that has been expressed in recent years in the problem of the broken home, it seemed appropriate to apply the investigative material on hand in developing data on the frequency of parental loss. It was particularly appropriate for this purpose, since the childhood and youth of my 208 probands had been thoroughly researched, and considerable information of many varied types had been accumulated about them in the process. Therefore I am convinced that the data on the loss of parents by my 208 probands is reliable. Furthermore, it was tempting to do an investigation on the parent losses of my probands, because previous investigations, as has just been demonstrated above, failed to supply answers to the problem of the frequency of such losses among schizophrenics in comparison to the normal population.

The previous investigations by other authors, however, do also raise rather weighty objections against tackling this specific problem anew. Here again it is obvious that it is easier to criticize than to improve. Anyone who remembers the criticism against the former statistics and wants to improve on them, soon sees himself confronted with a gigantic and, in the main, insurmountable task. The labor of years of a large staff of full-time co-workers would be required to achieve—maybe—the great dream of determining once and for all whether, to what extent, and in what respect, there are differences between the parent losses of later-onset schizophrenics and normal, healthy people.

For this reason alone I was on the verge of abandoning any attempt to carry through an investigation of parent losses among my probands, but in addition, still other objections turned up. It is, after all, our primary purpose to investigate the etiology of the schizophrenias, the statistics on premature parent loss, however, do not, as already explained,

tell us anything of primary importance on the etiology. Furthermore, it is also easy to heap contempt on the efforts to secure a better set of statistics on broken homes by ascertaining what anyone with any experience knows, namely, that schizophrenics as well as normal, healthy people can come from broken homes, just as they can come from normal, happy families—so why bother with any more figures and calculations?

If, despite all this, I proceeded to attack the problem, to work on the raw figures for the parental losses of my probands, it was not because I succumbed to the illusory hope of completely eliminating the statistical shortcomings that Gregory (1965) and I had censured. No, my expectations were a bit more modest. I felt that numerous statistics on a variety of groups of schizophrenics and representatives of the general population compared with one another, might yet be instructive, that such comparisons would be bound to reveal the more important sources of errors. And possibly, also, some light might be shed on the true origins of schizophrenias, if differences in the numbers and types of parent losses were to show up from comparisons of different subgroups of schizophrenics.

In order to impart real meaning to the data collected on my 208 principal schizophrenic probands, I had to gather a large number of subjects suitable for comparison. This was a task that consumed a great deal of time, that kept me busy for years, and that required a large staff of co-workers. I cannot be absolutely certain that all the time and effort devoted to the task were worthwhile.

To begin with, the findings for my schizophrenics had to be compared with findings for suitable representatives of the general population. One of the best sources for these was among the draftees eligible for military service. But the comparability of findings concerning premature parent loss among the 208 principal schizophrenic probands and among the 1505 draftees suffered, among other things, from the fact that the schizophrenic probands were all, on the average, several decades older than the draftees. The differences revealed by the investigation, therefore, had to be checked to make sure that they really were related to the schizophrenic condition of the probands or whether they were brought about or influenced by the age difference. It was not possible to investigate selected representatives of a normal population group that had the same birth dates as the schizophrenics.

But it was possible to study the parent losses of a new group of young schizophrenics whose birth years corresponded to those of the draftees. To further balance relationships, an additional group of schizophrenics were checked for premature parent loss—those whose birth years fell between those of the 208 principal schizophrenic probands at the one extreme and those of the above-mentioned draftees and the younger schizophrenics at the other.

In the meantime the surprising fact had been revealed that premature parent losses in the patient histories occurred more frequently among the schizophrenic women than among the schizophrenic men. However, this interesting indication discovered in studying the three above-mentioned groups of schizophrenics still was not statistically significant. In order to confirm or refute it, a supplemental investigation on parent losses was launched with a large number of additional schizophrenics.

A group of female schizophrenic probands from a private sanatorium was added to the study, so that the influence of childhood backgrounds of schizophrenics could be checked for frequency of early parent loss.

Among the 208 principal schizophrenic probands, I personally did the research on the childhood histories, gathering a great many different kinds of information in the process. At my direction a number of colleagues at the clinic took part in these supplemental investigations on early parent losses. All 1505 draftees were personally questioned by Drs. A. Hicklin or S. Rotach. The childhood histories of the four groups of schizophrenics that were added to supplement the principal investigations, were assembled for the most part from patient histories. Only when these lacked vitally needed data were additional interviews made. The major portion of this work was done by Mrs. Ruth Frey, who had had many years of psychiatric secretarial experience. Dr. Hicklin and I supervised her work, particularly in regard to the more difficult questions.

A total of 952 schizophrenics and 1505 draftees were investigated as to whether they had suffered premature parental loss.

In addition, however, I had been having several groups of schizophrenics studied for a number of years in respect to their childhood backgrounds. These groups were gathered by a number of colleagues, at the clinic by several different methods and their findings had been previously published (Huber 1954, Katharina Rubeli 1959, Illberg 1961, Doris Morf 1962).

By applying the requisite care, these findings could be used for comparisons.

Independently of the present study, findings on premature parent losses were published by our clinic on other than schizophrenic patients (by Angst 1966, Margrit Rotach-Fuchs 1968, and by me 1955). These also could be used for comparisons.

Table 2.5 was compiled as a survey of the groups of patients and normals, whose parental losses were specifically studied at our clinic and later compared among one another (see Table 2.5).

Establishment of Concepts and Definitions

In the following set of tables the first concept to be established was at what age of the late-onset schizophrenic the separation from the family community took place. Family disruptions were separately listed for each of the first three 5-year periods of life, for the 16th and 17th years, and for the 18th year. Then all family separations from birth to the end of the 15th year, and from birth to the end of the 18th year were listed.

In respect to the type or manner of family disruption, separate categories were listed for:
—death of one of the parents
—legal separation or divorce of the parents
—absence of long duration of one of the parents
—absence of the father subsequent to illegitimate birth
—placing the child outside the home for foster care.

The columns concerning the death of parents require no further explanation. Illegitimacy is used in the sense that the civil registry office uses it, that is, children born to parents out of wedlock whose parents marry after the birth of the child are entered as legitimate. Separation of parents implies a permanent separation, usually onc that a court of law has sanctioned. On the other hand, the temporary absence of a father on military service or temporarily in a travel status for his work was not registred as a separation, if family ties to him remained intact and the feelings of the family as a unit were undisturbed. Such "natural" absences of children from the home as attendance at schools, vocational training institutions, or jobs were not counted either. For instance, it is the custom in the Canton of Zürich to send young girls for one year to a boarding school or to a private household in the French-speaking part of Switzerland, or families living in

Table 2.5. Types of proband groups compared for parent loss by specific investigators

Type of proband	Abbreviated designation in the text	Investigator	No. of probands
Schizophrenics admitted to Burghölzli in 1942/43	Principal probands of this study	M. Bleuler	208
Schizophrenics born 1940/45; from admissions of 3 hospitals	Young schizophrenics	Hicklin & Mrs. Frey	150
Schizophrenics born 1915/30; from Burghölzli admissions	Middle-aged schizophrenics	M. Bleuler	130
Schizophrenics born 1940/45; from private sanatoria	Schizophrenic private patients	M. Bleuler	20
Schizophrenics admitted to Burghölzli in 1960/61	Supplemental schizophrenics	M. Bleuler & Mrs. Frey	444
Schizophrenic inpatients of Burghölzli in 1954	Huber schizophrenics	Huber	100
Schiz's. from admissions and inpatients of Breitenau clinic, 1930/45	Rubeli schizophrenics	Rubeli	102
Schizophrenics from admissions to Burghölzli in 1955	Illberg schizophrenics	Illberg	100
Schizophrenic foster-care patients admitted to Burghölzli in 1942/44	Morf schizophrenics	Morf	65
		Total schizophrenics:	1319
Draft-eligibles of 1945 from Canton of Zürich	Draftees	Rotach & Hicklin	1505
Alcoholics from Payne Whitney (N.Y.) and Burghölzli 1949/50	Alcoholics	M. Bleuler	100
Edogenous-depressives from Burghölzli admissions 1959/63	Depressives	Angst	331
Neurotics admitted to treatment station of Psychiatric Univ. Polyclinic of Zürich 1954/56	Neurotics	Rotach-Fuchs	100

the country send their sons away to learn a trade as an apprentice when no suitable master is available in the vicinity. Such children do not feel themselves to be cast out from their families; and indeed, they are not cast out, for contact with their parents is maintained, and they keep looking forward to coming home to their families when their stint away from home is finished.[9] There was no problem whatever in accounting for children who were completing their required schooling abroad (up to ages 15–16) in boarding schools or otherwise, for among our patients who were younger than this none had been sent to schools abroad. Contrary to customs in English-speaking countries, this practice is not in vogue in Switzerland.

It would have been desirable if our tables had contained nothing but objective and definite data. But at times some wholly unexpected questions developed as to definitions. For example, are we dealing with a broken home when a court decrees a divorce but the parents continue after the judgment to live

9. Listings on extended absences of the later schizophrenics (principal probands of this study) at ages 14–18, away from home for "natural" reasons, without separation from the family, that is, for apprenticeships or jobs, and among girls for a sojourn in the French-speaking sector of Switzerland (not included in Table 2.6):

Age during extended absence from home	Boys	Girls	Total
16 and 17 years old	6	2	8
18 and 19 years old	10	20	30

together with the child? On one occasion there were doubts as to whether the legal father was the actual father; another time an arbitrary decision had to be made as to whether a father traveled in his job only intermittently, or whether he was living and working abroad, permanently separated from his family. Such circumstances, which could be evaluated only subjectively, did not occur too frequently, however, so that their statistical value was insignificant. It would not be worthwhile to describe them in detail here.

Parent Losses among the 208 Principal Schizophrenic Probands

Table 2.6 shows the number of broken homes among the 208 principal schizophrenic probands. From it we learn that over one-third (36 percent) of all the schizophrenic probands came from families in which a separation occurred before the proband's 15th birthday; that is, from a broken home. By the time they had lived 18 years, as many as 40 percent had suffered either loss of, or separation from, one or both parents. The figure for parent losses accordingly seems high, so some additional figures on the average normal population will have to supplement the total impression.

Family disruptions are rather evenly distributed over the years of childhood and youth, showing that 23 percent fall in the first, 25 percent in the second, and 26 percent in the third five-year life-span.

Only in less than half the cases, did a family disruption occur because of death; in more than half, the cause was divorce or separation, illegitimate birth of the child, or his placement in foster care.

Loss of father by death is more frequent than loss of mother by death. Likewise, separation from the father predominates over separation from the mother, when the parents were divorced or legally separated. Both occur independently of later schizophrenia in the proband. On the average, fathers die earlier than mothers, because, on the average, fathers are older than mothers and, on the average, their life-spans are shorter.[10] In cases involving divorce or legal separation, the courts award the children to the mother in a vast majority of instances. The proportion between father-

10. Average life-span in the Canton of Zürich between 1901 and 1910 was 49.25 years for men, and 52.15 years for women; between 1959/61 the corresponding figures are 69.5 for men and 72.8 for women.

and mother-losses found to exist does not deviate significantly from what would have been expected quite independently of the schizophrenias of the probands. And, more especially, there is no sort of statistical basis for assuming that the loss of one's mother has any exceptionally great bearing on the onset of a schizophrenia in the child.

If after all this, Table 2.6 still does not show whether premature loss of one's parents places one in jeopardy of becoming schizophrenic as a consequence, the figures in this table will, however, suggest two indications: If premature parent loss does after all favor schizophrenic risk in the offspring, then (a) such danger is approximately the same at any stage in a child's life, and (b) loss of father has about the same significance as loss of mother. The figures do not prove the assumption that only the loss of a mother in the early years of childhood markedly increases the risk of a schizophrenic onset in the child.

Parent Losses among 1505 Draftees as Representatives of the General Population

The figures from Table 2.6 do not begin to become interesting until they are compared with the broken-home statistics of the general population. These were hitherto lacking in Switzerland, and broken-home statistics from other countries are in no way suitable for comparisons with those of our 208 principal schizophrenic probands. In the first place they are scarce. Then, they have been gathered from selected segments of the population, and their publication, only in rare exceptions, furnishes any precise description as to how the broken-home concept was arrived at in each individual case. Research on the frequency of the broken home among the average population of Zürich was a pressing need.

A marvelous source for just such research materialized in the questioning of the young men eligible for military service. All Swiss males are obligated to submit to examinations for fitness for military service when they reach age 20. The chief surgeon of our army, Dr. (Colonel) R. Käser, granted us permission to interview extensively all candidates reporting for this examination who were born in 1945, with respect to details of the relationships prevailing in their parental homes. These interviews were conducted in 1964 by my colleagues, Drs. S. Rotach and R. Hicklin, and their findings were published in 1965 in the *Vierteljahresschrift für Schweizerische Sanitätsoffiziere* (Quarterly for Swiss Medical Officers) (see

Table 2.6. Parent losses among all 208 principal probands

Totals of all probands with at least one parent loss[1]

Age spans in years

Parent loss by	0-4 11/12	5-9 11/12	10-14 11/12	15-16 11/12	17-18	0-14 11/12 No.	0-14 11/12 % of all probands	0-18 No.	0-18 % of all probands	Total parent losses[2] 0-18
Death of father	2	9	9(+1)	4(+1)	1	20(+1)	9.6	25(+2)	12	27
Death of mother	3	4	5(+2)	(+1)	1	12(+2)	5.7	13(+3)	6.25	16
Death of both parents	0	0	0	(+1)	0	0	0	(+1)	0	1
Separation or divorce										
Child lost father	5	4	4	0	0	13	6.25	13	6.25	13
Child lost mother	1	0	1	0	0	2	0.96	2	0.96	2
Child lost both parents	2	2(+1)	0	0	0	4(+1)	1.92	4(+1)	1.92	5
Long absence of one parent from home[3]	(+1)	2	3	0	0	5(+1)	2.4	5(+1)	2.4	6
Illegitimate birth										
Resulting in chaotic home	2	0	0	0	0	2	0.96	2	0.96	2
Resulting in happy home	4	0	0	0	0	4	1.92	4	1.92	4
Foster care[4]										
(a) Dissolution of family	(+7)	(+8)	(+8)	(+2)	0	(+23)	0	(+25)	0	25
(b) Despite family remaining intact	3	4(+1)	4(+1)	2	0	11(+2)	5.3	13(+2)	6.25	15
(c) Frequent shifting between foster home and parents	1	0	0	0	0	1	0.48	1	0.48	1
Total parent losses:	23(+8)	25(+10)	26(+12)	6(+5)	2	74(+30)	35.5	82(+35)	39.4	117

1. The numbers added in parentheses represent those probands who had already suffered an earlier, different loss of a parent, and who have been accounted for above or below that entry, under a different category. These figures are not represented in the percentage column that follows the (+) entries.

2. In the figures for total parent losses, loss of father and of mother are included even when they apply to the same proband while in the preceding column the probands are counted only once when they have lost both parents. The figures in this column are the sums of the figures in parentheses and those not in parentheses from the 8th column.

3. Extended absences of one parent include those parents who were away uninterruptedly for at least a year in a hospital or sanatorium.

4. Only those probands are counted as being in foster care (in foster homes or with strange families) who were so placed for at least a year. Probands away from their families for training or schooling were not included.

Bibliography). The study included 1505 draft-eligible young men from the Canton of Zürich, most of whom had been born in 1945 (a few in 1944 and 1946). The results appear in Table 2.7, which shows:

The general population of the Canton of Zürich also experiences rather frequent family disruptions, which amount to 24 percent before age 15 and 29 percent before age 18 among the draftees interviewed. Even so, our 208 principal schizophrenic probands more often come from broken homes than do the draftees, and the statistical evaluation of this difference reads as follows: The difference is set as certain for loss of parents by age 15 at $p < 0.001$, and by age 18 at $p < 0.01$.

The distribution by age groups of events leading to broken homes is less like that among the draftees than it is among the schizophrenic probands. During the first 5 years of their lives more disruptions occur than between ages 5 to 15. The difference is not statistically certain ($p < 0.1$).

It was worthy of note that family disruptions among the schizophrenic probands increase in comparison to those among the draftees in all five causal areas, but that the greatest difference of all occurs among those disruptions caused by death. Only in these cases is the difference significant ($p < 0.001$). If the attempt were made to relate the schizophrenias causally to a disturbed childhood, one ought to assume that the childhood history should reveal divorce, separation of the parents, or placement of the child away from home much more frequently than such events would occur among the normal population, whereas the death of one parent would play a lesser role. One is, to be sure, inclined to assume that separation from a father or a mother who is still living but has left the home induces far more anguish and is much more likely to produce illness than the mere process of getting over the death of a parent. But the findings seem to refute this expectation. The comparison between Tables 2.6 and 2.7 shows that the childhood histories of our 208 principal probands vis-à-vis those of the draftees reveal a greater frequency of parent loss by death than by divorce, separation, or abandonment of the child. Obviously this increase in deaths among the parents of our schizophrenics over those of the draftees is related to the fact that the latter belong to a much younger generation, and that the mortality rate drops in successive generations.[11] There is no reason to infer that this difference relates

to the fact that the one group is made up of schizophrenics and the other of mentally normal people.

As in the case of the schizophrenic probands, so also for the draftees up to age 15, the predominating cause for separation from parents, by a wide margin, is the death of the father. Among the schizophrenics the ratio is 20:12 and among the draftees 65:37, a difference that is not significant. This comparison should not be interpreted as an indication that the loss of a mother would be more conducive to the onset of schizophrenic psychoses than the loss of a father. Furthermore, the father's absence as the result of the child's being illegitimate also occurs with the same frequency in both groups.

If our 208 principal schizophrenic probands and the 1505 draftees were truly comparable groups that differed only as to the existence or absence of a schizophrenia, one could conclude that, by and large, parental separation is only a little more frequent among schizophrenics than it is among the general population, and that the increase occurs principally between 5 and 15 years of age of the child (not statistically verified).

But such conclusions are not certain, because only a limited comparability existed between the two groups. The group of schizophrenic probands quite obviously differs from that of the draftees in characteristics other than the fact of being or not being schizophrenic. The

---

11. The average life expectancy at birth during the listed years in the Canton of Zürich amounted to:

Birth-years	Males	Females
1881/88	43.3	45.7
1889/00	45.7	48.5
1901/10	49.25	52.15
1910/11	50.65	53.89
1920/21	54.48	57.50
1921/30	58.14	61.41
1929/32	59.17	63.05
1933/37	60.7	64.6
1931/41	60.93	64.84
1939/44	62.68	66.96
1941/50	64.10	68.28
1948/53	66.36	70.85
1959/61	69.5	74.8

But divorces and legal separations have also increased greatly, which is not revealed when comparing Tables 2.6 and 2.7. The number of divorces in the Canton of Zürich amounted to the following per 100,000 marriages:

1887–1890	293	1929–1932	671
1899–1902	325	1940–1943	594
1909–1912	384	1949–1952	699
1919–1922	542	1959–1962	585

Table 2.7. Parent losses among 1,505 draftees from Canton of Zürich, born between 1944–46, as representatives of the general population (by Hicklin and Rotach)

Totals of all probands having lost at least one parent[1]

Age spans in years

Separation from parents by	0–4 $\frac{11}{12}$	5–9 $\frac{11}{12}$	10–14 $\frac{11}{12}$	15–16 $\frac{11}{12}$	17–18	0–14 $\frac{11}{12}$ No.	0–14 $\frac{11}{12}$ % of all probands	0–18 No.	0–18 % of all probands	Total parent losses[2] 0–18
Death of father	23(+1)	15(+1)	27(+2)	22(+3)	12(+2)	65(+4)	4.3	99(+9)	6.5	108
Death of mother	12	15(+1)	10(+3)	8(+2)	4(+2)	37(+4)	2.5	49(+8)	3.3	57
Separation or divorce of parents	50(+1)	44(+2)	43(+2)	13(+2)	4	137(+5)	9.1	154(+7)	10.2	161
Long-term absence of one parent from home[3]	9(+2)	9(+2)	8	3	1	26(+4)	1.7	30(+4)	2	34
Illegitimate birth	33	0	0	0	0	33	2.2	33	2.2	33
In foster care[4]	15(+31)	23(+34)	24(+37)	7(+5)	4(+1)	62(+102)	4.1	73(+108)	4.9	181
Totals of parent losses:	142(+35)	106(+40)	112(+44)	53(+12)	25(+5)	360(+119)	23.9	438(+136)	29.1	574

1. The numbers added in parentheses represent those probands who had already suffered an earlier, different loss of a parent, and who have been accounted for above or below that entry, under a different category. These figures are not represented in the percentage column that follows the (+) entries.

2. In the figures for total parent losses, loss of father and of mother are included even when they apply to the same proband while in the preceding column the probands are counted only once when they have lost both parents. The figures in this column are the sums of the figures in parentheses and those not in parentheses from the 8th column.

3. Extended absences of one parent include those parents who were away uninterruptedly for at least a year in a hospital or sanatorium.

4. Only those probands are counted as being in foster care (in foster homes or with strange families) who were so placed for at least a year. Probands away from their families for training or schooling were not included.

first doubt is whether the statistical differences between the groups have anything at all to do with schizophrenic development, or whether they depend on other differences existing between the two groups. Such other differences may include:

(a) Sex differences. Both sexes are represented almost equally among the schizophrenic probands, but only men are draftees. The possibility that parental loss among the normal population might occur more or less frequently among children of one sex or the other is most unlikely.[12] On the other hand, it is possible to imagine that parent loss could affect the later development of boys differently than it does girls, and that for this reason the late-onset schizophrenic vulnerability is also different between boys and girls.

(b) Differences in birth years. The draftees were born between 1944 and 1946, most of them in 1945. The birth years of the schizophrenic probands are scattered between 1874 and 1927. Quite plainly this difference is of vital importance when comparing the two groups. The loss of parents must certainly decrease as life expectancy increases, but, on the contrary, divorces and separations have increased over the time span in question.

(c) Differences in locale of origin. There may perhaps be differences in the rates of parent losses among the general population coming from different locales in the Canton of Zürich, especially between those from urban and from rural sections.

(d) Differences in the type of questioning. The comment seems appropriate that the investigative techniques used for the two groups did not coincide, but that we may assume a reasonably comparable, reliable set of results from them. The investigative methods used for the 208 principal schizophrenic probands has already been described. Each one of the 1505 draftees was questioned in person in a private interview of 5- to 10-minute duration. They were informed that their statements would have no bearing whatsoever on their military evaluation and would in no way affect their personal lives. The result in every instance was an uninhibited, candid conversation in which the proband felt that his confidences

were safe. Both interviewers and I are convinced that, at the very least, the vast majority of premature parent losses among this group was revealed. There is a special advantage in personal questioning compared to methods using questionnaires. To be sure, the possibility that some few might attempt to conceal an unhappy childhood cannot be entirely eliminated, but they had no motive for doing so and besides, they were aware that the interviewers (who were familiar with the life circumstances of people in their particular locale) might very well have caught them in a falsehood. On the other hand, the methodology of accumulating data on parent losses among the 208 schizophrenic probands always had the advantage of verification from a number of different sources. But, again, contrary to this, was the fact that the youth of many of the latter subjects lay decades behind them, sometimes as far back as deep in the previous century.

The attempts properly to evaluate the significance of the differences in the birth years, in sex, and in childhood conditions as between the 208 principal schizophrenic probands and the draftees, required a great amount of laborious and meticulous effort, which is described in the following section.

Different Aspects of Parent Losses between the Sexes

In order to render the two sets of data on the 208 principal schizophrenic probands and the 1505 draftees, fit for comparison I at first considered setting up these two groups according to sex. To what extent would a true comparison be influenced by the fact that the schizophrenic probands were both men and women and that the draftees were men only?

The temptation arose to investigate not only male, but also female representatives of the general population as to premature parent loss, but such an investigation proved impossible. While the draftees were good, nonselected representatives of the average population of younger males, there is no group of young girls in similar numbers that would represent a nonselective youthful average population of females that was also accessible for questioning. It may be assumed as probable that premature loss of parents among men and women of the general population occurs with approximately equal frequency. The fact that the interviewed representatives of the general population are exclusively men will not appreciably disturb our comparisons

---

12. After the completion of the manuscript for this section, the study by Munro and Griffiths (1968) appeared from England about premature parent loss by patients of a polyclinic. According to expectations, parent losses were the same for men as for women; however, the study is based on just 49 women and 51 men.

between them and the schizophrenic probands.

In contrast to this, it was uncertain from the outset whether premature parent loss in the childhood histories was equally frequent among schizophrenic men and women. If such parent losses had any psychotraumatic significance, one could easily imagine that this would be different between boys and girls. And if such a psychic trauma resulting from parent loss had any relationship to the genesis of schizophrenias, one would also have to account for differences in the frequencies of early parent losses as between male and female schizophrenics. It is for this reason that the premature parent losses of male and female schizophrenics are separately determined, and then separately compared with the parent losses among the general population for both sexes. Table 2.8 summarizes the premature parent loss among the male, and Table 2.9 that among the female principal schizophrenic probands. The result of the comparison came as a surprise to me.

A comparison between Tables 2.8 and 2.9 shows that premature parent loss in the childhood histories of the female schizophrenic probands occurs more frequently than it does in the childhood histories of the male schizophrenic probands. To be sure, the differences are not statistically significant ($p > 0.1$). Parental loss before the 15th birthday occurs in only 29 percent of the schizophrenic men, but in 42 percent of the schizophrenic women. The corresponding percentages at age 18 are 33 percent and 46 percent, respectively.

In comparing the frequency of premature parent losses among the male schizophrenics with those among the draftees, there is no significant difference. Before age 15, 29 percent of the male schizophrenic probands had lost a parent, compared to 24 percent of the draftees. (The corresponding figures up to age 18 are 33 percent and 29 percent, respectively.)

May we now assume that the women among the general population born between 1944 and 1946 suffered the same proportional frequency of family disruption and in the same way as the draftees did? It is scarcely conceivable that parent losses through death or the absence of a father resulting from an illegitimate birth should occur more frequently to the children of one sex than to those of the other. And it makes as little sense that divorces or legal separations should occur more often among the parents who produced

daughters than among those who produced sons. It does seem logical, however, that the ratio between boys and girls may be different among children placed in foster care; but if there were differences in this area, they would have almost no effect on the overall statistics for parent losses.

From this particular viewpoint it is justifiable to compare the statistics of the female schizophrenic probands with those of the male representatives of the average population. There are no serious objections in this case arising from the differences in the sexes, but there may be such objections in respect to the differences in birth dates, which will be discussed again below. One of the comparisons of statistics of the schizophrenic females with that of the draftees, undertaken with this reservation in mind (see Tables 2.9 and 2.7), shows that girls who later become schizophrenic, much more frequently came from broken homes than did the draftees. In 42 percent of the girls who later became schizophrenic it was found that a family disruption had occurred before their 15th birthdays, while among the draftees it was 24 percent. The corresponding percentages for family disruption before age 18 were 46 percent and 29 percent, respectively. These differences are statistically significant ($p < 0.001$).

Parent losses by death, compared to all other categories of parent losses among the schizophrenic women occurred at a ratio of 23:26, and among the draftees at 148:290. The frequency of premature parent losses among the girls who later became schizophrenic, therefore, is more often caused by death than among the draftees (this has not been proved statistically). This, in turn, could be explained by the differences in birth dates between the two groups.

Among the schizophrenic women probands the relationship of loss of father to loss of mother by death is 12:11, among the draftees it is 99:49. Accordingly, loss of mother among the girls who later became schizophrenic occurs more frequently than among the draftees at $p < 0.1$ (not statistically verified).

But it must still be pointed out that the differences in parent losses between the male and the female schizophrenics were discovered for the first time only upon studying the 208 principal schizophrenic probands of this book. These first indications still do not make a definite statement as to whether the same differences would occur between the sexes among other groups of schizophrenics. There-

Table 2.8. Parent losses among the 100 male principal probands (breakdown of Table 2.6)

Totals of all probands with at least one parent loss[1]

Age spans in years

Parent losses by	$0-4\frac{11}{12}$	$5-9\frac{11}{12}$	$10-14\frac{11}{12}$	$15-16\frac{11}{12}$	$17-18$	$0-14\frac{11}{12}$ No.	$0-14\frac{11}{12}$ % of all probands	$0-18$ No.	$0-18$ % of all probands	Total parent losses[2] $0-18$
Death of father	2	4	4(+1)	2(+1)	1	10(+1)	10	13(+2)	13	15
Death of mother	1	1	0	(+1)	0	2	2	2(+1)	2	3
Death of both parents	0	0	0	(+1)	0	0	0	(+1)	0	1
Separation or divorce										
Child lost father	3	0	3	0	0	6	6	6	6	6
Child lost mother	0	0	1	0	0	1	1	1	1	1
Child lost both parents	2	1(+1)	0	0	0	3(+1)	3	3(+1)	3	4
Long absence of one parent[3]	0	2	2	0	0	4	4	4	4	4
Illegitimate Birth										
Resulting in chaotic home	0	0	0	0	0	0	0	0	0	0
Resulting in happy home	0	0	0	0	0	0	0	0	0	0
Foster care[4]										
Dissolution of family	(+2)	(+5)	(+3)	(+2)	0	(+10)	0	(+12)	0	12
Family remains intact	1	1(+1)	1(+1)	1	0	3(+2)	3	4(+2)	4	6
Frequent shifting between foster home and parents	0	0	0	0	0	0	0	0	0	0
Total parent losses:	9(+2)	9(+7)	11(+5)	3(+5)	1	29(+14)	29	33(+19)	33	52

1. The numbers added in parentheses represent those probands who had already suffered an earlier, different loss of a parent, and who have been accounted for above or below that entry, under a different category. These figures are not represented in the percentage column that follows the (+) entries.

2. In the figures for total parent losses, loss of father and of mother are included even when they apply to the same proband while in the preceding column the probands are counted only once when they have lost both parents. The figures in this column are the sums of the figures in parentheses and those not in parentheses from the 8th column.

3. Extended absences of one parent include those parents who were away uninterruptedly for at least a year in a hospital or sanatorium.

4. Only those probands are counted as being in foster care (in foster homes or with strange families) who were so placed for at least a year. Probands away from their families for training or schooling were not included.

Table 2.9. Parent losses among the 108 female principal probands (breakdown of Table 2.6)

Totals of all probands with at least one parent loss[1]

Age spans in years

Parent loss by	$0-4\frac{11}{12}$	$5-9\frac{11}{12}$	$10-14\frac{11}{12}$	$15-16\frac{11}{12}$	$17-18$	$0-14\frac{11}{12}$ No.	$0-14\frac{11}{12}$ % of all probands	$0-18$ No.	$0-18$ % of all probands	Total parent losses[2] $0-18$
Death of father	0	5	5	2	0	10	9.3	12	11.2	12
Death of mother	2	3	5(+2)	0	1	10(+2)	9.3	11(+2)	10.2	13
Death of both parents	0	0	0	0	0	0	0	0	0	0
Separation or divorce										
Child lost father	2	4	1	0	0	7	6.5	7	6.5	7
Child lost mother	1	0	0	0	0	1	0.93	1	0.93	1
Child lost both parents	0	1	0	0	0	1	0.93	1	0.93	1
Long absence of one parent from home[3]	(+1)	0	1	0	0	1(+)	0.93	1(+1)	0.93	2
Illegitimate birth										
Resulting in chaotic home	2	0	0	0	0	2	1.9	2	1.9	2
Resulting in happy home	4	0	0	0	0	4	3.7	4	3.7	4
Foster care[4]										
(a) Dissolution of family	(+5)	(+3)	(+5)	0	0	(+13)	0	(+13)	0	13
(b) Despite family remaining intact	2	3	3	1	0	8	7.4	9	8.4	9
(c) Frequent shifting between foster home and parents	1	0	0	0	0	1	0.93	1	0.93	1
Total parent losses:	14(+6)	16(+3)	15(+7)	3	1	45(+16)	41.8	49(+16)	45.6	65

1. The numbers added in parentheses represent those probands who had already suffered an earlier, different loss of a parent, and who have been accounted for above or below that entry, under a different category. These figures are not represented in the percentage column that follows the (+) entries.

2. In the figures for total parent losses, loss of father and of mother are included even when they apply to the same proband while in the preceding column the probands are counted only once when they have lost both parents. The figures in this column are the sums of the figures in parentheses and those not in parentheses from the 8th column.

3. Extended absences of one parent include those parents who were away uninterruptedly for at least a year in a hospital or sanatorium.

4. Only those probands are counted as being in foster care (in foster homes or with strange families) who were so placed for at least a year. Probands away from their families for training or schooling were not included.

fore, investigations of other such groups were urgently needed.

Such supplemental investigations were undertaken for three groups, designated briefly as "young schizophrenics" (Table 2.10), "middle-aged schizophrenics" (Table 2.13), and "supplemental schizophrenics" (Table 2.16). The groups of young schizophrenics and middle-aged schizophrenics were originally recruited in order to provide material for comparsions with the draftees. The methods for their selection and their suitability for comparisons with the draftees will be described below. The same groups are exceptionally well suited for determining the differences in the occurrence of premature parent losses as between male and female schizophrenics. No valid objections can be raised against the comparability between the men and women from each of these two groups.

Tables 2.11 and 2.12 provide comparisons between the frequency of early parent losses among young schizophrenic men and young schizophrenic women. As it was for the principal schizophrenic probands, here, too, the parent losses by schizophrenic women were more frequent than such losses by schizophrenic men, although the difference is slight and by no means significant ($p > 0.1$). Divorce and separation of the parents of the young schizophrenic women occurs more often than among the parents of young schizophrenic men. This difference is statistically not significant either. (The figures apply to premature parent loss before the 15th as well as before the 18th birthday.)

Tables 2.14 and 2.15 provide comparisons between the frequency of premature parent losses among schizophrenic men and women of middle age. Up to their 15th birthdays the number of parent losses among the women exceeds such losses among the men, but the difference is not by any means significant. But when parent losses are compiled up to age 18 for this group, the ratio is reversed between the sexes by a very small, statistically insignificant amount. Similarly, in contrast to the other groups, divorces and separations among the parents of middle-aged schizophrenic men occur more frequently than among middle-aged schizophrenic women, the difference being insignificant.

After the relationship between male and female schizophrenics as to frequency of premature parent loss had been compared for the 208 principal schizophrenic probands, for the 150 young, and the 130 middle-aged schizo-

phrenics, a disappointing situation seemed to have developed. The figures indicated a possibility that there might be a distinction between the sexes relative to the frequency of premature parent loss among schizophrenics, but these differences were so small that they could not be statistically verified.

I was not satisfied with such a result. Although it resulted in a delay in the completion of this book and the new studies required several additional months of work, I decided to recruit a fourth large group of additional schizophrenics and to study comparatively from it the differences in frequency of parent losses between men and women. I expected to find that this final investigation would provide some clarification as to whether the differences between the sexes shown in the preceding studies could be considered as general trends or not. I was pleased that these efforts rewarded my expectations.

We made probands of this group of supplementary schizophrenics, all those admitted to our clinic between 1960 and 1961, with the exception of those who came from abroad or patients who had already been included in one of the other groups. The group included 444 schizophrenics, 171 men and 273 women. As in the case of the groups of young and middle-aged schizophrenics, we relied principally for collecting the necessary data on the existing patient histories filed at our clinic. If these proved to be incomplete they were supplemented by new investigations. This task was again performed mostly by Mrs. Ruth Frey, who consulted with me on any and all doubtful or difficult decisions (Table 2.16).

There can hardly be any objections against the suitability of this material for comparison purposes to determine premature parent losses as between men and women. The comparisons can be made from Tables 2.17 and 2.18, which show that in this fourth group also, the women more frequently suffered premature parent losses than the men. In this fourth group the difference in parent losses through age 18 is significant. Up to age 15 the premature parent losses of the supplemental male schizophrenics amounted to 25.2 percent, among the females 34.4 percent ($p > 0.05$). Up to age 18 the corresponding figures are 29.8 cent and 40.6 percent, respectively ($p < 0.05$).

If all four groups are added together, the number of examined patients is quite substantial—407 men and 525 women. Schizophrenic women experienced considerably more premature parent losses than schizophrenic men, and at this point the difference assumes statistical significance. For parent loss before age 15 the significance is great: $p < 0.01$. The differences become even more meaningful, because for parent losses up to age 15 they show the same general trend in all four groups, and up to 18 they agree, in substance, in three out of the four groups.

Table 2.19 provides a summary of the premature parent losses among all four groups of schizophrenics and the degree of statistical significance of the differences as between men and women.

Our statistics prove with sufficient significance that in the Canton of Zürich and in our century more schizophrenic women than schizophrenic men come from broken homes. With statistical significance, but with some reservations as to the comparability among the groups, these statistics further show that, compared to the general population, the childhood background of a broken home predominates only among schizophrenic women, but not among schizophrenic men.

If we now generalize carefully, we are justified in saying that unmistakable indications have been discovered suggesting the possibility that schizophrenic women of our day and age and in our culture more frequently suffer premature parent losses than schizophrenic men do.

In the comparisons that follow, it is not worthwhile to consider separately the childhood conditions of all five groups of schizophrenics. (An additional group comprising the 20 female private patients and depitcted in Table 2.20 are included in addition to the four groups described in detail above.) I am discussing here only the joint statistics of the five groups taken together.

Further differences were revealed between the two sexes. The relationship of father-losses to mother-losses through death differs between the sexes. Among the male schizophrenics the ratio of father-loss to mother-loss by death before the patient's 15th birthday is $33:12 = 2.75$, and among schizophrenic females $53:35 = 1.51$[13] (absolute figures for all five groups of schizophrenic probands combined). According to this, the number of mothers who died prematurely (compared to that of the

fathers who died prematurely) is greater among the female schizophrenics than among the males. The difference calculated according to these absolute figures, however, is still not statistically significant $(p < 0.1)$.

It should also be determined at this point how many men and women had fathers and mothers who died prematurely. Among all the schizophrenic men (407) 8 percent (33) lost their fathers before they were 15 years old, as did 9.7 percent (53) of the 545 schizophrenic women. On the other hand, only 3 percent (12) of these schizophrenic men lost their mothers, as against 6.4 percent (35) of these schizophrenic women. If more schizophrenic women have lost their fathers than schizophrenic men have, the difference is not important (9.7 percent as against 8 percent), and not yet wholly significant statistically $(p = 0.05)$. On the other hand, many more women than men have lost their mothers prematurely by death (6.4 percent as against 3 percent), and this difference, in view of the large number of schizophrenics examined, is statistically significant $(p < 0.05)$.

Among our rather numerous and diversified group of probands, an unequivocal sex distinction is apparent in these schizophrenics with respect to the frequency of premature death of the mothers.

The difference is based mainly on the findings from studies of the 208 principal schizophrenic probands of this investigation. Among them the men up to their 15th birthdays revealed a ratio of 10:2 between father loss and mother loss, and the women, of 10:10. In the four other groups taken together, the corresponding figures are 23:10 and 43:25, respectively. Just as the sex difference in respect to the total figure for parent losses becomes particularly distinct only among the 208 principal schizophrenic probands, so also does the difference relative to father losses, as compared to mother losses. Among the draftees the same ratio as that between schizophrenic men and women is closer to that of the women (65:37).

The parent losses of schizophrenics are distributed fairly evenly over the first three five-year life spans (108:87:96). In them there was no apparent difference between the sexes.

---

13. The increase of father losses over mother losses by death among the schizophrenic men is highly significant as to reliability at $p < 0.005$. The frequency of father losses as compared to mother losses by death among schizophrenic women is significant at the critical level of

$p < 0.025$. The fact that schizophrenics lose their fathers prematurely more often than they lose their mothers is self-evident and of itself uninteresting, since fathers are on an average older than mothers.

Table 2.10. Parent losses among 150 young supplemental probands (born 1940–1945)

Totals of all probands with at least one parent loss[1]

Age spans in years

Parent loss by	$0-4\frac{11}{12}$	$5-9\frac{11}{12}$	$10-14\frac{11}{12}$	$15-16\frac{11}{12}$	$17-18$	$0-14\frac{11}{12}$ No.	$0-14\frac{11}{12}$ % of all probands	$0-18$ No.	$0-18$ % of all probands	Total parent losses[2] $0-18$
Death of father	1	3	1(+1)	2(+1)	2(+1)	5(+1)	3.3	9(+3)	5.94	12
Death of mother	0	(+1)	1(+1)	2	1	1(+2)	0.66	4(+2)	2.64	6
Death of both parents	0	0	0	1	0	0	0	1	0.66	1
Separation or divorce										
Child lost father	0	1(+1)	2	1	0	3(+1)	1.98	4(+1)	2.64	5
Child lost mother	0	0	0	0	0	0	0	0	0	0
Child lost both parents	3	2	1	0	1	6	3.96	7	4.62	7
Uncertain with whom child lived	0	3	0	0	1	3	1.98	4	2.64	4
Long absence of one parent from home[3]	1	0	0	(+1)	0	1	0.66	1(+1)	0.66	2
Illegitimate birth										
Resulting in chaotic home	0	0	0	0	0	0	0	0	0	0
Resulting in happy home	4	0	0	0	0	4	2.64	4	2.64	4
Foster care[4]										
(a) Dissolution of family	1(+4)	(+3)	0	0	0	1(+7)	0.66	1(+7)	0.66	8
(b) Despite family remaining intact	4(+2)	4(+1)	2(+1)	1	0	10(+4)	6.6	11(+4)	7.26	15
(c) Frequent shifting between foster home and parents	0	(+1)	0	1	0	(+1)	0	1(+1)	0.66	2
Total parent losses:	14(+6)	13(+7)	7(+3)	8(+2)	5(+1)	34(+16)	22.44	47(+19)	31.02	66

1. The numbers added in parentheses represent those probands who had already suffered an earlier, different loss of a parent, and who have been accounted for above or below that entry, under a different category. These figures are not represented in the percentage column that follows the (+) entries.

2. In the figures for total parent losses, loss of father and of mother are included even when they apply to the same proband while in the preceding column the probands are counted only once when they have lost both parents. The figures in this column are the sums of the figures in parentheses and those not in parentheses from the 8th column.

3. Extended absences of one parent include those parents who were away uninterruptedly for at least a year in a hospital or sanatorium.

4. Only those probands are counted as being in foster care (in foster homes or with strange families) who were so placed for at least a year. Probands away from their families for training or schooling were not included.

Table 2.11. Parent losses among 87 male young supplemental probands (born 1940–1945) (breakdown of Table 2.10)

Totals of all probands with at least one parent loss[1]

Age spans in years

Parent loss by	$0-4\tfrac{11}{12}$	$5-9\tfrac{11}{12}$	$10-14\tfrac{11}{12}$	$15-16\tfrac{11}{12}$	$17-18$	$0-14\tfrac{11}{12}$ No.	$0-14\tfrac{11}{12}$ % of all probands	$0-18$ No.	$0-18$ % of all probands	Total parent losses[2] $0-18$
Death of father	1	3	(+1)	1	0	4(+1)	4.6	5(+1)	5.8	6
Death of mother	0	0	1(+1)	1	1	1(+1)	1.2	3(+1)	3.4	4
Death of both parents	0	0	0	1	0	0	0	1	1.2	1
Separation or divorce										
Child lost father	0	(+1)	2	1	0	2(+1)	2.3	3(+1)	3.4	4
Child lost mother	0	0	0	0	0	0	0	0	0	0
Child lost both parents	1	2	1	0	0	4	4.6	4	4.6	4
Uncertain with whom child lived	0	0	0	0	1	0	0	1	1.2	1
Long absence of one parent from home[3]	1	0	0	(+1)	0	1	1.2	1(+1)	1.2	2
Illegitimate birth										
Resulting in chaotic home	0	0	0	0	0	0	0	0	0	0
Resulting in happy home	2	0	0	0	0	2	2.3	2	2.3	2
Foster care[4]										
(a) Dissolution of family	(+1)	(+2)	0	0	0	(+3)	0	(+3)	0	3
(b) Despite family remaining intact	1(+2)	3(+1)	1(+1)	1	0	5(+4)	5.8	6(+4)	6.9	10
(c) Frequent shifting between foster home and parents	0	(+1)	0	0	0	(+1)	0	(+1)	0	1
Total parent losses:	6(+3)	8(+5)	5(+3)	5(+1)	2	19(+11)	22	26(+12)	30	38

1. The numbers added in parentheses represent those probands who had already suffered an earlier, different loss of a parent, and who have been accounted for above or below that entry, under a different category. These figures are not represented in the percentage column that follows the (+) entries.

2. In the figures for total parent losses, loss of father and of mother are included even when they apply to the same proband while in the preceding column the probands are counted only once when they have lost both parents. The figures in this column are the sums of the figures in parentheses and those not in parentheses from the 8th column.

3. Extended absences of one parent include those parents who were away uninterruptedly for at least a year in a hospital or sanatorium.

4. Only those probands are counted as being in foster care (in foster homes or with strange families) who were so placed for at least a year. Probands away from their families for training or schooling were not included.

Table 2.12. Parent losses among 63 female young supplemental probands (born 1930–1945) (breakdown of Table 2.10)

Totals of all probands with at least one parent loss[1]

Age spans in years

Parent loss by	$0-4\frac{11}{12}$	$5-9\frac{11}{12}$	$10-14\frac{11}{12}$	$15-16\frac{11}{12}$	$17-18$	$0-14\frac{11}{12}$ No.	$0-14\frac{11}{12}$ % of all probands	$0-18$ No.	$0-18$ % of all probands	Total parent losses[2] $0-18$
Death of father	0	0	1	1(+1)	2(+1)	1	1.59	4(+2)	6.35	6
Death of mother	0	(+1)	0	1	0	(+1)	0	1(+1)	1.59	2
Death of both parents	0	0	0	0	0	0	0	0	0	0
Separation or divorce										
Child lost father	0	1	0	0	0	1	1.59	1	1.59	1
Child lost mother	0	0	0	0	0	0	0	0	0	0
Child lost both parents	2	0	0	0	1	2	3.17	3	4.76	3
Uncertain with whom child lived	0	3	0	0	0	3	4.76	3	4.76	3
Long absence of one parent from home[3]	0	0	0	0	0	0	0	0	0	0
Illegitimate birth										
Resulting in chaotic home	0	0	0	0	0	0	0	0	0	0
Resulting in happy home	2	0	0	0	0	2	3.17	2	3.17	2
Foster care[4]										
(a) Dissolution of family	1(+3)	(+1)	0	0	0	1(+4)	1.59	1(+4)	1.59	5
(b) Despite family remaining intact	3	1	1	0	0	5	7.94	5	7.94	5
(c) Frequent shifting between foster home and parents	0	0	0	1	1	0	0	1	1.59	1
Total parent losses:	8(+3)	5(+2)	2	3(+1)	3(+1)	15(+5)	23.81	21(+7)	33.34	28

1. The numbers added in parentheses represent those probands who had already suffered an earlier, different loss of a parent, and who have been accounted for above or below that entry, under a different category. These figures are not represented in the percentage column that follows the (+) entries.

2. In the figures for total parent losses, loss of father and of mother are included even when they apply to the same proband while in the preceding column the probands are counted only once when they have lost both parents. The figures in this column are the sums of the figures in parentheses and those not in parentheses from the 8th column.

3. Extended absences of one parent include those parents who were away uninterruptedly for at least a year in a hospital or sanatorium.

4. Only those probands are counted as being in foster care (in foster homes or with strange families) who were so placed for at least a year. Probands away from their families for training or schooling were not included.

Table 2.13. Parent losses among 130 middle-aged supplemental probands (born 1915–1930)

Totals of all probands with at least one parent loss[1]

Age spans in years

Parent loss by	0–4 $\frac{11}{12}$	5–9 $\frac{11}{12}$	10–14 $\frac{11}{12}$	15–16 $\frac{11}{12}$	17–18	0–14 $\frac{11}{12}$ No.	0–14 $\frac{11}{12}$ % of all probands	0–18 No.	0–18 % of all probands	Total parent losses[2] 0–18
Death of father	3	4(+2)	7	3(+1)	2	14(+2)	11	19(+3)	14.5	22
Death of mother	1	(+1)	1	1	(+1)	2(+1)	1.5	3(+2)	2	5
Death of both parents	0	0	0	0	0	0	0	0	0	0
Separation or divorce										
Child lost father	2(+1)	2	2	1	0	6(+1)	4.5	7(+1)	5.5	8
Child lost mother	0	0	0	1	0	0	0	1	1	1
Child lost both parents	2	2(+2)	(+2)	1	0	4(+3)	3	5(+3)	4	8
Long absence of one parent from home[3]	0	1	2(+1)	(+1)	0	3(+1)	2	3(+2)	2	5
Illegitimate birth										
Resulting in chaotic home	1	0	0	0	0	1	1	1	1	1
Resulting in happy home	5	0	0	0	0	5	4	5	4	5
Foster care[4]										
(a) Dissolution of family	(+8)	2(+2)	(+4)	(+1)	0	2(+14)	1.5	2(+15)	1.5	17
(b) Despite family remaining intact	2	2(+1)	0	0	0	4(+1)	3	4(+1)	3	5
(c) Frequent shifting between foster home and parents	0	0	0	0	0	0	0	0	0	0
Total parent losses:	16(+9)	13(+4)	12(+7)	7(+3)	2(+1)	41(+23)	31.5	50(+27)	38.5	77

1. The numbers added in parentheses represent those probands who had already suffered an earlier, different loss of a parent, and who have been accounted for above or below that entry, under a different category. These figures are not represented in the percentage column that follows the (+) entries.

2. In the figures for total parent losses, loss of father and of mother are included even when they apply to the same proband while in the preceding column the probands are counted only once when they have lost both parents. The figures in this column are the sums of the figures in parentheses and those not in parentheses from the 8th column.

3. Extended absences of one parent include those parents who were away uninterruptedly for at least a year in a hospital or sanatorium.

4. Only those probands are counted as being in foster care (in foster homes or with strange families) who were so placed for at least a year. Probands away from their families for training or schooling were not included.

Table 2.14. Parent losses among 49 male middle-aged supplemental probands (born 1915–1930) (breakdown of Table 2.13)

Totals of all probands with at least one parent loss[1]

Age spans in years

Parent loss by	$0-4\frac{11}{12}$	$5-9\frac{11}{12}$	$10-14\frac{11}{12}$	$15-16\frac{11}{12}$	17–18	0–14 $\frac{11}{12}$ No.	0–14 $\frac{11}{12}$ % of all probands	0–18 No.	0–18 % of all probands	Total parent losses[2] 0–18
Death of father	2	0	3	2	2	5	10.20	9	18.36	9
Death of mother	0	0	0	0	0	0	0	0	0	0
Death of both parents	0	0	0	0	0	0	0	0	0	0
Separation or divorce										
Child lost father	0	0	1	1	0	1	2.04	2	0.48	2
Child lost mother	0	0	0	0	0	0	0	0	0	0
Child lost both parents	2	2	(+2)	0	0	4(+2)	8.16	4(+2)	8.16	6
Long absence of one parent from home[3]	0	0	(+1)	0	0	(+1)	0	(+1)	0	1
Illegitimate birth										
Resulting in chaotic home	0	0	0	0	0	0	0	0	0	0
Resulting in happy home	2	0	0	0	0	2	4.08	2	4.08	2
Foster care[4]										
(a) Dissolution of family	(+4)	1(+1)	(+3)	0	0	1(+8)	2.04	1(+8)	2.04	9
(b) Despite family remaining intact	1	1(+1)	0	0	0	2(+1)	4.08	2(+1)	4.08	3
(c) Frequent shifting between foster home and parents	0	0	0	0	0	0	0	0	0	0
Total parent losses:	7(+4)	4(+2)	4(+6)	3	2	15(+12)	30.60	20(+12)	40.80	32

1. The numbers added in parentheses represent those probands who had already suffered an earlier, different loss of a parent, and who have been accounted for above or below that entry, under a different category. These figures are not represented in the percentage column that follows the (+) entries.

2. In the figures for total parent losses, loss of father and of mother are included even when they apply to the same proband, while in the preceding column the probands are counted only once when they have lost both parents. The figures in this column are the sums of the figures in parentheses and those not in parentheses from the 8th column.

3. Extended absences of one parent include those parents who were away uninterruptedly for at least a year in a hospital or sanatorium.

4. Only those probands are counted as being in foster care (in foster homes or with strange families) who were so placed for at least a year. Probands away from their families for training or schooling were not included.

Table 2.15. Parent losses among 81 female middle-aged supplemental probands (born 1915–1930) (breakdown of Table 2.13)

Totals of all probands with at least one parent loss[1]

Age spans in years

Parent loss by	$0-4\frac{11}{12}$	$5-9\frac{11}{12}$	$10-14\frac{11}{12}$	$15-16\frac{11}{12}$	$17-18$	$0-14\frac{11}{12}$ No.	% of all probands	$0-18$ No.	% of all probands	Total parent losses[2] $0-18$
Death of father	1	4(+2)	4	1(+1)	0	9(+2)	11.10	10(+3)	12.34	13
Death of mother	1	(+1)	1	1	(+1)	2(+1)	2.47	3(+2)	3.71	5
Death of both parents	0	0	0	0	0	0	0	0	0	0
Separation or divorce										
Child lost father	2(+1)	2	1	0	0	5(+1)	6.17	5(+1)	6.17	6
Child lost mother	0	0	0	1	0	0	0	1	1.23	1
Child lost both parents	0	(+1)	0	1	0	(+1)	0	1(+1)	1.23	2
Long absence of one parent from home[3]	0	1	2	(+1)	0	3	3.71	3(+1)	3.71	4
Illegitimate birth										
Resulting in chaotic home	1	0	0	0	0	1	1.23	1	1.23	1
Resulting in happy home	3	0	0	0	0	3	3.71	3	3.71	3
Foster care[4]										
(a) Dissolution of family	(+4)	1(+1)	(+1)	(+1)	0	1(+6)	1.23	1(+7)	1.23	8
(b) Despite family remaining intact	1	1	0	0	0	2	2.47	2	2.47	2
(c) Frequent shifting between foster home and parents	0	0	0	0	0	0	0	0	0	0
Total parent losses:	9(+5)	9(+5)	8(+1)	4(+3)	(+1)	26(+11)	32.09	30(+15)	37.03	45

1. The numbers added in parentheses represent those probands who had already suffered an earlier, different loss of a parent, and who have been accounted for above or below that entry, under a different category. These figures are not represented in the percentage column that follows the (+) entries.

2. In the figures for total parent losses, loss of father and of mother are included even when they apply to the same proband, while in the preceding column the probands are counted only once when they have lost both parents. The figures in this column are the sums of the figures in parentheses and those not in parentheses from the 8th column.

3. Extended absences of one parent include those parents who were away uninterruptedly for at least a year in a hospital or sanatorium.

4. Only those probands are counted as being in foster care (in foster homes or with strange families) who were so placed for at least a year. Probands away from their families for training or schooling were not included.

Table 2.16. Parent losses among 444 supplemental probands admitted in 1960–1961 (2 patient histories of female patients could not be located)

Totals of all probands with at least one parent loss[1]

Age spans in years

Parent loss by	0–4 11/12	5–9 11/12	10–14 11/12	15–16 11/12	17–18	0–14 11/12 No.	0–14 11/12 % of all probands	0–18 No.	0–18 % of all probands	Total parent losses[2] 0–18
Death of father	10(+1)	10(+6)	20(+3)	11(+4)	3(+2)	40(+10)	9	54(+16)	12.2	70
Death of mother	6(+3)	10(+2)	11	3(+1)	3	27(+5)	6.1	33(+6)	7.4	39
Death of both parents	0	3(+1)	2	2	0	5(+1)	1.1	7(+1)	1.6	8
Separation or divorce										
Child lost father	6(+1)	6	7(+1)	1	1	19(+2)	4.3	21(+2)	4.7	23
Child lost mother	1(+2)	1	3	1	0	5(+2)	1.1	6(+2)	1.3	8
Child lost both parents	2	0	0	0	0	2	0.5	2	0.5	2
Long absence of one parent from home[3]	1(+2)	3(+5)	1	(+1)	0	5(+7)	1.1	5(+8)	1.1	13
Illegitimate birth										
Resulting in chaotic home	5	0	0	0	0	5	1.1	5	1.1	5
Resulting in happy home	9	0	0	0	0	9	2	9	2	9
Foster care[4]										
(a) Dissolution of family	1(+18)	1(+10)	(+6)	(+1)	0	2(+34)	0.5	2(+35)	0.5	37
(b) Despite family remaining intact	10(+1)	2	5(+2)	0	(+1)	17(+3)	3.8	17(+4)	3.8	21
(c) Frequent shifting between foster home and parents	1	0	0	0	0	1	0.2	1	0.2	1
Total parent losses:	52(+28)	36(+24)	49(+12)	18(+7)	7(+3)	137(+64)	30.8	162(+74)	36.4	236

1. The numbers added in parentheses represent those probands who had already suffered an earlier, different loss of a parent, and who have been accounted for above or below that entry, under a different category. These figures are not represented in the percentage column that follows the (+) entries.

2. In the figures for total parent losses, loss of father and of mother are included even when they apply to the same proband while in the preceding column the probands are counted only once when they have lost both parents. The figures in this column are the sums of the figures in parentheses and those not in parentheses from the 8th column.

3. Extended absences of one parent include those parents who were away uninterruptedly for at least a year in a hospital or sanatorium.

4. Only those probands are counted as being in foster care (in foster homes or with strange families) who were so placed for at least a year. Probands away from their families for training or schooling were not included.

Table 2.17. Parent losses among 171 male supplemental probands hospitalized 1960–1961 (breakdown of Table 2.16)

Totals of all probands with at least one parent loss[1]

Age spans in years

Parent loss by	$0-4\frac{11}{12}$	$5-9\frac{11}{12}$	$10-14\frac{11}{12}$	$15-16\frac{11}{12}$	$17-18$	$0-14\frac{11}{12}$ No.	$0-14\frac{11}{12}$ % of all probands	$0-18$ No.	$0-18$ % of all probands	Total parent losses[2] $0-18$
Death of father	3(+1)	3(+1)	6(+1)	2(+1)	1(+1)	12(+3)	7	15(+5)	8.8	20
Death of mother	2	1(+1)	4	(+1)	2	7(+1)	4.1	9(+2)	5.3	11
Death of both parents	0	2	0	1	0	2	1.2	3	1.7	3
Separation or divorce										
Child lost father	3	1	3	0	1	7	4.1	8	4.7	8
Child lost mother	0(+1)	0	2	1	0	2(+1)	1.2	3(+1)	1.7	4
Child lost both parents	1	0	0	0	0	1	0.6	1	0.6	1
Long absence of one parent from home[3]	(+2)	(+1)	0	0	0	(+3)	0	(+3)	0	3
Illegitimate birth										
Resulting in chaotic home	2	0	0	0	0	2	1.2	2	1.2	2
Resulting in happy home	5	0	0	0	0	5	2.9	5	2.9	5
Foster care[4]										
(a) Dissolution of family	(+8)	(+5)	(+1)	(+1)	0	(+14)	0	(+15)	0	15
(b) Despite family remaining intact	3(+1)	0	2(+1)	0	0	5(+2)	2.9	5(+2)	2.9	7
(c) Frequent shifting between foster home and parents	0	0	0	0	0	0	0	0	0	0
Total parent losses:	19(+13)	7(+8)	17(+3)	4(+3)	4(+1)	43(+24)	25.2	51(+28)	29.8	79

1. The numbers added in parentheses represent those probands who had already suffered an earlier, different loss of a parent, and who have been accounted for above or below that entry, under a different category. These figures are not represented in the percentage column that follows the (+) entries.

2. In the figures for total parent losses, loss of father and of mother are included even when they apply to the same proband while in the preceding column the probands are counted only once when they have lost both parents. The figures in this column are the sums of the figures in parentheses and those not in parentheses from the 8th column.

3. Extended absences of one parent include those parents who were away uninterruptedly for at least a year in a hospital or sanatorium.

4. Only those probands are counted as being in foster care (in foster homes or with strange families) who were so placed for at least a year. Probands away from their families for training or schooling were not included.

Table 2.18. Parent losses among 273 female supplemental probands hospitalized 1960–1961 (breakdown of Table 2.16) (2 patient histories of female patients could not be located)

Totals of all probands with at least one parent loss[1]

Age spans in years

Parent loss by	$0-4\frac{11}{12}$	$5-9\frac{11}{12}$	$10-14\frac{11}{12}$	$15-16\frac{11}{12}$	$17-18$	$0-14\frac{11}{12}$ No.	$0-14\frac{11}{12}$ % of all probands	$0-18$ No.	$0-18$ % of all probands	Total parent losses[2] $0-18$
Death of father	7	7(+5)	14(+2)	9(+3)	2(+1)	28(+7)	10.2	39(+11)	14.2	50
Death of mother	4(+3)	9(+1)	7	3	1	20(+4)	7.3	24(+4)	8.8	28
Death of both parents	0	1(+1)	2	1	0	3(+1)	1.1	4(+1)	1.5	5
Separation or divorce										
Child lost father	3(+1)	5	4(+1)	1	0	12(+2)	4.4	13(+2)	4.7	15
Child lost mother	1(+1)	1	1	0	0	3(+1)	1.1	3(+1)	1.1	4
Child lost both parents	1	0	0	0	0	1	0.4	1	0.4	1
Long absence of one parent from home[3]	1	3(+4)	1	(+1)	0	5(+4)	1.8	5(+5)	1.8	10
Illegitimate birth										
Resulting in chaotic home	3	0	0	0	0	3	1.1	3	1.1	3
Resulting in happy home	4	0	0	0	0	4	1.5	4	1.5	4
Foster care[4]										
(a) Dissolution of family	1(+10)	1(+5)	(+5)	0	0	2(+20)	0.7	2(+20)	0.7	22
(b) Despite family remaining intact	7	2	3(+1)	0	(+1)	12(+1)	4.4	12(+2)	4.4	14
(c) Frequent shifting between foster home and parents	1	0	0	0	0	1	0.4	1	0.4	1
Total parent losses:	33(+15)	29(+16)	32(+9)	14(+4)	3(+2)	94(+40)	34.4	111(+46)	40.6	157

1. The numbers added in parentheses represent those probands who had already suffered an earlier, different loss of a parent, and who have been accounted for above or below that entry, under a different category. These figures are not represented in the percentage column that follows the (+) entries.

2. In the figures for total parent losses, loss of father and of mother are included even when they apply to the same proband while in the preceding column the probands are counted only once when they have lost both parents. The figures in this column are the sums of the figures in parentheses and those not in parentheses from the 8th column.

3. Extended absences of one parent include those parents who were away uninterruptedly for at least a year in a hospital or sanatorium.

4. Only those probands are counted as being in foster care (in foster homes or with strange families) who were so placed for at least a year. Probands away from their families for training or schooling were not included.

89

Table 2.19. Survey of parent losses for the four groups of probands differentiated by sex

Premature parent losses between the ages of

Proband groups	No. of probands			Men				Women				Difference in parent losses between men/women		Totals			
	Men	*Women*	*Total*	$0-14\frac{11}{12}$		$0-18$		$0-14\frac{11}{12}$		$0-18$		$0-14\frac{11}{12}$	$0-18$	$0-14\frac{11}{12}$		$0-18$	
				No.	%	*No.*	%	*No.*	%	*No.*	%			*No.*	%	*No.*	%
Principal schizo-phrenic probands	100	108	208	29	29.0	33	33.0	45	41.8	49	45.6	>0.1	>0.1	74	35.5	82	39.4
Young schizophrenics	87	63	150	19	22.0	26	30.0	15	23.8	21	33.3	>0.1	>0.1	34	22.4	47	31.0
Middle-aged schizophrenics	49	81	130	15	30.6	20	40.8	26	32.1	30	37.0	>0.1	>0.1	41	31.5	50	38.5
Supplemental schizophrenics	171	273	444	43	25.2	51	29.8	94	34.4	111	40.6	>0.05	<0.05	137	30.8	162	36.5
Totals	407	525	932	106	26.0	130	31.9	180	34.3	211	40.1	<0.01	<0.05	286	30.7	341	36.8

Table 2.20. Parent losses among 20 female probands from a private clinic

| | Age spans in years | | | | | Totals of all probands with at least one parent loss[1] | | | | |
| | 0–4 $\frac{11}{12}$ | 5–9 $\frac{11}{12}$ | 10–14 $\frac{11}{12}$ | 15–16 $\frac{11}{12}$ | 17–18 | 0–14 $\frac{11}{12}$ | | 0–18 | | Total parent losses[2] 0–18 |
Parent loss by						No.	% of all probands	No.	% of all probands	
Death of father	0	0	2	0	0	2	10	2	10	2
Death of mother	0	(+1)	0	0	0	(+1)	0	(+1)	0	1
Death of both parents	0	0	0	0	0	0	0	0	0	0
Separation or divorce										
Child lost father	0	(+1)	0	0	0	(+1)	0	(+1)	0	1
Child lost mother	0	0	0	0	0	0	0	0	0	0
Child lost both parents	0	0	0	0	0	0	0	0	0	0
Long absence of one parent from home[3]	0	0	0	0	0	0	0	0	0	0
Illegitimate birth										
Resulting in chaotic home	2	0	0	0	0	2	10	2	10	2
Resulting in happy home	1	0	0	0	0	1	5	1	5	1
Foster care[4]										
(a) Dissolution of family	(+2)	0	0	0	0	(+2)	0	(+2)	0	2
(b) Despite family remaining intact	0	0	0	0	0	0	0	0	0	0
(c) Frequent shifting between foster home and parents	(+1)	0	0	0	0	(+1)	0	(+1)	0	1
Total parent losses:	3(+3)	(+2)	2	0	0	5(+5)	25	5(+5)	25	10

1. The numbers added in parentheses represent those probands who had already suffered an earlier, different loss of a parent, and who have been accounted for above or below that entry, under a different category. These figures are not represented in the percentage column that follows the (+) entries.

2. In the figures for total parent losses, loss of father and of mother are included even when they apply to the same proband while in the preceding column the probands are counted only once when they have lost both parents. The figures in this column are the sums of the figures in parentheses and those not in parentheses from the 8th column.

3. Extended absences of one parent include those parents who were away uninterruptedly for at least a year in a hospital or sanatorium.

4. Only those probands are counted as being in foster care (in foster homes or with strange families) who were so placed for at least a year. Probands away from their families for training or schooling were not included.

Among the schizophrenic men the losses were 41:28:37, and for the women 67:59:59, for the three periods.

The relationship of parental loss by death on the one hand, and by divorce, separation, illegitimacy or the placing of the child in foster care, on the other, is about the same between men and women. The relationship of parental loss by death to other types of parental loss is $43:63 = 0.68$ among the men, but $85:100 = 0.85$ among the women, both calculated to their 15th birthdays. There is a difference in the relationship, but it is in no way statistically significant $(p < 1)$. Among the female probands as compared to the male probands there were a few more parental losses by causes other than death.

The attempt could be made to compile a number of various additional figures to illuminate the special meaning attached to the maternal losses among girls, but such attempts would prove little, in that they would merely show that there were either no significant differences between the male and the female schizophrenics, or else that the number of such differences would be too small to be distinguishable. For instance, one could calculate how the five major categories of family disruptions are distributed between the sexes up to their 18th birthdays. The table from such calculations for all five groups of schizophrenic probands would read as follows:

Parent loss by	Men	Women
Death	60	110
Divorce; separation	36	40
Temporary absence	5	9
Illegitimacy	11	22
Foster care	18	35

From this listing it can be seen once again that the women lose relatively more parents by death than the men do. Further, separate calculations can be made on family disruptions through divorce, legal separation, absence of a parent under one heading, and those resulting from illegitimacy or placement of the child in foster care, under another. The proportion for the men would then amount to 41:29 and for the women to 49:57. One might be reminded by this that divorces and legal separations of the parents most often place the child in care of its mother, but illegitimacy often leads to the child's placement in foster care. It would be tempting to draw the simple conclusion that loss of the mother's care imperils girls but not boys.

But this conclusion, based on the above calculation, is fraught with too many doubts and statistical inaccuracies to deserve serious consideration.

In the above-mentioned figures the criterion was mainly parent losses before the 15th birthday of the subject. In multiple events contributing to disruption of the family, only the first item is counted. Instead of the number of probands whose homes had been disrupted by one or several causes, one might also begin with the number of causal events as a basis and figure the statistics up to the 18th birthday instead of the 15th. It would be superfluous to load down the existing data with such additional calculations, because they would not change the conclusions.

All percentage figures have been rounded off to whole numbers, for the listing of fractions would represent a purported accuracy in that the mathematical accuracy shown would appear to be much greater than the facts would permit.

Differentiating Observations on Parent Losses of Schizophrenics with Widely Separated Birthdates

The comparability of the 208 principal schizophrenic probands with the draftees as representatives of the general population continues to suffer from the fact that the birth dates of members of the two groups differ sharply (the schizophrenics were born between 1874 and 1927, the draftees between 1944 and 1946, predominantly in 1945).

The gathering of material for statistics on premature parent losses among nonselected representatives of the average population with distribution of birth dates corresponding to those of the schizophrenics had proved to be impossible. Accordingly, the reverse procedure suggested itself, namely, of searching for schizophrenics born between 1944 and 1946, instead of searching for adequate representatives of the average population with birth years between 1874 and 1927. The problem then was to check whether the statistics on premature parent losses of these young schizophrenics differed from those of the (older) principal schizophrenic probands and from those of the draftees of the same age group. But a difficulty emerged immediately. The number of schizophrenics who had been born between 1944 and 1946 is small; therefore, the statistics were extended to include birth years between 1940 and 1945, and patients from two sister-clinics located not too far from Burghölzli, the Kilchberg Sanatorium and the canton's psychiatric clinic at Königsfelden near Brugg. At this point I wish to extend my sincere thanks to the chief physicians and directors of these clinics, Drs. U. M. Strub and P. Mohr, for granting us the use of their patients and facilities. But even with this addition of probands, only 150 not 208 young schizophrenics could be assembled for study. Table 2.10 shows these 150 schizophrenics born between 1940 and 1945 from Burghölzli, the Kilchberg Sanatorium, and the Königsfelden Clinic. To simplify matters they will be referred to below as the "young schizophrenics."

Only Swiss citizens are obligated for military service in Switzerland. The 208 principal schizophrenic probands of this study are mostly Swiss (89.5 percent), because during the time when they were selected the number of aliens in Switzerland was small.[14] Among the schizophrenics born between 1940 and 1946, who had been admitted by 1965 to one of the three above-mentioned clinics, there were considerably more aliens, because their number had increased appreciably since the war.[15] In the statistics of these young schizophrenics, therefore, only Swiss citizens were considered, not foreign laborers or other aliens.

The statistics on the young schizophrenics are based primarily on patient histories. If no definite information on the patient's childhood was available from these records, additional information was secured through interviews. We got the impression that all pertinent data were complete; but still, the childhood conditions of the 208 principal schizophrenic probands, with whom we were mainly concerned, were more intimately known to us. Their records also produced considerably more reports by other informants than was the case for the young schizophrenics. It is possible that comparability with the young schizophrenics is somewhat distorted because of the more precise information we had on the 208 older probands.

In one respect, however, the 208 principal schizophrenic probands and the young schizophrenics cannot be compared. The young schizophrenics are not only young according to their birthdates, but all of them also experienced their schizophrenic onset at an early age, whereas many of the 208 principal schizophrenic probands became ill later in life (see pp. 195–98).

First, let us compare the broken-home statistics of the young schizophrenics with those of the 208 principal schizophrenic probands (Tables 2.10 and 2.6). The comparison shows that the young schizophrenics more rarely experienced parent losses than did the much older principal schizophrenic probands of this study. However, for parent losses only up to age 15, the difference is barely significant statistically ($p < 0.05$). The smaller ratio of parent losses among the young schizophrenics is primarily due to the smaller number of parent deaths. Also, absences of long duration from home of one of the parents also occur more frequently among the older schizophrenic probands than among the younger ones (statistically extremely insignificant). On the other hand, divorce or legal separation of the parents occurs with approximately equal frequency in both groups.

The fact that there are fewer parental deaths in the records of the younger generation was to be expected. But what was unexpected was the equality of divorces and legal separations among the parents of the two groups, since official records show an increase in divorces among the total population over the intervening years.[16] The difference admits of a number of different interpretations. Perhaps the fact that fewer divorces and legal separations occur in the area served by the Königsfelden Clinic than that served by Burghölzli was responsible, although such a difference cannot be of great importance. It is also not entirely impossible that the difference occurred by mere chance, and that it was augmented by the fact that the interviews of the young schizophrenics simply did not yield as many data on broken homes as the more complete records of the 208 principal schizophrenic probands did.

Under these circumstances I became interested in gathering data on the premature parent losses among a group of schizophrenics whose ages ranged somewhere about midway between those of the principal probands and the young schizophrenics. For this purpose I selected all schizophrenics of Swiss nationality who had been admitted to our clinic between January 1, 1965 and February 28, 1966, who

14. In 1941, 37,946 or 5.6% of the 674,505 inhabitants of the Canton of Zürich were aliens. Among these aliens that portion who were permanent residents was greater then than it is today.

15. In 1965, 166,377 or 16% of the 1,039,200 inhabitants of the Canton of Zürich were aliens.

16. See footnote 18.

had been born between 1915 and 1930. These 49 men and 81 women I shall henceforth refer to as the "middle-aged schizophrenics."

For comparison purposes it should be noted that the group of middle-aged schizophrenics differs from the young schizophrenics in that the former include not only early-onset cases, but also patients who first became ill as late as age 51. It differs from the group of the 208 principal schizophrenic probands, on the average, by a lower onset age. The premature parent losses among the middle-aged schizophrenics are approximately equal to those of the young schizophrenics, as derived from patient histories which, when the records were incomplete, were supplemented by interviews. Nevertheless, the childhood histories of the 208 principal schizophrenic probands are more accurately and more extensively described. The middle-aged schizophrenics were hospitalized exclusively at our clinic, while, as mentioned above, the group of young schizophrenics was supplemented by patients from two other clinics. The distribution of sexes among the middle-aged schizophrenics shifts in favor of the females, in comparison to the other two groups. All these differences restrict the comparability, but have very little impact on the overall results.

As expected, the figures on premature parent losses among the middle-aged schizophrenics (Table 2.13) occupy approximately the middle ground between the figures for the 208 principal probands and those for the young schizophrenics. The number of parent losses before the 15th birthday diminishes, beginning with the group with the earliest birthdates, by way of the middle group and down to the youngest, at 36 percent, 32 percent, and 22 percent (the corresponding figures for parent losses up to age 18 are 39 percent, 39 percent, and 31 percent). This decrease is caused exclusively by the decrease in mortality rates of the parents (up to age 15 by 15 percent, to 13 percent, and to 4 percent, and up to age 18 by 18 percent to 17 percent, and to 9 percent). Parent losses caused by divorce or legal separation of the parents are relatively equal in all three groups, up to age 15, 9 percent, 8 percent, and 8 percent, and up to age 18, 9 percent, 11 percent, and 10 percent. There appears to be no uniform change of figures nor any statistical significance in the differences in illegitimate births or foster-care cases.

It still seemed worth the effort to check whether schizophrenics from the same area, but from different social strata than the previously studied patients would differ in frequency of broken-home childhoods.[17] For this investigation female patients from the Hohenegg Sanatorium in Meilen near Zürich were studied. This clinic serves chiefly female patients from the upper-middle class. All female schizophrenic patients were included, who were hospitalized at the Hohenegg Sanatorium in 1965 and who were born between 1940 and 1945, that is, women from the same age group as the patients of Table 2.10 and from an age group similar to that of the draftees. I should like to extend my sincere thanks also to chief physician of the Hohenegg Sanatorium, Dr. K. Ernst, for the courtesies he extended to me. There were, however, only 20 patients at the Hohenegg Sanatorium who met the necessary qualifications, and for this reason, the statistics on their childhood histories are potentially high in errors, due to the small number involved. There were no significant differences in parent losses among the young schizophrenics from the Hohenegg Sanatorium on the one hand, and the young schizophrenics from Burghölzli, the Kilchberg Sanatorium, and the Königsfelden Clinic on the other (cf. Tables 2.20 and 2.10). It would be permissible to regard the two groups as a single unit, whereby the median errors appearing in Table 2.19 would be reduced.

Differentiating Observations on Parent Losses according to the Locales of Origin of the Probands

The area in which the schizophrenics of this investigation and the representatives of the general population live, the Canton of Zürich, is small. It covers only 1723 sq. km. It can be crossed in any direction by car or train in under an hour. At the end of the last century there was a distinct difference in the life-styles of the two cities of Zürich and Winterthur, on the one hand, and the purely rural settlements on the other. Situated between urban and rural living conditions, however, even in those days, there were broad transitional areas of highly industrialized

17. Except for the fact that differences in the frequency of premature parent loss are accepted as matters of course among various social levels, a great number of statistics are available on them. For instance, in England, Ryle (1967) registered a 20 percent parent loss before the 15th birthday among a population composed of a number of different social levels, while Wardle (1960) came up with 35 percent for a similarly hetrogeneous group.

rural communities, in which life differed very little from that of the larger cities. Today the living conditions have become just about the same throughout the entire canton. Most of the rural communities have housing that can hardly be distinguished any longer from urban and suburban housing, and there is a constant bustle of people traveling back and forth between the cities and the rural community in which they live. There are, to be sure, still some few isolated farm settlements in the mountains where life moves at the pace it did centuries ago, but they are very rare. Their inhabitants hardly make a dent in the statistical population figures. There would probably not be a single one of these among all our probands. In the cities the various housing units are not distinguishable from one another to the same degree as is the case in other countries. There are no slums.

For this reason one would suspect that the broken-home statistics from various parts of the canton would at a certain period yield somewhat similar results, but this theory is not supported by the facts.

In Tables 2.21 and 2.22 the 1505 draftees who were questioned are arranged according to their places of origin, either from the City of Zürich or from a rural section. Quite unexpectedly some rather extraordinary—and statistically significant—differences appear in the frequency of parent losses ($p < 0.001$). The draftees from the cities more often came from broken homes than the draftees from the country; yet, the district representing the rural area from which they came is only 4 to 20 km away from the city! The differences did not result from parent deaths, but from parent divorces and legal separations,[18] and from illegitimate births. Despite that, the cause need not necessarily be based on the fact that there would have been more divorces and separations and more illegitimate births in the cities. It may possibly be based on the fact that young men from divorced or separated parents prefer to gravitate toward the cities

18. *Divorces per 100,000 existing marriages*

	Canton of Zürich	City of Zürich
1887/1890	293	343
1899/1902	325	459
1909/1912	384	602
1919/1922	542	850
1929/1932	671	992
1940/1943	594	824
1949/1952	699	960
1959/1962	585	747

rather than to remain marooned in a small rural community.

The difference in parent losses between the draftees from the city and those from the country would be thought-provoking, if one were tempted to consider as comparable the broken-home statistics of the two test groups, although they came from different environments.

During the youth of our 208 principal schizophrenic probands the rural population far outnumbered the city population in the Canton of Zürich. During the youth of the young schizophrenics, this difference had disappeared almost completely.[19] The young schizophrenics from the Königsfelden Clinic came predominantly from rural communities. If we have included in our statistics the draftees from the city and the country at a ratio of 1:2, the proportion approximates that between city and country backgrounds of the 208 principal schizophrenic probands, as well as that of the young and the middle-aged schizophrenics.

Differentiating Observations on Parent Losses among Schizophrenics with Different Onset Ages

During the attempt to draw conclusions from the differences between the sexes in the statistics on premature parent losses, one fact that is disturbing is that these differences vary among the different groups of schizophrenics. Among the principal schizophrenic probands and the supplemental schizophrenics they are greater than among the young and middle-aged schizophrenics (Table 2.5). Why is this? It must be remembered in this connection that the groups consisting of the 208 principal schizophrenic probands and of the supplemental schizophrenics include uniformly equal early- and late-onset schizophrenics, while the other two groups contain no late-onset cases, and partly only early-onset cases. Could this explain the difference? But this is certainly not the case. In Tables 2.23–2.28 the parent losses of the 208 principal schizophrenic probands of this study are shown separately, according to early- and late-onset of illness. (The 35th birthday was chosen as the limit between these two groups; any additional sub-

19. In 1900, in the two urban communities of Zürich and Winterthur there were 173,038 inhabitants, and in their combined rural communities 257,998. In 1960, the same combined populations amount to 520,522 for Zürich and Winterthur, and 431,782 for the rural communities.

Table 2.21. Parent losses among 505 Zürich city draftees born 1944–1946 (after Hicklin and Rotach) (breakdown of Table 2.7)

Totals of all probands having lost at least one parent[1]

Age spans in years

Parent loss by	$0-4\frac{11}{12}$	$5-9\frac{11}{12}$	$10-14\frac{11}{12}$	$15-16\frac{11}{12}$	$17-18$	$0-14\frac{11}{12}$		$0-18$		Total parent losses[2] $0-18$
						No.	% of all probands	No.	% of all probands	No.
Death of father	13(+1)	6	8	10(+1)	6(+1)	27(+1)	5.3	43(+3)	8.5	46
Death of mother	1	6(+1)	3(+3)	4	1(+1)	10(+4)	2.0	15(+5)	3.0	20
Separation or divorce of parents	22(+1)	24(+1)	23	6	1	69(+2)	13.7	76(+2)	15.0	78
Long-term absence from home of one parent[3]	4(+2)	5(+2)	5	0	0	14(+4)	2.8	14(+4)	2.8	18
Illegitimate birth	17	0	0	0	0	17	3.4	17	3.4	17
In foster care[4]	4(+16)	9(+15)	5(+7)	3(+3)	1(+1)	18(+38)	3.6	22(+42)	4.4	64
Totals of parent losses:	61(+20)	50(+19)	44(+10)	23(+4)	9(+3)	155(+49)	30.7	187(+56)	37	243

1. The numbers added in parentheses represent those probands who had already suffered an earlier, different loss of a parent, and who have been accounted for above or below that entry, under a different category. These figures are not represented in the percentage column that follows the (+) entries.

2. In the figures for total parent losses, loss of father and of mother are included even when they apply to the same proband while in the preceding column the probands are counted only once when they have lost both parents. The figures in this column are the sums of the figures in parentheses and those not in parentheses from the 8th column.

3. Extended absences of one parent include those parents who were away uninterruptedly for at least a year in a hospital or sanatorium.

4. Only those probands are counted as being in foster care (in foster homes or with strange families) who were so placed for at least a year. Probands away from their families for training or schooling were not included.

Table 2.22. Parent losses among 1,000 Zürich rural draftees born 1944–1946 (after Hicklin and Rotach) (breakdown of Table 2.7)

Totals of all probands having lost at least one parent[1]

Age spans in years

Parent loss by	$0-4\frac{11}{12}$	$5-9\frac{11}{12}$	$10-14\frac{11}{12}$	$15-16\frac{11}{12}$	$17-18$	$0-14\frac{11}{12}$		$0-18$		Total parent losses[2] $0-18$
						No.	% of all probands	No.	% of all probands	No.
Death of father	10	9(+1)	19(+2)	12(+2)	6(+1)	38(+3)	3.8	56(+6)	5.6	62
Death of mother	11	9	7	4(+2)	3(+1)	27	2.7	34(+3)	3.4	37
Separation or divorce of parents	28	20(+1)	20(+2)	7(+2)	3	68(+3)	6.8	78(+5)	7.8	83
Long-term absence from home of one parent[3]	5	4	3	3	1	12	1.2	16	1.6	16
Illegitimate birth	16	0	0	0	0	16	1.6	16	1.6	16
In foster care[4]	11(+15)	14(+19)	19(+30)	4(+2)	3	44(+64)	4.4	51(+66)	5.1	117
Totals of parent losses:	81(+15)	56(+21)	68(+34)	30(+8)	16(+2)	205(+70)	20.5	251(+80)	25.1	331

1. The numbers added in parentheses represent those probands who had already suffered an earlier, different loss of a parent, and who have been accounted for above or below that entry, under a different category. These figures are not represented in the percentage column that follows the (+) entries.

2. In the figures for total parent losses, loss of father and of mother are included even when they apply to the same proband while in the preceding column the probands are counted only once when they have lost both parents. The figures in this column are the sums of the figures in parentheses and those not in parentheses from the 8th column.

3. Extended absences of one parent include those parents who were away uninterruptedly for at least a year in a hospital or sanatorium.

4. Only those probands are counted as being in foster care (in foster homes or with strange families) who were so placed for at least a year. Probands away from their families for training or schooling were not included.

division according to other categories would have been useless because of the small numbers involved.) The tables reveal that the early- and the late-onset patients experienced parent losses at exactly the same rate, and also that sex differences between the two groups showed no differences in parent-loss figures either. Therefore, based on my investigation, I am unable to supply an answer to the problem as to why the sex differences are so distinct as to parent losses for the 208 principal schizophrenic probands and so very indistinct for the other groups of schizophrenic probands.

With respect to the type of parent loss, of course, there are some differences between the early- and the late-onset patients among the principal schizophrenic probands. In comparison to the early-onset patients, the late-onset probands more often suffer parent losses by death, especially among their mothers, and fewer parent losses from divorce or legal separation. But this difference must not be interpreted as an indication of differences in the presumed psychogenesis. It is readily explained differently, by realizing that the parents of the late-onset probands were born earlier than the parents of the early-onset probands. The time-span separating the average ages of the parents of these two groups is characterized by the fact that the mortality rate in general, and specifically the mortality rate among pregnancy and maternity cases, dropped while divorces increased.

In and of itself, it will be interesting in large-scale statistics to compare the frequency of parent losses between early- and late-onset schizophrenics. One would be inclined to assume that the loss of a parent would be more likely to have a traumatic effect on younger subjects than on those more advanced in years. In keeping with this theory, Jane Oltman et al. (1952, 1965) also discovered more parent losses among the early-onset patients than among the late-onset patients. Conversely, however, is it possible that the reverse may occur, for instance, that the premature parent loss of a female with late-onset schizophrenia (say after age 30 or 40) may have been contributory to the illness, rather than if she had become ill earlier in life? At a glance, this second supposition seems to be a paradox. But then, perhaps it is not such a paradox at all, perhaps it is a valid assumption, as Angst (1966) discovered in his studies on depressives. One might speculate that the premature absence of a mother would inhibit the development in the child's personality of the feminine

characteristics, which the mother had had. Such an inhibition will bear more weight when a woman has reached the age for motherhood than during puberty. The prototype of a pubescent girl may require less shaping by the mother than the prototype of a mature woman a few decades older. A daughter during her puberty, never really experiences her mother, but as a mature woman she does. Is it possible, therefore, that a disturbed family relationship might have a greater causal influence on the development of a schizophrenia in later life than it would in childhood during or shortly after puberty? It is conceivable, but here we are dealing with something highly speculative. I mention the possibility only in order to indicate that it would be interesting to check this facet in other patients.

Parent Losses of Schizophrenics According to Previous Studies from our Clinic

During the winter of 1953/54 Huber, studying 100 schizophrenics from our clinic, investigated whether or not they came from broken homes. For comparisons with the broken-home statistics of the 208 principal schizophrenic probands, Huber's (1954) statistics are suitable in some respects, but less so in others. They are comparable insofar as:
—parent losses were defined exactly as they are in this study
—Huber's (1954) schizophrenics come from the area served by the same clinic
—the diagnosis for schizophrenia was determined by the same standards
—the aliens from Huber's (1954) statistics are excluded
—the distribution of sexes is similar (40 males, 60 females)
—early- and late-onset schizophrenics are represented at approximately the same ratios.

The comparability of the two statistics, on the other hand, is limited because
—the birthdates of Huber's (1954) probands are, on the average, at least 10 years later
—Huber's (1954) schizophrenics were already residents at the clinic (not newly admitted), and therefore severe residual conditions are frequent among them
—Huber (1954) eliminated some patient histories that did not contain sufficient data on the childhood of the proband
—the young among Huber's (1954) schizophrenics were not as accurately documented as were the young among the 208 principal schizophrenic probands.

Table 2.23. Parent losses among 138 principal probands under 35 years old at schizophrenic onset

Totals of all probands with at least one parent loss[1]

Age spans in years

Parent loss by	$0-4\frac{11}{12}$	$5-9\frac{11}{12}$	$10-14\frac{11}{12}$	$15-16\frac{11}{12}$	$17-18$	$0-14\frac{11}{12}$ No.	$0-14\frac{11}{12}$ % of all probands	$0-18$ No.	$0-18$ % of all probands	Total parent losses[2] $0-18$
Death of father	2	6	6(+1)	2(+1)	1	14(+1)	10.14	17(+2)	12.31	19
Death of mother	1	1	4(+2)	(+1)	0	6(+2)	4.34	6(+3)	4.34	9
Death of both parents	0	0	0	(+1)	0	0	0	(+1)	0	1
Separation or divorce										
Child lost father	5	3	2	0	0	10	7.24	10	7.24	10
Child lost mother	1	0	1	0	0	2	1.45	2	1.45	2
Child lost both parents	2	1(+1)	0	0	0	3(+1)	2.17	3(+1)	2.17	4
Long absence of one parent from home[3]	(+1)	2	3	0	0	5(+1)	3.62	5(+1)	3.62	6
Illegitimate birth										
Resulting in chaotic home	2	0	0	0	0	2	1.45	2	1.45	2
Resulting in happy home	2	0	0	0	0	2	1.45	2	1.45	2
Foster care[4]										
(a) Dissolution of family	(+6)	(+5)	(+6)	(+2)	0	(+17)	0	(+19)	0	19
(b) Despite family remaining intact	0	2(+1)	2(+1)	2	0	4(+2)	2.89	6(+2)	4.34	8
(c) Frequent shifting between foster home and parents	1	0	0	0	0	1	0.72	1	0.72	1
Total parent losses:	16(+7)	15(+7)	18(+10)	4(+5)	1	49(+24)	35.47	54(+29)	39.09	83

1. The numbers added in parentheses represent those probands who had already suffered an earlier, different loss of a parent, and who have been accounted for above or below that entry, under a different category. These figures are not represented in the percentage column that follows the (+) entries.

2. In the figures for total parent losses, loss of father and of mother are included even when they apply to the same proband while in the preceding column the probands are counted only once when they have lost both parents. The figures in this column are the sums of the figures in parentheses and those not in parentheses from the 8th column.

3. Extended absences of one parent include those parents who were away uninterruptedly for at least a year in a hospital or sanatorium.

4. Only those probands are counted as being in foster care (in foster homes or with strange families) who were so placed for at least a year. Probands away from their families for training or schooling were not included.

Table 2.24. Parent losses among 76 male principal probands under 35 at schizophrenic onset (breakdown of Table 2.23)

Totals of all probands with at least one parent loss[1]

Age spans in years

Parent loss by	$0-4\frac{11}{12}$	$5-9\frac{11}{12}$	$10-14\frac{11}{12}$	$15-16\frac{11}{12}$	$17-18$	$0-14\frac{11}{12}$ No.	$0-14\frac{11}{12}$ % of all probands	$0-18$ No.	$0-18$ % of all probands	Total parent losses[2] $0-18$
Death of father	2	3	3(+1)	1(+1)	1	8(+1)	10.56	10(+2)	13.2	12
Death of mother	0	0	0	(+1)	0	0	0	(+1)	0	1
Death of both parents	0	0	0	(+1)	0	0	0	(+1)	0	1
Separation or divorce										
Child lost father	3	0	2	0	0	5	6.6	5	6.6	5
Child lost mother	0	0	1	0	0	1	1.32	1	1.32	1
Child lost both parents	2	1(+1)	0	0	0	3(+1)	3.96	3(+1)	3.96	4
Long absence of one parent from home[3]	0	2	2	0	0	4	5.28	4	5.28	4
Illegitimate birth										
Resulting in chaotic home	0	0	0	0	0	0	0	0	0	0
Resulting in happy home	0	0	0	0	0	0	0	0	0	0
Foster care[4]										
(a) Dissolution of family	(+2)	(+3)	(+3)	(+2)	0	(+8)	0	(+10)	0	10
(b) Despite family remaining intact	0	(+1)	1(+1)	1	0	1(+2)	1.32	2(+2)	2.64	4
(c) Frequent shifting between foster home and parents	0	0	0	0	0	0	0	0	0	0
Total parent losses:	7(+2)	6(+5)	9(+5)	2(+5)	1	22(+12)	29.04	25(+17)	33	42

1. The numbers added in parentheses represent those probands who had already suffered an earlier, different loss of a parent, and who have been accounted for above or below that entry, under a different category. These figures are not represented in the percentage column that follows the (+) entries.

2. In the figures for total parent losses, loss of father and of mother are included even when they apply to the same proband while in the preceding column the probands are counted only once when they have lost both parents. The figures in this column are the sums of the figures in parentheses and those not in parentheses from the 8th column.

3. Extended absences of one parent include those parents who were away uninterruptedly for at least a year in a hospital or sanatorium.

4. Only those probands are counted as being in foster care (in foster homes or with strange families) who were so placed for at least a year. Probands away from their families for training or schooling were not included.

Table 2.25. Parent losses among 62 female principal probands under 35 at schizophrenic onset (breakdown of Table 2.23)

Totals of all probands with at least one parent loss[1]

Age spans in years

Parent loss by	$0-4\frac{11}{12}$	$5-9\frac{11}{12}$	$10-14\frac{11}{12}$	$15-16\frac{11}{12}$	$17-18$	$0-14\frac{11}{12}$		$0-18$		Total parent losses[2] $0-18$
						No.	% of all probands	No.	% of all probands	
Death of father	0	3	3	1	0	6	9.66	7	11.27	7
Death of mother	1	1	4(+2)	0	0	6(+2)	9.66	6(+2)	9.66	8
Death of both parents	0	0	0	0	0	0	0	0	0	0
Separation or divorce										
Child lost father	2	3	0	0	0	5	8.05	5	8.05	5
Child lost mother	1	0	0	0	0	1	1.61	1	1.61	1
Child lost both parents	0	0	0	0	0	0	0	0	0	0
Long absence of one parent from home[3]	(+1)	0	1	0	0	1(+1)	1.61	1(+1)	1.61	2
Illegitimate birth										
Resulting in chaotic home	2	0	0	0	0	2	3.22	2	3.22	2
Resulting in happy home	2	0	0	0	0	2	3.22	2	3.22	2
Foster care[4]										
(a) Dissolution of family	(+4)	(+2)	(+3)	0	0	(+9)	0	(+9)	0	9
(b) Despite family remaining intact	0	2	1	1	0	3	4.83	4	6.44	4
(c) Frequent shifting between foster home and parents	1	0	0	0	0	1	1.61	1	1.61	1
Total parent losses:	9(+5)	9(+2)	9(+5)	2	0	27(+12)	43.47	29(+12)	46.69	41

1. The numbers added in parentheses represent those probands who had already suffered an earlier, different loss of a parent, and who have been accounted for above or below that entry, under a different category. These figures are not represented in the percentage column that follows the (+) entries.

2. In the figures for total parent losses, loss of father and of mother are included even when they apply to the same proband while in the preceding column the probands are counted only once when they have lost both parents. The figures in this column are the sums of the figures in parentheses and those not in parentheses from the 8th column.

3. Extended absences of one parent include those parents who were away uninterruptedly for at least a year in a hospital or sanatorium.

4. Only those probands are counted as being in foster care (in foster homes or with strange families) who were so placed for at least a year. Probands away from their families for training or schooling were not included.

Table 2.26. Parent losses among 70 principal probands over 35 years old at schizophrenic onset

Totals of all probands with at least one parent loss[1]

Age spans in years

Parent loss by	$0-4\frac{11}{12}$	$5-9\frac{11}{12}$	$10-14\frac{11}{12}$	$15-16\frac{11}{12}$	$17-18$	$0-14\frac{11}{12}$ No.	$0-14\frac{11}{12}$ % of all probands	$0-18$ No.	$0-18$ % of all probands	Total parent losses[2] $0-18$
Death of father	0	3	3	2	0	6	8.6	8	11.4	8
Death of mother	2	3	1	0	1	6	8.6	7	10	7
Death of both parents	0	0	0	0	0	0	0	0	0	0
Separation or divorce										
Child lost father	0	1	2	0	0	3	4.3	3	4.3	3
Child lost mother	0	0	0	0	0	0	0	1	0	0
Child lost both parents	0	1	0	0	0	1	1.4	1	1.4	1
Long absence of one parent from home[3]	0	0	0	0	0	0	0	0	0	0
Illegitimate birth										
Resulting in chaotic home	0	0	0	0	0	0	0	0	0	0
Resulting in happy home	2	0	0	0	0	2	2.9	2	2.9	2
Foster care[4]										
(a) Dissolution of family	(+2)	(+3)	(+2)	0	0	(+7)	0	(+7)	0	7
(b) Despite family remaining intact	3	2	2	0	0	7	10	7	10	7
(c) Frequent shifting between foster home and parents	0	0	0	0	0	0	0	0	0	0
Total parent losses:	7(+2)	10(+3)	8(+2)	2	1	25(+7)	35.8	28(+7)	40	35

1. The numbers added in parentheses represent those probands who had already suffered an earlier, different loss of a parent, and who have been accounted for above or below that entry, under a different category. These figures are not represented in the percentage column that follows the (+) entries.

2. In the figures for total parent losses, loss of father and of mother are included even when they apply to the same proband while in the preceding column the probands are counted only once when they have lost both parents. The figures in this column are the sums of the figures in parentheses and those not in parentheses from the 8th column.

3. Extended absences of one parent include those parents who were away uninterruptedly for at least a year in a hospital or sanatorium.

4. Only those probands are counted as being in foster care (in foster homes or with strange families) who were so placed for at least a year. Probands away from their families for training or schooling were not included.

Table 2.27. Parent losses among 24 male principal probands over 35 at schizophrenic onset (breakdown of Table 2.26)

Totals of all probands with at least one parent loss[1]

Age spans in years

Parent loss by	$0-4\frac{11}{12}$	$5-9\frac{11}{12}$	$10-14\frac{11}{12}$	$15-16\frac{11}{12}$	$17-18$	$0-14\frac{11}{12}$ No.	$0-14\frac{11}{12}$ % of all probands	$0-18$ No.	$0-18$ % of all probands	Total parent losses[2] $0-18$
Death of father	0	1	1	1	0	2	8.4	3	12.6	3
Death of mother	1	1	0	0	0	2	8.4	2	8.4	2
Death of both parents	0	0	0	0	0	0	0	0	0	0
Separation or divorce										
Child lost father	0	0	1	0	0	1	4.2	1	4.2	1
Child lost mother	0	0	0	0	0	0	0	0	0	0
Child lost both parents	0	0	0	0	0	0	0	0	0	0
Long absence of one parent from home[3]	0	0	0	0	0	0	0	0	0	0
Illegitimate birth										
Resulting in chaotic home	0	0	0	0	0	0	0	0	0	0
Resulting in happy home	0	0	0	0	0	0	0	0	0	0
Foster care[4]										
(a) Dissolution of family	(+1)	(+2)	0	0	0	(+3)	0	(+3)	0	3
(b) Despite family remaining intact	1	1	0	0	0	2	8.4	2	8.4	2
(c) Frequent shifting between foster home and parents	0	0	0	0	0	0	0	0	0	0
Total parent losses:	2(+1)	3(+2)	2	1	0	7(+3)	29.4	8(+3)	33.6	11

1. The numbers added in parentheses represent those probands who had already suffered an earlier, different loss of a parent, and who have been accounted for above or below that entry, under a different category. These figures are not represented in the percentage column that follows the (+) entries.

2. In the figures for total parent losses, loss of father and of mother are included even when they apply to the same proband while in the preceding column the probands are counted only once when they have lost both parents. The figures in this column are the sums of the figures in parentheses and those not in parentheses from the 8th column.

3. Extended absences of one parent include those parents who were away uninterruptedly for at least a year in a hospital or sanatorium.

4. Only those probands are counted as being in foster care (in foster homes or with strange families) who were so placed for at least a year. Probands away from their families for training or schooling were not included.

Table 2.28. Parent losses among 46 female principal probands over 35 at schizophrenic onset (breakdown of Table 2.26)

Totals of all probands with at least one parent loss[1]

Age spans in years

Parent loss by	$0-4\frac{11}{12}$	$5-9\frac{11}{12}$	$10-14\frac{11}{12}$	$15-16\frac{11}{12}$	$17-18$	$0-14\frac{11}{12}$ No.	$0-14\frac{11}{12}$ % of all probands	$0-18$ No.	$0-18$ % of all probands	Total parent losses[2] $0-18$
Death of father	0	2	2	1	0	4	8.8	5	11	5
Death of mother	1	2	1	0	1	4	8.8	5	11	5
Death of both parents	0	0	0	0	0	0	0	0	0	0
Separation or divorce										
Child lost father	0	1	1	0	0	2	4.4	2	4.4	2
Child lost mother	0	0	0	0	0	0	0	0	0	0
Child lost both parents	0	1	0	0	0	1	2.2	1	2.2	1
Long absence of one parent from home[3]	0	0	0	0	0	0	0	0	0	0
Illegitimate birth										
Resulting in chaotic home	0	0	0	0	0	0	0	0	0	0
Resulting in happy home	2	0	0	0	0	2	4.4	2	4.4	2
Foster care[4]										
(a) Dissolution of family	(+1)	(+1)	(+2)	0	0	(+4)	0	(+4)	0	4
(b) Despite family remaining intact	2	1	2	0	0	5	11	5	11	5
(c) Frequent shifting between foster home and parents	0	0	0	0	0	0	0	0	0	0
Total parent losses:	5(+1)	7(+1)	6(+2)	1	1	18(+4)	38.6	20(+4)	44	24

1. The numbers added in parentheses represent those probands who had already suffered an earlier, different loss of a parent, and who have been accounted for above or below that entry, under a different category. These figures are not represented in the percentage column that follows the (+) entries.

2. In the figures for total parent losses, loss of father and of mother are included even when they apply to the same proband while in the preceding column the probands are counted only once when they have lost both parents. The figures in this column are the sums of the figures in parentheses and those not in parentheses from the 8th column.

3. Extended absences of one parent include those parents who were away uninterruptedly for at least a year in a hospital or sanatorium.

4. Only those probands are counted as being in foster care (in foster homes or with strange families) who were so placed for at least a year. Probands away from their families for training or schooling were not included.

Despite these limitations on comparability, Huber (1954) found almost exactly the same number of parent losses as those shown for the 208 principal schizophrenic probands in Table 2.6, that is, before the 15th birthday for Huber's (1954) probands 39 percent, and for my 208 probands, 36 percent. In both sets of statistics, parent loss is distributed about equally over the first three 5-year periods of life, and in both sets, loss of father by death exceeds loss of mother by death.

In 1959 Katharina Rubeli reported on the anamneses and catamneses of 102 schizophrenics from the Schaffhausen psychiatric clinic at Breitenau. Her probands are suitable for comparison in that their parent losses are defined the same way as ours, and that the diagnosis for schizophrenia was made according to the same criteria. The birthdates of her probands are distributed similarly to those of the 208 principal probands of this study. Sex distribution is also similar (42 men to 59 women), and the young among this group have also been studied precisely and from numerous aspects. Patients admitted between 1930 and 1945 became probands for the study. In other respects, however, the comparability of results from the two groups is limited

—Katharina Rubeli's (1959) schizophrenics did not come from the Canton of Zürich, but from the neighboring Canton of Schaffhausen, and the author limited her research to residents of that canton (although the proportion of rural communities in the Canton of Schaffhausen is about the same as that of the Canton of Zürich);[20]

—the author excluded those patients from her study about whom too few anamnestic and catamnestic data were available.

Katharina Rubeli (1959) found a parent loss of 30 percent among her probands before their 15th birthdays, that is, somewhat less than the 36 percent found for the 208 principal schizophrenic probands, although the difference is not statistically significant. The percentage of deaths among parents is the same in both statistics, but there were fewer children in the Schaffhausen group whose parents had been divorced or legally separated. This lower figure for divorces corresponds to that of the Schaffhausen population as compared to figures for the Canton of Zürich.[21]

Doris Morf (1962) reported 65 parent losses among the schizophrenics hospitalized at Burghölzli for expert opinion between 1942 and 1944. Her probands were well suited for comparability with the principal schizophrenic probands because the same methods were used for determining the concepts of parent loss and schizophrenia, the area of origin was the same, and the distribution of ages was the same. On the other hand, comparability was imperfect because Doris Morf's (1962) cases were only those hospitalized for expert opinion, and the sex ratio for her probands leans heavily in favor of the males.

Among her probands only 23 percent had suffered parent losses before age 15, which is less than the percentage among the principal probands. The difference could easily be due to mere chance, partly perhaps also to the fact that most of her probands were males.

The results of an American author, Illberg (1961), deviate sharply from the series of statistics developed by others who studied those schizophrenics admitted to our clinic in 1955. He found parent losses before age 15 in 66 percent of his probands (as compared to 36 percent in my principal probands and even less among the young and the middle-aged schizophrenics). At that, his concepts for parent losses and for schizophrenia were derived according to the same methods as in the other studies at the clinic; his probands came from the same general locale, and the birth dates were within the limits of those of the statistics. What differed in this set of statistics was the fact that aliens had not been excluded, and that the sex ratio was slightly different from that of the 208 principal probands (52 men to 48 women). But all this is not enough fully to explain the marked difference in parent losses shown by Illberg's (1961) statistics. The confidence interval, with the possibility of error amounting to 1 percent, extends from 53 to 77 percent. The difference as compared to all other investigations can therefore scarcely be explained as the result of happenstance. There may, however, be a basis for assuming that this high percentage was due to an error in selection. Only about half of all the schizophrenics

---

20. The ratio of rural to urban population in 1910 amounted to 27,296; 18,801 in the Canton of Schaffhausen, and 287,932:215,983 in the Canton of Zürich.

21. In an average year between 1909 and 1912, out of 100,000 existing marriages, there were 384 divorces in the Canton of Zürich and 243 in the Canton of Schaffhausen. The corresponding figures for 1959 to 1962 read 585 and 427, respectively.

admitted to the clinic during this particular 6-month period were included in the statistics. Presumably those were selected whose childhood backgrounds were fully described in the patient histories. In routinely selected patient histories, childhood conditions are more likely to be recorded when parent losses occur than when the childhood runs a normal course.

Parent Losses among Nonschizophrenic Patients of our Clinic

In the years 1950–51 I studied 50 alcoholics admitted to Burghölzli, among other things, as to their backgrounds, by methods similar to those employed with the 208 principal schizophrenic probands. There were 38 men and 12 women, ranging in ages from 30 to over 70. The statistics on these alcoholics is comparable to those of the principal probands in that the same concepts of parent loss were applied, both groups came from the same general area, and their birthdates were scattered over the same time period. Of the 50 alcoholics, 21 came from families that were disrupted before the probands' 15th birthdays. However, the figure of 42 percent for this statistic has a high median error of almost 7, and does not differ at all significantly from the 36 percent of broken homes among the 208 schizophrenic probands. On the other hand, there is a purely numerical high significance in the higher parent losses among the alcoholics as compared to the draftees ($p < 0.01$). Some doubts about the significance of the difference, however, will result from the difference in birthdates between the alcoholics and the draftees. As was the case among the schizophrenic probands, family disruptions occur within the first three 5-year periods with about equal frequency in the lives of the alcoholics. There is a great preponderance of parent losses by death as compared to such losses from other causes, but they, too, are statistically not significant. A detailed description of investigative findings among alcoholics is also provided by Diethelm (1955).

Investigations of alcoholics according to the same methods and standards, undertaken at the Payne Whitney Clinic in New York, which admits mostly patients from high financial and intellectual levels, listed broken-home childhoods before age 15 at 31 percent.

In his investigations on manic-depressive states, Angst (1966) determined the frequency of premature parent losses among 331 depressives who had been admitted to our clinic between 1959 and 1963. Since, at their admission, they were older, on the average, than the 208 schizophrenic probands at the time of their admission, their birth dates are somewhat less than 20 years earlier than those of the latter group. Angst (1966) did not exclude aliens, a fact that of itself carries no statistical weight, since most of those aliens are young foreign laborers, among whom hospitalization for mental depressions is still rare. Angst (1966) limits the concept of parent loss the way it was done for the schizophrenic probands. Among his probands the women strongly outnumber the men (249:82).

Angst's (1966) findings on depressives are summarized in Tables 2.29–2.31. Before their 15th birthdays 33 percent of the depressives suffered broken homes, as compared to 36 percent among the 208 principal probands. The difference is statistically not significant. But it was unexpected that the deaths of parents before the probands' 15th birthdays should be more frequent among the depressives than among the schizophrenics (21 percent against 15.3 percent);[22] it was unexpected because the depressives were born later than the schizophrenics. Still, the difference is not statistically significant. In part it may be explained by a high suicide incidence among the parents of manic-depressives, or possibly also by increases in their mortality rate for other reasons. On the other hand, the number of divorces among the parents of schizophrenics is greater than it is among the parents of depressives (9.6 percent to 3.6 percent), a difference which is statistically insignificant. It deserves all the more attention, because divorces during the period between the birth dates of the schizophrenics and those of the depressives have increased among the average population.

The family disruptions suffered by depressives are not as evenly distributed among the first three 5-year periods in their lives as they were among the schizophrenics (52:27:31), but the differences are not statistically significant.

Angst (1966) set up separate statistics on broken homes for men and women, and found that they were about equal for both sexes (Tables 2.29–2.31).

22. As Table 2.29 shows, these percentages represent that portion of probands whose first parent loss was caused by death. If, instead, the figure for all parent losses by death were desired, that is, if the numbers added in parentheses were to be included, the disputed difference would be even greater.

Table 2.29. Parent losses among 331 depressives (from Angst)

Totals of all probands having lost at least one parent[1]

Ages spans in years

Parent loss by	0–4 $\frac{11}{12}$	5–9 $\frac{11}{12}$	10–14 $\frac{11}{12}$	15–18	0–14 $\frac{11}{12}$		0–18		Total parent losses[2] 0–18
					No.	% of all probands	No.	% of all probands	No.
Death of father	10(+2)	9(+2)	9(+2)	5(+1)	28(+6)	8.4	33(+7)	10.0	40
Death of mother	12(+1)	15	13(+3)	2	40(+4)	12.1	42(+4)	12.7	46
Separation or divorce of parents	6(+1)	2	4	1	12(+1)	3.6	13(+1)	3.9	14
Illegitimate birth	18	0	0	0	18	5.4	18	5.4	18
In foster care[3]	6(+12)	1(+6)	5(+9)	6	12(+27)	3.6	18(+27)	5.4	45
Totals of parent losses:	52(+16)	27(+8)	31(+14)	14(+1)	110(+38)	33.23	124(+39)	37.46	163

1. The numbers added in parentheses represent those probands who had already suffered an earlier, different loss of a parent, and who have been accounted for above or below that entry, under a different category. These figures are not represented in the percentage column that follows the (+) entries.

2. In the figures for total parent losses, loss of father and of mother are included even when they apply to the same proband while in the preceding column the probands are counted only once when they have lost both parents. The figures in this column are the sums of the figures in parentheses and those not in parentheses from the 8th column.

3. Only those probands are counted as being in foster care (in foster homes or with strange families) who were so placed for at least a year. Probands away from their families for training or schooling were not included.

Table 2.30. Parent losses among 82 male depressives (from Angst) (breakdown of Table 2.29)

Totals of all probands having lost at least one parent[1]

Age spans in years

Parent loss by	$0-4\frac{11}{12}$	$5-9\frac{11}{12}$	$10-14\frac{11}{12}$	15-18	0-14 $\frac{11}{12}$ No.	0-14 $\frac{11}{12}$ % of all probands	0-18 No.	0-18 % of all probands	Total parent losses[2] 0-18 No.
Death of father	1	2(+1)	0	3	3(+1)	3.6	6(+1)	7.3	7
Death of mother	3(+1)	5	2	0	10(+1)	12.2	10(+1)	12.2	11
Separation or divorce of parents	4	0	1	0	5	6.1	5	6.1	5
Illegitimate birth	5	0	0	0	5	6.1	5	6.1	5
In foster care[3]	2(+3)	(+1)	1(+1)	1	3(+5)	3.6	4(+5)	4.9	9
Totals of parent losses:	15(+4)	7(+2)	4(+1)	4	26(+7)	31.7	30(+7)	36.58	37

1. The numbers added in parentheses represent those probands who had already suffered an earlier, different loss of a parent, and who have been accounted for above or below that entry, under a different category. These figures are not represented in the percentage column that follows the (+) entries.

2. In the figures for total parent losses, loss of father and of mother are included even when they apply to the same proband while in the preceding column the probands are counted only once when they have lost both parents. The figures in this column are the sums of the figures in parentheses and those not in parentheses from the 8th column.

3. Only those probands are counted as being in foster care (in foster homes or with strange families) who were so placed for at least a year. Probands away from their families for training or schooling were not included.

Table 2.31. Parent losses among 249 female depressives (from Angst) (breakdown of Table 2.29)

Totals of all probands having lost at least one parent[1]

Age spans in years

Parent loss by	$0-4\frac{11}{12}$	$5-9\frac{11}{12}$	$10-14\frac{11}{12}$	$15-18$	$0-14\frac{11}{12}$		$0-18$		Total parent losses[2] $0-18$
					No.	% of all probands	No.	% of all probands	No.
Death of father	9(+2)	7(+1)	9(+2)	2(+1)	25(+5)	10.0	27(+6)	10.8	33
Death of mother	9	10	22(+3)	2	30(+3)	12.0	32(+3)	12.8	35
Separation or divorce of parents	2(+1)	2	3	1	7(+1)	2.8	8(+1)	3.2	9
Illegitimate birth	13	0	0	0	13	5.2	13	5.2	13
In foster care[3]	4(+9)	1(+5)	4(+8)	5	9(+22)	3.6	14(+22)	5.6	36
Totals of parent losses:	37(+12)	20(+6)	27(+13)	10(+1)	84(+31)	33.7	94(+32)	37.7	126

1. The numbers added in parentheses represent those probands who had already suffered an earlier, different loss of a parent, and who have been accounted for above or below that entry, under a different category. These figures are not represented in the percentage column that follows the (+) entries.

2. In the figures for total parent losses, loss of father and of mother are included even when they apply to the same proband while in the preceding column the probands are counted only once when they have lost both parents. The figures in this column are the sums of the figures in parentheses and those not in parentheses from the 8th column.

3. Only those probands are counted as being in foster care (in foster homes or with strange families) who were so placed for at least a year. Probands away from their families for training or schooling were not included.

Among the probands hospitalized at our clinic for consultation in 1942–1944, Doris Morf (1962) found parent losses before age 20 among 70 of the 154 psychopaths (45 percent) and among 10 of the 29 alcoholics (34 percent), in comparison to 18 parent losses among 65 of her schizophrenics (28 percent). The greater incidence of parent losses among the psychopaths vis-à-vis the schizophrenics is statistically significant ($p < 0.05$).

Margrit Rotach-Fuchs (1968) investigated the premature parent losses among 100 neurotic inpatients of our clinic. These were probands whose ages, on the average ranged, midway between those of the 208 principal probands of this study and the draftees. (Average age of the former in 1942/43 was 40, of the 100 neurotics in 1955/56, age 35, and of the draftees 19). Her selection included 105 patients, but catamneses for 5 of the aliens could not be obtained. The investigation includes only 100 patients, 30 men and 70 women. Premature parent loss was defined exactly as it had been for this study. Its frequency was exactly the same as it was for the draftees. The childhood environment of these neurotics was hardly any different from that of the normal population, in respect to early parent losses, but it is distinguished rather sharply from it in the frequency of abnormal personalities among the parents and in chaotic marriage relationships among them, without divorces or legal separations.

Discussion

If one were to disregard the errors due to small numbers, one could certainly formulate innumerable and confusing theories from the comparisons of parent losses among the various groups of probands. But in the following paragraphs, I intend to discuss only those findings that approach a reasonable statistical significance or that may be of special interest in other respects.

First I have to correct a point of view that was at the basis of many previous studies. This was that if the parent losses in any given group of schizophrenics are counted (for example, from patients hospitalized at a given clinic), one should not expect to be able to conclude from it an average rate for parent losses among schizophrenics in general, at all times, and from any given location. Just as little likely is the counting of premature parent losses for any given group representing the average population to yield a generally valid figure that could unequivocally be applied to

comparisons with findings for schizophrenics. This statement among others becomes rather impressive, supported, as it is, by an experience with the group of draftees from the Zürich area. The number of their parent losses is significantly different, depending on whether they live in the City of Zürich or a few kilometers distant from it! Differences in the frequency of parent losses do not result only from the fact that the members of one group are schizophrenic and those of other groups are not; a great variety of other factors have a stronger bearing on the phenomenon of parent loss, such as the period of time in which the probands were born, the locale of their homes, the social class to which they belong, and many other, partly puzzling and elusive factors. Rough changes may occur in the statistics through some minor changes in the method of questioning the probands about parent loss. These are conclusions that must be reached through the intensive study of the existing literature as well as the study and careful evaluation of one's own findings.

None of the numerous previous investigations, not those by other authors nor our own, have so far provided any irrefutable statistical proof for the theory that premature parent losses among schizophrenics occur with greater frequency than they do among normal people. It is certain that differences between parent losses among schizophrenics and those of normal people cannot be great, if they actually do exist at all.

It is, of course, possible that schizophrenics lose a parent during their childhood more frequently than normal people do. In this sense it is valid to say that the comparisons by other authors of parent losses as between schizophrenics and representatives of a normal population have always shown only that either the parent losses of both groups were equal or that they were higher among the schizophrenics. But there is not a single statistic that shows with even an approximation of statistical significance that there were fewer parent losses among schizophrenics than there were among normal people. But then, to be sure, this line of argument loses some power to convince by the fact that a number of investigators obviously made an effort statistically to prove their preconceived notion that parent losses either cause or favor schizophrenic onsets, and that they set about performing their investigations with this prejudice in mind.

As previously explained, a statistically significant preponderance of premature parent losses among the principal schizophrenic probands, as compared to the draftees as representatives of the general population, has, in fact, been achieved mathematically. However, the suitability for comparison between the two groups was limited.

If the number of premature parent losses is added for the five groups of schizophrenics studied in connection with this investigation, and is then compared with those of the draftees, the resultant difference is likewise statistically significant, showing that premature parent losses are greater among the schizophrenics.[23] Yet, here again, some weighty factors are to be found against a valid comparability. These have already been explained.

After it had become clear that I was unable to set up any groups of schizophrenics that could be compared unequivocally with our representatives of the general population, one additional consideration occurred to us. Groups of my schizophrenics recruited by totally different methods reveal totally different relationships as to their comparability with my representatives of the general population. If, now, the number of premature parent losses for most of the groups of schizophrenics exceeds that of the representatives for the general population, it is probable, after all, that the higher number of parent losses may have something to do with the schizophrenias of the probands (and not necessarily with other undesirable effects of selective processes). There are nine groups of schizophrenics from our clinic who have been studied for premature patent loss, if our previously published studies are also included. In seven of these nine groups of schizophrenics, the number of premature parent losses exceeds that of representatives for the general population.[24] This fact alone contains no conclusive proof to support

the assumption that schizophrenics lose their parents more frequently than normal people do, but it does constitute a rather clear indication that this may be the case.

Insofar as it can be assumed that a small excess of parent losses in the childhood histories of schizophrenics, as compared to those of the normal population, it certainly indicates nothing specific in connection with schizophrenia, for it is also true that an equal or higher frequency in parent losses is also detectable in the childhood histories of many other types of patients. But the qualifying statement must also be made here that a high concentration of parent losses among such other types of patients was just as little statistically completely significant as it was among the schizophrenics. But then, with a somewhat greater degree of probability than that with which an increase in premature parent losses among schizophrenics may be expected, such an increase may be expected among other types of patients, particularly among neurotics, psychopaths, antisocial individuals and addicts as they have been investigated by several other authors. And likewise, those alcoholics whom I investigated revealed a considerably higher incidence of parent losses before age 15 than did the figures representing the general population of Zürich.

The depressives belonging to the category of manic-depressives investigated by Angst (1966), however, apparently reveal a lower incidence of parent losses than the schizophrenics, although the difference is by no means significant. Still, from the older investigations by Pollock et al. (1939) also, a lower number of parent losses among depressives is to be assumed than among schizophrenics.

The statement often expressed in the literature, that early losses of mothers (in comparison with losses of fathers) generally appear in the records of childhood histories of schizophrenics more frequently, can be refuted with statistic certainly by our case records. The relationship between father loss and mother loss by death before age 15 among all five groups of schizophrenic probands combined, amounts to 81:42, and among the draftees to 65:37. (Here only the first parent loss is counted; that is, if after the father's death the mother also died, the death of that mother is not included in the figures.) The proportion of mother losses by death among all premature parent losses by death amounts to just 33 percent for the schizophrenics and to 36 percent for the draftees. The difference in

23. The five groups in question are: (a) the 208 principal schizophrenic probands, (b) the "young schizophrenics", (c) the "middle-aged schizophrenics", (d) the private schizophrenic patients, (e) the supplemental schizophrenics. Among the 952 schizophrenics of these groups, 291 parent losses occurred before age 15; that is, in 31 percent of the cases. Among the 1505 draftees there were 360 (24 percent) premature parent losses. The difference at $p < 0.001$ is, accordingly, highly significant.

24. The numerical series is 22, 23, 25, 30, 31, 32, 36, 39 and 66 percent, as compared to 24 percent among the draftees.

these percentages is statistically not significant, but the finding is valid that the loss of mothers by death compared to loss of fathers by death among schizophrenics cannot be appreciably greater than it is among the draftees. (The facts that the draftees are, on the average, younger than the schizophrenics and that they, of course, are all males, constitute no objections to a careful generalization of these findings.) The preponderance of father losses over mother losses is easily explained by the fact that men marry later and, on the average, die earlier than women do. The statistics in the literature, almost without exception, agree that a higher rate of father losses over mother losses exists in the childhood histories of schizophrenics.

The assumption that a parent loss during the first 5 years of life generally has a greater impact on schizophrenics than such a loss in the following two 5-year periods is likewise statistically refuted by the aforementioned findings. Nor are there any significant investigative results in the literature that would lend support to that assumption. Parent losses among schizophrenics are distributed evenly over the first three 5-year periods of life. Among all our five groups of schizophrenics combined, the parent losses in the first three 5-year periods of life amount to $108:87:96$. Using only the bare figures, there appears to be, rather, among the draftees, a greater number of parent losses in the first 5-year period of life $(142:106:112)$. These increased figures for the draftees are statistically not significant.

The statistical studies to date disagree on the question as to whether parent loss through divorce or legal separation of the parents or by eviction of the child from the home would exert a greater influence on the childhood development of a schizophrenic than such loss through death of the parent—a disagreement that was to be expected. My own investigation shows the reverse of this assumption to be true. The higher rate of parent losses among all four groups of our schizophrenics as compared to those among the draftees is exclusively due to the greater number of deaths among the parents of our schizophrenics. The schizophrenics had experienced just as many parental divorces or legal separations, long-term absences of parents from the home, or sojourns in foster care before their 15th birthdays as the draftees had! (Among the parents of the 952 schizophrenics of all five groups there were 130 (14

percent) divorces or separations of parents, long-lasting absences of a parent, or foster care, that the child had experienced before his 15th birthday. Among the 1505 draftees, the figure for the same types of family disruptions was 225 (15 percent), a confidence interval of $p > 0.1$, which means that there was no significant difference in the percentages of these types of separations, when the error due to small numbers is considered. There was, however, a difference in the death statistics of the parents for these two groups. While 128 (13 percent) of the 952 schizophrenics lost their parents by death before age 15, only 102 (7 percent) of the draftees lost theirs under the same condition. This difference is statistically highly significant at $p < 0.001$. In contrast to this, Oltman et al. (1952, 1965) as well as Brill and Liston (1966) found that it was specifically divorces that predominated among the parents of schizophrenics. Probably neither of the two results conforms to a sociological generality that would be truly typical for schizophrenics. Either the preponderance of divorces or their absence could hardly have anything to do with the schizophrenias of the probands; it might instead be the result of some peculiarity in the selection process.

Accordingly, it seems in retrospect that from all our laborious efforts in assembling statistics, all we have been able to show are negative conclusions that refute some widespread conceptions. In summarizing these the following appear to be valid:

—The frequency of premature parent loss among a group probands does not essentially depend on whether these probands are schizophrenic or normal, but certainly depends much more on a great many other factors, such as the age and regional origin of the probands.

—The frequency of parent losses among schizophrenics is certainly not much greater than it is among the general population, yet it can be assumed that it is slightly greater.

—If it should really be true that premature parent losses do occur more frequently among schizophrenics than they do among the general population, the phenomenon should by no means be regarded as something characteristic of schizophrenia, for it occurs even more frequently and with greater certainty among patients with psychopathic and neurotic personality developments.

—There is no general preponderance of mother losses over father losses through death, among schizophrenics.

—There is no general preponderance of parent losses during the first 5-year period of life over later 5-year periods among schizophrenics.

—Loss of parents through divorce or separation of parents, or placing the child in foster care does not occur in the childhood histories of schizophrenics at a greater rate than it does in the childhood histories of normal people, but loss of parents through death is more frequent among our schizophrenic probands.

We do achieve some positive results, however, if we now compare the number of parent losses in men and women separately. It has already been explained that among the 208 principal schizophrenic probands, parent losses among women occurred more frequently than among men, but that the difference was not yet statistically significant. Insofar as a difference in the number of parent losses among schizophrenics and among the normal population is assumed to exist, the excess among the schizophrenics occurs exclusively in parent losses among the schizophrenic women.

It has likewise already been noted that the parent losses up to the probands' 15th birthdays were greater among the women than among the men in all three additional groups of schizophrenics (the young, the middle-aged, and the supplemental schizophrenics), and that up to their 18th birthdays this occurred in only two of these three groups. If all groups of schizophrenics are considered together, the greater number of parent losses among the women over those of the men is statistically significant. If the groups are considered separately, statistical significance is reached only in the supplemental schizophrenics group for parent losses up to their 18th birthdays. But the near-equality as between the sexes among the four groups, for parent losses up to the 15th birthdays of the probands increases this significance. The differences found are certainly more probably genuine than they are illusions due merely to happenstance.

From the existing literature this difference between the sexes can neither be unequivocally supported nor refuted with any certainty. Brill and Liston's (1966) findings support them; those of Wahl (1954, 1956) oppose them.[25]

The findings form our own schizophrenics suggest the possibility that there may be a number of other differences to be discovered in the childhood backgrounds of schizophrenics that vary with the difference in sex. For the present, most of them have not yet been verified with sufficient statistical significance to be worthy of serious discussion. The differences between premature father- and mother-losses among the male and female schizophrenics do appear to be significant. In comparison to father losses, female schizophrenics more often lost their mothers through death than did the males. Male schizophrenics, on the other hand, more often lost their fathers.

Just what do these findings signify in terms of understanding schizophrenia? To begin with, they are negative. Premature parent loss predominates—if at all—only very little in the childhood backgrounds of schizophrenics as compared to the general population. Mental patients other than schizophrenics reveal parent losses in their early life histories just as often or even more frequently. It is therefore impossible to ascribe a role of any importance to the premature parent loss that would have any bearing on the genesis of schizophrenias in general. The statement is particularly insupportable that the premature loss of a mother in general has any decisive influence on the development of schizophrenias. As in relation to other illnesses as well, so also in relation to the schizophrenias, the mother-deprivation theory in its stark form is totally insupportable. It appears that there would be no evidence for a long time to upset these negative concepts, unless some completely new and unexpected discoveries were to be made.

If it is the case that late-onset schizophrenics do suffer premature parent losses at a somewhat higher rate than normal people, it may, in and of itself, be the result of a number of different reasons. One possible explanation may be that these parents die earlier, on the average, because of inherited (or even other) personality characteristics. For instance, it has been proved that relatives of schizophrenics from the preceding generation became ill of tuberculosis and died at a higher rate than the normal population because of generally

25. Barry and Lindemann (1960) discovered a similar phenomenon among the parents of neurotics. Premature loss of mothers occurred more frequently among their female neurotics than among their male neurotics. The premature loss of fathers appeared about equal among the male and female neurotics as it did among general patients.

unsanitary practices in their mode of living. Added factors include suicide and increased exposure to the risk of accidents. But it is also not impossible that the probable slight preponderance in parent losses in the childhood backgrounds of schizophrenics is brought about by separation from parents that favors a subsequent schizophrenic development.

The question arises, which explanation is the right one? Is the probable, slight preponderance in parent losses in the childhood backgrounds of schizophrenics—the importance of which has in the past so often been overestimated—an indication that the parents of schizophrenics have pathologically tainted personalities since they are genetically close to the schizophrenics, or does this parent loss mean a psychotraumatic predisposition for schizophrenia? Up to the present, almost no attempt has been made to find an answer to the question by way of statistics on these parent losses themselves. Instead, the attempt was made to evaluate the problem according to concepts one had developed from other experiences concerning the nature of schizophrenias. But now there seems to be a quite unexpected basis for answering this question on the basis of the statistics on parent losses, and it is this basis alone that is to be discussed in this chapter.

It is a statistically significant finding that among the probands studied in this investigation the schizophrenic women had more parent losses in their childhood backgrounds than the schizophrenic men had. It has furthermore been proved as statistically significant that only the schizophrenic women (and not the schizophrenic men) more frequently suffered parent losses in their childhood than did the representatives of the average population that we studied. Considering our investigative methods and the nature of our probands, we can attempt to superimpose the conclusions from our schizophrenic probands with reasonably valid probability on all the schizophrenics from our culture and our period in time. Until there is proof to the contrary, we may assume that it is part of the general characteristics of schizophrenias that in the childhood backgrounds of schizophrenic women more premature parent losses will be found than among schizophrenic men or among the general population. Furthermore, there have been (statistically significant) indications that mother-losses by death among schizophrenic women (as compared to father-losses by death among such women) occur

more frequently than they do among schizophrenic men.

If these findings are confirmed by series of new investigations, there would be but one probable explanation, namely, that premature parent-loss, and particularly maternal loss, favors a subsequent schizophrenic development in girls. The same would not be statistically evident for boys. It must be expressly emphasized that no evidence points to a probability that parental or especially maternal loss could be the single decisive factor causing schizophrenias in women. The statistics only enhance the probability that such a loss facilitates a schizophrenic development in girls. It poses a certain vulnerability—a disposition—toward schizophrenia in girls, which may have an etiological influence, but it is by no means the sole causative factor and in no way does it explain the origin of schizophrenia.

The positive conclusions from the above statistics, then, indicate that familial influences (in particular maternal loss), among girls may have an influence on the disposition to schizophrenia in girls rather than in boys. Actually it is easy to imagine that the development of girls may more readily depend on the intimate relationships in the family, particularly on the presence of the mother, than does that of boys. This entire question, however, is to be discussed below in greater detail in the context of totally different types of data that refer to the same problem (see pp. 425–28).

As regards future research, the findings presented here will scarcely inspire anyone, using the methods of most of the previous investigations, to make comparisons between the parent losses in certain groups of schizophrenics and those in certain representative groups of the general population. It has been shown that complete comparability of two such groups is impossible to achieve, at least not by any amount of effort and labor that lies within the realm of the possible.

Attempts to investigate more thoroughly the differences in the family backgrounds of schizophrenic men and women seem to hold forth promise of more rewarding dividends. Indeed, some rather plain indications were found that conclusions on individual lives could be drawn from such investigations that may signify predispositions toward schizophrenic onset.

Baxter (1966) arrives at a similar conclusion based on his studies of the existing literature on parent losses. He finds that schizophrenics are not markedly different as a group from other patients in respect to the incidence of parent loss. He suggests that in the future, comparisons should be attempted between groups of different types schizophrenics, specifically in the areas of the sexes, of different age groups, and of different courses of illness.

Overall Evaluation of Childhood Backgrounds

Introduction

By the counting of premature parent losses and the psychoses among the parents, the childhoods of our schizophrenic probands have been examined from one aspect only, and superficially and insufficiently at that. More important than the mere determining of the fact whether a child was raised by both parents is a description of what sort of care he received from either parents or foster parents. Presented with this problem, it soon becomes evident that it is relatively simple and rewarding to inspect in every single instance the childhood of the late-onset schizophrenics, but that it represents an exceedingly thorny, touchy, and unrewarding enterprise to set up statistically the varied, colorful data from many different childhood histories. The individual examination of a childhood always transmits a humanly moving set of images. However, the attempt at a statistical rendering of it usually ends up with a set of dry, inanimate facts, that really have little to say in their abstract formulations, and the real meaning of which is difficult to infer. A comparison suggests itself: The graphic representation of a human being by a great artist touches all our sensibilities most intimately; but if one attempted to stack 208 such representations on top of one another, and then retraced only the median lines of all the contours from them onto a sheet of paper, nothing but an absurd, meaningless figure would be the result.

The difficulties of grasping anything statistically are obvious, and yet in many scientific studies they are accorded too little attention. The data that we used to support ourselves are subjective. One reporter is more scrupulous than another, one has a better memory or ability to present facts than the next man. In many cases the data we elicit depend on the mood of the moment or the manner of questioning. Individual traits we mention always have real emotional and personal significance only when they are seen against the background of the whole situation. If the child goes through the experience of learning that his father is unfaithful to his mother and is having an extramarital affair outside the home, it will have an entirely different meaning according to whether his mother tolerates the father's philandering or not, depending on what set of morals prevail in that family, depending on how that father treats the child, and on many other considerations. The cryptic entry "Father was unfaithful" does not, by itself, summarize the picture of a childhood background. But if one neglects details, in search of broad, general evaluations, then the statistical set of data becomes even less satisfactory. The same qualifications do not necessarily mean that the same conditions prevail. The expression "It was horrible" as a summary statement on a childhood background in one case referred to an onset of silliness and meant something like: "You should have seen some of the capers my brothers and sisters used to pull off when we were kids"; but in another, the term "horrible" referred to years of brutal mistreatment by both parents to the point where the child's life was in constant jeopardy. Such extreme differences in meaning for one and the same expression can easily be correctly evaluated, but there are innumerable much more delicate nuances in the meaning of terms that in spite of all efforts toward accuracy lead to misinterpretations.

The bare summarizing, categorizing, and statistical processing of data from the childhood histories of our 208 principal probands is subject to even deeper pitfalls and difficulties than the mere unreliability of informants. Frequently we are confronted with highly ambivalent emotional experiences. Each one of us knows his own childhood best. But few of us would feel emotionally satisfied if we had to explain that it had been either good or sad. It was always both good and sad. Beautiful and sad experiences followed one another in a kaleidoscopic blending of events, and beyond that we experience many important happenings in childhood as beautiful in one sort of mood and as sad in another, and often even as both beautiful and sad or as delightful and repugnant at the same time. Not even all physicians could reply simply, plainly, unequivocally, and without some mental reservation to the questions, "Was your father strict and authoritarian?, Did your mother pamper you or was she strict with you?" etc. Statistics, however, demand inexorably a bare yes or no to such questions. Only one kind of answer could do justice to a description of the human condition. It would have to present a multifaceted picture of the attitude toward important childhood events that would also be able to express the internal conflicts, the lack of certainty, and the inner disunitedness. But then such a picture would no longer be useful for statistical purposes. Naturally, a person in my position finds it easy to emulate what many other investigators have done, namely, at the end, to render a decision after a lengthy interview with a patient or a member of his family, to the effect that his mother was "domineering" or that his father remained apart from the life of the family. But in the end I am not convinced that I have captured the entire truth of the situation in stating a summary judgment of that sort. And if I carefully allow the patient to continue to speak freely in a relaxed atmosphere, I find time and again that he himself begins, quietly or vehemently, to shake the carefully erected structure of every summary judgment, even though I had earlier skillfully obtained his complete agreement.

The ambivalent and often chaotic internal conflicts of the interviewed probands as to their childhood backgrounds are still not the most important of the insurmountable difficulties that stand in the way of a satisfactory set of statistical data on the childhood conditions among late-onset schizophrenics. In keeping with scientific tradition, we should like to evaluate the milieu itself independently of the child. In line with older methods of thinking we should like to know just how a particular set of conditions—and especially how the parents—influenced a certain child. We should like to assume that a child exists, that this child is placed in a particular environment, and that the child and the environment could exist independently of one another. But this very assumption is incorrect. The child has a part in creating the environment. The child is never merely placed into an environment that is totally independent of that child. And more particularly, the relationship between the parents and the child is not created solely by the parents, but also by the child. A cold, unloving relationship of a mother toward her child can, for example, have been partly brought on by the character of the child. It may be an error to conclude, from her unloving attitude toward a particular child, that a mother is incapable of maternal love. And once a mother's unloving behavior

has been entered on the record, one has no right to conclude from it without looking further that it is a causal basis for mental illness. Such behavior may just as well be the consequence of an existing pathological predisposition on the part of the child. In other words, only a portion of the childhood environment has anything like an impersonal implication. The more important part exists only in relation to the child itself. It could possibly have a meaning completely independent of the particular child when the mother permits the child to starve, or when the father, in a state of inebriation, beats the child regularly without otherwise having anything to do with the child. But if the child's inner feeling coexperiences the mother's internal or external distress, the shared experience of such distress can lead to a warm and intimate relationship between the two, just as the child might tolerate the father's beatings while he is intoxicated without emotional involvement, because the father is at other times kind and loving. Such situations are common in the childhood histories of my probands. The question now becomes: Did this child, have a horrible or a beautiful childhood? Were his father and mother unloving? Frequently the child provokes the father's punishment, just as sometimes a mother is more likely to let her child go hungry if it is given to tantrums at the dinner table. In such circumstances are the beatings or refusals to feed the child still aspects of the "childhood milieu," or are they not rather the necessary consequences of that child's immature behavior? Even in these extreme hyperschematized cases, such questions cannot be answered by a simple yes or no. The more one becomes absorbed in these human lives, the more one resists schematized answers.

Some shortcoming, then, is attached to every set of statistics on the "childhood backgrounds" of patients. It suggests that childhood backgrounds are something objective, but in reality to a great extent, they very extensively bear the outer imprint of the child's personality.

Despite all this, I admit that I should dislike having to work entirely without the benefit of statistical data. But I became convinced that statistics are all the more removed from fact, more arbitrary, more artificially contrived, and more without value, the more differentiated the subjective qualifications are on which they are based. Only the simplest and most basic qualifications lend themselves to statistical categorization. And even then, their results are to be applied only if the most scrupulous care is used. Statistics can never replace the detailed study of an individual family. Of much greater importance than any statistics is the impressionistic picture that is presented when a family is under treatment. Statistics only begin to meet the need of objectifying this subjective picture, and that is possible only in a few isolated facets and to a highly limited degree.

Attempt at a Statistical Evaluation

The childhood backgrounds were roughly characterized according to the concepts "normal," "doubtful," and "horrible."

They were considered "normal" when the following conditions were met: Parents or foster parents cared for the child according to standards acceptable in our society, with respect to food, shelter, schooling, and training at home. Parents or foster parents were people who adapted reasonably to their community without abnormal friction, that is, they did not posses the characteristics of criminals, or were antisocial or "nuts" to a degree where the child under their care would suffer considerably from the contrast between them and normal society. The parents or foster parents felt a responsibility for the child and accepted it emotionally—at least for the most part. As one necessary requisite to qualify as normal, the attitudes of the probands themselves during their childhoods must also be considered. Their childhood environment had to have been normal, not only according to descriptions by relatives, but also according to their own present-day evaluation of it.

Childhood backgrounds were termed "horrible" only after proof of long-term mistreatment or neglect existed according to commonly accepted standards. These included neglect in feeding and physical care in infancy to a health-menacing degree, regular beatings, or unreasonable punishment of the child (for instance, for bedwetting) or severe exploitation of the child by forcing it to work. The childhood background was also characterized as "horrible" when the child was regularly exposed to constant antisocial behavior on the part of the parents or foster parents, such as frequent drunkenness, with accompanying brutality by the father or overt prostitution by the mother. Or when the child was induced by the parents to beg or steal; when it was incestuously abused over a period of time, or when it was drawn into the defense against hallucinations or delusionary persecutions by schizophrenic parents or required to take part in the compulsive rituals of obsessively neurotic parents, etc. Such childhood "horrors," in order to qualify for the category of a "horrible" childhood background, had to be remembered and recounted by the later schizophrenic patient, and not simply taken from commonly accepted notations.

Any childhood background that did not unquivocally meet the qualifications for either "normal" or "horrible," was relegated to the median category of "doubtful." According to the way many of these conditions were circumscribed, we might have expected a preponderance of such doubful cases. But on the contrary, most of the cases could easily and unequivocally be categorized either as "normal" or as "horrible."

Conditions can change in the course of a childhood. A change from "normal" to "horrible" conditions most often occurred when the child was taken from the care of its parents and placed in foster care. Nor, conversely, was it rare that a child returned to its natural parents from foster care the worse for it. For this reason, separate categories were set up for children living with their parents and for those in foster care. But even during the continuous care by both parents childhood conditions can undergo changes. For the most part, only slight modifications occurred during any one childhood that would alter the qualification of family conditions as to care and home environment. Surprisingly often, the initial qualification held throughout the major part of a childhood, with only gradual deviations. If a significant, long-term change had occurred in the home environment, as it did in some exceptional cases, then two separate childhood histories were compiled. Short-term or less significant changes in childhood backgrounds were not recorded in the statistics.

Example of a horrible childhood in the parental home environment

Hans K. (Proband 29), born 1900

The proband's father (1858–1938) came from a poverty-stricken family of 10 children, of whom 6 died prematurely. Of the remaining 4, 2 (proband's father and one uncle) distinguished themselves by hard work and exceptional intelligence. Both became famous. Proband's father became a historian and even received an honorary doctorate from a foreign university. He had lived with a hearing problem since childhood, brought on by severe middle-ear infections, a problem that was aggravated as he grew older. For this reason he had had to refuse a university chair in his profession, shortly before proband was born. He was forced to raise his family of 8 children (of whom 2 died prematurely) as a mid-level civil service employee under rather stringent financial circumstances, which embittered him.

Proband's mother (1865–1937) came from an unpretentious home. Her father had lost his money in a small business venture that failed. She was a retiring, shy, and undemanding woman, who during the proband's childhood had experienced some rather extended periods of depression for which she had had to be hospitalized intermittently.

The proband himself was a physically weak child, somewhat retarded in both his physical and mental development. As a result, soon after his birth he was placed in various children's homes. Then he spent 5 years with a paternal aunt, a modest seamstress, who brought him up lovingly and raised him in the Catholic confession—although he had been baptized in the Reformed Church.

After he had failed his first year in elementary school his father took him back and attempted to teach him at home. During the following 8 years the proband remained with his parents and siblings, and it is this period in his life that was categorized as "horrible." His father attempted to overcome the son's "deficient mental activity" by the application of stern discipline. After work every day he would sit up with the proband with an abacus, would become extremely excited and irritated when the boy made mistakes, would slap him and pull his hair. For a number of years the same lamentable scene was reenacted evening after evening, during which the entire family suffered terribly. During the evening meal the father would ask his son again and again what answers he had given his teacher in school to various questions. For fear of physical punishment the son began to resort to lies, reporting that he had given a good recitation in school that day. His fear, the interrupted meals, his mother's and his siblings' tears had made everything inside him "sort of grow numb and stiff," and he reached the point where he was unable to answer even the simplest questions his father asked. The result would be renewed scoldings and slappings.

His mother had suffered through everything with him quietly and tearfully, day after day, but she had not possessed the courage to interfere. The father's tyranny continued unabated and dominated the lives of that family for years.

The mother had little to say in the family. The father had turned over authority and responsibility for operating the household to a housekeeper of resolute character, who had assumed the decisive female role in the household, taking precedence over the mother. Such were the reports given by the proband's siblings. The proband himself was incapable of making any statements at all concerning his father during the exploratory interviews. When he was questioned about his father he would fall into tense stupor. He spoke only about his mother, but even about her not in any tones of warm affection, but complaining that he had had to part from his aunt and had experienced difficulty in finding his way back to his mother. A portion of his curriculum vitae that he wrote in his questionnaire after becoming ill follows:

". . . then Dad himself came to take me home. There I now had to change myself over completely. I had to live with my mother, whom I actually did not really know. I had to learn to live together with my brothers and sisters. I had to go back again to the Reformed Church and change my faith over completely, too. Then I got into the second grade in school. But the teacher, Miss X, was such a terrible person that I was actually afraid of her. For instance, she did not mind, when she had to punish a boy, taking his pencil box and hitting him across the knuckles with it until they bled. This scared me so that I never got up the courage to say anything. . . ."

Among the 5 siblings who had survived infancy, the proband was the least intelligent. Later investigations showed that he was somewhat below normal intelligence, but by no means feebleminded. However, in spite of this, his scholastic progress was extremely limited under the described treatment by his father and his teacher. He was shy, monosyllabic, and a loner among his comrades. When he was released from the obligation of school at age 15 his father gave up hope of raising his capabilities to any sort of intellectual achievement and sent him into the country to work on a farm. With this event, the 8-year period of misery in his parental home came to an end.

None of his siblings, who had been less mistreated by their father because of their better scholastic prowess, but who were exposed for an even longer period to the evil atmosphere that dominated the family, became as ill as the proband himself. On the other hand, not one of them became a free and happy human being, either. All suffered from feelings of insecurity or depressions, and one brother actually became retarded. Another brother, as late as at age 60, suffered a schizophrenic psychosis from which he completely recovered.

Although it is extraneous to this context, it might be mentioned at this point that the schizophrenic psychosis of the proband himself began acutely the day of his father's funeral. He claimed to hear his deceased father knocking, spoke in confusion about a debt he owed him, and felt that he would be killed for that reason. He developed a state of increasing depressive-hallucinatory restlessness. But if one had believed to be observing a psychogenic rather than a schizophrenic psychosis, the further course of his illness showed that such an assumption was incorrect. What it was, was the onset of a severe schizophrenia that today has continued for over 24 years. Its course ran in acute hallucinatory depressive phases. Even after the first acute phase, there was never again any improvement. A severe residual state ensued, for which reason the proband was under psychiatric hospital treatment for $18\frac{1}{2}$ years. At present there is an unmistakable massive, permanent schizophrenic state, although it is still not a serious schizophrenic dementia.

Example of normal conditions in a childhood family background

Hanna J. (Proband 40), born 1913.

Proband's father, born 1877, died at age 87, was still robust until shortly before his expiration; he was a factory worker in a small manufacturing concern in the country where he worked all his life. He was competent and industrious, a respected citizen in his community, although a bit quiet and retiring. His life was steady, even, and uneventful.

Proband's mother died at age 68, when the proband was already fully mature. She had been a kind, friendly, and even-tempered person.

The proband grew up with her parents, together with a brother 3 years her senior, who later went to work in the same factory where his father worked, and where he is today, many years later, still employed and working steadily.

The family lived in an apartment provided by the factory for its employees. For this reason, the employer (whom I am personally acquainted with), as well as his coworkers had a good insight into the relationships within the family. According to their statements, these relationships were normal and happy, and the family was described as being quiet, orderly, and well respected. The father had come to our canton from a neighboring country, but had adapted easily to conditions in Switzerland, and there never was any evidence that the family, who later became citizens, might ever have had any difficulty because they had come to Switzerland as aliens.

The proband had encountered some difficulty in catching up in school and had to repeat one grade. There was no fuss made about it at home; in fact, her brother, who was questioned about it, did not even remember that it had occurred. After her formal schooling she successfully finished an apprenticeship as a dressmaker. After that she worked mostly in her parents' household, and in between at her trade and at a factory. She enjoyed being at home and substituting for her mother, who had often been hospitalized for thromboses during the proband's girlhood.

A brother of hers was the principal source of information on her childhood. He reported that as a child she had been quite mobile, happy, and outgoing. She had enjoyed playing with dolls and with other girls, but she also played ball, skipped rope, and spun tops. She had been easy to bring up and caused no problems in the family. She was rarely punished, usually only very mildly, after which she was usually ashamed of herself, although she did not bear a grudge for long. She got along well with her friends in school, was happy in their company, and especially enjoyed singing with them. The only oddity in her childhood that was referred to was a pronounced dislike for fish dishes, which made her ill just to smell them.

Example of a Proband whose childhood environment was characterized as doubtful, neither "Normal" nor "Horrible," Midway between Normal and Horrible

Heinrich G. (Proband 44), born 1901.

Proband's father (1851–1913), previously a shop foreman and later an innkeeper, was a brooding, melancholy sort of person. As long as he was head of the shop in a large factory he worked very well. At the time he was in no way conspicuous by his behavior. His first wife (not proband's mother) was an alcoholic, whom he divorced. At age 45, before the birth of proband, he took over a tavern, and from that time on he began to deteriorate. He became apathetic, gradually worked less and less in the business, and finally just sat around doing nothing and leaving everything in the business to his wife, the proband's mother. He grew extremely obese with advancing age and became an alcoholic. When intoxicated, he would instigate jealousy scenes with his wife, without any basis in fact. In other respects, even in old age, he remained good tempered and sensitive as he had been before. During the last years of his life he suffered from depression; his death of peritonitis followed quickly when proband was 12 years old.

He almost never actively spent time with his son, but he never mistreated him, either. The son must have sensed that his father was warmhearted and loving, despite his apathy.

Proband's mother (1872–1949) had suffered a delayed physical puberty, but had then developed normally in body and personality, except for the fact that, like her husband, she became extremely obese. As her husband continued to withdraw, she took active control of managing the tavern, finally assuming full charge and producing a living for the family from its operation. She became an excellent businesswoman and housekeeper, ever-tempered, kind, and sincere. While she passed through her menopause without complications, she did become sickly after age 60, but this was long after proband had become an adult. From then on, she suffered from asthma, headaches, and sciatica. When she died of myodegeneration, her son had already been hospitalized for many years.

The proband had an acromegaloid figure. His childhood was spent with his parents at the tavern. During his entire childhood he was listless and slovenly. Because of his indifference, apathy, superficiality, and laziness he had a hard time in school and had to repeat one grade. For the same reasons he was unable to complete an apprenticeship in a trade. He then remained at home and did small chores for his mother.

He enjoyed working at his parents' tavern and seemed to get along best when dealing with his mother. He was always willing and eager to do small services for her and cared for her devotedly when she was occasionally sick in bed. Especially during his mother's illnesses, he revealed his warm and loving

nature, so that the mother herself reported that she considered him to be a kind and dear person, in spite of his laziness. This sort of treatment was reciprocal in the home, and his shortcomings in working and efficiency never led to severe or certainly not to any cruel punishments.

Even before he was 20 the proband began to consume alcohol in quantity at his mother's tavern. Like his father, he proved to be intolerant of alcohol, and became excitable after drinking. His mental illness developed unnoticed and chronically, in that his general apathy and his autism gradually increased until delusions of persecution were added to them. It was not until age 37 that the actual psychosis emerged. Up to that point he had led a dull and sluggish life with his mother, had done little about helping at the tavern and, occasionally had indulged in alcoholic excesses. He never recovered from his psychosis, which developed into a permanent condition of almost complete apathy and extreme confused distraction, during which he could be cared for only in the special ward for the seriously ill. He died of thyroid carcinoma at age 59.

Table 2.32 shows the general finding that, with a shocking degree of frequency, schizophrenics come from backgrounds involving unfavorable childhoods, that is, broken homes or from "horrible" family circumstances. Nevertheless, a substantial minority of the schizophrenic probands do come from homes in which normal childhood conditions prevailed.

Table 2.32 shows in detail that among the 208 principal schizophrenics, only 59, about one quarter, had the good fortune of growing up with both parents in a reasonably normal family atmosphere. (The figures shown for probands who lived together with both parents under normal family circumstances until age 18 include those probands who left their homes during or after puberty in order to work or to serve apprenticeships, but who maintained a natural connection with their families.) Fifty of the probands experienced extremely unhappy, "horrible" conditions during childhood with their families, 12 with foster parents, and 9 with both parents as well as with foster families, a total of 71, or a good third of the total 208. The rest of the probands—over one-third—were living with their parents under conditions that could qualify neither as normal nor as horrible, or else they had suffered a parent loss that did not result in

Table 2.32. Childhoods of the 208 principal probands

Childhood conditions	No. of probands living with parents until age 18[1]	Probands who did not live with both parents until age 18		
		As long as they lived with both parents	In foster families, homes, or foster care facilities after parent loss	Never with both parents (illegitimate)
Normal	59	31	45	3
Doubtful	37	16	27	6
Horrible	30	29	21	0
Totals:	126	76	93[2]	9[3]

1. Includes those probands who were absent from home intermittently during or after puberty only to pursue jobs or training, without breaking family contacts.

2. Because of changes in care facilities, 15 of these probands are entered twice and 1 three times; that is, these 93 conditions were experienced by 76 probands.

3. Because of changes in care facilities, 3 of these probands are entered twice; that is, the 9 conditions apply to 6 probands.

actually "horrible" conditions at home.

Table 2.32 further shows that parent loss by death or by divorce or separation of the parents, in the majority of cases improved the family circumstances for the child,[26] obviously because the parent who usually left the family was the one who had been causing the disturbance and because sometimes a good foster family was found for the child. This finding is reminiscent of Haffter's discovery (1948) in his investigation of children with divorced parents. He emphasized that the divorce of a bad marriage more often than not improves the child's circumstances. But it also happened repeatedly that children were placed in foster families where they were exposed to the most appalling kind of mistreatment.

For a comparison I can make use of the childhood backgrounds of 50 alcoholics hospitalized at Burghölzli, which I investigated and evaluated by the same methods as those of the 208 principal probands. This was the same group of alcoholics that was previously used for comparisons with the broken-home statistics of schizophrenics. Only 10 of them (20 percent) grew up in homes with both parents under normal conditions, and 19 (more than one-third) had lived under horrible circumstances, either with their parents or after the loss of a parent. According to the absolute figures, the Zürich alcoholics have had even worse childhood backgrounds than the Zürich schizophrenics. If the small-sample error is taken into account, it is quite likely that this difference is a chance occurrence.

26. Barely significant: $0.1 > p > 0.05$.

Table 2.32 would lead one to believe that the family circumstances of our schizophrenics were a great deal worse during their childhood than those of a cross-section of the general Zürich population. This impression is confirmed when I include data pertaining to my former school friends and army comrades. But one must bear in mind that such improvised data are based on entirely different methods of research than those undertaken for these studies of schizophrenics; I should therefore like to disregard them. The assumption that the schizophrenics have had less favorable childhoods than the average population had, given the qualifications on which data in Table 2.32 are based, remains a mere probability.

Even if this probability were to be confirmed, the question would remain unanswered how such an unfavorable childhood is related to the schizophrenias of the probands. Did this unfavorable childhood pave the way for the genesis of the psychosis? Or was the unfavorable childhood a consequence of an unfavorable hereditary trait in the personality of the parents? Unexpectedly there emerges an indication toward an answer to this question from the comparison of childhoods as between schizophrenic males and females; for the female probands consistently come from even worse family circumstances than the males. Insofar as it is not the result of happenstance, this finding is difficult to explain with any sort of hereditary hypotheses, whereas it can easily be reconciled with psychogenetic hypotheses—assuming, for instance, that girls are more vulnerable to

Table 2.33. Childhoods of the 100 male principal probands (breakdown of Table 2.32)

Probands who did not live with both parents until age 18

Childhood conditions	No. of probands living with parents until age 18[1]	As long as they lived with both parents	In foster families, homes, or foster care facilities after parent loss
Normal	37	14	20
Doubtful	16		1
Horrible	14	12	7
Totals:	67	33	42[2]

1. Includes those probands who were absent from home intermittently during or after puberty only to pursue jobs or training, without breaking family contacts.

2. Because of changes in care facilities, 7 of these probands are entered twice and 1 three times; that is, the 42 conditions apply to 33 probands.

Table 2.34. Childhoods of the 108 female principal probands (breakdown of Table 2.32)

Probands who did not live with both parents until age 18

Childhood conditions	No. of probands living with parents until age 18[1]	As long as they lived with both parents	In foster families, homes, or foster care facilities after parent loss	Never with both parents (illegitimate)
Normal	22	17	25	3
Doubtful	21	9	12	6
Horrible	16	17	14	0
Totals:	59	43	51[2]	9[3]

1. Includes those probands who were absent from home intermittently during or after puberty only to pursue jobs or training, without breaking family contacts.

2. Because of changes in care facilities, 8 of these probands are entered twice; that is, the 51 conditions apply to 43 female probands.

3. Because of changes in care facilities, 3 of these probands are entered twice; that is, the 9 conditions were experienced by 6 illegitimate probands.

schizophrenic onset through unhappy childhood circumstances than boys are.

Tables 2.33 and 2.34 report the childhood conditions separately for the men and the women probands. The comparison shows that more male than female probands spent all their childhood and youth with their parents under normal conditions (37 of 100 males, and 22 of 108 females). The difference is statistically significant ($p < 0.01$).

Between the figures of Tables 2.33 and 2.34, a great number of other comparisons can be made, but these other differences are either nearly or totally insignificant. Still, it is interesting to note that such differences as do occur always occur in the same direction, that is, in raw figures the women always fare worse than the men, where childhoods are concerned.

The following comparisons, among others, can be drawn from these tables: Normal conditions for both parents relative to those probands who have at any time lived with both parents:

—Men: 51 of 100
—Women: 39 of 102
—p as to the difference: $0.1 > p > 0.05$.

Horrible conditions anywhere:
—Men: 33 of 100
—women: 47 of 102
—p as to the difference: $0.1 > p > 0.05$.

Horrible conditions in foster families or other foster homes relative to those probands who have ever been in any sort of foster care:
—Men: 7 of 33
—Women: 14 of 43;
—p as to the difference: $p > 0.3$.

Table 2.35. Principal probands' relationship to parents during their childhood

Type of relationship	All probands With father	All probands With mother	Male probands With father	Male probands With mother	Female probands With father	Female probands With mother
Normal	107	136	50	74	57	62
Poor	39	18	22	4	17	14
Neither-nor	36	35	19	15	17	20
No. of Probands with known relationships to parents[1]	182	189	91	93	91	96

1. These figures represent all probands except those who lost one parent soon after being born, and except those whose relationships with parents were not suffi- ciently well known. Figures for relationships to father exclude illegitimate females.

Horrible conditions among the parents relative to all probands who grew up only with their parents:
—Men: 14 of 67;
—Women: 16 of 59;
—p as to the difference:
   $p > 0.3$, etc.
Even though in the above investigation the childhood conditions of the schizophrenic women are shown to be worse than those of the schizophrenic men, one still has no right to formulate any kind of absolute generalities from them. The finding begins to acquire a meaning only in connection with other similar findings. The first thing to be remembered is that the sex differences on frequencies of broken homes were similar in context to those on the frequency of normal versus horrible childhoods, when the probands were living with parents or under other conditions. We note the following:
Female probands do not only have more frequent premature parent losses compared to males, but they also exceed the males in the proportion of horrible childhoods while living with both parents. Both findings are best interpreted by stating that unfavorable conditions in the childhoods of girls tend to predispose them to late-onsets of schizophrenia more often than such conditions would produce that probability in boys. It is to be noted that investigative results of a totally different nature indicate the same trend. It is only through the close study of all these investigative results that any serious, valid conclusions will emerge. The figures cited in this section do not as yet justify any such conclusions.
An additional attempt was made to depict in the broadest, most general terms the relationships of the future schizophrenics to their fathers and to their mothers during childhood (Table 2.35).
The relationships to parents could not be recorded for all 208 probands. Some of the probands had lost a father or a mother shortly after being born, so that no "relationships" with them could have been established. Furthermore, the illegitimate children were not included. For a very few individual probands the available data were too unreliable to attempt to draw any definite qualifications from them. For these reasons the relationships to just 182 fathers instead of 208, and to 189 mothers instead of 208, were recorded.
The qualifications "normal" and "poor" were applied according to the customary local usage. Requisites for the qualification "normal" included the following circumstances: The parents had to be sincerely motivated to assume full responsibility for food, clothing, shelter, education, and care of the child in such a way as to approach the standards of the average population in similar financial circumstances and holding similar social position. They would have to behave in such a way that no one could doubt their acceptance of the child, not just tolerating it as a necessary burden. No sort of deviant behavior should occur of the type described below to characterize "poor" relationships. By and large, the proband himself would have to regard his relationship to his parents as normal.
The qualification "poor" was applied only to relationships that were truly disturbed in the crassest sense, for instance, by continual, overt expression of hatred or repugnance on the part of a parent against the child, by continual physical mistreatment or neglect, by incestuous ties, by exploitation of the child

as a worker, or similar parental misconduct.
Examples:
—For a normal relationship with both parents: see this Chapter, Hanna J. Proband 40.
—For a normal relationship with mother: see this Chapter, Heinrich G., Proband 44.
—For a poor relationship with father: see this Chapter, Hans K., Proband 29.
—For neither a completely normal or a completely poor relationship with father: see above, Heinrich G., Proband 44

As Table 2.35 indicates, 107 out of 182 probands (slightly over half) had normal relationships with their fathers and 136 of 189 probands (almost 75 percent) had normal relationships with their mothers. For 39 probands (barely 25 percent) the relationships to fathers, and for 18 (nearly 10 percent) the relationships to their mothers were poor. On the average, relationships with fathers were more often troubled and more rarely good than were relationships with mothers. In part this difference is due to the fact that there were 49 alcoholics among the fathers, whose habituation spoiled their relationship to the child.

Table 2.35 also shows comparative relationships to the parents in childhood between schizophrenic male probands and schizophrenic female probands. For both men and women such relationships are better with mothers than with fathers, but the distinction is clear only for the men;[27] for the women the distinction is minimal and without significance. Normal relationships with parents for both sexes of schizophrenics predominate for the opposite sex, as opposed to those of the same sex,[28] and conversely, poor relationships are more frequent between parents and children of the same sex than between those of the opposite sex.[29]

There are no comparative figures available for representatives of the Zürich general

27. The statement for the men is statistically highly significant: $p < 0.001$.

28. The statement is statistically significant: $p < 0.05$.

29. The statement of this sentence only appears to contradict the statement of the previous sentence. The like-sexed relationship between father and son turns out to be a much unhappier relationship than the opposite-sex relationship of mother and son. The like-sexed relationship of mother to daughter does turn out more happily than that of father to daughter, but this difference is extremely small. The combined relationships of sons and daughters show that in general opposite-sex relationships are better than like-sex relationships.

population, but it is possible to use the figures of the 50 Zürich alcoholics from approximately the same generation for comparison. These figures showed among them an even greater proportion of poor relationships with fathers than did the schizophrenic probands. Only 14 of the 38 male alcoholics had normal relationships with their fathers during their childhood, as compared to 50 of the 91 schizophrenic males, and 14 of the 38 male alcoholics had severely disturbed relationships to their fathers, as compared to 22 of the 91 male schizophrenics. Of the 12 female alcoholics, only a single one had a normal relationship to her father, while 57 of the 91 female schizophrenics did have normal relationships. In contrast, the relationships of male alcoholics with their mothers, as among schizophrenics, was much better than with the fathers. Of the 38 male alcoholics, 24 had normal relationships to their mothers, as did 5 of the 12 female alcoholics. The reason for the excess of poor relationships to fathers in the childhoods of alcoholics is obvious. The number of alcoholics among the fathers of alcoholics is great, in fact much greater than among the parents of schizophrenics (more than one-third of the fathers of alcoholics in Switzerland are also alcoholics).

After it was determined that among the schizophrenic probands, premature parent losses and horrible childhood conditions were more frequent among the females than among the males, one would expect also to find a greater ratio of poor relationships to mothers in the childhoods of schizophrenic women than in the childhoods of schizophrenic men, and this was the case. The result is significant at $p < 0.05$. The sex difference is almost nonexistent in respect to relationships with fathers; it is clear only in relationships with mothers. On the average, the relationships in childhood of schizophrenic women to their mothers was worse than that relationship for schizophrenic men. We do not know whether the same ratio holds true for the general population. Therefore, we also cannot conclude that the relatively poor relationships toward their mothers of girls who later become schizophrenic would have anything to do with the pathogenesis of their schizophrenic psychoses. Such a connection acquires a certain probability only when girls who become schizophrenic are also found to have suffered premature parent losses and generally horrible childhoods more often than boys, and if findings of poor mother relationships fit into these two experiences as well. The limiting factors to be remembered here, as in so many other conclusions of this study, is that statistics relative to childhood conditions and the relationships to parents are based solely on my 208 principal schizophrenic probands. It is not certain that statistical findings from other groups of schizophrenics would show similar results.

Up to this point the statistics presented on relationships to parents of our probands is disappointing. It provides only extremely tenuous indications as to the genesis of schizophrenias. On the other hand it states definitely the significant role of alcoholism in the vitiating of the relationship between father and child. This fact, however, is well enough documented from numerous other psychiatric studies and really requires no further support.

relationships to their parents almost never changed, or at most only slightly so after puberty, when they deteriorated very slightly. It was different among the female probands where, on the average, relationships to parents usually were worse during their youth as compared to their childhoods. In accordance with this, the difference between the sexes also becomes greater with age with respect to parental relationships. A worse relationship with both parents, but particularly with the mother, is even more pronounced in female probands during their youth than during their childhood, although the difference does not attain statistical significance. This finding can be interpreted in various ways. It might be possible that in girls who do not become schizophrenic, the relationship to their mothers becomes just as poor, on the average,

Table 2.36. Principal probands' relationship to parents during their adolescence

Type of relationship	All probands		Male probands		Female probands	
	With father	With mother	With father	With mother	With father	With mother
Normal	87	115	43	69	44	46
Poor	41	24	19	5	22	19
Neither-nor	38	41	19	18	19	23
No. of probands with known relationships to parents during their youth[1]	166	180	81	92	85	88

1. These figures refer to all probands except those who lost mother or father in their youth, and except those whose relationships to their parents were not well enough known. Furthermore, relationships to fathers exclude 5 illegitimate female probands (one of the illegitimate females did know her father during her youth).

Table 2.36 shows in summary form the relationships to their parents of the schizophrenic probands, as they developed in the first years after their 18th birthdays, that is, during their youth. The total number of probands whose relationships to their parents during their youth could be determined is smaller than the number of those whose parental relationships during their childhood was recorded. That is to say, a number of the parents did not survive the 18th birthdays of their children, and in a few other cases the relationships to their parents had become so tenuous after either the parent or the child had moved away, that it was almost non-existent, and could not be characterized as either "poor" or "normal."

It is worthwhile to note that, on the average, during the youth of the male probands, the

after their 18th birthdays as we found it to be among our female schizophrenic probands. If this were true, the finding would have nothing to do with the psychopathology of schizophrenia, it would simply shed light on the development of mother-relationships during the youth of girls in general. But perhaps the average deterioration of relationships to mother among girls who later become schizophrenic does have some relationship to their later illness, although such a connection may be caused by different conditions. Such deterioration might be regarded as the symptom of a developing psychosis, as an autism, or as an injurious, illness-prone characteristic in the latent initial stages of the psychosis. But one can also recognize in it an indication of a disturbed mother-daughter relationship that predisposes toward schizophrenic illness. Possibly both views are correct. Be that as it may, in any event the observation does fit into the concept that a mother-daughter relationship is of greater significance in the genesis of schizophrenias than the relationship between a son and his parents is.

The attempt will also be made below to determine why so many schizophrenics reject their parents in reporting their childhood and youth. The motivations were summarily categorized in three separate groups:

1. The principal complaints of the probands were that their parents were too authoritarian, too harsh, too demanding, and too uncompromising, and that they lacked parental love and sympathy. Mothers were often described as being too masculine. In the statistics such types of parents are described as "too strong."

2. On the other hand, other probands complained that their parents themselves were too insecure, helpless and easy-going, so that they were unable to give their children support, guidance, or example. If such complaints applied to fathers, they were often described as effeminate. In the data such parents are described as "too weak."

3. Other probands complained that they had scarcely known their parents. Such parents either lived apart from their children, or they paid no attention to them because of professional commitments or social interests. In the statistics such parents are labelled as "too distant."

Scattered rejections of parents could not be evaluated in such simple terms. The ambivalence (for example, between love and fear) was so strong that none of the various attitudes could be listed as dominant. In a very few other cases a paradox type of "unfavorable" relationship prevailed. That is, the relationship to one of the parents appeared to be good, but good to such an excessive degree that it was regarded as highly detrimental. Expressed somewhat epigrammatically, these probands complained that their parents had shown them kindness and generosity in such measure that they were uncomfortably dependent on them and that their own development was inhibited.

The relationship of a person to his parents is not something stable; it fluctuates and is in a constant state of development. Regarded from this viewpoint, any attempt to assign labels in summary fashion to such a relationship as a one-time event is nonsense. And yet, it was possible to identify at least dominant

trends in parental relationships that remained relatively constant throughout life. I was really surprised that so many summary judgments could be made, without any pangs of conscience, on what characterized the dominant attitude to parents for a number of years before and after the eruption of the psychosis.

As Table 2.35 has already shown, the relationship to the father in 50 of the 91 male and 57 of the 91 female probands was, by and large, either favorable, or at least not definitely unfavorable. (In only 91 male and 91 female probands was it possible to form a judgment on the father-relationship, since 9 of the 100 male and 17 of the 108 female probands were omitted for the following reasons: The father had died before the child was old enough to know him, or it was an illegitimate father who had little or no relationship to the child, or only insufficient information on the relationship was available for determining what the conditions had been.)

The unfavorable relationships of 41 male and 34 female probands to their fathers can be characterized as follows:

	Probands	
Father concept	Male	Female
Too hard	23	14
Too weak	2	2
Too distant	11	16
Excessively idolized	0	1
Loved and feared	4	1
Loved and despised	1	0
	41	34

These figures are only an indication that fathers are perhaps more often regarded as authoritative, harsh, unloving, etc., by the male schizophrenic probands than by the females, although the figures do not approach anything like statistical significance. The principal reason for this unfavorable picture is alcoholism among the fathers.

Relationships to mothers were favorable in 74 of 93 male and 62 of 93 female probands (Table 2.35). (In 7 male and 12 female probands no decisions were made regarding this relationship for the same reasons as those mentioned above for father relationships.) The unfavorable relationships to their mothers of 19 male and 34 female probands are characterized in the table below.

The mother who is too authoritarian, too harsh, too masculine and unloving appears more frequently among schizophrenic women

| Mother concepts | Probands | |
	Male	Female
Too hard	3	10
Too weak	5	4
Too distant	8	15
Excessively loved and pitied	3	4
Ambivalently loved and feared	0	1
	19	34

than among schizophrenic men, but the figures are too small to attain any statistical significance.

Still, the indication that harsh and feared fathers are more detrimental to boys and the harsh and feared mothers more detrimental to girls coincides with the findings of other investigators and with the general experience not only among schizophrenics, but also among neurotics and all types of developmental retardates. However, in my previous investigations of alcoholics I did not detect any corresponding difference.

Impressions of the Childhoods of Schizophrenics

The observation of life's vicissitudes for statistical purposes either had to be limited to objectifiable external manifestations, or they were lost in vague, primitive value judgments that could scarcely be objectified. Just as in the evaluation of a collection of art works, so also the investigation and the reliving of a large number of childhood histories of schizophrenics leave behind an overall impression. Its nature is subjective, but possibly more illuminating than the results of trying to grasp such facts by means of statistics. What overall impression did I get from the processing of the childhood histories of my 208 schizophrenic probands? I cannot separate it from the impressions imparted to me in the process of investigating the childhood histories —and frequently coexperiencing together with my probands the subsequent life of countless schizophrenics other than only the probands of this particular study.

The strongest, most vivid impressions always came from the heart-rending sufferings that mostly confronted me when the schizophrenics themselves or their relatives told me the stories of their childhoods in simple, candid terms. It was rare that these childhood histories did not move me to profound feelings of sympathy. Exceptions to such suffering

were so rare that doubts arise as to whether the suffering was not simply being held back in such instances. In order to resolve these doubts, Ernst in 1956 studied these 8 exceptional cases at our clinic in minute detail, in which a previous careful routine study had left the impression of an untroubled, normal childhood. In 7 of the 8 cases he did finally discover indications of disturbing conditions that had not emerged during the earlier routine interviews.

To the impressions on the massive sufferings in the childhoods of our schizophrenic probands there is quickly added a second moving experience, which is that of our own impotence in interpreting this suffering by attempting to answer two specific questions: Does this suffering rather originate from the fact that the later schizophrenic creates a misery-prone environment, or is it that there was in the environment an unfavorable condition, independent of him, that affected the patient? And the second: Is the impact of such childhood suffering greater on schizophrenics than, for instance, on neurotics, on addicts, or on normal people?

As to the first question, many schizophrenics complain about either the cruelty or indifference of their fathers or mothers, and many of them support their statements with factual data, such as reports of punishment by beatings, deprivation of food, being locked out, being overloaded with work, etc. But once one becomes acquainted with the parents who have been thus described, or gets someone else's description of them, they are not always villains. Rather frequently others see them quite differently. Who is right? Certainly after lengthy new investigations it becomes clear sometimes that one of the contradictory descriptions is false, the other true—but all too often the question remains unresolved. The more intensively one searches, the less does one finally know whether misbehavior on the part of the parents or misinterpretation and misbehavior on the part of the child was the primary cause. Both develop simultaneously and mutually enhance each other. Often the behavior of the child and the condition of his environment cannot be accurately differentiated. They form an inseparable entity. We are confronted with an impenetrable secret if in every instance we ask: Is the child at fault, or is it his mother? And probably this puzzle remains insoluble because we asked our question on the basis of false premises. It is true, to be sure, that human relationships can be dominated by one partner or the other, but much more frequently the nature of the relationship is characterized only by the interplay between the partners.

Furthermore, the following questions arise: Is the childhood suffering of schizophrenics more severe than that of addicts, neurotics, or other patients? According to my impressions, it is not. Was the burden more severe than that which many normal people had to bear during their childhood? I do not believe that anyone would dare to answer this question definitely. In melancholy moods when people feel sorry for themselves or are depressed, many normal people will describe situations from their childhood that are just as affecting as those of many schizophrenics, in fact many healthy individuals report such stories when they are in a perfectly normal frame of mind. And here again we are confronted with a secret that is associated with yet another erroneous line of questioning. Suffering can be measured to only a limited extent. The measure of suffering, the intensity of it, is actually impossible to estimate. One must accept the fact that some quantities cannot be measured, and therefore one must also become reconciled to the fact that the effect of the environment on the genesis of a mental disturbance cannot be definitively and finally evaluated by the amount of human suffering endured.

But a more definite answer is within reach to the question as to whether—if not the measure of—at least the nature of unhappy childhood experiences among later schizophrenics might not have a special bearing on the problem. From impressions alone I would deny this. I have seen manifold childhood suffering in massive amounts in the histories of my schizophrenic patients. There is hardly a single kind of human suffering that the schizophrenics whom I got to know were spared in their childhoods. On the other hand, my schizophrenics did not experience any situation in their childhoods that had not been experienced by many others as well.

One conjecture, however, becomes admissible. The conditions under which schizophrenics existed during their childhood can be essentially characterized as such that would produce discords in the child's emotional perception. For example, the suffering of the child may consist of his inability to rid himself of loyalty to the way of life imposed by his deceased mother, while his stepmother tries to force on him conformity to a different way of life. Or the child suffers when the principles of commonly accepted morality are being imposed on him while his father is obviously unfaithful to his mother, or the mother is obviously engaging in prostitution. It is also a form of suffering for the child—as in the case of Hans K., Proband 29 (see above)—when his father appears as an epitome of moral virtue in the eyes of his wife and the community, while the child himself experiences nothing but cruelty from him, etc. Such experiences make it easy to reach premature conclusions based on genetics. The formula is downright seductive in its simplicity: disunified, highly ambitendent and therefore agonizing environmental conditions predispose to schizophrenia, for they foster the inner strife, disharmony, and division of mind that confront us in a schizophrenic psychosis. But such a thesis cannot be supported by such a subjective impression alone. Most of human suffering is suffering that tears us apart and generates an ambitendent disposition. Whether this occurs more often in the backgrounds of schizophrenics or in those of nonschizophrenics cannot be stated with certainty. Ambivalence is as impossible to measure and objectify as suffering is.

If one studies not only the childhood backgrounds of schizophrenics but also delves more deeply into their life history after childhood and the patient's subjective experience of the disease, there emerges yet another definite impression. In every instance the content of a later psychosis has something to do with the patient's childhood suffering. It is especially the case that the patient himself always senses a relationship between the development of his illness and his childhood suffering. In the subjective experience of a patient with whom one is well acquainted, the repetition, over and over again, of his preoccupation with his suffering in childhood is a common manifestation. Basically it is the same phenomenon so frequently observed since Freud's (1896) descriptions of neurotics. Hans K., Proband 29, was unmercifully tormented by his father for 8 long years because he did poor work in school; constantly the academically brilliant achievements of his father were displayed before him as an ideal example to be followed. At the beginning of the psychosis his father appeared to him as a phantom that pursued him, because he was a miserable wretch. Heinrich G., Proband 44, developed precisely the same pathological, passive and dependent role the father had occupied in the mother's household for years before his premature death. In his schizo-phrenic psychosis Heinrich clung tenaciously to this role.

If one wants to investigate the psychotrau-matic background of an illness, the first step is involuntarily to glance at all the negative qualities of the parents, at their failures as educators, at their irresponsibility, and their cruelty toward the child. All this is found in studying the childhood backgrounds of schizo-phrenics. But at the same time an opposite impression emerges that is just as strong. Quite often the parents exhibit an astounding measure of devotion to their families. The examples are numerous in which a difficult child who later becomes schizophrenic was brought up with the greatest understanding for his problems and was offered the fullest measure of patience and love.

Opinions on the Existing Literature

Since the terms "dementia praecox" and "schizophrenia" were conceptualized, atten-tive clinicians have always observed and often described that the later schizophrenics as well as their parents and other relatives are often difficult people, and that for this reason the childhood conditions of the later schizophre-nics are frequently unfavorable (Kraepelin 1899, 1912, Bleuler 1911, Kahn 1923, the Tübing School with Gaupp 1917, Hoffmann 1923, Kretschmer 1944, and many others). The personality disturbances so frequently discovered in the early histories of schizo-phrenics and their relatives were in the last century still labelled mainly as "neuroses," as "nervous illnesses," or as "character aberra-tions." Then the struggle began for terms that were to clarify their relationship to schizo-phrenia, and one began to speak of schizo-phrenia-like or schizophreniform personality deviations. It was often assumed that a "latent schizophrenia" or a partial tendency toward schizophrenia was operant (Kahn 1923). Finally the concept "schizoid"[30] replaced all

other designations, and the concept of a "schizoid constitution" became one of the most fundamental terms in Kretschmer's teachings.

During the first three decades of this century the expression of an inherited constitution was seen in the "schizoid" prepsychotic nature of schizophrenics as well as in the "schizoid" nature of their relatives. Searches were in-stituted for pathogenetic relationships be-tween the schizoid psychopathy and schizo-phrenia. In the process of formulating such hypotheses, too little attention was paid to the frictions between psychopathic parents and children, and the agony of such frictions was not sufficiently appreciated.

But if many of our modern authors believe that they are the ones who have discovered these frictions, they are mistaken. They forget to what a great extent the concept of the schizoid was developed, especially through the study of human relationships, and thus also the relationships between parents and their children. Already at the beginning of this century the authors mentioned and many more expressly emphasized what kind of excep-tional and unfavorable personal attitudes spoil the environment in which later schizo-phrenics have to live. Particularly Kretsch-mer (1944) described these traits superbly. For instance, he describes the characteristic attitudes of schizoids as follows: "brutally cutting or morose and dull, or ironically stinging or shy as a mollusk, or spineless and retiring"; or he speaks of "a facade of silence" that seems to reflect "nothing but debris, black rubble, yawning emotional emptiness or the cutting breath of the iciest soullessness."

But he does emphasize how, behind such behavior toward their fellowmen, an extreme sensitivity can be concealed that often ex-presses itself quite unexpectedly. Even the nature of the individual "schizoid" subforms he describes principally according to the personal attitudes of these people toward others as being antisocial, repressed, serious eccentrics, or that they are led by others with excessive ease and appear dull, indifferent, and impersonal. They are able timidly to avoid their fellowmen or to persecute them with cold, cruel persistence. The devious perversity of schizoids was already associated by Kretschmer (1944) with the delusionary bewilderment of schizophrenics.

E. Bleuler (1919, 1922) regarded the com-mon characteristics of schizophrenics and schizoids principally by using the concept of

30. As I remember it, the concept "schizoid" was first applied in the study done by a young assistant of E. Bleuler's, Kurt Binswanger (1920), "über schizoide Alkoholiker" (On Schizoid Alcoholics). Binswanger told me that at that time the term was in such common usage among the doctors at Burghölzli, he simply assumed that it had long been accepted as a formal medical term. When Dr. Maier reviewed his paper, Binswanger was informed for the first time that the expression up to this time was a colloquial term in use only at the hospital but was not in use in the formal literature.

autism. He observed how frequently there were people in the families of schizophrenics who led an inflexible, lonely inner existence by themselves, who could not open up to other family members, who were neither intellectually nor emotionally convincing, in short, people who would scarcely be fitting examples to their children that they would follow or emulate naturally and without difficulty.

It was often mentioned that such personality disorders affecting particularly the facility of human communications were also especially frequent among the parents of schizophrenics. Among the parents of the schizophrenic probands of my Pfäfers group there were 17 percent schizoid psychopaths.

The authors of the last 10 to 20 years have "discovered anew" the communications disorders in the parental families of later schizophrenics, without realizing the detailed thoroughness with which they had been described by the previous generations of clinicians. Their merit does not lie in having discovered the taciturn reserve, the inflexibility, the emotional frigidity, or the egocentricity in the parents of schizophrenics for the first time. Nor does it lie in the fact that they had observed for the first time how peculiar, how difficult to undestand, how ambiguous, and how misleading and deceptive the verbal and emotional expressions of the parents of schizophrenics often are, how such parents sometimes are totally inflexible and unyielding in the bringing up of their children, how they are unable to make allowances for the child's personality, how they attempt to shape its behavior according to their own distorted views, and how often they exist compartmentalized for themselves alone or fall into unhealthy dependencies or exhausting antagonisms toward one another. All these phenomena have already been seen and reported by the earlier clinicians.

The great merit of the young generation of schizophrenia investigators lies much rather in the fact that they no longer attempted to relate in one-sided partiality the difficulties and peculiarities of the parents of schizophrenics to a hypothetical theory of pathogenetics. They now directed their attention toward the agonizing and dangerous conditions in the child's development resulting from abnormal personality in the parents. We may thank this younger generation for no longer considering a schizoid personality from the very outset— as used to be the case—as an inherited personality constitution, but instead for checking seriously and carefully to what extent the effects and countereffects between the personalities of the child and of his parents influence the development of a schizoid personality in the child. If we discover a schizoid character trait in a father or a mother, our first thoughts today are no longer concerned with theories of heredity, but from the very first we sense painfully and sympathetically the difficulties and the suffering that result from such conditions for the parents and the children. The new method of observation has not only made possible new hypotheses, such as those about the psychogenesis of schizoid and schizophrenic backgrounds, but we must also be grateful to it that today's studies of childhood conditions reach the emotional level of understanding sooner, more intimately, and more frequently than ever before.

If the older generation of psychiatrists too often overlooked how much loneliness, insecurity, confusion, and suffering the pathological personalities of parents generated for their future-schizophrenic children (and for others involved), it certainly was not that their natures were colder than the natures of the younger one. The reason lay principally in the fact that the earlier psychiatrists, more than the modern ones, intermingled with adult schizophrenics in their communities. To the earlier ones the childhood of schizophrenics came only from third-hand reports out of the distant past. So, of course, it was natural that they turned their helpers' talents toward the present problems of their patients and regarded their childhoods from a purely theoretical viewpoint. To mention a prototype representing that past generation, E. Bleuler lived for 12 years in rural isolation and in the closest external and emotional communal relationships with his adult schizophrenics. Their relatives he saw very little, and he lacked the possibility of becoming as thoroughly acquainted with their childhoods and their family relationships as he was when he experienced the day-to-day joys and sorrows in their lives at the hospital. For him the childhood of schizophrenics was the dim and misty past; it was their immediate life that captured his interest. Accordingly, the discovery of the internal mental processes of schizophrenics and the psychodynamics of schizophrenia itself had to precede the discovery of the psychodynamic processes of childhood.

Some scattered studies on the behavior of parents and its significance for the pathogenesis of schizophrenia date back as far as several decades, as for instance, those by Kasanin (1934). It was not until approximately 1950 that "psychodynamic family studies" really came into vogue. From that time on they began to gain continually in depth and thoroughness. The mere evaluation of family conditions as taken from routine patient histories was replaced by planned, target-directed, and time-consuming interviews, and even by psychoanalytic investigations of the personalities of a number of family members. American groups of investigators assumed a leading role in these types of investigations from the very beginning. At the outset they were influenced by Meyer (1915) and his urgent demand to pay strict attention to the empirical data resulting from the studies of the pathogeneses of psychoses, and to avoid holding to illusive and speculative imaginary concepts. As an example of the latter, Meyer (1915) cites the assumption of a "schizophrenic pathological process" that pursues its course behind the scenes and out of reach of scientific observations. Furthermore, psychoanalytic developments in America exercised a monumental influence on family studies of schizophrenics. The principal interest in psychoanalytic treatment of patients and in psychoanalytic research had taken a turn away from limiting itself to internal development and toward interpersonal relationships. In this context increasing attempts were begun, to treat not only the mental patient coming to see the doctor for the first time, but his entire family. From that time on, it was but a small step to ignite the spark of interest in studying the immediate families of schizophrenics.

Since the beginning of the 1950s, Lidz and Fleck at Yale University played leading roles in the critical in-depth investigations of the parents of schizophrenics. A goodly number of students and colleagues has since joined forces with them. This research group did long-term psychoanalytic research and treatment of several members of the immediate families of schizophrenics. Unfortunately it was limited to such a small number of probands' families that even today a statistical evaluation is still not possible. Additional centers for investigation have been set up in Palo Alto, California (Bateson, Bowen, Jackson, Weakland et al.) and at the National Institutes of Health in Bethesda, Maryland (Rosenthal, Singer, Wynne et al.). To an increasing degree the Europeans, in particular the Scandinavian researchers have joined the new investigative trend, for example, Alanen in Finland, Delay, Green and Deniker in France, McGhie in England, Kisker and Stroetzel in Germany, Galachyan in Russia, and others. At our clinic, Ernst and Willi devoted themselves particularly to this type of investigation. Ernst (1956) showed that even a thoroughgoing anamnestic study within the framework of clinic routine was not always able to uncover the childhood tragedies of schizophrenics. Willi (1962) conducted thorough studies from precisely the opposite viewpoint from that which other authors were studying; that is, not the effects of parents on children who later become schizophrenic, but the effects of the developing schizophrenic problem child on his parents. The fate of such a child was deemed a terrible misfortune by most parents, one that threatened their self-esteem and their happiness over long periods of their lives, or sometimes even destroyed them. In close relationship to the child's onset of illness, the parents often became depressive, or they developed physical complaints rooted in emotional unhappiness, or they spun themselves into cocoons of eccentric delusionary fantasies. Others grew with their sufferings, accepted their fate and showed an active, never-to-be-extinguished love toward the patient. Willi (1964) discovered also how heavily the formation of theories by parents about the causes and treatment of the illness in their children depends on their own life experiences. As causes for the illness in their children they searched for psychotraumatic situations similar to the agonizing threats to their own mental well-being they had experienced in their own childhoods. What they had sensed as valuable advice toward improvement in themselves appeared to them to be the best possible therapy for their children.

Important indications for the significance of the immediate family in the psychodynamics of schizophrenias were also found in psychoanalytic research and the psychoanalytic treatment attempts pursued by so many therapists since the Second World War. At our own clinic, Sechehaye (1947), Benedetti (1954), and Müller (1953) were showing us with their impressive patient histories how intensively the schizophrenics themselves were experiencing the interconnections between their relationships to their parents and the development of their illnesses, and how pathologically they used to get along with their parents.

In the following section I should like to sketch briefly the development of research over the past 15 years concerning the families of schizophrenics. The important works by Alanen (1958, 1966) and Rosenthal (1959–63) I should like then to mention in particular. I believe they best represent the highly advanced state of the art and investigative methods up to the present day. I will still have the task of substantiating why I could not arrive at the same discriminating, clear-cut, and impressive conclusions from the patient histories of my 208 probands in respect to the importance of family conditions in the home, as many other authors have done.

First came the rediscovery of the schizoid personality of the parents of schizophrenics. In the beginning it was again being described but rather unilaterally in the case of mothers. In contrast to previous approaches, it was now being assessed almost exclusively for its impact on the child. For example, the picture of a mother emerged, who dominates her child authoritatively, who allows it no life of its own, who wants to shape it according to her own rigid norms, who isolates it, who regards it as an item of her own personal possessions, and who refuses to let it grow. Convincing data was presented on how, in connection with such an attitude on the part of the mother, the healthy development of the child's personality must suffer, how the child could develop well intellectually, but how it is inhibited in the entire process of maturation and remains frustrated in the development of its ability to give and receive love. It was accepted somewhat less convincingly although prematurely that such a stunted development was also causally related to the genesis of a psychosis, and in addition the rather unlovely and insufficiently supported concept of a "schizophrenogenic mother" was created. Soon it was revealed—what the older authors had long ago discovered—that the fathers of schizophrenics, too, were often difficult and pathologically inclined. The young authors especially frequently found that fathers were experienced by their children as weaklings who exercised no forceful control over or personal influence on their families. Often such fathers, residing under the same roof, not only managed to live in isolation from their families, but were also physically separated from their families in connection with their jobs. Naturally fathers

of schizophrenics, too, were observed who were tyrannical, authoritarian, or cruel toward their children. But these investigations never succeeded in discovering personality types that predominated exclusively among the parents of schizophrenics and that would not have been found as well among the parents of neurotics, addicts, or normal subjects. At the outside, some differences appeared as probable in the frequencies of certain peculiarities among parents of schizophrenics as compared to the general population. But pressure was mounting to find the origins of schizophrenias in the personalities of the parents. Such a demand for causality was not satisfied just to find more of certain peculiarities among the parents of schizophrenics than among the general population. The hope remained of finding "specific" peculiarities among parents that occurred predominantly among the parents of schizophrenics. But they were never found.

In the refinement of the investigations the focus now ceased to be directed unilaterally toward the person of the father or of the mother, but rather toward the internal relationships between parents and child in the family community. Less effort was expended to search exclusively for peculiarities in the personalities of parents, but rather for peculiarities of the entire psychological family structure that might be characteristic of the children's vulnerability to schizophrenia. The disturbed relationships were presented in convincing descriptions, as they frequently occurred in families from which schizophrenics had come. Many authors assume that such disturbed relationships were of decisive importance in the genesis of schizophrenias. Father or mother had often assumed rather unwillingly and unsatisfactorily the sex roles that nature and society had imposed upon them, and in connection with this, the child seemed to have difficulty in attaining a unified and harmonious relationship to its own sexuality. In other families the sense of generic succession has been lost. For instance, one parent treats the spouse rather like a child, does not take the partner seriously, sends him on minor household errands and generally looks down on him as if from above. If now the child identifies with the parent assuming the subordinated, dependent role, the development of his personality will be stunted. If he rather identifies with the dominant parent, he enters into a dangerously ambivalent relationship with the dominant parent that is laden with guilt and arrogance, that is just as detrimental to his development. "Schismatic" family relationships were thus characterized when the family split into two parties, that barely associated any longer with one another and gave only the external appearance of a family. Among other families a "skewed" adaptation of the normal parent to the ill parent occurred.[31] The normal parent took over the withdrawn, pathological attitudes of the other in an all-out effort to maintain some kind of communal relationship. Such developments may eventually lead to a folie-à-deux. In still other families the internal relationships could best be characterized by the expression "chaotic." In such instances there were no unifying relationships between the marriage partners. The father could allow himself to be dominated by the mother like a restless child under one given set of circumstances, while at another time, he would treat the mother with raw brutality, or the mother could pamper her child in one situation and completely neglect it in another.

If one wanted to trace back the genesis of schizophrenias to conditions in the parental relationships in the parental home, one would have to explain why in a family with several children other siblings from that same family did not all become schizophrenic, also. This line of questioning led to the idea of studying also the relationships of parents to their normal children and then comparing these to their relationship to the child who later becomes schizophrenic. Usually differences were revealed that caused one to believe that the future schizophrenic child was most directly affected by the unhealthy family relationships. That child was usually found to be the one on whom the parents had most intensively vented their inflexible, possessive attitudes, the one who had been most pampered and kept in a state of dependency, or the one who had been exposed to the most cruel bodily and mental mistreatment. And, too, the future schizophrenic child was often the one who had maintained the closest association with the more abnormal of the two parents. Often, as well, it had the most unfortunate position of birth order among its siblings in which the other siblings assumed toward the future schizophrenic the unhealthy dominant role of one of the parents, even augmenting that role's

intensity, and treating the child developing the illness accordingly.

In the course of this modern method of family research into the past histories of schizophrenics, the principal attention was first directed at the mothers of schizophrenics, then at the fathers, and then concentration of effort was directed more at personal relations than at individual personalities, and then finally and gradually the siblings, too, began to be included more and more.

Hand in hand with this shift of the research goal there followed one of a different sort. At first it was noticed how much suffering schizophrenics had endured during their childhood and how often this suffering seemed to be related to the personality of the parents. The inclination was to regard this entire burden of suffering as pathogenic. Later, attention was directed less toward suffering in general than toward the effects of the divisive and unhealthy attitudes of the parents on the development of the child, independent of whether such discordant attitudes were being perceived as being troublesome or not. Tests were made to determine whether disharmony in the family created prototypes for the patient's own personality or his selection of a mate, and the question arose whether under certain circumstances the predisposition toward schizophrenia might be contained in such disharmony. Most recent investigations also included especially any disturbances in the intellectual development of a child under the influence of abnormal thinking on the part of the parents. It was found that the thought processes of the parents of schizophrenics are frequently awkwardly unrealistic, distracted, and illogical, and even more, that both the spoken and the unspoken expressions of the parents of schizophrenics were bound to transmit an ambiguous, equivocal impression. The parents of schizophrenics do not always accompany their verbal speech with the appropriately harmonizing emotional gestures.[32] Many authors received the impression that this incongruity is the principal cause of the disturbed development of the child and that this disturbance enhances the predisposition toward schizophrenia.

Attention has thus shifted from an interest

31. The expressions "schismatic" and "skewed" were borrowed from the English as they had been introduced by Lidz.

32. All this has also been covered before by the older authors in the context of their descriptions of the schizoid personality, only it never occurred to the older authors to consider it as a cause or partial cause for schizophrenia in children.

in the stress of suffering in general to the more specific emotional experience with problematic parents, and from that point toward the "teaching of irrationality." While enlightenment on the psychopathology of schizophrenics had begun with Kraepelin's studies of intellectual disturbances, through which the discovery of basic emotional disorders later developed, we are confronted with the fact in the most recent investigations on the psychological backgrounds of families of schizophrenics, that these investigations took precisely the opposite turn when they considered first the emotional and only later the intellectual aspect of the person.

Like many of the great new concepts in psychiatry, these, too, on the importance of the immediate family to the genesis of schizophrenic psychoses, are impossible to "prove" objectively and unequivocally. They leave open loopholes to many a doubt. To do justice to their importance, criticism is needed. They could not be further developed or more solidly founded in the absence of such criticism. Some of the more important objections follow: Modern psychodynamic research did not succeed in assembling any sort of proof even approaching statistical validity for the connections between disturbances within the parental home and the genesis of schizophrenias. Nor, basically, can statistics alone have the final word on this matter. When such statistics are provided, they furnish indications, but not proof. What the reasoning that has been developed does state clearly to nearly everybody is that certain disturbances in the development of a child will result, if that child grows up in a pathological environment. It is considerably more difficult, however, to prove that these developmental disturbances prepare the way for schizophrenia. Some authors made it easy for themselves in that they did identify metioulously the developmental difficulties of children of pathological parents, but without ever having demonstrated the transition of these developmental difficulties into schizophrenia. They limited themselves to mere assertions in this regard. It is strange to realize that the specialists in "psychodynamics"—many of those investigators in the field of schizophrenia who interpret the emergence of schizophrenias purely "psychodynamically" and who compete among one another in deleting the importance of child development under given environmental influences—were inclined for a long time to regard the personalities of parents entirely by way of statistics. Specifically, they envisioned a "schizophrenogenic" mother, firmly set in her personality, under whose care the child developed abnormally. It scarcely occurred to them that the personal development of an individual is not static, that when the young girl has become a mother, her mother's personality also continues to develop. They forgot that not only is the personality of the child influenced by the mother, but that the mother's personality is also influenced by the child (and even the personality of the father as well). When difficulties in the parent-child relationship occurred, they saw problem parents who are set in their ways and malleable, as yet unmolded children. But a child is also a personality in and of itself, from the very beginning. The parents are not alone in creating the relationship to it; the child itself also helps to create that relationship from its first days in the cradle. An incorrect attitude on the part of the parents to that child may in part be provoked by the child. No matter how voluminous the case material on disturbed family relations in the home is, it will have little to say on how much such disturbed relations contribute causally to the emergence of a schizophrenia or to what degree they depend on the congenitally difficult nature of the child.

The concept prematurely popularized as secure knowledge, that the character and attitude of parents extensively explains the onset of schizophrenia had still another depressing result. Expressed somewhat pointedly, the parents were placed in the position of being the accused. In this context Alanen (1966) justifiably remarked that this was wholly unintentional. On the contrary, he explains, the parents were made partners in the psychological understanding and the medical eagerness to help, and it was the intention to allow the parents to benefit from the treatment concurrently with their schizophrenic child. In this statement he expressed an ideal that one can support wholeheartedly. But in real life the situation looks different. What mother does not perceive it as an accusation to be told that her attitude toward the child may be the reason for its schizophrenia? She would not feel cleansed before her own conscience when this attitude is regarded as pathological, even with the greatest psychological understanding and medical sympathy. But the schizophrenic's doctor, too, is a human being with human emotions. He has a great deal to put up with when he begins psychotherapeutic treatments with a schizophrenic. Usually he succeeds in mastering initial negative attitudes toward his patient. But in every one of his counseling sessions temptations arise for the psychotherapist, from the unavoidable tendency to identify with the patient, for him to find a scapegoat for all the misery. In the psychotherapist's irrational emotions, the parents often became those scapegoats, even when the therapist's rational thinking did not dictate that. The parents sense something of this and do not take it lightly. The truth must not be held back, because it could have unfavorable consequences; but mere assumptions about the truth should not be expressed in a way that might easily prove harmful.

In the following section I should like especially to discuss two great works that—although they were published several years ago—represent magnificently the modern state of research on the psychodynamic importance of the family home for the genesis of schizophrenia. They are those of David Rosenthal (1963) and Yrjö Alanen (1966). They contain comprehensive overviews of the literature as well as extensive investigations of their own. These authors have dulled the point on the lance of criticism in that they themselves take critical issue with their own views and in their formulation of justifiable objections, give careful consideration to these objections from various angles.

Rosenthal (1963), working with several colleagues at the National Institute of Mental Health in Bethesda near Washington, D.C., presented a family history dominated by monozygotic quadruplets who all became schizophrenic. The development of the relationships between the parents and each of the four children and among the children toward one another was pursued with a degree of thoroughness that had never before been achieved. Everyone who studies the reasoning presented will be convinced that the pathological behavior of the parents to one another and to the children rendered a normal development for the children impossible. Rosenthal further demonstrates with exceptional clarity that the particular child that was most mistreated and whose position in the family was the most unnatural, developed by far the worst psychosis. And conversely, the child that suffered the least under the pathological behavior of its parents and whose position in the family was the most natural, suffered a much milder psychosis from which there was a virtual recovery. Rosenthal is careful enough to leave open the question as to how much the child that had suffered the most had contributed to his misery by his own behavior.

Alanen (1966) investigated not only the relationships in the parental homes of schizophrenics, but also compared these results with studies of family relationships among neurotics. By so doing he explored the question as to the specificity of psychotraumatic manifestations in the childhood of future schizophrenics. His investigations encompassed 30 schizophrenics and 30 neurotics who were matched according to sex, age, and the social stratum from which they came. His findings largely confirm those of several previous American authors who had looked into the same problems. Of the 55 known parents of his schizophrenics, all except 1 were shown to be in some way pathological. Most of them (38) had personality disorders in the neurotic or psychopathic sense of the term, that were of many different types. The older European authors would have labelled most of them as schizoids, whereas Alanen emphasizes especially the differences in these deviations. Twelve parents were schizophrenic, and 5 suffered from manic-depressive or just schizophrenia-like psychoses. In contrast to many other authors, Alanen also already regards the pathology of the parents of his schizophrenics as something that has developed out of their life histories. He found that most of the mothers of schizophrenics were already caught up in a hostile relationship to their own mothers, while most of the fathers of schizophrenics had been excessively dependent on their parents. From his viewpoint, therefore, the pathogenesis of schizophrenia corresponds to an aggravation of the relationships among family members from generation to generation. Of the 29 parental families of schizophrenics whose internal structure could be carefully investigated, 14 proved to be torn with internal strife ("schismatic"), 7 lived in a "skewed" relationship, and 6 families had already been externally separated (terminology by Lidz and Fleck [1960]). Only 2 of these families appeared as a homogeneous, internally harmoneous units. Alanen (1966) not only characterized the relationships among individual members of the family in general, but also the predominating attitude of the parents toward their children. Ten of these he designated as "chaotic" and 11 as "rigid," while neither attitude predominated in the remaining 8 families. The mothers of schizophrenics were frequently authoritarian, possessive toward their children or downright hostile (the latter particularly toward daughters). Fathers were frequently absent from the family circle, or else they were passive, frightened, or personally insecure. For these reasons, fathers are generally described as lacking in authority and mothers as excessively authoritarian to the point of applying perverted rigidity and cruelty and being pathogenic to an excessive degree.

The childhood relationships of neurotics are seen by Alanen (1966) as differing in quantity rather than quality from those of schizophrenics. There are almost no psychotics among the parents of neurotics, fewer serious personality disorders, and more normals than among the parents of schizophrenics. The personality disorders among parents of neurotics are generally less severe. Also the relationships between the parents and between parents and children are considerably less severely disturbed in Alanen's group of neurotics than among his group of schizophrenics, even though the same type of disturbance occurs frequently in the families of neurotics. The excessive dependency on the parents is often limited to only certain specific activities among the neurotics, while among future schizophrenics it covers every aspect of living. Supported by these observations, Alanen surmises that no sort of psychodynamics specific to schizophrenia lies at the basis of schizophrenias, but that basically the same psychotraumatic childhood situations can lead to neurosis or to schizophrenia. He does not see a basic difference in the psychotraumatic childhood situation as decisive, but the degree of it. Conditions that favor neurotic development in the milder cases, he feels would in more severe cases favor the development of schizophrenic psychoses. But there are also differences in family backgrounds, in Alanen's opinion, that cannot be classified as merely quantitative. The tendencies of overprotective mothers to pamper their children he felt occurred more often among the mothers of neurotics, and the cold, cruel authoritarian type, among the mothers of schizophrenics. The parents of neurotics were more eager to raise their children under a system of conventional morality, while parents of schizophrenics are more inclined to set life's goals for their children that are eccentric, bizarre, and self-willed. Accordingly, he considers the wealth of ideas a little paler and more monotonous in the families of neurotics and a little more colorful and varied in the families of schizophrenics.

If the characterizations of parent personalities and the relationships among family members by Alanen (1966) and Rosenthal (1963) and a number of other authors were to be compared with those I have reported in this section about the probands of this study, a difference strikes one immediately. Namely, that Alanen, Rosenthal, and the other authors have succeeded in depicting extremely impressive, true-to-life character types, in respect both to behavior and attitude of the parents to interpersonal relationships; I was not that successful. In comparison to Alanen's characterizations, mine are dull, primitive, and colorless. Why this difference?

In the first place it is because of the different aims of the two studies and the different selection procedures for the probands. Alanen concentrated his efforts, as the title of his book reveals, on "The Family in the Pathogenesis of Schizophrenic and Neurotic Disorders," that is, on the importance of the parental home for the pathogenesis of schizophrenias. My principal aim was the long-term observation of adult schizophrenics and their next of kin. I wanted to observe schizophrenic patients for periods of more than 20 years and compare their destinies during this time span with that of their families. The investigation in retrospect of their childhoods occurred to me as a supplemental problem, whereas Alanen treated this as his principal investigative aim. Accordingly, the time spent on studies of the familial childhood conditions by Alanen (or particularly Rosenthal) is longer than mine, although on the whole I spent more time than he did on each of my probands during the period of over 20 years of the observation phase. And the same applies also to the selection of probands. Alanen chose his probands according to the possibility that they would supply useful data on their childhoods. For this reason he picked as probands only those schizophrenics who were between the ages of 15 and 40, who had several siblings of approximately the same age, and from families where at least one of the parents would be available for study. On the other hand, my probands were much older, on the average, their childhoods, on the average, lay decades behind the childhoods of his probands, many parents of my probands had died, could give no useful information because of their advanced age, or had lived together with their children for only short periods of time. It is therefore understandable that Alanen should have access to more impressive and more relevant data concerning his probands' childhoods than I had.

But the different evaluation has still other, more deep-seated reasons than that. From my viewpoint the personalities of the parents and the parent-child relationships were multi-layered and variable. I, too, saw mothers who were unequivocally cold-hearted and cruel, or fathers who were unequivocally weak and dependent, but doubts arose more frequently when I wanted to consider that type of characterization as my final judgment. There were sessions with parents in which suddenly, stirred to their deepest emotions, they were able to feel the warmest sympathy for the patient, whereas previously I had been inclined to characterize them as devoid of feeling. I saw parents whose attitude could certainly be described as rigid and possessive, but who at the same time, so arranged their lives that conditions would in their judgment be most advantageous for the child, who would deprive themselves of every pleasure in life in order to best serve only the well-being of their sick child—that is, according to their concepts. Should they, then, have been characterized as rigid and possessive, or as loving and self-sacrificing? I could not always decide. I also saw that many family relationships could have been designated as chaotic from a number of viewpoints, but often I saw the reverse. For example, that under the stress of the misfortune of schizophrenia in a child, the entire family would band together into a harmonious community that made almost superhuman sacrifices for their patient, or that the misfortune of illness in the family became the motivation for participating in some area of humanitarian service. For example, the 6 children of a family had made agreements with their parents that they would all remain single in order not to propagate the hereditary disease (their belief), that was the schizophrenia of one of their siblings. They did remain single, and each of them has left behind him a magnificent social accomplishment in a life that was rich in warmth and human kindness. It is true that the characterizations of parental family relationships are, in the final analysis, largely negative. But to me it appears that the suffering in these families awakened a great deal of love, generosity, and self-denial.

Furthermore, it seems to me as though Alanen (1966) and I look at the relationship of father or mother to the child, and vice versa, through a different set of spectacles, in a manner of speaking. I also see something in the personality of the child that is very little dependent on the parents or that influences the parents; while I include the influence of the child on his parents in my observation, Alanen (1966) observes for the most part only the influence of the parents on the child. I consider a reciprocal influence from parents to child and back again, while Alanen (1966), and along with him most of the modern authors, regard as important only the influence of the parents on the child. I often surmise that an unyielding, pampering, or cruel behavior of one of the parents may have been provoked by the child's difficult personality just as much or even more frequently than that the improper behavior of the parent had spoiled the child. As I listen to the parents, I must often ask myself, what attitude toward their difficult child should one expect from them? Or I must ask myself, could I muster a more favorable attitude toward this particular child? Although I love children, I would often have to reply in the negative to this question before my own conscience.

Well, who is right, now? Alanen and the authors who have developed data similar to his, who have characterized childhood conditions so superbly, or is it I, who because of excessive doubts and criticism is incapable of this? It would be possible to accuse Alanen and the others of overlooking the multi-faceted nature of events without adequate criticism, or I could be accused of losing sight of essentials because of excessive weighing of the pros and cons. I personally am inclined to believe that Alanen and his predecessors have made an eminently successful contribution. The meaning of these remarks is intended to be but an indication that the evaluation of similar concerns are largely dependent on subjective judgments. And one more indication occurs to me as being important. There are, to be sure, influences of parents on child and of child on parents, but it may not always be the thing to do to search for one or the other. Rather, parents and children adapt to one another and develop together, just as we shape our own environment and our environment shapes us. Perhaps, in studying such considerations we ought to put on a special set of spectacles that allows us to see the mother-child relationship (and the personality-environment relationship) more clearly than heretofore as an inseparable unity of action and reaction, and not always ask ourselves, to begin with, whether the mother affects the child or vice versa.

In quite a different way, investigators in psychology who work with tests come up against the same difficulties as I do. Jeanne Block (1969), for instance, attempted to confirm, by statistical evaluation of psychodiagnostic tests, the characteristics of the parents of schizophrenics whom Lidz (1958), Alanen (1966) and others had so graphically described. She compared the individual test results of the parents of schizophrenics with those of parents of other patients. But she succeeded as little as I did in demonstrating the peculiarities of the parents of schizophrenics. One of the reasons for the failure of such experiments lies in the very fact that the existence of most of the individual symptoms that were counted was ambivalently evaluated, and could just as easily have been confirmed or denied. A finding of "seeks assurance from others" can be assumed for as many parents of schizophrenics as it can be denied for. Whether it happens one way or the other depends on chance attitudes of the moment, and for this reason the results of statistics cannot grasp the psychological facts.

The Living Together of Principal Probands with Schizophrenic Parents

Posing the Questions

There is an old and widespread, misguided belief that psychoses are "contagious." If we learn in the daily pursuits of psychiatry how distorted the relationships of schizophrenic parents to their children are, the question as to whether children could suffer damage by living under the care of schizophrenic parents becomes a serious one. Possibly such damage may lie in an acquired disposition toward future schizophrenic development. Lately this possibility has been increasingly considered, and I, too, deem it worthy of careful investigation. But, on the other hand, I should like to issue a warning against the widespread temptation to represent mere assumptions about such dangers as facts already proved.

The care of children by schizophrenic parents could develop in various ways as a vulnerability for children with schizophrenic illnesses. Perhaps mistreatment, neglect, and suffering in the most general sense are in themselves detrimental. Such an assumption would agree with the theory on the effects of "nonspecific stress" on the development of schizo-

phrenias. But perhaps the essential damage does not derive altogether nonspecifically from any given suffering, but from the fact that the emotional world of the experiences of a child who lives in close proximity with a schizophrenic, cannot achieve any unity and therefore becomes strife-torn and conflictual. The very fact that a mother is supposed to be a maternal ideal, while she is at the same time schizophrenic, has simply got to disturb the disposition of the child. Nor does a schizophrenic parent provide any unifying emotions toward the child or the marriage partner. The divisiveness of the father or the mother toward the child simply must frustrate any attempts on the part of that child to bring forth any harmonious or unifying love toward his parents. And by the same token it is hardly possible for any unequivocal attitude toward the problems of sexuality to develop if the child is constantly exposed to the bickering of his parents about their feelings and judgments on this topic. It is possible to assume that the divisive attitudes transmitted by the parents to the child create a predisposition toward schizophrenia, for internal divisiveness is indeed something essential in a schizophrenic psychosis. Recently some people assume that the danger to a child with a schizophrenic parent might be predominantly in the area of its intellectual development. Perhaps the confused thinking of one of the parents, in which one and the same concept often has various meanings, facilitates the development of absent-minded distractedness in the child: what is called "teaching of irrationality."

Such obvious assumptions are opposed by the fact that most parents of future schizophrenics (93 percent among our probands) are not schizophrenics. (Among the 408 known parents of our 208 probands only 28 are definite or probable schizophrenics.) In order to deprive this objection of any force it is often proclaimed that an existing, latent schizophrenia of one of the parents already has a detrimental effect on the future development of the child. For that reason the attempt was made to diagnose such suspected, clinically latent schizophrenias, that do not emerge socially as psychoses, by means of projection tests. Such experiments must, however, be evaluated with extreme care. At this point the question of psychotraumatic effect of parental schizophrenias on the children is to be examined by quite different methods.

If even a clinically latent schizophrenia of one of the parents already had an important effect on the future schizophrenic development of the child, then, to be sure, a manifest schizophrenia would have even more of such an effect. Surely such a conclusion is not compelling. Yet it would require some quite complicated and contrived assumptions to label it a fallacy. Without such assumptions, one should be permitted to assume that even if obscure infliction of suffering, obscure chaotic affectivity, and obscure confusion in one of the parents would already predispose the child toward a future schizophrenia, how much greater would that predisposition be in the presence of full-blown psychotic behavior that is unbecoming to parents, of full-blown psychotic, emotional inner strife, and of full-blown psychotic confusion. If there were definite psychopathic influences emanating from a child's living together with a schizophrenic parent, one would have to assume further that such living together would occur frequently and over long periods of time. What about this line of questioning? The problem has rarely been studied in detail. The following sections show how often and how long our schizophrenic probands lived together with a schizophrenic parent and were under his or her care.

It was often assumed that unfavorable behavior of parents is most likely to predispose a child to schizophrenia if the child had been subjected to it particularly during the very first years of his life. We found also that unhappy circumstances among members of the immediate family would predispose girls rather than boys toward schizophrenia. In the following section, therefore, we also set out to examine whether schizophrenics have lived together with their schizophrenic parents with marked frequency during their earliest childhood, and whether such living together was more frequent in the childhood of schizophrenic women than in that of schizophrenic men.

The Living Together of Probands with Schizophrenic Parents up to Age 20

Tables 2.37 and 2.38 convey an impression of the frequency and duration of the living together of schizophrenic probands during their childhood with manifestly schizophrenic parents. Of the 408 known parents of the 208 probands, 28 were definite or probable schizophrenics. (In this section definite and probable schizophrenias will be counted together.) Two of these cases apply to both partners of one marriage, which means that

only 27 probands had schizophrenic parents. A glance at Table 40 and 41 will show that only a small portion of the childhood and youth of these 27 probands was spent in the family community with a schizophrenic parent. The data shown in the table can also be expressed in figures. We examined the first 20 years of life of the 27 probands living together with schizophrenic parents. Of the total of 540 years of childhood and youth of these schizophrenics only 16 cannot be taken into consideration, that is, for these 16 years only, no evidence could be discovered as to whether they were spent living in families with schizophrenic parents. Only 77 of the remaining 524 years of childhood and youth were spent living in families with a schizophrenic parent. Since the other 181 schizophrenic probands did not have schizophrenic parents, the result was that of 4144 known years of life of our schizophrenic probands up to age 20, only 77 years[33] were spent living in families with a schizophrenic parent, as against 4083 years in families without such a parent.

Confronted with figures such as these, would anyone dare to consider that living in a family with a schizophrenic parent is a decisive cause for future schizophrenia in the child? I believe not. Any noxious effect to which schizophrenics are as rarely and as briefly exposed as ours were, can be at best of subordinate, but never decisive, implication in the development of future schizophrenias. If we find it difficult to ascribe any great implication to even the manifest parental schizophrenias in the genesis of schizophrenias in the children, we should certainly have to approach with skepticism any attempts to regard latent schizophrenias in parents as highly important causes of schizophrenias in the children.

The preceding exposition considers only the years of living together with a manifestly schizophrenic parent on the part of future schizophrenics. Living together with a father or a mother who had once been schizophrenic, but who recovered from the psychosis, was not considered in the above. It might be admissible that possibly the recovery, in the

---

33. Ninety-three years, if the aforementioned 16 years of uncertainty are included. They concern one and the same female proband, who lived for 16 years with her father who was either schizophrenic at the time or became schizophrenic shortly thereafter. The exact time when his illness began could not be determined.

Table 2.37. Male principal probands living together with schizophrenic parent before, during, and after their illness (11 of the 100 male probands had 1 schizophrenic parent and 1 had 2)

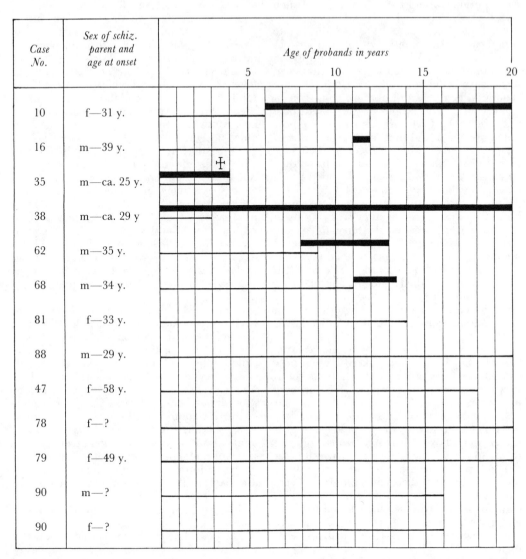

Case No.	Sex of schiz. parent and age at onset	Age of probands in years
10	f—31 y.	
16	m—39 y.	
35	m—ca. 25 y.	
38	m—ca. 29 y	
62	m—35 y.	
68	m—34 y.	
81	f—33 y.	
88	m—29 y.	
47	f—58 y.	
78	f—?	
79	f—49 y.	
90	m—?	
90	f—?	

Legend: Distance between 2 vertical lines = 1 year of life.
Heavy horizontal line = phase of manifestation of the schizophrenia in the parent.
Thin horizontal line = time proband lived together with a parent who had been schizophrenic at some time in his life, regardless of whether the time living together was concurrent with, preceding, or following manifestation of the psychosis.

No line = time during which proband did not live together with the parent who had ever been schizophrenic.

Translator's Note: y = age in years of male proband's parent
ca. = circa, approximately
† = stands for death of the parent.

Table 2.38. Female principal probands living together with schizophrenic parent before, during, and after their illness (15 of the 108 female probands had 1 schizophrenic parent)

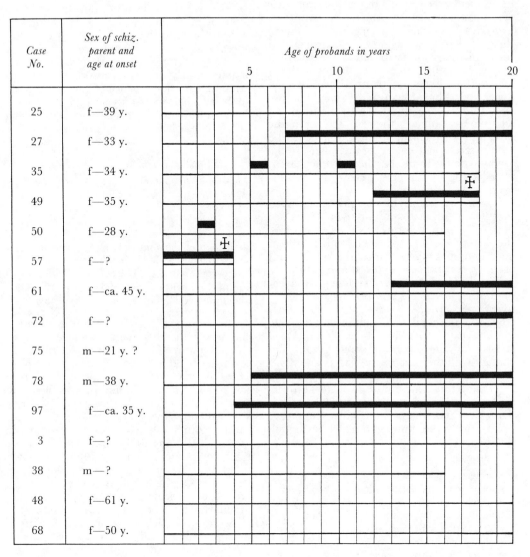

Case No.	Sex of schiz. parent and age at onset	Age of probands in years
25	f—39 y.	
27	f—33 y.	
35	f—34 y.	
49	f—35 y.	
50	f—28 y.	
57	f—?	
61	f—ca. 45 y.	
72	f—?	
75	m—21 y. ?	
78	m—38 y.	
97	f—ca. 35 y.	
3	f—?	
38	m—?	
48	f—61 y.	
68	f—50 y.	

Legend: Distance between 2 vertical lines = 1 year of life.

Heavy horizontal line = phase of manifestation of the schizophrenia in the parent.

Thin horizontal line = time proband lived together with a parent who had been schizophrenic at some time in his life, regardless of whether the time living together was concurrent with, preceding, or following manifestation of the psychosis.

No line = time during which proband did not live together with the parent who had ever been schizophrenic.

Translator's Note: y = age in years of female proband's parent
ca. = circa, approximately
† stands for death of the parent.

light of existing data, was not complete, and it might be assumed that specifically also from incompletely recovered parents some influence favoring schizophrenic vulnerability would be transmitted to the children. But even such thoughts lose meaning when we realize that the schizophrenic probands likewise spent only a very small portion of their childhood and youth in living together with parents who appeared to have recovered from their psychoses. Of the 524 known years of childhood and youth among the 27 schizophrenic probands with schizophrenic parents, only 66 years were spent in living together in the family with the formerly schizophrenic parent after he appeared to have recovered from his psychosis.

Insofar as schizophrenic probands lived together at all with parents who had once been schizophrenics, this was especially before the eruption of the parental schizophrenia, and amounted to 245 years of the known total of 524 years of their childhood and youth.

The schizophrenic probands whose father or mother became schizophrenic frequently lived apart from their parents without any contact with them at all. Of their total of 524 known years of childhood and youth, they spent 135 years in foster care without any contact with the parent who had been or was later to become schizophrenic.

These figures once more provide an overview of the above data: 27 of the 208 probands had 28 parents who became schizophrenic. A breakdown of the cumulative 540 years among them spent in childhood and youth appears below.

No living together with a schizophrenic parent	136 years
Living together with a parent who later became schizophrenic	245 years
Living together with a manifestly schizophrenic parent	77 years
Living together with a parent who appeared to have recovered from a previous schizophrenia	66 years
Undetermined relationships	16 years[34]

Quite obviously, these numbers would have had to be differently distributed, if the living together with the manifestly schizophrenic parent (or the previously schizophrenic parent) were of decisive importance in favoring the genesis of schizophrenias in these probands.

The Living Together of Probands with Schizophrenic Parents up to Age 5

What are the indications during the first 5 years of life? Did the future schizophrenics perhaps have to live with manifestly schizophrenic parents with exceptional frequency during their first 5 years? Would these years be particularly important in propagating the psychotraumatic influence of parental schizophrenia? The 135 first 5-year periods of life of the 27 future schizophrenics spent in living with a schizophrenic parent are distributed as follows:

No living together with a schizophrenic parent	9 years
Living together with a parent who only later became schizophrenic	96 years
Living together with a manifestly schizophrenic parent	13 years
Living together with a parent who appeared to have recovered from a previous schizophrenia	12 years
Undetermined relationships	5 years[35]

These figures do not support the assumption that living together with manifestly schizophrenic parents might be of decisive importance to the future development of a schizophrenia particularly during the future patient's first 5 years of life. In looking at the figures, it should not be forgotten that they represent only the years of those 27 schizophrenic probands who had schizophrenic parents; 181 of the 208 probands did not have a schizophrenic parent. Nothing is known about 16 years in the early childhood of the probands. Of the 1,024 known years in the lives of future schizophrenics, comprising the cumulative total of first 5-year periods, only 13 were spent living in a family with a schizophrenic parent, 7 with a schizophrenic father and 6 with a schizophrenic mother. Confronted by these figures, the assertion that living together with a manifestly schizophrenic mother during the first 5 years of life might be an important cause of future schizophrenia in the child is hardly acceptable. In assuming that living together with a manifestly schizophrenic mother would have to be more definitely pathogenic than living together with a merely latent schizophrenic mother, the dictum would have to be expanded. The transmission of schizophrenic feeling and

34. See footnote 33.

35. See footnote 33.

thinking in the first 5-year period of life cannot possibly be considered a generally valid, decisive causal factor in a future schizophrenia.

Furthermore, the conclusions from the above figures virtually annihilate the "mother deprivation theory" relative to schizophrenias. Of the 1,024 known years comprising the first 5-year periods in the lives of the 208 schizophrenic probands, 1,023 were spent under the care of a mother, and only a single one apart from the mother! Therefore, one really has no right to assume that depriving an infant of the care of his own mother might be operative in providing an essential or a frequent cause in the development of future schizophrenic onset in such a child.

The Living Together of Probands with Schizophrenic Parents up to Age 20, Considered Separately by Sex

Some interesting differences emerge when the living together with schizophrenic parents during childhood and youth is compared between male and female schizophrenic probands. Before age 20, the 100 male probands spent a total of 8 years living together with a manifestly schizophrenic parent, and the 108 female probands 69 years.[36] The apparently great difference, however, is statistically not significant.

That same difference can also be expressed in a different set of figures: 100 male schizophrenic probands spent 1,992 years of childhood and youth without living together in a family with a schizophrenic parent, and only 8 in such living together. The corresponding figures for female schizophrenic probands, however, read 2,075 years without such living together, and 69 years with.

Instead of calculating the years of living together with schizophrenics, one can merely count the male and female schizophrenics who have ever lived together with a schizophrenic parent. These figures are 3 of 100 men and 10 of 108 women—figures that are too small to attain statistical significance.

Since schizophrenic men spent less time than schizophrenic women in living together in a family with a schizophrenic parent, conversely they spent more time than did schizophrenic women growing up in families where they did not live together with a schizophrenic parent. These figures read: 100

male schizophrenic probands spent 80 years of their childhood and youth without living together in a family with a parent who sooner or later became schizophrenic. The corresponding number of years for the 108 schizophrenic women is 56.

Up to this point we have compared only how long schizophrenic men and women have lived together in a family with a manifestly schizophrenic parent, and how long they have lived apart from a parent who had been schizophrenic at any time. How long schizophrenic men and women lived together in a family with a parent who was not manifestly schizophrenic at the time they lived together but who had been manifestly schizophrenic earlier—or who became schizophrenic later —remains to be examined.[37]

Tables 2.37 and 2.38 and the other previously reported figures provide an impressive indication that female schizophrenics have more often than males lived in families with a schizophrenic parent to their 20th birthdays. The question of statistical significance of all assembled figures up to that point, however, has always had to be answered as being insufficient, or it posed mathematical problems that were too difficult to solve.

Dittrich, a professional psychologist, undertook the task of separating the principal problem of sex differences in respect to living together in a family with schizophrenic parents into separate partial problems, and of determining the significance of each of these separately. The results jointly indicate impressively the presence of a sex difference. The differences do achieve statistical significance in respect to the following findings:

More female than male schizophrenics witnessed a manifest schizophrenic episode in one of their parents before age 20 ($p < 0.05$).

No fully sufficient statistical significance was determined—although it is an indication

---

36. Eighty-five years, if the aforementioned 16 years of uncertainty are included; see also footnote 33.

37.	Men	Women
No. of years of childhood and youth spent living together with a parent who later became schizophrenic	110	135
No. of years of childhood and youth spent living together with a parent who appeared to have recovered from a schizophrenic psychosis	42	24
Total no. of years of childhood and youth about which conditions were known	2000	2144
No. of probands	100	108
The differences in the figures are not significant		

to be taken seriously—for the difference between male and female schizophrenics living together with a schizophrenic parent before age 20. It was an average of 2.7 years for males and 6.9 years for females.

Dittrich describes his calculations individually as follows:

Basis for questioning: Only a quarter ($N' = 3$) of the male schizophrenic probands with schizophrenic parents ($N = 12$) witnessed at least one schizophrenic episode of a parent by age 20. In contrast, two thirds ($N' = 10$) of the female schizophrenics with a schizophrenic parent ($N = 15$) witnessed at least one schizophrenic episode of a parent by age 20.

Result: This difference is significant at the critical level of $p < 0.05$. (χ^2-Test: $\chi^2 = 4.636$, $df = 1$; however, χ^2-Test with Yates' consistency correction: χ^2corr. $= 3.117$, $df = 1, 0.10 > p > 0.05$).

Basis for questioning: Male schizophrenics ($N = 3$) spent an average of 2.7 years living with one schizophrenic parent until age 20. Female schizophrenics ($N = 10$) spent an average of 6.9 years living with one schizophrenic parent until age 20.

Result: This difference at the critical level of $\leqslant 0.05$ is statistically not significant (Wilcoxon Ranked Totals Test: T_l [11] $< T$ [12.5] $< T_u$ [31]). If, as in the present case, the number of the fixed values exceeds 10 percent, the critical level will be underestimated by the Wilcoxon Ranked Totals Test. This fact, as well as the relative proximity of T_l to T, justifies the statement that there is a strong statistical tendency in favor of the significance of this difference.

Basis for questioning: Of the male schizophrenic probands whose parents were schizophrenic ($N = 12$), 75 percent spent at least 1 year *not* in the household of their parents before age 20. Of the female schizophrenic probands whose parents were schizophrenic ($N = 15$), 60 percent spent at least 1 year *not* in the household of their parents before they were 20.

Result: This difference is *not significant* at the critical level of $p \leqslant 0.05$ (χ^2-Test: $\chi^2 = 0.675$, $df = 1$).

Basis for questioning: For the male schizophrenic probands with one schizophrenic parent ($N = 9$) who did not live in their parents' household for at least 1 year before age 20, that average duration of absence amounts to 8.9 years. For the female schizophrenic probands with one schizophrenic parent ($N = 9$) who did not live in their parents' household for at least 1 year before age 20, the average

duration of absence amounts to 6.2 years.

Result: The difference is *not significant* at the critical level of $p \leqslant 0.05$ (Wilcoxon Ranked Totals Test: T_l [66] $< T$ [97] $< T_u$ [105]).

Basis for questioning: The 12 male schizophrenic probands who had one schizophrenic parent lived on an average of 13.3 years with their families until age 20, independent of whether the schizophrenic or probable schizophrenic psychosis of a parent had become manifest during the period of living together, erupted later, or there had been a recovery. The corresponding 15 female schizophrenic probands lived together with their families on an average of 16.3 years.

Result: The difference is *not significant* at the critical level of $p \leqslant 0.05$ (Wilcoxon Ranked Totals Test: T_l [133] $< T$ [143.5] $< T_u$ [203]).

How can the statistically rather uncertain finding be evaluated, that female schizophrenics have lived with a schizophrenic parent during their childhood and youth more frequently than male schizophrenics have? Regarded individually it has a number of different meanings. Among other things, it might be assumed that, for emotional, irrational reasons, the inclination is to prefer to take away a son rather than a daughter from parents who are developing a schizophrenia. But the reverse assumption appears to me to be more sensible, since living together with a schizophrenic parent seems to be more detrimental to girls than to boys and to predispose them to later schizophrenia. There are actually numerous other findings in support of this latter assumption. They will be compared and discussed later.

The Living Together of Probands with Schizophrenic Parents to Age 20, Differentiated as to Whether Father or Mother was Schizophrenic

Is the schizophrenic parent with whom the schizophrenic probands lived for a time during their childhood and youth more frequently a father or a mother? At first glance the answer is rather surprising. As already stated, the schizophrenic men spent only 8 years living together with a schizophrenic parent, and all 8 of those years were spent with a schizophrenic father; none with a schizophrenic mother. Conversely with schizophrenic women, they lived a total of 69 years[38] with a schizophrenic parent, of which only 15

38. Eighty-five or 31 years, if the above-mentioned uncertain 16 years are included. See also footnote 33.

were spent with a schizophrenic father, but 54 with a schizophrenic mother.

If these figures were to be uncritically accepted, the conclusion would have to be that a schizophrenic father endangers the mental well-being of a son, and the mother that of her daughter through his or her schizophrenia. In so doing, one would have arrived at a rather impressive conclusion, but unfortunately it cannot be drawn with any certainty from the figures. The figures representing the years schizophrenic men spent under the care of a schizophrenic parent are so minimal that it might have been a pure caprice of chance that this parent always happened to be a father. The fact that schizophrenic women were more often exposed to schizophrenic mothers than to schizophrenic fathers is partly ascribable to the fact that schizophrenics in general have more schizophrenic mothers than schizophrenic fathers, which is or may be a pure accident of selection. Just the same, the schizophrenic probands have just under twice as many schizophrenic mothers as fathers (18:10), while, on the other hand, the female schizophrenic probands had almost four times as many years of childhood and youth under the care of a schizophrenic mother than under a schizophrenic father (69:15). The difference is statistically not significant. To be sure, this difference does indicate a probability that the frequency of female probands under the care of schizophrenic mothers (in contrast to the rarity of care by schizophrenic fathers) is not caused alone by the fact that more mothers than fathers of schizophrenics were also schizophrenic themselves. An additional cause may also spring from the fact that girls under the care of schizophrenic mothers are more vulnerable to schizophrenia than if they were under the care of schizophrenic fathers. The figures mentioned above are not nearly enough to consider that assumption as probable. But we do come across reasons for this same assumption in a different context, and will discuss in summary the indications for this below.

After setting down the above information, Dittrich also broke down the line of questioning of this section into individual problems and processed each one statistically by itself. The following findings emerged with statistical significance: Female schizophrenic probands, before age 20, lived together longer with a schizophrenic mother than male schizophrenics did ($p < 0.05$). Conversely, male schizo-

phrenic probands before age 20 lived together longer with a schizophrenic father than female schizophrenics did ($p < 0.05$). Male schizophrenics more frequently had a schizophrenic father than female schizophrenics did ($p < 0.05$). Dittrich's calculations on these questions are given in detail below.

Basis for questioning: None of the male schizophrenics who witnessed a schizophrenic episode of one of their parents before age 20 ($N = 3$) lived at least 1 year in a family with a schizophrenic mother up to that time. The female schizophrenics who witnessed a schizophrenic episode of one of their parents before age 20 ($N = 10$) lived together with their schizophrenic mother during that time on an average of 5.4 years.

Result: This difference *is significant* at the critical level of $p \leqslant 0.05$ (Wilcoxon Ranked Totals Test: $T_l[11] > T[7.5] < T_u[31]$).

Basis for questioning: The male schizophrenic probands who witnessed a schizophrenic episode of one of their parents before age 20 ($N = 3$) up to that time lived together with their schizophrenic fathers an average of 2.7 years. The female schizophrenics who had witnessed a schizophrenic episode of one of their parents before they were 20 ($N = 10$) lived with their schizophrenic fathers an average of 1.5 years.

Result: This difference *is significant* at the critical level of $p \leqslant 0.05$ (Wilcoxon Ranked Totals Test: $T_l[11] < T[33] > T_u[31]$).

Basis for questioning: Of the 208 mothers of the schizophrenic probands 18 were themselves schizophrenic. Of the 208 fathers of the schizophrenic probands 10 were schizophrenic.

Result: This difference is *not significant* at the critical level of $p \leqslant 0.05$ (χ^2-Test: $\chi^2 = 2.450$, $df = 1, 0.20 > p > 0.10$).

Basis for questioning: Of the male schizophrenics who have at least one schizophrenic parent ($N = 12$), 6 have a mother who at some time, for example, even after the proband's 20th birthday, became schizophrenic. Of the corresponding 15 female schizophrenics, 12 have a schizophrenic mother.

Result: This difference is *not quite significant* at the critical level of $p = 0.05$ (χ^2-Test: $\chi^2 = 2.70, df = 1, 0.10 > p > 0.05$).

Basis for questioning: Of the male schizophrenics who have at least one schizophrenic parent ($N = 12$), 7 have a father who was at some time schizophrenic. Of the female schizophrenics who have at least one schizophrenic parent ($N = 15$), 3 have a father who was at some time schizophrenic.

Result: This difference *is significant* at the critical level of $p \leqslant 0.05$; that is, male schizophrenics probably have a schizophrenic father more often than female schizophrenics do (χ^2-Test: $\chi^2 = 4.201$, $df = 1$; the χ^2-Test with Yates' consistency correction, however: χ^2 corr. $= 2.718$, $0.10 > p > 0.05$).

The Living Together of Probands with Schizophrenic Parents up to Age 5, Considered Separately by Sex

Were our female schizophrenics exposed more to living together with a schizophrenic parent during their earliest childhood than were the male schizophrenics? That might be expected, at least if one were to believe the widespread hypothesis that unfavorable living conditions, especially during earliest childhood, are of decisive importance in the future development of a schizophrenia. The figures show, however, that the greater amount of time spent in living together with schizophrenic parents by females who later become schizophrenic does not occur during the first 5 years of life, but between ages 5 and 20.

Living together with a schizophrenic parent[39]	Schizophrenic	
	Men	Women
From birth to age 5	7	6 years
From age 5 to age 10	1	14 years
From age 10 to age 15	0	24 years
From age 15 to age 20	0	25 years

If the view is correct that the living together of a schizophrenic girl with a schizophrenic parent, particularly with a schizophrenic mother, predisposes her to schizophrenia, then according to this set of figures it would have to occur more often after her 5th, and especially after her 10th birthday, than during such living together before age 5. Of course, the raw figures could also be interpreted in an entirely different way: Very young girls are more readily taken from manifestly schizophrenic mothers than older ones. But this explanation misses the mark. It can be checked against information from our own female probands without much difficulty, since I was in a position to find out why the living together of each of our probands with his schizophrenic parent was stopped. Never was a child, either

39. Without taking into account the 16 uncertain years described in footnote 32. If these years were included, the figures under "women" would read: 11, 19, 29 and 26 years.

boy or girl, taken from a schizophrenic parent before he was 5 years old, if the possibility had existed of leaving him in the home of his parents. When a child did not live together with his manifestly schizophrenic parent before age 5, it was usually because the schizophrenia of the parent had not erupted until after the child was 5 years old. In 3 cases the parent recovered from the schizophrenia during the first 5 years of the child's life. One child lost his schizophrenic father early in life when his parents were divorced, another just as early by the death of this parent, a third had never had contact with his illegitimate father who was schizophrenic, and yet another lost his schizophrenic mother early by death.

According to this, the explanation certainly does not hold for our probands, that more older children than younger ones were exposed to the care of a schizophrenic mother, because the younger ones were taken away from their schizophrenic mothers sooner than were the older ones. The cause lies rather plainly in the fact that most of the mothers did not become schizophrenic until their children, our schizophrenic probands, were over 5 years old. It is therefore not admissible to draw any kind of conclusions from the differences in the amounts of time spent in living together with manifestly schizophrenic parents, on the question of whether living together with schizophrenic parents is more harmful in early or in later childhood. What may be stated is merely that our female schizophrenic probands, according to figures in the above listing, have on an average lived longer and more often with schizophrenic parents than the male schizophrenics. If this difference between the sexes is related to the theory that girls rather than boys are more vulnerable to later schizophrenic onset through living together with a schizophrenic parent, then such vulnerability was distinctly greater after age 5. The abovementioned set of figures neither confirms nor denies any such relationship before age 5.

General Childhood Conditions of Probands with Schizophrenic Parents

One additional observation seems worth noting. Probands who have lived together with manifestly schizophrenic parents were for the most part subjected to the most unhappy conditions in their childhood, regardless of the fact that their parents were schizophrenic.

Ten female schizophrenic probands lived in families with a manifestly schizophrenic parent during their childhood or youth. Six of these endured conditions during their childhood that qualify as horrible, and three others for whom conditions were not exactly horrible, certainly endured conditions that were not good. Conditions were good for only 1 of the 10, whose mother passed through just two brief manifestly schizophrenic episodes. Six male probands lived in families with a manifestly schizophrenic parent during their childhood. Three of them endured horrible conditions during childhood, and 1 other did not fare well at all. Conditions during childhood were good for 2 of them, and the father of 1 of these suffered a schizophrenic phase of only very short duration.

Under these conditions doubts arise against assuming that a mental disorder can be blamed solely on the fact of living together with a schizophrenic parent. A more general assumption agrees better with the actuality, namely that it is possible that, for girls who later become schizophrenic, their illness was slightly abetted by extremely poor conditions in the home during childhood if, in addition, they had to live together with a schizophrenic parent for a part of that time.

The Stepparents of Schizophrenics

Mental Health of the Stepparents

In this project, all those persons are considered stepparents who have ever been married to a parent of the proband, but who themselves are not parents of the proband. Foster parents or partners of probands' parents who produced illegitimate children with them were not considered stepparents.

We designate as actual stepparents those with whom the proband has lived together at any time before he was 20. Theoretical stepparents were those who had never lived together with the proband before he was 20. These were the spouses from previous marriages of probands' parents, if those probands were the offspring a subsequent marriage, or they were the second spouses of probands' parents who married these parents after the proband's 20th birthday.

The 208 principal probands of this project had a total of just 24 stepparents; 10 stepfathers and 14 stepmothers. Any findings with such small samples are without significance. Still, it is not entirely meaningless to become acquainted with the general health of the stepparents of schizophrenics, which has not been much studied up to this time. Information concerning the stepparents will also be indis-

pensable to the discussion of findings about the half-siblings of schizophrenics. For these reasons I have instigated a supplemental investigation of the stepparents of schizophrenics other than the 208 principal probands. It was carried out by our colleague, Dr. H. E. Gabriel, and supported by Mrs. Ruth Frey, who spent two months on related clerical duties. He selected all the stepparents of schizophrenics hospitalized on two target dates at our clinic, November 7, 1966 for the men, and October 27, 1966 for the women. All the 138 male and 129 female schizophrenics present at the hospital on these two days had 48 stepparents; 18 stepfathers and 30 stepmothers. These stepparents were designated as the stepparents of additional probands, to distinguish them from those of the 208 principal probands.

Gabriel and Ruth Frey first processed all patient histories of the additional probands. All information they contained was checked and supplemented by questioning the patient himself or at least someone of his family. If doubts remained about the actual marital status, copies from local court records of the home communities were procured. Gabriel is convinced that by his method all the stepparents were accounted for, and that he was fully informed about any and all psychoses among them.

Among all 72 stepparents there was not a single case of schizophrenia. The base figure of 72 does not require any age correction, since almost all stepparents (67 of 72) did not drop out of observation until they were over 40, and the other 5 dropped out between ages 30 and 40. The age correction coefficient derived in the customary way would have lowered the base figure to only 68.5.

If there were as many schizophrenics among the stepparents of schizophrenics as there are among their parents, we could have expected a probable approximation of 5 schizophrenics among them, since 7 percent of the parents were schizophrenic. Certainly, the difference is not sufficiently significant. Among 599 parents of the medical patients, as representatives of various groups of the population of Switzerland, there were 4 schizophrenics. If the frequency of schizophrenia among the stepparents of schizophrenics were equal to that of the representatives of the normal population who are parents, the greatest probability would also yield no schizophrenics—or at the utmost 1—among the 72 stepparents.

Two additional observations increase the

probability that the stepparents of schizophrenics are much less jeopardized by schizophrenia than are the parents of schizophrenics. Among the parents of the Pfäfers schizophrenic probands, 29 percent were psychopaths, and among these 16.5 percent were schizoid psychopaths (of 200 parents there were 58 psychopaths and 33 of these were schizoids). Among the 72 stepparents there were 2 schizoids and no psychopaths. So there are also considerably fewer psychopaths and schizoid psychopaths among the stepparents than among the parents of schizophrenics. On the other hand, however, the figure for psychopaths among the stepparents agrees almost exactly with expectations according to the greatest probability, if there were just as many psychopaths among the stepparents as among the parents of medical patients representing the general population. Among the 599 of the latter category, there were 18 = 3 percent psychopaths; of these 7 = 1.2 percent were schizoid psychopaths. Gabriel then also studied the closest relatives of the stepparents of his additional probands as to frequency of schizophrenias, but he found it to be slight. Among the parents and siblings of 48 stepparents there were only 2 cases of schizophrenia. (According to the greatest probability there would have been about 17 among parents and siblings of schizophrenics, and about 2 among the parents and siblings of the medical patients representing the general population.)

Under these circumstances it may be considered highly probable that stepparents of schizophrenics suffer much more rarely from schizophrenia than do the parents of schizophrenics. The occurrence of schizophrenias among the stepparents of schizophrenics is not markedly different from that among the parents of the general population.

But the stepparents of schizophrenics are healthier than the parents of schizophrenics in other respects as well.

There is no manic-depressive illness among the 72 stepparents, whereas 2–3 might have been expected among the parents of schizophrenics, with the greatest probability. Only 3 of the 28 stepparents were alcoholics, while we might have expected about 7 with the greatest probability, if alcoholism occurred at the same frequency among the stepfathers as it did among the fathers of our principal schizophrenic probands, and 5–6 if it were as frequent among the stepfathers as among the fathers of medical patients representing the general population.

There were no senile psychoses observed among the 72 stepparents. If they had occurred as frequently among the stepparents as they did among the parents of our principal schizophrenic probands, then at greatest probability we could have expected 6 senile psychoses among the 30 stepparents who had survived their 70th birthday.

There was 1 suicide among the 72 stepparents. If the frequency of suicides among the deceased stepparents had been as high as it was among the parents of the principal schizophrenic probands, the greatest probability of suicides to be expected among the stepparents was 1.6.

In relation to all other forms of mental illness also, the stepparents are no different from the average population.

Each of the above-mentioned differences in frequency of incidence of mental disturbances between the parents and the stepparents of schizophrenics is either statistically weak or insignificant. Taken together as a whole, however, they permit of the following statement: As there are fewer schizophrenias among the stepparents than among the parents of schizophrenics, so also the stepparents are generally physically healthier than the parents of schizophrenics.

This statement holds for the stepparents of the 208 principal schizophrenic probands, as well as for the stepparents of the 267 additional schizophrenic probands, as it does also for "actual" as well as "theoretical" stepparents.

The Mental Health of Parents Who Married More Than Once Compared to That of Their Spouses

We have just compared the frequency of mental disturbances among the stepparents of our probands with the frequency of mental disturbances among the parents of any schizophrenics. Another line of questioning suggests itself, and that is a comparison among the following three groups of parents: Group A—the stepparents of schizophrenic probands, Group B—parents of schizophrenic probands who married a stepparent, and Group C—parents of schizophrenic probands, who had not themselves married a stepparent, but whose spouse had married a stepparent.

The obvious and simple grouping, cast in these terms, looks as if it were complicated, but a simple sketch will show at a glance what is intended:

The three groups encompass 72, 62, and 62

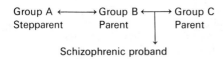

Fig 2.1 Diagram: relationship of stepparents

persons. (Since individual parents had sometimes married more than one stepparent, the number of stepparents is greater than that of each of the two groups of parents.) The age structure of the three groups is almost identical, with persons over 40 predominating. The schizophrenias are distributed among Groups A, B, and C in the ratio of 0:1:7. The fact that Group C must contain the most schizophrenics is plain: Divorces of parental marriages were usually requested by the healthier spouse because the other partner was schizophrenic. The healthy spouse remarried, and the sick one did not.

Additionally it is worth noting that among the 124 parents of schizophrenics (Groups B and C together) there were again about 7 percent schizophrenics (more precisely 6.5 percent). Since only a portion of these schizophrenics belonged to the principal probands group, the finding shows again that the frequency of schizophrenia always amounts to about 7 percent among the parents of the most varied groups of schizophrenics.

After Group C had produced more schizophrenics than Group B, according to expectations, one might suspect that there would also be more disturbed personalities in Group C than in Group B, but this is not the case. Severe personality disorders are distributed among the three Groups A, B, and C in the ratio of 2:9:8. Psychopathic and neurotic developments and alcoholism were counted in with severe personality disturbances, since a breakdown into these categories would have resulted in such low figures that they would have been meaningless.

The following line of thinking might be valid in respect to these findings, if they were to be confirmed by new series of investigations.

It is of sociological interest that Group B, whose members had married psychically imperiled spouses from Group C, found less psychically imperiled partners in a different marriage (with Group A). It has, to be sure, often been asserted that in the presence of certain mental disorders, one partner thus imperiled will invariably find his way to another partner afflicted the same way. This seems not to be the case with the schizo-

phrenias. Even though, according to this, the parents of schizophrenics who married several times chose a spouse imperiled with schizophrenia only one of these times, yet there is an indication that they are inclined to select partners in both marriages who are somehow pathological.

From the standpoint of forming pathogenetic hypotheses, these findings will hold interest if one assumes that pathological personality developments of all types emerge from the background of a partial disposition toward schizophrenia. These findings could then be better evaluated in the context of recessiveness rather than of dominance, because from the unions between parents of Groups B and C, at least one child always became schizophrenic, while marriages between parents from Groups A and B produced almost no schizophrenics at all. If the finding should be confirmed by using other probands, the presence of personality disturbances among the parents would present a danger to the children only if they occurred in both the mother and the father, not just in the mother or the father.

From the standpoint of psychogenetic hypothesizing, the findings indicate that a decisive psychotraumatic childhood situation is more likely to be developed when both parents have personality problems than when the pathological influence issues from just one parent.

But all these are at best untested indications. They are supported by nonsignificant figures that are too small and the interpretation of which is delicate and uncertain. I mention them only in order to generate interest in undertaking similar investigations with a greater number of probands.

The Living Together of Stepparents and Schizophrenic Probands

Of the 72 stepparents of schizophrenic probands, only 36 are "actual" stepparents, that is, stepparents with whom the proband lived in the same home before he was 20. Of the 24 stepparents of the 208 principal schizophrenic probands, 12 were "actual" stepparents, and of the 48 among the 267 additional schizophrenic probands, there were 24 "actual" stepparents.

A distinction according to sex reveals that.
—238 male schizophrenic probands had 7 actual stepfathers and 5 actual stepmothers
—237 female schizophrenic probands had 9 actual stepfathers and 15 actual stepmothers.

The 237 female probands, therefore, had more actual stepparents than did the 238 male probands. The ratio is 24:12. The difference is statistically not quite significant, but it does get close to the significance of $(0.1 > p > 0.05)$.

In contrast, the finding that female schizophrenics have more stepmothers than male schizophrenics have is statistically significant (χ^2-Test with Yates' consistency correction: $\chi^2 = 4.268$, $df = 1$, $p < 0.05$).

The male probands had a few more stepfathers than stepmothers, but the females, conversely, had more stepmothers than stepfathers, although the figures supporting this statement are by no means significant.

These figures might indicate that girls become more vulnerable to schizophrenia by living together with a stepmother than boys, and that living together with a stepmother would entail a greater risk for schizophrenia than living together with a stepfather. I mention this here only because some other, more significant findings in this study indicate the same relationship.

Instead of considering the number of schizophrenic probands who lived in families together with stepparents before they were 20 years old, the number of years spent in living together with stepparents before probands were 20 is now to be considered. This observation becomes somewhat complicated by the fact that for 1 male schizophrenic proband it was not possible to determine with any accuracy, despite all efforts to find out, how many years he had spent in his family together with his stepfather. At most it was 5 years, and probably less:

—The 238 male schizophrenics spent a total of 43 years[40] before they were 20 living in a family with a stepfather and 37 years in one with a stepmother

—The 237 female probands spent a total of 43 years in a family with a stepfather and 125 years in one with a stepmother before they were 20.

Without knowing the full statistical significance of the difference, it is obvious that female schizophrenic probands averaged more time living with a stepmother than did male probands. Male schizophrenic probands lived about the same amount of time with a stepfather as with a stepmother (or just a little more with a stepfather), but female probands lived longer with a stepmother than with a stepfather. The latter difference approaches statistical significance.

40. Five years at the utmost.

Dittrich also worked over the statistics of this chapter after its completion. He set out with the number of probands who had stepparents. In the above figures the starting point was the number of stepparents. It is somewhat larger than the number of probands with stepparents, since some probands had more than one stepparent; that is, one had 2 stepfathers, 3 had 2 stepmothers each, and one proband had 1 stepfather and 3 stepmothers.

At the level of $p < 0.05$, one difference proved to be significant: the female schizophrenics have more actual stepmothers than the male schizophrenics have.

For the remaining sets of differences the significance was insufficient at $p = 0.05$.

Dittrich's individual calculations follow:

Problem 1: Of 238 male schizophrenics, 10 (4.2 percent) have a stepfather. Of 237 female schizophrenics, 17 (7.2 percent) have a stepfather.

Result: This difference is not significant at a critical level of $p = 0.05$ (χ^2-Test: $\chi^2 = 1.956$, $df = 1$, $20 > p > 10$; χ^2-Test with Yates' correction: χ^2 corr. $= 1.441$, $df = 1$, $30 > p > 20$).

Problem 2: Of 238 male schizophrenics 13 (5.5 percent) have a stepmother. Of 237 female schizophrenics 26 (10.9 percent) have a stepmother.

Result: This difference is significant at the critical level of $p < 0.05$ (χ^2-Test: $\chi^2 = 4.780$, $df = 1$, $p < 0.05$; χ^2-Test with Yates' consistency correction: χ^2 corr. $= 4.078$, $p < 0.05$).

Problem 3: Of 10 schizophrenic men who have a stepfather, 7 (70 percent) live together with him. Of 17 schizophrenic women who have a stepfather, 9 (53 percent) live together with him.

Result: This difference is not significant at the critical level of $p = 0.05$ (χ^2-Test: $\chi^2 = 0.2168$, $df = 1$).

Problem 4: Of the 13 schizophrenic men who have a stepmother, 5 (38 percent) live together with her. Of the 26 schizophrenic women who have a stepmother, 15 (58 percent) live together with her.

Result: This difference is not significant at the critical level of $p = 0.05$ (χ^2-Test: $\chi^2 = 1.283$, $df = 1$, $0.30 > p > 0.20$; χ^2-Test with Yates' correction: χ^2 corr. $= 0.66$, $df = 1$).

Problem 5: Of 238 male schizophrenics 7 live together with a stepfather. Of 237 female schizophrenics 9 live together with a stepfather.

Result: This difference is not significant at the critical level of $p = 0.05$.

Problem 6: Of 238 male schizophrenics, 5 live together with their stepmother. Of 237 female schizophrenics, 15 live together with their stepmother.

Result: This difference is significant at the critical level of $p < 0.05$ (χ^2-Test: $\chi^2 = 5.28$, $df = 1$, $p < 0.05$; χ^2-Test with Yates' correction: χ^2 corr. $= 4.268$, $df = 1$, $p < 0.05$).

Problem 7: For 6 male schizophrenics who lived together with their stepfathers, the average duration of that living together lasted 7.2 years (the time of their living together for the 7th proband is unknown). For 9 female schizophrenics who lived together with their stepfathers the average duration of that living together lasted 4.8 years.

Result: This difference is not significant at the critical level of $p = 0.05$ (Wilcoxon Ranked Totals Test: T_l [33] $< T$ [57.5] $< T_u$ [63]).

Problem 8:   For the 5 male schizophrenics who lived together with their stepmother, the average duration of that living together was 7.4 years. For the 15 female Schizophrenics who lived together with their stepmother, the average duration of that living together was 8.3 years.

Result: This difference is not significant at the critical level of $p = 0.05$ (Wilcoxon Ranked Totals Test: T_l [33] $< T$ [46] $< T_u$ [72]).

Discussion

It would be a ridiculous undertaking to attempt to draw conclusions of general validity from an investigation of just 72 stepparents from only two groups of schizophrenic probands (208 and 267). Obviously the data from these two groups must be retested with a larger and more varied group of probands. However, considering the scarcity of investigations of stepparents of schizophrenics, the above findings do merit some attention. Assuming that they would be confirmed by findings from additional investigations, they deserve some serious thought in the following areas:

There are fewer schizophrenias[41] and fewer

41. As previously explained, schizophrenias occur with frequency only among those parents of schizophrenic probands with stepparents who married only once. Those who also married a stepparent are no more often schizophrenic than the stepparents and the representatives of the general population. This finding is brought about

pathological personality developments of all types among the stepparents of schizophrenics than among the parents of schizophrenics. As a group, the stepparents of schizophrenics are not noticeably to be distinguished in respect to their mental health from parents of the general population. Accordingly, the schizophrenic offspring can more probably be expected to come from a marriage of two psychopathological parents than from a union between one mentally ill and one normal parent. This assumption from our investigations of stepparents corresponds exactly to the old, well-known findings from the Munich School of Rüdin (1916), which were, however, obtained by entirely different methods. The Munich School customarily calculated the onset probability of the offspring of schizophrenic probands separately, according to whether both parents were mentally sound, whether one was mental ill and the other sound, or whether both were mentally ill. If pathogenetic causes are assumed to be fundamental, the findings support recessiveness of all sorts of traits, rather than dominance.[42] And they can just as easily be reconciled with the assumption of a disharmony of normal traits as an hereditary background of the schizophrenias. If psychotraumatic causes are assumed to be valid, the findings support the theory that the unfavorable influences of a pathological parent can be nullified through the favorable ones of the other parent. But these assumptions are a long way from being statistically supported by the data on these stepparents, and besides, the raw figures alone admit of some other interpretations as well.

More important, better supported and more interesting are the following findings:

Schizophrenic women lived with step-

entirely or in part by the fact that schizophrenias in one spouse often become the reason for divorce for the other, as well as the basis for yet another marriage.

42. The extended discussion about the pathogenetic influence of the data from stepparents of schizophrenics will be appreciably influenced by data on their half-siblings. If the probability for schizophrenic onset is minimal among them, it would indicate a recessiveness of pathogenic genes or a disharmony of healthy genes in the formation of a schizophrenia. Such findings could also have been reconciled with a theory of dominance, if the parents of schizophrenics who marry a second time had proved to be much healthier than those parents who did not marry a second time—which was not the case, with respect to pathological personality developments.

mothers during their childhood and youth more often and for longer periods of time than schizophrenic men did. If this result is supported by additional investigations, the simplest interpretation for it would be that living together with a stepmother was detrimental to girls and might predispose them to schizophrenia; this is not true of boys, or at least not to a degree that can be proved. Such an interpretation agrees with the findings from other sections; they will be discussed in detail later.

According to the findings presented here, girls rather than boys risk later schizophrenic onset by living together with a manifestly schizophrenic mother, as well as by living together with a mentally normal stepmother.

If this statement is true, we have achieved an impressive indication that the psychotraumatic experience with a mother is less specifically caused by her schizophrenic condition than by the disturbed relationship to that mother and the emotional burden on the girl engendered by this relationship. The indication is rather improbable that "teaching of irrationality" might be the single decisive factor in a psychotraumatic childhood situation that would later lead to schizophrenia. However, it is probable that the determining psychotraumatic situation most likely springs from the emotional experiences, be these in the form of emotional stress as such, or in the stresses peculiar to an ambivalent attitude toward the person of the mother.

3 The Personality of Schizophrenics before Their Illness

The Prepsychotic Character of the 208 Probands

The more intimately one gets to know one's probands, the more reluctant one would be to decide to categorize their characters for statistical purposes. Yet this is necessary for resolving the question whether there are typical prepsychotic personality traits interrelated with typical psychotraumatic conditions in life that normally precede the development toward schizophrenic psychoses. A good summary of prepsychotic character traits, however, is just as indispensable for any formulation of theories on hereditary pathogenesis. In future chapters I plan to address myself also to the problem of correlations between a prepsychotic character and the family history of schizophrenics, for which statistics also prove useful. There is practical value in studying the relationships between a prepsychotic character on the one hand, and the course and the therapeutic susceptibilities of the schizophrenias on the other.

During the past few decades, a great deal of statistical work has been done on the prepsychotic character of schizophrenics. Today there is no longer any doubt that the important and predominating character traits of future schizophrenics are easily categorized under the concept of the schizoid. To be sure, the term does not characterize all, but it does include the majority of the future schizophrenics. On the basis of these facts alone, that have been confirmed time and again by the experience of nearly half a century, all the problems concerning the prepsychotic personality of schizophrenics that could be processed by statistics have by no means been resolved. Comparisons of the prepsychotic characters of different groups of schizophrenics might, we should hope, be able to shed some light on the various aspects of the developmental history of the schizophrenias. Does the distribution of different psychotic characteristics vary at different periods of time, in different cultures, or among different social classes? How does it vary? To answer such questions we need statistics like those that follow, that consistently hold to the same interpretations of terms. The individual categorization of characteristics must be done

with a set of qualifications that can be applied to the majority of all probands without being force-fitted or arbitrarily assigned. These qualifications also have to correspond to those of other statistics. As in my previous studies, I applied the following simple breakdown that seems to meet the above-mentioned demands: (a) nonaberrant personality development, (b) aberrant personality development in the context of a schizoid nature within the norm, (c) otherwise aberrant personality development within the norm, (d) pathological personality development in the context of the schizoid nature, and (e) otherwise pathological personality development.

In order to avoid a clumsy, long-drawn text, and in the interest of brevity and clarity in inspecting tables, I have abbreviated the above

—Nonaberrant
—Schizoid aberrant within norm
—Otherwise aberrant within norm
—Schizoid-pathological
—otherwise pathological.

The distinction among "nonaberrant"— "aberrant within the norm"—"pathological" refers to the same condition as common usage of the terms imply, but in this section "pathological" refers consistently and expressly to the prepsychotic condition, since this section is exclusively concerned with the personality development before the onset of the psychosis. A reasonably satisfactory transscription of the three terms has been derived from the practice of forensic psychiatry in Switzerland, which also agrees closely with the concepts as they are used in everyday language. They cannot, however, be sharply and accurately distinguished from one another without the application of arbitrary, subjective judgment. "Nonaberrant" and "aberrant" personality developments would not in legal practice constitute reasons for accepting a reduction of personal accountability. According to the letter of the law in Switzerland, pathological personality development without mental illness would correspond approximately to the concepts akin to retarded mental development or impairment of mental health, and would, if illegal acts were committed in conjunction with them, constitute the postulates for

accepting reduction of personal accountability. Binder clearly described these concepts
for application in cases of involuntary commitment. Our own transcription of "pathological
personality development" applies similar criteria to those that Schneider introduced for
the transcription of the psychopathies, and
as they have become accepted in common
usage. He applies the term "psychopathic"
to those types of personalities that suffer from
their "abnormality" or under which "abnormality" society suffers. Again, of course, an
adjustment has to be made that conforms to
everyday experience and to subjective judgment, when the term "abnormal" is to be
applied and when estimates are to be made
as to what degree of suffering is under
discussion.

The characterization "aberrant within the
norm," of course, is bound to be subjective
and is distinguished from "nonaberrant"
when a certain amount of arbitrary discretion
is applied. Still, arbitrariness and subjectivity
are restricted by the fact that these characterizations stem from the consensus of a number
of people—one might almost say from a board
of qualified experts that includes a number
of the informants who have lived with the
proband, the proband himself, and from me,
based on anamnestic data from my studies.

The concept "schizoid" needs no further
transcription today; it has long ago won its
place in the vocabulary of psychiatry. It was
described with unsurpassable lucidity in the
older studies, particularly those by Kretschmer (1944), Hoffmann (1923) and E. Bleuler
(1911). I have cast it into a narrow mold for
this study. I characterized as "schizoid" only
those peculiarities of personality that the
majority of psychiatrists would also have
accepted as valid. Difficulties in personality
that had been labelled as "schizoid" by just a
few authors on the basis of theoretical considerations I did not refer to as "schizoid" in
the statistical categories, but I called them by
their proper name, as for instance, the an-
ancastic, obsessive-compulsive personalities.
Antisocial manifestations may have various
origins, and to me they were never in themselves a reason for assuming a schizophrenic
nature.

With the earlier authors the following
qualifications of the schizoid were, in my
opinion, applicable: Externally the schizoid
patient often appears rigid and impenetrable,
dull, and opathetic. He is taciturn or has little
regard for the effect on others of what he says.

Sometimes he appears tense and becomes
irritated by senseless provocation. He appears
as insincere and indirect in communication.
His behavior is aloof and devoid of human
warmth; yet, he does have a rich inner life.
In this sense he is introverted. He does not
seem rigid and unsympathetic because of
inner vacuousness, apathetic indifference, or
dull-wittedness, but he is unable to communicate coherently and sympathetically, because
the multiplicity of his mental images and
emotional surges disturb the coherence of his
senses and his ability to express himself.
Ambivalent moods are more pronounced in
the schizoid than in others, just as he distorts
the meanings of, and introduces excessive
doubts into, his own concepts. But on the
other hand, the schizoid is also capable of
pursuing his thoughts and of following his own
interests and drives, without giving enough
consideration to other people and to the
actual realities of life. He is autistic. The
better side of his autism reveals a sturdiness of
character, an inflexibility of purpose, an independence, and a predisposition to creativity.
The worse side of it becomes manifest in a
lack of consideration for others, unsociability,
a world-alien attitude, stubbornness, egocentricity, and occasionally even cruelty.

Most patients that I have characterized as
schizoids can be added to one of the schizoid
types described by Kretschmer (1944) and
others; they include the suspicious, the
hypersensitive eccentrics, the pedants, the
inconsiderate, the insensitive overambitious,
the paranoid, obstinate cranks, the excessively
shy and supersensitive, the fanatics, the
bigoted hypocrites, or the perverse.

The aberrant and the psychopaths who are
not schizoid fall into a number of varied
categories. When, in the tables, it seemed
appropriate they have been individually identified. Among them, the most numerous
groups and categories are formed, that is, the
intermittently or permanently discordant
(often included among the "affectives"); the
short-tempered and irritable reactives; the
callously unstable; then the infantile, among
them the alcoholics, are mentioned separately.
All other addicts who cannot be classified with
certainty as schizoid are counted as "other
than schizoid psychopaths."

Characterizing the prepsychotic personality
is done without regard to how the aberrant
or pathological traits began; that is, whether
they were character traits generated by neuroses or whether one was dealing with

psychopathic personalities. If, however, it was certain that personality disturbances were caused by a brain disease; that is, that they were posttraumatic or postencephalitic, the patient was not simply listed among the personality aberrations, but his problem was listed under "other mental disorders" and there specifically described. Among the 208 principal probands, by the way, there was not a single one with such a clearly organically caused personality disorder, but there were several in the statistics used in the comparisons.

If I speak in this chapter of prepsychotic characters rather than prepsychotic personalities, it is because I felt the need of separating the intellectual aspect statistically from the other aspects of a personality. The term "character" as applied in this chapter is thus intended in a broad sense. It encompasses almost all aspects of a personality with the exception of intellectual development.

As unsatisfactory as every attempt is for statistical purposes to interpret plainly and to distinguish sharply from one another every concept used in this chapter, one continues to be surprised that they turn out to be quite useful in practice after all. Simple experiences in life and the common usage of language have done more toward establishing accurate distinctions between the concepts "nonaberrant," "aberrant within the norm," "pathological," "schizoid," etc. than have all contrived attempts at scholarly definitions. Test samples have shown me that different adjudicators often agree in the applications of these concepts. Despite that, however, the significance of the figures must not be overestimated. One must never forget that subjective judgment was applied to derive the basic data for these statistics, and not objectively derived figures.

In order to show how the qualifications of characters that were applied were differentiated, the following paragraphs will contain some examples. The 5 descriptions are meant not only to show how the premorbid characters were qualified, but also to furnish the case material for the relationships between character and psychosis that will be discussed in future chapters. For this reason the brief sketch of the future schizophrenic psychosis of 5 of the 208 principal probands is here immediately attached to the character sketch. Several additional examples are given in my study on the Pfäfers schizophrenic probands.

If I compare the schizoids among my patients from the Canton of Zürich, from the St. Gallen mountains around Pfäfers, and from a private clinic in New York, I am struck by the similarity of how the schizoid personality manifests itself among the most diversified social groups. A wealthy New York banker, a poor St. Gallen farmer from the hills, and a factory worker from the industrial sector of Zürich may be schizoid in exactly the same way. The schizoid personality becomes distinctive in people, quite independent of their social status.

Example for the Characterization of a Prepsychotic Personality as "Nonaberrant"

Hans D. (Proband 12), born 1903

At age 5, Hans lost his father, who died of tuberulosis. He had been a painter, was an easy-going, happy sort of person, who had become well-liked by playing a hand organ in his leisure time. Proband's mother, who was still living at age 85 at the conclusion of the investigations, was a bit more retiring and somewhat phlegmatic. She was an excellent homemaker and a good mother.

Until he was 5, Hans was raised by both parents, in modest but adquate circumstances. After his father died, his mother had to board him at orphanages and place him in homes with farmers as a foster child, until she took him back home when she remarried. Despite these many changes in guardianship, and although the external circumstances had not always been ideal, Hans never caused any problems for his foster parents. He did well in school and stayed near the top of his classes.

His vocational training and activity were uneventful. Immediately upon finishing basic schooling, he entered an apprenticeship as a barber with his uncle, where he worked for 4 years after completing training. Then he worked for the next 15 years as a barber in another establishment. When he was 38 he stopped working there because of a civil lawsuit between him and his employer. Inspection of the court files showed that the fault of the quarrel was the employer's, who had found himself financially embarrassed and had refused to pay the employee his wages. The proband had agreed to cancel a large portion of his employer's debt, and the lawsuit ensued only because the employer had refused also to pay even the small remainder he owed him. As soon as he left that job, he took another position as a barber, where he remained until a year later when he became ill. How much his clientele liked him became evident when 70 of his former customers followed him to his new shop after he changed jobs.

Proband married at age 27 after a courtship of 3 years. For unknown reasons, there were no children from this marriage. It was an excellent marriage, in which no serious mis-understandings had occurred. An indication of this good relationship was the fact that his wife remained loyal to him throughout his psychosis, did everything possible for him, and when he improved treated him as though nothing had happened. Both spouses were hard workers, she as a saleswoman, and both enjoyed their work. They maintained a pleasant friendship with another couple.

The military life of the proband was as simple, as steady, and as favorable as his marital and his vocational careers had been. Until he became ill at age 39, he performed every duty required in his infantry unit, and spent the last $2\frac{1}{2}$ years in heavy active duty with a border-guard unit. He was promoted to corporal without the benefit of special training, based simply on his personal reliabli-ty to get along with his peers. As corporal he often had to assume leadership of a squad as though he were its sergeant. His superiors and his peers regarded him as an even-tempered man and a good buddy.

The proband had never attempted to achieve great aims. He had been raised in simple circumstances and felt at home and contented in them.

After his unit was recalled from active duty (proband was then 39) he complained to his wife that he could not work any longer. He felt uncertain about every task he at-tempted at the barber shop and when the job was finished kept worrying whether he had done the right thing. A few days later a serious psychosis erupted that left him in complete despair. He was not sure that he was the same person as before; touched various parts of his body in frenzied doubt that it was part of him-self. He spoke in total confusion. At the clinic he was diagnosed as an acute catatonic. With insulin treatment he rapidly improved. One attempt to release him ended in a few days with a relapse. At that time he was severely excited and distracted, and insisted that some-one was trying to poison him. Then a condition set in where he appeared to be submerged within himself; when spoken to, his replies were silly and confused. The psychosis lasted just under 6 months.

During the 13 years that followed the pro-

band was completely rational. People around him felt he was once again the same as before. At age 52 he began again to complain about being unable to do his work, and after several weeks was committed to a private clinic. His condition there was diagnosed as a hebe-phrenic schizophrenia. After several days he slipped away from the hospital, threw himself across the tracks and was killed by an oncom-ing train.

This patient's illness was categorized among those that would have been possible to call a schizophrenic-depressive mixed psychosis rather than a schizophrenia.

Example for the Characterization of the Premorbid Personality known as "Schizoid Aberrant Within the Norm"

Alice K. (Proband 17), born 1900

Alice's father was the son of a farmer who had lost his property and turned farmhand. Her father himself was a streetcar conductor, portly and good-natured. To outward appear-ances he took good care of his family, although he seldom shared their interests and, during Alice's childhood, engaged in several extra-marital affairs. At an advanced age, long after Alice had grown up and had been psychotic for a number of years, he suffered several attacks of apoplexy, a postapoplectic de-mentia, and died of cerebral arteriosclerosis at our clinic. Alice's mother was active and energetic and usually assumed the central position in her circle of friends. She was atten-tive in performing her duties, but self-assertive and tyrannical toward her family. When Alice was born she was 28, and her husband was 26.

Alice grew up with her parents in rather restricted and financially meager circum-stances, although the essentials of life were provided for. She had one slightly younger sister.

Alice drew away from both parents when she was still a small child. She learned to despise her father early in life because of his philandering, perceived her mother as cold and tyrannical, and maintained a distant relationship with her sister.

Her educational, intellectual, and voca-tional development was excellent. After ele-mentary and secondary schooling, she grad-uated from the municipal business school, passed her examinations for certification, and then became secretary to a well-known firm of attorneys. After she had completed her French language studies in the Romance-language sector of Switzerland, she worked in a good scretarial position abroad for the following 4 years (from age 20 to 24). Upon her return she became dissatisfied with secretarial work and wanted to advance her education. While she continued to earn her living doing office work, she attended night classes at the university. She acquired sufficient credit for her degree, and could have passed her examinations for it, according to reports from her teachers. However, she decided not to make the attempt, and instead accepted a good position in a large business (at age 28). Her position there gave her independence and responsible challenges which she proved able to meet. She kept this job for 14 years until she had to resign because of her psychosis (at age 42).

Alice had never fostered friendships, but she had one rather close girl-friend for a number of years. Her acquaintances regarded this friendship as something peculiar. Both young women took exceptional pride in their work and held equally fine positions; yet, despite their friendship, they seemed always to be competing against each other as rivals.

In her love life Alice had been unhappy and dissatisfied. In general she was somewhat retiring. During her work abroad (between ages 20-24), she maintained an intimate relationship with her married boss, but came back disappointed because, as she put it, he had jilted her. At the time she appeared to be "highly excitable" and had once suffered a fainting spell. In order to forget her unhappy love affair and to find complete fulfillment in her work, on the advice of her family physician she decided to complete her higher education. As already described, she pursued her studies with exceptional zeal, worked hard to the point of completing all requirements, and then gave it up.

According to statements by her relatives, as a child she did not scem like an ordinary girl. There was something of a tomboy about her, and this statement by informants meant that her demeanor was more calculating and intellectual than one would have expected from a girl. The family physician who knew Alice well described her as "an exceptionally fine, intelligent, industrious, thoroughly honest and respectable person." But he added, "All those years she had been too lonely, was incapable of assimilating her experiences, and had developed into a virtual monologuist through sheer loneliness." Her sister felt she had never been close to anyone, had remained independent, and had little sensitivity for her fellow men.

Her ideas were inflexible, and her development one-sidedly intellectual.

Her psychosis began insidiously and crept up slowly when Alice was 37. It developed at first as a delusion resulting from her sensitivity about her love relationship, as Kretschmer (1944) has described it. From "indications," or possibly also because of his silence, she had concluded that her employer was in love with her, indeed, that he was engaged to her. Her employer was a well known, ethical, highly respected, married man. There is no reason whatever to suspect that he had ever made the slightest advances toward her. Soon she began to complain that almost all her supervisors were molesting her with their coarse, erotic innuendos. She felt she was being ignored, mocked, ridiculed, and tormented because she refused their advances. She then claimed that wild sexual orgies were taking place in the business establishment where she worked. Actually it was a proper, orderly, and well-run place of business. She also believed she could detect the odor of urine about her person and that that was the reason for her quitting the job that she had held for many years. From that time on she remained doing nothing in her room, smoked incessantly, wrote formal complaints about the alleged bordello operation at her former place of employment, and finally procured a revolver to protect herself from her imagined pursuers. This was the reason for her hospitalization at our clinic. At the time she was 42.

In the period that followed, she turned out to be a rather difficult patient. She constantly voiced ideas about persecution, accused the chief physician and the nurses of having posted men wherever she went to observe her, even at her bath. Frequently she indulged in fits of scolding, became obstinate, unapproachable, and uncommunicative. She spoke distractedly and in confusion. In spite of that, for the most part, she performed the office duties assigned to her.

Until her death at age 66 she never recovered her mental health. After the full manifestation of her illness, a slight improvement took place that lasted just a few years, but then her condition took a menacing turn for the worse. When attempts were made to rehabilitate her at home, she mistreated and threatened her aging mother to the point where the latter's life was in danger. At the clinic she often stormed and raged and became violent. After many years of patiently administered work therapy, sudden release attempts, insulin treatments, and sleeping cures having resulted in only temporary improvements, a prefrontal lobotomy was attempted when proband was 51 years old. This surgery effected a marked improvement.

After this operation Alice was able to live outside hospitals until she died. She continued to live with her mother, and after the mother's death, with her sister. She did, however, continue to lead the life of a mental patient, spending almost all her time in her room reading, hardly speaking at all to her mother or sister, and never exchanging greetings with them. At times she stated explicitly that she was not a member of the family. She ate only once a day and cooked just for herself. She refused to do even the smallest household chores for her aging mother. Intermittently she did work again at her profession or took short vacations, staying with friends. Her death was sudden, at home, and since there was no autopsy, the cause was never established.

Evaluation: For this proband the term "schizoid-aberrant" quite obviously applies. Alice's schizoid nature is characterized by her emotional coldness which was noticeable externally; yet, any careful observer who knew her intimately would recognize the delicate sensitivity behind it. It is further marked by the disturbed communications with her family. Her enmity toward her parents is easy to understand, but not that toward her sister, who cared for her devotedly. To more casual acquaintances Alice appeared as a pure intellectual, lacking in human warmth and feminine charm. Her view of life was rigid and inflexible.

In contrast to Esther (Proband 22, below), however, I still characterized this schizoid development as being within the norm, and not as pathological. The principal reasons for classifying Esther's prepsychotic personality as pathological are lacking in Alice. Her intellectual and her vocational development were exceptionally good. She did not lack the capability to give and receive love, although she had only one great but unhappy love experience. Insofar as she suffered, her suffering was caused more by unhappy circumstances (the nature of her parents and feeling jilted by her lover) than by her own conduct.

In its beginning stages, Alice's psychosis, in the light of her life-long erotic frustrations and her increasing loneliness before her menopause, seems understandable in the same way

that the cases of sensitive affinity delusions described by Kretschmer (1918) do. It is tempting also to see the causal roots of a schizoid personality in the attitude of the parents toward the child.

Example of a Prepsychotic Personality as "Aberrant Other than Schizoid"

Walter L. (Proband 60), born 1904

Walter's father was a capable master grain miller, but the boy ran away from his father's mill and was disinherited for it. The father died when Walter was 9 years old. Walter's mother was married six times, and outlived all her six husbands. She was vigorous, vital, passionate, and impulsive where men were concerned. Until Walter's father died, the boy was raised in an apparently good and well-ordered household with his parents. After that, he was partly in orphan homes or with grandparents, and at times he was brutally mistreated and overburdened with work. He went only through elementary school.

After his basic schooling, he finished an apprenticeship as a gardener. Until his schizophrenia began, he worked in well-established greenhouses and nurseries and was a respected workman and employee.

From childhood on he had been good-natured, although difficult, too, because of his inclination simply to disappear. He would take a notion that he "just had to get away." Repeatedly and without apparent reason he would run away from his foster homes when he was a child, and later from his lodgings or job, just to travel or wander about for a while and then return. If he had no money he acquired it in some peculiar way, as for instance, by catching mice. In other respects, he was regarded as frugal, upright, and in no way aberrant in his behavior; he was gregarious and had good friends. His earnings were good, and he was a member of a religious youth group.

At age 25 he married a woman 10 years his senior. She was delicate and asthenic and had grown up under miserable circumstances with a father who was an alcoholic. She was extremely shy and anxious, and in constant fear of material distress or misery. Sexual relations between them were sparse, and there were no children. The wife felt as uncomfortable with her husband's easy manner as he did with her excessive concern over trifles. To her he seemed easily irritated, moody, unpredictable, and irresponsible. She therefore suffered when he started out on a vacation trip without enough funds and appeared not in the least worried about their finances.

The schizophrenic psychosis crept up slowly, beginning at age 32. Proband began working less and less efficiently and soon was unable to hold a job. He began to drink more and became interested in confusing philosophical and political dogmas, discussing these in a manner that soon branded him as "crazy" in the eyes of his associates. He engaged in irresponsible, debt-ridden business ventures. At home he defecated into fruit jars and placed these on the buffet for his wife to see. His reaction to any remonstrance about his behavior was generally one of silly, carefree flippancy. He would disappear with increasing frequency and would then be found in haylofts, in a filthy and unkempt condition.

Walter was first hospitalized when he was 38. At the clinic he persisted in displaying an asinine, gay exuberance. It was impossible to carry on a sensible conversation with him. Usually he gave monosyllabic, meaningless answers with frequent intermittent stoppages. He appeared to enjoy assigned tasks and, when questioned, insisted that he was completely happy with his lot. He reacted with complete indifference to his wife's request for a divorce. Personal hygiene was a problem that required constant admonition. The diagnosis was schizophrenia simplex.

In the 24 years that followed there was no appreciable change in Walter's condition. With his constant silly, slaphappy, and distracted behavior he seemed imbecilic to those around him. Nevertheless it was possible to place him in family care under medical supervision during this entire period; although these families' patience was often severely tried, especially because of his unclean personal habits. He now does only the simplest chores in the garden and the fields, and still runs away from time to time, hides in haylofts, where he is found, completely filthy.

Evaluation: The prepsychotic personality of the proband can be summarized as carefree, unruffled, and cheerful, with an unpredictable inclination to run away and to travel about. In this sense he was aberrant, but I did not choose to classify him as a psychopath. He had been a good, reliable worker in his job as a gardener, and until he married, he bothered nobody seriously with his behavior. The fact that his wife suffered severely under it before his psychosis began is mainly due to the irreconcilable differences in character

between the two, and only in small measure to the proband's personality. His compulsion to disappear is reminiscent of a poriomania, but primarily it seemed to be the consequence of his carefree, frivolous and exuberant attitude toward life. He was happy on his escapades, and considered his motivation to be something perfectly natural.

Typically schizoid characteristics include neither a frivolous, happy-go-lucky attitude nor phases of poriomanic wanderings; therefore I categorized the proband's premorbid personality as "aberrant, other than schizoid."

Example for Characterization of the Premorbid Personality as "Schizoid-Pathological"

Esther B. (Proband 22), born 1915

Esther's parents were from simple artisan families. She was raised at home with her parents, was well cared for; and yet, conditions during her childhood were not entirely favorable. For statistical purposes they were listed as neither good nor horrible. Her father had married late in life, after he had spent his early adult years as a typesetter in America and returned home with a small amount of savings. He had a hearing deficiency, was diabetic, and almost constantly depressive, and died of senile deterioration when the proband was 21. Her ties to him were not very close, and she easily recovered from his loss. Esther's mother had suffered with St. Vitus's dance as a child and was a timid, exceptionally nervous sort of person. She was friendly and kind and assumed her duties as mother and housekeeper with an attitude of meticulous precision. In her concern for the well-being of her only child she far exceeded the customary norms in shielding her from any sort of harm. For instance, at an age where any other girl is permitted to work with pointed scissors in doing needlework, Esther was permitted to use only scissors with rounded ends. Even when she was already going to school, her mother wanted her with her constantly, and limited her playtime with other children for fear that something might happen to her. She was not allowed to swim or to ride a bicycle. Her mother was given to complaining about life in general and to thinking anxiously and pessimistically about the future. In her old age she became demented with arteriosclerosis, and died at age 83, when proband was 45.

When Esther was born her father was 49 and her mother 38 years old. The couple, well along in years, wanted to care for and educate their only child as conscientiously as possible, but expected from her, in turn, some help and support when they became older and less able to care for themselves.

To outward appearances Esther's childhood and youth were uneventful. She went to public school as almost all other children did, and although she was not a good student, she never had to repeat a class. After basic schooling, she served an apprenticeship in a large grocery store as a salesgirl, but did not take her qualifying examinations. After her apprenticeship, at age 17, she took a job as housemaid in the French sector of Switzerland, as is customary for girls from the German sector when they reach that age. When she was 20 she came back home. From then on she worked as maid or servant in households, and as wardrobe checker, linen maid, or general houseworker in guest houses. She changed jobs frequently, because she always felt that she was being overworked, poorly paid, or just tired out. At times she lived with her mother, sometimes with her employers. When she prepared to leave her mother, quarrels and bickering developed between them, because her mother used every device possible to keep her living at home as much as possible.

Even before she started school her personality was already a peculiar combination of hurry, inquisitive curiosity, cheeky flippancy, general aimlessness, and restlessness. She was self-willed, and was often excitable and downright nasty. During free afternoons, according to her mother's explanation, she never wanted to go out with other children, but always only with her mother. According to her own, the reverse was true: she was not permitted to go out with other children, but only with her mother. She was never happy or gay during her time in school, as her friends were. She preferred to site quietly, more like an adult; she never acted as a child would be expected to act. During her 5th and 6th grades (at ages 12 and 13) her fidgety manner became conspicuous.

When she had come back from her sojourn in the French sector of Switzerland, she did not like it at home any more, although her mother made every possible attempt to please her. But she did not like conditions away from home either. For instance, sometimes she was afraid that she was going to be discharged when she had scarcely begun working in a new job.

She never kept company with boys. It is not known whether she ever had any interest in any of them, but she did masturbate frequently.

A number of years before her psychosis set in, the proband developed an exceptionally ambivalent attitude toward her mother, while she seemed indifferent toward her father. She held fast to this attitude in her psychosis until her mother died. On the one hand the proband complained that her mother was neglecting her and paid no attention to her, while in the same breath she complained that her mother was spending too much money on her and was spoiling her.

When she was 25, her psychosis began slowly to develop. Her suspicious nature became more pronounced; she claimed that everyone was cheating her and stealing from her. She finally lost her job because she voiced her prejudicial ideas with increasingly arrogant excitement. At age 26, when this had happened, she was medically examined for the first time. She was clearly distracted and full of crass contradictions in her long, wearisome verbal ramblings. In the following period, she could hold jobs for only a short time, and was first hospitalized in a private sanatorium. She then came to Burghölzli on June 6, 1942, at age 27, when she also became a proband for this study. The diagnosis of schizophrenia was supported by her distraction, her rigid autism, her lack of emotional flexibility, and her numerous delusionary ideas in a prejudicial sense.

The proband was hospitalized for only 9 months for her psychosis. During the first 24 years that she was known to us after 1942, she was able to make her own way outside the clinic by accepting simple jobs, but she remained eccentric and full of prejudicial ideas. After her mother fell ill of cerebral sclerosis and died, a marked improvement set in. At the end of this study she was 48 years old.

As long as her mother was alive, the proband complained about her constantly and felt in every way wronged and tormented by her. On the other hand, she never made a decision to break away from her mother, but always went back to her, seeking her help. The rest of her psychotic behavior may be characterized principally as a transference from her pathologically divisive attitude toward her mother to her attitude towards all doctors and others who attended to her needs. She continually scolded and complained vulgarly about the clinics and the doctors who had treated her; she felt that she was being destroyed by them, that they did not understand her, that they spent no time with her, and wanted just to torment her. On the other hand, she went back to those same doctors time and time again, seeking their protection and advice and requesting interviews and treatment. She was torn between her bitter refusal of any sort of help and her supplicant, pleading requests for it. Accordingly, her expression was at one time paranoic-aggressive, and the next time childish, kindly, and helpless.

When one has become immersed for years in a development such as the one just described, one is constrained to regard the dichotomous attitude of the subject toward her mother and the mother-substitute persons as the reflection of a dichotomous attitude of the parents toward their child. The aging parents had spoiled, overpampered, and shielded their child from external harm out of excessive concern and conscientiousness; yet, they constantly thought of their own infirmity with approaching old age, and saw in that same child the brave and strong young girl that would keep and care for her parents in their old age. In her psychosis the patient rebels against the unwarranted expectation that she came into the world in order to provide security for her parents' senescence. But motivated by helplessness and a sense of duty, she morbidly seeks contact and protection from her mother, her doctors, and her employers.

Evaluation: It seems plain that Esther B. can be prepsychotically designated as schizoid. She was always exceptionally lacking in human contacts, she did not play with other children, had no friends, no lovers, was cold and indifferent toward her father, even on the occasion of his death, and felt persecuted and prejudicially treated by all her employers. She was difficult to understand emotionally and generally gloomy and cheerless. Her attitude toward her mother was extremely dichotomous; she had been a child difficult to comprehend.

I felt much less secure in deciding whether Esther was to be classified as "schizoid aberrant within the norm" or as "pathologically schizoid." To me she seemed to be a borderline case. After much contemplation, I did decide to include her among the "schizoid-pathologicals." She herself, as well as her mother, constantly suffered severely because of her behavior. Her suspicious attitude toward her employers made impossible any advancement in her job that would be equal to her intelligence or her ability potentials. Her lack of any ability to give or receive love and her excessive masturbation also mark her erotic development as abnormal.

With the decision of schizoid and pathological in the case of Esther B., however, I did not intend to determine that hers was a case of constitutional schizoid psychopathy. It seems instead more likely, especially in the case of this patient, that her schizoid development was closely related to the unwholesome conditions generated by her parents during childhood.

Example for the Characterization of the Premorbid Personality as "Pathological Other than Schizoid"

Magdalena B. (Proband 1), born 1908

Proband is the 7th child of 10. Her father worked in a tannery, was a quiet, kindly man, a steady worker, who did the best he could in caring for his family, and remained stoical and somewhat aloof toward his wife's difficult personality and the family's poverty. He died at age 83 of arteriosclerosis, when Magdalena was already 46. The mother was described by some of the children as exemplary, while Magdalena reported a dismal picture of her. Her picture agreed with observations of the welfare authorities. It must be assumed as valid, therefore, that she was an industrious, although an inefficient worker around the home, that she was rude, domineering, and quarrelsome, and was careless about keeping her household clean. She was able to conceal her difficult personality from many, while others branded her as a gossip and a hypocrite. Her argumentive nature increased with time, until it led to a lawsuit. She died at age 76 of heart attack, when Magdalena was 40.

Magdalena grew up among her 6 siblings (3 had died early), almost ignored by her father and badly brought up by her mother, in virtual poverty. Nonetheless, the family had sufficient food, clothing, and shelter. In later examinations Magdalena's intelligence tested as below average, although not defective. She was different in every way from her siblings. While most of them got along well with their parents (surprisingly enough!), Magdalena was a rebel from her childhood on. As far back as she can remember, she hated her parents, and she did leave home early in life, and made a point of not caring anything about them. Up to the time of her death, she never knew whether or when her parents had died, and did not wish to know. She attended school only as long as the law prescribed; then she accepted the simplest and most irregular kind of employment with families and taverns, and not necessarily in good ones. After her puberty she became sexually promiscuous and bore an illegitimate child at 21. Thereupon her parents persuaded her to marry a feeble-minded farmhand. There were four children as offspring of this marriage, all of whom later became criminals and partly sexually promiscuous, and of whom 2 are feebleminded. Her oldest, the illegitimate child, whom she did not raise, developed normally. At age 27 Magdalena was sterilized.

As a consequence of the husband's feeble-mindedness and the difficult personality of the proband, the marriage relationship was appalling. The horror of it surpasses what an average human being could imagine as possible. The husband was such a poor worker that he could scarcely find employment even as a farmhand. He often soiled his clothing. Magdalena completely neglected her household. Intermittently the husband, then the wife, simply left home. Magdalena had frequent affairs with other men. With the passage of time, all 4 children became increasingly difficult to control. The family had to be supported on welfare, and the children were intermittently placed in foster care. Magdalena's behavior was irresponsible and shameless. She was in constant conflict with the authorities; then shamelessly demanded their support. When her children were taken from her, she argued and haggled, using every available means until she got them back. All her children, as they grew up, became sexually promiscuous without a shred of shame or inhibition. On one occasion the proband purposely led her feebleminded husband, 20 years older than she, into a compromising situation with strange children, whom he then molested. She then reported him to the police, and when he had been arrested, she was glad to be able to carry on her own extramarital affairs without interference. Through all this she remained garrulous, vivacious, extroverted, and excitable. She lied all the time. The unanimous judgment of her community was: "an appalling woman."

Under these circumstances the proband developed a slowly creeping hebephrenic schizophrenia when she was about 27 years old. She became completely silly in her behavior, and so distracted that it was almost impossible to carry on a conversation with her.

Between ages 27 and 36 she was six times committed to psychiatric hospitals, because her chronic psychotic condition was developing into acute episodes. During this period she spent a total of 23 months in psychiatric clinics. Her diagnoses indicated: "hebephrenic schizophrenic psychosis," and initially also "heboid." During these episodes the proband often had spells of silly excitement, reminiscent of a performing clown. During these times she was impossible to contact emotionally or intellectually. She expressed absurd ideas, partly just playful delusionary notions and partly fixed delusions (for instance, that the authorities had falsified her personal records). Intermittently, exceptional conditions of catatonia appeared. During one of these she lay on the floor and held her legs stretched rigidly upward.

After her sixth release from a hospital a divorce from her husband was granted. She then married a man with whom she had carried on an affair during her first marriage. Like the first husband, this one was also feeble-minded, but more domesticated and better able to work. During one of her catatonic episodes she had already claimed to be his wife, a statement that had been evaluated at the time as a delusionary idea. But now something amazing took place. After Magdalena's psychosis had undergone a chronic development when she was 27, and had had six acute exacerbations with psychiatric hospitalizations behind her, she remained with her second husband from age 36 to 54, until she died, experienced no further serious psychotic relapse; and although she did not completely recover her mental health, she certainly was improved and to a great extent socially rehabilitated. She lived with her second husband without ever again calling for aid from the authorities. A clergyman who ministered to her during these years, writes the following appropriate statement:

"She lied with the greatest of ease, but one couldn't be angry with her because she had to lie to make herself feel important. She was quick to hate anyone, especially those who dared to contradict her. She needed to assert herself, drank secretly, and when her husband died, she really wanted to die."

Evaluation: It seems obvious that in Magdalena's case a pathological personality development is the applicable term. The life she led made her incapable as a homemaker or a mother. She neglected her children in every way, especially from the standpoint of morals.

She herself ignored every vestige of human morals and could be spitefully malicious in the extreme. She was sexually so promiscuous that her sterilization, to which she agreed, seemed justified. She herself suffered under her constant hatred and prejudicial notions toward others.

I would, however, not care to label her pathological development as schizoid. Her personality is marked by her unbridled, instinctive nature, a need to assert her self-importance, her lack of inhibitions, her lack of consideration for others, and her disregard for obligations. In the main, the proband was extroverted; she vented her hatred by screaming at her adversary face-to-face; in a coarse way she was sensitive; she sought human contacts with a fierce passion.

A psychopathic personality is apparent in the subject, if one looks for it, and the same natural disposition in her mother and in her legitimate children might be regarded as indications of hereditary transmission. There also are, to be sure, weighty indications in

life the improvement from her psychosis was not the only amazing development; there was also her loyalty to her second husband. She, who had hated her parents, who wanted no more contact with her siblings, who had neglected and mistreated her children, who had persecuted her first husband with shocking maliciousness, who seemed to be devoid of human emotions, who had had countless paramours, now formed a close marital bond with a second man—a bond that lasted well over a decade. She was severely shaken by his death; in fact to such a degree that her minister actually wondered whether she had died of grief. She had died at home of severe dropsy with decubitus, and no autopsy was performed.

In the following paragraphs the prepsychotic characters of our 208 probands are first to be compared with those of 190 schizophrenic probands who were hospital admissions (not existing inpatients) among my New York and my Pfäfers probands:

Prepsychotic characters of probands	208 Principal Probands	New York and Pfäfers probands
Nonaberrant	62 = 30%	57 = 30%
Schizoid aberrant within the norm	59 = 28%	62 = 33%
Otherwise aberrant within the norm	9 = 4%	14 = 7%
Schizoid pathological	50 = 24%	47 = 25%
Otherwise pathological	28 = 13%	10 = 5%

support of the attempt to interpret the entire development as the result of neglect and a character neurosis. Magdalena's mother already had basically the same personality as she, though she was not nearly as antisocial. Magdalena had been poorly brought up; her mother was no fitting example for her to follow, and her father gave her no encouragement. She had not learned a trade. Her eccentric way of life from puberty on was partly the result of a spite reaction against her parents. Having to marry a feebleminded old moral delinquent after having borne someone else's illegitimate child was truly one of life's great injustices. Her continued decline into antisocial behavior can be partly interpreted as a reaction to that circumstance.

Magdalena's history may also serve as an expository example in the section on schizophrenic outcomes. In the last 15 years of her

The conformity of the figures is amazing, considering that the probands came from such widely different areas as the Canton of St. Gallen, the Canton of Zürich, and the area around New York, that the average ages of the three groups of probands were decades apart, and that the type and number of informants used for each of these groups were different. Particularly interesting is that the two most important sets of figures coincide exactly, the percentages of the nonaberrant, and the percentages of the schizoid pathological groups. Under these circumstances, the percentages of the different prepsychotic characters of all three groups of recent hospital admissions, from our own, the Pfäfers, and the New York clinics, may be calculated together, resulting in the following figures:

The prepsychotic characters of all 398 schizophrenics hospitalized in psychiatric clins break down as follows:

Nonaberrant	119 =	30%
Schizoid aberrant within the norm	121 =	30%
Otherwise aberrant within the norm	23 =	6%
Schizoid pathological	97 =	24%
Otherwise pathological	38 =	10%

To summarize, among schizophrenics being admitted to psychiatric hospitals, about $\frac{1}{3}$ are prepsychotically nonaberrant and schizoid aberrant within the norm, $\frac{1}{4}$ are schizoid pathological, and the rest, otherwise aberrant or otherwise pathological.

Information on siblings in Chapter 5 shows that among the schizophrenic siblings of probands, a few more were prepsychotically aberrant and fewer were schizoid than the above figures would indicate. The difference is not significant and could be by chance. It also could be explained by saying that the schizophrenias of the probands' siblings are milder than those of all the probands themselves (see p. 201 and Table 4.4), and that the schizophrenias of patients who were prepsychotically nonaberrant also were milder than those of the prepsychotic schizoids.

Neither among any groups of the average population, nor among any other given group of mentally ill, are there nearly as many schizoid aberrant and schizoid pathological prepsychotics as there are among schizophrenics. For comparison, the following may be mentioned: Among the 200 medical patients of the Liestal hospital, whom I personally examined and treated, I found, in accordance with the same criteria, 1 single schizoid psychopath; and among the 100 tubercular patients newly admitted under Rapoport (1935) and me, there were no schizoid pathological patients and just one schizoid aberrant.[1] With the introduction of

the concept "schizoid" after the turn of the century, the psychiatrists had the great good fortune of having available a handy term for characterizing the essential traits of the prepsychotic personality of schizophrenics. The accumulation of schizoid traits in the prepsychotic personality characterizes the schizophrenics as a group, but the frequency of broken homes does not. Accordingly, one loses the sense of proportion when in modern research the concept "schizoid" is omitted from discussions on the genesis of schizophrenias, and that on the broken home is placed prominently into the foreground. To be sure, only about half the schizophrenics have premorbid schizoid personality traits, while the other half certainly does not. The schizoid personality in the prepsychotic period cannot be assigned an absolute causative role in the genesis of the schizophrenias.

My own findings and those of previous authors about the great importance of the schizoid personality in the prepsychotic history of schizophrenics are being proved correct by the more recent twin studies. Kringlen (1968), among others, found that in a pair of twins, the one who becomes schizophrenic was the one who was more often, before his psychosis, reserved, lonely, hypersensitive, or obsessive-compulsive than the other one, who remains normal. The qualifications mentioned above include the same traits listed for the concept "schizoid," as the older authors understood it. Obedience and the strong dependency relationship to others, which Kringlen (1968) also found predominant in the premorbid history of the schizophrenic twin, apply less accurately to the concept "schizoid."

There is no difference in the breakdown of the prepsychotic characters as between schizophrenic men and women. The five categories

1. While investigating the entire population of a certain area in Sweden, Essen-Moeller (1956) found more schizoids among them than I did among the representatives of the Swiss population. But in Essen-Moeller's probands the frequency of schizoids among the general population is still much less than it is among future schizophrenics. Essen-Moeller distinguishes schizoids with major and with minor personality disorders. The minor personality disorders correspond approximately to the schizoids within the norm of this study, and the major personality disorders to the schizoid-pathologicals. Essen-Moeller found that the schizoid personality is more frequent among men than among women. Below are the figures for the general population group he studied:

	Men	Women
Schizoids with minor personality deviations	3.6%	1%
Schizoids with major personality deviations	2.4%	0.8%
Total schizoids	6%	1.8%

The greater frequency of schizoids among representatives of the average population studied by Essen-Moeller compared to that among my representatives of the average population might still be due to chance. It is possible, too, that Essen-Moeller has widened his definition of the concept "schizoid." It is less probable, however, that the differences in these findings reflect real differences between the Swiss and the Swedish populations.

are distributed among the 100 men in the ratio of 28:32:3:23:14, and among the 108 women as 34:27:6:27:14.[2]

But there is a difference in the frequency of schizoid psychopathies, if the statistics come from an inpatient clinic population instead of from hospital admissions. The most severe cases occur among this first group, and there is a positive correlation between prepsychotic schizoid psychopathy and adverse courses of illness. This correlation was first impressively demonstrated by the Kretschmer school. Among the Pfäfers and the New York probands, 190 became probands as clinical admissions, and 161 as clinic population (existing inpatients). Among the first group, 25 percent were schizoid psychopaths, and among the latter, 47 percent. Among my schizophrenics from the Basel University Clinic who had good remission under insulin- or cardiac-shock treatments, there were only 6 percent schizoid psychopaths (5 of 89). In my investigations of 130 late schizophrenics there were fewer schizoid psychopaths than among the majority of schizophrenics, although the difference was not significant.

My earlier investigations further showed that schizophrenics of above-average intelligence were more often schizoid psychopaths before their psychosis than those of average intelligence. Two causes may be contributory to bringing about this difference. Exceptional intelligence shows a positive correlation with exceptional character. Besides, the characteristic descriptions are more often applied to people from an intellectual environment than to people from a simple one, so that the qualification schizoid is more often applied to the intellectuals.

The Intelligence of the 208 Probands

The principal sources for checking the intelligence of the probands were their school records and an intelligence test administered

2. According to Essen-Moeller (1956) (see footnote 1), there are more schizoids among men than among women of the general population, a finding that is also supported by my own studies. Among the future schizophrenic men, however, suicides occur with equal frequency as among future schizophrenic women. Why this difference? It is possible to relate it to other findings. The schizoid personality under pressures of horrible childhood conditions seems to play a more important role in the schizophrenias of women than in those of men. This kind of explanation, of course is mere conjecture for the time being.

to them during their hospitalization. Educational standards in the Canton of Zürich during the childhood of these probands were relatively uniform in comparison to other regions and other periods in time. If one understood that school system well, the conclusions about intelligence derived from school records applied in the majority of cases. Such conclusions did have to be carefully evaluated and adjusted if the student had moved frequently, had been ill, or had had frequent character-involving disciplinary problems. But usually such exceptions were well documented. The intelligence test given at the clinic, in contrast to education and knowledge of the elementary basic subjects, such as reading, writing, and arithmetic, consisted of a test of practical understanding, such as the system of measurement, and a test of combined and abstract thinking capability, adminstered primarily by means of the patient's submission of stories and drawings. The IQ was determined in only a minority of cases. A few severe psychotic conditions made impossible any systematic attempts at intelligence testing during the proband's hospitalization. As a final check on describing the proband's intelligence, his efficiency on the job was always considered.

The principal indicators of an average intelligence included smooth progress in primary and secondary school and in the apprenticeship, but without special recognition of merit; the ability to perform adequately in a trade on the nonintellectual level; an estimated IQ near 100 (about 95–105). An above-average intelligence was assumed when the above-mentioned schools were passed with meritorious mention, or when high-school or college examinations were passed without difficulty, and the estimated IQ was over 105. Below-average intelligence was assumed when difficulty was encountered even at the basic educational level, that is, if one or two classes had to be repeated, if the proband was fit only for unskilled or menial jobs, and if the IQ was estimated between 90 and 95. Feeblemindedness was assumed when basic education was insurmountable (special classes, frequent repetitions), if job capability was such that even unskilled labor proved difficult because of intellectual insufficiency, and if the IQ was estimated between 70 and 90. Among the probands there were no instances of imbecility.

Among the 208 probands

38 = 18 percent were of above-average intelligence

104 = 50 percent were of average intelligence

51 = 25 percent were of below-average intelligence

15 = 7 percent were feebleminded.

There were more men of above-average intelligence than women (27 percent as against 10 percent), but there were more women of average intelligence than men (46 percent as against 54 percent). The reason for the difference is the manner of determining intelligence. Above-average intelligence was bound to be particularly conspicuous if the subject had had a higher education or distinguishing professional achievements were on record. But among the women, a much smaller percentage than men had enjoyed the benefits of a higher education, and a much smaller portion had the opportunity to achieve professional recognition. Quite often an exceptional degree of intelligence was found concealed behind the distractions and emotional changes during a psychosis, indicating that intelligence tests at the clinic fell far short of revealing all the outstanding intelligence levels among the women, who had not had the opportunity of being recognized for distinguished achievement in school or on the job.

The distribution of intelligence levels among the Pfäfers and the Basel schizophrenics of my earlier investigations agrees precisely with that of the men in this study, and most of that former group of probands were men. As a group, the New York schizophrenic probands had by far the most above-average intelligence patients.

Is the Determinant Factor a Congenital Schizoid Psychopathy or Abnormal Schizoid Behavior due to Environmental Stress?

During the first decades of this century the dominant inclination was to interpret the pathological schizoid character as an inherited, or a constitutional peculiarity, that is, as a psychopathy. In the same sense also, there seemed to be a correlation between the schizoid and an emaciated physique. In later years, however, a number of authors (Alanen 1966, Arieti 1955, Planansky 1966, and others) called attention to the other possibility that an unfavorable environment could drive a person to schizoid behavior that would become a permanent part of him. Autism and emotional rigidity may be interpreted as pro-

tective devices against intolerable experiences. Since we know that, according to Kretschmer, the different types of physiques are differently distributed among the different age groups, and that they are also dependent on the individual's habits and customs, the correlation between the schizoid and an emaciated physique is not really a decisive refutation of the assumption that the schizoid personality can be acquired.

In the beginning I attempted to check whether schizoid personality traits existed from earliest childhood on, or to what age their existence could be traced back. Alanen (1966) found that the schizoid personality is not necessarily always present from earliest childhood on, but that it often develops only later in life. Of course, the assumption would be false that the schizoid character has to be congenital or inherited if it is manifest in early childhood. It would be just as incorrect to assume the opposite, that a schizoid character was not necessarily hereditary, but was caused by the environment, if it did not become obvious until later in life. Unfavorable environmental influences could just as easily affect the character development early in life as later. An inherited trait does not necessarily have to become manifest in early childhood, but could also easily emerge later, for instance, during the physiological developmental crises at various stages in life. Despite this, it is important to a discussion of the genesis of the schizoid to know at what age the schizoid traits become evident.

On the basis of my data on the childhood development of the 208 principal probands of this study, I cannot with certainty answer the question as to the age at which the schizoid traits became evident. Data on the behavior of the probands during infancy and early childhood years are incomplete. Many of the parents were already dead at the beginning of the investigations, others were changed by senility, and others again were simply too nonliterate to be able to report on the early development of their children. For some of the probands that childhood occurred as long ago as the past century. But a clear set of data concerning their character during their school years and beyond, does exist for most of the probands.

As already shown, pathologically schizoid traits were found among 50 of the 208 probands. Most of the probands revealed them as early as during their early school years, that is, 37 of the 50. For 9 of the probands it was uncertain whether these traits had existed during their school years or had become evident only afterwards. For 4 probands it was certain that after an inconspicuous behavior pattern in childhood, the pathologically schizoid change first occurred during their adolescence or later. In mitigation of these facts, however, I must say that I did not include as schizoid character traits any personality changes that preceded the eruption of a schizophrenic psychosis by just a few weeks or months.

The finding that most of the pathological schizoid characters already became evident during the early school years applies equally to both sexes.

The data from our 208 probands become more revealing when they are extended to show whether the schizoid traits can be interpreted as a consequence of adverse environmental conditions.

Twenty-nine of the 50 probands with pathologically schizoid personalities had endured horrible childhoods and gave evidence of their schizoid traits early in childhood in a close time-relationship with their misery. "Horrible" is here meant in its fullest sense. These were cases of incredible childhood suffering, to a degree that most people would deem impossible to occur in this day and age. In contemplating these grief-laden childhood histories, it is hard to imagine how a child exposed to such misery could have developed otherwise than pathologically schizoid. The horror of the childhood environment of 25 probands was obvious to everyone who knew the child. These children were cruelly mistreated and neglected, or they were constantly being moved from one wretched foster care facility to one that was even worse. At the end of this section the childhood of Sigismund K. (Proband 84) is described as an example of an obviously gruesome, traumatizing childhood. The home environment of 4 of the probands appeared to outside observers to be normal and orderly. Not until the more detailed study of the actual emotional condition of the proband was undertaken, was the appalling distress discovered that these children had suffered during their childhood. Isidor R. (Proband 74) is an example of this, as is the childhood of Hans K. (Proband 29), described on pp. 117–19.

In 18 of the pathologically schizoid patients no childhood conditions were disclosed that would have been classified unequivocally as "horrible." In all these cases it can be argued whether pathogenic or psychotraumatic childhood conditions are to be considered, but in none of them would anyone be inclined to say that their childhoods were normal or unimpaired. Ominous shadows darkened each of these young lives, be it through the early loss of a parent, an onset of mental illness in one of the parents, poverty for which the parents were responsible, intellectual insufficiency on part of the child to the demands placed on him, the bitterness of a parent about his working conditions, or the unhappy marriage of his parents. In all these probands one can at least suspect that the adversity of conditions under which he had to live had something to do with the development of a pathologically schizoid personality. Rosmarie N. (Proband 13) and Ida A. (Proband 20), whose childhoods are described at the end of this section, belong to this group of patients for whom a psychotraumatic childhood environment seems probable, although to a lesser degree of certainty than was the case for the group with actually horrible childhood environments. Another example of this was Esther B. (Proband 22), who has been described above (pp. 159–61) as a pathological schizoid.

Three pathological-schizoid probands remain, for whom no basis was found for suspecting any mental damage during childhood. Of course, even these children had suffered stresses, and their childhoods were far removed from what one would consider ideal. According to all appearances, however, no psychotraumatic stresses were evident that would exceed what most people had to endure in their childhoods. In 1 of these patients the schizoid emerged under psychotraumatic conditions only after she had matured. In another the schizoid traits emerged after maturity without any psychotraumatic condition in evidence, just a few years before the onset of the psychosis. The question suggests itself whether the emergence of the schizoid traits might not have been the forerunners of the slowly developing psychosis.

Only 1 patient, in whom childhood conditions had been normal according to everything we knew about them, developed clearly discernible schizoid traits during his childhood. The question arises, was this a case of an unfavorable congenital developmental predisposition, or would a more thorough investigation have revealed an unknown psychotraumatic environment after all? The question cannot be answered.

Of the 23 schizoid-pathological men, 12

grew up under horrible childhood conditions; and of the 27 schizoid-pathological women, 17. So the women grew up under horrible childhood conditions somewhat more often than the men, although the difference is by no means significant.

Those probands who had schizoid-pathological traits before their psychosis, much more often grew up under horrible childhood conditions than those who were prepsychotically normal and nonaberrant,[3] as the following figures show.

Childhood conditions	Among 50 probands who were schizoid pathological before their psychosis	Among 62 probands who were prepsychotically nonaberrant
Normal, nonpsychotraumatic	3	25
Disturbed, possibly psychotraumatic	18	24
Horrible, severely psychotraumatic	29	13

These figures reveal a highly significant relationship between horrible childhood conditions and a schizoid-pathological personality: $p < 0.005 \cdot 2 \times 3$ area table, χ^2-Test with Yates' consistency correction $\chi^2_{corr.} = 10.85$, $df = 2$.

From this it may be concluded that, if a horrible, severely psychotraumatic environ-

---

3. Rodnick and Garmezy (1957, 1959), and after them Baxter et al. (1960, 1961, 1962, 1963, 1964 and 1966), compared data from the premorbid histories of schizophrenics with different prepsychotic personality traits, distinguishing between "good" and "poor" prepsychotic personalities. They hold the characteristics of a "good" personality to include the ability to make social contacts and to enjoy a satisfying sex life. They found that schizophrenics with a "good" prepsychotic personality most often came from families with a domineering father and a dominated mother. Conversely, the schizophrenics with a "poor" prepsychotic personality frequently had an excessively domineering mother and a weak father. Tension crises were especially frequent occurrences in these families.

It is doubtful that the findings of these authors would lend themselves to comparison with our material. Neither do the "poor" personalities of the American authors correspond exactly to my "schizoids," nor are the adverse family relationships described by the same criteria in the two sets of studies. Despite this, it is possible that the results of both investigations reflect the same basic psychological postulates, namely, that exceptional adversity and extremes in family conditions existed with greater frequency among schizophrenics who were unfit for life before their illness than among schizophrenics who appeared normal premorbidly.

ment in childhood really had a causal relationship to a future schizophrenia, it would usually at first produce a schizoid behavior, and the schizophrenic psychosis would develop out of that schizoid personality. The same idea could also be formulated: Insofar as childhood misery has any genetic relationship to a future schizophrenia, it is indirect, in that to begin with, it presupposes a schizoid personality change.

The fact of the strong correlation between horrible childhood conditions and a schizoid-pathological personality in childhood, however, in no way proves that the schizoid personality can be interpreted psychologically, and is not inherited. The horrible childhood conditions are by far most often the result of schizophrenia, schizoid-pathological personality, alcoholism, or other personality disturbances in the parents. To a lesser degree these same personality disorders play a part among the grandparents and the siblings. For this reason it is necessary to consider also an hypothesis of congenital pathology. If the schizoid personality is transmissible by heredity, the conditions under which children are raised and educated would also be tainted in those families where congenital personality disturbances are prominent. The miserable conditions of the children in such families would continue to be classified as "psychotraumatic," but the schizoid personality would not be the result of a mental trauma. In short, the correlation between the schizoid personality and wretched conditions in childhood can as easily be interpreted as resulting from congenital-pathological as from psychodynamic influences. This correlation agrees neatly with the assumption that schizophrenias may be interpreted as the interplay of congenital developmental tendencies of the personality and the human environment.

In the discussion of the genesis of schizoid personality changes, the data concerning the siblings of schizoids is obviously of primary importance. Of course, we are not certain how often siblings would have personality disorders if the schizoid personality change were hereditary, because the hereditary modus is not known. As Kahn (1923) explained it, it would presumably be dominant, so that at least about 50 percent schizoids could be expected among the siblings. Whether this percentage is valid cannot be accurately determined because of the imprecise definition of the schizoid personality. A somewhat more accurate prognosis of the findings on siblings can be made on the basis of the psychodynamic hypothesis concerning the origin of the schizoid personality. If it is not the congenital personality, but the wretched environmental conditions that bring about the schizoid behavior, then all siblings who grew up in the same adverse environment should theoretically, become schizoid in the same way. The most obvious flaw in this statement is that no two siblings ever grow up in exactly the same wretched circumstances. Their position in birth order, their sex, their appearance, and other factors invariably determine differences in the attitude of the parents toward them. Still one might presume that one ought to be able to recognize in the psychotraumatic genesis of a schizoid personality that the schizoids among a group of siblings were exposed to more deleterious influences than were the nonaberrant in that same group of siblings. Is that assumption justified?

It can now be determined that among those siblings of probands who grew up in an adverse environment and who manifested schizoid personalities early in life, as is to be expected, more personality disturbances occurred than among those siblings of probands who grew up in a normal environment and who revealed no personality aberrations in childhood. Nevertheless, there were many normal personalities in the first group, and also a number of pathological ones in the second.

This statement is based on the following figures: Adverse personality developments of all types (psychopathies, character neuroses, addictions, recidivist depressions of mild degree, or persistent mild depressions) occur
—among the siblings[4] of patients who were prepsychotically nonaberrant and who grew up under normal conditions (10 of 98 = 10 percent)
—among the siblings of patients who were prepsychotically schizoid-pathological and grew up under horrible conditions (19 of 69 = 28 percent).

The difference between 10 percent and 28 percent is statistically significant $(0.01 >$

$p > 0.001)$. If the depressive developments are excluded, the following figures apply
—for the siblings[4] of patients who were prepsychotically nonaberrant and who grew up under normal conditions (4 of 98 = 4 percent)
—for the siblings (see n. 4) of patients who were prepsychotically schizoid-pathological and grew up under horrible conditions (12 of 69 = 17 percent).

The difference between 4 percent and 17 percent is statistically significant $(0.01 > p_\chi > 0.001)$.

It would have been interesting, as was done for the probands, to count only the schizoid-pathological cases among the siblings, too, instead of considering all abnormal personality developments as a group. I had to abandon that refinement for two reasons: (a) the figure for schizoid-pathological siblings is so small that it is statistically insignificant, and (b) the siblings had not been as precisely investigated as the probands and I was uncertain, as I was also with the probands, whether the classification "schizoid-pathological" was justifiably indicated. On this occasion it occurred to me that the most diverse types of personality disturbances occurred after a childhood of adversities. One sibling may become addicted, another unstable, a third schizoid-eccentric, etc. There certainly is no single unequivocal relationship between childhood adversity and a schizoid-pathological development. Adverse conditions in childhood can at best comprise only one of a number of predispositions for a schizoid development. Anyone would already find convincing evidence for this conclusion in numerous other experiences from psychiatric practice.

Of course, I also wondered whether differences might be found in the frequency of actual schizophrenias among the siblings of the two groups of probands compared above (siblings of probands who were prepsychotically nonaberrant and grew up under normal conditions, and siblings of probands who were prepsychotically schizoid-pathological and grew up under horrible conditions). But no such differences exist among my probands. In the first-mentioned group there were 9 schizophrenics from a basic figure[5] of 90.5, that is,

4. Includes all siblings except those who died before age 10. The age distribution is similar in both groups.

5. The basic figure for schizophrenias is calculated in the usual way, as it was for other parts of the study. Siblings under 18 are not counted, siblings between 18

10 percent, and 6 schizophrenics in the second group from a basic figure of 64, that is, 9 percent. With a high degree of correlation between horrible childhoods and the genesis of schizophrenias, one would have expected to find differences. The figures are too small to reveal weak correlations in general.

It is noticeable, however, that schizophrenias occur more frequently among sisters of patients who grew up under horrible conditions than among their brothers, although the difference does not quite attain statisical significance.[6] If statistical significance had been attained, we could assume that while horrible childhood conditions predispose brothers and sisters of future schizophrenics equally to a variety of nonpsychotic personality disorders, these conditions predispose only their sisters to schizophrenic onset. Many arguments for and against this assumption could be raised. It means little, as long as it is based only on the described comparison; yet, it does agree with a number of other, more reliable findings among our data, according to which girls, rather than boys, are vulnerable to later schizophrenic onset when conditions in childhood were unhappy.

Further checks were made as to whether brothers and sisters behaved similarly in respect to the described comparisons, but there were no differences that even approached statistical significance.

Did the normal siblings of schizoid patients grow up under less adverse conditions than those probands themselves? Is there a relationship to be found between the degree of childhood misery that each sibling had to

---

and 40 are halved, and siblings over 40 are counted in full. Since the sibmates are in most cases quite old, the adjustment for age structure has little influence on the basic figure.

6. Among all the siblings of probands who grew up in a horrible environment, 136 were males and 126 females. Among the males 7, and among the females 14 were schizophrenic $(0.20 > p\ 0.10)$. If not all siblings of probands from horrible environments are included, but only those who were schizoid-pathological during childhood, there were 3 schizophrenics among 38 brothers and 3 among 31 sisters; all 38 brothers and 31 sisters were over 10 years old. By applying Weinberg's abbreviated method for age correction, the onset probability for schizophrenia among the brothers is calculated at 9 percent $(3:34.5)$, and among the sisters at 10 percent $(3:29.5)$. There is absolutely no statistical significance in the difference in these figures.

endure and his psychic state of mind?

The question cannot be answered unequivocally. Often one might suspect that the schizoid child was exposed to more severe psychotraumatic influences than his siblings who remained healthy. In many other cases no such correlation can be determined. If it cannot be determined, the same nagging, unanswerable question emerges: Could such a correlation be established if it were possible to study the family in even greater detail?

At first I attempted to count how often a correlation between the degree of psychotraumatic stress on the individual siblings and their psychic state of mind could be established. I soon had to stop counting. Those correlations are much too complicated and too variegated, and their evaluation is much too subjective, ever to be grasped by a set of figures. But I did determine that in many cases it is obvious that the proband who was schizoid in early childhood had more suffering to endure during that childhood than his nonschizoid siblings. Most often the reason was that the schizoid proband suffered greater stress because the others were intellectually more gifted. Often the schizoid was the least gifted. He grew up in the shadow of those superior to him intellectually, and was either less esteemed by his parents or even actively mistreated (Examples: Hans K., Proband 29 (mentioned earlier); Isidor R., Proband 74 (see below); Rosmarie N., Proband 13 (see below); Ida A., Proband 20 (see below). But in other, rarer cases, the schizoid was the most gifted among his siblings. He suffered most under the circumstance that, because of the parents' pathological lack of affection and sympathy or other adverse circumstances, neither he nor his siblings could be properly educated or trained in accordance with their abilities.

These statements are based on the study of individual cases. They could not be supported by statistics that compare the frequency of average intelligence among probands with nonaberrant personalities, who came from a normal environment, with those who were schizoid-pathological and came from a horrible environment. It is also less important whether a child's intelligence is different from that of the average population, than whether it is different from the intellectual norms prevailing in his family.

Additional schizoid probands grew up at a disadvantage in comparison to their siblings for the following reasons

—Often the proband was the youngest and lost one or both of his parents at a more tender age than his siblings
—Often the schizoid proband was in longer and closer contact with a pathological parent than his siblings
—One female proband was, as the only sibling of a psychopathic brother, gruesomely mistreated by him for a number of years
—One female proband was sexually assaulted by her father during her childhood
—One proband was predestined to spend his childhood on his parents' farm and was forced to remain in close contact with his pathological parents, while both his nonschizoid, nonschizophrenic sisters made contacts with other families early in life, and left home at an early age
—One female proband, being the oldest sister, had to take the place of the mother and homemaker at an early age, because her mother had been hospitalized for schizophrenia, and was overburdened with the problems inherent in these duties.
—One female proband was raised in a substandard orphanage after her family had broken up, while her siblings grew up in good foster homes.

Summarizing these facts, it can be stated that frequently—although by no means always—the childhood environment of the schizoid probands appeared to be more stress-laden than those of their siblings who were not schizoid and who did not become schizophrenic. But the kind of psychotraumatic stress of the future schizophrenic is manifold indeed. Alanen (1966) saw what an important role the close tie of a proband to his pathological parent played in his future mental development. My own experience yielded similar observations. But among my probands the close tie to a pathological parent did not by any means seem to be the only—nor even the most frequently encountered—additional stress on the early schizoid and later schizophrenic sibling.

The title of this subchapter poses the question: Is the pathologically schizoid personality described by the older authors a congenital psychopathy, or is it a behavior pattern forced on the patient by environmental stresses? In the paragraphs that follow I shall emphasize once again what contributions to an answer the described data supply or do not supply.

1. Alanen (1966) found among his own probands that the schizoid personality often occurs during the course of life, and is not predestined from early childhood on. This might be an indication—but by no means proof!—of its origin under environmental stresses. The schizoid-pathological character of most of the probands had already begun in childhood. Our information on the earliest childhoods of our probands is not thorough enough, however, so that I cannot decide whether pathological behavior existed during those very first years of life, or whether it began to emerge after the child entered school. Unlike Alanen (1966), therefore, I cannot contribute anything toward answering the question whether the development of the schizoid personality began with a "flaw" from a nonaberrant development, or whether it could be traced back to the very earliest years of life.

2. In contrast, experience with the probands of this study shows that a positive correlation does exist between a schizoid-pathological personality and horrible childhood conditions. At first glance, this indicates that a schizoid personality could be the consequence of a miserable childhood. But we must remember that horrible childhood conditions could also be the result of congenital personality disorders of the parents. Existing communication disturbances on the part of the child itself could aggravate them.

3. Proof of the positive correlation between a schizoid-pathological personality and childhood misery can be compared to another observation, namely that among the data on our probands there is no correlation between childhood misery and later schizophrenia among those probands who were not prepsychotically schizoid-pathological. If both observations apply, and if they are more generally valid than just among the probands specifically studied, the following conclusion would be admissible: Insofar as childhood misery has any causative influence on the later development of a schizophrenia, the correlation applies only when a schizoid personality develops first, and a schizophrenia is later superimposed on that schizoid background.

4. Among the siblings of the probands who grew up under horrible conditions during childhood, there are pathological—and also some schizoid-pathological—personality traits that occur more frequently than among the siblings of those probands who grew up under normal conditions. Therefore, not only does a correlation exist between personality problems and adverse childhood conditions among the schizophrenic probands them-

selves, but also among their siblings. In this, too, we may see an indication—but no proof —in support of the environmental influence in a difficult personality in general, and in a schizoid personality in particular.

5. Without achieving sufficient statistical significance, the above data revealed that sisters of schizophrenic probands who grow up under horrible childhood conditions more frequently become schizophrenic than do their brothers. If this finding were to be supported by additional investigative results, it would support several other observations described in other chapters. These include those that show that adverse childhood conditions more often predispose girls than boys to future schizophrenias. One might assume that adverse childhood conditions predispose boys and girls to schizoid and other disturbed-personality developments, but only girls to schizophrenia.

6. My studies support the definite impression (although it is not statistically supportable in figures) that among siblings who grew up under adverse childhood conditions, the one who develops a schizoid personality is the one among them whose misery was the most intense. This observation, too, supports the theory of environmental influences in the development of a schizoid personality. But not only schizoid, but a multitude of other disturbed-personality developments accumulate among the siblings of probands growing up under adverse childhood conditions. Horrible childhood conditions in general are therefore correlated with unfavorable personality developments in general, but scarcely with schizoid personality developments in particular.

Accordingly, the investigations here presented provide clear indications in support of the assumption that a schizoid personality must be regarded not only as a congenital psychopathy, but can also be, to a great extent, schizoid behavior, that has been developed under the stress of wretched environmental conditions.

The results that Kringlen (1968) among others, developed from the study of monozygotic twins can be interpreted in much the same sense. Prepsychotic personality disturbances, in particular those formerly labelled as schizoid peculiarities, occur frequently only to one of a pair of monozygotic twins, and particularly to the one who later becomes schizophrenic. For this reason also it is probable that environmental factors play a role in

the development of such disturbances. In that context, Kringlen's (1968) conclusions are excellent extensions of those from our studies. Conversely, our observations described above could, in turn, be regarded as extensions of Kringlen's (1968) findings. From the discordance of monozygotic twins with respect to schizoid personalities, Kringlen (1968) concludes that environmental influences were operative in their formation. The investigations here presented show that the expected detrimental environmental influences actually existed for many of the schizoids who lived in the families of the schizophrenic probands.

Here are the examples that were referred to in the above text.

Sigismund K. (*Proband* 84)

Sigismund was the 6th of 12 children of a small farmer. Two siblings were idiots and died early, 2 others died of tuberculosis, and 1 was feebleminded. The father was an alcoholic, who daily beat Sigismund with sticks. Sometimes the stick would break during the beatings. He kicked one of the little girls so hard in the back, that for several weeks all she could do was crawl, and she remained lame in one leg. Yet no doctor was called. The mother was overburdened with work. She did her best, but was unable to create an atmosphere of warmth in the home. Sigismund and his siblings were ridiculed, tormented, and rejected by their classmates in school, because their father had turned away from the village church that most of the community attended, and had become converted to a different confession. Most of Sigismund's childhood consisted of trying to hide from his father and his classmates, in order to avoid beatings. He was forced to work hard at an early age, and, for the rest, spent a great deal of time in haylofts and barns.

He was shy and unsociable from childhood on, was never able to play with other children, and was unable to make friends. When he came into contact with them he was partly shy and partly irritatable. In school he twice failed of promotion to the next grade, although he was just below average intelligence, not feebleminded.

As soon as his school obligation was finished, he left home; but he continued to lead the same kind of life as he had as a boy. Sporadically he went about to different farms, helping out as a farmhand and doing menial labor, until he became proficient in caring for the hooves of animals. He was never able to remain in a job, because he was restless, irritable, and easily offended. He had no close friendship with anyone. It is not known whether he ever had a girl friend; so it is to be assumed that he never had sexual relations, either. When questioned on this point, he answered with affecting sadness that he had always been too poor to have a girl.

Before his psychosis became manifest, he neglected himself atrociously. The psychosis then set in peracutely, in that he stripped down naked in his servant-chamber, raged, and broke up the furniture. After this serious catatonic episode, and a second one four years later, a residual state set in, during which for a number of years he did not require hospitalization. He is living the life of an eccentric and degenerate tramp, who makes disjointed, amusing speeches, and makes his way in life, in a primitive sort of way, partly by doing day labor on farms and partly by begging.

Discussion: Certainly Sigismund may be classified as pathologically schizoid from childhood on. He had kept no sort of close contacts, either with relatives with friends or with girls. He lived in complete isolation and loneliness. Inwardly he felt restless and harrassed. If any contact with him was attempted, he proved irritable and excessively sensitive. It may also be assumed with certainty that his schizoid behavior was the sequel to his miserable childhood. Everyone seemed to want to do him violence, he constantly had to flee and hide, nobody was kind to him, he was not given the opportunity to learn a trade, he felt much too inferior ever to court a girl and, terrible as this self-evaluation may be, that was how he turned out to be.

Isidor R. (Proband 74)

Isidor was the 4th of the 5 children of a railway station master. The family lived, to outward appearances, under well-ordered, bourgeois circumstances. The father was respected, assumed a rather taciturn, severe manner, but those who knew him better were aware of his gentleness and inner human warmth. The mother was a conscientious, hard-working homemaker. Isidor went through school and, living at home, finished an apprenticeship as a draftsman. He worked in this trade until his schizophrenic onset at age 21. As a small child he was aberrant in that he would flick his tongue in tic-like fashion. Furthermore, from earliest childhood on he had been excessively sensitive. Even

the slightest bit of teasing brought on lengthy crying spells. In his clumsy movements and in his relationships with others the impression he gave was droll and comical; in other respects, he caused no trouble and was obedient. For a time, because of his unusual sensitivity and his peculiar behavior, his parents sent him to a psychologist where psycho-analytic treatment was attempted. He had never made friends, and remained sexually completely unenlightened until well into maturity. Before the onset of his psychosis he had never had erotic or sexual relations with a girl.

This early information suggested a psychopathy that had persisted since early childhood. The schizoid-psychopathic behavior appeared in sharp contrast to his nonaberrant parents and their simple, orderly family household.

But a deeper, more precise study of the circumstances then revealed quite a different picture. It is best transmitted by citing a few passages from a letter of the proband's godmother, a frank, elderly woman who knew the family intimately.

She admitted that most people knew that this was a normal and forthright family — but: "The atmosphere there was a bit strained and the household quite perfect, indeed, a bit too perfect. One felt a chill there, and a lack of real contentment. The children always seemed to me as if they had been clamped in a vise. The mother was the absolute ruler, and everything in the home was under lock and key, wardrobes, bureau drawers, and the mailbox. She put out linens and clothing for everybody, and nobody was allowed to empty the mailbox. . . ." When the children were grown and had repeatedly and miserably failed in life, she reports that the mother by no means made any attempts to mitigate their misfortunes. "O no, she always found a scapegoat for everything. With Gottlieb it was the daughter-in-law, and with Ewald a teacher who had ruined him. No one was ever invited to the home as a guest. The boys had no friends. There were hardly any books . . ." Her grown children and the daughters-in-law had to account fully to the mother "about every visit, about everything they did, about every telephone conversation, and about every thought of theirs." According to the godmother's report, this mother even drew the bathwater for her grown children, measured the water temperature with a baby thermometer, then locked the door on the occupant and withdrew the key, and opened the door only after the bath was finished. She often said to one of her daughters-in-law, "You must work hard to become as we are. Just look at me, watch me, and then it'll be just fine." Furthermore, "The mother never read a book, never took a course or attended a lecture, and spoke only of her household, of cleaning, washing, and of personal perfection. . . . In spite of everything, I must mention in closing, that I always admired the patience and the courage with which these parents endured their lot. The father was lovable, kindly, and strictly correct in his behavior; I was very fond of him. . . . "

To all this should be added the fact that the mother treated the children quite unequally. Two of them, who were also more intelligent than the other 3, were her favorites. These other 3 could do nothing to please her, and the future schizophrenic, our proband, was in her opinion, the worst. "In the same conversation the mother would change her tone of voice, depending on which child she was talking to."

Not one of these 5 children became a healthy, normal, and free human being. The most intelligent son, who was his mother's favorite, developed best. He married a gregarious, very understanding, and warm-hearted woman, and had a successful career. At the end of this study he was 62 years old and had never been mentally ill. On the other hand, he did remain shy and personally insecure. The sister did not marry, suffered a lengthy neurotic depression during her menopause, and had to be hospitalized. Of the other sons whom the mother had rejected, 1 remained overly dependent and effeminate all his life; he married a widow, had no children, and died of a carcinoma at age 54. Another son incurred debts early in life, ran away, and went to America, where contact with him was lost. The third "rejected" son is our schizophrenic proband.

Discussion: Isidor may definitely be characterized as schizoid-pathological from childhood on. He was pathologically sensitive, was extremely clumsy and ungraceful in his movements, to the point where he appeared "droll," he was incapable of making or maintaining human contacts, had no friends, had no association with girls, suffered a tic, and was already referred for psychoanalytic treatment as a child because of his peculiar personality. In this case conditions in the family appeared to the outsider to be normal, and Isidor's unfavorable development appears to have no

causal basis. Only a more intimate understanding of conditions in the family forces the categorization of "horrible" on Isidor's childhood. His mother was the true prototype of a "schizophrenogenic mother." She created an agonizing emotional environment for all her children. In her eyes, Isidor was the black sheep of the family. One is justified in assuming that his schizoid behavior is connected with the moral mistreatment he received from his mother.

Rosmarie N. (*Proband* 13)

The father and the maternal grandfather of Rosmarie were teachers of philosophy, highly intellectual but impractical men. The father was described as "a religious-mystical character with one foot in another world." He was often irritatable and sensitive, took things hard, and always appeared to be depressed. The mother was a quiet, simple woman. The predominant atmosphere in the family was oppressive and seemed to emanate from the father. The mother, however, was incapable of changing it. Rosmarie was the eldest of 4; 2 of her 3 brothers were considered brilliant. Today both have a highly successful academic career behind them; one is an internationally renowned astronomer. The third brother suffered from spina bifida and was an idiot.

Rosmarie was of average intelligence, but was set off sharply and unfavorably as against her father and her two gifted brothers. She felt herself always in the shadow of these brothers.

In this situation, she created a peculiar role for herself in the family. She was shy vis-a-vis the male members of the family and also withdrew from her mother. But from her childhood on, she filled her life by caring for her younger idiot brother, a task in which she became totally absorbed. Her shyness toward her father and her other brothers she transferred to men in general. She had an inferiority complex in her contacts with boys, and was in constant fear of blushing when she spoke to them. She never had any close girl friends either. She was reserved and uncommunicative. Her mother reported that she had been easy to raise, had had good control of herself, but that she seemed excessively independent and inaccessible. She was always tired, depressed, dispirited, insecure, and not close to anyone. From her earliest youth she experienced feelings of alienation toward her environment.

As a young girl, Rosmarie was described by outsiders as "a tender blossom of a girl" or "a really pure little maiden." She had never had love relationships or sexual intercourse.

Her psychosis began subacutely at age 19, as a depressive state, in which she subjectively experienced the world and herself as barely existing, and simply remained in bed. In the course of the 10 years that followed, several exacerbations and improvements occurred, although this proband never fully recovered in the 33 years since her psychosis had first begun. For years she has been living in a large house together with relatives. She works hard and efficiently in that household, but keeps to herself and avoids human contacts.

Discussion: It certainly is possible to imagine how conditions in her family could have forced Rosmarie N. into her schizoid behavior. She had remained isolated in the family because she was not as intellectual as her father and brothers, and was unable to keep pace with them in her own world-alien frame of mind. Her mother was too shadowy a person to be able to supply the necessary warmth for communication, so Rosmarie shifted all her feminine energies onto the care of her idiot brother. In doing so she lost the capacity for human contact and her self-assurance, and became even more timid and withdrawn. Undoubtedly her own peculiarly unnatural position in life seemed strange and difficult to explain, even to herself. It is also interesting that she almost recovered from her psychosis, when she was able to be usefully employed in the home of her relatives, a condition that corresponded to her activities in childhood.

In spite of the adversity to which Rosmarie was exposed through her peculiar position in her family, her childhood cannot be simply classified as "horrible." In many respects these conditions were good. There was no material want, no hint of being mistreated, her parents and siblings were scrupulously moral, and the family lived on a high intellectual plane. Rosmarie is an example of a patient who by no means grew up in a horrible environment, but of whom a correlation between childhood conditions and a schizoid personality is still an admissible probability.

Ida A. (*Proband* 20)

Ida's father was a quiet, industrious, and kindly man, concerned about the welfare of his family. Unfortunately he enjoyed little success in his vocation, largely because of the years of economic crisis, but partly also be-

cause he was somewhat shy, was passive and modest when he applied for jobs or negotiated wages, gave an impression of being negative and unpretentious, and was therefore often passed over or held back. He had finished a business course, but usually worked in warehouses or stock rooms; and since he was often unemployed, he volunteered for auxiliary military service, sometimes for years at a time.

After many childbirths and the extraordinary demands made on her by the household and children, the mother became embittered, overworked, worn out, and irritable. She continually suffered hemorrhages, was frequently under doctors' care, and—when her daughters grew older—often went on extended vacations to "recuperate." Yet she was sincerely concerned about the welfare of her children.

Ida was the 7th of 8 children. The oldest sister contracted infantile paralysis early in life and remained an invalid. Two of the other siblings suffered from stomach ulcers and another from migraines. Except for Ida and the invalid sister, all the rest enjoyed generally good health, and became effective, useful human beings who got along well in life.

Ida herself was somehow different from the others from early childhood on. She was taciturn and withdrawn. When callers came to the house, she refused to appear, and when there were parties, she did not want to take part; when the family went on pleasure walks and outings, she would refuse to go along. She failed several classes in school, but at the expenditure of considerable effort finished a dress-making course. When she attempted to work at that trade, however, she proved incapable of it, and had to make her living as a servant. She was so slow and obviously so overly precise in her efforts at sewing, that she could not keep a job.

Despite poverty and the excessive work load on the mother, good relationships prevailed in the family. There was an atmosphere of affection and sincerity. The grown-up siblings were consistently concerned about one another, and all of them devotedly took care of Ida when she was ill.

Up to this point the impression was that her problem involved a typical "schizoid psychopathy." From earliest childhood, Ida had been different from her 7 siblings; she exhibited a difficult personality, and remained inaccessible. A more exacting study, however, reveals a more comprehensible picture of her personality.

An initial scanning of voluminous welfare records showed that the family was actually destitute through no fault of its own. But these records also showed that the family had been scandalously cheated and maladministered by the welfare agencies over a number of years. In all my life, I have never heard of such petty, trivial, rebellious opposition displayed by a welfare organization toward a family in need. Although the scant earnings of the father simply could not suffice to maintain even at a low level a family of 10 (at the time he was earning just 200 Fr. a month, although this was in the twenties), constant renewed investigations were undertaken. A check was made to make certain that meals were not too lavish, the father was confronted with an account of how much cider he consumed (although there was no question of alcoholic excesses), there was haggling about the quality of clothing; when one of the daughters, over 20 years old, went out on a date perfectly respectably with a decent escort, she was rebuked for it; in fact, the family was even reproached for taking walks on Sunday afternoons. In spite of all this, the support monies they were granted were minimal.

Investigation further revealed that Ida was the least intellectual one in the family. Her intelligence was rated at the borderline of feeblemindedness, while the rest of the family members were of average intelligence.

At age 24, after Ida had been seduced by a young fellow, she indulged in a number of other intimate relationships rather indiscriminantly, quite in contrast to her upbringing and to the behavior of the others in the family. She fell seriously in love with a young man, but he soon jilted her. Her serious psychosis began as a reactive depression from this disappointment in love. Within a short time, however, her condition developed into a typical catatonia, from which the proband never recovered in the 23 years that passed after her illness began. In her delusions she often accuses herself as being the cause of her mother's illness, and she considers her period of sexual promiscuity an abominable sin.

Discussion: Under these circumstances one can imagine how Ida was forced into the role of a schizoid psychopath—although without the chance of proving whether such genetic suppositions agree with the facts. While her father and siblings endured the family's material deprivation with stoical good grace and cheerful mien, Ida herself, because of her limitations, was less independent and more subject to its influence. She was more helpless in coping with her mother's tiresome whining and the sharp practices of the welfare agencies. While her siblings associated freely among their friends, showing little concern for the malevolent vigilance of the welfare authorities, Ida did not succeed in assuming a similar attitude. She met the demands of the welfare agency by associating with nobody, attending no entertainment functions, and playing to the hilt the Cinderella role the welfare agency expected of the family, that also corresponded with her mother's expectations. Was she then constitutionally schizoid and psychopathic? Or was she constitutionally merely somewhat limited and driven to schizoid behavior by the influence of her environment?

In this case also it would be an exaggeration to speak of "horrible" childhood conditions. The emotional relationships in the family were good. The parents were lovingly concerned about the children, and there was a good cohesive relationship among the children. A shadow was cast over Ida's childhood by the family's poverty and the unfathomable behavior of the welfare officials toward that family.

I include Ida, too, among those probands who did not grow up under "horrible" conditions, but for whom a correlation between childhood environment and a schizoid-pathological personality may be assumed.

Prepsychotic Vocational and Social Status of the 208 Probands

The listing of the probands according to their occupations has already appeared in Chapter 1. Insofar as small differences in social levels of the probands existed as compared to those of the general population, they would have to be related to the methods by which the probands were selected. In other respects the socio-occupational status of the 208 probands corresponded to that of the general population.

The following paragraphs are not intended as further comparisons of the status of the probands with that of the general population; but the occupational social status of the probands before their schizophrenic illness is to be compared to that of their fathers. The question then reads: Could the schizophrenic probands before they became ill achieve the same status as their fathers had? Could they rise higher vocationally? On the other hand, did they fail to reach the levels of their fathers?

I deliberately refused to set up an order of rank of the of various occupations and simply to count how many fathers and how many of the probands fit into each category. The doubtful aspects of such an operation would consist of the fact that workers with totally different levels of vocational training, occupational skills, and relative social status frequently make use of the identical label to identify their activity.

For example, the term "farmer" may be glibly applied to migrant day laborers in agriculture as well as to farmers who own their land, or to professors of the agricultural department of technical colleges of the Swiss Confederacy, etc. But the qualifications "large-scale" or "small-scale" farming operation would also not adequately identify the occupational level. Many of the farmers in our canton have other occupations on the side, such as factory worker, minor community civil servant, politician, etc. Their socio-occupational status cannot really be measured by the size of the farm on which they work. The same goes for many other job titles as, for instance, businessman, innkeeper, building contractor, taxi-owner etc.

So, in every individual case, the socio-occupational status of the proband was compared with that of his father. In the evaluation, the rank held in the job, the success in it, and the importance of jobs on the side were individually considered for each case, as were changes in jobs. By this method the error was avoided of assigning to a construction worker who had unsuccessfully tried his hand at jobbing for a few months, calling himself a "free-lance contractor," the same classification that one would assign to a legitimate, large-scale industrialist.

The setting up for the male probands of all these individual comparisons between their socio-occupational status and that of their fathers resulted in the following:

Proband compared to father	No. of cases
Increased his status	24
Remained at the same level	36
Decreased his status	36
Undetermined	4
Total:	100

Among the female probands who had married, the socio-occupational status of the proband's husband was compared with that of the proband's father:

Proband's husband compared to her father	No. of ca
Increased his status	14
Remained at the same level	19
Decreased his status	18
Undetermined	5
Total:	56

It was not possible to compare occupations of mothers with those of their daughters, because during the mothers' generation, women's occupations were interpreted quite differently from the way they are rated in the daughters' generation. But an attempt was made to compare the occupational status of the unmarried female probands with that of their fathers. This could not be accomplished without some arbitrary adjustment, since the occupational statuses of men and women were not considered socially equal—at least not during the period in question. The following figures are therefore very uncertain:

Unmarried female proband compared to her father	No. of cases
Increased her status	8
Remained at the same level	17
Decreased her status	24
Undetermined	3
Total:	52

The following paragraphs give examples that show what we mean by increases, remaining the same, and decreases in socio-occupational status:

Examples of increase in socio-occupational status

Male Proband 75: Father was Italian dye-works laborer; attempted independent operation of a grocery business which failed. Proband was self-taught and became a successful private teacher of languages.

Male Proband 91: Father was a mechanic, often unemployed, without making an effort to find a job. Proband independently operated a successful hardware business from the time he was 21 years old.

Female Proband 56: Father had been a farmer, who lost his property through a mortgage default; then worked as a lamp-lighter in the community. Proband became an elementary school teacher and married a successful teacher.

Examples of socio-occupational status remaining the same

Male Proband 20: Father was successful

shop foreman and lived a well-regulated existence. Proband was an efficient precision toolmaker and lived a well-regulated existence.

Female Proband 73: Father was a canton employee and an habitual absinthe drinker. Her husband was a part-time laborer and an alcoholic.

Examples of decrease in socio-occupational status

Male Proband 9: Father was a substantial, land-bound farmer; his son, the proband, a sporadic day laborer.

Male Proband 42: Father was a respected watchmaker with a variety of interests; proband was a door-to-door peddler.

Female Proband 12: Father was a high-school teacher; proband a servant doing simple household chores.

In evaluating the above figures, two conditions must be considered: Often the probands became ill early in life (Table 4.2). For many of them a promising career or apprenticeship was prematurely interrupted by the outbreak of their schizophrenia. If their illness had begun later in life, they might perhaps have attained a higher occupational level. Furthermore, it should be noted that the period in history during which most of the probands were passing through adolescence and their schizophrenic illness were times of economic crisis. During this period it was more difficult to progress upward on the occupational status ladder than it had been in previous decades, and much more difficult than it is today. The decisive periods between the final occupational success of the fathers and that of their sons were by no means distinguished by improved affluence or increased levels of education. Any improvement in finances and education occurred among the majority of the population only after the occupational level of most of the probands had already been established.

Considering these circumstances, it may be stated that the socio-occupational level of the probands was not markedly different from that of their fathers. There is absolutely no foundation for the notion that occupational failures often become schizophrenic. Those who become future schizophrenics are, as a whole, as efficient and reliable on their jobs as their fathers, and generally as efficient and reliable as the average of the general population.

This finding appears to contradict the findings of other authors, according to whom prepsychotic schizophrenics hold lower rank-

ing jobs and social positions than their fathers (Morrison 1959, among others, and summarized by Carstairs 1968). But the contradiction is resolved when consideration is given to the fact that the social status of probands investigated by other authors was evaluated at a different time in the patient's history than mine were. Other authors checked the social status of hospitalized schizophrenics before they were hospitalized. I checked mine before the probands fell ill. There is often a long period of time between the onset of schizophrenic illness and hospitalization for it, during which the patient's social and occupational levels declines. The occupational and social levels of the probands from this study had also dropped markedly below that of their fathers shortly before they were hospitalized.

The Erotic Life of Probands previous to Illness

The love life of an individual lends itself even less to expression in figures than does his personality. Still I found a way of fitting almost all the probands into summary categories, without leaving open too much room for doubt.

In the first group, investigation of the probands and their families and friends revealed that they had never had any kind of love relationships and, to all appearances, had never had any sexual relations. The abbreviated term applied to this group is in what follows "nonerotic."

A second group had natural love relationships, without major difficulties arising from them and without being conspicuous or embarrassing to outside observers. This group either had no sexual relations or practised them clandestinely, so that it was not apparent to others in the family and did not offend anyone. These are categorized as "discreet."

For a third group it was common knowledge that they maintained several intimate relationships, and that frequently difficulties developed in consequence of them. This group includes primarily probands with illegitimate children. These were categorized as "erotically active."

The fourth group consisted of sexual perverts and deviants.

A small group remained, on whom available information was either insufficient or too contradictory to be meaningfully categorized.

A summary overview of the erotic life of the 208 probands before eruption of their psychoses and before marriage is presented below:

	Men	Women
Nonerotic	24	40
Erotically discreet	43	14
Erotically active	16	42
Sexually perverted	2	1
Undetermined	15	11
Totals:	100	108

What strikes the eye immediately is the large number of nonerotics and the small number of sexual perverts. Among the latter, 1 was a voyeur, 1 a male homosexual, and the other a woman who practised incest with her brother for a number of years. Obviously, patients who had some homosexual tendencies along with heterosexual experiences or who had occasionally indulged in a homosexual experience in their youth were not included in this category. Only those patients were entered who were sexually deviant over long periods of time and for whom that deviance plainly dominated their overall behavior.

As for the large number of nonerotics, two facts need to be cleared up: how many remained without love relationships until maturity or advanced age, and how many became ill or married so early in life that the preceding absence of such relationships may be regarded as natural. The following listing presents an overview on these points:

No. of nonerotics compared to all probands :[7]

	Men	Women
Married or fell ill before age 20	6:11	5: 8
Married or fell ill between ages 20 and 29	11:44	22:48
Married or fell ill between ages 30 and 39	6:22	8:25
Unmarried before, and fell ill after age 40	1: 8	5:16

As expected, the number of probands without any love relationships decreases during the course of life. Among the late-onset schizophrenics there are relatively fewer nonerotics than among the early-onset patients. Still, 23 percent of the males and 41 percent of the females who had not married or become ill by the time they were 30, were nonerotic—and these figures are high.

It is also of interest to know the prepsychotic personality types of this group of nonerotic probands:

No. of nonerotics compared to all probands :[7]

	Men	Women
Of the nonaberrant	3:24	12:31
Of the schizoid-aberrant within the norm	12:28	12:22
Of the other-than-schizoid-abberant within norm	0: 3	2: 6
Of the schizoid-pathological group	6:19	11:25
Of the other-than-schizoid pathological group	3:11	3:13

7. The 22 probands on whom information concerning erotic behavior was incomplete are not included.

As expected, the listing shows that most of the nonerotics appear among the schizoids, but by no means exclusively so. There were men, and particularly some women with non-aberrant prepsychotic personalities, for whom no evidence of any love relationship could be discovered. This lack of known erotic behavior may be an aspect of the general incapacity for human contacts that often accompanies the schizoid personality, but it also occurs without any specific evidence of such incapacity.

Sixty-eight of the probands (28 men and 40 women) married before they became schizophrenic. An attempt was made to categorize summarily the husband-wife relationships into good, mediocre, and poor. It turned out that, based on existing data, the delimitation between "good" and "mediocre" was much easier to define than that between "mediocre" and "poor." A marriage was rated as "good" if the spouses lived together continuously, no incidents of infidelity were found, nothing was revealed about any sexual maladjustments, nobody had reported any serious quarrels, and both partners subjectively rated their marriage as happy and successful. Among the 28 marriages of the male patients, 11 were considered good in this sense, before eruption of their illness; among the 40 marriages of the women, 13 were considered good.

During the 289 years of marriage of the cumulative married period of the male probands, before eruption of their psychoses, there were 27 children. During the 600 years of marriage of the cumulative married period of the female probands, before eruption of their psychosis, there were 79 children. Of these 600 marriage years, 61 occurred after age 50 of the female probands. The 79 births, therefore, occurred during the 539 fertile years of marriage of the female patients, before onset of this illnesses. In addition, the males produced 3 and the females 8 illegitimate children, before onset of illness. The fertility of the probands before their psychosis agrees with the previous direct findings about their sexual activity.[8] The premarital sexual restraint and asexuality among the probands is as prominent as their low fertility in marriage is. In evaluating this conclusion it should also be remembered that modern contraceptive methods were little known and scarcely practised among the social groups and in the times that apply to these patients. It is not possible statistically to draw a comparison between the erotic activity of our 208 probands and that of the general population of Zürich for the same time period. Our figures are too small, and there are no figures for the general population available for comparison. Based on decades of medical experience with our indigenous population, which includes the 208 schizophrenic probands of this study as well as other schizophrenics and non-schizophrenic walk-in patients in search of medical advice, the following formulations appear to be justified:

The prepsychotic sexual life of schizophrenics does not differ appreciably from that of the average population. Insofar as differences do exist, they consist of a slightly higher frequency of nonerotic or sexually restrained behavior among future schizophrenics than among individuals of the average population. However, this difference is restricted to the men, and is nonexistent or negligible among the women. Sexual perversions are by no means more frequent among future schizophrenics, and probably less frequent there than among the general population. The total absence of any discernible sexuality is not counted as a sexual perversion. Many of the future schizophrenics were capable of normal love relationships and of generating happiness in a fulfilled marriage. If there should be some slight differences in this respect between future schizophrenics and members of the general population, they could not be meaningful.

Qualifying the above, it should be called to mind once more that the erotic life open to discussion here, is complete only to the extent to which it became accessible to us, and this was in retrospect, by way of testimony of the

probands themselves and their families. On the other hand, those testimonies were exhaustive and comprehensive.

It would prove interesting to compare the prepsychotic erotic lives of the schizophrenics with those of other types of mental patients. Unfortunately, the only material suitable for comparison available to me applies to the male alcoholics (see above). Of course, my figures are too small for any statistically valid comparisons, so I shall not repeat them here. On the other hand, they do correspond to experience and the general clinical impressions gleaned from hundreds of alcoholics. They can easily be formulated as follows:

Alcoholics more rarely achieved fulfillment in love relationships than did prepsychotic schizophrenics. There are more among alcoholics who are sexually impotent, more homosexuals, and more probands whose capability for love fails them when they are in need of sexual satisfaction, than among future schizophrenics. Of course, the sexual disturbances and sexuality in general of alcoholics are inseparably interwoven with the causes and the consequences of developing alcoholism; it is impossible to consider them separately.

Discussion

The conclusions drawn in this chapter about the personality of the probands may be grouped into two categories, according to their importance.

Group 1. The clearly defined data from the 208 probands, which correspond, in substance, to findings of most other authors using different probands and especially also to general clinical experience. These data represent nothing new. They merely contribute to the verification of existing, proved information from previous experience. What is new about them is at best the fact that they attempt to cast the old, established data into somewhat more precise figures; although such a procedure is risky and therefore open to question, because in the end it compiles figures that are composed not of objective, but largely of subjective judgments, and figures do possess the quality of feigning a degree of accuracy that does not really exist. This category includes the findings on the prepsychotic character, the intelligence, the erotic life, and the socio-occupational status of the probands.

Group 2. Findings from studies of the 208 probands that achieve only partial statistical significance, and that have not been recorded

8. The total fertility picture of the probands is discussed in a separate section in Chapter 5.

by any—or very few—other authors. These findings cannot yet be generalized. It is certainly possible that they cannot be verified by data from other groups of schizophrenics. These findings, in contrast to those of Group 1, do not merely verify, support, or improve the precision of known facts, they form the bases for new investigative hypotheses. They contain material that should be compared with subsequent findings. This category includes specifically those findings already mentioned, that were compiled investigating the genesis of the schizoid personality.

As to the first category, it includes primarily data on the prepsychotic character of the probands, character interpreted here in the special sense already described above. Psychiatrists from all over the world are agreed that schizoid personality traits and schizoid "psychopathy" are common occurrences in the premorbid histories of schizophrenics. But relatively few authors have made the attempt to record their frequency in sets of figures. Kretschmer (1944) himself, whom we revere for his excellent descriptions of the schizoid personality, did not record a count of their frequency among premorbid schizophrenics. He did record statistics on the types of constitutions among schizophrenics; he evaluated theoretically, impressively, and convincingly, the correlation between the schizoid personality, the asthenic habitus, and schizophrenia, but he did not determine them in figures with repect to the schizoid personality. Here he took over my data from the Pfäfers and the New York schizophrenics and applied them to his 15th Edition of *Körperbau und Charakter* (Body Build and Character). These data correspond to his clinical experience. He emphasizes that they also agree with "Luxenburger's (1939) final revisions of the Rüdin School's results."

In view of the concurrence of the figures with those of other authors in South Germany and with various other groups I had selected, we may assume that the given figures on the distribution of prepsychotic characters of schizophrenics are valid for all schizophrenics, or at least for those patients from the turn of the century and this century, and in Central Europe. Whether they would be valid for schizophrenics beyond that, from different cultures, for instance, is not at all certain. By impressions alone, I would like to assume that there arc fewer schizoids among African schizophrenics than among Central European ones. To be sure, in order to pursue the matter

a bit further, one would have to resolve the question whether a schizoid personality could be the same phenomenon in totally different cultures.

When barely $\frac{1}{3}$ of the schizophrenics were prepsychotically schizoid within the norm, and $\frac{1}{4}$ of them were even schizoid-pathological, it certainly supports the prevalent opinion that the schizoid personality is an important —in fact the only clearly proved—predisposition for schizophrenia. But one must never forget that a bare third of the schizophrenics is prepsychotically nonaberrant, and that a small portion prepsychotically reveals trends and personality disturbances that are aberrant, but that are quite different from schizoid aberrant behavior. Furthermore, it must not be forgotten, that not nearly all schizoids develop into schizophrenics. Whoever would prophesy the approach of a schizophrenia because of an existing schizoid personality, is, in my opinion, committing a technical error. In theorizing about schizophrenia, it should be kept foremost in mind that a schizoid personality is certainly the most important hitherto recognized predisposition for schizophrenia, but with equal certainty, it is not the only one.

The intelligence of the 208 probands is distributed among them in about the same pattern as among the population in general. This finding, too, agrees with the experience of many psychiatrists, and corresponds also to the statistics of the Rüdin school. To be sure. many modern authors encountered accumulations of schizophrenias among the lower social classes, among whom a below-average level of intelligence is also prevalent (Dunham 1964, Hollingshead and Redlich 1958, Faris and Dunham 1959, Goldberg and Morrison 1963, among others). I do not believe that the findings of these authors can be generalized in the sense that schizophrenias occur more frequently among the subintelligent than among the intelligent. I plan to come back to this point.

The findings about the erotic life of the 208 probands would also agree well with the experiences of most psychiatrists with their own schizophrenic patients. To be sure, there are very few studies that attempt to grasp erotic behavior by means of figures, as we have attempted to do in this chapter. The 208 probands do not appreciably differ qualitatively in their socially discernible erotic behavior from the average population. A probable difference may emerge from the fact that there are more nonerotics and erotically reserved, and fewer erotically active and sexual perverts among the schizophrenic probands than among the total population. Data that prove the contrary are unknown to me. Once more I should like to stress that I counted only manifest sexual perversions. My figures do not show any facts as to whether latent homosexual tendencies are frequent among schizophrenics (as many authors have assumed, and as I too have been tempted to believe from general clinical experience). My figures do not show either whether neurotic inhibitions have suppressed normal erotic behavior among the nonerotic or the erotically reserved, or whether their erotic instincts are simply underdeveloped from the outset.

It seems worthy of mention that the schizophrenic probands, before eruption of their psychosis, were generally capable of maintaining the socio-occupational status of their fathers and that of the general population. As will be explained later, in spite of all the suffering that the psychosis of the parents brought with it, the children of our schizophrenics showed no appreciable drop in socio-occupational status either. These findings agree with my psychiatric experience from the cantons of St. Gallen, Basel-City, and Zürich. It never became obvious to me that schizophrenics worked in simpler, less respected jobs before their illness than a corresponding average of the population did. Although, conversely, I often observed—and justifiably so—that after the onset of the psychosis, the socio-occupational status of the patient decreased.

During the course of decades, the prevailing opinions on how schizophrenics are distributed among various occupations and social classes have fluctuated considerably. Luxenburger (1939, 1940) from the Rüdin School concluded from his findings that "the specific sociological position of a schizophrenic family" was identifiable by the fact "that schizophrenia certainly occurs more frequently in the upper social classes than in the lower ones, while the middle classes revealed an average figure for onset of illness." Other authors before the second World War held the view that schizophrenia occurred with approximately equal frequency in all social classes.

During recent years, however, especially in the Anglo-Saxon literature, there were numerous reports that schizophrenia was most frequent among the poor, who were not trained for a specific occupation. Since Faris and Dunham first published such findings in 1939, several other authors have taken the same stand. Insofar as they were investigating the socio-occupational status of their patients during and after hospitalization, their data does not contradict mine. In this section I merely found that the socio-occupational status of my probands, before onset of their psychoses, corresponded to that of their fathers and the general population. It is a known fact, however, that many schizophrenics became ill long before they were hospitalized, and because of that dropped into a lower social status.

The instructive investigations by Goldberg and Morrison (1963) show that on the average, a socio-occupational decrease among schizophrenics actually does not take place until after onset of illness. According to their investigations, the average occupational level of the fathers of schizophrenics and of the schizophrenics themselves, before onset of illness, corresponds to that of the normal population, which, in turn, agrees with the findings on our probands.

The findings by Goldberg and Morrison (1963) and my own only appear to contradict the familiar studies by Hollingshead and Redlich (1958). These latter authors gathered their data expressly from schizophrenic inpatients, rather than from new admissions. It is obvious that the social status of newly admitted patients does not necessarily have to correspond to that of the inpatients. It is most probable that taking over patients for home care is not equally popular or customary among all social classes; and that therefore it is also probable that patients from certain specific social classes predominate among hospitalized inpatients.

Given these circumstances, I believe that modern authors should be more reticent in stating that there are more schizophrenics among the poor and the lower occupational classes than among the higher social levels. The truth of that statement has by no means been proved; it even seems to me rather improbable. If, for instance, records were compiled on how many schizophrenias had occurred in the palaces of the nobility of Europe, the statement that schizophrenias predominate among the poor would be regarded with considerable skepticism.

As to the second category of findings, involving the genesis of the schizoid personality, they do not reflect generally recognized, clinically proved facts, but they do indicate relationships that have not been extensively investigated, that are still uncertain, and that should be supported or refuted by additional studies.

The schizoid-personality development of my probands I could only begin to observe from their school age onward. I do not know whether its beginning might not already have occurred sometime during their infancy or early childhood years. However, it was easy to determine that among the principal probands the overwhelming majority of the schizoid probands revealed schizoid traits during their early school years and in time-correlation with horrible conditions at home. Only in a very small minority was a schizoid personality manifested for the first time during or after puberty, and then too, it was usually in correlation with an adverse home life—usually, although not always. There are exceptions to the rule, and they warn us to be careful in using generalities. My studies about the beginning of the schizoid personality are not nearly adequate for formulating final and definitive conclusions. Checks and rechecks are of the utmost urgency. Alanen (1966) was able to find considerably more beginnings of schizoid development after school age than I was.

The fact that those of our probands with pathologically schizoid personality traits much oftener came from horrible childhood conditions and much less frequently from normal ones than the prepsychotically non-aberrant probands, is a fairly new discovery. This finding requires confirmation. Only after that is in hand, may these temporary assumptions be considered to be valid. Insofar as childhood suffering has any genetic implications whatever for the future development of a schizophrenia, it often happens that the personality undergoes a change toward schizoid behavior, which, in turn, lays the foundation for the schizophrenia itself.

There are a number of observations recorded in the literature, according to which schizoid psychopaths grew up under poor conditions in the home. Among others, Kraft (1959) reports from Holland on 6 schizoid psychopaths, of whom 5 had unhappy relations with their parents. But none of these developed a schizophrenia, nor did any of the schizoid relatives of the probands either. There should certainly be no doubt about the fact that poor childhood conditions are frequent in the early histories of schizoids, just as they are in the early histories of neurotics and addicts. It may be suspected that poor relationships with parents favor the beginning of a schizoid development, quite independently of whether the schizoid personality later develops into schizophrenia or not. It may also be assumed that a schizoid psychopathy, correlated in some manner with poor relationships with parents, predisposes a patient for later schizophrenic onset. Naturally, it is not at all certain whether poor childhood conditions—if at all—imply such a predisposition to a schizophrenic psychosis only by way of a schizoid development.

The general finding that children who grow up under miserable circumstances are frequently impaired, agrees with general experience. Miserable circumstances in childhood might create a predisposition to schizoid development, but certainly they are not the only cause. We may be sure that such circumstances also predispose to a multitude of other personality disorders.

Only in modern times has the question really been seriously dealt with, as to why among siblings who grow up under the same disadvantages only 1, or very few, become schizophrenic. Up to now, most of the literature has emphasized that the child most closely involved with a pathological father or a pathological mother is the one most likely to become schizophrenic (Alanen 1966). I find these among my own probands, too. But my study points to the fact that the most varied types of damage are concentrated on that one among the siblings who becomes the later schizophrenic.

4 The Long-term Disease Courses of Schizophrenics

Difficulties and Errors of Previous Course Investigations

During the first years after the concept "dementia praecox" was instituted by Kraepelin, course studies of schizophrenics appeared to be of little interest. By definition the concept embraced the hopeless, incurable mental illnesses, the outcome of which was dementia. It soon became known that sometimes after "surges" of an illness, cessations would set in, that the disease did not run a straight-line course, that conditions alternated between better and worse; in fact, that phases occurred in which the disease just lay dormant or concealed, as common jargon used to express it. If released patients were able to remain for years active, capable of working, and scarcely aberrant in their behavior, an erroneous initial diagnosis was suspected, or there was mention of exceptions to the rule. Faith in the incurability of the disease was so firmly entrenched, that recoveries were misinterpreted by lines of reasoning that today would appear ridiculous to us. If a patient was released after a schizophrenic psychosis, and if he remained socially well integrated for many years, and finally died, it was suspected that he would eventually have become schizophrenically demented again, if he had only lived long enough. Such concepts as the merely practical recovery from an actually incurable psychosis" or the "latency reversion of a psychosis," were often marshaled in an effort to support the dogma of "incurability in principle."

One of the facts that motivated E. Bleuler (1908) to replace the concept "dementia praecox" with that of "the schizophrenias" arose from the observation that the symptomatology of "dementia praecox" also characterized those psychoses that healed. In classifying a psychosis as a schizophrenia, his most important yardsticks were the symptomatology and the psychological dynamics, but scarcely the course of the illness. Only after this change in conceptualization had taken place did course studies become meaningful. But many more years were to pass before the incurability concept was dropped as a diagnostic criterion in investigations of the courses of illness. Many more statistical data were generated that were ready-made to admit determinations of

adverse prognoses for schizophrenias from the very outset, mainly because only cases with an unfavorable prognosis were recognized as schizophrenias. After the introduction of insulin, cardiazol, and electroshock treatments during the years 1934–1937, the psychiatrists first became aware of how very little factual knowledge about the courses of schizophrenia was really available as yet. There were not enough valid statistics on untreated patients available for comparisons with statistics on the results of those who had been treated.

Then new pitfalls for errors opened up. It was considered correct procedure to compare the shock-treated patients with the untreated ones. What was overlooked was the fact that this was not a comparison between comparable terms. Most of the statistics on untreated cases already included many who had been released because of favorable outcome, since it had been assumed that a favorable course refuted the diagnosis of a schizophrenia. In the shock-treated cases, to be sure, a favorable course was considered the result of a recovery process; and those who recovered under shock treatment were, without further reflection, included with the schizophrenics. Following upon a good prognosis, an unintentional selection process evolved for the patients to be treated. The inclination was to treat especially the tense, highly excitable, and inwardly lively patients; that is, patients whose spontaneous prognoses were considered to be good from the very outset. The permission or refusal by the family for treatment by itself contributed to the fact that good prognoses predominated among the patients admitted for treatment. Soon after the treatments were introduced, the belief became popular that their efficacy for recovery was excellent if treatment was begun shortly after the onset of illness, and that the cures were ineffective only if they were initiated too late. In acute cases the tendency is to begin treatment at once, while the nature of a chronic development is such that the exact time of onset cannot be immediately determined and thus that treatment cannot begin immediately. The demand to administer shock treatment soon after onset of illness resulted unwittingly in treating acute cases as priorities, and in excluding most of the chronic cases from treatment entirely. It is a known fact, however, that the acute cases consistently have a better spontaneous prognosis than the chronic ones. This then became one more wrong way by which the curative value of shock treatments came to be overestimated. Another error evolved from the fact that temporary improvements after shock treatments were evaluated as permanent recoveries, on the basis of wishful thinking. Even before sufficient time had elapsed for adequate observation, a presumed conclusion was expressed, on the order of: Spontaneous remissions of schizophrenias are temporary; remissions resulting from shock treatment, are permanent.

By way of such theories, in the years before the outbreak of the last World War, the dogma of the incurability of schizophrenias without shock treatments was juxtaposed to the dogma of full recovery from almost all schizophrenias with early shock treatments. The awakening came swiftly and suddenly. It soon became obvious that many relapses occurred among the shock-treated recoveries. Already 10 years after the introduction of shock treatments, there were very few chronic patients left in the psychiatric hospitals who had not undergone shock treatment. After 1953, when the psychotherapy of schizophrenics began to be taken seriously again and the neuroleptic drugs had been introduced, the younger psychiatrists had almost forgotten that a decade or two before, the schizophrenias had already been pronounced as curable under early shock treatment.

My investigations on shock-treated schizophrenics, published in 1941, showed that successful treatment was achieved in the majority of patients who had a good spontaneous prognosis. Many of them had passed through several acute phases of the disease before shock treatment, and they had recovered from those earlier phases without the aid of shock treatment. In the period after treatment, new, acute, temporary phases emerged at about the same average frequency and in the same rhythm as they had before treatment. Some good phasic progress was noted among the untreated shizophrenic relatives of the shock-treated recoveries. Among patients with an unfavorable spontaneous diagnosis, with slow, creeping onsets and with strong psychotic symptoms during rationality, shock treatment usually had no effect, or achieved only a remission of short duration; but the long-term outcomes were equally unfavorable in these cases, whether they were shock-treated or not.

When these regrettable facts from my statistics of 1941 and 1943 became known, I received a generous measure of serious remonstrances. I was censured for having blocked the way to progress in healing schizophrenia. I had, however, never belittled the value of these treatments, neither at that time nor at present. As I shall explain later, I believe in their beneficial powers to improve and to temper and to speed the recovery process in many cases, especially when they are applied at the proper time in context with a general long-term care program. I only consider it a mistake to assume that any one or several physical cures, applied early, would be capable by themselves of turning an unfavorable prognosis into a favorable one in a large number of cases.

Since these errors that resulted from the first surge of enthusiasm about shock treatments have been corrected, a great number of studies on the courses of schizophrenias have been undertaken. Their results have been repeatedly summarized, as they have also been in the lectures on schizophrenia at our clinic in 1951, 1957, 1962, 1967, and 1969.

The modern disease-course investigations on schizophrenics have really only become possible and meaningful after the criterion of incurability was effectively excluded from the diagnostics. Once this great obstacle to disease-course studies was removed, however, new difficulties emerged that no one had ever thought of before. They were so serious that one was constrained to wonder whether there was any value at all in undertaking statistical investigations on the long-term courses of schizophrenias. An attitude of resigned reserve in this respect was understandable. In what follows I should like to mention some of the problems that still confront schizophrenic disease-course investigations, and to discuss whether these problems can be overcome or not.

The question of diagnostics has already been taken up in chapter 1.

How should the schizophrenic patients be selected, whose disease course is to be determined? Old statistics usually were based on the patient population of a psychiatric hospital. But obviously, it is the chronic cases that predominate among the patient populations of such hospitals, assuming at least that the chronic patients in need of hospitalization are not refused or consigned elsewhere. But if a clinic wants to deal with no chronic cases at all, it would have to amass an unthinkable proportion of benign cases among its patient population. Therefore, in order to reach a valid conclusion on the disease course independent of the influence of patient selection, one should begin with clinic admissions, and not with clinic populations. But should only first-time admissions be considered, or also those patients who had been previously admitted and then released? One would prefer to consider only the first-time admissions. Immediately then we realize that the term "first-time admission" is not quite as unequivocal as it might appear to be. How should those cases be counted that were first admitted under a different diagnosis (for example, as manics or psychopaths), and that now arrive as schizophrenics? Are these "first-time admissions" or not? How shall we consider patients who had been previously admitted to other clinics? One might decide to accept them only if earlier admissions had been to nonpsychiatric hospitals. But then the question arises: Are religious homes for problem people psychiatric hospitals? Are isolated hospitals that accept psychiatric emergency cases along with medical patients? and so on. Such questions are hard to answer objectively. It should further be considered that there are very few hospitals that accept all the schizophrenics from a given geographical area. Most of them apply a selective process, because admissions are often determined by circumstances other than the presence of schizophrenia symptoms alone. Such secondary circumstances may include the reputation of the clinic in the community it serves, the clinic's preference for acute or chronic, for serious or mild cases reflected in its admission policies, the relative costs of hospitalization, the economic circumstances of the patients, etc. Courses of illness of first-time admissions will never be representative of all schizophrenics in a given clinic. In addition, it should also be remembered that there are schizophrenics who are never hospitalized. I encountered this category not oo infrequently in a general practice in the mountain regions. These schizophrenics are picked up in family studies as the relatives of schizophrenic hospital cases. To be sure, there are also schizophrenics who have never been hospitalized, who have no close relatives that are hospitalized. Probably their psychoses develop along a different course than the average; but they are almost impossible to pick up.

In my opinion these problems can be overcome by just one general attitude: One must recognize the impossibility of assembling an ideal group of probands. It is an unattainable goal to gain control of a group of patients whose schizophrenias are characteristic with respect to the course of illness of all schizophrenias. On the other hand, it is possible to do course studies on the greatest number of different-type groups of schizophrenic probands, and to compare them. On the basis of such studies a determination can then be made within what limits the course statistics fluctuate for differently selected groups of probands. If, for instance, it is determined that after 20 years 25 percent among a certain designated group of schizophrenics has recovered, it should not be concluded that 25 percent of all schizophrenics recovered in that 20-year period; instead, the rate of recoveries should be tested with as many different types of proband groups as possible. After that one may justly say that, after a period of 20 years, 20–30 percent of all schizophrenic patients from a number of differently selected groups of probands will have recovered. A pattern of recovery rates deserving attention emerges from the threshold values of recovery rates among the variously selected group of probands. If these threshold values are close, they reflect the prognoses for recovery for all schizophrenics. If these threshold values differ widely, they indicate nothing specific about the disease courses of schizophrenias in general, but they do have a value in a different context: They can be studied to determine what kind of selective process influenced the course of illness.

For these reasons I undertook studies of disease courses of various groups of schizophrenics over a number of decades. I distinguished groups from different localities, patient populations from different hospitals and different backgrounds, first-time and multiple admissions, and hospitalized and nonhospitalized patients. In an effort to determine the limits within which different disease courses occurred in different selection groups of probands, I compared the findings for the different groups with one another.

A further problem arises as soon as the question occurs at what time-intervals reexaminations of schizophrenic patients should be scheduled in order to produce a valid picture of the overall course of schizophrenic psychoses. A simple procedure is to plan a reexamination after a predetermined lapse of time after the first examination; for instance,

1 year or 5 years thereafter. Most researchers actually do follow such a plan as this and as a result arrive at figures on recovery trends with relative ease. But they forget how very radically the patient's condition can change within 1 or 5 years; they forget further that a period of 5 years after the first hospitalization is not the same as "5 years after first onset," and that the latter point in time would be considerably more meaningful in many respects for determining the condition. An ideal demand, that would certainly be difficult to meet, would be to record the disease courses of many schizophrenics from first onset through their death. But even the statistics based on observations that ranged from the beginning of illness through the death of the patient cannot fully and adequately reflect the natural disease courses of schizophrenias. As a matter of fact, death often occurs before the schizophrenic psychosis has "run its course." Apparently very many schizophrenics whose psychosis would have run a favorable course, had they survived, die during acute catatonic seizures. It would therefore be illusory to suppose that the "average, natural disease course of a psychosis" could be determined from any studies that covered the period between onset and death. The results of such studies depend not only on the psychosis, but also on the vicissitudes the patient encountered in life, in at least a loose relationship to the psychosis. For instance, they depend on the average life-span of the population from which the patient originated. No matter what point in time is selected for determining the "total" course of the psychosis, there will always be objections that are difficult to resolve for any sort of generalization. In this respect also, then, there is no better choice open than to compare a number of investigations with varying catamnestic duration among one another, and to draw conclusions from them as to how the choice of timing the reexaminations will influence the resultant findings.

Another problem emerges in determining the degree of severity of a psychosis, particularly as to improvements and recoveries. Many statistics on the course of illness are considered satisfactory when they determine whether schizophrenic patients were still being hospitalized at a certain point in time or lived elsewhere outside the clinics. There should be no need to explain further that hospitalization depends on a great many other factors, than on the psychotic happening alone; for instance, on the release policies of the clinics and on the possibility of lodging and caring for the patient at home with his family. If the need for hospitalization is too inexact a criterion for establishing the patient's condition, then there is also a danger at the other extreme of applying excessively refined methods in determining recovery. As Uchtenhagen shows, in the framework of these studies, often test results reveal a normal, healthy person as schizophrenic. It would be a mistake not to regard the recovery of a schizophrenic as such, simply because it could not be determined by a projection test. As soon as the possibility is taken seriously that in every normal person's being there lie concealed some schizophrenic forms of life, considerably more care will be applied before considering every schizophrenic manifestiation in life as indication of a psychosis. The only doubts are not those arising from the test reports concerned with the assumption of schizophrenia, but also those arising from the overestimation of schizophrenia-like behavior, from a multitude of indications other than test results. To mention a few: the personal inner disposition toward beliefs, mysticism, or superstitions; a patient's behavior in a hostile environment or under conditions of reduced communications potential (partial deafness, for instance), or during other physical illness or impairment. Neither such a crude social criterion as hospitalization nor sporadic behavior under exceptional circumstances should be regarded as conclusive, not even when such exceptional incidents can reveal a schizophrenic inner life in healthy people. Nevertheless, it is necessary to attune an ear to the social behavior as well as to investigative results (the collection of which will always be fraught with some risks). But there will always be borderline cases. A schizophrenic may be nonaberrant in his own environment, but then become confused during reexamination when he is questioned about his former illness. Has he recovered or has he not recovered?

Then the question arises as to what is to consitute the healthy processing of a psychosis. Is the patient's complete insight into his illness always an indication of complete recovery? Or is it, on the contrary, an indication of an internal, pathological distancing by the patient from his own fate, in understanding something as unprecedented as an experienced psychosis, as if it were something to be shrugged off and forgotten? Complete insight into the mental disturbance certainly occurs also among recovered schizophrenics. Or is it necessarily pathological, when a schizophrenic who, judging by outward appearances, has recovered, makes confusing statements when he is asked to discuss his psychosis of recent experience? Perhaps it is an indication of recovery when the psychotic events of the past can be discussed only irrationally and autistically, while it does not necessarily indicate mental well-being when such shocking events are cast in clear, flowing language that could never correspond to subjective reality.

For all these reasons one easily becomes insecure and helpless when the attempt is made to determine the degree of improvement and recovery. Such qualifications simply are not possible without the application of arbitrary judgement, and the resulting figures are at best just indicators. They easily feign a nonexistent degree of precision.

But if we checked whether perhaps we are not accustomed to asking questions without having a realistic objective in mind, a great many difficulties inherent in the investigation of the courses of schizophrenias could be more accurately evaluated. We like to ask, what is the course of the disease that has befallen a person? But do we really know whether schizophrenia "befalls" an individual? Perhaps it is more of a phase or the result of a personal inner development. As often as similar trains of thought have been expressed, just as little have they become common usage in our clinical thinking or in the language. A radius fracture with all its implications can largely be investigated independently of the rest of the patient's life. We may ask what the "general" course of a radius fracture is, without becoming involved in extraneous problems. In cases of schizophrenia this may be different. This particular schizophrenia may correspond to the patient's struggle for harmony with his own ego, his inner existence, in the process of dealing with his environment. In such cases, schizophrenia does not endanger the personal fate of the patient from the outside, but it comes into being from the personal life-style of that individual. The development to maturity, goodness, or commonplace dullness in a healthy person is not forced on his personal fate either, but is an inherent part of that fate.

In the light of such reflections the concept "recovery from schizophrenia" is something quite different from that of recovery from other illnesses or injuries. When a schizo-phrenic recovers, it does not always mean that he is rid of a malady that attacked him from without, in the way that the injured patient is relieved of the incorrect position or mobility of one of his bones. The recovery from a schizophrenia denotes instead that his inner development has led him back into society as a unified person. If the schizophrenic does not recover, we may continue to refer to him objectively as ill; although we no longer feel constrained to determine that he has been sidetracked from the path of life intrinsic to his character by his "illness." Possibly his schizophrenic life is an inner necessity for him. The deeper we learn to feel our way into the schizophrenic, the less certain becomes our judgment as to what his recovery might mean, and whether a social readaptation would truly be the patient's own well-being—his own greatest personal achievement.

All these problems impose narrow limitats on the meaning of statistical studies of the course of illness. The point is to keep them in mind; although it is not necessary to capitulate before them. We need to have statistics on disease courses. We need them for prognoses, for the evaluation of our prophylactic and therapeutic methods, and we need them for research on the nature and origins of schizophrenias. The important fact is to evaluate them correctly; not to give them up.

Guidelines for Modern Course Investigations

It was over half a century before the problems inherent in course studies of schizophrenic psychoses became clearly defined. Only today is it possible to recognize clearly the procedural guidelines that may lead to a promising study of such courses, and only today can we avoid the pitfalls in which they so often foundered in the past. Some of the more important guidelines that I intend to follow in this exposition appear below.

1. The diagnosis of schizophrenias whose course one intends to investigate must not be adapted to, or made to depend on, that course. The diagnostic criteria inherent in this study have already been described.

2. The lives of schizophrenics are to be studied over long periods of time, over several decades. All of the 208 principal probands of this study I have observed from 1942 or 1943 either up to their deaths or for more than 20 years. The development of their psychoses had already been studied in retrospect from their

beginnings to 1942–1943.

3. The course of schizophrenic psychoses is to be considered longitudinally, as a continuous progressive curve. It is not valid to draw conclusions for the entire course from the data of a single reexamination, or as it were, from a cross-section of data. Accordingly, I have constructed graphs showing the progressive curves for all probands, from the beginnings of their illness to their deaths or over 20 years —frequently longer—after those beginnings.

4. The condition as to whether someone was hospitalized or not is an inadequate indication for determining the condition of a schizophrenic. In addition, his need for hospitalization, his performance efficiency, his ability to relate to others, and his total mental condition must be taken into consideration. This demand, too, I was able to satisfy.

5. The determination as to the recovery of a schizophrenic must be neither too superficial nor should it be adjudicated too narrow-mindedly, by criteria that are world-alien and excessively subtle. The criteria I apply are listed below.

6. Freedom of choice in the selection of probands is an impossibility. There is no group of schizophrenics whose disease course would be representative for all schizophrenics. For this reason the disease courses of many different groups of schizophrenics will be studied. By this process threshold values will be obtained, within which the disease courses of all schizophrenics will be included. With these demands in mind, I have examined the progress in a large variety of selected probands for several decades. These include patients from Pfäfers (Switzerland), New York, Basel, and Zürich; probands from city university clinics and one rural clinic; probands from different periods in time who had access to different treatment methods and facilities; and probands with different subcategories of schizophrenia. I compared the average courses of schizophrenias of all types with those of late schizophrenics, with schizophrenics who recovered under shock treatment, with schizophrenics with certain endocrinological stigmatization, etc.

Up to now there are very few studies on the disease courses of schizophrenics that follow those guidelines, as necessary as their observance may appear, since they have been derived from the experience of the past several decades. For this reason one might be inclined to expect completely new and spectacular results from investigations such as the ones described here. But our expectations become modest when we consider that the systematically scientific investigations on the courses of schizophrenias have largely been based on false postulates, but that there was a different—a higher—tribunal, that took all these guidelines into considerations all along, unwittingly, unconsciously, and without a great deal of fuss: it was simply the intuitive processing of life's experience. From their own life experiences the psychiatrists automatically arrived at the correct perspectives on the problem! Indeed, if one observes one's patients with a keen eye over a period of decades, one unwittingly adheres to all those guidelines that have so long been neglected by the customary planned research methods. The image of the prognosis of schizophrenia, as it took shape for psychiatrists over several generations, is closer to reality than the results of many statistics from studies of disease courses. When young research scientists published "new" and sensational results of course studies based on statistical investigations, their experienced colleagues regarded them with quiet smiles that implied "We know better,"—and they did know better.

If for this reason only modest results are to be expected from goal-directed statistical studies of disease courses, like the ones presented here, one still ought not to give up in defeat. It is meaningful intuitively to support scientifically and statistically any knowledge that comes to us from experience. And statistically derived data are by no means useless if all they do is to confirm intuitive knowledge. Beyond that, they can bring to light new facts, and in the process show the way to avoid dangers and dead ends and to plan for future research that would offer promising results. I often had to bear this in mind, when I no longer felt certain as to the value of the laborious pursuit of so many schizophrenics over so long a period.

Description of Concepts for Use in Statistical Application

It is rare that the beginning of a disease can be clinically observed. But it is usually possible to determine from the reports of the proband himself, his family, and his acquaintances, when he became psychotic, in the social definition of the term (see pp. 15–16), and when a clinical examination would first have permitted that diagnosis. It was almost always possible to determine that point in time, if in chronic cases not to the exact day at least to the exact period, within a few months. This point in time is henceforth called the "onset of illness." A mere change in behavior in the sense of eccentricities, pseudoneuroticism, or hypochondria may theoretically be assumed to constitute the "actual" onset of illness. As to the determination of the onset of illness for our statistics, however, personality changes that are not unequivocally psychotic are disregarded. An onset of illness is considered, rather, when the patient first expresses delusions or hallucinations, when he begins to talk in such confusion that he is regarded as mentally ill by people around him, when he begins to neglect his customary duties for no apparent reason, when he ceases to talk, refuses to eat, when he rants, etc.

An illustrative case is a patient who at age 15 became increasingly withdrawn, more rapturous, more irritable, and moodier than usual; although he continued his apprenticeship and continued to be employed, he was considered by the people in contact with him as eccentric but healthy. If, at age 24, within a few months' time he voiced with increased frequency and intensity his fears of persecution, prejudice, and injury, the onset was determined at age 24, and not at age 15.

I shall discuss the acute onset of illness or the acute recommencement of a phase of illness below, whenever the illness or phase of illness developed within a few days or weeks, or at the outside within a few months. If it is not possible to determine the onset of illness as having developed within the period of a few weeks or in a very few months, but the illness develops almost unnoticed over the course of several months, I assume a chronic onset. The concept of what is acute is thus expanded beyond its customary application in somatic medicine. It corresponds to the usual psychiatric application (the distinction between acute and chronic will be somewhat refined below, in this chapter).

When schizophrenics are observed over a period of decades, one may notice rather frequently that their condition stabilizes somewhat over several years before observations are stopped. The term "end state" is applied here, which would be attained after the active psychotic phases had run their course. In my previous studies I applied the same label, assuming that the "end state" might consist of a recovery, a mere defect, or a dementia. It so happens that one of the results of this and earlier studies is the finding that schizo-phrenic psychoses very rarely terminate in a fully stable condition that holds for several years. Instead, both the personality and the illness continue to develop further throughout life, and almost never remain entirely the same over a period of years. At least that conclusion is reached when probands are carefully observed. One is also amazed, time and again, when improvements or even recoveries still occur after many years of "dementias" and, conversely, when relapses occur many years after improvements or even recovery. Advanced age also seems to influence the schizophrenic condition. According to our present knowledge, there can no longer be any reference to the notion that schizophrenia would ever result in conditions that could be regarded as permanent. But if the "end state" is neither final nor permanent, it should no longer be called an "end state." Despite this, one does often see patients at the conclusion of decades of observation, whose condition has not changed in essence at least for a number of years. One might say of them that their condition has reached a plateau of long duration; or one might also speak of a "long-term, fairly constant condition at the end of observation." But such expressions, with their unwieldy wordiness, would embellish neither the text nor the captions of tables. How might they be replaced with a brief catchword? I should like in what follows to discuss "end states" by using quotation marks around the expression. It is intended to convey conditions existing at the conclusion of observations or before the death of the patient, that are of long duration and that run an even, constant course. The quotation marks are intended to warn the reader against accepting the term thoughtlessly and perhaps equating "end state" with "terminal condition" or with a final, permanent condition.

In the tabulations "end states" are recorded with the length of their duration. Only such conditions are considered as "end states" that have remained constant without interruption for over 5 years.

What, then, is the nature of the recorded "end states"?

The most severe among them may be identified as follows: They apply to probands who never carry on coherent, understandable conversations. They are either mutistic, or they speak in such confusion that, in response to simple questions, an occasionally applicable remark interspersed with confusing nonsense is the best one can expect in the way of a reply, although usually no sensible answers at all can be expected. They either do no work at all, or at best do purely mechanical chores, such as hauling a cart, plucking horse hair, etc., under intensively supervised work-therapy methods. They appear to disregard and to remain indifferent to their surroundings. Any human contact with them is impossible. They require constant care, and usually cause trouble for those who care for them by acts of violence, vocal abuses, noisy behavior, uncleanliness, or their inability to properly and independently care for their bodily needs, etc. Years ago such behavior was unthinkingly characterized as severe idiocy or dementia. But once we realize that seriously "demented" schizophrenics have not lost touch with a healthy psychic life, that in their case, healthy perception, memory, recall, judgment, and feeling are merely concealed behind their pathological behavior; that such probands actually do occasionally recover, then one begins to doubt the validity of the qualification of "idiocy." It has been pointed out, and with good reason, that the expression usually applied to conditions of severe cerebral atrophy should not also be applied to the most severe schizophrenic conditions that are so different in character. For these reasons I avoid the terms "idiocy" and "dementia" in the passages that follow, and use in their stead the expression "severe end states'."

"End states" that did not reach the severity of a dementia were formerly referred to as "schizophrenic defects"; in my earlier studies I distinguished between mild and severe defects. The term "defect" itself does not fully correspond any longer to present-day concepts. It indicates too strongly something unchangeable and irrevocable, and ignores the fact that behind the pathological condition healthy life lies concealed. These conditions do not indicate that anything has been permenently destroyed; pathological behavior simply replaces healthy behavior. I therefore avoid using the ominous expression "defect" in the material that follows, and apply "moderately severe" and "mild" schizophrenic "end states," in distinguishing from "severe end states."

The term moderately severe "end state" was applied to probands who generally behaved as did the seriously idiotic, except that in one respect or another they consistently proved that their mental equipment was better preserved than outward appearance would indicate. The concept includes probands who, for instance, behave like the seriously idiotic before their doctors and the subprofessional staff, but then regularly thaw out before certain visitors and give an impression that approaches normality. Or they are probands who, while, remaining totally uncommunicative, still perform hard work or become actively involved in caring for others, etc. Included in this group are also those who on certain occasions, for instance at a celebration or during a physical illness, suddenly thaw out and establish contact. Of the patients who reveal no such fluctuations, we include those in the group of moderately severe "end states" who unequivocally and regularly reveal thought disturbances, even in conversations on impersonal topics, but who can still communicate in such a way as to convey their thoughts on a subject with reasonable clarity. Their work performance in every instance is appreciably lower in comparison with what their performance was before the onset of illness.

A mild "end state" was entered for patients who can maintain a sensible conversation, at least about topics that do not concern their delusional or hallucinatory experiences, despite the fact that definite, schizophrenic symptoms do exist. Their overt behavior is generally normal, and their illness is not immediately obvious if one becomes involved in conversations. They perform useful work. They live either outside the institution or on quiet wards. This group includes also, among others, a number of probands whose delusional or hallucinatory ideas exist near the surface, without an actual deterioration of their personality being in evidence. It also includes some aged eccentrics who have rejected life, who scarcely manifest any normal interests, are incapable of performing even simple mechanical tasks, or who pursue any sort of whimsical idea.

To assume a proband had recovered, it was essential that he could be fully employed in gainful work, and that he could reassume his former role in society, particularly in the family as head of the family or, in women, as homemaker in the home. It was further required that his family accept him as "rational"; that is, that he was no longer considered by them as being mentally ill. Brief medical examinations should no longer reveal any psychotic symptoms. But probands were also considered recovered when a thorough medical examination uncovered some residues of delusional ideas, faulty perception relative to their former psychosis, eccentricity, or constriction in his fields of interest or activity. According to the statistics on the successful results of insulin treatments and the terminology applied in them in recent years (as for example, von Deussen 1937), my recoveries include the "total remissions" as well as the "good remissions"; and they include recovery in the medical as well as in the social context. The reasons why excessively strict demands on the concept of recovery of a schizophrenic psychosis seem unjustified to me have been previously explained: It is difficult to determine what would constitute the completely healthy processing of the outrageous experience of a schizophrenic psychosis. It often seems to me that it is more nearly pathological when a patient can discuss his former psychosis with unconcerned objectivity, and acts as if he had not been the victim of it, as if he considered the psychotic world valid as such, and his psychosis had merely matured him and made him introspective, or lonely and embittered.

The periods of illness that begin acutely and recede acutely I refer to as acute phases or undulations of a schizophrenic psychosis. They may involve a first-time or a repeated phase of illness, they may develop from a normal state of health or from a milder chronic condition, and then again they may revert to a recovery or to a milder chronic state. To qualify as an undulation, a phase must have lasted at least a week. Excitations of short duration, for instance, transitory orgies of scolding on the part of chronic probands, were not counted as undulations. Nor did we consider it an undulating phase of illness in the sense of our statistical terminology when a severe depressive or stuporous condition passed over into a severe manic-like state or one of extreme excitation.

It is patently obvious to any clinician that the given explanations of the concepts of onset of illness, acuteness, chronicity, "end state," recovery, and undulation are not adequate tools for defining a certain and objective delimitation of the various conditions, without the application of some arbitrary judgment. Again and again we come up against borderline cases which cannot be assigned to the existing definitions without the application of arbitrary judgment. This experience is depressing and dulls the pleasure of working. Of necessity one must be satisfied to find consolation in two thoughts: We are unsuccessful in formulating clearer and better

descriptions of the concepts; and experience shows that, even so, the great majority of cases will fit unobjectionably into the described concepts without forced, subjective decisions. Only a small minority are borderline cases. Examples for the determination of data that characterize the courses of illness can be derived from previously reported patient histories (to which we shall refer below), and from several others that follow.

The "Acute Onset"

Female Proband 71 (see pp. 20–23).

Her illusions of jealousy during pregnancy were aberrant, but were recognized as a first symptom of illness only in retrospect, for in the beginning they were not delusional. As a result, their beginning was not yet identified with the beginning of her psychosis.

The "Chronic Onset"

Male Proband 34, (see pp. 18–20).

"Chronic Onset" and "Severe End State"

Male Proband 82, Gottfried M.

The patient, born 1905, was beset at about age 23 by a lingering psychosis from which he never recovered. In general he has been in the same condition on an intensive care ward since 1951; that is, for 16 years between then and his last examination on April 26, 1967. He was characterized as "totally demented" in a number of patient histories, and in the statistics of this study his "end state" is classified as "severe, chronic schizophrenia."

He is the son of a fruit vendor, who was a hard worker, but who treated his family harshly and unlovingly. His mother, an intellectually limited, egocentric woman, developed an affection and devotion for the proband that was pathetic. She mothered him excessively, often took him home in his psychotic state against the advice of his doctors, and raved about his virtues long after he had been severely ill for many years, describing him as "a most wonderful person."

Even as a child he had been introverted and uncommunicative, had very few friends, but enjoyed the company of animals, which he treated with great affection. He grew up at home with his parents. He had little trouble acquiring a good secondary education. After his schooling he worked in his father's fruit business, usually as a truck driver, until he was hospitalized. He was as shy and withdrawn in feminine company as he was in his relationships with all other people; although he maintained a tenuous love relationship when he was 20 with a girl who left him about a year before his psychosis became evident.

His illness began as a lingering psychosis when he was 23, in that he became taciturn and sad. He first received psychocathartic treatments from a reputable practising freelance neurologist, with the diagnosis of a depression. From that point his condition deteriorated slowly. It soon became evident that his illness was by no means a simple depression. Increasingly he sat around listlessly, unconcerned, and bored; instead of working, he spoke in confusion, guffawed without provocation, and began more and more to withdraw from all human contacts, including that of his parents. From age 33 on he was hospitalized in a number of psychiatric clinics, was regularly retrieved by his mother against medical advice, but never showed any noteworthy improvement at home. Everywhere he was evaluated as an "apathetic, deteriorating catatonic." When he spoke, it was in total confusion. Often he complained about hearing voices, and at times he lapsed intermittently into states of violent excitability. He completely neglected his appearance. After probationary releases he threatened his parents and behaved absurdly and dangerously; for instance, he climbed about on rooftops without any apparent reason. Nobody was able to converse sensibly with him.

For about 11 years he has been on the same ward for the most severe, chronic mental patients, and his condition has since changed so little, that it is fair to classify his case as a "relatively stable, most serious chronic psychosis of more than 10-years' duration." The following paragraphs cite a few entries from his patient history:

August 17, 1956: Patient was transferred from a ward for quiet, severely ill patients to a ward for chronically restless patients, because he destroyed objects, ripped off the lattice work, and tore up all the paper he could get his hands on. He is agitated, ominously depressive and totally uncommunicative.

November 16, 1956: Condition unchanged. Demented patient who is intermittently restless, but poses no problems on the ward. He was especially helpful this fall in that he carefully picked up all fallen leaves in D-Quadrangle.

January 26, 1957: Patient is totally demented and leads a withdrawn and virtually sealed-off existence. Unable any longer to perform any useful work.

May 22, 1957: Patient unchanged but pleasant, constantly in motion. It is even an effort to keep him still while he eats. Does no work, but causes no problems otherwise.

July 26, 1957: A good-natured and willing patient; causes no trouble. His constant fidgety restlessness was somewhat suppressed with 2×4 mg reserpine. He does little work. Conversation with him is impossible because of his artificial speech.

October 16, 1957: This quiet, withdrawn patient seldom shows up during doctors' visits. Frequently mumbles autistically to himself. Poorly motivated for work. Takes notions to pull off anything movable; flowers, leaves, etc.

March 26, 1958: Patient remains unchanged on the ward. Walks briskly back and forth, stares grimly at the world, shakes hands mechanically without establishing any closer contact. Another reserpine cure is suggested because of his restlessness.

May 3, 1958: No appreciable change noted in patient after his treatment. He is somewhat less fidgety, intermittently he is pleasant and amiable; then again shut off from any contact, glowering, and restless.

June 25, 1958: Patient is occasionally cross, glowers malevolently at whomever he meets, refuses to answer, and runs away from people. On other days he is quite sociable, shakes hands, approaches me willingly and smiles. However, he is incapable of conversation, mumbles to himself, and gives no relevant answers. No care problems on the ward.

September 5, 1958: No change in condition of patient. Alternately moody and disagreeable, then again quite pleasant and sociable. Usually wants to shake hands when meeting him, but otherwise no contact.

January 21, 1966: In an attempt to engage patient in conversation, he repeatedly withdraws, signalling with his hands to desist. Permits only brief verbal interchange at 2–3 meters distance, and then only in short, conventional phrases, such as "How are you?" and so on. His mood is difficult to fathom; on occasions he suddenly sits down in a depressive attitude, his head down on his arms on the table, and then rubs his eyes; mostly he appears harrassed, yet as though running idle. Motor behavior is restless; occasionally attempts to escape when approached, as if pursued, leaping over tables and benches, and then disappears at the remote end of the hall. Sister and brother-in-law visit occasionally. According to attendant's report, he did good work caring for strappings, then with plastic syringes, also in housekeeping. No medication. Still retains his collector's instinct and picks up all manner of trash and odds and ends from the floor and puts them in his pockets.

Up to the time this report was written, April 28, 1967, nothing had changed materially. The patient is still under care in the same ward. He must be diligently admonished to keep himself clean, otherwise he would stay dirty. Nevertheless, he dresses himself, and washes himself when he is urged to. He can eat without assistance. Mechanically and under close supervision and apportionment of small tasks at a time (chopping kindling, assembling sections of toys, sorting straps according to length, etc.) he will perform work. He seldom rants any more. It is not ever possible to elicit any coherent, sensible speech from him. Mimic and facial gestures appear fixed and seem to express repugnance, resignation, and disgust with everything. The wrinkles in his face, carved there by years of discontent, have deepened with the passing of time. He often assumes peculiar poses, for instance, he tucks his right foot under his left thigh when he sits. His greeting is mechanical and stereotyped, in that he briefly glances at one, then boldly looks past, quickly and furtively extends his hand, makes contact without pressure, mumbles something unintelligible, and then turns and makes his getaway.

Thus he presents the picture of what used to be categorized as a most severe schizophrenic dementia. The fact that behind this exterior, intellectual faculties are still active and that the spirit has by no means been laid waste has been demonstrated. As an example, a year earlier, he was taken to the circus along with some other patients. Inadvertently or on purpose he lost himself in the crowd. He was paged, searched for, and reported to the police, but he was not found. Instead, he made his own way back to the clinic, where he arrived at night and reported himself in. He had not left the clinic for many years; but still he was able to find the distant, complicated route back by night. His family also reports that during the first few minutes of a visit, he asks perfectly clear and sensible questions about the well-being of relatives, but then quickly deteriorates into confused, unintelligible chatter. A talk I had with him yesterday showed plainly that he was able to grasp some rather complicated concepts fairly quickly. For instance, I asked him how the newly organized section of group psy-chotherapy was working out on his ward. His gestures showed that he knew instantly what I meant. Of course, he replied only with yes or no, but he got the idea of what it was about. His natural disposition is partly revealed by the following anecdote: As a child and a young boy he had loved animals. Aware of this, I gave him a guinea pig; his devotion to it is touching. He spends some time with it every day and speaks to it, using pet names such as "Potzy"; then his face brightens and his voice softens and vibrates with warmth, as if a normal person were talking to a child. He cannot take care of it by himself, but he watches over it zealously, making sure that one of his fellow inmates feeds it correctly; and he complains when his friend forgets.

Moderately Severe "End State"

Male Proband 34, described on pp. 18–20.

"Chronic Onset" and Mild "End State"

Male Proband 13, Georg Ch.

Proband was born in 1902, the son of an Italian bricklayer, who had immigrated and become adapted in Switzerland. He suffered a fatal accident when the proband was 3 years old. His mother raised him until 1911, and after that, she and her affluent second husband. Conditions appeared to be normal, from the perspective of observers. But a shadow of poverty lay over the adolescence and childhood of the proband and his two siblings, which was in stark contrast to the affluence of his stepfather and most of the other relatives. The proband was a gifted student in school, and was planning to study mathematics; but there was no money available for higher education. He became a mechanic and did excellent work in his field. From childhood on he was considered an eccentric, kept to himself, and appeared to be absent-minded. The other boys said of him, "He's not one of us."

While he was working abroad in 1926, representing his business firm, the first indications of prejudicial thinking began to appear, and these developed slowly into a persecution mania. He claimed everybody was "accusing" him of being a Freemason. He increasingly fell out of favor with his coworkers, whom he accused of all manner of imagined libels. In spite of his delusional condition, however, he was able to continue working for a number of years. Then his job performance began to deteriorate. His employers did not want to keep him abroad any longer, so they recalled him to Switzerland, where he just refused to do any work. Without having any real foundation, he claimed his employers owed him restitution, and made claims for outrageous sums of money from them. He would do no work at all and simply paraded about in his Sunday-clothes. He was suspected of being engaged in espionage (1941) for the Germans, since his appearance was rather sinister and he was not able to show a source of income. The investigation showed, however, that any activity in espionage was completely out of the question.

In 1942, without means, he was hospitalized at Burghölzli for mental illness. He gave the impression of the typical schizophrenic paranoic. He became distracted whenever the topic of conversation approached his condition. He clung tenaciously to incoherent delusional ideas, claiming, for instance, that he was being accused of practising Freemasonry, was being persecuted and mocked, and that his employer owed him large sums of money for various compensations. He kept away from all other patients; yet, externally, he adapted well to the routine of the clinic and did his work. On my initiative, legal permission was secured for his trial release after 2 months—a rather daring step. He moved into a furnished room, was given another job as a mechanic by his former employers, and was tactfully looked after by his legal guardian.

For the next 20 years, contrary to all misgivings, he got along well, until the observations for this study were suspended. For 18 years this former patient was capable of holding a job as mechanic, although he was often stubborn and overly sensitive. Two years before his normal time was up, he was pensioned, since he had begun at about that time to do careless work. He is able to live on his retirement income. His family and people who have known him for the past 20 years no longer regard him as mentally ill; instead, they consider him a bit of an eccentric, and somewhat embittered with life. His bitterness, he explains, stems from the fact that he was unable to advance his education, a reason that does deserve sympathy. He is rather monosyllabic in conversation and not very sociable; he lives alone and withdrawn. His eccentricity is rationalized by his family by the explanation that he is hungry for sunshine, meaning that he takes every advantage of every possible opportunity to expose himself to the sun. They do not like to go walking with him, because often he simply removes his shirt to expose his torso to the sun, and this may happen on a crowded street.

He no longer talks spontaneously about his delusional ideas; they seem to have disappeared into the background. During reexaminations, however, it soon became evident that he holds fast to them.

His interests center around doing kindnesses for the children of his relatives, and this is unanimously confirmed by anyone who testifies about him, describing his devotion to them as heart-warming. He is constantly concerned for their welfare. He regularly sends money in fairly large amounts, for which he stints himself, to a poverty-ridden sister and her son who live in America. He appears as a self-denying, generous, altruistic humanitarian.

Recovery

Female Proband 71, described on pp. 20–23.

Age of Patients at First Onset of Illness

Table 4.1 shows the age at onset of illness of the following groups of schizophrenic patients, arranged in order by decades: Groups A, B, F: the 208 principal probands of this study, categorized as males, females, and both sexes together; Groups C, D, G: 68 initial admissions at Burghölzli of the 208 principal probands of this study, categorized as men, women, and both sexes together (these initial admissions are included under the caption "all probands"); Group E: the 63 male and female schizophrenic siblings of the 208 probands; Group H: 208 male and female probands and 63 male and female siblings of those probands; that is, Groups E and F considered jointly.

There are comparison figures in Table 4.2, showing the age at onset of illness of the 208 schizophrenic probands and those of their 63 schizophrenic siblings (Group H from Table 4.1) in comparison with:

(a) the onset age of 459 hospitalized schizophrenics whose patient histories I had processed up to 1941. These were patients from Pfäfers, New York, and Basel, and their schizophrenic siblings (for details, see my study published on the subject in 1941). The statistics of

Table 4.1. Age of onset among principal probands and their siblings, listed by sex, and compared with initial admissions of all probands

Age group	A 100 male probands	B 108 female probands	C 32 first-time admissions of male probands	D 36 first-time admissions of female probands	E 63 siblings of probands	F All 208 probands	G All 68 first-time admissions	H All 208 probands and 63 siblings
15–19 Years	13 = 13% ±3.4	12 = 11% ±3	4 = 13% ±5.9	1 = 3% ±2.8	8 = 13% ±4.2	25 = 12% ±2.2	5 = 7% ±3.1	33 = 12% ±1.9
20–29 Years	43 = 43% ±4.9	36 = 33% ±4.5	12 = 38% ±8.6	9 = 25% ±7.2	20 = 32% ±5.9	79 = 38% ±3.4	21 = 31% ±5.6	99 = 37% ±2.9
30–39 Years	30 = 30% ±4.6	29 = 27% ±4.3	11 = 34% ±8.4	11 = 30% ±7.6	18 = 29% ±5.7	59 = 28% ±3.1	22 = 32% ±5.6	77 = 28% ±2.7
Over 40 Years	14 = 14% ±3.5	31 = 29% ±4.4	5 = 16% ±6.5	15 = 42% ±8.2	17 = 27% ±5.6	45 = 22% ±2.9	20 = 30% ±5.5	62 = 23% ±2.5
	100	108	32	36	63	208	68	271

older authors were used for additional comparisons:

(b) those by Kraepelin[1] on 1054 schizophrenic probands of the University Clinic of Munich;

(c) Schneider's (see n. 1) studies on 889 schizophrenic probands from the clinic at Arnsdorf;

(d) Schulz's[2] studies on 660 schizophrenic probands from the Munich clinic.

The tables show the median errors along with the percentage figures of my own investigations. They apply to the differences in the comparisons. Most of the differences lie within the threshold area of chance, although a study of the tables would permit the following statements:

1. The older investigations reveal more disease onset early in life than do the investigations from more recent years, and correspondingly fewer onsets later in life. The reasons are obvious: Kraepelin and Schulz (from the Kraepelin school) still regarded schizophrenia as an "early dementia." According to Kraepelin's conception, extreme skepticism was called for before categorizing late-onset illnesses as "praecox," even when their symptomatology was schizophrenic. Cases we regard today as late-onset schizophrenias were formerly regarded under diagnoses of paraphrenia, catatonic-like involutional psychoses, among others. These diagnostic differences may sufficiently explain the preponderance of early onsets, and the rarity of late onsets as reported by Kraepelin (see n. 1) and Schulz[2] in contrast to Schneider's findings (see n. 1) and mine. Besides, a shift in the age structure of a population is bound to occur over a period of several decades in relation to a proportional increase of onsets of illness later in life. At the time of the later investigations, older people were increasing among the population. This explains the increase of late-onset illnesses among the schizophrenics of this study in comparison to those among the schizophrenics I described in 1941. The differences between birthdates of the schizophrenics from the two studies is slight, but most of the patients discussed up to 1941 come

1. Figures from Mayer-Gross, W., "Die Klinik" in *Handbuch der Geisteskrankheiten*, (Handbook of Mental Illnesses) Vol. IX, O. Bumke, editor. Berlin, Springer, 1932.

2. Schulz, B., *Zentralblatt für die gesamte Neurologie und Psychiatrie* GXLIII, 175, 1933.

from an area in which exceptional longevity had not set in among the average of the population as it had in the area that was home to most of the probands of this study. Another reason for the lower figure of early onsets among the probands of this study as compared to those described in 1941—though an incidental one—related to the sex ratio. Among the schizophrenics of this study the ratio between men and women is almost equal, while among the schizophrenics described in 1941 the men outnumber the women; but most of the women were late onsets. Probably the tendency among the general population was the same because of a desire to spare children and young people the odium of living in a "madhouse." As already pointed out, for the Canton of Zürich, the area where most of the probands for this investigation originated, the result of this desire was that schizophrenic children were sometimes referred first to a private clinic, which meant that they could not become probands of this study. In the highlands around St. Gallen, where many of the probands studied up to 1941 originated, private clinics are located at more distance from the community; therefore the tendency is not as great. In the German university clinics, this tendency is not as great either as around Zürich, since the taboo of the "madhouse" is much less prevalent in those university clinics.

2. There were more late-onset patients among the schizophrenic women than among the schizophrenic men. Up to this time most investigations on late-onset schizophrenics have revealed an equally clear majority for women in this area, in keeping with our findings. For instance, among the late schizophrenics of my 1943 report, there were 32 men to 62 women.

3. There were more late-onset patients among first-time admissions than among all admissions. Insofar as this difference is not merely a caprice of chance, it is easy to explain: Early-onset patients stand a greater chance of multiple hospitalizations, and thereby becoming probands, than late-onset patients.

From inspecting Tables 4.1 and 4.2, we might summarize: The majority of schizophrenics ($\frac{2}{3}$ to $\frac{3}{4}$) became ill after maturity, between ages 20 and 40. Among the remainder ($\frac{1}{3}$ to $\frac{1}{4}$), the majority were early-onset cases (before age 20) a few decades ago; at that time only a small minority were late-onset cases (over age 40). Today the situation

Table 4.2. Age of onset among probands from other investigations

Age	Kraepelin's [1] 1054 patients	C. Schneider's [1] 889 patients	B. Schulz's [2] 660 patients	459 patients described by M. Bleuler in 1941		271 patients from the present study	
				Number	Percentage and standard deviation	Number	Percentage and standard deviation
10–20 Years	33.9%	20.4%	20.2%	91	19.8 ± 1.86	33	12 ± 1.97
20–30 Years	48.3%	43.8%	50.4%	211	46.0 ± 2.32	99	37 ± 2.93
30–40 Years	18.0%	24.1%	23.6%	89	19.4 ± 1.84	77	28 ± 2.72
Over 40 Years	5.8%	15.4%	5.6%	68	14.8 ± 1.65	62	23 ± 2.55

1. Figures from Mayer-Gross, W., "Die Klinik" in *Handbuch der Geisteskrankheiten*, vol. IX, ed. by O. Bumke. Berlin: Springer, 1932.

2. Schulz, B., *Zentralblatt für die gesamte Neurologie und Psychiatrie* vol. 143, p. 175, 1933.

is reversed. Among those schizophrenics who became ill outside the 20–40 age group, there are today many more late-onset and considerably fewer early-onset cases.

If within the last few decades the percentage of early-onset cases has decreased and that of late-onset cases has increased, the change is mainly due to the change in diagnostic practice, on the one hand, and to the difference in age structure of the population on the other. There are, accordingly, mitigating circumstances here that really do not concern the occurrence of the schizophrenic disease itself. As to the age of the patient at onset, the occurrence of the disease has remained constant over several decades, as was similarly the case in a number of different locales. Insofar as they can be evaluated in the context of the onset-age, the biological and psychological processes that lead to schizophrenia have remained remarkably stable. If changes in the frequency of either the late- or the early-onset of the disease have indeed been recorded, they do not indicate a change in the nature of the occurrence of schizophrenia; but they are brought about by variations of circumstances that occurred apart from the actual occurrence of the disease.

It will be necessary to redetermine the ratios of onset-ages of schizophrenics in later years and in different countries and cultures, and then to compare those results with the data on hand today.[3] We may hope to glean from

such comparisons some important conclusions on the genesis of schizophrenias. I see the most important value of these data on the onset of illness in presenting today's results for comparisons with the results of future investigations. Moreover, so much has been made known about the onset of illness in the past decades, that further studies about it could just as well have been omitted.

Acute and Chronic Onset

Below, the concept of an "acute" onset, as it was described on p. 190 will be further broken down into subcategories. A "peracute" beginning means an onset whose beginning can be determined accurately, within a few days; "acute" within a few weeks; and "subacute" when the disease becomes manifest within several months. Only those cases that begin almost unnoticed over periods of many months or years, making it impossible to determine their onset objectively, were classified as "chronic."

The results are contained in Table 4.3. The peracute, acute, and subacute cases were to the chronic cases as 129:79 = 62 percent: 38 percent. The differences between men and women, and between all probands and first-time admissions are not statistically significant. Nevertheless, they indicate, according to expectations, that according to general psychiatric experience, schizophrenic psy-

3. While this book was in press, an article by Larson and Nyman was published on this topic. It determines the onset of illness of 153 men born between 1881 and 1900, who were admitted to a clinic in southern Sweden.

The proportion of onsets after age 40 is exceptionally high at 30.7 percent; in fact, even higher than among my own probands. This high figure is due mainly to selection criteria according to birth date.

Table 4.3. Type of schizophrenic onset among 208 principal probands (listed separately by sex and by initial admission status or by all admission)

Type of onset	All male probands	Male probands initially hospitalized	All female probands	Female probands initially hospitalized	All probands hospitalized for the first time		All probands	
Peracute	2	1	2	1	2 =	3% ±2.06	4 =	2% ±0.97
Acute	36	13	43	14	27 =	40% ±5.94	79 =	38% ±3.36
Subacute	20	8	26	9	17 =	25% ±5.25	46 =	22% ±2.87
Chronic	42	10	37	12	22 =	32% ±5.65	79 =	38% ±3.36
	100	32	108	36	68		208	

choses among women are more often acute than they are among men.

It is interesting to note, however, that since the 1942 investigations the acute-onset states have by no means increased over the chronic ones. According to the bare figures alone, the contrary would be the case: In none of the various groups of schizophrenics whose beginnings of illness I had recorded in 1941 did the percentage of chronic developments come up to 38 percent. The highest rate among those early investigations came to 32 percent of schizophrenic psychoses with chronic development. The difference is not statistically significant, and can certainly not be generalized because of the operant selection factors. It remains remarkable, however, that in my present group of probands, the acute-disease developments have not increased, in contrast to those from previous investigations.

In recent years, in agreement with the findings of numerous authors and with the clinical impressions of most psychiatrists, that portion of those patients with acute schizophrenic episodes who needed hospitalization increased. But, on the other hand, from my own observations it can be assumed that acute onsets have not increased in frequency. It seems according to this, that acute phases are on the increase only during the course, and not at the beginnings of schizophrenic psychoses. In the last years, accordingly, the course of the illness rather than the onset of illness has undergone a change.

This finding supports the assumption that it was not changes in diagnostics or in the regularity in reporting hospitalized cases that brought about the increase of acute schizophrenic episodes in psychiatric hospitals. It is much more likely that influences that develop after onset of illness, and among these particularly the newer treatment methods, are causing the increased tendency toward a phasic development of the schizophrenias.

The Long-Term, Relatively Stable Schizophrenic States before Completion of Observation ("End States")

Of the 208 principal schizophrenic probands, 152 achieved a relatively stable condition that had held for over 5 years when observations were completed (after they had been probands for over 20 years). The remaining 56 probands either had expired during an acute phase of illness, were at the time in that state, or the stable condition they had achieved had not yet lasted a full 5 years.

The great majority of schizophrenic probands achieves a condition after a psychosis has run its course for several decades that is fairly stable for a number of years. The term "for decades" is no exaggeration of the specification "more than 20 years." Many of the probands had been schizophrenic for years before they became probands in this investigation.

Among the 61 siblings of probands, who also became schizophrenic and were hospitalized at least once, 35 attained a relatively stable condition after a course of illness of many years' duration.

Can a reasonably stable condition that lasts at least 5 years be considered an "end state" in the final sense, regarding it as a condition that will remain unchanged until the end of the proband's life? Daily routine clinical observation teaches us that this is not the case, if mild fluctuations in the proband's condition are also considered. A completely stable condition of a long-term schizophrenic state is even more rare than the complete stability of a healthy personality. The basic mood of the proband may change, they may abandon or develop anew any number of pathological behavior manfestations (for instance, while eating, dressing, or in respect to personal hygiene); they may manifest a more agitated or a more tranquil mood, or show a preference for one kind of work for a while and then change again to another, etc. Another section will show in detail that even in these "end states" some improvements and deteriorations still occur. But as changeable as any chronic schizophrenic state may be as to details of behavior and refinements in the proband's condition of health, it is still rare when a truly marked change occurs in a proband's condition that has, by and large, been stable over a number of years. Any changes that would call for a reassignment of the basic summary category (severe, moderately severe, or mild chronic states or recoveries) are rather rare after a lapse of so many years. It most often happens that a remission or a mild state that has persisted for many years will suddenly be interrupted by an acute episode of illness. Usually such an onset will quickly recede, and the state that has maintained itself over the long term becomes reestablished. There are other surprising changes also. It is one of the great events in the lives of all clinicians to witness the rare occurrence of the recovery of a patient who has lived through a most severe, stabilized schizophrenic state of many years' duration. The great majority of stabilized states of over 5 years' duration after a development of a number of years, are at best interrupted by acute episodes of illness until the patients expire; although little ever occurs to change the basic, principal categorizations. We are justified, therefore, in applying the abbreviated term "end state" to chronic, relatively stable states of long duration, in which the quotation marks should suffice to allay any misgivings as to semantic accuracy. The distribution ratios of long-term stable conditions (end states") of the 208 probands, of severe, moderately severe, and mild conditions and recoveries are shown in Table 4.4. They are differentiated as to sex, as to schizophrenic probands and their siblings, and as to whether the patients became probands during their first, or during subsequent hospitalizations.

The "end states" of at least 5 years' duration, which 152 of the 208 principal probands had attained at the end of the study, were distributed as follows:

errors, that prove very little. However, some answers on the progress of psychoses for all hospitalized schizophrenics after their first onset may be derived from studying the schizophrenic siblings of probands, who themselves had been hospitalized at least once in their lives. At least there is no selection process operating among them that categorized them according to multiple hospitalization cases, just as there is no such categorization among patients who became probands the first time they were hospitalized. In order to obtain larger figures and smaller median errors, the "end states" of probands' schizophrenic siblings who had been hospitalized at least once, and those patients who became probands after their first hospitalization were added together and considered as one group (Group H). Naturally there are some misgivings about such indiscriminate lumping. The most disturbing of these emerges from the assumption that schizophrenic psychoses that accumulate among the members of one sibship develop differently from those oc-

			Confidence interval at 95 percent[1]
Severe state	in 36	= 24 percent of cases	17–32 percent
Moderately severe state	in 36	= 24 percent of cases	17–32 percent
Mild state	in 50	= 33 percent of cases	26–41 percent
Recovery	in 30	= 20 percent of cases	15–28 percent

[1] According to *Documenta Geigy*, 6th Ed., p. 100. Decimals are ignored.

The figures here presented concerning all probands are, however, by no means the most interesting ones to be derived from Table 4.4. Not all probands were first-time admissions. It is not as interesting to know the distribution among all patients (initial and subsequent admissions) of their "end states," as it is to know the relative distribution of "end states" of all schizophrenics hospitalized for the first time, out of all probands observed over decades after they became ill. In order to arrive at this information, all patients who became probands after their initial hospitalization were listed separately (Group F, Table 4.4). There were 68, of which 47 progressed to an "end state." Sorting these 47 probands into four different categories of states of illness results in very small figures with large median

curring in only one member of a sibship. As will be shown later, however, only minimal differences could possibly apply between the two categories. On the average, multiple admissions are more seriously ill than patients admitted for the first time who became probands, and particularly more seriously ill than those who were picked up as siblings and hospitalized in the course of family studies. The more favorable "end states," therefore, predominate in Group H rather than in Group C.

The distribution of the "end states" of the schizophrenics from Group H, who became probands after their first hospitalization, and those schizophrenics who were siblings of probands, follows below:

			Confidence interval at 95 percent[1]
Severe state	in 12	= 15 percent cases	8–24 percent
Moderately severe state	in 14	= 17 percent cases	10–27 percent
Mild state	in 31	= 38 percent cases	27–49 percent
Recovery	in 25	= 30 percent cases	21–42 percent

[1] According to *Documenta Geigy*, 6th Ed., p. 94. Decimals are ignored.

Table 4.4 Stablized "end states" among principal probands

Col. A: All male probands
Col. B: All female probands
Col. C: All probands (both sexes) from Columns A and B
Col. D: Male subjects who became probands at first hospitalization
Col. E: Female subjects who became probands at first hospitalization
Col. F: All Ss who became probands at first hospitalization (Cols. D and E)
Col. G: Schizophrenic siblings of probands hospitalized at least once
Col. H: Columns of F and G combined

Column C permits conclusions on final prognoses of all schizophrenics admitted to a clinic
Column H permits conclusions on the prognosis of any beginning schizophrenia, if the patient must be hospitalized at the time

	A 100	B 108	C 208	D 32	E 36	F 68	G 61	H 129
No. of cases								
Of these, those which did not reach an "end state"	27	29	56	11	10	21	26	47
"End state"								
Severe chronic schizophrenia	19 = 26 % ± 5.13	17 = 22 % ± 4.66	36 = 24 % ± 3.42	3 = 14 % ± 7.57	4 = 15 % ± 7	7 = 15 % ± 5.21	5 = 14 % ± 5.86	12 = 15 % ± 3.94
Moderately severe chronic schizophrenia	15 = 21 % ± 4.76	21 = 27 % ± 6.83	36 = 24 % ± 3.47	3 = 14 % ± 7.57	6 = 23 % ± 8.25	9 = 19 % ± 5.72	5 = 14 % ± 5.86	14 = 17 % ± 4.14
Mild chronic schizophrenia	23 = 31 % ± 5.41	27 = 34 % ± 5.33	50 = 33 % ± 3.81	8 = 38 % ± 10.59	12 = 47 % ± 9.78	20 = 43 % ± 7.22	11 = 32 % ± 7.88	31 = 38 % ± 5.32
Recovery	16 = 22 % ± 4.85	14 = 17 % ± 4.22	30 = 20 % ± 3.24	7 = 33 % ± 10.26	4 = 15 % ± 7	11 = 23 % ± 6.14	14 = 40 % ± 8.28	25 = 30 % ± 5.06
Totals:	73	79	152	21	26	47	35	82

These figures constitute an approximate basis for indicating the distribution of the different "end states" among all schizophrenics in the Canton of Zürich in the middle of this century, who were ever in their lives hospitalized for mental illnesses and who attained any "end state" whatsoever.

But one must not conclude from these figures that only $\frac{1}{3}$ of all first admissions for schizophrenia recover and that a good $\frac{2}{3}$ of them become chronic. Such a conclusion would be too pessimistic, for $\frac{1}{3}$ of the initial admissions (47) never even achieved an "end state" that lasted 5 years or more. There were many phasic-benign forms among these 47 patients. Many of them were healthy during most of their lives, and only suffered brief psychotic episodes spaced far apart. More than 30 percent recovered among the categorized schizophrenics; however, just 30 percent recovered whose recovery state had lasted more than 5 years at the end of the observation period.

Table 4.4 furthermore shows that the "end states" are distributed almost equally among the male and female probands. The "end states" of the two extremes—recovery on the one hand, and severe chronic state on the other —occur somewhat more frequently among the men than among the women, as compared to the moderately severe states and the mild states among the women. But the difference is far from attaining statistical significance, as a glance at the median errors in the figures will show.

As explained in the Introduction, the developmental tendencies of schizophrenic illnesses cannot be derived from a single group of probands, if these tendencies are intended to be generally applicable. No single group of schizophrenic probands is representative of all schizophrenias; for each group is tainted with the individualities stemming from selection. Valid results must come from data gathered from many groups of schizophrenic probands. The minimal and maximal threshold values of these results are even more meaningful than the median values.

The figures of Tables 4.4 and 4.5 were drawn up with these stipulations in mind. Table 4.4 shows the "end states" of various groupings of schizophrenics from this project. They are broken down according to sex, and according to whether the patients became probands during their initial, or during subsequent hospitalizations. The "end states" of the probands themselves are compared with those of their siblings, who were hospitalized at least once in their lives. Table 4.5 shows the "end states" of various groupings of schizophrenics from the research material of the 1941 investigations.

The figures in Table 4.5 were derived from the following types of probands: the schizophrenic probands from my studies in New York and in Pfäfers who had become probands as initial admissions and not as parts of the existing clinic population of patients, as well as their schizophrenic relatives who had been hospitalized at least once. A total of 239 schizophrenic patients were checked as to whether they had attained an "end state," and if so, what type it was. An "end state" in the context of this exposition was achieved by 146 of the above-mentioned schizophrenics by the end of the observation period. In all of them it had endured over 5 years, and in 77 of them, over 10 years. The

Table 4.5. Stabilized "end states" among probands from 1941 investigations. The maximum and minimum values are those developed from various groups of schizophrenics (from Bleuler, M., *Krankheitsverlauf, Persönlichkeit und Verwandtschaft Schizophrener und ihre gegenseitige Beziehungen*. (Course of the Disease, Personality, and Relatives of Schizophrenics and their Interrelationships). Leipzig: Thieme, 1941)

	Maximum value of individual subgroups in percent	Minimum value of individual subgroups in percent	Result of all cases considered collectively in percent	Standard Deviation of preceding figures	Approximate limits within which the correct percentages will fall	Rough estimate of final percentage
Severe dementia[1]	36.4	27.4	28.8	± 3.7	25–35	30
Severe defect[1]	35.1	16.5	21.2	± 3.4	20–35	20
Mild defect[1]	24.8	13.5	21.9	± 3.4	15–25	20
Recovery[1]	30.3	21.6	28.1	± 3.7	20–30	30

1. These 1941 classifications correspond to the following in this text: severe "end state," moderately severe "end state," mild "end state," recovery.

subdivision of the 146 observed "end states" into groups was accomplished individually for several of these groups of schizophrenics. The groups were formed according to the following criteria: (a) whether they came from New York or from Pfäfers, (b) whether they were original probands or schizophrenic relatives of those probands who had been picked up in the course of family studies, (c) whether the qualification of "end state" was absolutely certain or beset with any doubts, and (d) whether their "end state" lasted more or less than 10 years. The minimal and maximal values of Table 4.5 refer to the different results from these different subgroups of schizophrenics from the studies published in 1941.

The following observations on the "end states" of schizophrenics, therefore, are based on investigations of a total of 508 schizophrenic psychoses, the evolution of which is well known, in the majority of cases, over the course of many years or of several decades. Of these, 333 had attained an "end state" at the conclusion of the observation period. Fourteen groups were formed according to the above-mentioned categories which lend themselves to comparisons among one another. In what follows, the first comparison to be made is between the groups of probands from the 1941 investigations and the group from the studies in this book (Tables 4.4 and 4.5). After that, an attempt will be made to gain a composite overview of the "end states" of schizophrenias in general, from the data of all groups, but especially from the groups of first-time hospitalizations and their siblings who were hospitalized at least once.

A comparison between the figures of Tables 4.4 and 4.5 is valid only with reservations and extreme caution. The groups under study are not only distinguished as to selection from totally different clinics and at totally different times (distinctions that are desirable, because we are attempting to check whether the long-term prognoses among schizophrenics from a variety of clinics and at different points in time would be the same); but there are other differences between these two groups as well, that seriously impair a valid comparability.

The most noxious of these pernicious differences are: (1) Men are in the vast majority among the probands from New York and Pfäfers, while in the present study the sex ratio among the principal probands is almost exactly equal. As previously mentioned, the final prognosis is not exactly equal for the two sexes, though it is very similar. (2) Among

the schizophrenics processed in 1941, the proportion of schizophrenic relatives among the probands is greater than it is among the principal probands of the present study. The prognoses of probands who were studied as a result of transfers from other clinics were different—less favorable—than those of probands who were picked up as schizophrenic relatives of principal probands in the course of family studies. (3) Among the probands described in 1941, no distinction was made as to which became probands on first, and which on subsequent, admission to a psychiatric hospital.

But these (and other adverse but less important) circumstances making a fair comparison difficult are opposed by other conditions that benefit comparisons in a way that rarely occurs in practice. The diagnosis of schizophrenias and the determination of the "end state" were all done by me in person, in uniform fashion. Usually the determinations of "end states" vary from one author to another, so that it is almost impossible to do comparisons between the various data from different authors.

The following evidence from Tables 4.4 and 4.5 permits a careful evaluation of the findings relative to long-term prognoses, from my 1941 studies as well as from the present ones. As previously explained, they are summaries of findings from various different groups of schizophrenics. I also take these individual findings into consideration in presenting this evidence. Table 4.5 is the composite of 6 tables from the 1941 publication. It contains the maximum, the minimum, and the average values of 6 different groups of schizophrenics from those 1941 studies.

The number of schizophrenics who attain an "end state" varies among different groups of schizophrenics under long-term study only between a good half and three quarters A greater variance might have been expected; for the groups differ markedly not only in their origins, age structure, and the years in which they became probands, but the duration of observation time among them is also quite different. As the next paragraph will show, the majority of schizophrenias that do not attain an "end state," progress as benign-phasic.

The proportion of schizophrenics who attained an "end state" amounts to 75 percent (109 of 145) among the relatives of the Pfäfers and the New York probands described in 1941; 73 percent (152 of 208) among the principal probands of this study; 69 percent (47 of 68) among the first-time admissions of the principal probands, and 57 percent (35 of 61) among the schizophrenic relatives of the 208 principal probands.

The Pfäfers and the American probands from the 1941 studies have to be excluded from this comparison, since so many of them were observed for such a short period that they could not have attained an "end state."

The most obvious result from the comparison of Tables 4.4 and 4.5 is that the frequency of severe and moderately severe "end states" decreased, but that the frequency of mild "end states" increased.

The frequency of severe "end states" fluctuates among the 1941 probands between 27 and 36 percent, but among the probands of this project, between 14 and 26 percent. Among the 1941 probands, the proportion of severe "end states" amounted to 30 percent, and among the probands of this project, to just 23 percent. Among the relatives of the 1941 probands, it was 28 percent, and among the relatives of our principal probands, only 14 percent.

The frequency of moderately severe "end states" among the 1941 probands ranges between 17 and 35 percent, and among those of this project, between 14 and 27 percent. Among the 1941 probands, the proportion of moderately severe "end states" amounted to 35 percent, and among the probands of this study, to only 24 percent. Among the relatives of the 1941 probands, it was 17 percent, and among the probands of this study, 14 percent.

In contrast to this, the increase in mild "end states" becomes clear. The frequency of mild "end states" ranges between 14 and 25 percent among the 1941 probands, but between 31 and 47 percent among our present probands. The proportion of mild "end states" was 14 percent among the 1941 probands, but 33 percent among our present probands. Among the relatives of the 1941 probands it was 25 percent, but among the relatives of probands from this study, 32 percent.

It would amount to overstressing the laws of probability to regard too seriously the value of p for the individual differences between the various chronic "end states" among the probands of the two groups. It has already been pointed out that the comparisons are somewhat faulty, since they were made between terms that were not exactly comparable. Even if the calculations show that the differences are most improbably due to chance,

they cannot be considered reliable because of the faulty comparability of the figures. The comparison of individual figures is not important here, but the uniform trend of the many numerical comparisons is significant. Nevertheless, the value of p for the following amounts are mentioned:

(1) Comparison on the one hand between the relatives of the 1941 probands hospitalized at least once (Group I), and on the other hand, the relatives of probands from the present study who were hospitalized at least once and those among the principal probands who became probands when they were hospitalized for the first time (Group II). The calculations for p were derived from the following figures:

"End state"	Group I	Group II
Severe chronic psychosis	31	12
Moderately severe chronic psychosis	18	14
Mild chronic psychosis	27	31
Recovery	33	25

The probability that taken as a whole the differences in these figures are entirely due to chance operation is less than $\frac{1}{10}$ ($p < 0.10$). It is equally unlikely that the differences in the frequencies of the most severe chronic psychoses came about by chance alone (for both differences $p < 0.10$).

(2) Comparison between those 1941 patients who became probands as hospital admissions (Group III), with all probands of the present study (Group IV):

"End state"	Group III	Group IV
Severe chronic psychosis	11	36
Moderately severe chronic psychosis	13	36
Mild chronic psychosis	5	50
Recovery	8	30

Again, the probability that the differences in these figures are entirely due to chance is less than $\frac{1}{10}$ ($p < 0.10$). The difference in the mild "end states" is statistically significant ($p < 0.05$).

All other differences in the figures of the two sets of comparisons may have depended on the operations of chance, particularly the differences in the number of "recoveries."

The above-mentioned calculations for p, however, are by no means the only indications of the validity of a difference in the proportion of severe and mild chronic psychoses between the 1941 probands and the principal probands of this study. These differences should be taken seriously, particularly because they continue to appear in the same proportion in numerous comparisons between the individual sub-groups, even when p is large for each of these comparisons.

The numerical shift in frequency discovered from severe to mild chronic conditions ("end states") corresponds to the experience from the practice of most clinicians. If comparisons were made from memory, between wards of schizophrenics as we saw them decades ago in most localities, and the schizophrenic wards of today, one is impressed by the obvious progress. On the wards for chronic schizophrenics there are more patients who are quiet, communicative, working, content, and not requiring restraint, than there were years ago. The same impression as that from Burghölzli emerges for a great many other clinics: While decades ago nearly all the wards for the most severely ill were almost always overcrowded, these wards today often contain empty beds, and space is scarce much more often in the wards for mild schizophrenic cases.

What are the causes for this shift in frequency from the severe to the milder chronic states? It should not be assumed that those clinics in which the probands from the 1941 studies were hospitalized were admitting patients with less favorable schizophrenic prognosis than the Zürich clinic did, from which the probands of this study were selected. The more favorable prognosis of today's probands can hardly be equated with their origin; instead, it is more probable that it is related to the difference in the time-period during which the two studies were carried out.

As is to be noted from Table 4.3 and has already been explained, over the course of years, late-onset schizophrenics have been steadily increasing among the patients I was investigating. Late-onset cases are often late paranoics, whose psychosis generally progresses to mild chronic states. For this reason we are inclined to assume that the increase of mild, stable chronic states among our principal probands is due to the fact that they include more late-onset paranoics than did the earlier investigations. But this assumption does not fit the facts. Among the 45 probands and the 17 probands' siblings whose schizophrenia began after their 40th birthday, there happened to be less—not more—mild, stable chronic states ("end states"), according to actual figures. To be sure, the figures are so small that the difference appears statistically entirely insignificant. Among the 45 late-onset

paranoids 6, and of the 17 late-onset paranoid siblings of probands, 5 attained a mild, stable chronic state. But in no case can the increase in frequency of mild, stable "end states" among the principal probands over that of the 1941 probands be ascribed to a shift in age structure of the probands.

Among all the conceivable circumstances that could explain the increase of the mild, and the decrease of the severe stable chronic states among the principal probands, as compared to those from the 1941 studies, the progress in modern treatment methods certainly rates among the most likely.

The fact that progress in treatment methods has had an important part in the decrease noted in severe and moderately severe chronic states becomes obvious even from daily clinical experience. Again and again we witness how the implementation of treatments in the most severe "end states" produces improvements. The selection of the three groups of patients who showed the improvement occurred in 1928/29, then in 1933–1936, and again in 1942/43. The end of the observation period for the first two groups was in 1937/38, and for the last-named group in 1966/67. Between 1928 and 1962 it became clear for the first time, how very significant the active hospital community can be for the treatment of schizophrenia. Nurses and ward attendants were scarcely aware of this in the early thirties. Medical interest in the clinics in question was concentrated increasingly on the treatment of schizophrenics during this period. If one has coexperienced this progress in general and in one's own therapeutic practice, one is less surprised to learn that the severity of the "end states" has decreased in intensity than that this tendency toward a decrease in intensity has not been expressed much more clearly by the figures. The reason for this may be that a reduced severity in general intensity of illness has emerged especially from within each of the three groups of severe, moderately severe, and mild states, in a way that the figures presented here cannot fully reflect.

As encouraging as statistical support of a decrease in severity of the long-term psychotic conditions over the course of years may be, it is as ominous and depressing to be confronted with the facts revealed in Tables 4.4 and 4.5, namely, that the long-lasting recoveries of schizophrenics have not increased markedly in the past 30 years. Among the probands of the 1941 investigations, the percentage of long-term recoveries in the various groups of schizophrenics ranges between 15 and 40 percent, and for the probands of this study, between 20 and 33 percent. The probands from the 1941 investigations themselves revealed even more long-term recoveries than those of this study; however, with a difference that is not statistically significant (22 and 20 percent). However, among the relatives of the probands, the relationship is reversed: there were 30 percent recoveries among probands from the earlier investigations, and 40 percent among those from the present study; although this difference is by no means statistically significant either.

These findings surely contradict the hopes of every clinician, but hardly his experience. He recognizes clearly that therapy produces improvement; but his routine experience does not teach him that it also produces long-term recoveries that affect statistics to a significant degree.

Among those schizophrenias with outcomes of long-term recoveries, those that progress multiphasically are in the majority. In a later section we show that familial influences are more pronounced among schizophrenias progressing in mild phases than among other types of schizophrenias. The fact that they are less susceptible to former treatment methods than other types can be related to this finding.

Supported by all these realizations, a prognosis evaluated by means of the "end states," as it was derived in 1941, can be adapted and defined by means of the more recent conditions (Table 4.6).

Easily one half to three quarters of all schizophrenics continue to attain a relatively stable "end state" of at least 5 years' duration within 20 or more years after onset of illness. The apportionment of these "end states" (from Tables 4.4 and 4.5) are depicted in Table 4.6.

While inspecting the data presented above, one must again keep in mind that they are merely classifications of the "end states." One quarter to nearly one half of all schizophrenias do not achieve an "end state" even after more than 10 years. The majority of this quarter to one-third are mild, phasic schizophrenias.

The figures, especially from column H of Table 4.4, provide important points of reference for the prognostications for 20–30 years after onset among recent-onset schizophrenics. The schizophrenias that qualify as "benign" are those that progress toward recovery over many years, that progress toward

mild, chronic psychoses, and those that still have some acute episodes with good prognoses.[4] In contrast, those that qualify as virulent are those that proceed as toward most severe or medium severe, chronic psychoses. Then it can be determined that approximately between two thirds and three fourths of the schizophrenias progress mildly over the long run. One fourth to one third of them, on the other hand, will run a virulent course.

This fundamental rule for prognoses contradicts the old—and unfortunately still prevalent—concept, according to which schizophrenias are much more malignant psychoses than these figures would indicate.

It would be an unjustifiable objection to argue that a relatively favorable prognosis may be derived from our figures because mild mental disorders that are not truly schizophrenias, were carelessly included as such in our statistics. I believe that this objection has been refuted by the descriptions of the concepts of schizophrenias that were given at the beginning, as well as by the numerous examples in the text. If anyone should still believe that my research material includes psychoses that most other clinicians would not include under the schizophrenias, I should like to suggest the following thought: In 1942, when most of the 208 principal probands became probands for this study, the number of schizophrenics among all admissions at Burghölzli amounted to 308 of 807 (38 percent). That is to say that at that time, even more than now, Burghölzli specialized in the treatment of severe cases of psychosis, that there were almost no severe cases of feeblemindedness, few epileptics, and few neurotics and mild depressives, and that at the time, during the war, the number of alcoholics was low as well. Other addictions besides alcoholism were not serious enough to warrant admission to a hospital. Seniles were discouraged because bed space was scarce. However, all schizophrenics who were referred were accepted. With this kind of an admission policy, the proportion of schizophrenics admitted to Burghölzli certainly does not exceed that of many other clinics all over the world. A set of data

4. According to column H, Table 4.4, 47 probands had not attained an "end state" at the conclusion of the observation period. They had dropped from the investigation for a variety of conditions at the time they left. During the summary calculations it was assumed that scarcely half of them would have had a good prognosis.

Table 4.6. "End states" before and after improved treatment methods (compare right and left columns), and between all admissions and initial admissions (compare middle and right columns)

1941 Probands[1] *(Patients who became probands with their hospital admission and whose relatives were hospitalized at least once*	*All 208 principal probands of this project*	*Initial hospitalizations among the 208 principal probands and their siblings, hospitalized at least once*
Half (or slightly more) of the cases with severe "end states" or recoveries	Long-term recoveries and severe "end states" combined, amount to somewhat less than half	Same
Recovery and severe "end states" occur at about the same frequency	Recovery is slightly more frequent than severe "end states"	Recovery occurs at about twice the rate of severe "end states"
About half the "end states" are moderately severe or mild chronic psychoses	Moderately severe and mild chronic psychoses amount to somewhat more than half all "end states"	Same
Moderately severe and mild "end states" are balanced nearly equally	Mild "end states" appear to be somewhat more frequent than moderately severe "end states"	Mild "end states" are considerably more frequent than moderately severe "end states"

1. Terms applied to designate "end states" in the 1941 investigations were: for severe "end states," severe idiocy; for moderately severe "end states," severe defects; and for mild "end states," mild defects.

on admissions, developed by Mayer-Gross (1932) shows a percentage range of schizophrenics admitted to five psychiatric clinics of between 42 and 55 percent. He determined that "the percentage of schizophrenics among admissions was approximately 40 percent." If my statistics on disease courses were markedly influenced by too broad diagnoses of schizophrenia, the Burghölzli clinic would have had a higher percentage of schizophrenics among its admissions than it actually had.

Even if the schizophrenias appear to be more benign in the light of the figures presented here, as was often assumed, they would still have to be categorized as terrible illnesses. About 9 percent of the patients regularly become severely psychotic, and would have been classified as "severely demented" not too many years ago (credibility limit of this 9 percent at 95 percent: 4–15 percent). And it is just as terrible that only 19 percent have long-term "end states" toward recovery (30 percent of those probands who have any kind of stable "end state" whatsoever) (confidence interval at 95 percent of the 19 percent: 13–27 percent, and of the 30 percent: 21–42 percent). Deaths occurring in peracute episodes are not even included in these statistics of human misery.

It is difficult to make comparisons of "end states" between my various groups of probands and statistics from the turn of the century, because diagnostics were different then. When in those times either no, or almost no recoveries were registered, it was partly due to the fact that acute psychoses and rapid recoveries were included as schizophrenias only with great reluctance and hesitation, even when their symptomatology in no way differed from that of the virulent schizophrenias.

On the other hand, those types of cases that never fully recovered, are the same today as they were in the past. Kraepelin (1913) determined—and reported in the 8th edition of his text—that, according to his own investigations, 75 percent of the "hebephrenic forms," and 59 percent of the "catatonics" proceeded to a state of profound idiocy (17 percent and 27 percent proceeded to "mild states of feeblemindedness"). Among others, he cites Mattauschek, who found between 54 and 67 percent "severe states of idiocy," compared to 9–14 percent "defective recoveries," and 21–25 percent "first-degree idiocy" among various forms of the disease. According to Albrecht (1905), the relationship between "severe idiocy," "simple idiocy," and "defective recovery" is 60:27:14 percent for hebephrenics, and 50:24:26 percent (?) for catatonics. According to Evensen (cited by Kraepelin, 1913), 70 percent of the hebephrenics and 50 percent of the catatonics became "completely idiotic." Among the paranoid forms, Kraepelin (1913) himself considered "about half the cases proceeding to milder states of feeblemindedness, and the other half to severe states of feeblemindedness." According to Mattauschek (cited by Kraepelin, 1913), "severe idiocy" occurs in 79 percent of these paranoid forms. Numerous other figures in the same context could be cited from the literature of the first two decades of this century. As an exception, Zablocka (1908) arrived at lesser percentages for "severe idiocy"; that is, between 21 and 29 percent for the various forms of schizophrenia. But Zablocka's (1908) study came from Burghölzli (under the guidance of E. Bleuler), at the time one of the very few university clinics to practice work-therapy and psychotherapy with schizophrenic patients, and also one of the very few to recommend "early releases" as a therapeutic and recovery measure.

When we realize from the personal descriptions of the previous generation of psychiatrists what conditions prevailed in the institutions of 50 years ago from which the above-mentioned statistics were gathered, we no longer doubt that such expressions as "profound—or severe idiocy," "most severe idiotic state," etc., represent conditions that were at least as serious as those I describe in this study as "severe end state."

A comparison between today's statistics and those of about half a century ago forces acceptance of the following conclusion: Among those schizophrenic psychoses that proceed to long-term, stable conditions, the most severe, chronic conditions of illness have become more rare, and the milder ones more frequent, in the past decades. As the comparison between my 1941 investigations and the present ones have shown, the shift from severe to mild chronic states is progressing with uniform regularity.

The Disease Courses

Up to 1941 I had learned from hundreds of long-term studies of the courses of schizophrenic psychoses, that over 90 percent of them could be classified in a natural, orderly arrangment, without the application of arbitrary and subjective compulsion (see Table 4.7).

Simple Courses

1. Acute to severe chronic "end states" ("idiocy"—"catastrophe schizophrenias" for some earlier authors)
2. Chronic to severe "end states" ("idiocy")
3. Acute to chronic moderately severe or mild "end states" ("defects")
4. Chronic to moderately severe or mild "end states" ("defects")

Undulating (Intermittent) Courses

5. Undulating to severe chronic "end states" ("idiocy")
6. Undulating to chronic, moderately severe or mild "end states" ("defect")
7. Undulating to recovery (includes the benign forms with either one single, or with several psychotic episodes)

Atypical Courses

Some misgivings against the expressions "end state," "dementia," and "defects" have already been pointed out.

Each of the seven subgroups formed according to type of disease course has its own particular relationship to the four known subgroups of the schizophrenias described according to symptomatology:

Group 1 (the "catastrophe-schizophrenias") includes the acute hebephrenic, as well as the catatonic states.

Group 2 (psychoses evolving to chronic, severe "end states") include primarily the hebephrenias, paranoid psychoses, and the schizophrenias simplex, as well as the catatonias without severe agitation and confusion.

Group 3 (psychoses proceeding acutely to moderately severe or mild "end states") includes so few cases, that one is tempted not to list them as a separate category; still, such psychoses do occur. They merit consideration in a system of disease-course types that is constructed to follow a natural order and to impress itself on the mind.

Group 4 (psychoses progressing chronically to moderately severe "end states") includes principally the late-onset paranoid schizophrenias.

Groups 5 and 6 (psychoses progressing in undulations to "end states" of varying degrees of severity) consist of hebephrenias, catatonias, and paranoid psychoses.

Group 7 (phasic-benign) includes principally the acute catatonias, acute delirious states, and schizophrenic states with admixtures of

Table 4.7. Frequency of course types, comparing principal probands and 1941 probands

a. Threshold values of findings in the 1941 probands

b. Findings in all probands of the present project. These findings permit conclusions on prognoses of all schizophrenias involving hospitalization

c. Findings in probands of this project, of all initial hospital admissions and in all probands' siblings. These findings permit conclusions as to the prognoses of beginning schizophrenias, insofar as they are severe enough to require at least one hospitalization

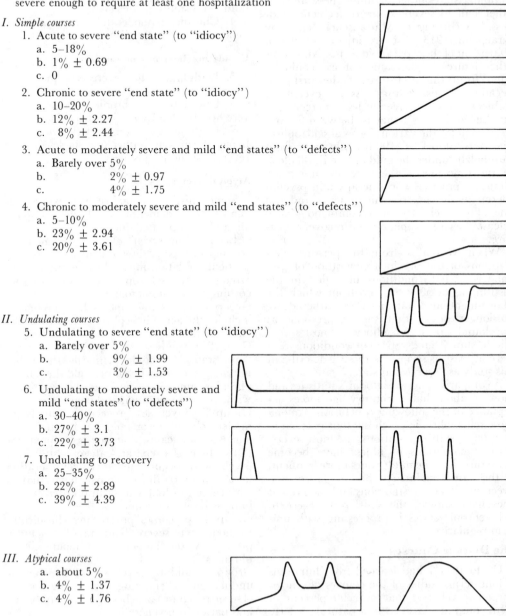

I. Simple courses

    1. Acute to severe "end state" (to "idiocy")
        a. 5–18%
        b. 1% ± 0.69
        c. 0

    2. Chronic to severe "end state" (to "idiocy")
        a. 10–20%
        b. 12% ± 2.27
        c. 8% ± 2.44

    3. Acute to moderately severe and mild "end states" (to "defects")
        a. Barely over 5%
        b.   2% ± 0.97
        c.   4% ± 1.75

    4. Chronic to moderately severe and mild "end states" (to "defects")
        a. 5–10%
        b. 23% ± 2.94
        c. 20% ± 3.61

II. Undulating courses

    5. Undulating to severe "end state" (to "idiocy")
        a. Barely over 5%
        b.   9% ± 1.99
        c.   3% ± 1.53

    6. Undulating to moderately severe and mild "end states" (to "defects")
        a. 30–40%
        b. 27% ± 3.1
        c. 22% ± 3.73

    7. Undulating to recovery
        a. 25–35%
        b. 22% ± 2.89
        c. 39% ± 4.39

III. Atypical courses
        a. about 5%
        b. 4% ± 1.37
        c. 4% ± 1.76

manic or depressive tendencies.

The typical schizophrenias, according to Langfeldt's (1956) definition, are principally those that correspond to my disease course types 1, 2, and 5, and a portion of them also correspond to types 3, 4 or 6. Langfeldt's atypical schizophrenias (schizophreniform psychoses) may assume any disease course described. Particularly those psychoses proceeding in the pattern of Group 7 belong to the group of "schizophreniform psychoses" described by Langfeldt (1956).

In addition to the above seven types of disease courses there are, naturally, numerous others. All of these "others" among the atypical courses considered together, however, occur in only 5–10 percent of all schizophrenias. They are so different, and each individual type is so unusual, that it is not worth the effort to subdivide them further. The most common among them are acute exacerbations that develop after a long-term chronic course. Then some improvements and recoveries occur not only among the undulating courses as shown in the outline, but also among courses with chronic beginnings; these, however, are rare.

In the course of years any of the types of courses may turn into one of the others, but again, such conversions are the exception. By far the majority continues to proceed along the course that becomes prominent and distinctive within a few years after the initial onset of illness.

For 3 of the 208 principal probands of this study, no regular course curve materialized, because they expired shortly after their illness had begun. Observations of the disease course extending beyond 20 years on the remaining 205 probands are on record, as are the notes on observations for at least 2–3 years on the probands who expired. It is possible that a few individual cases may still undergo a change in the type of disease course at some time in the future, despite the length of time they have remained under observation. These cases at best will be so few in number that they would not be statistically significant. The courses for 59[5] of the 63 schizophrenic siblings of probands were determined with the same

regularity and reliability. Four of the siblings in question had died soon after their illness had begun, or insufficient information in their records precluded completing the charting of their courses. The statistical data presented below for discussion, therefore, is based on the disease courses of a total of 264 schizophrenic patients from the present study, observed over a period of many years. They are suitable for comparison with the 187 courses from probands of the 1941 studies. Accordingly, the conclusions drawn from data of this section will be based on a total of 451 disease courses. This figure will be somewhat larger than the figure for "end states" of the previous section, because not all schizophrenics attained "end states" in the context of our definition.

Table 4.8 shows the distribution of types of disease courses. They are distinguished according to sex, according to principal probands and their schizophrenic siblings, and according to whether the patients became probands after their first, or after subsequent hospitalizations. Table 4.7 provides an outline of the various types of disease courses and shows the figures relating to their proportionate distribution among the various groups of schizophrenics, as follows:

A. Schizophrenic patients described in 1941 from New York and from Pfäfers and their relatives.[6]

B. All the probands from this study. They are valid for conclusions on the prognoses of all the schizophrenics admitted to psychiatric clinics.

C. Those probands from the present study, who became probands at the time of their initial hospitalization, and those of their schizophrenic siblings who were hospitalized at least once. These results would permit conclusions on the prognoses of all beginning schizophrenias, insofar as they are severe enough to require hospitalization once during the lifetime of the proband. These are the most important figures of the outline.

A comparison between the sexes shows that the undulating courses usually progress toward recovery in men, and toward mild chronic states in women. But this finding

5. Of these 59 disease courses, 2 that pertain to schizophrenics who have never been hospitalized have been excluded from Tables 4.7 and 4.9. The statistics are intended to show only the distribution of disease courses pertaining to those schizophrenics who have been hospitalized at least once in their lives.

6. These are 44 American probands and their relatives and 143 Pfäfers probands and their relatives. Probands include only those who became probands when they were admitted to clinics, and the relatives only those who were hospitalized at least once.

Table 4.8. Course types in groupings of principal probands

Col. A: All male probands
Col. B: All female probands
Col. C: All probands (Columns A and B)
Col. D: Male Ss who became probands at first hospitalization
Col. E: Female Ss who became probands at first hospitalization
Col. F: Male and female Ss who became probands at first hospitalization
Col. G: Schizophrenic siblings of probands, hospitalized at least once
Col. H: Columns F and G combined

Col. C permits conclusions on final prognoses of all schizophrenias involving hospitalization
Col. H permits conclusions on the prognosis of any beginning schizophrenia, if the patient ever had to be hospitalized for it

	A	B	C	D	E	F	G	H
No. of cases:	100	108	208	32	36	68	61	129
Of these, course undetermined[1]	1	2	3	0	2	2	4	6
Course types								
1. Acute to severe chronic "end states"	1 = 1 % ± 1	2 = 2 % ± 1.36	3 = 1 % ± 0.69	0	0	0	0	0
2. Chronic to sever chronic "end states"	14 = 14 % ± 3.48	10 = 9 % ± 2.78	24 = 12 % ± 2.27	2 = 6 % ± 4.19	3 = 9 % ± 4.9	5 = 8 % ± 3.34	5 = 9 % ± 3.79	10 = 8 % ± 2.44
3. Acute to milder chronic "end states"	3 = 3 % ± 1.71	2 = 2 % ± 1.36	5 = 2 % ± 0.97	3 = 9 % ± 5.06	1 = 3 % ± 2.92	4 = 6 % ± 2.92	1 = 2 % ± 1.85	5 = 4 % ± 1.76
4. Chronic to milder chronic "end states"	23 = 23 % ± 4.22	23 = 22 % ± 4.02	46 = 23 % ± 2.94	6 = 19 % ± 6.93	8 = 24 % ± 7.32	14 = 21 % ± 5.01	10 = 18 % ± 5.09	24 = 20 % ± 3.61
5. Undulating to severe chronic "end states"	9 = 9 % ± 2.87	10 = 9 % ± 2.78	19 = 9 % ± 1.99	1 = 3 % ± 3.01	2 = 6 % ± 4.07	3 = 5 % ± 2.68	1 = 2 % ± 1.85	4 = 3 % ± 1.53
6. Undulating to milder chronic "end states"	19 = 19 % ± 3.94	37 = 35 % ± 4.63	56 = 27 % ± 3.1	4 = 13 % ± 5.94	13 = 38 % ± 8.32	17 = 26 % ± 5.4	10 = 18 % ± 5.09	27 = 22 % ± 3.73
7. Undulating to recovery	25 = 25 % ± 4.35	19 = 18 % ± 3.73	44 = 22 % ± 2.89	14 = 44 % ± 8.87	6 = 18 % ± 6.59	20 = 30 % ± 5.64	28 = 49 % ± 6.62	48 = 39 % ± 4.39
8. Atypical	5 = 5 % ± 2.18	3 = 3 % ± 1.65	8 = 4 % ± 1.37	2 = 6 % ± 4.2	1 = 3 % ± 2.92	3 = 5 % ± 2.68	2 = 3 % ± 2.26	5 = 4 % ± 1.76
Totals:	99	106	205	32	34	66	57	123

1. Undetermined because patients died; records of 2 probands' siblings lacked sufficient data.

might still be ascribed to chance. It does correspond to the findings on "end states."

Theoretically there ought to be no difference between the disease courses of those patients who became probands during their initial hospitalization and those of the schizophrenic siblings of the probands. The majority of nearly all types of disease courses correspond to this expectation, except for those that run a phasic-benign course. But this difference, too, appears to be due mainly to a caprice of chance.

The comparison between the courses of all probands with the courses of patients who became probands at the time of their first hospitalization and the schizophrenic siblings of probands corresponds to expectations. The courses of the latter group are more favorable, since the more severely ill are more often hospitalized than are the milder cases.

The same problems encountered in the comparisons of "end states," as already discussed, are encountered in the comparisons of the disease courses of schizophrenics described in 1941 and those of this project.

This comparison shows first of all that, since 1941, the chronic disease courses to moderately severe and mild "end states" have increased. This increase was not caused by the fact that this study includes more late-onset patients than previous ones did.

Corresponding to the increase of the milder chronic types of courses (and probably reinforced by happenstance), most of the other types of courses occur more rarely among the probands of this study than among probands from the older investigations.

Up to this point, the results of the statistics on the evolution of the disease conform to expectations and have reported nothing new or previously unknown. However, the finding that the acute courses evolving to severe "end states" of long duration among Group 1 patients have significantly decreased, or even disappeared almost completely, is indeed a matter of great interest. The most important data in this context, from Tables 4.7 and 4.8, and supplemented by figures from individual descriptions of the 1941 studies, are outlined below.

Among the different subgroups of schizophrenic probands described in 1941, the frequency of catastrophe-schizophrenias ranges between 5–18 percent; but among the different subgroups of this study, they range between 0–1 percent.

There were some catastrophe-schizophre-

nias among all 6 subgroups of the 1941 probands, but only in 1 subgroup of the present study.

Among all probands from the 1941 studies, there were 5 of 65 catastrophe-schizophrenias (8 percent), and 3 among 208 ($1\frac{1}{2}$ percent) of all probands from this study. This difference is significant ($p < 0.05$).

Among all probands from the 1941 studies and their relatives combined, there were 10 percent catastrophe-schizophrenias (19 of 187), and among all probands from this study and their schizophrenic siblings, only 1 percent (3 of 262). The difference, at $p < 0.001$, is highly significant.

Among the schizophrenic relatives of the probands of 1941, 14 of 122 (11.5 percent) were catastrophe-schizophrenias, but among the 59 relatives of probands from this study there were none. The difference is significant ($p < 0.05$).[7]

Among the 68 disease-course types of first-time admissions of probands from this study there were no catastrophe-schizophrenias, and in the 1941 investigations no distinction was made between first-time or subsequent hospital admissions.

Additional subgroups were compared among one another, and all of them revealed a higher incidence of catastrophe-schizophrenias among the 1941 probands than among those of this study.

There are not sufficient reasons for assuming that the decrease in catastrophe-schizophrenias in the present investigative material was caused by errors in selection. It may be probable, however, that catastrophe-schizophrenias have actually decreased over the course of the last few decades.

The comparison among my three groups of probands seems to agree with these same findings. My first set of studies was done on a group of clinic patients hospitalized in 1929/30; the next on clinic patients hospitalized between 1933–1936; and the latest, the present one, includes patients hospitalized between 1942/43. The number of catastrophe-

7. There was a problem in calculating this value of p. In the χ-square test with the Yates consistency correction factor, one term is 0; therefore, in the strictest sense, the method cannot really be applied. As an experiment, the value 2 was inserted to replace the 0, and with this arbitrary adjustment, the statistical significance of $0.10 > p > 0.05$, mentioned above, resulted. Since in reality the empirical values 0 and 2 are not reckoned in, the actual significance is still somewhat greater than the one given.

schizophrenias decreases from one group to the next, as they run in sequence with time.[8] The clinical experiences of many other colleagues in the field, not only my own, conform in context to these findings as well. It is now quite a rare experience that an acute-onset schizophrenic, following an acute onset, remains severely psychotic and constantly on wards reserved for the most severely ill mental patients. Years ago it was a common occurrence.

The statistical studies of this section show any decrease in incidence over a period of time solely for those schizophrenias proceeding acutely to severe "end states"—that is, for the catastrophe-schizophrenias. For those schizophrenias proceeding chronically and in undulations to the most severe "end states" no clearly perceptible reduction of incidence has been observed. We may assume, therefore, that the influences that are exerted after onset of illness, and the influences of treatment as well, are most effective against those of the most severe psychoses that begin acutely and then without treatment, proceed quickly to severe "end states." There is much more doubt as to the external influences during the psychosis, including those that proceed definitely as chronic or undulating courses toward severe "end states." The statistics presented in this section are not the only indicators that therapeutic optimism is considerably more justified for the earlier cases of catastrophe-schizophrenia than for other severe forms of the disease. Furthermore, other studies also suggest strong indications that there are influences favoring the development of catastrophe-schizophrenias after onset of illness, and that this most outrageous course of the disease is also the one that can first be brought under control and overcome.

On the opposite page are listed some additional observations from the course studies of 1941, compared with those from the present study.

The differences between the first and second columns occur mainly because of improved treatment methods; and the differences between the second and third columns, because of the difference in prognoses between all hospital admissions and initial hospital admissions.

The number of the different "end states" in the previous section, which registers only the "end states" of long duration, and in this last section that registers the entire course of progress, cannot coincide. In the preceding section only those "end states" are counted that have remained constant for at least 5 years and that were stable at the conclusion of the observation period. In the preceding section on the course curves, "end states" of much shorter duration are included, but of the type that might be expected after decades of observation. For example: A proband has suffered through his first acute episode at age 18. Between ages 20 and 30 he again experiences three catatonic episodes of short duration, and he then remains healthy for a period of 12 years. At age 42 he again endures a brief catatonic phase, and then remains well again for the next 3 years, until the end of the investigation. This proband is not included in the statistics on "end states" of long duration, because his outcome to recovery had not lasted 5 years since his last psychotic episode. On the other hand, he is included in the statistics on courses of long-term duration, under the category of "undulating progress toward recovery." The concept of "end state" adheres more closely to its strict definition in the previous section than it does in this one.

Statistics on the frequency of the various types of courses that could be compared with mine were formerly never compiled. It is today no longer possible to determine whether these types of courses 50 years ago were distributed according to the same ratios or not.

But surely it is possible to determine from the earlier descriptions of the course of illness that many more "catastrophe-schizophrenias" were observed then than they are now. To be sure, there were no useful figures available in their support, but it is possible to conclude something about them from the descriptions, as for instance, Kraepelin's (1913) in the 8th edition of his text. He begins his exposition on the courses of psychoses as follows:

"The general progress of dementia praecox is an extremely varied one. On the one hand there are cases that bring about a very slow, lingering change in the personality, that are not too obvious to the outside observer, although they do inflict changes that are profound and far-reaching. On the other hand, the disease may strike suddenly, almost with-

8. To be sure, the three groups of schizophrenics also come from different clinics. A determination should be made as to whether the time period or the locale in which the data were assembled had any influence on the differences cited.

Among the schizophrenics of 1941 (all clinic admissions plus schizophrenic relatives)	Among all principal probands of this study	Among all first-time admissions of principal probands and their schizophrenic relatives
1. Schizophrenias more often proceed in undulations than uniformly	Same	Same
2. Undulating course rarely advances to severe pathological "end state"	Same	Same
3. The great majority of schizophrenias proceed on an undulating course advances toward recovery or toward moderately severe or mildly pathological "end states" at an approximately equal rate	Same	The same, but recoveries of long duration predominate over all pathological "end states" together
4. The majority of schizophrenias with chronic beginnings proceed to severe pathological "end states"	Usually only moderately severe or mildly pathological "end states" develop	Same
5. Severe pathological "end states" have developed most often after chronic onset of illness, almost as often as after the first acute episode, and least frequently after undulating course	Still most frequent after chronic onsets and much more rarely after undulating course, but almost never after the first acute episode	Same
6. Of the schizophrenias with acute beginnings, about one third advance to recovery of long duration	Similar	Over half advance to recoveries of long duration
7. Of the schizophrenias with acute beginnings about one fourth progress to severe pathological "end states"	With acute onsets, severe pathological "end states" occur in less than one quarter of cases	Occur extremely seldom

out noticeable warning symptoms, and produce a serious, incurable illness within just a few weeks or months. In the majority of cases with a clearly discernible beginning, a certain residual condition sets in, usually no later than 2–3 years after such a beginning, that bears the unmistakable marks of feeble-mindedness."

Surely he would not have mentioned "catastrophe-schizophrenias" immediately after the chronic-virulent forms, if he had not observed them much more frequently than they occur today.

The old texts reveal that lingering and undulating forms that led to illnesses of varying degrees of severity occurred frequently years ago, as they also occur frequently today. It is not possible to find out from these texts how the figures are distributed. It cannot be determined whether the undulating forms that progress toward recovery occurred earlier, or how often they occurred, since often

they were arbitrarily included with diagnoses other than dementia praecox.

The best comparison data on the frequency of catastrophe-schizophrenias come from Mauz's study that appeared in 1930 on the prognoses of endogenous psychoses. His patients came from Germany (Marburg) and were under observation from 1923 to 1928. Mauz (1930) describes the "schizophrenic catastrophe" as a form of schizophrenia in which, as early as 2–3 years after the first onset, a "severe and final deterioration" becomes discernible. "Catastrophe-schizophrenia" in the context of this present study and "schizophrenic catastrophe" as Mauz (1930) applied it do not mean exactly—although very nearly—the same form of progress. Among 1050 schizophrenics, Mauz (1930) discovered 180 disease courses in the sense of a "schizophrenic catastrophe"; that is, 15 percent (the median error of this percentage figure, I calculate at 1.1). According to this, there were many more catastrophe-schizo-phrenias among the research material of Mauz (1930) than among my 208 probands.

Late Course Characteristics of Schizophrenic Psychoses (25 to 35 Years after the Schizophrenic Onset)

Problems and Survey of Literature

A great number of studies have been published on the course of schizophrenic psychoses $\frac{1}{2}$ year, 1 year, 2, 5, or even 10 years after the initial onset of illness, or after hospitalization, or after completion of a certain treatment procedure. After introduction of the insulin cure, these studies increased dramatically in number. My colleagues and I had carefully studied over 200 of these papers, and had lectured about them, without claiming to have covered the subject exhaustively. But there is little available in the literature concerning the question of how schizophrenic psychoses proceed further, after they have persisted for 10, 20, or more years. Do they "proceed" at all after that much time? Or do they petrify into an "end state" in the narrowest sense of that concept; that is, into final, unchangeable residual states? If we still believe in the existence of a continuing process: Are we concerned with changes, with deterioration, or with improvement? And how often do these occur?

The experienced clinician knows more about the answers to such questions than is to be found in the literature. He knows that, in most clinics that do not simply refer patients to nursing institutions, an excessively large number of schizophrenic patients sojourn for years on the same wards and in approximately the same state of mental health. He will know many patient histories with the same notation entered repeatedly year after year: "Condition unchanged." He will know also from family social work and from outpatient practice, that many patients outside the clinic make about the same impression for decades on end. Of course, he also knows that not infrequently, although unpredictably—apparently spontaneously—changes do occur, for better or for worse. He has also learned that every newly devised treatment method that is introduced, often with great momentum and enthusiasm, will often effect improvements, and occasionally even recoveries, in many patients who have been ill for a long time. He has trouble overcoming a certain tired resignation, because he knows from sufficient experience

how often these improvements do not continue, and what a hard task it is to fan the fires of enthusiasm into life anew, if those improvements are to be stabilized. Nevertheless, he does enjoy some satisfaction, when in the course of his therapeutic efforts over a number of years he has in part succeeded in raising the overall social levels on all his wards.

Every clinician who knows and has treated schizophrenics over an extended period of time is fully aware that there are no completely unchanging "end states" that last for years. It is one of the most highly emotional, dramatic experiences in the daily routine of a psychiatric clinic, to sense again and again, that even the apparently dullest, most rigid, inert schizophrenics are internally alive and are somehow developing. Suddenly they are capable of expressing with touching sincerity a flash of happiness or a word of thanks. If they have neglected to greet us for years, they will suddenly begin to again, and continue to grow more cordial as they do. Almost all of them will thaw out somewhat in response to exceptionally patient efforts during recreation or work-therapy sessions, just as every new therapeutic method will bring about changes in the external behavior of many of them. But it is also an inherent part of the daily life of the clinician to suffer with disturbing frequency the disappointment of seeing such promising signs of an improvement and inner life vanish. Suddenly the patient begins to revile his doctor again, delusively, incoherently, without motivation, just when it was felt that a personal relationship had been established. Suddenly patients recede again into passive lethargy, just after they had been activated at the cost of monumental effort and patience. In sad resignation one sees the mannerisms and stereotypy regaining the upper hand on one of the wards, after believing these had been overcome. Reversals and retrogressions of all sorts seem endless.

Rümke (1963) impressively described the animation of long-term schizophrenics; accordingly he admonishes caution against asserting that their affectivity is bleak and flat. Older schizophrenics are more capable of an adequate mimical expression of their suffering. Their affectivity again is often less disturbed than that of newer patients. Occasionally they show signs of loving, warm-hearted affinity toward others. Even though older schizophrenics seldom laugh, they do smile on occasion. After years of illness they can still discuss their symptoms in detail, banter them about as if they were nothing but one of their whimsical ideas, and then adapt themselves in keeping with the effect of all this on the conversational partner. One patient remarked with regard to his symptoms: "It was partly my own choice, and partly it was repugnant to me." Schizophrenics learn no longer to live in the world of delusions, but to live with it; they no longer allow themselves to be driven by madness, but they work through it as part of themselves, in shaping their own will and manner of living, by considering and applying normal, healthy traits of human behavior.

Many of these changes in the conditions of older schizophrenic patients have an obvious relationship to the conditions for their care under which they have to live and the treatment methods that are used. If, for example, there are tensions and quarrels among the nurses on a ward, the patients' behavior begins to deteriorate; if there is harmony between the nurses and doctors and among themselves, the patients' behavior improves. Many cases of improvement are related to new treatment methods, and many aggravations and deteriorations are brought about by the fact that these methods are being mechanically applied and no longer hold any interest for the patient. It is not always possible to discern the reason for a change in a patient's condition.

While the clinician during his daily routine has learned a good deal about the late courses of schizophrenic psychoses, his experiences have so seldom been systematically processed and presented as complete, scientifically verified facts, that hypotheses alien to reality or mere speculations were much too often given credibility. Such hypotheses began with the characterization of the disease as "early dementia" and as "idiocy-psychosis." Both these characterizations unwittingly suggested the view that those psychoses labelled today as schizophrenias "actually" or "in principle" (as it used to be expressed) always led to a total deterioration of the psychic being, just as the mental diseases did in correlation with an irrevocably progressing cerebral atrophy. One is reminded of the maxim *"nomen est omen"* when one finds in the history of psychiatry how the relationships of terms, such as "dementia praecox" with "dementia paralytica" (before Wagner-Jauregg!), "dementia senilis or arteriosclerotica" and other dementias, would entice one to see a similar relationship between the schizophrenic "end states" and the organic dementias. The later concept of the "process-psychosis" which replaced the

one of "idiocy-psychosis" also radiated a suggestion that the disease progressed basically and virulently according to a predetermined "process." The widespread concept of a "surge" had the same general effect. It originated from the idea that acute schizophrenic phases basically proceed toward a virulent deterioration. Based on these lines of thinking it seemed justified and necessary to seek consistently in schizophrenias an anatomical-pathological manifestiation. But it seems less necessary today, since such an anatomical-pathological manifestation was never found, to speculate that it simply has to exist "with a priori certainty." The thrill and pleasure of observation, description, and scientific processing of the human emotionality of the schizophrenic, and his inner life, even in the "end states," were not exactly furthered by the emergence of the theory that schizophrenias and all psychoses are phenomena that— "at the core"—can neither be fathomed nor understood by way of the emotions.

In a modern way, the assumption of an organic process with a lasting, continuous tendency toward deterioration in the schizophrenic psychoses is suggested, in that the psychic adynamia, as it exists in cerebral atrophies, is regarded as an essential phenomenon of schizophrenias as well. The "adynamia," the reduction of the energy potential (Conrad 1958), the "dynamic depletion" (Janzarik 1959, 1963) are interpreted by some as the sequels to certain processes related to cerebral atrophy. Obviously, numerous schizophrenics are passive and give little evidence of activity, particularly little activity that is goal-directed and aimed at the successful accomplishment of a meaningful task. But let us not forget that the schizophrenic's activity is artificially inhibited. Years ago he was shackled, strapped to his bed, or isolated. Today, the entire pressure of social therapy and pharmacotherapy with psychotropic drugs and neuroleptics works out toward the same end. For this reason it may be said that the adynamia of the schizophrenic can be interpreted as the result of a partially successful therapeutic effort. Perhaps schizophrenics are not adynamic because their brains are atrophied and their internal energies exhausted, but because their dynamics are directed toward pathological behavior and we are able to suppress such behavior extensively, as we must. At any rate, it is certain that behind the adynamia of the schizophrenic, there is always in evidence a rich, active inner life; behind the adynamia of the demented organic brain patient, however, this is not the case. I cannot admit that the nature of the adynamia of schizophrenics and that of patients with manifest brain disease are one and the same.

All suspicions and assertions to the effect that schizophrenias are the manifestations of organic idiocy, a brain atrophy, a progressive process, or of an event that continues to propagate its own development that defies understanding or perception by the emotions, have created unfavorable presuppositions for the scientific exploitation of clinical experience with chronic schizophrenics. The clinician who discovered after years of observation that there was an improvement, and who found an abundance of inner life, of emotional perception, of human rationale in his chronic schizophrenic patient—rather than the expected inexorable progression of the disease—during certain periods in history almost had to be ashamed of his discoveries. On the other hand, he felt secure and in concert with the accepted hypotheses if he was able to record an increasingly severe state of idiocy and dehumanization of the patient.

All these factors contain the reason why we still know so little of what is generally accepted about the late course of schizophrenias (the continuing course after decades of illness), and why the literature still contains so little about it.

However, from one point of view the late conditions of schizophrenic psychoses have already been extensively studied. Among the aged of the clinic population, the influence of the senium and of senile dementia on schizophrenics have been investigated. The concepts of these studies were different from those of the present ones, in that I did not select aged schizophrenic clinical patients as my probands, but studied schizophrenics admitted to the clinic who were young, or at least not senile, for over 20 years, and observed some of them into their senility. My studies are therefore intended to yield information not only on the later periods of illness into senility, but also on the courses of the illness many years after onset, before the age of senility is reached. They were designed to encompass not only the hospitalized aged schizophrenics, but to check long-term courses, regardless of whether the patient was hospitalized or not.

During the last few decades, the former investigations on schizophrenias during old age have become more thorough and more extensive. It has always been common knowledge that individual schizophrenic psychoses in advanced age improve, while others deteriorate. In general, the older investigators considered improvements during advanced age a rare phenomenon. At times they argued, in pure speculation, against the possibility of such improvements, simply because it contradicted the established concept of the "process-psychosis." The later and more thorough studies have clearly supported the benevolent influence of advanced age on improvement in many cases.

Individual cases of improvement in advanced age did not entirely escape the keen perception of Kraepelin, although he maintained that, in general, a patient's psychosis in advanced age remained stationary or still continued to deteriorate.

E. Bleuler found that it was "the rule" that excitable schizophrenics became quieter with advancing age; that in many it amounted to an actual improvement, in that delusional ideas and hallucinations decreased. In others, again, the quieting down amounted to the predicted onset of idiocy. Many patients became accustomed to the psychotic manifestations, found themselves better able to cope with them as time went by, and could therefore occasionally do useful work again. He felt that senile dementia could in some cases become manifest along with schizophrenia, and that in other cases both diseases together made the patients totally uncommunicative and inaccessible; although sometimes the organic psychosis would again improve the accessibility of the patient.

Jaser (1928), Fleck (1928), Vié and Queron (1935), Riemer (1950), Bychowski (1952), and Barucci (1955) discovered in the senium of schizophrenics an unchanged or improved state of health, in varying frequencies and modifications, that was blended with amnestic symptoms.

We are indebted to Müller (1959) for the most recent systematic study. It was done with 101 schizophrenics over 65 years old, from the Psychiatric University Clinic of Lausanne. Müller (1959) in his psychiatric examinations differentiated improvements in social behavior in daily living from improvements in the psychopathological symptomatology. From the social aspect, 55 of his patients showed improvement in their old age, and only 14 deteriorated. The study of schizophrenic symptomatology revealed improvements in 27 patients, deterioration in another 27, and an unchanged state in the remaining 47. Müller (1959) warns us, on the basis of his experience, against interpreting the concepts "end state," "process," "dementia," and "defect" in such a way as to imply that an absolute endogenous illness leads to a totally unchangeable condition of inertness. Rather, he was impressed by how much even older schizophrenics were still involved in a continuing altercation with their own being and their environment. Among his patients, 10–20 percent showed indications of a senile or an arteriosclerotic dementia. The senile dementia had varied effects on the schizophrenias. It led to improvements in the sense of an overall sedative and syntonic effect, a modification of defensive attitudes and sublimations, and a peaceful resignation and adaptation to the environment. In other patients, senile dementia took an unfavorable turn, manifested by retrogression and withdrawal from all human contact. The general effect of the aging process was similar and comparable to the effect of neuroleptic drugs.

Findings similar to Müller's (1959) were also developed by Gamna et al. (1962), Wenger (1958), Wachsmuth (1960) and Zurabashvili (1967).

Janzarik (1959, 1963) described impressively how the "dynamic depletion"—which one was popularly inclined to regard as a final phenomenon rooted in physiological disorders—recedes again with approaching old age. Patients who, 5 years after the beginning of their psychosis, had to be described as cold, autistic, dull, vacuous, incapable of human contact, devastated, or "burned out," after another 10 years revealed themselves as interested, more sympathetic, and malleable. Janzarik (1959, 1963) interprets the "dynamic depletion" as a partial, premature phenomenon of aging. If later the general aging process were to make any further progress, this phenomenon would recede. He explains further, that the asynchronously preceding adynamia would be overtaken by the physiological aging process, beginning in the sixth decade of life, after which it becomes balanced again by way of a "rechronologization of the aging process." Many of my own observations could be interpreted in the same way. To be sure, Janzarik also observed patients, as I did, who persisted in their autism and their adynamia as if they were rigid and inert, well into advanced age and up to their deaths.

It seemed to me an important enterprise to determine for the 208 probands of this study,

to what extent the psychotic manifestations still undergo changes after a course that has proceeded for many years.

Investigations of the 208 Principal Probands

A time span of over 20 years elapsed for most of the principal probands between the first onset of schizophrenia and the cessation of observation in the years 1964/65, or their expiration. Only 32 probands died during the observation period, before the 20 years since their first schizophrenic onset had elapsed. This time span between first onset and their elimination from observation or their death is distributed for the remaining 176 probands as follows:

Years	No. of Probands
20–30	107
30–40	47
40–50	20
50–60	2
	176

The investigations of this section are divided into two parts: The first listing is to show, in the last 5 years of an observation period that is in excess of 20 years, how often major fluctuations still occur in the health of the proband, how often acute exacerbations, and how many dramatic cases of improvement have occurred. Observations were made on 176 probands over more than 20 years. The second listing is to include the more delicate refinements in changes that took place during the latter years of the observation period. This second listing included not only the principal probands who had been observed for over 20 years after their first onset of illness, but all probands who had not died during an acute episode or within 2 months thereafter. This listing was to check the tendencies of courses of the disease in the long-term chronic cases, and simultaneously those courses that seemed to proceed to a chronic state after an acute episode. Nineteen of the 208 probands died during an acute schizophrenic episode or within 2 months after it subsided. Thus, 189 probands qualified for the second listing of this section.

The first listing reveals that more than 20 years after first onset of illness, 176 probands were observed. Of these, 28 maintained a state of recovery uninterruptedly for the last 5 years of the observation period. During those last 5 years, 148 probands did not recover, or their recovery did not last for the full 5 years.

Within these 5 years, 35 of these probands (24 percent) experienced acute surges and dramatic improvements or recoveries from such surges. More than 20 years after onset of illness, therefore, there were still massive exacerbations among $\frac{1}{4}$ of the unhealed patients, that receded either entirely or appreciably.

If we were to believe that the percentage of such schizophrenics with acute dynamics would diminish, if not 20–30, then 30–60 years after first onset of illness, we would be mistaken. Sixty-nine probands were observed for more than 30 years. Of these, 8 sustained a state of recovery uninterruptedly for the last 5 years of the observation period, while 14 (23 percent) of the remaining 61 still experienced acute surges and dramatic improvements during this last 5-year period.

But if we now include those additional 22 cases that were observed more than 40 years, we find among them in that last 5-year observation period, 3 permanent recoveries, and 5 (26 percent) among the 19 nonrecovered with acute dynamics. If the margin of error due to the small figures is considered, the three percentages (24, 23, and 26 percent) do not differ significantly.

As previously determined, for about 2/3 of the probands, the schizophrenic psychosis began peracutely, acutely, or subacutely. About 10 years later, when the type of course of illness could be identified, a portion had proceeded to chronic types of courses, and another portion had recovered (Table 4.8). Another third remained that progressed in undulations to "end states." Of these, in the years that followed, some progressed to long-term "end states" without intervening acute episodes. Beginning with the 20th year after onset, those cases that still include acute episodes within 5 years do not diminish in number, but continue to amount to approximately $\frac{1}{4}$ of the nonrecovered patients.

The second listing concerns 145 probands. Of the 208 probands, two groups were eliminated from consideration: a) those who died during an acute episode of their psychosis or within 2 months thereafter (19 probands), and b) those who were either in a continuous state of recovery or who recovered intermittently during the last years of observation (44 probands).

The remaining 145 probands included in this listing, therefore, were those who had not recovered and those who had not, at the end of the observation period, been eliminated for

an acute episode. All of them had attained an "end state"; according to the former definitions, they were "idiotics" or "defectives." During the last years of observation, they registered no further changes that would have necessitated a reclassification from one of the three major groupings on "end states" to another (they remained within their group as severe, moderately severe, or mild "end states"). The checking that remains to be done is whether more delicate modifications in the probands' conditions took place, even though no major change had occurred in it.

Such delicate modifications did occur in 55 of the 145 cases near the conclusion of the observation period, that is, in well over a third of them. Of these, 47 improved and 8 deteriorated. The figure 55 in this result is a minimum. It is certain for all these 55 probands that their condition underwent a perceptible change near the end of the observation period, even if it was not of such a degree as to warrant their reassignment to one of the other four major categories of "end states." Very few of the original probands were left in our own clinic at the conclusion of the observation period; most of them had either transferred to other clinics or were under the care of their families. The course of illness of these probands was not always so closely observed that slight changes in condition would have been noticed.

Among those schizophrenics who had not recovered many years after the initial onset, and who are no longer undergoing intermittent, severe, acute phases of illness, many more, then, are still inclined to show at least a slight or partial improvement rather than regressive deterioration.

The conclusion of observation in which slight modifications were detected occurred in

No. of probands during the period	Years after first onset of illness
1	1–10
0	10–20
31	20–30
14	30–40
9	40–50

In the vast majority of cases (54 or 55), as shown above, the improvements and deteriorations at the end of the observation period occurred after a course of illness exceeding a duration of 20 years, and in 23 cases, the course of illness had run over 30 years.

There is no significant difference between

Table 4.9. Late fluctuations in condition, differentiated by sex

	Men	Women
Probands who had not recovered at end of the observation period, and who were not eliminated during an acute psychotic phase	67	78
Of these, showing improvement near end of observation	22	25
Of these, showing deterioration near end of observation	3	5

Table 4.10. Late fluctuations in condition, differentiated by course

	No. of cases	Improve-ments	Deteri-orations
1. Acute to severe "end states"	3	0	0
2. Chronic to severe "end states"	22	0	1
3. Acute to moderately severe or mild "end states"	5	3	0
4. Chronic to moderately severe or mild "end states"	42	17	1
5. Undulating to severe "end states"	14	3	3
6. Undulating to moderately severe or mild "end states"	51	19	3
7. Atypical cases	8	5	0
Totals:	145	47	8

the sexes as to their participation in late improvements or deteriorations.

The later, more delicate changes in condition are distributed over the different types of courses according to Table 4.10.

The compilation yields an impressive picture. There are improvements after some of all types of courses, with 1 exception. This exception consists of probands whose psychoses had developed chronically and had already stabilized as "severe end states." Among those probands with chronic, mild courses (which includes particularly the late paranoids), and those with phasic courses, late improvements still occur rather frequently. On the other hand, among the probands with chronic, unchecked courses ending in severe chronic states, there are no more late improvements recorded, once the dismal "end state" has been reached. According to the data presented, the capability for improvement from severe "end states" seems to depend on how these severe "end states" developed. If their development was chronic, the presented data from the probands on hand offers little hope for late improvement; although a great deal of hope is warranted if that development progressed in acute undulations.

Can the reasons for late improvements be determined? We must depend on mere conjecture for that answer. Such improvements emerge from timed coincidences between improvements and changes in the life style of the patient. Presumably those improvements are related to:

	No. of cases
Aging	12
Changes in care procedures	11
Resumption of active treatment measures	8
Serious physical illness	4
Death of a relative	2
Undetermined causes	10
Total	47

The listing shows that the causes of late improvement can usually be discovered. It is easily possible that, if every facet of life were known,—even of the 10 patients listed as "undetermined"—some additional causes might have been determined.

By far the most frequent supposition is that advancing age stands in a causal relationship with the improvement. Most improvements after age of 55 were regarded in this context. Our own findings agree with those of Müller (1959). In what way the aging process benefits the later courses of schizophrenias remains to be investigated. It must be remembered, that the cerebral aging process could have the effect of a lobotomy, in that it would mitigate the pathological activity and the emotional agitation in connection with the symptoms of the disease. Perhaps instead of this, or in addition to it, a purely psychological interpretation is also the correct approach, that is, the wisdom of advanced age, the improved capacity for distinguishing essentials from nonessentials, a resignation to more modest, realistic, and immediately effective possibilities, might also exercise a beneficial influence on the psychosis. Possibly even the helplessness, or the prospect of impending helplessness, plays a role and reinforces the necessity of a reintegration into human society.

In cases of changes in the methods of care which were followed by improvements, the following comments apply.

In the case of a chronic schizophrenic (Proband 13) a marked improvement set in, that lasted up to the end of the observation period, after he had been placed for a short time in a psychiatric clinic—but without active treatment—and then had been moved back to his original environment. Proband 36 improved after his wife, with whom he had lived in a poor marital relationship, had left him. Proband 37 improved after release from the clinic, when his second wife simply made all the necessary and natural preparations for their permanent living together. Proband 54 improved after his second marriage, although that wife had a neurotic, querulous personality. Proband 61 was well cared for by his mother after release from the clinic. Female proband 1 improved after she was divorced, and then married a man she had loved earlier. Female proband 30 improved when a friend of her mother's assumed responsibility for her care. Female proband 67 improved when she was given leave to return to her family, where she helped with work on the farm, as she had done as a young girl. Female proband 68 improved when she was able to live with her grown son, who took on her delusions. Female proband 84 improved after her release from the clinic after consistently being treated kindly by her husband. Female proband 100 (a debility case) improved when she found favorable placement in a home for underachievers.

The active treatment that was followed by improvement after many years, was a drug cure with neuroleptics for 6, and a prefrontal lobotomy for 2 probands. The serious physical illnesses followed by improvements were apoplexy in 2 probands, hypernephroma in 1, and a furunculosis in 1.

The two relatives, to whose deaths improvement was related, were mothers of probands.

The type of late mild improvement in many cases can be characterized by determining that it relates to the patients' attitudes toward individual persons and individual situations. Such situations, in which the behavior of chronic patients suddenly approaches a state of recovery, include, among others, the hours spent in specialized occupational therapy, parties at the clinic, walks for pleasure, leave periods at home, physical illnesses or accidents

that require treatment, rare opportunities to telephone someone, and the like. Some of these situations are amazing: One proband was granted home leave for several days after many years of hospitalization—under pressure of his family and with considerable misgivings on the part of his doctors. After several years he is now permitted such brief periods of leave regularly twice a year. His family reports candidly that he was contented and behaved nicely, and for three days no one would have known that he was mentally ill. On the second or third day he usually announces that he absolutely must return to the clinic. When he arrives at the clinic, it is in the same condition in which he left it when he began his leave, and the same condition he has been in for years at the clinic—a condition noted in his patient history as "scatterbrained idiocy." Many patients show improvement in that they establish closer contact with at least a few others. Frequently these chronic patients appear inside the clinic as uncommunicative, bewildered, delusional, and hallucinating while they are on the intensive care wards, but they begin gradually to become more communicative with one visitor or another, until they would scarcely be regognized as mental patients. Another peculiar indication of improvement is when patients begin write letters that sound almost normal, which are in sharp contrast to their usual confused way of speaking. Such types of partial improvement remind one of the selective mutism of children, who "can" speak to only certain people, while they remain incapable of any vocal utterance toward anyone else.

Discussion: In the last few paragraphs it was determined that many of the psychoses of the 208 probands take a favorable course (about $\frac{1}{4}$ of the 208 probands had maintained a state of recovery for over 5 years by the end of the observation period, and over $\frac{1}{3}$ of the first-onset cases progressed favorably as phasic-benign). In this section, the late courses among nonrecovery cases are investigated, unless they had died early during the observation period: During the last 5 years of an observation period that exceeded 20 years, about one quarter of them suffered acute phases of illness that receded again. An investigation of the nonrecovered patients (subtracting those who died in acute phases) for more delicate changes (and not only for the dramatically acute phases) at the end of the observation period (that is, more than 20 years after first onset of illness), reveals the remarkable fact that mild improvements still occur rather frequently, whereas further deteriorations are rare.

If the schizophrenias are observed in straight-line or undulating courses as process-psychoses leading to a final and definitely low level, one would expect that acute phases would cease when that level has been reached; that is, when schizophrenic "dementia" has been attained. According to this concept, the "process" would have to cease when there is nothing left to be destroyed or burned. Actually, the expression "burned-out" with respect to schizophrenias was fairly common years ago. This concept contradicts the fact that renewed, acute, and dramatic psychotic episodes still occur decades after the illness has set in. Suddenly the fire can begin to flare up again, where everything appeared to be burned out. Nor is there any congruity between the old concept of a regulated deteriorating process in the direction of a defect or a dementia and the observation that late improvements are still rather frequent in chronic states. Where everything seemed to be burned out, a shoot of life can sprout forth anew. In this respect, the schizophrenic courses of illness behave differently from those of brain diseases that lead to severe cerebral atrophies. Even the adynamia, the lack of inner tension and vitality, is not necessarily an irreversible phenomenon that endures for decades. Instead, real life energies remanifest themselves after decades of "adynamia."

Although the causes of late improvements are difficult to determine, one cannot assume that they happen "by themselves," or "from the inside." Actually, in a number of cases we can detect effects of the environment to which such improvements might be related. Schizophrenics can still be responsive to environmental influences, even after they have been ill for decades. One might indeed conclude that the task of attempting renewed treatment time and again, and of continuing to check on methods of care repeatedly and to attempt to improve them presents itself, not only with acute, but also with chronic schizophrenics.

Many psychiatrists of previous generations were inclined to assume that if all schizophrenics were to survive the natural course of the disease, they would all finally become idiotic. Based on modern research, however, it might more likely be assumed that if all schizophrenics were to survive the natural course of their disease, they would all eventually recover.

One serious misgiving, however, dims any excessive optimism. We are seriously concerned about those cases that proceed chronically and in a straight line to a severe, long-term state of psychosis. As was shown in this section, they did not markedly diminish in number after therapeutic methods had been modernized; nor do the newest discoveries indicate that any tendencies to late improvements are to be found among them. Is this now the core group of schizophrenias that has so often been postulated? Are these now the process-psychoses that develop "endogenously" toward a final state of idiocy, while all other groups were not really "genuine" schizophrenias? The statistics presented in this chapter do not provide answers to these questions. However, I can anticipate that in the families of those patients with chronic, uniform progression toward severe, long-term psychoses, benign psychoses will occur frequently. For this reason, perhaps, these forms are related in nature to the other forms, and therefore, perhaps, the hope is justified that even these most stubborn forms might eventually submit to treatment.

Examples of improvements after courses proceeding through decades

The tendencies for improvement in long-term psychoses are meaningful for the theory on schizophrenias, as well as for clinical practice in their treatment. But while beginning schizophrenias have been precisely described by any number of examples, the literature very rarely provides patient histories that illustrate improvements after courses of illness persisting over decades. For this reason I should like to select and illustrate below a few of the 44 patient histories of those probands whose psychosis progressed to a chronic state after several decades, and who still revealed some tendencies toward improvement.

Female Proband 12, Elsa Z., born in 1912.
To outward appearances, proband grew up in an orderly, normal household, although internally schismatic conditions prevailed. Her father, a basically contented and open-minded intellectual in the teaching profession, had become addicted to analgesics, partly because of severe headaches due to a previous accident, and partly also due to his whining, constantly complaining, and hysterical wife (mother of proband). In addition, proband's brother was an invalid from childhood on (Recklinghausen's disease), and she herself always felt inferior to her older, more intelligent sister.

Proband put forth exceptional energy to finish elementary and secondary school. From early childhood on, she had not been very articulate, and had kept close to her pathological mother's apron strings. She was a sensitive and ambitious child. During her last years in school she had become conspicuous by screaming out loud without any motivation. As a seamstress apprentice she worked with such diligence that she even denied herself her authorized snack break and hoarded her food for days. She needed recuperative leave; but when she returned, every effort to continue working at her apprenticeship failed. She finally ran away in the middle of a work period and wandered aimlessly about the forest.

During this period (about 1929) her psychosis began slowly to set in. Foster care did not work out, so the patient was first hospitalized in a private clinic when she was 19 (1931). The disease manifested itself partly as discordant moods of anxiety, a feeling that the environment around her was changing, and in numerous patently pathological utterances such as: "I'm going off to kill someone," "I know that I've been in this world before," "I'm carrying the spirit of God inside me," and the like. During onsets of delusions of grandeur and an augmented feeling of omnipotence as a "spirit of the sun," she threatened at times to "destroy" all the patients at the clinic. She also believed she was hearing voices. Her thought processes usually revealed themselves as inattentively absent-minded and at times also as totally distracted. The patient was transferred to our clinic after $2\frac{1}{2}$ years without improvement, where the previously rendered diagnosis of a schizophrenia was merely confirmed (1934).

From age 22 to 46 (1934–1958) she underwent a number of changes in care facilities, alternating in a confusing pattern between our clinic, a number of attempts in foster families under supervision, and in her own family with her mother. Proband continued to remain severely ill during this period. Even outside the clinic she behaved peculiarly and unpredictably and often expressed her delusional thoughts. She was never again able to do productive work, but just helped out occasionally about the household.

Since 1959, at age 47, the patient has remained hospitalized until today (June 1967). In 1959 she was transferred for the last time from a family-care situation under medical supervision to the clinic. Her delusional, hypochondriacal complaining had increased just before this, in that she claimed to be suffering from "brain catarrh" and that the printed letters seemed to be mixed up in confusion. She complained that she was being changed over to a different person during the night. She often beat and choked herself, screaming out loud as she did so. When the doctor came to visit, she sneaked away and hid in the woodshed. During the weeks that followed at the clinic, particularly detailed and thorough observations and examinations were undertaken. The summary of findings read: "Formal thought process shows a tendency toward fragmentation and dissociation. Capacity for judgment is impaired. Intellectual interests are lacking and limited to her delusional inner life. She experiences numerous disjointed delusions and auditory and somatic hallucinations. Her emotional state is flat and superficial; her emotional inner life is almost totally extinguished. She is poorly motivated, often entirely shut off from the world, although seldom actively negativistic." The experienced psychiatrist who wrote this summary also mentioned an "advanced intellectual defect, based on a still-active paranoid schizophrenia." At that time the subject was under long-term care on a women's ward for the most serious chronic patients.

To supplement a characterization of her thought processes, here follow a few lines of notes expressed in retrospect by one of her doctors:

To the question whether she felt sad: "I just don't follow you. I always have thoughts in my mind. I am something like a life spoiler. I always think I'm being persecuted, because I can't find any friends. I just never had the proper treatment. I've got something wrong down here in my intestines. Everything is all tangled up down there. I've simply been tormented, at home in the village. They don't want to believe that I am good, too. I do lots of good in private. I've always been alone with my thoughts. Then they'd tell me that what I said was wrong. They forced me to take on thoughts that did not come from inside of me. They're not just voices; it's my own broken will. My will is broken, because it can't live in freedom. . . . I believe devils are tormenting me. I always think I'm the evil one myself, and I torment everybody . . . "

In this condition the proband was transferred to a rural clinic for chronic patients at age 47, in 1959. As far as any of the older psychiatrists were concerned, she was now a well-advanced idiotic schizophrenic. The best hope for her in previous times would have been a "stabilization of the process," and an even more likely estimate would have been the "continuance of the process toward approaching idiocy."

But it turned out quite differently. The old condition persisted for another year or two. Then, for about 6 years, an increasingly marked improvement became evident. The proband became more communicative, more coherent in her thinking, always less delusional, and less hallucinating. Simultaneously, or somewhat later (at about age 50) a forgetfulness toward recently experienced events began to set in slowly, while her memory for events from her youth remained accurate. At present (1967) a diagnosis of a schizophrenia is no longer applicable to the 55-year-old proband. Physically and mentally she appears prematurely aged, and her memory is very much impaired for someone her age. But she is able to think clearly and no longer says anything about delusions or hallucinations. She particularly gives the impression of a kind and friendly person, and the nurses and ward personnel are genuinely fond of her. On the other hand, she regards her hospitalization as a matter of course, and shows no inclination whatever to want to resume a normal, independent life outside the clinic. Also, she is somewhat inclined to neglect her appearance.

In summary, the patient history of Elsa Z. is depicted graphically in Fig. 4.1: a lingering onset in 1919; a schizophrenic psychotic for 40 years, partly severe and partly mild; after 40 years schizophrenic symptoms recede almost completely, and somewhat later a premature amnestic aging syndrome develops.

Proband 2, Eduard S., born 1912.

Proband comes from an old, established, rather well-to-do family of mountain farmers, and is the youngest of 7 children. He had spent all his life at his family's farm-establishment, where he still lives today. Until 1932 he worked together with his father, then, after the father died, with his brother.

Conditions in the home were favorable, and relations with both parents were good. He had also been a good student. From childhood on he was somewhat withdrawn, quiet, and "an especially good child; the best behaved of all his siblings." He had few friends and had always been a bit shy with girls; only one very superficial relationship with a girl is on record. During the late summer of 1942 he was on active military duty. He was rated a good soldier, never appeared to be ill, and seemed to enjoy military service until one day, after a long, strenuous march along a sun-drenched country road, he reported for sick call. His behavior at the military aid station was extremely peculiar. He complained about "a stormy head," lay around in sick bay as through he were seriously ill, although no

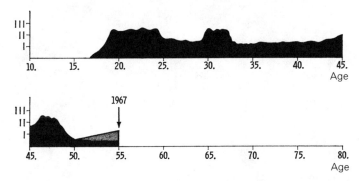

Fig. 4.1. Graphic overview of the disease course for Elsa Z. (Proband 12). The abscissa represents the age in years, the ordinate the approximate severity of the disease. Mere character changes without psychotic symptoms or obviously impaired capacity to work are not considered, either when they preceded the psychosis or when they followed a psychotic episode. The blackened areas in the diagram represent the degree and duration of schizophrenic-psychotic symptomatology; the shaded area, the degree and duration of the premature amnestic aging syndrome.

Level I: Not requiring hospitalization, usually able to work, and psychosis not immediately obvious in association with the patient.

Level III: Serious need for hospitalization, incapable of performing useful work, and contact with environment severely impaired, even under the simplest circumstances.

physical symptoms had been discovered, confided in no one, seemed completely without interest and apathetic, to the point that the military doctors had already at that time diagnosed a schizophrenia. But since the diagnosis had not been fully verified, he was first given temporary leave from active service. Once at home, he was no longer capable of performing any useful work. He customarily got up early in the morning, puttered about the yard without accomplishing anything useful, and then went back to bed or hid in some remote nook on the property. Sometimes he spent the night out in the open. He would do strange things. Once he took the buckboard down to the lake, launched its body onto the lake, and paddled around on it. Occasionally he would walk around the house and yard wearing his gas mask.

In September 1943 the proband was admitted to our clinic, age 31. Here he completely withdrew within himself, became passive, lost in reveries, and was plainly distracted in his thought processes. He expressed vague thoughts of having been poisoned. Electroshock treatments produced only temporary improvement.

From his release from our clinic in 1943 until the end of the observation period in 1965, proband remained at home, with one brief interruption at a private sanatorium, after having chopped down a number of freshly transplanted nursery trees. Until 1963 he accomplished nothing worth noting, was able to perform only the simplest tasks, and continued to show peculiar behavior stereotypies. For instance, every day he scrubbed three steps of a staircase. He voiced numerous delusional associations. If, for instance, an object was broken, he declared stereotypically that it could only be repaired if this or that person would live in a specified location or would die.

Beginning in 1963, that is, 21 years after onset of illness, a period of improvement set in. It seemed related to the death of his mother, although he had enjoyed a good relationship to her. The proband began to take an interest in many things; he began to read the newspapers again, which he had not done for many years, and especially, he speaks again with his relatives and has become their accepted and beloved family member again. His family no longer regards him as mentally ill, but simply as somewhat odd. After many years he again attends church with his family. To be sure, his case cannot be considered a complete recovery. He still voices delusional associations, as described, and leads a retired life limited to the confines of his family. This marked state of improvement has held for the past 2 years, to the conclusion of the observation period.

Evaluation: In respect to the type of course

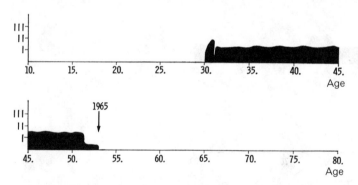

Fig. 4.2. Graphic overview of the disease course for Eduard S. (Proband 2). The abscissa represents the age in years, the ordinate the approximate severity of the disease. Mere character changes without psychotic symptoms or obviously impaired capacity to work are not considered, either when they preceded the psychosis or when they followed a psychotic episode. The blackened areas in the diagram represent the degree and duration of schizophrenic-psychotic symptomatology; the shaded area, the degree and duration of the premature amnestic aging syndrome.

Level I: Not requiring hospitalization, usually able to work, and psychosis not immediately obvious in association with the patient.

Level III: Serious need for hospitalization, incapable of performing useful work, and contact with environment severely impaired, even under the simplest circumstances.

(Fig. 4.2) of his illness, the case of Eduard S. is one of the rarest—one of an acute beginning, followed by a mild chronic psychosis. When the proband was at our clinic in 1943, we had set a rather poor prognosis for him, with his adynamia and his apathetic nature. After 10 years this prognosis had not materialized, in that his condition had remained stable. At that time it was assumed that it would almost surely remain stable; at least no one voiced any hope for his improvement. But in spite of that, he did improve and remained improved.

Proband 31, Johann Z., born 1910.

Proband grew up together with 6 siblings— 4 others had died in infancy—under poverty conditions aggravated by the father's alcohol addiction. His development started unfavorably, even as a young child. He was withdrawn, monosyllabic in his speech, although also an obstinate, stubborn bullhead; he revealed feelings of anxiety. He was a good student in school, but he just simply ran away from his apprenticeship in a machine shop after a short time. Then, living at home, he first worked as a helper, hiring out as a day-laborer, and then, after he was 20, moved to the city. At 21 he was forced to marry. Occupationally he had no success, for his escapade of leaving his apprenticeship branded him as unreliable; and as a helper in the construction trades he did not advance either, because, after starting a job, he would become intermittently ill, usually involving complaints that could not be objectively determined. They were marked down as fatigue, neuroses, or nervous prostration. His favorite pastime was puttering in his workshop until late at night. All too often he was unemployed—it was the time of the economic crisis of the thirties. So it came about that he and his family were mainly dependent on welfare organizations for their livelihood.

His psychosis became acutely manifest at age 29, in 1938. He had made unreasonable and ungrantable requests to a welfare agency. He had become excited to the point of threatening, unless his demands were met, to throw the office equipment of the welfare agency out into the street.

This was what brought about his first hospitalization at our clinic in 1938. Upon admission he seemed totally devoid of feelings, cold and stiff, and yet—completely in disharmony with the situation—sort of jolly with it all. His statements were unclear and incoherent. He developed distracted delusions,

claiming that he had been under a hypnotic spell, that someone wanted to kill him, that "a certain party or something of the sort" was behind it all; possibly also a neighbor woman or a fellow worker on the job were exercising control over him to test whether he was weak-willed, etc. (at the time he insisted, looking back, that similar ideas had occurred to him over the past few months). At the clinic he caused considerable trouble in the work-therapy sessions. But since no renewed states of excitability appeared, he was released after a 2-month stay, on probation.

Since that time he has never fully recovered.

After his first release he was able to stay out of clinics for $3\frac{1}{2}$ years, although he was never able to take on a regular job. He continued to feel persecuted by his comrades on the job, had hypochondriacal ideas and body hallucinations, and lived in a state of constant arguing and bickering with his wife. His wife, who was examined at our clinic, took on some of his ideas of persecution. At times it was a folie-à-deux between the two of them. He sent a number of threatening nonsensical letters to several agencies, in which he wrote, among other things: "Your silly little letter of August 12, 1941 really made me happiest of all; with your lies you can go to hell for all I care, but don't come to me. ... As to my activity at this time, I simply have no need of earning more since I'm only working for the fun of it, sort of, as a vacation. ... You can crawl up or down my back, as you please, with your silly repatriation, it just leaves me cold, there's a war going on, you know. It would be better for you if you made some sort of order in your paragraph mill and got some sense into your heads. ... But watch yourselves at Morgarten.* My guns are well aimed. ..." etc.

In 1942/43 the proband was hospitalized, after he had beaten his wife, and maintained the same condition for 11 months. He then remained at home again for 17 months, without showing any improvement.

From November 22, 1944 through June 2, 1958—for $13\frac{1}{2}$ years—he was continuously

---

* Battle of Morgarten (Nov. 15, 1315), background for the story of Wilhelm Tell, in which the cantons of Schwyz, Uri, and Unterwalden won their independence from Austria by defeating Leopold I. The famous battle, fought at the precipitous pass leading to the Schwyz mountains, marks the beginning of world fame and the brilliant career of the Swiss infantry, and strengthened the League and its confirmation of Louis IV.

in psychiatric hospitals. Except for minor fluctuations, his condition remained the same, as had already been observed in 1938. The notations below come from his long, rather uniformly similar, patient history: 1944: "Declares in rude, arrogant manner that he is unable to work." In letters he refers to himself as "Jurator, exploratus auctor." He sensed "something burning and pains in his heart, kidneys, and all over his body." Diagnosis after reexamination by different doctors: "Typical hebephrenia with malicious, irritable, and stiff and depressed mood." He insisted he was too weak to do manual labor, and that he was working "hand-in-hand with official agencies in the field of education and marital counseling." 1945: Again patient is described as exceedingly dull. 1946: Consistently withdrawn; writes memoranda to official agencies.

1947: From the report of a thorough reexamination: Proband speaks with affectation but incoherently; for instance, he says: "Only when I execute certain uniform movements, you know, as in mowing grain, that's when these symptoms of my hip-joint inflammation are reawakened, and that's when my leg goes lame on me again, that is what I picked up right here at Burghölzli." Or he says: "You've asked that of a lot of people; how am I supposed to explain it to you; I simply work on the revision of my legal commitment. And look now, I can tell you this right away, back in 1938 I purposely put that in the works, in order to get into my hands what I have in hand now. Look here, where do you suppose I would have learned that. . . . "

1948: Patient was transferred to a different psychiatric clinic. The diagnosis there reads: "Chronic hebephrenia, exceptionally cranky and vacuous." His condition there persisted for years as it had in the past.

In the spring of 1958 a largactil treatment series was instigated, which was complicated by a furunculosis. A slight improvement followed. This was 20 years after first onset, and 13½ years after uninterrupted psychiatric hospitalization.

Contrary to expectations, the improvement not only persisted, but further progress was realized. After dismissal, the patient lived for a short time with relatives, and then by himself. He attempted to make his living by tinkering and doing odd jobs, but did not succeed at it. Since it was necessary to support him largely from welfare sources, the agencies insisted that he enter an open home for the unemployable.

He has remained there until today—June 1967—9 years after his release. The amazing fact is, that his condition has been far better during the past few years than it has ever been, in fact, even better than it was before his onset of schizophrenia. He no longer gives any impression of being mentally ill. The house manager, who knows him well, says about him: "I know that he had something like schizophrenia some time ago, but we have observed nothing like that about him any more." He gets along well with his housemates and is considered a "likable follow." He has intellectual interests, keeps up with the times in journals and magazines, and is glad to explain things to his housemates. He rides a motorcycle, has had neither traffic warnings nor accidents with it, and takes long tours with it on Sundays.

In a recent reexamination that I decided to undertake personally, I was completely amazed about the change, in comparison with his condition in previous years. He was speaking clearly now, and was warmly, genuinely pleased to meet me again at the clinic, where he visited with lively interest the ward in which he had been a patient years before. He made no spontaneous utterances that were pathological. When he was questioned as to some of his farmer delusions, however, he still held to them and responded to such questions in the same confused and distracted manner as before.

Summary: The patient, coming from a difficult environmental background, was prepsychotically rated as a schizoid psychopath (extremely uncommunicative and taciturn, under constant treatment for asthenic complaints and hypochondria, not fully employable). The psychosis erupted at age 28 in an acute excitation, although possibly a few months before that there had been some expressions of delusions. The disease was characterized by a totally apathetic and world-alien attitude, distraction, manifold absentmindedly expressed delusions, and body- and auditory-hallucinations during full consciousness. The course was characterized as "beginning acutely, and progressing to a long-term moderately severe 'end state.'" This condition persisted for 20 years; the proband has been hospitalized without interruption for the last 13½ years. No one at this point in time would have expressed hope for any further improvement. From then on, however,—patient was 48 years old—a marked improvement began its course. In the last years of observation the proband certainly was not

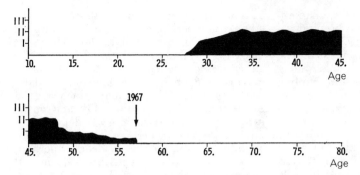

Fig. 4.3. Graphic overview of the disease course for Johann Z. (Proband 31). The abscissa represents the age in years, the ordinate the approximate severity of the disease. Mere character changes without psychotic symptoms or obviously impaired capacity to work are not considered, either when they preceded the psychosis or when they followed a psychotic episode. The blackened areas in the diagram represent the degree and duration of schizophrenic-psychotic symptomatology; the shaded area, the degree and duration of the premature amnestic aging syndrome.

Level I: Not requiring hospitalization, usually able to work, and psychosis not immediately obvious in association with the patient.

Level III: Serious need for hospitalization, incapable of performing useful work, and contact with environment severely impaired, even under the simplest circumstances.

completely recovered (he still thinks in delusion when questioned about it), but to outward appearances, he is not aberrant, and he is considerably better, by and large, than he was in his youth before onset of his illness. It should be specially emphasized, that this patient, now 57 years old, is more lively, more active, and more interested in realities than he ever was before; that his adynamia has receded; and that he, who was considered apathetic, malicious, and uncommunicative, is able to muster a warmth in his personality that would be ascribed to a normal healthy person (Fig. 4.3).

Proband 27, Robert R., born 1900.

Proband and his 8 older and 2 younger siblings (of whom the oldest brother had already died at age 4), spent their childhood and youth under the domination of a quick-tempered, brutal, alcoholic, and sectarian father, and a mother who was efficient and hard-working, although she was vengeful. She belonged to the same sect as the father. After her husband died she emigrated to America to live with a grown daughter, abandoning the rest of her children, most of whom were grown by that time.

Proband finished 9 years of elementary schooling and went into a mechanic's apprenticeship, which he had to interrupt for a year because of tuberculosis. After that he changed jobs often, attempted to improve his training by attending courses at a technical school, and then felt an urge to devote his time to music. He dropped his musical studies as spontaneously as he had begun them, to return to his previous occupation.

While looking for work, he spent some time in a city in the French sector of Switzerland, where he did not find a job, but went swimming in the lake at 2 o'clock in the morning, because, he said, it was so terribly hot; he then walked about the park totally naked carrying a sign inscribed "Prenez garde à la peinture" (Caution, wet paint). His arrest for this offense led to his first referral to a clinic. During his 8-day sojourn at a psychiatric university clinic in June 1925, he was diagnosed as "schizophrenic, delusions of grandeur and persecution." On instructions from his family, he was released, but already after one month his need for rehospitalization was evident. This time he was sent to a state institution, where he spent 6 months. For a little over 4 years, then, he was employable, generally nonaberrant, although consistently shy of people and uncommunicative. During this period he married a woman with good intentions, who was prone to indulge in idealistic ravings and inclined to reactive depressions.

Gradually the proband reverted to a distracted, restless, and finally severely agitated

state and, having upset a number of tomb-
stones in a cemetery, had to be hospitalized
in our clinic in the spring of 1931. The diagnosis of a schizophrenia was confirmed. The
patient was confused and delusional. Among
other activities, he busied himself attempting
to square a circle. After a stay of $4\frac{1}{2}$ months
in our clinic and a private hospital, he returned to his wife. Although his behavior did
not give rise to any serious complaints, he
never fully recovered after that. He acted
strangely at home, moody, lacking in interests
of any kind, and indifferent toward his wife
and child, so that he was finally divorced in
the fall of 1935.

A year later the patient again fell into a
state of manic-hebephrenic excitation, bothered and threatened his divorced wife, and as
a result was again hospitalized at our clinic.
Again the diagnosis was hebephrenia. Having
quieted down and improved, the patient was
released after 6 months.

His good state lasted for 4 years. During
this period the patient was socially nonaberrant, and even met his obligations toward
the child from his divorced marriage. The
court order for his commitment was rescinded.

Then a renewed onset of excitation, in
which he demolished furniture and shrubbery
in the garden, necessitated his third hospitalization in 1942, at which time he became a
proband of this study. He soon quieted down
again and was eligible for release 3 weeks
later.

Then followed long, undisturbed years with
the most variegated kinds of employment,
from air-defence service during the war, to
being a representative and a traveling salesman, then to an attempt at becoming independent by producing a bobbin-winding
machine, and finally by taking a job as
electrician at an electrical power plant. In
this job he suffered an accident. Three months
later he still felt unable to work, although
he had been considered fit, from a medical
viewpoint, by the surgical university clinic
and polyclinic. From May 1949 through June
1950 he came for outpatient appointments
to our clinic, where he proved to be at emotional neap tide, and his thought processes
were unclear and partly distracted. This condition intensified, until finally the proband
himself agreed to his hospitalization at the
clinic of his home canton (1950). After 15
months he was again released with the diagnosis of "surging schizophrenia with a moderately severe defect."

Since then, that is, until the end of the
observation period, for 13 years, the proband
required no further hospitalization. He makes
his living as a building caretaker, does all sorts
of services for the tenants in the way of minor
repairs, and on occasion goes out on dates
with a woman. He has maintained a good
relationship with our clinic. Off and on he
telephones and reports in great detail about
his day-to-day bickerings, about problems
with his heart, a bicycle accident, or perhaps
he explains how he orients his body in bed
according to the compass. In most conversations he is mildly distracted, though not to a
degree that would suggest mental illness to a
layman.

In our statistics this proband's psychosis is
carried as a phasic schizophrenia progressing
to a mild chronic state.

Twice in the life of this proband the course
of the illness has been more favorable than
we had feared. At age 37 he was in the middle
of his third severe acute "surge" of the disease.
Between the first and second, and between the
second and this third "surge" he had never
fully recovered, and the chronic pathological
condition had been considerably more severe
during the second interval than the first. At
the peak of the third acute episode one could
not have hoped for anything more favorable
than an improvement to the mild level of the
condition in the second interval between the
acute surges. But quite unexpectedly, he recovered almost fully from this third psychotic
episode. For approximately the next 10 years
—interrupted only by a fourth, short acute
psychotic episode—he remained well. The
fifth onset began at about the end of his 40s,
not acute, but subacute or chronic, and the
psychosis did not recede as quickly as it had
before. At his release from the clinic, the prognosis had been for a "moderately severe defect," and renewed, more acute episodes were
feared for the future. In the 13 years that have
elapsed since then, however, the chronic disturbance is milder than "moderately severe,"
and no additional episode has emerged. There
is no evidence of any "adynamia" nor any
"emotional desolation" (Fig. 4.4).

Proband 37, Edwin G., born 1898.

The happy parental home of this proband
was characterized in particular by the multifaceted interest in the arts of the father who
worked as a graphic painter, photographer,
and musician; the mother was a quiet, withdrawn woman.

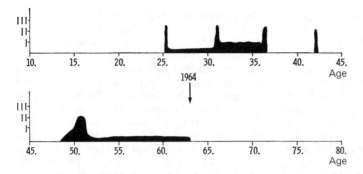

Fig. 4.4. Graphic overview of this disease course for Robert R. (Proband 27). The abscissa represents the age in years, the ordinate the approximate severity of the disease. Mere character changes without psychotic symptoms or obviously impaired capacity to work are not considered, either when they preceded the psychosis or when they followed a psychotic episode. The blackened areas in the diagram represent the degree and duration of schizophrenic-psychotic symptomatology; the shaded area, the degree and duration of the premature amnestic aging syndrome.

Level I: Not requiring hospitalization, usually able to work, and psychosis not immediately obvious in association with the patient.

Level III: Serious need for hospitalization, incapable of performing useful work, and contact with environment severely impaired, even under the simplest circumstances.

Proband was the 3rd of 4 sons, who all pursued careers involving poetry, painting, and music. As a child Edwin was already somewhat dreamy by nature. During his youth his chief interests were in the music and literature of romanticism. He began a business course, but did not finish it; instead he worked as a musician. He had few friends, most of them also musicians, and beginning with his last year in school he maintained a close friendship with a young woman who also studied music and later became his wife.

It spite of having failed to complete his musical education at a conservatory, the ambitious young man was successful. He was much in demand, was highly regarded as a violin teacher, and directed six choral singing groups. In the beginning, this marriage, consummated at age 23, was happy and successful. Then, under pretext of having to apply all his energies toward "intellectual accomplishment," he began to neglect his wife. Under the influence of Coué, he developed a considerable interest in public speaking, and wanted to "expand the arts with the aid of autosuggestion." During this period he began, as he reported later, to hear voices in his head, claiming at times that "they were cursing God." After 3 years of marriage, his wife obtained a divorce.

For a long time the proband was not able to cope with this fact, and had to be forcibly stopped by court order from continuing to send his former wife letters and gifts. To console himself he joined a religious sect, which later ostracised him. For years he lived with his mother, after his father had died in 1927. Religious thoughts occupied much of his time; in other ways his life seemed uneventful in teaching music.

In the fall of 1934 he awoke one morning hearing a loud voice, as if it were coming from the radio. At first, he said, it was as if someone had opened a damper somewhere inside of him, but then it seemed as if his thoughts were merely being expressed out loud. Then he felt that a "certain gift of spiritual communication" had come to him. Six months later the patient had to be hospitalized, after having wanted to "drive out the hypnotic forces of a magnetizer." Later he himself, reported that he felt he was undergoing the splitting of his personality, that it was as if two of him were struggling with each other. A similar feeling had occurred to him in the fall of the same year, which was the reason he turned himself in to a private clinic. During the interview at that clinic he also reported that he had been hearing voices as early as 1925, and that images like pictures in a cinema moved before his eyes. In 1935, he said, suddenly a strange, oriental language issued from his mouth. According to the reports of one of his brothers, the patient had been aberrant for years before his first hospitalization. Instead of giving music lessons, he prayed with his students and placed his hands on them. Voices had nearly driven him to suicide. In both these hospital admissions he was diagnosed as a schizophrenic.

In 1936 the proband married for the second time; he met his second wife shortly before his first hospitalization. He directed small religious groups, wanting to minister spiritually to resort guests with religious singing, looked in vain for music pupils and, although he had 3 children, followed soon thereafter by a 4th, traveled from one town to another, earning virtually nothing and living off the proceeds of an inheritance.

In the summer of 1942 he checked in to our clinic of his own free will, wanting a thorough examination. He complained that recently he had felt compelled to write lengthy letters, not only to his wife and brother, but also to a number of government agencies. Voices had directed him to our clinic. His behavior at the clinic was coherent and quiet. He was able to discuss impersonal topics rationally. When his personal problems were discussed, he became confused and bewildered. Then he described queer ideas about religion, the occult, his special gift of "spiritual communication," that he did not want to refer to as fortune-telling, and the like. He complained of hearing his thoughts, numerous phonemes, and automated speech and action.

The proband was released after a 6-day stay at the clinic. Although he was partially aware of the nature of his illness, he still held to ideas that were unrealistic as to the continuation of his life style and the financial security of his family. Since that time, and until the end of the observation period 22 years later, he has enjoyed a happy family life, in which his simple, unpretentious and natural wife plays a major role. He is active as a private music teacher. We gained a good impression of the degree of his social recovery in a personal interview a few years before the observation period ended, in which he was content and cordial in giving rational and coherent answers. About 4 years later we got the same impression during a house visit. Naturally we cannot say that his chronic paranoid disturbance has completely left him. In some of his emotional expressions, the former patient seems somewhat monotonous and flat. He still holds to some rather quaint, unusual philosophical convictions that are difficult to follow. He also has some peculiar body sensations, at times feeling "vibrations" in his body. He claims that he must purge

"blasphemous thoughts" that come to him, with his religious thoughts. At age 66 he feels that he is already an old man without a future. However, considered as a whole, he could not by any standard be regarded as psychotic for a number of years past. He is a bit odd and eccentric, but he is not mentally ill.

Summary: Beginning in his middle twenties, a lingering, paranoid schizophrenic psychosis developed in Edwin G. After a duration of 17 years, when it had reached its peak, the patient voluntarily requested hospitalization, which made him a proband of our study. Thereafter an amazing, unprecedented improvement set in, which held to the end of the observation period 22 years later. It is possible that the natural and loving personality of his wife contributed to the favorable outcome for this former patient (Fig. 4.5).

Proband 66, Klara E., born 1890.

Proband comes from a city in southern Germany, in which she grew up together with 3 sisters in a simple but normal family environment. Nevertheless, even as a venerable old woman, she still cannot restrain her tears when she talks about how mean her father was when he was drinking. As a young girl she had maintained an intimate liaison with a Swiss foreigner who lived in her city, and whom she married after her second pregnancy by him. During the First World War, this man went back to Switzerland for his military service, and in 1918 the proband with 2 of their children also moved to Switzerland. The older illegitimate daughter remained in Germany with her grandparents; in Switzerland 2 more children were born to them. With the husband's low income as a porter and newspaper vendor, the family endured a life of poverty. The proband found it virtually impossible to adapt to the Swiss way of life. She maintained her German dialect, which caused both her and the children to be generally looked down on. The proband was hard on her children. She seemed to delight in refusing their wishes out of hand, although she usually fulfilled them later on. Her husband, on the other hand, was a kind and gentle father. When the Second World War began, the proband was already a mean and querulous woman with a sharp tongue, who had alienated all her neighbors. Then, in addition, she slowly turned delusional as well. She felt she was being persecuted by her neighbors. She regarded the early German successes in battle as a personal vindication and as punishment

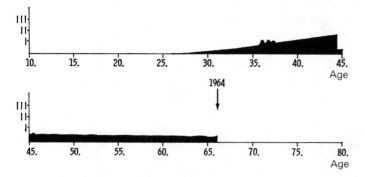

Fig. 4.5. Graphic overview of the disease course for Edwin G. (Proband 37). The abscissa represents the age in years, the ordinate the approximate severity of the disease. Mere character changes without psychotic symptoms or obviously impaired capacity to work are not considered, either when they preceded the psychosis or when they followed a psychotic episode. The blackened areas in the diagram represent the degree and duration of schizophrenic-psychotic symptomatology; the shaded area, the degree and duration of the premature amnestic aging syndrome.

Level I: Not requiring hospitalization, usually able to work, and psychosis not immediately obvious in association with the patient.

Level III: Serious need for hospitalization, incapable of performing useful work, and contact with environment severely impaired, even under the simplest circumstances.

for all the wrongs that had been done her. In the divorce proceedings, instigated by her husband in 1940, she was obviously psychotic. Her oldest son, who had since married, took her in to live with his family. In the spring of 1942, an aggravated acute condition set in. She became confused, felt herself persecuted because she was German, felt that she was magnetized and electrified, and had "divine infusions." She sat down in someone's automobile, clutched the wheel and refused to let go, whereupon she was referred to our clinic.

The proband stayed at our clinic for 2 months, maintaining the same scolding and raving behavior. Then she was released as improved, but had to be rehospitalized 4 weeks later, with a renewed onset of excitation. Her condition was hardly changed at all at the clinic. She remained a wrathful, scolding woman, who even slapped her grown son's face when he came to visit. During acute periods of excitation she threatened to destroy everything, and even attacked nurses and fellow patients. She was transferred to a private clinic, where she is still characterized as a "primitive chronic paranoid pyknic," who "with her lively affectivity and based on her systematic delusions is inclined to displays of explosive temper." During the last 8 years, that is, from age 65 on, an unexpected improvement set in. The patient had become an endearing, scarcely aberrant, diligent little granny. She tends to the children of the

clinic's employees with total devotion, although she is unable to establish any relationship with her own children, whom she treats with cold indifference when they come to visit.[9]

At the conclusion of the observation period, I personally undertook this proband's re-examination. Compared to her condition of years ago, she just would not be recognized. She was carefully groomed; no psychotic symptoms were in evidence. Of course, there was no spark of insight into her own previously endured, severe psychosis. When confronted with those previous symptoms, she disputed their happening and made light of them. She is quite content with treatment at the psychiatric hospital, but has no initiative to reshape her life into something useful, active, and independent.

Summary: Even before onset of her psychosis, Klara E. at best had a difficult character; and besides she lived in depressing circumstances. Her paranoid schizophrenia became chronic at age 49, although later in the course of the disease, two severe acute

9. Five years after the completion of the manuscript of this chapter, but before the manuscript of the entire book was finished, I did another catamnesis on this proband. At the end of 1968, at age 78, she is still doing well. The duration of this state is now 13 years rather than 8, as reported in the text.

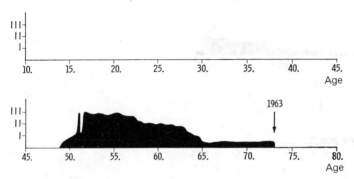

Fig. 4.6. Graphic overview of the disease course for Klara E. (Proband 66). The abscissa represents the age in years, the ordinate the approximate severity of the disease. Mere character changes without psychotic symptoms or obviously impaired capacity to work are not considered, either when they preceded the psychosis or when they followed a psychotic episode. The blackened areas in the diagram represent the degree and duration of schizophrenic-psychotic symptomatology; the shaded area, the degree and duration of the premature amnestic aging syndrome.

Level I: Not requiring hospitalization, usually able to work, and psychosis not immediately obvious in association with the patient.

Level III: Serious need for hospitalization, incapable of performing useful work, and contact with environment severely impaired, even under the simplest circumstances.

episodes emerged. Along with the second episode, the proband was a severely ill schizophrenic, who would have been categorized as "idiotic" without any misgivings, according to the terminology of previous times. In spite of that, after a long-term duration of many years of the severe condition, an improvement was noted after a 5-year period, and after 10 years an even much more extensive improvement set in. In the past 8 years (see n. 9) the proband is nonaberrant to all outward appearances, displays no more schizophrenic tendencies, but has lost the initiative for a normal life and has no insight into the illness she has endured (Fig. 4.6).

Long-Term Courses of Illness Evaluated as to Frequency and Duration of Hospitalizations

By far the greatest number of the many previous investigations on the courses of schizophrenic psychoses consider as the only or as the primary catamnestic criterion, the mere fact whether a patient was hospitalized or whether he lived outside a psychiatric hospital. Actually the criterion of hospitalization at a given point in time is the simplest, the clearest, and the most convenient method for evaluating the courses of psychoses, but it is also a method that tells us very little about the natural course of the illness. All too often it is forgotten that the hospitalization of schizophrenics never gives us an accurate picture

of their condition. After all, their hospitalization in no way depends on their condition alone, but just as much (among many other circumstances) on social conditions, that have little or nothing to do with their mental condition. To a great extent it depends on the admission and release policies of the hospitals in question whether a patient is admitted and when he is released. There are doctors in hospitals who take pride in seeing how soon they can release their patients, and there are others who see an advantage in keeping mildly ill patients hospitalized as long as possible because such patients feel more secure there than out in open society. For instance, the idea that the psychiatric hospital might also be a nursing home for the aged who have improved or recovered appeals to one clinician, but not to another. Furthermore, the availability of bed space allocated to psychiatric patients influences the number and the duration of hospitalizations in all countries. Just as much as the hospitalization of the mentally ill depends on the whims and attitudes of the hospital's doctors and on available hospital facilities, so also it depends on the whims and attitudes of the patients' families and of the local population. It depends on whether families have the will and the capability of taking in their mentally ill relatives, whether sufficient and adequate facilities for the public care of the mentally ill are available, and what sort of opinions and prejudices in respect to the mentally ill prevail in the community. Besides, whether a mental patient is hospitalized or not does not really reflect his actual state of health. There are mildly ill schizophrenics who are hospitalized, and there are severely ill schizophrenics moving about freely in society.

In fact, it is amazing how often, and over how many years one has seriously accepted the criterion of hospitalization in the evaluation of the courses of schizophrenic psychoses, despite the obvious objections cited above. This can only be explained by saying that many investigators simply found it impossible to make an accurate evaluation of the mental condition of patients after they were hospitalized. As a result, they had to lean on the dubious criterion of hospitalization per se.

Even while planning these investigations (as also in planning the Pfäfers investigations of 1941) I made a special effort not to evaluate the long-term courses at all—or at least not primarily—on the basis of hospitalization data, but according to the "true" condition of the patient. The previous chapters are written with this problem in mind. However, in this chapter a closer look at the various hospitalizations of the 208 probands is called for. Even if the study of such data will permit only summary conclusions as to the courses of the illness, they still are of significant interest, in that they may stimulate interest in making comparisons of treatment results and hospital admission policies of various locales and at various times. This type of research has recently become popular, among other places in England, and has yielded some important results. Statistics on the hospitalization of schizophrenics are furthermore suited to comparisons with the course statistics that do not employ hospitalization as one of the criteria for determining the condition of patients.

Table 4.11 indicates how many of the probands, after their first hospitalization, until they died or until the observation period was ended,

—remained hospitalized uninterruptedly
—were released once and remained hospitalized without interruption after their second hospitalization
—were released and remained unhospitalized
—were released more than once and rehospitalized more than once, for more than 22 years (or at best 44 years) thereafter.

Those probands whose admission that qualified them as probands was not their first hospitalization, of course, more often belong to the last group than do those who became probands along with their first hospitalization. The former probands are naturally and automatically selectious because of their inclination toward undulating courses.

About half the probands first hospitalized in 1942/43 were released more than once and readmitted more than once after this hospitalization, within over 20 years or until they died. For brevity's sake, this type of patient will be referred to in the text that follows as "pendular." Among all probands, that is, all schizophrenics admitted to our clinic in 1942/43, barely $\frac{1}{4}$ are pendular cases. But among those schizophrenics who were entering as readmissions at that time, they were by far the majority, that is, over $\frac{3}{4}$.

In the light of information from Table 4.11, one is shocked to note that 6 percent of the schizophrenics admitted to our clinic in 1942/43 remained hospitalized continuously from their first admission[10] through more than 20 years or until they died. This was the case in 13 of the 208 probands. What was the reason for their tragic fate?

In order to examine this question, the histories of these 13 patients will be investigated more closely.

—Two patients died during an attack of acute excitation, without having developed to a chronic state.

—Nine patients had already been schizophrenic for a number of years (6–29 years) before they were admitted to our clinic in 1942/43 to become probands. Of these 9, 6 had a lingering development with extremely poor prognosis from the very beginning, while 3 had suffered an acute onset with a syndrome that suggested a "schizophrenic reaction."

—Two patients had been schizophrenic only a short time (3 and 5 years) before they became probands through admission at our clinic. The one psychosis had a lingering development; the other became manifest in a first-time acute episode without hospitalization, while the second acute episode led to permanent hospitalization.

10. The hospitalization at our clinic, that made the patient a proband, was the first hospitalization for schizophrenia in only 68 cases. In 140 cases, patients had required hospitalization for schizophrenic psychosis before that time. A portion of this latter group was transferred to our clinic from other clinics in 1942/43.

Table 4.11. Incidence frequency of hospitalization among principal probands

Time from first hospitalization to end of observation period or to patient's death	*All probands*		*Ss who became probands at first hospitalization*		*Ss who became probands at subsequent hospitalization*	
	No.	*%*[1]	*No.*	*%*[1]	*No.*	*%*[1]
Hospitalized without interruption	13	6.3 (4–11 %)	6	8.8 (3–18 %)	7	5 (2–10 %)
Released once, rehospitalized and remained hospitalized	22[2]	10.6 (7–16 %)	9	13.2 (6–24 %)	13	9.3 (5–15 %)
Released and remained unhospitalized	21	10.1 (7–16 %)	21	30.9 (20–43 %)	0	—
Released more than once and rehospitalized more than once.	152	73 (68–81 %)	32	47.1 (55–60 %)	120	85.7 (79–91 %)
Totals:	208		68		140	

1. Applying the confidence interval at the level of 95%, according to *Documenta Geigy*, 7th Ed, p. 90, ff. (disregarding decimals).

2. Three of these patients died in an acute psychotic state soon after the second hospitalization.

—A total of 13 patients were never again released after their first psychiatric hospitalization until the end of the observation period (that is, 22 years after they were first hospitalized) or until they died, in contrast to 195 patients who were relased after their first admission to a hospital (although some were rehospitalized after that first admission).

Two of the 13 did not attain a chronic state; they died in a most severe state of acute excitation, one within 8 days, and the other within 22 months after first hospitalization. In both cases the prognosis for the courses of their psychosis had been favorable. The first patient (Male proband 50) died shortly after admission with symptoms of an "acute delirium." The second, (Female proband 50) was in a state of extreme excitation for a number of months. Her prognosis seemed favorable, because her hebephrenic symptoms were blended with a manic syndrome, and because her mother and one sister had experienced similar manic-like hebephrenic states and had recovered. Neither of these two cases proves anything about long-term courses.

Nine of the 13 cases had already been schizophrenic for over 5 years without interruption when they became probands with their admission to our clinic in 1942/43. The duration of the psychoses before admission to our clinic amounted to 6, 9, 10, 13, 13, 13, 17, 22, and 29 years. They became probands as chronic schizophrenics. Three of them had

been former inpatients of ours when they were admitted; the duration of their hospitalization in other clinics had amounted to 7, 10, and 13 years. Two of them had spent 3 years and 3 months, and 5 months, respectively, in other clinics before admission in our clinic.

Six of these 9 cases had a poor prognosis from the outset, in that their psychoses underwent a lingering-progressive development, and the probands had remained rational for a long time (3 of these 6 were chronic paranoid late-schizophrenics, and 1 was a case of schizophrenia simplex). All these probands had been treated in clinics where they received no active therapy at all or very little of it for a number of years (some before, and some after the 1942/43 hospitalization). Actually, the patients were not neglected in these clinics. All these clinics had introduced work-therapy, even if it was not always up to optimum standards. And if one digs a little deeper for additional reasons for the unfavorable courses of illness, he will be confronted repeatedly by the fact that the patients, had they been released, simply would have found no family, no home, and no job outside the clinic. Proband 47, for instance, had an alcoholic father, who abandoned his family early, and a mother severely psychopathic and incapable of love, who developed a paranoia late in life. He had only 2 brothers, who were both psychopaths and paid scarcely any attention to him. Proband himself was a cretin, who was conspicuous by his exceptionally large head and his typically cretin-like figure. He was born in 1888 in an area where endogenous cretinism was still prevalent at the time. It spite of his cretinism, his intelligence was good and, contrary to most cretins, he had erotic desires. His appearance impaired his chances for recognition on the job or for marriage. Embittered, he left Switzerland, and soon began to develop a persecution complex. Another patient (Proband 65) is the son of a poverty-ridden alcoholic, who was unable to find a job and scarcely able to keep a roof over his head during the crisis years, became a vagabond and as such, gradually developed a schizophrenia simplex. A female patient, Proband 9, came from a family of Russian nobles, but in a moment of capricious, romantic impulsiveness, had married a Swiss commoner who had been working in Russia. She moved to Switzerland with him, where she felt totally uprooted, quarreled constantly with her husband, divorced him, lost all contact with the children, and became completely solitary. In grotesque overestimation of her own abilities, she felt that she could make her way as an artist. She attempted to surround herself with artist friends, who did express compassion for her, but who showed no sort of recognition for her efforts. Feeling completely forsaken, and impoverished, she developed a love-mania for a well-known musician, from which there developed a lingering, severe schizophrenia with full-blown autism.

None of the other 6 patients would have had any sort of family or job to return to, if they had been released from the clinic. It is, therefore, reasonable to assume, that the chronicity of the beginnings in all 6 of these cases, the insufficiency of therapeutic intervention, and the stress of social hardships in case they were to be released from the hospital, were the principal causes for their lengthy hospitalization, from their first admission to the end of the observation period, that is, more than 20 years.

The 3 cases that began acutely, under circumstances that suggested a schizophrenic reaction in the beginning, are of exceptional interest. In these 3 cases the unfavorable course followed a favorable prognosis after initial hospitalization. Their patient histories deserve our attention:

Heinrich E. (Proband 39) became ill under the typical syndrome of a prison psychosis, which began acutely in 1923, at age 23. He had been arrested for theft, along with two brothers-in-law. He exhibited a silliness-syndrome, but E. Bleuler, who had determined upon his legal commitment at the time, found that the simulated silliness-syndrome was a manifestiation upon the background of a schizophrenia with its primary initial symptoms. The patient never recovered. His acute condition quickly progressed to a most severe, chronic schizophrenic state that has remained for the past 40 years. Since that time, any form of conversation with him is impossible. He mumbles something unintelligible or confusing to himself, and insofar as his words can be understood, he is talking incoherently about the Japanese and the yellow peril, and insists that his wife and child have gone to join the Foreign Legion, and so on. He has massive acoustic and olfactory hallucinations, and is on a ward for the most severely ill.

This proband was already in a hopeless life situation before he became ill. He was the son of an alcoholic who had to be committed. The father mistreated his family when he was drunk, but when sober, he was kind and warm-hearted. Patient's mother had to work as a cleaning woman. The patient completed a business apprenticeship and later worked as a clerk. He was an even-tempered, likable person, but easily influenced by others and completely incapable of independent action or decision. At age 21 he married a totally unstable woman, because he felt sorry for her. She had come from an appalling family environment, and was habitually unfaithful to him. He bought her everything that she demanded until he became absolutely destitute. In this condition he was persuaded by his wife's brothers to accompany them on their thieving expeditions. After his arrest the psychosis emerged. A divorce followed; he never knew what had become of his daughter. If he had recovered and been released, he would have stood alone in the world, lonesome, disgraced, and uprooted.

Margrit G. (Proband 43) had an irresponsible alcoholic for a father, whose nature was as happy-go-lucky as that of her mother. In complete contrast to both, the daughter was rather quiet, withdrawn, and phlegmatic. She was helpful and kind toward others, but rather taciturn. She made her living working as a servant in hotels and private families. She was a plain, insignificant looking girl, not at all attractive. For 14 years, from age 18 to 32, she was seriously in love with a young man who worked out of town for the most part, and whom she sometimes did not see for years at a time. When he had been away for a long time, she would travel long distances to visit him, but he had lost interest in her. At age 32 the psychosis emerged subacutely. She became despondent and began to neglect herself. When she entered the clinic, she had already torn out most of her hair, and kept lamenting the loss of her sweetheart. Very quickly she became completely uncommunicative, then began scolding wildly and aggressively. Between such onsets she was mutistic for extended periods of time. Usually she could be motivated to do simple chores. She referred to herself as a dog. Her disappointment in the love affair at the beginning of her illness was probably related to the fact that she was almost constantly in an erotic state and masturbated frequently, often wanted to undress, and kept raising her skirts. The most severe catatonic state endured beyond the end of the observation period, 21 years after its beginnings. It looks in this case as if the collapse of her hopes for a love relationship, that had become her only aim in life, was related to the unhappy course of her illness.

Germaine K. (Proband 56) differed from Heinrich E. and Margrit G. in that her condition did not after her first acute onset deteriorate to a most severe chronic state. In the beginning she suffered a mild schizophrenic episode from which she recovered without hospitalization, and later several mild depressive episodes that did not require hospitalization either. At age 54, she became subacutely severely ill, was hospitalized, and remained hospitalized as a severely ill patient for the next 13 years, until she died. While the courses of the last two patients referred to were type-categorized as "acute to severe chronic 'end states'" the illness of Germaine K. belongs to the typology of an "undulating course to severe chronic 'end state.'" Germaine's father lived from 1850 to 1893. He came from the Alsace region, where he had lost a handsome agricultural estate as the result of a mortgage litigation. He had come to the Zürich suburbs to make his living, working as a lamplighter and operating a small farm. He married a girl from Zürich, who came from a family of doughty, respected citizens in good social standing. After the early death of her father, when Germaine was 7 years old, her mother had been left in dire financial straits with the 5 children. The mother, however, managed to sustain the family by

providing the barest necessities through an immense personal effort and industrious self-application. Germaine's family felt itself ostracised from the social status to which it had been accustomed. Even when both parents were living, they felt socially uprooted in their financially difficult circumstances, and continually strove—with little success—to keep up a position commensurate with the standards of their family origins. The same attitude—but augmented to extremes—was assumed by Germaine. She was a proud and beautiful girl with a regal bearing, who looked for the "higher things" in life. People used to say that she liked "playing the queen." She completed enough education to become a teacher, but that position did not suffice for her. She believed in higher callings, and attempted to train herself as a therapist. Primarily, she pursued an artistic bent in a style that was deemed rather extravagant at the time. At about the turn of the century she was beginning to attempt abstract painting. She wanted to marry an intellectual, was unable to find any promising love relationship, and finally entered into an affair with a married clergyman. Between 1912 and 1931 she was married to a teacher. She strove incessantly to make an academician of her husband. During her only pregnancy at age 27, she endured a mild schizophrenic episode, remaining at home. She spoiled both her husband and her son. As a whole, the marriage was a good one, although she tyrannized her husband, and occasionally kept up the relationship with the clergyman. After her husband's sudden death (pulmonary embolism, 1931), she found it difficult to adjust to the life of a widow, although from time to time she did some teaching. Serious quarrels developed between her and her only son, who had become a musician, but who was an eccentric and a neurasthenic. She made attempts at being a philanthopist by making extravagent gifts to her mother-in-law, but at the same time damaged that relationship by her authoriatarian attitude toward her. After another unsuccessful relationship with a man, she picked up her old affair with the clergyman, whose wife had since died, expecting that he would marry her. In the end, however, he informed her that she would never become a proper homemaker, and married someone else in 1940. At this point Germaine found herself in a hopeless situation. Her dreams of accomplishing something extraordinary in the field of art or of education were effectively shattered. Her husband was dead, her raltionships to her son and other relatives had been spoiled by her bickering, and her siblings had accomplished as little in life as she had. Her love affair that had been nurtured over decades—and that contained the fond hope of finally raising her "status" in life—lay in ruins, just after she might finally have expected its fulfillment. She was confronting a sad and lonesome old age. In this condition she retreated to an attic room, quickly developed delusions of persecution, and began completely to neglect herself. At age 55, in 1941, she was hospitalized at our clinic and became a proband of this study. However, she had to be transferred to another psychiatric clinic. For the following 11 years, until she died in 1953 of a coronary infarct, she remained hospitalized as a most severe schizophrenic, requiring maximum care. Confused excitations alternated with stuporous states of long duration. One got the impression that Germaine's first schizophrenic onset was related to her becoming a mother under conditions that did not meet her high standards. At the time, however, she still had possibilities of realizing some of the goals she had set for herself. After that first onset, she recovered quickly. But she became permanently and severely ill, without the prospects of returning to a normal way of life, when all her fondest hopes were finally and irreparably shattered.

Of the 13 cases that remained constantly hospitalized from their first admission to the conclusion of the observation period or until they died, we have discussed 11. Two died prematurely in acute states, 9 had come to our clinic as chronic schizophrenics and became probands of this research project. Two cases remain, whose psychoses had lasted for 3 and 5 years, respectively, before they were referred to our clinic, and neither one was ever released again up to the end of the observation period. It is worthwhile to sketch briefly these 2 patient histories also, in order to hazard at least an estimate as to what might have precluded their recoveries.

Regine I. (Proband 24), born 1908, came to us from Germany. Her father, a common laborer, at times indulged in alcoholism, whereas her mother was a hard-working housewife. At age 17, the proband was sent to Switzerland because chances for employment were better there, where she continued working as a servant until she married. From childhood on she was quiet and retiring and

found it difficult to establish contact with others. She entered into a close relationship with her future husband, that lasted for 6 years before she married him, in 1933. There were no children because of a tubercular epididymis in the husband. Regine herself proved to be a good housewife. She was dependent wholly on her husband, who was stingy, and treated her as a nonentity. From the outset of the marriage she ran into problems in her neighborhood, being a German national married to a Swiss citizen. At the time considerable antipathy prevailed in Switzerland against the National Socialist regime in Germany. German women married to Swiss nationals in Switzerland were regarded with considerable mistrust and contempt, and were subjected to all sorts of verbal abuse in their contacts with the general public. Every contact with her parents and siblings had been broken off. As a result, Regine was lonely not only because of her own taciturn nature, but also because of unhappy external circumstances. Her psychosis developed slowly, beginning in 1937, at the same time that her husband's tuberculosis became aggravated. Delusions of persecution and of manipulation by others emerged, shortly after which she had to be hospitalized. In her absurd and manifold delusional existence, Hitler played a primary part. She lived in erotic and political relationship with him, feeling that she was elevated to higher spheres by the experience. Accordingly, she ranted and scolded in vulgar and hatred-laden terms against Switzerland and her specific lot in it, and in that context, patently resisted any therapeutic attempts on her behalf. During those times it often happened that Germans living in Switzerland began to develop sympathies for the National Socialist movement because of the pressures of mistrust that prevailed against the Germans. Since that time—for 21 years—Regine has remained a seriously ill paranoid. She has confusing ideas of coming from a family of German nobility, of persecutions, and of sexual influences. She has become so estranged from her family that her siblings, living in Germany, did not even bother to inform her of the death of her parents. She has no family in Switzerland. She is under care at a clinic, without any active therapy being attempted. At the beginning of her psychosis, the patient had lost her parents, a husband, social position, her home, and her security, without any hope of recovering any of them. In her madness, it seemed as if she was clinging to Hitler, in order to enjoy some form of revenge for the gross injustices of fate she had suffered in Switzerland, and in order to find in him a sublimated symbol in substitution for her lost home, her lost stability, her lost husband, and her lost parents.

The psychosis of Klara A. (Proband 91) developed under particularly ominous environmental conditions. She had come from Austria. Her father was a simple quarry laborer, addicted to alcohol. Her mother was intelligent and industrious, but was not accepted by her husband's family because of her own illegitimacy. Klara, born in 1899, was forced to earn her living as a factory worker at an early age. As a worker she was always considered to be difficult, obstinate, and irregular in her productive efforts. In 1922 she was summoned to her married sister's in Switzerland to help care for her sister's child, suffering from osteomyelitis. An intimate relationship evolved between her and her brother-in-law. In 1928 Klara gave illegitimate birth to a child, presumably sired by the brother-in-law. Two years later she got married, although she did not live quite a year with her husband. The couple quarreled and beat each other, and during the divorce proceedings Klara was forced to admit to the relationship between herself and her brother-in-law. After the divorce became final, her general living conditions became even more disastrous. She began living together with her sister and brother-in-law in a triangular relationship, where she was supposed to help raise her own child and her sister's children. Her son turned out to be debilitated and epileptic. Her sister is also debilitated and "peculiar in the same way that Klara is herself." In addition, her difficult position in the community as a foreigner in Switzerland (described above in the history of Regine I., particularly during the period before the war), aggravated the pressure of circumstances. In this condition she suffered through her first brief psychotic episode at home in 1939, when she was 40. The psychosis was characterized as a hallucinatory phase with visions of devils and religious delusions. She quieted down after that, and was able to work as a newspaper vendor.

But now she was even more eccentric than before. Three years later, in 1942, her condition deteriorated, in that her brother-in-law had to return to Germany and her son had

to be hospitalized with a long-term prognosis. At this point a severe psychosis erupted acutely, from which she has not recovered in 21 years, that is, to the end of the observation period. She is in a moderately severe chronic state, in which a confused persecution mania, demons, rapes, and the murder of her son became manifest in kaleidoscopic confusion. Emotionally she is still able to communicate. There are times in which she can be motivated to do work at the clinic, but it is interrupted by wild vituperative attacks. Her relatives did not show any concern for her. She is under care at a clinic out of town that has limited facilities for active therapy. This proband is another for whom it is difficult to imagine how she would make her way in life if she were released, even if she had recovered. Her internal and her external existences were so intertwined with self-perpetrated misfortune, that she really would not be able to find her way out of the dilemma.

On the basis of these patient histories one might easily assume some reasons why these 13 probands could not be released after their first hospitalization up to the time they died or to the end of the observation period (over 22 and up to 44 years later). Two patients died prematurely during acute episodes, and several reasons in combination applied to the other 11:

(1) In all of them schizophrenia had become manifest at least 2 years before they were hospitalized for the first time, and in 9 of the 11 it was more than 5 years before. During this period before the initial hospitalization they had not received any treatment.

(2) Seven of the 11 patients had become involved in really serious life tragedies at the time of initial onset of their psychosis, from which a disentanglement was not only objectively extremely difficult, but subjectively apparently impossible. In the 4 remaining cases the general conditions of life were also poor at the time their psychosis began, although not to the same degree of hopelessness as in the other 7.

(3) None of these probands had had any active, long-term therapy after being hospitalized.

(4) Ten of the 11 probands were either completely (7 cases) or largely (3 cases) abandoned by their families while they were hospitalized. None of them, had they been released, would have been able to find tolerable conditions on the outside in respect to family, employment, society, and welfare support. In no case did a family member show

any real, serious concern for the hospitalized patient.

Many have assumed that relationships between stressful circumstances in life and the eruption of a schizophrenia would be favorable to the prognosis. To be sure, in the existing literature numerous cases of a great many contradictory experiences have been documented. Among the 13 probands who could not be released after their initial hospitalization, there is a concentration of cases in which the beginning of the disease was accompanied by the most unbearable, crushing, and 'exhausting of such conditions. These were circumstances in which every shimmer of hope for life outside the clinic appeared to be effectively extinguished. Based on this experience (as well as a number of others), the statement that psychotraumatic living conditions at the beginning of a schizophrenia are indications of a favorable future will no longer be justified. The following assumption will more nearly correspond to the facts: If a schizophrenia erupts in a person who is mired down in excessively difficult, insoluble misfortune, that is an indication for a poor course of his psychosis; and if his situation at the beginning of his psychosis is tortuous, but a hope exists for tolerable circumstances in the future, then, such a situation, which might have been called a "concomitant psychogenic cause," would be a good omen for the future.

One might have presumed that those probands who were not released after their initial hospitalization would have had a particularly unfavorable prognosis from the very beginning; that is, that they were probands with a chronic beginning and with severely pathological prepsychotic personalities. These two important criteria for an unfavorable prognosis, however, applied to only a portion of these 11 probands, and they hardly occurred with any significant frequency, judging by the findings among all 208 principal probands (chronic beginnings in 7, and acute beginnings in 4 cases; nonaberrant prepsychotic personalities in 2, schizoid within the norm in 5, other than schizoid aberrations within the norm in none, schizoid psychopathy in 1, and other psychopathies in 3 cases). Also the distribution between normal, doubtful, and horrible childhood conditions corresponds in these 11 probands approximately to that of all probands (3:4:4). The figures are too small to assume statistical significance. In spite of that, we can state that neither chronic beginnings, nor unfavorable prepsychotic person-

alities, nor exceptionally unhappy childhoods are in themselves indications that they might have played a causal role in the wretched long-term hospitalizations of these probands.

On the other hand, the findings in these 11 probands do suggest that external influences at the time of onset and immediately thereafter were decisive factors in the continuous hospitalization for over 20 years after the first hospitalization, for 11 of the total of 208 probands. At the onset of illness they were involved in personal problems and so entangled in tragic life situations that any escape from them seemed impossible; they were confronted with the impossibility of entering into any feasible family, employment, or care arrangement upon their release, if such release had been forthcoming; and they lacked any intensive[11], long-term, active therapeutic treatment.

The thought that these 11 probands did not get any better care than they did can be most depressing; although the indication derived from this sad experience may, after all, bear some hope for the future. It might be assumed that long-term hospitalization after an initial admission can be avoided, if an intensive[11], long-term, active treatment program (see n. 11) is instigated, and if families, relatives, and care-service organizations become actively, devotedly, and selflessly involved in adequately preparing the patient's road back into society.

We should therefore insist on long-term active therapy and on active preparatory measures for returning the released patient to society. Neither of these demands is new, but in the course of the last few decades they have often been considered as trifles or entirely forgotten. In the 30's of this century, after the introduction of insulin and electroshock therapy, the impression was prevalent that such therapy was effective only in the initial or very early stages of the disease, while later applications of it were scarcely of any use. The fact that many apparent successes of early treatment were merely illusory successes had not yet been fully understood, since most of such successes of early treatment occurred in patients whose schizophrenia would have run a favorable course even without the intervention of a physical cure. According to modern experience, a constant, or a frequently re-

11. An explanation of what I mean by intensive, long-term treatment appears in Chapter 7, under Conclusions for Routine Medical Practice.

peated therapeutic program in cases of schizophrenias is just as important as early treatment. This feature, more than any other, is what was lacking in those unfortunate cases cited above, while the acute cases among them were treated actively, although without success. These questions will, however, be discussed in greater detail in the section on treatment methods. That a positive effort to release schizophrenic patients as early as possible and to organize a care program with the patient's family, are beneficial, are ideas that E. Bleuler had frequently stressed as early as 1905 and 1914. In recent years the demand for early release and for active preparations for the released patient's social needs have been recognized and met on an international level, and particularly so in the Anglo-Saxon countries. A number of English authors have also described experiences attesting to how schizophrenias threaten to become chronic, if the families do not make an effort to reintegrate their patients into their midst (Harris et al. 1956, and others).

If adequate treatment and aftercare appear to be salient causes for early release of first-time-hospitalization schizophrenics, and would increase their chance of avoiding permanent hospitalization, it must not be assumed that this conclusion can be expanded to include recovery or nonrecovery as such. The avoidance of permanent hospitalization of itself cannot be equated with recovery. Convincing proof is lacking that those measures that might be effective in preventing permanent hospitalization would convert all incurable schizophrenias into curable ones. On the contrary, the described findings suggest the unpleasant likelihood that we are almost incapable of producing recoveries in chronic schizophrenias that develop progressively chronic; we are able merely to alleviate their severity and to achieve some improvements.

Nevertheless, some rather weighty clues already emerged years ago, that those "catastrophe-schizophrenias" with acute development that progress to severe chronic states without remission, are artefacts that could be avoided. Among all 208 probands I found 3 such catastrophe-schizophrenias (Table 4.7). These 3 catastrophe-schizophrenias are included in the 11 cases described above; they were never released after their first hospitalization. The great hope is justified that permanent hospitalization after a first admission and catastrophe-schizophrenias will not occur any

more in the future, if two conditions are met: 1) that we give our schizophrenics careful and long-term treatment and 2) that we keep open the road back from the hospital into a society, or that we reopen it, if we find it blocked.

There is one objection to this line of thought. From investigations done in England, we find, in spite of a much better developed aftercare program, that just about as many first-time admissions for schizophrenia as in this study remain continuously hospitalized during the observation period. To be sure, the observation period in all these studies from England is much less than 20 years. In the study by Brown et al. (1966), 7 percent of the 111 first-time admissions remained hospitalized without interruption during the 5-year observation period, as compared to 9 percent among our own probands. It is probable that not all patients from the English studies who remained hospitalized for 5 years after their initial admission would have remained hospitalized more than 20 years. It is also probable that the better quality of aftercare in England was after all decisive in keeping down the number of schizophrenics who remained hospitalized without interruption. But be that as it may, the study of the patient histories of our probands who remained hospitalized without interruption after their initial admission does show the discouraging fact, with unmistakable, unequivocal clarity, that more should have been done for these patients! They had need for more intensive care, and a much greater effort should have been made to attempt their resocialization.

Sixty-eight patients were hospitalized for the first time when they became probands at our clinic in 1942 and 1943. Table 4.11 shows that almost $\frac{1}{3}$ of the probands hospitalized for the first time at our clinic never had to be rehospitalized after their first release before they died or up to the end of the observation period, that is, 22 years later. It is doubtful that any statistics would be available that could be used for comparison. The catamnestic studies done up to this time all covered less than 20 years, although there are many statistics with shorter catamneses. For example, let me mention again those done by Brown et al. (1966). Among 111 schizophrenics admitted for the first time in 1956 to three hospitals in England and released, 72 percent were not rehospitalized within 5 years. But it should be remembered that there are many recidivists requiring hospitalization more than 5 years after their first release. They are particularly frequent when many patients are still visibly ill at the time of their release, a fact that applies to the statistics from England. These statistics do not include alcoholic or feebleminded schizophrenics, while mine do. Such a selective bias is bound to have improved the English results. Along the same lines, it was favorable that there were no private hospitals in the jurisdictional area of the English clinics, which prefer to accept patients with good prognoses, while there are a number of such private hospitals in the jurisdictional area of Burghölzli. In addition, the English investigators emphasized that there were no settlements in the jurisdictional area of their hospitals in which "patients with particularly difficult problems were concentrated." No such settlements are excluded from the jurisdictional area of Burghölzli. If these and some further differences between the two sets of studies are taken into account, the difference between 31 percent and 72 percent can be explained. It is not a serious indication that the better, more individually goal-oriented aftercare in England might have prevented the need for rehospitalization; and it goes without saying that many other reasons speak for an aftercare program that is thoroughly planned and organized.

Table 4.12 shows how many of the 208 probands were rehospitalized in some psychiatric hospital 2, 5, 10, and 20 years after their first hospitalization, or not at all. The table distinguishes between all 208 probands and those among them who became probands along with their first hospitalization (68), it also distinguishes between the sexes. It is very probably the first time that anyone succeeded in compiling that kind of data without any important selective bias.

The remarkable feature of Table 4.12 is less the absolute percentages, than the comparison of the percentages of hospitalized patients 2, 5, 10, and 20 years after their first hospitalization. In the course of years, the percentage of hospitalized patients does not increase. Insofar as this percentage varies over the years, it does so within the limits that could be expected to occur by chance.

According to concepts that prevailed to the middle of this century, a schizophrenia was regarded as a "process-psychosis" that basically proceeded to a state of idiocy, even though the rate of that process may have varied. The data of Table 4.12 are in the sharpest contrast to this concept. Even 20 years after first hospitalization, there are no more schizophrenics still or again in need of hospitalization than 2 years thereafter. In validating this fact it ought also to be mentioned that only a small minority of probands from each of the key periods (2, 5, 10, and 20 years after initial hospitalization) were still among those hospitalized. Many hospitalized probands are "pendular" patients, who may be among those released in one of the key periods and among those hospitalized in another such period.

The resultant figures on hospitalizations in the four key periods after initial hospitalization correspond—and must correspond—to the findings on "end states" and on disease courses earlier in this chapter. There it was set forth that the earlier expectation was in error when it assumed that schizophrenic psychoses would usually or "characteristically" intensify in severity with the passing of time. It goes without saying that "end states" and "course types" as we described them, are much more precise criteria for the course of the psychosis than "hospitalized" or "not hospitalized." To be sure, the criteria are more dependent on subjective judgment than is the criterion of hospitalization. This was another reason why I welcomed the opportunity to check the results of the various course studies against the more objective criterion of hospitalization data.

Table 4.12 does not reveal any statistically significant differences in the need for hospitalization as between men and women; nor are there such differences between all principal probands and the initial hospitalizations of 1942/43. One might at first suspect that the percentage of later rehospitalizations after first admissions would have to be less than it would be after subsequent multiple admissions, since first-time admissions include also patients who remain recovered after a single schizophrenic episode. But in multiple-admission cases the reverse is true, because the multiple admission cases include the "pendular" cases, and these spend long periods of time outside hospitals.

If we now evaluate the number of cases from Table 4.12 and consider the absolute confidence interval, we find that 2, 5, 10, and 20 years after their first hospitalization for schizophrenia, a good one third of the living probands were still hospitalized, while two thirds live outside of hospitals. Within the range of variance between a scant third and a scant half, the number of hospitalized patients could easily have been determined by happenstance.

Table 4.12. Hospitalized and nonhospitalized probands compared 2, 5, 10, and 20 years after first hospitalization, listed separately by sex. In the first spaces all 208 probands are considered; in the last three, only those who became probands at their first hospitalization. Percentages are calculated according to the number surviving at the given point in time

Abbreviations: h = hospitalized; P = proband; m = male; f = female; I = subjects initially hospitalized when they became probands

	2 years after first hospitalization		5 years after first hospitalization		10 years after first hospitalization		20 years after first hospitalization	
	h	not h	h	not h	h	not h	h	not h
All m Ps	28 = 29 %	70 = 71 %	37 = 39 %	59 = 61 %	32 = 35 %	59 = 65 %	34 = 44 % (32–55 %)	44 = 56 % (45–68 %)
All f Ps	41 = 39 %	64 = 61 %	44 = 43 %	58 = 57 %	45 = 47 %	51 = 53 %	28 = 35 % (24–46 %)	53 = 65 % (54–76 %)
m and f Ps	69 = 34 %	134 = 66 %	81 = 41 %	117 = 59 %	77 = 41 %	110 = 59 %	62 = 39 % (31–47 %)	97 = 61 % (53–68 %)[1]
Total living Ps	203		198		187		159	
Total deceased Ps	5		10		21		49	
Grand total:	208		208		208		208	
All m I	8 = 26 %	23 = 74 %	6 = 21 %	23 = 79 %	5 = 18 %	23 = 82 %	6 = 22 % (9–42 %)	21 = 78 % (58–91 %)
All f I	14 = 42 %	19 = 58 %	16 = 48 %	17 = 52 %	14 = 45 %	17 = 55 %	6 = 26 % (10–48 %)	17 = 74 % (52–90 %)
m and f I	22 = 34 %	42 = 66 %	22 = 35 %	40 = 65 %	19 = 32 %	40 = 68 %	12 = 24 % (13–38 %)	38 = 76 % (62–87 %)
Total living I	64		62		59		50	
Total deceased I	4		6		9		18	
Grand total:	68		68		68		68	

Figures in parentheses apply to confidence interval[1] at 95%, according to *Documenta Geigy*; they are applied only for the most important figures to avoid cluttering the tables. (Decimals are omitted; the last digit before the decimal is rounded off to the closest figure in the Geigy table, so it may be very slightly inaccurate.)

1. To avoid unnecessary conversions confidence intervals were taken from the tables at $N = 160$.

But with the high probability of 1:19, we are justified in assuming the number of hospitalized patients after all these years is significantly less than half. Among the initial hospitalizations of our probands, the confidence interval of the percentage of hospitalized patients after 10 and 20 years even drops to 20 percent and 13 percent.[12]

Table 4.13 compares the number of hospitzlized probands with that of nonhospitalized probands 2, 5, 10, and 20 years after their admissions to Burghölzli in 1942 or 1943. The figures in this table are of lesser interest than those of Table 4.12. The initial hospitalization has a direct relationship to the actual occurrence of the disease; on the other hand, the point in time at which a schizophrenic patient was rehospitalized at Burghölzli is, by and large, dependent on circumstances that are only indirectly related to the occurrence of the disease. Among these, for example, is whether the family have moved to the Canton of Zürich from another canton, or on how the various welfare agencies of the different cantons with legal jurisdiction agree as to the cost of taking on a patient whose residence and home of record are not the same. Table 4.13 thus does not reveal anything about how many schizophrenics are hospitalized at a certain point in time after their initial hospitalization, but only about how many are hospitalized after that particular point in time at which they happened to have been admitted specifically to Burghölzli. Still, Table 4.13 does supplement the information

12. In America, years ago, the proportion between hospitalized schizophrenics and (recovered or non-recovered) schizophrenics who lived outside hospitals after a period of hospitalization, was incorrectly estimated. It was assumed that it was 1:1. Deming attempted to get a more accurate answer by careful, laborious calculations based on initial admissions in New York hospitals in 1960. In so doing, he could not work with precise figures exclusively, but was compelled to use some less reliable assumptions. He arrived at the conclusion that for one hospitalized schizophrenic three (recovered or unrecovered) schizophrenics who had at some time been hospitalized were living outside psychiatric hospitals. According to his calculations the percentage of patients still hospitalized (of all patients hospitalized for schizophrenia at least once) amounted to 24 percent in the State of New York in 1960. It corresponds precisely to the percentage of my probands still living at the end of the observation period, who were still—or again—hospitalized 20 years after their first hospitalization (Table 4.12).

of Table 4.12 that is interesting in one respect. It contains data on most of its probands at a much later point in time than Table 4.12 does, and a great deal of time had passed for many probands between the initial hospitalization and the 1942/43 admissions that made them probands. While Table 4.12 stops at fixing the number of hospitalized patients 20 years after their initial hospitalization, Table 4.13 also indicates whether the number of hospitalized patients increases or decreases in more than 20 years after initial hospitalization.

This indication is clear and unequivocal, namely, that the number of hospitalized probands surviving after more than 20 years beyond their first hospitalization does not increase. Further, after a duration of the schizophrenia of over 20 years (and sometimes considerably longer—even up to 30 years more) since the first hospitalization, only a good third of all surviving probands are still hospitalized (confidence interval is a scant third to a scant half). The corresponding number of patients who became probands upon initial admission amounts to just a quarter (confidence intervals from one eighth to one third).

It is further noteworthy that among the 55 probands still hospitalized after more than 20 years since their admission after 1942/43, there are still some for whom their hospitalization was not at all or only partly related to their actual schizophrenic condition. In that context, for 6 of the hospitalized probands schizophrenia was in evidence in a very mild form or not at all. At the end of the observation period these 6 patients were over 65 years old. For them their hospitalization was a nursing-home service for the aged, and not a hospitalization for psychiatric care. Eight other, younger patients had remained hospitalized with a mild "end state," for which they might have received care outside a psychiatric hospital. Two patients were "pendular" cases, who happened to be temporarily hospitalized on the key date. According to this, only 39 of the 55 hospitalized patients were obviously in need of hospitalization because of their schizophrenic psychoses (in a severe or moderately severe chronic state) 20 years after 1942/43. If one should wonder how many schizophrenics still require hospitalization for schizophrenia after more than 20 years after their first hospitalization, the percentage would then amount to less than that of the patients actually hospitalized, as appears above. To be sure, this conclusion results from

Table 4.13. Hospitalized and nonhospitalized probands compared 2, 5, 10, and 20 years after becoming principal probands in this project on admission to Burghölzli in 1942/43, listed separately by sex. In the first space all 208 probands are covered; in the last three, only those who became probands along with their initial hospitalization. Percentages are calculated according to the surviving patients at the specified point in time

Abbreviations: h = hospitalized; P = probands; m = male; f = female; I = patients who became probands at time of initial hospitalization

Point in time after Ss became probands since 1942/43 on initial admission to Burghölzli

	2 years		5 years		10 years		20 years	
	h	not h	h	not h	h	not h	h	not h
All m Ps	36 = 38 %	59 = 62 %	41 = 45 %	50 = 55 %	37 = 44 %	47 = 56 %	26 = 38 % (26–50 %)	43 = 62 % (50–74 %)
All f Ps	46 = 46 %	55 = 54 %	48 = 48 %	51 = 52 %	45 = 49 %	46 = 51 %	29 = 39 % (28–51 %)	45 = 61 % (49–72 %)
m and f Ps	82 = 42 %	114 = 58 %	89 = 47 %	101 = 53 %	82 = 47 %	93 = 53 %	55 = 38 % (31–48 %)	88 = 62 % (54–71 %)[1]
Total living Ps	196		190		175		143	
Deceased Ps	12		18		33		65	
Total:	208		208		208		208	
All m Is	8 = 26 %	23 = 74 %	6 = 21 %	23 = 79 %	5 = 18 %	23 = 82 %	6 = 22 % (9–42 %)	21 = 78 % (58–91 %)
All f Is	12 = 36 %	21 = 64 %	14 = 42 %	19 = 58 %	11 = 35 %	20 = 65 %	6 = 26 % (10–48 %)	17 = 74 % (52–90 %)
m and f Is	20 = 31 %	44 = 69 %	20 = 32 %	42 = 68 %	16 = 27 %	43 = 73 %	12 = 24 % (13–38 %)	38 = 76 % (62–87 %)
Total living Is	64		62		59		50	
Deceased Is	4		6		9		18	
Total:	68		68		68		68	

Amounts in parentheses represent confidence intervals at 95% according to *Documenta Geigy*, entered only for the most important figures to keep the table uncluttered. (Decimals are omitted; the last digit before the decimal is rounded off in keeping with the *Geigy* tables; it may therefore be very slightly inaccurate.)

1. Confidence intervals were taken from the tables at *n* = 140 in order to avoid unnecessary recalculations.

the probably valid assumption that there are none among the nonhospitalized who would be in serious need of hospitalization.

Tables 4.12 and 4.13, discussed above, compare the hospitalized and the nonhospitalized patients 2, 5, 10, and 20 years after their first hospitalization (Table 4.12), and the hospitalization that made probands of them (Table 4.13). Table 4.14, on the other hand, begins at the point in time when the proband first became schizophrenic, and shows how many probands are hospitalized and how many are not hospitalized, after lapses of 2, 5, 10, and 20 years beyond their first schizophrenic onset —not beyond their first hospitalization.

It would be easy to assume that the need for hospitalization at certain points in time after the first onset of illness would reveal important information about the "natural" and "true" course of the disease, independent of external influences, rather than such need at certain points in time after the first hospitalization. However, closer inspection of the facts reveals that just those statistics that begin from the first onset of illness are particularly fraught with uncertainties, selection biases, and the effects of other external influences. To begin with, the exact date of the onset of illness cannot be as accurately determined as the date of the initial hospitalization. In cases that develop chronically, it sometimes proved to be arbitrary whether the beginning of the illness was to be recorded as, for instance, September of a given year of February of the following year. But it is important to keep in mind that, as a result of the selection of probands, all probands were hospitalized at least once after the onset of their illness. According to this, the number of hospitalized probands, according to Table 4.14, is bound to increase over the course of many years. The time spans between first onset and first hospitalization do amount to a considerable number of years for many probands. On the other hand, the number of hospitalized probands decreases rather dramatically during the first few years after the first onset, by the number of probands who are then released from the hospital. The bare figures of Table 4.14, therefore, do not show any valid indication as to how many of the nonhospitalized patients had not ever been hospitalized 2, 5, 10, and 20 years after their first onset of illness, nor how many had been released after they had been hospitalized.

The time span between first onset and first hospitalization is distributed as follows among the 208 principal probands:

Time span		No. of probands
Less than 1 year		105
1–10	⎫	86
10–20	⎬ years	13
over 20	⎭	4

The point in time of the first hospitalization, as well as the time of release from the hospital are heavily influenced by conditions that result from sources independent of the psychosis of the proband (fear of the stigma of a "mental institution" on the part of family, bed space available in hospitals, release policies of the hospital's doctors, etc.). One should therefore have no illusions as to what the categorization of hospitalized probands a few years after their first onset of illness is really able to tell us about the natural course of schizophrenias. The statistics on long-term chronic states ("end states") and the types of courses of illness gave us an incomparably clearer insight into the natural tendencies of schizophrenia courses.

Nevertheless, the data on the number of hospitalized probands at various points in time after first onset (Table 4.14) are not entirely without interest. Ten years after first onset, there are only a few probands who had never been hospitalized before, and 20 years thereafter it dwindles down to just a scattered few. The two last columns of Table 4.14, disregarding the few very late hospitalizations, accordingly tell us that, among those probands once hospitalized at Burghölzli for schizophrenia in 1942/43, at most half, and probably less than half are still hospitalized 10 and 20 years after their first onset of illness. From the 5th year after the first onset of illness, the number of hospitalized probands does not increase appreciably any more up to the 20th year. We are again confronted with the same contradiction of facts in the assumption that schizophrenia is for the most part an irreversible, progressive "process-disease," with which we were confronted in the preceding accumulation of data.

One might become interested in the size of the percentages of hospitalized probands not only 20, but 30 and 40 years after the onset of illness. My own calculations in that context are so ambiguous that I shall forego displaying them here. The ambiguity results from the fact that, beginning with the 20th year after first onset, probands begin to die off rapidly. The numbers of survivors beyond 20 years after first onset, accordingly, are so small that they provide no statistical significance. Besides,

Table 4.14. Hospitalized and nonhospitalized probands compared 2, 5, 10, and 20 years after first onset of schizophrenia, listed separately by sex. Percentages are calculated according to the number of probands surviving at the specified point in time

Abbreviations: h = hospitalized; P = probands; m = male; f = female

Point in time after first onset of schizophrenia

	2 years		5 years		10 years		20 years	
	h	*not h*	*h*	*not h*	*h*	*not h*	*h*	*not h*
All m Ps	24 = 24.5 %	74 = 75.5 %	35 = 36 %	62 = 64 %	34 = 37 %	58 = 63 %	40 = 47.5 %	44 = 52.5 %
All f Ps	34 = 32 %	71 = 68 %	38 = 36.5 %	66 = 63.5 %	37 = 37 %	64 = 63 %	34 = 37 %	57 = 63 %
m and f Ps	58 = 28.5 %	145 = 71.5 %	73 = 36 % (29–43 %)	128 = 64 % (57–71 %)	71 = 37 % (30–44 %)	122 = 63 % (56–70 %)	74 = 42 % (36–50 %)	101 = 58 % (51–66 %)
Total living Ps	203		201[1]		193[2]		175[3]	
Deceased Ps	5		7		15		33	
Total:	208		208		208		208	

Amounts in parentheses represent confidence intervals at 95% according to *Documenta Geigy*, entered only for the most important figures to keep the table uncluttered. (Decimals are omitted; the last digit before the decimal is rounded off in keeping with the *Geigy* tables; it may therefore be very slightly inaccurate.)

1. Confidence intervals were taken from the tables at $n = 200$, to avoid unnecessary recalculations.
2. Confidence intervals were taken from the tables at $n = 190$, to avoid un-

3. Confidence intervals were taken from the tables at $n = 170$, to avoid unnecessary recalculations.

necessary recalculations.

interpretation of the figures would be impaired, because the time of death would be causally linked to factors related and unrelated to schizophrenia in such confusion as to render any meaningful evaluation impossible.

Up to this point we have observed the number of hospitalizations in the life histories of the 208 probands; further, we have recorded how many were still hospitalized at a certain point in time after onset of illness, after their first hospitalization, and after their admission to Burghölzli which made them probands of this study. But our patient histories also yield precise information as to the duration of the probands' hospitalization. A sizable string of figures can be compiled on that subject. To begin with, we shall explain several of the figures that make up the following set of data; then we shall point out what it is that is interesting about them.

Among others, the following data were compiled on the 208 probands:

—138 probands survived the entire observation period from 1942/43 through 1964/65
—After they became probands, as a group, they lived through a total of 2984 years and 10 $\frac{1}{2}$ months
—70 probands, dying prematurely, survived only a portion of the entire observation period
—Those probands who died prematurely, lived a total of 745 years and 4 months after they became probands
—All 208 lived a total* of 1836 years and 10 months from the time they became ill until they were made probands (of this number, the 70 who died prematurely lived 808 years and 11$\frac{1}{2}$ months in the same period)
—After their first onset of illness until the end of the observation period, all 208 probands lived a total of 5567 years and 1 month (of this number, the 70 who died prematurely lived 1554 years and 3$\frac{1}{2}$ months over the same period of time)
—On the average, each proband lived 26$\frac{3}{4}$ years between the onset of his schizophrenic illness and the end of the observation period
—After their first onset of illness, but before they became probands, the 208 probands were hospitalized for a total of 324 years
—The 138 probands who survived the entire observation period were hospitalized for a

total of 1196$\frac{1}{2}$ years from the time they became probands to the end of the observation period
—The 70 probands who died prematurely were hospitalized for a total of 446 years and 6$\frac{1}{2}$ months from the time they became probands until they died
—Since their schizophrenias began, all 208 probands were hospitalized for a total of 1967 years and 1 month (594 years and 1$\frac{1}{2}$ months of this time was lived by the 70 who died prematurely)
—The proportional number of years spent in hospitals after the first onset of schizophrenia to the end of the observation period as compared to the total number of years lived in the same period, for all probands: 1967 years to 5567 years, or 35.33 percent
—The proportional number of years spent in hospitals after the first onset of schizophrenia to the end of the observation period as compared to the total number of years lived in the same period, for all probands who survived the entire observation period: 1373 years to 4013 years, or 34.21 percent
—Each one of the probands who survived the entire observation period of 21–22 years was hospitalized on an average of 8$\frac{1}{2}$ years during that period.

One of the first answers that these figures supply is to a question that has not been previously answered, namely: what is the proportion of years of hospitalization compared to all the years a proband has lived, for two or more decades after the first onset of schizophrenia? Or, the same question in reverse: How many years do schizophrenics live outside of clinics several decades after onset of illness? Our 208 probands lived a total of 5567 years and 1 month from the first onset of schizophrenia until they died or until the end of the observation period was reached. Of this time, they were hospitalized for a total of 1967 years and 1 month, and they lived a total of 3600 years outside of clinics. On the average, our schizophrenics spent 35 percent of the first few decades after their schizophrenic onset in hospitals, and 65 percent of that time outside them. If the patients who died during that observation period were eliminated from the calculations, the proportion would not change materially (the proportionate amount of time spent in hospitals drops from 35 percent to 34 percent).

There is another way of expressing the same relationship: From the beginning of their schizophrenias until they died, or until the

*In 4 cases the date of onset could not be precisely determined, and it might be possible that the onset occurred a few years earlier than we assumed in making the calculations.

end of the observation period, the 208 probands lived an average of $26\frac{3}{4}$ years. Of this time, they spent an average of $9\frac{1}{2}$ years in psychiatric hospitals, and $17\frac{1}{4}$ years outside such hospitals (if patients who died prematurely are omitted, the figures change very little). These figures apply to our 208 probands. They cannot without considerable misgivings be superimposed on schizophrenics from other places and at other times, since the conditions existing in our hospitals, that is, the number of beds for psychiatric patients, the type of clinical treatment, the dismissal policies, and the aftercare program, all contributed greatly to supplying those very figures. A great deal less dependent on time, place, and conditions, however, is the finding that even when schizophrenia is evaluated according to the criterion of hospitalization time, it is not a process-psychosis that in the majority of cases would increase in severity toward the end of life.

Long-Term Courses of Illness Evaluated by Social Status at End of Observation Period

Up to this point, the long-term courses of illness have been evaluated in 10-year periods, according to the psychopathological syndromes of reasonably constant chronic conditions, at the end of the observation period ("end states"), according to the type of disease, and finally according to periods of hospitalization. The remaining aspect to be recorded is the social status of the patient after a long-term illness (Table 4.15). The following points are to be considered:
—Capability of earning a living outside a clinic, as opposed to the inability to do so
—Independence of the patient, as opposed to his need for nursing care after release. Not only were those released schizophrenics listed in the category of "cared-for" schizophrenics who were in constant need of medical attention, the assistance of a guardian, or a social worker, but also those whose families performed regularly scheduled care services
—Residence either alone or with members of the family or relatives as compared to living in nursing homes, and as compared to living in a psychiatric hospital
—Probands staying in psychiatric hospitals were listed as to whether they were assigned to wards for the mildly, the moderately, or the severely ill. Among the conditions in probands determining their ward assignment in hospitals, for the mildly ill one qualification

was almost always that they still should be able to perform useful work, and that they require a minimum of supervision or help in performing it. Patients on wards for the severely ill work in a framework of work-therapy only, in which the economic value of what they do is close to zero, compared to the costs and the effort invested in their care and therapy. Patients on wards for cases of moderate severity fall between these two categories in respect to work achievement.

The key time-period for making this determination was the last 5 years before the probands died or before the end of the observation period. Those patients who did not die during the observation period had all been ill for more than 22 years at the end of the 5-year period in question, and a considerable number of them for much longer.

The social status that was reported for evaluation was the one that had been maintained by the proband during this 5-year key period. If, for instance, a proband on a ward for mild cases had been on probational release once or twice during this 5-year period, despite this, he still came under the category of "patients hospitalized in a psychiatric clinic, ward for mildly ill." On the other hand, if a patient had been employed gainfully during most of that 5-year period, and was not in need of supportive care, although he had visited a psychiatric polyclinic on several occasions because he was low in spirits or could not sleep, he was categorized as being capable of earning a living outside the clinic. The social status of the majority of the probands during this key 5-year period was remarkably steady, so much so in fact, that the assignment to categories could be undertaken without misgivings, and subjective judgment played much less a part than I had at first feared it might. Those few probands whose social status varied a great deal during the key period, making it difficult to fit them into the established pattern, are appropriately noted.

Evaluating the condition of patients as to their social status is something quite different from evaluating their "end states." The "end state" was evaluated primarily according to the psychopathological findings which are not directly considered in evaluating the social status. Of course, they do play a major role indirectly, since they determine the social position of the proband. For example, a proband who lives independently, is actively employed, and does not require care, but who hallucinates and has delusional thoughts, is categorized in one set of statistics as "employable outside clinics, not dependent on care facilities," while in another set he is categorized as being in a "moderately severe chronic state." A proband who has made his home in a psychiatric clinic and is not interested in leaving it, even though nothing in the examination indicated any schizophrenic symptoms, will be carried in one set of statistics as "hospitalized, on a ward for mildly ill," and in the other as "recovered."

Comparing the number of hospitalized probands in the data from this section with that from data from the preceding one (Tables 4.15 and 4.13), a discrepancy occurs, because Table 4.13 depicts hospitalization covering 20 years after admission in 1942/43, while Table 4.15 shows hospitalizations to the end of the observation period, that is, 2–3 years later. Besides, probands who had died in the interim are not considered in Table 4.13, but they are considered in Table 4.15.

To render the data in Table 4.15 more easily readable, the confidence intervals of percentage figures are omitted. With the small number of probands in the individual columns these percentage figures are quite far apart. In the following discussion of Table 4.15, I shall also mention these confidence intervals with the given percentages.

At the end of the observation period, that is, more than 22–23 years (and often much longer) after onset of illness, or when the proband had died, 31 percent of all probands and 40 percent of the probands first hospitalized in 1942/43 were employable and did not require care, living outside a clinic (confidence intervals at 95 percent for the 31 percent are 26 percent–40 percent, and for the 40 percent, 28 percent–52 percent). According to this, after many years since the onset of their schizophrenias, between one fourth and a good one third of schizophrenics are employable, living outside clinics, and not in need of care. For obvious reasons the proportionate figure is greater for the initial hospitalization cases than it is for all probands; however, the difference is not even statistically significant.

The figures correspond to those of the hospitalized probands 20 years after their initial hospitalization of 1942/43 (Table 4.13). They are greater (and almost significant) than the number of recoveries in Table 4.4. and the number of the "undulating course types progressing to recovery" in Table 4.8. In addition to other reasons for this difference, a primary one is the fact that there are quite a few among

the probands who are living at home, not requiring care, and fully employable, who are not recovered; for example, paranoids who still harbor full-blown delusional ideas.

At the end of the observation period or at death, 21 percent of all probands and 13 percent of the initial hospitalization cases are inpatients on wards for the severely ill (confidence interval at 95 percent for the 21 percent: 16 percent–28 percent[13], and the 13 percent: 6 percent–23 percent. Accordingly, after many years since their onset of schizophrenia, scarcely a quarter of all probands and between one twentieth and a scant quarter of the probands initially hospitalized in 1942/43 are on wards for severely ill patients.

Therefore, 22–30 and more years after onset of illness, the number of schizophrenics living outside hospitals, employable, and not requiring care, is greater than the number of schizophrenics who are inpatients on wards for the severely ill. (The difference for all probands is on the border of statistical significance, and that for the initial hospitalization cases is significant.) What an unexpected result this is for the older psychiatrists who, along with Kraepelin, saw in schizophrenia a process-disease that runs a course of constant deterioration over the years, until it reaches dementia!

Probands who were hospitalized when they died or when the observation period ended are distributed approximately on a ratio of $1:1:2$ on wards for the mild, the moderate, and the severe cases. The proportion corresponds to the actual distribution of chronic schizophrenics on these wards, respectively.

The terms applied to wards for mild, moderately severe, and severe cases, are accurately defined in contracts between the local government of Zürich and the clinics, for Burghölzli as well as for most of the clinics into which chronic patients from Burghölzli were to be transferred. Wards for severe cases might be described summarily approximately as follows: They are closed wards; patients in them are under constant care of two nurses or wardmen in dayrooms; patients are kept busy, but produce little useful work. Wards for mild cases are generally open wards, the patients in them are not under constant supervision, and in general they produce useful work. Wards for moderately severe cases

13. For the sake of convenience $N = 200$ was applied instead of the more accurate $N = 208$. The difference is totally insignificant.

fall between these two.

Comparisons with statistics developed by other authors would be most desirable, but no statistics exist that would really lend themselves to such comparisons. Whatever other statistics I might want to use, there are always possibilities for explaining the resultant differences, so that it is as useless to draw conclusions from them as it would be from a single equation with several unknowns.

Among several possibilities, a comparison might be attempted with the catamnestic investigations by Harris et al. (1956). They studied the catamneses of 123 schizophrenics initially hospitalized in England 5 years after their release following insulin treatments, in the years 1945–1950. The hospitalization of their probands in England occurred just a few years after that of my probands. In contrast, however, their catamneses were completed after 5 years, while mine ended 22–23 years after initial hospitalization. Despite that, an amazing similarity in the social status of probands came to light between the English probands and mine at the conclusion of the catamneses:

	123 English Ps by Harris et al.	68 Initial hospitalizations among my own probands
Independent, outside the clinic, recovered, or improved[1]	45%	40%
Hospitalized	34%	29%
Dependent, outside the clinic[1]	21%	29%

[1]Six patients from Harris et al. (1956), representing 5 percent of their patients, lived "independently," but their condition was unchanged or worse than it was when they were hospitalized. Since they were in obvious need of care, they had to be counted as "dependent on care" in order to render Harris's figures comparable to mine, just as had been done by Brown et al. (1966).

Each of these differences is well within the limits of chance deviations that might be expected. For example, the confidence range of the 45 percent of the probands from Harris et al. (1956) is approximately 36 percent–54 percent; and the 40 percent of my own probands, 28 percent–52 percent. But it would be illusory to conclude from the agreement of figures that the social status of the probands from the investigation by Harris et al. (1956), 5 years after their initial hospital-

ization, was the same as that of my probands. The figures, although similar, were derived by totally different methods. The description of social status is not the same in the two sets of statistics, a different system for recording the prematurely deceased patients was applied, and there are other differences. The striking similarity of figures between the two sets of statistics may be primarily due to happenstance.

In their investigations, also done in England on schizophrenics initially hospitalized in 1956, 5 years later Brown et al. (1966) developed statistics that were much more favorable as to probands' social status than those by Harris et al. (1956) or by me. The differences, however, have either no, or very little statistical significance.

Among the schizophrenics who in 1956 became probands after readmission for Brown et al. (1966), there were almost exactly as many employable probands outside of clinics 5 years later, as there were among all my 208 probands, 22–23 years after their admission in 1942/43 (30 percent and 31 percent). On the other hand, among the probands observed by Brown et al. (1966), there are considerably fewer hospitalized probands at the end of the catamneses than among mine (20 percent and 45 percent), and on the other hand, more whose condition is not satisfactory live outside clinics. But the comparisons of these figures do not permit valid conclusions either.

There is an agreement, however, with the extensive investigations by Marinow (1959) of Bulgaria, of chronic schizophrenics. Many years after onset of illness the average of patients' capability to work does not decline any further; instead, it improves, at least with appropriate treatment procedures including primarily work-therapy, active rehabilitation efforts, and neuroleptic drugs.

Table 4.15 embraces all probands, even including those who died prematurely. Table 4.16, on the other hand, considers only those 138 probands who survived to the end of the observation period. All of them were observed for at least 22 years after having become probands in 1942/43. For a great many of them, a number of years elapsed between first onset of schizophrenia and their hospitalization in 1942/43. Accordingly, Table 4.16 includes 138 probands who were still alive in 1964, at least 22 years, and at most 44 years after their first onset of illness.

The results from Table 4.16 are even more

Table 4.15. Social status of all princiapl probands through end of project. Percentages are calculated for all 208 probands and for all 68 initial admissions, not only patients who survived the entire observation period

Abbreviations: P = proband; m = male; f = female; I = initial hospitalizations when they became probands.

Probands whose social status had stabilized for at least 5 years at the end of observation period	mPs	$-fPs$	*m and f Ps*	$mI's$	$fI's$	*m and f I's*
Employable, outside a clinic, not requiring care	32	32	64 = 31%	16	11	27 = 40%
Employable, outside a clinic, requiring care	6	0	6 = 3%	3	0	3 = 4%
Requiring care in home or with family; partially employable	5	14	19 = 9%	0	6	6 = 9%
Requiring care in home or with family; unemployable	6	6	12 = 6%	3	2	5 = 7%
Requiring care for physical disability only; not employable	1	1	2 = 1%	1	0	1 = 1%
Partly employable; requiring care part-time outside a clinic	0	2	2 = 1%	0	0	0
In psychiatric clinic on ward for mild cases	14	11	25 = 12%	2	2	4 = 6%
In psychiatric clinic on ward for moderately severe cases	16	9	25 = 12%	3	4	7 = 10%
In psychiatric clinic on ward for severe cases	19	24	43 = 21%	3	6	9 = 13%
Alternating between inpatient and outpatient care; partly employable	0	4	4 = 2%	0	3	3 = 4%
Patients with undetermined social position at end of observation period	1[1]	5[2]	6 = 3%	1[1]	2[2]	3 = 4%
Totals	100	108	208	32	36	68

1. Suicide outside the clinic.
2. One with variable status, hospitalized; 1 with variable status outside the clinic; 1 suicide outside the clinic;

1 deceased at the clinic; 1 deceased in a medical hospital after suicide attempt.

favorable than those from Table 4.15, for rather obvious reasons. Among the patients who died are those who died in a state of peracute excitation of their chronic illness while they were living on wards for the severely ill. They include also those probands who were inpatients in a psychiatric hospital because of advanced age or for physical complaints while mild psychotic symptoms persisted.

The most noteworthy features from Table 4.16 appear below. Percentages shown in parentheses are the confidence intervals at 95 percent, rounded off according to *Documenta Geigy*:

The rate of surviving probands who work productively in open society without the need for care, in proportion to probands on wards for the severely ill is 3:1. With those patients who became probands on their first hospitalization, the rate is as much as 8:1. The view of schizophrenia as a progressive psychosis toward idiocy has led to the assumption, persisting well into this century, that after a schizophrenic course running into several decades, the great majority of schizophrenics will end on wards for the severely ill in a state of idiocy. Such an assumption is false.

Social status of probands 22 or more years after first onset	*Percentage of all surviving probands*	*Percentage of surviving probands who became probands on first admission*
Employed, outside clinics, and not requiring care	40.5% (32–49%)	50% (35–65%)
Inpatients on wards for severely ill patients	13% (8–20%)	6% (1–17%)
Total in psychiatric hospitals	35.6% (29–45%)	22.5% (12–37%)

Table 4.16. Social status of principal probands surviving at end of project

Abbreviations: P = Proband; m = male; f = female; I = initially hospitalized when they became probands

Probands whose social status had stabilized for at least 5 years at the end of the observation period	*mPs*	*fPs*	*m and f Ps*	*mI's*	*fI's*	*m and f I's*
Employable outside a clinic; not requiring care	29	27	56 = 40.5 % (32–49 %)	15	9	24 = 50 % (35–65 %)
Employable outside a clinic requiring care	4	0	4 = 3 %	2	0	2 = 4 %
Requiring care in home or with family; partially employable	4	11	15 = 11 %	0	5	5 = 10.5 %
Requiring care in home or with family; unemployable	5	2	7 = 5%	3	2	5 = 10.5 %
Requiring care for physical disability only; not employable	1	0	1 = 0.5 %	1	0	1 = 2 %
Partly employable; requiring care part-time outside a clinic	0	2	2 = 1 %	0	0	0
In psychiatric clinic, on ward for mild cases	10	8	18 = 13 %	1	1	2 = 4 %
In psychiatric clinic, on ward for moderately severe cases	8	6	14 = 10.5 %	3	3	6 = 12.5 %
In psychiatric clinic, on ward for severe cases	7	11	18 = 13 % (8–20 %)	1	2	3 = 6 % (1–17 %)
Alternating between inpatient and outpatient care; partly employable	0	1	1 = 0.5 %	0	0	0
Patients with undetermined social status at end of observation period	0	2	2 = 1 %	0	0	0
Totals:	68	70	138[1]	26	22	48

Values in parentheses represent confidence interval[1] at 95% according to *Documenta Geigy*, entered only for the most important values. Decimals are omitted; last digit is rounded off according to closest figure in the *Geigy* table. It may therefore be slightly inaccurate.

1. Confidence interval was taken from tables at N = 140 to avoid laborious recalculations.

Course of Illness and Background

Table 4.17 and 4.18 show the frequency of the different "end states" and of course types in comparison with different family backgrounds. The descriptions of "end state" and course type conform to the criteria already given. The type of background was divided into three groups

—Childhood before age 18 spent in a broken home or under horrible conditions with both parents

—Childhood spent with both parents under conditions ranging between "normal" and "horrible"

—Childhood spent under reasonably normal conditions with both parents.

The criteria for childhood conditions labelled "broken home," "normal," and "horrible" have already been explained. Further breakdown of categories of childhood conditions for statistical purposes would be meaningless, since the resulting figures would be so small as to eliminate from the outset any kind of statistical significance.

It has often been suspected, although never proved, that a proband's childhood background influences the course of his illness. The assumption that unfavorable childhood conditions might cause an unfavorable course of illness is especially suggestive. Of course, the contrary may also be assumed, that severe psychoses erupt, independently of unfavorable

Table 4.17. Background and "end state" compared. The standard deviations are not given, to keep the table readable; they are usually so great that the differences are statistically not significant (for exceptions that approach statistical significance see this Chapter, footnote 17)

Childhood background for 100 male probands	Severe "end state"	Moderately severe "end state"	Mild "end state"	Recovery	No "end state" attained	Total
Normal	4 = 11 %	6 = 16 %	14 = 38 %	9 = 24 %	4 = 11 %	37
Between normal and horrible	5 = 31 %	1 = 6 %	3 = 19 %	6 = 37.5 %	1 = 6 %	16
Horrible or broken home	14 = 30 %	9 = 19 %	14 = 30 %	9 = 19 %	1 = 2 %	47
Total:	23 = 33 %	16 = 16 %	31 = 31 %	24 = 24 %	6 = 6 %	100
Childhood background for 108 female probands						
Normal	5 = 22.5 %	6 = 27 %	6 = 27 %	4 = 18 %	1 = 4.5 %	22
Between normal and horrible	4 = 19 %	5 = 24 %	8 = 38 %	3 = 14 %	1 = 4.5 %	21
Horrible or broken home	11 = 17 %	14 = 21.5 %	22 = 34 %	10 = 15 %	8 = 12 %	65
Total:	20 = 18.5 %	25 = 23 %	36 = 33 %	17 = 16 %	10 = 9.5 %	108
Childhood background for all 208 probands						
Normal	9 = 15 %	12 = 20 %	20 = 34 %	13 = 22 %	5 = 8.5 %	59
Between normal and horrible	9 = 24 %	6 = 16 %	11 = 30 %	9 = 24 %	2 = 5 %	37
Horrible or broken home	25 = 22 %	23 = 20.5 %	36 = 32 %	19 = 17 %	9 = 8 %	112
Total:	43 = 20.5 %	41 = 20 %	67 = 32 %	41 = 20 %	16 = 8 %	208

Table 4.18. Background and course type compared. To keep the table readable, the standard deviations have not been included. Usually they are too great for the differences to be statistically significant (exception that approaches statistical significance appears in footnote 17, this Chapter)

	Acute to severe "end state"	Chronic to severe "end state"	Acute to mild "end state"	Chronic to mild "end state"	Undulating to severe "end state"	Undulating to mild "end state"	Undulating to recovery	Atypical course	Died before type of course was determined	Total
Childhood of 100 male probands										
Normal	0	2 = 5 %	1 = 3 %	8 = 22 %	3 = 8 %	10 = 27 %	10 = 27 %	2 = 5 %	1 = 3 %	37
Between normal and horrible	0	3 = 19 %	1 = 6 %	2 = 12.5 %	1 = 6 %	2 = 12.5	6 = 37.5 %	1 = 6 %	0	16
Horrible or broken home	1 = 2 %	9 = 19 %	1 = 2 %	13 = 28 %	5 = 11 %	7 = 15 %	9 = 19 %	2 = 4 %	0	47
Total :	1 = 1 %	14 = 14 %	3 = 3 %	23 = 23 %	9 = 9 %	19 = 19 %	25 = 25 %	5 = 5 %	1 = 1 %	100
Childhood of 108 female Ps										
Normal	0	2 = 9.5 %	0	6 = 27 %	2 = 9.5 %	7 = 32 %	4 = 18 %	1 = 4.5 %	0	22
Between normal and horrible	1 = 5 %	2 = 9.5 %	1 = 5 %	5 = 24 %	1 = 5 %	7 = 33 %	3 = 14 %	1 = 5 %	0	21
Horrible or broken home	1 = 1.5 %	6 = 9 %	1 = 1.5 %	12 = 18.5 %	7 = 11 %	23 = 35 %	12 = 18.5 %	1 = 1.5 %	2 = 3 %	65
Total:	2 = 2 %	10 = 9 %	2 = 2 %	23 = 21 %	10 = 9 %	37 = 34 %	19 = 17.5 %	3 = 3 %	2 = 2 %	108
Childhood of all 208 Ps										
Normal	0	4 = 6 %	1 = 1.5 %	14 = 24 %	5 = 8.5 %	17 = 29 %	14 = 24 %	3 = 5 %	1 = 1.5 %	59
Between normal and horrible	1 = 3 %	5 = 13.5 %	2 = 5.5 %	7 = 19 %	2 = 5.5 %	9 = 24 %	9 = 24 %	2 = 5.5 %	0	37
Horrible or broken home	2 = 2 %	15 = 13 %	2 = 2 %	25 = 22 %	12 = 10.5 %	30 = 27 %	21 = 19 %	3 = 2.5 %	2 = 2 %	112
Totals:	3 = 1.5 %	24 = 11.5 %	5 = 2.5 %	46 = 22 %	19 = 9 %	56 = 27 %	44 = 21 %	8 = 4 %	3 = 1.5 %	208

childhood conditions, while an unfavorable childhood in addition to these severe psychoses might even promote the development of benign psychoses. If this were the case, the most favorable courses would have to be most frequent among patients with unfavorable childhoods.

Tables 4.17 and 4.18 show clearly that there certainly is no high degree of dependence on childhood background for the course of illness. This corresponds to clinical experience, for we have observed daily the most variegated types of disease courses in patients from both favorable and unfavorable backgrounds.

Among female schizophrenics there is not the slightest indication of any sort of relationship between disease course and background. On the other hand, among the males there is a slight, although insignificant indication to that effect. There is only an indication of a correlation between horrible childhood conditions and a poor "end state" among schizophrenic males. Other correlations among schizophrenic males point in the same direction, but fail to achieve statistical significance to an even lesser degree.[14]

In order to be sure that the difference for the sexes that has been uncovered has any general validity, the existing basic data would have to come from a larger number of probands. What value would it have to know that there actually were no correlations between childhood conditions and the courses of schizophrenic psychoses in women that are distinct enough to show up in statistics, while, on

the contrary, among schizophrenic men a horrible childhood and premature parent loss showed a correlation with an unfavorable course of illness? I shall mention the most obvious answer that occurs to me among a number of possible interpretations, namely that it lends support to the experience that schizophrenic women more often had unfavorable childhoods than schizophrenic men did. But then, perhaps, those schizophrenias that are somehow related causally to an unhappy childhood are on the whole the more benign forms of schizophrenias. While among both men and women an unfavorable childhood is rather likely to have an unfavorable influence on their schizophrenia, this unfavorable influence might have been concealed in the women's statistics, because their unfavorable childhood backgrounds might also have induced mild schizophrenias in them. A great number of arguments could be presented both for and against such assumptions. Lacking statistical significance for the differences in the figures from Tables 4.17 and 4.18, however, the discussion of any of these arguments is premature.

Does the childhood history of probands have any relationship to the age at which they suffer a schizophrenic onset? It would seem that it does. Specifically, it is possible that the background from a horrible childhood among early-onset cases occurs more frequently than it does in late-onset cases. A glance at Table 4.19 shows that this is not the case. Insofar as we can determine from our 208 probands, there is no relationship between the quality of a proband's childhood and his age at onset of his schizophrenia. The differences in the figures of Table 4.19 lie within the range where chance operation must often play a weighty role. In particular the percentage of those who became ill before age 20 is about the same for men and women as it is for all probands (between 9.5 percent and 16 percent), whether their childhood was normal or horrible.

Angst (1966) made the unexpected, statistically significant discovery in phasic-depressives, that late-onset cases (after age 50) come from broken homes much more frequently—this is statistically significant—than do phasic-depressives with an onset before age 50. A corresponding difference for schizophrenics could only be checked statistically if the number of probands were to contain more late-onset schizophrenics than our present one does.

14. Among the 37 male schizophrenics with normal childhood backgrounds, 4 had developed a chronic, severe "end state," but among 47 male schizophrenics who had come from broken homes or horrible childhood backgrounds in the homes of their parents, the number was 14.

The difference at $p < 0.10$ is not sufficiently significant.

Among the same 37 male schizophrenics with normal childhood backgrounds, 10 ran a course that was undulating and progressed to recovery, while among 47 male schizophrenics coming from broken homes or a horrible childhood milieu with their parents, there were 9.

At $0.6 > p > 0.5$, the difference is by no means significant.

Among the same 37 male schizophrenics with normal childhoods, 2 became uniformly chronic, severely schizophrenic (according to course types I and II), and among the 47 male schizophrenics from broken homes or horrible childhood environments with their parents, the number was 10.

The difference at $0.1 > p > 0.05$ is not significant.

Table 4.19. Background and age at onset compared. The confidence intervals, rounded off according to *Documenta Geigy*, appear next to the percentages

Age at onset of illness (years)

Childhood background	15–19		20–29		30–39		Over 40		Total
Childhood background for 100 male probands									
Normal	6 = 16 %	(6–32 %)	12 = 32 %	(18–50 %)	8 = 21.5 %	(10–38 %)	11 = 30 %	(16–47 %)	37
Between normal and horrible	2 = 12.5 %	(2–38 %)	12 = 75 %	(48–93 %)	2 = 12.5 %	(2–38 %)	0		16
Horrible or broken home	5 = 11 %	(4–23 %)	19 = 40.5 %	(26–56 %)	20 = 42.5 %	(28–58 %)	3 = 6 %	(1–18 %)	47
Totals:	13 = 13 %	(7–21 %)	43 = 43 %	(33–53 %)	30 = 30 %	(21–40 %)	14 = 14 %	(8–22 %)	100
Childhood background for 108 female probands									
Normal	2 = 9.5 %	(1–29 %)	8 = 36 %	(15–59 %)	6 = 27 %	(11–50 %)	6 = 27 %	(11–50 %)	22
Between normal and horrible	3 = 14 %	(3–36 %)	7 = 33 %	(15–57 %)	7 = 33 %	(15–57 %)	4 = 19 %	(5–42 %)	21
Horrible or broken home	7 = 10.5 %	(4–21 %)	21 = 32 %	(21–45 %)	16 = 24.5 %	(15–37 %)	21 = 32 %	(21–45 %)	65
Totals:	12 = 11 %	(6–18 %)	36 = 33 %	(24–42 %)	29 = 27 %	(18–36 %)	31 = 29 %	(20–38 %)	108[1]
Childhood background for all 208 probands									
Normal	8 = 13.5 %	(6–25 %)	20 = 34 %	(22–47 %)	14 = 23.5 %	(14–37 %)	17 = 29 %	(18–42 %)	59
Between normal and horrible	5 = 13.5 %	(5–29 %)	19 = 51 %	(34–68 %)	9 = 24 %	(12–41 %)	4 = 11 %	(3–25 %)	37
Horrible or broken home	12 = 11.5 %	(6–19 %)	40 = 35.5 %	(27–46 %)	36 = 32 %	(24–42 %)	24 = 21 %	(15–31 %)	112[1]
Totals:	25 = 12 %	(8–18 %)	79 = 38 %	(33–47 %)	59 = 28 %	(24–37 %)	45 = 22 %	(17–29 %)	208[2]

1. Confidence intervals were taken from the tables at N = 110 to avoid laborious recalculations.   2. Confidence intervals were taken from the tables at N = 200 to avoid laborious recalculations.

Course of Illness and Prepsychotic Personality

In the 20's and 30's of this century a number of investigations were published on the significance of the prepsychotic personality for the prognosis of schizophrenias. Since that time, questions concerning prognoses that motivated most investigators have shifted their emphasis. There is now less interest in how the prepsychotic personality might influence the prognosis, than in how treatment, aftercare, and relationships with family members might affect it. This shift in the direction of questioning is based on sound reasons. It is important to know whether what we can do for the schizophrenic, what can be manipulated, really helps. In contrast, for two decades it seemed rather hopeless to study whether something we cannot control, that is solidly, irrevocably cast in the past, might possibly exert an influence. The prepsychotic personality was for much too long regarded as something that was merely statistical, that was something that had been poured, cast, solidified, and rendered unalterably permanent and incapable of being influenced or manipulated. Today we know that such a prepsychotic personality unfolds along with life experiences, that it is in a continuous process of shaping and reshaping. With this in mind, the study of prepsychotic personalities has again become a matter of interest. If psychopathic—and particularly schizoid—behavior patterns have an influence on the courses of schizophrenias, then measures that tend to inhibit such behavior are also prophylactic measures for severe courses of schizophrenias.

Unfavorable relationships to family members can force children into unfavorable personality and behavior patterns. If such prepsychotic behavior aggravates the course of schizophrenia, then concern for the family's mental hygiene involves also a commitment in the struggle against schizophrenic onsets. In brief, a study of the relationships between prepsychotic personalities and the courses of schizophrenias is not merely scientific theory, but at the same time it pursues medical, social, and humanitarian goals as well.

It has been a well-established, assured fact for a number of decades that for psychopaths, and particularly for schizoid psychopaths, schizophrenic psychoses on the average run a less favorable course than they do for those who had led useful and productive lives, were

adaptable, and behaved in nonaberrant fashion before the schizophrenic onset. This prognostic rule-of-thumb corresponds to the experience of most clinicians. It was first demonstrated in exhaustive investigations by Mauz (1930). Since then a sizeable number of investigations have in the main verified and supported his conclusions.[15]

In my paper published in 1941, I compared the prepsychotic personalities of 405 schizophrenics with their "end states," and those of 332 schizophrenics with their types of disease courses (they were schizophrenics from St. Pirminsberg in Pfäfers, from Bloomingdale Hospital in White Plains, New York, and from Friedmatt in Basel, along with their schizophrenic relatives). In general, at that time the findings confirmed our expectations (see Table 4.5 concerning the 1941 studies). Among the "end states," recovery was more frequent for those who have been prepsychotically nonaberrant, and more rare for the schizoid psychopaths than for all probands combined. On the other hand, the most severe chronic states occurred somewhat more rarely among the nonaberrant, and more frequently among the schizoid psychopaths than among all probands. The course type "undulating to recovery," accordingly, was more frequent among the prepsychotically nonaberrant, and less frequent among the schizoid and other types of psychopaths than among all the probands. Compared to all probands, there were fewer psychoses with acute or lingering courses evolving to severe chronic states among the nonaberrant, and more of them among the schizoid psychopaths. It is an interesting observation that the "undulating courses proceeding to severe chronic states", on the contrary, occur with less frequency among the nonaberrant and the schizoid psychopaths—a direct reversal of the distribution for "acute or uniformly chronic, progressing to severe chronic states" type. The distribution between "undulating, proceeding to severe chronic 'end states'" and "undulating, progressing to recovery" types of courses was about equal.

The above-mentioned—and numerous other—positive and negative correlations reached statistical significance in only a few cases. When all cases were considered jointly, the differences were greater than the median error in the empirical figures in just a few of the comparisons, and never greater than three times the median error. Calculations for the coefficients of correlation r were made according to Bravais' method with the following results:

"Between recovery and prepsychotic nonaberration r is well within twice the standard deviation at 0.13 ± 0.05. Between schizoid psychopathy and recovery, r is -0.11 ± 0.05. On the other hand, r between schizoid psychopathy and a poor outcome (dementia + severe defect) is 0.11 ± 0.05. These figures, too, seem to point out clearly that there are more unfavorable "end states" among the prepsychotic schizoid psychopaths, and more favorable "end states" among the prepsychotically nonaberrant. As we have likewise emphasized, the undulating course evolving to dementia behaves oppositely from other forms leading simply to dementia, in that it reveals no negative correlation to prepsychotic nonaberration; in this instance, r is 0.04 ± 0.05."

The correlations that attained even a weak statistical significance in the study of all cases combined were found to be nearly equal for the different groups of probands, so that they deserved to be taken more seriously statistically than the combined study of all probands might have indicated.

We can observe, by inspecting column A1 of Table 4.20, how often the various "end states" of our 208 probands occur among the nonaberrant, the schizoid- and otherwise-aberrant within the norm, and among the schizoid and other types of psychopaths. Column B1 indicates how often each of the "end states" would have occurred in each of these personality types, if the various "end states" were equally distributed among all personality types. Table 4.21 shows similar data, but applied to course types rather than to "end states."

Tables 4.20 and 4.21 show that the correlations that might have been expected, judging from general experience and the findings from my own previous studies, are either partly nonexistent or only very weakly indicated in the 208 probands of this project. But it is also immediately apparent that the individual entries are so small, that any statistical significance is scarcely possible either. The figure 208 simply does not represent enough probands to show up the relationships between "end states" and course types on the one hand,

and prepsychotic personalities on the other.

If the correlations expected from general experience were clearly revealed in my previous probands, but were less clearly revealed in studies of my 208 principal probands, the probabilities of chance may possibly be the principal cause. There is no statistical significance in the difference between the two sets of data. But there may be another reason for these apparent differences. As has been previously explained, today I set the boundaries between schizoid and nonaberrant somewhat differently than I did in 1941. I no longer seek to qualify a personality independently of the proband's life history, but I attempt to relate the proband's behavior to the effect of suffering to which that proband has been exposed, more than I did before. If someone has been mistreated and neglected throughout his entire childhood, I hesitate before I classify him as a "schizoid psychopath," even when his behavior is such as would have to be designated as psychopathic, had he lived under favorable circumstances. In such cases the question bothers me, whether the retrogression into an autistic behavior pattern is not often a behavior pattern that has been imposed on the otherwise nonaberrant person by circumstances. Perhaps this line of thinking resulted in my conception of psychopathy and the schizoid, that has a less positive relationship to the courses of schizophrenic psychoses than the older concepts had.

In this situation, I added the data from my 1941 probands to those from this investigation, to establish or refute statistical significance. This combined set of data amounted to a considerable volume (see Tables 4.20 and 4.21). The "end states" can be subjected to comparison in 613 cases, and the course types in 529 cases, with the prepsychotic personalities (cases for which a course type was not established by the time the proband died or by the end of the observation period were omitted, as were cases with an atypical course of illness).

Tables 4.20 and 4.21 show that among the probands of this study, the expected relationships between "end states" and course types on the one hand, and prepsychotic character traits on the other, can be detected, but the correlations are but weakly defined, and few achieve any statistical significance.

In order not to overload Tables 4.20 and 4.21 with data to the point where they would become cluttered, the median errors are given for only one line of figures, that is, for the

Table 4.20. Prepsychotic personality and "end state" compared. Summary of conclusions published in 1941 for the 405 schizophrenics and for the 208 probands of this project

Vertical columns A1: Number of combinations observed for the 208 principal probands
B1: Number of combinations that would result if there were no interdependency between prepsychotic personality and "end state" (for the 208 principal probands)
A2: Number of combinations observed for all 613 probands investigated
B2: Number of combinations that would result if there were no interdependency between prepsychotic personality and "end state" (for all 613 probands investigated)
C: Standard deviation
D: Proportion of A2:B2

Prepsychotic personality

	Nonaberrant						Schizoid aberrant within norm						Otherwise aberrant within norm						Schizoid psychopaths						Other psychopaths					
	A1	B1	A2	B2	C	D	A1	B1	A2	B2	C	D	A1	B1	A2	B2	C	D	A1	B1	A2	B2	C	D	A1	B1	A2	B2	C	D
Severe "end state"	10	12.8	38	43.2	6.3	0.9	13	12.2	39	38.4	6.0	1.0	1	1.9	7	7.0	2.6	1.0	10	10.3	44	40.7	6.2	1.1	9	5.8	13	11.7	3.4	1.1
Moderately severe "end state"	14	12.2	28	32.1	5.5	0.9	10	11.6	24	28.7	5.2	0.8	1	1.8	2	5.1	2.2	0.4	11	9.9	38	30	5.3	1.3	5	5.5	13	9.1	3.0	1.4
Mild "end state"	21	20	47	40.2	6.1	1.2	16	19	31	36.3	5.8	0.8	5	2.9	7	6.3	2.5	1.1	16	16.1	36	36.5	5.8	1.0	9	9	11	12.7	3.5	0.9
Recovery	13	12.2	38	30.4	5.4	1.2	14	11.6	29	26.9	5.1	1.1	1	1.8	3	4.8	2.2	0.6	9	9.9	22	28.6	5.2	0.8	4	5.5	7	8.2	2.8	0.8
Did not attain an "end state"	4	4.8	37	42.1	6.3	0.9	6	4.5	44	36.5	5.8	1.2	1	0.7	11	6.9	2.6	1.6	4	3.9	37	41.5	6.2	0.9	1	2.1	7	8.9	2.9	0.8

Table 4.21. Prepsychotic personality and course type compared. Summary of investigations of 332 schizophrenics published in 1941 and the 208 principal probands of this project[1]

Vertical columns A1: Number of observed combinations in 197 probands of this project
B1: Number of combinations that would result if there were no interdependency between prepsychotic personality and course type (for the 197 probands of this project)
A2: Number of observed combinations for all 529 schizophrenics under investigation
B2: Number of combinations that would result if there were no interdependency between prepsychotic personality and course type (among all 529 schizophrenics investigated)
C: Standard deviation for B2
D: Proportion of A2:B2

Course types	Prepsychotic personality																													
	Nonaberrant						Schizoid aberrant within norm						Otherwise aberrant within norm						Schizoid psychopaths						Other psychopaths					
	A1	B1	A2	B2	C	D	A1	B1	A2	B2	C	D	A1	B1	A2	B2	C	D	A1	B1	A2	B2	C	D	A1	B1	A2	B2	C	D
Acute to severe "end state"	1	0.9	11	12.8	3.5	0.8	1	0.9	13	11	3.3	1.2	0	0.1	3	2.0	1.4	1.5	0	0.7	14	13.4	3.6	1.0	1	0.4	1	2.9	1.7	0.3
Chronic to severe "end state"	7	7.2	18	24.5	4.8	0.7	9	6.8	25	21.6	4.5	1.1	2	1	2	3.7	1.9	0.5	2	5.8	25	24.3	4.8	1.0	6	3.2	11	6.8	2.6	1.6
Acute to mild "end state"	1	1.5	7	4.5	2.1	1.5	1	1.4	3	4.0	2.0	0.7	0	0.2	0	0.7	0.8	0	1	1.2	3	4.5	2.1	0.7	2	0.7	2	1.3	1.1	1.5
Chronic to mild "end state"	13	13.7	20	22.2	4.6	0.9	13	13	17	20.2	4.4	0.8	4	2	4	3.3	1.8	1.2	9	11.1	21	20.2	4.4	1.0	7	6.2	12	8.0	2.8	1.5
Undulating to severe "end state"	4	5.7	13	13.3	3.6	1.0	5	5.4	11	11.9	3.4	0.9	1	0.8	1	2.0	1.4	0.5	7	4.6	16	12.7	3.5	1.2	2	2.5	3	4.1	2.0	0.7
Undulating to mild "end state"	18	16.7	44	45.9	6.5	0.9	11	15.9	38	40.8	6.1	0.9	3	2.4	10	7.0	2.6	1.4	18	13.5	48	44.7	6.4	1.1	6	7.5	12	13.6	3.6	0.9
Undulating to recovery	15	13.1	47	36.5	5.8	1.3	16	12.6	35	32.6	5.5	1.1	1	1.9	5	5.6	2.3	0.9	8	10.5	26	35.6	5.8	0.7	4	5.9	8	10.7	3.2	0.7

1. Eight of the 208 probands had an atypical course; 3 died before the course type was identified. These cases are not included, nor are the corresponding cases from the 1941 studies.

figures of all calculated combinations between prepsychotic personality on the one hand, and "end state" and course type on the other, which would result if personality and course of illness were independent of one another. The most important correlations, indicating their degree of significance, will be discussed in detail below.

1. Among the prepsychotically nonaberrant probands, the "end states" are distributed differently than among all probands, but the difference is not statistically significant (0.20 > p > 0.10). The difference indicates that a recovery outcome is more frequent, and that severe "end states" are more rare among nonaberrant prepsychotics than among all probands described in both tables.

2. Among the prepsychotic schizoid and the otherwise aberrant within the norm, the "end states" are distributed about the same way as for all probands. The value of p for the difference in these comparisons is just less than 0.5 and 0.3.

3. Among the prepsychotic schizoid- and other psychopaths, the "end states" are distributed in clearly different proportion than they are among all probands. In this comparison the difference attains a significance of p < 0.05. We may regard as probable that among the prepsychotic psychopaths (schizoid

tia" are less frequent than among all schizophrenics combined.

5. Among the prepsychotic schizoid- and otherwise aberrant within the norm, the course types are distributed about the same way as they are for all probands. The value of p for the differences in these comparisons is only less than 0.8 and 0.5.

6. Among the prepsychotic schizoid- and other psychopaths, the course types are distributed differently than they are for all probands. The difference does not attain statistical significance, although it does not fail by much. Schizophrenias proceeding "undulating to recovery" are rarer among these psychopathic personalities than among all probands combined.[16]

The salient points are also illustrated in the following listing; they refer to the abbreviations from Table 4.20.

Comparisons are presented of the observed number of combinations between "end states" and personality type, and the calculated number; that is, that figure which would most probably result if the different "end states" were equally distributed among all personality types.

The observed and the calculated numbers for the "end states" behave for the nonaberrant-character personalities as shown below:

With severe chronic "end states"	as 38:43 = 0.88
With moderately severe and mild chronic "end states"	as 75:72 = 1.04
With recoveries	as 38:30 = 1.26
The same relationship for the schizoid- and otherwise aberrant:	
With severe chronic "end states"	as 46:45 = 1.02
With moderately severe and mild chronic "end states"	as 64:76 = 0.84
With recoveries	as 32:32 = 1.00
The same relationship for the schizoid- and other psychopaths:	
With severe chronic "end states"	as 57:52 = 1.10
With moderately severe and mild chronic "end states"	as 98:88 = 1.1
With recoveries	as 29:37 = 0.78

and others), a recovery outcome is rarer, and an outcome to severe chronic states more frequent, than among all probands combined.

4. Among the prepsychotically nonaberrant probands, the distribution of course types is different from what it is among all probands. This difference is statistically almost significant at p < 0.1. It indicates that the course type "undulating, proceeding to recovery" is more frequent among the prepsychotically nonaberrant, and, on the contrary, the types "acute to dementia" and "lingering to demen-

16. The comparisons under 1–6 might be made somewhat differently, too. Instead of comparing the individual estimates of the patient's prepsychotic condition with the course of illness of all probands, it might be compared with the courses of only those probands whose prepsychotic condition was evaluated differently. Such a comparison would have a greater significance than the comparisons described above.

These figures show clearly how a positive correlation exists between the "nonaberrant" personality and a good course, and a negative correlation between the "nonaberrant" personality and a poor course. For the psychopaths, the correlations are reversed. There is no correlation between an "aberrant" personality and the "end states."

From the 9 relationships selected and all individual figures considered jointly, it may be stated that, according to expectations, schizophrenias progress to recovery more frequently for the prepsychotically nonaberrant than they do for schizoid- and other psychopaths.

There are no further positive or negative correlations that even approach statistical significance in the combined data from investigations shown in Tables 4.20 and 4.21. In the studies of 1941, such correlations appeared to emerge, but their significance was reduced when the research material was increased.

Quite different listings, appearing elsewhere, also support the finding that there is a positive correlation between good disease courses and a nonaberrant prepsychotic personality, just as there is a negative correlation between poor disease courses and a schizoid personality. On the average, the psychoses run a worse course for probands who were taken into the study when they were already hospitalized than for those who became probands along with some other condition of hospitalization; however, the prognoses of the latter category is, in turn, worse than the prognosis for schizophrenias among the relatives of schizophrenic probands, who were picked up in the course of studies of families. Corresponding to this, the least probands with nonaberrant prepsychotic personalities occur among those of the first group, more among those of the second, and most among those of the third group; and, conversely, there are more schizoids in the first group than in the second, and more in the second than in the third group.

Contrary to expectations, however, is the finding that the correlation between a healthy prepsychotic personality and a benign course in schizophrenias is extremely uncertain. Most clinicians would rather have expected a more clearly defined correlation, on the basis of the existing literature and their own experience. On the other hand, we are aware that the research material as it has been assembled for the data in Tables 4.20 and 4.21 is extensive, and is based on knowledge gained from long-term courses and thorough studies of the probands. There would scarcely be a set of statistics capable of challenging the findings shown in Tables 4.20 and 4.21.

We must conclude, therefore, that the course of schizophrenic psychoses is only very minimally affected by the prepsychotic personality of the probands. Factors other than the prepsychotic personality must be much more influential in shaping the course of schizophrenia. Modestly and restrictively, however, we might add that this conclusion is valid only in respect to those personality peculiarities that could be crudely and summarily categorized in our own terms (nonaberrant, schizoid- or otherwise aberrant, and schizoid-psychopathic or otherwise psychopathic). Beyond that, as to whether there are more subtle personality peculiarities that influence the course of schizophrenias more decisively, our investigation has nothing to say. Nor does it make a statement as to whether there may be congenital tendencies rooted in the character that do not become manifest in the personality, that might influence the course of schizophrenias.

The disappointment that the relationships between (classifiable) prepsychotic personalities and schizophrenic courses are so minimal should, however, constitute an incentive for the active continuation of investigations on the long-term influence of treatment methods, aftercare, and the restoration of family relationships, as they are practised in most modern clinics.

Course of Illness and Multiple Occurrences of Schizophrenia in Families

Do schizophrenias proceed along a different course if additional cases of it emerge among relatives of the proband than when they occur as a single catastrophe in only one family member?

For more than a century the inclination was to answer the question according to preconceived opinions. The primary assumptions concerning it go back to the "degeneration theory" of the last century, as represented by Morel (1860), among others. According to this theory, entire families would progressively "degenerate" under the most diversified kinds of adversity. The accumulation of cases of schizophrenia within a family would constitute proof of the high degree of degeneration and thereby predestine the unfavorable course.

Later a different attitude was the reason for the still prevailing assumption that a "familial hereditary taint" was cause for an unfavorable prognosis. It was assumed that a "hereditary taint" always had only hereditary causes, but it was forgotten that there are also external damaging influences that may affect several members of a family in common. It was further assumed that psychoses springing from hereditary causes ran unfavorable courses and that acquired ones, ran favorable courses; neither of which must necessarily be the case.

Numerous indications in the literature, even in recent years, concerning severe courses with a "familial hereditary taint" are not in any way based on research, but are speculative theories based on the "degeneration theory" or on the fallacious equating of terms such as "familial = hereditary = progressive and incurable."

But for over 30 years a great number of investigations have been published on the disease courses of schizophrenias occurring in families and in isolated individuals, that do merit serious attention. The results differ, however. One investigator found less favorable prognoses in the isolated cases, while another found the opposite to be true. The differences in the prognoses are not great. Only one conclusion can be drawn from all these investigations, and that is that there is no statistically valid correlation between the severity of the course of a psychosis and the incidence or absence of secondary cases within the family. If such a criterion should nevertheless exist, it could certainly only be to a minimal degree.

Among the most important findings indicating a positive correlation between the severity of a schizophrenic psychosis and the frequency of schizophrenic incidence within a family, are without a doubt those by Kallmann (1938, 1946). He distinguishes a "core group" and a "peripheral group" of schizophrenics, referring to the latter also as "S-group or simplex group." But Kallmann (1938, 1946) is being misquoted if his findings are credited with showing that a stronger "hereditary taint" is prevalent in the virulent schizophrenias than in the milder ones. To be sure, those schizophrenias that he includes in his "core group" are schizophrenias that progress unfavorably, but those of the "peripheral group" are by no means benign types with recovery outcomes, but primarily those with a

somewhat less unfavorable course than the ones from the "core group." Because of the peculiarities of his probands and his own concept of schizophrenia, none or only very few "recovered" schizophrenics appear in his investigative material. As to some further details I did attempt some other comparisons between these findings of Kallmann's (1938, 1946) studies and my own, in my 1941 paper on the Pfäfers schizophrenics already referred to in Chapter 2.

Wittermans and Schulz (1950) studied 50 "probable" schizophrenics, whose psychoses had lasted less than 1 year, and had remained recovered for over 8 years. They found fewer schizophrenics among the parents, children, and siblings of these probands than they usually found among these same relatives of all schizophrenics combined. Again it would be incorrect to generalize this very specific investigation by claiming that there are fewer schizophrenics among the relatives of recovered schizophrenics than among the relatives of incurable schizophrenics. As the authors themselves have stressed, the number of probands in their investigation is too small to permit that sort of generalization. A primary consideration is, however, that among the recovered schizophrenics of most other studies, as of my own, there are numerous probands who have passed through several or many psychotic phases, but among the probands of Wittermans and Schulz, only probands are included who have passed through a single psychotic phase. On the average, the courses of schizophrenia in relatives are inclined to be similar. For this reason it is probable that similar mild cases are common among the relatives of schizophrenics, who rapidly recovered from a one-time psychotic episode. Such types of mild, very brief onsets of schizophrenia escape inclusion in catamneses much more often than do cases with several phases or an unfavorable outcome.

The findings of Hallgren and Sjoegren (1959) indicate a favorable course of a schizophrenic psychosis in the absence of schizophrenias among the relatives. Welner and Stroemgren (1958) investigated "schizophrenia-like benign psychoses" and found very few schizophrenias among their relatives.

Many other authors, on the other hand, found no correlation between favorable courses and low incidence of schizophrenia among relatives or even, on the contrary, they actually found a positive correlation between a favorable course and a high frequency of schizophrenias in the families. Principally, there were many secondary schizophrenias among the rather benign "atypical" or "unsystematic" schizophrenias of the Kleist (1953) school and among the "schizophrenic-like psychoses" of Langfeldt's (1956) school. To be sure, among these "atypical" and "schizophrenic-like" psychoses there are not only recoverable psychoses, but also a great many more recovered and improved cases than among the schizophrenic "core groups," with which they were compared (Schwab 1938, Schulz and Leonhard 1940, Leonhard 1956, Ambrumova 1957, Leonhard 1964, von Trostorff 1964, etc.). Other authors who found a similar or greater number of secondary cases among relatives of patients with favorable rather than unfavorable courses of schizophrenias are, for example, Galatschjan (1937), Gerloff (1937), Kraulis (1939), Mitsuda (1941/67), Kant (1942), Selma Siegfried (1943), Szewczyk (1950), Zolan and Bigelow (1950), Mitsuda (1957), Inouye (1959/70), and Jansson and Alstroem (1967).

In each of these above-mentioned papers there are, however, serious objections against generalizations, which would be too cumbersome to explain in detail. No matter how many other papers one were to study that concern this problem, my initially mentioned conclusion holds that, up to this point, there is no statistically proved correlation between the severity of the course of a schizophrenic psychosis and the frequency—or the absence—of secondary cases in members of the proband's family. In my opinion, the most nearly admissible assumption justifiable from findings of previous studies is that schizophrenias occurring in number within a family, average a somewhat better prognosis than those occurring as isolated, individual cases.

It is very impressive to note how in the reports of cases in the literature there are descriptions of numerous schizophrenic psychoses with favorable courses, although there are several cases of schizophrenias manifest within the families in question. In my own experience as well, there have been numerous recoveries among multiple cases of schizophrenia within a family. There are even schizophrenias with favorable courses among the children of two schizophrenics and among some twins of schizophrenics (Schulz 1940, Rosenthal 1961, Gastager and Hofmann 1962, and a number of others). It is certain that one may not formulate a statement to the effect that multiple cases of schizophrenias within

families are usually severe schizophrenias.

In my own 1941 studies, I arrived at certain conclusions about the courses of schizophrenic psychoses among the "tainted" and the "untainted." There were by no means any more of the severe chronic "end states" among the "tainted" than among the "untainted." The contrary appears to be a more permissible assumption.

The expression "hereditary taint" should at this time be purged from the modern professional vocabulary and replaced by "repetition of a certain disorder within a family or a sibship." The expression "tainted" is pejorative; it is attended by a twilight type of emotional connotation; it does not specify any objective set of circumstances, but rather suggests the dangerous concept that illnesses within a family group always impose a "taint" or disposition toward that illness on the proband and, in a sense, always predestine him to misfortune from the very start. In fact, this is by no means always the case. For that reason I now apply the terms "taint" and "the tainted" only in quotation marks and only when I am quoting from the older literature. The quotation marks are intended to warn the reader against making incorrect interpretations.

I pursued the same question in this present group of probands. No new information was discovered in that study; the old conclusions were confirmed.

Table 4.22 shows a comparison between the "end states" and the course types of the schizophrenic probands among whose close family relatives schizophrenias have also occurred, with those schizophrenic probands among whose close relatives there are no schizophrenias. A glance at Table 4.22 will show that there are no differences that approach statistical significance. The figures do not even permit the assumption that whether schizophrenia occurs within a family in an individual has any bearing whatsoever on the course or the outcome of the psychosis in a given proband.

To be sure, Table 4.22 does leave open some room for more specific questions. Among other considerations, it is perhaps incorrect to group probands with one schizophrenic sibling together with probands who had one schizophrenic parent. Perhaps, among other things, the finding is different if only the psychoses of certain relatives are compared. For this reason, the same question will be considered again from a slightly different angle

Table 4.22. "End states" and course types compared in probands with and without schizophrenic relatives

Group A: 77 probands with schizophrenics among parents, siblings, children, or nephews and nieces
Group B: 131 probands without schizophrenics among close relatives

"End state"	Group A			Group B		
	No.	%	Conf. Interv.	No.	%	Conf. Interv.
Severe "end state"	20	26	(17–37%)	23	17.5	(12–25%)
Moderately severe "end state"	10	13	(6–23%)	31	24	(17–32%)
Mild "end state"	27	35	(25–47%)	40	30	(22–39%)
Recovery	14	18	(10–29%)	27	20.5	(14–29%)
No "end state" attained	6	8	(3–16%)	10	8	(4–14%)
Totals:	77			131[1]		

Course type						
Acute to severe "end state"	1	1	(0–7%)	2	1.5	(0–5%)
Chronic to severe "end state"	11	14	(7–24%)	13	10	(5–17%)
Acute to mild "end state"	3	4	(1–11%)	2	1.5	(0–5%)
Chronic to mild "end state"	12	15.5	(8–26%)	34	26	(19–35%)
Undulating to severe "end state"	9	12	(5–21%)	10	7	(4–14%)
Undulating to mild "end state"	22	28.5	(19–40%)	34	26	(19–35%)
Undulating to recovery	14	18	(10–29%)	30	23	(16–31%)
Atypical	3	4	(1–11%)	5	4	(1–9%)
Deceased before course was determined	2	2.5	(0–9%)	1	1	(0–4%)
Totals:	77			131[1]		

Figures in parentheses = confidence intervals[1] at 95%, rounded off according to *Documenta Geigy*.

1. Confidence intervals were taken from the tables at $N = 130$, to avoid unnecessary recalculations.

in the study on the siblings of probands.

But we are setting out now not only to check whether schizophrenias occuring among several family members run a different course from those occurring individually, but also another closely related question. Do schizophrenias among close relatives run a similar course? And if they do, do all different course types and "end states" among relatives reveal similar tendencies? Or is it just a few individual cases among them; and if so, which do and which do not run a similar course?

Table 4.23 shows how the courses of schizophrenic relatives of the probands run, in comparison to the courses of the schizophrenic probands themselves. What the table brings out primarily is the fact that in one and the same family different "end states" often occur. Among the schizophrenic relatives of the 20 probands whose "end states" correspond to severe chronic psychoses ("schizophrenic dementia"), there were 5 cases of long-term

recovery and 10 cases with mild "end states." On the other hand, however, among those relatives of probands who recovered, there was no case of outcome to a severe or a moderately severe chronic state. Rather, among the 18 schizophrenic relatives of the 14 probands who recovered from their schizophrenias, there were only complete recoveries (14) and mild "end states" (4) (except for 3 patients who had not reached an "end state" at the end of the observation period).

It is often doubted that the most severe cases of schizophrenia and also recoveries from schizophrenia occur in one and the same family, although there are many instances of it in the literature. Some authors who nosologically separate the severe chronic courses of schizophrenia from the recoveries, discover for themselves that there are among their probands those with both, the most and the least favorable prognoses, although they do believe that this is an exception. But when

Table 4.23. Comparison of "end states" of probands with those of their schizophrenic relatives, i.e., parents, siblings, children, or nephews and nieces. Seventy-seven probands had a total of 108 schizophrenic relatives in this category

"End state" of probands	"End state" of relatives	No.	
Severe "end state" (20 patients)	Severe "end state"	4	
	Moderately severe "end state"	0	
	Mild "end state"	10	
	Recovery	5	
	No "end state" attained	3	Total: 22
Moderately severe "end state" (10 patients)	Severe "end state"	2	
	Moderately severe "end state"	6	
	Mild "end state"	6	
	Recovery	1	
	No "end state" attained	1	
	"End state" undetermined	1	Total: 17
Mild "end state" (27 patients)	Severe "end state"	7	
	Moderately severe "end state"	2	
	Mild "end state"	11	
	Recovery	12	
	No "end state" attained	6	
	"End state" undetermined	2	Total: 40
Recovery (14 patients)	Severe "end state"	0	
	Moderately severe "end state"	0	
	Mild "end state"	4	
	Recovery	14	
	No "end state" attained	3	Total: 21
No "end state" attained (6 patients)	Severe "end state"	0	
	Moderately severe "end state"	0	
	Mild "end state"	0	
	Recovery	5	
	No "end state" attained	3	Total: 8

they do happen to discover such a concurrence of events, they surmise that it is a coincidental combination of two different psychoses. For this reason, it is worthwhile to illuminate in detail a few examples of extremely severe and of favorable courses of schizophrenia occurring within the same families of our present probands. Among these 5 cases are to be mentioned.

Hans F. (Proband 42), born 1880, grew up as the son of an impoverished watchmaker in miserable circumstances. The father had little tolerance for his economic misfortune, and was often depressed. The mother was idealized by the family.

As a child the proband suffered severely with scrofulosis. He had trouble passing his grades in school. Already as a child he was quiet and introverted, and suffered from his compulsion to masturbate. He lacked vitality and was lethargic. When he was 20, he joined the Salvation Army. He did not learn a trade,

but earned his living by door-to-door peddling. In spite of the unfavorable conditions at home, two of his siblings developed splendidly.

Hans became ill in 1904, at age 24, with a subacute onset, hearing voices that accused him of masturbation. He was then hospitalized for the first time over a 10-month period, in 1903/04. There he began to report grotesque physical and other general delusions of depressive content, although he usually was not at all depressive while he talked, but smiled rather indifferently. He thought of himself as the devil who could no longer pray; found that his hands were devoid of blood, and described peculiar experiences in a peculiar way, for instance, that he "had heard people praying for him in church, but that he had run away instead of having his devils exorcised."

Upon his release from the clinic, he reassumed his life as a peddler and an eccentric. For a long time he was not precisely observed by anyone. From 1920–1924, when he was between 40 and 44, and from 1928 to 1933, when he was between 48 and 53 years old, he suffered severe psychotic episodes at the clinic, that were similar to the first episode described above.

After the fourth episode in 1943, at age 63, he never recovered. He was last admitted to a psychiatric clinic after having, in broad daylight, defecated out the window of a general hospital where he had been interned for an indolent leg ulcer. Thereafter, until his death, the syndrome remained uniform. Usually his attitude was rigid and catatonic; he kept repeating the same sayings in stereotype fashion; he indulged himself by finger-painting objects with feces. Intermittently he had onsets of raging anger, during which he struck out brutally at himself or the care personnel. One of his unshakable ideas was that he was immortal. He was placed under care on a ward for severe cases in a psychiatric care institution. In 1951, at age 71, he suddenly and unexpectedly expired. Without any attempt being made to determine the exact cause of death, a "sudden heart failure" was assumed. The severe state of illness, which the clinic had called "schizophrenic dementia," had persisted without interruption for 8 years before his death.

The proband's brother Fritz, 9 years younger, had developed splendidly despite the adverse home background. He became shop foreman in a large plant, was happily married, and raised two healthy, successful daughters. He was an industrious, hard-working, open-minded, and engaging sort of person, although he was excessively "soft-hearted"; that is, he was not resilient to life's vicissitudes, and he showed it. At age 45 he suffered a severe psychosis that lasted several months. He suddenly felt that he was a prophet, and claimed, among other things, to be able to forecast the future of Austria. He clamied to be receiving messages from God about the future of the world. Around 1934 he developed a terrible fear of Hitler. He claimed his family had sold him; one of his acquaintances was the second Lord Jesus; his heart was on fire; the Nazis were concealed about his house; and he mistook the identity of people from his neighborhood in fantastically distorted ways. At times he was depressive in his psychosis, but then again, in spite of his grotesque delusional experiences and delusional ideas of depressive content, he would be quite jolly. The acute severity of his psychosis lasted only a few weeks. When it subsided, he was the way he had been before. At age 72, 27 years later, he died of apoplexy, without any intervening incident of mental illness.

Andreas C. (Proband 8), an Italian, born 1910, grew up under difficult circumstances at home. He is the son of an honest, doughty tailor, who barely managed to make his way by hard work. The family was poor and often close to starvation. Often there were quarrels between the father and the whining mother, who complained constantly about their misery. After emigrating to Switzerland, the family found it had little in common with the existing coustoms and conditions. They felt rejected because of their Italian heritage and suffered constantly under that stigma.

As a child the proband was well behaved, although sad and lonely, and lacking in human contacts. His illness began at age 15 with a lingering development. He continued to grow more apathetic and more shy. He never learned a trade or became employable, but just helped his father with simple chores in his tailoring business. Beginning at age 22 he ceased doing anything at all, just remained mute and inactive in his parents' home, and finally became totally mutistic and remained in bed all day.

In this condition he was admitted to Burghölzli in 1942, at age 32, and became a proband for this project. The prominent syndrome at the time was a stuporous catatonia with mutism. Off and on he again spoke vaguely of hearing voices. Insofar as he could be moved to talk at all, he was distracted, and indicated a persecution mania. He was only minimally activated after 6 months of treatments; after that, his parents asked to have him sent home. In the beginning, he helped a little about the house, but soon relapsed into his former apathetic state.

At age 33 he was rehospitalized at Burghölzli, again for the most part in a state of catatonic stupor. At times, however, he would become excited, noisy, and violent. Insofar as he could be brought to talk, his delusional ideas were much more clearly expressed now than earlier. He claimed he was being persecuted; someone unseen was touching him; he had remained a child. At night he ranted with hallucinated pursuers; he stuffed paper into his ears in order to get rid of the "voices." He felt that his environment was "not natural any more"; he lacked any ability to establish contact.

Soon after his second hospitalization he had

to be transferred to an institution in Italy. At the end of the observation period, when proband was 54, his stay there had lasted for 19 years. He is apathetic, hallucinates frequently, and is considered a completely "demented" schizophrenic.

His older sister had developed better intellectually. She had done well in school, although she usually felt physically fatigued and weak. Her family described her as "nervous"; that is, sensitive and excitable. She worked hard in her parents' tailor shop and was a valuable support to them.

At age 21 she came to the clinic voluntarily for the first time, reporting that suddenly she was indifferent to everything, that she did not care about working, she was no longer a Christian, and that she forgot everything. She claimed that indescribable feelings in her abdomen were taking away all her strength; that she had changed, was not herself any more; that she felt empty; her train of thought was suddenly interrupted; that she no longer had feelings, and that this made her "an old woman."

In the period that followed, a state of negativism developed. She became totally mutistic, grimaced a great deal, and hid herself in the toilet. For a long time she refused food and had to be fed by tube. When she began again to talk a little, she mentioned, among other things, that she "had been in the world forever." After such remarks, she usually fell back again into a stuporous state.

At the clinic there was not a single physician who had the slightest doubt that her diagnosis was that of a typical schizophrenia.

After 6 weeks at the hospital her parents requested to take her home in her stuporous state, and did so against all medical advice.

Once she was home, much to the surprise of everyone, her condition improved rapidly. At the end of the observation period this proband had remained recovered for a total of 34 consecutive years. I personally undertook a check-up examination, and detected nothing psychotic about her. She continues to work as a tailor, earning her living independently. She never married. Of course, her personality had clearly changed since her psychosis. She became somewhat flat emotionally, and is inclined to engage in idle, vacuous chatter.

Her younger sister suffered from tuberculosis as a child and accordingly was placed in a sanatorium. Just like her older sister, she was always considered excitable, but she did maintain good contacts with other girls. After basic schooling, she also worked in her parents' shop. At age 21, 3 years before her illness, she became mildly depressive after a male friend had moved away and had neglected to write to her.

Her severe psychosis erupted peracutely, after her father had become seriously ill physically. A few days after the onset of his illness, the subject came to our clinic and became a proband at age 24. At first she asserted that her father had been poisoned; then, that everything was poisoned. She persisted in assuming peculiarly distorted poses. Without any external reason, she spoke only in indistinct, mumbling tones. Then quickly she passed into a state of most severe catatonic excitation, in which she became intermittently raving mad, struck out all about her, shouted noisily, spat at the doctors and nurses, and was totally deranged in her thought processes. Successively, electroshock, sleep, and fever treatments, and one insulin treatment were carried out. After each set of treatments mild improvements were noted, but none of them were lasting. After the insulin treatments, administered 7 months after first admission, she was released in good condition to go home.

Since then, to the end of the observation period 22 years later, this proband was never again severely psychotic. However, at age 29, 5 years after dismissal from the hospital, we had to treat her again as an outpatient for a reactive depression caused by an extramarital pregnancy. At that time, however, she did not appear to be merely straightforwardly depressive, but rather as confused, emotionally inert, and perpetually amazed. If one was familiar with her first catatonic episode, one would have to assume a mild, subclinical and different schizophrenic phase.

Notwithstanding, she continued to remain mentally well since her dismissal from the clinic, although her personality had changed. She is now garrulous with little emotional modulation, and complains excessively, for example, about the noisy students living in her parents' house. She is working again as a dressmaker now.

Table 4.24 shows the course type in the same way that Table 4.23 shows the "end state." The numbers in this table are small; so small under most headings, in fact, that they really do not signify anything. Statistical significance is never attained; yet, from this table, certain indications may be derived.

The type of disease course that is most in-

Table 4.24. Comparison of course types of probands with those of their schizophrenic relatives, i.e., parents, siblings, children, and nephews and nieces. Seventy-seven probands have a total of 108 such schizophrenic relatives.

Course types of probands	Course types of relatives	No.	
Acute to severe "end state" (1 patient)	Acute to mild "end state"	1	Total: 1
Chronic to severe "end state" (11 patients)	Chronic to severe "end state"	5	
	Acute to mild "end state"	1	
	Chronic to mild "end state"	6	
	Undulating to recovery	4	Total: 16
Acute to mild "end state" (3 patients)	Undulating to mild "end state"	2	
	Undulating to recovery	2	Total: 4
Chronic to mild "end state" (12 patients)	Chronic to severe "end state"	3	
	Chronic to mild "end state"	7	
	Undulating to severe "end state"	1	
	Undulating to mild "end state"	2	
	Undulating to recovery	8	
	Deceased before course was identified	1	Total: 22
Undulating to severe "end state" (9 patients)	Chronic to mild "end state"	3	
	Undulating to mild "end state"	2	
	Undulating to recovery	3	
	Atypical course	1	Total: 9
Undulating to mild "end state" (22 patients)	Chronic to mild "end state"	2	
	Undulating to severe "end state"	3	
	Undulating to mild "end state"	7	
	Undulating to recovery	10	
	Deceased before course was identified	1	
	Atypical course	2	
	Unknown	2	Total: 27
Undulating to recovery (14 patients)	Undulating to mild "end state"	1	
	Undulating to recovery	17	
	Atypical course	1	
	Unknown	1	Total: 20
Atypical course (3 patients)	Acute to severe "end state"	1	
	Chronic to mild "end state"	1	
	Undulating to mild "end state"	2	
	Undulating to recovery	1	Total: 5
Deceased before course was identified (2 patients)	Undulating to recovery	4	Total: 4

clined to be the same within the same family is the "undulating to recovery" type. Of the 208 probands, 77 have schizophrenic close relatives. In 14 of these 77 probands, the course of their schizophrenia runs "undulating to recovery." These 14 probands have in the immediate family 19 schizophrenic relatives for whom we know the course type of their illness; of these 17 also had a course type that ran "undulating to recovery," and those of the 2 others progressed according to types that were related to it.

Among all my probands there were no families with two schizophrenic members, both of whom developed acutely to severe "end states" in one or more surges. Nor were there any families with two schizophrenic members whose disease developed "undulating to severe 'end states'." Among those schizophrenic family relatives of probands, on the other hand, whose schizophrenia proceeded uniformly to most severe chronic states, a few are to be found with the same course type, although of these there are only 5 of 11.

In addition, there are also many different

Table 4.25. Comparison of "end states" among schizophrenic relatives of probands. Included are only relatives of probands related to one another, not probands themselves. For comparison there are 39 possible combinations

"End states" of relatives of the first instance	"End states" of relatives of the second and third instance	No.	
Severe "end state" (5 patients)	Moderately severe "end state"	1	
	Mild "end state"	2	
	Recovery	2	
	No "end state" attained	1	Total: 6
Moderately severe "end state" (4 patients)	Severe "end state"	1	
	Moderately severe "end state"	2	
	Mild "end state"	3	Total: 6
Mild "end state" (7 patients)	Severe "end state"	2	
	Moderately severe "end state"	2	
	Recovery	5	
	No "end state" attained	1	Total: 10
Recovery (12 patients)	Mild "end state"	2	
	Recovery	10	
	No "end state" attained	2	Total: 14
No "end state" attained (2 patients)	Mild "end state"	1	
	Recovery	1	Total: 2
"End state" undetermined (1 patient)	No "end state" attained	1	Total: 1

Table 4.26. Comparison of course types among schizophrenic relatives of probands. Included are only relatives of probands related to one another; not the probands themselves. For comparison there are 39 possible combinations

Course type of relatives of the first instance	Course type of relatives of the second and third instances	No.	
Acute to severe "end state" (1 patient)	Undulating to recovery	1	Total: 1
Chronic to severe "end state" (2 patients)	Acute to mild "end state"	1	
	Chronic to mild "end state"	2	Total: 3
Chronic to mild "end state" (8 patients)	Chronic to severe "end state"	2	
	Chronic to mild "end state"	4	
	Undulating to mild "end state"	1	
	Undulating to recovery	4	Total: 11
Undulating to severe "end state" (2 patients)	Undulating to recovery	2	Total: 2
Undulating to mild "end state" (2 patients)	Chronic to severe "end state"	1	
	Chronic to mild "end state"	2	
	Undulating to mild "end state"	1	Total: 4
Undulating to recovery (14 patients)	Undulating to mild "end state"	2	
	Undulating to recovery	12	
	Deceased before course was identified	2	Total: 16
Deceased before course was identified (1 patient)	Chronic to mild "end state"	1	Total: 1
Unknown (1 patient)	Undulating to recovery	1	Total: 1

varieties of course types occurring in schizo-phrenias in the same family, among them:
—Acute or chronic-uniform to most severe states, and in acute phases to recoveries (4 of these)
—Uniform-chronic to severe chronic state and uniform-chronic to mild chronic state (9 of these), etc.

Up to this point, the schizophrenias of the probands themselves were compared with those of their close relatives. Among the parents, siblings, children, nephews and nieces of 24 of the probands, there is more than 1 additional case of schizophrenia. The com-parisons of schizophrenias of probands them-selves with those of their close relatives will, in what follows, be further supplemented by comparisons between the schizophrenias of two relatives related to each other and, in turn, to the relative of a proband. Eighteen probands have 2 schizophrenic relatives each, 5 have 3, and 1 has 4 schizophrenic relatives. In all, 39 combinations of schizophrenic psychoses occur among the close relatives of probands' relatives. They are shown on Tables 4.25 and 4.26. They fully and com-pletely support the findings from the 77 com-parisons between the probands themselves and their schizophrenic relatives.

Tables 4.25 and 4.26 show specific findings in support of previous data from comparisons of "end states" and course types between two interrelated schizophrenics who are relatives of schizophrenic probands.
—Again cases of schizophrenic psychoses with totally different "end states" are found to occur in one and the same family.
—Again we find several combinations of most severe chronic "end states" and long-term recovery states (2 cases).
—Again we find that several combinations with similar course types among the relatives of schizophrenics most commonly run an "undulating to recovery" type of course (12 of these).
—Again we find not one single incident in which two relatives were both subjected to an "acute (progressing in one or several surges) to most severe chronic state" type of course.
In comparing probands and their relatives there were 19 "chronic to severe 'end states'," in which the same "end state" occurred 5 times in partners who were related. In the comparison to be discussed below, among the relatives of probands' relatives, the corre-sponding figures are 5 and 0. If it were still

feasible, after the above-mentioned set of data, to suspect a tendency toward familial simi-larity in the chronic, most severe courses, the second set of data should invalidate this suspicion, even though these data are too small seriously to refute the assumption.

From the 116 comparisons shown between the schizophrenic psychoses of close relatives, the following conclusions are drawn:
—The most variegated course types and "end states" occur frequently among schizophrenic relatives.
—There is a certain tendency, however, for schizophrenias to run similar courses among relatives.
—Most frequently the phasic types of courses with recovery outcomes tend to repeat them-selves among close schizophrenic relatives.
—On the other hand, two acute types of psychoses proceeding to severe chronic "end states" after single or multiple surges do not occur among close relatives, or do so very rarely (there were none among the probands of this study).

These findings may be generalized without any hesitation, because they occurred not only in this study, but also in a large number of previous ones.

The investigations published in 1941 in-cluded 367 pairs of related schizophrenics. Among the 7 types of courses, 28 different combinations are possible. All these 28 pos-sible combinations of course types actually occurred. Among all the pairs, 261 combina-tions had different, and 106 had similar types of courses. The most frequent among all the combinations were those of 2 phasic types of courses with recovery outcomes (50 in all). On the other hand, there were only 19 com-binations of 2 severe chronic "end states." Among this latter group, those most severe chronic states with an acute onset and pro-ceeding in one single or several surges were particularly rare (they were repeated only 3 times among the 368 pairs of relatives). The most frequent combinations of 2 severe chronic "end states" (16) were those that had been reached by a chronic process.

In another study—on 89 schizophrenics recovered after shock treatment (1941)—the great frequency with which two family-psychoses proceed in phases and time and again progress toward recovery is illustrated with particular clarity. Among 17 schizo-phrenic siblings with long-term recovery records, 12 had recovered after acute-phasic courses.

Among the relatives of late-onset schizophrenics, I likewise discovered (1943) the most variegated forms of schizophrenias.

It ought to be unnecessary to explain that the most variegated course types of schizophrenias are found among the close relatives of schizophrenics. After all, it is a part of the amazing everyday experience of the clinician to find, in the histories of the relatives of schizophrenics, those with a totally different course from the one of his own proband. If it was possible for the concept of schizophrenia, as it was conceived by E. Bleuler (1911) at the turn of the century, to remain relatively unchanged in spite of all the objections and attacks to which it was exposed, then it was particularly so because often different courses of illness were discovered in the same family, that all agreed with that concept. In spite of that, authors even in the most recent studies repeatedly express doubts that acute, benign schizophrenias and the malignant, incurable types have something in common in their nature. In view of these doubts it seemed worthwhile to illuminate the findings about the different courses of schizophrenias in our present probands.

The continuation of the question treated above, however, is one that has had little attention in previous research and literature. It is the question whether among schizophrenic relatives, certain types of courses occur in the same way more frequently than other types. Very rarely has it been noted, up to this time, to how frequently the schizophrenias of the relatives of probands with phasic benign courses, also undergo a phasic benign development. Even less often has attention been given to the fact that, in contrast, the combination of most severe courses among the relatives of schizophrenics is less frequent. No attention at all has been given by other authors to the fact that particularly the acute onsets proceeding in one or more surges to most severe chronic states are extremely rare in two related individuals.

To be sure, the deliberations on which the latter conclusions are based must be critically examined. A familial tendency toward a certain type of course was assumed from the frequency of incidence of one and the same course type in two related individuals. Against this assumption, it might be argued that the frequency of combinations of similar course types in two related individuals does not depend exclusively on a hypothetic familial tendency toward this particular course type.

It depends also on other factors, among them, particularly on how frequently the course type in question occurs at all. If it is frequent, then combinations of that same course type must also be frequent—quite independently of any familial tendency toward the same course type. However, the above considerations were carefully formulated, with this objection in mind. With the given frequencies in the existing probands, the very high incidence of the combination "phasic benign course in both relatives," in contrast to the low incidence of the combination "acutely attained, most severe states of dementia in both relatives," cannot be exclusively ascribed to the mere distribution of the different course types among the probands. In the section on siblings of the probands this relationship will be treated in greater detail.

How are the findings of the above section to be applied to our concept about schizophrenias?

In the first place, they deny that the schizophrenias that run a favorable and those that run an unfavorable course can be separately treated as diseases of a different nature. The concurrence of favorable and unfavorable forms among close relatives is so frequent that the similarity in the nature of these two types of psychoses is an established certainty.[17] This

17. The data assembled here on the course types of schizophrenias among relatives coincide with experiences of the clinical subtypes of schizophrenias among relatives, as they have been recorded for decades. That is, that among relatives of patients who suffer from one of the subtypes of schizophrenia (catatonic, hebephrenic, or paranoid), there are frequent occurrences of all the other of these subtypes. The family studies thus confirm the theory that all these clinical subtypes have some kind of close genetic relationship. Despite this, the tendency persists to combine one and the same subtype in the relatives of schizophrenics. Schulz (1933), who had earlier published some meticulously detailed studies on this subject, reports among other things: "If we check whether there is a relationship between the clinical subgroups of the secondary cases and those of the corresponding groups of probands, we find here a positive correlation in the three pure groups" (the intended meaning here is the purely catatonic, hebephrenic, and paranoid subtypes) ... "Furthermore, however, it seems that ... there are more schizophrenics with any given subtype among the siblings of schizophrenics with any of the given subtypes than there are among the siblings of normals; for example, there will be more cases of catatonia among the siblings of hebephrenics than among the siblings of normals ..." These findings have often

similarity had first occurred to E. Bleuler (1911) in a different way over half a century ago through his researches in psychopathology. He was the first to emphasize that the psychopathology of benign and malignant schizophrenias could not be differentiated. The conclusion of this psychopathological research is confirmed in the studies of the families of his schizophrenic probands.

The most widely different "end states" and course types combine in so many different ways among closely related schizophrenics that it is justifiable to state that the "group of schizophrenias," as it was diagnostically described at the beginning and as it is still described in many clinics, are actually a collection of psychoses that are internally related.

By the application of the term "dementia praecox," Kraepelin (1899) suggested the idea that the "dementia" was something intrinsic to the occurrence of schizophrenia, that it might be, in a sense, the "core-syndrome." A number of schools subscribe to that concept to the present day. Many surmised in addition, that just this "core-syndrome" in particular was hereditary and immune to external influences. E. Bleuler (1911) took the opposite stand. He had found so many possibilities of social and psychotherapeutic influences among "demented" schizophrenics, that the progress-toward-idiocy concept for schizophrenics simply did not appear to him to be the quintessence of the disease course. He conceived of the "development toward dementia" as being a secondary development, in which a vicious circle between the patient's behavior and the reactions of his environment plays the principal role. The results of the family studies stand in sharp, virtually indisputable contrast to the old concept that a hereditary progress toward idiocy was the central disturbance in actual schizophrenias, and that the benign schizophrenias were primarily only pseudo-schizophrenias, that is, exogenous psychoses. "Dementia" in particular is poorly represented among families. Much rather decisive familial causes are to be presumed, particularly in the benign phasic types of schizophrenias. If the schizophrenias of close relatives develop according to the same course types, it is in the vast majority of cases the type that runs "in phases to final recovery."

The most severe chronic states (dementias), however, do have different relationships to familial or individual causes, according to the course of the disease. The severe chronic "end states" that emerge from one or several acute phases can hardly have familial causes. It is precisely these forms of dementia, then, that depend on external influences. They are the very ones in which it can be expected that incorrect treatment would favor their genesis and that, with correct treatment, they would not even get started. In contrast, internal, familial influences are more likely to be implicated in the development of those severe chronic states that develop chronically and proceed steadily. These conclusions from the findings described in the foregoing section correspond exactly to those from a totally different set of observations described elsewhere.[18]

Course of Illness and Death of Father or Mother

Is the course of schizophrenic psychoses influenced by the major events that make up the tragic milestones in the course of a life, such as the serious illness or death of close relatives, loss of a job or the means of earning a living, loss of status of the family, or the disruption of a marriage? Surely every clinician has concerned himself with this question and has come to approximately the same conclusion on the basis of his experience. For the most part, such events take place without any timely or otherwise recognizable causal relationship to the onset, the improvement, the recovery, or the dramatic aggravation of the disease. But every clinician has also experienced exceptions to this pattern. He is well aware of dramatic changes in the psychotic manifestation in relation to severe mental stresses, and he is amazed how unpredictably, sometimes an onset or an aggravation, sometimes a recovery or an improvement will follow such stresses. If he knows his patients. he could easily construct a psychological novel around the theme of why one and the same event in the life of a patient can cause the eruption or the aggravation of his schizophrenia in one, and the recovery from his schizophrenia in

---

been comfirmed, and they correspond with my own as well. For this reason it was not necessary to undertake new investigations on this question for this project.

18. It has already been explained in this chapter that, very probably, the most severe acute cases proceeding toward dementia can be avoided by good therapeutic intervention.

another. But this experience has made him humble, and he would not be so presumptious as to regard his psychological explanation as infallible. To wit, he would not dare to predict how one patient or another might react in the future to a given unusual event. If he were to succumb to making such "prophecies," he would frequently later on have to admit his error.

The clinician must smile indulgently at any attempts to attach new data to his own experiences through "statistics." He knows well that nothing much can come of that. Even now I have to smile at myself, because I too, despite this, used to count. Nor could I resist the temptation to look at the ready-made data on the long-term courses of my 208 probands in terms of figures in this respect. The result is modest. But perhaps it is worthwhile anyway to communicate some of the figures discovered.

Among those strokes of fate that lend themselves to numerical reckoning, the first to be considered is the death of a parent. The applicable figures follow.

	Fathers	Mothers
Known:	204	208
Unknown (extramarital):	4	0
At the end of observation period:		
Living	17	30
Deceased	187	178
Dead long before proband's illness	89	65
Died shortly before or during proband's first onset	4	5
Died after proband's illness began	94	108

In 34 cases there was a close time relationship between major changes in the proband's mental condition and the death of one of his parents, so that a causal relationship might be suspected. Table 4.27 gives an overview, broken down by sex.

Possibly these figures do supplement, after all, what is already common knowledge from clinical experience, particularly the fact that

relationships between the courses of illness and the vicissitudes of life are more frequent among female than among male schizophrenics. The proportion among our probands is 9:25. The finding agrees with previous ones, according to which the loss of a parent or living at home with a psychotic parent or stepparent occurs more often in the childhood of girls who become schizophrenic than in that of boys who become schizophrenic. The relationship to parents seems to play a more important role in the occurrence of schizophrenia in women than it does in men.

The discovery that after the loss of a parent a decline is more frequent than an improvement in the proband's condition supports the expectations from clinical experience. However, I could not from general clinical experience have answered the question whether a change in the proband's condition might more often be expected after the loss of a father than after the loss of a mother. Theoretically one might have surmised that the loss of a father would be more detrimental to the social and economic position of the family, and for that reason would also have a greater influence on the state of mental well-being of its members. But among the present group of probands, the loss of mothers more frequently affected the course of illness.

It would be simple to state in figures the statistical significance of the comparisons under discussion, but we were not given precise figures anyway. The onset of the disease, improvement, or aggravation, cannot be fixed precisely in time; and it is even less feasible to delimit the significant or insignificant modifications in a proband's state of health. Given these uncertainties in the figures, the attempted comparisons surely cannot have any statistical significance. They may be accepted merely as indications, but can never be applied as statistical proof.

It was exciting to pursue the question of whether it would be possible to detect the individual reaction to parent loss from the individual psychological makeup of each patient. First, let us briefly evaluate the improve-

Table 4.27. Change in mental condition after parent loss, broken down by sexes

Condition after	Death of father		Death of mother		Total
	Improved	Deteriorated	Improved	Deteriorated	
Male probands	0	3	1	5	9
Female probands	1	10	5	9	25
Totals:	1	13	6	14	34

ments.

The patient history of Eduard S. (Proband 2) has already been referred to in this chapter as an example of improvement after a course of decades. When his mother died, he had already lived on his parents' farm for 23 years as a schizophrenic eccentric. He had always had a good ralationship with his mother. After her death, his condition improved markedly, although nothing else in his daily life had changed. It is possible to assume that his pathological autism had become stereotyped in the family relationships. Perhaps his mother's attitude is partly to blame for this, because she regarded her son's condition as the result of his overexertion while in the military service on border patrol duty, and consequently (although to a mild degree), similar to a combat injury. After her death, the son's "duty" to play the part of the wounded soldier ceased, and the shock of her death was in itself a motivation to relinquish his stereotypic behavior.

A psychologically convincing line of reasoning for the improvement of Alwine M. (Proband 8) after the death of her mother emerges from her patient history. Between ages 22 and 43, Alwine suffered 6 acute, severe psychotic schizophrenic episodes. In the interim periods her personality had been plainly altered by schizophrenia. Immediately following her 6th psychotic episode, when she was 43, her mother died. In the 10 years that followed, until the end of the observation period, the proband had no more acute psychotic episodes, and her condition was markedly better than it had been for the preceding 21 years. Alwine's father, a lathe hand and truck farmer, was an eccentric, respected in the neighborhood, but a terror in the family. He drank heavily, was taciturn and mean, and slowly developed a state of senile dementia in which he became even more difficult than he had been for 21 years before. The formerly nonaberrant, cheerful mother gradually grew slowly embittered with her marriage, became tyrannical, and contracted a functional heart ailment and a colitis ulcerosa, which became aggravated by the prevailing emotional tensions in the home. The marriage produced 4 daughters and no sons; only 1 of Alwine's sisters managed to escape the depressing family milieu, at age 22, when she became happily married and subsequently raised 9 children. The other 3 daughters— one of them Alwine—continued to suffer miserably under the depressing conditions at home, but made only inadequate attempts to extricate themselves from it.

One of these sisters remained unmarried at home, was moody and obsessive-compulsive, deteriorated completely with respect to her own life interests, and, as her mother had, contracted colitis ulcerosa. The second sister became the tyrant in the home and continually nagged and tormented Alwine and her illegitimate child. She got married, and naturally should have wanted to leave the family; instead, she married an invalid whom she took into the home. A third sister suffered a depression. She married an eccentric, who cared little about her and barely made a living, so that he also had to live with her in the parental home. Alwine herself was constantly torn between an exaggerated loyalty to her mother and dramatic, although totally futile attempts to escape from the family. She was afraid of her father, loved her mother, and—even after she was fully grown —suffered miserably from homesickness when she left the family. In a fit of indignation she finally did make plans to leave the home for good and to marry, although the prospective groom was an alcoholic. As she had expected, her parents disapproved and refused their permission. She accepted that decision, but then became pregnant by another alcoholic, where there was no possibility of a marriage. Now she was doomed to live in her parents' home with her illegitimate child. For years she was looked upon as the disobedient, sinful daughter, who was supposed to show gratitude for being tolerated by her parents. In this general situation Alewine's schizophrenic illness ran its course for many years. When her illness became more severe, her mother's colitis and heart neurosis became aggravated, and vice versa. Alwine's psychosis and her mother's illnesses progressed in close time-relationships. With the death of her mother, the primary source of Alwine's emotional tension was gone. She had no more acute psychotic episodes, and her chronic schizophrenic state improved to such a degree that I might well have included her among the "recovered" patients. When she was 49, she married and, although her husband is debilitated, she is living with him in a satisfactory marriage.

The patient history of Esther B. (Proband 22) has also been described earlier, as an example of characterizing the premorbid personality "schizoid-aberrant." She was the only daughter of rather elderly parents. On the one hand, her mother expected her to support her parents in their old age, and on the other, she kept her daughter tied to her apron strings and pampered her like a small child. The same ambivalence was reflected in Esther's psychosis: On the one hand, she had ideas of persecution and personal harm toward her mother (and later toward her physicians), and on the other, she did everything possible to remain dependent on her mother (and later on her physicians). After her mother's serious illness of cerebral sclerosis, and after the mother's death, a clear improvement took place in Esther's mild chronic schizophrenic state that had persisted for years. In this case an assumption similar to the one for Alwine M. (see above) suggests itself, namely, that her psychosis developed in connection with the irreconcilable ambivalence and ambitendency in respect to her mother, and in her psychosis this ambitendency dilemma became manifest in her delusions. After the death of her mother, the psychotic process was deprived of something that might possibly be called its "field of action."

In connection with the psychological situation, the improvement of Anna K. (Proband 25) after her mother's death is particularly impressive. Her father was a farmer's son from a simple, respectable family. He is the village constable, a quiet, content, agreeable man of pyknic proportions. His wife, Anna's mother, was the daughter of a degenerate alcoholic, who together with his wife, Anna's maternal grandmother, had committed double suicide after a business failure. Anna's mother had always been given to quarreling, hysterics, and incessant nagging. Her difficult personality finally led to a separation, when Anna was 9 years old, and later to a divorce. From then on Anna was totally dependent on her pathological mother. She turned into a superficial, insensitive girl, lacking in human warmth, independence, and initiative, and had to be evaluated as a schizoid psychopath. After her parents were divorced, when Anna was 11, both mother and daughter developed a psychosis, in the form of a "folie-à-deux." First the mother became ill, developing delusions of quarreling and persecution at first against her former husband, then against official agencies and doctors, and then delusions of grandeur, feeling that she was capable of doing anything, writing poetry or painting, that she had been spiritualized, and that she was outstanding in every respect. She was 39 at the time, and she never recovered from her paranoid schizophrenia. She died at age 72. Against the background of a chronic manic psychosis, 3 more acute episodes with distraction developed. Shortly after her mother's onset, Anna suffered a depression; then she slowly ceased to be critical of her mother's delusions. Many years later she suffered an acute onset of a severe catatonic episode accompanied by total distraction, hallucinations, and delusions. Until her mother died, when Anna was 44, she was admitted temporarily on 17 different occasions to psychiatric hospitals for such acute exacerbations, where she became the terror of all the nurses because of her excessively violent behavior. She suffered through a number of other acute episodes at home. During the interim periods she was outwardly calm, but shared her mother's delusions. Shortly after her mother's death, Anna suffered 2 more mild acute episodes, and since then, for the past 3 years, she has been living outside a clinic, is able to earn her living, and has improved markedly. The death of her paranoid mother, who had induced the illness in the daughter, had brought about the improvement.

Manuela E. (Proband 52) is the daughter of a man with many dramatic social successes and failures. His father had been in the civil service, and he became a businessman with a number of different enterprises, vacillating abruptly between wealth and such poverty that his family often went hungry. From his first marriage he had two sons; both of them went to college, but both committed suicide. His second wife, an internationally known dancer, was Manuela's mother. For a long time this family had no home, but lived in hotels as they travelled from one city to another. Manuela is the youngest of 4 children from the second marriage. She was terribly pampered by her mother but, in turn, unmercifully tormented by her envious sister. Manuela never had sufficient schooling, partly because the family was constantly on the move, with no permanent home, and partly because she was a sickly child. She was totally dependent on her mother, incapable of independent thought or action. She became subacutely ill at age 23 and has not recovered since; at the end of the observation period she was 54. Her psychosis began with a pathological moodishness and violent behavior toward her mother. Then her course became variegated and changeable. Often Manuela was manic-like and distracted, then again stuporous, and again extremely excitable and violent. Along with other delusional ideas, she often claimed that she was a princess, and actually she had mockingly been called a princess by her sister because her mother was pampering her. After major somatic treatments there were usually marked improvements in her condition. Frequently her mother would have her released from the hospital to come home, against the advice of her physicians. She had been hospitalized on 32 different occasions, and released a total of 31 times. When she was at home, quarrels and physical violence generally broke out again between her and her mother. Sometimes Manuela made feeble attempts to take a job, but most of them faltered quickly. Among other things she had attempted door-to-door selling, serving as a waitress, as a housemaid, and at times she had worked as a prostitute. During the last years of the observation period she remained hospitalized. After the death of her mother, when Manuela was 40, was the first time a temporary marked improvement in her condition had occurred. A few years later that improvement became lasting, and during the past 9 years she has been outwardly normal and on a ward for mild cases. Her condition since then has been evaluated as a mild chronic schizophrenic state. From her childhood on, Manuela had been totally dependent on her mother and was raised under completely unnatural circumstances. Her psychosis developed (and propagated itself) as a running argument with her mother. After the death of her mother, at first a temporary, then much later, a final considerable improvement set in.

In the case of Vera R. (Proband 82), neither the correlation of the improvement after the death of her mother, nor its psychological interpretation are quite as convincing as they are in the above cases. Between her schizophrenic onset at age 17 until the end of the observation period, when she was 58, the patient suffered through numerous schizophrenic episodes, some manic-like, some more depressive, and then again catatonic ones. She was hospitalized 17 times, but other episodes occurred at home also. During the intervals of widely varying duration, she never quite recovered in the latter years. She lost her mother at age 23 during a severe psychotic episode. When she first received news of her mother's death, she was firmly convinced in her delusion that it was a lie. Five days thereafter, however, she seemed to realize the truth of the matter and fell into a healthy state of

grief about it. Shortly thereafter she recovered from the psychotic episode.

Vera had lost her father when she was 5. Her mother, a doughty and loving woman, raised her 5 children (plus a 6th one who died at age 6) from her skimpy earnings as a midwife in a remote valley. Vera was the youngest, and had suffered a serious cranial injury when she fell while herding sheep, had a hard time keeping up in school, and had to be cared for by her mother. Her first psychotic episode had developed like a schizophrenic reaction, when Vera suffered through a pregnancy phobia during an unhappy love affair, and came into conflict with her mother. It is certain that she had been very close to her mother for many years, and it is probable that ambivalently she also regarded her mother as an obstacle to her love life. However, this is merely a speculative indication as to the causal effect of the death in bringing about a recovery from one single acute-psychotic episode, that probably suggests itself by the timely coincidence of the two events.

Agnes I (Proband 63) is the only one among the 208 probands who showed a marked improvement after the death of a father. Her schizophrenia had begun acutely when she was 18, and had run a course of several highly psychotic episodes between which only mild psychotic symptoms persisted. After Agnes had lost her father, at age 38, the course of her disease was mild for the next 15 years, that is, to the end of the observation period. Agnes's father had walked with a limp since childhood, the result of an accident. He was a mechanic, but had to be satisfied with modest jobs, since he lacked the self-confidence and initiative to make an effort to improve himself. But he expressed his dissatisfaction all the more around the home. Particularly during the onset of Agnes's mental illness he indulged in depressive moodiness and outbursts of violent anger. He tortured his wife, who had brought two illegitimate children into the marriage from previous affairs with other men, with accusations about this "family disgrace." On the whole, he showed little concern for his family. He showed them kindness only ofter he had mistreated them in a state of drunkenness and his conscience happened to plague him the next day. The proband's mother came from a miserable family background, and had twice become pregnant before her marriage. After marriage she became a hard-working, industrious homemaker and a loving, warm-hearted mother. She bore up stoically under her husband's slanderous invectives, even though she suffered under them inwardly. Agnes grew up as a well-liked, happy, and friendly child, although her intelligence was below average and she had a hard time getting through school. For years she had to take pneumothorax treatments for pulmonary tuberculosis. As a young girl she was the prettiest of her sisters, enjoyed going to dances, found great pleasure in pretty dresses, and was smitten with a number of movie actors. She never did have a happy relationship with a young man. She had a job in a watch factory. From age 13 and for the next 10 years, until her psychosis erupted, she had to share her room with her older catatonic half-sister. At times this half-sister was in a stupor, and then again she hallucinated for nights on end, which was terribly disturbing to Agnes. Agnes had been planning to emigrate to America just before her psychosis began. At the outset this psychosis appeared to be merely a "schizophrenic reaction"; the prognosis was good. It seems she had received all sorts of hocus-pocus treatment from a charlatan to whom she had turned to cure a tubercular anal fistula. This quack sexually abused her in appalling fashion, forcing her to allow him and his friends to touch her. He frightened her with the treat that spirits would drive her crazy if she mentioned anything about what had happened. In this situation Agnes first became frightened and wept a lot. She expressed thoughts of having sinned, and then became confused and agitated. In the hospital she behaved childishly, screamed, and urinated in the room. She felt she was hypnotized, and hallucinated vividly. At times she acted like a dog and bit the nurses, saying she had to sleep in a kennel. Then again she became sexually uninhibited and exhibited her nude body. Soon a marked improvement set in, although she never fully recovered from her psychosis. The later acute episodes were usually—but not always—preceded by recognizable emotional stresses, such as a re-encounter with the quack, the surgical cure of her fistula, etc. When the acute episodes were beginning, she launched forth in violent accusations against her parents and her older siblings. During the intervening periods of calm her prejudicial ideas remained, and she suffered recurrent depressive or spitefully malicious moods.

Gradually the oldest brother, who had done a great deal to care for the family, assumed the father role toward her and cared for her devotedly. Repeatedly she suffered aggravations of her mental condition when this brother had to be away because of illness or vacations. Conditions within the family continued to be peculiar and agonizing for everyone involved. The family suffered under the father's personality, under the oppressive enslavement the older half-sisters imposed on the younger sisters, under the fact that the husband of one of these half-sisters was sexually molesting his sisters-in-law, and under the further fact that there were two mental patients (Agnes and one of her half-sisters) in the family to be cared for. Despite all this, the family held together, and its members helped one another as much as they could. All of Agnes's siblings made something of themselves, and one brother even completed a college education, the expenses of which were largely borne by his siblings. But all of them later became embittered people, depressive, moody, and insecure within themselves.

Agnes's father died when she was 38, 15 years after the onset of her psychosis. From that time on, her psychosis became milder; she began working again in a watch factory, and her brother looks after her properly. Every year for about a month she becomes continuously moody, rails or weeps, is afraid to be left alone, laughs without apparent cause, and talks to herself. It is not hard to imagine why the death of her father had a beneficial influence on Agnes's schizophrenia. There had been an obviously intense ambivalence in that her father, who should have been the head of a closely integrated family community, had totally failed in that task. The paternal duties he should have fulfilled for Agnes were, in effect, taken over by her brother. For this reason, the father had become superfluous; he was just in the way. It is also probable that the blind trust Agnes had placed in the vulgar quack also stemmed from a need for paternal protection, and that her later justified repugnance for this man, in turn, was in part transferred to her father. Certain, however, is the intense ambivalence of Alice toward her father, whom she often wanted to leave, but to whom she continued to remain tied at least externally as she had always been. His death removed the worst thorn of this ambivalence.

By scanning through the patient histories, the psychological situation in which the death of a parent is followed by the patient's improvement from a schizophrenic psychosis does reveal itself rather clearly. In these cases there is an exceptionally strong tie to that father or mother, although it is fraught with an agonzing ambivalence. In the psychotic experience the patient is in a constant state of conflict with this stressful relationship. With the death of the parent who is the source of this love-hate conflict, that long inner conflict seems to have been deprived of its principal nourishing soil.

The great majority of those patients, however, whose condition became aggravated in a close time-relationship with the death of a parent, were in a quite different psychological relationship with their parents. These patients were internally, externally, and in every other respect intensely dependent on the parent who died. The parent's death left them unsteady and unprotected—and sometimes, even, without security for their existence—as lonely and forsaken creatures in the world. Often these were people whose character development was already stunted prior to the eruption of their schizophrenic psychosis, whose interests were limited, and who were by nature helpless and wholly dependent on others. Many of them had been half-orphans, and their situation was aggravated by the death of the remaining parent who had raised them. Often their psychosis began with an apathetic self-negligence that led to total neglect and deterioration. In that situation, or a similar one in varying manifestations is where 22 of the 27 patients found themselves, whose condition had worsened after the death of their father or mother. It is not feasible to describe all 22 of these cases individually, but 5 have been selected as examples and are described below:

Züse R. (Proband 86) is the daughter of a truck farmer, who worked extremely hard under near-poverty conditions to make ends meet for his family of 10 children. He was a strict disciplinarian, but at the same time religious, honest, and righteous. He occupied some of his time praying for the sick and bedridden. The mother was equally industrious and unselfish. In addition to its poverty, the family was pursued by misfortune, in that 2 of the 10 children died during early childhood, and 2 more during their youth. From the very beginning, Züse's intelligence had been below average, but she was not retarded or feebleminded. Her nature was gregarious, always friendly, and willing to help others. Only once was she seriously in love with a young man, and he jilted her. She never got over it but continued to mourn his loss for a

long time. She had not learned a trade, and worked only sporadically in factories and in other people's households. Otherwise she continued to live at home and help with the farm chores. She was 21 when her mother died, and Züse immediately took over the mother's position in the family. Her younger sister, who had remained well, also stayed at home, but she worked independently as a dressmaker. Züse now relinquished all personal interests and dedicated herself completely to the tasks in the household and the care of her aging father. The older sister worked outside the home as a housekeeper and became schizophrenic, and the 3 brothers followed in their father's footsteps, took on small farms, and worked excessively hard to wrest a bare living from them. When Züse was 40, her father, whose household had occupied her entire existence, died at age 83. According to her own description, she was in a state of confusion after her father's death, and in her confusion, managed to relate his death to an imaginary transgression of her own. She could never rid herself of such thoughts, but the actual psychosis did not begin until $1\frac{1}{2}$ years later, when she indulged in sudden outbursts of weeping and lamenting that could not be stopped. She developed massive delusions of persecution and sinful transgressions. At times she was stuporous. Her illness, diagnosed as a catatonia, lasted over a year, with one brief interruption; then Züse recovered again. She ascribed her illness entirely to the loss of her father.

She then went to live with one of her brothers, where she remained for 20 years, as withdrawn from life as she had been before. Although she kept house for her brother and worked like a slave for him in the household, she received almost no wages for her labors. Finally she decided to move away and take a job for wages. While preparing for such a move, she fell ill again with a most severe psychosis. She was 64 at the time. From this psychosis she never recovered; it persisted for the next 14 years, until she died. In all these years she had been the very picture of misery, sitting around slumped over, often in a stuporous state, and had to be tube-fed. She lacked any ability for human contact. Between her spells of silence she ranted and railed at everyone, asserting that her siblings "were at fault for all the misery in the world." When she was released on probation for home care to members of her family, she attacked her sister-in-law with a hatchet. At other times she would plead to be beheaded, or complained, insisting that her parents had been buried alive. In between, there were always days in which she appeared lucid, fully conscious, and almost nonaberrant. All therapeutic efforts that were attempted were in vain, including electroshock, chlorpromazine, and reserpine cures. Her psychosis was included among those 9 cases for which some schools would have diagnosed not a schizophrenia, but rather a depressive catatonic mixed psychosis. In her final years, Züse also contracted glaucoma. She died in a state of marasmus of pneumonia and multiple pulmonary embolisms. Until she was 40, she had oriented her entire life toward the care of her father's household and had allowed all other interests to wither away completely. After her father died, her life lacked substance, and in this situation she suffered her first onset of illness. A clear indication that there is some sort of relationship between this first onset and her life situation may be derived from her situation at the time of her second onset. At that time, to be sure, she lost no one by death, but for good reasons she had decided to leave her brother, for whom she had worked for a period of 20 years, similarly to the way in which she had worked for her father earlier. She was so completely integrated with housekeeping and her related duties to it, that the separation from her brother was to her something like a plunge into the bottomless void of the unknown.

Gotthilf H. (Proband 41) was a frightened, modest, and upright man, who suffered through 6 episodes of schizophrenia with manic features between the ages of 38 and 53. He had grown up under truly gruesome circumstances as the son of a frightfully brutal, pugnacious alcoholic, given to fits of excessive jealousy. His mother had brought up 6 children with a maximum of effort and ability; 2 others had died in early childhood. While the proband had always felt rejected by his father (and justifiably so), he revered and loved his mother (again, with justification) in spite of her somewhat rough-hewn nature. When she died, he was 48 years old and was in the midst of a full remission after a psychotic episode. Shortly thereafter he became pathologically unstable emotionally and began to hallucinate. In particular, he saw flowers in the eyes of his dead mother. Six months later a new acute psychotic episode erupted. It is easy to imagine why the death of his mother was an especially shocking

event in the life of this man, and why he idealized his mother in his schizophrenic experience.

Zoe A. (Proband 3) comes from an exceptionally unfortunate family background. Her father committed suicide after his construction business had declined and he had succumbed to alcoholism. Before he ended his life, he had also suffered from aphasia. A statement by one of the relatives aptly summarizes the conditions prevailing in the family: "He was brought to disaster by his wife, who had lied to him, telling him she was rich; then had piled up debts on him. He was the 'best son-of-a-gun ever,' who just led the life of a martyr around his wife." When he died, Zoe was 26. Zoe's mother lived in high style, accumulated a lot of debts, and actually was a swindler as well. She gradually became disorderly, completely confused, and distracted in her thinking, so that Zoe's doctors, who had to have dealings with her, at times thought of her as being schizophrenic. She herself, however, was never hospitalized or examined psychiatrically, so that I must not include her among the definite schizophrenics. Zoe herself, who had no siblings, was constantly exposed to the everlasting quarrels and bickerings of the parents when she was a child, and had to experience with them the gross changes between high-level standards and actual privation. She became an extremely withdrawn, introverted young girl. Occupationally she was successful and worked in well-paid office jobs. In the quarrels between her parents she was wholly on the mother's side. During her mother's illness she remained totally dependent on her and turned a deaf ear to her shortcomings. She had one major love affair, but her suitor, unable to cope with the mother's personality, dissolved the relationship. Shortly thereafter she made a dangerous suicide attempt. Her father's death did not noticeably affect her. Between ages 29 and 32, she passed through 2 brief but violent episodes of paranoid confusion. After her mother's death she became ill a third time, at age 33. In the 21 years that have elapsed since then, she has never recovered. Zoe has remained on a ward for severe cases. Usually she is mutistic.

After Zoe had recovered from 2 schizophrenic episodes, she became ill a third time after her mother died, and remained severely ill for the rest of her life. From her childhood on, she had been completely oriented toward her mother in all her interests, and in spite—

or possibly because—of her mother's pathological personality, completely dependent on her. The only attempt to break that tie to her mother by marriage was frustrated specifically by her mother's personality. After her mother died, Zoe stood alone in the world, isolated from all other human contacts and all interests. In this situation she became permanently ill.

The situation was somewhat different in the case of Hans K. (Proband 29), whose prepsychotic life has already been described as an example of a horrible childhood. He was continually tormented and abused most cruelly by a tyrannical father and, on the very day of his father's death, suffered the onset of a severe, long-term illness. He claimed to hear his deceased father knocking at his door, felt even more obligated toward him than he had been when his father was alive (his father had constantly reminded him of Hans's debt to him), and felt that he was to be killed. His father, who actually had persecuted him while he was alive, persecuted him after his death in the guise of a phantom. This too was a manifestation of a pathological dependence on his father, although Hans was not bound to him by any bond of love, but by a bond of terrible fear.

Lena I. (Proband 7) developed her 4th severe schizophrenic phase of illness in connection with the death of her father. She was not bound to her father by love either, but by economic necessity. Her home life had been miserable. Her father was an alcoholic, who tyrannized over his family and was morose and embitted about his failures in life. Her mother, the daughter of a criminal, had grown up working outside her home as a hired girl on contract. She was a semi-invalid with a clubfoot, who suffered her lot in silence, but exuded no sort of human warmth. Lena grew up with an attitude of opposition to both her parents. She had a quick temper and a sharp tongue, but before she became ill had been communicative, happy, and full of original ideas. She did sewing for wages at home, where she soon assumed the leading role, completely bypassing her mother in decisions affecting the household. She permitted no interference from her parents, railed at her mother when she was not clean enough, and plainly reversed the usual mother-daughter relationship. When her father died, she was 32, had suffered 3 acute schizophrenic episodes since the age of 18, and had never fully recovered from the 3rd of these. Now she

expressed a terrible fear of becoming dependent on her siblings, with whom she did not get along at all. Her fear was justified. In this situation her 4th severe schizophrenic episode erupted. She virtually recovered from this and the following onset, but from her 6th acute episode she developed a severe chronic schizophrenic state that lasted for 20 years, to the very end of the observation period.

In 5 additional probands of the 27 whose condition deteriorated after the death of a parent, one would hardly claim a very special dependency on the deceased father or mother. The psychological relationships between the experiencing of the death and the deterioration of the patient's condition seem to be different, or else can scarcely be guessed at.

The connection between the onset of the schizophrenic psychosis in the case of Germaine Q. (Proband 27) and the death of her mother was something quite unexpected. For Germaine had become totally estranged from her mother from earliest childhood. Her mother contracted tuberculosis when Germaine was still a small child, and for that reason was absent from the home a great deal. When Germaine was 7, a schizophrenia began its lingering development in the mother, and from the time Germaine was 14, her mother was almost continually hospitalized for her psychosis. The situation in the home in the interval between the mother's hospitalization for tuberculosis and her hospitalization for schizophrenia, before Germaine was 14, was described to us as follows: "The mother often ran away from home ... especially at night ... flirted with the laborers to the point where she became a laughing stock ... ranted, using the coarsest language imaginable, if someone tried to hold her back ... threatened she would leave for good ... didn't care a thing about her two children ... pestered the neighbors day and night ... threatened to kill people ... put scraps of paper on the windows to keep out bad odors...." Relatives reported that "Germaine virtually brought herself up, so to speak, since her mother was always in hospitals." Nevertheless, her father, a businessman, was a kind man and concerned about her. Originally Germaine had been a happy child, but she began to withdraw after her mother's illness began. She had learned to be a seamstress, but did not work at that occupation; instead, she managed the household for her father and her only brother, a schizoid psychopath. The same year that her mother died at a psychiatric clinic, in a state of total

idiocy, Germaine developed a chronic schizophrenia that began as a paranoia. It began
with hallucinatory altercations with a delusional lover. The progression of her psychosis
was slow and uniform, to a most severe chronic
schizophrenic state that has persisted to the
very end of the observation period, that is,
for 21 years. It is marked primarily by apathy,
mutism, and personal uncleanliness; at times
the mutism is interrupted by senseless, unprovoked screaming. Is it permissible to apply
psychology in this case? Is it admissible to
assume that Germaine had suffered guilt
feelings at her mother's death, after she had
been forced to take her mother's place when
she had not really accepted her as a mother
even in childhood? Or are the concurrent
events of her beginning schizophrenia in the
same year that her mother died a mere coincidence? Perhaps these questions cannot be
answered.

Discussion

The findings reported in the preceding
section were compiled in connection with the
old and important question: Do events of
severe traumatic psychological impact have
an influence on the emergence or the course
of schizophrenic psychoses? How often, to
what degree, in what sense, and under what
circumstances? The time-relationships between the deaths of parents and changes in
the patient's condition seem to warrant attention in a discussion of this topic.

Our 208 probands had lost a total of 211
parents either immediately before or after the
beginning of their illness. In 34 cases a time-
relationship was discernible with the onset,
an aggravation or an improvement of, or a
recovery from their psychosis. It could not be
expected from the outset that the death of a
parent would have any connection whatsoever
with the change of condition in most of the
schizophrenic probands. Everyday clinical
experience alone thus excludes any marked
influence of such a parent loss. Most schizophrenics experience the onset, improvements,
setbacks, or recoveries while both their parents remain alive. For most of the probands
the onset of schizophrenic illness did not show
any definite reaction to the death of either
parent. The fact that such a reaction was,
after all, observed in 34 cases primarily confirms again only the same everyday clinical
experience according to which one is occasionally surprised to find a change in the course of
illness after a death in the family.

Based on the figures alone, the incidence of
34 changes in the course of illness among 211
parent losses might well be a coincidence. I
was tempted to compile a set of figures on the
phenomenon, but soon had to give it up. The
relation in time between a particular happening and the onset of illness, the data on the
onset of illness, the degree of change in the
condition, etc. can at best be only inaccurately
assessed. To develop precise figures on these
could be done only arbitrarily, and would
feign a degree of precision that was nonexistent.

The question as to whether there might be
not only a timely, but also a causal relationship between the loss of a parent and the
schizophrenic event, cannot really be proved
by figures, but only by psychological examination of each individual case.

Such examinations have led to certain conclusions. Improvements in a schizophrenic
psychosis have usually occurred when the
proband was dominated by a highly affect-
laden ambivalence toward the deceased, and
when this ambivalence also played a major
role in the psychotic experience. One might
assume that in such cases the death of the
parent released the internal tension, depriving the psychosis of the necessary environment in which to flourish. Aggravations of
the schizophrenic psychosis occurred for the
most part when a highly unnatural dependency relationship existed between the proband and the deceased parent, and the proband felt after his parent died that he had no
support, no purpose, and no aim in life, that
he was alone and forsaken in the world. To
be sure, there are individual cases in which
other psychological relationships might be
suspected between the experience of the death
of a parent and the course of his psychosis.
Again there are other cases in which such an
interrelationship is not at all evident without
the application of arbitrary, subjective judgments.

It seems, accordingly, that the changes in
a proband's schizophrenic condition after the
death of a father or mother can often be
interpreted psychologically. This is a reason
for assuming that not only timely, but also
causal relationships exist when in a minority
of courses of schizophrenia the death of a
parent marks the turning point.

A less careful formulation, I dare not attempt. Oddly enough, it has been the custom
for a long time to present psychological
relationships in which one believes as the

absolute truth. I do not share such a conviction of clairvoyance for myself. On the contrary, I am constantly plagued by doubts in the presence of psychological interpretations. Unfortunately, I cannot say, "If a schizophrenic patient was in a highly frustrating ambivalence toward his father or mother, and this father or mother dies, this death might alleviate his psychosis." I can only say, "It seems to me that ...".

The fact that we cannot always deal with psychological relationships objectively should not prevent our being concerned with them. If we allowed this to inhibit our efforts, dynamic psychopathology and many types of psychotherapy would surely wither on the vine. Psychological relationships are important, even if they cannot be objectively proved. We are not able either to "prove" in a healthy person that there is not only a timely, but also a causal connection between the effect of the death of a close relative and his own inner development. However, we count on it, although it cannot be objectively demonstrated. I have no objections to drawing conclusions from psychological intuition; I believe, however, that the time has finally come in which such conclusions should not be presented as if they were provable or proved facts.

Accordingly, let me formulate the more important conclusions of this section approximately to the effect that there are subjectively convincing indications for the assumption that the internal mental dealing with the loss of a parent will, under certain circumstances, influence the development of schizophrenics —just as they will influence the development of many healthy people. Based on the same criteria of recognition and with approximately same proability as we assume the influence of external events to have on the development of our own personalities, we may also assume that such influences exist for schizophrenic developments.

Course of Illness and Relationships in Family after Onset of Illness

What is the effect on the course of illness of the schizophrenic patient of the continuation or the cessation of relationships to family members? This is a question to which clinicians have tried for a long time to find some answers and for a long time they have depended on general impressions from their own clinical experience for such answers. Until recently there were no precisely developed ground rules to help them in their judgment, and even today such ground rules are still insufficient. This lack is all the more lamentable, since important decisions for the care and treatment of patients often depend on what might be expected from the continuation of close relationships with members of the immediate family.

The first directors of the Burghölzli clinic, von Gudden and Hitzig (1870–1879) were of the opinion that the removal of patients from their families, as it occurs when a patient is hospitalized, had a generally salutary effect. For this reason there was also the tendency to limit the visiting hours; in fact, to prohibit visits for many patients. E. Bleuler, the director of the clinic from 1898 through 1927, on the other hand, was convinced that isolation from the family frequently had an adverse effect on the course of the patient's illness. He believed that close ties maintained with the next-of-kin would enhance improvement and the recovery process in schizophrenics, and would forestall the solidification of acute states which are generally more amenable to improvement. For this reason, he advocated the early release of schizophrenics from the clinic to the care of their families. Of course, he also knew patients who did not benefit from family care, and this was one of the reasons why he actively organized the care of released schizophrenics in suitable foster families under the supervision of appropriate physicians and social workers. The family-care program at Burghölzli has since 1909 become such an important auxiliary activity that, in the course of time, about half as many schizophrenics under the care of foster families are being seen by the doctors and social workers of Burghölzli as there are hospitalized patients in the clinic.

Since that time the attitude of the clinic has for decades remained about the same. By and large, an effort is made to release patients to their families for care as early as possible. Often at the same time arrangements are made for regular house calls by doctors or social workers. If, however, there is no immediate family to accept the recovered patient for care, arrangements are made to place him with a foster family. The same procedure is followed when there is constant friction between the patient and his family.

The development of modern hospital policies in many other hospitals both at home and abroad seems to be similar.

In the literature the question concerning

the influence of families on the course of schizophrenias only began to get increased attention since about the middle of the 50's. Hollingshead and Redlich (1958) were the first to call attention with impressive and well-founded data to the importance of this influence. Since then many others have concerned themselves with the question, in particular British and American researchers, among them Orr et al (1955), Brun (1956), Brown (1959), Tybring and Kusuda (1959), Deykin (1961), Gordon and Groth (1961), Brown et al. (1962), Brooks et al. (1963), Wessler and Kahn (1963), Gillis and Keet (1965), Scott (1965), Leyberg (1965), and Jilek (1968). In general they have come to the conclusion that the willing collaboration and understanding of family members have a beneficial influence, and that coldness and rejection have an adverse effect on the course of schizophrenias. But often the course of illness was evaluated only according to the need for hospitalization, without taking into account the actual condition of the patient.

The material of some authors reveals some noteworthy indications of details concerning the influences of families on patients that really begin to make this summary discovery interesting. Brooks et al. (1963) found that conflicting attitudes toward the patient on the part of family members are more harmful than out-and-out rejection. According to their experience, good relationships with siblings were even more salutary than good relationships with parents. Brown et al. (1962) studied patients who had been accepted in their homes after release, but who were treated in loveless fashion by their families and looked down upon. Their development was less favorable than that of patients who were accepted with warmth and understanding. Jilek (1968) made the interesting discovery that among his schizophrenics those who were accepted and cared for by their families exhibited mostly almost symptom-free, adynamic long-term states, whereas patients who were rejected by their families were inclined to hold fast to grossly psychotic symptoms.

An alarming discovery cited by Meyer (1969) in a rectorial address, based on investigations by Jonas et al. (1969), reads: "Among 350 schizophrenic patients hospitalized over 5 years in a psychiatric state hospital in the Federal Republic of Germany, 40 percent of the men and 30 percent of the women received neither visitors nor mail in the course of one year."

It was exceedingly difficult, in fact virtually impossible, to pursue these questions statistically with our probands. In most cases I became helpless when I attempted to show in figures the multifaceted relationships to families, as they were revealed to me by my patient histories. Mostly it was not merely a matter an unambiguous acceptance or rejection of the proband, but a number of attitudes that lay between these or were ambivalent. Besides, most of the probands had several "family members," and often their attitudes toward the proband were not the same. And finally, over the course of years and decades, changes occurred in the relationships of the families toward the probands.

At the beginning I attempted to quantify the relationships to families by methods similar to those employed by other authors, in that I determined whether—or how often —the proband received visitors at the clinic. In the time during which our principal probands were hospitalized, a visitors' register was, for the most part, being maintained. With the increasing relaxation of controls and more liberal operation of the clinics such registration became an impossible task. Besides, the formerly maintained visitors' registers by no means always revealed the visitor's relationship to the patient. It was not always clear whether they were members of the family, officials, friends, or even possibly creditors; so I had to give up the use of visitors' registers.

In order to obtain an overview equivalent to statistics I selected a different method. I looked for the extreme cases among the 208 probands. On the one hand, patients whose parents, spouses, siblings, or children looked after them for a number of years after their illness, who willingly accepted responsibility for their care, who loved them, and who also did everything possible to maintain a comfortable relationship with them. These I contrasted with the extreme cases of rejection by the family community, such as patients whose families had not been concerned about them for years. With the aid of individual patient histories, I then attempted to formulate a judgment as to whether the personality of the patient was clearly determining the behavior of his family toward him, or whether the behavior of the families showed no relationship to the patient's behavior. The problem, then, was to determine whether the family kept a close relationship to the patient who was receptive to and grateful for their efforts, or whether their concern was wasted

Table 4.28. Family concern for patient (probands)

"End states"	"Devotedly cared for"	"Rejected"
Severe "end state"	17	7
Moderately severe "end state"	8	7
Mild "end state"	19	10
Recovery	10	1
No "end state" attained	4	2
Totals:	58	27

Course types		
Acute to severe "end state"	0	1
Chronic to severe "end state"	8	5
Acute to mild "end state"	2	1
Chronic to mild "end state"	9	10
Undulating to severe "end state"	10	2
Undulating to mild "end state"	14	7
Undulating to recovery	13	1
Atypical course	2	0
Totals:	58	27

on a patient who continually rejected them and who did not perceptibly react to their efforts on his behalf.

The results of these studies are sparse. Table 4.28 shows how the different course types and "end states" are distributed over the two groups of probands categorized as "devotedly cared for" and "rejected."

1. "Devoted care" by the immediate family accrues to male schizophrenics more often than the female ones; among our probands to 36 of 100 males, but to only 22 of 108 females; the difference is not statistually significant ($p < 0.02$). If it is not merely a coincidence showing an illusory difference, it would be easy to explain. Healthy wives are more likely to accept the care of schizophrenic husbands than healthy husbands are to accept the responsibilities for the care of their schizophrenic wives. Mothers more readily accept the care of schizophrenic sons than of schizophrenic daughters. Hower, the same number of schizophrenic men and women seem to be totally rejected.

2. (Under the conditions given) schizo-

phrenics much more frequently receive devoted care from their families than they are neglected and rejected by them (58:27). This picture corresponds to our everyday experience at Burghölzli. It does happen according to public opinion and sometimes in the literature that a contrary opinion predominates.

3. "Devoted care" by families over a period of many years cannot always prevent solidification in a portion of the schizophrenics to a severely psychotic chronic permanent state (an "'end state' of severe dementia," according to the former definition).

4. Nevertheless, the courses run somewhat better, on the average, when the patient is under "devoted care" than when he is "rejected." In particular, there are more long-term recoveries among probands under "devoted care" than among the "rejected." However, neither finding is statistically significant.

5. Just as under the "end states" recoveries were more frequent among probands receiving "devoted care" than there were among those "rejected," so also under the course types, the phasic-benign courses are more frequent among probands receiving "devoted care." At $p < 0.1$, however, the difference is still not sufficiently significant. Among probands "devotedly cared for," the phasic courses progressing to severe "end states" also occur more frequently than they do among the "rejected," as does the total figure for all three phasic course types. This latter difference does attain statistical significance at $p < 0.05$.

We conclude, therefore, that there does exist a loose, nonsignificant, but positive correlation between devoted care and phasic-benign courses, and conversely, between rejection and unfavorable, severe courses. There is a significant positive correlation between devoted care and all phasic types of courses considered jointly. The finding corresponds to expectations.

On the basis of my probands I was not able to distinguish cause and effect. In almost all cases the question remained open as to whether the "devoted care" accorded the proband was the result of kind concern for that proband in his improved state, or whether it was the cause that brought about his benign course. The more I became involved in experiments in an effort to clarify this causal relationship, the more impossible it seemed, to me to derive results from such an undertaking. This is another case in which the question of an either-or might be misplaced, as so often is the case in research on schizophrenia. The concern of families does not determine the course of the patient's illness, and the family's willingness to help is not decisively dependent on a predestined course of illness. There is, instead, a constant interaction between the condition of the patient and the concern or nonconcern of his family. This interaction is virtually impossible to determine by means of statistics. It is something one senses as soon as one becomes submerged in the individual patient histories. Schweizer (1954) did an excellent job of describing this interaction in a female patient at our clinic. It was also described convincingly in a uniquely thorough paper on quadruplets by Rosenthal (1963). This interaction has also been considered in earlier sections of this work.

The next section shows some additional experiences with the same type of problem. In modern family treatment of schizophrenics, the same urgently recurring problem continues to emerge. Kaufmann and Müller (1969) among others have summarized their own conclusions and those of other authors on this subject.

Some Other Emotional Influences on the Course of Illness

It has long been known that psychoses that are today classed as schizophrenias frequently occur in connection with some kind of severe emotional shock, and that recovery is much rarer in connection with such an experience. The school of psychiatrists known as "psychics," popular in the first half of the past century, thoughtlessly concluded that there was a causal relationship in such timely co-incidences. After the turn of the century, the "endogenous" psychoses were strictly and dogmatically distinguished from the reactive ones, so that the psychiatrist who adhered to the prevailing dogma was virtually forbidden to give serious consideration to such time-relationships. He was restricted to considering them as mere coincidences, or to assume a causality which was the reverse of the one professed by the "psychics." He was forced to assume that the patient had become involved in cumbersome difficulties as a result of his psychosis, and not that the difficulties had caused the psychosis. After the works of Jung (1907), E. Bleuler (1908), Kretschmer (1918), Klaesi (1922), and many others with them and after them, renewed emphasis was given to the idea that events of severe emotional stress to the patient often exert an influence on the course of his schizophrenia. The fact that such events might at least bring about the emergence of schizophrenic psychoses, that they might mitigate, aggravate, or force them into a state of latency, or that at the very least their "secondary symptoms" might be significantly influenced by them, could soon be convincingly demonstrated. The main questions still remaining open were whether acute psychic stresses really constituted a primary cause for the emergence of the disease, and whether they could play an essential role in the complete recovery of the patient.

The selection and processing of the probands employed in this set of studies was not specifically oriented for checking the meaning of individual events of an emotional nature in connection with schizophrenias. In order to make a systematic study of such phenomena, one would have to begin by investigating, for example, subjects with schizophrenic puerperal or prison psychoses. In the preceding section the death of father or mother was selected, from the entire range of questions. In the section to follow, there will be a discussion of still other important events of emotional impact that seemed to influence changes in the course of illness of our probands.

In order to retain control over the whole picture, I have counted these events. But I shall be wary indeed of ascribing values to precise figures on such concepts, for these figures could easily simulate a precision as to facts that does not exist. It is impossible to define precisely what is emotionally charged and what is not. If after a big love affair a girl is jilted by her lover, then this is unequivocally a severe emotional stress. If some other girl has a different affair every month and is jilted by one of her lovers immediately before eruption of the psychosis, this loss of a lover cannot be regarded as being an important emotional stress. But where to draw the line? And how can we set a definite date for the breakup when, as so often is the case, it comes about gradually? In order to determine whether the psychosis was aggravated in a time-relationship with this event, one would have to know the exact dates. In short, the experiences related to the problem cannot be expressed in absolute figures. Relative figures are more revealing in such cases as, for instance, comparisons between the sexes or comparisons between the different types of psychic traumatization.

A survey of the emotionally significant events in the lives of our probands, that are followed by changes in the courses of their illness, reveals scarcely anything more than what any practicing clinician would already have accepted as a matter of course. Clinical experience will show anyone today, as it has shown for decades, that emotional shocks often precede the onset, the improvement, the aggravation of, or the recovery from schizophrenic psychoses, but such changes in condition of the patient occur with even greater frequency as apparently "spontaneous," or at least without any emotional shocks of any importance being discovered in a time-relationship with them. For this reason specifically, the concept "endogenous" has only a limited justification for existence. When time-relationships are in evidence between emotionally important events and changes in the condition of the patient, experience shows that the possibility of mere coincidence can hardly ever be excluded from consideration. For the most part, it is not possible to distinguish either whether the traumatic event is only a partial cause of the change in the patient's condition, or whether the reverse is true—at least as long as one is not thoroughly acquainted with one's patients. Common experience furthermore agrees with the finding that the most various events conceivable will occur in a time-relationship with changes in the patient's condition, and then again, and frequently, that they reveal not the slightest trace of change in the schizophrenic course of illness. All these possibilities have also actually occurred in the lives of the 208 principal probands.

A comparison between male and female probands shows that psychotraumatic experiences in connection with changes in the patient's condition occur more frequently among female than among male probands, in fact at about twice the rate. This, too, was expected on the basis of general experience.[19] The difference is primarily based not only on postpartum schizophrenias, schizophrenias during pregnancy, or after abortions (there were only 4 schizophrenias that erupted or became aggravated after childbirth). The primary difference occurs with respect to

19. Corroborative findings apply not only to schizophrenics, but also to many other types of patients, such as sufferers from Basedow's disease and phasic depressives (Angst, 1966).

being jilted by a spouse or a lover. Among my female probands this latter experience occurred in connection with the eruption or aggravation of a schizophrenia at 3 times the rate for male probands. This also was to be expected, on the basis of general past experience. On the other hand, the finding that more women than men experienced aggravation of their psychotic condition after losing a member of the immediate family was not expected (among our probands the ratio was 8 : 1). In this case members of the immediate family do not include parents; the reaction to their death has been discussed in the preceding section. Cases of death that were followed by unfavorable reactions in the development of our female probands involved 3 husbands, and 1 each of an only child, 1 favorite aunt, 1 uncle, 1 grandfather, and 1 foster mother. The sole death that affected the condition of a male proband unfavorably concerned a buddy on the job, who died of an accident in the presence of the proband. It seems that the same tendency emerges here that was determined in the preceding section. According to it, the death of a father or mother seems to play a more important part in the course of schizophrenic development of women than of men, and in addition we may conclude, at least insofar as the 208 probands of this project are concerned, that the death of close relatives, among them those who approach the concept of the parental image, more readily influences schizophrenic developments in women than in men. An interesting observation is that among the events experienced emotionally that occurred more frequently in women than in men before aggravation of their condition, are the marriages of close relatives, and this seems to apply exclusively to siblings (the ratio is 5 : 1). In 1 case it was a double wedding of two siblings; in another, the wedding of the favorite brother, and 2 cases of a sister's wedding. In the only case of the male proband it was also the sister's wedding.

The individual figures covering the differences between male and female probands, insofar as they have been mentioned, are ridiculously small. If all the events were added together in which the loss of a person is involved who was emotionally close to the patient, they would be considerable. What was summarized was how often changes were clearly evident in the course of schizophrenia of men and of women after the following events.

—Death of father or mother (see pp. 275 and

276)
—Death of a different close relative
—Divorce
—Loss of a sweetheart
—Loss of a brother or sister through marriage

These events occur 58 times among the 108 female probands and 16 times among the 100 male probands in a time-relationship to the onset of or to a change in, the course of their schizophrenias. The absolute figures are not to be taken seriously, for the reasons already outlined, although the comparison may readily be. The difference in the figures is statistically highly significant ($p < 0.005$). We may conclude that, among our female probands, changes in the course of schizophrenic psychoses after the loss of a close relative or loved one occurs more frequently than among male probands.

Another finding may possibly be pure coincidence, but may also be testimony in support of the same trend. Five male and 4 female probands have undergone marked changes in their condition in a timely relationship with their own engagement or marriage. For all 4 female probands that change was an improvement, but in 4 of the 5 male probands their condition deteriorated. If one were inclined to take these small figures seriously, one might assume that, just as in the course of a schizophrenia in women the loss of a loved one predisposes an aggravation, so the acquisition of such a person will predispose an improvement.

The greatest number of emotionally important events in time-relationships with drastic changes in the courses of schizophrenia in men are related to military service, instead of to the loss of a loved one, as they are in women. Among the 100 male probands, however, there were only 10 for whom the onset of schizophrenia, its marked aggravation or improvement was time-related to induction into, release from, or particularly difficult experiences within the military service. These 10 cases make up almost a quarter of all the emotionally significant events in the lives of men that were in a definite time-relationship to changes in their courses of illness. There were 9 onsets or aggravations and 1 improvement of the psychosis in connection with experiences as soldiers. Part of this service involved active duty on border patrol during the World War II, and part was military training during peace time.

I had previously done investigations on the interrelationship between the Swiss military service and the course of schizophrenia (M. Bleuler et al. 1962). We reached the conclusion that in Switzerland the concurrence in time between induction into the service, release from the service, or particularly hazardous or strenuous duties, and the changes in the course of schizophrenia was usually not a causal, but merely a coincidental relationship. We could prove neither for active duty nor for training assignments that schizophrenias had occurred more frequently in connection with military service. I personally did not come across a single case of schizophrenia in my long experience as batallion surgeon in active service. Insofar as the training assignments in peacetime were concerned, in 1960, for example, 318,420 men served a total of 9,017,638 days. The military medical service had knowledge of only 21 cases of schizophrenia from this group during that period, and among them were cases that had existed previously but had not been identified until the trainee had been examined in the service. As a matter of fact, the Swiss training assignment is by no means a psychic trauma, even for the average man. Active duty did impose some rather strict demands, but much less taxing than the military service in other armies. The majority of our male probands had done service either in active duty or in a training assignment. The fact that 10 cases revealed a time-relationship between such service and the eruption, aggravation, or improvement of their schizophrenias might well have been a coincidence. It is certain, of course, that there are men, even in the Swiss military service, with personal hypersensitivity problems, although these generally include the homosexual tendencies that are experienced as inner disharmonies. These types of disorders are similar to those Kempf (1921, 1949) so lucidly described as "homosexual panic." [20]

20. Kempf (1921, 1949) regards this as an acute psychosis that might belong to the schizophrenias, but that in certain other cases might be categorized along with the psychogenic states. The condition is interpreted as the conflict with homosexual tendencies that are vehemently rejected. In a psychosis, these tendencies become hallucinations and delusions that get correlated with filth, dust, and poison. The patient undergoes a struggle with the symbols of homosexuality that is fraught with fear and sometimes with sexual excitement. Kempf (1921, 1949) observed disorders of this type particularly in men exposed to homosexually provocative conditions, for instance, among young sailors on sea duty.

An example of these is Karl A. (Proband 23). He grew up the son of a street constable, who was kind and understanding when he was sober, but who was an alcoholic. Intoxicated, he was a pitiful specimen of a man, who spent so much money on alcohol that his family suffered under it. Karl had ambivalent feelings toward him, and was deeply attached to his mother. He had been a model child, excessively obedient and industrious, and became a clerk in a business. In puberty he was homosexually seduced and for a short time was homosexually active. His relationships with girls were only superficial and temporary. He liked to say that he "preferred to eat a good meal rather than waste his money on girls." He did not marry. After he had come through his military training period and his first active duty assignments without any particular difficulties, he was reassigned as a military medic on active duty during the war. On the day of his reinduction he suffered an acute onset of a severe catatonia under extreme agitation and confusion. After 4 months of insulin treatments he improved and could be released from the hospital. On his release, however, he was not rated as recovered, particularly because of his affective rigidity and incapacity to communicate. After his release, this residual state lasted for another year, and then Karl became the same person he had been before. Four years later, no longer in the military service, he suffered a similar episode, and then remained completely well for the next 12 years. From that point forward, when Karl was 41 years old, catatonic states with brief intervening remissions recurred in great number over the next 4 years, until the very end of the observation period.

In his psychosis after entering active military service, the proband spoke completely distractedly about delusional and hallucinatory experiences, brought up absurd ideas, or uttered expressions that were totally unintelligible. When he did this, many ideas turned up that might have been connected with his homosexual tendencies and that would correspond to the symptoms described by Kempf (1921, 1949). Thus, for example, he had the illusion that the dishes were clumsy and dirty. He imagined he was being poisoned. With a peculiarly stiff, paramimic smile he would remark: "I've always wanted to have my father come and live with me, if I ever had my own income.... Dad always had such large, beautiful eyes...." Then again it seemed to him as if "Hitler was coming to

Switzerland to look for someone, coming first to see me and then perhaps going on to see others—I don't know that he'd rid himself of any vices.... I've felt all along that Hitler perhaps did become weaker through his constant nonimmunity to things. I thought I would find a way to render the human brain non-infectuous to anything. And I also thought that certain sides of my father were clean, whereas mine were soiled. ... " Immunity, poisoning, infection, soiling occurred often, sometimes as desirable, and sometimes as repugnant, and often in relationship to his father or to Hitler. At that time Hitler was being interwoven into schizophrenic thinking by many patients in an ambivalent way, as a supermasculine or superpaternal figure, both in a good and in an evil context. Frequently, in delusions, he then became the homosexual or heterosexual seducer, experienced ambivalently by the patient.

One might argue that the military service could not have played a decisive causative role, because the proband had suffered other schizophrenic phases totally independent of his military service, and because, on the other hand, he had performed his military duties without any concurrent illness. In my opinion this argument is valid, if one were to consider the military service as the only cause for the existing schizophrenia. But this cannot possibly be the case. At best it could only have been a partial cause among many, under certain given predispositions of the particular proband. In other phases of the illness, other combinations of causes may have been operative. I know of no long-term, observed case of schizophrenia, for which the same psychic trauma could always be related to every acute episode that occurred.

Among the 9 probands in whom schizophrenia either erupted or became aggravated in connection with their induction into military service, there were 2 others in whom we might suspect an uncommonly high degree of sensitivity toward experiences in the military service because of possible latent homosexual tendencies.

Consistent with our own experience, very few other authors ascribe any general importance to the military service in the onset or the course of schizophrenic psychoses. Psychiatrists are reacting to the powerful impression they received from the experiences of the great wars. Everywhere they found evidence to show that schizophrenias were not increasing, either among front-line combat troops or among the suffering population. This experience from the very beginning prevented any interest in investigating the influence of peacetime military service. If not even active combat duty had a clear influence on schizophrenias, one could hardly expect such an influence from peacetime service. Nevertheless, a number of authors did discover an increase in schizophrenia cases in the military service anyway, but the degree of this increase was minimal, and great difficulties with the statistics had to be overcome. Steinberg and Durell (1968), for example, discovered new onsets of schizophrenia in the United States, especially at the beginning of entering military service in peacetime. They conclude from this that a partial causative relationship did exist. If the above-mentioned experiences of Kempf (1921, 1949) are considered, which correspond to my own modest findings on this relationship, using the principal probands of this study and other schizophrenics, one would be permitted to assume —as long as no contradicting data is in evidence—that military duty, such as that in the Swiss Army in the past few decades, by and large, has no decisive influence on the onset or the course of schizophrenias. In certain specific individual cases of predisposition it might assume such an influence. Among these cases of personal predisposition, the most important seems to be that of latent, ambivalently experienced homosexuality.

If the cases involving military service were eliminated, and only the other emotionally stressful events were considered in connection with changes in the courses of schizophrenias in men, there would be no such single event that occurred with any frequency. No specific, characteristic traumatic situation has been discovered that could be applied in men to a causal relationship with the fluctuations of the course of illness. Men in particular experience the most variegated emotional stresses on an individual basis, as for instance, physical illnesses, incarceration, extramarital sex relationships, loss of job, the job-related accident of a colleague, etc.

Here is a summary of the above comparisons between men and women in respect to psychotraumatic influences on the courses of illness.

1. Psychotraumatic influences on the courses of schizophrenia may more often be suspected in women than in men.

2. Among such influences, those predominating in women are losses of close relatives or sweethearts. In men there is no predominance of evidence of this specific traumatic experience.

3. Among men there is in some instances a time-relationship between military duty and a change in the course of illness. In most cases, however, that relationship is merely a coincidence in time, and not necessarily a causal one. In only very few cases, and when there is a personal predisposition for it, such as an ambitendently experienced homosexual tendency, might a causal relationship be justifiably suspected.

In the preceding chapter it was already shown that the meaning of a psychic trauma (loss of a parent) might often be understood in its relationship to the psychosis if one knows the patient very well. I found the same phenomenon again in a few individual males, whose aggravated condition has a connection to the activation, in military service, of their concealed homosexual tendencies. In numerous other cases of time-related connections between changes in the course of illness and disturbing emotional experiences, it appears that they would be understandable psychologically if the patient were intimately known; and the more accurately he is understood, the better that patient is known. Of course, this does not by any means apply to all cases. At times it remains completely puzzling why a certain patient is particularly overwhelmed by a certain experience and why his psychosis underwent a change, while a similar experience in a number of other patients produces no reactions whatever. Was it that these patients were too superficially known, so that meaningful psychological relationships remained hidden? Or were there simply no psychological relationships existent in these cases? A real answer to these questions is still not possible. They confront us with mysteries that still leave us baffled.

Two examples are included below that show that the impact of an experience that influences the course of illness can be psychologically "understood." Attention is invited again, however, to problems inherent in such psychological understanding. Whether one has only autistically contrived an interesting novel with nonrealistic substance and confused it with "understanding," or whether "understanding" actually reveals internal processes, are questions that have never been settled. The revelation of internal processes can only be modestly surmised or hoped for; it can never be asserted with authority.

Kaspar H. (Proband 35) was profoundly shocked when he accidentally witnessed the retrieval of a female corpse from the water. Immediately thereafter he became schizophrenic. There was, therefore, a time-relationship between the onset of his illness and an event that might have shocked a number of people temporarily, but that would seriously harm the very least of them. Here are the facts of the case.

Kaspar was raised in an emotionally unhealthy environment. His father, an employee at a bank, had forced some unusual sexual demands on his wife-to-be during their courtship that were so repugnant to the young girl, that she felt she had to wash out her mouth after every kiss. When once he had overcome her resistance and had, before marriage, impregnated the girl, a sudden and permanent change took place in his sexuality. He told her that he was like "ice and snow," and, after that, engaged in sexual intercourse with her only on rare occasions and in an indifferent, loveless manner. He tried to persuade her "to turn over the child (Kaspar) to the French Army," and to keep the child's birth a secret. In the end, however, he was persuaded to marry her and did show considerable love and devotion toward the child after all. However, he died of the flu when Kaspar was only 4 years old. The mother's attitude toward the boy was one of ambivalence. This was revealed in part by the fact that she gave him to his paternal grandparents to raise for a number of years, although she detested her father-in-law (the child's grandfather), describing him as one of the most horrible people imaginable.

Under these circumstances Kaspar from childhood on, developed into a schizoid eccentric. Intellectually he was gifted and rated above average, and was able to pass his final high school examinations without difficulty. On the other hand, he had begun to isolate himself from others when he first started school. Even as a child he began to develop peculiar ideas, for instance, that he had to hold his head over the stove in order to warm up his cold brain. At the age of 5, he made coarse incestuous demands on his mother, and developed guilt feelings as a result. He had never entered into an amorous relationship with a girl. He kept putting off his studies in philosophy at the university. Then he became an active exhibitionist on occasion, expecially as a voyeur. On occasion he would swim under the dividing nets of the public baths into the women's section to observe them while they changed their clothes, or he would swim under the women to touch their genitals. For this reason he was in constant fear of being apprehended, sooner or later, by the police.

At this stage, at age 23, he was taking a harmless walk, before attending a lecture, along the shores of the same river where he had succumbed to his perverted inclinations. By chance he happened on the scene where the police were recovering the body of a drowned woman from the waters.

His psychosis set in immediately. He was beset by the delusion that the police were accusing him of the murder of this woman. He turned himself in to the police voluntarily to protest in confusion the false "accusation" against him.

His schizophrenic psychosis ran a severe course and he never recovered. The proband was often completely confused and delusional. Sometimes he demanded to be put in jail, because he had killed a young boy. Then again he exhibited catatonic attitudes and became substuporous. He was almost completely inaccessible. Two slight temporary improvements occurred, during which he could be released on probation. On both occasions he was able to remain outside the clinic for only a short time. He died, $6\frac{1}{2}$ years after his first onset, of a pulmonary infarct during a sleep cure that had been instigated for the treatment of his catatonic state.

The psychological relationships in this case seemed obvious. The young man had felt guilty because of his perverted sexual activities and expected sooner or later to have to submit to a criminal investigation. Now he came into close proximity to the place where he had committed his misdemeanors in the water against women bathing, and by mere chance was confronted with the body of a drowned woman. Although he had had nothing to do with the death of this woman, who had drowned, his natural guilt feelings were suddenly converted to the delusion that he had murdered her. Perhaps he was further traumatized along the same line because he had earlier imposed incestuous acts on his mother.

Gerhard M. (Proband 55) became ill gradually at age 37 in connection with an accusation of the alleged murder of his wife, although the court had cleared him as completely innocent. His wife was burned to death in his presence, when their house burned down.

Gerhard's father was a respected farmer,

and both parents were able, healthy people. Gerhard's development in school was excellent. But he never trained for any specific job, although his background and good intelligence indicated that he should have. He worked rather sporadically in factories and for farmers, proving to be adroit and skillful when he did so. Except for his future wife, he did not associate with girls, but instead leaned toward acquaintances with boys, which suggested homoerotic tendencies. At age 23 he married a woman who became severely schizophrenic one year later and never recovered. He cared for her devotedly at home, sacrificing both his time and money, and never regretted expenses for both good doctors and quacks in an effort to help her. From age 30 on, however, he maintained simultaneously a close, peculiar friendship to a man, in which homoerotic tendencies certainly played a part, although no physical homosexual relationship was ever proved. When his house burned down, and his mentally ill wife lost her life in the flames, he was 33 years old. About 2 years later, quarrels developed between him and his friend. In the course of these arguments, his friend falsely accused him of being guilty of his wife's death in the fire, but the proband was declared innocent by the court and exonerated.

Gerhard then immediately filed suit against his friend for damages, that seemed reasonable in the beginning, but his demands soon increased to the point of absurdity and had to be refused by the court. This motivated him to .sue the courts, claiming that they were against him and had entered into a conspiracy with his opponent. He virtually flooded the courts and the authorities with confusing, unreasonable demands and threats. He was 37 when his psychosis began. At first it appeared as if his was a case of paranoia in Kraepelin's sense. Soon he began to develop totally unsystematic delusions and at times became totally distracted in his thinking. His demeanor seemed unnatural, as if it were "frozen," sweet-eager, and condescending. He formulated his delusions in the most diverse ways; for example, he claimed to be "exposed to the hidden influences of others," or that he had the ability "to persecute his enemies by a control system and penetrate their secret nature." For a long time he nurtured the delusion that he was everywhere being falsely accused of being a homosexual, which he was not. He expressed this idea long before he had been identified as a true homosexual by

his illegal, punishable acts with young boys.

Gerhard never recovered from his paranoid-schizophrenic psychosis, nor did it become more aggravated after the first few years. At the end of the observation period Gerhard was 65 years old. The 28 years since his illness began, he had spent partly in psychiatric clinics, partly in punitive confinement for his sexual offenses against young boys, partly in state-supported and organized family care, but in part also at liberty and dependent only on himself. He never again relinquished his hold on his confused delusions, his pathological assertions, and his threats. Outside of clinics he did odd jobs, and turned up here and there with different relatives and friends, where he was usually an unwelcome guest, because people were always afraid that he would come forth with obscene innuendos or homosexual advances. He did, however, retain his ability to work and could render reasonable judgments in matters that did not concern him personally.

In this case, too, it is obvious that the emotion-laden experiences before his psychosis must have had an exceptional internal impact on this proband. For many years he devoted himself completely to caring for his schizophrenic wife, which was in itself an emotionally stressful experience. But the severe internal conflicts had developed principally because he was a homosexual, who had concealed and controlled his physical homosexuality before the eruption of his psychosis. On the other hand, a homoerotically tainted, pathological relationship to a man had developed, that disturbed the marriage. The tragic and dramatic death of his wife undoubtedly shocked him not only in the obvious way, but certainly must also have assumed pathogenic proportions because he experienced it in ambivalent fashion. It conformed to the proband's own secretive tendencies. His friend, who was familiar with these tendencies, hurt him in an extremely sensitive spot with his false accusation. Gerhard's subsequent delusions all hovered around this same tragedy. He began making demands on his former friend, that exceeded his justifiable claim many times over. It seemed as if he was demanding restitution not only for the false accusation against him in court, but also for the fact that his friend had played a decisive role in the unhappy development of his life, or for the fact that he could never enter into any natural, happy relationships because of his homosexual tendencies. In his own mind he converted his actual homosexuality into malicious slander accusing him of being a homosexual. He acted as if the courts, the state, and all agencies involved were responsible for his misfortune that had resulted from his own pathologically sensual way of life.

If we take a closer look at those probands whose psychosis runs an undulating course, it becomes obvious what a totally different part emotional stresses play in it. There are patients who seem to be sensitive only to certain specific emotional stresses, others who seem sensitive to the greatest variety of emotional stresses, and again others whose psychosis rises and wanes without any time-related emotional stress being in evidence. This experience with our own probands conforms to general clinical experience. In respect to the assumption that emotional stresses influence the course of illness, every clinician must be tormented by doubts when he observes cases that develop without any discernible emotional stresses, that recover, recur, improve, or become aggravated in the absence of any such experience being visible on the patient's record. If he then inspects many other cases more closely, the time- and subjective relationships between the illness and the emotional experience are so impressive that he simply cannot ignore them. Both findings considered together admit of only one interpretation, namely that emotional stresses are bound in many cases to play an important part in the origin and the course development of schizophrenic psychoses. But they alone cannot be the only decisive factor; other influences are involved. Whether these are unidentified emotional stresses or influences of an entirely different nature remains a mystery.

Example of a case in which emotionally stressful experiences, a different one in each instance, occurred preceding a number of different schizophrenic psychotic episodes.

Hanna W. (Proband 102). Her schizophrenic psychosis ran an acute course in violent hebephrenic phases. After the last of these she recovered for 2 years, until she died at age 55. In her psychotic phases Hanna was in a highly agitated state, confused, and silly in her demeanor. She railed at everyone and felt herself persecuted and tormented. She labelled the nurses as "lust-murderers," felt she was being poisoned, that she was shackled into a "sterilization machine," wrote letters to agencies in Moscow complaining

about conditions at home, heard voices, etc. Her father had campaigned for a socialistic type of social order. In her psychosis she extended his ideas in a confused and absurd manner. In between her psychotic phases she was a simple domestic employee, but decidedly unfeminine. After her mother had harshly chided her for having engaged in some harmless petting with a boy when she was 14, she never again displayed any erotic tendencies for the rest of her life.

In Hanna's case, her psychotic episodes were in close time-relationships with certain emotionally stressful events
—The beginning of her menstrual periods which was late (at age 18) and, with the rejection of her femininity, was an agonizing experience
—The marriage at age 34 of her twin brother, to whom she had felt very close
—A goiter operation she dreaded, at age 40
—Suicide of her employer's daughter, at age 47
—The death of her mother, when Hanna was 53.

The idea suggests itself that those schizophrenic psychoses, the course of which is in a close time-relationship with emotionally stressful experiences may be of a different nature than those that develop and progress independently of visible influences. Therefore I checked whether psychoses with and without visible relationships to emotionally stressful experiences could be distinguished from one another. Like many other clinicians, I discovered no such distinguishing features. Most especially, I found that schizophrenias with malignant progressions occur also in cases in which a psychogenic release or multiple causality may be involved; and on the other hand, among schizophrenias with recovery outcomes there are some for which no kind of basis for any psychotraumatic release can be detected. Of course, the entire group of schizophrenias cannot be subdivided as to whether they might reveal psychotraumatic causes or not. Just like most clinicians, I, too, came to these conclusions with my probands and by daily experience with all the schizophrenics under my care.

Course of Illness and Treatment Methods

The preceding findings of this chapter have shown clearly that the course of catastrophe-schizophrenias—those psychoses that after an acute onset proceed to long-term, severe chronic states—may be influenced in a beneficial way by life circumstances as well as by therapy. Contrary to that concept, the preceding investigations have shown no indications that there is no hope for recovery from the chronic-malignant types of psychoses; although, as general experience shows, there can be alleviation and improvement by treatment. Our findings do not refute this experience.

I have already discussed earlier the methods by which our 208 probands were treated. In summary, all patients were subjected to work-therapy in the clinics, and their free time was organized with therapeutic aims in view. Constant checks were made for the possibility of releases, also for early releases where possible, and subsequent open-care arrangements, frequently in conjunction with the courts or welfare agencies. This therapeutic activity was relatively standardized in the different clinics charged with the care of our probands, even though its application varied somewhat in its intensity and quality. On the average, therapeutic activity increased progressively during the observation period. Up to 1953 only the traditional sedatives and soporifics were employed during states of agitation. After 1953, neuroleptics of all kinds were used, primarily chlorphromazine, reserpine, and mellaril. In the beginning these were given only in large doses as part of an overall cure, and often in conjunction with bedrest; then later in smaller doses and without bedrest. As a whole, we were much more conservative than the majority of other clinics in the administration of neuroleptic drugs. All patients were influenced psychotherapeutically, in that at least their immediate concerns, their needs, and their wishes were discussed with them during the daily ward visits, and often also in special psychotherapeutic sessions. Skill and the expenditure of time employed in such psychotherapeutic efforts varied considerably from time to time and among the various clinics. Psychoanalyses were not done on our probands. Table 4.29 shows the "great" somatic cures undertaken.

A special feature of treatment in our clinics as compared to most clinics in other countries is the frequency with which sleep cures are administered according to Klaesi's method (long-term anesthesia up to 10 days). The compounds of the classic soporifics employed varied. The "twilight cures" were administered with the classic soporifics until 1953; then with neuroleptics, and partly these in

Table 4.29. Somatic therapies of probands

	No. of cures	No. of probands
Sleep cures	85[1]	51
Twilight cures	38	18
Insulin cures	99[1]	69
Electroshock cures	227[1]	99
Lobotomies	9	8[2]
No somatic treatment	9	74[3]

1. Minimal figures. In a few severe cases these 3 cures were administered two or more times in succession at intervals that varied according to the physical condition of the patient. For this reason it was arbitrary whether the series of treatments was to be a single cure (with interruptions) or was to be considered as a sequence of several cures. Here it is considered as one single cure.

2. One patient was lobotomized twice.

3. Sum of the number of patients exceeds 208, because many patients underwent several cures.

combination with soporifics. "Twilight cures" were those treatments in which the patient was under a drug that caused him to sleep or doze during most of the day, but the dosage was administered and measured so that the patient would awaken two or three times a day to partake of liquids or other light nourishment. Patients undergoing "sleep cures" slept through and were fed rectally or intravenously. Insulin cures were administered according to the original regulations set up by Sakel. The frequency of the individual shocks in cardiazol and electroshock treatments varied, but was generally less than that in many clinics of other countries. While no lobotomies were performed on schizophrenics at our clinic before 1944, and almost none since 1955, 8 of our probands underwent lobotomies. The percentage of 3.8 lobotomies among the schizophrenic probands of this study happens to be a great deal higher than in any other given group of schizophrenics that have ever been at our clinic.

The idea occurs to one to set up statistics as to how often improvements or recoveries followed each type of treatment. I did compile such a set of data; however, it would be useless to present it here. Statistics of this type show only that the psychoses run a less favorable course the more frequently the patients were treated by cures of all types. The conclusion would be senseless, for treatments by the great cures rendered the prognosis gloomy. Rather, the truth was the reverse: The more adverse the course of the psychosis, the more frequently and intensively it had to be treated.

The present study of the 208 probands does not permit of statistical representations about the results of one therapeutic method or the other, nor were any statistics ever planned that would adequately resolve this type of question.

For the sake of completeness, however, I should like to mention what overall impression I got about therapeutic methods with schizophrenics, as I look back over the many years of experience with the 208 probands of this project, together with my lifetime of experience with all the schizophrenics I have treated. Many of the individual problems in those decades of daily experience with schizophrenics were scientifically worked on before.

During my tenure as chief physician at the Basel University Clinic at Friedmatt, numerous papers on the effectiveness of insulin treatments were published under the direction of Dr. J.E. Staehelin by Plattner and Frölicher (1938), Plattner (1939), M. Bleuler (1941), Ramer (1943), and Siegfried (1943). I personally witnessed the beginnings and progress of all these papers. Since I took over the direction of the Zürich Psychiatric University Clinic of Burghölzli, numerous papers have been published about the success of individual treatment methods with schizophrenics; to wit, on prefrontal lobotomies by Tuor-Winkler (1948), Condrau (1950), Rorschach (1951), Stoffel (1952), Stoll (1954), Krayenbühl and Stoll (1956), and M. Bleuler (1961); on pharmacotherapy by Baer (1946, 1947), Walther-Büel (1953, 1954), Ernst (1954), Weber (1954), Mielke (1955, 1956, 1957), M. Bleuler (1955, 1956, 1964), Stoll (1955, 1957), Avenarius (1956), Vogt (1956), Benedetti (1956, 1957), Angst (1960, 1961, 1963, 1965), von Brauchitsch and Bukowczyk (1962), Kirchgraber (1963), Angst and Pöldinger (1963, 1964, 1965), Kind (1964), and Hicklin and Angst (1967); and on the psychoanalysis of schizophrenics by Benedetti (1954, 1955, 1956, 1964) and Müller (1958, 1959, 1961).

All these results indicated to me the following basic concepts about the treatment of schizophrenics:

The essential element to keep in mind in the treatment of schizophrenics is consistently and indefatigably, in spite of and because of his psychosis, to appeal to the healthy ingredient of the schizophrenic's nature. This principle can be applied in a great number of different ways—by consistently speaking to the patient in an friendly, intimate tone of voice, even when he does not react to it; by making a constant effort to give in to his immediate desires and to sympathize with his concerns, and to discuss these with him, no matter how strained that conversation may become; by not ever assuming a purely observing attitude, but always maintaining that of a sympathetic human being and of the caring physician who has been summoned to help, no matter how difficult the patient may make it to do so; by always granting the patient as much responsibility as he can cope with; by trusting him, through the organization of the clinic, to take an active part in helping to care for the community; by expecting from him, as one does from anyone, that he wants to accomplish something and to be effective, and by making him realize that for this reason he is engaging in work-therapy on a regular and full-time basis; by expecting of him that he should want to spend his recreation and free time in the same way as a healthy person would want to, and by giving him as many opportunities for this as possible; and primarily by seeking continually to reestablish or to replace the human relationships that have been interrupted by his illness.

The second principle involves shock and surprise, sudden changes or transfers, sudden involvement with responsibility, sudden early dismissal, and physical therapeutic intervention.

A third principle involves calming and soothing the patient. It is necessary, in part, because patients have got to live in a community, and this community simply cannot tolerate a great deal of excitement and agitation. The best calming is done by soothing speech, by distraction, by involving the patient in something specific to do. Since there are not enough aides available, the neuroleptic drugs assume great importance in this respect.

In many cases special measures must be added to the three treatment principles outlined above. Vital and drastic measures are indicated when an acute schizophrenic phase progresses to an acute delirium, and there is danger that it may turn into a "fatal catatonia." When it is indicated, water and electrolyte, electroshock, or cortisone are administered. If depressive symptoms are prominent, the well-known medications by which depressions are sometimes alleviated, can be administered. In apathetic states it is rare for stimulants to be effective.

I am convinced that there are no "specific" treatment methods for schizophrenia. All the effective treatment methods are directed toward the basic treatment feasibilities—and each in a totally different way. They include stimulating and appealing to the patient's healthy element, in particular to his need to make contact with others; surprises and shocks; and when necessary, tranquilization. The same therapeutic methods are effective for a number of psychic disorders other than schizophrenia, insofar as these do not respond to specific treatments directed at the cause.

But the influences that are favorable to the schizophrenic are not only identical to those that are beneficial for many other types of patients. Rather, they are in essence the same forces that develop a healthy personality from childhood on, and that keep it healthy. They include active participation in the community of his fellowmen and the natural unfolding of the abilities with which the patient was endowed; the concentration of all his energies in case of danger or violence; and in between, rest and quiet.

It is hardly necessary to point out that all psychotherapies applied to schizophrenics can be interpreted along these lines. But all effective somatic treatments to which schizophrenics are subjected also follow these same principles. They create human contacts in a natural way by causing the patient to become dependent on physical care; he needs to be fed, bedded down, and kept clean and dry. These therapies shock the physical state to the point of subjectively threatening his existence. They surprise the patient psychologically in that he suddenly sees himself projected into an entirely different relationship to the people treating him and caring for him, than he is accustomed to. In addition, they tranquilize the agitated patient and help to calm him.

In my opinion, one of the primary reasons compelling us to accept this sort of concept of treatment principles lies in the very fact that there is no known technique for the treatment of schizophrenias that could be replaced by any other without some adverse effect on the patient. This fact is plainly and unequivocally demonstrated in the 208 probands of the present study. The insulin-, electroshock-, sleep-, and fever-cures, the twilight cure with one anesthetic or the other, the highly intensive activity- or work-therapies, and the therapeutic adaptation of free time, have all been effective or noneffective in a colorful kaleidoscope of confusion. What proved useless for one patient, was suddenly a dramatic success for another. An overview of treatment methods, as they have been practised in different decades and at different clinics in different countries, gives us the large-scale view of what I experienced on a small scale with my 208 probands and several hundred other schizophrenics, namely, that treatment results can be achieved or may not be achieved by the most widely diverse methods. For example, it would be downright absurd to insist that one clinic had better treatment results than another because it administered more insulin cures than twilight cures with neuroleptics, or vice versa.

The special indications for one or another specific treatment technique do not arise from any standards by which one such technique or the other would be more suitable or more "specifically oriented toward any given basic schizophrenic process." They depend on entirely different sets of circumstances, most particularly on the individual hypersensitivity and the tolerance capacity of the patient. The patient's physical condition plays a major role, and more frequently, the psychic attitude of the patient is decisive in the selection of the treatment method; the patient's faith in the effectiveness of a given medication or his stubborn refusal of it (or even such refusals by members of his family) must be considered. The relationship of the bedridden patient who requires intensive care to those who administer that care are not helpful if they fan into flame his internal struggle with homosexual desires, without resolving it. Shocks and surprises cease to be shocks and surprises if they are repeated too often. In general, only the agitated patient needs to be tranquilized, but passive patients may have the same need if they are under internal tension—and many other similar matters-of-course apply in the selection of therapeutic methods. That selection, however, will also depend a great deal on the physician, his training, and his predilections, as well as on the care facilities available for the patient. The more skillful, well-trained nurses, ward attendants, and occupational therapists there are available with good backgrounds in treating schizophrenics, the more physical treatments can be eliminated.

The interchangeability of the greatest variety of treatment methods for schizophrenics is not the only reason that shakes one's faith in a "specific treatment method." Another reason lies in the observation of the extent to which the effectiveness of every method depends on the enthusiasm with which it is administered; that is, an active enthusiasm that becomes manifest in a close and skillful relationship to the patient. If the physical cures are administered without personal interest, without exchanging a word, or without exhibiting the least bit of personal warmth or sympathy in the process, even if they are executed with somatic exactitude, little can be accomplished by them. Nor did this information come from my probands alone; numerous other authors from a great variety of clinics have described the same thing.

Almost every new method recommended for the treatment of schizophrenics was reputedly the most effective if it was applied as soon after the onset of illness as possible. Former investigations by my colleagues and me taught me that this is true to a limited extent only. The need for further qualifying this statement is demonstrated in the findings from our present probands. It is correct to say that after treatment by all the various methods, remissions are most frequently observed when the treatments were applied soon after the onset of illness. But it should be added that most of these remissions occurring soon after the initiation of a given treatment method would also have occurred with any other method or without any treatment at all. It is only possible to apply treatment soon after onset of illness if the illness is promptly diagnosed. An early diagnosis is the more feasible, the more acutely the psychosis begins. In cases of psychoses that develop very slowly, over periods of months and years, it will only seldom be possible to initiate an effective treatment shortly after their onset. That is why most of the schizophrenias treated soon after onset are in the majority of instances schizophrenias with acute onsets; that is, schizophrenias with a good prognosis, without regard to the specific treatment method applied. Numerous serious errors have occurred because treatment results from acute-benign schizophrenias were unwittingly compared to those of the unfavorable courses of chronic-malignant schizophrenias. It was assumed that the differences in types of course were the results of early treatment, although they came about only because the benign psychoses were treated sooner than the malignant ones. The investigations of "shock-cured" schizophrenics revealed the benign character of the successfully treated schizophrenias not by their acute beginnings alone, but rather by the fact that most of the patients who underwent successful shock treatments had suffered acute schizophrenic episodes before or after such shock treatments, from which they recovered without shock treatment. Furthermore, the schizophrenias from which the patient recovered after shock treatment revealed themselves to have been selectively benign insofar as they had developed among healthier personalities on the average than nonselective schizophrenias. The schizophrenic psychoses among the relatives of shock-cured patients also more often averaged a phasic-benign course than the general average of schizophrenias, and this without shock treatment (in one case even in a monozygotic twin).

It is not only the insulin and the electroshock treatments that are particularly successful for those schizophrenias that by their nature incline toward a phasic-benign course; the same holds true for all treatment methods.

It is certain, however, that the conversion of a schizophrenia into a "catastrophe-schizophrenia" (a psychosis proceeding after an acute onset into a most severe, lifetime, chronic state) can usually be avoided by intensive treatment. But the impressive retrogression of such "catastrope-schizophrenias," insofar as it can be determined, is not dependent on one specific method, but evolved slowly and deliberately, over the course of decades, in which a variety of therapeutic measures were intensified (as was the case in the probands of this study). Whether those psychoses that would have developed into "catastrophe-schizophrenias" under unskilled treatment would have ended in recovery, or whether they would have converted to the phasic-to-mild chronic types of course under skillful treatment is still uncertain. It is also uncertain whether the decimation of the "catastrophe-schizophrenias" may be set down as the successful outcome of active treatment, or whether it should merely be ascribed to the absence of deleterious hospital conditions. Such conditions would have existed in the absence of activity and human contact for the patient, as was often customary in institutions with a poor staff. Perhaps it was only the elimination of the bed-straps and long-term isolation that brought about the virtual disappearance of "catastrophe-schizoprenias."

While former investigators overestimated the effect of early treatment, they often underestimated how effective any treatment can be even after the illness has run a course over many years. In this respect the experience with the probands of this study has shown some encouraging results. Even patients who have been ill a long time are subject to influences and have the capacity to improve. In chronic schizophrenics it is worthwhile to initiate treatments years and even decades after onset. Improvements are often achieved this way, although rarely complete remissions. These general experiences are corroborated by the data on our own probands.

The literature much more frequently puts emphasis on the urgency of early treatment than on the urgency of later treatment at the appropriate time. Still, there are also impressive recommendations for late treatment, as for instance by Howard (1960).

Time-dependent treatment methods conclude the treatment effort for only a portion of schizophrenics, mainly for that portion that tends toward a benign course, even without treatment. Most schizophrenics are ill over periods of years and decades, and for this reason long-term treatment is essential.

Neuroleptic drugs were introduced in our clinic at about the middle of the 22-23-year observation period of our probands. In the last 9–10 years of that observation period they were already in common use. For many patients these drugs had their beneficial effect not only in the acute phases, but also in chronic states over extended periods of time, among both the in- and outpatients of our clinic, and this corresponds to experiences on the international scene. But most of these patients sooner or later reached a state in which they fared as well or better without the drugs than with them.[21] Many requested that medication be stopped because of undesirable side-effects or for the sake of convenience, and many others just simply did not take their prescribed medication for the same reasons. The dis-

21. In the course of recent years a great deal of data has been accumulated on the fact that the importance of long-term maintenance with neuroleptics has been much overrated. In many cases long-term medication can be reduced or eliminated without the risk of aggravation (Ekblom and Lassenius (1964), Simon et al. (1965), Cawley (1967), Letemendia and Harris (1967), Pritchard (1967), Abenson (1969), and Zocchi (1969). In concurrence with my own findings, newer authors are also discovering that most released schizophrenics who remain outside of clinics are not subjected to regular drug maintenance programs (Herjanic et al 1969).

pensing of medication was by no means the only help nor even the most important one that could be given to chronic patients.

Based on the experience with our probands, the overall picture as to the prophylactic effects of neuroleptic drugs is unfavorable, considering the relapses into acute psychotic phases from states of recovery or virtual recovery from schizophrenia. Not one single patient living outside the clinic for years or permanently, in a state of recovery or improvement, ever took medication over extended periods of time. In the majority of cases, medication was not prescribed to ambulatory patients; and if it was, the prescription was for short periods only. On the other hand, many inpatients while living at the clinic or after probationary releases suffered relapses under neuroleptic drugs.

If we relied only on experience with our own 208 probands, we would arrive at a negative conclusion about the prophylactic value of neuroleptic drugs for released schizophrenics. However, such a negative judgment would be incorrect. Like all clinicians, I am acquainted with other schizophrenics who often suffered relapses after the cessation of neuroleptic drugs, but who can be maintained outside the clinic with long-term medication of neuroleptics. I am reluctant to advise against the prescription of long-term medication with neuroleptics for prophylactic purposes in every case of schizophrenic remission.

Nevertheless, my experiences with the principal probands are a clear indication that the value of any—and particularly of prophylactic—long-term maintenance with neuroleptics of remitted or partially remitted schizophrenics must not be overestimated. The assumption that the majority of improved schizophrenics would remain improved only under neuroleptics for any length of time is an error. It is especially erroneous to assume that cases with advance indication of acute relapses after remissions can in most instances be prevented by neuroleptic medication. There are great numbers of long-term remissions without neuroleptics, and an equally great number of relapses that occurred while the patient was under treatment with neuroleptics.

Beyond this, the disadvantages of long-term maintenance with neuroleptics must be kept in mind. One of these disadvantages in particular is receiving too little attention: Numerous patients who are given long-term prescriptions for neuroleptics simply do not take them, and for various reasons. The most frequent of these is pure indifference; then there are the unpleasant side-effects, such as fatigue, dizziness, or dryness of the mouth. Sometimes medications are not taken for eccentric personal reasons or delusional prejudices. When a doctor prescribes medications that the patient does not want to take, a distorted situation may develop. Either the ambulatory patient ceases to go to that doctor, or the doctor must continually admonish the patient to follow his counsel, or the patient becomes dishonest and lies about no longer taking his prescribed medication. Over a number of years I have collected data on how often long-term medications of all kinds are not taken. I am acquainted with scientific papers on the effects of drugs that were prescribed, to be sure, but actually never taken. All these situations are distressing.

The long-term dispensing of neuroleptic drugs is a measure I strive to avoid because it also often dampens the vitality and the initiative of a person. Patients under such long-term medication are sometimes more impersonal, more "adynamic," and less sharply defined in personality—this, to be sure, by no means always, but sometimes. So we see that long-term maintenance with neuroleptics is fraught with some of the same disadvantages that are ascribed to lobotomies. In addition, there are the dangers of permanent physical damage, although these are not yet sufficiently well known. One of such dangers is that the neurological effects of such drugs are often not only temporarily troublesome and offensive, but that they lead to permanent damage. This I did not witness among my probands, but then I could not have seen it, because none of them were treated with strong neuroleptic drugs over extended periods. Among my other patients, too, I witnessed, but fortunately only once, a severe case of dyskinesia that persisted a number of months after cessation of drug treatment. Several have been described in the literature. Mild cases of dyskinesia, such as twitching of the mouth, often persist over long periods. The question of permanent damage in all cases to the cornea, the retina, and the liver has still not been sufficiently explained. Many patients also incur danger from drugs when they drive cars against medical advice, and especially if they do not realize that the effect of alcohol is intensified by the drugs.

For all these reasons, it seems to me that long-term drug treatment is not indicated for all remitting schizophrenics, but only when it is certain that regression is threatened after withdrawal of the drug. Much more often a prompt reduction in the dispensation of drugs, rather than long-term treatment, proved helpful for threatening cases of regression, both in our probands and in other patients.

For probands released from the clinic who were receiving medical treatment, drug treatment was not the primary method; the indulgent counseling of the probands and of their families in matters of their day-to-day concerns and difficulties was far more important. Many of our probands lived at home contentedly for long periods of time, under such a care program, administered by general practitioners or specialists. These probands were not the types of patients who were subjected to intensive aftercare programs, with group therapy sessions including themselves and their families, in ex-patient clubs, or by other similar methods.

One experience in the context of the modern trend toward aftercare seems worth mentioning. As valuable and important as long-term aftercare for released schizophrenics may be, and as welcome as the modern development of this aftercare has come to be, it can be just as helpful to many schizophrenics to be released from aftercare at the appropriate point in time and to be allowed to stand independently on their own feet. It was advantageous to many of our probands to be suddenly or gradually left to depend on themselves. It usually turned out then that the capacity of the patient to bring about his own recovery was greater than it had been estimated to be. At times the patients would reorganize their lives in an eccentric or even a pathological fashion; yet, in such a way that they really fared better than under the circumstances that would have been deemed appropriate by the doctors and the social workers. Several of my patients joined religious sectarian groups, others joined small political extremist groups that had gathered around the influence of an oppositionally oriented or a querulous eccentric, and, surprisingly, to their own advantage. A young, academically inclined and well-educated girl from an intellectual and affluent family, who was not able to improve in her environment at home, began working under substandard employment conditions as house- and kitchen maid, had the feeling that by so doing she would come closer to reality and make herself useful by her personal dedication, and under these conditions she actually recovered. The most peculiar kind of therapeutic adaptation came to my attention through one of our female patients, Proband 90.

She was married to a loving husband (to be sure, he had come from an entirely different background than hers), but she fell ill at age 24. After a lingering onset, she suffered a great number of schizophrenic exacerbations during the 10 years that followed. Even during the better interim periods she never fully recovered. As a mother, wife, and homemaker she had become impossible and had to be quickly rehospitalized after every trial release. After she was divorced, numerous attempts were made to place her in foster families for both medical and social work care, but all these attempts failed. Then she withdrew from aftercare. She ceased to come back to the clinic, and I had a great deal of trouble locating her for the catamnesis. When I did, an amazing change had taken place. She had found peace as the housekeeper of her divorced husband. While she had made the marriage impossible with her psychosis, and while she was unable to maintain herself in what appeared to be the most suitable foster families, she was now working for her former husband, just as if she were his hired housekeeper, living in the maid's quarters, serving at table when guests were invited, and generally keeping her distance, as any house employee would. She had remained autistic, eccentric, and enigmatically delusional, but in the social sense she had recovered. The patient had understood how to create a salutary milieu for herself; the doctors and social workers had not.

In addition to these examples of peculiar and pathological, but yet successful adaptations, there are also many more normal ones. I know patients who unexpectedly secured and held jobs after they had been released or had escaped from organized care, while they had remained psychotic in the social sense under the most carefully administered aftercare.

Just as in former times the tendency persisted to keep schizophrenics hospitalized if they did not recover, so today the tendency prevails to maintain them under care outside the clinics. According to my experience this tendency, in the main, has a favorable effect. But just as there are on the record some individual releases of unrecovered patients from clinics, so also are there individual releases of unrecovered patients from outpatient care.

Such releases are usually troublesome. As is the case with early releases from the clinic, these overburden the physician with a great deal of added responsibility. It is necessary to study in great detail the early history of such patients before recommending their early release.

Frequently release from aftercare becomes difficult for financial reasons, since it involves the loss of sickness benefits. I know patients who justifiably complain, "I am not permitted to work." What they really mean is they must not regain their health, because they would lose their sickness benefits if they did; and this was indeed the fact. These sickness benefits often serve to shackle the patient in golden chains that prohibit his recovery. An arrangement ought to be made so that patients in probational employment situations do not jeopardize their income from sickness benefits, and that both patient and his family should be made to grasp what good fortune it is to recover one's health and the ability of earning a living, even when the support income has to be given up.

The experiences worth mentioning with therapeutic methods with the principal probands—which I cannot really separate from those with other schizophrenics—may be summarized as follows:

1. Intensified therapeutic methods applied in recent decades have been able to combat with considerable success the "catastrophe-schizophrenias" (schizophrenias that convert to lifelong, severe chronic states without remissions after acute beginnings). But there are no indications for assuming that therapeutic methods have to date been capable of eliminating unfavorable outcomes in the progressive chronic schizophrenias.

No evidence is available as to whether those cases that formerly would have developed into "catastrophe-schizophrenias" could have ended in recovery today, or whether they convert to other forms that simply do not have remissions any more after intermittent exacerbations.

2. The majority of cases reported as "recovered" under active treatment methods applied early after initial onset concern schizophrenic psychoses with a good initial prognosis.

Whereas the successes of early treatment used to be overestimated, the more recent inclination is to underestimate the therapeutic efficacy of repeated treatments after a course of long duration.

3. Improvements are to be expected from skillful treatment for all schizophrenic psychoses.

4. No treatment method directed specifically toward schizophrenia has so far been identified. All effective treatment methods consider three basic therapeutic requirements in various combinations.

—Reintegration of the patient into the active community and provision for space and facilities for his healthy activities

—Surprise and shock

—When needed, tranquilization (special indications in individual cases, as in acute delirium, in frequent depressions, etc.).

The success of a treatment method depends less on any specific technique than on the constant, skillful, and patient pursuit of the above-mentioned therapeutic objectives.

5. As a time-limited treatment method in acute schizophrenic psychoses, treatment with neuroleptic drugs for tranquilizing and for facilitating the patient's reintegration into the community has proved to be effective in our clinic as well as everywhere else. Even in chronic cases such drugs often produced improvement over extended periods. Then again, the patient fared better without neuroleptics, after a period of time that varied with each case.

Long-term states of improvement or recovery without medication of schizophrenics after hospital release are far more frequent than some statements in the modern literature would lead one to expect. On the other hand, retrogressions into acute episodes despite the application of neuroleptics are also more frequent than many recommendations on prophylactic long-term treatment methods would indicate. Medication after recovery has been achieved is only indicated when the individual case demands it, because aggravations threaten after the medication is withdrawn. Long-term treatment with neuroleptics requires exceptional care, because numerous dangers and adverse reactions must be weighed against any possible advantages.

6. Even more important than drug treatments for released schizophrenics have been the long-term psychotherapeutic and social welfare counseling sessions with the patient and his family.

Just as the early release policies for schizophrenics from their clinics have become an important therapeutic measure, so also are there indications for the release from aftercare of nonrecovered schizophrenics. Some individual patients develop unsuspected powers to heal themselves during certain phases of their illness, if they are left to themselves, (on probation, and carefully time-controlled).

Causes of Death

There are numerous statistics on the causes of death of schizophrenics who died while they were inpatients at a hospital, and on the causes of death among the general population. On the other hand, there are no statistics on the causes of death of schizophrenics who died within 22–26 years after their hospitalization. A survey of the causes of death of the 70 principal probands is of limited value, since there is no material on hand for comparisons.

Despite this, I felt that there was a certain value in looking into the causes of their deaths, particularly because so very little is still known about the causes of death of schizophrenics who have been released from hospitals for a long time.

Of the 208 probands, 70 died during the observation period, between 1942/43 and 1964/65. The causes of death are shown in Table 4.30.

There are no statistically significant differences in the causes of death between men and women; besides, the figures are too small. For this reason, the causes of death will be discussed jointly for both sexes.

The most frequent cases of death (12 of 70) occurred in immediate or remote relationship to treatment in severe psychotic states, either in acute psychoses or in exacerbations of chronic psychoses. Individually considered, these 12 cases were ascribed to the following causes:

Deaths not related to treatment as a possible cause

—Suddenly dropped dead in a state of catatonic agitation, and autopsy did not reveal definite cause

—Sudden collapse and death after the severely catatonic patient was lifted from his bath, and autopsy did not reveal definite cause.

Deaths concurrent with electroshock treatment

—Femoral fracture during electroshock therapy, nailing repair under anesthetic, then collapse—diagnosis of the pathologist was "heart failure with dilatation"

—Violent vomiting attacks, collapse; sudden death one day after electroshock therapy; autopsy did not reveal definite cause.

Deaths concurrent with sleep therapy

—Pulmonary infarction

Table 4.30. Causes of death of principal probands

	Men	Women	Total
Malignant tumors	5	3	8
Cardiac infarct	4	3	7
Myodegeneratio cordis	1	2	3
Apoplexy	0	2	2
Sudden death at over 65 years of age, without autopsy (certificate registers heart attack or stroke)	1	3	4
Marasmus—general weakness and senility over age 75	1	4	5
Pulmonary tuberculosis	6	2	8
Renal tuberculosis	0	1	1
Pneumonia at advanced age	0	2	2
Pulmonary embolism	0	1	1
Pharyngeal abscess	1	0	1
Volvulus	0	1	1
Bleeding duodenal ulcer	1	0	1
Strangulated hernia	0	1	1
Diabetic coma	0	1	1
Found dead in bed (at advanced age); no autopsy	0	1	1
Death in immediate or related connection with treatment in acute psychotic states	7	5	12
Suicide	4	5	9
Accidental	1	1	2
	32	38	70

—Pulmonary abscess, probably caused by aspiration during vomiting under sleep therapy (2 cases); sudden death during sleep therapy, and autopsy did not reveal cause of death (2 cases).

Deaths concurrent with twilight therapy
—Pneumonia.

Death concurrent with brain surgery
—Cerebral hemorrhage during transcortical lobotomy
—Prefrontal lobotomy, followed by attacks of epilepsy, and heart infarct during one of these.

Most of these cases of death occurred either during, or shortly after the war, and under circumstances that were favorable to neither the treatment nor the determination of the cause of death. For instance, there was no penicillin available for the treatment of pneumonias; the modern methods for keeping open the breathing passages during unconsciousness had not yet been introduced; brain surgery was attempted more frequently before the introduction of neuroleptics than they are today, and partly by surgeons who lacked experience in using them; there was a lack of medical personnel during the mobilization period; and in some of the clinics, autopsies were not always performed by trained pathologists, so that probably the more delicate changes remained undetected.

In 5 of the 12 cases, neither clinical observation nor the autopsy adequately revealed the cause of death. Naturally there was no lack of minor findings (congestion of organs, myodegeneration, mild brain swelling, mild pulmonary hypostasis, and the like), but there were no findings that would unequivocally have explained the death. The psychiatrist who treats the most severe cases of mental illness is often depressed by the deaths of his patients, which occur in a state of hyperagitation and for which the pathologist has no adequate explanation. They occur in states of acute delirium, in extended comas caused by insulin cures and tranquilizer therapies of all kinds, and they occur also whether tranquilizers have been dispensed or not. The "fatal catatonias" of former times are no longer encountered today, because suspected cases are promptly arrested by intensive treatment. After the patient has died one is never quite certain whether death occurred in spite of the treatment, or whether it should be ascribed to the treatment, in particular to poisoning by the medication.

Suicide ranks second among the causes of death in the 208 schizophrenic probands of

Table 4.31. Suicide and tuberculosis as cause of death compared with population of Switzerland (For comparison see frequency of suicide and tuberculosis as cause of death among probands, Table 4.30)

Switzerland	All deaths				Suicides				Death of tuberculosis			
	Total		Deaths at age 30 or later		Total		Deaths at age 30 or later		Total		Deaths at age 30 or later	
	Men	Women	Men	Women	Men	Women	Men	Women	Men	Women	Men	Women
1940 in figures	25721	25038	21500	22310	751	245	576	204	1761	1542	1272	1005
Percentage of all deaths in the appropriate category					2.9%	1.0%	2.7%	0.9%	6.8%	6.2%	5.9%	4.5%
1950 in figures	24178	23194	21239	21161	787	314	665	250	950	696	777	557
Percentage of all deaths in the appropriate category					3.3%	1.4%	3.1%	1.2%	3.9%	3.0%	3.7%	2.6%
1960 in figures	27032	25062	24544	23590	718	298	583	243	383	245	371	234
Percentage of all deaths in the appropriate category					2.7%	1.2%	2.4%	1.0%	1.4%	1.0%	1.5%	1.0%

this study. Nine of the 70 who died during our observation period were suicides, or 13 percent (with a confidence interval at 95 percent = 6 percent–23 percent). The figure significantly exceeds the frequency of suicides among the general population. Our probands died between 1942 and 1965. During this period the proportion of suicides among all causes of death in Switzerland for males was about 3 percent, and for females a little over 1 percent. But since all suicides of our probands occurred when they were over 30 years old, only those cases of suicide of people over 30 among the general population should be used in the comparisons. However, suicide as a cause of death in people over 30 among the entire population occurs at about the same frequency as it does among all cases of death— just slightly less. The precise comparisons for the average population are shown in Table 4.31.

In inspecting Table 4.31, the following is to be noted. The statistics apply to the whole of Switzerland. There are no separate statistics for causes of death for the Canton of Zürich alone. Deaths of our probands occurred between 1943 and 1965, while the key years for figures for the entire population, taken from the statistical records, were 1940, 1950, and 1960. While suicides among the total population were twice as frequent for men as for women, among our present probands they were almost equal for both sexes (men 12 percent and women 13 percent).

It is common knowledge that schizophrenias include the danger of suicide. The assumption that suicides from schizophrenias occur most frequently at the beginning of the psychosis is common, but experience with our probands contradicts this assumption. One single female patient committed suicide at the beginning of her psychosis (one month after onset); for the other 8 suicides 2 to 32 years intervened between the beginning of their illness and their act. Time intervals for the 4 men were 2, 4, 13, and 32 years, and for the 5 women, 1 month, 3, 14, 16½, and 30 years. From my own general clinical experience I know and fear the danger of suicide late in the course of schizophrenias. The older view corresponded to the concept that in the course of time the inner life of schizophrenics "was extinguished, dulled, or burned out," and that in time they would lose their "internal dynamics" and their capacity to suffer. But the fact that years and decades after onset of illness suicides continue to occur

points to the fallacy of that outdated assumption. It is also placed in doubt by many findings in our probands, in several other chapters.

Schulz (1949) found a slightly greater frequency of suicides among the causes of death of schizophrenic men than among those of schizophrenic women. There is no such difference apparent in the present study.

The third most frequent cause of death among the 208 schizophrenic probands is pulmonary tuberculosis (8 probands). One female proband died of renal tuberculosis. Accordingly, of the 70 probands who died during the observation period, 13 percent (credibility limit at 95 percent = 6 percent– 23 percent) died of tuberculosis: 6 men (18 percent of the male deaths) and 3 women (8 percent of the female deaths). The difference between the sexes is not significant, although it corresponds to the sex ratio for the general population.

Any comparison between the mortality rates from tuberculosis among our probands and those of the general population is risky. Since the beginning of this study in 1942, the mortality from tuberculosis has decreased appreciably. In 1940 6.8 percent of all deaths in Switzerland were still caused by tuberculosis, and in 1960, only 1.4 percent; the corresponding figures for women were 6.2 percent and 1.0 percent, respectively. Besides, the rate of deaths caused by tuberculosis is different among different age groups. In order to be able to make a valid comparison, one would have to know in what year and at what age the tubercular patient died of this disease. The death years of the 9 tubercular probands were 1943, 1943, 1946, 1946, 1948, 1949, 1954, 1955, and 1956. Their ages were 38, 48, 52, 54, 58, 60, 64, 67, and 74 years. For this reason, none of the figures in Table 4.31 should be used for comparison without close inspection. The best comparison figure results from considering the deaths in 1950 in the age group 40–70. Among these cases of death in the population of Switzerland, tuberculosis caused 5.1 percent of them in men and 3.6 percent in women. Accordingly, tuberculosis as the cause of death occurred 2 to 4 times as frequently among our probands who died, as among the general population. The difference, however, considering the small figures of the causes of death statistically, just barely approaches the limits of significance.

Kraepelin (1909) calculated that, among schizophrenic inpatients of institutions, tuberculosis occurs 4 to 5 times more frequently than among the general population. Meyer (1943) discovered that the mortality rate of tuberculosis in schizophrenics was 4.5 times that of the general population. The statistics by Schulz (1949) reveal a slightly smaller difference. Oddly enough, the preponderance of tuberculosis deaths that prevailed in many clinics about the turn of the century did not occur at Burghölzli. E. Bleuler wrote about this in 1911 as follows:

"In our clinic no more schizophrenics died of phthisis than in the population around us. According to some authors this disease seems to be a particularly frequent complication of dementia praecox."

The authors mentioned derived most of their findings from hospitalized schizophrenics. In our present probands, a portion of those who died had been released from the hospital long before their deaths. According to my knowledge, there are no reliable statistics available on the causes of death of schizophrenics long after their release from clinics.

A comparison of the frequency of tuberculosis as a cause of death between our probands and the average population, as shown in Table 4.31, is furthermore not feasible because almost all our probands died in the Canton of Zürich, but the comparison figures representing the population exist only for the whole of Switzerland.

Here is a careful interpretation of the 9 deaths from tuberculosis. For definite conclusions the figures are much too small. However, they may support the assumptions that
—The frequency of tuberculosis as a cause of death of schizophrenics has markedly decreased in recent decades, just as its frequency has as a cause of death among the general population.
—Tuberculosis as a cause of death among schizophrenics is still occurring at a greater frequency than among the general population.

Just as many probands (9) died of malignant tumors as of suicide and of tuberculosis. Among the general population, deaths caused by malignant tumors occur at several times the frequency as deaths caused by tuberculosis and also by suicide. In this respect the causes of death among our probands as compared to those among the general population occur at a markedly distorted ratio.

The frequency of malignant tumors, tuberculosis, and suicides as causes of death occurs for our probands at a ratio of 9:9:9, and for the entire population of Switzerland in 1940, as 7437:3303:996, in 1950, as 8397:1646:1101; in 1960, as 9441:628:1016.

The low proportion of malignant tumors as a cause of death among our probands is largely due to the fact that three other causes of death occur at a greater frequency among them than they do among the general population—the sudden death during severe acute psychoses, death from tuberculosis, and suicides. It would be important to determine whether there are still other causes for the rarity of malignomes as causes of death among the schizophrenic probands. The probands of this study are not suited for the exploration of this question.

All other causes of death beyond the four discussed above were individual cases among our probands. In this context a detailed discussion of these would not be fruitful.

5 Siblings, Half-Siblings, and Offspring of Siblings of Schizophrenics

Number of Siblings and Frequency of Twin Births

We succeeded in collecting data on all the siblings of the principal schizophrenic probands, and in constructing a summary picture of the course of their lives and their mental health until they died or to the end of the observation period.

The 208 principal probands had a total of 818 siblings, of whom 144 (17.6 percent) died early, that is, before their 18th birthday, and in most cases in their infancy. The average number of siblings of our probands was 3.9.

The corresponding averages in some other studies used for comparisons were
—For the 100 Pfäfers schizophrenics from my 1941 investigation, 4.9
—For the 100 American schizophrenics from my 1930 investigation, 3.5
—For the 89 shock-treated and recovered Basel schizophrenics from my 1941 investigation, 4.1
—For the 65 Basel schizophrenics from my 1943 investigation, 4.1
—For the 200 Danish schizophrenics reported by Smith (1936), 5.3
—For the 200 general patients from my 1932 investigations in the rural sectors around Basel, 5.6
—For the 100 Zürich tuberculosis patients from my 1935 investigations, 4.8

The averages listed cannot be compared directly with one another, because the probands come from different localities and from different periods of time. Besides, there are a number of parents among the schizophrenics from Pfäfers and the United States, and especially among the general patients from the rural environs of Basel and the tuberculosis patients from Zürich, who may possibly have had children after the end of the observation period, which means that the given averages for their children represent a minimum. After careful study, however, the above listings do show that the sibships of schizophrenics are no larger than those of general patients. This fact will be discussed again in the context of the investigations on the fertility of schizophrenics.

The differences in the number of siblings among the different groups of schizophrenics

that I investigated are easily explained. The minimal average of siblings (3.5) was for the American schizophrenics, that is, patients who primarily came from urban homes, and whose parents were still so young that they could still have more children. The maximal average (4.9) was for the Pfäfers schizophrenics, who came from a completely rural environment, in which the number of children in families was greater than in the cities of Zürich and Basel during that period. The number of siblings of the principal probands, however, lies between that of the American and the Pfäfers probands, just as the probands of this study also came partly from rural and partly from urban communities.

There were 11 sets of twins among the probands and their siblings together. Three pairs were like-sexed, 8 opposite-sexed, and 7 probands were themselves one of a pair of twins. For 92 births, therefore, there was one twin birth.[1] According to the most favorable probability, one twin birth may be expected for about 82 total births. The difference lies within the probabilities of chance, and is by no means significant.

For decades it has been an established fact that there is no predominance of twins among schizophrenics or their siblings.[2] It would have made no sense to repeat the count of the pairs of twins, just to prove that truism all over again. On the other hand, it is a criterion of reliability for the data on a group of probands, to know whether the expected number of twin births conforms to the actual findings. The test was passed with respect to the data on our our sibships. In one case, 1 of the like-sexed twins died shortly after birth; another case was very probably one involving monozygotic twins that is, 2 mentally perfectly normal brothers of a female schizophrenic proband;

1. Customarily the birth of twins is counted as a single birth and related as such to all births of a mother. The number of births by proband mothers corresponds to the number of probands (208), plus the number of probands' siblings (818), minus half the number of twins (11). It amounts to 1015.

2. Previous findings on this subject have been summarized, among others by Rosenthal (1961), and Kringlen (1968) reconfirmed the old findings by his twin studies.

Table 5.1. Mental disorders among siblings of male probands, arranged according to whether they were alive or dead at the end of the observation period, according to sex, and according to age when they died or at the end of the observation period

Types of mental disorders among all Male probands' siblings

Age group	Living or dead	Sex	All siblings	Schizophrenia	Probable schizophrenia	Manic-depressive illness	Epilepsy	Senile psychosis	Other psychoses	Feeblemindedness	Schizoid psychopathy	Alcoholism	Other disorders	Suicides
0–18	Dead	m	35							1[9]				
		f	22											
		?	1											
19–39	Living	m	7	1										
		f	10										1[11]	
	Dead	m	17		1[4]					1	1		1[12]	6
		f	13					1		1				2
40–59	Living	m	56	9[2]							1	1	8[13]	
		f	52	8[3]		1							6[14]	
	Dead	m	17[1]	2						1		2[10]	2[15]	4
		f	17	3					1[6]	1			2[16]	
60–79	Living	m	44	2	2[5]					1	1	1	3[17]	
		f	55	7		1			1[7]				8[18]	
	Dead	m	15	1		1	1		1[8]			1	1[19]	
		f	8					2		1				
80 or over	Living	m	2											
		f	3											
	Dead	m	3										2[20]	
		f	2											
Totals:			379	33	3	3	1	3	3	7	3	5	34	12

1. Age had to be estimated for 1 of these. He was living abroad; exact dates of birth and death could not be determined (Proband 98).

2. 2 of these, mixed psychoses with mania.

3. 1 of these, manic-depressive mixed psychosis

4. Brother committed suicide at age 34. Before that, an excessively conscientious but efficient gardener with a great sense of responsibility. Suicide was committed during an acute psychosis, that was, according to our estimate, a depressive catatonia rather than a pure depression (Proband 79).

5. A 78-year-old man, never hospitalized. He had always been eccentric, alcoholic, sullen, uncommunicative, and a loner. He committed a number of exhibitionist offenses, for which he was placed under the guardianship of a well-known private neurologist. The latter reported that, beginning at about age 37, this patient developed a mild chronic schizophrenia, with an obstinate attitude toward official and administrative agencies, intense negativism, delusional mistrust, and eccentric behavior (for instance, for a long time he carried live squirrels about under his clothing). However, his guardian did not specify any definite, tangible psychotic symptoms of this patient (Proband 25).

A 76-year-old man, never hospitalized. In childhood he had been a young genius, highly intelligent; passed both highschool and college examinations with outstanding marks. Beginning at age 22, however, a complete "loafer," never holding a proper job. Wanted to compose or to study philology, but accomplished nothing. Had a delusional attitude of protest against many. For a number of years has lived in solitude in a single room, where he cooks his own meals. Was pronounced a "hebephrenic simpleton" by one examining physician (Proband 48).

6. Psychosis of unknown type, quick-tempered, had been institutionalized in the United States.

7. Chorea (Huntington's?), depressive, compulsive neurotic, organic psychosyndrome.

8. Delirium tremens, although only an occasional light social drinker.

(Continuation of footnotes of Table 5.1)

9. Hydrocephalus; died at birth.

10. 1 of these: psychopath, confused thought processes.

11. Submanic.

12. Severe poriomania.

13. 2 eccentrics; 1 reactive depressive; 1 stunted development; 1 unstable psychopath; 1 difficult personality, unsteady; 2 stutterers.

14. 1 often depressed; 1 mild depressive; 1 one-time depression 1 neurotic depression; 1 querulous psychopath (female); 1 hospitalized as a child for attacks of hysteria.

15. 1 stutterer; one Parkinson's disease (postencephalitic).

16. 1 excitable (female) psychopath; 1 rigid eccentric.

17. 2 eccentrics; 1 criminal (embezzlement).

18. 1 with attacks of melancholia; 2 reactive depressives; 2 mild depressives; 1 depressive, (female) querulous psychopath; 1 criminal, unstable (female) psychopath; 1 unstable (female) criminal (theft).

19. Multiple sclerosis, sexual delinquent.

20. 1 cretinoid, but not debilitated; 1 phasic heart- and anxiety-neurosis with phasic depressions.

and the third case involved a female proband and her twin sister. The extreme difference in appearance and the exceptionally higher degree of debility in the twin sister of the proband suggest that they were dizygotic. Among our probands there were no monozygotic twins of whom one or both became schizophrenic.

Mental Disorders among the Siblings of Schizophrenics

A survey of the mental disorders among the the 818 siblings of the 208 principal probands of this study is provided in Tables 5.1 and 5.2. Table 5.4 provides data for comparisons.

Schizophrenias

Among the 818 siblings of our probands, there are 57 certain, and 6 probable schizophrenics (Tables 5.1 and 5.2).

If the probability is taken into account that at the conclusion of the observation period not all siblings who will ever be schizophrenic had already become schizophrenic, by applying Weinberg's[3] abbreviated method, we

3. The raw percentages of schizophrenics within a population group depend on the age structure of that population. If that group contains a large number of young people, many of these could still become schizophrenic after the time at which the schizophrenics were counted. But if the age structure of that population and the average onset-age are known, the true "schizophrenia-onset probability" can be calculated (that is, the percentage of schizophrenics to be expected at a certain point in time at which all who are going to be ill have, in fact, become ill). For an accurate calculation, the distribution of schizophrenic onset for every year of life would have to be taken into consideration, and this is done in Stroemgren's method. To simplify the calculations, we assume, according to Weinberg's method, that half of those who will be schizophrenic at all have already become schizophrenic during the period of maximum susceptibility. The number to which the number of actual schizophrenics

arrive at an onset probability of 9.0 percent for the siblings of probands, counting only the definite schizophrenics, and of 9.9 percent if the probable schizophrenics are included.

These percentages were calculated on the assumption that the age of vulnerability for schizophrenic onset extends from ages 18 to 40. The great majority of the siblings, however, drop out of observation at an advanced age. The probability for onset remains the same, however, whether the age of vulnerability is fixed to begin at ages 15, 16, or 20, or at 18. But if the end of the vulnerability period were shifted to age 45 (instead of the customary 40, as it was in the above calculations), the percentages will be a little higher.

Thanks to the good offices of Prof. E. Stroemgren on my behalf, his colleague, Dr. Nils Engkilde, in Aarhus, Denmark, calculated the onset probabilities of the siblings for me, according to Stroemgren's more accurate method. It turned out that the figures according to the abbreviated Weinberg method and the accurate Stroemgren method used in the present investigation are almost identical. The onset probability for schizophrenia among the 818 siblings of probands amounts to 9.0 percent by Weinberg's method, and to 9.9 percent by Stroemgren's. When the figures are broken down by sexes, and also when the probable cases of schizophrenia are

is to be related (the base figure) is calculated according to the formula: Half the total population who are at the age of susceptibility plus all members of the population who have passed the age of susceptibility. Those members of the population who have not reached the age of susceptibility are not taken into consideration. Unfortunately, the age of susceptibility for schizophrenia is not always placed at the same level in all investigations. Sometimes that age is fixed at 15, then again at 16, at 18, or at 20 years. For the most part, the final age is fixed at 40, and by a few authors at 45 or at 50 years.

Table 5.2. Mental disorders among siblings of female probands categorized as to whether they were living or dead at the end of the observation period, by sex, and by age at time of death or end of observation period

Types of disorders among all female probands' siblings

Age group	Living or dead	Sex	All siblings	Schizophrenia	Probable Schizophrenia	Epilepsy	Senile psychosis	Other psychoses	Feeblemindedness	Schizoid Psychopathy	Alcoholism	Other disorders	Suicides
0–18	Dead	m	46						1				
		f	36									1[14]	
		?	4										
19–39	Living	m	3										
		f	1										
	Dead	m	18	1					1		1	2[15]	2
		f	11[1]	2	1[5]	1			1[11]				1
40–59	Living	m	55[2]	1	1[6]	1		2[8]	4	2	1	7[16]	
		f	63[3]	6[4]				1[9]	5	2		8[17]	
	Dead	m	25	1					1		4[13]	1[18]	4
		f	14	4	1[7]			1[10]				1[19]	
60–79	Living	m	44	1			3		4[12]		4	4[20]	
		f	60	5			2		4	1		4[21]	
	Dead	m	25	1			2			1	2	4[22]	
		f	19	2						2		3[23]	
80 and over	Living	m	4				1		1		1		
		f	5										
	Dead	m	3							1			
		f	3										
Totals:			439	24	3	2	8	4	22	9	13	35	7

There were no cases of manic-depressive illness among the female probands.

1. 1 of these:⎫ Age was estimated. Six siblings are
2. 1 of these:⎬ involved. They live abroad; exact
3. 4 of these:⎭ birthdates could not be determined.
   (Proband 4)
4. 1 of these, Basedow's disease.
5. Sister died of influenza at age 21. She was a high-strung, peculiar young girl, who was treated in a clinic abroad for "delirium," but the clinic never sent me convincing data about a diagnosis of schizophrenia on her (Proband 54).
6. Brother was twice punitively interned by court order on testimony of expert witnesses and diagnosed as schizophrenic. When I scanned the records, however, I found that the psychopathological data was so poorly described that, in retrospect, I am no longer certain of the diagnosis (Proband 54).
7. Sister lived from 1868–1921, and before she died was hospitalized at a private psychiatric clinic, where the diagnosis was hallucinatory paranoia (the patient record was lost). She had been a housekeeper, reclusive, and given to religious fanaticism. Her psychosis began about one year before her death, at age 52, and she did not recover (Proband 86).

8. 1 unknown psychosis (hospitalized in Poland, and disappeared); 1 Huntington's chorea, gradual lapse into psychic ihiocy.
9. 1 unknown psychosis (totally withdrawn, speaks and laughs to herself).
10. Chromophobic hypophyseal adenoma, psycho-organically changed, almost blind.
11. Spina bifida.
12. 1 of these a deaf-mute; the other a sex offender.
13. 1 of these an unstable psychopath.
14. Enuresis; highly sensitive.
15. 1 Recklinghausen's disease; 1 an unstable psychopath.
16. 1 with apoplexy and unilateral paralysis; 1 with endogenous or reactive depression; 1 deaf-mute following meningitis; 1 difficult personality, psychopathic; 1 post-traumatic encephalosis; 1 irritable psychopath; 1 with neurotic-depressive personality development.
17. 1 pedantic-compulsive and colitis ulcerosa; 1 psychasthenic; 1 endogenous depression; 1 mild phobic neurosis and Basedow's disease; 1 melancholic and

(*Continuation of footnotes of Table 5.2*)
moody; 1 with mild depressive phases; 1 with encephalitis lethargica, Parkinson's disease; and one female highly changeable and moody.

18. Excitable, stubborn psychopath.
19. Schizoid.
20. 1 schizoid; 2 deaf-mutes; 1 difficult personality

with "nervous trembling."

21. 1 infantilistic, unrealistic; 1 neurotic; 1 stunted development; 1 constantly suffering from mild depression.

22. 1 difficult personality, frightened; 2 schizoid eccentrics; one unstable psychopath.

23. 1 mildly psychoorganic; 1 schizoid; 1 with chronic nephritis, depressive.

---

included, the differences between the calculated percentages by the two methods are quite minimal.

Since the basic figures are large, the confidence intervals and median errors for the stated percentages are small. The median error for the probability of diagnostically certain schizophrenic onset of 9 percent is 1.1, and that for the combined diagnostically certain and probable schizophrenias, 1.2. The confidence interval per *Documenta Geigy* (rounded off to the closest figure in the tables) is 7–11 percent for the 9 percent, and 7–12 percent for the 9.9 percent probability.

The conformity in onset probability of the siblings of the Pfäfers probands and our own is remarkable; that is, 9.0 percent onset probability among the siblings of our present probands, and 10.1 percent for those of the Pfäfers probands. And if the probable schizophrenias are included, the corresponding figures read 9.9 percent and 12.5 percent, respectively. Zerbin-Rüdin (1967) figured out the percentages of onset probability for schizophrenia among the siblings of schizophrenics from all previously published investigations on the subject, and came up with the average of 10.4 percent ± 0.3. Thus, the findings for our present probands conform to those of other authors.

Table 5.3 is a partial reconstruction of one by Zerbin-Rüdin (1967), except for details that we added from our own findings. Two papers—one by Smith (1936) of Denmark and my own New York paper (1930)—were not considered, because of the low onset probability they revealed. Smith himself estimates the reason to be the fact that, among the siblings, he counted a number of undiagnosed psychoses of which some may have been schizophrenias. In the case of my New York probands, the reason lies in the admission policies of private clinics, as I explained in that same paper. In the remaining investigations, for the 12 groups of schizophrenics investigated by 9 authors, the onset probabilities fluctuate between the extremes of 5.4 percent and 14.3 percent.

These comparisons justify certain conclusion, namely, that the probability for schizophrenic onset among the siblings of schizophrenics is about the same at close to 9–10 percent, when it is figured for schizophrenic probands from different countries and in different decades of this century.[4] A similar conclusion was reached for the parents of schizophrenics (see p. 54).

As a comparison between Tables 5.1 and 5.2 shows, there are more schizophrenics among the siblings of the male probands than among those of the female probands, but the difference is not at all statistically significant ($p < 0.3$). There are no indications in the literature either that would claim significance for this difference. Until something new is discovered in this area, this fact will have to be disregarded.

The courses of schizophrenias among the siblings of probands have already been compared in Tables 4.1, 4.4, and 4.8, with those of the probands themselves, and in particular with those patients who entered the research program as probands at their first hospitalization. Because of selection biases, the courses for the siblings are bound to be milder, on the average, than those of the probands themselves. There were patients among the siblings of schizophrenics who were never hospitalized for schizophrenias (although only 2), whereas all of the probands became probands through their hospitalizations. Many of them (140 of

4. In a paper from New York State, published after this manuscript was ready for press, Pollack et al. (1969) again discovered a similar frequency of schizophrenia among the siblings of schizophrenics. Among 64 siblings of schizophrenics, there were 5 = 8 percent. To be sure, the median error of the figure is great (confidence interval at 95 percent is from 2.6 to 17.3 percent). Besides, these authors made no provision for an age-correction factor, which would increase the percentage considerably. A very recent paper by Larson and Nyman concurred closely with my findings, namely, that among the siblings of their 153 male schizophrenics from southern Sweden, 11.6 percent were schizophrenic, with age correction included.

Table 5.3. Onset probability for schizophrenia in siblings of various proband groups investigated by the author and comparative data from other authors (the latter from compilations by Zerbin-Rüdin (1967). Sibships are included even if parents were not schizophrenic. The simple standard deviations appear after the percentages

Investigator	Publication year	Probands' locale of origin	No. of probands	Base figure	Schizophrenia among the siblings Diagnostically certain cases only	Certain and probable cases combined
Bleuler	1930	New York	100	B 188	9 = 4.8% ± 1.6	12 = 6.4% ± 1.8
Bleuler	1941	Pfäfers	100	B 257	26 = 10.1% ± 1.9	32 = 12.5% ± 2.1
Bleuler	1972	Zürich/Men	100	F 297.5	33 = 11.1% ± 1.8	36 = 12.1% ± 1.9
Bleuler	1972	Zürich/Women	108	F 336.5	24 = 7.1% ± 1.4	27 = 8.0% ± 1.5
Bleuler	1972	Zürich/Men and women combined	208	F 634	57 = 9.0% ± 1.1	63 = 9.9% ± 1.2
Brugger	1928	Basel City	85[1]	A 252	26 = 10.3% ± 1.9	29 = 11.5% ± 2.0
Schulz	1932	Bavaria	660	A 1959.5	131 = 6.7% ± 0.6	163 = 8.3% ± 0.6
Luxenburger	1936	Germany	118[2]	A 278	21 = 7.6% ± 1.6	32 = 11.5% ± 1.9
Smith	1936	Denmark	200	A 611.5	20 = 3.3% ± 0.7	25 = 4.1% ± 0.8
Galatschjan	1937	Moscow	214	A 322	45 = 14.0% ± 1.9	
Kallmann	1938	Berlin	886	C 1996.5	149 = 7.5% ± 0.6	230 = 11.5% ± 0.7
Kallmann	1946	New York	691[2]	C 1434	205 = 14.3% ± 0.9	
Böök	1953	Sweden	78	D 277	27 = 9.7% ± 1.8	
Slater	1953	England	158[2]	A 481		26 = 5.4% ± 1.0
Garrone	1962	Geneva	227	E 452.5		39 = 8.6% ± 1.3

1. Grafted schizophrenia.
2. Twin probands.

Susceptibility periods:

A	15–40	E	15–70
B	20–40	F	Same results with 15–40 and 20–40
C	15–45		
D	15–50		

208) had already been hospitalized a number of times before they came into this research program. For this reason they represent a selection bias by being the types of cases that usually require hospitalization. Two groups of schizophrenias, however, should run exactly the same courses, those of siblings who had been hospitalized at least once, and those of our probands who entered this research project along with their first hospitalization. As Tables 4.1, 4.4, and and 4.8 show, this assumption, within chance variations, corresponds to our findings. To be sure, there is hardly any significant difference, in that there were more recoveries and more early onsets among the schizophrenic siblings who were hospitalized at least once than among those probands who entered the research project along with their first hospitalization. If this increase of recoveries and early-onset schizophrenias among the psychoses of these siblings is due to something other than mere coincidence, the reason should be sought in the hospitalization policies of the Canton of Zürich, where very mild cases and schizophrenias in children are more often referred to private clinics than to the University Clinic, and would therefore easily be underrepresented as probands among the clinic's inpatients.

It would be of interest to know the average courses of schizophrenias that never require hospitalization. By their nature it would be difficult to follow them nonselectively in significant numbers; this would most likely be possible in the course of family studies. Among the 63 schizophrenic siblings of probands, only 2 had never hospitalized by the end of the observation period. At the conclusion of that period, their dates of onset lay 41 and 39 years behind them. After this long a course, it would be most improbable that these 2 would ever at any time in the future be hospitalized for schizophrenia; they were then 76 and 78 years old. The psychoses of these 2 patients ran a chronic course, in one case to a medium severe, and in the other a mild, long-term chronic state.

Among the Pfäfers (1941) probands, I found among the relatives of the schizophrenic probands 19 cases of diagnostically certain schizophrenias that had never led to hospitalization. Among these were 6 cases whose onset, at the end of the observation period lay but a few years or months behind them, so that the actual course could not be finally determined. If the remaining 13 cases of the

Pfäfers probands were to be combined with the 2 cases of the present investigation, the courses for the relatives of schizophrenics with definite schizophrenias who had never been hospitalized would show that all 15 schizophrenias ran a chronic course, proceeding as follows

—To severe chronic psychoses, 0
—To moderately severe chronic psychoses, 2
—To mild chronic psychoses, 11
—To long-term recoveries, 2.

Accordingly, it may be assumed that the preponderant majority of nonhospitalized schizophrenias that could be diagnosed took on a chronic course that proceeded to mild chronic psychoses (mild "end states"). The fact that there were no severe, and only a few moderately severe chronic psychoses among them is obvious, since those types almost always lead to hospitalization under our prevailing policies. It is also clear why there were so few recoveries among these schizophrenics who had never been hospitalized. If a case of schizophrenia recovers that was so mild as not to have required hospitalization, it has usually not been recognized as such.

Most of the statistics on the long-term courses of schizophrenic psychoses usually apply to schizophrenias that led to hospitalization. If one were to attempt to write something like a comprehensive "Natural History of all Schizophrenias," and to evaluate in it the courses of "all" schizophrenias, one would naturally have to include in the investigation as well all patients who had never been hospitalized. If that were done, the number of chronic psychoses progressing to mild "end states" would obviously increase in the statistics, although not markedly so, for the family studies show that the number of schizophrenics never hospitalized is quite small in comparison to the number of hospitalized schizophrenics.

The number of schizophrenics who have never been hospitalized in their whole lives has never been precisely determined, and is usually overestimated. Among the siblings of the 208 principal schizophrenic probands of this project, the proportion of schizophrenics who were hospitalized to those never hospitalized is, as already mentioned, 63:2. The percentage of the 3.2 nonhospitalized schizophrenics among these siblings ought to be close to that for all nonhospitalized schizophrenics, since neither group of nonhospitalized schizophrenics is likely to be hospitalized at any time in the future. Besides, it is unlikely that the rate of hospitalization for those schizophrenics who have schizophrenic siblings would be markedly different from the rate of those schizophrenics who do not have any schizophrenic siblings.

Whether there are nondiagnosed schizophrenics among the population that are not detected even by careful family studies remains one of the mysteries in the science of schizophrenia. If schizophrenia is a disturbance in the relationships of patients to their material and human environment, there could hardly be schizophrenias that could not be diagnosed. On the other hand, if a schizophrenic psychosis is merely an aspect of a basic physical disorder that has not been identified, we shall be able to investigate the courses of those schizophrenias that cannot be diagnosed today, when such disorders have been discovered.

Of the prepsychotic personalities of the 63 schizophrenic siblings of our probands, 57 can without any difficulty be fitted into the classification system previously outlined and applied. They are distributed as
—Nonaberrant, 24
—Schizoid-aberrant within the norm, 15
—Otherwise aberrant within the norm, 4
—Schizoid-pathological, 9;
—Pathological other than schizoid, 5.

Among 398 probands, the distribution, in keeping with the statistics from the preceding sections showed that nearly $\frac{1}{3}$ were prepsychotically nonaberrant and schizoid-aberrant within the norm, and that $\frac{1}{4}$ were schizoid-pathological; the rest were otherwise aberrant and otherwise pathological.

Among the schizophrenic siblings of probands of this study, there were prepsychotically, more nonaberrant and fewer schizoid-aberrant and schizoid-pathological than among the probands themselves. With the small samplings, the difference may be coincidental. But it is more likely because the siblings of probands have a more favorable course in their schizophrenias than all probands put together, and that there are more prepsychotically nonaberrant patients than prepsychotic schizoids among the schizophrenias that run a benign course.

The fact that the frequency of schizophrenias in the siblings of schizophrenic twins, as it appears to have been established for decades, had to be reevaluated in the light of more recent studies, has received a great deal of attention (Tienari 1963, Kringlen 1964, Harvald and Hauge 1965, and Gottesman and Shields 1966). On the other hand, the

investigations of parents and siblings of this study reveal that the onset probabilities calculated 30 and 40 years ago are still valid. A nagging question emerges as to why the onset probabilities among twin siblings of schizophrenics were different in the old and the new investigations, but not among their parents or ordinary siblings. If the error ascribed to the small numbers is considered for both cases, the answer seems simple. That error is many times greater in the twin studies than in the studies of parents and ordinary siblings, and for this reason the investigative findings for twins are bound to be farther apart than for parents or ordinary siblings. In the lively discussions on the wide separation of data for the old and the new twin studies this simple fact has been given too little attention. Certainly other causes may have been operative that already have been convincingly explained by other authors (selection errors, omission of considering the sexes of the twins, the influence of concordance by the genes, or by the environment of the patient).

Other than Schizophrenic Psychoses and Feeblemindedness

The incidence of manic-depressive states, epilepsy, senile psychoses, other psychoses, and of feeblemindedness is to be found in Tables 5.1 and 5.2. Table 5.4 provides data for comparison of the different psychoses and feeblemindedness among the siblings of the 208 principal probands of this project with the same psychoses and feeblemindedness among
—The siblings of the Pfäfers schizophrenics (1941)
—The parents of the principal schizophrenic probands of this project and the parents of the Pfäfers schizophrenics;
—The representatives of various average population groups, among them of two investigations involving the Swiss population that I personally conducted, employing the same diagnostic principles and investigative methods that I used in the investigations of schizophrenics.

The frequency of psychoses other than schizophrenic and of feeblemindedness among the siblings of the 208 principal probands of this study and that of the Pfäfers probands corresponds. Insofar as differences exist, they lie within the expected range of variation ascribable to chance. The fact that senile psychoses occur among the siblings of our present probands but not among the siblings

Table 5.4. Onset probability for certain psychoses in siblings of probands and comparative figures from other investigations

Investigative material		Schizophrenia[1]	Manic-depressive illness	Senile psychoses	Other psychoses	Epilepsy	Feeble-mindedness	Paralysis
Siblings of the 208 principal schizophrenic probands	Corrected base figure	634	569.5	295	634	689	689	0
	Corrected percentage	9.9	0.5	4.0	1.1	0.4	4.2	
	Standard deviation	±1.2	±0.3	±1.1	±0.4	±0.2	±0.8	
Siblings of the 100 Pfäfers probands; M. Bleuler 1941	Corrected base figure	257	210.5	27	257	392	392	0
	Corrected percentage	12.5	0	0	1.6	1.5	4.1	
	Standard deviation	±2.1			±0.8	±0.6	±1.0	
Parents of the 208 principal schizophrenic probands	Corrected base figure	405.5	393	323	405.5	412	412	0
	Corrected percentage	7.0	2.3	14.2	0.7	0	2.2	
	Standard deviation	±1.3	±0.8	±1.9	±0.4		0.7	
Parents of the 100 Pfäfers probands; M. Bleuler 1941	Corrected base figure	195.5	183.5	121	195.5	200	200	0
	Corrected percentage	6.1	2.2	9.1	1.5	0	2.5	
	Standard deviation	±1.7	±1.1	±2.6	±0.8		±1.1	
Groups representing the average population: siblings of tubercular patients; M. Bleuler and Rapoport 1935	Corrected base figure	248.5	196.5	17.5	248.5[2]	390[2]	390	146
	Corrected percentage	0.8	0	0	0	0.5	1.0	0
	Standard deviation	±0.6				±0.4	±0.5	
Siblings of general patients in the rural Basel area; M. Bleuler 1932	Corrected base figure	507.5	422	24.5	507.5[2]	866[2]	866	295.5
	Corrected percentage	1.2	0.2	0	0.2	0.5	1.6	0
	Standard deviation	±0.5	±0.2		±0.2	±0.2	±0.4	
Siblings of general patients in Munich; Schulz 1931	Corrected base figure	262.5	219.5	31.5	262.5[2]	373	373	176.5
	Corrected percentage	0.8	0	0	0.4	0.3	0.5[3]	0
	Standard deviation	±0.5			±0.4	±0.3	±0.4	
Siblings of spouses of organic psychotics in Basel; Brugger 1929	Corrected base figure	391	317	73.5	391[2]	460	460	299.5
	Corrected percentage	1.5	0	0	0.3	0.2	0.4[3]	0
	Standard deviation	±0.6			±0.3	±0.2	±0.3	

Table 5.4 (continued)

Siblings of spouses of organic psychotics in Munich; Luxenburger and Schulz 1928							
Corrected base figure	590.5	494	70.5	590.5	695	695	463
Corrected percentage	0.8	0.4	1.4	0.3	0.3	0.6[3]	1.7
Standard deviation	±0.4	±0.3	±0.4	±0.2	±0.2	±0.3	±0.2

Calculations for the base figure

For schizophrenics 19–39 years old figures are halved; all 40 years old and over are fully counted; for **M. Bleuler's** 1941 studies, ages 16–40 are halved, all over 40 are fully counted.

For manic-depressive illness: 19–49 years old are halved; all over 50 years old are fully counted.

For senile psychoses: age 60 and over, all fully counted.

For other psychoses: as for schizophrenia.

For epilepsy: 19 years old and over, all fully counted.

For feeblemindedness: 10 years old and over, all fully counted.

1. In studies encompassing diagnostically certain and probable schizophrenias, both categories are included.

2. Base figure from **Bleuler** and **Rapoport** (Table 4) 1935 was altered to conform to present calculation.

3. Not directly comparable because of a narrower specification of the concept.

Table 5.5. Manic-depressive states among parents and siblings of schizophrenics from three studies by M. Bleuler[1]

	Manic-depressives among the	
	Parents of Probands	Siblings of Probands
Present principal probands	9 : 393 = 2.3% ± 0.7	3 : 569.5 = 0.5% ± 0.3
Pfäfers probands	4 : 183.5 = 2.2% ± 1.1	0 : 210.5 = 0
American probands	3[1] : 177.5 = 1.7% ± 1.0	0 : 150.5 = 0
	16 : 754.0 = 2.1% ± 0.2	3 : 930.5 = 0.3% ± 0.2

The absolute number relates to a derivative figure.

1. These 3 cases are not diagnostically certain, although they are probable; in the original study they were entered under "depressions of doubtful nature occurring at advanced age."

of the Pfäfers probands is due to the age structure.

At the close of the observation period 295 of the 818 siblings of our probands were over 60 years old (36 percent), and only 27 of the 492 siblings of the Pfäfers probands (5.5 percent) had reached that age. A comparison with the siblings of my American probands does not approach any statistical significance whatsoever either in the differences of the incidence of other than schizophrenic psychoses. Feeblemindedness was a rare occurrence among the siblings of the American probands, but this was due to a selection bias, for during that period, Bloomingdale Hospital did not accept any cases of feeblemindedness.

Manic-depressive states occur with no greater frequency among the siblings of these or of former schizophrenic probands than among the general population; although the rate is higher among their parents. The onset probability for manic-depressive states as already stated is 2.3 percent ± 0.7 among their parents, but only 0.5 percent ± 0.3 among their siblings. This difference is not significant. But now it is repeated for my Pfäfers and my American probands, as shown in Table 5.5.

The observation is not new that there are more manic-depressives among the parents than among the siblings of schizophrenics. It agrees with most statistics on the frequency of psychoses among the relatives of schizophrenics, for instance, those by Slater (1953) and Hallgren and Sjögren (1959). There are, to be sure, also statistics that do not reveal this difference for example, Kallmann (1938), but scarcely any that show the opposite difference. The investigations on children of manic-depressives often also reveal more schizophrenics than is common among the general population, and particularly among the children of two manic-

depressive parents (Schulz 1940, Elsässer 1952). Again in the same context, clinical experience shows that in the course of years of practice most clinicians have come across a number of schizophrenics with manic-depressive parents, as we have at Burghölzli as well.

These three sets of experiences combined (my own statistics summarized above, the statistics of other investigators, and general clinical experience) permit the assumption that the combination of manic-depressive states in a parent and schizophrenia in the child occur more frequently than mere coincidence could produce. This assumption is awkward if one considers schizophrenia and manic-depressive illness as two separate and sharply distinct illnesses, or even if one goes so far as to assume that they are the products of different specific hereditary predispositions.[5] Proceeding from this concept, one might assume that the diagnosis for one of the partners was in error. This is conceivable, for it is certainly possible that a specific disease may occasionally emerge in an atypical form. But if one suspects that the predisposition for schizophrenia existed primarily in a disharmony of the psychic developmental potential, it would be understandable why manic-depressive parents have schizophrenic children much more often than vice versa. It also seems possible that the manic-depressive psychosis of the parent has a similar psychotraumatic impact on the child as a schizophrenia in the parent would have, and that a predisposition for schizophrenic illness would be enhanced by such an experience. It is most

5. Schulz (1940) suggested the possibility that two optional dominant hereditary factors for schizophrenia would become so modified by a third dominant hereditary factor, that a manic-depressive state would develop. But he did not hold fast to this assumption.

likely that all these conditions are jointly responsible.

The findings on the frequency of manic-depressive illness among representatives of the general population have varied. The precise delimitation of the diagnosis in this area is even more difficult than for schizophrenia. In addition, manic-depressive illness actually occurs at different rates among different population groups. In 1935 I calculated the onset probability from the combined data on the subjects investigated by Luxenburger (1927), Schulz (1927), Brugger (1929) and myself (1932, 1935), for probands supposed to represent the general population, and arrived at 0.2 percent. Since then a great number of investigations have been published with higher percentages (Slater 1953, 0.5–0.8 percent, Sjögren 1948, 0.6–0.8 percent, Fremming 1951, 1.2–1.6 percent, and Thomasson 1938 as high as 7 percent). A few scattered investigators came up with even lower frequencies (Böök 1953, 0.07 percent). In short, there are no real indications that manic-depressive illness among the siblings of schizophrenics occurs more frequently than among the general population; although earlier studies revealed that manic-depressive illness among the parents of schizophrenics was somewhat more frequent than among the average population.

Senile psychoses are found in 11 of the 295 siblings over 60 years old, or in 3.7 percent ± 1.1 (A description of the concept "senile psychoses" in the context of these statistics appears in Chapter 2, under Senile psychoses). The fact that we had fewer senile psychoses among the siblings than among the parents of our probands[6] is easily explained: Most of the siblings over 60 are not much older than 60, whereas a great number of the parents are much older than 60. The siblings of the Pfäfers and the American probands were too young to have seniles among them. Among the 58 siblings of the general patients of my own investigations, who were over 60 years old, there were no senile psychoses.

The difference in the proportions of 11:295 and 0:58 is obviously statistically not significant. I should not even have mentioned it, if there had not been other findings in support of the theory that schizophrenias and senile psychoses occur somewhat more often among the relatives of schizophrenics than mere

---

6. Among 323 parents over 60 years old there were 46 senile psychoses or 14 percent ± 1.9.

---

coincidence would allow us to expect. Among the parents of our probands (see Chapter 2, Table 2.6), we were confronted with the same preponderance of seniles as among the parents of general patients, although also without any statistical significance. But then, it has come to my attention for decades, both through study of the literature and through my own clinical experience, how often schizophrenics are found among the relatives of seniles. Among others, Meggendorfer (1925) already discovered an increased onset risk for schizophrenia among the children of the senile demented. He surmised that late-schizophrenics were concealed among his senile-demented patients. Schulz (1930) found eccentrics and schizophrenics among the relatives of patients with "paranoid tainted aging-psychoses" that exceeded the frequency that might have been expected from the general population, although this difference was quite small.

But the findings by Schulz (1932) from Rüdin's exceptionally large sampling of schizophrenics does merit special attention. As previously mentioned, among these schizophrenic probands there was a frequency of senile dementia of 1.9 percent among the parents aged over 60. Among the representatives of the average population assembled by Schulz for comparison, it amounted to just 0.25 percent and 0.67 percent. Schulz did not calculate the statistical significance of this difference. The median error of the 1.9 percent, however, amounts to almost 0.5. Among the parents of senile dementia cases, along with 1.8 percent of senile dements, Cresseri (1948) discovered 20 percent of "various mental illnesses."

It does not fit neatly into the usual concepts of psychiatry that senile psychoses and schizophrenias should appear in combination among relatives at a greater frequency than coincidence would provide. But one is easily dissuaded from dealing with facts that seem awkward and appear unexpectedly. This specifically was the fear that caused me to emphasize the frequency of senile psychoses among the parents and siblings of my schizophrenic probands, although it was perhaps due to nothing but the caprice of chance.

If the observation had been statistically significant, the first question to be asked would have been whether there might not be schizophrenias that do not become manifest until old age, and that are usually confused with senile psychoses. This possibility has already been indicated. Commonly we include the psychoses of aging with schizophrenia-like symptoms, with the senile psychoses, without further ado, if they occur in the presence of symptoms of the amnestic psychosyndrome. Perhaps a portion of these, however, are primarily schizophrenias occurring in certain individuals who suffer from an impairment of memory from physiological or mildly pathological causes. Many scientists have been attracted to this question. Jacob (1968) remarks in regard to it: "It must certainly be a part of the peculiarities of psychiatric disorders in advanced age, that brain-organic, exogenous, and endogenous psychosyndromes occur with uncommon frequency and in close proximity to one another."

After the question was raised, whether the psychoses of age among the relatives of schizophrenics might not be disguised forms of schizophrenia, the problem arises of investigating more thoroughly the psychopathology of these psychoses common in advanced age. I attempted to do this, but the attempt foundered with the present probands. Most of the patient histories that showed the presence of psychoses in old age were too inexact to be useful in the more detailed psychopathological studies. In going over them, however, the previous experience was confirmed, that psychoses in advanced age are not being studied with the same meticulous attention in most clinics as are the psychoses of younger patients. Check-up examinations were omitted in a great many cases, simply because many of the relatives with ailments related to age were already dead when the investigations were undertaken. Many of the parents and siblings of probands with psychoses related to age were suffering from cerebrovascular sclerosis with hemiplegia and aphasia following brain insults. Others were described as typical senile dementias. Actual schizophrenias could be suspected with greatest likelihood in the presence of confused states in advanced age. I only found a total of 11 cases among the 57 psychoses in connection with old age, in the parents and siblings of our probands, in which the symptomatology might in some way suggest the possibility of schizophrenic disorders in advanced age.

The question of a general relationship between senile and schizophrenic psychoses has already been broached in our descriptions of the parents of our probands (see Chapter 2, Table 2.20). Below in Chapter 5 on the frequency of schizophrenias among the children of senile psychotics, I shall return to this topic again.

Epilepsies and other psychoses occur very rarely among the siblings of probands. There is no indication that such disturbances might occur among the siblings of schizophrenics at any different rate than they do among the average population.

The frequency of feeblemindedness among the siblings of schizophrenics also concurs with our experience for the average population.

Schizoid Psychopathy, Alcoholism, Various Other Personality Developments, and Suicide

I encountered more "schizoid psychopaths" among the siblings of my Pfäfers probands than among the siblings of the 208 principal probands of this project. This is due to my subjective evaluation. In the investigations of my Pfäfers probands I was virtually unable to consider the life histories of the siblings; whereas for the probands of this study I did this extensively. But if ever the assumption suggested itself that a schizoid-psychopathic attitude was imposed on the patient by agonizing vicissitudes of life, I could no longer categorize it as a "schizoid psychopathy," as I have mentioned earlier. Nevertheless, I must emphasize that, despite my extreme reluctance to diagnose a "schizoid psychopathy" during the present research project, and despite my very liberal diagnosis of it for the siblings of general patients, there are many more "schizoid psychopaths" among the siblings of our probands than among the siblings of the general patients. There is no doubt that schizoid psychopathies or schizoid-pathological personality attitudes are high among the siblings of schizophrenics in comparison to the general population. There is no need to prove this point again.

Table 5.6 compares the incidence of alcoholism among the brothers of the 208 schizophrenic probands of this study with that among the brothers of other schizophrenic probands, of alcoholics, and of general patients. A description of the concept "alcoholism" for the purpose of these statistics has already appeared. Among the sisters, alcoholism is so rare that statistical comparisons cannot be considered. Table 5.6 confirms what has been said about alcoholism among the parents of our probands. As little as any frequency of alcoholism can be demonstrated among the parents of schizophrenics, just as little is it to be found among their siblings. Biological relationship to schizophrenics does not predispose to alcohol addiction, nor vice versa.

Suicides among the siblings of the principal

Table 5.6. Alcoholism among brothers of various proband groups compared with brothers of other schizophrenic probands, brothers of alcoholics, and brothers of general patients

Brothers of	No. of brothers over 40	No. of alcoholics among them		
		No.	%	±
208 Principal probands of this study	293	18	6.1	1.4
100 Probands of the Pfäfers study (1941)	55	6	10.9	4.2
100 Probands from New York (1930)	54	0	0	0
50 Alcoholics from Zürich (1955)	49	6	12.2	4.7
50 Alcoholics from New York (1955)	27	6	22.2	8.0
84 Alcoholics from Basel and Munich by Brugger (1929)	83	23	27.7	4.9
200 Basel area general patients (1932)	144	20	13.9	2.9
100 Zürich tubercular patients (1935)	67	6	9.0	3.5

Table 5.7. Suicides among siblings of various proband groups compared with siblings of other schizophrenic probands and of general patients

Siblings of	No. of Deaths	No. of Suicides	%	±
208 Principal probands of this study	210	19	9.0	2.0
100 Pfäfers schizophrenics	40	2	5.0	3.4
100 American schizophrenics	28	2	7.1	4.8
200 Liestal general patients	94	2	2.1	1.5
100 Zürich tubercular patients	43	0		

schizophrenic probands occur more frequently than among all other groups of probands' siblings. In Table 5.7 the number of suicides is related to the total number of deaths of persons over 20 years old.

It appears as if suicides among the siblings of schizophrenics occurred more frequently than among the average population, however, without any statistical significance being applicable to this finding. A corresponding difference between the parents of schizophrenics and the general patients could not be detected, or was not plainly in evidence.

Among the siblings of our probands, there were, in addition, 68 other mental disorders. They were of varying types that simply defy all efforts to include them in any sort of statistics. It is certain, however, that this total among the siblings of schizophrenics is considerably greater than among the siblings of general patients. The figure 68 came from a total of 674 siblings of schizophrenics who had passed their 18th birthday, as compared to only 20 such cases among the 1077 siblings of general patients over 20 years old, from my previous investigations. As may be seen from the commentaries appended to Tables 5.1 and 5.2, most of these were the types of disturbances that might develop from neurotic or psychopathic disorders or from personal degeneration. Only very few of these are dis-

turbances that probably developed independently of either the patient's hereditary constitution or his life experiences. The frequency of other disorders among the siblings of schizophrenics can thus be easily explained, either by way of unfavorable traits in the personality development or by way of unfavorable experiences living with the families of schizophrenics.

Comparisons of the Schizophrenic Psychoses among Siblings

Comparisons between the schizophrenias of siblings (and other relatives) shed light on a number of questions.

Do schizophrenias of different types occur in combinations among siblings? If so, does it mean that the different types of schizophrenias are somehow related to one another, or are there individual types of schizophrenias that never, or very rarely, occur in two siblings? If so, is it likely that influences other than familial ones bring about this particular type of schizophrenia?

Or are there, perhaps, individual types of schizophrenias that occur at an exceptionally high rate in two siblings? If so, it is probable that familial influences are of significance in their formation.

The expression "familial influence" is again applied independently of whether it applies to hereditary traits of development or to an experience in the life of the individual that may apply jointly to both siblings. In the latter case, it would most likely apply to experiences in childhood, for similar influences in the environment that would affect two sibling simultaneously would be more likely to affect both of them during their childhood than later on in life.

This entire set of problems has already been partly discussed in the section on the course of illness of schizophrenia and its frequency in families (see pp. 264–75). In the present section we shall attempt to come back to these problems by way of somewhat different, more detailed calculations, and with a greater number of probands.

The probands from the 1941[7] investigations and the 208 probands of this project are to be considered jointly. In order not to clutter the study with an endless number of tables, only those are reproduced in which the present probands and those from the 1941 studies are treated jointly. For the same reason I am eliminating those tables that depict only the diagnostically certain schizophrenias, and reproducing only those that encompass both the certain and the probable cases together. To forestall misunderstanding, therefore, the principles emphasized in the text may be gleaned from all these tables individually, those from the Pfäfers investigations and the present ones, and from those that either include or exclude the probable schizophrenias. In the collective tables reproduced here, the great and troublesome errors occurring in the individual tables due to the small numbers will be proportionately smaller.

The first comparisons to be undertaken are the "end states" (see pp. 189–91, 200) and the course types (see p. 209) of schizophrenic siblings. Included in the tables are comparisons between the original schizophrenic probands with their schizophrenic siblings, some

of whom were discovered in the course of family studies, as well as comparisons between two schizophrenic siblings of the probands.

The number of pairs of schizophrenic siblings in which both partners were accessible for comparison amounts to[8]

	For the "end states"	For the course types
From the Pfäfers studies	151	111
From the present study	77	64
Totals:	228	175

The following is an explanation for the process applied in comparing the "end states." The course types are compared with one another by the same kind of statistics. The two siblings of a pair were arbitrarily categorized as primary and secondary siblings, in which the primary sibling was the proband, and the secondary one was the sibling observed by way of a family study through which he came to our attention. When two schizophrenic siblings are compared who had both become accessible through a family study, the older one was designated the primary sibling. At the outset a list was set up showing the distribution of the five types of "end states"[9] among the primary siblings, which was in the ratio of 49:31:63:39:46. The same proportion of "end states" was determined for the secondary siblings, which was in the ratio of 37:25:61: 62:43. The two sets of proportions do not agree exactly. If we are to assume that the "end states" for two schizophrenic siblings were independent of one another, then the "end states" for the secondary siblings would consistently be distributed among them in the same proportion, if the primary siblings were broken down according to their different "end states." This means, for instance, that among the primary siblings whose psychosis progressed to a long-term recovery, such recoveries should not occur in greater proportion than they did among all secondary siblings.

By simple rule-of-three calculations, the distribution of "end states" can be determined

7. In order to reduce the errors due to small numbers, in our 1941 studies we used data not only pertaining to the schizophrenic siblings of the Pfäfers and the American probands, but supplemented these by data from investigations at the Basel University Clinic. Comparisons were made not only between schizophrenias of the probands and those of their siblings, but also with the schizophrenias among siblings of more distant relatives. In addition, comparisons were undertaken of schizophrenias in two relatives other than siblings. Those investigations encompassed a total of 547 comparisons between two schizophrenic psychoses of blood relatives.

8. Siblings with atypical course types are not included; there are, therefore, more comparisons for the "end states" than for the course types.

9. The five "end states" are severe, moderately severe, or mild-chronic schizophrenias, recovery states of long duration, or no "end state" has yet been reached.

for the siblings of schizophrenics with a certain "end state" that could most likely be expected, if the operations of chance were given free reign. If among the primary siblings with a certain "end state" more schizophrenics are found with the same "end state" than the calculation has indicated, that may be taken as an indication that familial influences were involved in bringing about this particular "end state." The relationship of the actual number to the calculated number of the specific "end state" in the secondary siblings will indicate the degree of correlation between two given "end states" among siblings.

Example: There are 39 among the primary siblings whose "end state" was evaluated as long-term recovery. If the operations of chance were given free play, the "recoveries" among the 39 primary siblings could most probably be expected to occur in the same proportion as among all secondary siblings. This ratio is 62:228. The number of the expected recoveries among the 39 secondary siblings of the primary ones who recovered from their psychoses, would therefore amount to $X:39 = 62:228$ where $X = 10.6$, if chance were given free play. Actually, however, it was 19, almost twice as many as chance operation would be expected to produce. This can be taken as an indication that familial influences play their part in bringing about the tendency toward long-term recoveries. To be sure, the significance of this difference must still be checked. A summary representation of it is given by the calculation of the median error of this difference. It amounts to

$$\sqrt{\frac{(10.6)\,(217.4)}{228} + \frac{(19)\,(207)}{228}} = 5.2;$$

that is, the difference can easily tolerate the single standard deviation, but hardly the doubled one. However, $p < 0.05$ ($\chi^2 = 6.3182$), that is, the difference is almost significant at the 1 percent level.

There are some possible objections to the statistical method described above, but they do not seem to me to be of such importance as to shatter appreciably the carefully phrased summary conclusions that are to be drawn from the statistics to follow. As early as 1941 I had already checked out this method empirically. I put together at random 820 pairs of schizophrenics who were not related to one another, and compared their different course types (Table 5.8). The psychoses for 180 of the primary siblings ran a course, for example, of "acute to severe chronic psychosis" (demen-

tia). Further, the percentage of the same course type was calculated for all secondary siblings. If the course types among primary and secondary siblings are independent of each other, then the type "acute to dementia" would have to occur in the same ratio among the secondary siblings who are the partners of the 180 primary siblings with the same course type. There would have to be 188.2 such cases; actually there are 190. The expectation that the calculated figures (within limits of chance fluctuations) should agree with the actual ones has been fulfilled. Table 5.8 shows how perfectly the calculated and the actual figures coincide (within chance deviations) for all combinations, that is, their quotient is always near 1. As expected, the courses of psychoses between the random-paired schizophrenics of two nonrelated probands proved to be totally independent of each other, upon application of the above-described method. However, a glance at Tables 5.9 and 5.10 will show that, contrary to the above findings, the "end states" and the course types of schizophrenias among the siblings are in part much more similar to one another than the happenstance of chance would indicate.

The following reflections may give rise to some objections against the above-outlined statistical procedure. If, for example, a familial tendency existed, according to which, course type X develops in siblings, it would show up in our statistics by an accumulation of the combination XX in siblings. However, assuming that a prankster had gotten hold of the patient histories of the schizophrenic sibships in my probands, and had mischievously removed some of the records containing the descriptions of course type X, then the sought-after tendency could no longer be discovered in my statistics, although it did exist. The role of such a spoilsport could now be assumed by an unconscious selection of the probands. If, now, my scientific zeal had misdirected the admission policies of our clinic to a point where I would prefer to admit a patient whose sibling had a similar type of illness rather than one whose sibling's illness was different, the statistics for this section would become meaningless. This is not the case. What is most likely to have happened is that disturbing selection biases resulted from the fact that in reality the recruitment of the probands followed a different procedure than that of their siblings. The probands entered the research project by way of their being hospitalized, while their siblings came to our attention

Table 5.8. Comparison of course types among nonrelated schizophrenics. The table serves merely as an empirical test for the usability of the method that was applied for comparing the course types of the psychoses of two siblings. As expected, the numbers shown on Table 5.8 correspond to those most likely to occur when the courses of both psychoses are independent of each other (from M. Bleuler, *Disease Course, Personality, and Kinships of Schizophrenics and their Interrelationships.* Leipzig, Thieme, 1941)

Comparisons of 820 course types between nonrelated schizophrenics: combinations	A Observed cases	B Most probable figure by coincidence	A : B
Both psychoses run acutely to dementia[1]	10	12 ± 3.4	0.8
Both psychoses run lingeringly to dementia[1]	45	48.4 ± 6.7	0.9
Both psychoses run acutely to defect[1]	0	0.5 ± 0.7	0
Both psychoses run lingeringly to defect[1]	3	4.3 ± 2.1	0.7
Both psychoses run phasically to dementia[1]	1	0.5 ± 0.7	0
Both psychoses run phasically to defect[1]	66	69.7 ± 8.0	0.9
Both psychoses run phasically to recovery	28	29.3 ± 5.3	1.0
One psychosis runs acutely; the other lingeringly to dementia[1]	50	48.2 ± 6.7	1.0
One psychosis runs acutely to dementia[1]; the other acutely to defect[1]	5	4.8 ± 2.2	1.0
One psychosis runs acutely to dementia[1]; the other lingeringly to defect[1]	15	14.9 ± 3.8	1.0
One psychosis runs acutely to dementia[1]; the other phasically to dementia[1]	10	8.6 ± 2.9	1.2
One psychosis runs acutely to dementia[1]; the other phasically to defect[1]	60	59.3 ± 7.4	1.0
One psychosis runs acutely to dementia[1]; the other phasically to recovery	40	40.4 ± 6.2	1.0
One psychosis runs lingeringly to demantia[1]; the other acutely to defect[1]	10	9.6 ± 3.1	1.0
One psychosis runs lingeringly to dementia[1]; the other lingeringly to defect[1]	30	29.5 ± 5.3	1.0
One psychosis runs lingeringly to dementia[1]; the other phasically to dementia[1]	20	18.0 ± 4.2	1.1
One psychosis runs lingeringly to dementia[1]; the other phasically to defect[1]	120	118.1 ± 10.1	1.0
One psychosis runs lingeringly to dementia[1]; the other phasically to recovery	80	79.8 ± 8.5	1.0
One psychosis runs acutely to defect[1]; the other lingeringly to defect[1]	3	3.2 ± 1.8	0.9
One psychosis runs acutely to defect[1]; the other phasically to dementia[1]	2	1.7 ± 1.3	1.1
One psychosis runs acutely to defect[1]; the other phasically to defect[1]	12	11.8 ± 3.4	1.0
One psychosis runs acutely to defect[1]; the other phasically to recovery	8	8.0 ± 2.8	1.0
One psychosis runs lingeringly to defect[1]; the other phasically to dementia[1]	6	6.3 ± 2.5	1.0
One psychosis runs lingeringly to defect[1]; the other phasically to defect[1]	36	34.6 ± 5.8	1.0
One psychosis runs lingeringly to defect[1]; the other phasically to recovery	24	22.7 ± 4.7	1.1
One psychosis runs phasically to dementia[1]; the other phasically to defect[1]	24	25.2 ± 4.9	1.0
One psychosis runs phasically to dementia[1]; the other phasically to recovery	16	18.9 ± 4.3	0.8
One psychosis runs phasically to defect[1]; the other phasically to recovery	96	91.5 ± 9.0	1.0

Total: 820   819.8

1. In conformity with the older designations, the table uses "dementia" instead of long-term, severe chronic psychosis and "defect" instead of long-term, moderately severe or mild chronic psychosis.

through family studies. If my informants had rather had a special interest in reporting to me the similar psychoses of siblings in preference to the dissimilar ones, the statistics would have been distorted. But the family studies were done so thoroughly that this was not possible. The distribution of the different courses among the siblings—as previously shown—was not exactly the same as that among the probands, for obvious reasons, although it was similar. The preceding sections have contained discussions on this topic, which is one of the reasons why I do not believe that any selective biases have seriously distorted the statistics of this section.

It is not possible to determine from the bare figures of the statistics whether the accumulation of the XX combination comes into being because familial tendencies favor a predisposition to a similar course development of the type X, or whether the opposite is true, that some kind of familial influences favor opposing course types, for instance, XY, among siblings, which would be the case in dominant vs. submissive behavior in twins. But only contrived reasons seem to indicate that familial influences apply in the formation of opposing schizophrenic courses in siblings, and this possibility I can safely eliminate from consideration.

Besides, a single familial tendency toward similar courses, for instance toward an XX course type, is bound to increase not only the frequency of the XX combination, but would certainly change the entire distribution pattern of the most variegated combinations that could be expected to occur through any given coincidence. Then it would become more difficult to decide which is the primary influence and which is the mere consequence of it.

This distinction I was unable to determine mathematically, but a number of opportunities for checking this out developed from the many tables on the subgroups of all the probands. For instance, by studying them it is possible to find out whether an accumulation of XX disturbs the combination NM consistently or only occasionally, or possibly another time disturbs the combination YZ. But, primarily, careful attention must be paid to which figures among those closest to what coincidence might provide, might sensibly justify the assumption of a familial influence.

In a table I have not reproduced here I compared all "end states" of the primary siblings of the 208 principal probands with all "end states" of the secondary siblings. A clear tendency emerged toward equal or similar "end states" among schizophrenic siblings. The standard deviations in the individual entries of the table, however, are so great, that it is not worthwhile to reproduce them in print.

Table 5.9 summarizes the data from a number of individual tables. It is based on 192 combinations of sibling-psychoses from the probands of the 1941 investigations and from those of the present study. At the end of the observation period the psychosis of one sibling or another of the pair had not yet progressed to a chronic state in 41 cases, and these 41 cases are not included in the table. These combinations were counted as "similar 'end states'": a. Severe chronic psychosis in one, and medium severe in the other sibling; b. Medium-severe chronic psychosis in one, and mild in the other sibling; c. Recovery in one, and mild chronic psychosis in the other sibling.

Table 5.9 shows unequivocally that totally different "end states" are rather frequent

Table 5.9. Comparison of "end states" of schizophrenic psychoses among siblings. The frequency of the combinations of sibling psychoses with equal, similar, or different "end states" (cases of definite and probable schizophrenias are combined, but cases that had not attained an "end state" are omitted).[1] The comparison was made from 228 courses of sibling psychoses, 151 from the probands of the 1941 investigation, and 77 from the present 208 principal probands of this study

"End states" among the 228 combinations of sibling schizophrenias	A Actually observed figure	B Most likely figure chance would provide	Standard deviation for B	A : B
Same "end states"	62	39.2	± 5.64	1.6
Similar "end states"	54	53.7	± 6.37	1.0
Vastly different "end states"	35	55.4	± 6.45	0.6

1. Calculations for the figures under B were done for a table that is not reproduced, which includes the cases without "end states." For this reason the figures under A and B are not exactly equal.

Table 5.10. Comparison of course types of schizophrenic psychoses among siblings. The frequency of combinations of sibling-psychoses with similarities and differences in course type (including cases of diagnosticaticly certain and of probable schizophrenia, but not the atypical or unidentifiable courses). Comparison was made for 175 courses of sibling-psychoses, 111 from the probands of the 1941 investigations, and 64 from the family histories of the 208 principal probands of this project

Combinations of course types of sibling-schizophrenias as to similarity or dissimilarity	A Observed cases	B Most probable figure by coincidence	Median error of B	A : B	p for Difference between A and B
(1a) Course types similar in every respect	79	37.9	±5.46	2.1	$p < 0.001$
(1b) Course types dissimilar in every respect	20	55.7	±6.18	0.4	$p < 0.001$
(2a) Similarity only as to uniformity and phasic development	48	53.1	±6.10	0.9	No difference
(2b) Dissimilarity as to uniformity and phasic development	48	84.6	±6.63	0.6	$p < 0.001$
(3a) Similarity only as to acute or chronic onset	58	60.8	±6.32	1.0	No difference
(3b) Dissimilarity as to acute or chronic onset	38	76.9	±6.59	0.5	$p < 0.001$
(4a) Similarity only as to outcome	21	21.6	±4.36	1.0	No difference
(4b) Dissimilarity only as to outcome	75	116.1	±6.29	0.6	$p < 0.001$

among siblings; although it does occur more frequently than we might expect by chance that both siblings attain the same "end state." On the other hand, totally different "end states" occur more rarely than they might have by mere chance. This finding is statistically highly significant: $p < 0.001$.

The course types were broken down into the frequently mentioned seven characteristic forms; to these were added some uncharacteristic and a few undefinable forms. These nine different groupings yield 45 possible combinations. A total of 239 comparisons were made between the different course types occurring in siblings. In the 45 individual entries of the table, the absolute figures are so small that their median error is often larger than they themselves are. For this reason it would be useless to reproduce the entire table dealing with these comparisons. Based on that table, the following should be remembered: The combination "acute to severe chronic states" never occurs in both siblings. On the other hand, the combination of long-term recovery in both siblings is by far the most frequent one, occurring 39 times. The combination "chronic course to severe chronic psychoses occurs 13 times.

Table 5.10 is a summary of entries from the unpublished table about the combinations of 238 schizophrenic psychoses among siblings. In this table the atypical and the undetermined courses have been omitted. Vertical column A contains the actual count of combinations, and column B the theoretical number of combinations that would most probably occur if chance were given free play. In the horizontal spaces certain comparisons are listed:

Space 1 shows comparisons between
—Combinations of courses in complete concordance; that is, the courses of sibling schizophrenias equal in every respect
—Combinations of sibling schizophrenias with courses totally different in every respect (complete discordance).

Space 2 shows comparison between
—Combinations of courses of sibling-schizophrenias that are concordant only in respect to whether the course was uniform or undulating (partial concordance)
—Those combinations that are discordant in respect to the same course characteristics (partial discordance).

Space 3 shows comparisons between
—Combinations of courses of sibling-schizo-

phrenias that are concordant only in respect to whether the beginning was acute or chronic (partial concordance)

—Those combinations that are discordant in respect to the same course characteristics (partial discordance).

Space 4 shows comparison between

—Combinations of courses of sibling-schizophrenias that are concordant only in respect to their outcome ("end state") (partial concordance)

—Those combinations that are discordant in respect to the same characteristics (partial discordance).

In evaluating Table 5.10, the important aspect is the proportions of the figures under A and those under B. For the differences, if any, p is given in a separate column. The quotient will provide a summary orientation about it. However, special attention must be given to the differences in the quotients for the figures in columns A and B for horizontal listings in spaces 2–4.

The greatest—and the only statistically highly significant—difference occurs between the expected and the actual figures for "courses that were equal and unequal in every respect" (complete concordance and complete discordance). The familial tendency to produce concordant course types in two siblings may be regarded as primary. For this reason, all or a portion of the remaining combinations are bound to occur much less frequently than they would through mere coincidence, that is, if there were no family tendencies operating in favor of the combination of similar courses. Hence, if, for instance, the combination "similarity only in respect to a uniform or an undulating course" occurs more rarely then the calculated probability for mere coincidence would indicate (48 instead of 53.1), then, insofar as it is no mere happenstance, this must be just a consequence of the fact that the combination between "courses running concordant in every respect" is so frequent. For this reason, the difference in these figures does not tell us anything. Instead, we discover that the shortage of actual cases found with the combination "inequality with respect to a uniform or an undulating course" is still considerably greater than the above-mentioned shortage of the combination "equality only in respect to a uniform or an undulating course." The excess of the combinations "congruent in every respect" is thus compensated for to a much greater extent by the shortage in "inequality in respect to uniform or undulating courses" than by the shortage in "equality in respect to uniform or undulating courses." This suggests the conclusion that familial influences are also operative in favoring the combination "equality only in respect to uniform or undulating forms," insofar as the differences are not merely coincidental. Similar reflections are also valid for spaces 3 and 4.

Here are the essential findings resulting from the comparisons of this table.

1. The tendency toward concordance of the course types in respect to all 3 of their essential characteristics together, is unmistakably a matter of fact in the schizophrenias of siblings. These 3 characteristics are a phasic evolution or uniformity of the entire course, acuity or chronicity of its beginning, and the outcome in most severe chronic psychoses, in mild chronic psychoses, or in recovery.

2. There is a tendency toward concordance in respect to each of the 3 characteristics in the course types of schizophrenias among siblings.

3. In respect to the outcome of the psychosis, the tendency toward concordance in the psychoses of siblings is certainly not greater than it is in respect to uniformity or undulating evolution, and in respect to acuity or chronicity of its beginning.

In my 1941 publication I compared not only the psychoses of schizophrenic siblings, but also the psychoses of more distant relatives. Among the probands of these investigations there were 363 combinations in respect to "end states" and 256 in respect to course types among the relatives who were not siblings. As I explained in detail in 1941, the comparisons of the courses among relatives other than siblings and the courses of the siblings yielded approximately the same ratios. For this reason, the findings ascertained from siblings take on an increased importance. To be sure, the discovered tendencies toward concordance and discordance of "end states" and course types in more distant relatives were, according to expectations, not as pronounced among these family members as among siblings. But in the evaluation of all the probands, we by no means relied solely on the summary tables. On the contrary, these 164 individual tables on which the summary tables are based, were constantly being compared among one another. The median errors of the individual figures in the entries of these individual tables are so great that no absolute value can be assigned to them. However, there was some value in checking whether despite the small numbers of the individual tables the same indications could be derived from most of them jountly, and this was indeed the case. Without a clear similarity in the tendencies revealed by the 164 individual tables, I should hardly have dared to consider seriously the data derived from the summary tables. All these data were further supplemented by the comparisons of disease courses among schizophrenics who were not related to one another (see Table 5.8).

Proof has existed for a long time that there is a loose, positive correlation between the age of onset among closely related schizophrenics. Stroemgren (1935) discovered it between schizophrenic siblings, and Schulz (1940) between schizophrenic parents and their schizophrenic children. Among my own probands described in 1941 it turned up once more, primarily in the siblings, but then also between more distant relatives.[10] The investigation at that time was based on a comparison of 147 combinations of two schizophrenias in siblings and 428 combinations of two schizophrenias in other relatives.

The same correlation between the onset age of schizophrenic siblings was also revealed among our present probands, in 76 combinations of two sibling-schizophrenias. The standard deviations of the correlations with such a small number are, of course, great. Therefore, in Table 5.11. I am summarizing the data from the 1941 investigations and the present ones. The table shows 223 combinations of sibling-schizophrenias. The figures occurring with the greatest probability by sheer coincidence were calculated by the same method for similarity or dissimilarity of onset age as they were for the "end states" and course types described earlier in this chapter. Table 5.11 shows a statistically significant correlation between the age of onset in schizophrenic siblings.

Among the 223 combinations of sibling-schizophrenias the proportions of those sibships in which both partners became ill in the same decade, became ill in adjacent decades, and became ill in nonadjacent decades are in

the ratio of 87:94:42.

If there were no correlation between the onset ages, the corresponding ratio would be 70.6:92.1:60.2, and p for that difference $<$ 0.01 ($\chi^2 = 9.35$ see Table 5.11).

The great merit in contemplating the correlation of the onset ages in the schizophrenic relatives of schizophrenics has not always received the attention it deserves. In the process of formulating theories on the genesis of schizophrenias it should not be neglected as badly as it has been in the past. We might ask whether it is brought about by the common childhood experiences of the siblings. We should like to assume that it is, if it were valid specifically only for the early-onset schizophrenias. But this correlation seems to appear with even greater frequency among the later onsets. It is difficult to imagine that the common childhood experience should still exert an influence on the onset of a schizophrenia after age 30. The concordant correlations of onset ages between parents and children, and between the more distant relatives further refute any theory about the environmental influence on the correlations among siblings. Somehow, it does seem to be rooted in the hereditary background. But it is almost impossible to imagine that different genes could exist for the earlier or later eruption of schizophrenias. So the cause for the correlation of the onset ages would most likely be found by investigating the entire gene environment. As one's personal nature and disposition exerts its influence on the "end states" and the course types of the psychosis, so also it affects the age of schizophrenic onset.

It can be said that the course of the psychosis in schizophrenias is heavily dependent on the personal nature that relatives have in common. But by that alone, only very few of all the aspects of a psychosis are being included that have a familial implication in the statistics on the correlations of types of illness, on "end states," and on age of onset. Perhaps, if we undertook still more differentiated comparisons of the psychoses of schizophrenic siblings, it might occur to us to regard the influences of the personality on the psychosis with even greater importance than we do today. If we did, the patient's personal nature vis-à-vis the impersonal illness would then gain increasing importance in a practical sense.

For a comparison between the prepsychotic personalities of schizophrenic relatives, I was able to compile 87 combinations of schizo-

10. The correlation coefficient turned out to be positive for all age groups tested. For the onset-age span of 20–30 years, however, it was no greater than its median error. For onset ages over 30, however, it was twice, and sometimes three times the amount of its median error, that is, for onset-age group 30–40 among siblings it was 0.16 ± 0.08, and for siblings over 40, 0.32 ± 0.07.

Table 5.11. Comparison of onset age in schizophrenic siblings. Condensed comparisons from the 1941 probands and from the family histories of the 208 principal probands of this project ($147 + 76^1 = 223$)

Age spans of the 223 combinations of sibling schizophrenias	A Observed cases	B Most probable figure by coincidence	Median error of B	A : B
A. Both comparison partners in the same decade				
Between 10–19 years old	8	6.8	±2.56	1.2
Between 20–29 years old	51	46.5	±6.06	1.1
Between 30–39 years old	14	11.1	±3.24	1.3
Over 40 years old	14	6.2	±2.45	2.3
Totals:	87	70.6	±6.94	1.2
B. Both comparison partners in adjacent decades				
Between 10–19 and 20–29	41	36.2	±5.50	1.1
Between 20–29 and 30–39	37	39.4	±5.69	0.9
Between 30–39 and over 40	16	16.5	±3.90	1.0
Totals:	94	92.1	±7.35	1.0
C. The two comparison partners in nonadjacent decades				
Between 10–19 and 30–39	13	15.5	±3.80	0.8
Between 10–19 and over 40	8	12.4	±3.42	0.6
Between 20–29 and over 40	21	32.3	±5.25	0.8
Totals:	42	60.2	±6.62	0.7

1. One case for which onset age was uncertain was omitted.

phrenic siblings and 314 combinations of other schizophrenic relatives from among the probands of the 1941 investigation. At that time I came to the conclusion that, if a schizophrenic patient was prepsychotically a schizoid psychopath, then the schizophrenics among his relatives would have developed a schizoid psychopathy prepsychotically much more often than is the case among schizophrenics in general. Accordingly, prepsychotically nonaberrant personalities are very rare among the schizophrenic relatives of a schizoid psychopath who became schizophrenic. If a schizophrenic was prepsychotically nonaberrant, then the schizophrenics among his relatives are also prepsychotically non-aberrant more often than usual.[11]

The comparisons between the prepsychotic personalities of the schizophrenic siblings of

11. For the personality characteristic "nonaberrant," the correlation coefficient according to Bravais amounted to 0.34 ± 0.09 among schizophrenic siblings, and to 0.17 ± 0.05 among all relatives. For the characteristic "schizoid psychopathy" among siblings it was 0.62 ± 0.07, and among all relatives, 0.36 ± 0.05.

our probands point to exactly the same conditions. But these amount to only 72 comparisons, so that the errors of the small number are excessive. Table 5.12 therefore is a summary of the data on the prepsychotic personalities of schizophrenic siblings from the 1941 and the present studies combined. They reveal significantly that the premorbid personalities of schizophrenic siblings are correlated.

Table 5.12 shows, among 159 combinations of sibling-schizophrenias, that the proportions of the sibships for those that concur in all personality traits, those that concur in some of them, and those that differ in all of them are in the ratio of 77 :65 :17. If the prepsychotic personalities were distributed without correlation, those same proportions would be in the ratio of 46 :73.2 :40. The differences of the two sets of proportions are significant at $p < 0.01$.

According to earlier descriptions (see Chapter 3) the prepsychotic personalities are broken down into categories; on the one hand, schizoid-aberrant within the norm and schizoid-psychopathic, and, on the other, aberrant (other than schizoid) within the norm and

Table 5.12. Comparison of prepsychotic personalities in schizophrenic siblings. Summarized comparisons from the 1941 studies and from family histories of the 208 principal probands (87 + 72 = 159[1])

Prepsychotic personality combinations among the 159 schizophrenic sibling pairs	A No. of cases observed	B Most probable figure by coincidence	Median error of B	A : B
Personality of both was the same:				
Nonaberrant	38	27.0	±4.73	1.4
Schizoid-aberrant (within the norm)	13	8.1	±2.77	1.6
Otherwise aberrant (within the norm)	1	0.5	±0.70	2.0
Schizoid psychopathic	21	9.4	±2.97	2.2
Otherwise psychopathic	4	1.0	±0.99	4.0
Totals:	77	46.0	±5.71	1.7
Personality of both was aberrant and similar as to type, but different as to degree:				
Schizoid-aberrant within the norm/schizoid psychopathic	10	15.0	±3.68	0.7
Otherwise aberrant within the norm/otherwise psychopathic	2	1.5	±1.21	1.3
Totals:	12	16.5	±3.84	0.7
Both were aberrant and similar as to degree, but different as to type of aberrance:				
Schizoid-aberrant/otherwise aberrant, both within norm	1	4.5	±2.09	0.2
Schizoid-psychopathic/otherwise psychopathic	3	4.4	±2.10	0.7
Totals:	4	8.9	±2.89	0.4
One sibling nonaberrant; the other schizoid or otherwise aberrant within the norm:				
Nonaberrant/schizoid-aberrant within the norm	28	28.5	±4.81	1.0
Nonaberrant/otherwise aberrant within the norm	11	8.7	±2.86	1.3
Totals:	39	37.2	±5.33	1.1
Both were aberrant, but different in type and degree:				
Schizoid-aberrant within the norm/otherwise psychopathic	5	5.5	±2.30	0.9
Otherwise aberrant within the norm/schizoid psychopathic	5	5.1	±2.22	1.0
Totals:	10	10.6	±3.14	0.9
One sibling nonaberrant; the other psychopathic:				
Nonaberrant/schizoid psychopathic	15	31.0	±4.99	0.5
Nonaberrant/otherwise psychopathic	2	9.0	±2.91	0.2
Totals:	17	40.0	±5.47	0.4

1. Personalities of siblings that could not be determined with certainty were omitted from the statistics.

otherwise psychopathic. One might ask the question, is the correlation between the prepsychotic personalities caused by the correlation of schizoid natures, or is it more probably caused only by the degree of some kind of disturbance in the personality? Table 5.12 is so arranged that it would answer this question, if the figures in it were large enough —which, however, they are not. They permit only the assumption, an uncertain indication, that a schizoid nature rather than the degree

of deviation from the norm has a causative influence on the correlation between schizophrenic siblings.

At any rate, it is to be considered a fact that the correlation between schizoid and schizophrenia differs in different families. Just as not every schizophrenic was premorbidly schizoid, so also every family does not have the tendency that all schizophrenias occurring in it are based on a schizoid predisposition.

Here are the conclusions that may be drawn

from all this information.

1. It is again shown, that among the schizophrenias occurring in two schizophrenic relatives, frequent combinations occur in which the "end states" and the course types are totally different. This lends renewed impetus to the need for summarizing the psychoses of schizophrenic symptomatology under one all-inclusive concept—that of schizophrenias in general—despite the variety of their courses.

2. But it is just as certain that there is a definite tendency toward concordance in the age of onset, the "end states," and the course types of schizophrenias of two relatives. The courses of schizophrenic psychoses are subject to familial influences, be they hereditary or environmental, even though such familial influences are by no means the only decisive ones.

3. The only course type that is almost never common to two schizophrenic relatives is the "schizophrenic catastrophe," the course type of "acute onset and rapid evolution to a severe chronic schizophrenic psychosis." This observation alone suggests the conclusion that this course type is either least of all or not at all bound to occur by way of familial causes. Investigations of an entirely different nature on the matter of course types, earlier indicated the same conclusion. These investigations demonstrate that the frequency of this course type has dropped in recent decades, probably in connection with the advances in treatment methods. I consider as valid the determination that holds that "schizophrenic catastrophes" are primarily artifacts. They are determined neither by any personal, hereditary predisposition nor by any unfavorable childhood conditions, but primarily by the living conditions of the patient after the eruption of the psychosis.

4. Of all the course types, the one that is found in combination by far most frequently in relatives, is the phasic course with a long-term recovery outcome. Insofar as familial influences have any effect on the courses at all, they are most pronounced in the psychoses with recovery outcomes following acute phases. The concept that childhood experiences in the family home have a causal influence on the series of intermittent acute schizophrenic psychoses occurring in maturity may present some problems. The familial influences that do have an effect in this area are probably hereditary. They are reminiscent of the familial influences in manic-depressive illnesses, which very few have found reason to dispute. From the data of this section the only conclusion that can be drawn is that familial (possibly hereditary) influences in respect to shaping the course of illness to a phasic-benign course do have significant implications. But these data do suggest the question whether these familial influences are also operative in the genesis of the disease, and not only in shaping its characteristic type. The investigations already discussed in preceding sections yielded no definite indications for an affirmative answer to this question, but they do justify the assumption that would favor an affirmative reply. The recognition that familial influences play a major role in determining the benign-phasic forms of schizophrenias actually came from different investigations, namely from those that described the effects of schizophrenia therapy. They showed unequivocally that the natural tendency toward benign-phasic courses cannot be increased at all, or not appreciably, by the hitherto applied methods of schizophrenia therapy. In sharp contrast to the above finding on "catastrophe schizophrenias" it can be stated unequivocally that the phasic-benign course of schizophrenias is more often determined by factors that are in existence long before the onset of illness, and less—if at all—by factors that begin to affect the patient after onset of his illness.

5. Outcomes to most severe chronic psychoses after chronic beginnings or after multiple acute episodes show a certain tendency toward concordance among relatives. But this tendency is no more pronounced than the tendency toward other course types, and is decidedly weaker than the concordance in respect to phasic-benign courses. These findings cannot be reconciled with the former speculation, according to which those schizophrenic psychoses with outcomes to most severe chronic states were thought to form the "actual hereditary nucleus" of the schizophrenias. The influences from hereditary developmental predisposition do not by any means exert a greater influence on the unfavorable outcomes than on the favorable ones.

As early as 1908, E. Bleuler discovered on the basis of his psychodynamic investigations that the evolution toward a "state of idiocy" in schizophrenics could not be a primary disease course. It had been regarded as such, as the labelling of the illness as "dementia praecox" plainly indicated, and is still regarded as such by many to the present day.

E. Bleuler believed he could establish the fact that a development toward a "state of idiocy" corresponds to a retreat from one's environment into one's self, which is rendered psychologically comprehensible by the primary symptoms of the disease and by the attitude the patient assumes toward his fellowmen. In his monograph of 1911 he wrote about this as follows:

> After we have characterized as secondary the most important elements that comprise the schizophrenic dementia, it follows naturally that this schizophrenic dementia itself should also be essentially regarded as secondary. Possibly some few individual primary symptoms play a part in the total syndrome, but usually we do not recognize them. It is also quite possible that sometime in the future, improved methods of observation will reveal to us in severe cases a primary idiocy behind the secondary one. For the time being, we see only that the patients split their thoughts, that they block off their affectivity, that they turn away from the world of reality. We see, furthermore, that no existing intellectual substance is destroyed; in fact, our experience with many individual cases makes it highly probable that in all chronic states, even the power of deliberate reasoning in complicated matters does not cease entirely, but is essentially only suppressed secondarily and inhibited by the cleavage.[12] Therefore, we cannot exclude from any stage of the illness the possibility of temporary or permanent improvements. The fact that possibly one third of the institutionalized cases actually never—or only temporarily—improve from a state of idiocy is, naturally, in no way evidence against the secondary nature of the phenomenon. Even healthy people occasionally become obsessed with a given idea. How much more often would this be the case in the schizoprenic, who systematically separates himself from the mitigating influences of reality and the power of reason, and who is already in possession of a tendency toward the perpetuation of psychic functions.

---

12. In plans for a second edition that was never published, E. Bleuler replaced the expression "cleavage" by "weak integration."

The data assembled by psychodynamic investigation, according to which the "state of idiocy" cannot be the hereditary, primary basic process in becoming schizophrenic, is revealed also in family studies. The process toward a "state of idiocy" is either not at all dependent on heredity (idiocy as an outcome after a one-time schizophrenic catastrophe) or not more than all other possible course types of psychoses (idiocy as an outcome after a long-term course).

6. The familial influences that condition the correlation of age in the onset of illness among siblings are most probably hereditary developmental predispositions of the personality, or the entire "gene-milieu." The familial tendency toward benign-recidivist course types is probably also rooted primarily in heredity. Insofar as correlations between the other course types and the "end states" exist, they might just as easily have been caused by childhood experiences in the family as by heredity.

Under no circumstances can one assume that there is a variety of "schizophrenia genes," that would lead partly toward one age of onset or another, or to any specific type of course or "end state." Such an assumption is already invalidated by the above-mentioned fact that among the relatives of schizophrenics with certain characteristic course types, there are often schizophrenics with other characteristic types. The personality, as it has been shaped by hereditary influences and the childhood experiences in the family home, has an influence on the course of schizophrenias. In former times the formulation used to read: The internal and the external environment determine the manner in which a psychosis manifests itself—and "psychosis" in this context meant something impersonal that assails the personality. In contrast to this idea, one might ask whether the course of illness is not shaped by the personality to a much greater extent than the comparisons of the schizophrenias in siblings would indicate. If this were the case, then, under extreme circumstances, a psychosis that imposes itself on the person as something alien could no longer even be postulated, for the illness would lie rooted in the patient's personality.

7. There is a correlation between the premorbid personalities of schizophrenic relatives. Not in every family do most schizophrenias arise from a schizoid nature in that family. There are different and special familial

predispositions to schizophrenias. Just as there are families with schizoids but without schizophrenics, so also are there families with schizophrenics but without schizoids. This observation contradicts the concept of the schizoid as a partial manifestiation or a partial tendency to an impersonal disease—schizophrenia.

The fact that schizophrenics frequently exhibit a schizoid nature before the eruption of their psychosis was a true and an important discovery. But for a long time it blinded scientific research to families in which schizophrenias grow out of specific familial difficulties, that are either falsely or insufficiently labelled as "schizoid." In my 1941 monograph I described a family in which schizophrenias and paranoic psychoses suspected of being schizophrenic occurred in connection with attitudes of jealously. An internal predisposition and reasons stemming from the specific personal background worked together in the development of the jealousy situation. In another family, several members of it suffered from very similar abnormal reactions to alcoholism. The proband became schizophrenic following a pathological intoxication, and after that, a relapse of his catatonia after recovery occurred only under the effect of alcohol. Karlsson (1968) demonstrated by way of a family tree of a large family, how the predisposition toward schizophrenia was related to a high degree of intelligence.

Here is a summary of answers to the questions posed at the beginning of this chapter:

Among siblings schizophrenias of widely differing varieties occur in combination. This is an indication that the different varieties of schizophrenias are, in their nature, related to one another.

There is a type of schizophrenia that never or very rarely occurs in siblings; it is the type that begins acutely and evolves acutely to a severe, long-term chronic psychosis. It is to be assumed that other than familial influences bring about the frightfulness of this catastrophe-schizophrenia.

On the other hand, there are types of schizophrenias that occur with exceptional frequency in two siblings, they are the ones with a phasic-benign outcome. It may be assumed that familial influences play a major role in their origin.

An objection to the investigations of this section might be that all the questions raised might be answered better and more clearly from comparisons of the schizophrenic psychoses of monozygotic twins than from comparisons of such psychoses in siblings. For that reason alone I would not have attempted to seek the answers to these questions from these data that are best suited for the purpose. The objection is basically correct. In rebuttal, however, I should point out that the present comparisons between the psychoses of siblings do have some significant advantages over the comparisons offered in the literature on twins. Among siblings the problem can be studied with a much larger number of cases. The combinations between sibling-schizophrenias among the present probands alone amount to about the same number as that of schizophrenias in monozygotic twins in the entire world literature. But it is even more important to realize the fact that the literature on schizophrenic twins contains precise data on the courses of illness in only a small minority of cases. The courses of illness in schizophrenic twins have not been observed nearly as often over many years and decades as they have for the schizophrenic siblings described here.

On the whole, the findings in twins yield about the same results as the findings in siblings. In particular they show that the schizophrenias of two monozygotic twins can be very different (Kringlen 1964, and others). Among the monozygotic quadruplets described by Rosenthal (1963) the courses were likewise dissimilar. Nor is the nonschizophrenic monozygotic partner of a schizophrenic twin always typically schizoid. Moreover, he might be nonaberrant or aberrant in a different way. These findings confirm the evidence that the family background of schizophrenias is by no means always described correctly by the term "schizoid."

A good concurrence resulted between my comparison of schizophrenias in siblings and the comparison of schizophrenias in monozygotic twins, as Inouye reported it. Just as schizophrenias in siblings occur in different combinations of the widest variety, so also do schizophrenias in monozygotic twins. Among others, there was one pair of monozygotic twins among Inouye's probands, one partner of which developed a chronic progressive schizophrenia, and the other "schizophrenia-like psychotic episodes." To be sure, not all possible combinations of schizophrenic courses occur among these probands of Inouye's. But that was hardly to be expected, for the number of his twin pairs (58) is much too small for such a possibility to materialize. Just as among the sibling-schizophrenias, so also among the schizophrenias of monozygotic twins, concordance in respect to periodic courses occurs most frequently.

Gottesman and Shields (1966) emphasized that the concordance in monozygotic twins with severe schizophrenias is greater than the concordance in those with milder forms. In this statement one might suspect a contradiction to my own findings to the effect that the greatest concordance occurred particularly among the phasic-benign courses of schizophrenic siblings, and that there was almost never a concordance in schizophrenic catastrophes. However, this contradiction might very well appear only because other authors described the degree of severity of schizophrenic psychoses quite differently from the way I did in the present study. Gottesman and Shields (1966) use primarily only the duration of hospitalization for determining the severity of the psychosis, and further, they apply it without regard to the duration of the observed course of illness. If, for instance, they label as "severe" schizophrenia cases that had been hospitalized longer than 52 weeks, it is quite possible that many are included among them that I would have categorized as "phasic-benign," in my investigations. On the other hand, it is just as possible that among the twins described by Gottesman and Shields (1966), whom they classified as cases of "mild" schizophrenias because they had been hospitalized less than 52 weeks when their observation period ended, there are many who, according to my conceptualization, became "severe chronic schizophrenias" a few years later. It will only be possible to make meaningful comparisons between the data from the twins of Gottesman and Shields (1966) and those of my siblings when enough of such data on the twin-schizophrenias have been collected to extend over several decades.

The Sexes of Two Schizophrenic Siblings

Line of questioning, as it develops from previous findings in symbionic psychoses and in twin-schizophrenias

Are the combinations brother-brother, brother-sister, and sister-sister distributed among schizophrenic siblings according to the laws of chance, or do men or women, or like-sexed or opposite-sexed combinations occur more frequently among them than might be ascribed to chance? If this were the case, one would have to assume some sort of influences being operative in the onset processes of

schizophrenic psychoses, that affect each sex differently. It would then be an intriguing task for schizophrenia research to disclose their nature.

What has aroused the interest in the sexes of schizophrenic sibling pairs was the experience from investigations of folie-à-deux cases, the symbionic psychoses (Scharfetter, 1971). It had long been obvious, that women are stricken with this type of psychosis much more often than men (Joerger 1889, Wollenberg 1889, Kröner 1891, Marandon 1894, Kraepelin 1909, and Gralnick 1942). In 1962 Rosenthal again pointed out the same phenomenon.

Scarcely anyone doubts that the living together in a close relationship of the two people with folie-à-deux delusions would have caused or contributed to the cause of the development of the psychosis in at least one of the partners. In former times the formulation was even bolder: The assumption was considered valid that the psychosis of the one partner—the "inducer"—had developed independently of the second partner, and that the psychosis of the second partner—the "induced"—was regarded as an unequivocal result of his living together with the inducer. Such simplistic assumptions no longer conform to our present-day knowledge about the multiplicity of backgrounds for psychotic developments. A number of investigators—at our clinic Edith Bernhard (1969) and Scharfetter, (1971)—also discovered all sorts of influences that play a part in the formation of symbionic psychoses. Each partner influences the other, even though often the influence of one over the other may predominate. Specifically for this reason Scharfetter (1971) coined the expression "symbionic psychosis." And there are other experiences in their lives besides those concerning the partnership they have in common, that affect both the inducer and the induced. It has been demonstrated with exceptional clarity that the personal constitution and the family relationships of the induced partner—not only of the inducer—deviate from the average norm (Scharfetter, 1971). In former times the speculation was popular that a prevalence of "endogenous" psychoses occurred only in the families of the inducer, and not in those of the induced. Actually, however, such a difference does not exist. Constitutional influences also affect the induced psychosis.

Important influences, even if they are not the only conditions that favor the development of symbionic psychoses, are the relationships between the partners of such psychoses. The assumption that women developed symbionic psychoses more often than men, because unhealthy, close, and long-lasting communal relationships are more dangerous for women than for men, may be well founded. This determination tempts one to apply it to schizophrenia research. If long-term, unhealthy, and close associations are important in the onset processes of schizophrenias, it ought to show up as a preponderance of women among the schizophrenics. It is also possible that unhealthy associations only play an important part in the genetics of certain specific types of schizophrenias, in which event we could expect a preponderance of women in at least those specific cases.

Scharfetter (1971), determined the proportions of sexes for the symbionic cases at our clinic with more probands and more accurately than had ever been possible before. The number of probands with symbionic psychoses of a single investigator or a single clinic is too small to be suitable for statistical studies. For this reason, Scharfetter (1971) took on himself the laborious task of working through the international literature on these psychoses. Including his own probands, he found a total of 240 partnerships with 562 psychotic partners that were suitable for statistical processing. His resultant data turned up more of the induced than of inducers, because many inducers had induced more than just one partner. Scharfetter (1971) collected not only descriptions of the folie-à-deux, but—borrowing from the old expression—also folie-à-trois and -à-quatre. His results appear in Table 5.13.

The women predominate significantly among the induced, as was to be expected from the impressions of all clinicians. But they also predominate just as much among the inducers, which was not known before and was scarcely expected.

The frequency of women among the induced for the symbionic psychoses in siblings alone is greater than for all other symbionic psychoses combined. The difference is largely due to the fact that not only the mother-daughter partnerships, but also mother-son partnerships are often involved in the formation of psychoses.

The preponderance of women among the induced was formerly explained by simply relating it to woman's greater susceptibility to influences. But after the finding that there are also many women among the inducers, this interpretation is no longer quite so simple. Today, however, we know that, in general, the inducer's illness is not entirely independent of his induced partner, but rather that there are also influences operating from the so-called induced on the inducer that are important. The psychoses in both partners are much more likely to develop simultaneously, rather than having the psychosis of one partner emerge solely from the psychosis of the other. The susceptibility of women might therefore also be a reason for finding so many women among the inducers. However, it also seems possible or probable, that women in intimate association with a partner often exert a stronger influence on that partner than men do.

Today it would be careless simply to state that the preponderance of women among patients with symbionic psychoses can be related to the greater susceptibility of women in close association with a psychotic. A more correct formulation would be the statement that the preponderance of women among partners of symbionic psychoses is an indication that close, long-term, unhealthy associa-

Table 5.13. Sex of patients with symbionic psychoses (from Scharfetter, 1971)

	Males			Females			Ratio of male to female partners
	No.	%	Conf. Interv.[1]	No.	%	Conf. Interv.[1]	
Among all inducers	67 = 28.0%		(23–33%)	173 = 72.0%		(66–76%)	1:2.6
Among all induced	130 = 40.3%		(35–46%)	192 = 59.7%		(54–65%)	1:1.5
Among all inducing siblings	26 = 29.9%		(21–41%)	61 = 70.1%		(60–79%)	1:2.3
Among all induced siblings	21 = 24.1%		(16–35%)	66 = 75.9%		(64–86%)	1:3.1

1. Confidence intervals shown in parentheses at 95 percent.

tions jeopardize women more than they do men.

Rosenthal (1962) and others, however, noticed not only the excess of women among all symbionic patients, but even more the preponderance of two female over two male partners. In an unpublished paper by Greenberg (1961)[13] Rosenthal found the best group of nonselected probands on this theme. The figures about the sexes of partnerships of symbionic psychoses among close relatives by Scharfetter and Greenberg (1961) in juxtaposed comparison yield the following picture:

Sexes of partnerships	Scharfetter (1971)	Greenberg (1961)
Two brothers	14	3
Two sisters	54	18
Brother-sister	19	3
Father-son	9	2
Father-daughter	19	0
Mother-son	22	6
Mother-daughter	59	13

The two sets of figures, so differently compiled, correspond remarkably. What does strike the eye, though, is that there are more father-daughter partnerships in the world literature than in Greenberg's (1961) data. Except for that, there are no significant differences.

In contrast to Greenberg (1961),[14] Scharfetter (1971) distinguished the induced from the inducer in his partnerships:

Among the 19 brother-sister partnerships, 12 brothers and 7 sisters are the inducers. Among the 9 father-son partnerships, 7 fathers and 2 sons are the inducers. Among the 19 father-daughter partnerships, 6 fathers and 13 daughters are the inducers. Among the 22 mother-son partnerships, 21 mothers and 1 son are the inducers. Among the 59 mother-daughter partnerships, 35 mothers and 24 daughters are the inducers.

It is striking that more daughters induce their fathers than vice versa. In the parent-

13. At least insofar as can be determined from Rosenthal's (1962) figures and Greenberg's (1961) unpublished paper.

14. Greenberg (1961) worked from the admission records of psychiatric hospitals in England and Wales. He was looking for relatives and spouses who were admitted in close succession as patients. He came up with 114 cases of relatives and spouses admitted in close succession, and a total of 234 of such patients. In 60 partnerships, involving 124 patients, he diagnosed folie-à-deux, -à-trois, or -à-quatre.

child combinations, the women seem to have the leading role rather than the men, no matter whether they are the mother or the daughter. But, on the other hand, in the pathological relationship between father and son, the father is dominant, as expected. Among the siblings, however, the female partner is not more often the inducer.

One might ask, are there more women among the symbionic psychotic patients because there are more partnerships involving females? Or reversed: Are there more partnerships involving females because there are more women among all symbionic psychotics? Related to the development of symbionic psychoses, the questions mean: Do unhealthy associations primarily lead to illnesses only between two women? Or are women especially susceptible in any given unfavorable association, even with men? Based on the figures presented, one might assume that most likely both are true.

A definite decision of the question would be easy in the two extreme cases: (1) If there were an equal number of men and women among all symbionic psychotics, but there were only pairs of the same sex, then it would be certain that the unhealthy associations were affecting only the like-sexed partners. (2) If there were a pronounced preponderance of women, and if, despite that, there were just as many man-woman partnerships as the highest probability would provide, considering the given preponderance of women, it might be concluded that women are much more susceptible in any unfavorable partnership than men are. These two extreme cases, that would permit a straight answer, just do not exist.

It is now possible to calculate how, for a given number of men and women, the three combinations (man-man, woman-woman, and man-woman) are distributed, according to the highest probability among the probands with symbionic psychoses. Then what remains to be checked is whether the proportions actually encountered differ from the calculated probabilities. The most probable distribution may be calculated according to the following formula:

$$\frac{m(m-1)}{2(t-1)} : \frac{w(w-1)}{2(t-1)} : \frac{mw}{t-1};$$

in which

m = number of male patients = 56
w = number of women patients = 166
t = $m + w$ (total 222)

(Figures from Scharfetter [1971] and Greenberg [1961] are combined.)

The proportion of combinations man-man, woman-woman, and man-woman amounts to 7:62:42 according to greatest expected probability, and to 17:72:22 according to actual count.

The like-sexed pairs outnumber the opposite-sexed pairs, and this observation is highly significant ($\chi^2 = 25.42$, $p < 0.005$).

Both in expected probability and by actual count, the predominance of like-sexed pairs over opposite-sexed pairs occurs not only for the woman-woman combinations, but for the man-man combinations as well (in men 17 over 7, and in women 72 over 62).

Insofar as these findings are significant, they may be interpreted as follows: (1) Unhealthy long-term companionships endanger the mental health of women more severely than that of men. (2) An unhealthy long-term companionship is more likely to produce illness if it occurs between two like-sexed partners than between two opposite-sexed partners. The assumption is not warranted that women in like-sexed unhealthy partnerships would fall ill sooner than men in such partnerships in the same situation. These statistical results are psychologically meaningful. As viewed from the day-to-day experience in psychology, it is quite possible that women are more sensitive to close companionships than men; and it seems just as possible that the influences favoring the onset of illness in both like-sexed partners are more often as effective as in opposite-sexed partnerships; and finally, it is also possible that in an existing unhealthy association among them the sameness of sex in two men or two women would bring about illness.

For two reasons I placed these data on the symbionic psychoses before the investigations on the sex ratios among two schizophrenic siblings. In the first place, it has been demonstrated by a kind of model (the symbionic psychoses themselves), that the sex ratio among psychotic partners can be related to causally important influences, if these influences affect the two sexes to different degrees of intensity. In preceding chapters repeated reference has been made to data that indicate the varieties in the genesis of schizophrenic psychosis in men and in women. In the present chapter these findings are to be checked against the sex ratios among schizophrenic sibling pairs. But then, the symbionic psychoses themselves are, for the most part, to be included under the paranoid schizophrenias.[15]

According to findings derived by totally different methods, which have been described in other chapters, one might assume that familial influences in women exert a greater influence on the development of schizophrenias than they do in men. The special subtype of the symbionic schizophrenias illustrates this sex difference with exceptional emphasis and clarity.

The schizophrenias of monozygotic twins are usually not included in the symbionic schizophrenias. To be sure, there was not always a close relationship between twins before the eruption of the psychosis, although it usually did exist in childhood. Similar psychodynamic processes in symbionic schizophrenias and in twin schizophrenias are possible. Actually, a number of investigations revealed the striking fact that concordance in respect to schizophrenic psychoses occurs more often in monozygotic twin sisters than in monozygotic twin brothers. Rosenthal (1962) in particular directed our attention to this phenomenon. He worked out a breakdown of the concordance figures of monozygotic twins for schizophrenia according to their sexes, using the data from twin studies that were accessible at the time. He found that these studies concerned more female than male twin sets, and that the concordance of the female twins was greater than that of the males.

Rosenthal's (1962) data is based on the well-known twin studies by Luxenburger (1928), Rosanoff et al. (1934), Essen-Moeller (1941), and Slater (1953). Rosenthal (1962) was not able to use Kallmann's (1946) investigations, since they did not indicate the sexes of his twins. Of the 60 female monozygotic twin pairs among the four studies, 47, or 78 percent were concordant, and of the 42 male pairs, only 23, or 55 percent. The confidence intervals of the two mentioned percentages at 95 percent amount to 66–88 percent and 39–70 percent.

The findings on monozygotic twins published after 1961 resulted in indications both

---

15. Years ago only the psychoses of inducers were counted as schizophrenias. The psychoses of the induced were considered as purely psychogenic. Actually, however, there is no sharp or basic difference in the nature of paranoid psychoses between inducers and the induced. According to more modern concepts, paranoid psychoses with a schizophrenic symptomatology are simply schizophrenias, although they are schizophrenias with their own particular dynamics.

for and against the assumption of a higher concordance in female than in male pairs. Thus, up to the present day, there is no valid decision as to which assumption applies.

In two groups of all-male monozygotic twins, there were only very few (Kringlen 1964), or no (Tienari 1968) concordant pairs. One had to assume that this was an expression of a low propensity for concordance in male monozygotic pairs, in respect to schizophrenia. However, other explanations for these findings suggested themselves as well. The investigations by Kringlen (1968), with a different and larger group of twins, and by Shields (1968), in a research project at Maudsley Hospital, result in opposite findings.

In the groups assembled by Rosenthal (1962), however, he found a higher concordance in female than in male monozygotic twins, and in the dizygotic twins as well.

In the combined groups by Rosanoff et al. (1934) and Slater (1953), there are only 5 pairs among the male dizygotic pairs out of 32 (15.6%) who are concordant, against 16 out of 83 female pairs (19.3 percent). The confidence intervals at 95 percent are 5.3–32.8 percent for the 15.6 percent, and 11–49 percent for 19.3 percent. The differences are statistically not sufficiently significant.

In the more recent series by Kringlen (1968) and by Shields (1968) these sex differences in discordant twins do not occur, and they must be regarded as questionable.

Rosenthal (1962) further compared the sex ratios in pairs of schizophrenic siblings who were not twins. The only research material along these lines available to him, however, were the findings by Schulz (1933) from Munich and by Zehnder (1941) from central Switzerland. These two groupings combined resulted in the following breakdown

Totals in figures and percentages of all 203 pairs with a confidence interval of the percentage at 95%

Two schizophrenic brothers	50 = 24.6% (19–31%)
Two schizophrenic sisters	68 = 33.5% (27–41%)
One brother and one sister, both schizophrenic	85 = 41.9% (35–49%)

Again, the differences are not sufficiently significant. Shields (1968) objects to Zehnder's (1941) findings because her schizophre-

nic siblings were assembled as patients from a hospital. Possibly there were more sisters in this type of group, because their brothers, rather than they, were more likely to have moved to other localities.

In summary, we find that among symbionic psychoses in which unhealthy personal associations played an important role, the women predominate impressively. Among schizophrenias of monozygotic twins, for whom the question of unhealthy personal associations as a causal background is to be answered, the women also seem to be predominant. Among schizophrenias of dizygotic twins and siblings who are not twins, for whom the same question is posed, a preponderance of women was at first suspected, but has not yet been made probable.

At this point I intended to begin my investigations. I wanted to answer the question whether two sisters rather than two brothers from the same family were at greater risk of becoming schizophrenic, by studying the family histories of the 208 principal schizophrenic probands, supplemented by the family histories of other schizophrenics. Let us anticipate by reporting that, despite the laborious efforts to gather sibling-schizophrenias, the question could not be answered unequivocally.

My Investigations on the Sexes of Two Schizophrenic Siblings

The attempt is to be made to answer two questions, based on the investigations of the 208 principal probands and additional information from other schizophrenics at Burghölzli.

1. Is the proportion of schizophrenic women who have schizophrenic siblings the same as among all schizophrenics and among the general population? Or is it greater, as it is for the symbionic psychoses?

2. Are the combinations brother-brother, sister-sister, and brother-sister in two schizophrenic siblings distributed according to the laws of chance, if a definite proportion of the sexes occurs among all schizophrenics with siblings?[16] Or are the combinations of two

16. The following hypothetical example may serve to explain the difference between questions 1 and 2. Keeping in mind question 1, let us assume a preponderance of women. Among 100 combinations of sibling psychoses, there are 50 men and 150 women. This combination patently suggests that woman-woman pairs must occur more frequently than man-man pairs (the latter is possi-

women predominant over those of two men (as they are for symbionic psychoses), and do the like-sexed combinations exceed those of the opposite-sexed combinations?

If among schizophrenic siblings differences can be proved that favor the absolute number of women, the combinations of woman-woman, and of like-sexed pairs, they can probably be interpreted in the same sense as the symbionic psychoses, that is, the differences suggest that in the development of schizophrenias close personal association between siblings plays a greater role in women than it does in men. From this proportion as between the sexes a factor that is contributory to schizophrenia in women might be established.

To be sure, a close relationship between two schizophrenic sisters does not imply the same thing as the close relationship of the partners of symbionic psychoses. The latter of these refers to the close association of the partners during the years before onset of the illness. Such a relationship is rare between two schizophrenic sisters. On the other hand, such close relationships are fairly common in sisters during childhood. Favorable or unfavorable influences in the parental home might have the same effect on two sisters, in fact even more so than on a brother-and-sister combination. Besides, it may be assumed that two sisters are more often dependent on one another in the same family, and suffer with and for each other more than two brothers would.

In considering the first question, one frightening difficulty is immediately encountered. The sex ratios of schizophrenics with siblings should be compared with those for all schizophrenics. But nobody knows how schizophrenias are distributed between men and women. There are any number of statistics on this, but none that was free of selection bias. One set of these statistics shows a slight preponderance of men; the other, a slight preponderance of women. Still, most of them agree that there cannot be any great difference between the number of male and of female schizophrenics.

Most statistics on the sex ratios of schizophrenics are based on the admissions or the population statistics of psychiatric hospitals. But it is doubtful whether the sex ratios among hospitalized schizophrenics and those never or rarely hospitalized are the same. Besides, most psychiatric clinics must adjust their admissions according to the number of available beds. This number of beds available for men or for women patients, however, is different, because other illnesses besides schizophrenias occur at different rates in the two sexes (such as alcoholism, manic-depressive illness, etc.). Additional factors interfering with a free selection are almost endless in most of the existing statistics on the distribution of schizophrenias between the two sexes.

The actual conditions are more closely approached by avoiding clinic admissions and clinic populations, and by concentrating on schizophrenics who are picked up as siblings of nonschizophrenics, in censuses of an entire population, or as nonselected representatives of the general population. These types of investigations are the ones to be reported below.

I am certainly aware that even this type of investigation is not entirely free of some selection bias. For example, it must be borne in mind that the nonhospitalized schizophrenics are more easily overlooked than the hospitalized ones, even in these investigations, and that one sex or the other might be the majority among the nonhospitalized who were overlooked.

Fifteen studies in which the incidence of schizophrenia among the general population was investigated, revealed a ratio of 205 male to 222 female schizophrenics. The proportion of the sexes amounts to 205 = 48 percent (43–53 percent) : 222 = 52 percent (47–57 percent).[17]

Six of the above studies concern general patients; the mental health of their siblings was investigated by Luxenburger (1928), Brugger (1929), Schulz (1931), M. Bleuler (1932, 1935), and Panse (1936). Two of these studies concerned investigations of subjects taken at random from birth registers as representatives of the general population (Klemperer 1933, and Helgason 1964). Seven of

---

ble at a maximum of 25 times, and the former, at a minimum of 50 times). What is to be checked is whether, and to what degree, the three different sex combinations deviate from the one with the greatest probability of occurrence. The most probable ratio of man-man, woman-woman, and man-woman amounts to 6.1 : 56.2 : 37.7 A predominance of the combination woman-woman existing for a given sex ratio among all schizophrenics with siblings could only be assumed if the combination woman-woman occurred more often than 57 times, and if, besides, the difference were also significant.

17. Confidence intervals at 95 percent, according to Geigy tables.

them included investigations of the total population at the time they were done (Brugger 1931, 1933, and 1938; Sjoegren 1935, 1948; Stroemgren 1938; and Essen-Moeller 1956).

The study on the frequency of schizophrenias among the population with the greatest number of probands was done by Kaila (1942). He found a total of 1791 schizophrenics in a district in Finland with 418,472 inhabitants. The number of schizophrenics established by Kaila (1942) within a population group is therefore more than four times greater than the number of schizophrenics established by all other authors combined. In order not to assign too much importance to this one investigation in comparison to all the others, I shall first discuss it separately. Among the schizophrenics established by Kaila (1942), there were 873 men and 918 women, that is, the ratios of men to women amounted to 48.8:51.2 percent.[18] Surprisingly, this ratio corresponds almost exactly to that of the probands of the other 15 authors already mentioned, even though Kaila's (1942) data were collected by different methods and in a different country.

If the figures obtained by the 15 previously mentioned authors and those by Kaila (1942) are combined, the confidence intervals of the sex ratios among schizophrenics in the general population become very close, in fact, much closer than they could be derived from the figures of the 15 above-mentioned authors alone. Instead of a confidence interval at 95 percent, the following formula shows twice the standard deviation:

$$48.6 \text{ percent} \pm 2 \times 1.05 :$$
$$51.4 \text{ percent} \pm 2 \times 1.05$$

This again shows that schizophrenias in men and in women occur at nearly the same frequency. The difference in the greater number among women is not significant. However, it should be pointed out that it would have to become greater if the age structure were taken into account, since schizophrenic women suffered their onset later in life, on an average, than schizophrenic men did.

The sex ratios of contemporary populations from which schizophrenics were identified is not precisely known. For this reason, it is not

possible to make an exact comparison of sex ratios of schizophrenics and those of the general population. These two ratios, however, would differ very little, if at all.

The next comparison is made between the sex ratios of the schizophrenics among representatives of the general population and those of schizophrenics who have schizophrenic siblings.

In the 8 papers on sibships among schizophrenic probands, there were 175 male schizophrenics with schizophrenic siblings, as against 222 females with schizophrenic siblings. The ratio between the sexes is 44 percent (42–47 percent)[19] : 55 percent (53–59 percent.)[19]

Among the 8 papers from which the above-mentioned figures were compiled, the present study of the 208 principal schizophrenic probands is included (Tables 5.1 and 5.4). The 208 probands have a total of 24 male and 39 female schizophrenic siblings. Furthermore, the findings from my New York (1930) and my Pfäfers (1941) schizophrenics were included. Investigative results by other authors drawn upon include those by Schulz (1932), Luxenburger (1936), Stroemgren (cross section 1938), Slater (1953), and Hallgren and Sjoegren (1959). Several other authors who counted the schizophrenic siblings of schizophrenics did not differentiate these by sex.

The result is, therefore, that among all schizophrenics selected free of bias who had schizophrenic siblings, the women outnumber the men. The difference is small, but still significant. The preponderance of women among schizophrenics with schizophrenic siblings is greater than the preponderance of women among all schizophrenics. This latter difference, however, is not so great as to be significant.

The lack of significance of this difference in the sex ratios among all schizophrenics and the schizophrenics with schizophrenic siblings is already obvious from the above-mentioned confidence intervals, and shows up even more accurately from the equation: $\chi^2 = 1.1246$, $p < 0.30$.

For determining answers to the second question posed at the beginning of this section, certain experiences and calculations were useful.

All sibships with more than one schizo-

---

18. These figures are not actually contained in Kaila's (1942) paper; although they can be calculated from his data. In the process it is possible for small errors to occur in the decimals.

19. Confidence intervals at 95 percent, according to Geigy tables.

phrenic were used that came from the following groups of schizophrenic probands already described

—The 208 principal schizophrenic probands of this project
—The 100 probands from Pfäfers
—The 100 probands from New York
—The 150 "young schizophrenics"
—The 106 "middle-aged schizophrenics"[20]
—The 400 "supplemental schizophrenics"[21]
—The 239 schizophrenics present as inpatients at Burghölzli in May/June 1965—a total of 1303 probands.

The "young schizophrenics," "middle-aged schizophrenics," and the "supplemental schizophrenics" are the same groups of probands whose backgrounds were studied, and who were earlier used for the statistics on premature parent losses. But all these groups of probands produced such a small number of schizophrenic siblings, that it seemed prudent to increase the total number of probands still more, so as to reduce the median error. So the 116 male schizophrenics who were inpatients at Burghölzli on the key date, May 31, 1965, and the 123 female schizophrenics who were present there on the key date, June 11 of that year, were included as supplemental probands for this investigation. A check was made to find out whether these 239 schizophrenics had schizophrenic siblings and what the sex ratio was among these schizophrenic siblings.

The data on siblings of the 208 principal probands and that of the remaining 1095 other probands will be considered separately below. The latter group was identified as "supplemental schizophrenics." The data reproduced below represent the distribution of the sexes and the combinations of sexes among all schizophrenics who have at least 1 schizophrenic sibling. Below is a key to the abbreviated entries

20. In earlier data, 130 "middle-aged" schizophrenics are accounted for, but here only 106. The reason for this difference is that, among the schizophrenic patients present at Burghölzli in May/June of 1965, more of them from research groups of previous investigations had been included, and that these were omitted from that category for this set of data.

21. In earlier figures, 444 "supplemental" schizophrenics are counted, while here it is just 400. Reason for the difference, as in footnote 20 above.

m = Number of male schizophrenics with 1 or more schizophrenic siblings
f = Number of female schizophrenics with 1 or more schizophrenic siblings
mm = Number of pairs of schizophrenic brothers
ff = Number of pairs of schizophrenic sisters
mf = Number of sibling pairs with 1 schizophrenic brother and 1 schizophrenic sister
1 = data on sibships among the 208 principal probands
2 = data on sibships among the 1095 supplemental schizophrenics;
3 = data on sibships among the principal and the supplemental probands combined.

Here are the resultant numbers for the categories

	1	2	3
m	71	178	249
f	83	176	259
mm	21	45	66
ff	27	44	71
mf	29	88	117

The distribution according to the highest probability was determined separately for 1, 2, and 3, showing the relationships for each given figure of males and females in the three sex combinations (mm, ff, and mf). The calculation was done by application of the formula already mentioned,

Most probable number of mm
$$= \frac{m(m-1)}{2(m+f-1)}$$
Most probable number of ff
$$= \frac{f(f-1)}{2(m+f-1)}$$
Most probable number of $mf = \dfrac{mf}{m+f-1}$

The comparison between the actual numbers of sex combinations and the calculated ones according to the above formula appear below for mm, ff, and mf:

	For 1	For 2	For 3
By count:	21 :27 :29	45 :44 :88	66 :71 :117
By calculation:	16.2:22.2:38.5	44.6:43.6:88.7	58.9:65.9:127.2

The difference between the counted and the calculated sex combinations is close to significance for 1 ($0.1 > p > 0.05$), insufficiently significant for 3, and there is no difference at all for 2. For 1 the values are shown in percentages below, with confidence intervals at 95 percent. The ratios mm:ff:mf amount to:

first, that they do affect women, and second, that they affect women more often than men, if they affect men at all.

From our experience with symbionic psychoses, we are constrained to assume that the proved preponderance of women attests to a genetic implication of close associations in men and women both, but that the signifi-

By count:	27.3 percent (18–39 percent) : 35.1 percent (25–47 percent) : 37.6 percent (27–49 percent)
By calculation:	21.1 percent (12–32 percent) : 28.8 percent (19–40 percent) : 50.0 percent (39–62 percent)

All confidence intervals overlap considerably.

The figures show that, with a given preponderance of women among schizophrenics with schizophrenic siblings, the combinations brother-brother, sister-sister, and brother-sister are distributed in accordance with the greatest chance probability. There is no proof that a sister-sister combination or like-sexed pairs outnumber others (considering the preponderance of women), as is the case in symbionic psychoses.[22]

In summary, the investigations on the sex ratios of schizophrenic sibling pairs have not yielded any decisive results, and they were hardly worth the expenditure of time and effort required. Nevertheless, they did show significantly that among schizophrenics who have schizophrenic siblings women outnumber the men.

If one is aware of the preponderance of women among symbionic psychoses and the numerous indications that unfavorable conditions in the homes of schizophrenics favor the development of schizophrenias in the women, then one might regard the predominance of women among schizophrenics who have schizophrenic siblings as an additional indication in the same direction.

If, for the time being, it has been shown only for women that unfavorable long-term personal associations play a part in the development of schizophrenias in women, this does not mean that such associations have no effect on men. Up to now we know only,

22. Pollack et al. (1969) likewise reach the conclusion that neither sisters nor like-sexed pairs predominate among two schizophrenic siblings—although it should be mentioned that their investigation encompassed only 10 schizophrenics with siblings.

cance of this implication is greater in women than in men. In symbionic psychoses this preponderance of women may certainly be interpreted in this sense.

The preponderance of women among schizophrenics with schizophrenic siblings is greater in the probands already investigated than among all schizophrenics, although the difference is below the limits of significance. This observation, too, agrees with the assumption that unfavorable personal ties play a certain role in the genesis of schizophrenias in women.

But we were not able to demonstrate with any degree of certainty that, with the existing preponderance of women among schizophrenics with schizophrenic siblings, the schizophrenic sister-sister pairs outnumbered the schizophrenic brother-brother pairs. Nor do the like-sexed pairs outnumber the opposite-sexed pairs. Accordingly, we found no valid indications that girls are more likely to become schizophrenic together with girls than with boys, but only that girls with brothers or sisters more readily become ill together than boys do.

In interpreting the greater number of women among schizophrenics with schizophrenic siblings, the psychogenetic basis that has been discussed seems to me to be the most probable one. But other interpretations are possible, as well. Among the heredity-pathological theories the most acceptable one is that the predisposition to schizophrenia is more often manifested in women than in men, which is possibly true for the phasic depressions. But then, a preponderance of women would have to be found among all schizophrenics, and not only among those schizophrenics with schizophrenic siblings. A shift in the sex ratios might be the result of a selection bias. For examples, such a shift in the natural sex ratio would come about, if not all schizophrenic men, but all schizophrenic women had been included in the investigation. This would happen if, for instance, probands for an investigation were picked from local psychotics rather than from patients who had left their homes, and if there were more men in the latter group. The same selection bias would occur if families were more inclined to be secretive about the psychoses of their men rather than about those of their women. The family histories of the 208 principal probands certainly do not include such—or similar—selection errors, and for most of the supplemental schizophrenic probands they can most probably be considered nonexistent.

Mathematical and Statistical Appendix

The calculations of this chapter present some difficult and complicated mathematical problems. At my request, Dr. Erwin Hansert of the Max Planck Institute for Psychiatry in Munich checked them over for me while the book was in press. He performed his calculations by using improved methods.

The essential result of his effort was the assurance that the significance of figures in this chapter had not in any instance been overestimated. It had been determined with adequate, and in some instances even with excessive caution.

Based on Dr. Hansert's calculations, some of the recent entries should be discussed in a new light. They show a contrast between the findings in the 208 principal probands and in the supplemental probands. Among the former group, the like-sexed pairs outnumber the opposite-sexed pairs significantly, and among the latter group, the like- and opposite-sexed pairs are distributed according to the calculations for greatest probability. Why this difference? The families of the 208 principal probands are more accurately documented than the families of the supplemental probands. The assumption is therefore likely that like-sexed schizophrenic siblings in the families of supplemental probands were overlooked. It is almost inconceivable that like-sexed pairs were overlooked more often than opposite-sexed pairs, although there appears to be a plausible explanation, namely that there actually is a slight tendency toward like-sexed,

female schizophrenic siblings among the principal probands, who happened to outnumber those of all schizophrenic probands. A certain support for the plausibility of this explanation is the fact that the threshold value for the total number of probands (calculated by a method to be explained later) amounts to 12.4 percent; that is, it is also relatively small.

Dr. Hansert's calculations are important, not only as a criticism of my own methodology, but especially also as a point of departure for future statistical processing of the same material. They are therefore reproduced verbatim below.

I.

From the theoretical-statistical problems emerging from the preceding chapter, let us first select the one that can be outlined in a general and abstract form as follows:

From a population of objects, a certain object-type is to be investigated (in this instance, psychotics or schizophrenics). As a symbol for the object-type under consideration, let the letter A be used. Suppose A occurs in two varieties that are to be distinguished in this investigation (to wit: male and female), which might be further symbolized as Aa and Ab. Of the A actually existing during a certain investigative time-span and in a certain investigative locality, a certain portion comes to the attention of the investigator through certain selective processes, the statistical properties of which would have to be discussed separately. The investigator is furthermore interested specifically in those A's that belong together in a certain way as pairs (in this instance, as siblings), which means that a sampling should be taken with the following possible distinctions per case:

$$x_1 : Aa,\ Aa$$
$$x_2 : Aa,\ Ab$$
$$x_3 : Ab,\ Ab$$

The investigator will find in his material the raw numerical frequencies: $f(x_1)$, $f(x_2)$, $f(x_3)$.

The frequency of Aa or Ab among the given pairs is, therefore

$$(1)\quad \begin{aligned} y_1 &= 2f(x_1) + f(x_2) & (Aa) \\ y_2 &= f(x_2) + 2f(x_3) & (Ab) \end{aligned}$$

The problem treated below is a hypothetical one. If y_1 and y_2 are given, do the frequencies

$f(x_1)$ correspond to "coincidence"?

The solution of this problem is the basis for the results already obtained. Before a solution can be attempted in the formulation of this problem, the terms "correspond" and "coincidence" must be precisely defined.

According to previous explanations, the following conception of the term "coincidence" seems to apply to the above problem.

The two numerical values y_1 and y_2 being given, let y_1 combine objects Aa and y_2 objects Ab into pairs, in such a way that the process of pairing would give the same probability to every possible combination of such pairs. Imagine, for instance, an urn, in which y_1 Aa's and y_2 Ab's are mixed together, and that these objects are successively removed, at random, two at a time, without ever replacing any, and remixing the remaining content after each withdrawal, until the urn is empty. One combinatory deliberation shows that in such a case the probability for

$(2a)\ f(x_1) = f_1, f(x_2) = f_2, f(x_3) = f_3$

has the following value:

(3a)

$$w(f_1, f_2, f_3) = 2^{f_2} \frac{\dbinom{(y_1 + y_2)/2}{f_1, f_2, f_3}}{\dbinom{y_1 + y_2}{y_1}}$$

It is to be observed, however, that the equation system (1) admits only one sole degree of freedom; that is, one sole, independent solution. Therefore, it is enough in (2a) to depict only one of the three values, since the other two are determined from it. If we label the above-described process "chance pairing," we can thus also say: In the process of chance pairing, the probability for, for instance,

$(2b)\ f(x_1) = f$ has the following value:

$$(3b)\ w(f) = 2^{y_1 - 2f} \frac{\dbinom{(y_1 + y_2)/2}{f, y_1 - 2f, y_2 - y_1 \over 2 + f}}{\dbinom{y_1 + y_2}{y_1}}$$

in which the following must hold true:

$$(4)\qquad \frac{y_1 - y_2}{2} \leqslant f \leqslant \frac{y_1}{2}$$

In addition, three other important values of probability distribution are briefly indicated that were defined by the probabilities from (3b):

The most probable value (that is, the value with the maximum probability) of $f(x_1)$ is the next higher whole number of

$$(5a)\ f_o = \frac{y_1^2 + y_1 - 2y_2 - 4}{2y_1 + 2y_2 + 6}$$

$$= \frac{y_1(y_1 - 1) + 2(y_1 - y_2) - 4}{2(y_1 + y_2 + 3)}$$

If f_o itself is already a whole number, then f_o and $f_o + 1$ will both have the same maximum probability.

The expected value (the theoretical mean) of $f(x_1)$ is equal to

$$(5b)\qquad E_1 = \frac{y_1(y_1 - 1)}{2(y_1 + y_2 - 1)}$$

(This value is very close to the most probable value, if y_1 and y_2 are not too radically different.)

The variance (the theoretical distribution) of $f(x_1)$ is finally equal to

$$(5c)\ \sigma_1^2 = \frac{y_1(y_1 - 1)y_2(y_2 - 1)}{2(y_1 + y_2 - 1)^2(y_1 + y_2 - 3)}$$

II.

What we now interpret as "corresponding" to chance can be determined on the basis of the preceding deliberations by application of the principles of mathematical statistical procedure: one of the values $f(x_1), f(x_2), f(x_3)$ is selected, and the totality of their possible values is separated into two parts, of which one has an extremely high probability under "chance," and the remainder, which has an extremely low probability under "chance." This remainder is selected so as to have a relatively high probability under "not-chance." In the previously cited cases, where from the outset we expect that pair type x_1 (that is, in this instance, female-female) occurs with exceptional frequency, we would accordingly select $f(x_1)$, and determine a number z in such a way as to have (6a) $f(x_1) \leqslant z$ "corresponding" to "chance," while (6b) $f(x_1) > z$ not "corresponding" to "chance." A handier, more understandable, although less precise way of stating it would be, for instance, in the case of (6b): "x_1 is significant to a high frequency."

Before we now, in turn, proceed to deal with the series according to the concrete figures earlier in this chapter, it should be pointed out that the χ^2-method applied there cannot do full justice to the problem, for the simple reason that at this point it requires two degrees of freedom (any type of chance calculation other than the one defined above could, of course, provide the proper solution despite an inadequate methodology).

(a) On p. 336 the number of female probands was given as 166, that of male probands as 56. Utilizing these figures, the given values are

$$y_1 = f = 166$$
$$y_2 = m = 56$$

The expected value of $f(x_1)$ (there called the "most probable value," in contrast to common usage here) amounts to 62, and $f(x_1)$ assumes the value of 72. The standard deviation (that is, the positive square root of the variance) of $f(x_1)$ equals 2—see formula (5c). The difference between the actual $f(x_1)$ and its expected value, accordingly, is five times that of the standard deviation, which in itself is a valid criterion for ignoring chance pairing.

The possible values for $f(x_1)$, according to formula (4), are the whole numbers between 55 and 83, inclusive. In Chart I the probabilities under "chance" are given for the possible values between 65 and 83, rounded off to three decimals. This chart shows that if the traditional testing level of 5 percent is used as a basis, then a value of 65 should be selected for z from formulas (6a) and (6b). A more accurate calculation shows that the so-called threshold value, that is, that probability which —selected as a test level—just barely leads to a repudiation of the chance-assumption, amounts in our case to a probability for $f(x_1) \geqslant 72$ of $1.9 \cdot 10^{-6}$. Accordingly, chance pairing as an explanation for the great number of pairs discovered is virtually out of the question.

Note: By the χ^2-method, at a test level of 5 percent, the value to be selected for z would be 66, and the threshold value is equal to $3.0 \cdot 10^{-6}$, in which, to be sure, it should still be remembered that the χ^2-test is a bilateral test.

(b) Although, seen as a whole, the data on p. 338 are not as weighty as those from cases cited on pp. 336 and 341—possibly because of the objections raised by Shields—we shall apply them once again to serve as a model case for the methodology:

They are $y_1 = 221$, and $y_2 = 185$
Expected value of $f(x_1) = 60.0$
Expected value of $f(x_2) = 101.0$
Expected value of $f(x_3) = 42.0$

Chart 1. Probabilities for possible frequencies greater than or equal to 65 of a female/female combination

f	Probability
65	0.062
66	0.027
67	0.009
68	0.003
69	0.001
70	0.000
83	0.000

Chart II. Probabilities for possible frequencies greater than or equal to 66 of a female/female combination

f	Probability
66	0.027
67	0.016
68	0.009
69	0.005
70	0.002
71	0.001
72	0.000
110	0.000

Chart III. Probabilities for possible frequencies greater than or equal to 26 of a female/female combination

f	Probability
26	0.042
27	0.017
28	0.006
29	0.001
30	0.000
41	0.000

For a test level of 5 percent the χ^2-method for rejection of chance-pairing would require $f(x_1) > 68$, actually, $f(x_1) = 68$. The pertinent threshold value amounts to 8 percent. Chart II shows, rounded off to three decimals, the chance probabilities for the values $f(x_1) \geqslant 66$. From this, at the 5 percent test level, it follows that $z = 66$ (see [6a] and [6b]), and for the threshold value, 1.7 percent. Even when the fact is considered that the χ^2-test is a bilateral test, the obvious difference between the two methods is readily apparent.

Besides, according to formula (5c) the standard deviation σ_1 of $f(x_1$ is equal to approximately 3.5, that is, the difference between the actual value and the expected value is more than twice its value, which means that a significance at 5 percent might well be assumed from this calculation.

(c) If now the figures given on p.   are considered, it is immediately evident that there can be no significance for Case 2. The evaluation of formula (5c) also reveals immediately that no significance can be expected for Case 3 either, for the standard deviation of $f(x_1)$ amounts to 4.0, and the difference of the observed $f(x_1)$—namely, 71, and its respective expected value—namely 65.9—are very little larger. However, for Case 1 it is different: The corresponding standard deviation is equal to 2.2, and the corresponding difference is equal to 4.8, and that is more than twice the standard deviation. As a matter of fact, Chart III reveals a value of 26 as the critical z-value according to (6a) and (6b), and for the test level of 5 percent, and the threshold value for $f(x_1) = 27$ amounts to 2.5 percent.

Of course, in interpreting this result as well as the previous ones, we should consider whether some postulates might exist that would render Type "x_1" more comprehensible. Naturally, with materials from different sources, these postulates might well be different too, and in combining such materials, the effect might well be strengthened or weakened.

A final remark on the χ^2-method: As may be readily proved by way of the formulas under I, the expected value of the χ^2-test statistics under "chance" is, for practical purposes, equal to 1. For this reason it may be assumed that an improvement of this method could be achieved by taking one degree of freedom as a basis. The calculation showed that this is also true for cases II (b) and II (c) as well, although the problem will not be pursued further at this point.

III.

An additional remaining problem concerns that area of inquiry which reads approximately: Is the element "feminine" (or stated in the language of I, the element Aa) represented with greater frequency in a given kind of research material than the element "masculine" (that is, the element Ab)? Let us limit ourselves for the time being to pairs (namely, x_1, x_2, x_3 from I), then the equations (1) show that the above question is equivalent to the question whether female pairs are observed with significantly greater frequency than male pairs [or whether the frequency $f(x_1)$ is significantly greater than the frequency $f(x_3)$]. Phrased in this way, an exact means for an answer is provided by the so-called (unilateral) binominal test (see, for example, [1]). This method is particularly applicable when individual cases (nonsymbionic) are investigated in respect to the frequency of the "feminine" and the "masculine." As to the results achieved by this method, only for the data on p. 336 can one say that "feminine" was observed with greater frequency than "masculine", and there it was highly significant for both the sibling pairs as well as for the parent-child pairs. The feminine pairs for the data on p. 338 (threshold value 5.9 percent) are almost significantly more frequent, at 5 percent. The critical level for the combined data on p. 340 amounts to 9.8 percent, but the thresholds for all other data pp. 340 and 341 are considerably higher than 10 percent. Unfortunately the data from p. 341, col. 1, cannot be analyzed any further, since they are not broken down by pairs.

The Half-Siblings

In theory, information on the half-siblings of schizophrenics would be important if schizophrenia were propagated by heredity according to a mendelian formula, that could be easily cross-checked by the frequency of schizophrenias among the half-siblings of schizophrenics. If the childhood environment alone played the decisive role, it should again be obvious in the findings of these half-siblings. For half-siblings of the schizophrenic probands who grow up under the same adversities as the probands themselves should frequently become schizophrenic, but half-siblings who grow up in a different, more favorable environment should seldom become schizophrenic.

Important as information about the half-siblings would be, they have been but little studied up to the present time. So far only three systematic investigations on the half-siblings of schizophrenics have been undertaken (Rüdin 1916, Kallmann 1938 and

1946). Of these, only the series done by Rüdin (1916) is large enough to have statistical value (the number for schizophrenias is 175.5), whereas the two series by Kallmann (1938 and 1946) are actually too small for statistics (the numbers are 78.5 and 57). Besides, the frequency of schizophrenia in Kallmann's (1938 and 1946) series is 10–12 times greater than that of Rüdin's (1916), which gives rise to doubt as to the validity of the results.

Everyone who does family studies knows why the half-siblings of schizophrenics have been so inadequately investigated up to now. Mainly it is because half-siblings occur much more rarely than siblings. The ratio of siblings to half-siblings among the 208 principal proband of this study, for instance, amounts to 818:112. If we have found about 800 siblings among some 200 probands, we would have to look at 1600 subject families to get as many half-siblings. But there are still more, even weightier obstacles in the way of successful research on half-siblings. Families with half-siblings are more often the separated and unsteady types of families. While most researchers consider it a matter of course to know all the siblings in a family and to be able to pursue their history, this does not hold true in studying families with half-siblings. Frequently family secrets and interfamily feuds keep people apart who have only one parent in common. Furthermore, unmarried parents or the untimely death of one parent is more often a bar to investigation of half-siblings than of siblings.

The investigations presented here provide a better opportunity for the reliable evaluation of the frequency of schizophrenic psychoses among the half-siblings of schizophrenics than has been possible heretofore. On the other hand, the number of half-siblings is too small to be further subdivided for statistical purposes (for instance, into half-siblings, with and without schizophrenias). Such a breakdown would be necessary, however, in order to deal with the many questions important to the study of schizophrenia.

Thirty-six of the 208 principal schizophrenic probands have half-siblings, and of these there are 112. In order to achieve any meaningful, significant results whatever, two additional groups of half-siblings were added, a total of 63 half-sibships with a total of 146 half-siblings. The following data, therefore, are based on a total of 258 half-siblings of schizophrenics.

Here is the makeup of the two additional groups of half-siblings.

1. In the family histories of the 100 Pfäfers probands whom I described in 1941 there were 14 half-sibships with a total of 46 half-siblings. They were not mentioned in the 1941 monograph, because the results from such small figures would have been meaningless.

2. The patient histories of all schizophrenic inpatients present at Burghölzli were checked twice, ten years apart, as to whether they had half-siblings (Vogt and Dinkelkamp), and 49 of them were found to have half-siblings. Where it was necessary, the data in the patient histories were supplemented with information from renewed inquiries about the half-siblings. By this process, 49 half-sibships with a total of 100 half-siblings were identified.

Table 5.14 shows the age distribution of these above-mentioned half-siblings and the incidence of mental disorders among them.

The schizophrenia onset probability, calculated in the usual way[23] (see Chapter 5), and compared with the studies previously published,[24] produces the data of Table 5.15.

Today we may assume, with a high degree of probability, that the schizophrenia-onset probability for half-siblings of schizophrenics ranges somewhere around 2 percent and 7 percent, and most probably around 5 percent. Thus, it lies somewhere between the figures of Rüdin (1916) and those of Kallmann (1938 and 1946), closer to Kallmann's (1938 and 1946). It is several times greater than the onset probability for the general population, although only about half as large as the onset probability for siblings.

Among the parents of my 258 half-siblings only 1 is schizophrenic. This schizophrenic mother, however, has only healthy children, and no schizophrenic ones. This alone would not change the percentages in my investigations as they appear in the above table; that is, if only the half-siblings with nonschizophrenic parents were counted.

Mental disorders other than schizophrenia occur only sporadically among the half-

23. In my study, the period of susceptibility for deriving the base figure is between 18–40, in Rüdin's (1916) between 20–40, and in Kallmann's (1938, 1946) between 15–45 years of age. The differences do not affect the calculations.

24. The comparison is a reconstruction of a table by E. Zerbin-Rüdin, in P. E. Becker, *Humangenetik*, vol. V/2. Stuttgart: Georg Thieme, 1967.

Table 5.14. Mental disorders among half-siblings of various proband groups (100 probands from the 1941 study, and 49 schizophrenics from the Psychiatric University Clinic at Burghölzli), listed according to whether they were alive or dead at the conclusion of the study, by sex, and by age at death or at the end of the study

Age group	Living or dead	Sex	No. of all half-siblings	Types of disorders among all half-siblings							
				Schizophrenia	Probable schizophrenia	Other psychoses	Feeblemindedness	Schizoid psychopathy	Alcoholism	Other disorders	Suicides
0–18	Liv.	m	7								
		f	6				1				
	Dead	m	12								
		f	12				1				
19–39	Liv.	m	26	1			2	1		1 [6]	
		f	23				1	1		1 [7]	
	Dead	m	9							1 [8]	
		f	7				1				
40–59	Liv.	m	53 [1]	2	1	1 [2]		1			
		f	52		1			2		3 [9]	
	Dead	m	8 [1]			1 [3]			1		3 [1]
		f	5	3							
60–79	Liv.	m	8						1 [4]		
		f	19	1						2 [10]	
	Dead	m	5						2 [5]		
		f	3								
80 +	Liv.	m	2								
	Dead	f	1		1						
Totals:			258	7	3	2	6	5	4	8	3

1. Age had to be estimated for 1 of these.
2. Very brief, undetermined psychosis.
3. Severe organic psychosis from CS_2-poisoning.
4. Also an unstable psychopath and swindler.
5. 1 of these also suffered from sclerosis of the brain vessels.
6. Deaf-mute; hyperexcitable.

7. Inclined to reactive depressions.
8. Somnolence and kleptomania.
9. 1 cretionid psychasthenic with stunted development; 2 inclined to reactive depressions.
10. 1 with hearing defect and distrustful; one hypersensitive and hyperexcitable.

siblings of schizophrenics. Their frequency can scarcely be distinguished from that of the general population.

After these summary findings we reach the point at which the actual study of half-siblings ought to begin. For all the questions to be discussed, the general data on half-siblings ought to be further subdivided. But as soon as I begin to break down these 212 half-siblings, the individual groups become too small for statistical studies. If, below, I attempt to make such a breakdown despite that, it is for two good reasons: Should an investigator in the future again undertake to

study series of half-siblings, then the data presented here can be combined with his own, so as to reduce the amount of error due to small numbers. Also, even the small numbers will yield some indications as to significance of certain familial causations.

For the following types of information, only the data on the half-siblings of the principal probands and the supplemental probands from Burghölzli are of any use. The origins of the half-siblings of the Pfäfers probands are too inaccurately documented for these purposes. They involved 46 half-siblings from 14 Pfäfers probands, of whom 3 were schizo-

Table 5.15. Probability of schizophrenic onset among half-siblings of schizophrenics. Author's own findings compared with those of others[1]

| | | Number of schizophrenics and schizophrenia-onset probability | |
Probands	Base figure[2]	Certain cases only	Certain and probable cases combined
1. Principal probands of this project	82	2 = 2.4% ± 1.7	3 = 3.7% ± 2.1
2. Supplemental probands from this project	106.5	5 = 4.7% ± 2.1	7 = 6.6% ± 2.4
3. 1 and 2 Combined	188.5	7 = 3.7% ± 1.4	10 = 5.3% ± 1.6
4. By Rüdin (1916), Bavaria	175.5	1 = 0.6% ± 0.6	1 = 0.6% ± 0.6
5. By Kallmann (1938), Berlin	78.5	5 = 6.4% ± 2.8	6 = 7.6% ± 3.0
6. By Kallmann (1946)	57	4 = 7.0% ± 3.4	4 = 7.0% ± 3.4
7. 4 and 6 Combined	311	10 = 3.2% ± 1	11 = 3.5% ± 1.0

1. The comparison is a reconstruction of a table by Zerbin-Rüdin, E. that appeared in P. E. Becker, *Humangenetik*, vol. V/2, Stuttgart: Georg Thieme, 1967.

2. In my study the period of susceptibility for deriving the base figure is between 18–40, in Rüdin's (1916) between 20–40, and in Kallmann's (1938, 1946) between 15–45 years of age. The differences do not affect the calculations.

phrenic.

If a search is made for a "hereditary cause" of schizophrenias, some of the following questions will arise:

Is the common parent[25] of 1 schizophrenic proband and 1 half-sibling frequently schizophrenic? In all 7 cases of diagnostically certain or probable schizophrenia in one of the half-siblings, the common parent is not schizophrenic. In 2 of the 7 cases, however, that parent reveals neurotic or psychopathic personality traits or addictions. The ratio of 2:7, however, does not differ markedly from that expected in the general population.

Is the common parent of a schizophrenic proband and a healthy half-sibship healthier, on the average, than the sole parent (see n. 25) of the schizophrenic proband? Among 88 common parents of healthy half-siblings and schizophrenic probands, 4 are schizophrenic[26], but among 89 known parents of schizophrenic probands who are not parents of the healthy half-siblings, there are 6. There is no real difference recognizable in the frequency with numbers as small as this.

The same question can be varied by asking not only for schizophrenias, but also for any other types of pathological personality developments such as neuroses, psychopathies, or developments of addictions. No clear differences result from such a line of questioning, either. Among the common parents of the healthy half-siblings and the schizophrenic probands, the ratio of mentally ill (in the broad sense outlined above) to healthy is 20:68, but among those parents of schizophrenic probands who are not also parents of the half-siblings, it is 18:71.

25. Illustration of the expressions "common parent" and "sole parent"

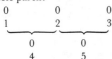

4 = Schizophrenic proband

5 = Half-sibling of the schizophrenic proband

1 = Parent of only the schizophrenic proband, but not of his half-sibling = sole parent of the schizophrenic proband

2 = Parent of the schizophrenic proband as well as of his half-sibling = common parent of schizophrenic proband and his half-sibling

3 = Parent of only the half-sibling, but not of the schizophrenic proband = sole parent of half-sibling

26. According to earlier data, the probands used for the investigation, without considering the Pfäfers probands, consist of 85 half-sibships. In the above text, 88 common parents of mentally healthy half-siblings are referred to. This difference occurs because, on the one hand, the common parent of the half-sibship consisting only of the proband and 1 schizophrenic half-brother is subtracted from 85, and on the other, 4 probands' parents with 2 different spouses have produced half-sibships.

If a check were to be made on the influence of childhood conditions on the genesis of schizophrenias, the following additional questions would emerge:

Do the half-siblings of schizophrenics also become schizophrenic if they grow up under worse conditions than the schizophrenic probands? Only 2 of the half-siblings grew up under worse conditions than the schizophrenic probands. One of these also became schizophrenic, and the other remained healthy.

How often do half-siblings become schizophrenic, who grew up under the same or similar conditions as the schizophrenic probands? Fifty-six half-siblings grew up under the same or similar conditions as the schizophrenic probands, and of them 4 became schizophrenic.

Summarizing the last three findings, the relationship of schizophrenics to nonschizophrenics among the half-siblings, under the given conditions, is as follows.

If the half-siblings were raised under worse conditions than the schizophrenic probands, it is $1:1$; if the half-siblings were raised under similar conditions, it is $4:52$; and if the half-siblings were raised under better conditions, it is $0:19$.

If the raw figures were several times greater than they are, and if the cited proportions were the same, one would be tempted, out of hand, to consider the causal significance of the childhood conditions. But the above-mentioned figures are naturally small and not significant. If they were significant, the question would arise: Why are the environmental conditions different for the half-siblings than for the principal probands? The answer might well come from considering the differences in personality between the sole parent of the half-sibling and the sole parent of the schizophrenic proband. If the former is healthy and the latter pathological, the childhood conditions of the half-siblings were more favorable than those of the schizophrenic proband—although at the same time, the half-siblings had a much better hereditary prognosis from the outset. For this reason, the question as to whether inherited traits or childhood environment played the greater role in the difference of mental well-being between the half-siblings and the full sibship of the proband remains open.

A valid reply to the questions for every individual case was impossible just because of the small figures. In looking over the entire scope of the specific questions, along with a few other similar ones that occur in the same context, and considering all the insignificant, individual results combined, there is, after all, something to be learned: Certain of the chance-findings can be related to one, and certain others to another of a hypothetical mendelian hereditary process of schizophrenia "as such"; although most of them really cannot, without tampering with the facts. One set of findings points to the importance of heredity; others, to the importance of childhood experiences. A survey of the entire set of data suggests that life experiences and heredity work together in an irregular, individually different way, and that any great importance of a mendelian law is simply out of the question.

The same conclusion emerges even more impressively from the careful study of individual family histories than from the above-mentioned scanty statistical indications. Examples below should demonstrate how the study of one family history might suggest the power of heredity, and another, the impact of life experiences in childhood:

Joseph S., born in 1925 (one of the supplemental probands with half-siblings), was the son of an impoverished woodchopper from a nearby mountain valley. This father was an unstable, unloving, unfeeling man, who could be called a schizoid psychopath. He died while chopping wood, when Joseph was 11 years old. Joseph's mother was a hard-working, affable woman, idealized by her children. She gave birth to 14 children, of whom 7 died early. She did her best to keep the family together, and to make her living by sewing; despite this, after his father died, she could not avoid placing Joseph in foster homes, each one of which was worse than the other. After his schooling, Joseph often did no work at all, becoming a burden on his mother, or else he sometimes earned pittances as an errand boy, farmhand, or kitchen helper. He became an unsteady, secretive eccentric as his father had been, and soon succumbed to alcoholism.

At age 42 he became a subacute paranoid schizophrenic, and has never fully recovered. He came to the clinic in a totally confused state, in which he performed peculiar dances and made stereotyped defensive gestures. He hallucinated continually and developed delusions of persecution. He indicated that spirits wanted to do him harm and complained about a double who used his name and who needed psychiatric care. During the $1\frac{1}{2}$ years since his admission, he calmed down and showed some improvement. Regarded externally, he is no longer aberrant, but has become indifferent and apathetic. He works slowly and superficially, and stops intermittently in amazement to admire his work. He continues to hallucinate voices, but these no longer impress him very much.

His three brothers did not become schizophrenic, although they are similarly unstable, indifferent, and secretive eccentrics just as their father and as Joseph had been before his schizophrenic onset. One of them was for many years in charity institutions.

Joseph also has a half-brother, Max, a child of his mother's first marriage. Max's father was an industrious, competent, even-tempered man, an electrician by trade. This father was killed in an accident shortly before Max was born. Soon after that, his mother married Joseph's father "in order to provide a father for her orphaned son." Thus Max grew up as the older half-brother of his 14 half-siblings, with his mother and his stepfather, under truly horrible circumstances. Often the family went hungry, and the mother simply could not cope in any way with the difficulties of raising the unruly sons from her second marriage. When Max was only 14, he had to take a job in a factory to earn his own living.

In spite of this adverse childhood, Max developed remarkably well. He insists—and justifiably so—that he turned out like his father, and not like his stepfather. Still, he had never seen his father, and all through his childhood was exposed to his stepfather, who was incapable of raising him. Today Max is a much sought-after and highly specialized technician. He leads a normal family life with his wife and 3 children. It is easy to assume in this case that Joseph and his brothers inherited their schizoid nature and with it, their disposition for schizophrenia, from their father, while Max inherited the disposition for a favorable development from his natural father, and that the same miserable childhood conditions that shaped Joseph's illness and his brothers' schizoid, difficult personalities had no effect on Max.

Again, from a different aspect, the family history of Joseph could be interpreted as an indication of the importance of childhood experience on the development of the personality. Joseph and his 3 brothers all turned out more or less bad, following the example set by their psychopathic father, while their 3 sisters, following the example of their courageous and affable mother, all made something of themselves.

The following case might be applied to illustrate the impact of a childhood experience, and in particular, of a tragic mother-daughter relationship:

Anneliese K. (Proband 64), who was 47 at the conclusion of the observation period, has 3 half-sisters. All 4 of the half-sisters share the same mother, but each has a different father. The mother bore 1 child from her first marriage, and 2 illegitimate children from different fathers while she was married to her first husband. The marriage ended in divorce after the second adulterous pregnancy. She bore the 4th and last daughter during her second marriage. Her first husband, (father of half-sister Hedwig) was a successful businessman, active and full of life, although at times given to alcoholic abuse. Her second husband was also a healthy, competent person. The two illegitimate fathers could not be located. The mother herself was pretty as a young woman and highly spirited, although she later developed as a serious psychopath. She became increasingly stingy, petty, and argumentive. She put on pious airs, although her family thought of her as a hypocrite because in general she lied glibly and was overly egotistical. She enjoyed evoking pity and help, complained a great deal, but never concerned herself about the welfare of others. In money matters she was signally careless. In her old age (she was 72 at the end of the observation period), she experienced a mild psychoorganic change following an attack of apoplexy. Among her 18 siblings there were no psychoses nor any personality developments quite as unfortunate as the ones she herself experienced.

Of the 4 half-sisters, Anneliese is the only one who developed pathologically, but she is also the one who suffered most severely by far from the unfortunate personality of her mother, and the one whose whole childhood was the most depressing because of it.

Anneliese was born during the divorce proceedings that had been initiated because her mother was pregnant with her by a man other than her husband. She spent the first seven years of her life in foster care under normal conditions. Meanwhile, her mother remarried, at which time Anneliese, unwanted and unloved, was returned to the home of her mother and stepfather. During this period there began that lifelong, terrible dissension with her mother that led, in turn, to a lifelong hatred of monumental proportions against her mother. The child became hyperexcitable and moody, gave vent to exaggerated spite-reactions, and lied and stole to excess. Even during her early school days Anneliese became sexually aware and, for example, falsely accused men in dangerous fashion of having molested her. Efforts to raise her at home soon became impossible, and Anneliese had to be committed to institutional residential homes on repeated occasions. Beginning at age 21, a phasic schizophrenic psychosis began to emerge that gradually increased in severity. Anneliese developed periodic states of delusional confusion with terrifying outbursts of rage. Her delusions centered principally around her mother. Even after she was hospitalized, she believed that she was being severely tormented by her mother, and continued intermittently to hear her mother's threatening voice. Often she threatened her mother with death, that shocked anyone who heard her because of the violent hate-laden attitude she displayed. But reactive experiences of a different nature, such as thought transmissions and the sense of being hypnotized, also occurred. In the more benign phases she remained suspicious and distrustful, and gave vent to violent fits of anger when she was contradicted. She was evaluated as suffering from "early schizophrenic dementia." Contrary to all expectations, however, an increasing improvement set in after many years of hospitalization. During the last seven years the proband revealed no more psychotic symptoms and has been able to earn her own living.

Her half-sister Hedwig, 4 years older, born in wedlock during her mother's first marriage, lived the first 11 years of her life with her paternal grandmother. Then she lived intermittently with her father and his second wife, her stepmother. Her stepmother treated her badly, and for this reason she was soon placed in a foster home, where she received proper treatment. She remained healthy, and presently, at age 51, earns her living by ironing.

Her half-sister Frieda, two years older and begotten illegitimately during her mother's first marriage, was adopted by her mother's husband and accepted with warmth and inner feeling. She was a beautiful, intelligent, and accommodating child. While her mother rejected Anneliese, she favored Frieda. Anne-

liese had every reason to be jealous. Her mother took Frieda along into the home with her second husband, who turned out to be a good stepfather to her. Frieda remained healthy, and today manages her home as a good wife and mother.

Anneliese's half-sister Anna, 9 years younger than she, was the legitimate child of her mother's second marriage. She grew up with both her parents. She got along well with her father, and her relationship to her mother was at least not especially bad. She developed favorably, became a teacher of needlework, and married and academician.

In many other examples, one might just as readily assume the major influence as being hereditary as well as childhood-environmental:

Marie K. (Proband 74) was the daughter of a healthy, active, and successful father and a pathological, continually depressive mother. Her mother was in a constant state of unhealthy tensions with her sisters-in-law, who shared the home with her. When in 1914 the father had to enter active military service, she hanged herself for fear of having to live by herself with her sisters-in-law. Marie, 10 years old at the time, was the first to discover her mother's body. Soon after that, Marie assumed the position of housekeeper, from which she was displaced at age 16, because her father remarried. She soon became alienated from both her stepmother and her father, and married a psychopathic eccentric, who treated her more like an immature child than a grown-up woman. After the birth of her only child, at age 30, she first suffered a schizophrenic episode, from which she never recovered. She remained severely ill, suffering additional acute episodes later. Her half-brother, 17 years younger than she, grew up with both parents under favorable conditions and developed splendidly. He is a skilled mechanic, is active in politics where he represents social and humanitarian ideals, and holds a seat in the legislature of his home district.

In view of this family history, one might equally assume either of two processes. The pathological (although not schizophrenic) mother might have transmitted a personal disposition toward schizophrenia to her daughter, a trait that was lacking in her half-brother, or else Marie grew up under dissimilar circumstances from her half-brother, "for this reason" she became schizophrenic while her half-brother did not.

There are also examples that do not give rise to any theories about the geneses of illnesses, for instance, those in which family members are not pathological and in which conditions in the home were healthy.

The Offspring of Siblings

The onset probabilities of siblings' children (that is, of nephews and nieces) of schizophrenics have been determined by Schulz (1926), Luxenburger (1939), Kallmann (1946), and Sjögren (1957), and compared with the findings of other investigators in summary form. The findings of these authors vary between 1.4 percent and 3.9 percent; on the average they amount to 2.6 percent ± 0.3, as calculated by Zerbin-Rüdin, 1967.

Rather frequently the siblings of schizophrenics ask us whether their children are vulnerable to schizophrenia, and for this reason the knowledge of the onset probability for schizophrenia of the siblings' children is of practical importance. It is desirable to supplement the previous findings on this subject with new data. The determination of onset probability from as many different selections as possible, at different times and in different locales, is furthermore meaningful because significant differences in all types of different cases are important to the formulation of theories on the nature of schizophrenia in general.

In 202 of the 208 principal schizophrenic probands of this project either all children of siblings are known (for 153 probands), or we know that they have no siblings (49 probands). Six probands remain whose siblings' children are not all known. To avoid selection errors, these have been omitted from the following sets of data.

The 153 principal schizophrenic probands whose siblings' children are fully known have a total of 937 sibling children. Among these, 6 are diagnostically certain schizophrenics, and 1 is a probable schizophrenic. The base figure for schizophrenia, calculated in the usual way, amounts to 469. Thus we obtain a schizophrenia-onset probability of 1.3 percent ± 0.5, including only the diagnostically certain cases, and of 1.5 percent ± 0.6, including also the probable case. These percentages are close to the lower limits of previous findings.

The 464 siblings' children of the Pfäfers probands are, in the majority, still quite young. The base figure for schizophrenia is only 86.5. In the 1941 paper I omitted a description of the siblings' children because their number was so small. Today I can make the attempt of considering them in conjunction with the siblings' children of the principal probands of this work. Seven of the Pfäfers siblings' children are schizophrenic. There is an amazingly high onset probability at 8.1 percent ± 2.8. In view of the great difference in the onset probability between the Pfäfers probands and the principal probands of this project, we are constrained to ask whether this is a true difference, or whether one of the two studies is inaccurate. However, if one considers the error due to the small number, the misgivings vanish. The difference between the two percentages (that is, between 1.3 percent and 8.1 percent) amounts to 6.8 ± 3. Thus, it is only twice the size of its median error, and a happenstance figure is certainly possible. In keeping with that, the confidence intervals of the two percentages at 95 percent are very close, and those at 99 percent overlap. Furthermore, the high percentage of 8.1 was a chance figure for yet another reason. 99 of the Pfäfers probands do not have any siblings' children whatever; all 7 siblings' children of that group come from just the one proband, and this was a family with an exceptional frequency of schizophrenia.

Combining the Pfäfers and the present probands (Table 5.16), the figure for schizophrenia-onset probability among the siblings' children of schizophrenics amounts to 2.3 percent ± 0.6, counting only the diagnostically certain cases, and to 2.5 percent ± 0.7, including the 1 probable case.

These figures agree remarkably well with those of Zerbin-Rüdin (1967), at which she arrived by compiling the data of former authors. They confirm again that the onset probabilities, as the Munich school calculated them after publication of Rüdin's great monograph in 1916, were correct, even decades later and rechecked with probands from different countries. The minor fluctuations of figures among the investigations remain within the range of error due to small numbers, or they can be rationalized with ease by the differences in the selection of the probands.

The data on psychic disorders other than schizophrenia among the siblings' children of the schizophrenic probands reveals nothing that could be regarded as characteristic. Their number is extremely small, and does not differ markedly from that of the general population. We can safely exclude the possibility that mental disorders other than schizophrenias occur in great numbers among the siblings' children of schizophrenics.

Table 5.16. Mental disorders among siblings' offspring of two proband groups (this project and the 100 probands from 1941)[1], arranged according to whether they were dead or alive at the end of the investigation, according to sex, and according to age at time of death or at end of the investigation

				No. of cases among all siblings' children								
Age group	Living or dead	Sex	All siblings' children	Schizophrenia	Probable Schizophrenia	Epilepsy	Feeblemindedness	Schizoid psychopathy	Alcoholism	Other disorders	Suicides
0–18	Living	m	249			2	4[2]			8[5]	
		f	239			1	1			4[6]	
		?	4								
	Dead	m	30								
		f	34								
		?	17								
19–39	Living	m	272	1			5[3]	1	4[4]	9[7]	
		f	270	3			4		1	12[8]	
		?	6								
	Dead	m	14		1						
		f	10	2			1				
40–59	Living	m	107	4			2		2	3[9]	
		f	115	2		1	1	1		7[10]	
	Dead	m	3								
		f	3								1
60 and over	Living	m	9	1						1[11]	
		f	7								
	?	m	2								
?		f	8								
		?	2								
Totals			1401	13	1	4	18	3	6	44	1

1. Siblings' children of 6 principal probands on whom insufficient data was collected were omitted.

2. 1 of these, semi-annual meningitis.

3. 1 of these, a deaf-mute.

4. 1 of these, criminal.

5. 2 problem children; 1 stutterer (possible epileptic); 1 stutterer, not troublesome; 1 personality neurotic; 1 enuretic; 2 "nervous."

6. 1 deaf-mute; 1 with psychosomatic complaints; 1 sexual neurotic; 1 schizoid neurasthenic.

7. 1 eccentric; 1 psychopath, peculiarly lazy and personally unclean; 1 unstable psychopath; 1 habitual criminal (theft); 2 deaf-mutes; 1 embittered; 1 inventor; 1 with encephalitis lethargica.

8. 1 mild hypothyreosis, psychically unchanged; 2 with Werdnig-Hoffmann's type of muscular atrophy; 2 unstable; 1 female psychopath, transvestite; 1 irritable, impulsive; 1 hyperexcitable; 1 moody psychopath of low intellect; 1 prostitute; 1 with difficult personality; 1 deaf-mute.

9. 1 committed by court, afraid of work; 1 unstable; 1 asocial psychopath.

10. 1 depressive; 1 psychasthenic 1 addict, hysterical psychopath; 3 psychopaths; 1 argumentive.

11. Involutional depression.

6 The Offspring of Schizophrenics

Number of Children

All children born from the marriages of the 208 probands and all children born to the female probands out of wedlock, were studied. Of course, there is no certainty that all the children born out of wedlock to the male probands were identified. At least we know from studies of the life histories of the male probands, that they certainly cannot have had a large number of illegitimate children. The number of those that do exist is small enough not to influence significantly the statistics that follow. This certainly small—although unknown—figure of illegitimate offspring of male probands had to be disregarded in the data that follow. Of all the children studied, it was possible to gain a good insight into their personality and development up to the time of their deaths or to the end of this project. An overview of the number, sex, and age of the offspring is provided in Table 6.1.

Our 208 probands had 184 children, an average of 0.9 children for each proband. Exactly half the probands remained unmarried. From the marriages of these 104 probands, 169 children were born; accordingly, an average of 1.6 children was born to each married proband.

Fifteen children were born out of wedlock; that is, 8.2 percent of all children. Each proband, therefore, had an average of 0.07 illegitimate children. The confidence interval at 95 percent for the 8.2 percent illegitimate children amounts to 4.7–13.4 percent. In the probands' fertile years during their observation period (1891–1963), the percentage of children born out of wedlock among all children born in the Canton of Zürich fluctuated between 4.7 percent and 7.9 percent. So the proportion of illegitimate children of all the children born to our probands is not significantly different from that of a corresponding portion of the entire Canton of Zürich.

Table 6.1 shows the differences in fertility between male and female probands. The proportion between married and widowed probands is about the same for the males as for the females (34 percent and 32.4 percent). The number of divorces is greater among the females than among the males (19.4 percent and 14 percent), although the difference is not statistically significant (confidence intervals at 95 percent for the 19.4 percent lie between 13 percent and 29 percent, and for the 14 percent, between 8 percent and 22 percent). The female probands have more children than the males. (108 women have 118 children. To compare this with the 100 men, we must calculate how many children would be born to 100 women, and that would be 110. These 110 children from 100 women compare with 66 children from 100 men. The average number of children from female married probands is proportionately greater than that of male married probands. The female pro-

Table 6.1. Sex, marital status, and number of children of principal probands

	Married or widowed			Divorced			Unmarried		No. of legitimate children	Average no. of children per marriage (including divorced)	Average no. of children per proband	No. of illegitimate children	Average no. of illegitimate children per proband
	Probands		No. of children	Probands		No. of children							
	Number	Percent		Number	Percent		Number	Percent					
Men	31	31	46	17	17	15	52	52	61	1.3	0.6	5	0.05
Women	35	32.4	66	21	19.4	42	52	48.2	108	1.9	1.0	10	0.1
All probands	66	31.7	112	38	18.3	57	104	50	169	1.6	0.9	15	0.07

Three children of male probands died before they were 4; ten children of female probands died before they were 4.

bands also have more illegitimate children than the males—insofar as the illegitimate children of males can be accounted for).

The most important reasons for the greater fertility of schizophrenic women compared to schizophrenic men are obvious. On the average, the women marry earlier than the men, and on the average, the women develop mental illness later than the men. The fertile years of a marriage before onset of the psychosis are, therefore, more numerous for women than for men.

The later onset of mental illness in female probands was shown in Table 4.1, and their earlier age of marriage in the following listing:

	Probands	
Age when first married	*Male*	*Female*
19–20 years old	31	40
30–39	14	12
40–49	3	3
50–53	0	1

It may be assumed that, in addition, fertility is influenced by psychological differences between men and women. Schizophrenic autism frequently inhibits or prevents men from seizing the initiative in choosing a sexual partner. The same autism in schizophrenic women might be a lesser barrier to propagation, if they allow themselves to become the sexual partners of normal, active men, without a great deal of effort on their part. Besides, sexuality is considerably stronger in hospitalized schizophrenic women than in such men.

The finding, according to which schizophrenic women have more children than schizophrenic men corresponds to the previous finding that shows schizophrenics more often have schizophrenic mothers than schizophrenic fathers.

Determining the number of children of the probands would be of little significance, if their fertility period had not been completed at the conclusion of the investigation. Actually, however, the fertility period of probands may, for practical purposes, be considered as finished at the conclusion of the investigation. If any more births can be expected after that time, they will be very few.

This finding is based on the fact that at the conclusion of the investigation, only 2 of the married female probands were still under 50 years old and not chronically hospitalized (all other female probands who were married and under 50, either had died or were long-term

hospital patients, probably for the rest of their lives). Considering their ages (42 and 45), it is unlikely that these only remaining married women probands, still capable of reproduction, would have children. Among the unmarried female probands, at the end of the investigation, 3 are still living, are under 50, and are not chronically hospitalized. Considering their ages (38, 45, and 47), and considering especially their previous life styles, it is again most improbable that they will still conceive. It is more likely that some few of the male probands might still produce a few children. There are 10 among them who are married, under 60 years old, and, after conclusion of the investigation, not chronically hospitalized. However, at the same time, their wives are already 39, 40, 40, 44, 44, 44, 45, 52, and 54 years old at the end of the study, and 1, whose age cannot be definitely determined, is certainly over 40. In addition, there are 12 single, divorced, or widowed men under 60, who are not chronically hospitalized. In view of their ages and their former life styles, however, it is most improbable that they would produce offspring hereafter, and if they did, certainly not in any large number.

We know, therefore, that our 208 principal schizophrenic probands have produced at least 184 children during their lifetimes, that they will only produce very few more, if any, and that the average number of children per proband amounts finally to 0.9 (or very few more).

Strange to say, in the literature, figures suitable for comparison are almost entirely lacking. The best possible thing to do was to use the conclusions by Kallmann (1938) from Berlin. His 1087 schizophrenic probands were selected, as ours were, without regard to whether they had children or not. At the end of his study, they had reached ages at which no—or very few—more children could be expected. They had a total of 2,120 children. At the end of their fertility periods, an average of twice the number of children was assigned to each schizophrenic proband (that is, 1.9) that was found in my own research (0.9). On the other hand, the death rate for the children of Kallmann's probands is much higher than for mine (more than half the children of Kallmann's probands died before age 20, while less than one-tenth that number of my probands' children died that early. These vast differences obviously are tied to the different period of time in which Kallmann's probands and mine were fertile. Kallmann's probands were born between 1820 and 1887, while mine were born between 1874 and 1929. In the meantime, in Europe the average number of children and the child mortality rate have declined significantly. Furthermore, the difference in locale between the two studies (Berlin and Zürich) may have influenced this difference.

Furthermore, despite diligent searching, I did not find any study that would have contained any figures suitable for comparison. Most papers on the children of schizophrenics are not suitable for determining the fertility of schizophrenics, since the probands were specifically selected because they had children that could be studied, or because their period of fertility had not terminated by the end of the observation period (Hoffmann 1921, Schulz 1926, Juda 1928, Oppler 1932, Luxenburger 1939, 1940, and Garrone 1962).

Fertility of Schizophrenics Compared to Fertility of Population

The fertility of our schizophrenic probands compared to the fertility of their nonschizophrenic relatives and of the population of Zürich.

A comparison between the fertility of our schizophrenic probands and that of the general public would be of great importance. Figures that would produce accurate and meaningful comparisons, however, are hard to come by. Statistical offices are not able to supply average figures on how many children are produced by an inhabitant whose period of fertility has ended. Furthermore, such figures would still have to be precisely defined, if they were to be of value in providing exact comparisons. For instance, the times in which the person lived, the age at which he died, whether he lived in the city or in the country, are among a few of the considerations that would have to be taken into account. Although no accurate comparisons are feasible, here are some summary ones.

The 208 probands and their spouses would have to produce 416 children for the generation of children to remain the same in number as their own—however, they produced only 184. The period during which they were born falls into a time of sharp increases in births in our Canton (in 1891 the population of the Canton of Zürich was 347,000; in 1963 it was 1,023,000). This increase in population is based mainly on an increase in births, and not exclusively on immigration and longevity. The assumption can be made that, during the decades between 1891 and 1963, the

schizophrenics in the Canton of Zürich were at least half as fertile as the general population.

Furthermore, the fertility of the siblings of probands can be used for a comparison, with the following data pertaining to that study.

The 818 siblings of probands had 937 children, but the children of 6 of their siblings were excluded from the count, because their legitimacy could not be accurately established. For our calculations, the following should be subtracted from the 818 probands' siblings:

Schizophrenic siblings of probands	63
Probands' siblings who were eliminated from the project before reaching fertility age (assumed to be age 18)	144
Siblings of probands without fully established offspring	6
Total:	213

Of the 937 children of siblings, those with 1 schizophrenic parent should be subtracted, that is, 33.

Accordingly, six hundred and five nonschizophrenic siblings of probands over 18 years old had 904 children. They should have had 1,210 children, if the children's generation had been the same proportionate size as their parents' generation. The difference between the actual number of children and the number that would be needed to keep up the size of the generation, according to these figures, is much smaller among the nonschizophrenic siblings than among the schizophrenic probands. But the fact that for many siblings of probands the end of their fertility period is still a long way off, and that almost all probands themselves have, indeed, reached it, must be taken into account. In summary it may be stated that in men of ages from 19 to 60, and in women of ages ranging from 19 to 40, approximately half the children born during their entire lifetime had already been born at the conclusion of this study. Two hundred and twenty-two of the siblings of probands are in this age group. For purposes of comparison, then, half of them (111) must still be subtracted from the 605 siblings of probands considered above. For the comparison, we may assume that 494 siblings of probands produced 904 children. The offspring of nonschizophrenic siblings of probands are almost as numerous as the siblings of the probands themselves and their spouses, combined. This is not true of the schizophrenic probands. The number of their offspring is not even half that of their number and that of their spouses combined. In other words, the nonschizo-phrenic siblings of probands produce so many children that their second generation almost matches the number of the first. This is not true of the schizophrenic probands. The num-ber of the probands' children is so low that their second generation is barely half the size of the first. Their low fertility is in sharp contrast to the population increase of the average citizenry. Finally, the fact that even the siblings of schizophrenics produce fewer children than the general population must be taken into consideration.

The markedly reduced fertility rate among the siblings of schizophrenic probands is also in evidence. Sixty-three of them have only 33 children, that is, about a quarter the number that would be necessary to produce a genera-tion of children as numerous as that of their parents.

Based on the comparison between the ferti-lity of schizophrenic probands and that of their nonschizophrenic siblings and of the popula-tion, one reaches the same conclusion as the one already drawn; namely, that the fertility of schizophrenics is not more than half as great as that of the general population. To be sure, we are once again relying on just a summary comparison based on rough estimates.

The question arises, whether a reduced fertility rate among schizophrenics can be proved, not only in the generation of the principal probands, but also in that of their parents. In such a comparison, many effects based on selection bias must be considered. They become manifest as a reduction of an overall difference in the fertility of normal people and of schizophrenics. But this com-parison, too, supports the finding that the fertility among schizophrenics is considerably less than among normal subjects.

Six of the 1,026 children of probands' parents were born out of wedlock and are not taken into consideration in the following figures. Of 25 marriages with 1 schizophrenic partner and 1 marriage with both partners schizophrenic, an average of 3.9 children were produced, while from marriages of 176 coup-les, of whom neither partner was schizo-phrenic, 5.2 children resulted (absolute figures: 102 and 918).

These parents were included as parents of schizophrenic probands. For this reason, only fertile marriages are considered among the marriages of parents. Already for this reason, the average number of children from these marriages must be greater than from non-selected marriages—as indeed they are. The fact that the probability is greater of finding a schizophrenic (that is, a proband) among a large group of siblings rather than a small one, is another manifestation of this same thing. More cases of schizophrenia occur among the offspring from marriages with 1 schizophrenic partner than among the offspring from marri-ages of two non-schizophrenics. If the parents are considered because of having a schizo-phrenic child, (as is the case here), the effect of selection bias in favor of prolific marriages, for that reason, is bound to be greater in marriages with 1 schizophrenic partner than in marriages with 2 nonschizophrenics.

Still other circumstances indicate that in this study on the fertility of parents of pro-bands, the difference between the fertility of schizophrenics and of nonschizophrenics is bound to appear much smaller than it actually is. As we shall show below, the lower fertility among schizophrenics is, above all, the result of fewer marriages and the small number of children by schizophrenic men. In the above comparison the unmarried are simply not counted. Since, among the probands' parents, there are more schizophrenic mothers than schizophrenic fathers, the presented compari-son between the fertility of male and female schizophrenics combined and the fertility of married nonschizophrenics reveals a much smaller difference.

It would be a bit too much to attempt to express these generalized findings in figures. Even from the general data and the studies presented here, certain facts are clear; namely, that the difference of 3.9:5.2 children from marriages with 1 schizophrenic partner and from marriages with 2 nonschizophrenics has to be much smaller than the overall difference in fertility between schizophrenics and non-schizophrenics, because the probands were selected. Tests of the offspring of probands' parents agree with the previous findings, according to which the fertility of schizo-phrenics is low.

Further possibilities for comparisons in fertilities of our schizophrenic probands em-erge from the results of the censuses of the Canton of Zürich in 1941, 1950, and 1960. These figures primarily enable us to gain reference data for understanding how the low fertility of probands comes about. Is it low because of a lower fertility in marriage, is it lower in marriages of long or of short duration, in marriages of the male or the female pro-bands, because of the lower rate of illegitimate offspring, or because of the higher rate of celibacy among the schizophrenics?

Good possibilities for comparisons arise in respect to the fertility of completed marriages. In conformity to statistics of census figures, "completed" marriages refer in what follows to marriages that have lasted at least 25 years, and from which, because of the wife's menopause, no more—or, if any, very few more —children are expected, after conclusion of the investigation. The result of this comparison is that from "completed" marriages of the female schizophrenic probands, an average of about the same number of children is produced as from completed marriages among the total population of Zürich. From the completed marriages of male schizophrenic probands, however, considerably fewer children are produced than from the same category of the general population. The postulates and deliberations that led to these conclusions are explained below.

The census figures encompass the entire Canton of Zürich, that is, exactly the same area from which our probands were selected. The figures were gathered during the same years in which our probands were alive.

In these censuses it was established how many married women had children, and the figures were differentiated according to the duration of the marriage. After 25 years of a marriage it is very rare that more offspring can be expected; so rare, in fact, that this possibility may be omitted from the accounts that follow.

Official statistics list only the number of children of those women who were married in the period when the census was taken. The children of unmarried women, widows, divorcees, and of women who had died during the time of the investigation were not included. Furthermore, only the children from marriages existing during the time the census was taken are considered. The children of former marriages of married couples or their illegitimate children are not counted. On the other hand, all children that had been born alive to existing marriages are counted, including those who had died by the time the census was taken.

The three censuses yielded the following figures for women married 25 years or more and their children.
—In 1941, 36,188 women bore 105,511 children; that is, each woman averaged 2.9 children
—In 1950, 47,256 women bore 112,638 children; that is, each woman averaged 2.4 children
—In 1960, 61,792 women bore 129,802 children; that is, each woman averaged 2.1 children
—Combined, 145,236 women bore 347,951 children; that is, each woman averaged 2.4 children.

In contrast to this, the following figures apply to the schizophrenic probands over the same period of time, coming from the same general population, and considering "completed" marriages in exactly the same sense:

	No. of probands	No. of children	No. of children per marriage
Male probands	16	20	1.25
Female probands	20	56	2.8
Total probands	36	76	2.1

Accordingly, the fertility of male schizophrenic probands in completed marriages is reduced by about half, and that of female schizophrenics is not reduced at all. This finding is valid for the principal probands of this study. It would be unwise to transfer these figures to schizophrenics in general, because of the small sampling. These figures will be adequately taken into consideration in the more carefully formulated data to be presented later. Nevertheless, this latter finding agrees with previous conclusions. The low figure for offspring of schizophrenics is easily explained without its being necessary to take into account the reduced fertility of schizophrenic women in completed marriages. It is important, however, that these findings correspond to those in the existing literature, or at least that they do not contradict them. This point will be discussed later.

The comparison between fertility of schizophrenics in "uncompleted" marriages and fertility in such marriages of the normal population is not as simple as the comparison for completed marriages. The disturbing factor is the dissimilarity in duration of uncompleted marriages of the schizophrenic probands and the population. On the average, the uncompleted marriages of schizophrenics last longer than those of the population, in which marriages of just one or very few years are included. In such a comparison, no reduction in fertility has been determined among the uncompleted marriages of schizophrenics. Roughly estimated, the fertility in uncompleted marriages of schizophrenic probands is approximately equal to that of uncompleted marriages in the normal population. Here are the figures and deliberations to support this fact.

At the conclusion of the observation period of this study, 43 probands were spouses in a marriage that had lasted less than 25 years, or else they were widowed or divorced before 25 years of their marriage had elapsed, and before the study was completed. From these 44 "uncompleted marriages,"[1] 93 children were born; that is, an average of 2.1 children resulted from each marriage. In contrast, according to the three censuses, 402,734 women in uncompleted marriages bore 582,843 children, or 1.4 children for every uncompleted marriage of the general population. This should not suggest, however, that the uncompleted marriages of our schizophrenics were more fertile than those of the population. Many of the uncompleted marriages among the population lasted only one or very few years, while the uncompleted marriages of schizophrenics lasted considerably longer, on the average. Since the number of schizophrenic probands is so very small there would be no sense in compiling a table showing a comparison between probands and the population with the exact length of time of the marriages. The result of an estimate shows that the number of children from uncompleted marriages is about the same among our probands as it is among the population.

Separate listings by sex of uncompleted marriages of men and women probands is also useless, because of the relatively small numbers of our probands involved.

Most of the probands' uncompleted marriages ended in divorce; 27 of these produced 55 children. Eight marriages that lasted less than 25 years were terminated by the death of one of the partners, and these marriages had produced 19 children. Nine marriages presently in force had lasted less than 25 years before the end of this study and produced 19 children. These figures show that the average fertility in marriages that had lasted less than 25 years and those that were ended by divorce or death, is about equal. Again, however, the figures are too small to be significant.

It is certain that the number of the married among the schizophrenic probands in this study is much smaller than that of the population. Among the probands, 50 percent re-

1. One female proband has two incomplete marriages on her record.

mained single (confidence interval at 95 percent lies between 43 percent and 57 percent). Considering the age of the unmarried probands, the type of the illness they have, and their life styles, it is highly unlikely that any—or at any rate very few—more marriages will be consummated after the end of this research project.

Tables 6.2, 6.3, 6.4, 6.5 show comparisons between the marital status of probands and that of the total population of Zürich. Despite the small number of probands, the marital status is shown separately for both sexes, for various age groups, and for both living and deceased probands. The ages of our probands fit best into the census figures for 1960; the same census was also used for comparative data (the results would have been no different if the 1950 census figures had been used).

In the tables, the numbers of probands in the breakdowns are so small that they appear insignificant in their fields. On the other hand, the tables do show significantly that, comparatively, the percentage of the unmarried is considerably higher among the probands than among the population.

The large number of unmarried schizophrenic probands corresponds to their relatively small number of married and widowed probands. On the other hand, there is no real difference between the percentage of divorcees among the probands and that of the general population. The absolute number of divorced schizophrenic probands (19), however, is so small, that comparing it to that of the population is virtually meaningless.

It was to be assumed from the outset that very probably the distribution of marital status among the 208 probands would be representative of all schizophrenia patients admitted to Burghölzli over the same period. At least, there seems to be no good reason for assuming the contrary, and when I checked the facts, I found the assumption to be true. In making this check, the marital status of all schizophrenics admitted to Burghölzli during 1962 and 1963 was recorded. There were 223 first-time admissions and 437 readmissions in the group. Tables 6.6 and 6.7 show the distribution of marital status classified according to first admissions and readmissions, age grouping, and sex. The marital status of probands is compared with that of corresponding age groups in the general population.

The individual fields in Tables 6.6 and 6.7 are numbered. By themselves these figures

Table 6.2. Marital status of surviving male probands at conclusion of project (1963–1965), compared with the marital status of surviving males from the population of Zürich (Swiss only) at census taken December 1, 1960. (From: *Statistische Quellenwerke der Schweiz*, No. 357, Bern, 1963)

Age	Single				Married				Widowed				Divorced			
	Population		Probands		Population		Probands		Population		Probands		Population		Probands	
	Number	%	Number	%	Number	%	Number	%	Number	%	Number	%	Number	%	Number	%
20–39	43,952	40	1	50	64,911	59	1	50	109	0	0	0	1,785	1	0	0
40–49	4,900	10	7	60	43,374	86	5	40	288	0	0	0	1,810	4	0	0
50–59	4,627	9	12	57	46,069	86	5	24	906	2	0	0	1,967	3	4	19
60–69	2,888	8	10	50	28,889	82	4	20	2,140	6	0	0	1,239	4	6	30
70 and over	1,658	8	5	38	13,313	63	4	31	5,838	26	3	23	608	3	1	8
Total:	58,025	21	35	52	196,556	73	19	28	8,826	3	3	4	7,409	3	11	16

Table 6.3. Marital status of surviving female probands at conclusion of project (1963–1965), compared with the marital status of surviving females of the total living population of Zürich (Swiss only) at census taken December 1, 1960. (From: *Statistische Quellenwerke der Schweiz*, No. 357, Bern, 1963)

Age	Single				Married				Widowed				Divorced			
	Population		Probands		Population		Probands		Population		Probands		Population		Probands	
	Number	%	Number	%	Number	%	Number	%	Number	%	Number	%	Number	%	Number	%
20–39	33,308	28	1	100	81,851	69	0	0	629	0	0	0	3,278	3	0	0
40–49	7,822	14	9	82	43,801	77	2	18	1,867	3	0	0	3,300	6	0	0
50–59	9,511	15	12	45	43,160	69	6	22	5,937	9	3	11	4,087	7	6	22
60–69	8,010	17	10	53	24,331	52	3	16	11,615	25	1	5	2,966	6	5	26
70 and over	5,422	16	4	33	8,273	24	1	9	18,356	54	3	25	1,880	6	4	33
Total:	64,073	20	36	52	201,416	63	12	17	38,404	12	7	10	15,511	5	15	21

Table 6.4. Marital status of deceased male probands at conclusion of project (1963–1965), compared with marital status of the deceased from the total male population of Zürich (Swiss only). (Average span of years 1959–1962, according to figures from the Statistics Office of the Canton of Zürich of May 9, 1969)

	Single				Married				Widowed				Divorced			
	Population		Probands		Population		Probands		Population		Probands		Population		Probands	
Age	Number	%	Number	%	Number	%	Number	%	Number	%	Number	%	Number	%	Number	%
20–39	117	55	6	86	91	42	0	0	1	0	0	0	6	3	1	14
40–49	37	18	3	75	155	74	1	25	2	1	0	0	15	7	0	0
50–59	80	13	6	67	488	77	2	22	19	3	0	0	45	7	1	11
60–69	96	9	0	0	772	75	3	50	98	10	1	17	59	6	2	33
70 and over	167	8	2	40	1,094	54	2	40	700	34	0	0	75	4	1	20
Total:	497	12	17	55	2,600	63	8	26	820	20	1	3	200	5	5	16

Table 6.5. Marital status of deceased female probands at conclusion of project (1963–1965), compared with marital status of females deceased among the total population of Zürich (Swiss only). (Average span of years 1959–1962, according to figures from the Statistics Office of the Canton of Zürich from May 9, 1969)

	Single				Married				Widowed				Divorced			
	Population		Probands		Population		Probands		Population		Probands		Population		Probands	
Age	Number	%	Number	%	Number	%	Number	%	Number	%	Number	%	Number	%	Number	%
20–39	38	35	1	50	64	59	1	50	1	1	0	0	6	5	0	0
40–49	24	17	4	67	98	71	2	33	4	3	0	0	12	9	0	0
50–59	66	18	3	38	231	63	2	25	46	12	1	12	27	7	2	25
60–69	139	18	3	50	371	47	0	0	220	28	1	17	54	7	2	33
70 and over	419	16	5	31	426	16	2	13	1,671	63	7	43	145	5	2	13
Total:	686	17	16	42	1,190	29	7	18	1,942	48	9	24	244	6	6	16

Table 6.6. Age and marital status of male admissions for schizophrenia at Burghölzli during 1962 and 1963 and of the total male population (Swiss only), according to census of December 1, 1960

	Single						Married					
	First admissions		Re- admissions		Total population		First admissions		Re- admissions		Total population	
Age	Number	%	Number	%	Number	%	Number	%	Number	%	Number	%
20–39	44	78	67	84	43,942	40	11	20	13	16	64,911	59
40–49	6	38	14	50	4,900	10	8	50	12	43	43,374	86
50–59	2	17	5	20	4,627	9	7	58	17	68	46,069	86
60–69	3	100	2	33	2,888	8	0	0	3	50	28,889	82
70 and over	0	0	2	33	1,658	8	0	0	3	50	13,313	63
Total:	55	63	90	62	58,025	21	26	30	48	33	196,556	73

	Widowed						Divorced					
	First admissions		Re- admissions		Total population		First admissions		Re- admissions		Total population	
Age	Number	%	Number	%	Number	%	Number	%	Number	%	Number	%
20–39	0	0	0	0	109	0	1	2	0	0	1,785	1
40–49	1	6	0	0	288	0	1	6	2	7	1,810	4
50–59	0	0	0	0	906	2	3	25	3	12	1,967	3
60–69	0	0	1	17	2,140	6	0	0	0	0	1,239	4
70 and over	0	0	0	0	5,383	26	0	0	1	17	608	3
Total:	1	1	1	1	8,826	3	5	6	6	4	7,409	3

are meaningless. But the tables show significantly and unequivocally that the schizophrenics accepted at Burghölzli in 1962 and 1963 also remained single in much larger numbers than is true under corresponding conditions among the population of Zürich. Celibacy among the population is about the same that it is among the 208 principal probands. With this additional data, it is also clear that divorces are more frequent among schizophrenics than among the general population; however, this finding is not sufficiently significant. These findings apply to both first-time admissions and readmissions of schizophrenics.

Could the high incidence of unmarried schizophrenics among the principal and the supplemental probands be the result of a selection bias? This would be the case, if the unmarried probands were hospitalized rather than the married ones, and theoretically, this possibility must be considered. Perhaps husbands or wives undertake the home care of their spouses more readily than any other individual would, for a single person. The effect of such a selection factor, however, can-

not be regarded as important.[2] For we do know that the number of schizophrenics who have never been hospitalized is quite small, compared to that of schizophrenics who have been hospitalized one or more times. For that reason, there are also very few married schizophrenics who have never been hospitalized. If they could be counted, the proportion of unmarried schizophrenics among the probands of our statistics would not be appreciably reduced.

The deficit in offspring among our schizophrenics, which is the result of their low motivation for marriage, is certainly not compensated for by extramarital fertility, as has already been shown.

In a study of first-time hospitalizations for mental disorders in Ireland, Walsh (1969) was surprised, as was I in Zürich, at the large

2. Based on the calculations of others, Essen-Möller (1936) arrives at the same conclusion. He investigated the marriage rate among schizophrenics who were turned up in family studies, not as clinical patients. There were not many more unmarried among them than among the schizophrenics in clinical studies.

Table 6.7. Age and marital status of female admissions for schizophrenia at Burghölzli during 1962 and 1963, and of the total female population (Swiss only), according to census of December 1, 1960

	Single						Married					
	First admissions		Re- admissions		Total population		First admissions		Re- admissions		Total population	
Age	Number	%	Number	%	Number	%	Number	%	Number	%	Number	%
20–39	28	48	67	56	33,308	28	25	42	34	29	81,851	69
40–49	11	33	23	37	7,822	14	15	46	22	35	43,801	77
50–59	6	23	27	38	9,511	15	11	42	23	32	43,160	69
60–69	9	64	12	35	8,010	17	1	7	12	35	24,331	52
70 and over	3	75	2	40	5,422	16	0	0	0	0	8,273	24
Total:	57	42	131	45	64,073	20	52	38	91	31	201,416	63

	Widowed						Divorced					
	First admissions		Re- admissions		Total population		First admissions		Re- admissions		Total population	
Age	Number	%	Number	%	Number	%	Number	%	Number	%	Number	%
20–39	0	0	1	1	629	0	6	10	17	14	3,278	3
40–49	0	0	1	2	1,867	3	7	21	16	26	3,300	6
50–59	2	8	5	7	5,937	9	7	27	17	23	4,087	7
60–69	3	22	7	21	11,615	25	1	7	3	9	2,966	6
70 and over	1	25	2	40	18,356	54	0	0	1	20	1,880	6
Total:	6	4	16	5	38,404	12	21	16	54	19	15,511	5

number of unmarried patients among the first-time admissions of male schizophrenics.

To summarize, the comparisons of relative fertility among schizophrenic probands with that of the population confirm that the fertility of the probands is appreciably lower. These comparisons make it possible to formulate reasons for this reduced fertility. It is principally due to the fact that schizophrenics remain single more frequently than nonschizophrenics do. The fact that male schizophrenics are less fertile in completed marriages is probably a contributory factor. On the other hand, it is not certain whether their lower fertility can also be ascribed to a reduced fertility in completed marriages of schizophrenic women or to a reduced fertility in all uncompleted marriages of schizophrenics. Nor is any reduction in extramarital fertility recorded for our schizophrenics.

In discussing the reduced fertility of schizophrenics, it is easy to explain it as the consequence of long-term hospitalizations of married schizophrenics. That is why it is really surprising that, in the completed marriages of our female probands and in the uncomplet-

ed marriages of all our probands, the number of children compared to those of the population is not demonstrably lower. There is good evidence to indicate that the figures discussed above do not show the inhibiting influence of hospitalization on procreation. On the one hand, the total time of hospitalization compared to the life spans of schizophrenics is much less than expected. The time spent outside clinics (in contrast to time spent being hospitalized) is much greater among married schizophrenics than among unmarried ones. Many of our schizophrenics were late-onset schizophrenics, who were not hospitalized until they had approached or passed the end of their procreative period. Schizophrenic disorders become more numerous during childbirth, and in women especially after the birth of their children.

These facts take on meaning when it is feared that early dismissals from hospitals would lead to increased propagation among the married schizophrenics. They show that this danger, even when it exists, does not carry much weight in the statistics. The most significant reason for the reduction in fertility among schizophrenics is not their hospitalization, but a lack of interest in marriage among many of those who become schizophrenic late in life.

In connection with the discussion on the probands' sex lives, I already presented figures showing how many births occur among married probands during their marriages and before the onset of their psychoses. In a total of 289 years of married life before onset of illness, the male probands produced only 27 children. Since we are discussing here those years of married life at the very beginning of the union (for it is after this that the probands became ill), the average number of years in which a birth occurs—nearly 11—is large, indeed. A similar picture applies to the female probands. Before onset of the psychosis and before reaching age 50, the women had a total of 539 fertile years in their marriages. During this time, they bore a total of 79 children, or an average of less than 1 child every 7 years. It certainly becomes unequivocally clearer from these figures, rather than from the previous ones, that the fertility of married probands is less than that of the total population.

Of the 184 children of our probands, born before the onset of psychosis, 117 were born in, and 12 were born out of, wedlock. Of the remaining 55 children, 14 were born in, and 1 was born out of wedlock during the period between the onset of illness and the initial hospitalization. After hospitalization, 38 were born in and 2 out of wedlock, that is, 22 percent of all the children that were born. Up to this point, the proportion of children born after initial hospitalization (compared to those born before) was small. The increase in births because of frequent early releases would have to be enormous in order in the future to balance out the total low fertility rate among schizophrenics. According to studies so far, it has been quite small.

The significance of the reduced fertility among the schizophrenic probands is derived from the fact that 14.4 percent (30 of 208) of the proband-families had died childless during the period of the investigation (30 probands and their siblings and half-siblings died childless, or they had reached an age too far advanced to bear children). It can be estimated with certainty, that many more proband-families will die out in the next generation. Kallmann (1932) also pointed out that the number of families from the proband generation that die out will increase rapidly during the coming generation.

Comparisons of Fertility of Schizophrenics with Fertility of the Population by Other Authors

The question whether the fertility of schizophrenics as compared to that of the general population is markedly less, is of great importance to the study of the genesis of schizophrenia. An ailment occurring as frequently as schizophrenia could only have originated by the mutation of one or of a few genes, if the lower fertility of schizophrenics were meaningless (or if all the carriers of recessive characteristics were to reproduce beyond their expected averages). The degree of reduction in fertility among schizophrenics must also be taken into account when dealing with the question of whether in the genesis of schizophrenia the new formation of the pathogenic mutations or the consistent transmittal of the mutated genes is more important in the hereditary process. If a truly significant reduction in fertility among schizophrenics could be proved with certainty, the transmittal of a hereditary schizophrenic characteristic could no longer be important in the genesis of the disease. In such cases, only new mutations or personal experiences could be significant for the genesis of schizophrenias, and the following question would demand our attention: What noxae, in what areas, and at what specific times are so consistent that the frequency of schizophrenia cases always remains just about the same?

The results of a comparison showing a lower fertility among our probands than among the population of Zürich must not yet be accepted as conclusive evidence that there is a reduced fertility in general among schizophrenics. Such a conclusion can only be admitted when, at different times and in other locations, completed investigations have led to the same result.

In what follows, therefore, the findings from the study of our schizophrenic probands and their relatives, and those from other investigators will be compared.

It must be obvious, how rarely the very important question of fertility among schizophrenics has been treated in the international literature. Up to the end of the 1920s, it was virtually impossible to do research on the fertility of schizophrenics, for the concept of the schizophrenias was not really conceived until the beginning of the century. It took a long time after that before it was accepted. The growing up of the children of schizophrenics who were diagnosed on the basis of this new concept took decades. Accordingly, the important investigations on this topic did not appear until about 1930.

In 1927 Ostmann, remarking on the fertility of schizophrenics in Schleswig, found that it was exceptionally low. Only 30 percent of the schizophrenics he had hospitalized within the preceding decade had been married. Only 2 children were born, on the average, to each marriage involving a schizophrenic. Surprisingly, these findings agree with mine, which evolved in such different times and in a different locale.[3]

In 1929, Bowman, my teacher at the time, together with Raymond from the United States, compared the fertility of schizophrenics with that of manic-depressives. All the schizophrenics combined had fewer children than all the manic-depressives. But when the authors excluded from their totals all those patients without children, and counted only the children of patients who had at least 1 child, the number of children among schizophrenics was no smaller than it was among manic-depressives. These findings might corroborate the experiences I had with my probands, among whom the lowness in fertility derives from their disinclination to marry, and not—or not as definitely—from a diminished fertility in marriages with more than 1 child.

In 1932 and 1933, Nissen in Norway determined among 322 hospitalized schizophrenics that their fertility and their marriage frequency were lower than those of the population. These findings agreed with mine. On the other hand, Nissen (1932–33) found an increase in extramarital fertility among schizophrenics, which was not found among my probands.

In 1933, Dahlberg was opposing the popular concept that had become widespread in

3. I did not have access to Ostmann's original paper. The above data were taken from F. J. Kallmann, *The Genetics of Schizophrenia*. New York: Augustin Publishers, 1938. Kallmann (1938) refers to Ostmann's paper (1927), which reference I included in my bibliography. But this reference of Kallmann's (1938) is incorrect, for Ostmann's (1927) paper does not contain these same figures. I am unable to determine where Kallmann obtained them. The search for these figures in other writings by Ostmann yielded nothing. Apparently Kallmann knew Ostmann well and, considering the degree of conscientiousness with which Kallmann worked, it may be assumed that he published reliable figures from Ostmann, even though he gave erroneous references for their origins.

the eugenics literature of the time, that the mentally ill propagated more prolifically than the normal population. But he made no statement expressly about the fertility of schizophrenics; instead, he discussed the fertility of all female patients from a psychiatric clinic in Uppsala (2138 female patients). Since we may assume that there were a considerable number of schizophrenics among them, his findings should be mentioned here. In all age groups over age 20, the number of children of female mental patients was much lower, even at the time of hospitalization, than the number of children by women from the entire population. The number of children of Dahlberg's (1933) mental patients is barely two thirds that of the corresponding normal population, and this is even true at the time of hospitalization. The difference would have to be even greater if it were calculated at the end of the patients' fertility period. The small numbers of offspring among the patients is mainly ascribable to the large number of unmarried and the childless marriages among them. On the other hand, those women who have children at all, have about as many as comparable numbers among the population have. Insofar as the findings of Dahlberg (1933) about all mental patients could be applied to schizophrenics alone, they would nearly correspond to mine. Both investigations reveal a drop in fertility among mental patients, which can essentially be related to their low marriage rate. In both investigations, the difference in fertility between patients and normals is less when the average is taken of children that result from one marriage, than when the average is taken of those children born to one proband.

The first major and thorough investigation on the fertility of schizophrenics, however, came from Essen-Moeller (1935). It is unsurpassed in volume of research material and statistical accuracy. The probands came from Bavaria and were selected at the German Psychiatric Research Institute. Their fertility rate was checked in 2366 diagnostically certain and 599 probable schizophrenics of various ages, and was compared to that of manic-depressives, epileptics, and nonselectively chosen representatives of the general population. The principal conclusions by Essen-Moeller (1935) were that

1. The overall fertility of schizophrenics compared to that of the normal population is markedly lower—in fact less than half.

2. This decline is based on a sharply reduced marriage frequency among schizo-

phrenics, as well as on a sharply reduced fertility in the marriages of schizophrenics. The higher death rate among schizophrenics plays a very minor, subordinate role in this phenomenon, although, after onset of the disease, it is triple that of the population. The extramarital fertility of schizophrenics is about the same as that of the normal population, and is also related to the high number of unmarried schizophrenics.

3. In the last decades of the past century, from which most of the probands of this author originated, the total number of births dropped with the increasing distribution of birth control measures. This drop was more pronounced among the normal population than among schizophrenics. With the increasing use of contraceptives, the fertility of schizophrenics approached that of the average population.

I regard the following data which are derived from the numerous figures by Essen-Moeller (1935), as the most significant for the purpose of this study.

range between 27 ± 9.5 percent and 1 ± 8.9 percent.) Based on this new study, Essen-Moeller now assumes a marriage frequency among schizophrenics that amounts to only $\frac{1}{3}$ that of the normal population, rather than a good $\frac{1}{2}$, as he had previously done. The total propagation of schizophrenics he now estimates at "somewhere between $\frac{1}{5}$ and $\frac{2}{5}$, and at its highest, between $\frac{1}{4}$ and $\frac{1}{2}$ that of the normal population, instead of the range between $\frac{1}{3}$ and $\frac{2}{3}$ that he had assumed earlier, depending on the status of the overall drop in births."

Essen-Moeller's (1935) findings from Bavaria agree, in essence, with mine from the Canton of Zürich, although not in a few supplemental details. Both studies agree that the fertility of schizophrenics, compared to that of a corresponding population, is much lower, amounting to less than half. There is also agreement that the fertility reduction among schizophrenics is largely due to their lower marriage rate. The loss in offspring resulting from this, is in no way compensated

Fertility in Marriage	In population not practicing birth control	In population practicing birth control
Schizophrenic men:	Less than half	$\frac{2}{3}$ to $\frac{3}{4}$
Schizophrenic women:	$\frac{1}{4}$	$\frac{1}{2}$
	of the average population	

Marriage frequency
Before onset of schizophrenia: Half that of the average population
After onset of schizophrenia: $\frac{1}{6}$ that of the average population

Professor Dr. Essen-Moeller was responsible for giving me the hint, that had occurred to him in subsequent studies, that the above-mentioned figures, used for the fertility of schizophrenics, may be somewhat high. In his monograph, which was the source for these figures, he supposed that unmarried schizophrenics are hospitalized much more frequently than married ones. In reporting the figures pertaining to unmarried probands and to fertility, he had corrected this error that had resulted from this selection bias. In a later paper (1936), to which I did not have access at first, he had undertaken specific investigations on the frequency of hospitalization among married and among unmarried schizophrenics. He checked the frequency of hospitalization in married and single schizophrenics who had come to his attention not as clinical patients, but as their siblings. In this study he found that the difference in the frequency of their hospitalization was not as great as he had surmised. (It was found to

for by an increase in extramarital fertility. Differences in the findings concern the fertility of married schizophrenics. It is markedly low in Essen-Moeller's probands; among mine it is not as low or only slightly lower. There is also a difference in the marital fertility of schizophrenic men and schizophrenic women. Compared to the normal population, it is lower in schizophrenic women than in schizophrenic men. In my findings, there is no such difference. Based on his investigations, Essen-Moeller's probands and their corresponding of schizophrenics would drop even further with the increasing use of contraceptives. He assumed that contraceptive measures were introduced to late schizophrenics later than to the general population. It is true, of course, that birth control measures gained in importance among my probands and their corresponding population more than among Essen-Moeller's probands and their corresponding population. His study was done on a predominantly Catholic population, and mine on a predominantly Reformed Church one. Besides, Essen-Moeller's studies were done a number of years earlier than mine. The reduction in the deficit of offspring among schizophrenics, as expected by Essen-Moeller, however, did not occur. But perhaps his expectations were validated at least among the married schizophrenics, whose low fertility rate was established among his own probands, although not in mine.

The second major—and statistically valid—study on the propagation of schizophrenics came from Kallmann (1938). Although it was published three years after Essen-Moeller's (1935), the schizophrenics whose fertility was investigated were born before those of Essen-Moeller (1935); that is, between 1853 and 1871. The figures include all patients treated at the Berlin Herzberge Clinic between 1893 and 1902, who were diagnosed as certain schizophrenics. Five hundred and sixty-two of the 1087 schizophrenics had no children, and the remaining 525 had 2,120 children, of whom only 1,038 survived their 20th birthdays. (As an afterthought, the author later excluded 40 cases from his study, because he was not completely certain about their diagnosis. The remaining 1047 schizophrenics had 2000 children.)

Summarizing, Kallmann (1938) reached the conclusion that the fertility rate of schizophrenics is appreciably lower than that of the average population. Kallmann (1938) emphasized that his conclusion agreed with that of Essen-Moeller (1935). Both investigators also agree in the finding that the lower fertility rate of schizophrenics is related to lower marriage rate as well as to a lower number of children from their marriages.

Kallmann (1938) found the fertility rate in his "core group" of schizophrenics, that is, cases of catatonic and hebephrenic dementia, much lower than in his "fringe group"—among which he considers the paranoics and the more benign phasic forms without dementia. In the "core group," the marriage rate is half that of the general population, and, on the average, only about 1 child is born for each proband. The marriage rate among the "fringe group" cases is greater, and so also is their fertility rate. Still, even the fertility rate of the fringe group amounts to just $\frac{2}{3}$ of that of the general population.

Kallmann's (1938) figures, however, are difficult to interpret because he had no access to accurately comparable figures from a corresponding average population. He calculated that, among schizophrenics, an average of 3.2 children are born per completed marriage, and an average of 4.8 children per completed marriage in a corresponding average population group from a somewhat later period. Since the fertility rate among the population dropped during the period in question, an even greater difference has to be expected. When Kallmann (1938) calculated the number of children for all probands (including the unmarried and the childless married couples), he arrived at the figure of 1.9 children for each schizophrenic, a figure that is obviously much smaller than the average number of children per representative from the general population at a time when the birthrate was obviously exceeding the norms. He mentions that no contraceptives were yet in use during the fertility period of his probands.

Kallmann (1938) further amplifies his data on the low fertility rate of schizophrenics with percentage figures on the extinction of each generation. In the generation of probands from the "core group," 13.3 percent of the families became extinct; that is, in 13.3 percent, neither the probands, their siblings, nor their half-siblings produced any offspring. In the following generation, the figure is already up to 56.3 percent. The corresponding figures for the "fringe group" are 5.3 percent and 35.5 percent, respectively.

Seventy percent of the children were born before their schizophrenic parent had been hospitalized for the first time, and 61.5 percent before the first onset of the parent's illness.

Like Essen-Moeller (1935), Kallmann (1938) also emphasized that birth control measures were less effective among schizophrenics than among the general population. The basis for this finding stems from a comparison between two generations. He compares the fertility rate among the siblings of his probands with that of the children and nieces and nephews of these same probands. The latter were at a fertile age during a period when birth control measures were already exerting their influence. Normal siblings of these probands had an average of 1.8 children more than their mentally sound children and nephews did; however, the difference in the number of births among the women of the two generations amounted to only 0.8.

The fertility rate of schizoid-psychopathic women among Kallmann's (1938) probands is lower than that of the general population, but still higher than that of schizophrenics.

Kallmann's (1938) studies again agree in

essence with mine. According to his findings, too, the fertility rate among schizophrenics compared to that of the general population from which they came, is markedly lower. Both studies show that the low marriage rate among schizophrenics plays an important part in their low fertility rate. On the other hand, the difference in the fertility rate of married schizophrenics is clear only in Kallmann's (1938) studies, but not in mine. I did not verify the differences between Kallmann's (1938) "core groups" and "fringe groups" of schizophrenics. They are quite credible, however, because the mild phasic cases of schizophrenia and the paranoic schizophrenia were, in fact, concentrated in this "fringe group" of Kallmann's (1938). The latter often become ill late in life and often marry long before onset of their illness.

Mertens (1939) investigated the marital status of 564 schizophrenics from the patient population of the Heil- und Pflegeanstalt of Lohr am Main in West Germany. He compared this with that of manic-depressives and of tubercular patients in the sanatorium. He regarded the latter group as representing the average population. His conclusion was that among schizophrenics the proportion of unmarried members of all age groups is much larger than among manic-depressives and, as he assumes, among the general population. The siblings of schizophrenics also remain unmarried more often than do the siblings of manic-depressives.

The final result of Mertens' (1939) investigations agrees completely with my own findings. In certain cases the figures do not lend themselves to individual comparisons because, among other factors, Mertens' (1939) schizophrenics came from the populations of the Lohr Clinic, and because former patients who had already expired were also included.

Mertens' (1939) most important figures were: The percentage of unmarried schizophrenic men drops from 97.5 percent to 56 percent between the ages of 25 and 55, and among schizophrenic women, from 91.4 percent to 46 percent. The corresponding figures for manic-depressives (and for tubercular patients) are: for men 77 percent–5 percent (44.8 percent to 4 percent), and for women 55.7 percent–14 percent (39.3 percent–6.8 percent).

Zuring calculated that only 42 percent of the schizophrenics he knew were married. This portion he contrasted with the 72.9 percent of the general population of Amsterdam who were married. (He does not indicate how he dealt with the age structure in this comparison.) According to his calculations, the married schizophrenics had an average of 2.3 children per marriage, while 14.5 percent of these marriages resulted in no children. There is no indication as to whether "completed" marriages were considered. Zuring (1948) established that the average number of children " . . . surely is not greater than the average number of births among the population." Accordingly, Zuring came to the same conclusion in Holland as I did in the Canton of Zürich.

In 1953, Böök determined at a Swedish isolation hospital that the fertility rate of schizophrenics was 70 percent that of the population. His findings apply to a narrowly limited group of the population and are not suitable for drawing general conclusions.[4]

Roth collected his data in Switzerland (Geneva) and published them in 1959. Because of the locale and the time of his study, they are particularly well suited for comparison with mine. However, Roth proceeds from different lines of questioning than I do. In agreement with my findings, he reports that many schizophrenics remain unmarried (he differentiates 28 percent of the paranoid schizophrenics and 67 percent of all other schizophrenics). The unmarried ones constitute one half of his schizophrenics. Roth (1959) studied the overall fertility rate of schizophrenics using only a selected group of patients: 60 paranoid-schizophrenic women who had been hospitalized for the first time after age 45. One has to assume that the fertility rate is greater in such a selected group than in the majority of schizophrenics (for these women, contrary to most female schizophrenics, had never been hospitalized during their most fertile years). Despite this, the fertility rate of these 60 paranoics as compared to the fertility rate of the population was lower by half—corresponding to my findings in my own schizophrenic probands. The reasons for the low fertility rate reported for Roth's paranoics, however, were different from mine for my probands: The principal reasons for Roth's findings were childless marriages and a low birthrate from fertile marriages (married

4. Many young women from this group of the population emigrated, so that most of the remaining women did marry, even when they were schizophrenics. This fact increased the number of children among schizophrenics for the group that was studied.

females had an average of 1.14 children, which he compared to a figure of 3.13 children per married woman over 45 in the general population). The proportion of unmarried probands among Roth's paranoics was also large (28 percent), although not quite so large as that of the schizophrenics of all the subgroups combined that I studied. These differences are easily explained by the peculiarities of the life histories of the paranoid schizophrenics as compared to those of all other schizophrenics. (In his efforts to get figures for comparison from the general population, Roth met with the same difficulties that I did, which stem from the peculiarities of the Swiss methods of census-taking.) Roth emphasizes that his findings on the number of children among paranoid women contradict Kallmann's (1938) views, according to which the fertility rate among parnoics (compared to that of the entire population) is only slightly lower.

The fertility rate of the mothers of schizophrenics (who were studied as the mothers of his schizophrenic probands) amounts to an average of 4.5 children per mother from the 300 mothers of Roth's (1959) probands—and almost the same among mine, that is, 4.8 children. Roth takes his figure (3.7) from the census data for comparison, but points out, as I do, that this figure is too small for comparison, since only the number of children from existing marriages is given in the census data (but not the ones from previous marriages or from pregnancies of unmarried partners).

In 1962 Garrone published an extensive study about the schizophrenics in Geneva. He also checked their fertility rates. His probands were the same ones that Roth (1959) used. Garrone arrives at the same conclusion, namely, that the number of children among schizophrenics is reduced to half that of the population. For this reduction there are a number of reasons. The prevailing celibacy among schizophrenics, the frequency of nonfertile marriages, and a low birth rate in the productive marriages. The parents of schizophrenics, however, are just as fertile as the population. In essence, these findings agree with mine.

In her studies in England in 1964, MacSorley found that the fertility rate of the mentally ill, and particularly of schizophrenics, is much lower than that of their mentally sound siblings or of the population. The reduction in fertility, according to her findings, is due to the frequency of celibacy as well as to reduced fertility in marriage. Her investigations draw upon 155 schizophrenics, groups of other mental patients, controls of general patients, and the population census data.

Among 100 schizophrenics (50 male and 50 female) studied by Janzarik in Germany, only one third after an average duration of illness of 35 years were married.

A short time ago, W. Hartmann (1969), studying long-term hospitalized schizophrenics in Germany (Lower Saxony), found that more than half of them had remained single all their lives. In their "final" hospitalization, 73.3 percent of the men and 52.3 percent of the women among the 1,373 patients were still unmarried, and only 15.5 percent of the men and 16.4 percent of the women had married. The remainder was divorced or widowed, not including 2.5 percent whose marital status could not be determined. It is obvious that, with such a low percentage of marriages, the fertility rate must be low.

Barbara Stevens studied the fertility rate of 811 schizophrenic women who had been admitted to a hospital in London in 1969. In agreement with my findings in Switzerland, she found a marked reduction in marriages among schizophrenic women, but only slightly lower fertility in marriage. She calculated the marriage rate of schizophrenic women, before their first hospitalization, amounted to $\frac{3}{4}$ and to $\frac{1}{3}$ after that, in comparison to the population. On the average, a married schizophrenic woman had 1.36 children, as compared to 1.54 children for the average woman in the population.

In recent times the fear has persisted that the more liberal treatment conditions of schizophrenics are the cause of increased births among them, and that, therefore, schizophrenia cases would increase among the next generation. A number of publications report on the fertility rates of schizophrenics who have been admitted to state hospitals in the State of New York. These papers report comparisons between schizophrenics hospitalized between 1934 and 1936, and schizophrenics admitted between 1954 and 1956 (Erlenmeyer-Kimling et al. in 1966, and Rainer and Erlenmeyer-Kimling et al. in 1969). Both groups of schizophrenics show a lower fertility rate than the general population. Still, the fertility rate of schizophrenics hospitalized between 1954 and 1956 is considerably higher than that of schizophrenics admitted between 1934 and 1936. But the overall fertility of the total population also increased over those two decades, although to a lesser degree by far than that of schizophrenics. The increase in fertility among schizophrenics is caused mainly by an increase in the marriage rate, and not by increased fertility within existing marriages. Male schizophrenics play a greater role in the increased fertility than do female schizophrenics. The authors assume that the increase in hospital releases and the more tolerant attitude of the population toward released mental patients have made the increase in marriages possible.

It is not difinitely known whether this increase in fertility among schizophrenics between the thirties and fifties is limited to the State of New York or whether it has shown up in other areas as well. It is certain, however, that the effects of neuroleptics introduced between the 30s and the mid-50s were greater on the conditions in psychiatric hospitals in the State of New York than in many other places, for instance, in Europe. For this reason alone, it seems doubtful that similar calculations made in Europe would yield the same results.

It has already been pointed out that most of the children of our probands were born before these probands were first hospitalized (71 percent). The same finding holds true for Kallmann's (1938) probands. (Of the 2000 children from his 1047 probands, 1,230 were born before their parent's schizophrenic onset, 165 between the parent's onset of illness and inital hospitalization, and only 605 after the parent's first hospitalization.) According to these figures, fertility after the initial hospitalization plays a lesser role in comparison with fertility before the initial hospitalization. In view of the more liberal treatment methods, the inherently low fertility rate of schizophrenics after initial hospitalization would have to increase considerably in order to balance out the total deficit in the propagation of schizophrenics, indeed, more dramatically than the figures cited by Erlenmeyer-Kimling et al. (1969) have indicated.

From a check of the existing literature certain conclusions can be drawn.

1. An important drop in the fertility of schizophrenics compared to that of their non-schizophrenic relatives and of the normal population is found not alone in my studies, but also in the studies of all other authors who have concerned themselves with this question.

2. All the authors encountered enormous difficulties, as I did, when they attempted to make accurate quantitative comparisons between the fertility rate of the population and that of schizophrenics—difficulties that Essen-Moeller (1935) alone succeeded in overcoming to a great extent. From all the studies combined, however, the assumption arises that in the countries of our culture, and within the last 100 years or so, the fertility rate of schizophrenics compared to that of the population from which they came, was reduced to less than half.

3. The reduction in fertility of schizophrenics is certainly caused to a great extent by the fact that schizophrenics more often remain unmarried than the normal population does. It is furthermore certain that the deficit in offspring of schizophrenics, caused by their greater celibacy, is not balanced out by increased extramarital fertility.

4. For the time being, it remains uncertain to what extent the fertility rate among married schizophrenics has been lowered. In this respect different authors have come to different conclusions. It is also uncertain exactly how the reduced fertility among married schizophrenics comes about. Is it due to a limited number of children among the male or among the female schizophrenics, or to a combination of both? Is it due to a lower number of children because of more divorces or of later marriages?

5. For decades now it has been assumed—and often feared—that the difference in the fertility rates of schizophrenics and of the normal population was narrowing. The assumed increase in fertility among schizophrenics was formerly ascribed to the increased use of birth control among the population, but more recently rather to the more liberal treatment of schizophrenics. For the time being, very few authors record findings of a lowering in the difference between the fertility rates of schizophrenics and those of the population. It is still absolutely uncertain whether such a reduction applies generally or only in certain scattered locations and at specific times.

The small number of children of schizophrenics can be related to the predominance of weakened or lacking psychosexuality. Some findings on this topic have already been noted. It is a fact, however, that the degree of sexuality has been estimated partly according to the frequency of celibacy and partly according to the number of offspring. In this respect, the conclusions of this chapter and those of the chapter on psychosexuality are based on the same observations, and do not supplement one another. Still, the marital status and the number of children were not the only criteria applied for determining the psychosexuality of schizophrenics.

The determination of the number of offspring of schizophrenics is of great importance, as already noted, because on it depends the determination of the mutation rate which would be necessary in a mendelian study of heredity in schizophrenics in order to keep the frequency of these offspring approximately the same. When individual studies indicate that the fertility rate of schizophrenics might increase during our time, it does not meaningfully influence the previous findings of low fertility rates among schizophrenics. In recent decades the lower fertility rates among schizophrenics and the increase of schizophrenias remained the sames. These findings suffice to determine the hypothetical mutation rate of schizophrenia derived from them (assuming the mendelian heredity law), and to determine whether they may be regarded as probable. Such a conclusion is admissible, quite independently of whether the fertility rate of schizophrenics is on the rise today or not. In future decades they will surely have to be checked again, when it has once been established how the fertility rate of schizophrenics and the frequency of schizophrenia interrelate in the future.

6. The number of children of the parents of schizophrenics is no greater than that of the general population. The single contradictory finding, reported by Böök (1953), is based on a severely circumscribed isolated study.

Mental Disorders among the Offspring of Schizophrenics

A survey of the mental disorders among the 184 children of the 208 principal schizophrenic probands is provided in Table 6.10.

Schizophrenias

Ten of the 184 children of probands are definite schizophrenics; only cases of probable schizophrenia are lacking among them.

Considering the age structure of the children (by the same criteria already used in the statistics on siblings), figures on the expectancy of schizophrenia among them were calculated (Table 6.8)

According to Table 6.8, we are presented with an expectancy figure for schizophrenia among the children of schizophrenics of around 8–10 percent. Here the standard deviation is considerable. Despite this, the percentage remains within the minimal and maximal values reported by earlier investigators. It lies somewhat below the average of the findings by earlier authors, although the difference is not significant.

In 1967, Zerbin-Rüdin summarized the findings of earlier authors about the onset probability for schizophrenia among children of schizophrenics (Table 6.9). The average from all studies amounts to 13.7 percent ± 1.0, the maximum to 16.9 percent, and the minimum to 7 percent.

Even during the investigation of the parents and siblings of schizophrenics it became apparent that the onset probability for schizophrenia was calculated to be about the same by various authors from different countries (although all of them did represent Western culture), and in different decades. The same holds true for the offspring of schizophrenics.

The percentages for onset expectancy calculated by Stroemgren's or by Weinberg's method for the offspring, as well as for the parents or for the siblings of schizophrenics do not markedly differ from one another, even when different age limits are assigned

Table 6.8. Schizophrenics among the 184 offspring of principal probands

	Base figure	Schizophrenics among them No. %	Standard deviation	Confidence interval to 95%[1]
According to Weinberg:				
Vulnerability ages 18–40	106.5	10 = 9.4%	2.8	4.7–16.9%
Vulnerability ages 20–40	104	10 = 9.6%	2.9	4.7–16.9%
Vulnerability ages 18–45	129.5	10 = 7.7%	2.3	3.7–13.7%
According to Stroemgren[2]	115.8	10 = 8.7%	2.6	4.9–16.6%

1. From *Documenta Geigy*.

2. I am grateful to Prof. Dr. Stroemgren and Dr. N. Engkilde in Aarhus, Denmark for these calculations.

Table 6.9 Onset expectancies in offspring of schizophrenics according to different authors (compiled by Zerbin-Rüdin)

Investigator, Year of publication, Origin of probands	Number of schizophrenic probands	Base figure	No. of schizophrenic children	Standard deviation
Hoffmann, 1921, Munich	51	85.5	8 = 9.4%	3.2
Oppler, 1932, Silesia	109	289.5	28 = 9.7%	1.7
Gengnagel, 1933, Munich	44	96	8 = 8.3%	2.8
Kallmann, 1938, Berlin	525	678.5	111 = 16.4%	1.4
Garrone, 1962, Geneva	27	77	13 = 16.9%	4.3

Diagnostically certain and probable schizophrenias are consolidated. Hoffmann (1921) and Gengnagel (1933) considered a vulnerability period for schizophrenia between ages 15 and 40, Oppler (1932) between 20 and 40, Kallmann (1938) between 15 and 45, and Garrone between 15 and 70.

to the vulnerability periods. I should now like to define the different types of psychoses of the schizophrenic children of schizophrenics, and to compare them to the types of schizophrenia of their parents and to all types of schizophrenia in general. Actual statistics cannot be set up, because there were only 10 cases. To increase the number of probands, I cannot reach back for the New York or the Pfäfers probands, since most of their children at the end of the observation period were still too young to have become schizophrenic. The results from the data below about the schizophrenias of the probands' offspring are by no means statistically significant, yet, they do provide a rough idea as to general tendencies.

The premorbid personality[5] of the schizophrenic offspring of probands was non-aberrant in 3 of the children, schizoid-aberrant within the norm in 4, abberrant other than schizoid within the norm in 2, and schizoid-psychopathic in 1. In 2 cases the premorbid personality of the probands and of their offspring were considered to be equal, in 6 combinations to be similar, and in 2 to be totally different. In 4 proband-child combinations the premorbid personality of the parent was better than that of the child, and in 4, the reverse was true.

These figures deserve to be mentioned only to show that there is no definite trend toward a high frequency of premorbid schizoid-psychopathic personalities among the schizophrenic offspring of schizophrenics; instead, the findings seem to indicate the contrary, for in only 1 of the 10 schizophrenic children of my probands could a schizoid-psychopathy be diagnosed.

From the very beginning, one must expect, on the average, to find a much higher onset age[6] among the schizophrenic probands who have children, than that among all schizophrenics or among the probands' schizophrenic children. On the other hand, it must be expected, among the probands' children, that there would be relatively many early-onset cases. (Late-onset schizophrenics are more apt to have children than early-onset cases, and the generation of probands' offspring are still so young that it would be impossible for many late-onset cases to figure among them.) These expectations are in fact met. The ratio of onsets before age 30 to onsets after 30 is 2:8 for schizophrenic probands with schizophrenic children, but for those schizophrenic children it is 8:2. The onset ages of probands and of their offspring are 5–10 years apart in 4 cases, 10–20 years apart in 3 cases, and over 20 years apart in 3 other cases.

The period of long duration into which the psychoses of the probands' children developed, the so-called "end state,"[7] ended in recovery for 5, and in a mild, chronic schizophrenic state for 3. One offspring entered an acute phase as late as near the end of the observation period. Only one developed a moderately severe chronic schizophrenic state, but none could ever be rated as "severe" cases. In 4 cases, both parent and offspring recovered from the psychosis, and in 1, it evolved for both in to a mild chronic state. In 3 cases the "end states" of parent and child were not exactly the same, although they were similar.

5. A description of the qualifications that constitute a "premorbid personality" was given in Chapter 2.

6. A description of the concept "onset age" as it is applied here was given on p. 190.

7. A description and critique of the concept "end state" was given on pp. 189–91 and 200.

In 2 of these cases the parent proceeded to a moderately chronic state and the child to a mild one, and in 1 parent his chronic state was severe and the child's was moderate. In one parent-child pair the outcomes of their psychoses were totally different, in that the parent's proceeded to a severe chronic state while the offspring recovered from his pychosis.

The significant fact about these figures is that the schizophrenias of the probands' children do not evolve more severely, but rather more benignly than those of their parents. The final prognosis on the schizophrenias of father or mother and child are frequently, but not always similar.

Among the 10 schizophrenias of both a parent and a child, the combination recovery –recovery occurs 4 times, and the combination of 2 mild chronic states 1 time, while only 6 combinations occurred of the other 14 combinations that were possible. The combinations of both severe or both moderately severe "end states" did not occur in any pairs of schizophrenic parent and his schizophrenic child. The combination severe "end state" and moderately severe "end state" occurred 1 time. From the comparison of the schizophrenias of parents and their children, we derive a new indication of the value of the comparisons of the schizophrenias of two siblings, where there is a much larger sampling and there are significant results. The trend toward favorable outcomes is quite familial; on the other hand, there is no such familial trend toward an outcome to severe "end states" (total idiocy). As already emphasized, this finding contradicts the older theories that claimed to detect the inevitable effects of heredity in the "regression toward idiocy," and which accordingly credited environmental or acquired influences for any improvements in the patient or a more benign course of the disease. A close look at the course type[8] confirms and differentiates what was previously said about the "end state."

Six of the 10 schizophrenias of the probands' children run a benign phasic course with recoveries between the phases, and in 5 cases the recovery had persisted through the end of the observation period and was considered permanent. In 1 case the observation period ended while an acute phase was in progress, but judging from the favorable course of the

8. A description of the concept "course type" was given on pp. 209–10.

previous episodes, a recovery could again be expected. Two of the schizophrenias of probands' children evolved to a mild and a moderately severe chronic state; 1 acutely to a mild chronic state, and 1 chronic to a severe state.

Seven of the courses of parent-child schizophrenias are phasic. Four are benign-phasic (with recovery outcomes) for both, proceeding in 2 cases in both partners to mild or moderately severe chronic states, and in 1 case for the parent to a severe chronic psychosis and in the child to recovery. For one parent-child pair, both psychoses proceeded chronically to severe "end states." The psychosis of 1 parent proceeded chronically to a severe "end state" and that of the child, acutely to a mild "end state." One last combination was a chronic course, progressing to a mild chronic state in the parent and to a mild phasic course ending in recovery for the offspring.

From these figures, also, the same tendencies can be derived as those developed from studies in far greater numbers of combinations of schizophrenics and their siblings, for instance, the tendency toward phasic— and particularly the benign-phasic—courses, which is extremely familial. On the other hand, there is no definite tendency toward the common occurrence of severe and chronic courses. Among the parent-child schizophrenias there are just as few combinations of 2 catastrophe-schizophrenias (acute onsets with immediate evolution to chronic, severe psychoses) as there are among the schizophrenias of siblings.

An overview of comparisons of the premorbid character, the age of onset, the "end state," and the course type among the schizophrenias of parents and their schizophrenic children, leads to the assumption that different forms of schizophrenia can occur among close relatives of schizophrenics. Herein lies the justification for a general concept of "schizophrenias" from which all schizophrenic psychoses can be derived. Schizophrenias among close relatives—no matter how diversified their courses may run—still show a common tendency, on the average, of proceeding along courses more nearly similar than those of nonrelated schizophrenics. This tendency toward similarity in schizophrenias in relatives, as just emphasized, concerns mainly the phasic-benign courses, and certainly not the catastrophe-schizophrenias. The comparisons between the schizophrenias of the probands and those of their children—

although insignificant because of the small number of probands and probands' children —do indicate basic conditions similar to those found to be significant in the results of comparisons between the types of schizophrenias in siblings.

Five of the children of schizophrenic probands are offspring of a schizophrenic male, and 5 of a schizophrenic female parent; 3 are sons and 7 are daughters. In one instance a father-son combination is involved, 4 times the combination is father and daughter, 2 times, mother and son, and 3 times, mother and daughter. These figures on the sex breakdowns are really too small to warrant discussion.

Mental Disorders Other Than Schizophrenias among the Probands' Children

Whereas a glance at Table 6.10 immediately convinces one that schizophrenias among the probands' offspring are numerous, the differences in the frequency of other mental disorders are less easily apparent.

Psychoses other than schizophrenias simply do not occur in their offspring. This was to be expected, for no one found—or seriously suspected—that such other psychoses were more frequent among the children of schizophrenics than among the entire population. Among 184 persons from the general population (with the same age structure as that of our probands' children), one would expect to find no—or in all probability very few—other types of psychoses. The offspring of probands are not only too few in number, but also too young to be suitable subjects for an accurate study on the frequency of manic-depressive states or especially of age-related psychoses. A case of epilepsy among these children of probands corresponds to what might have been expected according to findings among the population. Two cases of feeblemindedness is less than corresponds to this expectation; however, the difference is obviously not significant.

However, it is striking that there are more mentally sound offspring among our probands than was to be expected from earlier studies. The difference is based primarily on the fact that among the offspring of our probands there were fewer eccentrics or psychopaths—and especially fewer schizoid-psychopaths—than among the offspring of other authors' probands. First, I would like to show that these differences are significant, and then discuss the reasons why they are.

Exact figures for these claims are not easy to come by. Every author expressed the various mental disorders in different terms in accordance with his personal judgment. Even the authors who worked under Rüdin's direction did not achieve complete uniformity in their diagnostic descriptions. Besides, the treatment of the age structure is handled differently by different authors.

The first important paper on the offspring of schizophrenics is Hoffmann's (1921). However, he set out to solve an entirely different problem than the counting of types of mental disorders. His chief aim was to determine, by studying the families, the relationships between the schizoid symptoms and the schizophrenias. Luxenburger (1940) reworked Hoffmann's (1921) data in order to achieve a more precise, empirical determination of the hereditary prognosis. I derived the following data from Luxenburger's (1940) restudy, and from Hoffmann's (1921) publication. By the way, the differences are unimportant.

Hoffmann's schizophrenic probands came from Munich. He selected 51 schizophrenics who had a total of 126 children. Among these there are none between the ages of 16 and 20, which means that the percentages for the patients remain the same, no matter whether all probands' children over 15 or those over 20 are to be considered.

Among the 102 probands' children (over 15 or over 20 years old), Hoffmann found 49 "schizoid psychopaths" = 48.0 percent $\pm$ 4.9. Among my probands' children (Table 6.10), the corresponding personality types appear partly under "schizoid psychopaths," partly under "otherwise aberrant." In this latter category I include 1 each from Table 6.10nn. 3, 5, and 7–9, as corresponding to Hoffmann's (1921) psychopaths. Among my 143 probands' offspring over 20, I find only 8 = 5.6 percent $\pm$ 1.9. The difference is significant at $p < 0.0005$. If I had included the probands' children over 15 years old, 8 of 153 would have been "schizoid psychopaths," and the percentage would have been 5.2 percent.

Among the 102 probands' offspring of Hoffmann's (over 15 or over 20), 38 = 37.2 percent $\pm$ 4.7 were nonaberrant, whereas among my probands' children over 20, 104 of 143 = 72.7 percent $\pm$ 3.7 were so classified. The difference is significant at $p < 0.0005$.

Schulz (1926) developed some highly accurate data on the offspring of schizophrenic probands. He was most interested, however, in nieces and nephews. Only 55 of the 85 probands' children that he studied were over

Table 6.10. Mental disorders among offspring of principal probands, arranged according to whether they were living or dead at the conclusion of the study, according to sex, age at death or at the end of the study

Age	Living or dead	Sex	All children	Schizophrenia	Epilepsy	Feeblemindedness	Schizoid psychopaths	Alcoholic	Other disorders or eccentricities	Suicides
Less than 20	Living	m	11						1[2]	
		f	14							
	Dead	m	8							1
		f	8							
20–29	Living	m	15	1					6[3]	
		f	15			1[1]	1		1[4]	
	Dead	m	2		1					
		f	1							
30–39	Living	m	23	1				1	4[5]	
		f	21	3			1		2[6]	
	Dead	m	0							
		f	1		1					
40–59	Living	m	29	1			1		2[7]	
		f	30						4[8]	
	Dead	m	2						1[9]	1[11]
		f	2						1[10]	
Over 60	Living	m	1							
		f	1							
Total:			184	10	1	2	3	1	22	2

1. Also unstable.

2. Neurotic manifestations in childhood.

3. One Addison's disease; 1 unmanageable as a child, and once abnormally drugged; 1 habitual embezzler; 1 anorchus, fidgety; 1 schizothymic; 1 with depressive anxiety and moodiness.

4. Spiteful in childhood, suicide attempt at puberty, good development as an adult.

5. One induced by prejudicial ideas from the mother; 1 duodenal ulcer, excitable and sexually unstable as a youth; 1 depressive personality; 1 insensitive, emotionless and primitive.

6. One puerperal depression; 1 unstable.

7. One schizoid-quarrelsome development in involution; 1 deaf-mute.

8. One with emotional gastrointestinal disorders; 1 schizoid; one neurasthenic, neurotic depressive; 1 sound through age 52, then postapoplectic.

9. Schizoid eccentric in childhood and youth.

10. Sexually unstable.

11. Psychopath, committed suicide at age 47 after financial difficulties.

Among those 41 proband children who dropped out of the investigation before age 20, 5 are 18–20 years old

Among the 63 proband children who dropped out of the investigation between 40 and 59, 24 are 40–45 years old.

17. Of these, he listed 10 = 18.2 percent ± 5.2 as eccentrics, assuming that these eccentrics would correspond to those called schizoid by other authors. Applying the meticulous workmanship so typical of him, Schulz (1926) did, however, emphasize that to state such a correspondence was fraught with uncertainties. My comparable data read 8 of 148 = 5.4 percent ± 1.8.[9]

Among Schulz's 55 offspring of schizophrenic probands over 17, 31 = 56.4 percent ± 6.7 were "normal," while among mine it was 107 of 148 = 72.3 percent ± 3.7.

9. Schulz's (1926) figures are based on the over-17-year-old group, while mine are based on the probands' children over 18. The discrepancy resulting from this comparison is quite meaningless.

According to this, Schulz's results as well reveal more schizoids and fewer normals than mine did. Because of the small number of probands' children in Schulz's work, the differences are affected by too large a median error to be significant. At that, the differences are smaller than those between Hoffmann's (1921) findings, those of other authors still to be cited, and my own.

I should like to compare my findings from the children of my 208 principal probands also with those of Oppler (1932) and the children of his 109 schizophrenic probands from Silesia. Oppler used fewer probands than I did, but his probands had more offspring; that is, 488 instead of 184, as my probands did. He selected as probands for his study only those schizophrenics who had children, while children played no part at all in the selection of my probands.

There follow, now, comparisons between schizoids, those with personality disorders, and the nonaberrant among the children of schizophrenics that Oppler and I observed.

Oppler lists the schizoids of other authors as "eccentrics." He comments: "These are people who, in some respects, have schizophrenia-like tendencies, but no definite schizophrenic characteristics." To be sure, some of them might be schizophrenics undergoing a mild course of the disease. The differentiation between them might not always be certain. "There are among them, then, (that is, among the eccentrics) people who deviate only slightly from the normal, and then again others who are almost psychotic, with all the typical transitional gradations. Furthermore, this group, together with Schneider's includes the stubborn, the obstinate, and the autistic."

Among my probands' children, Oppler's eccentrics correspond to the same personality types that I used for comparisons with Hoffmann's (1921) "schizoid psychopaths."

Among all of Oppler's 344 probands' offspring, who, being over 20 were excluded from the study, there were 45 eccentrics, that is, 13.1 percent $\pm$ 1.8. Among my 143 probands' offspring over 20, there were 8, or 5.6 percent $\pm$ 1.9, who corresponded to Oppler's eccentrics. The difference is significant (0.025 $> p >$ 0.01).

For all the probands' children over 10 years old, the following data apply: For Oppler, 48 among 372 = 12.9 percent $\pm$ 1.7; for me, 8 among 165 = 4.8 percent $\pm$ 1.6. The difference is significant (0.01 $> p >$ 0.005).

All probands' children with personality disorders observed by Oppler are divided by him into 5 categories: eccentrics, hysterics, criminal delinquents, psychopaths, and alcoholics. In my Table 6.10 they are categorized as schizoid psychopaths, alcoholics, otherwise aberrant, and suicides.

Among all 344 probands' offspring of Oppler's, who were dropped from the study after age 20, 131 are classified under these personality disorders, that is, 38.4 percent $\pm$ 2.6 of them.

Among my 143 probands' offspring who were dropped from the study, after age 20, 26 are classified under such personality disorders, that is, 18.2 percent $\pm$ 3.2. The difference is significant at $p <$ 0.005.

For all probands' children over 10 years old, Oppler's figures read 135 of 372 = 36.3 percent $\pm$ 2.4, and mine, 28 of 165 = 17.0 percent $\pm$ 2.9. The difference is significant at $p <$ 0.005.

The category "nonaberrant" from both Oppler's data and mine is applied uniformly to all offspring of schizophrenic probands combined, who have not been diagnosed as either mentally ill or suffering from personality disorders.

Among all 344 probands' offspring of Oppler's who were omitted from the study because they were over age 20, 153 are nonaberrant, that is, 44.5 percent $\pm$ 2.6.

Among my 143 probands' offspring who were omitted from the study because they were over age 20, 104 were nonaberrant, that is, 72.7 percent $\pm$ 3.7. The difference is significant at $p <$ 0.005.

For all probands' children over 10 years old, Oppler's figures are 170 of 372 = 45.7 percent $\pm$ 2.5, and mine, 124 of 165 = 75.2 percent $\pm$ 3.3. The difference is significant at $p <$ 0.005.

All these figures show significantly that there are more mentally sound children among my probands' offspring than among Oppler's (1932). The difference becomes even greater when we consider Oppler's (1932) remark that accompanied his listing of psychopaths: "The figures shown here are more likely to be too low than too high."

Oppler compared a portion of the above-mentioned figures with previous findings involving fewer subjects: Luxenburger (1939) had assumed that the number of "nonaberrant" children of schizophrenics ranged between 43 percent and 48 percent, that is, just as low as Oppler did.

In studying the 197 children of 44 schizophrenics from Bavaria in respect to schizoid-psychopathic tendencies, Gengnagel (1933) arrived at conclusions totally different from Hoffmann's (1921) and Oppler's (1932), and also different from Kallmann's (1938) conclusions, which will be discussed below. Among Gengnagel's 138 probands' children over age 15, there were only 10 "eccentrics," that is, 7.2 percent $\pm$ 2.2. This figure is quite similar to my 5.6 percent (see above). The term "eccentric" has the same definition here as it had for Oppler, who encountered so many more of them.

Among the 138 children of schizophrenics studied by Gengnagel (1933) over age 15, 106 are nonaberrant, or 76.8 percent $\pm$ 3.6. Among my 153 children of schizophrenics over 15, I found 112 who were nonaberrant (73.2 percent $\pm$ 3.6), which amounts to about the same ratio.

Kallmann (1938) assembled and studied by far the largest number of probands' children of schizophrenics. His 1,047 schizophrenic probands were hospitalized at a psychiatric clinic in Berlin between 1893 and 1902, and had produced 2000 children.[10]

In his statistics, Kallmann (1938) distinguishes between "schizophrenia" and "schizoidia." The "schizoidia" group he subdivides into "eccentric borderline cases" and "schizoid psychopaths." He considers that the term "borderline" denotes the demarcation between psychopathy and schizophrenic psychosis. Theoretically he regards both groups, the eccentrics and the schizoid psychopaths, as carriers of a single "schizophrenia gene," and not of two genes. He claims that they are genetically heterozygotic. Quite obviously Kallmann (1938) includes among his eccentrics those cases of whom he is not really certain whether they are not indeed schizophrenics whose psychosis is running a benign course. On the other hand, he feels sure that his schizoid psychopaths are not homozygotic —meaning not schizophrenic, either. According to his theory on the recessive heredity of schizophrenia, only homozygotics can be schizophrenic. Besides, it is not clear exactly

how Kallmann (1938) differentiates among his eccentrics, the schizophrenics, and the schizoid psychopaths, and the latter from other psychopaths and from healthy subjects. About this he has very little to say. The most important part of it reads:

> Our concept of schizoid psychopaths therefore embraces unsociable, cold-hearted, indecisive and fanatic types regarded by Schneider as prototypes of the catanoid, heboid, schizoid and paranoid cases, respectively, as well as Hoffmann's bullheaded oafs, malicious tyrants, queer cranks, overpedantic schemers, prudish "model children" and daydreamers out of all touch with reality.

Kallmann (1938) assumed he was encountering "schizoidia" in 326 of the 1,000 children of schizophrenics over 15 years of age, that is, in 32.6 percent $\pm$ 1.4.

Of the children of my schizophrenic probands, 153 reached the age of 15. Among them I found 8 that Kallman would probably have classified as schizoids (this figure 8 was compiled from the data of Table 6.10).

Kallmann's percentage of 32.6 $\pm$ 1.4, therefore, must be compared with mine of 5.2 $\pm$ 1.7. The difference is significant at $p < 0.0005$.

Among the 1,000 children of his schizophrenics over age 15, Kallmann included another 170 psychopaths in addition to the 111 diagnostically certain and probable schizophrenia cases and the 326 cases of "schizoidia." These figures give a percentage for "schizoidia" and psychopathy of 49.6 percent $\pm$ 1.5. This percentage may be compared to mine of 18.3 $\pm$ 3.1, which was arrived at from a total that included schizoid psychopaths, alcoholics, otherwise aberrant patients, and suicides among my probands' offspring over age 15 (28 of 153). The difference is significant at $p < 0.0005$.

The great difference in the number of schizoids among Kallmann's probands' children and mine is thus by no means the result of my just having listed a large number of Kallmann's (1938) schizoids under the category of "otherwise aberrant."

Kallmann individually calculated the probabilities for onset of schizophrenia, "schizoidia," psychopathy, feeblemindedness, epilepsy, and neurosyphilis according to the abbreviated Weinberg method and totalled the results. From his total of onset probabilities he concludes that more than $\frac{2}{3}$ of the children

---

10. On p. 368 the figures for Kallmann's (1938) probands and probands' children are shown to be somewhat higher, at 1087 and 2120, respectively. The reason for this difference is that, during the course of his study, Kallmann eliminated an additional 40 probands. He discusses the fertility of 1087 probands, but the offspring of only 1047 of them.

of schizophrenics will at some time in their lives suffer from a mental disorder. He summarizes this idea as follows:

"On the score of total psychopathologic taint, we find that more than two thirds of the proband-children ... might be regarded as 'eugenically doubtful' types."

The method by which Kallmann arrives at the figure two thirds, by adding the different onset probabilities, is open to criticism. He is not dealing with an accurate figure, although it does reveal something about the distribution of numbers. If, despite all misgivings, I were to proceed as Kallmann did, I would come up with an onset probability of only one third.

Kraule (1969), working in Russia, found that among 54 children of schizophrenics, considerably more than half were likewise in some way mentally ill (5 schizophrenic, 26 neurotic, and 9 feebleminded).

These comparisons show adequately that three earlier authors, basing their findings on extensive research, came up with a much higher number of eccentrics and psychopaths, particularly of schizoid eccentrics and psychopaths, among the offspring of schizophrenics, than I did. The studies by these earlier authors and my own do result in approximately the same onset probabilities for schizophrenia among the children of schizophrenics. All these studies also agree in that psychoses other than schizophrenia do not occur more frequently among the offspring of schizophrenics than they do among the children of the general population. Only the most diversified types of mental disorders, especially the schizoids (although not the psychoses) are more prevalent among the children of the schizophrenics observed by the most important other authors than among the children of my probands. As a whole, among the children of my probands, there are many more mentally sound ("nonaberrant") than among the children of the schizophrenics of these other authors. Of these earlier authors, only Gengnagel (1933) arrives at the same figures as I did.

The findings of Hoffmann (1921), Oppler (1932), and Kallmann (1938), based on a large number of probands, as assembled, among others by Luxenburger (1939), have been incorporated into textbooks and handbooks. They have become the basis of a widely accepted pedagogic opinion that is interpreted in a number of variations, but which reads, in substance, that among the offspring of schizophrenics, only 10 percent–15 percent will probably again become schizophrenic, but a large number of the nonschizophrenics are not considered to be mentally sound, either. About half or two-thirds of all the children of schizophrenics have some sort of mental disorder and are, therefore, "eugenically undesirable." Less than half the offspring of schizophrenics are really healthy.[11]

This is the picture that has been officially presented to many who sought an answer to the question of the probability of onset of mental illness among the children of schizophrenics.

According to my findings, this current popular concept is in error, for there are more mentally sound children among the offspring of schizophrenics than was formerly assumed.

Which opinion is now the right one? Is the current doctrine correct? Or can my contradictory evidence be applied as generally valid?

In view of the importance of the question, an exact check must be made to determine the reasons for these differences.

From the outset it becomes obvious that the high percentages of schizoids and the low percentages of normal children were derived from data much more exhaustive than my contradictory ones (Hoffmann 1921, Oppler 1932, and Kallmann 1938 between them reported on 2,614 children of schizophrenics, whereas my probands had only 184 children). It would be tempting to accept as more accurate the findings by three different authors from a much larger number of probands, and to disregard those from a single author—mine—based on a smaller number of probands.

To be sure, Gengnagel (1933) also found

---

11. Luxenburger (1939), in the addendum to Bumke's (1939) *Handbook of Mental Diseases*, comments, for example, that among the offspring of schizophrenics, 16.4 percent were schizophrenic, and 32.6 percent were schizoid-psychopaths. In so doing, he accepts Kallmann's (1938) figures, but he lists Kallmann's eccentrics under the schizoid psychopaths. In his textbook, Bumke (1939) employs these same figures as basic references. He claims, therefore, that 49 percent of the offspring of schizophrenics will, in turn, become schizophrenic or schizoid-psychopathic. He assumes additionally that all other forms of mental or emotional disturbance may still appear among the remaining 51 percent, which includes the feebleminded, bizarre personalities other than schizoid-psychopathic, alcoholics, etc. It is from this data, therefore, that the conclusion may be drawn that considerably fewer than half the children of schizophrenics stand a chance of remaining mentally sound.

just about as few abnormal personalities among his 197 offspring of schizophrenics as I did. Gengnagel (1933) and I studied a combined total of 381 probands' children, which is still a modest figure compared to the 2,614 studied by the three other authors.

But it does prove instructive now to investigate the reasons for the differences between the findings of Hoffmann (1921), Oppler (1932), and Kallmann (1938) on the one hand, and Gengnagel's (1933) and mine on the other. By and large, the difference is based on a different method of classifying the concepts "schizoid," "psychopathic," and "non-aberrant," and on the different age-level structure of the probands' children under study.

Obviously, schizophrenics and other psychotics are far easier to distinguish diagnostically than "eccentrics," "psychopaths," or other behavioral deviates.

When all authors estimate the frequency of schizophrenias and other psychoses in complete agreement, but disagree on that of "eccentrics," etc., it is in itself a reason for suspecting that such a disagreement is the result of differing diagnostic concepts. This assumption is supported by a closer examination of the various studies. Hoffmann (1921), for his part, had very little interest in the precise differentiation between psychotic, psychopathic, otherwise aberrant, or healthy personalities. He was interested in the schizoid manifestations, no matter whether they appeared in a psychopath or in a healthy individual. This is another reason why his findings do not permit any valid conclusions about the frequency of healthy children among the offspring of schizophrenics.

Hoffmann (1921), Oppler (1932), and Kallmann (1938) became acquainted with their probands' offspring for purely scientific purposes. I, on the other hand, became acquainted with the majority of mine as the physician of their parents. Many of these probands' children I had to counsel professionally, principally because of the distress that the psychosis of their parents had caused them. I shared with these children their concern for the sick parents when things went bad for them—and their joy and pleasure when their parents improved. I have often seen these probands' children weep,[12] I have

met them on the stairs and in the halls of the clinic, bearing flowers and gifts as they went to visit their parents. And I saw them again repeatedly, sometimes years apart, or heard of them and their fates for years, while visiting other patients. From this different way of meeting them, I was bound to come up with a different evaluation of their personalities. Personality phenomena that appeared to an exclusively scientific investigator to be firmly set prototypes of eccentrics or psychotics, appeared to me as the physician (and perhaps sometimes as a personal friend as well) of the probands' children, much more as perfectly natural behavior patterns for a healthy individual undergoing difficult circumstances in connection with his family. In the course of their purely scientific interest, the earlier investigators aimed specifically at deviant personality characteristics. I searched for these, too, but I saw primarily also the good and the normal aspects. I saw how children worried about their parents, how they struggled against it when their parents were to be transferred to other clinics because, perhaps, visiting them would be more difficult then. I found out how many of these children of my patients made economic sacrifices or interrupted their professional training in order to help their parents, or how a son might undertake to manage the household to take the place of his hospitalized mother. A school-age girl cleverly evaded the truant officer in order to be able to care devotedly for her smaller siblings, necessarily neglected by the sick mother. And I saw frequently, too, how these children were confused in their relations to the opposite sex, because of the schizophrenia of their father or mother. Invariably they felt guilty toward a love partner; they worried whether, faced with the probability of becoming ill or of their future offspring becoming ill, marriage would be a responsible step to take. What appeared to be a form of schizoid autism in an erotic situation, without knowing their internal sufferings, was actually the understandable, rather dramatic reaction of a warm-hearted, sensitive human being. In short, it was inevitable that I should find considerably more mentally sound and fewer psychopaths than I would have, if I had seen my probands' children in but a single

---

12. In order to avoid misunderstanding, most of these "probands' children" were not really children any more according to their age while I was acquainted with them.

The expression "child" as employed here is in the sense that one remains a child to his father or mother as long as he lives.

interview and only for the purpose of scientific inquiry.

The same factor can also be illustrated from a different viewpoint. The investigator who attempts to determine an empirical prognosis for heredity will ask relatives about symptoms of abnormality. Then personality profiles are drawn up, as they appear in Oppler's (1932) study, for example:

"Male, age 25; learning difficulties, excitable, uncommunicative, inclined to temper tantrums, usually a loner"—or

"Male, age 24; idealistic, a dreamer, very exacting, meticulous, quiet nature"—or

"Female, age 11; poor appearance, undernourished, exceptionally quiet and retiring."

Perhaps it is justified that—based on these descriptions—such children should be categorized as "eccentrics." But whether they are "psychopaths" or "abnormal"—or, indeed, "eugenically undesirable"—is more than a mere question. For example, it is quite reasonable for an 11–year-old girl in the custody of her schizophrenic mother to have a poor appearance, to be undernourished, and to be quiet and retiring, even if by nature she was a sweet, communicative, and perfectly healthy child. In submitting my findings, I took care to determine whether such a child had become undernourished or taciturn during a time when a sick mother was caring for her, or through other tangible negative circumstances. If the former was true, the child would appear to me as being normal, much more so than she would to Oppler (1932).

A second reason why I listed more normal probands' children than Hoffmann (1921), Oppler (1932), or Kallmann (1938) did, was the difference in age groups. The probands' children of these authors were older on the average than mine. For example, the ratio of the over-40-year-olds to all probands' children among Oppler's (1932) patients was 224:466, and among mine, 65:184. Some form of pathological personalities seems to be particularly numerous among the older offspring of the probands of these other authors (among Oppler's [1932] 224 probands' offspring over 40, 135 or 60.3 percent, were somehow pathological, while among my 120 probands' offspring between 20 and 40, 55 or 45.8 percent, are in some way pathological).

Who is right? Hoffman (1921), Oppler (1932), and Kallmann (1938) combined, or I? Or are the right ones possibly the two authors whose results lie somewhere between those of Hoffmann (1921), Oppler (1932), and Kallmann (1938) on the one extreme and mine on the other; that is, Schulz and Gengnagel (1933)?

I believe both parties are right, but each in a different sense from the others. The three authors who present few healthy or normal cases among the children of their schizophrenic probands are right, if any digression from an idealized way of life and manner of giving one's self under all circumstances is considered abnormal. They are right if "schizoid psychopathy" and a "schizoid personality" are regarded as something that is part of a human being by nature, and cannot be considered a sound state of health, even under miserable living conditions. On the other hand, I would be right if one chose to recognize the fact that a person who is by nature healthy and mentally sound can assume a schizoid posture or apparently psychopathic behavior characteristics under extremely torturous living conditions, without necessarily having to be classified as abnormal.

If the hitherto prevailing dogma, based on the studies of Hoffmann (1921), Oppler (1932), and Kallmann (1938), is to be retained, to the effect that over half the children of schizophrenics are in some way abnormal (and therefore basically "undesirable"), it is in serious need of more exacting definitions. These children can only fit that classification if "abnormal," "pathological," or "undesirable" are terms to be applied even to those whose behavior becomes different from and more difficult than that of their basic nature because of an added stressful situation. They will not fit that classification if the normal person is permitted to exhibit behavior traits in stressful situations that might be difficult to distinguish from abnormal or psychopathic behavior patterns.

A considerable number of offspring of schizophrenic probands of earlier authors, characterized as somehow abnormal, aberrant, or eccentric, have passed their 40th birthdays. The younger ones among them were in the minority. Personality disorders that do not show up until the second half of a normal life span were those most often listed as the abnormal conditions among the offspring of schizophrenics studied by these authors. In the oft-repeated statement, that less than half the children of schizophrenics were normal and healthy, lay the unspoken suggestion that the shockingly high figure for disorders among these offspring was mainly caused by the schizophrenic disorders in one of their parents.

This is the way the statement was often interpreted. Of course, there is the possibility that the effects of the psychoses of the parents do not become manifest in the child until later in life. But it is also true that disorders related to unfavorable hereditary developmental characteristics as well as those that originate from unfavorable conditions in childhood could just as easily not become manifest until later in life. And again, in mitigation, it is true that many of the personality disorders that begin late in life are caused by damage incurred late in life (the sequels of all sorts of diseases, early cerebral involutions, partial deafness, changes in social status, etc.). The hitherto accepted dogma has unjustifiably supported the concept that the schizophrenia of the father or mother would somehow alter pathologically the personality of half to two-thirds of their children. Even if the cited ratios of the offspring of schizophrenics who are somehow abnormal were correctly calculated, many of the personality disorders of these offspring would have to have originated independently of the disorders in the parents.

Based on the misfortunes in life of the children of my 208 probands and on a critical evaluation of the findings from earlier authors concerning the offspring of schizophrenics, I should like to issue a serious warning not to accept as valid without qualification, any future findings that determine that half to two–thirds of the offspring of schizophrenics are somehow abnormal. The depressing conclusion, however, that 8–10 percent of these offspring will, in turn, become schizophrenic, remains a fact. But beyond that, the prognosis for the mental well-being of the children of schizophrenics is a much less pessimistic one than it formerly was. It is certain that many more than half the children of schizophrenics remain mentally sound, and possibly it may even run as high as three-quarters. Among those offspring that do manifest personality disorders, there is still quite a number whose abnormal development has no or no unequivocal connection with the schizophrenia of their parents, or at least no such connection that is scientifically traceable.

These findings are encouraging for all those who are treating or caring for the families of schizophrenics. They should be helpful to many who are depressed because a relative of theirs is schizophrenic—but they are not necessarily suitable for banishing completely the fear of familial illnesses. Furthermore, in an entirely different sense, glossing over facts

is out of place. Even if the psychotic disorder of a father or a mother does not bring on a mental illness or an abnormality in their offspring, it still does cause them suffering and harm. I shall discuss below in detail the shadows that are cast over the lives of many children of schizophrenic parents.

Theoretically, the study of the offspring of schizophrenics leads to a certain unequivocal conclusion. Determining the frequency of "eccentrics," "schizoids," and "psychopaths" among the offspring of schizophrenics is highly dependent on the subjective judgment of the investigator and on the type of investigation. No precise figures have been uncovered, and most probably never will be. Earlier authors have attempted to formulate hypotheses about the hereditary aspects of schizophrenia, according to a certain mendelian theory of heredity. In so doing, they assumed two postulates as valid. (1) That the number of schizoids or eccentrics among the offspring of schizophrenics was an exactly known quantity, and (2) that one could assume that schizoids or eccentrics were the carriers of a partial or a latent predisposition for schizophrenia. Both these postulates are invalid. Hereditary hypotheses that assume a definite number of carriers of hidden or partial tendencies among the offspring of schizophrenics do not merit our confidence.

The mental disorders and aberrations other than schizophrenia in the offspring of schizophrenics are still to be compared to those of the general population. An exact comparison is impossible. Questioning people from the general population about themselves and about their relatives results in an entirely different relationship to the people questioned than does the questioning of the relatives of schizophrenics. But the evaluation of a personality depends on this relationship between the questioned subject and the interviewer. The counting of "aberrants," of "eccentrics," of "psychopaths," or of the "otherwise aberrant," depends to an even greater degree on this relationship than does the counting of severe psychoses or physical illnesses. It has already been mentioned that there were no differences in the frequencies of psychoses other than schizophrenia, epilepsy, or feeblemindedness between the probands' children and those of the population, and that our probands' children were too few in number and too young to reveal more precise differences. However, differences are assumed to exist in relation to the criteria "nonaberrant" and "mentally sound."

Of the 143 offspring of my schizophrenics over age 20, 104 = 72.7 percent ± 3.7 are "nonaberrant and sound." Among the two population groups representing the Swiss population which I studied, the corresponding percentage is 92.0 percent ± 0.8 (991 of 1,077). The difference is not significant at $0.10 > p > 0.05$.

The offspring of my schizophrenic probands do appear to be healthy and "nonaberrant" less frequently than one might expect from a similar sampling of the population.

But the difference is still not significant at the level of $p < 0.05$. The comparison is furthermore inaccurate, since the population from which the probands' offspring came differed, partly as to time and partly as to locale, from those representing the two population groups used for comparisons in the studies.

The difference is only partly the result of the increase in incidence of schizophrenia among the probands' children (onset probability of schizophrenia in probands' children was 9.4 percent, and in the two groups representing the population, 1.1 percent). The difference is also partly due to listing jointly all unfavorable personality developments and eccentricities (except for psychoses, feeblemindedness, and epilepsy).

In all the offspring of my schizophrenic probands over 20, there were 18.2 percent ± 3.2 (26 of 143) of such unfavorable personality developments and eccentrics. Among the two population groups I studied, the corresponding percentage amounts to just 4.8 percent ± 0.7 (52 of 1,077). The difference is highly significant at $p < 0.005$.

The absolute figures are much too small to answer the question that would now demand attention: What personality disorders (with the exception of psychoses, feeblemindedness and epilepsy) occur more frequently among the offspring of schizophrenics than among the general population? Only the fact that the sum of all these personality disorders is more frequent among these offspring has statistical significance. In respect to the schizoid there is a difference in the absolute figures, but these are so small that they do not prove anything.

The mental health of the offspring of schizophrenic probands will now be compared to that of the siblings of schizophrenic probands. Schizophrenias occur at about the same rate in both groups (9–10 percent). Much to our surprise, the number of unfavor-able personality developments (with the exception of psychoses, feeblemindedness, and epilepsy) is also about the same among the probands' offspring and their siblings.

Of the 148 offspring of my probands over age 18, 28, that is, 18.9 percent ± 3.2, have such types of adverse personality developments and eccentricities. Among the probands' siblings over age 18, it was 17.4 percent ± 1.5 (117 of 674).[13]

Many of the previous assumptions that were based on heredity theories are refuted when the overall state of health of the offspring and the siblings of schizophrenics is found to be equal. This also refutes every one of the mendelian laws of "heredity" of schizophrenia (or of the schizophrenias and the nonpsychotic personality disorders in general). With simple recidivism, there would have to be more abnormals among the siblings than among the offspring. The fact that these findings are similar might be explained by the theory of simple dominance; but that is out of the question here, since most schizophrenics did not come close to having 50 percent of schizophrenic offspring.

If one assumes that upbringing by (living together with) a psychotic or otherwise abnormal parent had any bearing on producing schizophrenia in the offspring, then the findings indicate that statistically, schizophrenia in one of the parents does not have any worse effects than other disorders do in the parental families of schizophrenics, in which schizophrenia in the father or mother is a rare occurrence.

In any case, it is impossible to determine any valid statistical drop in the overall mental health picture from one generation of schizo-

13. I can spare the reader a lot of lengthy and involved data, which is why I chose as a base figure the number of probands' offspring over 18 in one instance, and the number over 20 years old in another, in the discussions of their adverse personality developments. It is a true reflection of the fact that the base figures were often treated quite differently in the literature. At times the number of personality disorders were related to all probands, then again just to those over 10, then over 14, over 17, over 18, or over 20 years old. The differences in the figures given when the 18–20-year-old age group either is or is not included are meaningless. I have selected the base figures in such a way that comparisons between them and those in the literature can be made, but that the senseless subdivision by age groups would not have to be pursued unless it was necessary. In the data on siblings the boundary line was drawn at age 18.

phrenics to the generation of their children. If the old theory of degeneration of schizophrenia had not already been refuted long ago, we would have the proof here how false that theory was.

The Spouses of Schizophrenics

In determining data on the offspring of schizophrenics, a sound knowledge of both the parents of these offspring is important, that is, not only of the schizophrenic probands themselves, but also of their spouses. Within the framework of the hereditary-pathological studies of the Rüdin School in Munich, there were three important studies between 1938 and 1943 on the selection of marriage partners by schizophrenics. One by Leistenschneider in 1938, one by Egger in 1942, and one by Früh in 1943. Information about the spouses of schizophrenics is important also for determining the living conditions under which the children of schizophrenics grew up and sometimes became ill.

A survey of the spouses of the 208 principal probands of this study appears in Table 6.11.

The onset probability for schizophrenia

(susceptible age from 18 to 40) amounts to 2.6 percent $\pm$ 1.5 (1 case of probable schizophrenia included). According to that, there is no significant difference in susceptibility to schizophrenia in comparison to that of the entire population, where it is estimated to be about 1 percent.

For comparison with the findings of other authors, see Table 6.12 (set up by Zerbin-Rüdin in 1963).

From all these four studies combined, the onset probability does not deviate significantly from that of the entire population either, although it is somewhat higher when the cases of probable schizophrenia are included.

In the studies by earlier authors, minor hints indicate that schizophrenics do perhaps have a mild tendency of preferring schizophrenics or persons vulnerable to schizophrenia as marriage partners after all. Früh (1943) found a number of schizoids among the spouses of schizophrenics and, just as Leistenschneider (1938) had, a slight increase of schizophrenias among the siblings of these marriage partners. This increase, however, is by no means statistically significant.

Table 6.11. Spouses of principal probands

Types of disorders among all spouses of probands

Age group	Sex	All probands' spouses	Schizophrenia	Probable schizophrenia	Senile psychoses	Feeble-mindedness	Schizoid psychopathy	Alcoholism	Other disorders	Suicides
30–39	m	7	1					1		1
	f	3	1							
40–59	m	25[1]				3		6	2[2]	2
	f	28		1		2			3[3]	
60–79	m	28			1	2	1	2	3[4]	
	f	20							5[5]	
80 +	m	3							1[6]	
	f	2			1					
Age undetermined	m	4								
Total:		120	2	1	2	7	1	9	14	3

1. Age of one of these had to be estimated.

2. One unstable, primitive; 1 probable organic psychosyndrome.

3. One infantile, psychasthenic depressive; 1 neurotic; 1 neurasthenic psychopath (female).

4. One homosexual; 1 eccentric (schizoid-aberrant); 1 certain case of induced insanity.

5. One hyperthyreosis without psychic disorders; 1 sexually unstable; 1 sexually unstable female psychopath; 1 mild depressive (bizarre personality); 1 female hysteriform psychopath.

6. One psychopath, a cranky, secretive individual with an hypocritical air.

Table 6.12. Onset expectancy in spouses of schizophrenics, according to various authors (compiled by Zerbin-Rüdin)

Probands of:	Diagnostically certain schizophrenics	Certain and probable schizophrenics combined
This project	2:115 = 1.7% ± 1.2	3:115 = 2.6% ± 1.5
Leistenschneider (1938)	0:114 = —	2:114 = 1.4% ± 1.1
Egger (1942)	2:78.5 = 2.4% ± 1.7	4:78.5 = 4.8 ± 2.4
Früh (1943)	0:91.5 = —	0:91.5 = —
4 Authors combined	4:399 = 1.0 ± 0.5	9:399 = 2.3% ± 0.7

Among the spouses of my probands, the feebleminded, alcoholics, and suicides appear somewhat more frequently than would correspond to conditions in the average population. The difference is not significant. But even Egger (1942)[14] and Früh (1943) found slightly more feebleminded among the spouses of schizophrenics than calculations from the average population would have indicated.

In summary, then, schizophrenics select marriage partners who, from a statistical aspect, are not at all—or not appreciably—different from the average population in respect to their mental health. Perhaps there are a few more schizophrenics and feebleminded among the spouses of schizophrenics than among married couples of the general population, but the difference is not significant.

The Offspring of the Marriages of Two Schizophrenics

Two spouses of our schizophrenic probands were diagnostically certain schizophrenics, and 1 was a probable schizophrenic (Table 6.11).

These 3 couples have 5 offspring, ages 30, 33, 38, 52 and 54. None of the offspring became schizophrenic, but 1 qualified as a schizoid psychopath, 1 was a severe neurotic, and 1 suffered a mild schizoid development. Two are healthy and lead useful lives. The daughter with mild schizoid tendencies is, nevertheless, getting splendid results in her nursing of idiots. Three of the 5 children, therefore, are worthy, useful citizens in their communities. The development of these children is worth discussing in detail.

Proband 31, Johann Z., has already been described as an example of a "late improvment." His wife had come to our clinic as a girl of 17 (5 years before she married). She complained that a boyfriend had left her, but

she made such an impression of being eccentric and unapproachable, that her diagnosis sheet was marked: "Psychopath, schizophrenia?" At age 22 and pregnant, she married Johann Z. The marriage was a bad one. Husband and wife had little in common, and they constantly picked and nagged at each other. Despite this, divorce was farthest from the woman's mind. She remarked once that she would rather get a daily thrashing from her husband than consider a separation. The family suffered severe economic privation, since the father had only a sporadic income or none at all. In 1933 the mother came to our clinic again, this time seeking official approval for an abortion. However, before the interviews were finished, she ran out of the clinic railing pathologically and shrieking. On the occasion of our treating one of her children when she was 29, she became known to us as a client of our psychiatric children's clinic. At that time, she was definitely a maniac. She felt she was being pursued by detectives, and rationalized the idea by stating, among other things, that she had seen a policeman looking at his watch. At the time there were grave doubts as to the wisdom of continuing to entrust the children to her—but they stayed with her nonetheless. In the decades that followed, she became quieter, but she never fully recovered. Finally she got a divorce. When she was 49, her husband was released from the clinic after a 16-year stay (with one interruption). The divorced couple now lived separate lives. During a house visit shortly before this project was ended, the woman, who was then 55, seemed to distrust us, but was not clearly psychotic. Her house was in the greatest disorder. Her husband, who was still seeing her occasionally, thought that she was still "not quite normal." He wondered whether it would be necessary to have her placed in legal custody, although she was working and earning, living as a maid in a hospital.

This woman was never clinically evaluated.

14. Egger's (1942) findings are of little value, since his probands come from an area in which feeblemindedness is prevalent.

A diagnosis of paranoid schizophrenia seemed very probable to me, as it did to other doctors who knew her. I am listing this patient as a probable schizophrenic only, because from the standpoint of differential diagnostics a temporarily induced state of manic delusion in a psychopathic woman was the case confronting us.

The pregnancy that had induced the marriage of the proband to this sick woman produced one daughter, Maria. At the conclusion of the study Maria was 34 years old. The first 11 years of her life she spent with both her parents. During this time, both parents were pathological. Until Maria was 6, her father was an unstable, ill-adjusted, jobless psychopath. He then suffered a schizophrenic psychosis marked by childish silliness, delusions of persecution, and hypochondria. His psychosis developed simultaneously with Maria's mother's as a folie-à-deux. From her 11th birthday on, Maria lived with her mother only. During her father's lengthy hospitalization, her mother obtained a divorce. After the father was released as improved, he lived alone, apart from the family. The mother was continually given to eccentric behavior, partly exhibiting her distrustful, egocentric personality, and partly giving way to overt delusional behavior.

Maria's childhood was a gruesome one, spent in poverty and under the care of two sick and often totally psychotic parents.

Shortly after her father had become psychotic, Maria, at the age of 7, was suffering from nocturnal terror attacks and depressive states. She was treated at our children's clinic. She was able to go to school and to finish an apprenticeship as a salesgirl. Now she works in that job. She is unsociable, unpopular, and secretive, and lives with her mother, although she does not get along with her. At 19 she bore an illegitimate child. Her behavior before that was abnormal, in that she took a passive attitude toward her pregnancy and made no sort of preparation for the child's birth.

During the mother's pregnancy with Maria's brother Karl, she tried to get legal permission for an abortion, but then did not go through with the necessary medical examinations for no apparent—but possibly pathological—reasons. Karl lived only for his first 7 years together with his sick parents, and not 11, as Maria had done. Then he spent one year with an aunt in a healthy environment. From age 9 on he then stayed with his mother again, as Maria had done. He attended elementary school and completed an apprenticeship as a bricklayer, a trade he has worked at since. At the end of the study he was 30 years old, still single, and mentally sound.

Summary: Two siblings spent their childhoods under the care either of both their pathological parents or of only their pathological mother. An extremely adverse home environment was marked by poverty because of the father's world-alien personality, the bickering between the parents, and the persecution complex of both parents. The girl developed a schizoid personality, while the boy remained nonaberrant and healthy. Why the difference? One might assume that the boy was exposed to his completely psychotic father for a shorter time than the girl was. Also, that during his early school years he lived temporarily in healthy surroundings. Probably he is also less sensitive and less intelligent than his sister.

The schizophrenic psychosis of Gerhard M. (Proband 55) has already been described, as an example of emotional influences on the course of the disease. When his only daughter Eva was born, he still was not psychotic, although he had already shown some homoerotic tendencies and led a rather disorganized existence, considering his high intelligence. He worked only at odd jobs as a common laborer. Eva spent the first 4 years of her life with both parents; during this period her mother was still healthy. Then the mother developed a lingering paranoid schizophrenia, from which she never recovered. From age 4 to 6, Eva was raised by her schizophrenic mother and her psychopathic father. Then her mother was burned to death in a fire. After that the child was under the temporary care of foster parents and, until age 9, stayed with her psychopathic father alone. The father then married a healthy woman, who as her stepmother took over Eva's care. Shortly after that, the father developed his paranoid psychosis. Eva was fully 17 years old before her father was hospitalized, where he remained for a number of years. During this period, the second marriage ended in divorce.

From age 14 on, Eva worked as a household servant. She was married and became a good homemaker, remaining completely healthy. At the end of the study she was 38 years old. One of her children is an epileptic and suffers from psychomotor attacks.

Summary: The daughter of a schizophrenic couple was exposed to both sick parents until she was 6 years old and then, except for one interruption, to her schizophrenic father alone until she was 14. From age 9, however, she had a stepmother who was normal. The daughter remained completely healthy.

Proband 33, Annemarie S., was prepsychotically nonaberrant and worked unselfishly and happily as a seamstress. At age 30 she married a 28-year-old, overly serious, hyper-conscientious, solid clerical employee and at the outset lived with him in reasonable contentment. But just a few years after the marriage, the husband had to be hospitalized for an acute schizophrenic episode. He was later released to go home, but never fully recovered. He remained abnormally pious and peculiar. After sporadic, mild, phasic regressions, he suffered a severe relapse at age 37 and had to be rehospitalized. Before a year had passed, he died of pneumonia, in the midst of a severe psychosis.

The proband, Annemarie, herself became ill at age 49, when the disease crept on lingeringly, slowly and steadily, almost unnoticed by the people who knew her, at about the time when her husband had his last relapse. She suffered from phonemes, delusions of witchcraft, and other hallucinations that all seemed related to an idea that her children had a "different spirit" within them. She grew frightened and excessively religious. She became extremely strict in disciplining her daughters and often threatened them with committing them to an orphanage, if they did not behave. She wanted to teach them "humility." When their father died, she scolded them for grieving. According to her, the daughters "had no right to quarrel with God," which is the way she interpreted their mourning. At age 64, this proband's chronic paranoid psychosis took a turn for the worse and became a case of extremely severe catatonia. Until her death at age 75, she remained hospitalized in a severe psychotic state.

Her older daughter Magda was born 1 year after the father had his onset of schizophrenia. Until age 7, she lived with her sick father and her mother, who was still healthy then. When her father died, she continued to live with her latently psychotic mother until she was 16. The mother did not become seriously psychotic until Magda was 32.

At first, Magda was employed as a houseworker. For a number of years now, she has been nursing and caring for idiots at an institution. She has remained unmarried. Her personality is rather peculiar, almost schizoid,

but not to the degree or of the type that would classify her as psychopathic. At the conclusion of the study she was 54 years old.

The younger daughter, Madeleine, was born 3 years after the onset of the father's illness. Until age 4, she lived mostly with her sick father and her mother, who was then still healthy. After the death of her father, she remained with her latently psychotic mother, not as Magda had, who left home when she was 16, but until she was 30 years old. Madeleine remained wholly dependent on her mother and suffered a retarded personality development because of it. She learned no trade, and although she is industrious and intelligent, she constantly feels tired and weak. At age 24 she was treated in a private psychiatric hospital with a diagnosis of "neurasthenia." From her 40s on (she was 52 at the end of the study) she has been under constant medical outpatient treatment for insomnia, "nervous heart ailments," bothersome sexual "pressures," attacks of depression, and periodic compulsive symptoms. In her case there is no indication whatever of a psychosis.

Summary: Both daughters were exposed to their schizophrenic father during their early childhood years, while the mother was still healthy. Thereafter they stayed with their latently schizophrenic mother. The older daughter left the unhealthy maternal environment at age 16 and became an unselfish, diligent nurse, although retaining schizoid tendencies. The younger one remained with her mother and fully dependent on her well into middle age. She developed as a severe neurotic in the psychasthenic-depressive-anancastic sense, but not psychotic.

What do these three family histories have to teach us? They cannot be evaluated statistically. It could actually be a coincidence that no one of my 5 probands' children from 2 schizophrenic parents turned schizophrenic, even though, according to previous authors, the onset probability ranges somewhere around 50 percent.

But I was impressed by the fact that even long-term close association with two schizophrenic parents, and being raised by them under most adverse circumstances, does not necessarily mean that a child needs to become schizophrenic, but may well remain healthy and become a useful human being. This surprised me even more than the observation that 2 of the 5 children of two schizophrenic parents did develop abnormal personalities under these difficult childhood conditions and that a third became schizoid (within the norm).

These findings fit into the concept that a clinician would readily accept, to the effect that adverse childhood conditions resulting from psychoses of the parents jeopardize the personality development of the children—but even under extremely unfavorable conditions, the children may still remain healthy.

Previous investigations showed a vulnerability for schizophrenic onset in the children of two schizophrenic parents ranging between $\frac{1}{3}$ and $\frac{2}{3}$ (Kallmann 1938, Schulz 1940, Elsaesser 1952, and Sjoegren 1959). One might assume that the healthy children of two schizophrenic parents were those who did not have to live—or at least not live long—together with such parents, but from my family histories there is no basis to support that assumption. A normal development can prevail in spite of total neglect, of copious "teaching of irrationality," and of the complete degeneration of the imaginative world of the parents. Nothing in these statements is directed against the true pathogenic significance of all these adverse influences; on the contrary, I am quite convinced of their pathogenic validity. But on the other hand, I cannot assert that these psychopathological influences (individually or combined) would be a decisive cause by themselves.

The Grandchildren of Schizophrenics

At the conclusion of the study, the 208 probands had only 205 grandchildren. Table 6.13 shows their age groupings and their mental disorders. One grandchild is a diagnostically certain, and 1 other a probable schizophrenic. But most of the grandchildren still have not reached the age of greatest susceptibility to schizophrenia, which we again estimate to be between 18 and 40. For this reason the base figure amounts to just 26.5. The onset probability for the grandchildren of my probands amounts to 1:26.5 = 3.8 percent ± 3.7 for diagnostically certain schizophrenia alone, and 2:26.5 ± 7.6 percent ± 5.1 for certain and probable schizophrenia combined. The standard deviations are so great that the figures as such are virtually meaningless. They are of some value, however, for comparing the findings of other authors. They do fall within the extremes of these findings, although close to the upper extremes. These extremes of the earlier authors range between 1.8 percent and 8.1 percent, with a mean average of 3.5 percent ± 0.7, including the probable

Table 6.13. Mental disorders among grandchildren of principal probands, showing whether they were living or dead at the conclusion of the project, their sex, and their age at the time they died or the end of the project

Age	Living or dead	Sex	All grandchildren of the 208 proband	Schizophrenics	Epileptics	Other types of disorders
0–9	Living	m	39			1[5]
	Living	f	40		1[4]	2[6]
	Dead	m	3			1[7]
	Dead	f	2			
	Living	?	4[1]			
10–15	Living	m	26			2[8]
	Living	f	23			3[9]
	Dead	m	1			
	Dead	f	0			
16–18	Living	m	9			1[10]
	Living	f	5			
19–20	Living	m	6			1[11]
	Living	f	2			
21–40	Living	m	19[2]		1	2[12]
	Living	f	26[2]	2[3]		1[13]
Total			205	2	2	14

1. Infants living in foreign countries, data on sex uncertain.

2. The age of one in each sex category had to be estimated.

3. One probable schizophrenia; 1 hybrid schizophrenia.

4. Psychomotor epilepsy, completely recovered for 2 years (since 1962).

5. Imbecile, special-school pupil.

6. One enuretic; 1 retardate.

7. Died at age 2–1/2 of hydrocephalus.

8. Both debilitated.

9. Two retarded; 1 a "bundle of nerves."

10. Difficult child (restless, sensitive, lacking self-confidence, inhibited).

11. Juvenile delinquent, gang burglar.

12. One brooding lone wolf; 1 rash, irresponsible.

13. Grew up in foster homes and institutions; sexually unstable, divorced.

Table 6.14. Onset expectancy in grandchildren of schizophrenics. Comparison of findings by various authors

Probands of:	Diagnostically certain schizophrenias	Certain and probable schizophrenias combined
This study	1: 26.5 = 3.8% ± 3.7	2: 26.5 = 7.6% ± 5.1
Juda (1928), Basel	4: 62 = 6.5% ± 3.1	5: 62 = 8.1% ± 3.5
Juda (1928), Munich	2:113.5 = 1.8% ± 1.3	2:113.5 = 1.8% ± 1.3
Oppler (1932), Silesia	6:244 = 2.5% ± 1.0	6:244 = 2.5% ± 1.0
Kallmann (1938), Berlin	8:293.5 = 2.7% ± 0.9	12:293.5 = 4.2% ± 1.2[1]
Authors combined:	21:739.5 = 2.8% ± 0.6	27:739.5 = 3.6% ± 0.7

1. Farther along in the text, Kallmann (1938) reports 4.3%; from a combination of the data by Zerbin-Rüdin (1963) and that of his own table it is 4.2%.

cases (compilation by Zerbin-Rüdin, 1963). In order to arrive at averages with a somewhat lower standard deviation than before, my figures could be combined with those of the three previous authors (Table 6.14).

One of the 2 schizophrenic grandchildren of one of my probands has a schizophrenic mother. Eleven of the 25 schizophrenic grandchildren of the other authors have either a schizophrenic mother or a schizophrenic father. It would be meaningful to be able to differentiate the onset probability for schizophrenia in the grandchildren of schizophrenics as to whether their fathers or their mothers were schizophrenic or normal. The data from earlier authors are not sufficiently detailed to yield an accurate set of figures for this differentiation. Still, the figures presented do permit the statement that the onset probability for schizophrenia for the grandchildren of schizophrenics, if both the parents of these grandchildren were sound, is not significantly different from that of the population. But for the grandchildren of schizophrenics who had either a schizophrenic father or a schizophrenic mother, it is not much different from the onset probability for schizophrenia of the children of other schizophrenics.

Zerbin-Rüdin (1963) arrived at the same conclusion, based on Kallmann's (1938) data. For Kallmann's (1938) probands' grandchildren with 2 nonschizophrenic parents, the onset probability for schizophrenia amounts to just 0.9 percent, and for the grandchildren with 1 schizophrenic parent, 18.5 percent.

The fact is meaningful when one has the children of schizophrenics under his care.

They are often tortured by the fear that their children, in turn, may become mentally ill. But if they themselves have remained healthy and useful in society, have reached a mature age and the danger that they may become ill has diminished, then the probability of their own children becoming schizophrenic is no greater than that of the general population. What is meant here by a "mature age" is, of course, subjective. In practice I construe it to mean beyond the age of 25. Naturally, this assumption becomes easier for me every year that an inquiring client has passed his 25th birthday. One might also consider that a definite correlation exists between the onset age for schizophrenia among close relatives, although such a correlation has not been specifically established for the relationship of parents to their children (presumably because the factors attending selection have blurred the accuracy of the data). When the father or the mother of a prospective client has become psychotic early in life, and that client is as old as 30, his vulnerability may be estimated to be considerably lower than if the parent had become ill later in life. It is improbable that the offspring of schizophrenics, who have become "mature" in the sense described above, and who have neither a transient mental disturbance, nor a schizoid personality characteristic, nor any other kind of psychopathic symptoms, should still be susceptible to schizophrenia. The danger of becoming schizophrenic amounts to just a small fraction of that 9 percent with which all children of schizophrenics are threatened.

But what about the risk of becoming schizoid? Of the 205 grandchildren of my

208 probands, only 2 can be clearly and un-equivocally designated as "schizoid psycho-paths" (listed under comments 10 and 12 of Table 6.13). Two others have undergone an abnormal personality development, but these cannot really be declared as schizoids (comments 11 and 13 of Table 6.13). Of the 67 grandchildren over age 15, 2 = 3 percent are schizoid psychopaths (confidence interval at 95 percent: 0.4 percent to 10.4 percent).

In contrast to this, Kallmann (1938) found 22.8 percent of the grandchildren of his probands with "schizoidia," his concept of which has already been explained (p. 378). The difference is significant. Where does it come from? I would not attempt to explain it in the main at once, as I did the difference in the figures for "schizoid" between the children of Kallmann's probands and mine. I knew the grandchildren of my probands less intimately than I knew their children. A portion of this difference might be ascribed to the difference in age grouping between the two sets of grand-children. His probands' grandchildren were older than mine (ratio between the over- and under-20-year-olds of the grandchildren of Kallmann's probands was 560:456, and of mine, 45:160). Insofar as the number of schizoid psychopaths increases with age, Kall-mann's figures should approach reality more closely than mine. On the other hand, one begins to feel less certain when an attempt is made to interrelate the "schizoid" in the child with schizophrenia in one of the parents, the later in life the schizophrenia becomes mani-fest. Probably Kallmann's (1938) concepts of "schizoidia" is more inclusive than my cir-cumscription of schizoid eccentricities and schizoid psychopathies. Herein may lie the principal reason for the difference in our findings.

Here is Kallmann's summary of his find-ings on the grandchildren of schizophrenics.

"Without any differentiation, the expect-ancy figures in a collective group of grand-children of schizophrenics are 4.3 percent for schizophrenia and 22.8 percent for schizo-idia."

If we are certain that Kallmann (1938) bases his "schizoidia" on heredity and con-ceives it as being closely related to schizophre-nia, his statement means that at least $\frac{1}{4}$ of the grandchildren of his schizophrenics will clear-ly bear the clinical earmarks of their psy-chopathic heritage. Since mental disorders other than schizophrenia or schizoid disorders will become manifest among grandchildren

of schizophrenics, according to Kallmann, far more than $\frac{1}{4}$ of all the grandchildren of schizo-phrenics who survive the vulnerability period would have to be in some way mentally ill.

These statistics have often been applied in counseling the children of schizophrenics who seek advice about the dangers of their pro-jected marriages and the expectancy and probability of hereditary mental illnesses in their own children.

My own figures contradict Kallmann's. Oppler's (1932) and Juda's (1928) findings do not agree with Kallmann's (1938) either, but with mine. Only 4.8 percent and 4.7 percent of the schizophrenics' grandchildren over age 15 of these authors are "eccentrics," that is, aberrant or abnormal personalities that could possibly fit the description "schizoidia" of Kallmann (1938). It would really serve no purpose to determine that Kallmann's (1938) findings were "incorrect," and Oppler's (1932), Juda's (1928), and mine were "correct." The latter findings, however, must give rise to serious doubts as to whether the depressing predictions indicated by Kall-mann's figures about the future of the grand-children of schizophrenics actually do apply. I certainly feel justified in regarding the future of the grandchildren of schizophrenics with considerably more optimism than that.

For the time being—until the contrary has been proved—the following assumption seems justified. The grandchildren of schizophrenics whose parents have remained completely mentally sound until a mature age are not significantly more vulnerable to schizophrenia or schizoid psychopathy than the entire popu-lation is. The mental health prognosis of a person in respect to schizophrenia and schizo-phrenia-like disorders is influenced clearly and directly by the health of his parents, but not clearly and only indirectly by the health of his grandparents.

The schizophrenic and the probably schizo-phrenic granddaughter among the grand-children of my probands share the same schizophrenic grandmother (Proband 55); that is, they are cousins. One of them has a schizophrenic mother (daughter of Proband 55). This is the only instance within the ex-perience of my 208 probands that 3 successive generations in the same family have been schizophrenic.

But there are other mental disorders among the offspring of Proband 55. Only 1 of her 4 children remained mentally sound through maturity (2 of them died young). One daughter became schizophrenic, 1 sexually unstable and, in her forties, irritable and unhappy. One son also became sexually unstable, showed little responsibility toward his family, suffered excessive fear of cancer, and committed suicide after several acts of embezzlement. In that third generation, 1 granddaughter is healthy; she is the daughter of the proband's healthy son. Among the 6 grandchildren with 1 pathological parent, 2 developed normally; 2 granddaughters became schizophrenic (1 of these is a probable schizophrenic); 1 grandson became a moody, retiring lone wolf, and one was sexually unstable.

Of immediate interest is the type of schizophrenia this proband had, the one who had so many pathological offspring. It was a lingering, late-onset schizophrenia with a paranoid beginning, at age 44, that turned into a chronic psychotic state of moderate severity. In her daughter, schizophrenia set in at age 19 and ran an acute phasic course, with intermittent recoveries each time between peaks. At the conclusion of the study this daughter was acutely ill. In 1 granddaughter a schizophrenia which turned into a mild chronic psychosis, began chronically in her early 20s. The second granddaughter—originally feebleminded—when she was age 32, developed acute schizophrenic episodes, between which a pathological state of moderate severity persisted.

The 4 schizophrenias in this family thus ran their different courses. The matriarch had a type of schizophrenia that Kallmann (1938) would not have listed in his core group as occurring with any special frequency within families.

On the other hand, one may regard this family history—if one were so inclined—as an example of the idea that adverse conditions in childhood promote unfavorable personality developments. The oldest son of this proband, born out of wedlock, was raised in foster families and, just like his daughter, developed splendidly. Two other children of this proband who reached maturity grew up under frightful conditions at home. Before their mother became schizophrenic, she was intellectually handicapped, slovenly about herself and the household, and enjoyed loitering idly about the neighborhood, gossiping. The father had to look after the household; but he became an alcoholic, had frequent fits of temper, often beat his wife, and became a senile dement. The proband even took foster children into this household, but she exploited them, did not feed them adequately, and squandered the payments for their board. When the mother became paranoid, 1 of her own children was 17 years old, the other 15. The son is the schizoid, the daughter the schizophrenic. The last daughter was brought up for the most part by good foster parents, but she became sexually unstable. Of the proband's 7 grandchildren, the 4 who were raised by pathological parents developed pathologically, and the 2 raised by normal parents or foster parents remained normal themselves. The other one, whose mother was sexually unstable, also remained normal.

The rest of the mental illnesses (except for schizophrenias and schizoid developments) are within the bounds of what might be expected from the average population. However, the figures are so small that only great differences would be discernible. Nor is the figure of 6 cases of feeblemindedness among the grandchildren markedly different from what the average population would yield.

Social and Familial Status of the Offspring of Schizophrenics

It proved to be an impossible task to compare the occupations of the probands' children with those of the normal population. These "children" were much too diversified in age for that, and usually too young. Their occupations usually could not be accurately described, either, and they also fluctuated a great deal.

I did achieve some relevant results, however, by two comparisons of jobs and occupations of the probands' children. First, the education and vocational training of each one was compared to his proficiency on the job, and then a comparison between the father and his child was made between the occupation and proficiency in each case. Only those children of probands were considered in the comparisons who had passed their 20th birthdays; of these there were 72 sons and 71 daughters. Here is the comparison of education and vocational training.

	Sons	Daughters	Total
Occupational improvement	32	13	45
Occupational proficiency[15]	30	45	75

15. (Translator's footnote)

"Proficiency" in this context includes the willingness and initiative to accept a job, self-application to it, and reasonably acceptable performance, attendance, and accomplishment in it.

Top-ranked at end of training period	2	5	7
Failure because of onset of schizophrenia	2	3	5
Failure because of feeblemindedness, epilepsy, or congenital syphilis	1	2	3
Failure for other reasons	4	2	6
Determination uncertain	1	1	2

The most arbitrary of these data are the estimates concerned with the occupation of married women who were not gainfully employed outside the home. The proper care for a household with children was entered under "occupational proficiency." Married women were listed under "occupational improvement" when they had worked for and achieved promotions in their occupations before they were married, and then later took on the responsible managment of a household.

One hundred and twenty of the 143 sons and daughters fulfilled the hopes that were expected of them in line with their training, or they surpassed them. To be sure, their activity in occupations occurred at a time when the economy was at a peak, during which improvement on the job was easier than it had been before. Despite that, it registers a monumental accomplishment in job proficiency for these offspring. They are even more deserving of our admiration when we consider how many of them (about one fourth) had some form of character or personality disorder, and how many of them were at a distinct emotional and economic disadvantage through the psychoses of their fathers or mothers, and were, therefore, in constant danger of social ostracism.

In comparison with their parents, the offspring's social and occupational prowess showed

	Offspring of male schizophrenic Ps.	Offspring of female schizophrenic Ps.	Total
Increase	21	64	85
Remained at same level	21	21	42
Decrease	1	9	10
Undetermined	4	2	6

Again it is surprising to note how many children of the probands were able to maintain or even improve on the occupational and social levels of their parents. An improve-

ment of the occupational and social status might have been expected from the children of schizophrenic fathers rather than from the children of schizophrenic mothers. It might be assumed that, because of an oncoming schizophrenia or a prepsychotic psychopathy, the schizophrenic fathers had shown little progress in their occupations, making it comparatively easy for the children to exceed their development in occupational proficiency. But the figures do not correspond to such an assumption. On the contrary, more children from schizophrenic mothers succeeded in social and occupational upward mobility more often than did the children of schizophrenic fathers. It is possible that in such cases, the favorable example of a normal father was responsible, one who remained productive and useful in his occupation, despite the psychosis of his wife and her influence on the family.

The fates of the marriages of our probands' children were also investigated, and are shown in Table 6.15. Of course, in this study it was not possible to become involved in the more subtle psychology and the intimate relationships of a given marriage. Generalities and estimated judgments had to suffice for our statistics. Marriages were rated as successful and happy if they took a normal course or if they were reputedly happy as reported by the partners themselves or by their relatives. They were rated as unsuccessful if they ended in divorce or if there were obviously, perceptibly distressing circumstances; that is, if gross infidelity, acts of violence between the partners, or a lack of familial responsibility on the part of the husband were in evidence or reported spontaneously, candidly and quickly by one or both of the partners.

Of the 143 probands' offspring over 20, 101 were married. Among the 65 probands' offspring over 40, 56 were married. A study of marriages of the probands' married children yielded the data shown in Table 6.15.

The great majority of the married children of probands have proved capable of sustaining a happy and successful marriage relationship. A similar table on the marriages among the general population would very probably look no better.

The marriages of the children of the female schizophrenics were just a little bit better than those of the children of the male schizophrenics. By the same token, the marriages of all the daughters of the probands were just

Table 6.15. Marriages of offspring of principal probands

Rating of marriage	Offspring of male probands	Offspring of female probands	Sons from all probands	Daughters from all probands	All probands' offspring
Happy	26	55	43	38	81
1st marriage divorced; 2nd happy	0	3	1	2	3
Unhappy	2	6	4	4	8
Undetermined	2	7	4	5	9
Total:	30	71	52	49	101

a bit less successful than those of the sons of these probands. But the differences are minimal and statistically quite insignificant. As fascinating as it might be, the insignificance of this difference prohibits our drawing any meaningful psychological conclusions from these figures.

Offspring of Schizophrenics Living Together with Their Schizophrenic Parents

Based on the family histories of the 208 probands, we shall in this section attempt to determine how often, how long, and at what ages the offspring of schizophrenics were living in households together with their schizophrenic parents, and whether any connection is to be found between the frequency of disorders among the probands' children and their maintaining contact with their schizophrenic parents.

The childhood histories of the probands' children are to be compared with the childhood histories of the probands' siblings.

If the findings concerning the probands' families could be generalized, a great deal would be gained toward forming hypotheses on the effects of living conditions in childhood and the influence of such conditions on subsequent schizophrenic illness. In and of themselves, the family histories of our probands are well suited to such studies. But unfortunately, the number of probands' children who had attained maturity at the conclusion of our project is too small to permit general and valid conclusions. Nonetheless, these findings can provide indications, and they can form the basis for the collection of new data.

Of the 184 children of our probands, scarcely half (85) ever lived together with their manifestly schizophrenic parents for any significant length of time before their 20th birthdays. Twelve probands' children died at

a very early age. Eighty-seven probands' children who survived infancy never lived together with their psychotic father or mother before they were 20. Thirty-six of them were over 20 years old when one of their parents suffered a schizophrenic onset. Eleven probands' children born out of wedlock lived in foster homes from the time they were born. Twenty-five of them never lived together with their schizophrenic mother or father, because they were committed to foster care during the psychotic phases of their parent, or because the schizophrenic mother or father had been removed from the home. The sick parent of 15 of the probands' children had recovered from his or her schizophrenia when the children were living with him.

Table 6.16 gives an overview of the situation for the 85 children of probands who had lived together with their schizophrenic parent at some time before their 20th birthdays. It shows during which years of its life the child had lived with such a parent (by different age groups), and which of these children later became schizophrenic or suffered an unfavorable personality development.[16] The 85 probands' children are shown in Table 6.16 under 175 different entries, because many of them lived with their schizophrenic parent during more than one period in their lives. The table indicates whether the children were sons or

16. "Unfavorable personality development" was the general condition assumed to prevail among the proband children depicted in Table 6.10, under the subcategories of "schizoid psychopathy," "alcoholism," "other disorders," and "suicide." What was included under "other disorders" appears in the commentaries under Table 6.10 in abbreviated form. Thus the most diversified unfavorable types of personality development are listed under one single term. An accurate breakdown into subcategories would have been desirable, although rather meaningless, because the figures were so small.

daughters, and whether the mother or the father was the schizophrenic proband.

Table 6.17 shows the total number of years during which the probands' children of various age groups lived together with their schizophrenic parents. Just as in Table 6.16, the figures are differentiated according to the sexes the children and the schizophrenic parent in question.

Is there any connection between living together with a schizophrenic parent and a subsequent onset of schizophrenia?[17] In order to approach an answer to this question, it was first necessary to determine how many children became schizophrenic who had lived in the households of their schizophrenic parents. That number must be compared to the number of schizophrenic children who never lived under such conditions. Among those probands' children who had lived together with their schizophrenic parents, more became schizophrenic than among those who had always lived apart from them. This finding—if the figures were large enough—would support the assumption that living together with a schizophrenic parent enhances a

17. It is tempting to ignore this question as totally irrelevant and as one long ago refuted. According to studies so far, only 5–7 percent of all schizophrenics have schizophrenic parents; therefore, considering the small number of schizophrenics, the living together with schizophrenic parents can at best play a causative role among this minority of children alone. The objection is justified. But despite that, a thorough investigation of the effective role that the living together of children with their schizophrenic parents plays is still founded on good reasoning. Many authors today assume that, except for the 5–7 percent of the parents who were obviously schizophrenic, there is a goodly number of parents of schizophrenics who suffered from a hidden type of schizophrenia. They ascribe a considerable causative function to this hidden schizophrenia for the manifestiation of schizophrenia in their children (Lidz 1958, Singer and Wynne 1963, Alanen 1966, etc.). Their suspicions increase in probability the more definitely a certain symptom predisposing to schizophrenia can be traced to the manifest schizophrenia in the parent. Time and again statements appear in the literature asserting that the living together of children with any schizophrenic relative during their childhood (if not, indeed, the living together with a schizophrenic parent) will favor a predisposition for schizophrenia. This assertion—still lacking any proof—also becomes more or less probable according to whether a stronger or a weaker implication of the living together with schizophrenic parents can be assigned to their predisposition for schizophrenia.

predisposition for schizophrenia. But the figures are not large enough. The differences are a long way from approaching any degree of significance.

Here are the figures on which this statement is based. Of 85 probands' children who have ever lived together with a schizophrenic parent, 7 have become schizophrenic. But of the 87 children of probands who never lived with a schizophrenic parent, only 3 became schizophrenic. The age structure of the two groups is so similar, that a comparison is feasible without age corrections (the 12 probands' children who died very young have been omitted).

Even if, because of this paucity of numbers, I cannot significantly prove that children's living together with their schizophrenic parents enhances a disposition for schizophrenia in them, I do feel that the theories about these relationships are justified. They are today being seriously discussed at the international level. They are being supported mainly by experiences from human contacts within specific families that produced schizophrenics. I could add many examples to these from the early histories of my probands. One indication (again not a statistically significant one) of the schizophrenia-prone implications of the living together of girls with their schizophrenic parents already came to light from studies about the geographic origins of the probands on p. 146.

The question whether the living together in a household with schizophrenic parents increases the probability for onset of schizophrenia in the child will very likely be decided within the next few years by investigations that presently occupy the efforts, among others, of entire teams of researchers. These scientists are determining the frequency of schizophrenia in those children who were taken over by foster parents shortly after their birth, without ever having lived together with their schizophrenic parents (Kety, Rosenthal, Wender, Schulsinger 1968, and Uchtenhagen). Nevertheless, the family histories of our probands show data even today that already provide some basic reference points as to how highly significant living together with schizophrenic parents can be in enhancing a predisposition for schizophrenia. As previously found, of 184 probands' children, each of 85 lived together with a schizophrenic parent for a cumulative total of 518 years. This figure springs to life when it is contrasted against the total number of years these chil-

Table 6.16. Probands' offspring living together with schizophrenic parent, by age groups

Probands' children living with 1 schizophrenic parent	No. of children of male probands	Among these: a: schizophrenic	Among these: b: abnormal personality development	No. of children of female probands	Among these: a: schizophrenic	Among these: b: abnormal personality development	No. of children of all probands	Among these: a: schizophrenic	Among these: b: abnormal personality development
To age 1									
Male	3	1	1	7	0	3	10	1	4
Female	8	0	1	7	1	1	15	1	2
Age 1–3									
Male	2	1	0	9	0	3	11	1	3
Female	9	0	1	7	0	0	16	0	1
Age 3–6									
Male	3	1	0	7	0	2	10	1	2
Female	11	1	1	10	1	0	21	2	1
Age 6–14									
Male	6	0	0	22	1	4	28	1	4
Female	10	2	2	10	1	1	20	3	3
Age 14–20									
Male	4	0	0	20	1	4	24	1	4
Female	8	2	1	12	2	0	20	4	1
Total:	64	8	7	111	7	18	175	15	25

Among all of probands' children, only 85 lived together with one schizophrenic parent before age 20, and this was in 175 phases of life, as shown in the table. In addition to the figure for children who spent 1 phase of their lives living with 1 schizophrenic parent, there are figures on how many of these children later became schizophrenic or underwent a nonpsychotic, abnormal personality development. Significance of this concept is explained in Table 6.10.

dren have lived. All of them combined lived a total of 3,231½ years, from birth to their 20th birthdays, or to the time before their 20th birthdays when they dropped out of the investigation. This figure includes the total number of years those probands' children lived who had never lived together with their schizophrenic parents. Those probands' children who lived at least once with their schizophrenics parents, lived for a cumulative total of 1688 years to their 20th birthdays or until they dropped out of the investigation.

Almost half of the probands' children, therefore, lived in homes with a schizophrenic mother or father—an average of ⅓ of their first two decades of life—and still, the expectancy for schizophrenia onset for all probands' children amounts to no more than 8–10 percent. Even if we should want to make the irrational assumption that the schizophrenias of the probands' children had no sort of hereditary-pathological correlation with those of

their parents, the figures presented here do show that the long-term living together with schizophrenic parents cannot be regarded as a general and decisively causative factor for schizophrenia in the children. The great majority of the children who have lived together with their schizophrenic parents for many years do not necessarily become schizophrenic. But one may assume with confidence that the children of schizophrenics do not become schizophrenic solely because of adverse environmental conditions, but only under the influence of unfavorable tendencies and unfavorable living conditions, in their general, all-embracing context. If one agrees with this statement, then, in the face of these findings on the probands' children, the possibility of seeing a true causative relationship between the children's living together with schizophrenic parents and their susceptibility to schizophrenia is even more greatly reduced. Our findings do permit the statement

Table 6.17. Total years probands' offspring lived together with schizophrenic parent, by sex and various age groups

Probands' children living with 1 schizophrenic parent	No. of years with schizophrenic fathers	*Of these:* No. of children who became schizophrenic	No. of children with abnormal personality development	No. of years with schizophrenic mothers	*Of these:* No. of children who became schizophrenic	No. of children with abnormal personality development	No. of years with schizophrenic fathers or mothers	*Of these:* No. of children who became schizophrenic	No. of children with abnormal personality development
To age 1									
Male	3	1	1	7	0	6	10	1	7
Female	8	0	1	6	1/2	1	14	1/2	2
Age 1–3									
Male	4	2	0	14.5	0	7	18.5	2	7
Female	18	0	2	11.5	0	0	29.5	0	2
Age 3–6									
Male	7	1	0	21	0	5	28	1	5
Female	23.5	3	3	21.5	1	0	45	4	3
Age 6–14									
Male	20	0	0	81.5	8	17	101.5	8	17
Female	53	11	11	47.5	4	3	100.5	15	14
Age 14–20									
Male	20	0	0	75.5	6	14.5	95.5	6	14.5
Female	38	8	6	37.5	7	0	75.5	15	6
Total:	194.5	26	24	323.5	26.5	53.5	518	52.5	77.5

Among all probands' children, only 85 ever lived together with their schizophrenic parents before age 20. The table shows the no. of years probands' children lived together with their schizophrenic parents during the given phase of their lives. In addition, the table shows the no. of years such children lived with schizophrenic parents, who themselves became schizophrenic and those who had abnormal personality developments of a nonpsychotic nature (see Table 6.10 for definition of this concept). Table 6.16 shows the no. of children for each age group and the total no. of years spent with their schizophrenic parent.

that close contact in the home with their schizophrenic parents cannot have any important or decisive causative significance for a later onset of schizophrenia in the children. The figures cited, however, do not exclude the possibility that such living together, in isolated cases, could be contributory to a disposition for schizophrenia, if many other kinds of mental damage or disorder are also present.

Wynne and Singer (1963) and other American authors, employing investigative methods such as Rorschach's and other testing procedures, found certain irrational responses from the parents of schizophrenics, which they considered to be tantamount to schizophrenic thought disturbances. But they discovered that these parents were, in fact, not psychotic or schizophrenic in the common definition of

these terms. I personally speak of schizophrenia only as a manifest psychosis (as I pointed out at the beginning of this book). The findings presented above really say nothing decisive in contradiction to Wynne and others concerning the meaning of "the teaching of irrationality" in the genesis of the schizophrenias.

It has been shown (p. 139) that the schizophrenic probands lived together with one schizophrenic parent, a total of only 77 years out of a total of 4,144 cumulative years of their childhood and youth. The probands became schizophrenic even though not even one fifth of their cumulative years of childhood and youth had been spent with schizophrenic parents. On the other hand, only 8–10 percent of the probands' children became schizophrenic, although almost one-sixth[18] of these years were spent with schizophrenic parents—surely a clear indication of the fact that living together with schizophrenic parents is no decisive cause for the genesis of schizophrenia in the offspring.

We should like to make one more differentiating comparison: The probands' children are a selective group, because they all had schizophrenic parents and, since this is so, all of them had the possibility of living together with schizophrenic parents. We are aware of the expectancy for onset of schizophrenia for them. We should like to compare their expectancy for schizophrenic onset with that of the children who did not come to us for observation as children of schizophrenics and who, for that reason, much more rarely spent time living together with schizophrenic parents. For a comparison, we used data on the siblings of our probands. According to Weinberg's method, we must eliminate from consideration those among them who were our schizophrenic probands. I did not calculate exactly how many years the siblings of our probands lived together with schizophrenic parents, but it is impossible that the proportion of years that siblings of probands lived together with schizophrenic parents during their childhood and youth, as compared to the total number of years of their childhood and youth, should be appreciably greater than the corresponding proportion for the probands themselves. In either case it has to be less than 1:50.

It might be deduced that siblings of probands spent less than one-fiftieth of their childhood and youth with schizophrenic parents, and that 9–10 percent of them became schizophrenic. The probands' children spent a much larger portion of their childhood and youth ($\frac{1}{6}$) with schizophrenic parents, and their onset expectancy is about the same (8–10 percent). The fact that our probands' children spent more time living with schizophrenic parents than their siblings did, does not appreciably raise the onset expectancy for these children. This certainly is a valid figure for refuting the assumption that living together with schizophrenic parents is a decisive cause of schizophrenic onset.

According to the first tentative results of Wynne and Singer (1963), who are presently examining children of schizophrenics who are being raised by foster parents, another extensive concurrence with the conclusions based on my findings may be expected. Living together with schizophrenic parents as a cause for the onset of schizophrenia can only be of subordinate significance.

It has often been assumed, and sometimes even directly asserted, that especially for very young children, being in close association with schizophrenic mothers is dangerous, at least more dangerous than for children somewhat older. To answer this question, Table 6.16 offers the following contribution.

Whenever children of our schizophrenics lived together with manifestly schizophrenic parents, they did so most frequently during the very earliest years of their lives. The older the children became, the more rarely did they spend time with a schizophrenic mother or a schizophrenic father. During the first year of life, 25 children lived together with a schizophrenic parent. This figure drops steadily during the following years to an average of $6\frac{2}{3}$ years at ages 14–20. The reasons for this are numerous. The schizophrenic parents did not become schizophrenic and hospitalized until some time after the birth of their children; the normal partner usually separated from the schizophrenic one and took charge of the children; the children were placed in foster care; older children left home at an early age and sought employment away from home, because they could not bear conditions there, etc. Only to a very small degree are their decreasing ranks influenced by the fact that some children were not quite 20 years old at the conclusion of the study.

The total number of years during which the probands' children of every age lived together with a schizophrenic parent does not decrease from year to year (see Table 6.17). Such a decrease was discovered just now in the number of children who had lived together with a schizophrenic parent. This means that during the later years of childhood, fewer children live for extended periods of time with their schizophrenic parents than they do in the earlier childhood years.

At whatever age the probands' children lived together with their schizophrenic parents, the frequency of subsequent onsets of schizophrenia in these children always re-

18. The value $\frac{1}{6}$ results when the years spent with schizophrenic parents are brought into relationship to the total cumulative years that all proband children have lived. When we mentioned above in this context the value of $\frac{1}{3}$, that ratio involved only those proband children who had lived together with schizophrenic parents, but not all probands' children.

mains about the same—at least, the figures from Table 6.16 reveal nothing different. They show no significant differences in the frequency of schizophrenia for the different groups of probands' children, as they are broken down by age groups during which they lived together with one schizophrenic parent. To be sure, the individual figures are small, and their mean errors enormous. Only if the age at which the child lived together with schizophrenic parents had tremendous significance for the subsequent onset of his schizophrenia could my small numbers reveal this phenomenon. It is worth mentioning, however, that these figures indicate the same basic law that was suggested from the study of the probands themselves, namely, that for the later onset of even the schizophrenia of the probands it is not significant whether the child lives together with schizophrenic parents early in life or later.

Differences between sons and daughters, or between the children of schizophrenic fathers and schizophrenic mothers were not shown in Tables 6.16 and 6.17. The figures are so small, that any such differences, if they were to show any significance at all, would have to be large.

In the search for significant data, I have studied Tables 6.16 and 6.17 from a number of totally different viewpoints. In so doing, I took into consideration the ages at which the children dropped out of observation. Table 6.10 contains only summary information on this point. It was a fruitless effort. I was unable to develop any data that was in any way meaningful. As an example, the years that boys and girls spent together with their schizophrenic parents did not differ with any significance.

Overall Evaluation of the Childhood Conditions in the Offspring of Schizophrenics

Among the conditions relating to raising and caring for the probands' children, those specific ones were selected that could be unequivocally regarded as "normal" and those that could without challenge be rated as "horrible." One large category remained, that could not be entered under either heading without some misgivings. The delimitations of the terms "normal" and "horrible" have already been defined in detail on p. 117.

During the first decades of these children's lives, the circumstances of their care at home changed rather frequently. The 172 probands'

children (omitting those who had died early) experienced a total of 270 individually defined child-care conditions. For only 88 of these probands' children did the care conditions remain the same throughout their childhood and their youth. Of course, conditions did change for these children in a number of details during the course of 20 years, but the general classification of "normal," "horrible," or "neither one nor the other" remained the same for them, in spite of some alterations in the external aspects of the general condition.

Tables 6.18 and 6.19 give an overview of the 90 instances of care conditions for the 63 children of the male probands (Table 6.18), and the 180 instances of care conditions for the 109 children of the female probands (Table 6.19). Relatively more of the children of male probands lived their entire childhoods together with both parents than did the children of female probands. It is easier for the normal, healthy wife to care for a sick husband and for the children and to keep the family together than is the case for the husband. As expected, more children of female probands lived together with just their fathers during their youth than did the children of male probands. A comparison of Tables 6.18 and 6.19 shows further that, on the average, the children of male probands grow up under more favorable circumstances than the children of female probands. A normal, healthy mother with a sick husband is in better position to shape the milieu and the living conditions of her children than is a healthy father whose wife is sick.

Of the 172 probands' children, only 49, that is, a little over one-fourth of them, were fortunate enough to spend their entire childhood and youth under the care of both their parents, under reasonably normal conditions. Over $\frac{3}{4}$ of these probands' children grew up lacking one parent either all or part of their youth ("premature parent loss" and "broken homes" have been explained on pp. 70–71. Thirty-two, or almost $\frac{1}{5}$ of the probands' offspring suffered under the most gruesome experiences, either the entire first 20 years of their lives or during a substantial portion of it. As already indicated, the childhood conditions for the probands' children are comparable to those experienced by the probands themselves and their siblings. For the siblings of probands it must be assumed that, on the average—and considered as a group—their childhood was similar to that of their children. That portion of the probands' children who

Table 6.18. Childhood quality of 63 offspring of male probands (3 who died early are omitted).

Childhood condition	Always with both parents		Years with both parents		If not always with both parents:									Total
					With mother only		With father only		In foster homes or families		Never with either parent (illegitimate or in care since childhood)			
	Sons	Daughters	Sons	Daughters	Sons	Daughters	Sons	Daughters	Sons	Daughters	Sons	Daughters	
"Normal"	10[1]	19[2]	2	2	2	6[6]	0	0	7[9]	3[10]	5[11]	5	61
Neither "normal" nor "horrible"	3[3]	3[4]	0	2	0	0	0	0	0	0	0	2[12]	10
"Horrible"	0	0	5	5	3[5]	1	2[7]	2[8]	0	1	0	0	19
Total:	13	22	7	9	5	7	2	2	7	4	5	7	90

1. Of these, 4 children are only 11, 9, 12, and 11 years old.

2. Of these, 6 children are only 6, 16, 9, 15, 12, and 11 years old.

3. Of these, 2 children are only 16 and 13 years old.

4. Of these, 1 child is 15, and 1 died at age 8.

5. Of these, 1 child lives with mother and stepfather.

6. Of these, 1 child lives with mother and grandparents.

7. Both children live with father and stepmother.

8. At times with stepmother too; 1 of them never with mother.

9. Of these, 2 are only 16 and 13 years old.

10. Of these, 1 child is only 15 years old.

11. 1 child mostly in homes and with foster parents; from age 14, with mother only.

12. Of these, 1 child with mother and stepfather.

spent their entire childhood under normal conditions together with both parents, is just as small as the corresponding portion for their siblings and for the probands themselves. Truly gruesome conditions throughout their entire childhood or a portion of it prevailed somewhat more frequently among the probands and their siblings than among their children (about one-third to one-fifth, by comparison). On the other hand, the children of probands changed parental care more often than their parents had done.

It can be determined that, regarded as a whole (according to whether they experienced early parent loss or not, and according to the overall characterization of "normal" or "horrible"), the childhoods of our probands' children were spent, on the average, under similarly hazardous conditions as those of their siblings. However, the probands' children much more often lived together with their schizophrenic parents than did the probands' siblings. The expectancy of schizophrenia in the probands children and the probands siblings, however, is about the same.

If we consider seriously the assumption that the overall childhood conditions (in the sense described above) as well as the living together

with schizophrenic parents in childhood might increase a predisposition for a later onset of schizophrenia, then we could draw a conclusion from the above data about the relative significance of these two psychotraumatic childhood conditions, namely, that in all probability, the overall living conditions during childhood are more influential for the subsequent onset of schizophrenia than the mere living together with manifestly schizophrenic parents. If this were not true, it would be difficult to explain how children with similar overall childhood conditions become schizophrenic at the same rate, although the frequency of their living together with schizophrenic parents is quite different.

In this rather carefully worded formulation I consider the conclusion as valid. But it must not be expressed in terms any more definite than these. In addition to the explanation given, others are possible as to why those children of probands who are exposed to their schizophrenic parents for longer periods do not more often become schizophrenic than their siblings, who are less frequently exposed to such parents. It would be conceivable that the inherited predisposition of the probands' siblings is less favorable than that of their

Table 6.19. Childhood quality of 109 offspring of female probands (9 who died early are omitted)

| | Always with both parents | | Years with both | | If not always with both parents : | | | | | | | | | |
| | | | | | With mother only | | With father only | | In foster homes or with families | | Never with either parent (illegitimate or in care since childhood) | | |
Childhood conditions	Sons	Daughters	Sons	Daughters	Sons	Daughters	Sons	Daughters	Sons	Daughters	Sons	Daughters	Total
"Normal"	11[1]	9[2]	3	7	3[5]	3	8[8]	2[10]	11	11	4	1	69
Neither "normal" nor "horrible"	8[3]	7	19	10	8	4	10[9]	3[11]	3	3	2	3	80
"Horrible"	1	2[4]	10	9	4[6]	5[7]	0	0	0	0	0	0	31
Total:	20	18	32	26	15	12	14	5	14	14	6	4	180

1. Of these, 1 died at age 11; of these, 2 children only 11 and 19 years old.

2. Of these, 1 died at age 3; of these, 2 children only 19 and 14 years old.

3. Of these, 1 child only a few months old.

4. Of these, 1 child only 13 years old.

5. Of these, 1 intermittently with stepfather; 2 never with father.

6. Of these, 2 children intermittently with stepfather.

7. Of these, 2 children intermittently with stepfather.

8. Of these, 2 children together with stepfather.

9. Of these, 7 children together with stepmother; 1 never with mother (suicide at age 18).

10. Together with stepmother.

11. Of these, 2 children together with stepmother.

children. Such a hereditary predisposition in the siblings of probands might be more important than the advantage they have by the infrequency of their living together with their schizophrenic parents, but that is just a possibility derived purely by speculation.

The comparison further assumes that the overall evaluation of childhood conditions of the probands themselves and of their siblings would have to yield the same results. This approaches the truth—but, to be sure, it only approaches it. According to Weinberg's method, the onset expectancy for schizophrenia among the probands' siblings—excluding the probands themselves—has already been indicated. I do not know of any serious objections to this procedure, and less important misgivings are admissible, but they would not markedly influence these conclusions.

In order not to overburden this book with figures, no adjustment has been made in the comparison for the fact that the childhood and youth of the probands' siblings extend in the tables only through their 18th birthday, while those of their offspring extend through their 20th. The fact that all the probands had passed their 18th birthdays, but all their off-

spring had not, was not taken into consideration, either. The corrections necessary to equalize these differences in the comparison studies, however, would change nothing in the summary conclusions that were drawn.

It would be interesting to check whether schizophrenia in the probands' offspring who were raised under various childhood conditions occurs at different frequencies. It might be possible to assume that the children raised by both parents under normal conditions were less frequently beset by schizophrenia than those raised under atrocious conditions. However, in such a rendition as this, the figures would be about as minimally insignificant as their median error was enormous. For a meaningful study of this question my probands are not suitable.

Nor are the figures from my family studies sufficiently large for discovering the obvious differences in relation to the summarily judged childhood conditions of the sons and daughters of my probands.

A Comparison: The Offspring of Psychotic Seniles

As previously shown, there were more cases of senile psychosis among the probands' parents and siblings than one would expect to find in the entire population. I have cited other authors who had discovered similar facts. Neither among the data of these authors, nor in my own, are these differences significant.[19] But they do stimulate a scientific interest as to whether schizophrenias occur more frequently among the relatives of senile psychotics than they do among the general population.

Uchtenhagen shows in his study, contained in the German edition of this book, that the Rorschach results from many relatives of senile psychotics are similar to those of schizophrenics. This finding also incites investigative interest in the frequency of schizophrenias among the relatives of seniles.

Whoever collects statistics and believes he is finding typical data in them, is plagued by doubts as to whether he has not, indeed, been caught in the trap of some malicious circumstance or of an unconscious selection bias. He is not pacified by the statistical calculation and the standard deviation, if he has any sensitivity as to the reckoning of probability. All too often such calculations are based on uncertain postulates. Plagued by such doubts myself, I felt the constant need to add comparative data to the statistical findings and, among other things, to compare such findings on the offspring of schizophrenics with those of the offspring of other types of mental patients.

Besides, there are few studies about the offspring of senile dements. Usually they arrive at contradictory conclusions about the frequency of schizophrenia among such offspring. Meggendorfer (1925, 1926),[20] as well as Constantinidis et al. (1962),[21] find more schizophrenics among the offspring of senile psychotics than among the population. But these differences do not reach statistical significance. On the other hand, Larsson et al. (1963) emphasize that the offspring of seniles in Stockholm become schizophrenic at no higher rate than those of the population. Meggendorfer (1925, 1926) was surprised by the large number among the offspring of seniles, whose personalities could be characterized as schizoid. But he suspects that the schizoid nature of these offspring does not quite correspond to the characteristic nature of schizoids among the relatives of schizophrenics.

Under these circumstances, I welcomed the opportunity for an investigation of the offspring of seniles, that had materialized at our clinic in 1969. The need existed for questioning the grown offspring of our senile clinical patients, as to whether they were satisfied with the care and treatment of their senile parents, or whether they had any kind of criticism or suggestion to offer. Within the framework of this line of questioning, it was a simple and natural process to establish contact with the grown children of our seniles, to become more closely acquainted with many of them, and to get reliable information from them about themselves and their siblings. The work was made all the easier, since most of these sources of information were indeed satisfied with the care of their fathers or mothers. The investigations were carried out by Dr. R. Nagel, a woman coworker at our clinic.

The study included 169 offspring of the 75 hospitalized patients with senile psychoses. These senile psychoses included those with sclerosis of the cerebral bloodvessels, senile dementia, and Alzheimer's disease (presenile psychosis). Without exception, ours were cases of severe psychoses with a serious need for hospitalization and care, and usually with accompanying total disorientation. In all these psychoses, the amnestic psychosyndrome was prominent (at least for as long as conversation with the patient could be sustained). Frequently conversation became complicated by moodiness or manic delusions. The precise

---

19. Disregarding the lack of significance of these calculations, the data on the frequency of senile psychoses among the parents and siblings of schizophrenics is unreliable for yet another reason. As especially Larsson et al. (1963) have proved, the frequency of senile psychoses between the ages of 60 and 90 increases rapidly from year to year. The age structure of seniles over 60 should therefore be taken into consideration. I could not concern myself with it, because the figures were much too small, and because in the population census concerning seniles, which was used for the comparison, these age groups were not accurately broken down either.

20. Meggendorfer (1925, 1926) reports 2.1 percent schizophrenics among the offspring of his senile probands. The figure would be even higher if he had made the corrections according to the age structure of his probands.

21. For the offspring of patients with senile, "mixed," and arteriosclerotic dementia, these authors calculated a frequency of schizophrenia at 4.4 percent to 4.8 percent, of 4 percent and of 2.9 percent, while they calculated the schizophrenia frequency for the entire population of Geneva at 2.4 percent.

Table 6.20. Offspring of senile psychotics, arranged according to whether they were dead or alive at the conclusion of the study, their sex, their age at the time of death or the end of the investigation, and the frequencies of mental disorders among them

				Incidence among all children of:				
Age	Living or dead	Sex	All children	Schizophrenia	Probable Schizophrenia	Depression	Alcoholism	Suicide
0–18	Dead	m	5					
		f	2					
		?	1¹					
19–39	Living	m	20					
		f	15					
	Dead	m	5					
		f	2					1
40–59	Living	m	47	1	1		1	
		f	40					
	Dead	m	4					
		f	5	1				2²
60 +	Living	m	11	1				
		f	11		1	1		
	Dead	m	0					
		f	1					
Total:			169	3	2	1	1	3

1. Sex not recorded; died very early.

2. One of these had already been registred as a schizophrenic patient; she later committed suicide.

data on the observations and findings for all these seniles are preserved in the records. Dr. Nagel personally saw over three-fourths of these offspring, and carried on a conversation with them for at least a half hour.

As to the choice of proband in the summer of 1969, there were 58 senile psychotics at our psychiatric university clinic in Burghölzli, who had children (including some who had already died). The only children of 2 patients could not be contacted (1 son was missing; 1 daughter refused our every effort to establish contact). One hundred and twenty-three offspring of the 56 patients were thoroughly studied (26 male seniles had 56, and 30 female seniles had 67 children). In order to increase the sampling, the studies were extended to two private psychiatric clinics in the suburbs of Zürich (Hohenegg-Meilen and Kilchberg).²² According to reports from the administrations of these two sanatoria, there were 24 senile psychotic patients during the

22. I wish to express my thanks to the chief physicians of these two clinics, Doctors S. Rotach and U. M. Strub, for their permission to conduct these studies on their patients.

summer of 1969 who had children. The offspring of 5 patients could not be contacted. Nineteen seniles had 46 children (3 male seniles had 8, and 16 females, 38). All senile probands are either married or widowed, and there were no illegitimate children of any of the senile probands who were hospitalized at the time of the investigation. All proband marriages were "completed marriages" (as defined on p. 359), that is, no more children can be expected from any of them. The number of children per marriage is 2.3. It is not significantly different from the number of children from the completed marriages in the population.

Table 6.20 shows an overview of the 169 offspring of the 75 senile probands. It shows their distribution according to sex and age, and whether they were dead or alive at the time of the investigation. It follows the pattern of Table 6.10 on the children of schizophrenic probands. It shows the mental disorders of the offspring.

Among the offspring of the senile probands, there were 3 certain and 2 probable cases of schizophrenia. If only the diagnostically certain cases are considered, and the age of vulnerability ranges between 18 and 40, by employing the abbreviated Weinberg method, we arrive at an expectancy figure for schizophrenic onset of 2.1 percent $\pm$ 1.2. By including also the probable cases, the figure is 3.6 percent $\pm$ 1.6.

The frequency of schizophrenia among the offspring of senile psychotics in this test group is considerably lower than among the offspring of schizophrenics, but higher than among the general population. This latter difference, however, is by no means significant. For that reason it could be disregarded, except for the initially mentioned data that support it: For, among the siblings and parents of the schizophrenic probands, there were more senile psychotics than among the population (the difference is not significant). In addition, there are the previously mentioned supporting data of Meggendorfer (1925, 1926), of Constantinidis et al. (1962), and of Schulz (1933). All these data taken together constitute an indication that schizophrenia and senile psychoses occur more frequently among close relatives than could be expected by mere coincidence. The causes of this loose correlation are today still not identifiable in any way.

The assumption of an internal relationship between the schizophrenias and senile psychoses disturbs and offends our nosological thinking. According to currently accepted theories, these two illnesses have nothing in common in their basic natures. Concern with the question: "Have hidden schizophrenias been included in the study that are misdiagnosed cases of senile dementia?" is unnecessary. The question already came up during the studies of the large number of seniles among the parents of the schizophrenic probands. It could not be properly answered for them, because the available clinical data about most of them were insufficient. But this was the very reason for my intensified interest in the supplemental investigation of the offspring of seniles that is being reported in this chapter. We know these seniles from our own precise clinical studies and observations. Is it possible, then, that these were cases of schizophrenia, misdiagnosed as senile psychoses— because these patients were not hospitalized until they had reached an advanced age? Such a suspicion must be rejected as unfounded, on the basis of the symptomatology. All these patients had records of an indisputable psychoorganic syndrome with its amnestic symptoms, and in severe stages at that.

Nor does the time of onset of their illness provide any evidence against the diagnosis of senile psychosis. In all 5 senile parents with schizophrenic or probably schizophrenic offspring, the psychosis did not set in until an advanced age had been reached (at ages 70, 71, 78, 81, and 90 years). If, on the other hand, we look closely at the prepsychotic personality, we note that, in the case of the senile psychotic father of a probably schizophrenic daughter, there is a strong indication of a bland, chronic schizophrenia. He was an impractical, moody sort of a lone wolf, out of touch with reality and given to hallucinations, similar to his daughter's, who was a suspected schizophrenic. Based on the fact that a single 1 of the 5 senile patients with schizophrenic or probable schizophrenic offspring may possibly have been schizophrenic, the question of the nature of the relationship between schizophrenic and senile psychoses, of course, cannot be resolved.

It would be quite revolutionary, however, to pose an entirely different question as a basis for this working hypothesis: "Could the same psychopathological processes that produce schizophrenias in youth and in old age, have senile psychoses as their result? And could, therefore, a symptomatologically typical senile psychosis, by its nature, be a type of schizophrenia brought on by the aging process?" The question is a daring one and cannot as yet be answered today, but it is not pure nonsense either, considering the rather loose correlation between senile psychopathology and the senile cerebral changes. It is conceivable (but in no way intended to be indicated as probable) that the same internal processes that lie at the basis of schizophrenia in young people, lead to a cerebral decompensation in the aged, which would camouflage the customary schizophrenic symptomatology. These are, however, only speculations. Today we still do not know why there is probably more schizophrenia in the families of seniles, and why there are probably more seniles in the families of schizophrenics, than is the case for corresponding conditions in the general population.

In addition to those already mentioned, there are a goodly number of psychodynamic and pathogenetic theories that can be discussed in connection with these types of problems. It is possible that the emotional stress on the mother or the father of a schizophrenic child promotes a disposition for senile psychosis. The reverse seems less probable, yet, there are a few family histories that could be interpreted as indicating that the stress on a mature individual caused by the developing senile psychosis in his father or mother contributed to the onset of his own schizophrenic illness. For instance, the personality of a daughter degenerated markedly, as did her interest in the care of her sick mother, when she felt driven to despair by her mother's progressive senile decline, went into total isolation, and became schizophrenic. It is easy to imagine, from the standpoint of pathogenesis, that there is a weak predisposition for mental illnesses of all types that would lead to schizophrenic as well as to senile disorders. In the olden days it was not uncommon to give voice to such generalities of hereditary predisposition for all kinds of mental disturbances. But since it has been proved that heredity cannot possibly play an important role in that process, and that there are certain definite hereditary predispositions for certain specific mental illnesses, this old assumption has ceased to be discussed. But it has never been completely refuted. It is conceivable, of course, that the selective process has biased our findings. If the readiness for hospitalization in families with schizophrenias and senile psychoses were greater than in other families, the disputed correlation would have to show up numerically, without the existence of any internal relationship between these two illnesses. In part, these probabilities were already being discussed by Meggendorfer in 1926.

The 5 (certain and probable) schizophrenias of the offspring of seniles, in no sense aroused the suspicion that these might be cases of disguised senile psychoses. One of the 3 diagnostically certain schizophrenias progressed to a severe, long-term chronic "end state." In the second schizophrenia, a female,[23] the disease set in at age 18, accompanied by the feeling of a complete internal collapse and the "conviction" of something demonic within her, that would henceforth determine the course of her life. She was treated for years as a neurotic with symptoms of depersonalization, communication disorders, and constant dysphoria. From approximately the age of 26 on, her paranoid-schizophrenic psychosis became manifest; for instance, the patient believed, simultaneously, that she was Christ and Satan. The subsequent long-term

23. Her father was also schizophrenic. Her mother was the proband with senile dementia.

state remained constant at a stage of moderate severity, as that term has been previously defined. The third schizophrenic offspring, son of a senile mother was someone I treated and counseled myself, for a period of $4\frac{1}{2}$ years up to the present. He developed a chronic mania of persecution and jealousy which was, at times, similar to Kraepelin's definition of a paranoia. However, he continued to regress into completely nonsensical thought-relations that approached total mania. He completely isolated himself and left his family in dire straits. After a long-term illness, he was hospitalized at age 54 at our clinic, where one of the most surprising improvements took place that I have ever witnessed. The patient got over his mania, resumed his employment —successfully—and reestablished his shattered family relationships. He was grateful for the clinical treatment he had received and has maintained an active contact with me until today, 5 years after his first hospitalization, he even assists in counseling in a number of situations. To be sure, since his illness, he has been an overly sensitive, mistrusting, and insecure individual.

One of the 2 probable schizophrenics among the offspring of our seniles became well known to us in the course of two treatments at our clinic. This lonely, withdrawn man became acutely ill at age 35, sustaining a manic-depressive psychosis with persecution and guilt-of-sin notions. At the time, the assumed diagnosis for his case was paranoid schizophrenia. After several months he improved appreciably, but remained the same retiring, excessively parent-bound man he had already been earlier. Nine years later, at age 44, he was again hospitalized at our clinic. This time it was in the main a case of simple depression, and the symptoms of a paranoid schizophrenia remained very much in the background. He recovered almost completely from this depression, too. One daughter, a suspected schizophrenic, emigrated overseas. She tried repeatedly to study psychology (from her youth until age 63) but without success. She had broken off all contact with her relatives many years before, refusing even to open their letters. While abroad she became mentally ill, but no definite diagnosis was obtainable.

Other mental disorders among the offspring of senile psychotics were listed only sporadically. There was 1 case of involutional depression, 1 of alcoholism, and 2 suicides for unknown reasons. Also, 1 of the schizophrenics committed suicide.

There were no cases of epilepsy, feeblemindedness, or discernible personality aberrations. The children of the seniles we examined were on the whole sounder and healthier than the children of schizophrenics. Except for the true schizophrenics, they were even healthier than those representatives of the general population I had examined; however, this difference was by no means significant. The offspring of our senile-psychotic probands were not old enough at the time of the study for any of them to be classified as senile psychotics.

Childhood Suffering

In the quest for a mendelian law of heredity among schizophrenics, and for the purpose of determining the "hereditary prognosis," the offspring of schizophrenics were studied systematically as early as the 20s, 30s, and 40s of this century. But at that time the focus was limited principally to determining how many of these children would also become schizophrenic or schizoid-psychotic. The authors spent their main efforts on the state of well-being of the already grown "children" of schizophrenics. Scarcely any attention whatever was paid to the sufferings they had had to bear during their childhoods. And yet, there would have been sufficient reasons in the evidence to justify such attention.

For decades people had been writing about how many schizophrenics were living at home, unimproved, both before and after discharge from psychiatric hospitals, how often they still suffered attacks, caused confusion and noisy, railing scenes, and how often they failed in communication attempts and became apathetic. It had also been known for a long time how often they neglected their family responsibilities. And again, it had long been common knowledge how many schizophrenics were alienated from reality and eccentric, both before and after becoming ill. Many of these were then classified as "psychopathic," fanatic, autistic, cruel, emotionless, querulous, or argumentative.

How was it possible for such a long time to bypass thinking about the effects on the children of all these disorders? The reasons, of course, are manifold. Child psychiatry was late in developing. The clinical psychiatrist in the "institution" of bygone days was not permitted to have the children of his patients even come into his clinic. Stone walls as well as social barriers stood between him and them.

The patients themselves were usually of the opinion that the raising of their children was quite in order, and they tended to form negative thought-hallucinations about the physical and moral mishandlings their children must be enduring. The less capable the natural or foster parents are in dealing with the problems of children, the less they are usually inclined to accept advice on, or to admit to, the existence of any problems. However, the principal reason seems to lie in the children themselves. All too often they remain silent about their sufferings and can seldom be moved to discuss them. Even after they have grown up, they much prefer to keep to themselves everything terrible and disagreeable that happened to them. Somehow they consider it a disgrace to have suffered so much misery at the hands of their own parents. It actually happens that the misery of a neglected child, caused by the psychosis of his father or mother, is the cause of ridicule and disgrace, not only at the hands of his schoolmates, but also of people who ought to know better, for instance, his teachers. Moving and pathetic descriptions of what sufferings schizophrenics had to endure in their childhood under their pathological parents are then revealed in psychoanalytic or phenomenologically oriented interviews (see, for example, Sechehaye, 1947).

Not until much later were the childhood conditions of the offspring of schizophrenics examined more thoroughly and more frequently, and not only in retrospect, that is, looking back at the childhoods of adults, but by actually examining the childhoods of children themselves.[24] Corboz (1959) published an overview paper on this subject at our psychiatric polyclinic for children and youth, and Wilhelm (1964) described 4 different childhood histories in great detail. Other important papers were prepared by Zuring (1947/1948), Cowie (1961), Sobel (1961), Brock (1962), Ladewig (1965), Suworina (1965), Biermann (1966), Rutter (1966), and Yarden and Nevo (1968). Although all these studies by 12 authors come from six different countries on two continents, their findings are in essence the same.

Many children of schizophrenics have to

24. Some sporadic papers appeared a little earlier, for instance, those by Canavan and Clark (1923, 1936), Preston and Antin (1933), and others. In part they anticipate newer data. Insofar as they disagree, all sorts of objections are possible.

endure appalling childhoods. Not only do they suffer often, and quite directly, under their sick parents, but often they are entrusted to foster parents who are not by any standards suited to that role. Sometimes a healthy father or mother has little understanding of how to bring up a child unassisted. The children of schizophrenics quite ordinarily exhibit pathological behavior or development during their childhoods that only seldom attain the magnitude of psychoses. In small children especially, fear is at the very forefront of their existence. At times bodily manifestations of fear dominate the picture. As the child grows older, increasing communication disorders are added to the fear. The children grow shy, inept at human contacts, retiring, sensitive, and either provocative and aggressive or apathetic. Their mood is depressed and unhappy. Often the children withdraw into fantasies and daydreaming. A number of authors combine such personality changes into a general category they call "schizoid." Children may also take on the hallucinatory ideas of their parents, establishing a specific type of folie-à-deux.

Of course, not nearly all offspring of schizophrenics experience an adverse childhood development. There are vast numbers of examples that show how even schizophrenic parents can be good parents. Some children learn to distinguish what it is about their father or mother that is peculiar or sick, and what is good and lovable about him or her. Sometimes gifted, warm-hearted spouses are able to nullify all the evil influences of the other partner who is schizophrenic. In one isolated report the statement is made that no damaging influences on the children of schizophrenics were observed, but that particular paper (by Sussex et al., 1963) covers only 16 children.

The demand for improved care of the children of schizophrenics is a unanimous one. So far, none of the existing care facilities in a number of countries has been capable of preventing or alleviating the suffering of such children.

Most authors regard the behavior disorders they describe mainly as reactions by the children to the abnormal behavior of the mother or to their whole unfavorable environment, even when they do not expressly point them out. Neurotic developments are even more rarely mentioned. Cowie (1961) even found that indications of neuroses in the psychodiagnostic tests of the children of schizophrenics are rare. In recent years, in Denmark, Mednick and Schulsinger (1968) began a series of extensive investigations. They want, over a period of 20 years, to compare the development of 207 children of schizophrenics with that of 104 children from the general population. At the latest publication by these authors, the children averaged 15 years of age. The children with schizophrenic parents had greater difficulty in making friends, they lived a more lonely existence, were more irritable, and revealed more uncertain thought-processes than the other children. The girls with schizophrenic parents more often had a constrained, depressive, and moody personality than did the children of normal parents. The authors classify many of the disorders of the children of schizophrenics as "schizoid." In an association test, these children more often revealed dissociated ideas, and in the psychogalvanic test, their reactions showed up as variable.

It was repeatedly observed how quickly the behavioral disorders of the children of schizophrenics began to diappear when good care was substituted for poor care. But the course of the disorders found in children has hardly ever been studied and followed through to the children's maturity. The abovementioned investigations by Mednick and Schulsinger (1968), however, do promise some decisive conclusions for the future.

The family histories of my 208 probands contain a wealth of material about the development of their children, and about the conditions under which these developments took place. In most respects these data agree with those mentioned by other authors. The fact becomes reinforced repeatedly that these data have a rather generally valid significane. Studies of my probands' children facilitate the pursuit of their development farther into maturity than is true for previous studies. The childhood conditions of the probands' children can also be compared with their later development. In many cases something else can be observed, too, that has hitherto been virtually ignored; that is the fact that childhood suffering may have its aftereffects, even when no clinical symptoms of it are evident.

To begin with, here are some examples.

The husband of the schizophrenic daughter of Proband 20 reports on conditions in their household as follows: There are days when nothing is right. For years now, no Sunday has been just right. My wife keeps nagging all the time at table when someone's arm or fork is in an improper position. Then she shoves her 16-year-old son with her elbow, or punches him, until he gets up and leaves the table. If she hits him, he hits back. He has had to repeat one class in secondary school because he could not concentrate on his school work. The 13-year-old daughter is good in secondary school, but she is a regular "bundle of nerves." He (husband of the schizophrenic) sometimes loses control at home when his wife continues to nag without end. Sundays he had to start the fires himself and prepare breakfast; and this, from his wife's viewpoint, was quite as it should be. In spite of that, she did not let up until there was a serious argument. If, for example, a child spilled the milk, her nastiness boiled up to the very point of explosion. She would then slam doors and cry out, "Today you can do your own cooking."—In this family, the healthy father (reporter of the above-cited incidents) could not succeed in neutralizing the abnormal behavior of his wife. His sister-in-law states about him, that he becomes "disgracefully" angry with the children if they don't obey him exactly according to his pedantic demands. Then he rants as if he were "crazy," leaves the house, and starts to talk about suicide. When he's like that, he doesn't know what he's doing. The children say, "Mommy fusses a lot, but then she's real good again, but Daddy—he starts it all over again."

From the report of the illegitimate daughter of Proband 15 (she was 40 years old when she made the report): "My mother came from a poor, but a good family of 8. She was 20 when I was born. Before or after that she never was with any other man than my father" (who had not married her). "And, when I was 16, she died of grief and disappointment" (more accurately, of cerebral meningitis). "My father never stopped nagging her the whole time." After the death of her mother, she was raised by her grandmother, and later by an aunt. "My 'beloved' father didn't even stop pulling his tricks on my relatives after that. He adopted me when I was 8, and I was given his name. The reason was to threaten my grandparents, implying that he had a right to take me to live with him." With the stipulation that he be relieved from paying for her support, he left the daughter with her grandparents. He often bragged that he had accomplished what he wanted to by this maneuver. The daughter continues: "I can only remember with horror how frightened I was when he came to visit, about once a year." This

daughter developed splendidly. She was at the head of her class in school. Although she was unable to learn a trade because of her poverty, she worked up successfully in the innkeeping business. At 20 she married. From modest beginnings this couple, working together, built up a rather handsome middle-sized industrial business. The marriage was a happy one; it produced two children. But still a shadow is cast across this woman's life: "My only fear is, really, whether our children will be somehow tainted by heredity through my father."

The fate of the children of Proband 36 is told by one of them (at age 40) as follows: Parents were divorced when he was 2 years old. He was first given into the care of his natural mother who, in turn, passed him on to the mentally ill father and his second wife. He remained there until he was 9. He reports about this period as follows: "My stepmother was a mean and cruel woman. She showed great favoritism toward her own children; we stepchildren were absolute nobodies; my brother and I had to go to a child care center, but she didn't give us anything to eat when we came back at supper time; our half-siblings made fun of us and laughed at us. She beat us—and we really could have stood that—but she didn't give us anything to eat; she really cast us out; we were just nobody to her."

From age 9 to 12 this son stayed with foster parents, and from 12 to 14, with his mother and stepfather. With the latter couple, the old miseries of cold and hunger returned. From age 16 on, he had to earn his own way by working as a farmhand. In spite of this, his development was fortunate. He became a printer, and holds a respected job as foreman. He has 4 children, all healthy—but: "One can never be completely happy after such a childhood as I had."

The only daughter of Proband 41 (discussed on p. 282) grew up under the care of a loving mother and her schizophrenic father, who was often depressive between his acute episodes. His manic ideas often took on incestuous tendencies toward his daughter. Despite this, the family stayed together, and the parents and child were close to one another. The daughter felt herself sheltered and protected. During her 20th year she became somewhat annoyed with her father. Later, she became a dedicated nurse—for after all, marriage was out of the question "if one has an abnormal father."

The only daughter of Proband 39 was born

two years before the onset of her father's psychosis. Her mother was a sexually unstable woman. From age 2, neither her parents nor her grandparents showed any interest in her. For the following 4 years, she stayed with a foster family under atrocious conditions. She was frequently beaten, spent much of her time locked up in the cellar, and was never permitted to eat at the family table. She was not accepted in school, because she did not have proper clothing and was infested with lice. Then, until she was 15, she was placed with good foster parents in well-ordered circumstances, but where there was no human warmth. From age 15 on she had to earn her own way, working as a servant. Slowly she worked her way up to a better position. Now she is the head of a large branch office of a business and is doing well. But marriage seemed to be out of the question for her, too. "I'd never be able to tell a man what happened with my parents." Besides, she has somatic complaints with emotional overtones. For instance, she cannot bear to drink milk, and if she tries to anyway, she has to think of the watered milk her foster parents used to give her.

Proband 43 was a tiny, goitered, cretinoid, debilitated dwarf. He married a wicked, loose woman, who gave herself regularly to her boarders. During this marriage, the proband at first became an alcoholic, and developed an alcoholic hallucinosis, which progressed to a permanent schizophrenic-paranoic psychosis. At the onset of his psychosis, his son was already 20. The marriage of his parents had already ended in divorce when he was 13. He was awarded to his mother by the court. The son continued to maintain a warm relationship with his father. In spite of the father's alcoholism and the psychosis following it, he evaluates his father as a kind-hearted man. His greatest sorrow was that he had been assigned to his mother and stepfather, rather than to his father. The loneliness of his father moved him to pity and compassion, while he thinks of his mother always as an "evil whore." He served a successful occupational apprenticeship, has an exceptionally good marriage, and is raising two normal, healthy children.

Proband 18 was a young girl, full of zest for life, but still quite debilitated from her very beginning. A good, robust laborer married her, but he "fathered" her to excess, checked all her expenditures carefully (which was necessary), was quite stingy, and finally threatened to bring his mother into the household to watch over her even more. After this threat, at age 40, she suffered an acute onset of a depressively colored, severe paranoid schizophrenia. One month after her release from our clinic, she committed suicide at home by inhaling gas. It was precisely this experience that impressed most profoundly the younger of her sons, who was 12 at the time and very fond of his mother. He had the feeling as though he had dropped a grade in school and was being held in contempt by his classmates. The stepmother he acquired 3 years later was adequate, but she was not loving as a mother would be. That was why he became secretive and always found guilt in himself rather than in others. In spite of all this, he became quite successful in his job as a machinist, is happily married, and the father of two boys. While talking to him, a warm-hearted personal nature penetrates his mask of isolation. His brother, 3 years older, works in a chemical plant. He chose a wife who is very similar to his mother—our proband. He often is unfaithful to her.

A number of different concepts have to be employed to describe the prepsychotic personality of Proband 37. She was talkative, lacked concentration, was odd and egotistical, lacked emotional warmth, was stingy, and disciplined her children excessively. By the time all of this had culminated in the actual eruption of her psychosis, her daughter was 17, and her son was 12 years old. Before her children were grown up, the proband experienced a brief attack of manic agitation and a severe manic-like catatonic episode. Her husband was an alcoholic. Today her daughter is a 61-year-old, competent, happily married homemaker with a healthy daughter of her own, who is a teacher. The 56-year-old son is a successful master saddler and interior decorator, and has two healthy sons. Both these children suffered a great deal under their sick mother; still they developed splendidly, although they are somewhat puritannical and phlegmatic. Both of them admit to feeling closer to their father, in spite of his drunkenness, and insist they were raised principally by a most "wonderful" motherly grandmother.

The following example shows how the aftereffects of abnormal parental behavior can still manifest itself out of the unconscious, even after decades.

The two daughters of Proband 39 are normal, healthy, successful, and happily married middle-aged women. The son, now 47, is a fully healthy, although somewhat plump and uncouth sort of man, who earns his living as a shop foreman. He continued to reveal a persistent emotional participation in his mother's misfortune, as the following episode illustrates. The mother's schizophrenia began with an extramarital relationship with a man who played a leading role in the nudist culture movement. This relationship was completely contrary to the father's conservative traditions. At the beginning of the catatonia, the mother felt herself to be under the hypnotic spell of her lover. The son remembered nothing whatever of the term "nudist culture" when it came up in the exploratory interview. He was quite embarrassed when he attempted to define the term, and finally stammered his definition: "I can't say that word any more—something like a friends-of-nature group, but they are not friends of nature as we usually know them."

These few examples should suffice; they could be multiplied with little effort. They show that the suffering of children is a direct or indirect sequel to schizophrenias and psychotic personality disorders of their parents. They show especially that much more should have been done for these children than was done.

The data from these probands corresponds to my own from my experience with other schizophrenics. The childhood conditions of their children are often appalling. Few bother to pay attention to this fact. Even in a well-administered government, whose principal, self-imposed mission is to provide help to the sick and infirm, the sufferings of children are all too often not recognized by anyone.

What are the consequences of this type of childhood misery?

Only a minority of the children of schizophrenics who have lived an unfavorable childhood develop abnormally thereafter; however, it is quite a substantial minority. In some isolated cases, a study of the family histories leads to the subjective conviction that the unfavorable childhood has been the principal—undesirable—causative factor in the unfavorable personality development in later life. Frequently it seems more probable, however, that unfavorable hereditary developmental potentials and unfavorable environmental conditions work hand-in-hand, and that it is impossible to distinguish between them. Perhaps some statistical data could contribute to the clarification of this problem.

A check could be made to determine whether there were more particularly adverse personality developments among those probands' children with extremely poor childhoods, or whether more of them occur among children whose childhoods more nearly approached the normal. The children of the 208 schizophrenic probands of this study are too few in number to provide any significant results in such statistics. We can only say, with any certainty, that the offspring of schizophrenics often endure childhood adversities. But one must never (as used to be the custom) simply and unequivocally conclude that heredity transmits to them a partial vulnerability for schizophrenia. One must consider seriously the possibility that the unfavorable environment plays some part in an unfavorable personality development.

But here it must be emphasized, that only a minority of the children of schizophrenics are in any way abnormal or socially incompetent. The majority of them are healthy and socially competent, even though many of them have lived through miserable childhoods, and even though there are reasons to suspect adverse hereditary taints in many of them. Keeping an eye on the favorable development of the majority of these children is just as important as observing the sick minority. It is surprising to note that their spirit is not broken, even of children who have suffered severe adversities for many years. In studying a number of the family histories, one is even left with the impression that pain and suffering has a steeling—a hardening—effect on the personalities of some children, making them capable of mastering their lives with all its obstacles, in defiance of all their disadvantages.

The observations of the children of my probands confirm the child-psychiatric postulate, that many abnormal attitudes of children are simple, direct reactions to the abnormalities in their parents—symptoms that will diminish with the passing of time. These immediate reactions do not by any means always introduce long-term neurotic developments. Nor should they be classified as schizoid, if schizoid aberrations are to be regarded as hereditary characteristics.[25] Children without unfavorable characteristics can

25. If we were to assign the adjective "schizoid" a definition purely for the purpose of qualifying symptoms, we might correctly refer to "temporarily schizoid children."

take on abnormal behavior under abnormal environmental conditions. In some cases this can be observed in the foster children of schizophrenics. There is no use, of course, to count these instances of aberrant behavior in order to apply them as bases for theories on heredity.

The fact that most children of schizophrenics remain normal, in spite of the horror and misery they experienced in childhood, must not be regarded as a reason for ignoring such miseries, either. The danger of passing over this problem is ever-present. If years ago this danger was caused by the concentration of interest in hereditary theories, it is just as real today for other reasons. For instance, if the personality structure is unilaterally considered only in respect to learning theories, and if the intellectual aspect of "teaching irrationality" is emphasized too strongly, it would be very easy to pay too little attention to the suffering of the children.

Although only a minority of the children become schizophrenic or otherwise mentally ill, and although the suffering that children endure in their childhood may not influence their health in later life, we doctors in all countries are still obligated to do a great deal more to alleviate the sufferings of the children of the mentally ill.

One of the most lasting impressions brought home to me by the family studies of our probands is the fact that even normal children who are successful in life can never fully free themselves of the pressures imposed on them by memories of their schizophrenic parents and their childhoods. Once one knows them more intimately, it is not rare that one perceives from the depth of their hearts a long-drawn sigh, something like: "When you've been through that . . . you can never really be happy; you can never laugh as others do; you always have to be ashamed of yourself and take care not to break down yourself." Schizophrenia in the parents particularly burdens their growing children with the crushing feeling that they will be incompetent as partners in love or marriage, and that they could never assume the awesome responsibility of putting children of their own into the world. Many—but by no means all—overcome such inhibitions; others never do. They plunge into their jobs and reject a normal family life.

In short, the sufferings that children of schizophrenics endure can continue to affect their lives, even when they do not interfere with their health and their occupational advancement. Any horrible experience remembered from childhood can continue to hurt and to cast its shadow over their lives and their happiness.

7   Results

Documentation

In the course of planning this project, our first task was to compile data on the course of illness, the origins, and the family relationships of a group of schizophrenics who lived during a certain specified period and under certain social and cultural conditions. The resultant figures were meant to provide us with material for comparisons with groups of schizophrenics who had lived at different periods and under different conditions. Such comparisons promise insights into the typical and characteristic beginnings and evolution of the disease, and from these, some indications as to therapeutic possibilities.

The most important data depicted in the tables concern
—The course of the disease; that is, the onset of illness, the state of the patient after more than 20 years of observation (based on and estimated by his general condition, his need for hospitalization, and his social capabilities), the entire course of the disease over more than 20 years, and the cause of death
—The influences affecting the course of the disease, such as death of parents, other types of emotional shocks, or pampering or neglect and or abandonment by the family during the illness
—The family backgrounds of schizophrenics, measured by early parent losses (compared to that of the population), by normal or horrible childhood conditions, and by the living together with stepparents or schizophrenic parents
—The prepsychotic personality and the identifiable expressions of the prepsychotic sex lives of schizophrenics
—The frequency of psychic disorders, and particularly of schizophrenias in parents, siblings, stepparents, half-siblings, siblings' children, spouses, children and grandchildren of schizophrenics, compared with the frequency of psychic disorders among the population
—The frequency with which similar course types of schizophrenia occur among close relatives
—The fertility rate of schizophrenics compared with that of the population
—The childhoods of the offspring of schizophrenics
—Comparisons among several of the data, for instance, comparisons between the backgrounds and prepsychotic personalities and the disease courses of schizophrenics.

These and other data are intended particularly to serve research in the future. Some results, among others, from comparisons of previously developed data that can already be applied today are that the average course of the disease has undergone some unmistakable changes during the course of the last few decades. On this topic more specific information is contained in the following section. Furthermore, that the disease course is similar in schizophrenics from three different regions of Switzerland and in schizophrenics from certain social groups in New York State.

On the other hand, the average course of schizophrenic psychoses in Switzerland is different from that in several countries in Africa. Jilek-Aall (1964) from our clinic published his experiences with schizophrenic psychoses in parts of Tanganyika. I personally was able to compile some data on them in Morocco, but they were published only in summary. In these countries, more than in Switzerland, are to be found the most severely acute schizophrenic psychoses, from which many patients recover, but many of these psychoses also terminate in death. In the above-mentioned African countries there are also many more obvious correlations between the illness and the depressing mode of life than is the case in Switzerland. The comparison with our clinic's African experience will be mentioned only briefly here. It has not been included in detail in this book.

Comparisons with earlier papers show that the onset expectancy for schizophrenia in most relatives of schizophrenics has remained about the same in various countries of European culture for a number of decades. This finding shows also that the concept of schizophrenias, as it has been applied for a number of decades by different investigations in different localities and as it is applied in this text, has been described with sufficient accuracy to make the figures comparable.

On the other hand, the comparisons show that the concept of the schizoid personality and that of schizoid psychopathy is so differently interpreted by different authors, that figures about them simply cannot be accorded any general applicability.

I have put forth a great deal of effort studying many different groups of schizophrenics and of representatives of the population to learn whether they have suffered an early parent loss (broken-home statistics).

My own findings were compared among one another and with those of other authors. This revealed that there had been no previous statistics that could prove with any reliability that the early loss of a parent occurred more frequently in the childhoods of schizophrenics than it did in the general population. The frequency of premature parent loss depends to a much greater degree than was previously suspected on the time period in which the probands were born, and on the locality and the social background from which they came. When differences were found in the frequency of premature parent loss between schizophrenics and representatives of a given population, they might have resulted from the contingency that the backgrounds of the schizophrenics and those of the population were not alike in many respects. On the other hand, the comparisons of premature parent losses among various groups of schizophrenics showed differences that deserve futher study, which even today are already making helpful contributions in the formation of theories on the factors governing the onset of schizophrenias.

The comparison between the social standing of schizophrenics and their siblings with that of their offspring shows that the close relatives of schizophrenics can generally succeed in the struggle for existence, despite the terrible stress to which they are exposed as a consequence of the psychosis of a relative.

We shall come back to all these findings in a different context a bit later.

The Essential Conclusions on the Long-term Disease Courses

In planning the present project, the investigation of the long-term courses of schizophrenic illnesses was my first and most important aim.

Up to the 30s of this century there were in existence only very few studies about the courses of illness, and these contained many shortcomings. After the introduction of insulin- and cardiazole-shock treatments, treatment results were frequently described, but these descriptions contained only brief catamneses of several months' duration, or at best, they extended over a very few years. Even the studies consulted for comparisons about the courses that did not involve treatment, seldom covered more than very short periods. On the courses of schizophrenias over many years or decades, only a very one-sided concept was possible, and it was principally inferred from experiences with patients who

were permanently hospitalized or who were rehospitalized after intermittent remissions. But nothing was really known about the fates of the great numbers of patients with whom, after their release, the doctor lost contact.

I wanted to fill in the gaps of our knowledge on this topic. In order to obtain reliable results, an important task was to avoid the numerous errors found in previous course statistics. I had to impose stricter demands upon my investigations than had ever been done before. Of these demands the most important were:

1. The diagnosis for schizophrenia had to be uniform and stated according to clear, unequivocal concepts. It could never be made dependent on observations of former courses, or on the assumptions of future courses.

2. The selection of probands was to be determined by no other criterion than the fact that they had been admitted to the Burghölzli Psychiatric University Clinic as schizophrenics during a predetermined time period.

3. I was to have examined every patient personally and to have observed his future myself over a given number of years, and if it should happen that I personally lost track of such a patient, I was to form my own opinion on his condition on the basis of reliable reports.

4. At least 200 patients were to be included in the study.

5. The greatest effort was to be put forth not to lose contact with any, or with as few, patients as possible. From the outset my projected goal was to remain fully and continuously informed on the course and condition of at least 95 percent of all original probands until they died or until the study was completed 20 years or more later.

6. Not only was their condition to be checked at specified points in time after the beginning of the study, but the full, continuous, and uninterrupted course was to be sketched on the evolution of illness for every single patient.

7. The condition of a patient was by no means to be characterized only as to whether he had or had not been hospitalized, but his overall state of health and his total situation in life were to be considered.

8. Beginning with the patient's hospitalization that first brought him into the study project as a proband, right through to his death or at least 20 years after that first hospitalization, the course of his illness should

be fully charted and explained. Since many patients had been psychotic long before they were hospitalized, the course for those probands had been studied for well over 20 years.

9. The catamnestic data should be supported by more than a single inquiry. In every case, medical reports, personally administered follow-up examinations, or multiple reports from a number of different informants were to be required.

I was able to meet all these demands for my studies throughout the 27 years it took to accomplish them. In the course of time I even supplemented them with data exceeding these norms. This additional information was useful not only because it reduced the impact of the errors of small numbers; it also provided material for comparisons with experiences from other times and other clinics. It provided indications that the findings from the 208 principal probands have validity beyond their local significance.

Two of these findings seem to exceed all the others in importance: Five to ten years after onset, the relationship between recoveries, chronic-mild, moderate, and severe cases seems to have remained about the same for years and even decades, up to the deaths of these patients. But in order to be able to evaluate this finding correctly, a second finding should be considered simultaneously.

In the course of years it is not always the same patient whose conditions show recovery, improvement, no change, or deterioration. This stability indicated in the findings relates only to the numerical relationship of recovery, improvement, unchanged condition, or deterioration that is common to all patients, but not to the individual proband. For a substantial minority, the disease is still in process. Patients are constantly changing back and forth between states of recovery, improvement, nonimprovement, or deterioration.

These bare facts will have little meaning for anyone who is not familiar with the history of the theory of schizophrenia. However, they seem revolutionary when compared with the schizophrenic theory of a continuous regressive process toward a state of idiocy. Fortunately this theory has outlived its blossom; although now, as then, it exerts its paralyzing influence on therapeutic initiative, and in its own secretive, insidious way, promotes hopelessness and resignation among doctors, nurses, families, and among the patients themselves. This theory still holds sway in wide circles of the population and administrative jurisdictions, suggesting the idea that only those funds should be spent on the insane that are left over after facilities for general patients have been adequately equipped. This concept, that the schizophrenias are irrevocable processes that lead to idiocy, does agree rather neatly with the interpretation of schizophrenias as brain processes and chronic metabolic diseases from "inborn errors of metabolism." Hypotheses in this vein, however, are most difficult to reconcile with the fact that, on the average, the schizophrenias do not by any means necessarily take a chronic-progressive course, and that in many cases schizophrenics can still change, improve, and occasionally even recover years and decades after onset.

From 1886 to 1898, E. Bleuler dedicated himself completely to his community of schizophrenics as director of the remote psychiatric clinic of Rheinau, which was then in an isolated, rural sector of Switzerland. Two decades later, during and after the First World War, he went back to Rheinau to visit about once a year, usually when the weather was fine during the summer. His former schizophrenic patients always greeted him warmly and enthusiastically. Much as these greetings pleased him, he usually made the painful observation, "Most of them did seem to have deteriorated." Then, depressed, he would ask, "Is there really nothing that can stop this disease?" If he spent all his life wrestling with the question whether there was an "organic process" at the basis of schizophrenia, it was mainly because of experiences like the above. But E. Bleuler did not know how many improved patients were out for their Sunday walks during his visits, and certainly not how many had been released and were living at home, recovered. Had he known, and if he had not continued to meet only the most severe cases among his old problem children, his assessment of the schizophrenias would have been strongly influenced. A number of generations of clinical psychiatrists had experiences similar to his.

In order to evaluate the course of all schizophrenic psychoses in general, one attempts to develop unequivocal data that characterize the "natural" course of the disease. It is impossible to do full justice to this effort. Even considering the strict criteria that I had set myself in planning these investigations, none of the figures concerning the course of the disease can be rated as truly "unequivocal," and the assumption that one has seized upon the "natural" course of the disease is equally easy to refute. First of all, the results depend on whether all hospitalized patients or only initially hospitalized patients are considered, or whether the probands are schizophrenics encountered during family studies. They depend on whether or not patients who die before senility are included in the statistics; on how strictly the criteria are drawn in respect to "outcomes" of the disease, for instance, how strictly one judges "recoveries," and on the other hand, the "severe chronic states," and on how much observation is considered adequate before justifiably assuming the existence of a reasonably stable condition that could be the "final outcome." In every case reasons can be formulated for and against one calculation method or another. The thing to remember is that every figure has its median error and with it, its limits of credibility.

It is not the purpose of this chapter to present again the multitude of calculations in their entire unsurveyable hodgepodge. Nor is it intended to reiterate the errors of small numbers, the confidence intervals, or the degrees of significance. These appear in the main text. Here the intention is merely to summarize in easily surveyable form the most essential conclusions from that multitude of figures. The terms used have been described in detail, with appropriate examples in chapter 4.

Easily half to three-quarters of all schizophrenics about ten or more years after onset, attain reasonably stable states that last for many years. Such states then undergo no more dramatic changes. Formerly they were summarily regarded as end states. There are two objections to the use of this expression: Even in these states, all sorts of minor changes constantly do occur. Further, no matter how long a "long-term, reasonably stable state" has persisted, there is still the possibility that some dramatic changes may take place. For the sake of brevity, I continue to use the expression "end state" consistently, but I put it in quotation marks to indicate that there is much in it that can be objected to. I consider as "end states" only those that have persisted for at least 5 years by the time of the patient's death or at the end of the observation period.

If the long-term recovery periods, the recoveries that are interrupted only by brief psychotic episodes, and the mild chronic "end states" are regarded as characteristic of benign schizophrenias, and the moderate and severe "end states" as characteristic of malignant ones, the following general rule applies: Some two-thirds to three-fourths of schizophrenias are benign, and only about one-third or less are malignant. In addition, the frequency of the two opposing types of "end states" should be mentioned. About one-fourth to one-third of the "end states" are long-term recoveries, and about one-tenth to one-fifth are the severe chronic psychoses. Confronted by the actual figures, the reader must be reminded that they include only those cases that had a long-term, relatively stable outcome over many years, that is, an "end state" by our definition. That particular quarter or scant half of all schizophrenias that never attain an "end state" is not even included in these figures. They include a good many cases that proceed in phases to intermittent recoveries. The prognosis of all schizophrenias combined is therefore better than the prognosis that is limited to schizophrenias progressing to an "end state."

At the middle of this century, the frequency of the different course types lay within these limits

—Acute onset–rapid conversion to severe chronic psychoses: almost none at all.
—Chronic onset and chronic conversion to severe chronic psychoses: 3–28 percent
—Acute onset–rapid conversion to chronic moderate or mild psychoses: statistically insignificant, very few
—Chronic onset and chronic conversion to chronic moderate or mild psychoses: 13–27 percent
—Acute phases with outcomes to severe chronic psychoses: statistically insignificant, a very low percentage
—Acute phases with outcomes to moderate or mild chronic psychoses: 15–29 percent
—Acute phases with recovery outcomes: 29–49 percent
—Various atypical courses: statistically insignificant, a very low percentage.

Some rather obvious formulations can be derived from these figures. Most frequently, schizophrenia runs in acute phases with intermittent recoveries (a good third of all cases). About a quarter of all schizophrenias run in phases, and end in mild or moderate chronic psychoses. Third in the order of frequency are the schizophrenias with chronic beginnings and outcomes in moderate or mild chronic states (about one-fifth). Then follow the schizophrenias with chronic courses to severe chronic psychoses. Each of the remaining course types occurs only in a very low percentage of all cases.

Or else the schizophrenias somewhat more

often take a phasic course than a uniform one. Among the schizophrenias with phasic courses, about the same number end in recovery as in chronic psychoses. The majority of the chronic types of courses end in moderate and mild chronic psychoses, and only a minority in severe ones.

These figures apply to patients who, when they became probands, were hospitalized for the first time. The figures for all patients admitted to the clinic remain in about the same relation, but they are somewhat more unfavorable.

Comparisons between the findings from my previous probands and from the 208 probands of this project reveal some remarkable differences in the distribution of "end states" and course types. The psychoses with acute beginnings and rapid conversion to severe chronic states (catastrophe-schizophrenias) are disappearing. Mild "end states" have increased in frequency and severe ones have declined However, the number of recoveries has shown no marked increase, at least not to a degree that my data would reveal statistically.

Many experiences indicate a general validity for all these trends, and in particular for the steady, consistent decline within the past half century of the catastrophe-schizophrenias. Very probably the main reason for this decline is the improvement of treatment methods, or at least the avoidance of ineffective measures.

The late-onset schizophrenias have increased in comparison to the rate of former times, partly because of diagnostic changes and partly because of an overaging population.

The experiences with the 208 probands of this project, for the first time permit the publication of figures on the very late-course trends of schizophrenic psychoses. Up to this point, only very one-sided information was available on the course of schizophrenias in the third and subsequent decades after onset. Customarily the later periods of courses were assessed only on the basis of daily experience with patients who remained at the clinic. There were almost no statistics available that were not based on selection bias. Now we have learned that a quarter of the schizophrenias that have not experienced recovery after more than 23 years, still undergo impressive changes in the patient's condition, whether they be acute, phasic deteriorations, improvements, or—though rarely—even recoveries. Schizophrenia does not "burn itself

out," nor does it lead irrevocably to mental oblivion. Even among patients whose psychosis had lasted over 40 years, some marked changes still occurred in the conditions of a quarter of them (5 of 22). The percentage of schizophrenias progressing in acute phases does not drop any more, but remains constant after the 20th year and beyond.

The course studies of probands who have neither recovered nor revealed any acute episodes of illness by the end of the observation period led to some interesting conclusions. These were the types of cases that had hitherto been popularly referred to as "defects" or "dementias," whose conditions would not undergo further changes. Near the end of the observation period (that is, more than 23 years, and for 2 patients more than 60 years after onset), at least one-third of the patients (55 of 145) still experienced marked changes in their conditions. But what is even more remarkable is that these changes involve many more improvements than regressions (47 remissions and 8 regressions). Anyone who looks upon schizophrenia as a progressive brain disease must be surprised by these data.

Late remissions occurred especially in those schizophrenics whose disease had run in acute phases. The most severe psychoses, that had been chronic from their very beginnings, showed no further improvement.

Up to this time, the long-term courses had been judged according to the overall state of health of the patient. We shall now present a summary overview of these courses when they are assessed by the frequency and duration of hospitalization and according to the social position of the patient. Considering the sojourn as inpatients of the probands 2, 5, 10, and 20 years after their initial hospitalization, it turns out that the percentage of hospitalized patients remains about the same. It does not increase over the years. Beginning with the second year after initial admission, a little over half of the formerly hospitalized patients are living outside of clinics, but not by any means always the same ones. After more than 20 years, the ratio of the hospitalized to the nonhospitalized is even more favorable; that is, 24:76, and here again only those are included who became probands along with their initial hospitalization.

From their initial onset to their death or to the end of the observation period, the 208 probands spent a total of 3600 years outside, and only 1967 years (35 percent) inside of hospitals.

Barely one-third of all the probands were capable of earning their living outside a clinic by the time they died or at the end of the observation period, and about one-fifth of them were hospitalized on closed wards for the severely ill. For those probands exclusively who became probands at the time of their initial hospitalization and who were still alive at the end of the observation period, these figures are even much more favorable, that is, half the patients living outside and earning their own existence, and just about one-twentieth hospitalized on closed wards for the most severe cases.

I spent a great deal of effort (with only modest results) checking what kinds of influences shape the course of the disease. Between the course of the illness and a background of horrible or favorable childhoods, and with or without premature parent loss, I found no really significant correlations. Between a favorable course and prepsychotic health and usefulness there was a positive correlation, as there was also between an unfavorable course and prepsychotic psychopathy. However, that correlation was weaker than popular opinion might suggest.

Between the course and frequency of schizophrenia in the family, I discovered no significant correlations on the whole. If, nevertheless, in two related persons, schizophrenias do occur that are similar as to course type, it is most commonly the phasic-benign variety of course, and most rarely the type with acute onset and evolution to severe chronic psychoses.

Does the death of a father or a mother influence the course of schizophrenic psychoses? Among the 211 deaths of parents while probands were suffering their psychoses, 34 cases appeared to be related in time to a marked change in the patient's condition. It occurred more frequently among the female than among the male schizophrenics. Patients with remissions after the death of a parent appeared to suffer from an exaggerated ambivalence toward the deceased parent. On the other hand, those patients whose condition deteriorated after the death of their parent had lived in exaggerated dependency on their parents.

There were slightly more phasic and benign psychoses among patients devotedly cared for by their families than among those who were neglected. However, whether the patient's condition influenced his rapport with his relatives or whether their behavior affected his well-being remains an open question.

One set of data that could not be statistically supported, but that continues to surface from individual family histories suggests the major influence of a tragic lot in life on the course of the disease, namely, the duration of hospitalization required. If the disease develops in a tragic environment that has a chance of improving, it is a good omen for the future of the patient; but if the disease develops in an environment of hopeless tragedy (complete loneliness—without any possibility of reintegration into society), the duration of the need for hospitalization is extended.

Still other influences of severe psychic stresses seem to affect women more frequently than men. In particular, the loss of a lover or spouse or anyone else considered to be very close, seems to occur in schizophrenic women more often than in men in a close time-correlation and in a subjectively felt relationship to a relapse. And conversely, the establishment of a close human relationship occasionally occurs in a close time-correlation and subjective relationship to a turn for improvement in women.

If a schizophrenia erupts or worsens after a psychic trauma, it often turns out that this specific trauma had a very special personal meaning for that particular patient.

As already mentioned, there are statistical indications that the improvement in treatment is eliminating the types of courses that begin acutely and proceed to most severe, lifetime psychoses without intervening remissions. Similarly, therapy can alleviate any chronic condition. On the other hand, there are no statistical indicators showing that the progress of therapeutic methods in recent decades had increased the number of long-term recovery periods and had reduced the number of severe chronic courses.

It cannot be determined whether any specific one of the traditional therapeutic techniques exceeds another in effectiveness to any great degree. Other findings on therapy are summarized below in the section in this chapter on the results of everyday medical experience.

From the study of causes of death among the present probands the following indications emerge:

When the diagnosis has been carefully arrived at, an autopsy never—or at best in very rare, exceptional cases—discloses a physical illness that would suggest a symptomatic psychosis to follow.

Cases of death with insufficiently specific, vague diagnoses still occur frequently even today, in acute phases of schizophrenia. In earlier times many of these were designated as lethal catatonia; although we have to fear that a goodly number of them were caused by improper therapies. It becomes increasingly clear, however, that many different causes are contributory, such as complications of the pulmonary apparatus, of the fluid and the ion system, and of the urinary tract, decubitus, exhaustion due to excitation, etc. Suicides and tuberculosis, rather than other malignancies seem to be the cause of death more often among schizophrenics than among the general population.

The So-called Schizophrenic "Dementia"

For a long time now the expression schizophrenic "dementia" has no longer been understood in its original literal sense, either in clinical practice or in the field of psychopathological research. Even at the time the concept "dementia praecox" was introduced, the type of dementia it brought to mind was similar to what is known as "dementia senilis." One thought of it as a perpetual state of being "out-of-one's-mind"—a final, irrevocable loss of one's mental existence. Kraepelin, however, already corrected this misconception and, among other things proved that one's primary thinking capacity remains intact in dementia praecox. In 1911 E. Bleuler regarded dementia as one of the combining and secondary symptoms of schizophrenia. He described this at the time: "In no disease is the disturbance of the intellect as inadequately defined by the words 'idiocy and dementia' as it is in schizophrenia." He emphasized that, in schizophrenic dementia, all intellectual functions continue to operate covertly. He felt that this was the principal distinction between schizophrenic dementia and the dementia related to brain diseases, and that the difference was easily distinguished by the results of intelligence tests, in which brain-diseased dementia cases could solve only the simpler test questions, whereas the schizophrenic dementia cases had less trouble solving the difficult problems than the easier ones.

So it happened that the clinician became increasingly accustomed to seeing in his schizophrenic dementia cases an autistic attitude on the part of the patient. The patient and those who were healthy had ceased to understand one another. The patient gives up, in abject resignation or total embitterment, any effort to make himself understood. He either no longer says anything or says nothing intelligible. In so doing, the naive observer declares, out of hand, that the patient has lost his reasoning powers. But it is quite possible to discover his reasoning, if the patient is treated with sufficient skill, perseverance, and a great deal of sympathetic understanding.

One of the inexplicable phenomena in the history of psychiatry is that in the field of hereditary biology the conversion of meaning that "dementia" has undergone has scarcely been acknowledged up to the present day. In many studies on problems of heredity, schizophrenic dementia is still being interpreted as if it reflected the "actual process of the disease" in its purest form, and as if it were the most direct expression of a hereditary pathological predisposition. In this context scientists write of the "demented" forms of schizophrenia as being the "core-syndrome" of the disease, to which related psychoses that do not end in dementia are appended. Many researchers in the field of heredity suspect that these are something other than the true, genuine schizophrenias, or at least that they are only manifestiations of "schizophrenic predispositions."

In planning this project I also included among my goals a recheck of the question of schizophrenic dementia, that is, can it be proved that the evolution toward schizophrenic dementia is actually determined to a greater extent by heredity than other course types of the disease? Are they more difficult to characterize in the course of a life than other forms are? In contradiction to the clinicians, are the researchers in the field of heredity correct when they style dementia as a hereditary "core-syndrome" of schizophrenia?

To answer these questions I wanted especially to apply my family studies and my observations that extended over many years of long-term courses in patients. The direct observations of schizophrenic dements have certainly been described so often that I do not need to restate them in this context.

The most essential data on the question of dementia from the life and family histories of the 208 schizophrenic probands, augmented by the 100 from Pfäfers and the 100 from New York (and for a portion of the studies of additional patient histories of other schizophrenics from Burghölzli) follow.

1. Among the relatives of schizophrenic dements there are no more schizophrenics than among the relatives of recovered schizophrenics or of all schizophrenics (see Table 4.22).

2. The course types of schizophrenic psychoses most frequently observed in common in two schizophrenic siblings are by no means types that proceeded to dementia. On the contrary, they are the benign phasic types of courses.

3. Schizophrenias running an acute course to dementia without intermission very rarely are found in combination in siblings (see Table 5.12).

4. The number of acute schizophrenias proceeding to dementia without intermission has declined sharply over the past decades, apparently because of the use of improved treatment methods (or because unfavorable measures were avoided).

5. The condition of many schizophrenics who have been "demented" for many years can still improve appreciably, even decades after the initial onset of their illness.

From these data the following conclusions are unequivocal. Schizophrenic "dementia" is by no means always a permanent state. It is accessible to influences from the environment. It is not the "core-syndrome" of a hereditary destructive disease process.

There are, to be sure, findings that suggest the existence of two distinct types of dementias in schizophrenia. One of these would then, in fact, be the "core-syndrome" of a hereditary disease unresponsive to environmental influences, while the other would be a kind of nongenuine "pseudodementia." These findings include late remissions after long-term dementia that occur among my probands only in those who became demented after one—or more frequently—after several acute phases of illness. I know of no patient who became a schizophrenic dement in slow, gradual stages over the course of many years, whose dementia did not recede appreciably again at a later time. There is a second experience of a similar nature. The frequency of only those malignant types of schizophrenia clearly diminished in number within recent decades in which dementia emerged after the initial acute illness had begun. On the other hand, neither I nor any other author has to any noticeable extent observed a reduction in the frequency of the malignant chronic schizophrenias (as compared to all other course types). It might therefore be assumed that the schizophrenic dementia with a chronic development, by its very nature, is something other than the one that manifests itself in acute surges. The first is a true, incurable, and final dementia. The second is similar to it only in symptomatology. In its basic nature it is different. It reacts to external influences. The first type would indicate an internal destructive process; the second type alone would correspond to the concept of dementia as an autistic attitude on the part of the patient, as an aspect of his struggle with his environment.

I do not support the theory of the existence of two types of schizophrenic dementia, that are totally different in essence. While it is true that every patient presents a unique and personal picture, it has been impossible to distinguish two different symptomatological types of which one became manifest after an acute, the other after a chronic course, no matter how meticulous the investigation that was conducted. A much simpler explanation of the phenomenon suggests itself to me, namely, that as a general rule, acute changes in personality are much more apt to be temporary and regressive than those that develop slowly over the course of many years. It is justifiable, therefore, to distinguish a psychic reaction from a long-term psychic development, in both of which all transitions occur. The first is generally reversible; the second is usually not reversible, although both are similar in nature. Why should the same prognostic laws not apply to the same schizophrenic developments? In a basic study, Ernst (1959) singled out the common implications of these basic laws for neuroses and schizophrenias. I, too, believe that the resistance to external influence of the dementia with slow, lingering development, and the susceptibility to such influences of the dementia that has become manifest after an acute psychotic episode, are scarcely valid indicators of a fundamentally different nature of these types of dementia. It is, instead, natural that the susceptibility is related to the acuity or the chronicity of the development.

The belief that a "familial taint" would adversely affect any psychiatric prognosis extends far back into the past century. Its origin was speculative. Despite that, it has had its aftereffects in respect to schizophrenia, right up to modern times. Even lacking any basis of clinical experience, it is tempting to assume, purely by "intuition," that a schizophrenia would run a worse course, the more schizophrenic relatives the patient had. My findings contradict this speculative assumption. In my experience, it is specifically the benign-phasic types that were least shaped by environmental influences, and were most likely to be determined by familial and possibly hereditary factors. On the other hand, I had to assume that particularly many of the most severe types had been responsive to environmental influences.

However, my conclusions are not only contradictory to speculative assertions, but—at least apparently—they are contradictory also to some other impressive findings, particularly those by Kallmann (1938) and by Gottesman and Shields (1966, 1967). Kallmann (1938) discovered that one "core group" of schizophrenics with severe disease courses had more schizophrenics among its close relatives than did a "fringe group." His findings led many authors to assume that familial incidence and the "force of heredity" were particularly strong in the most severe types of schizophrenia, and weaker for the mild types. In my study of 1942, I cited detailed reasons why Kallmann's (1938) figures in no way supported such a generalization, and why they only seemed to contradict my conclusions. Among a number of other reasons, the following deserve attention: Kallmann has an entirely different concept of the diagnosis of schizophrenia from the one in common use today, and as I applied it. Among the probands of his 1938 paper, there were no schizophrenias whatever with a phasic-benign course and a recovery outcome. For this reason, the schizophrenias of his "fringe group" are by no means comparable or summarily to be equated with the mild and benign schizophrenias. As a matter of fact, most of them evolved into chronic psychoses. Among them there were also exceptionally many late-schizophrenics; a proper calculation of their onset-expectancy would have required an age-correction factor different from the one that Kallmann (1938) used. Among monozygotic twins studied by Gottesman and Shields (1966, 1967) there was a higher concordance figure for schizophrenia among the malignant types than among the more benign types. But these authors defined malignancy in types of courses by completely different standards and much more summarily than I did. The essential qualifying characteristic for malignancy in schizophrenia for Gottesman and Shields (1966, 1967) is only the relationship of the time since onset to the time of hospitalization for schizophrenia. For this reason alone their findings are not suitable for comparison with mine.

But other authors as well have turned up numerous findings according to which familial influences emerged with exceptional clarity, particularly among the milder schizophrenias. Perhaps the most impressive finding is that of Langfeldt (1956), who noted an exceptional number of his "schizophreniform" psychoses with familial implications. (According to the conceptualization applied in this study, these were principally benign schizophrenias.) Among the authors of twin studies, Kringlen (1968) in particular emphasizes that not only monozygotic twins with mild schizophrenias, but those with malignant ones as well, may have normal twin partners.

In the literature there are numerous other examples showing whether it is the benign or the malignant types of schizophrenia that occur most often in familial settings. The findings contradict one another. It would be excessive to mention them all individually here. They show that the differences in the incidence rate of schizophrenia among the relatives of patients with a benign or a malignant schizophrenia are not great—if they exist at all. Nor do my own findings reveal any unequivocal differences in this respect, either. More instructive, and considerably more decisive for the formulations reported, were my comparisons between the long-term courses of schizophrenic psychoses in two siblings. The literature is still scarce in this field. It lacks particularly any data that would refute my findings.

Is it still permissible today to apply the expression "schizophrenic dementia"? It is doubtful, and the doubt is justified. If a healthy mental existence is still dormant, however concealed it may be behind a great need for care and a total lack of human accessibility, as is the case with schizophrenics, then they simply are not demented or idiotic in the common definitions of those terms. And in a similar vein, the old concept is refuted by the findings that the patient's attitude toward his environment is reflected in his dementia, and that the conditions of "dements" do, in fact, often improve and are not necessarily always final. For that reason it would be pleasant simply to avoid the concept of dementia in the description of schizophrenics. The difficulty, however, lies in the fact that it still cannot be replaced by a brief and fitting alternative concept that is easily remembered. The term "pseudodementia" that has been suggested is already being used for states of hysteria. I sometimes use the expression "severe chronic schizophrenic psychosis," although the expression is unwieldy, and the clinician must remind himself what is meant by it, whereas the old term "schizophrenic dementia" gives him the idea in a flash.

Whether the concept "dementia" for the most severe schizophrenic psychoses can be given up and adequately replaced, only the future will tell. To me it seems permissible to continue to use it for the time being, but only with the proviso that it must be clearly stated that it is a dementia in a particular and unusual context. In places where I should need to indicate this condition briefly, I shall use "dementia," but I will place it in quotation marks.

Correlations between Life Experiences and the Genesis of Schizophrenias

There is hardly any endeavor more emotionally touching than the study of the life histories of schizophrenics. Often in the process there is disclosed a series of unfortunate developments, sometimes beginning in childhood, and sometimes not until just before the onset of their illness. If one becomes involved in the history of such misfortunes, one begins to feel that he, too, would have been inundated by it, had he been subjected to the same experience. Often the living conditions of the later schizophrenics were of such a nature that any person would have rated them abominable; but even more often they were patently horrible in the light of the patient's individuality and his most personal needs and inherent sensibilities.

Correlations between life experiences and the onset of illness can be estimated, sensed, or intuitively felt to be true just as well—or just as poorly—for many schizophrenics as for neurotics, addicts, or normal persons. Nevertheless, we proceed more carefully with schizophrenics, and are more reluctant than we are in the case of neurotics, addicts, and the normal, to trust our intuitive faculties in concluding that a causal correlation exists. This is probably so because schizophrenia is a kind of "madness" that defies intuitive feeling—a disease that one would not suspect of being capable of attacking one's own self as a result of life's adversities, whereas it is easy to imagine one's self becoming neurotic

or addicted under stress. The argument is subjective. Whether it is valid is doubtful. Be that as it may, the awesome fear of grasping sympathetically something as shocking as schizophrenia does exist. It plays a major role in the history of schizophrenia research. It springs from elementary emotions that intrude, independently of any rationalization. If one broods a lot over many patient histories of schizophrenics, one soon runs across facts that seem to justify an irrational fear of discussing the schizophrenic illnesses in a psychological vein. Rather often one finds a patient history that defies any sort of psychological interpretation.

We see people become schizophrenic whose lives leave little to be desired, at least not more than do the lives of most normal people. Such experiences suggest our fears that we may be imagining a nonexistent psychogenesis, when in other cases we are correlating psychic traumas and illnesses.

From my own experiences with the disgraceful conditions of patients from one of Ernst's (1956) studies, I do know, however, that many of the gruesome conditions can be concealed behind our seemingly reliable data regarding a well-ordered home life. Ernst (1956) examined 43 schizophrenics according to the careful standards of our own clinic. He discovered some extremely stressful conditions in the lives of 35 of them. Thereafter he spent further months in attempting to decide whether his judgment concerning a "harmonious and orderly childhood" for the remaining 8 schizophrenics could be supported, by launching an additional, more detailed investigation—with considerable expenditure of time. He finally did discover a shocking picture of previously concealed misery for 6 of these 8 schizophrenics.

The life histories of my 208 probands are well known. Despite that, I would not dare to insist that every aspect of severe, long-term suffering had been discovered. It is doubtful whether there are, in fact, no psychological correlations, just because no such correlations are discovered.

If one ponders the question whether favorable life histories of schizophrenics were reliable, one would still encounter obstacles other than merely the one that personal misery is preferably kept to one's self. One should not only seek out the adversities, but rather attempt to place into proper relationship the adverse with the good that a person experiences in his home life. A sad experience has a diffent meaning when it occurs in the presence of a number of happy ones, than if it were the only experience in an otherwise empty existence. But most especially, suffering and good fortune take on a highly personalized interpretation for the individual. It is doubtful that we could adequately assess their impact from the perspective of our own personal emotions. We therefore come upon an unrevealed secret of psychiatry, when we attempt to grasp and empathize with the life experiences of a patient with increasing accuracy and thoroughness. Often the feeling of insecurity becomes greater the more we know about a patient.[1]

Thus we continue to be confronted time and again by puzzles and difficulties if we attempt to live vicariously the sufferings of schizophrenics, in order to derive from their experience some viable, scientifically useful conclusions. Perhaps the scientific researcher in schizophrenia will find consolation in the fact that he is not alone in his frustrations. Modern historians and sociologists are confronted with the same dilemma in their search after the correlations between personal developments and acts of historical or social importance.

It is outside the scope I had set for myself in this project to describe individual histories of schizophrenics in detail. It would be simple to describe for each case why they arouse so much compassion and why they leave behind the impression that the origin of their illness can be psychologically understood. Some indications of this nature are contained in a few of the summarized proband histories in the text. Detailed patient histories that transmit an understanding have also been studied from psychoanalytical as well as from phenomenological viewpoints, and are contained in the literature (Sechehaye 1947, Binswanger 1944, 1945, 1946, 1947, 1949, 1952, 1953, and others). But I was constrained to indicate at least in general terms that the problem of schizophrenia can be approached not only by way of descriptions, by counting, and by the search for statistically valid correlations, but also by the effort of coexperiencing the fate of the individual patient with him, and in this way of understanding it. This subjective aspect of schizophrenia research must not be neglected. The most fruitful lines of questioning addressed to the so-called

exacting research activities that are oriented to methods of the natural scientist arise from it.

One principal task of the present investigation is the attempt to support subjective assumptions on the significance of psychological processes for the genesis of schizophrenias, by the most objective data possible, or to refute, supplement, or refine such data. Jaspers distinguishes between genetic understanding, imparted to the mind by mentally assuming the role of the patient, and the acquisition of objective, causal facts. Such acquisition discloses regular patterns, because certain elements of data are repeatedly related to one another. I should now like to summarize what correlations of objective facts from the patient- and life-histories of the 208 probands reveal individual relationships between the intuitive, subjective, and the objective type of schizophrenia research.

1. The life histories of the 208 probands show clearly that disturbances in the home life of the most varied kinds occur with exceptional frequency in the childhood and youth of schizophrenics, but that no particular adversity exceeds another type of adversity in frequency. The first finding supports the assumption resulting from empathizing by way of the patient histories, according to which adversity in living conditions is somehow related to the genesis of schizophrenia. The second finding contradicts the numerous psychogenetic theories that have continued to appear in the literature for decades, according to which there is supposed to be a special and rather specific type of living condition that plays a major role in the genesis of schizophrenia. But it coincides with the experiences of many other clinicians and with my own experiences, gleaned from numerous schizophrenic probands other than the 208 of this project.

The following judgments concerning environmental conditions of the childhood and youth of schizophrenics appeared to me to be highly objective: Premature loss of father or mother, or of both, by death, divorce, or long-term separation; being reared in foster homes; and the categorization of living conditions that anyone would consider under the general heading of "horrible" or "normal." Between these extremes there were many conditions that did not neatly fit the categories of either horrible or normal. The most important result of this investigation, described in detail earlier, was that only a little over a fourth of all schizophrenic probands had the

1. Bleuler, M., "Aspects secrets de la psychiatrie," *Evolution Psychiatrique*, 1, (1956), 45–50.

good fortune to grow up under normal conditions with both parents, and again that about a fourth suffered under extremely unfavorable—even horrible—conditions during their childhood, either at home with their parents or with foster families. For a good third of them conditions were neither definitely normal nor definitely horrible.

We have no reason to assume that the childhood histories of other schizophrenics from similar cultural backgrounds and from a comparable period would be markedly different from those of the 208 probands. In the course of decades I have become acquainted with many schizophrenics who were hospitalized elsewhere (in Pfäfers, in Basel, in Boston, and in New York), and their childhood histories, without noticing any appreciable differences in them.

The most likely explanation for the frequency of adverse childhoods among schizophrenics lies in the assumption that such adversities promote the emergence of a schizophrenia. But there are also other explanations that are just as feasible. The difficult personalities of later schizophrenics could be a partial cause of adverse, "horrible" environmental conditions. Or the horrible conditions might be the result of hereditary personality disorders in the parents of the schizophrenics. I believe that in some singular isolated cases such correlations may apply. But I do not believe that they alone are an explanation for the phenomenon. To be sure, I can furnish no "proof" in support of this opinion. It is an inference that resulted from the study of individual family histories.

Since the concept of schizophrenia has been defined, many have regarded it as a specific disease, and have therefore undertaken a search for its specific causes. Such a tendency still plays a major role today in the psychogenetic research effort in schizophrenia. My probands, however, have revealed quite uniquely that misery of all descriptions is rather common in the childhoods of schizophrenics. Despite all my careful searching, I was not successful in discovering any specific burdens that were particularly numerous in the early life histories of schizophrenics. Most especially, there was no indication that those circumstances that were assigned a special importance according to one or the other of the early hypotheses occurred in any great number in their childhood histories.

Thus, there was no indication that disturbances in the child's relationship to his mother during the first few months of his life had any sort of influence on him. A separation from his mother, occurring at any time or during any specific phase of his life, was not experienced with any greater frequency by schizophrenics than by representatives of the general population. The living together with a schizophrenic father or mother is so rare in late schizophrenics and so frequent in the children of schizophrenics who never become schizophrenic, that one is not justified in suspecting that there lies in this phenomenon a predisposition for schizophrenias. Mothers who have been identified as "schizophrenogenic" do, indeed, bear many schizophrenic children, but by no means are all their children schizophrenic, and many of these mothers have no schizophrenic children at all. The love life of schizophrenics during and after puberty is often stunted, but no more and no differently than in the early life histories of addicts or neurotics.

Based on experiences to date, therefore, a specificity of any psychotraumatic situation as being contributory to the genesis of schizophrenias is simply out of the question. It is especially important that one keep uppermost in mind, again and again, the one elementary truth, whenever the temptation arises to designate a certain psychotraumatic situation as significantly predisposing or causal to schizophrenia that no such specific psychotaumatic situation occurs in all, or in most, schizophrenias, and that all these same specific situations are experienced by countless numbers of people who never become schizophrenic, but perhaps neurotic, addicted, afflicted with personality disorders, or who simply remain normal—at least insofar as previous experience and my investigations indicate.

Most certainly the last word has not yet been uttered on this topic. It certainly is permissible to continue to search after specific processes with pathogenic implications for schizophrenia. Just such research is in process even now. It concerns principally the possibility that socially healthy, externally nonaberrant parents are particularly contradictory, ambiguous, uncertain, and unclear in their expression, and that they do not sense or express with sufficient clarity such concepts as the roles of the sexes and of the generations (Lidz 1962, Singer and Wynne 1963, 1965, and others). The results of my own research efforts in no sense contradict those of these authors, but they do raise some doubts that will have to be resolved. For instance, information from my probands showed definitely that the fact of living together with schizophrenic parents cannot dispose to producing schizophrenia. From this, some doubts must arise as to whether the living together with parents who are not manifestly schizophrenic, but who do show some schizophrenia-like thought disorders, can really be so influential. In addition, the investigations by Uchtenhagen (and other data as well) show how the results of projection tests become altered by the effect of living conditions that have emotional overtones. The test interpretation by Singer and Wynne (1963, 1965) and others do deviate somewhat from the customary one and from Uchtenhagen's. In spite of that, Uchtenhagen's experiences with the Rorschach Test applied to family members of senile patients call for a recheck of the test results of these above-mentioned authors. A check should be made to determine how much these results depend on the test situation itself.

2. The life histories of the probands reveal a correlation between adversity in childhood and later onset of schizophrenia. In respect to a causal correlation between childhood misery and later schizophrenia, it has to be an indirect one, since childhood misery, to begin with, engenders a schizoid attitude, and this schizoid attitude predisposes to schizophrenia. Actually, there is a statistically significant correlation between childhood misery and the pathological, schizoid personality of later schizophrenics. Insofar as a correlation between childhood misery and schizophrenic onset can be ascertained, it is limited to those schizophrenics who were schizoid before. I find no evidence in my probands who were not also prepsychotic schizoids, to indicate a relationship between childhood misery and schizophrenia. That in itself is no proof in refutation of the existence of such a relationship. It does become clear, however, that relationships between childhood misery and schizophrenia appear especially when schizoid personality traits appear during a miserable childhood.

These findings do indicate that assumptions about psychogenetic processes in the emergence of schizophrenias have a relationship to objective experience. In any case, the importance of the type of childhood for a later schizophrenia seems more credible when one is aware that under the stresses of a miserable childhood, the personality is first distorted into becoming schizoid, and one then accepts the assumption that the schizoid development

predisposes to a schizophrenia.

To be sure, research experience shows unequivocally that childhood misery, even among prepsychotic schizoids, can be only one among many weighty conditions favoring schizophrenic onset. Studies of the siblings of schizophrenics who were raised under adverse circumstances reveal the psychotraumatic impact of such conditions in that they frequently continue to develop unfavorably in some way, although such continued unfavorable development does not by any means always take the direction of a schizoid psychopathy. Something other than childhood misery must be operant that directs the particular course of the later schizophrenic toward the schizoid. To date we can only assume what the nature of this "other" influence may be. It could be inherent in congenital developmental propensities.

3. Frequently, as has been shown, there are close time-correlations between emotional traumata and the onset, the worsening, the improvement, or the total remission of the disease. This is the experience of every clinician, and a number of figures have been compiled on it from the life histories of my probands (see pp. 288–95). But more important than these bare figures is the observation how often it is not only the time-relationship that indicates inner implications; rather, many patients subjectively experience a causal correlation between what happens in their illness and their life experiences. Of course, such a judgment is, again, largely subjective and difficult to consider objectively. It was impressive to note that the loss of father or mother had a beneficial effect when the proband's relationship to the deceased parent was a highly ambivalent one, and a pernicious effect—in some isolated cases even initiating the onset of the disease—when the patient's relationship to his deceased parent was a highly dependent one.

But influences on the course of illness cannot just simply be identified with influences on the onset of the disease. The assumption that they are at least partly identical does, however, suggest itself. At any rate, one does find the same time-correlations between shocking experiences and the onset of the disease as between shocking experiences and changes in its course.

However, the emotional trauma cannot possibly be the only decisive and consistent influence in every instance. Often the disease begins or changes its course without being preceded by such an experience. And even much more frequently, such a traumatic experience is not followed by the eruption of the disease or by any change whatsoever in its course.

4. A convincing indication of the significance of psychic experiences for the schizophrenias has long been evident from psychotherapeutic experience. My own corresponding experiences with the 208 principal probands constitute such a minimal portion of all my other psychotherapeutic experiences with schizophrenics, that I shall just touch upon it briefly in the framework of this project. It was all the easier for me to keep it short since there is a wealth of material available on the subject in the international literature. For the sake of completeness only, therefore, let me call to mind that often very sudden, unexpected improvements or recoveries occur in connection with the most diverse therapeutic measures, and that these are the very measures that could only be effective by way of the psyche. These recoveries are observed most frequently after surprise therapies and after introducing the patient to normal activity in the community. It happens during the course of any skillful and long-term psychoanalytic effort with schizophrenics, that at least phases occur in which the disease symptoms disappear. If one is inclined to believe, as I do, that the effect of shock treatments is principally based on violent psychic shock, then these treatments also belong in the same general category. Even an unfavorable psychological influence can have its definite effect on the disease, just as a favorable one can. It is especially true that human isolation has a deleterious effect on the course of the illness.

Again, it might be objected that influences on the course of the illness do not necessarily imply binding conclusions as to influences on the eruption of the disease. And most especially, despite all psychotherapeutic sucesses, the majority of schizophrenias are not completely curable, and insofar as there is full recovery from some schizophrenias, it is uncertain whether therapy was the essential underlying cause of that recovery.

The formulation will have to be carefully phrased to the effect that experiences with psychotherapy prove a strong influence of psychological processes on the course of the disease and suggest the possibility that such an influence may also be operant in its genesis. But these experiences by no means justify the assumption that any and all occurrences in schizophrenia are principally based on psychogenetic processes.

5. An additional experience gained from the study of the probands of this project should be brought up in this connection. As shown, convincing observations suggest that the phasic-benign schizophrenias are by far the most contingent on hereditary developmental predispositions. This implies that the schizophrenic psychoses of two close relatives run this same type of course with unexpected frequency. The study of our patient histories (in concurrence with other experiences) does indicate that in the great majority of cases, no psychogenetic correlations are indicated for just these phasic-benign types.

In cases where the stamping of the entire disease by hereditary developmental predispositions is most clearly in evidence, we find no psychodynamics. We find it most prevalent among the course types in which the hereditary influence is not so plainly evident. Could this not mean that the subjective intuitive empathy for the genetic implications of psychological processes for the schizophrenias might not be completely utopian after all?

6. I myself was most surprised by the differences in the life histories between the male and the female schizophrenics. I can scarcely interpret them in any other way than by saying that disturbances in the relationships to close relatives or friends play a more easily observable role in the development of schizophrenias in women. I intend to report about this phenomenon in the following section.

Apart from everything else that has been reported up to this point, the twin studies in which I personally was not able to take part, had long before uncovered a decisive fact, namely that the monozygotic partner of a schizophrenic twin does not by any means always become schizophrenic. Research on twins has not discovered anything conclusive about the importance of heredity for the schizophrenias, although it did on the importance of life experiences. It has proved that acquired damages play an important part in the genesis of the schizophrenias. Among the environmental noxae, however, by far the greatest majority of them are purely psychological ones. The theories about acquired somatic damage rest on even less secure foundations.

Today the gap between the results from intuitive, psychologically based schizophrenia research and that based on objective relationships is a long way from being bridged. Nevertheless, I do believe that a few fragile footbridges have been thrown across this gap. Objective factual data indicate that some of the assumptions that suggest themselves in the process of careful, sensitive empathizing into the life histories of one's schizophrenic patients might be correct.

Differences in the Family Histories of Schizophrenic Men and Women and Their Significance

In my previous studies of schizophrenics and in planning the present project, it had scarcely occurred to me to break down the data on family backgrounds according to sex. Quite by chance I began to count premature parent losses among the men, and only later, among the women as well. I was surprised to come upon different results for the two sexes. From then on, I made an effort to distinguish between them on data concerning their backgrounds, and found rather consistently that there were differences under a number of different conditions.

A few years ago, Rosenthal (1962) pointed out that there were more women than men among closely related schizophrenics. From this he concluded that the significance of communal family life in childhood had a bearing on the emergence of schizophrenic psychoses in women. But his conclusions were based on the findings of earlier authors, and it was doubtful that they were in every instance free of selection bias. Rosenthal (1962) stimulated my interest in probing deeper into findings on sex differences in the backgrounds of schizophrenics, and I set out to determine the ratios of men to women among schizophrenic relatives.

Schizophrenic women more often experienced stressful conditions during their childhood in their parental homes than schizophrenic men did. They also show more frequent changes in the course of illness when they gain or lose people to whom they feel close.

In part, these findings about such sex differences are significant, and, in part, they are not. They ought to be taken seriously because all of them always point in the same direction, indicating that certain familial conditions exerted a greater influence on schizophrenic psychoses in women than they did in men.

Here is a brief summary of these findings.

1. Premature parent loss (broken home) occurs more often in the childhood histories of schizophrenic women than of schizophrenic men (statistically significant).

2. Premature parent loss occurs more often in the childhood histories of schizophrenic women than among the general population (statistically significant). A corresponding difference between the childhood histories of schizophrenic men and representatives of the general population cannot be determined.

3. If the living conditions at home during childhood are subdivided into normal, horrible, and a category between these two, it turns out that schizophrenic women more often grew up with adverse childhood backgrounds than schizophrenic men did (statistically significant).

4. In girls who later become schizophrenic, the relationship to their mothers is more often a disturbed one than is true of boys in the same situation (statistically significant).

5. The poor relationships to the mother in the childhoods of girls who later become schizophrenic often deteriorate further during the process of growing up.

6. Girls who later become schizophrenic more often lived together with a schizophrenic father or a schizophrenic mother before their illness became manifest, than did boys who later became schizophrenic (statistically significant).

7. Girls who later become schizophrenic more often live together with a schizophrenic mother than with a schizophrenic father— in contrast to boys (statistically not significant).

8. Girls who later become schizophrenic more often lived together with stepparents before manifestation of their illness, and particularly with stepmothers, than boys did (statistically significant).

9. Among the sisters of schizophrenics coming from horrible childhoods there are more schizophrenics than among brothers of schizophrenics from such childhoods (statistically not significant).

10. A relationship between fluctuations in the course of schizophrenias and the death of a father or a mother occurs more frequently in schizophrenic women than in schizophrenic men (without significance).

11. In women, a great many other psychotraumatic experiences can more often be related to a deterioration of the state of mental health than in men (statistically significant). This includes, (except for the loss of father or mother), in particular the loss of a lover, a

husband, or other person regarded as emotionally close.

12. On the other hand, improvements occur more often in women than in men, when they establish contact with a person they love (statistically not significant).

13. Among two partners of a symbionic psychosis (folie à deux) more women are involved than men (statistically significant). Many of these psychoses are schizophrenias. In these cases the preponderance of women is obviously brought about by the fact that women, rather than men, get sick from the detrimental effects of an unfavorable intimate relationship.

14. Among schizophrenics who have schizophrenic siblings, there are also more women than men (statistically significant).

While this book was in press, another investigation appeared, that by Larson and Nyman, who studied 153 schizophrenics in Sweden. They found no correlations between the onset ages of 2 schizophrenic brothers, but they did find such a correlation between the onset ages of 2 schizophrenic sisters ($r = 0.82 \pm 0.11$). If this finding can be confirmed on the basis of a larger sampling, it will indicate that sharing a common life in the parental home has a greater influence on the courses of schizophrenias in 2 sisters than on the courses of schizophrenias of 2 brothers.

How can all these findings be best interpreted? Each of them indicates that personal relationships—in childhood toward the parents, and later toward others to whom one feels close—in women have an influence upon the genesis and the course of schizophrenic psychoses. Only a few scattered findings could with some effort be explained by way of far-fetched hereditary-pathological theories.

However, none of the findings reported above indicate whether the detrimental influences emanating from a disturbed family relationship also affect the schizophrenias of men. My statistics merely indicate that either such influences play a more significant role in the genesis of schizophrenias in women than they do in the genesis of schizophrenias in men, or else that they play such a role only in women. General psychological and psychopathological experiences (not my statistics) point to the first assumption, namely, that my figures do reveal the significant influence of psychotraumatic family conditions on women, but that they are too inexact a means for perceiving such influences in men, in whom they are less pronounced. Based on

our general knowledge of human nature, we could easily imagine that girls are more sensitive in reacting to disturbances in the family than boys are, but it is quite inconceivable that boys would not react to them at all. The psychological differences between the two sexes are assuredly not as great as that. Only a difference as to the degree and the type of influence of family misery is actually conceivable. Besides, the study of the individual life histories of a good number of schizophrenic men revealed a time-related and subjectively felt causal correlation between agonizing experiences with others and their own psychoses.

When one understands the psychopathology of schizophrenics, the presumptions about what psychotraumatic experiences are most important among men emerge rather easily. In comparison to the importance to men of their next-of-kin, it appears that their relationship to a fellow employee, a competitor, and to other men plays an important part during the process of their social integration. Beginning with his school years, a boy measures his own self-worth by the strength of his body, and his courage in the course of his altercations with his friends and his successes in school studies. A girl, on the other hand, measures her self-worth by whether she is attractive, charming, and desirable—qualities with which she assures for herself the approval of her family, and later of young men. In the imaginary world of schizophrenic men, a major role is played by the persecution by other men, in particular by homosexuals, altercations with men, as well as their occupational accomplishment. On the other hand, for women, altercations with members of the family and questions concerning sex predominate. Topics involve wanted or unwanted motherhood and a sexual partnership, one's own immaculate conception, virginity, or even holiness on the one hand, as opposed to their innate "prostitute nature" on the other. The statistical findings about the worse types of family situations for women indicate that sort of psychological mood. Later statistics will have to determine whether among schizophrenic men, psychotraumatic experiences different from those among women have accumulated in great number, as I would expect they have.

It seems to me to be worth noting that we did successfully prove, by way of rather laborious though basically simple statistics, an influence of life experiences on the emergence of schizophrenias. To be sure, it is only an influence of limited significance. It has been proved as being operant only in women, and nothing indicates that by itself it would be a decisive, or even a necessary or important prerequisite to the emergence of a schizophrenic psychosis. Still, statistics do basically show that psychogenetic influences on the schizophrenias merit serious consideration. In the past 20 years a great many fallacies for the psychogenic origins of the schizophrenias have appeared in print that were based on totally uncritical statistics. Statistics that set such goals for themselves have come into disrepute. On the other hand, it does seem to me that the proper evaluation of a large amount of research material—carefully undertaken—can yield some valid indications on the problem of psychogenesis.

On the one hand, my statistical findings are an indication of the influence of life experiences on the emergence of schizophrenias, although at the same time they also convey a warning. It is the warning to exercise caution in overevaluating and in generalizing and considering as absolute, experiences from life, and in particular, certain individual or specific experiences. The literature of the past two decades contains many such overevaluations. Especially the influence on the emergence of a schizophrenia of the loss of a mother at a particularly early age was most grotesquely overrated. Based on totally inadequate statistics, the "mother deprivation theory" was for some time placed in the foreground of schizophrenic onset. When my figures point to psychological correlations between the onset of schizophrenia in women and "mother deprivation," they also show, with unmistakable clarity, that "mother deprivation" can be only one among many other more important requisites for the onset of a psychosis. My figures showed quite plainly, that even those psychotraumatic experiences that are most frequently named as "causes" for the schizophrenias, are not found at all among schizophrenic men, and that they appear among schizophrenic women only slightly more often than they do among the general population. The most popular of these is the broken home in all its aspects.

By way of statistics we succeeded at least in proving that certain of life's experiences do have an influence on the emergence and the shaping of the course of schizophrenias in women. This is at the same time an indication of the importance of psychogenetic processes for the emergence of schizophrenias in general. However, the statistics clearly show that even the obviously traumatizing life experiences cannot exert any decisive, but only a subordinate influence on the emergence of schizophrenia.

The findings here presented agree with the theory of the multifactorial genesis of the schizophrenias. One single psychogenetic factor has emerged with clarity from these statistical labors. At the same time it has become clear that it cannot all by itself have a decisive influence on the schizophrenias.

The skeptic—and first of all, the skeptic I myself am—having absorbed these expositions, will ask with a bitter smile what purpose these years of schizophrenia research have served. All they disclosed was what any physician knows from the experience of his own practice, namely, that an adverse childhood is not exactly one of the most favorable backgrounds for a harmonious development, that it jeopardizes the future of child, and that girls are somewhat more sensitive to it than boys. In order to find that out, the statistics that cost many years of the labor of secretaries, colleagues, and of myself were not worth the effort.

Why do I hope that it was somewhat worthwhile anyway? In the process of painstakingly studying the life histories of schizophrenics individually (and this process was one of my principal endeavors for a number of decades), I continued to be confronted again and again with correlations between crushing life experiences of the patient with his fellowman, and his illness. Pathological ideas, confusing judgments, hallucinations, autistic attitudes (to mention but a few) fall into place in relationship to his life experiences. This relationship is subjectively felt by the patient as well. Often time-related correlations also appear. Such experiences make it easy for me to conjure up an image before my mind's eye of the most realistic psychogenesis for the psychoses of most patients. This psychogenesis is just as convincing (or as unconvincing) to me, as the psychogenesis of the development of a neurosis or the attitude of a normal person. Something on the order of a novel emerges about the development of a schizophrenia, that is just as gripping and as convincing as a classical novel written by a gifted author. If I tell it to my students, they are at once surprised and disappointed, if I do not draw the same conclusion that they worked out by themselves, namely, that the tragic story of tortured human relations brought on the schizophrenic illness. I myself am tormented by doubts as soon as I am tempted to draw this conclusion; for then I am not entirely certain whether I have invented a "novel," or whether I have discovered one.

In the state of this dilemma I yearn for a statistical foundation for my psychogenetic ("romantic") assumptions that I draw from the patient histories. But statistics have shed light on just one tiny area of the psychogenetic assumptions. They did show, however, that assumed correlations between the adverse family relations and the schizophrenia actually do exist. As far as I am concerned, the laborious statistical effort with few results —but with some results, after all—was worthwhile. I presume that I am not the only one contemplating the origins of schizophrenia who is tormented by doubts. And I hope that the findings presented here will be of some help to someone else when he wrestles with that enormous question of whether the correlations between the origin of the schizophrenias and a tragic fate in life, that one suspects upon first confrontation with the patient, really do have a causative significance.

As I had previously mentioned, so far as I know, these problems were first worked over in their essence by Rosenthal (1962). I was not able to find statistics that would lend themselves to direct comparison with mine. Nevertheless, some statistics do marginally approach some similar problems. Thus, Birtchell (1970) investigated the early backgrounds of 500 mental patients with varying diagnoses, in respect to premature parent loss. There are 259 depressives, but only 65 schizophrenics among his patients, so that his findings apply rather to depressives than to schizophrenics. He discovered that his patients, aged from 20 to 40 years, experienced the death of a parent within the first 5 years preceding their hospitalization, more often than the control subjects did. The difference was greater for female patients than for males. It is possible that the loss of a parent predisposes more women than men for depression as well as for schizophrenia.

Data on the Theory of the Hereditary Backgrounds of Schizophrenia

1. The fertility of the schizophrenic probands and their schizophrenic relatives has decreased to less than half that of the population. The fertility of the nonschizophrenic

parents and siblings of the probands is no greater. These findings from my probands agree with those of previous authors.

In theorizing about the heredity factor in schizophrenia, the reduced fertility of schizophrenics ought to be taken into account much more than it used to be. Even after the publication of the first convincing findings on this subject, it has been largely disregarded by many theorists, and even at the present time, it receives only brief mention. It should be kept in mind in any discussion concerning the place of heredity in schizophrenia, however. If schizophrenics propagate at a much lesser rate than the rest of the population, but the frequency of schizophrenic psychoses remains the same in spite of it, then it follows that schizophrenia must always be coming into being anew. The question as to the reasons for this new formation gains in importance from this aspect, while the question as to the process of hereditary transmission recedes in importance. Unfortunately, however, research on the matter of heredity has invested half a century exclusively in pursuit of this latter question of secondary importance, while the first, the more important one, has never been seriously dealt with.

If one holds fast to the speculative belief that mutant genes constitute the hereditary basis of the schizophrenias, then mutations would continually have to be generated anew. But at this point such a hereditary theory of the schizophrenias begins to run into insurmountable difficulties; for with the low fertility rate of schizophrenics, the mutation rate would have to be improbably high.

An objection raised to this statement was that the reduced fertility of schizophrenics would perhaps be somehow compensated for by an increased fertility among the carriers of latent hereditary tendencies. These assumptions were apparently supported by an exacting study by Böök (1953). But they were done with isolated subjects, among whom emigration played a particular role. Their results must not be generalized. My own figures and those of many other authors show the contrary to be true, that the fertility previously among the nonschizophrenic parents and siblings, is not at all higher. Indeed, no one (except the monozygotic twin of a schizophrenic) could more definitely be the carrier of latent hereditary tendencies for schizophrenia than specifically the nonschizophrenic parent or sibling of a schizophrenic.

If only as the result of the above deliberations, the old, accepted assumption that the schizophrenias could be based essentially on one single, or on a few individual mutant genes for their principal hereditary disposition, must be rejected out of hand. But a great deal of additional evidence of a different type refutes that assumption, and one might even add, that nothing really supports it, except, perhaps, the preconceived conviction that that is just the way it has to be.

This preconceived conviction, as it began to take shape under the enormously convincing impression of the new discovery that came into existence from the mendelian doctrine at the beginning of this century, persuaded even so eminent a hereditary scientist as Rüdin (1916). He declared with absolute certainty that the frequency of psychoses in families was a result of the hereditary process, and that the transmission of mental disorders was bound to proceed according to a mendelian pattern. He did not think of the possibilities of environmental factors that influence all the members of a family, and he forgot—and along with him, almost two generations of psychiatrists also forgot—that, actually, not one single purely mental disturbance was ever traced to a mendelian hereditary process, but that only a number of physical defects and characteristics were so traced. And furthermore, it was forgotten that in addition to a hereditary process according to simple mendelian laws (as was already recognized at the time) there was a multifactorial type of hereditary process to which the mendelian laws cannot be applied in practice. One of the most important aspects not considered was the fact that disturbances could develop from the incompatibility of hereditary tendencies, and that individually healthy genes in unfavorable combinations could jeopardize the capacity for life itself. This is readily understood, insofar as it involves physical development. In fact, it is already revealed rather neatly in the fact that crossbreeding of races or species usually does not produce offspring capable of sustaining life.[2] It took modern psychology to prove that the unity of a person is not a matter of course, but that it is based on postulates of heredity and experience, that may exist or may not exist sufficiently. A healthy personality development presupposes a harmony of the propensities for psychic development. In many neurotic developments and in pathological

personality developments of later schizophrenics it can be demonstrated that there are operant within the patient, internal antitheses and tensions that are partly rooted in hereditary tendencies.

The most likely explanation for the fact that the frequency of the incidence of schizophrenia remains the same in spite of reduced fertility among schizophrenics, lies in the assumption that the hereditary predisposition for schizophrenia does not consist of individually mutating, pathogenic genes, but rather in a disharmony of the congenital tendencies for personal development.

2. The studies presented here confirm that the findings developed by Rüdin and his school since 1916, about the frequency of schizophrenias in the parents, siblings, and offspring of schizophrenics, have a validity beyond the confines of the times and locales in which they appeared. This statement has a special meaning, because the former figures about the frequency of schizophrenia in the partners of schizophrenic monozygotic twins have been proved unreliable. It is not justifiable to transfer the mistrust in respect to the old data from twin studies to the old data on the frequency of schizophrenia in the parents, siblings, and offspring of schizophrenics. Unfortunately this is what did happen. The findings concerning the close relatives of my probands confirm the practical hereditary prognoses of the old figures of Rüdin's school, with respect to marriage counseling.

It is certain that in our century, under Western cultural conditions, the frequency of schizophrenia among parents of schizophrenics is about 7 percent, and for the siblings and offspring of schizophrenics, about 9 percent for each, assuming that all parents, siblings, and offspring survive the age of vulnerability for schizophrenic onset.

Studies on the frequency of schizophrenias among the half-sibs and offspring of the children of schizophrenics are extremely scarce in the literature. It was most desirable to increase the knowledge on this subject through the use of the family histories of my 208 probands. My figures on the subject are also in general agreement with the previous findings. The incidence of schizophrenia among half-sibs and siblings' offspring still needs further verification in spite of that, although it is more feasible now than earlier to state with certainty that for the half-sibs it is approximately at 5 percent (certainly within the extremes of 2–7 percent), and for the

2. This point will be discussed in detail on pp. 463–74.

offspring of siblings, between 2–3 percent. I made no attempt to determine the incidence of schizophrenia for the siblings of parents or for the cousins of the 208 schizophrenic probands, although I was able to determine such ratios from the large-scale experiences of my 1930 investigations with New York schizophrenics and from my 1942 investigations with the Pfäfers schizophrenics. In addition, there are investigations by Weinberg (1928), Smith (1936), and Galatschjan (1937) on those types of relatives. Each of these categories shows an incidence rate for schizophrenia of 2–4 percent.

A recheck of the spouses of the 208 schizophrenic probands confirmed previous findings to the effect that psychic disturbances among them are certainly not much more numerous than among the population. A suspicion remains that schizophrenias might occur just a little more frequently among them than among the population.

The above-mentioned figures on the incidence of schizophrenia among the relatives of schizophrenics are meaningful for the practice of marriage counseling. In addition, they will always and forever constitute one of the principal bases for the hereditary theories on schizophrenia. It is obvious that the onset frequencies among the various relatives of schizophrenics are not reconcilable with the assumptions concerning any simple sort of mendelian hereditary process.

Of course, it is easy to speculate that "schizophrenia-genes" could have a number of different manifestation probabilities, or that their manifestation probability could differ according to the entire hereditary syndrome (the entire "genic" environment) or according to the individual life experience. The speculative assumptions as to how many latent hereditary carriers there are and whether schizoids are hereditary carriers, however, are just as easy to make. One can also call upon statistics on mortality rates, which are not generally valid, in an effort to adapt the empirically determined incidence rates of illness to the ones theoretically calculated. If one persists patiently in such speculations, it is always possible to find some sort of intricate hereditary modus that will appear to correspond halfway to the empirical figures. But hereditary moduses derived by this method have never proved to be plausible. The very fact alone, that so many totally different hereditary theories on latent hereditary carriers have been set up that were based

on manipulations of the manifestation probability and of the changing mortality rates of schizophrenics, rob such attempts of any credibility.

3. Theories on the mendelian law of heredity in respect to the tendency for schizophrenia were often formulated on figures about the incidence of schizoid psychopaths or schizoid eccentrics. People who are designated as "schizoid" occur frequently among the relatives of schizophrenics. This research project of mine, along with many others, pointed out with great clarity that it is impossible to count schizoid psychopaths and schizoid eccentrics accurately. The schizoid personality that is congenital differs almost imperceptibly from schizoid behavior patterns of basically healthy individuals in a difficult human environment. All the many theories about the hereditary aspects of schizophrenia, that deal in precise figures with the frequency of hereditary schizoid psychopathies, from the very outset merit no confidence. More details in respect to the schizoid personality appear below in the summary discussions on the conclusions of my investigations. (see p. 434).

4. Simple mendelian hereditary processes are recognized not only by way of voluminous statistics on the incidence of disease among the relatives of the congenitally diseased, but they appear also when a large enough number of the family trees of congenitally ill patients are studied and compared to one another. For instance, not too many of such family trees need to be inspected to realize that Huntington's chorea is transmitted by simple dominance, and Friedreich's ataxia by simple recessiveness.

I have on file a number of the family trees of the Pfäfers schizophrenics, still unpublished, each of which includes well over 100 individuals. I have spent considerable time studying them. It has proved impossible, however, to make plausible any sort of mendelian law from them. When one believes one has found an indication of such a law in a family tree, such assumptions are soon refuted by others from the same source. In keeping with this, no sort of mendelian transmission modus for schizophrenias has been identified from the family-tree studies of other authors, either. When an author had postulated such a law on the basis of some individual family-tree studies, another author discovered a different one based on other family trees. A large-scale family-tree study was recently carried out in Iceland (Karlsson 1968). However, the assumptions suggested by the Icelandic family trees about a certain mendelian type of propagation of schizophrenia, are by no means confirmed by the data from my family trees. It is quite possible that the suspected congenital pathological correlations operate only for certain Icelandic families.

During the course of this research project, an excellent opportunity presented itself for family-tree studies of the probands with half-siblings. It should be possible to identify the universally applicable mendelian laws of heredity, if the ancestors and the offspring of the half-siblings of hereditary carriers are known. I was most disappointed in this expectation of mine from the study of my family trees. Schizophrenics emerged and failed to emerge with distressing irregularity, where, according to a mendelian theory, they were —or were not—expected.

In short, studies of family trees of schizophrenics, as well as the statistical findings on the incidence of schizophrenias among the relatives of schizophrenics, decisively refute the assumption that a certain simple mendelian law has any validity in the hereditary transmission of a hypothetical propensity for schizophrenia.

5. The preceding discussions (1–4) resulted from the unexpressed assumption that heredity is influential in the genesis of the schizophrenias. Quite properly, this presumption is not an indisputable fact for modern psychiatrists, as it was for the older ones. Today proof must be submitted as to why hereditary postulates for the emergence of schizophrenia are formulated. Supported by my general clinical experience and supplemented by the findings from the family histories of my schizophrenic probands, I should like to summarize these arguments below for the acceptance of hereditary backgrounds of schizophrenias that seem to me most convincing.

The frequent occurrence of schizophrenias among the blood relatives of schizophrenics is a matter of fact beyond any doubt. This was proved anew by the findings of studies of the family histories of my probands. But those findings also show unequivocally that this frequency cannot be traced primarily to "psychic contagion" among relatives, as it has sometimes been stated. A large portion of the schizophrenics have never lived together with schizophrenics before the eruption of their psychosis. Especially weighty arguments emerge from these investigations against the assumption that living together with schizophrenic parents is an essential prerequisite for the onset of schizophrenias. Only a very small minority of the schizophrenic probands (27 of 208) ever lived together with a schizophrenic parent before they were 20. The number of years of such living together during the first two decades of life is small in comparison with all the cumulative years of life (77 of 540). Our family histories encompass a total of 4,144 known years of childhood and youth of schizophrenics, of which only 77 were spent in close relationship with schizophrenic parents. The children of the probands spent a great deal more time in living together with schizophrenic parents than the schizophrenic probands themselves or their siblings did; about half of these children spent an average of one-third of their childhood and youth with schizophrenic parents. These offspring of the probands, who frequently lived together with schizophrenic parents, became schizophrenic at no greater rate than the proband sibs, who seldom lived together with schizophrenic parents. In the light of these findings, it is quite impossible to ascribe any great influence on the emergence of schizophrenia to living together with schizophrenic parents. One qualification, however, has to be stated and that is, that when I speak of schizophrenias, I mean psychoses in the currently accepted sense. If, now, socially and medically healthy individuals with certain characteristics in test situations were also regarded as schizophrenic, these above-mentioned deliberations would no longer be valid.

Diseases that originate from "contagion" occur frequently not only among the blood relatives of patients, but also among their relatives by marriage. In the area of psychiatry I was able to check this expectation through the study of alcoholics. Spouses and stepparents of alcoholics are often alcoholics, too, but the spouses and stepparents of schizophrenics are not often also schizophrenic.

The frequent occurrence of schizophrenias in families—that cannot have originated from "contagion"—constitutes a positive argument for accepting the importance of heredity as one thing disposing for schizophrenias. But there is just as valid a negative argument, namely that there is no psychological theory for the onset of schizophrenia deserving serious consideration that does not require support from an acceptable theory of special hereditary dispositions. If one were inclined to assume that schizophrenic psychoses were principally traceable to unhealthy relationships with other people, one should also have been able to prove that such relationships are indeed unfavorable, either in a special way or to a special degree. The contrary has been proved. That is, that whatever aspect of unhealthy human relationships has been blamed as a cause of schizophrenias has also been found in the childhood histories of many neurotics, human derelicts, antisocials, addicts, and even among many healthy people. It has never been proved that a certain type of biographical noxa occurs only in the childhood of schizophrenics. No type of stress that can befall a person will always—or even mostly—imply a subsequent schizophrenic psychosis. Psychotraumatic situations can therefore be influential only in the onset of schizophrenias in connection with personal, and very probably, hereditary susceptibilities.

It might be expected that investigations into the fates of children of schizophrenics, who grew up from birth with healthy adoptive parents, disclose additional important facts concerning the influence of hereditary dispositions. For the time being, it appears as though they will uncover renewed support for the influence of heredity.

For a long time, high concordance figures for schizophrenic onset in monozygotic twins were regarded as the "absolute scientific proof" for the great importance of heredity. As I have emphasized for many years and in many places, the line of reasoning of such rigorous precision is based on a fallacy. It was assumed—probably correctly—that the hereditary traits in monozygotic twins were equal, and that in dizygotic twins they were quite different; but incorrectly, it was also assumed that the human environment of two monozygotic twins would also be equal or differ to the same degree as the human environment of two dizygotic twins. The conclusion was that the higher concordance in the monozygotic twins could not be caused by the environment, but only by hereditary factors. But the fact that two monozygotic twins might live in a more similar environment than two dizygotic twins was forgotten. Personal characteristics (for instance, a homely or a pleasing appearance), that actually have nothing to do with the hereditary implications of schizophrenia, are, in fact, usually the same in monozygotic twins and usually different in dizygotic twins. They evoke the same type of behavioral reactions from others toward the two monozygotics. When monozygotics reveal high concordance figures for

psychic disturbances, it could be caused just as easily by the great similarity in hereditary factors as by the great similarity in their human environment. Quite arbitrarily, for a long time, the first of these possibilities was blamed as the major culprit.

The hereditary influence on schizophrenia, therefore, is by no means established by the fact that the concordance figure for schizophrenia in monozygotic twins is higher than it is in dizygotics. Nevertheless, one might carefully formulate that the finding is reconcilable with the assumption that heredity does play a part in the genesis of schizophrenias.

6. Up to now almost nothing was known about whether hereditary dispositions had different influences on the different course types of schizophrenia. The studies of the family histories of the 208 principal probands and of numerous other schizophrenics added later, shed some light on this problem.

One comparison shows that the course types of schizophrenic psychoses in two siblings certainly do not combine according to the laws of chance. Rather, it appears that there is a tendency toward similar course types of schizophrenic psychoses in siblings and in other relatives. What occurs by far most frequently, much more frequently than mere chance would provide, is that two sibs contract schizophrenic psychoses that run a phasic-benign course. It can be considered certain that there is a familial tendency for such course types. It is difficult to imagine that environmental influences that affect whole families are the cause of the phasic-benign course. Actually, psychological schizophrenia research shows that the recurring acute schizophrenic phases specifically can almost never be correlated with psychological processes—with environmental experience—in a convincing way. It is most probable, therefore, that the familial influences on the genesis of the phasic-benign schizophrenias are hereditary.

Inherited dispositions play a role in the benign-phasic schizophrenias, and it is a more important role than in all other course types of schizophrenia.

The analogy to manic-depressive illness suggests itself, for in manic-depressive illnesses the phases of illness also frequently emerge in families. Up to now they also eluded any satisfactory explanation based on psychological factors. Should we therefore include the phasic-benign schizophrenias among the manic-depressive illnesses? I believe not. Those phasic-benign schizophrenias I have in mind have a definite schizophrenic symptomatology, and most importantly, among the relatives of patients with these types of schizophrenias, there is by no means any frequency of manic-depressives, but most especially similar types of schizophrenics, and secondly, patients with other types of schizophrenia.

In contrast to the phasic-benign types of schizophrenia, there are almost never combinations in siblings of the catastrophe-schizophrenias, (those that begin acutely and without remission proceed to severe long-term psychoses). In the same vein, it could also be demonstrated that the treatment and other environmental influences have an effect on these psychoses. There is no evidence for hereditary tendencies for catastrophe-schizophrenias.

The frequency of combinations of similar and different course types in two siblings lies between the two above-mentioned extremes; they do not occur as often as combinations of phasic-benign types, but they occur more frequently than combinations of catastrophe-schizophrenias.

The findings here presented seem to contradict previous ones from twin studies to the effect that in monozygotic twins the concordance in respect to schizophrenia is greater when the twin who became the proband was severely ill than when he was mildly ill. (These data from twin studies had already been compiled by Rosenthal 1961, among others.) According to my studies, however, a familial frequency is least evident specifically in the "catastrophe-schizophrenias"[3] and is most obvious for the phasic-benign types. But this contradiction is resolved readily when one considers that my "catastrophe-schizophrenias" cannot be equated with the group of severe schizophrenias of the twin studies either, nor can my phasic-benign types be equated with the milder schizophrenias described in twin studies. The severe schizophrenias of the twin studies are not only the "catastrophe-schizophrenias," but also many other types of schizophrenias that evolved slowly or in several phases to a chronic, severe state. The mild schizophrenias of the twin studies are not mainly phasic-benign types, but chronic mild ones. Kallmann (1946)

3. Here again, the "catastrophe-schizophrenias" are those that begin acutely, proceed to the most severe chronic psychoses without intervening remissions, and persist for the rest of the patient's life.

probably did not include many of my phasic-benign types in his twin studies, because of his specialized concept of schizophrenia.

Besides, solely as a result of the selection process of the probands, decided differences in the concordance figures for schizophrenia in twins with severe and mild forms of illness were to be expected. On the average, it has been demonstrated that there is a tendency for similarity in course types of schizophrenia in a set of monozygotic twins. Patients with malignant schizophrenias are generally hospitalized longer and earlier than patients with benign forms. Twin studies use those twins as probands who are admitted during a certain period of time at a certain hospital, or who are being treated there. Twins with severe psychoses, therefore, are more often included in studies than twins of whom one or the other suffers a mild psychosis. This in itself would not disturb the relationship of the concordance of severe and of mild forms. But now some of the investigators engaged in twin studies (among them Kallmann 1946) calculate the concordance figure by the proband method. He counts twin pairs twice in his statistics if both partners were picked up as probands (that is, if they were hospitalized in the specified time-period in the hospital in question). For this reason, his concordance figure for the severe cases of schizophrenia is artificially higher compared to his concordance figure for the milder cases.

In still another way the manner of processing the probands leads to similar illusions. If a twin proband is only mildly schizophrenic, there is a high probability that the other partner has an even milder form of schizophrenia (at least that probability is much greater than for a twin whose partner's schizophrenia is severe). That partner will often be so mildly schizophrenic that his psychosis is much more likely to escape detection than the psychosis averaging a greater severity in the partner of a severely ill schizophrenic. The first psychotic episode of the partner of a mild case of schizophrenia might have been so mild that hospitalization was not necessary, and that it could hardly be detected from the interviews with family members. Or it might also have taken a chronic mild course, so that under favorable living conditions it would not be noticed. The twin with a mild psychosis is also apt to be the one to have emigrated or otherwise become inaccessible to the investigator, rather than the one who is constantly hospitalized with a severe psychosis.

Accordingly, it is certain that the differences in the concordance of schizophrenia in monozygotic twins with mild schizophrenias and those with severe schizophrenias are largely artificial. They are the results of differences in the methods of acquiring and of processing the probands. For the time being, it has by no means been proved that a concordance in nonselected twins with severe schizophrenias occurs more frequently than it does in those with mild schizophrenias. Surprisingly, this line of reasoning is still extremely scanty in the literature. Research supported a preconceived notion when it appeared to indicate that heredity played a more important role in the severe schizophrenias than it did in the milder ones.

The Schizoid Personality and Schizoid Psychopathy

The concept of the schizoid personality is already an unfamiliar one to many young psychiatrists, and almost unknown to some. For this reason I am constrained to preface my contributions on the "schizoid"[4] with some remarks about its evolution. It is strange and worth mentioning how quickly the concept of the schizoid assumed importance, how for a time it impregnated and dominated the whole of psychiatric thought, and how interest in it gradually vanished—all within half a century.

The concept of the schizoid personality itself and the term took shape in conversations among the doctors of Burghölzli in connection with the expression "schizophrenia" around 1910. For a long time there was no mention of it in publications, or it was only briefly referred to. Its prime time flourished after 1921, when Kretschmer and the Tübing psychiatric school popularized it.

4. "The schizoid" (or, according to Kallmann, "schizoidia") is a convenient—though homely—abbreviated form, laden with ambiguity. At times it is understood to mean schizoid personality traits, sometimes it is a somewhat peculiar term for an illness connoting schizoid psychopathy and schizoid abberation combined. The schizoid personality within the norm Kretschmer called "schizothymic," and he reserved the expression "schizoid" for the psychopathies. The distinction is no longer customary, so that I use the term "schizoid-aberrant within the norm" instead of schizothymic. According to the view E. Bleuler (1922) set forth, there are also nonabberant healthy people that might be called schizoid; in fact, every person has possibilities of existing as a schizoid.

What was it that gave this doctrine its great importance? At the beginning, it neatly summarized all the peculiarities that every psychiatrist had observed in his daily routine in the relatives of his schizophrenics, and that he derived anamnestically as characteristics of many of his schizophrenic patients before their illness. But it was a real pioneering achievement for the development of psychiatry when the concept of the schizoid personality suggested the idea of recognizing something in the phenomenon of psychoses that was generally human. To anyone who had accepted the concept, much of what constitutes the essence of schizophrenia was bound to appear to him as not quite so "crazy" psychologically. The magic touch of the concept lay in the fact that it brought the mental patient closer to the heart and to the understanding of his doctor. It helped to establish a clear pathway to a "psychodynamic" schizophrenia theory and to a sympathetic meeting with the mentally ill patient that was unencumbered by the hard, cold dogmas depicting the mental patient as something different, inaccessible, and beyond the reach of human empathy. No matter how "dynamically" the concept of the schizoid personality seemed to manifest itself in some respects, in others, it turned to something "static." By implication the schizoid personality and schizoid psychopathy came to be regarded as something constitutional in the context of heredity and as something constant. It was presumed that it characterized a person by nature, and for life. After Kretschmer (1944) had brought the schizoid personality traits into relationship with the physical constitutions (the asthenic and other types of physiques) that also used to be regarded as purely hereditary, it seemed for a long time to be a matter of course to accept the schizoid personality as a hereditary manifestation that was in no need of further discussion.

In the past two decades all talk about the concept of the schizoid personality has lapsed into silence. Its importance as a bridge to psychological understanding of schizophrenias was forgotten. The whole concept of a firmly established, inherited personality structure became alien to a generation that was chiefly interested in the shaping of character by the experiences of life. When even Kretschmer's body-structure types could no longer be regarded as exclusively the expression of a hereditary constitution, after it had been shown how they, too, were dependent on the age and the life-style of the patient, the doctrine of the schizoid of the 20s had lost another firm support. In addition, the concept seemed a little too indefinite to suit the younger psychiatrists. Indeed, it becomes difficult to recognize something common and characteristic in descriptions such as "bizarre, cold, fanatic, sensitive," etc., if one doesn't constantly call to mind the descriptions of schizoid patients as Kretschmer provided them, written with all the poetic flair of a gifted literary master. It was necessary to hold on to the essentials of the concept, but this, expressed in dry scientific terms, seemed too abstract and not sufficiently impressive. In the intellectual life of the schizoid the shackles of common, conventional thought are broken. His individual life experiences are brought into new relationships. The world he experiences undergoes a constant, renewed mental readaptation. What is good about it is that such an inner life is creative; it is the kind of life that generates new things, and that is necessary for cultural development. In the adverse sense it means egocentric crankiness, alienation from the world, and a crafty, complicated, and unnatural personality. Raised to a pathological level, it becomes schizophrenic distractedness. As regards feelings, this type of intellectual life corresponds to a differentiation of the emotions. Feelings, when they might be called for, do not emerge consistently. Vague and distant products of the imagination take on an emotional value with which not everyone could empathize. Different, multivarious emotional stirrings exist side by side. The ambivalence is difficult to overcome. In the good sense all this takes on the aspect of self-reliant independence; in the bad, of a bizarre, uncompromising, and stubborn nature. Augmented to a pathological level, it is closely related to schizophrenic autism.

My years as a medical student fell into the period when the introduction of the concept "schizoid" seemed to be one of the most important achievements of psychiatry. Accordingly, I applied it in the same way that the Tübing school did, and thereafter, as the school of hereditary pathology of Rüdin had done. I then succeeded in showing statistically for the first time, using the family histories of my Pfäfers schizophrenics, that (in accord with the expectations of those times) abberant schizoids and schizoid psychopaths were found much more frequently among close relatives of schizophrenics than among the general population.

The relatives of my 208 principal probands I came to know much more intimately and over a longer period than I had known the relatives of probands of previous studies. But I found it by no means easier to classify them as schizoid or nonschizoid—on the contrary, I found it much more difficult, and in some cases quite impossible. The difficulty came from the fact that I could not distinguish between schizoid attitudes and a constitutionally schizoid personality. The more accurately I came to know the relatives of my schizophrenic patients, the more often I seemed to realize that they were secretive, cold, unpredictable, or bizarre. I further discovered that their personalities underwent changes. When I approached them, they seemed capable of dropping their "schizoid" personality. It was especially difficult for me to label the children of schizophrenics simply as schizoid. I could empathize with them, as they told their stories, and experience together with them what it meant for them to have sick parents. The son of a paranoid mother with delusions of jealousy had been trained to yell out to his father, as he came home evenings, "Well, you whoremaster! Where have you been wenching again tonight?" Another had to take wide detours on his way to school in order to evade imagined persecution. Other children were kept out of school for extended periods or kept in complete isolation from their school comrades. Many had to live through the torment of seeing their sick father or mother become the butt of mockery and derision in their neighborhoods. Others were present when their raging father had to be overpowered in a melee of fisticuffs, and hauled off to the hospital. Again others found their mother who had severed an artery lying in a pool of blood, or their father dangling from a rope in the attic. So to me it seemed quite natural, human, and comprehensible, when such experiences left behind lasting impressions, that such children could not be as other children were who had enjoyed a normal, orderly childhood. The fact that they were frightened, spiteful, insecure, shy, insolent, or excessively hard through overcompensation—was this a hereditary, solidly impressed personality disturbance? Did it not conform more readily to the development that particularly a warm, sensitive, and healthy person was bound to undergo, under the given circumstances?

These were questions I could no longer answer. The concept of the schizoid personality and of schizoid psychopathy seems to dissolve, once one knows about the life experiences of "schizoids."

Such experiences teach us impressively that it is intrinsically wrong to regard the schizoid personality from the outset as something traditional and inherited. A schizoid peculiarity may be the natural sequel to life's experiences. We know of a temporary schizoid attitude under the stress of emotional shock. And certainly there are long-term schizoid developments under the pressures of stressful life experiences. This modification of the concept is a recognized characteristic of the development of psychiatry over the past decades. It is not only the concept of schizoid psychopathy that has undergone a change in this sense, but the concepts of most of the other types of psychopathy have done the same. In this sense, my own experiences in the application of the concept "schizoid" have come to conform to those changes that most of the psychiatrists of my generation have made in one way or another.

The only new thing resulting from my investigations on this subject was one single piece of information. It supports the assumption that the schizoid personality does not necessarily have to be inherited, but that it can also be acquired. There was one statistically significant correlation between a schizoid pathological personality and a horrible childhood that emerged from the study of the 208 principal probands. Among all the probands there was just 1 who, under apparently normal conditions at home, was pathologically schizoid as a child. It would be naive to conclude from this single instance, that an unhealthy schizoid development was unequivocally caused by a horrible childhood in every one of the remaining cases. Not every child becomes schizoid under horrible childhood conditions. The horrors of a childhood are not entirely independent of the child himself. A difficult personality in the child disturbs the harmony of his environment. Dependent on his personality, the child reacts to what others may regard as horrible. But despite that, the evidence that a prepsychotic schizoid personality usually develops under the stress of miserable childhood conditions, impressively illustrates what the modern theory of human development suggests anyway, namely that a schizoid personality must not be simply and unequivocally evaluated as a constitutionally inherited characteristic.

A pathological, schizoid personality ("schizoid psychopathy") had evolved in one-fourth (50) of my 208 schizophrenic probands, long before the eruption of their psychosis. In 13 of these probands, the disturbance did not emerge until after school age. It was not present from the beginning; it developed. Exactly when this disturbance emerged in the remaining 37 probands, whether it was before or during their school years, does not emerge from my investigations.

Unfavorable personality developments of a schizoid or other type (psychopathies, character neuroses, addictions, depressive personalities) occur with considerable frequency among the siblings of probands who grew up under horrible conditions and became schizoid early in life. They occurred more frequently among them, with statistical significance, than among the siblings of those probands who grew up under normal conditions and who were prepsychotically nonaberrant. On the one hand, this finding indicates that the horrible conditions did, in fact, have the suspected psychotraumatic influence on the personality development. On the other hand, it shows that additional reasons must be found why this misery caused the probands to become specifically schizoid. After all, their siblings often became otherwise aberrant or psychopathic. Theoretical explanations readily present themselves, but so far none has been proved, or even seems highly probable.

There is a warning to be heard from all these experiences of intimate acquaintance with the concept "schizoid personality." It is that precise counting of schizoid psychopaths and of the schizoid-aberrant is an impossibility. Figures about them must not be overestimated as to their significance. Such overestimations have occurred in the past. Many attempts to prove the hereditary theories for schizophrenia contain precise figures about the carriers of "characteristic schizoid genes." Hereditary theories that use figures of this type in support of themselves do not deserve any confidence. All too often it is quite arbitrary whether schizoid psychopathy or a schizoid attitude forced on the patient by environmental circumstances are under discussion. Just how unreliable the figures on the frequency of schizoid personality disorders really are, comes out clearly in the comparisons of my findings on the children of schizophrenics and the findings of other authors.

As I have demonstrated in detail, the difference is principally caused by the fact that the inclination to assume the existence of a schizoid psychopathy declines appreciably as one's knowledge of the probands' lives increases.

My investigations further confirm what everybody knows so well that it scarcely needs any further verification, namely, that if one has a good anamnestic picture in mind of the prepsychotic personality of schizophrenics, the term "schizoid" aptly characterizes most of them. Without a doubt or having to have pangs of conscience about it, I could label over half my schizophrenic probands before their psychoses as schizoid; that is, one-third as schizoid-aberrant within the norm, and one-fourth as schizoid-psychopathic.[5] But it would be incorrect to consider a schizoid personality type as the only disposition for schizophrenia. Almost half of all future schizophrenics are unequivocally not schizoid, and one-third in no way whatever aberrant in their personality. It is interesting that there are families whose schizophrenic members were all prepsychotically schizoid. But there are also families in which no schizophrenic member had ever been schizoid. And there are even families whose schizophrenic members all had totally different personalities; for instance, some were infantile. It does seem as if a schizoid personality does constitute a disposition for schizophrenia in certain families, yet in others it does not. One other experience is a warning not to overestimate the schizoid personality as a disposition

5. Different calculations with different probands at different times always yielded the same frequencies of schizoid personalities and schizoid psychopathies in the backgrounds of schizophrenics. However, I did not always encounter the same frequency of schizoids among the relatives. Where does the difference come from? I consider two explanations to be probable. Later schizophrenics might be more clearly schizoid than their relatives who never become schizophrenic. Schizoids who did not become psychotic were often able to give me a detailed picture of their development that made their personalities appear plausible. In their cases, I became uncertain whether to classify them as schizoid. However, with schizophrenics it was usually more difficult to find convincing correlations between their life experience and their personal development in retrospect over many years, from their own reports and from those of their families. An arbitrary distinction between a congenital personality and an acquired attitude was less frequently necessary for them.

for schizophrenia. Only a small portion of the schizoid-aberrant and the schizoid-psychopaths become schizophrenic. This is clearly demonstrated in the schizoid relatives of my schizophrenic probands, and it agrees with general clinical experience.

One of the many reasons that rendered the concept of the schizoid personality useful lies in its importance for the prognosis. The Tübing school has demonstrated in a number of investigations, that have also been supported by others, that the prognosis is less favorable for prepsychotically schizoid schizophrenics. This general rule is confirmed by my own research material. To be sure, the correlation between schizoid psychopathy and an unfavorable course is only minimal among my probands. Even as a prognostic devic for schizophrenia, schizoid psychopathy must not be overestimated.

Thus my investigations contribute a great deal to show that the concept of the schizoid personality must be carefully applied and that its importance must not be overrated. They show that it was an incorrect and preconceived notion to regard the schizoid personality as something hereditary, imposed by nature; they show that development toward a schizoid personality or a schizoid psychopathy can also be partly or entirely caused by the pressures of adverse conditions in life; they show that figures on the frequency of schizoids have only a limited significance; they show that the schizoid personality certainly cannot always be regarded in all families as a disposition for schizophrenia; and, finally, they show that the schizoid personality is only of minor importance in prognoses.

Having said this, I do not mean to say that the time is anywhere near at hand to abandon the concept. It simply has not yet been replaced by a better one. There still is no better term that includes all the kinds of aberrant psychiatric morbidity shared by the later schizophrenics and by many of their relatives, than that of the schizoid personality. The concept of the schizoid personality still implies a challenge to search for something healthy and comprehensible in the schizophrenic mental patient, and to approach him by that means. Accordingly, the concept of the schizoid contains within itself the stimulus for us to search within ourselves for that which is in essence comparable to the nature of the schizophrenic.

The young research scientist is still too

unaware of how many of the most important new developments had already been anticipated by the concept of the schizoid, although its definition was still somewhat imprecise. Today's research effort is justifiably directed at determining whether the "teaching of irrationality" plays a part in the origin of schizophrenia. The fact that the parents of schizophrenics are often schizoid has long been established. This implies that by their own nature, the influence on their children is an unhealthy one—by the "teaching of irrationality." It is a part of the schizoid concept that ambiguous terminology is used, that the emphasis on the affectivity of a concept contradicts its own content, that talk about it is indefinite and in a questioning mood, and that the traditional attitudes toward one's own sexuality and toward one's own heterogenesis are experienced somewhat diffusely. All discoveries concerning these matters fit neatly into the old concept of the schizoid personality. One of the great achievements of modern research has been to identify more precisely described, individual behavior patterns on the basis of the schizoid behavior of parents, and to check their influence on the development of the children. But there is still no decision as to whether certain of these specific traits have a specific influence, or whether the decisive influence emanates from the schizoid parents and is transmitted to the child from their total schizoid nature in its multiplicity.

Does the Knowledge of Long-term Courses and Family Histories Help to Break down the Group of Schizophrenias into Various Etiologically Independent Diseases?

Kraepelin and E. Bleuler were convinced that their descriptions "dementia praecox" and "the group of schizophrenias" included all types of mental disorders, the essential symptoms of which were common, and the great majority of which differed in symptomatology from all other types of psychoses. Originally Kraepelin also assumed that the course of all these disorders was uniform and typical. He felt that the disease was incurable and evolved in the direction toward a particular type of dementia of varying severity. But then Kraepelin himself soon observed that many patients recovered, although in the beginning their symptomatology was the same as that of the malignant cases. E. Bleuler stated even more emphatically that among his schizophrenics

recoveries were not rare exceptions. Despite this, he determined nonetheless that the disease courses in a certain sense were all similar to one another. He formulated that the disease might be static, might recede, or might progress along its course; but when it advanced, it was always in the same direction of a chronic psychosis of quite an exceptional type. Also, that its symptomatology was different from that of all other types of chronic psychoses.

The basic common features in the symptomatology and a limited uniformity in the courses of all schizophrenics, however, still do not constitute proof of a common etiology for all schizophrenias. This is a truth that E. Bleuler (1911) especially stated emphatically. The title of his monograph on "The Group of Schizophrenias" should have a thought-provoking effect. It should encourage all doctors to look for diseases with a specific etiology within the group of schizophrenias.

When over 30 years ago I began to collect family histories, I was in hopes of getting a step closer to this goal. I expected to find some specific schizophrenic diseases that would be distinguished by a specific set of family characteristics that would set them apart from all others. I wanted particularly to separate schizophrenic illnesses with frequent occurrences among relatives from those that did not occur in this way. I wanted further to investigate whether I could find indications that certain subgroups of schizophrenic psychoses would be transmitted more easily according to one mendelian hereditary theory, and others according to another.

But such hopes remained unrealized. Many psychiatrists of my generation expected at the time, along with me, that the next great forward step in the field of psychiatry would consist of a subdivision of the group of schizophrenias, into individual illnesses each of which had its own particular etiology. But progress in this vein was not forthcoming to other authors either. Slater (1963) was one exception. He was studying the psychoses of epileptics with a schizophrenia-like symptomatology. He succeeded in proving that these types of psychoses, according to their nature, have nothing to do with schizophrenia. In the main, the psychoses that E. Bleuler (1911) had summarized as a group of schizophrenias, up to the present day, still defy subdivision acording to specific etiologies.

The patient- and family-histories of my probands confirmed anew that those psychoses that are considered as a homogenous group have natural relationships to one another.

This fact was definitely established from studies of the long-term courses as well as from studies of the family histories. During the course of years, one and the same patient often exhibited the most varied schizophrenic states. Catatonic, hebephrenic, and paranoid manifestations would follow one another in irregular succession and then interchange with states that correspond to the syndrome of schizophrenia simplex. Under therapy (or simply in the course of time and without therapy), states of excitation and moodiness, catatonic and hebephrenic symptoms most usually recede. If recovery is not forthcoming, paranoid states are frequent. The persistence of the illness may also reveal itself by the patient's distracedness, by an introverted, day-dreaming attitude, or by loss of interest in natural activities. To be sure, there are many patients who reveal no marked changes in schizophrenic symptoms over many years. By and large, however, one is impressed with the variability of the manifestations, more than with their consistency. I have tried in vain to get accurate data in order to prove this type of evidence, but I had to abandon it, because I could only make subjective judgments as to whether the case in question concerned a clear-cut, definite change or merely an insignificant change in symptomatology.

Meanwhile precise figures that illuminate the problem came from the family histories. No matter how the probands were subdivided according to the course type of the psychosis, there were also schizophrenics among their relatives whose psychoses evolved quite differently. Of course, there are individual families, in which one course type or another prevails; but there are also families in which a number of different course types are combined. If a large number of schizophrenics were to be assembled under every possible course type, the number of relatives with schizophrenias of other course types is always greater than the data for a corresponding group of the general population would indicate.

For this reason it still makes sense today to hold to the inclusive concept for the group of schizophrenias. All schizophrenias, no matter of how many different course types, have a great deal in common, not only in their symptomatology, but also in common family backgrounds.

To be sure, these declarations must be immediately qualified. Even if schizophrenics with different course types occur frequently among the relatives of a schizophrenic with a certain specific course type, there is still a certain tendency for family psychoses to evolve similarly. Among the relatives of a schizophrenic with a specific course type, the schizophrenics do not necessarily always evolve with the same course type, although chiefly that same course type would predominate.[6]

So it is possible to recognize a familial tendency for contracting any type of schizophrenia, just as there is such a tendency to contract a certain definite type of it. Such types of "contingent uniformity" of diseases running in families occur frequently.[7] It is a

6. Russian scientists arrive at similar interpretations. They subdivide the schizophrenias according to their courses, much as I have done. They distinguish chronic-progressive schizophrenias from those proceeding in surges and in phases. According to their investigations, however, there are also numerous intermediate forms. Thus, the Russian investigations, which were carried out quite differently from mine, reveal the facts that subforms of schizophrenia, classified according to their course, can be identified that are partially independent, but that all belong together under the overall concept of the schizophrenias (Nadzharov 1969, Sneznewsky 1969).

7. Pupillatonia, for example, sometimes occurs in families as a syndrome that encompasses the failure to react to light, delay in contraction of the pupil for close focusing, and the unrounding of the pupil. Among the relatives of carriers of this characteristic, however, the symptoms also occur separately, although only sporadically and in different combinations, as for instance, frequent and slight delays of contraction in focusing for close vision under normal lighting. In other cases only an unrounding or unevenness of the pupil takes place. One case was observed that lacked the principal characteristic (stiff pupil), but all other characteristics were represented (André-van Leeuwen 1948).

The masculine stigmatization of women occurs very frequently in many families. Often women of such families are masculine in their total personalities; then again, there is only a single masculine characteristic, such as facial hair, masculine body hair, a deep voice, a masculine distribution of fat over the body, or the like. On the one hand, one must assume that the manifestation according to the overall concept of masculinity is a family characteristic, and on the other, that the overall concept can also be broken down into specific

phenomenon that has received much too little attention, considering its prevalence.

The findings summarized here make no statement as to whether the tendencies occurring in families are hereditary or acquired because of shared destinies. The only certainty is that the phasic-benign types of courses show an unmistakable tendency to occur among schizophrenics who are related to one another. It is hard to imagine that this one form specifically is shaped by shared family experience. The familial disposition for a phasic-benign course is probably of hereditary origin, and the same is assumed about the phasic psychoses of the manic-depressive family of disorders, that seem somehow to be related to the phasic-benign schizophrenias.

A great many authors, particularly the French and the Scandinavians, attempt to distinguish between the benign ("schizophreniform") and the malignant ("genuine") schizophrenias. Langfeldt described some extensive investigations on this subject. In favor of such a subdivision one might say that recovery from psychoses with acute beginnings, along with moodiness, excitation, or confusion, occurs much more frequently than recovery from psychoses with chronic beginnings, along with schizophrenic symptoms and full presence of mind. The phasic-benign schizophrenias of my investigations correspond almost entirely to the first group. The fact that two schizophrenics related to one another both frequently manifest the same phasic-benign courses, justifies the distinction between benign and malignant forms. The two forms are not influenced by exactly the same familial background. Nonetheless, family studies also reveal that there are no precise boundaries between the two forms. It is true that among relatives schizophrenias of similar course types predominate, but frequently there are also schizophrenias of different course types. Accordingly, it is possible to draw only probable—but not certain —conclusions for a prognosis from the type

---

categories. In one family the one, and in another family one of the other subcategories will predominate. There are many such examples of "contingent uniformity," of a characteristic with a familial predominance. In one case, "familial" can be equated with "hereditary," and in another, it can be better equated with "acquired by family tradition," but for the most part, the two are closely related (M. Bleuler 1949).

of beginning and the symptomatology of a fresh onset. Recently Stephens compiled new data on this subject. The matter is best served by the following formulation: Benign and malignant schizophrenias are two types of one and the same disease, and between them numerous transitional forms are possible.

It is a matter of interest that there are psychoses of schizophrenic symptomatology to which—in contrast to schizophrenias— very definite etiological causes or secondary causes may be ascribed, yet whose general familial image is nevertheless close to that of the schizophrenias. The investigations on this type of psychosis have not been included here. At our clinic, Scharfetter (1970) for the symbionic psychoses, Rohr (1961, 1964) for the schizophrenic reactions, and Benedetti (1952) for certain chronic alcoholic hallucinations, have determined that among the close relatives of patients there were more schizophrenics than in the general population, but still not quite as many as among the relatives of schizophrenics. For many other diseases with a schizophrenia-like symptomatology, systematic family investigations would be indicated that might perhaps turn up similar findings. They would probably be Caesarian insanity or the schizophrenia-like psychoses occurring after the abuse of stimulants.

For the time being, this information is best interpreted by the application of an old, established assumption, namely, that different noxae that are harmful to the psyche can trigger the eruption of a schizophrenia-like psychosis in the presence of a mild familial tendency for schizophrenia.

Conclusions for Ordinary Medical Practice

The treatment of schizophrenics is unquestionably a worthwhile endeavor. It is a great, a beautiful, and an important task, however laborious and difficult it may be. In any condition and at any stage of progress, treatment can bring about improvement or remission, even when a full recovery cannot be achieved. It is worthwhile, even independently of the objective successes. In the course of skillful treatment (sometimes sooner, sometimes later, and often even very late), the wall suddenly collapses that had for so long frustrated every natural communal relationship with the patient. Whether it be only for moments, for days, weeks, months, or for good, suddenly conversation with the patient can be reestablished as though he were normal, and he reveals his desires and needs clearly, as a healthy person would. More than this, one is taken aback by the patient's distress, by his gratitude, his helplessness, his modesty, or his confident self-complacency—in brief, one can empathize with him again. At least for the time being, everything that marked him as pathological is gone, as if by the waving of a magic wand. It is as if we had penetrated into a dungeon and had been able to spend a few moments with the prisoner, in pleasant, comfortable communion with him.

These are the elementary medical experiences, not only with my 208 principal probands, but also with the several thousand other schizophrenics that I have treated, or whose treatment I was allowed to direct. They are the experiences common to every clinician. There is no need for me to describe them any more fully, although I should explain how the above-presented investigations shed new light on existing knowledge.

Working with the probands, it was possible to observe therapeutic efforts extending over decades, while the literature usually reports the results of therapies over brief periods only, over months, or possibly over a few years. The long-term experience gleaned from my probands revealed one fact most impressively, namely that successful results can be achieved through totally different methods.[8] Any one of the known therapeutic methods can easily be replaced by any other. No single method, in comparison with others, has so much better chances for success that it alone would deserve to be the method of choice. With all methods the result is often disappointment, and many

of them often lead to success. Regarded externally and technically, the effective therapies for schizophrenia exist in virtually overwhelming multiplicity. They extend all the way from psychoanalysis to brain surgery, from sleep therapy to the employment of the patient in a factory; and yet, there must be something of therapeutic essence in all of them, that all these therapeutic methods have in common. This much has been established. But whatever it is that they have in common is open to discussion. I personally became convinced that the well-tried and proved therapeutic methods for schizophrenia are effective because they establish, or violently affect, or quiet down active communal relationships. In the long view, it is essential to distribute or to combine these three goals of methodology at the appropriate time and in an appropriate manner.

The active communal relationship seems to me to be the most important principle of treatment. It consists of a communal relationship with the doctor, with the nurses and warders, with other patients, with the family members, or with anyone at all, depending on the condition of the patient and on the given external circumstances. The need to lean upon a kind, helpful person in one's own state of distress should be assuaged, as should the need to take one's place as a friend among friends, as well as the need to help those more helpless than one is oneself. In a communal relationship, the patient's own talents, strengths, and interests should unfold and have their being. Often a first communal relationship comes about with the doctor in conversations about the patient's needs and desires. In other cases, the physical treatment methods generate a care-dependent communal relationship. Life on the ward of the hospital should be planned to enhance communal relationships for the well-being of all. Important means for establishing such relationships include work- and occupational therapy, planned leisure, and group psychotherapy in the narrower sense. Outside the clinic, opportunities for social contact are provided by clubs, among workers in therapeutic industrial settings, and—best of them all—in the patients' own families.

Violent shocks of all kinds awaken the psychic forces. These include sudden changes from one environment to another, sudden unexpected trust with responsibility, etc. In an analytically conceived psychotherapy this is dealing with unexpected, direct manifesta-

---

8. Applied methods have already been discussed in Chapter 4. All methods were actually applied that were current and recognized in Europe while the probands suffered their psychoses (that is, from 1904 to 1964). The best developed were the work-therapy sessions and clinical milieu-therapies. We applied sleep therapy by Klaesi's method more often than most of the other clinics did. Our clinic was reluctant to apply eletroshock treatments. In the use of neuroleptics, dosages were kept lower and prescription time shorter than in many other clinics. Medical and social aftercare were available to any patient who requested them or whose family arranged for them. On the other hand, there was no organization to follow up expatients automatically without specific arrangements being made—except that I personally did it in connection with the present research project.

tions. The physical shock methods presumably take effect by the reaction to shock, up to a subjectively perceived threat to life itself.

Sedation and the relaxation of tensions are often necessary to make possible the establishment of any therapeutic community at all. It is probable that they have an additional immediate "antipsychotic" effect as well. Excitation, tension, and surges of repugnant emotions constitute the essential aspects of many psychotic phases. Beyond the simplest and most effective means of tranquilizing—by neuroleptics—the relaxing effect of psychic influences should not be overlooked. A powerful suggestive influence emanates from the self-assured, relaxed attitude of the physician and his assistants. Organization and regularity in the daily program contribute to inner tranquility; in fact, even neatness in the rooms the patients occupy makes such a contribution. Of course, besides these general aims in therapy, a great number of additional therapeutic considerations are indicated, depending on the individual case (for instance, special measures in cases of depression, when there are physical complications, refusal of food, or the need for social welfare).

The concept sketched here of the nature of treatment measures for schizophrenics is, of course, not based entirely only on our experiences with the 208 principal schizophrenic probands, but it is confirmed and supported by these experiences.

But I learned something else from just these experiences of decades of observation of my probands. This is that the possibilities for therapeutic success with schizophrenia are not limited as to time. A schizophrenia may have persisted for decades and have frustrated every therapeutic attempt, yet, after years on end, it may again become therapeutically accessible. Of course, this does not mean to say that every chronic schizophrenic can be made to recover or to improve. But with surprising frequency one does observe marked improvements that closely approach recovery when one begins to work with chronic schizophrenics with renewed zeal and dedication.

The inner life of older schizophrenics is often revealed, among other things, by the facts that they still undergo acute episodes, that their condition can still change for the better or worse, and that they can still be seized by despair and driven to suicide. In the course of a close relationship with them, one is often deeply impressed by the richness of their inner life, in a morbid as well as a

normal way. For the physician's medical routine the following dictum applies: The inner life of the schizophrenic is never "burnt out." It always continues on its way. When ceaseless attempts are made to establish contact with him as with a normal person, and he is not left to stand aside like an outsider, a communal relationship is established that means a great deal to both the patient and the doctor.

During the thirties, after introduction of insulin- and cardiazole-shock treatments, the opinion gained ground that, if treatment is begun early, it is usually successful; if it is begun late, it can never be successful. This opinion was erroneous. It was based on the contingency that the treated patients unwittingly represented a selection bias for cases with a good initial prognosis, and that only short catamneses were compiled. Investigations by a number of authors, my own previous investigations, and my experiences with the present 208 probands reveal unanimously that opinions on the effects of early treatment were too optimistic in the past. What were interpreted as successes of new methods were, at least in part, spontaneous remissions. Besides, some of the so-called "recovered" suffered renewed onsets. Insofar as late treatments were concerned, however, the opinion was too pessimistic. Late treatments can be worth the effort.

The present findings allow for a judgment as to what progress improved therapeutic methods have achieved over those of the past decades. They have succeeded in causing the disappearance of the catastrophe-schizophrenias (acute beginnings followed without interim remissions by lifelong, severe chronic psychoses). They have succeeded in improving all schizophrenic states. Mild chronic psychoses are taking the place of severe ones. They have not been successful so far in reducing the chronically-proceeding types of courses to a degree that would show up statistically. And they were scarcely successful in increasing the number of recoveries to a degree that would show up statistically.

The experiences with my probands contributed to the question on long-term maintenance with neuroleptics. Not a single one of the 208 principal probands received any medication outside the clinic on long-term prescription. All probands who remained recovered over a long period did so without long-term medication. During the cumulative 3600 years that probands spent outside of hospitals in the first two to three decades after onset of their illness, they were usually without any medication whatsoever; only a scattered few were given drugs on a brief, temporary basis.

These facts cast some light on the importance of long-term medication. Recoveries and improvements among the probands were achieved without resorting to long-term medication. In order to render acceptable the theory that long-term medication definitely increases the number of recoveries, it would have to be demonstrated that long-term recoveries were more frequent under long-term medication than they are according to present statistics. So far, this has not been the case. Furthermore, it appears that it cannot be expected in the future either. In recent years the idea has been expressed from time to time that long-term medication is indicated for every schizophrenic after hospital release, for the prevention of relapses. Experiences with the probands refute such a theory. I do not consider a general indication for long-term medication to be appropriate for every recovered or improved schizophrenic. On the other hand, I certainly recognize individual indications in specific cases. Long-term medication is indicated when observation has shown a propensity for relapse without medication, and when the stability of the improved state with medication has been established. In the light of my own experience, such indications prevail only for a minority of schizophrenics released from clinics. Many patients regard the prescription of medications as a nuisance, while others suffer from the well-known side effects. In addition, the danger exists of sustaining permanent damage from the medication (loss of energy and happiness, loss of the ability to establish or sustain friendships or love relationships while under medication, the danger of irreversible dyskinesia, etc.). I consider it a welcome discovery that reasons sufficiently weighty to cause long-term medication to be prescribed, in spite of all misgivings, apply to only a small minority of released schizophrenics.

Many countries have organized a systematic aftercare program for all schizophrenics released from clinics. In respect to such a generally systematized aftercare program, we in the Canton of Zürich are behind a number of other states. To be sure, we do have good treatment and counseling facilities for patients who need help after their release, if they seek it themselves or are encouraged by their families to accept it. Only court-committed cases or patients in permanent financial distress receive constant care under our system, without any action on their part. This, however, is only a small minority of the patients released from hospitals. I personally believe in the need for a more effective aftercare program for schizophrenics than the one presently being followed. However, in evaluating the success of a systematized aftercare program, it should be kept in mind that many patients are quite able to sustain themselves out in society without such assistance. Only after generally applied aftercare programs have increased the number of permanent releasees from clinics beyond the rate indicated by the findings in my probands, will their value and the justification for their application be considered established.

Certain of my probands suddenly and unexpectedly experienced a marked improvement when they withdrew from aftercare. Without a doubt, the cessation of any type of care can at times be salutary. In certain rare phases of the disease, not only is early release from the hospital a therapeutic measure, but early cessation of any sort of care is, too.

The experiences with the 208 probands provide some useful hints for medical counseling in education, marriage, and sex counseling. The prognosis for the children of schizophrenics is not nearly as dismal as it once was assumed to be. However, the sad fact that the onset expectancy for schizophrenia in such offspring is about ten times that of the normal population remains valid. Approximately 9 percent of the offspring of schizophrenics become schizophrenic, if they do not expire prematurely. But the assumption that more than half of these offspring somehow are morbid or abnormal has been disproved. Today, it is no longer possible to say that over half such children are somehow "eugenically undesirable"—an expression that should not have been applied even when it was. Over one-half, or rather about three-fourths of these children are healthy, useful citizens. To be sure, the suffering that they endured through the illness of their parents did cast shadows over their happiness. For this reason I consider it appropriate now, as I did then, to advise medically against the procreation of schizophrenics. The prohibition by law of marriage for the mentally ill does have some humanitarian merits in this context. After clinic releases of schizophrenics, contraceptive means and practices are often in order. If however, as often happens, children are born to schizophrenics without or contrary to medical counsel, their future is certainly prospectively brighter than it was formerly, when the fear prevailed that half of them would turn out to be "eugenically undesirable."

Digressive and justifiably forgotten was the expectation that the incidence of schizophrenia could be reduced or eliminated if all schizophrenics were to be sterilized. Aside from the fact that this would be impossible, undesirable, and illegal, it would not eradicate schizophrenia. The fertility rate among schizophrenics is low. Even if we wanted to assume that schizophrenia was based on one or several mutating, pathological genes, the new formation of mutations would be more important to the frequency of schizophrenia than the hereditary transmission of the mutant gene. If one believes, as I do, that unfavorable combinations of traits that are in and of themselves nonpathological may be shaping the hereditary background for schizophrenias, then the eradication of schizophrenia by rendering unfertile the "hereditary carriers" is absolutely unthinkable.

An important indication for the clinician evolves from the knowledge of the suffering that many children of schizophrenics have to endure. The alleviation of this suffering is a monumental task in which doctors have a part to play. For decades this suffering received insufficient attention. The children of schizophrenics ought to be accorded the benefits of welfare and assistance. Often they are in need of child-psychiatric treatment. At times foster care is indicated. The doctor or the social worker ought always to be concerned about the children's well-being. It has not been proved, although the possibility cannot be entirely rejected, that even the onset expectancy for schizophrenia in these children could be reduced, if they were spared a portion of the unfavorable influences from a schizophrenic father or mother.

One of the great sources of affliction of the children of schizophrenics is often the fear that their own children (as grandchildren of schizophrenic grandparents) would, in their turn, become somehow pathological. In these days they ought to be relieved of this fear. If these children of schizophrenics have themselves reached a mature age and remained healthy, happy, and useful in life, insofar as we know today, there is no greater expectancy for psychic disturbances among their children (the grandchildren of schizophrenics) than that which exists for any other person.

My investigations of the nephews and nieces of schizophrenics have confirmed the previous findings of the Munich school, according to which, if their own parents were normal, they are not much more vulnerable to mental disorders than any other person. The siblings of schizophrenics, who reach a mature age and remain healthy, happy, and useful in life, need not be counseled against propagation because of the illness of a sibling of theirs.

An incidence of schizophrenia is popularly regarded as a disgrace for the family in which it occurs. For a long time, even doctors were inclined to regard schizophrenia as a "degenerative disease," that stamped the family in which it occurred as inferior. The prognosis for the children and children's children was estimated too unfavorably. Even modern investigations still suggest to many that they consider the family members of schizophrenics as undesirable. The expression a "schizophrenogenic mother" easily becomes a derogatory invective in unscientific thinking. Even the information that the "teaching of irrationality" by the parents might contribute to the genesis of schizophrenia could lead to a reproachful attitude toward the parents—even though it would be unfair. In addition, we psychiatrists are often bothered and attacked by the families of schizophrenics. All this contributes to the fact that even today whole families of schizophrenics are still tacitly and thoughtlessly being regarded with suspicion and contempt. Our new experience should teach us better. If we as doctors stop looking at only the sickness and weakness in our patients, but also pay attention to the evidence of their health and strength, quite a different image of the schizophrenics and their families will evolve. This new image I experienced most impressively with my probands and their families. Schizophrenics and their families do not only torment, nag, fight, and harm one another, but much more frequently they help one another. Quite often they represent a formidable combat team against their unkind fate. As a unit, the families of schizophrenics are capable of dealing with life. In spite of the severe obstacles imposed by the mental illness of one of their number, they generally manage to keep up the social, cultural, and human levels of their family.

Schizophrenia is a terrible disease. But on the basis of more recent knowledge, the prognosis, the therapeutic possibilities, and the entire range of life's expectations for schizophrenics and their families may be more optimistically assessed than formerly, when schizophrenia was labelled as dementia praecox and regarded as a hereditary, degenerative disease that leads irrevocably to idiocy. Besides, we have observed with amazement what a one-sided picture resulted, when in former times mainly only the sick, the weak, and the evil elements of the schizophrenic himself and of the families of schizophrenics were considered and described. We had to become fully acquainted with the schizophrenic and find out that he can remain a warm-hearted human being. And we had to become acquainted with the families of schizophrenics from many points of view in order to appreciate the great deeds and sacrifices practiced on behalf of their sick relative, and what they accomplish to maintain the same standards as more fortunate families do. Today's doctor, who is aware of all this and who has experienced it all with open heart and mind, is better equipped to approach with confidence the treatment and the counseling of schizophrenics and their families than his predecessors were. And accordingly, he is in a better position to help them than was the doctor of former decades.

Critique

When I feel constrained—as I often do —to exercise as harsh a criticism of my book as I possibly can, I find that it consists of a peculiar admixture of feelings and statistics, in which the statistics do not render the feelings more impressive, and the feelings do not support the statistics. Surely both are in need of support, the feelings because they are subjective, and the statistics because they never rest on really secure foundations. Of course, the numbers as given are correct, and the calculations of the standard deviation and of p are also certain. But what always remains uncertain, is whether, in comparisons, truly equal terms are being compared (if, for instance, the representatives of the general population with whom the schizophrenics are being compared actually come from the same type of population group as the schizophrenics do.)

This objection cannot be refuted. I can only offer the excuse that the subject matter of this book must necessarily be treated in a completely distinctive manner. It is an inherent feature of the medical profession that the doctor should empathize with his patient, that he should assess his patient's aches and complaints by feeling the effects of the illness vicariously in his own body— and that, simultaneously, he should retain the capability of building his diagnosis, his therapeutic program, and his etiological research on a sound scientific foundation. By the same token, the problem of schizophrenia cannot be approached either, if both conditions are not met, that is, to empathize mentally and emotionally with the condition of the patient, to experience it as if it were one's own—and yet to look for objective data. In brief, one must recognize the validity of emotions and statistics that exist side by side. No matter how peculiar the manifestation of this side-by-side existence of the two methodologies, it does make sense. Every now and then subjective empathizing with the disease will produce a concrete line of questioning for the statistics, and every now and then the statistics will confirm an idea that originated from empathy. When we succeed in discovering such concordances, we are amply rewarded for the great effort it takes to keep changing over again and again from the objective to the empathetic type of investigation.

At times it seems immodest and unscientific of me to apply emotional expressions in my descriptions, such as "horrible," "oppressive," "splendid," and the like. Is it permissible to communicate how deeply one sympathizes with disaster and what respect one feels when patients and their families alike bear and manipulate their misfortune continuously, bravely, and successfully without losing heart and their zest for life? Minkowski (1966) gave us an unequivocal answer when he said that it is a paradox to undertake to attempt to describe empathetic psychopathology and yet to conceal one's own emotions in the process. If one sets out to be a physician to the patient and apply medical experience, there is nothing wrong with empathizing. Of course, the emotions must not gain the upper hand, and they must step down when the purely scientific labors begin.

I have been accused of yet another shortcoming, namely, of being "ambivalent" in that I acknowledge neither heredity nor psychogenesis as the decisive factor in the formation of schizophrenic psychoses. I believe this ambivalence corresponds with the facts, namely, with the circumstance that hereditary developmental traits are closely interwoven with life's experiences to produce the illness.

My finding that the hereditary disposition for schizophrenia is by no means traceable to any mendelian hereditary process involving one or more specific pathological hereditary factors has been accused of being unscientific. For several decades, clinical research in heredity registered its great successes only through the exposure of mendelian hereditary processes. Multifactorial heredity had been known for just as long a time, although it did not capture the interest of clinicians quite as frequently. On the other hand, considering the cooperative interplay of various hereditary factors during development is a concept of more recent origin. Both phenomena are biological facts. There is multifactorial heredity, and the harmony or disharmony of the developmental traits exert their influence on the development of every living being. It is not unscientific to delve into this matter, although it will require a revision of thinking in family research.

I have been reproached analogously in respect to my findings on the psychological backgrounds of schizophrenia. It was established that research had the task of revealing specific traumatic situations or disturbances in specific developmental phases as postulates for a specific disease, that it would be highly unscientific to neglect such an effort. To this I can only reply that no one has been able to find such a specific psychological cause for schizophrenia. To affirm that there is such a cause when it cannot be found is out of place here. On the contrary, one does find that the entire psychotraumatic life history—and within it probably certain individual unfavorable experiences more than others—does have something to do with a disposition for schizophrenia. To become aware of this and to continue working on the basis of this stipulation, does not seem to me to be an unscientific endeavor.

I must excuse myself once more, if a reader should reprove me for excessive repetitions in the book. The explanation is my constant effort to make every chapter readable independently.

Addendum: While the book was in press, Rolf Lindelius's great piece of work was published. Between 1900 and 1910 he studied the lives of 270 schizophrenics who had been admitted to a Swedish clinic, together with those of their families. His findings are extremely well suited for comparisons with mine, and correspond to them in all essential aspects.[9]

The fertility of these Swedish schizophrenics (evaluated at the end of the observation period and thus also at the end of their fertile period) amounted to only about one-third that of the population. The reason lay chiefly in the fact that there were many unmarried among them. The fertility of married schizophrenics was only slightly lower.

The fertility of the siblings of schizophrenics proved to be by no means higher, but slightly lower.

These findings confirm that the theory that the deficiency in offspring of schizophrenics can be explained by the assumption of one or a few pathogenic genes as the major cause of schizophrenia is untenable.

The course of illness for the schizophrenics hospitalized at the turn of the century was much less favorable than for my probands. The prognosis of schizophrenia has clearly improved over the course of this century.

The onset expectancy for schizophrenia of the children, of the siblings, and of the children of the siblings of schizophrenics corresponds with remarkable accuracy to the research material of Lindelius and to my own calculations. (To be sure, Lindelius recorded many undiagnosed psychoses and had to estimate the number of schizophrenias among them.) Among the parents of the Swedish schizophrenics, however, fewer schizophrenics were discovered than the findings of most other authors and my own findings would lead one to expect. (The reason probably lay in the fact that psychoses that emerged way back in the past century are very difficult to reconstruct in retrospect.)

9. Rolf Lindelius, "A Study of Schizophrenia," *Acta Psychiatrica Scandinavica*, Supplement 216, Copenhagen: Munksgaard, 1970.

8 Theories: Thoughts and Assumptions concerning the Nature of the Schizophrenias

Are the Schizophrenias Physical Illnesses?

The temptation to interpret schizophrenia as an aspect of physical diseases, even when no physical diseases are in evidence

As a physician, one is accustomed to assume the presence of physical diseases when physical symptoms are in evidence. When they are absent, one is most reluctant to make authoritative statements that some physical illness lies concealed behind any sort of complaints or behavioral disturbances. At the utmost, a hidden physical illness might then be suspected, but one would never dare to represent it as a certainty in such a case. Amazingly, up to now, these fundamentals were barely valid for the field of schizophrenia. Through to the present day, many clinicians and researchers are fully convinced that primary physical disorders (functional or structural) constitute the most essential onset conditions for schizophrenia, although they are unable to identify any clear symptoms indicating such supposed physical disorders. At certain times, researchers were even in danger of being reproached for having an unscientific, uncritial mentality, of being insulted and ostracized if they did not conform by "admitting" that there were physical explanations for schizophrenia. In a peculiar reversal of otherwise valid norms, assumptions used to be declared "scientific" that resulted from pure speculation or emotional needs, and any attempt to consider only information that could actually be proved was rejected as "unscientific."

Such tendencies were partly a consequence of the fact that psychiatry was becoming more and more a part of the field of general medicine, especially around the middle of the last century. The concept of "mental illness" displaced the older concepts of craziness and of being possessed. Methods of working, thinking, and doing research in medicine at that time were best suited to seeking a pathological-anatomic or pathological-physiological, tangible, bodily disorder for every "disease"—which, in popular opinion, the schizophrenias had turned out to be. Not until most recently has the concept gained respect in the field of medicine, that the doctor often has to be concerned about complaints that cannot by existing modern methods be brought into causal relationship with physical changes, complaints, which, however, have their origins in the patient's mental development and his emotional life. This concept was long and slow in gaining recognition in the field of schizophrenia.

While the faith of many in tangible physical causes of the schizophrenias remained steady, unshakable, and intact, assertions and presumptions changed constantly about the kind of physical causes that were involved.

In the middle of the last century, the hypotheses kept leaning for support on the degeneration theory. According to this concept, all conceivable psychic and physical noxae inherent in civilized life first undermined mental health, then physical health and, in the course of generations, this damage to health attacked the hereditary legacy. In this degenerative process there appeared, late in life, inherited "processes toward idiocy," near the end of the tragic chain which is idiocy. Many of these processes we today include among the schizophrenias. This degeneration theory began to recede into the background by the end of the last century and has virtually disappeared as a subject of discussion since the beginning of the 20s. After dementia praecox had been conceived as a specific "unit of illness," the idea prevailed, just before and after the turn of the century, that the specific syndrome for this disease had to be based on a specific brain pathology. The doctors of that period were being supported in this idea by the successes of brain pathology in neurological diseases. Between the two World Wars (in connection with progress in pathological physiology) the hopes of schizophrenia researchers were centered on pathological metabolic disorders. Frequently at that time the formulation used to read that the "psychosis schizophrenia" may be interpreted as a "schizophrenic somatosis," which was basically a metabolic disorder. The sweeping advances in endocrinology during the past three decades were followed immediately by working hypotheses on schizophrenia that were endocrinologically oriented. After medical knowledge had become immensely enriched through the elucidation of a number of disease syndromes as hereditary enzyme deficiencies, today "inborn errors of metabolism" occupy the foreground in discussions on the somatic foundations of the schizophrenias.

The conviction that physical bases exist as backgrounds to schizophrenia, however, does not stem solely from the speculative transferral to schizophrenia theory of every new and great medical discovery, but rather it corresponds also to our own natural feelings—our own emotional shock—in the face of the schizophrenic catastrophe. A schizophrenia fundamentally changes the personality of our fellowman. It seems to us as though we have suddenly come up against a wall, when we try to understand him and empathize with him as we understand and empathize with our own nature and that of our healthy fellowmen. We are amazed and overcome by something incomprehensible, unfamiliar and eerie, when we encounter a schizophrenic. In this emotional state we intuitively refuse to accept any trite explanation based on mere routine psychological experience. We consider it inappropriate, insulting, almost cynical, to base an erupting elementary catastrophe on something commonplace. With this dread of psychological interpretations, the very conceptualizations of mental illness, of the psychosis, and of insanity have close relations. Such concepts were created in order to confront the incomprehensible with the comprehensible. However, as soon as we exclude any comprehensible psychological causes from discussions, the idea of physical disorders as the cause of psychic catastrophes intrudes on the mind of modern man—who does not believe in demons. This immediate experience with the incomprehensibility of a psychosis is the background against which magnificent philosophical edifices have been erected to the impossibility of psychological interpretations of the schizophrenias. But the modest "intuitive" conviction of many, requiring no contemplation, that physical reasons for the schizophrenias may be assumed, quite independently of whether we could discover them by our research methods or not, also stems from the same source. It was this type of mental attitude that prevailed when Luxenburger wrote in the 30s that the existence of a "schizophrenic somatosis" may be assumed "with a priori certainty."

When one reads many reports about physiological schizophrenia research impartially, one continues to be surprised with what levity serious researchers conclude that they have discovered physical causes for schizophrenias on the basis of insignificant information and a minimal number of schizophrenics. This line of thinking becomes easier to understand if one is familiar with the tendency to postulate "with a priori certainty" physiologically provable foundations for schizophrenia. Doubtful physiological indications become even more credible if one is convinced of physical causes of schizophrenia than if one believes in the possibility that schizophrenic manifestiations are correlated with the vital processes, that are just as inaccessible to modern somatic research as are the mental and emotional processes of the healthy individual.

Is the schizophrenic physically ill, according to the clinicians?

Routine clinical experience teaches us that the overwhelming majority of schizophrenics are in the prime of physical health, if they receive proper care and if they care properly for themselves. Just like healthy people, they either tolerate physical stresses or they are susceptible to physical diseases. Most of them reach an advanced age. Death is caused by complications of physical illnesses of the same kinds that cause the deaths of healthy people.

Naturally, these assertions apply in broad generalities only. A multitude of minor objections of one kind or another could be raised. It would be possible to establish "microfacts" at the borderline of normality and other distributions of frequency for one disease or another, and to interpret them as valid objections against the given findings. But anyone rooted in active medical practice would think twice before allowing his efforts to be diverted from essentials in order to pursue that sort of trivia. He would have found out that there is no medical determination about a patient's state of health or illness in which secondary facts have not given rise to doubts. He knows that medically one can only arrive at a judgment or a decision by sticking to decisive and essential facts. The essential element in the clinical observation of the physical condition of schizophrenics is their physical health. Any doubts about it assume a position of quite secondary importance. But the attitude of the researcher who dedicates himself to special studies of schizophrenics, applying sophisticated methods, must needs be different from that of the practising clinician. When he discovers facts, he does not compare them to general medical experience and, evaluated by him alone, they are bound to appear more meaningful to him than to the practising physician. In the process of theorizing about any consistent physical genesis of the schizophrenias, more allowance should be made for the great difference in viewpoints between the research specialist and the doctor with clinical experience. The experiences of one ought to support and supplement those of the other. Today the specialized researcher pays less attention to the experiences of the clinician than vice versa. This practice results in an overestimation of the importance of odd or unusual minor facts.

Nevertheless, there are individual experiences that even the clinician has, that cause him to wonder whether they are not indeed significant indicators of physical illness in schizophrenics. The most important among these emerge from the observation of the so-called "lethal catatonia," of tuberculosis in schizophrenics, and from the successes from physical treatments. In the following paragraphs I should like to explain briefly why I cannot regard these experiences as proof of physical disease, which would be the principal postulate for many—or all—of the schizophrenias.

Lethal catatonia runs its course under the syndrome of the "delirium acutum." But today we know that the "delirium acutum" that was formerly frequently noted is not a characteristic manifestation or course type of schizophrenia. A delirium acutum is encountered the same way as it is in schizophrenias, for example, in cases of poisoning and in the encephalitides of all kinds. Today it is probable that in cases of fatal catatonia a syndrome is operant for which no mysterious specific schizophrenic process is responsible. It becomes manifest in states of extreme agitation, complicated by the most diverse kinds of physical noxae which exert their influence, in part independently and in part as a consequence of the agitation. The most frequent among these are dehydration; imbalance of the electrolytic equilibrium; retention of urine with increasing pyelitis (with and without previous catheterization); congestions in the respiratory system with faulty expectoration, in part under the effects of soporifics; poisoning resulting from excessively strong medication, as this becomes necessary to quell extremely severe agitation; infections emanating from decubitus; general exhaustion and

circulatory insufficiency; thromboses and embolisms in connection with changes in therapeutic anesthesia and agitation. Pathologic-anatomical as well as therapeutic experiences offer support for this explanation of lethal catatonia as an unspecific sequel to agitation with manifold, complicated physical noxae. The pathologic-anatomical findings are entirely unspecific. There has not been a single specific remedy that has proved to be therapeutically effective, whereas all measures that either suppress the agitation or are aimed at the physical complications are all the more effective. The most effective among them are indulgent, skillful psychotherapeutic care in the presence of the patient, and occupational therapy; sedation by drugs, insofar as it succeeds without complicating manifestations of poisoning; interruption of the agitation by shock effects in electroshock treatment. The simultaneous consideration of physical manifestations is of the greatest importance, in particular those that result from the continual checking of the fluids and the electrolyte systems; maintenance of respiration; drug therapy for infectuous complications, especially from the respiratory organs and the urinary tract; support of the circulatory system; and the unspecific treatment with adrenal hormones.

In the 30s of this century, many assumed that the combination of schizophrenia and tuberculosis, so often observed at the time, could indicate a physical weakness common to both. Luxenburger (1927) assumed a "weakness of the connective tissue" for both diseases. At the time, both schizophrenics and their close relatives were often designated as tubercular, although I was soon able to show (1935) that, on the contrary, schizophrenia did not appear frequently among the families of tubercular patients. This was opposed to the theory that a hereditary pathological process was an essential postulate common to both diseases. It supported the theory that the epidemiological causes, poor hygiene, and contagion among the family members were increasing the frequency of tuberculosis among schizophrenics and persons in their immediate surroundings. Actually, we know today that prophylactic measures against tuberculosis are just as effective for schizophrenics as they are among the general population. The former spread of tuberculosis among schizophrenics and their families is attributable to epidemiological causes, and not to any hereditary physical weakness at the basis of the two diseases.

After the introduction of sleep therapy, of cardiazole-, insulin-, and electroshock therapies for schizophrenics, the argument was often raised that the discovery of a specific physical therapy indicated a specific physical disease. Subsequent experience effectively refuted such assumptions. Today we know that the somatic therapeutic methods for schizophrenics cannot be regarded as anything specific for schizophrenia alone. They are clearly effective only for a relatively small portion of all schizophrenics and only in certain phases of schizophrenia and, on the other side of the coin, they are likewise effective for symptomatically similar conditions in the course of other diseases. Brain surgery and neuroleptic medications are impressively effective against many types of schizophrenia, although in those cases it is particularly obvious that just as often—or even more often—they would be equally effective under totally different conditions. In these types of treatment, the thought of any specific effect hardly ever occurred any more. The effectiveness of nonspecific drug treatment, however, has nothing in common with the effectiveness of former somatic therapeutic methods. This experience alone has frustrated the former hopes that in insulin therapy a specific treatment method had been discovered for a specific schizophrenic somatosis. Insofar as we understand the nature of physical treatments for schizophrenia, it amounts to a combination of the following effects: sedation for agitation or stimulation for lack of motivation; effect on the central nervous system as a means of suppressing emotional outbursts from perceived or imagined excitations; simplification of thought and indifference in an organic psychosyndrome, which is marked—usually intermittently—by epileptic attacks and extended unsconsciousness. Psychological therapeutic effects are concurrent with those that affect the central nervous system. A dangerous vicious circle is interrupted, that is, the chain of causality: psychotic behavior—reaction of the healthy family members or care personnel with shock, surprise, fear, pity, or repugnance, causing the natural tone of voice to change in conversation with the patient—reaction of the patient with feelings of loneliness, rancor, hatred, anger, and aggression—the total incapacity on the part of family or care personnel to see or to sense a fellow human being in the patient—their attitude toward protection, defense, etc. This unfortunate chain of causality is interrupted by physical methods. When the patient awakens from shock, he finds himself in a changed human atmosphere; he himself has changed in that he has placed his internal struggles and tortures at a distance, and his memory of them has been dimmed; he is physically helpless and in need of care; the care personnel are no longer afraid of him, for they are full of happy expectations of seeing him awaken improved. His need for care during the treatment phase offers an excellent opportunity for reviving, human relations that are natural and warm. In addition, it might be assumed that the life-threatening experience during shock may mobilize natural healing forces, as it is often capable of doing when life is threatened.

Our experiences with the 208 principal probands are quite in line with these general clinical experiences. At the time of their recruitment, the probands were for the most part, in good general physical health, and most of them have remained so until today, in spite of advanced age. When they did become physically ill or died, it was of the same diseases that befall the mentally sound. The long-term catamneses show impressively that the long-term schizophrenia courses are independent of any specific therapeutic technique or method, but that, instead, a general, long-term, constant care program is effective, and for certain special indications, the application of a wide variety of methods is valuable (see pp. 295–303 and 440–42).

Have special research groups succeeded in proving physical disorders to be the basis for the schizophrenias?

It was a great and an urgent scientific project to supplement the existing clinical knowledge about the physical condition of schizophrenics by undertaking special investigations. A number of generations of researchers have already accomplished meritorious results with this problem. In most recent times, it is being attacked with ever-increasing resources of personnel and technology. As far back as the last century, thoroughgoing pathological-anatomic studies of the brain and—to a lesser extent—the other organs were being undertaken. Earlier supplemental physical investigations were still being carried out with simple measures. Thus, the reflexes and sensitivity were thoroughly checked, or series of studies were undertaken on the cerebrospinal fluid, basic metabolism, morphological studies of the blood, and drops in blood pressure in schizophrenics. In keeping with progress in medical diagnostics, most of the newest technical advances for the complete examination of schizophrenics were utilized, among them air-encephalography, electroencephalography, and especially biochemical and endocrinological methods. The repeatedly suspected toxicity of the body fluids of schizophrenics was checked and studied by a multitude of methods. In fact, they went so far as to investigate in schizophrenics, the carbohydrate metabolism of blood corpuscles in the plasma and to check the metabolism of neuroactive substances, such as 5-hydroxytryptamine and the catecholamines.

It is not within the scope of this presentation to describe these studies in detail and to examine them critically. That was the task of literature surveys at our clinic, and will soon become the subject matter for a handbook. I should like merely to summarize briefly what of significance for the knowledge of schizophrenia came out of an overview of all these studies. Unfortunately, I myself did not have the opportunity to participate actively in any of the specialized somatic research studies of schizophrenics. My own personal knowledge about them is that of a bookworm, supplemented by many discussions with active researchers. An actual summary overview is what has been lacking, that would focus on what is important to the clinician. Besides, most of the researchers have become so involved in the minutiae of special problems, that only very few of them have shown any concern at all for the efforts of others. Most of the somatic studies of schizophrenics are planned and described in such a way as to imply that only very few others in that area had been carried out.

The essential conclusions of former specialized somatic schizophrenia research can today be summarized in a few simple sentences.

No physical findings were discovered that were common to all—or even most—schizophrenics. Insofar as data on physical conditions of schizophrenics were gathered, they are those that would also be in evidence among numerous other types of patients or even among healthy persons. Accordingly, all the laborious research efforts expended have not come near the goal of discovering a specific physical disorder, a specific schizophrenic somatosis, as the essential prerequisite for the onset of schizophrenic psychoses. Nor have any physical manifestations been discovered that appear with all the schizophrenias of a specific subgroup. Up to now, no specific physical bases for psychopathologically described subgroups of the schizophrenias have been discovered.

Emotional agitations and tensions have similar physiological effects in schizophrenics as in normals. Many physical manifestations that were first determined as being typical for the schizophrenias can today be traced to emotional upset (for instance, changes in the function of the adrenals).

It was determined that many kinds of peculiarities in the body build and the body functions of schizophrenics are distributed differently, on the average, than they are in normal people. Limits of norms (though in different directions) are more frequent in schizophrenics than in normals. Thus, the usual proportions between individual characteristics are less rigid in schizophrenics (as for instance the proportions between individual physical measurements or the sequence in time of the development of certain indicators of puberty). But one may by no means assume that these represent any essential onset criteria for the schizophrenias. Many schizophrenics lack these peculiarities, and on the other hand, they are found in a great many nonschizophrenics (for instance, in the feebleminded).

Many kinds of physical findings in schizophrenics used to be interpreted as causes or partial causes of psychoses, about which we know today that they are attributable to bad eating habits or a lack of general hygiene (examples: pathological findings while checking on the function of the liver; tuberculosis. Parin [1953] showed with patients of our clinic that the obesity of many schizophrenics, formerly claimed as an indication of an enigmatic peculiarity of metabolism, depends unequivocally on the quantity of food consumed).

Many of the assertions about pathological metabolic manifestations in schizophrenics are based on faulty investigative methodology that cannot stand up against criticism. Without a doubt, some psychiatrists overextended themselves when they set out on the search for some kind of metabolic disorder in schizophrenics by applying self-conceived, extremely questionable techniques. Indeed, almost no one has any interest in pointing out the technical shortcomings in the workmanship of these authors by publishing them. However, if one engages in private discussions with real experts in the field of pathological physiology, it is depressing to note how much doubt they express about the findings in the literature about a pathological metabolism in schizophrenics. Many publications can also be criticized for declaring certain findings as pathological that possibly still lie within the norm.

Insofar as pathological somatic manifestations have been disclosed in some individual schizophrenic or some individual groups of schizophrenics, it still cannot be clearly determined whether, and in what manner, they may have a pathogenetic relationship.

Are there physical disorders whose syndrome includes schizophrenic psychoses?

The question whether physical disorders comprise an essential prerequisite for the schizophrenias can be answered from two different viewpoints. One may ask whether somatic disturbances occur with schizophrenias that are the decisive cause, and this question I have already answered in the negative. The opposing line of questioning reads: Are there any kinds of physical disorders that are regularly accompanied by psychoses that might be considered as belonging to the schizophrenias?

I have been in pursuit of an answer to this question for decades, studying endorcrine disorders, since for a long time they were the prime suspects as the physical prerequisite for schizophrenias. Actually, there are frequent references in the older literature, indicating that one type of endocrine disorder or another (for instance, acromegaly) would lead to schizophrenic illnesses or, at least, to psychoses that can barely be distinguished from schizophrenia. My colleagues and I checked the personalities of hundreds of endocrine patients, some with milder forms of endocrine disorders, and of several thousands of their relatives. The results of these investigations are easily summarized. As the overwhelming majority of schizophrenics has no endocrine disorders, so the overwhelming majority of endocrine patients is not schizophrenic. Schizophrenia does not occur any more frequently among the relatives of patients with endocrine disorders than it does among the population in general. To be sure, almost all patients whose endocrine system is severely disturbed over longer periods undergo a personality change, and in the most severe cases they become psychotic.

The mental disorders of such patients, however, are distinctly different from the schizophrenias. They resemble personality and mental disorders accompanying brain diseases, and their genesis has by now been clarified in broad terms. Endocrine and certain central nervous system functions also depend on one another, both functionally and structurally. Endocrine disorders first lead to functional changes that are limited to individual systems, and later to structural and diffuse changes in the central nervous system. It is no wonder, therefore, that they manifest themselves as brain diseases do. Time and again new assertions appear that claim one endocrine function or another is ailing and constitutes an essential condition favoring the onset of schizophrenia. Such assertions can no longer be taken seriously when one knows the patients who actually have the endocrine functional disorders that are only suspected of existing in schizophrenics. One realizes then that they are, in fact, not schizophrenic. In our time, no further endocrinological schizophrenia theories ought to be postulated without considering the knowledge we have concerning the psychopathology of the endocrine diseases.

The manifold concomitant psychic symptoms that accompany all kinds of acute, severe physical disorders can all be listed under one large, all-inclusive category according to Bonhoefer (1912), namely that of the "acute exogenous reactive type." Do schizophrenias or schizophrenia-like psychoses occur within the framework of the acute exogenous reactive type? The less this is the case, the more unlikely it is that acute, severe physical disorders are the causes of acute schizophrenic psychoses. A great volume of literature is dedicated to this question. At our clinic, E. Bühler (1951), Walther-Büel (1966), Willi (1966), I (1966), and others, too, have spent years working on this problem. The results of all this research are easily summarized by saying that the symptomatology of the acute exogenous reactive type may be conveniently subdivided into three categories:
—Reduction of one's psychic existence, down to its very extinction, that is, all possible states between mild dizziness and apathy to total unconsciousness.
—Disorder of one's psychic existence, that is, shifts in consciousness to twilight states, deliria, and confusion
—Simplification in the order of one's psychic existence with loss of the more delicate

differentiations and depletion of content (amnestic of Korsakoff's syndrome).

The symptoms of these three categories of syndromes usually combine in the acute cases.

Reduction of consciousness and amnestic psychosyndrome, that is, disorders of the first and the third categories above, are quite common manifestations in somatic patients with acute psychic changes, but never in schizophrenics. However, the symptomatology of syndromes of second category very often overlaps with that of schizophrenias. The confusion of somatic patients cannot always be distinguished from the giddy absent-mindedness of schizophrenics. The dream experiences, perceptual illusions, and delusional ideas may be the same in both cases, although they may differ as to certain nuances. Accordingly, there assuredly exist symptoms and phenomena that are identical in patients with acute organic disorders and in those with acute schizophrenias. On the other hand, however, it must be emphasized as well that in the great majority of cases the two can be readily distinguished. Our studies confirm what, after the turn of the century, classical psychiatry labeled as one of its fundamental doctrines and what also agrees with the experience of most researchers, namely that it is definitely possible to draw a line between the acute schizophrenias and the acute organic mental disorders. In discussions about whether the schizophrenias are rooted in somatic disorders, more attention should be given to this fact of experience than is usually the case.

Quite unfairly the so-called experimental psychoses that emerge after administration of LSD and the other hallucinogenic substances have been designated as schizophrenic. They belong to the types of disturbances in the category of the acute exogenous reactive type, not only according to their etiology but also to their psychosymptomatology. While it is true that certain features can be picked out of the overall clinical syndrome that cannot be distinguished from certain individual schizophrenic symptoms, this is true not exclusively of these "experimental psychoses," but also of many other types of disturbances within the category of the acute exogenous reactive type. The hallucinations in these types of disturbances are principally elementary optical hallucinations of the type that usually recede in frequency among schizophrenics, as compared to others. Only slight manifestations of schizophrenic confusion and

schizophrenic affective disturbance of these noxious effects ever occur. It is also dangerous to equate with the schizophrenias any manifestations that last only a few hours. This practice could easily lead to interpreting as "schizophrenias" any common day- or nighttime dreams, an abnormal alcoholic intoxication, or any state of high agitation under anesthesia.

What about the distinction between the chronic schizophrenias and the chronic organic psychoses? In the overwhelming majority of cases—of the mild as well as of the severe ones—we are confronted with an impressive difference between schizophrenic and organic psychoses. In the organic psychoses, depletion, simplification, and the inability to distinguish detail—in the schizophrenic psychoses, an unbelievably disintegrated inner life, overabundant in the most incredible imaginings, experiences, and emotions. In the organic psychoses, in severe chronic cases, the final breakdown of the primary functions of memory, perception, judgment[1], and the more delicately modulated emotions. In the schizophrenic psychoses, however, the old intellectual competence, warmth, and emotional depth are discernible behind every serious state of morbidity, time and time again. These differences are almost universally acknowledged today. I felt constrained to mention them only because they are too often shunted aside in discussions on the somatic backgrounds of the schizophrenias. Erroneously, the exceptions from what is common are all the more emphasized.

There are such exceptions, and they are generally known. During the years after the discovery of the treatment of fevers of progressive paralysis, paralyses of schizophrenia-like symptomatology stood in the foreground of the discussions. They were labeled as "malaria-paranoid," because at first it was

1. It is a well-known fact that these primary intellectual disorders are lacking in many psychic illnesses that are the result of localized failures in the brain, the most striking examples of which are the effects of encephalitis lethargica. But such disorders are then distinguished sharply from the schizophrenias, in that they lack the distractedness and a number of other common schizophrenia symptoms. The disorders in mood, drive, and motivation in the psychosyndromes localized in the brain may at times resemble those of schizophrenias. On the whole, however, the psychosyndrome localized in the brain is unmistakably distinguishable from schizophrenic symptomatology.

believed that they emerged only after malaria treatments; but they also emerge in cases of untreated or differently treated paralyses. The most frequent and the most acute forms of alcohol hallucinosis are obviously contingent on toxic causes, although there are the much-discussed forms that can no longer be distinguished from the schizophrenias in their final stages. In 1963, Slater et al. lucidly described schizophrenia-like chronic psychoses in epilepsies, especially in cases of temporal-lobe epilepsies. Syndromes that appear identical to schizophrenia syndromes —at least in certain phases—are also observed as exceptions in many other types of brain disorders and poisonings, as, for instance, in brain tumors, sclerosis of the brain vessels, systemic diseases of the brain, in poisoning by amphetamines, and in rare cases even after brain injuries.

When a pathological organic event can bring about schizophrenia-like disturbances, one simply must assume—so runs the argument—that all schizophrenias are based on a somatic illness—which, to be sure, has still to be discovered. Such a line of argument simply does not appear convincing to me in any way. In the first place, it does not consider the frequency relationships. It is rare indeed when paralysis, or cases of chronic psychosis with alcoholism, of amphetamine addiction, of epilepsy, or of other organic diseases reveal the same symptomatology as schizophrenias do. Mostly they can be distinguished from schizophrenias, so that the overwhelming majority of information plainly indicates that identifiable organic disorders do not, in fact, lead to schizophrenias. A portion of the schizophrenia-like syndromes in organic diseases can be explained as a combination of schizophrenias (or of a susceptibility to schizophrenia) together with a somatic illness. Walther-Büel (1951) succeeded in validating this explanation for certain individual psychoses in the case of brain tumors. But such an explanation does not hold for all cases. For instance, Slater et al. (1963) have shown through extensive family studies, that there is no real family syndrome in the schizophrenia-like psychoses of epileptics that would be similar to that of schizophrenics.

The findings from their investigation reported by Slater et al. (1963) suggest that whenever disorders in the temporal lobe in epileptics lead to schizophrenia-like psychoses, it might be an indication that the schizophrenias themselves were based on a disorder of the temporal lobe. However, this line of argument can be countered by the fact that no schizophrenia-like psychoses are found along with most disorders in the temporal lobe, and that no disorders in the temporal lobe have been discovered in conjunction with schizophrenias. The conclusiveness of this theory, however, is again in doubt when we remember that not only do temporal-lobe lesions occasionally lead to schizophrenias, but so do brain lesions in other localities, and general poisonings as well. What if we now transfer our deliberations on schizophrenia-like psychoses from temporal-lobe lesions to those from other types of lesions? If such psychoses occur with a frontal-lobe lesion (which does happen), one would have the same right to conclude that a frontal-lobe disorder causes schizophrenias; if they occurred with the consumption of amphetamines, we might assume that an abnormal metabolic product resembling the amphetamines was affecting the schizophrenias, and so on.

The fact that schizophrenia-like syndromes can emerge along with the most varied types of somatic disorders will be temporarily set aside for a later detailed discussion of the fact that psychic experiences, too, can reveal manifestations that can hardly be distinguished from a schizophrenic existence, or even that processes are concealed in the lives of healthy individuals that resemble a schizophrenic existence. The assumption, therefore, seems to suggest that the most varied influences can manifest a usually concealed life inherent in human nature that resembles the inner life of the schizophrenic. The symptomatic similarity of some psychoses in temporal-lobe epilepsy to schizophrenias seems to apply in the light of these deliberations, because a change in the function of the temporal lobe (just as many other cerebral disorders do) causes certain forms of life to burst forth that are always present—and that would also burst forth in actual schizophrenic psychoses without any changes in the functions of the temporal lobe.

Almost incomprehensibly, the newly developed information on inborn errors of metabolism is today being regarded as an indication that schizophrenias may also come into existence against the background of a transferred disorder in metabolism. It is pointed out that many inborn errors of metabolism have led to mental disturbances, and the conclusion is drawn that the schizophrenias would also have to be based on such "errors." Such a line of reasoning is completely misleading, because the "inborn errors of metabolism"—insofar as they affect the personality—lead to idiocy and to epilepsy, but definitely not to schizophrenia. Insofar as assumptions on the genesis of schizophrenia can be related to experiences with the "inborn errors of metabolism," they must serve as an indication that the schizophrenias simply are not based on any "inborn error of metabolism," because they lead to entirely different disorders, but never to schizophrenias. It is strange that this obvious conclusion is given so little consideration.

In summary, I come to the conclusion that most schizophrenias do not produce any somatic changes that could be brought into relationship with their genesis, and that, on the other hand, most of the physical diseases are not accompanied by schizophrenia-like psychoses. It is worth noting, however, that there are exceptions, namely, somatic illnesses with certain schizophrenia-like manifestations, and even those whose accompanying psychoses cannot be distinguished symptomatologically from schizophrenias. Since the most varied somatic illnesses in exceptional cases occasionally lead to accompanying schizophrenic psychoses, it cannot be assumed that a specific somatic disease process would be the prerequisite for a schizophrenia. The assumption is much more likely that different disease processes lead to the same psychopathological syndromes because they allow a psychic life to overflow that under better concealment runs its natural course in every person. Since up to the present time, and in spite of all efforts, no true indications have been discovered to the effect that somatic disorders exist along with the actual schizophrenic psychoses, other causes will have to be sought after.

The concept of the "somatic" from a philosophical and an empirical-clinical point of view

If—on the basis of our existing knowledge —I find it impossible to see any diseases in the schizophrenias, whose prerequisite would be a somatic disorder, and therefore refuse to include the schizophrenias in the category of "organic" psychic disturbances, then I certainly must explain what is meant by "somatic" or "organic" disturbance. The concepts were derived from common usage of the language and from direct experience. There are mental patients with recognizable physical changes, and those in whom no physical changes can be detected. The mental disorders of the first group may be designated as "organic," and those of the latter as "functional." In functional disorders one may assume that they manifest themselves in the same dimensions as do most psychic processes for which there are no somatic correlates as, for instance, memory, thought, and discriminatory perception. The conjecture as to whether these normal psychological processes and the "functional" pathological ones might possibly be somatic processes after all, is not in the least predetermined by the trite distinction between the concepts "functional" and "organic." The qualification of the schizophrenias as "nonsomatic" or "nonorganic" psychoses merely attests to the fact that no demonstrable somatic disorders are their necessary prerequisites, and that their genesis probably manifests itself in processes that, like most of the normal psychological processes, do not perceptibly reveal any somatic correlates.

If, on the basis of philosophic and ideological deliberations, the unity and the inseparability of mind and body should become established, assuredly all the "functional" pathological processes and the common psychological ones would, in the end, become accepted as somatic and organic processes, as would also the emergence of schizophrenic illness. But then the terms "somatic" and "organic" take on a totally different connotation from that of everyday language. In one case, organic and somatic appear in an all-encompassing, general context, and in another, only in the context of our present-day, limited human insight into the existence of two types of psychopathological processes namely, those with demonstrable somatic correlates, and those without such demonstrable somatic correlates. I believe that a very common and dangerous error lies in the practice of postulating tangible anatomic or physiological changes from mere philosophical deductions, while the philosophical deductions actually apply only to the fundamental identity of the essentials in the nature of the somatic and the psychic. If we declare the schizophrenias to be nonorganic and nonfunctional, this means only that we do not expect to find in them, as we do in the organic mental disorders, any pathological-anatomic or pathophysiological factors in a causal relationship with them. This statement, however, leaves the way completely open to the possibility that everything that is schizophrenic, together with everything that is functional, may be somehow identical to somatic processes.

Indeed, sometimes, the knowledge that something is hereditary leads to the conclusion that it is somatic. To be sure, such a line of reasoning is correct, insofar as we have to assume that everything hereditary in material structures, whose chemical nature can already be partially determined today, is passed on from generation to generation. There are, however, hereditary characteristics that manifest themselves somatically during or at the end of the development, and some that never react this way (at least not so far as our present knowledge extends). Important developmental foundations of the intellect are certainly hereditary, and their somatic roots can be logically traced by the fact that they are hereditary, and for many other good reasons. Despite this, linguistic usage separates intellectual life as something specifically "mental" from the "somatic." In the context of experience and in line with such linguistic usage, there exists also a heredity of nonsomatic properties or—more precisely expressed—of characteristics the corporeality of which we infer by way of logical reasoning at best, but which we are unable to render perceptible. For this reason it is no contradiction when one accepts certain hereditary postulates for the schizophrenias—as I do—and still never sees a somatic or an organic psychosis in them.

From the dual meaning of the concepts "somatic" and "organic," no further misunderstandings should ensue. We must reconcile ourselves to the fact that our colloquial speech contains the same expressions for two different concepts about somatic and organic factors: the narrow concept, of calling somatic and organic only that which appears perceptibly as a physiological manifestation, and the other, more extensive concept, that takes its place above the imaginary world of dualism and does not concern itself with the criterion of sensual perceptibility of what is physical.

The distinction between "somatic" or "organic" on the one hand, and "functional" on the other, as I apply them, is in keeping with long-established psychiatric tradition. It is precisely described and substantiated in a paper by Jaspers (1923), who comments about it as follows:

"The so-called *functional* mental disorders . . . are so named because *nothing whatsoever* is found in the brain, neither any direct, nor any other more specious foundations. Despite this, no expert would doubt that every peculiar mental process *also* had its own peculiar somatic prerequisites. Although this somatic foundation, in psychopathic personalities, in hysteria, in many of the psychoses, is still being regarded as dementia praecox (psychic processes) and the like, it is not conceivable in any way other than as the somatic foundation in the brain with all the variety of characters and talents; that is, we are a *long way off* from considering them even as a *possible* object of investigation" (italics by Jaspers).

In spite of this clear description in a paper that is considered a classic, errors still occur today in the description and the distinction between somatic and functional. For this reason it was necessary to elucidate what is meant by these terms in this book.

Deductions and Conclusions

This section highlights the following findings:

Traditional habits of thought and emotional needs together tempt the researcher to regard the schizophrenias as "organic" mental diseases, and to postulate the conditions for their onset in somatic, physiological changes, even when such changes have not been determined with any certainty. Actually, of course, they certainly are not proved, despite the fact that generations of psychiatrists have tirelessly searched for such evidence. Clinical experience shows that most schizophrenics are physically healthy, and that most patients with somatic diseases are not schizophrenic. Even the most sophisticated methods applied in the examination of somatic patients revealed no somatic disorders that occurred in all schizophrenics or only in schizophrenics. No somatic disease is accompanied with any regularity by schizophrenic psychoses.

I do not in any way mean to imply by this that research to discover somatic causes of schizophrenia is any less urgent today than it was heretofore. What has not been discovered up to now, might be discovered tomorrow. We ought to recognize the courage of researchers who continue to pursue research of the somatic aspects of schizophrenia, despite all the sad disappointments suffered by their predecessors.

However, today we must learn to count seriously on the other possibility, that somatic correlates of the schizophrenias will never be detected because they escape detection by the senses in a way similar to the way the somatic correlates of mental processes and of the differentiated human emotional processes do. It is possible, and even probable, that schizophrenic illness is staged in the same general spheres of life where the neuroses are formed, and in which the human personality is shaped in a constant interplay between hereditary developmental tendencies and environmental experience. From a distant and philosophical viewpoint, one might designate as "somatic" and as related to bodily functions whatever takes place in these spheres, based on the fact that everything living is bound to something material. But it lies outside the realm of the somatic to the extent that we cannot directly relate it to any perceptible physical processes.

That is why the research on hereditary psychic developmental tendencies, a disturbed relationship among these tendencies toward one another and toward life's experiences is on a par with somatic schizophrenia research, that is, with the psychodynamic schizophrenia research that is unable to turn up any discernible somatic correlates.

Present-day concepts of schizophrenia must be built on our present-day knowledge. What we do not know but would only like very much to assume as true is better omitted from any provisional theorizing. We know nothing about somatic developmental postulates for the schizophrenias; we know a great deal, however, about those that repose in the cogenital personality and in the development of the personality in conjunction with life's experiences. For this reason, I believe it is incumbent on us, for the time being, to formulate a temporary picture as to the nature of the schizophrenias that is supported by demonstrable disturbances in personal development.

On the basis of such a picture, new lines of questioning emerge for any schizophrenia research endeavor in the future. As I shall emphasize later, there will emerge, a new evaluation especially for the therapy of schizophrenics. We can trust in the therapeutic methods for schizophrenics that have proved to be empirically effective. We are not considering a therapy that is causally directed against a somatic disease, but a therapy that consists of effects that are similar in nature to those that develop, stabilize, and harmonize any given personality.

The Role of Heredity

What my own investigations have individually contributed to the doctrine on hereditary backgrounds of the schizophrenias has already been explained on pp. 428–34. In the formulation of theories on the nature of the schizophrenias the view as to the implication of heredity plays an important role. In the discussion on this theorizing, I shall summarize and supplement previous material in a slightly different context.

Are there hereditary postulates for the formation of schizophrenias?

I am accustomed to answering the question as to what is most convincing to me about the significance of heredity for the manifestation of schizophrenic psychoses somewhat differently from the way most of my colleagues have done until just a few years ago. They cited the greater incidence of schizophrenias among the partners of schizophrenic monozygotic twins than among schizophrenic dizygotic partners as decisive "proof" for the importance of heredity. I cannot admit that it was specifically the previous effort in twin research that presented definite proof for the hereditary implications of schizophrenia. It is true that monozygotic twins (probably!) share exactly the same biological heritage, and the same kinds of illnesses could possibly be the consequence of this; but monozygotic twins also create a more similar environment for themselves than dizygotic twins do. Similar illnesses could, therefore, also be the consequence of their extremely similar human environment.

Many might deem it a paradox when I affirm that nothing is quite as unequivocally convincing to me of the hereditary basis for the onset of schizophrenias as the experiences of psychological research. If one follows impartially the inner development of schizophrenics from infancy to the time of manifestation of the disease, one must bear in mind that schizophrenics for the most part have been exposed to extremely severe psychic stresses, but never to stresses any different from those suffered by many others who did not become schizophrenic.[2] Something is

2. I know of but one single objection to this finding: It stems from the interesting investigations by Wynne and Singer (1963, 1965) on apparently specific psychological test-results from the parents of schizophrenics. Discussion is still in progress concerning to what extent

bound to be inherent in the nature of later schizophrenics that makes them particularly sensitive to their environment to an exceptional degree and in an exceptional manner. And furthermore, later schizophrenics have rarely been exposed to psychic stresses that arose, absolutely independently of their own personalities. The later schizophrenics have a way of maneuvering themselves into unfavorable circumstances in life, in accordance with their personalities, that strike back at them. In brief, if one follows the early life histories of schizophrenics "psychodynamically" (whether by psychoanalytic or by some simpler technique), one begins to understand their illnesses consistently only as the effect of the reciprocal interchange between a person and his living conditions, but never as the effect of these living conditions alone.

Then too, one is worried about every patient for whose psychotic catastrophe one cannot find a plausible, psychologically convincing explanation even after a great expenditure of effort. These are primarily the patients with phasic, catatonic-confusion types of schizophrenia. Their psychoses reveal to a greater or lesser degree characteristics of manic-depressive illness. Especially in cases like theirs, attempts to clarify their condition by psychological or by somatic means often fail, while there are a number of them within families. The assumption of hereditary requisites for the onset of schizophrenia suggests itself most urgently for these types.

the irrational thought-processes revealed by these findings might be the consequence, rather than the cause of schizophrenia in the children. Supposing that it was actually the cause, one might assume—somewhat summarily expressed—that manifest schizophrenias developed from the condition that latently schizophrenic parents (whose irrationality is not expressed in the form of a psychosis in the accepted sense) transmit to their children a manner of thinking and perception that would dispose them to schizophrenia. Even if such an assumption were correct, however, the significance of heredity in the origin of schizophrenias would by no means be patently refuted. For immediately the question would arise: How does it come about that the parents of manifestly schizophrenic children became latently schizophrenic? There is no indication whatever that their "irrationality" might have arisen from a different specific environmental experience than, in turn, from the "irrationality" of their own parents. But in that case there would again be good reasons for postulating the influences of hereditary tendencies for their origin in any of their ancestors.

Along with the new reasons for the assumption of hereditary onset-conditions for the schizophrenias that emerge from psychodynamic research, the most important among the older reasons are still valid.

The incidence of schizophrenia increases in number among the blood relatives of schizophrenics a great deal more than it does among the general population, and more than among the relatives by marriage. For over a hundred years this ratio was suspected, without the benefit of precise research. Koller (1895) and Diem (1905) attempted for the first time to prove it numerically although they applied methods that were still inadequate. Rüdin (1916) and his students succeeded in proving it statistically, and their basic findings have since been repeatedly confirmed. However, the question has been justifiably raised, whether this frequency of schizophrenias in families might not be explained by environmental influences, to which members of families were commonly exposed, rather than by hereditary ones. Anyone who has collected as many family trees of schizophrenics as I have (my collection includes a number of them having well over 100 members), would never acknowledge that the familial frequency of schizophrenias is a manifestation solely of sharing a common detrimental environment. Schizophrenias are encountered with fair frequency even among relatives who have lived under totally different conditions. In particular, we often find schizophrenics in the families of schizophrenics who have never lived together with a sick relative, and who also never even had any personal contact with one. The psychic "contagion" from a sick to a well person may possibly play a role in the formation of many schizophrenias, although exclusively by itself, it cannot be applied as an explanation for the accumulation of schizophrenias in families.

The new, large-scale investigations of children of schizophrenics who grow up in foster families, and of monozygotic twins who grow up apart from each other, will further clarify the questions on hereditary dispositions for schizophrenia. The temporary results on hand suggest the hope that they will provide the proof of their positive implication (Rosenthal et al. 1968).

Quite often, and for many years, the assumption of hereditary preconditions for schizophrenia was opposed not for scientifically objective reasons, but on the basis of the honest conviction that hereditary theories would stand in the way of the treatment of schizophrenics. As a matter of fact, in the past decades the formulas "inherited = incurable" and "acquired = curable" lay painfully close to credibility. Today those formulas are unequivocally obsolete. Even many consequences of hereditary metabolic disorders have become curable, and research on the treatment of hereditary illness, for example, has become one of the principal tasks of pediatrics. Obviously, inherited and experienced causal conditions work hand-in-hand in the formation of schizophrenias. Acknowledgement of the former excludes the possibility of prevention and treatment as little as it excludes them for neuroses and other unfavorable personality developments, the formation of which usually also includes hereditary preconditions.

Incorrect deductions from mistaken theories of heredity used to lead to inhumane measures, such as forced sterilization of schizophrenics. It is understandable that a great many, after the immediate shock of contemplating such measures, wanted nothing more to do with heredity. But for that reason to want to ignore the hereditary backgrounds of the schizophrenias today is no longer justified. Ignoring this problem would stop the progress in gaining any real understanding of the patient; it would make more difficult any effort to help the schizophrenic patient by way of an intimate approach to him.

The concept has long been outdated that it was the doddering old men who would spend their time on research of the hereditary aspects of schizophrenia and that the bright, future-oriented young ones would spend theirs on psychological research. The pioneers of research on heredity, like those of psychological research, already belong to the penultimate generation.

Today we must learn to deal with hereditary postulates for the onset of schizophrenias, whether we like them or not. There is a need to investigate what they consist of, how their sequelae affect the formation of a human environment, and how the person disposed to schizophrenia experiences and tolerates his environment.

Does the hereditary disposition for schizophrenia consist of one or of several pathogenic genes, and is it transmitted according to a simple and tangible mendelian hereditary process?

The mendelian hereditary theory was introduced into psychiatry as a working hypothesis by Rüdin (1916) during the first World War. During certain intermittent periods that followed, many believed almost dogmatically that schizophrenia, as such, could be traced back to a pathogenic gene (or possibly two or three such genes). At the time, the only possibility of checking out the mendelian hereditary hypotheses of schizophrenias was by way of family studies. Today the situation has changed. The phenomenal development of our knowledge about the biochemical and enzymatic processes inherent in the developed organism, somewhere between the transfer of the pathogenic heritage during impregnation and the manifest hereditary disease, has had a tremendous influence on psychiatric research. Many consider it a matter of fact today that every kind of biological heritage takes effect by way of precisely described enzymatic and metabolic processes. In research on heredity, metabolism research has taken its place alongside family research. So it is expected that investigations of the metabolism in schizophrenics would lead to the discovery of an "inborn error of metabolism" and to a clarification of the hereditary process of schizophrenia.

Up to now, probably too little emphasis has been put on how great a shift in ideas about pathological genes as the hypothetical basic causes of schizophrenia has taken place within the last years. Most of today's schizophrenia researchers can hardly imagine anything else when considering mendelian heredity in schizophrenia except the hereditary transmission of an "inborn error of metabolism." The ideas of most schizophrenia researchers between the two World Wars and up to just a few years ago were quite different, however. Their concept was "hereditary transmission of a characteristic," and they operated with this, independently of any concept of an "inborn error of metabolism." They usually worked with it without even thinking of metabolic disorders. To be sure, they knew that certain disorders of metabolism were hereditary, but it did not occur to them that every pathological gene became evident exclusively by way of demonstrable enzymatic and metabolic processes. Instead, they counted on the possibility that the schizophrenogenic heritage could be transmitted by hereditary processes without any somatic correlates that would be subject to research. Even at that time a good deal was already known about the hereditary aspects of human character, without even the hope of discovering detectable somatic functions or structures on which intelligence and character depended.

Naturally, it was necessary to carry over the new ideas into the doctrine of heredity of schizophrenia, although the excessive emphasis they were given was less necessary. The present-day concept that is gaining in popularity, undoubtedly a manifestation of such excessive emphasis, has it that if schizophrenia were hereditary, one should also be able to find a metabolic disorder, analogous, for instance, with phenylketonuria or with galactosemia; and if this was not the case, schizophrenia could not be hereditary, either. Whoever makes such a statement should be confronted with the problem of identifying the enzymatic and metabolic chain reaction in human development that corresponds to the multifactorial hereditary strain that governs intelligence. Although all hereditary processes may involve metabolic processes, he will fail in solving this problem, and thereby admit that there may be operant on the mental level a hereditary process, the biochemical foundations of which elude analysis, as they will for a long time to come. This fact shows that the older concept of hereditary moduli that still defy analysis as to their biochemical foundations, should not yet be unceremoniously discarded. Schizophrenia may be hereditary, even though no metabolic disorder on which it may be based can be discovered.

Today it is possible to declare simply and briefly that the old method of family research did not succeed in discovering for schizophrenia a mendelian hereditary process by which to trace it back to a mutation in the biological heritage. Certainly ample attempts to accomplish just that have not been lacking. In experiments of this type, the onset-expectancy first had to be derived from empirical figures on the frequency of schizophrenias among the different relatives of schizophrenics. Rüdin (1916) and his disciples, as well as British and Scandinavian scientists—Slater (1953), Stroemgren (1935), and others—worked out a rather subtle technique for calculating the onset-expectancy from empirical figures on the frequency of incidence. These rates of onset-expectancy are actually quite useful in practice. But they were also developed in order to check whether they agreed in any way with any mendelian hereditary process. Obviously, this was not the case for the simple-recessive, the simple-

dominant, and other very simple mendelian hereditary processes. In the speculative conviction that some type of mendelian process would be discovered despite such evidence to the contrary, calculations were now undertaken as to what frequency rates could be expected for various degrees of kinship in the more complicated hereditary processes. An enormous number of such hereditary processes is conceivable under the working hypothesis of assuming several genes, and considering imperfect penetrability (or other possibilities of hereditary pathology) for each of them as possible hereditary bases for schizophrenia. It soon proved an easy task to find some hereditary process at random and from it to calculate the expectancy of incidence for a number of degrees of kinship that would agree with the derived figures on these onset-expectancies in the relatives of schizophrenics. In some papers the numerical correlation between the figures calculated for a certain complicated hereditary modulus and the derived rates of incidence was more precise than the median error of the latter! Even that had to be critically correct. Then one was confronted with the revelation that the incidence-expectancies determined by different authors varied to such a degree, that every author's figures suggested some different hereditary process. And finally, after more information had been amassed, the simple truth emerged that each of the laboriously calculated, complicated mendelian hereditary hypotheses could be refuted as soon as new information had become available from different kinship degrees and was critically evaluated.[3] So the mendelian hereditary research for schizophrenia, cross-checked by way of a monumental mathematical effort, actually came to naught, except, perhaps, to prove that a mendelian hereditary process for schizophrenia could not be proved.

At this point, research on metabolism should have taken over. When the psychiatric

3. New findings from twin studies provide an excellent example of this. Most of the former hereditary hypotheses on schizophrenia relied on a manifestation probability of about 80 percent, as it was derived from the older twin studies. New Scandinavian studies show, however, that this figure is too high, and that, perhaps, there is a difference in the concordance between male and female monozygotic twins that contradicts all the simpler hereditary theories. Based on these new findings, many of the previous assumptions about certain hereditary moduli can no longer be considered.

disease syndrome of schizophrenia is too imprecisely described to provide an exact count by which to express the mutation of genes, then the metabolic disorders inherent to the disease—as many expected—should be precisely identifiable and subject to count. But such metabolic disorders have not been discovered. Just as family research was incapable of tracing schizophrenia to a mutation of genes with a definite hereditary process, so also the modern, metabolism-oriented research was unsuccessful in achieving this aim. This finding is all the more painful, since the laborious research effort expended, in its quest for a hereditary enzymatic and metabolic set of disorders, does deserve the highest laudatory recognition. However, insofar as its results are intended to relate to a schizophrenia-specific metabolic disorder, such an interpretation still cannot hold its own in the face of critical judgment. This has already been discussed. The expectations of a discovery of a hereditary metabolic disorder as an essential onset-postulate for the schizophrenias was supported by a completely misleading line of argument, to the effect that since some hereditary metabolic disorders led to mental disorders, schizophrenia was bound to be traceable to a metabolic disorder. With this line of reasoning, many had disregarded the sobering fact that the only known mental disorders in connection with "inborn errors of metabolism" were feeblemindedness and epilepsy, but definitely not schizophrenic psychoses.

After it was revealed that the schizophrenias could not be traced back to a mutation of genes that would be transmitted according to a simple mendelian hereditary process, it was also easy to find theoretical bases for the empirically derived facts concerning the case.

First of all, the inaccuracy in classifying the schizophrenias should be pointed out, as has already been mentioned. Family studies can only disclose mendelian laws for characteristics that can be clearly described and counted. In schizophrenias various descriptions are possible, depending on the diagnostic criteria applied. Dependent on whether schizophreniform senile psychoses, paranoid developments, mixed psychoses with manic-depressive infusion, schizoid psychopathic personality problems are included with the schizophrenias or not, different rates of incidence occur among the relatives. If, moreover, the attempt was made to distinguish a "dementia core group" from a "fringe group" of schizo-

phrenics that run a benign course, one was confronted with so many transitory forms that both the subdivision and the counting became completely arbitrary.

The old and simple mendelian laws can be applied only to characteristics of a certain degree of independence and autonomy from all the remaining development of the organism. As soon as the manifestation of a gene begins to blend closely with the whole environment of genes and with the total personality development, family studies can no longer reveal anything about the hereditary process. But now clinical observation particularly supports the concept that, from the very beginning, schizophrenic developments are inseparably tied to the entire personality development. The manifestation and course of the schizophrenias, on the one hand, and the personality development, on the other, are in a constant state of inextricable reciprocal interaction. The concept is justified that for most patients schizophrenia is much more a pathological personality development than the intrusion of a disease onto a healthy personality. When one knows schizophrenics thoroughly, every delusional idea, every derailment of thought, every hallucination, every illusion of memory, every stereotypy, and every abnormal emotional manifestation can be brought into a relationship with corresponding normal-psychological phenomena from the days of sound mental health. The more accurately we have followed the details of a developing schizophrenic psychosis, the less are we able to describe the natural limits between the communications disorders of the child, puberty crises, deviations in the personality development toward the schizoid-psychopathic, development of the forerunners of the disease, and the development of the "actual" psychosis. It is easier to draw limits in relation to the social impact of the pathological manifestations than as to where something new, special, strange, and pathological breaks into something that was regarded as healthy from a biological point of view. Nor are we able to decide, after the course of a schizophrenic phase, whether the personality changes it leaves behind are still "residues of the psychosis," and thereby, something alien to the natural personality and the healthy biological heritage, or whether they correspond to a natural developmental process that a healthy personality undergoes in working through the outrageous experiences it suffered and in its difficult reentry into society. If these and similar experiences are kept in mind, it is hard to believe that we might have seized upon something in the description of the schizophrenias that should correspond specifically to one gene and that would transmit itself genetically as readily as the color of a blossom, as albinism, or as a certain blood type.

In the research material used for this presentation, the expectancy of incidence among parents, siblings, and children of the probands do not agree with any simple mendelian hereditary process, either. On the other hand, it would be easy to discover such a complicated one that would coincide with these expectations. But then again, it could be easily refuted, if one were to cross-check it against the experiences of other authors, especially in twin studies. When I looked over the individual family histories for the incidence of schizophrenia, there was a confusing kaleidoscope of facts. Now, schizophrenias and character disturbances were totally absent in the families, and then, they occurred in mass accumulation, and then again sporadically; now, generations were skipped over entirely, then, the disease would manifest itself in the proband, in one of his grandparents and his parents, as also in one of his children, so that it seemed to be propagating itself over four generations.

And there is still another deliberation that bars the way to the assumption that schizophrenias developed essentially as the result of one or a few mutations of genes. Among all peoples and in all ages the schizophrenias, when they were counted, have proved to be frequent occurrences. Insofar as we know up to this point, their frequency is the same everywhere. But frequently it was also found that the fertility of schizophrenics is much lower than that of the average population. If a mutant gene were the principal postulate of schizophrenias, the rate of mutation would have to be enormous. It would be improbably high, in fact it would be greater than any that had ever been discovered. Since, as a result of the reduced fertility, the mutated heritage would be constantly and regularly dropping out of the entire human hereditary mass at a rapid rate, the essence for the genesis of schizophrenia would no longer be heredity, but the formation of new mutations. Paradoxically, it is specifically an overstated mendelian hereditary theory, according to which schizophrenia would be based on a mutant biological heritage, that had to lead to the conclusion that the origin of the mutation

is more significant than its transmission, that is, that the new contraction of the disease is more important than its hereditary acquisition! This conclusion is inescapable if the assumption of a mutation is considered simultaneously with the reduced fertility of schizophrenics.[4]

4. Repeated attempts have been made to calculate the mutation frequency of a hypothetical "schizophrenia gene" according to a formula by Haldane. The application of his formula presupposes that the hereditary process of the illness is known or at least suspected. If one believes in a definite hereditary process for a "hereditary" schizophrenia, the simple-recessive process is the most probable one that would apply (or better yet, it is the least improbable). The rate of mutation (relationship of the number of new mutants to the number of alleles of the same gene locus in the population) could then be found according to the formula $(1-f) \cdot X$, in which f is the relative fertility of schizophrenics (assuming a fertility factor $= 1$ in the general population), and X the number of schizophrenics in comparison to the total population. X is known fairly accurately, and amounts to 1 percent. Under the hypothetical assumption that the fertility of schizophrenics is lower by 1/20, Vogel calculates a mutation rate of $5 \cdot 10^{-4}$ ($1/20 \cdot 1/100 = 5 \cdot 10^{-4}$). He remarks in this connection the mutation rate is higher to the 10th power above the previously known mutation rates. According to the investigations described in the preceding chapters, however, the fertility of schizophrenics is a great deal lower than his estimated 1/20; in fact, it is lower by more than half. If we substitute this actual fertility (instead of the hypothetical one) in the above formula, the result is a mutation rate for the "schizophrenia gene" (assuming a simple-recessive hereditary process) of $5 \cdot 10^{-3}$—a mutation rate 100 times greater than any discovered for any known disease.

Vogel has, however, conscientiously described all possible objections that might be valid against the application of Haldane's formula in the simple-recessive hereditary process. They are to be taken so seriously that he recommends not using the formula at all for the recessive process. However, he does add that the two most important objections need not be considered in calculations for schizophrenia; that actually, no recession of incest can be involved in schizophrenia, since the frequency of schizophrenia in populations with varying degrees of incest is about equal. Nor is an increased fertility of heterozygotics involved. According to many findings, including my own, it does not exist.

Despite this, objections can be raised against the described method of calculation. It would have to follow even if other types of hereditary processes were substituted. But when such substitutions are made, an

Here are the conclusions we arrive at. Neither during the course of family research nor during the course of metabolic research was it possible to prove or even to depict as probable, according to a mendelian pattern, the hereditary transmission of a trait for schizophrenia. Even theoretically such a transmission would be improbable, because schizophrenia simply is not distinguished

---

incredibly high mutation rate appears for the hypothetical "schizophrenia gene."

In view of the uncertain foundations for their calculation, it is simpler to omit from discussions precise figures on the mutation rate, and to be satisfied with the fact that we know of no disease that is transmissible according to any simple mendelian hereditary scheme, that occurs as frequently as schizophrenia and still limits fertility as drastically as schizophrenia does. This fact is established. It is sufficient for rendering quite unbelievable the hypothesis, according to which schizophrenia is a hereditary disease that transmits itself by way of a simple mendelian process.

While this book was in press, Professor Dr. G. Röhrborn of the Institute for Human Genetics and Anthropology in Heidelberg transmitted to me, through the professional mathematician Jens Krueger yet another method of calculation: "If it were important to show that the hypothesis of a simple hereditary process required the assumption of a mutation rate that is markedly higher than commonly known mutation rates, I would calculate the mutation rate for those monogenic heredity hypotheses with the lowest expected mutation rate, and that is the one with a dominant hereditary process, with a possibly incomplete manifestation among the heterozygotics (whereas the disease does become manifest in all homozygotics). By a minor modification of the formula by Haldane, the mutation rate for this case would amount to $\mu = (1\text{-}f)\,(X\text{-}d \cdot p)$, in which

X = relative frequency of patients in the population
f = fertility of patients (assuming a value of 1 for normals)
d = frequency of dominant gene responsible for the disease
p = expectancy of manifestation (penetration factor) of the heterozygotics.

For the fixed values of f and X, the mutation rate μ, calculated according to this formula, assumes a maximum value at $p = 0$ (recessive hereditary process as an extreme), and its minimum value at $p = 1$ (complete dominance). The lowest value is

$\mu \approx 1/2 \cdot (1\text{-}f) \cdot X$.

At $f = 50\%$ and $X = 1\%$, the following downward estimate of the mutation rate μ can be expected:

$\mu \geqslant 2.5 \cdot 10^{-3}$,

and that is still a very high rate.

---

sharply as a describable characteristic from the personality development. Mitigating decisively against the assumption of a single pathological gene as the hereditary cause of schizophrenia, is the fact that the fertility of schizophrenics is amazingly low, while the frequency of schizophrenia incidence has remained the same throughout decades. What is it, then, that supports a mendelian process for the hereditary transmission of schizophrenia? I believe one might truthfully answer: Nothing at all! And still, the doctrine has emanated from many departments of psychiatry in many countries and throughout decades, that schizophrenia must be a hereditary disease according to mendelian laws, possibly one transmitted according to a simple-recessive mendelian hereditary process. Only preconceived ideas could have led to such an opinion that arose from the mental attunement of the times. There were three such prejudicial misconceptions
—that schizophrenia was a homogenous disease unit;
—that it was entirely—or principally—dependent on heredity;
—that the hereditary transmission of a mental disease could take place only according to a mendelian process, as for example, Huntington's chorea or hemophilia. One of the most amazing aspects of it all was that hereditary hypotheses could spread far and wide without the benefit of any empirical foundation, and that this took place during a period in which psychiatry aspired to its proudest achievement by joining forces with the exact natural sciences.

Of what do the hereditary postulates for the onset of schizophrenic psychoses consist?

If the deliberations here presented are correct, then research on heredity must finally reconcile itself to accepting two basic facts that have appeared to many to be contradictory for much too long, namely, that there are hereditary onset conditions for the schizophrenias, but that there is no hereditary transmission of the schizophrenias according to a simple mendelian formula. There is nothing in support—and everything in opposition—to the theory that the essential onset postulates for the schizophrenias are contained within one or very few pathogenic genes, and that a schizophrenic psychosis is the symptom of a tangible hereditary disorder of the metabolism. But then, of what do these hereditary onset conditions consist?

It is not too difficult to imagine what they might be or what they probably actually are. The disposition for schizophrenia might elude concrete perception, just as the dispositions for the mental unfolding of a person do. And such a disposition might be the result of either the total of a number of genes, or of the lack of a reconciliation, that is, of a disharmony between a variety of individually normal, healthy, psychic developmental tendencies. It is amazing how long and to what extent these likely assumptions have escaped consideration, and how research—without any convincing indications on hand—has doggedly held fast to the concept that a mendelian hereditary process for the schizophrenias could be discovered, yes, and even one for a hypothetical metabolic disorder fundamental to the schizophrenias.

No one would dispute that there are hereditary traits for types of mental development that we are unable to grasp materially. The traits inherent in intelligence and in certain talents, for instance, for music, draughtsmanship, or mathematics, belong to the same category. Very probably many release mechanisms for emotions and motivations are hereditary, as for instance, for smiling or for crying in infants and for the corresponding emotional reactions of the mother, without being able to establish any relationship between the hereditary disposition (as for instance, the presence of these mechanisms in the person) and any kind of physical manifestation. Most especially, the doctrine on personal character development cannot get along without assuming the existence of materially imperceptible traits, as for instance in respect to the ability to relate to one's fellowman, to practical interests, or to a temperamental moodiness in one direction or another. Nothing says that the hereditary traits for the schizophrenias cannot exist in the same spheres as the hereditary traits for other expressions of mental life. Actually, the schizophrenic phenomenon does take place specifically in the mental spheres. The biological foundations of the psyche, that we have in common with the animals, and that can be investigated by studies of the metabolism and the electrical activities in the brain, concern consciousness, elemental drives, moods, and motivations, and how they proceed in time. But disorders of consciousness, drives, moods, and motivations are by no means among the essential symptoms of schizophrenia. The disorders of these types of life processes, on the other hand, are to be found in the endocrine and cerebral diseases. The basic disturbances of schizophrenics, in contrast, relate to the mental and intellectual attitude toward the world, in the manner by which the affective and the emotional entities fail to attune to and balance one another, in the overevaluation of symbols, etc.—in brief, to the mental sphere. Under these circumstances, why should we not look for the hereditary dispositions for schizophrenia within the same realm as for the hereditary dispositions for mental development?

One could argue against these deliberations by pointing out that everything that is passed on by heredity is bound to a hereditary substance, and is, accordingly, something concrete. For this reason, schizophrenia, insofar as it is hereditary, is a somatic disease. Certainly this line of reasoning is unassailable, but we must reckon with the actual facts. There is a hereditary process of diseases in which research techniques can trace the somatic hereditary processes. These are diseases that can be traced to a single gene. We can attempt to localize that gene. For many of these diseases we can also attempt to ferret out the connections between the primary material manifestations in the hereditary substance, down to the manifestation of the disposition for that disease. It is quite different, however, for the hereditary developmental traits in one's mental life. In this area we are a long way from postulating individual genes, and even from investigating metabolic processes that, separated from their gene, have a certain specific effect on the mental processes. With our modern, sophisticated research methods, it would be positively ridiculous if someone were to attempt to find an answer as to what specific gene governs hereditary mathematical proficiency, or what changes in metabolism are released by this gene that enhance mathematical thought-processes. On the other hand, the same question in respect, for instance, to phenylketonuria is anything but ridiculous, in fact, it expresses a concrete, modern research problem in a simple formula.

In the state of our present knowledge, we are, accordingly, permitted to distinguish between hereditary processes that we can pursue by way of somatic research and those that can in no way be approached by that means. Instead of explaining laboriously each time, that we have been unable so far to explain this latter type somatically, we may briefly state that they belong to a sphere of life that is not the physical one.[5]

The polygenic inheritance of the disposition for the development of schizophrenia is today considered as probable by most researchers. This polygenic inheritance may be conceived of in two different ways, combinative or additive. A disposition for schizophrenia might depend on the chance that a number of genes were present in a certain combination. Each of these genes would constitute a certain definite part of the Gestalt-type disposition which we can perceive as the hereditary disposition for schizophrenia. Every gene would then correspond to a single piece of a jigsaw puzzle. Putting together this puzzle into a whole Gestalt would now be possible only if all the necessary genes were present. No matter how many of a single gene partially involved in causing the disease were present, they still, in the absence of all the others, would not yet constitute the disposition for schizophrenia. However, the

5. However, today, the first hints of ideas on how to bridge this gap between bodily and mental hereditary processes are being vaguely foreshadowed. They emerge from researches on the bases of thought-processes in the ribonucleic acid of nerve cells. According to the principles of mnemonic theory (Hering 1870, Semon 1904, E. Bleuler 1925), the hereditary psychic predispositions would be similar in nature to the individual faculty of memory. Among other possibilities, it might be assumed that the "collective unconscious" of Jung, the hereditary-tendencies patterns, and the acquired memory traces had the same material bases. If the assumptions on tangible material bases of memory were to become established in the ribonucleic acid or in other information carriers of the nerve cells, and if the theory of mnemonics were to be proved reliable and correct under modern investigative methods, it might be possible, after all, to approach the hereditary backgrounds of mental activity and of schizophrenic development by scientific methods. Any speculations beyond this are out of place here. Insofar as we can foresee now, any research aimed in that direction will at best lead to a possible discovery of a general material basis of memory and hereditary dispositions for mental developments. On the other hand, there is today not the slightest indication on record as to how the individual memory and the individual inherited developmental tendency can be correlated with certain individual processes in the carrier-substance of memory and psychic development. If the capability existed to do that, one would immediately be confronted by yet another, more formidable puzzle, namely, how can the countless material carriers of mental developmental tendencies and memory traces influence one another in such a way as to produce a composite whole?

process is different for the simple additive polygenic hereditary concept. In this case, each of the genes contributory to the disposition for the disease would be qualitatively equal to the others. In order to constitute the disposition for the disease, it would simply be a matter of having a sufficient number of the disease-producing genes come together.

Gottesman and Shields (1967) and Shields (1968) were first credited with having accurately checked whether the simple additive hereditary theory is applicable to the schizophrenias. They arrived at an affirmative answer. Among other objections, they had to combat the protest that polygenic heredity was valid only for characteristics and diseases attended by the smooth transitions from the mildest to the most severe manifestations. No one was accustomed, up to that time, to assuming the possibility of polygenic heredity in characteristics and diseases that either existed or did not exist—without revealing a quantitative difference. Researchers were possessed by the concept that in this type of hereditary process, a few pathological genes would represent a mild syndrome of the disease, and many of them, a severe one. But the schizophrenias do not belong to those diseases whose severity lends itself to measurement. In general, one may say about a person that he is or is not schizophrenic. But one would soon be embarrassed if one was asked to determine whether that person is more or is less schizophrenic. To be sure, there are borderline cases. But such borderline cases are few in number, although one was inclined to assume that, according to the polygenic hereditary theory, specifically the milder borderline cases were bound to outnumber the severe ones by a considerable margin. Gottesman and Shields (1967) showed that an additive polygenic hereditary process applied also to characteristics and diseases that either exist or do not exist, and for which the milder forms do not necessarily predominate over the more severe ones. One need only take into account the possibility of a threshold value of the effect of many pathologic genes. Below such an established threshold value, the pathologic genes would remain undetected, and above that figure the disposition for a disease would become a reality (the steadily falling drop of water makes no impact, so long as the glass is not already full, but it does make an impact if it causes the glass to overflow). According to the method outlined by Edwards (1960) and Falconer

(1965), Gottesman and Shields (1967) were still mathematically checking the possibility of an additive polygenic hereditary process for schizophrenia. If, by this method, we place the incidence-expectancy among various relatives of schizophrenics in relationship to the manifestation-expectancy (as the results of twin studies had suggested) and to a given frequency of the disease among the population, the calculated figures will correspond approximately to what might be expected from an additive polygenic hereditary process. This by no means constitutes any proof of the validity for this type of hereditary process. But the finding has merit, at least since it cannot be refuted because of its mathematical calculations.

Dalén has recently attacked the theory of polygenic heredity by an ingenious line of argument. He objects to it on the grounds that it has little to say and cannot be refuted —and justifiably so; although he forgets that experiments in biology have proved the existence of numerous polygenic hereditary systems, and that beyond that, there are interrelationships in nature that are not directly "provable," yet they do exist. He holds that the monogenic theory of heredity deserves more credit because we can try to refute it—and this, too, is justified. But he forgets that this theory has already been disproved. Among other such refutations, he does not mention the most important one, namely, the one derived from the low fertility among schizophrenics along with a consistently high incidence rate of schizophrenia.

The explanations that follow are intended as an expansion of the theory of a polygenic cause of schizophrenia.

In the field of biology it has long been known and described how malformations and diseases originate when the developmental tendencies of the paternal and the maternal heritage are in poor harmonious relationship to each other. Disorders rooted in heredity can be caused by tendencies that in themselves have a life-threatening effect; however, they may also be caused by tendencies that have no particular adverse implication in most of their possible combinations, but that in combination with other (themselves quite healthy) developmental tendencies lead to a disharmonious development, to malformations, or to diseases.[6] The observation of lacking or limited viability of certain hybrids has demonstrated this impressively through the ages.

Even if copulation and conception take place between the representatives of two different species, the offspring is seldom able to sustain life. If the offspring do not die prematurely, hybrids develop who—if they retain their health—sometimes develop completely new characteristics that are different from those of the parents. Often they suffer from some kinds of disorders that limit their viability, although the parents may have been of completely healthy stock. They are not afflicted with any hereditary characteristics that would of themselves dispose to a given disease, but rather they became ill from an adverse combination of individually favorable hereditary developmental tendencies.

One of the most commonplace observations of disorders common to hybrids is their infertility. Thus, male and female mules are infertile because the spermatogenesis fails with the second meiosis (Lang 1914).

A frequent hereditary disorder that comes about from a disharmony of tendencies (even among racial hybrids) is the imperfect meshing of the upper and lower mandibles in mammals, denying them the capability of chewing. In crossing Pekinese and Saloniki dogs, for instance, it turns out that the tendencies of the upper and the lower mandibles are independent of one another. If they do not compensate one another in hybrids, malformations of life-threatening implications ensue from individually normal tendencies (James 1941).

Here is an example of the emergence of a new characteristic. By crossing a racially pure, wild white mouse and a racially pure black mouse, grey mice are produced. The reason is that when the gene for black hair coloring is combined with a speckling gene (My), light-colored rings are formed around the black hairs and, to the observer, the entire pelt looks grey instead of black. The gene for black hair coloring, however, melanogen (M), is not individually capable of producing the black hair coloring, if a general coloring

---

6. Prof. Dr. E. Hadorn, who was kind enough to check my statements on the hereditary bases of schizophrenia, advises me against the use of the expression "totally normal developmental tendencies," on the ground that there are almost no genes in existence that promote or assure a harmonious development in any genetic milieu. A hereditary trait, imbedded in an unfortunate combination with other traits, may produce adverse effects, while in combination with a different grouping its effect would be quite normal and healthy.

factor—a gene for chromogenic substance (C) —is not simultaneously present, as well. All mice without this gene are white. If we indicate the presence or the absence of a certain gene by capital and lower-case letters, respectively, the hereditary formulae may be written

For the wild, white
   parental animal: cc, MyMy, MM
For the black
   parental animal: CC, mymy, MM
For the hybrids: Cc, Mymy, MM

Since C is dominant over c, and My over my, the generation of hybrids is grey (according to Lang 1914).

The example is a very simple model for the way in which new—and in this case healthy —characteristics develop from new combinations of genes. Why could not such a new characteristic turn out to be a disease on some occasions?

Examples of how malformations and diseases in the offspring might emerge from crossing healthy individuals derive, among others, from the experience of crossbreeding of various kinds of dogs. If a dachshund is crossbred with a St. Bernard, the results are "veritable monstrosities: heavy body structures typical of the St. Bernard on short, crooked legs" (Lang 1914, describing experiments by Heim).

Even some very old experiments revealed that disorders in temperament and behavior emerge in hybrids whose parents were pure of race and of acceptable temperament. In that vein, Gates (1909) described how hybrids with the most varied temperaments were produced from crossing a "very gentle and timid" English bobtailed shepherd female with a lively, playfully aggressive Scotch shepherd male, some of which revealed an exaggerated aggressiveness. The phenomenon has virtually no explanation other than saying that with a specific combination of hereditary tendencies, such a high degree of aggressivity developed that it manifested itself as an illness (example cited from Lang 1914).

Large-scale crossbreeding experiments with dogs that considered body form, the endocrine system, and behavior were conducted by Stockard et al. (1941). He shows impressively how hereditary disharmonies result from crossbreeding, that affect the body structure as well as the behavior. Here are just a few examples. By interbreeding basset

hounds with German shepherds, hybrids result that reveal an admixture of the characteristics of both parents. When these hybrids are, in turn, crossbred among one another, various kinds of animals result, among them some that have the bodies of shepherd dogs but the more passive behavior of the basset hound, and vice versa. Disharmonies ensue, because form and behavior no longer match. The form and behavior of the basset hound are attuned to make him a proficient hunter. He has an exceptionally keen sense of smell and, in contrast to the German shepherd, is not easily diverted, once he picks up a trace. Many hybrids retain just a few individual characteristics that make them proficient in hunting. Their functional fitness has been disturbed by an adverse blending of hereditary tendencies.

The breed called the English bulldog, according to James (1941) was the result of crossbreeding racially pure dogs, and he owes his unfavorable characteristics to adverse combinations of genes. "The English bulldog also deviates from the normal type in general behavior. The hunting reaction in these dogs has been completely lost. In many members, the maternal reaction is distorted. The puppies are often neglected after whelping, and in some cases there is a peculiar abnormal reaction during whelping, in that the bitch, instead of eating the amnion and biting it off at the proper place, chews it off too close to the body of the puppy, leading to hemorrhage or later infection. Besides these abnormal maternal reactions, the animal is noted for undue tenacity and ferocity during excitement and is, in fact, supposed to have been inbred to emphasize this tendency."

By mixing hereditary tendencies it is possible that not only animals with disturbed viability and defects in their functioning are produced, but also occasionally some that are capable of better accomplishments than their racially pure ancestors. James (1941) remarked about hybrids of the first generation from cross-breeding basset hounds with German shepherds:

"They are better balanced dogs and make a more satisfactory adjustment in any situation than either the basset hound or shepherd parent. This suggests that there is a blending of the behavior factors, as seems also to be the case in the head and body factors."

In other hybrids the behavior types of the two parent animals may be observed in a state of imbalance to one another. Now one behavior pattern emerges, and then the other:

"It was found that not only could the physical form and behavioral nature be modified,[7] but that the same dog may behave like both the grandparental types under different conditions."[8]

It is easy to speculate that this sort of inconsistency in the behavior of an animal that lives in complete freedom is unfavorable, and may manifest itself as a disease. Considered as such a hereditary disease, the animal would be suffering from a type of ambivalence, although this "ambivalence" would be something quite different from what we understand by that term as applied to man.

James (1941) emphasizes repeatedly that new characteristics in dogs may be based on two different causes:

"It may be assumed that there are two basic factors influencing the constitutional complex. One is the combination and patterning of the genes which determine bone, glands and the nervous structures[9] of the body, and the other is the action of mutations."

In a summary the same author gives the following beautiful description of the disorders that emerge as a result of unfavorable mixtures of hereditary tendencies in dogs:

"It has been shown that within the specific reaction systems studied in the experiments there are differences in quality and degree of activity. It may be assumed that in the two pure behavioral types the genetics of each system is different, and the interaction between the genetic factors and the glandular processes also differs. Within the pure behavioral types there is a harmonious relationship between behavioral systems and the other bodily organs. This holds both for the inactive and the active types. Among the hybrids, however, in which there is mixed physical form, there is also disharmonious relationship between the bodily organs and

7. Modification by crossbreeding experiments is what is intended here.

8. In another place James (1941) describes the unusual observation as follows: "Under experimental conditions it was found that some animals" (the implication is hybrids) "could not be included within the range of normal behavior. These animals also have a mixed nature, in that they may conform to an inhibited type in one situation and to an excitable type in another."

9. The "nervous structure" referred to is an estimated condition that the author derived from behavior. This is not anatomic data scientifically developed from the nervous system.

the reaction systems. For example, one system may be easily excited, yet others may be extremely difficult to excite. The animal may be overtly disturbed in situations involving pain, yet entirely undisturbed in another situation. Again the muscular systems of the limbs may be well developed, yet action limited because of a low energy factor. The factors which influence behavior become mixed and varied, just as do those which determine physical form. In the mixed types, the harmonious relationship found within each pure behavioral type is broken up, and the result is a disharmony among the systems."

In man, poorly reconcilable hereditary tendencies may often be suspected as bases for psychopathic and neurotic personality developments. At times, for instance, one gets the impression that increased activity and hyperactivity in one of the parents and a lack of facility for human contacts and personal warmth in the other, would dispose the child to antisocial activity that was alien to the father as well as to the mother. But these are still only presumptions. It appears that v. Baeyer (1935) came closest to establishing a demonstrable argument. He established a relationship between the hereditary postulates for pathological lying and cheating, with a dangerous combination of various hereditary, individually harmless traits and developmental tendencies. Some of these, among others, were a lack of self-restraint, a strong sense of self-importance, and an active imagination. In the ascendancy of the "conditional-feebleminded," we occasionally see, on the one hand, intellectual underachievement, and on the other, energy and a sense of self-importance.

Such examples from the field of biology could be multiplied ad infinitum. These suffice, however, to demonstrate that in biology, scientists have long accepted the fact that disorders can come about by imperfect blending; that is, by the disharmony of polygenic hereditary tendencies. Animal experiments even provide examples showing that changes in emotional excitability and in instinctive behavior may be caused by an unfavorable blending of hereditary tendencies.

Beyond this, we know today that genes frequently work together in groups. The type and the timely sequence of this cooperative effort of genes in the formation of transcriptions for the formation of certain ribonucleic acids (and later of certain proteins) is determined by certain genes, the so-called operator-genes. The genes they in turn influence are called "structural genes." There are also "regulator genes," that in turn affect the "operator genes." This latter influence can be controlled by "inductors" that originate in the environment, for instance, by substances in the culture medium of bacteria. The inductors may in other cases be formed by yet another special gene, the "inductor gene." Up to this point, the hypothetical "schizophrenia gene" has unwillingly been imagined as a more or less independent structural gene in psychiatric genetics. No one had yet thought of the possibility that regulator, operator, or inductor genes, and especially a cooperation among these, may be important in formulating the biological postulates for the unity of the person—and for its disorders.[10]

The new doctrine on the cooperation of various genes, to be sure, was first discovered principally from studies of lower forms of life. But if even in bacteria the mutual cooperation of genes and the influences of the environment are important, it is reasonable to assume that the harmony of the cooperative effect of various genes among one another and with the environment would have an even greater influence on the formation of higher forms of life. It certainly is no absurd assumption that this harmony may be decisive, particularly for the ontogeny of biological postulates in the personality of humans. Surely it will no longer seem absurd, once one has become thoroughly acquainted with the importance of harmony in personality, in biology on the one hand, and in its developmental process on the other.

It is really amazing how psychiatric research in heredity for nearly half a century disregarded the possibility that tendencies for

---

10. The psychiatrist who does not want to go deeply into the modern doctrine of the regulation of genes could easily be instructed from numerous citations in the literature on genetics how important the cooperative effect of genes can be, for instance: "The cell contains a sufficient number of genes so that 10–30 regulator genes each affect every structural gene, which then, in turn, codifies an enzyme." Or: "Even more complicated cycles for the regulation of genes have been suggested. For instance, 2 genes might activate each other by way of their gene-products. The two genes would then be dependent on each other. Neither of the two could function independently if the other were not also functioning." (Citation from J. Butler).

mental illness might be the consequences of unfavorable mixtures of tendencies that are themselves not necessarily pathogenic. The reason may be that the mendelian discoveries and their application to chromosome research were truly revolutionary discoveries in the biology of heredity. After Rüdin (1916) had introduced the mendelian theory into psychiatry with an astounding degree of methodical care and inspired enthusiasm, the attention of all psychiatrists remained focused on him. Almost no one conceived the possibility that, alongside heredity which is revealed by the mendelian formulae, there is an intermediary polygenic heredity and a formation of new characteristics governed by the blending of genes. Few psychiatrists realized that these other forms played an important part in biology, and that in recent years they have reassumed considerable recognition. Of course, anyone who studied in Zürich during the first or second decade of this century was influenced by the great hereditary scientists, Lang and Standfuss, who also acknowledged the importance of intermediary heredity and the formation of characteristics by the blending of hereditary tendencies, after Mendel's discoveries had become known.

Of course, the proof that hereditary disorders may occur through unfavorable combinations of individually "healthy" hereditary tendencies, still does not yet attest to the theory that specifically the hereditary dispositions for schizophrenia are based on an unfavorable combination of hereditary tendencies. What does attest to that theory? I believe that quite a lot of weighty evidence does.

As already pointed out, the existence of hereditary onset-conditions for the schizophrenias in the absence of hereditary postulates in accordance with comprehensible mendelian laws indicates a multifactorial type of heredity in which unfavorable combinations of genes could be decisive. There are considerations that support the expansion of the polygenic theory by means of the disharmony-theory.

1. As previously discussed, the markedly lowered fertility of schizophrenics while the incidence rate of schizophrenia remains the same, is irreconcilable with the assumption that one gene or a few pathogenic genes constituted the principal onset-conditions for the schizophrenias. A hereditary process based on the total of a great number of pathogenic genes could possibly be reconciled with the

lower fertility rate. Still, the best explanation for the consistency of the incidence rate in spite of the reduced fertility of schizophrenics is the assumption of a disharmony in hereditary tendencies.

2. In the theory of multifactorial heredity by means of a total of pathogenic genes, the assumption would have to be among the offspring of related parents that the number of schizophrenics would accumulate at a greater rate than is really the case. The slight influence of inbreeding in the hereditary disposition for schizophrenia more probably indicates that its origins depend on a disharmony between normal tendencies. There is no evidence indicating that a disposition for schizophrenia could be "pure-bred" in a culture medium of inbreeding. We observe, on the other hand, that schizophrenia occurs unexpectedly in families where none had occurred for generations. Of course, the same is possible in any recessive hereditary process and in any new formation of mutations. At all events, there is no evidence to show that families could emerge from the union of two nonschizophrenics who have no longer been vulnerable to schizophrenia for a number of generations.

3. Insofar as a personal psychic disposition for schizophrenia can be identified, it rests in the schizoid personality. The schizoid personality is identifiable by a difficulty in reconciling the tendencies, drives, and emotions of a person. For this reason, a schizoid personality corresponds exactly to what we theoretically expect from a disposition, whenever a faulty reconciliation of psychic tendencies constitutes the hereditary causes for schizophrenias.

4. The physique and metabolism of schizophrenics show extreme, discernible characteristics in different directions, more often than the norm would indicate. Such manifestations are observed in hybrids of various strains in the second filial generation, in which the individual hereditary characteristics are poorly combined to form a whole. Schizophrenics also often reveal unusual proportions of certain body measurements and various metabolic data, as might be expected whenever hereditary traits are mixed that are difficult to combine into a harmonious whole.

5. The elementary phenomena of the schizophrenic psychosis itself lie in the cleavage of various psychic life processes. These processes run concurrently to a greater degree than in normal individuals, without uniting into a whole. This is true of the schizophrenic's volition (he demands opposites simultaneously), of his actions (he speaks, but he does not speak so that he can be understood); he extends his hand, although he applies no pressure, etc.); it is true also of his feelings (drastically illuminated by that contradictory aspect of his expression often referred to as a "lack of grace"), of his mental imagery (memory, imagination, and perception are not brought into proper temporal order, and memories are experienced as perceptions); of his thinking (symbols and symbolized concepts run along parallel lines and share the same meaning), and of his entire intellectual being (a "double set of books"). Keeping in mind all these psychopathological manifestations, it does not seem to be too far off the mark to trace the hereditary basis of a psychosis that is characterized by a lack of unity of the inner life, back to a faulty reconciliation of mental developmental tendencies.

6. Treatment methods that have proved their worth with schizophrenics utilize the same influences that, in the course of an individual's development, promote a unity of the personality—the development of the ego. They consist of emphasizing the distinction between "I" and "we," and between "you" and "all-of-you," in an active communal relationship, and in the mobilization of all forces for an unequivocal confrontation with threats of all kinds. If influences that favor the unity of the personality have a beneficial effect on the schizophrenias, it is not surprising that a lack of unity, that is, a disharmony, should be among the postulates for the emergence of schizophrenias.

None of these constitute proof for the assumption of a disharmony in the hereditary tendencies for the formation of schizophrenia, although they are indications—some of them quite clear, others more obfuscated. But rather than support our theories with indications, we should like to depend on proofs. No way has been found to secure such proofs. We may have to admit that it is impossible ever to depict the nature of the hereditary disposition for schizophrenia with the desired degree of assurance. One might take exception to the idea that this assumption cannot be proved. Some critics have gone so far as to reject it because it could not be proved. I hardly believe that psychological or psychopathological theories have to be rejected out of hand because they cannot be perceptibly demonstrated or proved mathematically or statistically. There are psychological and psychopathological facts whose very nature defies "proof," and that can, by their very nature, only be rendered as probable. It is unscientific to designate psychological and psychopathological phenomena as nonexistent, simply because they cannot be proved.

Their inprovability applies to the assumption of a polygenic heredity for schizophrenia just as it does to the assumption of a disharmony in the tendencies as hereditary postulates for the onset of schizophrenia. Neither can be refuted, nor can they be proved; they are simply more or less probable.

The two theories—the polygenic hereditary theory for schizophrenia and the coming into being of a disposition to schizophrenia by a disharmony of developmental tendencies inherited from the parents—form a unit. Up to a certain degree it amounts merely to a difference in the formulation, and not to a difference in the thing itself. If, according to the polygenic theory, the many genes responsible for the pathogenic condition contribute harmlessly toward the development of a healthy person in most combinations, but just by blending in a certain different combination they become pathogenic, then anyone at all should be at liberty to refer to a disharmony of tendencies. The concept can also be supported that there is no gene that is in itself pathological (and would not be pathological in most combinations, either), that schizophrenia originates rather whenever the total of certain individually healthy genes did not tolerate one another well. Of course, based on other deliberations, one would hardly identify the polygenic hereditary theory with the theory of disharmony. Speculatively, one could imagine that there are deleterious tendencies that take no essential part in shaping a healthy personality; they would manifest themselves merely as mischievous dispositional spoilers if they existed in a person in sufficient number or in a suitable combination. In that case it would hardly be justifiable to talk about a disposition for schizophrenia from unfavorable combinations of normal tendencies. In that case the (objectionable) assumption of a total of "pathogenic" genes would be more acceptable. It is possible, therefore, to conceive of the polygenic hereditary theory of schizophrenia just as easily as being identical to the theory of disharmony as the opposite; as though it were something totally different. Between these, all sorts of transitions are conceivable. For the time being, any discussion of them would be fruitless.

Just like the polygenic theory, the disharmony theory must assume that in the families of schizophrenics unfavorable genes must be present as a condition, and present in large numbers. In the first instance they would themselves be unfavorable or pathogenic, and in the second, they would first lead to disharmonies in a certain genotypic environment.

In discussions with professional colleagues, three objections against the disharmony theory emerged.

1. The combining of irreconcilable developmental tendencies would be most likely to occur—so ran the argument—when two people of different races, and also of different skin coloring, produced children. But so far, no one has demonstrated any accumulation of schizophrenias among half-castes with any regularity. The objection is thought-provoking, although not fully convincing. We do not know what psychic developmental tendencies are compatible or incompatible with one another. No one can predict theoretically whether the inherited mental developmental tendencies of two people of different races pose favorable or unfavorable conditions for the formation of a strong, unified ego. We do not even know whether the difference in the mental life of the different races is based on hereditary causes or whether it is brought about by growing up under different cultural conditions. Perhaps the human races are less different in respect to their hereditary mental developmental tendencies than they are in respect to their skin coloring or their facial configuration. If, however, they should also be different in respect to their inherited mental developmental tendencies, it would be just as conceivable that the differing tendencies supported one another favorably than that they should lead to disharmony.

2. Further serious objection against the disharmony theory is aimed at the fact that this theory does not explain the accumulation of schizophrenias among most of the relatives of schizophrenics. Based on that theory, only the established frequency of schizophrenias among the siblings could be accounted for, but hardly that among the children or other relatives of schizophrenics. The objection would be correct if the disharmony theory were dependent on unfavorable combinations of just a few genes. But that the combination of a certain specific number of genes should accumulate to such an extent among certain degrees of kinship (except among siblings) as the schizophrenias actually do accumulate, is

most unlikely. Such a contradiction between theory and facts could only be bridged over by the construction of arbitrary and meaningless auxiliary hypotheses. But the disharmony theory does not count on it that the essence in hereditary dispositions for schizophrenia might consist of the combination of a definite countable number of certain genes. The essence is, rather, the total design of the personality structure that, in the course of the ontogenesis, is shaped with greater or lesser facility into a comprehensive whole out of the sum total of the individual tendencies. A group of hereditary developmental tendencies can be more or less detrimental to the whole.[11] If conditions are such, the disharmony theory does not permit of any prediction in figures as to the frequency of schizophrenia among certain relatives of schizophrenics. On the other hand, the fact that schizophrenia occurs all the more frequently among the relatives of schizophrenics the closer the relationship is compatible with the theory.

3. The disharmony theory does not explain the fact that the disease manifests itself rather equally among the most varied kinship groups (at least so uniformly that the same diagnosis —schizophrenia—is the most obvious one). This argument may be countered by the concept of the threshold value. Gottesman and Shields (1967) have already used it in defense of the additive polygenic heredity theory. One might imagine that the unity of the person disintegrates or does not disintegrate. If it does, the nature of the consequences no longer depends on the type of disharmony that brought about its disintegration. It then depends on how the irrational, autistic thinking, that has now burst forth from its confinement, is personalized in the specific instance. It further depends on whether the new life experiences enhance or damage the health and the unity of the individual.

Do the theories about polygenic heredity and about the nonreconciliation of hereditary tendencies erode the firm foundations of

hereditary research in the field of psychiatry? Are they merely academic declamations from somewhere in the clouds? Or do they have concrete significance after all?

Unfortunately, it is true that both theories disappoint many hopes—namely, the hopes of describing clearly and succinctly the disposition for schizophrenia by means of statistical methods and by studies of the metabolism. Despite this, I believe that some tangible benefits can be forthcoming if both these theories are finally taken seriously. Below I point out this forthcoming benefit.

Both theories set new goals for research. On the basis of the disharmony theory, promising research projects can be planned. Are certain disharmonies evident in the personalities of the parents of schizophrenics? Important research results on this question are already on the record. A schizoid personality in the parent predestines the child to schizophrenia, but not every type of schizoid personality. How, then, is the type of schizoid personality that jeopardizes the offspring with schizophrenia distinguished from the type that does not so jeopardize it? General clinical observation teaches us that a schizoid personality in one of the parents is by no means neutralized in its unfavorable influence on the children by a cyclothymic personality of the other parent, as was once surmised. In clinical practice one gets the impression, rather, that the two characteristics in their noxious effect on the health of the offspring support one another. This point, however, is in need of more accurate investigation.

The findings from projection tests on parents of schizophrenics are important for research. In projection tests (particularly of the Rorschach variety) and performance tests (object sorting) many ambiguities were revealed in the expression, the thinking, the conceptualization, and the emotional attunement of the parents of schizophrenics (Wynne et al. 1958; Lidz 1958, 1962, 1968; McConaghy 1959; Singer and Wynne 1963, 1965; Wynne and Singer 1963; Wild 1965; Wynne 1968; and Schopler and Loftin 1969). Up to the present, they had principally been regarded merely in respect to their psychotraumatic influence on the children. To what extent these ambiguities develop under the stress to which parents of a schizophrenic child are subjected, and to what extent they magnify peculiarities of the parents that are independent of the actual psychic stresses remain to be investigated (Schopler and Loftin

---

11. A simple deliberation will illustrate what is meant. Imagine the problem of rearranging all the essential elements from two different idyllic landscape paintings into one new composite painting that is also idyllic and harmonious. If the two originals contained mostly similar elements, this would be possible. But the pictures may also contain such vastly different elements that it would become impossible. A certain element may go well with the new composite version, but it would be irreconcilable with some other version.

1969; Uchtenhagen in the original German edition of this volume). These types of tests used to be applied only in psychodynamics research; they ought also to become the instrument for hereditary research in the future. To what extent are the discovered disharmonies in the personalities of the father or the mother of schizophrenics active as disharmonious hereditary developmental tendencies in the children? To what extent do they provides an unfavorable influence for the child through heredity, and to what extent—as previously postulated—through the "teaching of irrationality"? Do disharmonies in thought and perception really predominate only in the father or mother considered individually? Do they not much more probably result also from a disharmony in conceptualization and in the emotional tone between the father and the mother? For instance, does not overemphasized sexuality on the part of the one parent and an underemphasized one on the part of the other have as great an influence on the child as when one of the parents alone is ambiguous as to his sex role? Could an overemphasized sex consciousness in one, and an underdeveloped such consciousness in the other parent not also somehow be rooted in the hereditary developmental tendencies? Could an unfavorable hereditary disposition result for the child as a result of such a combination? All these questions are waiting to be resolved, and in the process, test experiments conducted simultaneously with both parents, among others, will play an important part. Willi (1962, 1964, 1968, 1969) has worked them out as an instrument for the processing of similar problems.

Psychodynamic schizophrenia research has already been intensively engaged in studying the contradictory nature of the prepsychotic personality of later schizophrenics. There is no longer any doubt about this contradictory aspect. However, in the future it will be important to find out what areas of the inner life exist with what other areas at the greatest frequency and in a particularly irreconcilable contrast, before the schizophrenia erupted. Furthermore, it will be important to trace the development of such contrasts back to earliest childhood, and to investigate whether this antagonism in the later patient has any relationship to those of both parents or their stand-ins.

These remarks should suffice to point out that research on the heredity of schizophrenias does not cease with the acceptance of the disharmony theory; it begins on a new foundation.

But the disharmony theory is not significant just for research alone. Beyond that, it is not exactly inconsequential in the treatment of schizophrenics, in counseling their families, and in governing what to do and what not to do in practical medicine.

Whoever deals seriously with this theory will not be tempted to try to eradicate schizophrenia by sterilizing all schizophrenics. He will hold to his belief that families in which schizophrenias have occurred do not necessarily have to degenerate, do not necessarily carry within them any inherent "hereditary danger" to the entire population, and that the misfortune of today's generation and the preceding ones will not fatalistically afflict future generations of that family. If one knows schizophrenics and their families well, it is sometimes a matter for despair to see how much they suffer under the terrible concept of "familial tainting." Like a sinister shadow it darkens the lives of many people and of entire families. The stifling, uncertain fear of coming from an "inferior breed," of carrying within one's self the seeds of something pathological, morbid, and evil (I am speaking in the jargon the afflicted apply to themselves), like a curse that you must pass on to someone else, causes oppressive feelings of inferiority. We must confront the bitter truth that rash, premature, thoughtless pronouncements by doctors and the popularization of such pronouncements have been the partial cause for this lowering of morale in the families of schizophrenics. In the last century it was the "degeneration theory" by Morel (1860) that —born of the fear and the prejudices of the people—in its turn propagated these fears and prejudices for its own sake. Today the aftereffect is still with us. Later, the happiness of the families of schizophrenics was not really encouraged when they were told that the illness of their problem child was based on recessive pathological genes; whereupon they would deduce that such genes were also present in the "manifestly healthy" relatives, and that the disease would certainly emerge again in one or the other offspring. They were told such things much too often, and all too often the speaker did not really know whether it was true. Today the mind of the population has retained what formerly doctors had thoughtlessly declared, without the necessity of hearing it restated.

Perhaps the disharmony theory will one

day have a more beneficial effect on the relationship between the doctor and the schizophrenic or between the doctor and the family of the schizophrenic than did the theories about a mendelian hereditary process of schizophrenia or hereditary metabolic disorders. If a patient could not be approached, if therapy took no effect, if the patient completely withdrew into himself, it was popular for a long time to form the autistic chain-reaction of thought: Well, then he's just simply schizophrenic, then he has a hereditary disease, and then I just can't help it that I don't understand him and can't treat him. (That is irrational thinking, but it is natural to human frailty.) I have always felt good when I could say to myself in this kind of situation: "He is a human being endowed with the same developmental tendencies inherent in all of us who are healthy, including myself, although he is unable to overcome his inner disruption." At times families were pleased to hear that they had no unhealthy genes and no familial illness, but rather that a misfortune could befall any family with normal tendencies in unfavorable combinations and in unfavorable cooperation with the environment. At some time, under certain conditions, the disharmony theory may contribute to making the relationship between the patient, his family, and his doctor more natural, more sincere, and more human. This is sentimental, wishful thinking, however. It is not necessary to spell out that these are not arguments in support of a hereditary theory. It is scientifically immaterial whether a theory pleases the patient and us or not. A hereditary theory must be made scientifically probable in order to merit discussion. In the final analysis, concepts founded on lies and wishful thinking have no substance in the intercourse between doctor and patient either. But all this does not keep the doctor from feeling some degree of pleasure when scientific knowledge supports his specific vocation, and thereby is also helpful to his patients.

In summarizing this subchapter I should like to establish that

—Hereditary developmental tendencies are definitely operant in the formation of schizophrenias

—The schizophrenias definitely are not hereditary according to any simple mendelian formula

—Probably the disposition for schizophrenia may be propagated by polygenic heredity (additive or combinative)

—The disposition for schizophrenia may emerge from a disharmony of psychic developmental tendencies that were inherited from the father or the mother.

The Role of Psychotraumatic Experiences

The role that psychotraumatic experiences play in the genesis of schizophrenias and the role of heredity were developed by similar methods. Just like the implications of heredity, the implications of psychotraumatic experiences in life were posited as "self-evident facts" at certain times, while at others they were just as self-evidently ignored. During certain periods, heated passionate arguments developed for their recognition—as they did for the recognition of heredity. There were times and cultural groups within which the recognition of the implications of life experiences in the development of schizophrenia would jeopardize the academic advancement of a psychiatrist, and there were times and cultural groups within which the circumstances were reversed, that is, an admission of "psychodynamic" interpretation of schizophrenia was then the mark of professional standing. In more recent years these views have begun to approach each other. Today most psychiatrists acknowledge that psychotraumatic experiences do play an important role in the genesis of schizophrenia, but that by themselves, without considering also hereditary developmental tendencies, they do not provide a complete picture of the evolutionary process of the psychosis. To promote mutual understanding of this subject, the Second International Congress for Psychiatry, held in Zürich in 1957, that was dedicated to the schizophrenias, was one of several bodies to make some major contributions.

As research on heredity sought out specific hereditary damage, so also psychological schizophrenia research for a long time posed the problem for itself of discovering specific psychotraumatic experiences in connection with schizophrenia. Both research areas, that in other respects emanated from totally different fundamental concepts, agreed that schizophrenia was a specific disease, and as such it would have to have specific causes. Just as research in heredity, so also psychodynamic research must reconcile itself to the frustrating truth that specific causal damage relating to schizophrenia will never be discovered, because it does not exist.

In our day and age the recognition has

prevailed that we can only understand the hereditary dispositions for schizophrenia as developmental tendencies. They tend to inhibit the formation of harmonious relationships of future patients with others, and simultaneously to render such future patients particularly sensitive to disturbances in their human environment, in a special way and to an exceptional degree. Accordingly, we understand the influence of psychotraumatic experiences only in relationship to hereditary developmental tendencies. The unfavorable hereditary dispositions, as well as the adverse experiences, are not individually specific in their nature. However, in combination they jeopardize the formation of a strong personality, of a strong ego, that is capable of prevailing in a unified way and a goal-directed manner in its own world.

I should like now to enumerate briefly the most important experiences that compel us to acknowledge the significant role of psychotraumatic experiences in the origins of the schizophrenias.

When we really become closely acquainted with a schizophrenic in the course of treatment, we can always think our way into the origins of the disease's elements, and often into the origin of the entire disease, just as we often believe to be able to feel our way into and to understand subjectively—yes, even to "explain"—the origins of neuroses and the shaping of every human destiny, including our own. In addition we learn from the patient how often he himself feels that his illness was the necessary consequence of the kind of life he has had. All this has been amply described, and it requires no further elucidation in this book.

We often see correlations in time between the beginning of a psychosis and changes in its course, along with changes in the conditions imposed on the patient by life. Some of these correlations, as routine daily clinical practice has shown them, I have already attempted to support with statistics in Chapter 1 of this book.

The frequent successes of our psychotherapeutic efforts suggest that if psychic influences in the therapy changes the aspect of the disease, adverse psychic influences almost certainly play a part in the formation of that disease.

Especially the most terrible schizophrenic conditions, that have been labelled "dementias," and that were long regarded as the "core syndrome" of the schizophrenias, can largely be understood in the context of reactions to adverse environmental influences. This has been elucidated on pp. 417–20.

The attempts to establish statistically the psychogenetic influences on the formation of the schizophrenias yielded only scanty results in the beginning. A significant portion of the investigations presented in Chapter 4 had a part in establishing them.

The totality of the arguments presented seems to me to constitute a compelling reason for accepting the significance of psychotraumatic experience for schizophrenia. I feel no need to go further into detail about it.

I should like, however, to explain somewhat more fully why, in my opinion, the concept should be rejected that there are specific psychotraumatic experiences that are essential for the formation of schizophrenias. Neither in the course of the investigations presented here, nor in the course of my general clinical experience, was I able to find indications of the existence of such experiences. The assumption of a fully specific psychotraumatization of future schizophrenics, in my opinion, is conclusively refuted by merely enumerating the views of different authors at different times, and realizing how widely they disagreed on the subject. Almost every conceivable psychotraumatization has already been accused of being the specific cause of schizophrenia. Again and again, good reasons were presented for the implication of a certain traumatization, but never have there been sufficient reasons for their exclusive implication. The deduction suggests itself that a great variety of adverse experiences may be involved.

For a long time, investigators searched expressly for specific critical time-phases that were exclusively responsible for the preparation for subsequent schizophrenic development. In so doing, they had in mind Freud's concepts as to the phasic development of sexuality and as to the special significance of every developmental phase in shaping the personality and in developing neuroses. The supposition arose that the critical time for the emergence of schizophrenias lay still farther back in childhood than that of the neuroses, because schizophrenia leads to an extensive disintegration of the personality, whereas neuroses leaves the basic personality structures intact. The concept that the libido of later schizophrenics was incapable of establishing object-relationships was itself a decisive indication of the significance of earliest infancy for the psychodynamic preparation of a schizophrenia. Since then many authors have come to regard disturbances during breast-feeding as a basic psychotrauma for schizophrenia. Sechehaye (1947) and Rosen (1953), among others, held similar views. Individual analyses suggested interpreting the pathological fantasies of schizophrenics as expressions of disturbed relationships to the mother's lactating breast, and in some individual patients objective indications of such a disturbed relationship in childhood were evident. However, in the overwhelming majority of schizophrenics there were no indications whatsoever for assuming disturbances in the early breast-feeding of the patient, and on the other hand, doctors know of countless children whose breast-feeding was attended by most severe disturbances, at times to the point of jeopardizing survival, without such children having later become schizophrenic. Under these circumstances the concept that the "oral phase" alone was critical for the psychodynamics of schizophrenia lost considerable cogency. In the period that followed, almost all phases of life, from birth to senility were regarded as critical in the formation of all or certain specific schizophrenias, by one author or another. Especially puberty, and then the beginning of vocational life, the beginning of sexual activity, and the birth of children were considered as especially critical. The experience of the menopause or of involution were considered causative in the later eruption of schizophrenias. A persistent contradiction in opinions existed in the evaluation of the implications of childhood experiences and those of mature life prior to the onset of the illness. This contradiction in the field of schizophrenia corresponded to that concerning neurosis. Genetic theories that emphasized the implications of the current situation were then developed by, for instance, Kretschmer (1918) in respect to sensitivity delusions of reference and Kempf (1921, 1949) in respect to "homosexual flight."

Not with respect to the time period, but with respect to the kind of critical traumatizing experiences, there is an almost total agreement among all authors that such experiences are best sought in disturbed relationships to one's fellowmen. Often, according to Sullivan (1953, 1956), the erotic partners of future patients, for instance, homosexual seducers, were considered as the significant persons—the destiny figures—for the evolu-

tion of the illness. But increasingly the interest of most authors shifted to a concentration on relationships to the parents. As time wore on, the significance of the erotic partner came to be regarded as secondary, corresponding to how it developed from earlier experiences within the family community. Consideration of relationships to one's fellowmen in shaping the personality goes back largely to Meyer (1915). He personally had become aware of it during his youth through the philosophy of his grandfather, who in his turn had been conditioned along these lines by an 18th-century country philosopher. Among the authors who regarded the implications of human relationships as significant for the shaping of personalities, Meyer's disciple, Sullivan, occupies first rank.

The overwhelming majority of the earlier authors assumed that an adverse influence by the mother was the most detrimental. What the special traumatizing aspect of mothers was, however, was estimated entirely differently by every one of them. To many it was blamed on unfavorable attitudes during the breast-feeding of the infant, for others, on an egocentric, dichotomous conditioning through elementary schooling and vocational training of the child, as well as on his erotic maturation. Most often a very specific and wretched attitude toward the child, rooted deep in the character of the mother, was held accountable. The concept of the "schizophrenogenic mother," as it is universally known today, became popular, and was considered by some as the appropriate code word for an important, established fact, although it was smiled upon by others indulgently as an unrealistic, hyperbolic fad-expression. The "schizophrenogenic mother" has been described in multifarious variations. Usually her egocentric personality occupies the foreground in these descriptions, as do her unbridled efforts to mold the child according to her own eccentric precepts, her incapacity to grant him freedom of action and independence, her lack of sincere maternal love and warmth, and her obsession for overcompensating for these shortcomings by her incessant, pedantic control of unimportant externals. Others did not consider an unfavorable attitude by the mother toward her child as important, but rather the absence of a mother or mother-substitute with a true maternally adaptable personality. After they had emphasized the influence of a distorted attitude on the part of the mother, the role of the father also received some attention. Very often the onset conditioning for schizophrenias was related to the subject's experiences with a weak, effeminate, or absent father. From the mother and father as individuals, the principal interest shifted over to the relationships within the close parental family community. For instance, an influence enhancing the development of schizophrenia was assumed when one of the parents did not live up to his natural sex role, in situations where the father preferred to assume a femine attitude or the mother, a masculine one. A detrimental condition with similar effect was seen in the condition where the father does not assume a mature erotic attitude toward his wife, but instead, behavior with erotic overtones toward a daughter begins to surface.

The psychotraumatic situations that were regarded as favoring schizophrenic development were considered until just a short time ago to be principally situations that involved suffering and renunciation. It was assumed to be self-evident that the abysses opening between burning desires and their fulfillment, or between contradicting aspirations, would be perceived as something intolerable from which schizophrenic development would ensue. In contrast, today, individual intellectual processes are considered to be the principal causes by some, as for instance, the "teaching of irrationality." It is assumed that one of the parents is latently schizophrenic and carried on conversations with his child that were ambiguous, in which "yes" from such a sick parent did not mean yes, and "no" did not mean no. According to this concept, owing to the schizophrenic ambivalence of the father or mother, the development of an unequivocal manner of thinking or speaking that leads to normal communication for the child would be impossible. If this were the case, of course, the schizophrenia of the child could always evolve only from the schizophrenia of one of the parents. The advocates of that kind of hypothesis, so far as I know, have never considered that, as a result of the reduced fertility of schizophrenics, the disease would soon become extinct, if schizophrenic thinking by the parents alone would lead to schizophrenia in the child. This is also a striking example of how long-forgotten concepts abandoned as obsolete manage to turn up again as modern. One has to reach far back into the past century before finding acceptance of the concept that learning or mislearning from a sick parent

may be causative of a psychotic way of life and thought. At that time the unanimous conviction prevailed for many years that emphasis on the affectivity of the person would brand the experience as psychotraumatic. Only in the last few years did the old concept reemerge that a primary pathogenic process consisted of something intellectual, in the learning of incorrect conceptualizations. In this context, it is thought-disturbance that is again regarded as the essential factor in schizophrenic existence. The learning process is closely related to the formation of conditioned reflexes that form the basis of Pavlov's concepts of schizophrenia.

By critically surveying the wealth of literature that takes a stand on the question of specifically dangerous developmental phases or specific psychotraumatic situations, the essence of the arguments can be briefly outlined as follows:

1. There are few psychotraumatic situations that have not been discovered in the early histories of schizophrenics, and that have not also been considered characteristic of the development of schizophrenias. Their very multiplicity and the contradiction of opinions about them show that there is no psychotraumatic situation that is in and of itself of critical importance for the formation of schizophrenias.

2. Many statements about anything specific in the early lives of schizophrenics are speculative deductions. They have been ingeniously derived from one psychoanalytic theory or another, which theory was derived, in turn, from experiences with either neurotics or normal subjects. They have scarcely been tested on schizophrenics themselves, nor do they claim to be in any sense fully objective. This goes, among other things, for many statements claiming that adverse experiences in life are important for a subsequent schizophrenia only in a certain specific phase of life. To many who set up hypotheses on this topic, the thought never occurred of cross-checking their suppositions by, for instance, collecting data from a number of different sources about the actual living conditions during the supposedly critical phase of life.

3. Almost all statements about anything specific in the premorbid period of schizophrenics depend on subjective judgment. They could not tolerate objective scrutiny. Thus, the attempt was made to interpret the schizophrenic world of imagination as symbolic of life's problems during a certain time

phase in life, namely the oral one. But such interpretations depend entirely on the judgment of the analyst. Then, too, different analysts offer different interpretations. The symbolic significance of every individual schizophrenic imaginary idea is manifold. It is quite arbitrary which one will be acknowledged as the critical one.

4. In all these investigations one runs across yet another treacherous and discouraging problem, namely, that one believes to have discovered an adverse trait of character in the parents or something otherwise psychotraumatic; one zealously pursues this discovery and finds, as expected, the same psychotraumatic situation in the premorbid history of many schizophrenics—ah! but then the disappointing discovery is made of having found something in schizophrenics that cannot be excluded from the lives of normals. This is a problem of methodology, to which many fall victim. It receives far too little attention in scientific planning and discussions.[12] One cannot help but reproach former schizophrenia research for having depicted something as characteristic of schizophrenia that is also in evidence in most normal people. For example, it is virtual child's play to find character traits in any mother that fit neatly into some of the many characterizations of a "schizophrenogenic mother." What mother would not want to adapt her child to her own wishful images, either consciously or unconsciously? Is there a child-rearing situation in which this is not the case? For what mother could we not discover that she either pampers her child excessively or sometimes neglects it, in order to compensate for not fully meeting the ideal standards expected of a good mother? What motherliness is total and perfect, beyond the reach of all criticism?—Or another example: In the genesis of "homosexual flight," which includes—according to many sources—most of the acute schizophre-

12. This is the same phenomenon that can be so grotesquely overevaluated in naive interpretations of projection tests. Characteristics are identified from the test that match those of the experimental subject with amazing accuracy—only afterwards the critical observer must come to the disappointing conclusion that he cannot imagine anyone to whom these same characteristics would not also apply ("easily lapses into dejection and moodiness, lacks self-assurance when confronted with difficult problems, and compensates for this insecurity by attempting to conceal it from himself and from others ...").

nias of young men, the sudden need for living in close contact with many other men is supposed to signify something essential. With this concept as a working hypothesis, one actually finds in nearly every young schizophrenic that before and during the onset period he was exposed to the "trauma" of sensing homosexual temptation in the company of men. But then, what young man does not experience this "trauma" in military service, in vacation camps, in boys' boarding schools, etc.?

5. Among the few possibilities existing of rendering objective the conjectures about relationships between certain psychotraumatic situations and schizophrenias, investigations on the premature loss of a parent by death, separation, or divorce play the most important role. These types of studies were described in detail in Chapter 2. They showed that premature parent loss does not occur with any greater frequency in the premorbid history of schizophrenics than in that of neurotics, psychopaths, and other types of patients. For male schizophrenics it is no more frequent than among the average population. It does not grow more frequent in any definite phase of life. Along with the propagation of Bowlby's (1954) statements on the deprivation of maternal care, numerous other investigations have been carried out on the consequences of the lack of maternal care (for example, by Ainsworth et al. 1962). Years ago schizophrenia was still being mentioned as a consequence of such losses, although only occasionally and as a contention, without supporting that contention by the results of observations. It is worth noting that the theory on schizophrenia as a sequel to deprivation of maternal care has dropped out of discussion almost entirely in recent years. Among these consequences, today lagging intellectual development, poor capacity for contact with others, and dysphoric moodiness have become probable, but not schizophrenias. In short, few assumptions about specific implications of psychotraumatic experience can be objectively checked. Premature parent loss can be depicted statistically, although such figures will show that it has no generally valid significance for the formation of schizophrenias.

So none of the assumptions about the incidence of fully specific and solely decisive psychotraumatic conditions for the formation of schizophrenias have been confirmed. We must assume that the most diverse types of psychic traumas play a role in the genesis of the schizophrenias. Countless people who never become schizophrenic are also exposed to all the psychotraumatic effects that are found in the premorbid histories of schizophrenics. Between the schizophrenic catastrophe and other forms of human destiny there is a vast difference, but this difference is not reflected in qualitative or quantitative differences of psychotraumatic stresses. We may deduce that, insofar as psychotraumatic situations in life play a pathogenic role in the schizophrenic illnesses, they do so only in the presence of specific susceptibilities.

The findings described in the present research material lie wholly within this summary of general experience in life and of previous schizophrenia research. The great majority of our probands had been exposed to severe and agonizing experiences. However these were all quite different as to their nature and occurred during totally different phases of time, anywhere between birth and the onset of illness. They are really no different from the sufferings and misfortunes that fall to the lot of all mankind.

If there are no fully specific traumas in a human existence that are solely responsible for the formation of schizophrenias, that does not necessarily exclude the possibility that there are certain such traumas that do constitute a greater danger of the formation of a later schizophrenia than others do. To be able to recognize such dangers will remain one of the great assignments for schizophrenia research in the years to come.

After many years of close contact with schizophrenics, it seems to me personally at times that their psychotraumatic experience does have something about it that is relatively characteristic of them. It is not the type of experience that is characteristic, however, but the accumulation of discordant experiences that suggest a confused goal-directedness. When the later schizophrenic patients pursue a goal, a drive, or a desire in life, they experience a conflict with these that is self-contradictory. Some of the discordant aspects that I frequently found, that seemed to explain confused behavior were, for instance, a contrast between externally displayed morality for the sake of outward appearances and an immoral way of life on the part of the parents of schizophrenics, who themselves exhibited excessive impulsiveness and inhibitions within one and the same person; contrasts between the life ideals of a deceased mother and those of the stepmother; contrasts between background and original morality of a father and his actual social status in life, etc. But the criticism that I apply to the assumptions of others, I must apply to my own as well namely, that the above-mentioned impressions are not completely objective. When one coexperiences the evolution of neuroses, one encounters the same discordant experiences as the ones that impressed me among my schizophrenics. At times one can even find them in the lives of normal people. Therefore, I must not assert as an assured fact that the contrasts and discords in life contain something psychotraumatic that is characteristic of schizophrenic development. Such an experience in life would imply a fully generalized endangering of the personality development, and there is no proof that any kind of "specific" traumatization of future schizophrenics is implied. There are merely suppositions to that effect.

To be sure, such suppositions do happen to agree with the psychopathology of schizophrenics, which is dominated by unresolved ambivalences and ambitendencies. The following determination might occur to us: If contradictory experiences that permit the same experience to be simultaneously feared and hoped for, force their way into the ambivalence, then the person thus beset is vulnerable to a psychosis in which that ambivalence plays a significant role. Because such formulations seem so perfectly plausible, however, caution and skepticism are required. One might easily be tempted to find discordant experiences in the lives of schizophrenics because that is where one expects to find them.

The disturbances in family relationships that have been described in recent years by Bateson, Fleck, and Lidz (1962), Singer and Wynne (1965), Alanen (1966), among others, and to which I have already referred, probably belong among the most dangerous types of life's experiences that have special implications for schizophrenia. They are the ambiguities and contradictions occurring in relationships between the sexes and between the generations, and the ambiguous and contradictory demeanor of parents in communicating with one another and with the children. Recently Kaufmann and Müller (1969) wrote a summary paper on their own experiences and those of other authors, based on family research. Among other points, they emphasize the peculiar incestuous tendencies of fathers toward their schizophrenic daughters. The erotic behavior of the father is not directed toward a unified goal; it reflects his equivocal demeanor. It is supposed to impart to his daughter something like:

"1. You see, I'm close to you, and if necessary, I can provide sexual gratification for you, too (concession to the biological maturity of the child). 2. But please don't think of this trifle as something sexual." 3. (Not a demonstrated communication, but one that is inferred from it:) "No matter what happens, you and I—we're staying together."

The disturbed communications are characterized by the authors as follows:

1. Difficulties in terminating, resolving, and ending; disqualification of the communication by the communication itself. 2. Commonplace disturbances such as garbled speech or too soft a tone to be understood. 3. Fragmentation by skipping to different subject matter. . . .

Kaufmann and Müller (1969) found the concept of Boszormenyi-Nagy and Framo (1965) particularly helpful in therapy. It was that the superego in the families of schizophrenics is less prone to condemn the sexual and other instinctual drives than the autonomy of the individual person is ("Examples: Sexuality in a young person experiencing puberty is neither praised nor positively opposed or tabooed, but simply nullified.")

All these depressing happenings in the families of schizophrenics are characterized as undisguised manifestations of discord: between paternal and sexual love; between the desire to express something and not to express it; between the tendencies of being an independent person or a family member. These findings and many others similar in essence, by other modern scholars in family research, as well as by me, suggest the formulation that discord, inner disruption, and ambitendencies in the life of the schizophrenic (particularly in experiences within the family community) inhibit the development of a strong, unified personality. They render impossible a unified, personal attitude in one's life, the development of a will and energy aimed at personal self-assertion in one's life, and an adaptation to the hard demands imposed by the environment. All these are ideas derived from personal empathy with the patients and from relationships with their families that can hardly be "proved."

The Normal Aspect in Schizophrenics and the Schizophrenic Aspect in Normals

The fact that a normal life is running its course parallel to and behind the schizophrenic life is undoubtedly one of psychiatry's important and assured realizations. Kind-natured care personnel of schizophrenics have probably always known this, although the fact did not become one of the formulated doctrines of many schools of psychiatry until the past half century.

Almost everywhere, everyone agrees today that the severe chronic states of schizophrenics, that used to be called "schizophrenic dementia" and that are still often referred to that way today, are a totally different type of dementia than those occurring with diffuse chronic atrophy of the brain. The essential difference lies specifically in the fact that with skillful, indulgent and prolonged association with the schizophrenic dement, one always encounters indications of intact intellectual capacity and normal, healthy emotional impulses; whereas, by contrast, the organic dement has become permanently incapacitated in his intellectual capacity and his emotions, and is forever impoverished in his imaginary world. Under these circumstances, many no longer refer to the severe chronic schizophrenic states as "dementias"; but if we do insist on retaining the term, we must bear in mind that a very specific kind of dementia is the one under discussion.

No doubt, every clinician has had the emotionally stirring, moving experience of seeing a patient in a rare, uncommon situation suddenly and abruptly give an indication that he can feel and think as we can, after he has lived for years in a totally strange world that was inaccessible to us. Of course, there are no situations in life in which this would always occur, but there are situations in which it is more likely to occur than during the common everyday routine of living. For ages it has been an impressive experience when, in the dramatic course of catastrophic processes, schizophrenics suddenly behave like normals —or might one perhaps say "unexpectedly recover"? This kind of phenomenon has been observed after serious accidents, on patient's death bed, or during the sudden evacuation of a hospital under bombardment in wartime. One of the experiences E. Bleuler had as a young man concerned the behavior of a few schizophrenics judged to be totally demented, during a severe typhus epidemic at the rural Rheinau Clinic. "Demented" patients unexpectedly took over the duties of care personnel and did an excellent job.

Even more important than the observations under such rare and unusual circumstances are those that every clinician and every nurse can make almost routinely. Examples: A schizophrenic who never utters a sensible word in his customary daily intercourse with others suddenly carries on a normal conversation with an unexpected visitor (and often, thereafter, that visitor will find it hard to believe that this patient is still in need of hospitalization). An apparently obtuse, totally insensitive patient succeeds in making his escape from the clinic by way of a sophisticated, cleverly devised plan. After one such escape, the patient unobtrusively joined the waiting line of inpatients outside my consultation office and, when interviewed, complained about a persistent headache, in such rational terms that for a long time. I did not recognize him. After unexpected transfers from one clinic to another or after unexpected releases, every vestige of schizophrenia may suddenly disappear in the patient for a time —and, in one instance, even permanently. When one suddenly approaches the patient in a totally different manner, the same thing may occur; for instance, when a patient who was previously feared as being violent and brutal is suddenly approached without any accompanying security precautions, without the show of any fear or inhibition, or when another patient who seemed to be completely helpless is suddenly entrusted with a serious responsibility that would usually be given only to a normal person, such a patient may easily reveal such a dramatic change. Some illustrative examples of such phenomena were published from our clinic by Klaesi (1922). It is a touching emotional experience when the torpid, immobile face of an apparently apathetic patient suddenly lights up with shared joy and pleasure, as she warmly congratulates her physician on his becoming a father. Others, who customarily exhibit a stony, scowling, or withdrawn demeanor, may unexpectedly express sincere gratitude for extra help or a special kindness accorded them. Some patients, who appeared to be completely idiotic, suddenly write a coherent, perfectly sensible letter.

Similar revelations emerge in projection tests. Quite commonly, even severe cases of schizophrenia reveal occasional reactions that show a capacity for discrimination as if they emanated from normal subjects. Not too rarely, test results reveal no pathological symptoms at all, not even in the most severe cases.

The most convincing experiences indicating that a normal, healthy life continues to exist in schizophrenics are revealed during therapy. Under many therapeutic procedures, schizophrenics—even those who had been severely ill for decades—succeed in reestablishing communication, at least for a time, and often to the point where they can converse sensibly and empathize with us emotionally. Such observations have been made after the introduction of sleeping cures and insulin- and electroshock treatments in a number of different clinics. Modern experiences with the newer psychoanalytical methods are of immense importance in learning about the nature of the schizophrenias. In the course of such psychoanalytical experiences with patients, phases continue to emerge in which patients unexpectedly become as we are and appear not to be sick at all any more. These good phases are, in the chronic cases, for the most part of short duration. Nevertheless, the observation that they do occur at all does, in turn, establish the fact that normalcy in schizophrenics has not been entirely eradicated, and that it is basically possible to establish contact and to communicate with a schizophrenic as with a normal, healthy person.

A long-term, severe organic dementia does not recede. However, the careful clinician will always be on guard against making a similar statement with certainty about a severe schizophrenic dementia. For it does happen that schizophrenics who had been —or had appeared to be—demented over many years, do recover, sometimes in connection with a treatment method, sometimes in connection with abrupt changes in life styles, and sometimes simply "all by themselves."

One of the easiest and most certain determinations about schizophrenics is that their faculty of memory is not primarily disturbed. Often it is secondarily disturbed in that recollections become fragmentary or falsified by delusion. Under this surface, however, normal conceptualization and an efficient memory are easily discernible. There are severely ill schizophrenics who are more capable of recalling the critical dates in their life histories than most normal people are. Schizophrenics apparently totally submerged within themselves and completely barren of any other interests can pick up an astounding amount of information from snatches of conversation about the personal lives of their doctors and care personnel, and about tensions existing among them. The concealed capacity for rational deliberation and judgment is more difficult to assess.

One fact that did not come to light until recent years is that even severely ill schizophrenics are able not only to retain normal, healthy intellectual capacities, but are also capable of the most delicate, discriminating emotional manifestations. This area is specifically where psychoanalytic experience has recorded observations of critical significance.

A few clinicians (Conrad 1958 and others) had the impression in recent years that chronic schizophrenic are, after all, irrevocably altered in one respect in that they suffered from a permanent adynamia, from an incapacity to prevail as individual personalities, and from the inability to develop a normal pattern of activity. There is certainly no doubt that this observation applies to most schizophrenics. I suggest, however, that this "adynamia" must not be confused with the adynamia attending brain diseases—as has been done. Rather, a comparison with the "end states" of neuroses is instructive. Ernst (1959, 1965, 1968) has described these convincingly. He concludes that the same type of adynamia that has been characterized as a central phenomenon of schizophrenic and organic "end states" characterizes many residual conditions of neurotics. I should like to add that they also constitute the essence of the simple-mindedness of the bourgeois, narrow-minded townsman. Adynamia characterizes the lives of many who have survived years of imprisonment or the deprivation of concentration camps. Persistent lack of motivation, loneliness, uprootedness, or the incapacity to be active and involved according to one's desires, might produce adynamia. All of this has contributed to the fate of schizophrenics. I therefore do not believe that something in adynamia, in reduced mental elasticity, can be interpreted as being contradictory to the view that a healthy, normal life remains active, concealed behind the schizophrenic one. Ernst (1959, 1965, 1968) goes so far as to describe how the affected, forced, peculiar, and stereotypic antics occur in the same way in the residual states of schizophrenics and neurotics.

Just as the schizophrenic does not permanently lose his normal inner life, so the normal person also is no total stranger to a schizophrenic inner life.

The dream experiences of normal people do perhaps differ in some details and nuances from the symbolic thinking and imagination of schizophrenics, but certainly only in details and nuances. For example, in dreams of normals, the visual hallucinations outnumber the acoustic ones, and certain symbolic concepts occur with varying frequency in dreams and in schizophrenic thinking. The similarity between the dream life of normal people and schizophrenic existence, however, is so close that Jung was fully justified in formulating his famous sentence: If the dreamer could speak and act, he could not be distinguished from the schizophrenic.[13] Both the normal dreamer and the schizophrenic have in common the formation of symbols, condensation, confusion, depersonalization, and autism. Even Freud was impressed with this similarity. However, he paid less attention to how similar the emotional life in dreams can be to that of many schizophrenic states. Just as the dreamer can experience the most terrifying events without feeling anything emotional about them, so also the emotional reactions of the schizophrenic can become petrified, although in his imagination he suffers immeasurable torment. In both, however, it is also possible that fear, anger, repugnance, despair, delight, or ecstasy become inflated out of all proportion, and often without any relationship to the image content that would make sense in normal, everyday reasoning. The dreamer, like the schizophrenic, can "slip out of his skin"—in a manner of speaking—and observe himself from afar, as an impartial observer, and can simultaneously feel the moods and emotions he would feel in his original role as himself. The dismemberment of his ego and the simultaneous, parallel existence of various contradictory emotions reach such extremes that both become totally unfathomable and inconceivable when regarded in the light of sober judgment and from a state of wakefulness. In a dream one can feel himself pursued, and the pursuer can be simultaneously a beast, a bandit, or just a disliked neighbor; one can kill the pursuer, chase him away, or shoot at him, and at the same time feel oneself in the role of the pursuer, who is, in turn, beset by all the fears of the pursued. The schizophrenic has experiences that are essentially similar. Jung (1907) and Storch (1922)

13. Comparisons between dream life and the inner life of the mentally ill have been drawn through the ages. So also Moreau de Tours (1855) was convinced of "l'dentité du rêve et de la folie."

dedicated a large portion of their lifework to establishing that the magical and archaic way of thinking and perceiving at various times and in different cultures are processes governed by the same principles and the same kind of symbolism as those of schizophrenics. The enormous accomplishment of these researchers has been checked by a great many others and has been criticized from a number of different aspects. The determination of a congruence in the symbolism as between the schizophrenic and the magical, archaic realm of imagination, however, has withstood every kind of criticism.

To be sure, the fine works of abstract art are distinguished from the artistic renditions by schizophrenics by their beauty, but both depict a basically similar world. Accordingly, the abstract artistic efforts of nonproficient normals cannot really be distinguished from those of schizophrenics either. Nor can the works of artistically gifted schizophrenics really be distinguished from those of professional artists in abstract art. The correlations between schizophrenia and art have been presented by Navratil (1965). He emphasizes, correctly, that the creativity in artists and in schizophrenics is not ego-directed. In the creative processes of both artists and schizophrenics, they were primarily struggling to discover that ego that would itself subsequently confront the world. Such indications by Navratil (1965) provide an excellent illustration of the essential similarities between artistic and schizophrenic expression. In the process of discovering an ego by attempting to reproduce the disorderly, chaotic backgrounds of their conscious egos, they first put some distance between themselves and the everyday norms that regulate our social order. At the outset, in order to remain themselves, they deviate from all norms, and they isolate themselves and retreat from society in loneliness. Despite this, their aim to find that ego is also an expression of their desire to establish contact with the world, for the ego implies a confrontation with others. But that specifically is what we perceive so strongly in schizophrenics, namely that they separate themselves from the commonly accepted norms of intercourse and of thinking that have substance and validity in everyday life. They distance themselves from society, yet at the same time they seek to establish contact with us in their type of quest for the ego. And herein lies a truly pitiful experience in the association with schizophrenics. Much as they attempt to break away from contacts with others in their schizophrenic world, their very nature always reveals also an ardent longing and groping for relationships with others. In this specific phenomenon we are presented with a point of contact for psychotherapy. The artist and the schizophrenic share the same dark and dimly perceived tendency in turning away from reality, society, and everyday life, with the ultimate aim, after all, of reestablishing contact with their fellowmen. They try to represent themselves as they are, and they want to be accepted in this representation of themselves.

Artistic expression, that revolves around the search for and the finding of an ego, as do the lives of schizophrenics, is by no means a manifestation of modern art alone. In its manneristic form, for example, it goes back to centuries before Christ. Here is a quotation from Navratil (1965) about this art form.

> The human figure, in any manneristic representation of it, loses the true-to-nature form established for it by the rules of classical art. Grotesquely crass foreshortening and excessive expansion appear. An ideal style is created which, reminiscent of the Gothic, distorts the sagittal axis to a "figura serpentinata." Bodies become elongated, with tiny heads.... The figures have no solid relationship to the ground, they appear to hover. Often they are shown with limbs running out to elongated points. The attitudes of the figures are stilted, affected, and distorted. Frequently they appear in animated motion, or else as if suddenly frozen in space.... Sudden changes from darkness to light occur, or the entire painting is bathed in a shadowless, painful brightness. The color tones often appear broken, irridescent, or restlessly glittering. Preferred manneristic themes include the spiral, the mask, time, the clock, and death; and besides that, the single eye, a body fragment, and the anatomic representation, the Janus face and the anthropomorphic landscape (landscape with human faces). There is evident a predilection for the unusual, the abnormal, the abstruse, an interest in hieroglyphics, puzzles, secret doctrines, secret writings, heraldic emblems, election slogans, peculiarities and monstrosities in nature, but an interest

also in the automatons and "wonder-machines" developed by man.... Contents of paintings become painted dreams. ... Objects that do not belong together are united in fantastic combinations.... In the "Arcimbolesques," on the other hand, unified objects or people are dissolved into a multitude of different objects (for example, a librarian consisting of nothing but books). This drive for deformation is opposed by an inanimate, soulless constructivism. The mask-like, impenetrable, enigmatic face corresponds to the labyrinth as an allegorical symbol of the unknown....

What is said here about manneristic art applies likewise to descriptions of schizophrenic representations, and even to the inner lives of schizophrenics, as well.

In projection tests the same phenomenon turns up again. There are normal individuals who "project" into the formation of the unformed that facet of their personality that is undistinguishable from the schizophrenic. There are "schizophrenic" test results without the presence of schizophrenia. This, too, should be an indication that the schizophrenic nature is latently inherent in the normal. In the original German edition of this volume Uchtenhagen presents experiences from the relatives of our probands on this very matter.

For the clinician, however, it is the observations of mental disorders following acute physical damage that show in simplest terms how latent schizophrenic life styles can unexpectedly gain the upper hand in nonschizophrenics. As already set forth after severe physical insults to the brain, a series of three kinds of psychopathological phenomena run their course, either concurrently or successively. Reduction of consciousness (particularly at the beginning of the disorder) and the psychoorganic simplification of the inner life (particularly as an end phase) have really nothing to do with a schizophrenic existence. But between them lie a series of the twilight and delirious shifts in consciousness, along with confusions and dream experiences, that cannot be clearly distinguished from a schizophrenic existence. The somatic background of such psychoses can be recognized only by its intertwining with indications of reduced consciousness or of the psychoorganic disorder and by the physical manifestations. Still, they can hardly be distinguished from the schizophrenias at all, or not with any certainty, if only the shift in consciousness is observed.

It is common knowledge how carefully one must proceed in the diagnosis of schizophrenic delusions, as soon as the ideas suspected of being delusional concern a belief, a superstition, or a philosophy. Whenever the subject's thinking runs along such areas of thought, it becomes difficult to separate schizophrenic thought from bizarre attitudes within the norm. These are areas in human mentality in which the limits remain undefinably fluid. E. Bleuler (1919) pursued attitudes, convictions, memory- and perception-falsifications that a normal person develops in defense of his self-esteem, and that in their extreme manifestation cannot be clearly distinguished from schizophrenic thinking. They belong to the realm of what he called "autistic, undisciplined thinking."

It seems to me that the deductive conclusion from all these experiences is inescapable. It is that schizophrenic life exists in normal people —sometimes dormant and concealed beneath the surface, but still a part of our personality and constantly helping to shape that personality. I do know, however, that such a conclusion is self-evident to many, while others indignantly reject it. For the first group it will evolve compulsively from the basic dictum that a disease does not create anything new. A process of illness will only take away something and may expose something that lay under it or that was inhibited; but in a disease, defensive processes emerge in addition. We owe Jackson a debt of gratitude for having worked out this concept and introduced it into the field of neurology, and Ey (1954) for having given it renewed impetus and full respectability in modern psychiatry. According to the concepts of these authors, something is liberated in schizophrenia and in the other psychoses as well, that had always been there. It is released because organization and the proper guidance have been weakened; nothing is newly created. With this concept I can readily agree. On the other hand, the assumption of schizophrenic elements in healthy individuals is not reconcilable with the extremes of possible endogenetics nor with a deductively derived conviction that something endogenous has to be something original and absolutely incomprehensible. If any schizophrenic aspects do exist latently in normal people, careful attempts seem to be justified for becoming deeply involved in the evolutionary process of the schizophrenias to the same extent as in the evolutionary processes of normal and of neurotic developments. Whoever refuses to engage in the study of the schizophrenias to that extent, will also find it difficult to acknowledge the existence of latent schizophrenic life in normal individuals.

On Psychopathology

Our knowledge of the psychopathology of schizophrenics developed in phases from various aims and a number of different methods. Today the results of this multitude of research projects that used to run their separate ways are slowly beginning to come together to form an imposing unified picture.

In the beginning the symptoms had to be described and categorized. In this effort Kraepelin saw one of his principal missions, as also in the investigation of disease courses. From the turn of the century on, through the successive editions of his textbook, he succeeded in explaining the doctrine of symptoms with increasing clarity and in developing them to such an extent that finally there was but little left to be altered, added, or supplemented. What renders his later expositions on symptomatology particularly interesting is his theory on symptomatic changes. The severe catatonic symptoms become less frequent, and patients express fewer delusions and hallucinations in less colorful and grotesque detail than before. Instead, more bland, apathetic, querulous, and pseudoneurasthenic symptoms occur more frequently. The contents of the patients' imaginary material begin to adapt to their cultural development; depersonalization, for instance, is experienced more as submission to evaluation than as being possessed or under the spell of hypnosis, and the end-of-the-world experience is seen rather as the detonation of an atomic weapon than as a form of God's final judgment.

Just a few years after Kraepelin's doctrine on symptomatology had begun to flourish, a psychological understanding was achieved, at least about the subject content of imaginings and about a portion of the symptoms—the so-called "secondary symptoms."[14] At the time, to be sure, one was still wary of declaring positively that the disease in its entirety could be interpreted psychologically. The origins of "primary" disorders, against the background of which the "secondary" disorders might be understood, still lay shrouded in darkness. Estimates about them included primarily distraction and affective disorders among these "primary" symptoms, for which no attempt had yet been made to relate them to any of the already understood psychic processes.

It was discovered that hallucinations, delusions, eccentric expressions, stereotypies, and many other symptoms were reflections of fears, emotional tensions, hopes, expectations, and struggles with frustrations that had been experienced, and with other internal problems. Many symptoms now appeared as symbols or as expressions of "complexes," as the "affect-oriented sets of imaginings" were then called. As separate phenomena it was possible to empathize with them. However, it remained incomprehensible why they manifest themselves in a way that threatened the social existence of the patient, that branded him as "crazy," and that frustrated the patient's every effort to take a unified stand in his own world. It also seemed incomprehensible why patients expressed themselves in self-contradictions, and why, much more often than in normal people, love and hatred or acceptance and aversion should coexist simultaneously. One was confronted by the phenomenon of the disintegration of mental life, and classified it as one of the primary symptoms that could not as yet be fully explained. But even in those days, the leading scholars were interpreting specifically the "dementia" of schizophrenics largely as the understandable consequence of the patient's own disturbed attitude toward his environment. When the tensions between him and his fellowmen could no longer be resolved—

---

14. The distinction between "primary" and "secondary" symptoms was introduced into the doctrine on schizophrenia by the following statement:

"In a disease like osteomalacia, the chemical and physiological processes, including decalcification of the bones, constitute the process of the disease; the lack of resistance of the bones is a direct consequence of changes in the bones; a curvature or a fracture of the bone, however, occurs only after an external influence; these latter manifestations are not the consequences of the disease process itself, but the consequences of altered behavior of the bones in the presence of accessory influences. . . . The primary symptoms are necessary partial manifestations of a disease; the secondary ones may, at least potentially, be lacking or change, without the disease process being simultaneously changed as well. Almost all of the symptomatology for dementia praecox described up to the present is a secondary one, based in a sense on chance" (E. Bleuler 1911, who had published studies on the genesis of osteomalacia before he dedicated himself wholly to schizophrenia research.)

so it was assumed—he had to withdraw within himself and, as a result, appear externally as bleak, petrified, mentally dead—simply as "demented"—even when a rich inner life continued to remain active under the surface. The psychologically empathic and understanding brand of psychopathology of the "secondary" symptoms goes back to E. Bleuler, Jung, and Klaesi, who were followed by many other clinicians.

The differentiated psychoanalytic research of schizophrenics was initiated by Freud himself in one of his patients as early as 1896, although he had not formulated a specific diagnosis for the disease at the time. Since Freud considered ties to other people, and especially any transmissions of emotion by schizophrenics to their psychotherapist, as an impossibility, he did not hope for any therapeutic successes to be forthcoming from the psychoanalyses of schizophrenics. This attitude did nothing to fan the fires of enthusiasm for the psychoanalysis of schizophrenics. That is why psychoanalytic research progressed only slowly and did not really get under way until decades later. It achieved full-blown recognition in the period after World War II. It then became evident that some degree of transference is possible after all, by the application of newer techniques and a great expenditure of time and the personal dedication of the therapist. The transference is just more difficult to control and to overcome than for neurotics. If the schizophrenic begins to bring out and express his feelings for the psychotherapist, the danger emerges that he will unrealistically seek to confirm his awakening confidence in the physician. He will demand what is impossible to grant, for instance, erotic love in place of medical interest. After denial of such requests he often becomes set in his amorous delusion, which is closely followed by a delusion of persecution. These are developments experienced by psychoanalysts of the past as well as the present generation. What is new, however, is that the delusional transferences in the continuing communication with the doctor can also recede again. In order to achieve this development, to be sure, an almost superhuman measure of personal inner firmness, patience, kindness, tact, and psychotherapeutic skill on the part of the doctor are required. In the course of modern psychoanalytic research in schizophrenia, however, it was not only the feelings schizophrenics impart to their analysts that were discovered. Beyond that, a great

sensitivity in intercourse with others came to light, along with a susceptibility for suggestion that no one had had any idea existed before. Analysts who merit special laudatory mention for developing these facts include: Sullivan, Lidz, Fromm-Reichmann, Rosen, Sechehaye, Benedetti, and Mueller.

Even shortly after World War I, existential research on the psychopathology of schizophrenics was beginning. It began just before the second wave of psychoanalytic research in schizophrenia, but did not arouse international interest until later. The analysis of life does not require a clarification of the causes of phenomena. Despite that, the presentations of existentialist analysts have made important contributions to what is today encouraging us to get to know and depict the essence of the disease and its origins. They discovered that the psychic life of schizophrenics is by no means just chaos, rather that it is structured, that the internal processes combine to form into something whole and Gestalt-like. The different life processes come to relate to one another. Regarded longitudinally, they become a drama in which no player acts alone, but in which each player has a meaning for the others. In cross-section, although with a multitude of sharp contrasts, a composite picture emerges rather than a mass of details unrelated to one another. What in former observations appeared as chaotic, fragmented, splintered, confused, and totally lacking in any correlation, begins to fuse into an amazing single impression under the improved empathy and enlightenment of existential analysis. We then see a human being who is engaged in a struggle with the fateful contradictions within himself and his position among other human beings, and who fashions the contradictions of his own experiences and struggles into graphic mental images that he confronts with one another.[15] We no longer

15. The effort to establish order in a disintegrated world is markedly illustrated in the art works of schizophrenics. Winkler (1966) and Marinov (1967), among others, remark as follows about them:

"Paintings by schizophrenics are attempts on the part of the patient to establish order out of schizophrenic chaos, to express something abstract that cannot be described verbally, and to establish a form of preverbal communication with their present world that has become their environment" (Marinov citing Winkler). Or: "The geometric renditions of figures by schizophrenics is a completely prerational reaction and springs from the tendency to reestablish a form of order from the ground up."

see the person whose life is dismembered into unrelated fragments.

In a picture or a drama that can be co-experienced existentially, we hardly distinguish between primary and secondary symptoms. We recognize only one whole human destiny. Every disease symptom and every expression by the patient is yet another brush stroke of a complete Gestalt, and is not independently discernible as a consequence or a cause of one of the others.

Modern psychopathology that not only describes, but that also attempts to find correlations, revolves primarily around the big question: Can the entire psychosis be rendered comprehensible as a struggle within one's self and with one's environment? Or are there, as was assumed during the beginnings of psychoanalytic research, primary symptoms without any correlation to life experiences and to internal struggles, that can really be distinguished and separated out from the secondary ones, that lend themselves to understanding and to empathy?

All the results from the many different former psychopathological studies jointly and individually, each in its own way, suggest this question. When comprehensive psychological research began, shortly after the turn of the century, very few schizophrenic expressions were psychologically comprehensible. With the intensification of this type of research, the amount of it rapidly increased, and the psychological interpretations became increasingly convincing. While at the beginning of the century only a few sporadic ones among the vast multitude of psychopathological phenomena were felt to be understandable in a psychological context, very few remain today for which we cannot as yet perceive such an understanding. An effort should be made, therefore, to gain a psychological understanding of the remaining symptoms.

In quite a different way existential analysis confronts us with the same problem. When an existential confrontation with a schizophrenic imparts the impression of a self-contained, unified inner life, it does not necessarily also give us indications for distinguishing primary from secondary symptoms. Instead, the results suggest psychological explanations for the self-contained psychological picture as a whole.

Psychopathological and psychodynamic research has not arrived at any clear and generally acknowledged decision as to whether the mental life of schizophrenics could really be understood psychologically as a whole, or whether an understanding was possible only for some part of the symptoms, namely the secondary ones. After all, we are not really interested in interpretations that can be rendered objective and can be "proved" in respect to their own nature, but only in those that are capable of being rendered more or less credible.

At all events, a magnificent concept of schizophrenic man has evolved from the most recent efforts of psychopathological research. This is that the schizophrenic wants to be the way he really is. He cannot and will not any longer submit to the pressures to overcome his inner discords and to take his place in society alongside his fellowmen as a conventional person. His mental life flicks by in pictures of his own inner life and in pictures of a world, that suits his nature better than the real one does.

In words somewhat too erudite for common understanding, the assumptions were often formulated thus: The search for an ego in confrontation of one's self with others is impossible for the schizophrenic in his struggle for existence. He cannot locate his ego, for he will not submit to submerging a portion of himself nor to adapting other parts of his self to his environment. He seeks his ego by materializing his own internal contradictions into realities for himself, and by ignoring the world around him that does not understand him.

The same thought can also be expressed in simpler terms: The schizophrenic has grown weary of internal and external pressures; he lives out everything that is on his mind, regardless of any benefits to his existence. He cannot exist in a conventional adaptation to the real world, but struggles for the concept of a world that would adapt to him. Or, in a somewhat loose, oversimplified statement it might be said that schizophrenia is the extreme rejection of established convention.

The lack of adaptation to his own internal contradictions and to his conflict with the world around him, as well as his ruthless bent to live his life according to his own nature, constitute a rejection of contact with others and signify schizophrenic autism.

Up to this point I have summarized the suppositions of many. More rarely, something else has been brought forth in today's tentative concept of schizophrenia that seriously engages my personal interest. It is that if the retreat to a schizophrenic life is an autistic rejection of one's environment, then simultaneously existing opposing tendencies are its basis. The patient, who cannot succeed in establishing contact by conventional behavior, in schizophrenia presents himself vulnerable, in a way, in his whole unconventional life. In all his autistic withdrawal from others and from the world of reality, he simultaneously is voicing an appeal—sometimes softly and then again louder. Put into words it might read: "Please—O please!—for God's sake, accept me as I am." When the schizophrenic draws away from rational thinking and from a communal feeling with others and retreats to his own world, it is not always only to be alone with himself for evermore, but with the faint hope in the background: "If I present myself candidly, as I am, perhaps they'll understand me better than behind a mask of conventionality that alienates me from my own nature." It seems as if he suspected that his trust in displaying himself honestly and openly might awaken the trust of others in him. To a very slight degree there is something inherent in the schizophrenic that resembles the contradictory behavior of a child who runs away, howling and full of spite, from its scolding mother in order to be rid of her—but also to let his mother catch up with him and enfold that same naughty child in her loving arms. The longing of the schizophrenic for communal relationships in spite of all his flight from the community is the aspect that continues to sustain the hope of all of us doctors, that we might be able to help him.

Schizophrenics who have recovered often tell us about the deep longing they have felt for communion with others as they lay helpless in a catatonic stupor or a delirium. During psychoanalytic treatment they refer to that same kind of longing. Quite obviously the verbal requests of schizophrenics for sexual intercourse with the therapist is not always supported by the patient's sexual desires. For him sexual relationship is much more often the symbol for the reestablishment of a comforting communal relationship.

Ever since long ago the "paranoid glance" has been identified as a symptom of schizophrenia. It is that glance that immediately imparts the distrust and the hatred that the mentally ill feel for others. It strikes one like the thrust of a dagger, and it hurts. However, the fact that only the paranoid glance of schizophrenics is described verbally and in writing and no other glances of theirs, is an indication that, for much too long a time, one has been much too prone to seek out only the pathological and the evil aspects of mental patients, without noticing their healthy and good features. For otherwise we would know that schizophrenics are capable of quite different glances than just the paranoid one. They also have a look that shows us the patient as a poor, wounded creature who seems to be begging for help from one, although he feels that one is not actually able to give it to him. In these past years I have seen this helpless, imploring glance more often than the paranoid one.

The mimicry of schizophrenics is commonly described as rigid, stiff, distorted, impenetrable, and grotesquely queer-looking. It is common knowledge that they rarely can laugh naturally. Usually they do not laugh at all, but when they do, their laughter is hollow and artificially forced. But what has been accorded too little attention, considering its importance, is the smile of schizophrenics. Similar to the glance, the smile belongs to the originally naive means of expression in human relations that can be relied upon. Schizophrenics that one is concerned about smile often. They can smile in a soulful, expressive way. Their smile tells us something like: "Dear friend, it's all just an act. Somehow, in some other world, we'll get along with one another." I believe that this kind of smile should be counted among the important signs of life in schizophrenics. I was never deceived by it. Always when I experienced it, I later encountered additional signs of the need for help and contact. If I saw it flash up in a schizophrenic patient who seemed sinister and charged with anger, of whom everyone feared he would explode any minute and start lashing out, I knew I could take him by the hand, in utter confidence that nothing untoward would happen.

The most puzzling of all schizophrenic characteristics was for decades the phenomenon of dissociation, of distraction in thinking. To understand it psychologically was initially not even attempted. Instead, from the very outset it was regarded as the fundamental, primary characteristic of the disease. Yet, it had long been common knowledge that, along with distracted thinking, the schizophrenic retains the capability of coherent thinking as well. But too little attention was previously paid to exactly when the patient changed over from distracted to coherent thinking and back again. To be sure, this change-over cannot always be understood; however, if one watches for it carefully, one can often bring it into connection with the patient's attitude toward the conversation theme or into relation with the conversational partner. It seems as if the patient enjoys talking distractedly when he is rejecting human contacts, but enjoys talking coherently when he is desirous of them. This is most commonly in evidence when patients plead their case for dismissal from the clinic. Severely ill patients suddenly possess the capability of delivering a convincing speech to relatives or even strangers, about how depressing life is at the hospital and what pressing problems they have, to be taken care of outside the hospital.[16] They can expose these thoughts so lucidly that the listener is quick to believe that dismissal has been too long delayed. But as soon as the doctor begins to discuss the actual difficulties, the patient becomes incapable of uttering a single coherent, comprehensible sentence. Or, there are schizophrenics who speak rationally with people whom they like, but irrationally with people whom they reject. This phenomenon, for example, is often the cause of tensions and jealousy among the nurses when the patients are discussed in professional conferences. The reverse also occurs. Schizophrenics will talk irrationally just to people who like them. One gets the impression then that they are overreacting to protect themselves from overwhelming emotions. Schizophrenics who had not uttered anything sensible or understandable for a long time can suddenly speak like normal people if they are asked to dance at a hospital party, or if one talks to them as their physician, in treating a somatic ailment. In gathering data for the premorbid history one often notices that the patients are able to give information logically on their physical histories and other external facts, but not on the history of their mental illness. But if the doctor's questions bore them, they answer distractedly. Another common experience is that if a schizophrenia ward is operated on the "covert principle," that is, by discussing with the patients in a conventional tone, primarily only everyday occurrences, it may happen that the inmates of that ward will speak almost only in rational terms, although they will revert to a fully confused demeanor in a different environment.

16. A representative of a welfare agency remarked: "No matter how crazy you are, you retain a mind sharp enough to explain to people that you're not crazy."

With many observations such as these, the following question demands attention: Is the distractedness an expression of the patients' autism? Can they apply distracted speech at will when they want to avoid contact, and avoid it when they want to communicate? There are patients who will tell us quite candidly to our face that they can and they do. Today such a possibility must at least receive consideration.

Often we fancy we are able to understand the absurd statements of schizophrenics in much the same way as the formal thought-disturbances we see in them. If the patients express themselves in total delusion, for instance, claiming they are the owners of the clinic, and simultaneously the Lord God, and simultaneously also the persecuted little nobody, anyone would accept that this is something totally incomprehensible. But when one begins to empathize with the autism of the patient, it is quite possible to approach a degree of understanding. Absurd utterances defy discussion. Why then should the patient not express himself absurdly if he wants no further discussion, but wants instead to withdraw into his own inner imagery? If we sense in the patient a vague effort to show himself in his despairing inner distress as totally changed, as lost, and as being completely helpless, how could he do it better than by expressing absurd ideas?

Another phenomenon that seemed to defy any sort of understanding is delusional assertiveness. If we see in the patient someone who struggles for the reality of his own kind of human nature, and particularly for his inner discordant self, who does not want to be rejected as a fool, but wants to be taken seriously in spite of himself, who indeed takes himself seriously, and whose mental images have become his real life as he deeply perceives it, then one is certainly tempted to empathize with a kind of delusional assertiveness. It becomes all the easier to do this if we remember that this delusional assertiveness is not something entirely absolute. In one instance, the schizophrenic relies on his delusions, but the next time he will do without them. He can see in me the concocter of poisons, his murderer, Satan himself, and morally spit at me; yet at the same time, he will point out his aching tooth to me, and cooperate fully by positioning his jaw for local anesthesia and the extraction, and then thank me as warmly as any normal person would. As with his distractedness, with his absurd notions, as well as with other kinds of symptoms, the schizophrenic can manipulate and use his delusions as the expressions of his attitude toward his environment. Only in old textbooks is the schizophrenic delusion depicted as an unalterable, rigid condition; in reality, it adapts itself to the patient's inner needs and desires. Is this relative delusional assertiveness really a phenomenon for which it is forbidden to seek psychological understanding?

If we pay close attention to the expressions of schizophrenics, many confirm the picture of their nature as I have attempted to describe it. From the vast number of such expressions in my notes I shall cite a few:

"I am what the outside world has lost."

"Body and soul don't belong together; there's no unity."

"When I feel my body, I am constrained to take my own life."

"My signature is being taken apart. It is not good when everything is taken apart; then one is crazy."

"For me the substance has become spirit."

"The sum total of the spirit is constant, and the crazy thing about it is that it adds up to zero."

If one knows the correlations, the most plausible meaning of such expressions lies in the indication that the patient exists in a constant state of inner struggle (the signature is dismembered), and that the sense of belonging to a world, to substance, and to a body has been lost. It is not good that way, but that is the way it has to be. A return to harmony with the body would be tantamount to suicide, that is, to throttling the patient's true inner nature. The sum of the spirit, to which matter is converted, is always the same, and in the last analysis, it is nothing. Specifically this "nothing" is what schizophrenic mentality is for the real world. It is the element that identifies it as crazy. Of course, there is no way of proving the reliability of such interpretations. But when one hears expressions that match these interpretations repeatedly and over a number of years, it becomes tempting to make use of them when one is making the effort to gain access to the inner world of schizophrenics.

Less equivocal are the communications of many patients to the effect that they have discovered something like an inner freedom—their own identity—in their psychoses, and that they feel themselves liberated from the restraints of the conventional obligations of the mentally healthy. A case in point: I want to transfer a female patient from a ward for the severely confused into one that is quiet and orderly. She refuses to be moved, remarking, "Now I'm able not to relate to others, but over there I'm going to have to." She seemed to have a need to protect herself by her own confused talking from having, as a normal person, to enter into discussions with others. The same patient explained further: "When I perceive my body, I feel obligated to be around those others." She would like to live only in spirit and to withdraw from the community.

The following remarks by schizophrenics are completely lucid:

"In my world I am omnipotent; in yours I practice diplomacy." Or, from the personal letter of a different female patient:

> I'm enjoying so much wonderful freedom in my mental illness, that I would be ever so much worse off at liberty, at liberty and mentally well. Besides, it sometimes suits my purposes to have the privilege of being mad. It is so comfortable to be able to remain aloof from the need for exemplary conduct before one's own self. Since one must live according to one's own individual mentality, or be declared a fake, one must live in a healthy spirit, since one is declared mentally defective anyway. . . .
> The life of a mental patient means being a prince, with all its freedoms and thoughts, in its freedom revolving around the obligations to one's fellowmen. . . .

Just as submersion into the mental world of schizophrenia can be felt as spelling happiness and freedom, it can also be fraught with considerable anxiety and fear of terrifying magnitude. "I've been delivered over to fear." "I'm always being swallowed at long-distance and beheaded at long-distance." Such expressions of fear have been amply described in the literature. However, many of the descriptions in the literature create the erroneous impression that fear alone dominates the schizophrenic. Outstripping the conventional ego in a schizophrenic search after a more "genuine" ego is a conflicting, schismatic experience, that is at once fraught with a tinge of happiness and with fear.

Such a picture of schizophrenic life is by no means new. Most papers on the psychopathology of schizophrenia have drawn some fragmentary lines for this picture, or they draw it in its entirety—in a multitude of variations, to be sure. My own variation distinguishes itself merely by the different placement of some highlights. To me, more than to other authors, the observation seems important as to how often and how intensely the autistic aversion combines with a longing for acceptance. Differing in many new ideas, although in concurrence with the older authors, I find that I cannot concur in ascribing as much critical importance to fear in the schizophrenia syndrome as Sullivan (1953) did. It seems to me that in a torrent of emotions, fear is but one of many that are equally powerful. Here just a few examples on this theme from the literature:

Kraepelin's descriptions are still primarily listings of individual symptoms, although even he had begun to look for a "commonly applicable characteristic." His description reads: "A peculiar destruction of the inner cohesiveness of the psychic personality with predominant damage to the emotional life and the will."

Freud expressed himself, in line with his doctrine on human drives, as follows: "The libido of the schizophrenic withdraws from the outer world onto its own ego." E. Bleuler saw the disturbance in the cohesiveness primarily in thought and in the emotions. With the introduction of the concept "autism," he was already making the transition over to the later concept, namely, that the essence lay in the turning away from the community.

Probably for the first time, Bornsztajn (1927) identified autism as the essential factor of schizophrenic life.

On a broad scope, explicitly, and convincingly, Minkowski (1927) was one of the earliest to construct a unified picture of schizophrenia. In his opinion the essence is the turning away from the community and from reality, the submerging oneself into an autistic life, that applies with some limitations also to normal individuals. His formulation of the idea follows:

"All the troubles" (concerning the schizophrenics) "seem to converge upon one single notion, that of the loss of vital contact with reality." He goes on to explain how a feeling of harmony with life develops in the normal individual when his life springs from internal sources and continually adapts itself to the environment of the external world.

It is from within ourselves that we seek to draw on life forces for our activities and our labors. But if we thus find within ourselves the source of the loftiest manifestations of our personality, do we not then, by this same process, endeavor to eliminate all outside influences? Definitely not. On the contrary, we allow the environment to act upon us, we would even like to enfold it in its entirety; nonetheless, we remold all the outside elements within the crucible of our intimate life, to use them as the substance of our own activities. While isolating ourselves in this way, we remain in contact with our environment. But then it seems of interest to specify, on the one hand, to what extent we do allow outside influence to act upon us, and on the other, how far should the isolation from our environment be attempted, in an effort to safeguard one's originality? No categorical answer to such a proposition is possible. No precept of mental health could resolve it. Basically, the essential element which acts as a regulator in such cases cannot be intellectualized. It is one of life's irrational elements. We can call it the feeling of harmony with life. In an intellectual sense, the formula becomes "I feel myself in harmony with life and with myself."

In contrast to this sort of description for a normal individual, the one for a schizophrenic reads:

His personal inner drive does not seek to identify with reality, but becomes like an empty slate. In a sense it rather obliterates reality and hence, deprived of its natural support, becomes lost in the clouds, drowned in philosophical reflections. To think and act, without taking into account the ideas of others or without outside contingencies, leads to intellectual errors and, in practice, to the absurd.

Every coercion applied to find one's way back from the autistic world to the one of reality is torture for the schizophrenic. One of Minkowski's (1927) patients phrased it, after having been persuaded to contribute a little toward the support of his aged parents, as follows:

"From my viewpoint, all my rights of initiative seemed voided, and I had the frightful feeling of suffocating." To this, Minkowski (1927) remarks: Briefly outlined, such is the attitude of our patient. In accord with this antithetical attitude, he considers any alien force coming from the outside and acting to exert influence on the individual as an effront to his personality. When he experiences such an attack on himself, he feels himself swept toward what he sees as a catastrophe.

Minkowska (1925), wife and coworker of Minkowski, made the following formulation of the difference between schizophrenics and normals: "For the schizophrenic, the life of the imagination supersedes reality, and thought supersedes experience."

Minkowski (1927) distinguishes between a rich and a poor autism in schizophrenics. In the rich variety, the inner life resembles colorful dreams; in the poor variety, it drains off into rigid systems that seek symmetry, into mathematical formulae, and into images that run out on infinite lines or rails—that are cold, impersonal, timeless, and that cannot be influenced. Minkowski (1927) indicates that the schizophrenic lost in autism is not necessarily barred from finding his way back to reality:

"The concept of loss of contact with reality implies the idea that such a contact can be reestablished either totally or at least in part." And, "We find that we have no affective contact with the schizophrenic. Does this not mean that we ought to try to establish such a contact?"

In regarding schizophrenia as a process toward idiocy, the way to recovery is effectively barred. The new concept involving faith in a potential recovery is in itself a beneficial effect.

As Minkowski (1927) had done, Binswanger (1944–1949, 1952, 1953, 1958) also set out from the phenomenology in his schizophrenia investigations. The two were friends. They both looked back on their work together at Burghölzli, and their studies extended and supported each other. At the Second International Congress of Psychiatry, held in Zürich in 1957, Binswanger summarized his epoch-making schizophrenia research in particularly well-turned sentences. Among them, the following are of interest:

"The primary aim of our research with schizophrenics is also in this endeavor to retrieve human beings from the conceptual systems, the theories, and the accustomed thought-processes of psychopathology and of clinical psychiatry into a form of human existence of world-awareness." He claims that for the "revision of the structural system" of the schizophrenic form of existence, motive forces are responsible that jeopardize the consistency or the sequential order of previous experience. "Experience does not always seem to be confirmed in every instance, and it must never rest on established laurels. As a consequence, contradictions and rigid alternatives of experience, and with them the disintegration of the inner world, will prevail for schizophrenics. But this spells, at the same time, "no way out"; that is, "the impossibility of consummating a way of life."

What we call experience is consistent and has coherence in a natural sequential order. Where this order fails or breaks down, a place remains vacant in the total experience, in a manner of speaking. Therefore, every effort must be made to find out where these voids are and what the schizophrenics do to fill them in; in other words, what sort of solutions they find to escape from the inescapable and the nonfeasibility of dealing with life. This specifically schizophrenic solution reveals itself in that, in place of a normal, undisturbed, sequential order of experiences, a cleavage in the consummation of the act of living takes place, leaving just certain alternatives and often even a mere, rigid, unequivocal either-or. These alternatives lack the capacity of dealing adequately with the life situation in question, as possible solutions for the dilemma. As a consequence, the schizophrenic does not know which way to turn, nor whether to move forward or backward in life; nevertheless, he keeps on trying to make his way anyhow ... with his alternatives—his either-or. In so doing, he becomes ever more inextricably enmeshed in his alternatives, not in any consistent mode of experience, but in a contradictory manner.

With these words (and even much more explicitly in some of his later works) Binswanger (1957) characterized something that can be expressed in a sentence: The schizophrenic becomes rigid in his internal struggle with the contradictory aspects of his nature and of his experience in life.

In this process of rigidity, however, he does not remain in just one chaos; rather, the schizophrenic succeeds in structuring his own contradictoriness. In Binswanger's (1957) words: "His incapacity for consummating the course of his life" manifests itself in an "overly ambitious formation of ideals," in a "'mis-carried' way of life that is precisely predetermined in its structural order."

Wyrsch (1941, 1949, 1956, 1960), who had worked at Burghölzli as Minkowski and Binswanger had, further extended the phenomenological viewpoint of the psychopathology of schizophrenics and enriched it with many accurately conceived formulations. He arrived at conceptions similar to theirs.

Morselli (1930, 1958), from an entirely different school, arrived at very similar results. He held schizophrenia to be far more than a mere derailed psychic function; the schizophrenic strives for an equilibrium—to be sure, for a nonbiological one (he tends "vers un équilibre biologiquement inédit"). The complete slipping away into autism, Morselli (1930, 1958) calls a "metamorphosis." He illustrates it with his experiences with a patient named Elena, a young pianist, who told him:

> Now I am in the other life—in the other world—where I sometimes see angels and hear music. But I feel that it is not right, that it is something like the world of madness. I would not want to retreat from real life, but I am drawn by something that is stronger than I am. I seem to split and become two people, and I understand that. I cannot live life that way, so I bury myself in the other one. In truth, I am closer to the soul, to Dante's Paradise in that world, but I feel removed from life, devoid of emotion, and detached from everything.

In schizophrenic autism, the concept of the world, as Morselli (1930, 1958) emphasizes, is not only dissolved, but at the same time also newly refashioned. "The schizophrenic autistic experience . . . is also fundamentally a way sui generis of relating to reality where the personality reveals a structuring without analogy in the normal psychic world." I personally should like especially to emphasize that the schizophrenic striving after a "rapport avec le réel" means, above all, a striving after a human relationship that is compatible with his nature.

Ey (1956) arrives at a similar concept in his great clinical studies. It is summarized, for instance, in the sentence: "For the schizophrenic . . . schizophrenia is tantamount to the building of a world based on the principle of strangeness; that is to say, a system of values to which he adapts his existence, and which is, in turn, an existence for him."

Schindler (1965) described a number of different types of the long-term autism of schizophrenics: The "dismemberment" of an "ego-component" in which parts of the inner existence are isolated, displaced, or manically "talked out of existence"; the "chrysalis" type, in which the patient regresses externally to childishness and puts on a primitive front; the delusional fixation and its embodiment in hypochondria and in motor peculiarities. From Schindler's (1965) exposition we see again that symptoms which used to be regarded as primary are better considered in correlation with inner tendencies. The "manic talking-out-of-existence" is a distracted kind of talk which Schindler (1965) lucidly correlates with the autistic tendency of denying the truth of what one is discussing.

Rümke (1963) identifies the autistic life of schizophrenics as the "exposure" of the inner existence through the loss of comprehension of the "signal systems of others."

Arieti (1959, 1965) describes how the schizophrenic, in his frightened state of insecurity, is first beset by moods of indefinite distrust or unbearable self-contempt; how these develop into a need for more definite, more concrete types of distress that one can combat; and how this need can then be appeased by delusions and deceptive hallucinations. In the state of distraction it is easier to symbolize and to compress than in logical thinking; it is conducive to converting the dreaded unknown into something tangible (Binswanger [1957] said, into something familiar).

In 1965 Benedetti impressively described a number of the elementary contradictions that tend to allow schizophrenic behavior to be understood as a form of regression, namely, the craving to be an adult and the desire to recover the ties and securities of childhood force the patient into an attitude in which he simultaneously plays the child but reproaches others for not regarding him as an adult. The same result, regression, might emerge from the extreme need to submit to authority, after having lost one's self-confidence as an adult.

Avenarius (1966) observed in another example how the confused speech of schizophrenics meets an inner need. He noted how schizophrenics expressed the crassest, most grandiose ideas in absolute confusion. They were able to converse about other topics clearly and coherently. According to his impression, their extreme "megalomaniacal disposition" was something primary. The urgency existed for the formation of grandiose ideas. If these grandiose ideas had been clearly expressed, they would have been open to criticism by the patient himself and others around him. Presented in confusion, they do not subject the patient to the embarrassing position of having to evaluate his pathological disposition critically. I, too, had similar impressions quite often. Delusional patients begin to become confused when they get into a situation where they have to substantiate their mood, their behavior, or their aberration. The confusion eliminates any possibility for critical observation.

Wieser (1969) discusses the impact of public opinion on the mental patient. If the schizophrenic is made to feel different from everyone else, he feels himself in opposition to public opinion. If he cannot tolerate the thought of his own problems, the public is blamed for its opposition to him, and he feels himself persecuted by it.

In a large-scale research project, still unpublished, Matte-Blanco sees what is essential from a completely new and different viewpoint, namely, in the inclination to convert relationships that are actually asymmetrical into symmetric ones. For instance, a symmetrical relationship exists in the fact that Anna and Hans are in love; Anna loves Hans, and Hans loves Anna. But there is no symmetry expressed in the statement: "I love Anna." The schizophrenic, however, easily translates this to mean: "I love Anna, and Anna loves me."

Amazing as Matte-Blanco's interpretation seems to be at first glance, under more careful scrutiny it does illuminate the real essence of schizophrenia. Schizophrenics lack organization, equilibrium, and symmetry in their thoughts and evaluative faculties. A multitude of contradictory conditions plague the patient. His struggle for organization and symmetry corresponds to his struggle for the recovery of unity in thought, in feeling, and in action. In particular, he must seek to establish a harmony between his own personality and his life experiences. In his autism (one might also say, his "fool's freedom"), he longs for equilibrium between himself and the outer world. Symmetry provides it for him, for instance, according to the pattern: "I hate them—they hate me," or "I look at the world

—the world looks at me."

With these few examples we still do not have an overview of the important modern contributions to the psychopathology of schizophrenia. The studies cited were selected from a large number of others which might just as easily have supported what seems important to me. The most widely differing authors from the most varied schools today incline toward a similar concept of what schizophrenic life is.

The breakdown of schizophrenic symptoms into primary categories (not yet understandable) and secondary categories (psychologically understandable by way of the primary ones), has fulfilled an important mission in medical history. It is only on the basis of these breakdowns that a comprehensive psychopathology began to develop. Is it still relevant today? Or has it become obsolete, since we envisage schizophrenic life today as being entangled in autism? I should think that, although the distinction has lost its importance and should be adapted to newer concepts, the existence of the distinction is still justified.

As I had attempted to establish it, it is no longer so certain, that distractedness is the most important primary symptom. Today it is more probably autism, as Minkowski (1927) had emphasized. The fact that distractedness may be based on psychologically comprehensible factors is a probability today, but there is no proof that it is always and exclusively based on psychologically understandable factors. But even now we already anticipate in autism a personality development based on irreconcilable tendencies and irreconcilable life experiences. If this concept is correct, autism itself would be secondary to it, and the total of the rest of the symptoms would be third, in comparison.

We must hold fast to the concept with the utmost certainty, that there are symptoms which, in comparison to others are (relatively) secondary. If a schizophrenic patient, who has mistakenly been isolated, begins to soil himself and to become violent in his isolation, this is plainly a secondary symptom, in comparison to the disease that led to his hospitalization. If a patient becomes rigid and assumes an attitude toward his doctor of being in love with him or persecuted by him, that, too, is a secondary symptom, in comparison to the basic illness that necessitated treatment. In treatment it is of great importance to recognize such gradations. We must not grow weary of searching for them. Deterioration, which is a condition we used to be inclined to call dementia, a process toward idiocy, or a vegetative pining away, is also a secondary development, based on the symptoms of the disease, which has deeper foundations and is far more difficult to explain. Such findings constitute an important part of schizophrenia research today, as they did long ago.

The Nature of the Schizophrenic Mental Illnesses

Today we know a great many things about the schizophrenias. Our knowledge about countless details makes more difficult our understanding of the essentials and of the whole. Stroemgren (1938) justly insisted that research be undertaken and financed not only on some individual aspects of the entire problem, but rather that a schizophrenia researcher should finally be permitted to survey all the details deliberately and undisturbedly and to contemplate thoroughly the basic essentials.

If we want to grasp this essential element and to achieve an overview, we have to separate the essentials from ancillary factors, consider the schizophrenia doctrine as a whole, and launch our investigative efforts on the basis of what we really know. We should ignore preconceived opinions that have no basis in fact and whatever is mere statement, presumption, or hope.

These requirements seem so obvious that one ought to be ashamed to have to spell them out—if they had not been so blatantly ignored for such a long time. The doctrine of schizophrenia has developed along devious paths. One of the first to point out the right path was Adolf Meyer (1915). He continued to insist that, in explaining the schizophrenias, we set out from premises that we can determine and prove, and not from something that is merely suspected. For much too long a time his warning voice of caution was ignored.

In retrospect, it seems almost incredible how one-sided theories on the schizophrenias, upheld entirely by wishful thinking and unsupported by empirical fact, could propagate themselves. It is most peculiar that, for decades, new doctrines on schizophrenia could continue to emerge, creating the impression of being products of exacting scientific research—while, in fact, they lacked any sort of foundation that could withstand precise scientific criticism. For instance, the belief is still prevalent that the schizophrenias are

founded on a progressively destructive brain process, despite the fact that no one has ever seen such a process in a schizophrenic brain, and that patients with progressively destructive brain processes are not schizophrenic. Who, in the presence of other diseases, would assume a severe brain disorder without specific evidence of it? Many hold the opinion that schizophrenia can be explained via some "inborn error of metabolism," undeterred by the fact that no one has discovered any metabolic disorders as a basis for the schizophrenias, and undisturbed, further, by the fact that "inborn errors of metabolism" do not cause schizophrenias (but do cause feeblemindedness, organic dementia, or epilepsy). The belief that the schizophrenias could be traced back to one or to a few specific genes was being taught from a number of psychiatry chairs for decades as the great discovery, without sufficient evidence ever having been found for such an assumption. Psychological theories on the schizophrenias were set up just as frequently, and with as little evidence to back them up as the biological ones. Even laymen with some experience in life ought to know that countless children are deprived of their mothers at an early age without becoming schizophrenic afterward, and that the fewest of schizophrenics lost their mothers prematurely. In spite of that, a "mother deprivation" theory on schizophrenia gained popularity, at least among laymen. Such examples could easily be multiplied.

The many obsolete theories on schizophrenia without empirical foundations were not merely harmless assertions; they caused a great deal of harm. Anyone who has been involved in the ills that they propagated, can hardly discuss them without a note of bitterness entering in. The assertion that schizophrenia has to be transmissible by a simple mendelian process, combined with the asinine conviction that hereditary disorders were not amenable to treatment, lay for decades like a stifling frost over the enthusiasm of every therapeutic endeavor. If a destructive brain process was suspected to be lurking in the background of a schizophrenic psychosis, that was certainly no motivation for trying to communicate with that schizophrenic as a human being who feels and thinks the way everyone else does—and that specifically is what is so very important for therapeutic success. As a result of the preconceived notion that schizophrenia had to be based on an adrenal malfunction, the adrenal glands of schizophrenics were removed. But that did not cure these patients; it merely converted them into schizophrenics with Addison's disease. There were nurses who dangerously overdid the Bowlby hypotheses (1954, 1962). They held the opinion that the World Health Organization, under whose name Bowlby (1954, 1962) published his papers, had "determined" that every child deprived of his mother's care early in life would later develop as a schizophrenic or a criminal. So they put up considerable resistance to placing a child with foster parents, even if that child was being tormented by his own ailing mother to the point of endangering his life.

The essential results of schizophrenia research, which we must keep in mind when formulating our opinions on the nature of the schizophrenic mental disorders, have been outlined in the preceding sections. Here is a summary of these results.

1. Most somatic patients are not schizophrenic, and most schizophrenics are not physically ill. A somatic disorder of critical significance as the cause for the formation of the schizophrenias has not been identified up to now.

2. The discord between the patient's experience in life and his own personality is regarded subjectively by the patient as the cause of his illness. When we get to know schizophrenics and their life histories accurately, we are able to sense the interrelationships between their life experiences on the one hand, and personality and disease development on the other; we come to believe that we understand these interrelationships. At least we understand them as well (or as poorly) as the personality development of a neurotic or of a normal person. Such subjectively conceived psychic processes cannot be "accurately" proved in respect to their nature. Despite that, we have to realize that they exist. We are the more justified in acknowledging their existence, since there are, indeed, some objective indications of their importance. Among these are time correlations between suspected psychotraumatic experiences and the development of symptoms of illness.

3. Just as we can establish a correlation between the longitudinal development of schizophrenia as a discordance within the patient's own difficult personality and his life experiences, so also schizophrenic life—studied cross-sectionally—can be interpreted as the same discordance. The schizophrenic

symptoms can be correlated meaningfully with the patient's own schismatic personality and his schismatic experience.

4. We had no success, however, in recognizing any specific psychotraumatic event that always occurred in the backgrounds of schizophrenics, but never in the backgrounds of nonschizophrenics. Accordingly, a schizophrenia theory that is supported solely by the patient's experiences cannot be self-sufficient. Still other factors than adverse experiences must contribute to the onset of the illness.

5. Among these other factors, hereditary developmental tendencies in the personality have to be postulated. The significance of heredity is strongly suggested by the frequency of schizophrenias among the family members of schizophrenics. This accumulation of the incidence of schizophrenia in families cannot be traced back entirely to external damage by the environment that affects the entire family. To be sure, schizophrenic illness cannot in any case be traced back to any single or to just a few pathological genes. Many unfavorable traits or, rather, a disharmony among individually healthy traits may constitute the hereditary disposition for the schizophrenic illnesses. There is nothing to indicate that the inherited traits for schizophrenia become prominent by way of known metabolic characteristics. But a great deal does indicate that, according to their nature, these traits correspond to developmental aspects of the mind and the character, that we find just as impossible to correlate with any metabolic processes.

6. Insofar as a psychic disposition for schizophrenia can be identified, it consists of a lack of harmony in the life processes. This lack is characteristic of the "schizoid" personality. Insofar as a somatic disposition can be identified, it consists of a disturbance in the harmony of structures and functions.

7. Schizophrenic life is covertly inherent in the normal person, and a normal life is covertly retained in the schizophrenic.

8. During the course of schizophrenic illness, the mental life of the patient is neither simplified nor dismantled, as it is in the course of progressive brain diseases. The schizophrenic retains a great store of thought-content and a capacity for intellectual and emotional creativity, while the brain-diseased patient becomes impoverished in thought-content, and his creative capacity is diminished. Schizophrenic "dementia" is not

an organic dementia. Actually, schizophrenics never become "demented" or idiotic; they only seem to, since their rich inner life remains hidden because of their inability to communicate.

9. After a 5-year duration of the illness, schizophrenics do not generally deteriorate any further. Instead, from then on, tendencies for improvement prevail over tendencies for deterioration.

10. In all treatment methods that have proved effective in the treatment of schizophrenics, the same kinds of influences are brought to bear as those that develop and keep alive the personality of the normal person.

This is most clearly illustrated in the course of modern family therapy. In these group sessions the relationships between family members are clarified and placed in their proper perspective; independence and the feeling of belonging to the family should no longer be experienced as contradictory, but as harmonious, so that one member becomes the necessary extension of the other. Kaufmann and Müller (1969) mention a "communications sorting-out" in connection with group therapy with families. They try to "seize by the scruff of the neck and to signalize confused, contradictory, bewildered, verbalized communications" and to "point the finger at the lacunae in communications." As a goal for their "communications sorting-out" they state: "... consistently to signalize the limit between the personal and the interpersonal. We constantly appeal to the ego of the family members, calling reality to our aid." In a similar way, the small child finds the delimitation between I, you, and we. Enfolded in the bosom of his family, he experiences the communal relationship, and gradually also the necessity of finding his own ego in the community.

If these fundamental results of schizophrenia research are accepted, a simple and illustrative picture emerges of the causes and the nature of the schizophrenic mental disorders.

Hereditary factors striving in opposite directions in the development of a personality are obstacles for the later schizophrenic in the way of establishing a unified position in life in his struggle for existence. The development toward a strong personality that can take a unified, goal-directed stand in the world becomes inhibited. Because of the multiplicity, the disunity, and the disharmony of his inner

being, his relationships to other human beings become indefinite and ambiguous. Independently of his own personality, additional external problems develop that disturb his efforts at finding his own ultimate self. His development presses on toward a critical breaking point. This is reached when new and special demands are made upon his independence and his capacity for self-assertion. Then the person who has become ill intensifies the struggle with his own internal contradictions and with the contradictions of the world, as he has been experiencing it. His inner life flicks by in images of his own personality, and creates for itself images of a world that would correspond to his personality. Anything that lives and works in our dream lives, our wishful thinking, and our mythological thinking spills over its dams, achieves exaggerated implications, and breaks through to the realm of conscious life. The patient's effort to adapt to reality becomes impossible for him in many respects. His natural relationships to his fellowmen are destroyed, and the state of isolation into which the patient gets, further augments his autism. If the effort to motivate him to act toward unfolding his full potentials in society is successful, and if he is shocked at the auspicious moment to the point where he feels his very existence is threatened, the chances are that he can recover a unified, realistic attitude toward the world and find his way back to his own personal ego.

The same thought can also be expressed by a shorter formula: In the later schizophrenic a disintegration of his own personality and a disintegration of his experience with the environment develop in conjunction with and in support of each other. When the psychosis erupts, the inner conflicts have become so insurmountable that any natural relationship to the outer world is lost, and the patient loses himself in the imagery of a world of inner mental pictures. He can again become reconciled with reality when threats and distress awaken his defensive forces and when he can function in an active community.

Shortened even further and oversimplified: The schizophrenic loses himself in the discord between the disharmony of his own personality and the disharmony of his environment.

What is new about such formulations? Really, not very much at all. Most of my thoughts on the nature of the schizophrenias have already been expressed by many authors and in many variations. The fact that there are two kinds of psychic life with different rules and different goals, is something Jung, among others, described as far back as 1911 in his exposition "On Two Kinds of Thinking." He contrasted "directed thinking" with dreaming and imagining and characterized the distinction as follows:

"The former creates new acquisition and adaptation, imitates reality, and strives also to act upon it. The latter turns away from reality, liberates subjective desires, and is totally unproductive in respect to adaptation."

E. Bleuler (1912) contrasted realistic and "autistic" thinking:

When autistic thinking seeks to produce images that correspond to an inner inclination, a momentary mood, or any kind of personal bent, it does not necessarily have to have any consideration for reality. Whether something is actually real, possible, or conceivable is immaterial in these processes; they relate to reality only insofar as reality has provided and continues to provide them with imaginary materials to which the autistic mechanisms relate, or with which they operate.

In this way autistic thinking is capable of expressing all sorts of tendencies and drives from within. Since the logic that reproduces relationship to reality has no validity for autistics, the most varied desires can coexist simultaneously, regardless of whether they contradict one another, whether consciousness rejects them or not. In realistic thinking, in living and acting, a great number of drives and desires are ignored or suppressed in favor of the subjectively important ones; of many of these we are virtually never conscious. In autism, anything can be expressed. To be a child again, to be able to enjoy anything without inhibitions, and to be a mature man, whose desires for accomplishment, power, and an important position in life have been fulfilled. To live forever, and to have exchanged this doleful existence for Nirvana. To possess the woman one loves and simultaneously to retain one's freedom, or to engage in homosexual and heterosexual activities, etc. Such contradictions can find expression side by side, specifically in autistic thinking. . . .

Anyone who knows life and knows himself will have to acknowledge that, in the sense of Jung (1911) and E. Bleuler (1912), there are two distinct forms of psychic existence, although they may have been described and characterized differently by every author, in accordance with his personal predilection. In acknowledging the two distinct forms of psychic life, one acknowledges also that in normal individuals a state of equilibrium must exist between the two. With that established, the concept logically emerges that this equilibrium can become disturbed. This disturbance of the equilibrium—the outweighing of autism over realism—can be directly observed in the schizophrenic. The autistic, or fantastic-dream-like kind of thinking discernible even in most normals emerges in every good clinical description of the inner life of schizophrenics. I certainly do not imply, therefore, that there is anything new in my formulation to the effect that in schizophrenics the hidden psychic life of normals spills over its natural dams and takes on an immense importance for their entire inner life.

The evolution to schizophrenia, as I have summarized it, was also described by many great clinicians a long time ago. Agreeing in principle on most facets of it, they describe the personality peculiarity one frequently finds in the backgrounds of schizophrenics and their families, which often persists in more severely distorted form, after the schizophrenic psychosis has subsided. Whether this peculiarity were to be called introversion, schizoidia, eccentricity, or anything else, its essence still is the internal multiplicity and the disharmony that inhibit a complete, fulfilling, and harmonious devotion to the opportunity of the moment, to a frame of mind, to others, and to the entire world of reality. This personality contains the inclination to sensualize, to negate reality, to wishful thinking, and to autism. E. Bleuler (1922) had the following to say about it:

The schizoid retains his independence in the face of his environment; he seeks to withdraw from the affective influences of the animate and the inanimate environment and to pursue his own aims. This leads to . . . a shutting oneself off from reality, to a deliberate reshaping of it, or to an adaptation to it by way of inventions. . . . The lack of respect for reality and for what exists leads, on the one hand, to an effort to change this condition in some way, and on the other, to turn inward toward oneself. But not even here does the schizoid find a harmony of the syntonic; contradictory forces struggle and suppress one another without weakening in their own inherent drives. Thus, the patient is compelled to go to work on himself. . . .

In summary it might be added that this process of going to work on one's self is primarily an autistic one, in that one's own personal symbolic world is blithely created, while reality is bypassed.

The fact that tensions toward others are bound to result from the schizoid personality could be readily postulated, even if it were not obvious from any given patient history. A great deal has been written about this, for instance, by Sechehaye (1947), in his patient history of Renée. The patient histories also show, as expected, how the communications difficulties, in which the later schizophrenic becomes enmeshed because of his personality, force him farther away from reality and from his fellowmen, and thereby reinforce his autism. To this he adds independently developed involvements that have the same effect. Lidz (1962) and his students describe, for example, unnatural personal relationships of the parents to one another which harmfully affect the child.

With my description of the later schizophrenic as a person disrupted, disharmonious, and insecure within himself, I mean about the same condition the American psychiatrists have long described as an "ego-weakness." Similar ideas already formed the bases of many older concepts, for instance, that of the "intrapsychic ataxia" of Stransky (1904), that of the "disorders of association tensions" of E. Bleuler (1919), or that of the "hypotension of the energy source" of Rümke (1963). Primarily I know that I am also in agreement with Sullivan's (1953, 1956) formulations as well, when he spoke about an insufficiency in the "self-system" of schizophrenics, which he explains more fully in the concepts of "paratactic distortions" and the loss of "consensual validation." By the term "paratactic distortion," Sullivan understands something similar to my concept of an autistic interpretation of the world of human relations. By the loss of "consensual validation" he means the loss of proper understanding of the patient's own statements by others. So even Sullivan placed into the foreground the back-and-forth shifting between the inner

development and the human environment. But I cannot follow him in his one-sided emphasis on the fear that accompanies the disturbance in relationships. Of course, I, too, learned of the fear of schizophrenics as they became mired in their autism; but I also took note of many other emotions, of anger and hatred, of love, of helplessness, of a crippling of the emotions, of hope for redemption and possibly the good fortune of escaping into new worlds and finally enjoying the privilege of being oneself.

The picture of a critical breaking point, which the developing schizophrenic would have reached at the eruption of his psychosis, suggests itself to many clinicians. It would be reached when autism takes over in the principal facets of life, when the communications bridges are destroyed, and when one's close associates are under the impression that the person in question had become a stranger to them, had withdrawn from them to an unreachably distant place and had become marooned there. Usually it takes another additional stressful event until the "breaking point" is reached. Freud's description of his paranoid Schreber (1911) was already based on just such a concept. The dependency on the doctor who treated him was for Schreber the stressful situation that brought him to the "breaking point," to spilling over, and to bogging down in unrestrained, delusional autism, following the inner struggles with his homosexual tendencies. Kempf (1921) conceived the development of "homosexual flight" in quite the same way. After an inner disintegration following variously directed sexual tendencies, the psychosis erupts in situations in which homosexual seduction is suspected. In his exposition on the relationship-association delusion, Kretschmer (1918) also gave a good illustrative description of this breaking point and spilling over. We see in everyday practice how, during puberty, during pregnancy, before sudden increased occupational responsibilities, or at the beginning of their involution, our patients were exposed to new stresses that brought them close to that breaking point.

According to all this, the essential components of my concept of the nature of schizophrenia are old and long-established, acknowledged facts. Somewhat new is my concept of the systematic selection of what is essential in the doctrine of schizophrenia. The sequential order of the important data are
—The hereditary disposition for schizophre-

nic onset is multifarious; it is most readily conceived as the disharmony of hereditary developmental traits.
—The disharmony in the personality development is reflected in a disharmony in human relations.
—Adverse environmental experiences independent of the personality have the same effect.
—The adversity of the environment intensifies the disharmony of the personality.
—With increased stresses the development reaches a breaking point in which the essential adaptation to others and an understanding with others becomes impossible.
—In the schizophrenic psychosis autistic thinking exceeds its normal limits. The schizophrenic sets up an altercation with his personality by means of mental images and shapes a world for himself according to his own liking.
—Effective therapy in schizophrenia utilizes the same forces that contribute to a harmonious development of the personality.

The details that seem important to me for the modern concept of schizophrenia, however, are relatively new. They include the idea that the hereditary disposition is more likely to depend on a disharmony among basically normal genes, rather than on the sum of several pathogenic ones; a strong emphasis on the theory that an adverse personality and an adverse environment develop in mutual support of each other and with each other, and primarily that they are not independent of one another; the concept that effective therapy consists of participation in an active community, of shock, and of sedation, so that it applies the same forces that shape the personality and keep it alive and strong.

What is new is the consideration of long-term disease courses, which exposes the problem inherent in the old idea of a long-term, "progressive worsening" of the disease. For theorizing, it is important to keep in mind that, after an average duration of 5 years, the condition does not deteriorate any further, but rather that it may improve, and that it can be demonstrated that the patients, even in the most severe chronic states, remain mentally alive.

Possibly it is also new that I take today's knowledge seriously as a basis for our concepts, and that I disregard the expectations by which something essential or sensational, of which we have no knowledge as yet, is still waiting to be discovered.

In my opinion, the schizophrenic happening takes place in the realms of the mind and the emotions, that is, in mental spheres that exist only in man. It is inaccessible to direct influences by elementary physical processes. Like the mind and the emotions, of course, it, too, somehow has its somatic postulates. The emotions of the schizophrenic have no different interaction with physical processes than those of the normal individual have. No one has ever reported a schizophrenia in an animal, and it is, indeed, unthinkable. In some animal behavior we can detect simple models for the pathological reactions and developments inherent in man. In animals we note changes in motivation, in moods, in drives, and in inner periodicity, as we sometimes find them in man with endocrine or cerebral damage. The rich mental life, with the fullness of its imagery and symbols, however, that characterizes the schizophrenic, we are unable to ascribe to any animal.

The demarcation of the schizophrenias in contrast to normality and to other mental disorders emerges clearly and naturally from the already sketched concept of their nature. In the genesis of the schizophrenias, just as in the genesis of the neuroses, effect and countereffect of congenital developmental tendencies of the personality and life experiences are of critial importance. But to formulate, on this basis, that the schizophrenias are neuroses, would indeed be nonsense. The effects of the interaction of one's personal nature with the experience of living are quite different in the two cases. In the popular, as in the forensic interpretation, the schizophrenic is a case of mental illness, whereas the neurotic is not. The mental and emotional life of the schizophrenic have undergone such a complete change, that a normal person finds it impossible any longer to approach him directly as his equal. Disease symptoms, prognoses, the social impact of the schizophrenic's illness, and his therapeutic needs are something entirely different from those of the neurotic. The neurotic has by no means consummated his venture into the autistic world so inclusively and so completely as the schizophrenic. He has not been overwhelmed by conflicting tendencies; he does not have to reshape mentally the great insurmountable world, nor adapt it to himself in his mind, and he is not totally submerged in his autism. In the main, he is still able to present his entire personality to his environment. Schizophrenic development, furthermore, differs from a normal and from a psychopathic personality development, in that it is a psychosis—a mental illness.

The schizophrenic reaction is a schizophrenia in which the unleashing of the psychic shock—in comparison to a lingering psychic cleavage—is of extreme importance. Accordingly, there are flowing transitions between schizophrenic reactions and typical schizophrenias.

The organic origin of mental disturbances as phenomena accompanying acute somatic diseases can usually be identified by the patient's drowsiness, by a reduction of his consciousness, by reflex hallucinations, or by amnestic disorders. However, delirium and twilight states of a schizophrenic or an organic nature are often deceptively similar in their symptoms, if the somatic illness is not taken into account. But such a finding does not disturb the concept of the schizophrenias at which we have arrived. If schizophrenic life is concealed in the normal individual, it may come to light for a number of different reasons in the presence of acute somatic illnesses. The cerebral functional disorders imply a disturbance in the order, in Jackson's meaning. It may be surmised that within the framework of a general loss of order the equilibrium between rational and irrational thinking is also disturbed. The kind of irrational life that in the physically healthy person overflows out of inner necessity would come to light for physical reasons in an organic delirium or twilight state. But severe physical illnesses also often produce severe stresses on the patient's self-awareness. They frequently shatter the social status of the patient. They can provide the cause of a schizophrenic reaction. In organic deliria and twilight states, therefore, we are confronted with an interblending of the direct consequences of cerebral functional disorders and the sequelae of psychodynamic processes. Actually it has been demonstrated that deliria and twilight states appear frequently when the general patient has been exposed to a mentally stressful situation, and particularly if the illness separates him from human contacts (Willi in M. Bleuler et al., 1966, among others).

Chronic diffuse brain diseases usually bring on an impoverishment, a devastation, and a simplification of mental life—something quite different from what occurs in schizophrenia. It is only in rare cases that psychoses that are difficult to distinguish symptomatologically from the schizophrenias that occur with chronic brain damage, (as, for instance, the chronic, schizophrenia-like alcohol hallucinations, schizophrenia-like psychoses in temporal-lobe epilepsies, and in brain tumors the so-called "malaria-paranoid," chronic toxic psychoses from amphetamine addiction, and others). Just as in deliria and twilight states in the acute somatic illnesses, so also in these cases, cerebral and psychodynamic processes may be operating together.

There is, of course, no overall picture of the true nature of the schizophrenias that would accommodate every clinical case neatly and unequivocally. My picture, too, is in need of further amplification. Probably the most important phenomena in need of further explanation are the schizophrenias with a phasic-benign evolution, that is, those that evolve similarly to the manic-depressive psychoses, but that present a schizophrenic symptomatology. In many of these, it is impossible to find correlations between the individual, acute catastrophes and life's experiences. In these types of schizophrenia, I believe that metabolic disorders, with their effects on periodicity and agitation, are possible or probable, just as I do in cases of manic-depressive psychoses. It is to be hoped that in the course of the large-scale research projects now in progress, about water, electrolyte, and catecholamine metabolism in manic-depressives, something new may also be discovered on the nature of the phasic-benign schizophrenic psychoses.

The concept of the schizophrenic disorders at which I arrived, by a path similar to that of others among my contemporaries, is of only modest importance. It is a picture that evolves almost by itself, by piecing together today's certain and nearly certain knowledge about the schizophrenias, and by omitting only mild suspicions, unfounded assertions, and mere hopes. The picture is neither complete nor final. As early as tomorrow, a great new discovery may appear that reveals this picture as an illusion, or that shows the need for resketching it, after all. But despite all uncertainties as to its permanence, such a picture is useful for the time being. Schizophrenia research is in danger of losing itself in thousands of minor details, if it is not held together by one leading, central idea. Such a leading idea must not submit to the temptation of striving merely to be supported or amplified by future research. It should also be a challenge for research scientists to muster their best effort to refute it. But in performing our research, let us not forget that we are doctors. As doctors at the patient's bedside we need the broad, summary overviews of present-day knowledge in order, supported by such knowledge, to be able to act with conviction and assurance. We must act with conviction, even when we know perfectly well that this conviction is based on mere human knowledge, which is always incomplete, and which continues to change with advancing research.

The validity of a theory surely cannot be supported merely by expounding its usefulness. But as doctors, we can be glad when a theory conceived independently of its usefulness helps us in the treatment of our patients. Perhaps the picture of the nature of the schizophrenias that can be drawn today can sometimes mitigate the lot of our patients and their families a little after all, at least more than most of the previous hypotheses. According to our present-day concept, schizophrenics founder under the same difficulties with which all of us struggle all our lives. In spite of our own inner discords, our ambivalences, and our ambitendencies, all of us must find ways and means for establishing an awareness of our own egos and of confronting the world with our own wills. As long as we recognize in the schizophrenic a fellow sufferer and comrade-in-arms, he remains one of us. But when we see in him someone whom a pathological heritage or a degenerate brain has rendered inaccessible, inhuman, different, or strange, we involuntarily turn away from

him.—Yet it is so very beneficial to the schizophrenic for us to stay close to him!

According to my concept, the schizophrenic and his family may well rid themselves of the tormenting idea that they are carriers of an evil heritage, or that they are, as they have been accused of being, "eugenically undesirable individuals". It is very likely that their hereditary factors are not at all pathological; they may simply possess normal traits in unfavorable combination.

Primarily, the concept of the nature of schizophrenics, as it is depicted here, should serve to rekindle anew the flames of enthusiasm for their treatment. It shows us that we are acting correctly when we continually expand with increasing care and indefatigable persistence those treatment methods which our experience shows to be most effective, and which is the treatment that reintegrates the patient into an active community, which sometimes shocks him to awaken his dormant faculties, and which at other times tranquilizes him in his agitation and helps him to reestablish his inner consciousness. Our present-day concept of the schizophrenias frees us from the crippling accusation that our therapeutic practice does not get at the cause, but is merely superficial and symptomatic, and that it will be replaced by a true, great, causal kind of therapy as soon as the cause of the disease is discovered. We may rest assured that we are on the right track with our therapeutic methods, and that it is worthwhile to put forth our best, most vigorous effort for the treatment of schizophrenics.

Bibliography

Aall, Louise M.: Erfahrungen zum Thema in Tanganjika (Symposium über schizophrenieartige Psychosen und Ätiologie der Schizophrenie). Schweiz. Arch. Neurol. Neurochir. Psychiat. 93 (1964) 377–379

Abenson, M. H.: Drug withdrawal in male and female chronic schizophrenics. Brit. J. Psychiat. 115 (1969) 961–962

Ainsworth, Mary D., R. G. Andry, R. G. Harlow, S. Lebovici, Margaret Mead, D. G. Prugh, Barbara Wootton: La carence de soins maternels: réévaluation de ses effets. Org. mond. Santé Cah. Santé publ. No. 14 (1962) 168 pages

Alanen, Y. O.: The mothers of schizophrenic patients. Acta psychiat. scand. Suppl. 124 (1958) 1–361

Alanen, Y. O.: The family in the pathogenesis of schizophrenic and neurotic disorders. Acta psychiat. scand. Suppl. 189 (1966) 1–654

Alanen, Y. O.: From the mothers of schizophrenic patients to interactional family dynamics. In: The transmission of schizophrenia, hrsg. von *D. Rosenthal, S. S. Kety;* Pergamon Press, Oxford 1968 (S. 201–212)

Albrecht: Zur Symptomatologie der Dementia praecox. Allg. Z. Psychiat. 62 (1905) 659–686

Ambrumowa, A. G.: Zur Frage der sogenannten „familiären" Schizophrenien. Zh. Nevropat. Psikhiat. 67 (1957) 1101–1105

André-van Leeuwen, Maria: Aspects cliniques et problèmes du terrain de la pupillotonie, Bd. V. Institut Bunge, Antwerpen 1948

Andry, R. G.: Paternal and maternal roles and deliquency. In: Deprivation of maternal care, hrsg. von *J. Bowlby;* Wld Hlth Org. Publ. Hlth Pap. No. 14 1962

Angst, J.: Begleiterscheinungen und Nebenwirkungen moderner Psychopharmaka. Praxis 49 (1960) 506–511

Angst, J.: Tofranil: A Clinical analysis. In: Proceedings of the 3rd world congress of psychiatry, Bd. II; Univ. of Toronto Press, McGill Univ. Press, Montreal 1961 (S. 1383 bis 1387)

Angst, J.: Psychopharmakologie und Familienforschung. Schweiz. Arch. Neurol. Neurochir. Psychiat. 91 (1963) 267 bis 272

Angst, J.: Intoxikation mit Psychopharmaka. Ther. Umsch. 22 (1965) 178–180

Angst, J.: Zur Ätiologie und Nosologie endogener depressiver Psychosen. Eine genetische, soziologische und klinische Studie. Springer, Berlin 1966

Angst, J.: Psychiatrische Pharmakogenetik. Klinische Psychopharmakologie. Mod. Probl. Pharmakopsychiat. Bd. I. Karger, Basel 1968 (S. 260–272)

Angst, J.: Neuere Entwicklungen der Pharmako-Psychiatrie. Praxis 57 (1968) 143–148

Angst, J.: Die somatische Therapie der Schizophrenie. Thieme, Stuttgart 1969

Angst, J., C. Perris: Zur Nosologie endogener Depressionen. Arch. Psychiat. Nervenkr. 210 (1968) 373–386

Angst, J., W. Pöldinger: Klinische Erfahrungen mit dem Butyrophenonderivat Methylperidol (Luvatren). Vergleichender Beitrag zur Methodik pharmakopsychiatrischer Untersuchungen. Praxis 52 (1963) 1348–1354

Angst, J., W. Pöldinger: Klinische Erfahrungen mit Protriptylin (MK-240); vorläufiger Bericht. Schweiz. Arch. Neurol. Neurochir. Psychiat. 94 (1964) 480–481

Angst, J., W. Pöldinger: Psychopharmaka. Ther. Umsch. 22 (1965) 222–230

Anthony, E. J.: A clinical evaluation of children with psychotic parents. Amer. J. Psychiat. 126 (1969) 177–184

Arieti, S.: Interpretation of schizophrenia. Brunner, New York 1955

Arieti, S.; American handbook of psychiatry, Bd. II. Basic Books, New York 1959

Arieti, S.: The schizophrenic patient in office treatment. In: Psychothérapie de la schizophrénie, hrsg. von *C. Müller, G. Benedetti;* Karger, Basel 1965

Avenarius, R.: Zur Wirkungsweise von Rauwolfiaalkaloiden und Phenothiazinderivaten bei Schizophrenen. Nervenarzt 27 (1956) 454–458

Avenarius, R.: Über Größenwahn und Sprachverwirrtheit. Nervenarzt 37 (1966) 349

Baer, H.: Psychophysische Erregungszustände und ihre Behandlung durch neue Schlafmittelkombinationen. Schweiz. med. Wsch. 76 (1946) 582

Baer, H.: Psychotische Erregungszustände und ihre Bekämpfung durch Schlafmittel. Schweiz. Arch. Neurol. Neurochir. Psychiat. 60 (1947) 1–47

Barich, Doris: Zur Frage der Beziehungen zwischen dyskrinem und schizophrenem Krankheitsgeschehen: Infantil stigmatisierte Schizophrene und ihre Verwandten. Arch. Klaus-Stift. Vererb.-Forsch. 21 (1946) 1–36

Barry, H., E. Lindemann: Critical ages for maternal bereavement. Psychosom. Med. 22 (1960) 166–181

Barucci, M.: La vecchiaia degli schizofrenici. Riv. Pat. nerv. ment. 76 (1955) 257

Bateson, G., D. D. Jackson, J. Haley, J. H. Wakland: Toward a theory of schizophrenia. Behav. Sci. 1 (1956) 251–264

Baxter, J. C.: Family relationship variables in schizophrenia. Acta psychiat. scand. 42 (1966) 362–391

Baxter, J. C., Sonya Arthur, Constance G. Flood, Bethy Hedgepeth: Conflict patterns in the families of schizophrenics. J. nerv. ment. Dis. 135 (1962) 419–424

Baxter, J. C., J. Becker: Anxiety and avoidance behavior in schizophrenics in response to parental figures. J. abnorm. soc. Psychol. 64 (1962) 432–437

Baxter, J. C., J. Becker: Defensive style in the families of schizophrenics and controls in response to parental figures. J. abnorm. soc. Psychol. 64 (1964) 432

Baxter, J. C., J. Becker, W. Hooks: Defensive style in the families of schizophrenics and controls. J. abnorm. soc. Psychol. 66 (1963) 512–518

Baxter, J. C., Sonya Cornell Arthur: Conflict in families of schizophrenics as a function of premorbid adjustment and social class. Family Process 3 (1964) 273–279

Baxter, J. C., J. Williams, S. Zerof: Child-rearing attitudes and disciplinary phantasies of parents of schizophrenics and controls. J. nerv. ment. Dis. 141 (1966) 567–579

von Baeyer, W.: Zur Genealogie pathologischer Schwindler und Lügner. Thieme, Leipzig 1935

Beck, S. J.: Personality Structure in Schizophrenia. Nerv. ment. dis. Mongr. 1938, 63

Beck, S. J.: The six schizophrenias. American Orthopsychiatric Ass., New York 1954

Beck, S. J.: Review of Skalweit's „Konstitution und Prozeß in der Schizophrenie". Amer. J. Psychol. 47 (1935) 717–719

Benedetti, G.: Die Alkoholhalluzinosen. Thieme, Stuttgart 1952

Benedetti, G.: Psychotherapie der Schizophrenie. Nervenarzt 25 (1954) 197–201

Benedetti, G.: Psychotherapie einer Schizophrenen. Psyche (Heidelberg) 8 (1954) 1–16

Benedetti, G.: Die Welt des Schizophrenen und deren psychotherapeutische Zugänglichkeit. Schweiz. med. Wschr. 84 (1954) 1029

Benedetti, G.: Möglichkeiten und Grenzen der Psychotherapie Schizophrener. Bull. Schweiz. Akad. med. Wiss. 11 (1955) 142–159

Benedetti, G.: A propos de l'accès psychothérapeutique au monde du schizophrène. Evolut. psychiat. 1955/I, 145–157

Benedetti, G.: Psychotherapie eines Schizophrenen. Psyche (Heidelberg) 9 (1955) 23–41

Benedetti, G.: Il problema della coscienza nelle allucinazioni degli schizofrenici. Arch. Psicol. Neurol. Psichiat. 16 (1955) 287–312

Benedetti, G.: Analisi dei processi di miglioramento e di guarigione nel corso della psicoterapia. Arch. Psicol. Neurol. Psichiat. 17 (1956) 971–988

Benedetti, G.: Terapia reserpinica in psichiatria. In: Symposium nazionale sulla reserpina e cloropromazina in neuropsichiatria. „Vita e Pensiero", Mailand 1956 (S. 183)

Benedetti, G.: Psychotherapie der Psychosen. In: Lehrbuch der Psychiatrie, hrsg. von *H. Hoff;* Schwabe, Basel 1956

Benedetti, G.: Possibilità e limiti della terapia reserpinica in psichiatria. In Psychotropic drugs, hrsg. von *S. Garattini, V. Ghetti;* Elsevier, Amsterdam 1957, S. 527–533

Benedetti, G.: Klinische Psychotherapie. Huber, Bern 1964

Benedetti, G.: Le problème de la régression psychotique dans la psychothérapie individuelle. In: Psychothérapie de la schizophrénie, hrsg. von *C. Muller, G. Benedetti;* Karger, Basel 1965

Benedetti G., H. Kind, A. S. Johansson (unter Mitarbeit von P. F. Galli): Forschungen zur Schizophrenielehre 1956 bis 1961. Fortschr. Neurol. Psychiat. 30 (1962) 341–505

Benedetti, G., H. Kind, F. Mielke: Forschungen zur Schizophrenielehre 1951–1955. Fortschr. Neurol. Psychiat. 25 (1957) 101–179

Benedetti, G., H. Kind, Verena Wenger: Forschungen zur Schizophrenielehre 1961–1965. Übersicht. Teil I und II. Fortschr. Neurol. Psychiat. 35 (1967) 1–34, 41–121

Berkowitz, M., J. Levine: Rorschach scoring categories as diagnostic signs. J. cons. Psychol. 17 (1953) 110–112

Bernhard, Edith: Katamnestische Studien über die „Folie à deux". Diss. Zürich 1969

Bessière, R., J. Fusswerk: Constitution et processus dans la schizophrénie. Ann. méd.-psychol. 112 (1954/II) 504–522

Biermann, G.: Die seelische Entwicklung des Kindes im Familienmilieu Schizophrener. Schweiz. Arch. Neurol. Neurochir. Psychiat. 97 (1966) 87–133

Binder, H.: Die Geisteskrankheit im Recht. Schulthess, Zürich 1952

Binder, H.: Der Begriff der Geistesschwäche im Schweizerischen Zivilgesetzbuch. Mschr. Psychiat. Neurol. 129 (1955) 9–18

Binder, H.: Die Urteilsfähigkeit in psychologischer, psychiatrischer und juristischer Sicht. Schulthess, Zürich 1964

Binder, H.: persönliche Mitteilungen

Binswanger, K.: Über schizoide Alkoholiker. Z. ges. Neurol. Psychiat. 60 (1920) 127–159

Binswanger, L.: Der Fall Ellen West. Eine anthropologisch-klinische Studie, Teil I, II und III. Schweiz. Arch. Neurol. Neurochir. Psychiat. 53 (1944) 255–277; 54 (1944) 69–117; 55 (1945) 16–40

Binswanger, L.: Studien zum Schizophrenieproblem. Zweite Studie: Der Fall Jürg Zünd. Schweiz. Arch. Neurol. Neurochir. Psychiat. 56 (1946) 191–220; 58 (1947) 1–43; 59 (1947) 21–36

Binswanger, L.: Studien zum Schizophrenieproblem. Dritte Studie: Der Fall Lola Voss. Schweiz. Arch. Neurol. Neurochir. Psychiat. 63 (1949) 29–97

Binswanger, L.: Studien zum Schizophrenieproblem. Vierte Studie: Der Fall Suzanne Urban. Schweiz. Arch. Neurol. Neurochir. Psychiat. 69 (1952) 36–77; 70 (1952) 1–32; 71 (1953) 57–96

Binswanger, L.: Daseinsanalyse, Psychiatrie, Schizophrenie. Schweiz. Arch. Neurol. Neurochir. Psychiat. 81 (1958) 1–8

Binswanger, W.: Über den Rorschach'schen Formdeutversuch bei akuten Schizophrenien. Schweiz. Arch. Neurol. Neurochir. Psychiat. 53 (1944) 101–121

Birtchell, J.: Parental deprivation. Brit. J. Psychiat. 116 (1970) 281

Birtchell, J.: Recent parental death and mental illness. Brit. J. Psychiat. 116 (1970) 289

Bleuler, E.: Frühe Entlassungen. Psychiat.-neurol. Wschr. 6 (1905) 441

Bleuler, E.: Die Prognose der Dementia praecox (Schizophreniegruppe). Allg. Z. Psychiat. 65 (1908) 436

Bleuler, E.: Dementia praecox oder Die Gruppe der Schizophrenien. In: Handbuch der Psychiatrie, hrsg. von *G. Aschaffenburg;* Deuticke, Leipzig 1911

Bleuler, E.: Das autistische Denken. Jb. psychoanalyt. psychopathol. Forsch. 4 (1912) 1–39

Bleuler, E.: Frühe Entlassungen. Wien. med. Wschr. 64 (1914) 2499–2504

Bleuler, E.: Störung der Assoziations-Spannung, ein Elementarsymptom der Schizophrenien. Eine Hypothese. Allg. Z. Psychiat. 74 (1919) 1

Bleuler, E.: Das autistisch-undisziplinierte Denken in der Medizin und seine Überwindung. Springer, Berlin 1919 (und spätere Auflagen)

Bleuler, E.: Die Probleme der Schizoidie und der Syntonie. Z. ges. Neurol. Psychiat. 78 (1922) 373–399

Bleuler, E.: Die Psychoide als Prinzip der organischen Entwicklung. Springer, Berlin 1925

Bleuler, E.: Lehrbuch der Psychiatrie, 11. Aufl. Springer, Berlin. 1.–6. Aufl., 1916–1937. Bearbeitung der 7.–11. Aufl., 1943–1969, und Nachtrag zum Neudruck der 10. Aufl. 1966, von *M. Bleuler*

Bleuler, M.: s. S. 61 f.

Bleuler, M. (mit Beiträgen von H. Baer, G. Condrau, D. I. Jacobs, H. K. Knoepfel, W. Stoll, H. Wipf, Delia Wolf, W. Zueblin): Untersuchungen aus dem Grenzgebiet zwischen Psychopathologie und Endokrinologie. Arch. Psychiat. Nervenkr. 180 (1948) 271–528

Bleuler, M., G. Benedetti: Schizofrenia. Enciclopedia Medica Italiana. Sansoni, Florenz 1956 (S. 1476–1510)

Bleuler, M., M. Müller, G. Schneider: Probleme der Schizophrenie im Versicherungsrecht. Schweiz. Arch. Neurol. Neurchir. Psychiat. 89 (1962) 359–383

Bleuler, M., L. Rapoport: Untersuchungen über die konstitutionelle Verwandtschaft von Tuberkulose und Geisteskrankheiten. Z. ges. Neurol. Psychiat. 153 (1935) 649–679

Bleuler, M., W. A. Stoll: Clinical use of reserpine in psychiatry: comparison with chlorpromazine. Ann. N. Y. Acad. Sci. 61 (1955) 167–173

Bleuler, M., J. Willi, H. R. Bühler: Akute psychische Begleiterscheinungen körperlicher Krankheiten. „Akuter exogener Reaktionstypus" – Übersicht und neue Forschungen. Thieme, Stuttgart 1966

Bleuler, M., B. A. Zurgilgen: Tuberkulose und Schizophrenie. Wien. med. Wschr. 99 (1949) 357

Block, Jeanne: Parents of schizophrenic, neurotic, asthmatic, and congenitally ill children. Arch. gen. Psychiat. 20 (1969) 659–674

Böcher, W.: Die Brauchbarkeit des Rorschachtests als klinische Untersuchungsmethode. Fortschr. Neurol. Psychiat. 30 (1962) 1–60

Bochner, Ruth, Florence Halpern: The clinical application of the Rorschach test. Grune & Stratton New York 1945

Bohm, E.: Lehrbuch der Rorschach-Psychodiagnostik. Huber, Bern 1951

Bonhoeffer, K.: Die Psychosen im Gefolge von akuten Infektionen, Allgemeinerkrankungen und innere Erkrankungen. In: Handbuch der Psychiatrie, hrsg. von *G. Aschaffenburg;* Deuticke, Leipzig 1912 (S. 1–118)

Böök, J. A.: A genetic and neuropsychiatric investigation of a North-Swedish population. Acta genet. (Basel 4 (1953) 1–100

Bornsztajn, M.: Der klinische Standpunkt der Schizophrenie und eine neue Theorie ihrer Pathogenese. Roczn. psychiat. (1927) 79–92; ref. in: Zbl. ges. Neurol. Psychiat. 48 (1928) 364

Borowitz, G.: 337 consecutive alcoholics. (Personal communication) zit. von *Brown, F.:* Brit. J. Psychiat. 112 (1966) 1035–1041

Bosia, G.: Zur Frage der Beziehungen zwischen dyskrinem und schizophrenem Krankheitsgeschehen. Eine maskuline schizophrene Frau und ihre Verwandtschaft. Arch. Klaus-Stift. Vererb.-Forsch. 25 (1950) 269

Boszormenyi-Nagy, I., J. L. Framo: Intensive family therapy. Harper & Roy, New York 1965

Bowen, M.: A family concept of schizophrenia. In: The etiology of schizophrenia, hrsg. von *D. D. Jackson;* Basic Books, New York 1960

Bowen, M., R. H. Dysinger, W. M. Brodey, B. W. Basamania: The family as the unit of study and treatment. Amer. J. Orthopsychiat. 31 (1961) 40–86

Bowlby, J.: Soins maternels et santé mentale, 2. Aufl. Org.

mond. Santé Sér. Monogr. No. 2, 1954

Bowlby, J.: Deprivation of maternal care. Wld. Hlth Org. Publ. Hlth Pap. No. 14, 1962

Bowman, K. M., Alice F. Raymond: Physical findings in schizophrenia. Amer. J. Psychiat. 8 (1929) 901–913

Von Brauchitsch, H. K.: Neuere Untersuchungen über die organische Natur der Schizophrenie. Diss. Zürich 1960

von Brauchitsch, H.: Endokrinologische Aspekte des Wirkungsmechanismus neuroplegischer Medikamente. Psychopharmacologia (Berl.) 2 (1961) 1–21

von Brauchitsch, H.: Erfahrungen mit dem Methylaminbenzodiazepinderivat „Librium" in der psychiatrischen Poliklinik. Dtsch. med. Wschr. 86 (1961) 1669

von Brauchitsch, H.: The influence of Thyroxine and Insulin on the clinical effects of some neuroplegic drugs. In: Neuro-psychopharmacology, Bd. II, hrsg. von E. Rothlin; Elsevier, Amsterdam 1961 (S. 230–235)

von Brauchitsch H., A. Bukowczyk: Zur Frage der Verwendung des Chlorprothixen („Taractan") im psychiatrischen Hospital. Schweiz. Arch. Neurol. Neurochir. Psychiat. 90 (1962) 104–117

Brill, N. Q., E. H. Liston: Parental loss in adults with emotional disorders. Arch. gen. Psychiat. 14 (1966) 307

Brock, Helene: Untersuchungen über die Entwicklung der Kinder nervenkranker Mütter. Acta paedopsychiat. 29 (1962) 116–123

Brooks, G. W., W. N. Deane, R. C. Lagor, B. B. Curtis: Varieties of family participation in the rehabilitation of released chronic schizophrenic patients. J. Nerv. ment. Dis. 136 (1963) 432–444

Brown, F.: Childhood bereavement and subsequent psychiatric disorder. Brit. J. Psychiat. 112 (1966) 1035–1041

Brown, F., Phyliss Epps: Childhood bereavement and subsequent crime. Brit. J. Psychiat. 112 (1966) 1043

Brown, G. W.: Social factors influencing length of hospital stay of schizophrenic patients. Brit. med. J. 1959/II, 1300 bis 1302

Brown, G. W., Margaret Bone, Bridget Dalison, J. K. Wing: Schizophrenia and social care. Oxford University Press, London 1966

Brown, G. W., E. M. Monck, G. M. Carstairs, J. K. Wing: Influence of family life on the course of schizophrenic illness. Brit. J. prev. soc. Med. 16 (1962) 55–82

Brugger, C.: Zur Frage einer Belastungsstatistik der Durchschnittsbevölkerung. Z. ges. Neurol. Psychiat 118 (1929) 459

Brugger, C.: Versuch einer Geisteskrankenzählung in Thüringen. Z. ges. Neurol. Psychiat. 133 (1931) 352

Brugger, C.: Psychiatrische Ergebnisse einer medizinischen, anthropologischen und soziologischen Bevölkerungsuntersuchung. Z. ges. Neurol. Psychiat. 146 (1933) 489

Brugger, C.: Familienuntersuchungen bei chronischen Alkoholikern. Z. ges. Neurol. Psychiat. 151 (1934) 103

Brugger, C.: Psychiatrische Bestandesaufnahme im Gebiet eines medizinisch-anthropologischen Zensus in der Nähe von Rosenheim. Z. ges. Neurol. Psychiat. 160 (1938) 187

Brun, O.: Schwere schizophrene Verläufe. Diss. Zürich 1956

von Brunn, Ruth, W. L. von Brunn: Infantil stigmatisierte Schizophrene. Arch. Psychiat. Nervenkr. 189 (1952) 324–340

Bukowczyk, A.: Weitere Infantile mit psychischen Erkrankungen und ihre Familien. Diss. Zürich 1962

Bumke, O.: Schizophrene Erkrankungen. In: Lehrbuch der Geisteskrankheiten, 5. Aufl., hrsg. von O. Bumke; Bergmann, München 1942 (S. 532–621)

Bychowsky, G.: Schizophrenia in the period of involution. Dis. nerv. Syst. 13 (1952) 150

Canavan, M. M., R. Clark: The mental health of 463 children from dementia praecox stock. Ment. Hyg. (N. Y.) 7 (1923) 137; 20 (1936) 463

Cancro, R. A. A. Sugerman: Classification and outcome in process-reactive schizophrenia. Comprehens. Psychiat. 9 (1968) 227–232

Carstairs, G. M.: Social factors influencing the genesis and outcome of schizophrenia. In: The origins of schizophrenia, hrsg. von J. Romano; Excerpta Medica Foundation, Amsterdam 1968 (S. 270–275)

Cawley, R. H.: The present status of physical methods of treatment of schizophrenia. In: Recent advances in schizophrenia, hrsg. von A. Coppen, A. Walk; Headley Brothers, Ashford, Kent 1967

Chase, L. S., S. Silverman: Prognostic criteria in schizophrenia – a critical survey of the literature. Amer. J. Psychiat. 98 (1941/2) 360

Chase, L. S., S. Silverman: Prognosis in schizophrenia – an analysis of prognostic criteria in 150 schizophrenics treated with metrazol or insulin. J. nerv. ment. Dis. 98 (1943) 464

Cheney, Clarence O., H. E. Clow: Prognostic factors in insulin shock therapy. Amer. J. Psychiat. 97 (1941) 1029

Condrau, G.: Die präfrontale Leukotomie. Schweiz. med. Wschr. 80 (1950) 783

Conrad, K.: Die beginnende Schizophrenie. Versuch einer Gestaltanalyse des Wahns. Thieme, Stuttgart 1958

Constantinidis, J., G. Garrone, J. de Ajuriaguerra: L'hérédité des démences de l'âge avancé. Encéphale 51 (1962) 301–344

Corboz, J. R.: Reaktive Störungen bei Kindern schizophrener Eltern. Congr. Rep., IInd Internat. Congr. Psychiat. Zürich 1957, Bd. III; Orell Füssli, Zürich 1959 (S. 457–462)

Corboz, R. J.: Les psychoses endogènes de l'adolescent. 6ième Congr. Internat. Psychiat. Infantile, Symp.: Syndrômes psychiatriques spécifiques à l'adolescence, Edinburgh 1966

Corboz, R. J.: Psychopharmaka im Kindesalter. Landarzt 44 (1968) 922–928

Corboz, R. J.: La psychopharmacothérapie de l'enfant et de l'adolescent. Expériences cliniques. In: Concilium Paedopsychiatricum, Verh. 3. Europ. Kongr. Pädopsychiat., Wiesbaden 1967; Karger, Basel 1968 (S. 295–306)

Corboz, R. J.: Endogenous psychoses of the adolescent. In: Adolescence: Psychosocial perspectives, hrsg. von G. Caplan, S. Lebovici, Basic Books, New York 1968 (S. 275 bis 279)

Cowie, Valerie: The incidence of neurosis in the children of psychotics. Acta psychiat. scand. 37 (1961) 37–71

Cresseri, A.: L'ereditarietà della demenza senile. Boll. Soc. ital. Biol. sper. 24 (1948) 200

Dahlberg, G.: Sélection dans les populations humaines. Zool. Bidr. (Uppsala) 25 (1947) 21–32

Dalén, P.: One, two or many? In: Genetic factors in schizophrenia, hersg. von A. R. Kaplan; Thomas, Springfield im Druck

Delay, J., P. Pichot, J. Perse: Le test de Rorschach et le diagnostic de la schizophrénie. Beih. Schweiz. Z. Psychol. Anwendg. 35, Rorschachiana VI, 66 ff.

Delay, J., P. Deniker, A. Green: Essai de description et de définition psycho-pathologique des parents de schizophrènes. Congr. Rep., IInd Internat. Congr. Psychiat. Zürich 1957, Bd. IV; Orell Füssli, Zürich 1959 (S. 49–56)

Delay, J., P. Deniker, A. Green: Le milieu familial des schizophrènes. Encéphale 51 (1962) 1–73

Deming, W. E.: A recursion formula for the proportion of persons having a first admission as schizophrenic. Behav. Sci. 13 (1969) 467

Dennehy, Constance M.: Childhood bereavement and psychiatric illness. Brit. J. Psychiat. 112 (1966) 1049–1069

Deussen, J.: Methodisches zur Insulinschock-Therapie. Allg. Z. Psychiat. 106 (1937) 339

Deykin, E.: The reintegration of the chronic schizophrenic patient discharged to his family and community as perceived by the family. Ment. Hyg. (N. Y.) 45 (1961) 235–246

Diem, O.: Die psycho-neurotische erbliche Belastung der Geistesgesunden und der Geisteskranken. Arch. Rassenu. Gesellsch.-biologie 2 (1905) 215–252 und 336–368

Diethelm, O.: Etiology of chronic alcoholism. Thomas, Springfield 1955

Dunham, H. W.: Social class and schizophrenia. Amer. J. Orthopsychiat. 34 (1964) 634

Edwards, J. H.: The simulation of mendelism. Acta genet. (Basel) 10 (1960) 63

Egger, H.: Zum Problem der Gattenwahl Schizophrener. Z. ges. Neurol. Psychiat. 174 (1942) 353–396

Ekblom, B., B. Lassenius: A follow up examination of patients with chronic schizophrenia, who were treated during a long period with psychopharmacological drugs. Acta psychiat. scand. 40 (1964) 249

Elsässer, G.: Die Nachkommen geisteskranker Elternpaare. Thieme, Stuttgart 1952

Erlenmeyer-Kimling, L., Susan Nicol, J. D. Rainer, W. E. Deming: Changes in fertility rates of schizophrenic patients in New York State. Amer. J. Psychiat. 125 (1969) 916–927

Erlenmeyer-Kimling, L., J. D. Rainer, F. J. Kallmann: Current reproductive trends in schizophrenia. In: Psychopathology of Schizophrenia, hrsg. von *P. H. Hoch, J. Zubin;* Grune & Stratton, New York 1966 (S. 252–276)

Ernst, K.: Psychopathologische Wirkungen des Phenothiazinderivates „Largactil" (= Megaphen) im Selbstversuch und bei Kranken. Arch. Psychiat. Nervenkr. 192 (1954) 573–590

Ernst, K.: „Geordnete Familienverhältnisse" späterer Schizophrener im Lichte einer Nachuntersuchung. Arch. Psychiat. Nervenkr. 194 (1956) 355–367

Ernst, K.: Die Prognose der Neurosen. Springer, Berlin 1959

Ernst, K.: Wann besteht Verdacht auf eine schizophrene Psychose? Schweiz. med. Wschr. 94 (1964) 776–780

Ernst, K.: Die psychiatrische Behandlung im Rückblick von Patient und Nachuntersucher. 20jährige Katamnesen von 70 hospitalisierten und 120 ambulanten Neurosekranken. Nervenarzt 35 (1964) 248–256

Ernst, K. (unter Mitarb. von *Cécile Ernst*): Ergebnisse der Verlaufsforschung bei Neurosen. Eine vergleichende Literaturübersicht. In: Ergebnisse der Verlaufsforschung bei Neurosen, hrsg. von *K. Ernst, H. Kind, Margrit Rotach-Fuchs;* Springer, Berlin 1968, (S. 1–106)

Ernst, K., Cécile Ernst: 70 zwanzigjährige Katamnesen hospitalisierter neurotischer Patientinnen. Schweiz. Arch. Neurol. Neurochir. 95 (1965) 359–415

Essen-Möller, E.: Untersuchung über die Fruchtbarkeit gewisser Gruppen von Geisteskranken. Acta. psychiat. scand. Suppl. 8 (1935) 1–314

Essen-Möller, E.: Die Heiratshäufigkeit der Geschwister von Schizophrenen. Arch. Rassen- u. Gesellsch.-biologie 30 (1936) 367–379

Essen-Möller, E.: Psychiatrische Untersuchungen an einer Serie von Zwillingen. Munksgaard, Copenhagen 1941

Essen-Möller, E.: Individual traits and morbidity in a Swedish rural population. Acta psychiat. scand. (1956) Suppl. 100 1–160

Essen-Möller, E.: Mating and fertility patterns in families with schizophrenia. Eugen. Quart. 6 (1959) 142–147

Essen-Möller, E.: Über die Schizophreniehäufigkeit bei Müttern von Schizophrenen. Schweiz. Arch. Neurol. Neurochir. Psychiat. 91 (1963) 260–266

Evensen: zit. von *E. Kraepelin* in: Psychiatrie, 8. Aufl.; Barth, Leipzig 1913

Ey, H.: Etudes psychiatriques: Structure des psychoses aigües et déstructuration de la conscience. De Brouwer, Paris 1954

Ey, H.: Groupe des psychoses schizophréniques et des psychoses délirantes chroniques. Encyclopédie médico-chirurgicale, Psychiatrie, 2. publié sous la direction de H. Ey. Paris 1955

Ey, H.: Le problème de la définition et de la délimitation du groupe des schizophrénies. Congr. Rep., IInd Congr. Internat. Psychiat. Zürich 1957, Bd. I; Orell Füssli, Zürich 1959 (S. 144–151)

Falconer, D. S.: The inheritance of liability to certain diseases, estimated from the incidence among relatives. Ann. hum. Genet. 29 (1965) 51

Farina, A.: Patterns of dominance and conflict in parents of schizophrenic patients. J. abnorm. soc. Psychol. 61 (1960) 31

Farina, A., R. M. Dunham: Measurement of family relationships and their effects. Arch. gen. Psychiat. 9 (1963) 64

Faris, R. E. L., H. W. Dunham: Mental disorders in urban areas. Univ. Chicago Press, Chicago 1939

Fleck, U.: Über Beobachtungen bei alten Fällen von Schizophrenie. Arch. Psychiat. Nervenkr. 85 (1928) 705

Forrest, A. D., R. H. Fraser, R. G. Priest: Environmental factors in depressive illness. Brit. J. Psychiat. 111 (1965) 243–253

Fremming, K. H.: The expectation of mental infirmity in a sample of the Danish population. Eug. Soc. Occasional Papers on Eugenics, Nr. 7; Cassell, London 1951

Freud, S.: Weitere Bemerkungen über die Abwehrneuropsychosen. In: Gesammelte Werke, Bd. I; Imago Publishing, London 1892–1899 (Erstpublikation in Neurol. Centralblatt 1896, Nr. 10)

Freud, S.: Psychoanalytische Bemerkungen über einen autobiographisch beschriebenen Fall von Paranoia. Jb. psychoanalyt. psychopathol. Forsch. 3 (1911) 9–68

Früh, Liselotte: Über die Belastung von Ehegatten Schizophrener. Z. ges. Neurol. Psychiat. 176 (1943) 695–741

Galachyan, A. G.: The basic aetiological factor in the development of schizophrenia. Ref. in: Excerpta med. (Amst.) Sect. VIII (1963) No. 3642

Galatschjan, A.: Die Vererbung der Schizophrenie. Schweiz. Arch. Neurol. Psychiat. 39 (1937) 291–315

Gamna, G., N. Attisani, L. Ferrio: Considerazioni statistico-cliniche e psicopatologiche su un gruppo di schizofreniche pervenute ad età senile. G. Psichiat. Neuropat. 40 (1962) 767

Gardner, G. E., S. Aaron: Childhood and adolescent adjustment of negro psychiatric casualties. Amer. J. Orthopsychiat. 16 (1946) 481–495

Gardner, G. E., N. Goldman: Childhood and adolescent adjustment of naval successes and failures. Amer. J. Orthopsychiat. 15 (1945) 584–596

Garmezy, N., A. R. Clarke, Carol Stockner: Child-rearing attitudes of mothers and fathers as reported by schizophrenic and normal control patients. J. abnorm. soc. Psychol. 63 (1961) 176

Garrone, G.: Etude statistique et génétique de la schizophrénie à Genève de 1901 à 1950. J. Génét. hum. 11 (1962) 89–219

Gastager, H., G. Hofmann: Psychiatrische Verlaufsuntersuchungen an konkordanten eineiigen schizophrenen Zwillingspaaren. Wien. Z. Nervenheilk. 29 (1962) 466

Gaupp, R.: Über den Begriff der psychopathischen Konstitution. Z. ärztl. Fortbild. 14 (1917) 565–569

Gengnagel, E.: Beitrag zum Problem der Erbprognosebestimmung. Über die Erkrankungsaussichten der Kinder von Schizophrenen. Z. ges. Neurol. Psychiat. 145 (1933) 52–61

Gerloff, W.: Über Verlauf und Prognose der Schizophrenie. Arch. Psychiat. Nervenkr. 106 (1937) 585

Gillis, L. S., M. Keet: Factors underlying the retention in the community of chronic unhospitalized schizophrenics. Brit. J. Psychiat. 3 (1965) 1057–1067

Glueck, S., E. T. Glueck: Unraveling juvenile delinquency. Harvard University Press, Boston, Mass. 1950

Goldberg, E. M., S. L. Morrison: Schizophrenia and social class. Brit. J. Psychiat. 109 (1963) 785–802

Gordon, H. L., Groth: Mental patients wanting to stay in the hospital. Arch. gen. Psychiat. 4 (1961) 124–130

Gottesman, I. I., J. Shields: Schizophrenia in twins: 16 years' consecutive admissions to a psychiatric clinic. Brit. J. Psychiat. 112 (1966) 908

Gottesman, I. I., J. Shields: Contributions of twin studies to perspectives on schizophrenia. In: Progress in experimental personality research., Bd. III, hrsg. von *B. A. Maher;* Academic Press New York 1966 (S. 1–84)

Gottesman, I. I., J. Shields: A polygenic theory of schizophrenia. Proc. nat. Acad. sci. (Wash.) 58 (1967) 199–205

Gottlieb, B. S.: Prognostic criteria in hebephrenia. The importance of age, sex, condition and marital status. Amer. J. Psychiat. 97 (1940) 332

Gralnick, A.: Folie à deux: The psychosis of association. Psychiat. Quart. 16 (1942) 230–263

Granville-Grossman, K. L.: Early bereavement and schizophrenia. Brit. J. Psychiat. 112 (1966) 1027–1034

Greenberg, H. P.: Folie à deux: An historical and clinical study. Unpublished Thesis Sidney 1961

Gregory, I.: Studies of parental deprivation in psychiatric patients. Amer. J. Psychiat. 115 (1958) 432–442

Gregory, I.: Retrospective estimates of orphanhood from generation life tables. Milbank mem. Fd Quart. 43 (1965) 323–348

Haffter, C.: Kinder aus geschiedenen Ehen. Huber, Bern 1948

Hallgren, B., T. Sjoegren: A clinical and geneto-statistical study of schizophrenia and low-grade mental deficiency in a large Swedish rural population. Acta psychiat. scand. Suppl. 140 (1959)

Harris A., Inge Linker, Vera Norris, M. Shepherd: Schizophrenia: A prognostic and social study. Brit. J. soc. Med. 10 (1956) 107–114

Hartmann, W.: Statistische Untersuchungen an langjährigen Schizophrenen. Soc. Psychiat. 4 (1969) 101

Harvald, B., M. Hauge: Hereditary factors elucidated by twin studies. In: Genetics and the epidemiology of chronic diseases, hrsg. von *J. V. Neel, MW. Shaw, W. J. Schull;* U. S. Dept. of Health, Education and Welfare, Washington, D. C. 1965

Hegg, J. J.: Vergleich psychiatrisch und internistisch behandelter Mißbraucher von phenazetinhaltigen Analgetica. Z. Unfallmed. Berufskr. 55 (1962) 258–290

Helgason, T.: Epidemiology of mental disorders in Iceland. Acta psychiat. scand. Suppl. 173 (1964) 11–258

Hering: Über das Gedächtnis als allgemeine Funktion der organischen Materie. Wien 1870

Herjanic, M., R. C. Hales, A. Stewart: Does it pay to discharge the chronic patient? A 2 year follow-up of 338 chronic patients. Acta psychiat. scand. 45 (1969) 53–61

Hicklin, A., J. Angst: Retrospektive und prospektive Studie über die klinische Wirkung von Clopenthixol (Sordinol) bei endogenen Psychosen. Schweiz. med. Wschr. 97 (1967) 615–621

Hilgard, Josefine R., Martha F. Newman: Early parental deprivation as functional factor in etiology of schizophrenia and alcoholism. Amer. J. Orthopsychiat. 33 (1963) 409 bis 420

Hilgard, Josefine R., Martha F. Newman: Parental loss by death in childhood as etiological factor among schizophrenic and alcoholic patients compared with non-patient community sample. J. nerv. ment. Dis. 137 (1963) 14–28

Hoffmann, H.: Studien über Vererbung und Entstehung geistiger Störungen. II. Die Nachkommenschaft bei endogenen Psychosen. Springer, Berlin 1921

Hoffmann, H.: Schizothym-Cyklothym. Z. ges. Neurol. Psychiat. 82 (1923) 93–104

Hollingshead, A. B., F. C. Redlich: Social class and mental illness. Wiley & Sons, New York 1958

Howard, B. F.: An optimistic report on total rehabilitative potential of chronic schizophrenics. Arch. gen. Psychiat. 3 (1960) 345–356

Huber, H. U.: Statistische Untersuchungen über die Lebensverhältnisse späterer Schizophrener in ihrer Kindheit. Diss. Zürich 1954

Hurschler, H., H. Perrier: Schizophrenie und Tuberkulose. Schweiz. med. Wschr. 76 (1946) 95

Illberg, P.: Statistische Untersuchungen über die Lebensverhältnisse späterer Schizophrener in ihrer Kindheit. Diss. Zürich 1961

Ingham, H. V.: Statistical study of family relationships in psychoneurosis. Amer. J. Psychiat. 106 (1949) 91–98

Jackson, D. D., J. H. Weakland: Schizophrenic symptom and family interaction. Arch. gen. Psychiat. 1 (1959) 618 bis 621

Jackson, D. D., J. H. Weakland: Conjoint Family Therapy: Some Considerations on Theory, Technique, and results. Psychiatry Suppl. 2 (1961) 30–45

Jacob, H.: Psychiatrische Aspekte des Alterns- und Aufbrauchkrankheiten des Gehirns. Verh. dtsch. Ges. Path., 52. Tagung 1968, Fischer, Stuttgart 1968 (S. 21–32)

James, W. T.: Morphologic form and its relation to behavior. In: The genetic and endocrinic basis for differences in form and behavior, hrsg. von *C. R. Stockard;* Wistar Institute of Anatomy and Biology, Philadelphia 1941 (S. 525–634)

Jansson, B., J. Alstroem: The relation between prognosis, symtoms and background factors in suspected schizophrenic illnesses in young people. Acta psychiat. scand. Suppl. 198 (1967) 1–96

Janzarik, W.: Dynamische Grundkonstellationen in endogenen Psychosen. Springer, Berlin 1959

Janzarik, W.: Der Aufbau schizophrener Psychosen in der Längsschnittbetrachtung. Nervenarzt 34 (1963) 58–61

Janzarik, W.: Schizophrene Verläufe; eine strukturdynamische Interpretation. Springer, Berlin 1968

Jaser, R.: Über den Einfluß des Greisenalters auf die Gestaltung schizophrener Prozesse. Allg. Z. Psychiat. 89 (1928) 1

Jaspers, K.: Allgemeine Psychopathologie, 3. Aufl., Springer, Berlin 1923

Jilek, W. G.: The residual dimension. A study of residual syndromes in veterans with chronic psychiatric illness. Psychiat. Clinica 1 (1968) 175–191

Jilek-Aall, Louise: Geisteskrankheiten und Epilepsie im tropischen Afrika. Fortschr. Neurol. Psychiat. 32 (1964) 213–259

Jonas, R., H. E. Oberdalhoff, H. H. Schulze: Die Besuchsfrequenz an psychiatrischen und nichtpsychiatrischen Krankenhäusern. Soc. Psychiat. 2 (1969) 69

Johanson, Eva: A Study of schizophrenia in the male. Acta psychiat. scand. Suppl. 125 (1958) 1–132

Jörger, J.: Das induzierte Irresein. Allg. Z. Psychiat. 45 (1889) 307–363

Juda, A.: Zum Problem der empirischen Erbprognosebestimmung. Über die Erkrankungsaussichten der Enkel Schizophrener. Z. ges. Neurol. Psychiat. 113 (1928) 487 bis 517

Jung, C. G.: Über die Psychologie der Dementia praecox. Marhold, Halle/Saale 1907

Jung, C. G.: Über die zwei Arten des Denkens. Jb. psychoanalyt. psychopathol. Forsch. 3 (1911) 124

Kahn, E.: Schizoid und Schizophrenie im Erbgang. Springer, Berlin 1923

Kaila, M.: Über die Durchschnittshäufigkeit der Geisteskrankheiten und des Schwachsinns in Finnland. Acta psychiat. scand. 17 (1942) 47–67

Kallmann, F. J.: The genetics of schizophrenia. Augustin, New York 1938

Kallmann, F. J.: The genetic theory of schizophrenia. An analysis of 691 schizophrenic twin index families. Amer. J. Psychiat. 103 (1946) 309

Kant, O.: A comparative study of recovered and deteriorated schizophrenic patients. J. nerv. ment. Dis. 93 (1941) 616

Kant, O.: The incidence of psychoses and other mental abnormalities in the families of recovered and deteriorated schizophrenic patients. Psychiat. Quart. 16 (1942) 176

Karlsson, J. L.: Genealogic studies of schizophrenia. In: The transmission of schizophrenia, hrsg. von *D. Rosenthal, S. S. Kety;* Pergamon Press, Oxford 1968 (S. 85–94)

Kasanin, J., E. Knight, P. Sage: The parent-child relationship in schizophrenia. I. Over-protection – rejection. J. nerv. ment. Dis. 79 (1934) 249–263

Katz, H.: Untersuchungen an insulinbehandelten Schizophrenen mit dem Rorschachschen Formdeutversuch. Mschr.

Psychiat. Neurol. 104 (1941) 15–33

Kaufmann, J.: Zur Frage der Beziehungen zwischen dyskrinem und schizophrenem Krankheitsgeschehen: Maskulin stigmatisierte Frauen und ihre nächste Verwandtschaft. Arch. Klaus-Stift. Vererb.-Forsch. 18 (1943) 439

Kaufmann, L., C. Müller: Über Familienforschung und Therapie bei Schizophrenen. Nervenarzt 40 (1969) 302

Kempf, E. J.: Psychopathology. Kimpton, London 1921

Kempf, E. J.: Bisexual factors in curable schizophrenia. J. abnorm. soc. Psychol. 44 (1949)

Kendig, I. V.: Rorschach indications for the diagnosis of schizophrenia. J. project. Techn. 13 (1949) 142–149

Kety, S. S., D. Rosenthal, P. H. Wender, F. Schulsinger: The types and prevalence of mental illness in the biological and adoptive families of adoptes schizophrenics. In: The transmission of schizophrenia, hrsg. von *D. Rosenthal, S. S. Kety;* Pergamon Press, Oxford 1968 (S. 345 bis 362)

Kind, H.: Familienuntersuchung zur Frage des Zusammenhangs von Schilddrüsenfunktionsstörungen, Struma und Psychose. Schweiz. Arch. Neurol. Neurochir. Psychiat. 78 (1956) 138–158

Kind, H.: Psychopharmaka in der täglichen Sprechstunde. Praxis 53 (1964) 863–866

Kind, H.: Welche Fakten stützen heute eine psychogenetische Theorie der Schizophrenie? Psyche (Heidelberg) 19 (1965/66) 188–218

Kind, H.: The psychogenesis of schizophrenia. Brit. J. Psychiat. 112 (1966) 333–349

Kind, H.: Prognosis. In: The schizophrenic syndrome, hrsg. von *L. Bellak, L. Loeb.* Grune & Stratton, New York 1969 (S. 714–734)

Kind, H., Margrit Rotach-Fuchs: Die Bedeutung der psychotherapeutischen und medikamentösen stationären Behandlung im langen Verlauf neurotischer Syndrome. In: Ergebnisse der Verlaufsforschung bei Neurosen, hrsg. von *K. Ernst, H. Kind, Margrit Rotach-Fuchs;* Springer, Berlin 1968 (S. 137–164)

Kirchgraber, D.: Klinik der Nebenerscheinungen eines „milden" und doch wirksamen neuroleptischen Mittels (Melleril). Schweiz. Arch. Neurol. Neurochir. Psychiat. 91 (1963) 412–445

Kisker, G. W., N. Michael: A Rorschach study of psychotic personality. J. nerv. ment. Dis. 94 (1941) 461–465

Kisker, K. P.: Schizophrenie und Familie. Nervenarzt 33 (1962) 13–21

Kisker, K. P., L. Strötzel: Zur vergleichenden Situationsanalyse beginnender Schizophrenien und erlebnisreaktiver Fehlentwicklungen bei Jugendlichen. Arch. Psychiat. Nervenkr. 202 (1961) 1–30; 203 (1962) 26–60

Klaesi, J.: Über die Bedeutung der Stereotypien. Karger, Berlin 1922

Kleist, K.: Die Gliederung der neuropsychischen Erkrankungen. Mschr. Psychiat. Neurol. 125 (1953) 526

Klemperer, J.: Zur Belastungsstatistik der Durchschnittsbevölkerung: Psychosenhäufigkeit unter 1000 stichprobenmäßig aus den Geburtsregistern der Stadt München (Jahrgang 1881–1890) ausgelesenen Probanden. Z. ges. Neurol. Psychiat. 146 (1933) 227

Koller, Jenny: Beitrag zur Erblichkeitsstatistik der Geisteskranken im Canton Zürich; Vergleichung derselben mit der erblichen Belastung gesunder Menschen durch Geistesstörungen u. dergl. – Arch. Psychiat. Nervenkr. 27 (1895) 268–294

Kraepelin, E.: Psychiatrie, 8. Aufl. Barth, Leipzig 1909–1915

Kraft, Th. B.: Gibt es eine familiäre degenerative (schizoide?) Psychopathie? Schweiz. Arch. Neurol. Neurochir. Psychiat. 84 (1959) 110

Kraule, I. V.: Children of schizophrenic parents. Zh. Nevropat. Psikhiat. 69 (1969) 239–242

Kraulis, W.: Zur Klinik von Erbpsychosen. Allg. Z. Psychiat. 113 (1939) 32

Krayenbühl, H., W. A. Stoll: Chirurgische Eingriffe in der Psychiatrie. In: Lehrbuch der Psychiatrie, hrsg. von *H.*

Hoff; Schwabe, Basel 1956

Kretschmer, E.: Der sensitive Beziehungswahn. Springer, Berlin 1918

Kretschmer, E.: Körperbau und Charakter, 18. Aufl. Springer, Berlin 1944

Kringlen, E.: A psychiatric twin study. Preliminary findings. Acta psychiat. scand. Suppl. 180 (1964) 313–315

Kringlen, E.: Discordance with respect to schizophrenia in monozygotic male twins. Some genetic aspects. J. nerv. ment. Dis. 138 (1964) 26

Kringlen, E.: An epidemiological-clinical twin study on schizophrenia. In: The transmission of schizophrenia, hrsg. von *D. Rosenthal, S. S. Kety,* Pergamon Press, Oxford 1968 (S. 49–63)

Kröner, E.: Die folie à deux. Allg. Z. Psychiat. 46 (1891) 634–662

Ladewig, D.: Über schizophrene Mütter und ihre Kinder. Diss. Heidelberg 1963

Lang, A.: Experimentelle Vererbungslehre in der Zoologic seit 1900. Fischer, Jena 1914

Langfeldt, G.: The prognosis in schizophrenia. Acta psychiat. scand. Suppl. 110 (1956) 1–66

Larsson, T., T. Sjögren, G. Jacobson: Senile Dementia. A clinical, sociomedical and genetic study. Acta psychiat. scand. Supp. 167 (1963) 1–259

Leistenschneider, P.: Beitrag zur Frage des Heiratskreises der Schizophrenen. Z. ges. Neurol. Psychiat. 162 (1938) 289–326

Leonhard, K.: Einteilung und Prognose der endogenen Psychosen. Zbl. ges. Neurol. Psychiat. 178 (1964) 104

Letemendia, F. J. J., A. D. Harris: Chlorpromazine and the untreated chronic schizophrenic. Brit. J. Psychiat. 113 (1967) 950

Leyberg, J. T.: A follow-up study on some schizophrenic patients. Brit. J. Psychiat. 111 (1965) 617

Lidz, Ruth, T. Lidz: The family environment of schizophrenic patients. Amer. J. Psychiat. 106 (1949) 332–345

Lidz, Ruth, T. Lidz: Therapeutic considerations arising from the intense symbiotic needs of schizophrenic patients. In: Psychotherapy with Schizophrenics, hrsg. von *E. Brody, F. Redlich,* Int. Univ. Press, New York 1952

Lidz, T.: Intrafamilial environment of the schizophrenic patient: VI. The transmission of irrationality. Arch. Neurol. Psychiat. (Chic.) 79 (1958) 305–316

Lidz, T.: Schizophrenia and the Family. Psychiatry 21 (1958) 21–28

Lidz, T.: The relevance of family studies to psychoanalytic theory. J. nerv. ment. Dis. 135 (1962) 105–112

Lidz, T.: Thought disorders in the parents of schizophrenic patients: A study utilizing the object sorting test. J. psychiat. Res. 1 (1962) 193–200

Lidz, T.: The family, language, and the transmission of schizophrenia. In: The transmission of schizophrenia, hrsg. von *D. Rosenthal, S. S. Kety,* Pergamon Press, Oxford 1968 (S. 175–184)

Lidz, T., Alice Cornelison, S. Fleck, Dorothy Terry: The intrafamilial environment of the schizophrenic patient. I. The father. Psychiatry 20 (1957) 329–342

Lidz, T., Alice Cornelison, S. Fleck, Dorothy Terry: the intrafamilial environment of the schizophrenic patient. II. Marital schism and marital skew. Amer. J. Psychiat. 114 (1957) 241–248

Lidz, T., Alice Cornelison, S. Fleck, Dorothy Terry: The intrafamilial environment of the schizophrenic patient. VI. The transmission of irrationality. Arch. Neurol. Psychiat. (Chig.) 79 (1958) 305–316

Lidz, T., S. Fleck: Schizophrenia, human integration, and the role of the family. In: The etiology of schizophrenia, hrsg. von *D. D. Jackson;* Basic Books, New York 1960

Lidz, T., S. Fleck, Y. O. Alanen, Alice Cornelison: Schizophrenic patients and their siblings. Psychiatry 26 (1963) 1–18

Lidz, T., S. Schafer, S. Fleck, Alice Cornelison, Dorothy Terry: Ego differentiation and schizophrenic symptom formation in identical twins. J. Amer. psychoanal. Ass. 70 (1962) 74–90

Lidz, T., C. Wild, S. Schafer, B. Rosman, S. Fleck: Thought disorders in the parents of schizophrenic patients: A study utilizing the object sorting test. J. psychiat. Res. 1 (1962) 193–200

Lutz, J.: Einige Bemerkungen zur Frage der kindlichen Schizophrenie. Z. Kinderpsychiat. 11 (1945) 161–180

Lutz, J.: Über akute Begleitpsychosen körperlicher Erkrankungen und Schizophrenie im Kindesalter. Schweiz. med. Wschr. 80 (1950) 774

Luxenburger, H.: Tuberkulose als Todesursache in den Geschwisterschaften Schizophrener, Manisch-Depressiver und der Durchschnittsbevölkerung. Z. ges. Neurol. Psychiat. 109 (1927) 313–340

Luxenburger, H.: Demographische und psychiatrische Untersuchungen in der engeren biologischen Familie von Paralytikerehegatten (Versuch einer Belastungsstatistik der Durchschnittsbevölkerung). Z. ges. Neurol. Psychiat. 112 (1928) 331–491

Luxenburger, H.: Vorläufiger Bericht über psychiatrische Serienuntersuchungen an Zwillingen. Z. ges. Neurol. Psychiat. 116 (1928) 297–326

Luxenburger, H.: Untersuchungen an schizophrenen Zwillingen und ihren Geschwistern zur Prüfung der Realität von Manifestationsschwankungen. Mit einigen Bemerkungen über den Begriff und die Bedeutung der zytoplasmatischen Umwelt im Rahmen des Gesamtmilieus. Z. ges. Neurol. Psychiat. 154 (1936) 351

Luxenburger, H.: Die Schizophrenie und ihr Erbkreis. In: Handbuch der Erbbiologie des Menschen, hrsg. von G. *Just;* Springer, Berlin 1939

Luxenburger, H.: Der schizophrene Erbkreis. (Die Schizophrenie.) In: Handbuch der Geisteskrankheiten, Ergänz.-bd. Teil I, hrsg. von O. *Bumke;* Springer, Berlin 1939 (S. 74–100)

Luxenburger, H.: Erbpathologie der Schizophrenie. In: Handbuch der Erbkrankheiten, Bd. II, hrsg. von A. *Gütt;* Thieme, Leipzig 1940 (S. 191–294)

MacSorley, K.: An investigation into the fertility rates of mentally ill patients. Ann. hum. Genet. 27 (1964) 247–256

Madow, L., S. E. Hardy: Incidence and analysis of the broken family in the background of neurosis. Amer. J. Orthopsychiat. 17 (1947) 521–528

Marandon de Montyel, E.: Des conditions de la contagion mentale morbide. Ann. méd.-psychol. 19 (1894) 266–293

Marinow, A.: Über den Verlauf und Endzustand bei der Schizophrenie. Psychiat. Neurol. med. Psychol. 11 (1959) 368

Marinow, A.: Der malende Schizophrene und der schizophrene Maler. Z. Psychother. med. Psychol. 17 (1967) 231

Marinow, A.: Schizophrene „Endstadien". Erscheint demnächst, Zitat gemäß Manuskript.

Matte Blanco, I.: Research theories on schizophrenia. Subtile characterization of schizophrenia with the help of symbolic thinking. Erscheint demnächst. Zitat gemäß Manuskript

Mattauschek: zit. von E. *Kraepelin* in: Psychiatrie, 8. Aufl. Barth, Leipzig 1913

Mauz, F.: Die Prognostik der endogenen Psychosen. Thieme, Leipzig 1930

Mayer-Gross, W.: Ätiologische Probleme. In: Handbuch der Geisteskrankheiten, Bd. 9, Spez. Teil V, hrsg. von O. *Bumke;* Springer, Berlin 1932

Mayer-Gross, W.: Die Klinik. In: Handbuch der Geisteskrankheiten, Bd. 9, Spez. Teil V, hrsg. von O. *Bumke;* Springer, Berlin 1932 (S. 538)

McConaghy, N.: The use of an object sorting test in elucidating the hereditary factor in schizophrenia. J. Neurol. Psychiat. 22 (1959) 243–246

McGhie, A.: A Comparative study of the mother-child relationship in schizophrenia. I. The interview. II. Psychological testing. Brit. J. med. Psychol. 34 (1961) 195–221

Mednick, S. A., F. Schulsinger: Some premorbid characteristics related to breakdown in children with schizophrenic mothers. In: The transmission of schizophrenia, hrsg. von D. *Rosenthal, S. S. Kety;* Pergamon Press, Oxford 1968 (S. 267–291)

Meggendorfer, F.: Über familiengeschichtliche Untersuchungen bei arteriosklerotischer und seniler Demenz. Zbl. ges. Neurol. Psychiat. 40 (1925) 359

Meggendorfer, F.: Über die hereditäre. Disposition zur Dementia senilis. Z. ges. Neurol. Psychiat. 101 (1926) 387 bis 405

Meier, A. R.: Schizophrenie und Panik. Diss. Zürich 1958

Mertens, K.: Untersuchungen über die Heiratshäufigkeit der Schizophrenen und der Manisch-Depressiven sowie deren Geschwister. Diss. Würzburg 1939

Meyer, A.: Objective psychology or psychobiology with subordination of the medically useless contrast of mental and physical. J. Amer. med. Ass. 65 (1915) 860–863

Meyer, H.: Besteht bei vererbbaren Geisteskrankheiten, insbesondere bei Schizophrenie und manisch-depressivem Irresein, ferner bei genuiner Epilepsie und Schwachsinn, eine erhöhte Sterblichkeit, in dem Sinne, daß die Fortpflanzung der Kranken vermindert wird? Allg. Z. Psychiat. 100 (1933) 46–61

Meyer, J. E.: Die Gesellschaft und ihre psychisch Kranken. Universitas 24 (1969) 1167

Mielke, F. A.: Übersicht der klinischen Erfahrungen mit Serpasil am Burghölzli. In: Das zweite Serpasil-Symposium in der psychiatrischen Universitätsklinik Burghölzli, Zürich, Schweiz. med. Wschr. 85 (1955) 439–444

Mielke, F. A.: Über die medikamentöse und psychotherapeutische Führung der Serpasilkur. Schweiz. med. Wschr. 86 (1956) 162–165

Mielke, .F A.: Über das Rauwolfia-Alkaloid Reserpin (Serpasil) in der Psychiatrie. Arch. Psychiat. Nervenkr. 193 (1956) 263–288

Mielke, F. A.: Anamnese und Katamnese Reserpin-behandelter Schizophrener. Nervenarzt 28 (1957) 111–119

Mielke, F. A.: Methods employed and results obtained in our psychiatric studies with new drugs acting on the brain-stem. Amer. J. Psychiat. 114 (1957) 134–139

Minkowska, Françoise: Troubles essentiels de la schizophrénie dans leurs rapports avec les données de la psychologie et de la biologie modernes. Evolut. psychiat. 1925/I, 127–141

Minkowski, E.: La schizophrénie. Psychopathologie des schizoides et des schizophrènes. Payot, Paris 1927

Minkowski, E.: Traité de psychopatologie. Presses Univesitaires de France, Paris 1966

Mitsuda, H.: Klinisch-erbbiologische Untersuchung der endogenen Psychosen. Acta genet. (Basel) 7 (1957) 371

Mittelholzer, K. W.: Konstitutionsanalytische Familienuntersuchung zur Frage der Korrelation von Struma und Psychose. Diss. Zürich 1957

Morel, B. A.: Traité des maladies mentales. 1860

Morf, Doris: Das Herkommen von psychiatrischen Exploranden. Diss. Zürich 1962

Morrison, S. L.: Principles and methods of epidemiological research and their application to psychiatric illness. J. ment. Sci. 105 (1959) 999–1011

Morselli, G. E.: Sulla dissociazione mentale. Riv. sper. Freniat. 54 (1930) 209–322

Morselli, G. E.: Aspect psychopathologique de la schizophrénie. Évolut. psychiat. 1958/III 539–548

Müller, Chr.: Der Übergang von Zwangsneurose in Schizophrenie im Lichte der Katamnese. Schweiz. Arch. Neurol. Neurochir. Psychiat. 72 (1953) 218–225

Müller, Chr.: Die Pioniere der psychoanalytischen Behandlung Schizophrener. Nervenarzt 29 (1958) 456–462

Müller, Chr.: Psychotherapie der Psychosen. In: Die Psychotherapie der Gegenwart, hrsg. von E. *Stern;* Rascher, Zürich 1958 (S. 350–367)

Müller, Chr.: Über das Senium der Schizophrenen. S. Karger, Basel 1959

Müller, Chr.: Die Psychotherapie der Psychosen. Fortschr.

Neurol. Psychiat. 27 (1959) 363–391

Müller, Chr.: Die psychiatrische Klinik und die Psychotherapie der Schizophrenen. IInd Int. Symp. Psychother. Schizophrenie, Zürich 1959, Bd. II; Karger, Basel 1960 (S. 291–296)

Müller, Chr.: Die Psychotherapie Schizophrener an der Zürcher Klinik. Nervenarzt 32 (1961) 354–368

Müller, Jenny: Schizophrenes und endokrines Krankheitsgeschehen: Übersicht über die bisherigen Arbeiten. Arch. Klaus-Stift. Vererb.-Forsch. 19 (1944) 53–156

Müller, M.: Der Rorschachsche Formdeutversuch, seine Schwierigkeiten und Ergebnisse. Z. ges. Neurol. Psychiat. 118 (1929) 598–620

Müller, U. G.: Gesunde Familien Schizophrener im Rorschach-Versuch. Nervenarzt 21 (1950) 29

Munro, A.: Parental deprivation in depressive patients. Brit. J. Psychiat. 112 (1966) 443–457

Munro, A., A. B. Griffiths: Further data on childhood parent-loss in psychiatric normals. Acta psychiat. scand. 44 (1968) 385–400

Nadzharov, R. A.: The clinical picture. Main stages in the study of schizophrenia and its clinical varieties. In: Schizophrenia. The clinical picture and pathogenesis, hrsg. von *A. V. Sneznewsky;* Verlag „Medizina", Moskau 1969

Navratil, L.: Schizophrenie und Kunst. Deutscher Taschenbuch Verlag, München 1965

Navratil, L.: Schizophrenie und Sprache. Deutscher Taschenbuch Verlag, München 1966

Nielsen, C. K.: The Childhood of Schizophrenics. Acta psychiat. scand. 29 (1954) 281

Nissen, A. J.: On de Schizophrenes Fruktbar Hetsforhold. Nord. Med. 4 (1932) 929–934; 5 (1933) 374–375

Oltman, Jane E., S. Friedman: Report on parental deprivation in psychiatric disorders. I.: In schizophrenia. Arch. gen. Psychiat. 12 (1965) 46–56

Oltman, Jane E., J. J. McGarry, S. Friedman: Parental deprivation and the broken home in Dementia praecox and other related mental disorders. Amer. J. Psychiat. 108 (1952) 685–694

Oppler, W.: Zum Problem der Erbprognosebestimmung. Z. ges. Neurol. Psychiat. 141 (1932) 548

Orr, W. F., Ruth B. Anderson, Margaret P. Martin, D. F. Philport: Factors influencing discharge of female patients from a state mental hospital. Amer. J. Psychiat. 111 (1955) 576–582

Ostmann: Untersuchungen über die Tuberkulose als Todesursache in der Heilanstalt Schleswig. Allg. Z. Psychiat. Psych. gerichtl. Med. 85 (1927) 459–473

Ott-Schaub, Edith: Zur Frage der Beziehungen zwischen dyskrinem und schizophrenem Krankheitsgeschehen. Ein fettdysplastischer, kretinoider Schizophrener und seine Familie. Arch. Klaus-Stift. Vererb.-Forsch. 18 (1943) 411

Panse, F.: Beitrag zur Belastungsstatistik einer Durchschnittsbevölkerung. Z. ges. Neurol. Psychiat. 154 (1936) 194

Parin, P.: Über abnorme Ernährungszustände bei Schizophrenen. Schweiz. Arch. Neurol. Neurochir. Psychiat. 72 (1953) 231–243

Perris, C.: A study of bipolar (Manic-Depressive) and unipolar recurrent depressive psychoses. Acta psychiat. scand. Suppl. 194 (1966) 1–188

Piotrowski, Z. A., N. D. C. Lewis: An experimental Rorschach diagnostic aid for some forms of schizophrenia. Amer. J. Psychiat. 107 (1950) 360–366

Pitts, F. N., J. Meyer, M. Brooks, G. Winokur: Adult psychiatric illness assessed for childhood parental loss, and psychiatric illness in family members – A study of 748 patients and 250 controls. Amer. J. Psychiat. 121, Suppl. (1964/65) 1–19

Petursson, E.: A study of parental deprivation and illness in 291 psychiatric patients. Int. J. soc. Psychiat. 7 (1961) 97

Planansky, K.: Conceptual boundaries of schizoidness:

Suggestions for epidemiological and genetic research. J. nerv. ment. Dis. 142 (1966) 318

Plattner, P.: Klinische Erfahrungen mit der Insulinschockbehandlung von 145 Schizophrenen. Allg. Z. Psychiat. 111 (1939) 325

Plattner, P., Frölicher: Zur Insulinschockbehandlung der Schizophrenie. Z. ges. Neurol. Psychiat. 160 (1938) 735

Pollack, M., Margaret G. Woerner, Ph. Goldberg, D. F. Klein: Siblings of schizophrenic and nonschizophrenic psychiatric patients: Psychopathology and gender concordance. Arch. gen. Psychiat. 20 (1969) 652–658

Pollock, H. M., B. Malzberg, R. G. Fuller: Hereditary and environmental factors in the causation of manic-depressive psychoses and Dementia praecox. State Hosp. Press, Utica, N. Y.1939

Preston, G., R. Antin: A study of children of psychotic parents. Amer. J. Orthopsychiat. 2 (1933) 231

Pritchard, M.: Prognosis of schizophrenia before and after pharmacotherapy. I. Short term outcome. II. Three year follow-up. Brit. J. Psychiat. 113 (1967) 1345

Rainer, J. D., L. Erlenmeyer-Kimling: Studies on marriage and fertility in schizophrenia. 11th Annual Meeting, Majorca, September 14, 1966. Eastern Psychiatric Research Association

Ramer, P.: Die präpsychotische Persönlichkeit schockresistenter Schizophrener. Schweiz. Arch. Neurol. Neurochir. Psychiat. 50 (1945) 93–107

Ramer, T.: The prognosis of mentally retarded children. Acta psychiat. scand., Suppl. 41 (1946) 1–142

Rapaport, D.: Diagnostic psychological testing. The Menninger Clinic Monogr. Series Nr. 4, Bd. II; Year Book Publ. Chicago 1946

Rattner, J.: Das Wesen der schizophrenen Reaktion. Diss. Zürich 1963

Rickers-Ovsiankina, M.: The Rorschach-test as applied to normal and schizophrenic subjects. Brit. J. med. Psychol. 17 (1938) 227–257

Rieman, G. W.: The effectiveness of Rorschach elements in the discrimination between neurotic and ambulatory schizophrenic subjects. J. cons. Psychol. 17 (1953) 25–31

Riemer, M. D.: A study of the mental status of schizophrenics hospitalized for over 25 years into their senium. Psychiat. Quart. 24 (1950) 309

Rodnick, E. H., N. Garmezy: An experimental approach to the study of motivation in schizophrenia. In: Nebraska symposium on motivation, hrsg. von *M. R. Jones;* Univ. Nebraska Press, Lincoln 1957 (S. 109–184)

Rodnick, E. H., N. Garmezy: Premorbid adjustment and schizophrenia. J. nerv. ment. Dis. 129 (1959) 450

Rohr, K.: Beitrag zur Kenntnis der sogenannten schizophrenen Reaktion – Familienbild und Katamnesen. Arch. Psychiat. Nervenkr. 201 (1961) 626–647

Rohr, K.: Untersuchungen über die schizophrenen Reaktionen (Symposium über schizophrenieartige Psychosen und Ätiologie der Schizophrenie). Schweiz. Arch. Neurol. Neurochir. Psychiat. 93 (1964) 381–385

Rorschach, H.: Psychodiagnostik. Huber, Bern 1921

Rorschach, W. U.: Zürcher Erfahrungen an leukotomierten Schizophrenen. Schweiz. Arch. Neurol. Neurochir. Psychiat. 67 (1951) 355–364

Rosanoff, A. J., L. M. Handy, I. R. Plesset, S. Brush: The etiology of so-called schizophrenic psychoses. Amer. J. Psychiat. 91 (1934/35) 247–286

Rosen, J. N.: Direct analysis (selected papers). Grune & Stratton, New York 1953

Rosenthal, D.: Some factors assosiated with concordance and discordance with respect to schizophrenia in identical twins. J. nerv. ment. Dis. 129 (1959) 1–10

Rosenthal, D.: Confusion of identity and the frequency of schizophrenia in twins. Arch. gen. Psychiat. 3 (1960) 297 bis 304

Rosenthal, D.: Sex distribution and severity of illness among samples of schizophrenic twins. J. psychiat. Res. 1 (1961) 26–36

Rosenthal, D.: Problems of sampling and diagnosis in the major twin studies of schizophrenia. J. psychiat. Res. 1 (1961) 116

Rosenthal, D.: Familiar concordance by sex with respect to schizophrenia. Psychol. Bull. 59 (1962) 401–421

Rosenthal D.: The Genain quadruplets. Basic Books, New York 1963

Rosenthal, D., P. H. Wender, S. S. Kety, F. Schulsinger, J. Welner, Lise Østergaard: Schizophrenics' offspring reared in adoptive homes. In: The transmission of schizophrenia, hrsg. von D. Rosenthal, S. S. Kety; Pergamon Press, Oxford 1968 (S. 377–391)

Rosman, B.: Thought disorders in the parents of schizophrenic patients: A further study utilizing the object sorting test. J. psychiat. Res. 2 (1964) 211–221

Rotach, S.: Erfahrungen zum Thema im Kongo (Symposium über schizophrenieartige Psychosen und Ätiologie der Schizophrenie). Schweiz. Arch. Neurol. Neurochir. Psychiat. 93 (1964) 385

Rotach, S., A. Hicklin: Mitteilung über Broken home-Untersuchungen bei Stellungspflichtigen. Vjschr. schweiz. Sanit-Off. 42 (1965) 125–129

Rotach-Fuchs, Margrit: Hundert zehnjährige Katamnesen von stationär behandelten Neurosekranken. In: Ergebnisse der Verlaufsforschung bei Neurosen, hrsg. von K. Ernst, H. Kind, Margrit Rotach-Fuchs; Springer, Berlin 1968 (S. 107 bis 136)

Roth, G.: Etude de la fertilité de 300 mères de schizophrènes. Thèse Genève 1959

Rubeli, Katharina S. D.: Untersuchung von Familienbild und Milieuverhältnissen bei 102 Schizophrenen unter spezieller Berücksichtigung des Einflusses dieser Faktoren auf den Verlauf der Psychose. Diss. Zürich 1959

Rubin, M., M. Lonstein: A cross-validation of suggested Rorschach patterns associated with schizophrenia. J. cons. Psychol. 17 (1953) 371–372

Rüdin, E.: Studien über Vererbung und Entstehung geistiger Störungen. I. Zur Vererbung und Neuentstehung der Dementia praecox. Monogr. Neur. Psych., Bd. XII; Springer, Berlin 1916

Rümke, H. C.: Über alte Schizophrene. Schweiz. Arch. Neurol. Neurochir. Psychiat. 91 (1963) 201–210 (Festschr. M. Bleuler)

Rutter, M.: Children of sick parents. Oxford University Press, London 1966

Ryle, A.: Neurosis in the ordinary family. Tavistock Publications, J. B. Lippincott, Worcester 1967

Scharfetter, Chr.: Symbiontische Psychosen. Huber, Bern 1971

Schindler, R.: Das psychodynamische Problem beim sogenannten schizophrenen Defekt. In: IInd Internat. Symp. über die Psychotherapie der Schizophrenie Zürich 1959, hrsg. von G. Benedetti, C. Mueller; Karger, Basel 1960 (S. 276–288)

Schollenberger, W.: Schizophrenie und Hypothyreose in ihrer Wechselbeziehung. Diss. Zürich 1966

Schopler, E., Julie Loftin: Thought disorders in parents of psychotic children. Arch. gen. Psychiat. 20 (1969) 174–181

Schulz, B.: Zum Problem der Erbprognosebestimmung. Die Erkrankungsaussichten von Neffen und Nichten von Schizophrenen. Z. ges. Neurol. Psychiat. 102 (1926) 1–37

Schulz, B.: Zur Frage einer Belastungsstatistik der Durchschnittsbevölkerung. Geschwisterschaften und Elternschaften von 100 Hirnarteriosklerotiker-Ehegatten. Z. ges. Neurol. Psychiat. 109 (1927) 15–48

Schulz, B.: Über die hereditären Beziehungen paranoid gefärbter Alterspsychosen. Z. ges. Neurol. Psychiat. 129 (1930) 147

Schulz, B.: Zur Belastungsstatistik der Durchschnittsbevölkerung (Geschwister und Eltern von 100 Krankenhauspatienten). Z. ges. Neurol. Psychiat. 136 (1931) 386

Schulz, B.: Zur Erbpathologie der Schizophrenie. Z. ges. Neurol. Psychiat. 143 (1933) 175–293

Schulz, B.: Kinder schizophrener Elternpaare. Z. ges. Neu-

rol. Psychiat. 168 (1940) 332

Schulz, B.: Erkrankungsalter schizophrener Eltern und Kinder. Z. ges. Neurol. Psychiat. 168 (1940) 709

Schulz, B.: Sterblichkeit endogen Geisteskranker und ihrer Eltern. Z. menschl. Vererb.- u. Konstit.-Lehre 29 (1949) 338–367

Schulz, B.: Die Schizophreniegefährdung der Verwandten Schizophrener. Ärztl. Mh. berufl. Fortb. 5 (1949/50) 299

Schulz, B., K. Leonhard: Erbbiologisch-klinische Untersuchungen an insgesamt 99 im Sinne Leonhards typischen bzw. atypischen Schizophrenien. Z. ges. Neurol. Psychiat. 168 (1940) 587

Schwab, H.: Die Katatonie auf Grund katamnestischer Untersuchungen. II. Teil: Die Erblichkeit der eigentlichen Katatonie. Z. ges. Neurol. Psychiat. 168 (1938) 441

Schweizer, Erica M.: Entwicklungsgeschichte eines frühverstorbenen schizophrenen Mädchens. Diss. Zürich 1954

Scott, J. C.: The work of a resettlement committee in a mental hospital and a pilot study of aftercare. Int. J. soc. Psychiat. 11 (1965) 197–203

Sechehaye, Marguerite: La réalisation symbolique. Huber, Bern 1947

Seiler, E.: Ein akromegaloider Schizophrener und seine Verwandtschaft. Diss. Zürich 1953

Semon, R.: Die Mneme. Engelmann, Leipzig 1904

Shields, J.: Summary of the genetic evidence. In: The transmission of schizophrenia, hrsg. von D. Rosenthal, S. S. Kety; Pergamon Press, Oxford 1968 (S. 95–126)

Siegfried, Selma: Untersuchungen über Krankheitsverlauf und Familienbild bei schockresistenten Schizophrenen. Schweiz. Arch. Neurol. Psychiat. 50 (1943) 108–121

Simon, W., A. L. Wirt, W. V. Halloran: Long term follow up study of schizophrenia patients. Arch. gen. Psychiat. 12 (1965) 510

Singer, M. T., L. C. Wynne: Differentiation characteristics of the parents of childhood schizophrenics, childhood neurotics, and young adult schizophrenics. Amer. J. Psychiat. 120 (1963) 234–243

Singer, M. T., L. C. Wynne: Thought disorders and family relations of schizophrenics. III–IV. Arch. gen. Psychiat. 12 (1965) 187–212

Sjögren, T.: Investigations of the heredity of psychoses and mental deficiency in two North Swedish paushes. Ann. Eugen. (Lond.) 6 (1935) 253

Sjögren, T.: Genetic-statistical and psychiatric investigations of a West Swedish population. Acta psychiat. scand. Suppl. 52 (1948) 1

Sjögren, T.: The genetics of schizophrenia. Congr. Rep., IInd Internat. Congr. Psychiat. Zürich 1957, Bd. I; Orell Füssli, Zürich 1959 (S. 312)

Skalweit, B.: Konstitution und Prozeß in der Schizophrenie. Sammlg. psychiatr. neurol. Einzeldarst. Bd. V, Thieme, Leipzig 1934

Slater, E.: Psychiatry. In: Clinical genetics, hrsg. von A. Sorsby; Butterworth, London 1953

Slater, E.: Psychotic and neurotic illnesses in twins. Spec. Rep. Ser. med. Res. Con. (Lond.) Nr. 278, 1953

Slater, E.: The monogenetic theory of schizophrenia. Acta genet. (Basel) 8 (1958) 60

Slater, E., A. W. Beard, E. Glithero: The schizophrenialike psychoses of epilepsy. Brit. J. Psychiat. 109 (1963) 95–150

Smith, J. Ch.: Dementia-praecox-Probleme. Z. ges. Neurol. Psychiat. 156 (1936) 361

Sneznewsky, A. V.: Symptomatology and nosology. In: Schizophrenia. The clinical picture and pathogenesis, hrsg. von A. V. Sneznewsky; Verlag „Medizina", Moskau 1969

Sobel, D.: Children of schizophrenic patients: preliminary observations on early development. Amer. J. Psychiat. 118 (1961) 512

Staehelin, B.: Aus der Psychotherapie einer Schizophrenie. Acta psychother. (Basel) 3 (1955) 341–360

Statistische Quellenwerke der Schweiz. Heft 104 (1942), 157 (1946), 247 (1953), 276 (1955), 336 (1963), 357 (1963) Bern

Steinberg, H. R., J. Durell: A stressful social situation as a precipitant of schizophrenic symptoms: An epidemiological study. Brit. J. Psychiat. 114 (1968) 1097–1105

Stenstedt, A.: A study in manic-depressive Psychoses. Acta psychiat. scand. Suppl. 79 (1952) 1–111

Stenstedt, A.: Involutional melancholia. Acta psychiat. scand. Suppl. 127 (1959) 1–71

Stockard, Ch. R.: The genetic and endocrinic basis for differences in form and behavior. The Wistar Institute of Anatomy and Biology, Philadelphia 1941

Stockmann, Maria: Zur Frage der Beziehungen zwischen dyskrinem und schizophrenem Krankheitsgeschehen: Weitere maskulin stigmatisierte schizophrene Frauen und ihre Verwandten. Arch. Klaus-Stift. Vererb.-Forsch. 21 (1946) 171

Stoffel, A.: Zürcher Erfahrungen mit der präfrontalen Leukotomie. Diss. Zürich 1952

Stokvis, B.: Die Bedeutung des Rorschachtests als diagnostisches Hilfsmittel bei der Differenzierung beginnender Schizophrenie und zwangsneurotischer Reaktionsformen. Psyche (Heidelberg) 4 (1951) 552–560

Stoll, W. A.: Leukotomie-Erfahrungen der Psychiatrischen Universitätsklinik Zürich. Nervenarzt 25 (1954) 195–197

Stoll, W. A.: „Conference on reserpine in the treatment of neuropsychiatric, neurological, and related clinical problems", New York, 3.–4. Febr. 1955. – Tagungsbericht am 2. Serpasil-Symposium der psychiatrischen Universitätsklinik Burghölzli, Zürich, 4. März 1955. Schweiz. med. Wschr. 85 (1955) 439–440

Stoll, W. A.: Jodtraceruntersuchungen der Schilddrüse nach *Reiss* bei chronischer Schizophrenie. Schweiz. Arch. Neurol. Psychiat. 77 (1956) 310–329

Stoll, W. A.: Schizophreniebehandlung mit neuen Medikamenten. Neue Zürcher Zeitung 1. Sept. 1957, Sonntags-Ausgabe

Stoll, W. A.: Die Pharmakotherapie und das psychiatrische Krankenhaus. Bull. schweiz. Akad. med. Wiss. 15 (1959) 278–285

Storch, A.: Das archaisch-primitive Erleben und Denken der Schizophrenen. Springer, Berlin 1922

Stotsky, B. A.: A comparison of remitting and non-remitting schizophrenics on psychological tests. J. abnorm. soc. Psychol. 47 (1952) 489–496

Stransky, E.: Zur Auffassung gewisser Symptome der Dementia praecox. Neurol. Zbl. 1904, 1074, 1140

Stroemgren, E.: Zum Ersatz des Weinbergschen „abgekürzten Verfahrens". Z. ges. Neurol. Psychiat. 153 (1935) 784

Stroemgren, E.: Beiträge zur psychiatrischen Erblehre. Munksgaard, Kopenhagen 1938

Sullivan, H. St.: The interpersonal theory of psychiatry. Norton, New York 1953

Sullivan, H. St.: Clinical studies in psychiatry. Norton, New York 1956

Sulzer, H.: Zur Frage der Beziehungen zwischen dyskrinem und schizophrenem Krankheitsgeschehen: Ein akromegaloider Schizophrener und seine Familie. Arch. Klaus-Stift. Vererb.-Forsch. 18 (1943) 461

Sussex, J. N., F. Gassman, S. C. Raffel: Adjustment of children with psychotic mothers in the home. Amer. J. Orthopsychiat. 33 (1963) 849–854

Suworina, N. A.: Über die Familienschizophrenie. In: Probleme der Neurologie und Psychiatrie. Samml. wissenschaftl. Arb. Ges. Neuropath. u. Psychiat. Chabarowsk (Festschr. *J. S. Galant*), Chabarowsk 1965

Szewczyk, H.: Die Remissionen Schizophrener und ihre Abhängigkeit von Belastung, Konstitution und präpsychotischem Charakter. Psychiat. Neurol. med. Psychol. 2 (1950) 304

Thiesen, J. W.: A pattern analysis of structural characteristics of the Rorschach test in schizophrenia. J. cons. Psychol. 16 (1952) 365–370

Tienari, P.: Psychiatric illness in identical twins. Acta psychiat. scand. Suppl. 171 (1963) 39

Tienari, P.: Schizophrenia in monozygotic male twins. In: The transmission of schizophrenia, hrsg. von *D. Rosenthal, S. S. Kety,* Pergamon Press, Oxford 1968 (S. 27–36)

Tomasson, H.: Further investigations on manic-depressive psychosis. Acta psychiat. (Kbh.) 13 (1938) 517

von Trostorff, S.: Unsystematische Schizophrenien und cycloide Psychosen im Familienbild. Zbl. ges. Neurol. Psychiat. 178 (1964) 106

Tschudin, A.: Chronische Schizophrenien im Rorschachschen Versuch. Schweiz. Arch. Neurol. Neurochir. Psychiat. 53 (1944) 79–100

Tuor-Winkler, Lina: Zur Frage der Beeinflussung der Schizophrenie durch die präfrontale Leukotomie nach *Moniz.* Diss. Zürich 1948

Tybring, G. B., P. H. Kusuda: Influences upon adjustment in patients released on tranquilizing drugs. Detroit Divisional Meet. Amer. Psychiat. Ass. 1959

Uchtenhagen, A.: (Untersuchungen bei Adoptivkindern, in Vorbereitung)

Vaillant, G. E.: The prediction of recovery in schizophrenia. J. nerv. ment. Dis. 135 (1962) 534–543

Vié, J., P. Queron: La vieillesse de quelques déments précoces. Ann. méd.-psychol. 93 (1935) 190

Vogt, W.: Beitrag zum klinischen Vergleich der Wirkung von Largactil und Serpasil. Schweiz. Arch. Neurol. Neurochir. Psychiat. 77 (1956) 330–336

Voser, H.: Fettdysplastische Schizophrene und ihre Verwandtschaft. Diss. Zürich 1951

Wachsmuth, R.: Der Schizophrene im Alter. In: Geriatrie und Fortbildung, hrsg. von *W. Doberauer;* Bergland Druckerei, Wien 1960 (S. 383–392)

Wahl, C. W.: Some antecedent factors in family histories of 392 schizophrenics. Amer. J. Psychiat. 110 (1954) 668 bis 676

Wahl, C. W.: Some antecedent factors in family histories of 568 male schizophrenics of United States Navy. Amer. J. Psychiat. 113 (1956) 201–210

Walsh, D.: Mental illness in Dublin – First admissions. Brit. J. Psychiat. 115 (1969) 449–456

Walther Büel, H.: Die Psychiatrie der Hirngeschwülste und die cerebralen Grundlagen psychischer Vorgänge. Acta neurochir. (Wien) Suppl. 2 (1951) 1–226

Walther Büel, H.: Uber Pharmakopsychiatrie. Schweiz med. Wschr. 83 (1953) 483

Walther Büel, H.: Drei Dezennien Narkotherapie. Mschr. Psychiat. Neurol. (Basel) 125 (1953) 718–731 (Festschrift *Klaesi*)

Walther Büel, H.: Zur klinischen Therapie der endogenen Psychosen. Nervenarzt 25 (1954) 191–194

Wander-Voegelin, Margrit: Schizophrenes und endokrines Krankheitsgeschehen: Akromegaloide Schizophrene und ihre Familien. Arch. Klaus-Stift. Vererb.-Forsch. 20 (1945) 257–305

Wardle, C. J.: Two generations of broken homes in the genesis of conduct and behaviour disorders in children. Brit. med. J. 1960/II, 349

Weakland, J. H., W. F. Fry: Letters of mothers of schizophrenics. Amer. J. Orthopsychiat. 32 (1962) 604–623

Weber, E.: Ein Rauwolfiaalkaloid in der Psychiatrie: seine Wirkungsähnlichkeit mit Chlorpromazin. Schweiz. med. Wschr. 84 (1954) 968–970

Weber, H. J.: Beispiel einer konstitutionsanalytischen Untersuchung an einem Fall von schizophrenen und manisch-depressiven Mischsymptomen, Struma, *Adieschem* Syndrom und orthostatischem Kollaps. Arch. Klaus-Stift. Vererb.-Forsch. 25 (1950) 243

Weinberg, I.: Zum Problem der Erbprognosebestimmung. Erkrankungsaussichten der Vettern und Basen von Schizophrenen. Z. ges. Neurol. Psychiat. 113 (1928) 101

Welner, J., E. Stroemgren: Clinical and genetic studies on benign schizophrenieform psychosis based on a follow-up. Acta psychiat. scand. 33 (1958) 377

Wenger, P.: A comparative study of the aging process in groups of schizophrenic and mentally well veteran. Geriatrics 13 (1958) 367–370

Werner, A.: La schizophrénie (rappel de quelques notions). Rev. méd. Suisse rom. 64 (1944) 896–905

Wessler, M. M., V. L. Kahn: Can the chronic schizophrenic patient remain in the community? A follow-up study of twenty-four longterm hospitalized patients returned to the community. J. nerv. ment. Dis. 136 (1963) 455–463

Wieser, St.: Aspekte des paranoischen Mechanismus. Nervenarzt 40 (1969) 101

Wild, C.: Some implications. In: Schizophrenia and the family, Int. Univ. Press, New York 1965

Wild, C.: Disturbed styles of thinking: Implications of disturbed styles of thinking manifested on the object sorting test by the parents of schizophrenic patients. Arch. gen. Psychiat. 13 (1965) 464–470

Wilhelm, Elsa: Kinder schizophrener Mütter. Acta paedopsychiat. 32 (1965) 203–222

Willi, J.: Die Schizophrenie in ihrer Auswirkung auf die Eltern. Schweiz. Arch. Neurol. Neurochir. Psychiat. 89 (1962) 426–463

Willi, J.: Untersuchungen über die Gemeinsamkeiten von Schizophrenen und ihren Angehörigen (Symposium über schizophrenieartige Psychosen und Ätiologie der Schizophrenie). Schweiz. Arch. Neurol. Neurochir. Psychiat. 94 (1964) 386–388

Willi, J.: Der Gemeinsame Rorschach--Versuch, ein diagno--stisches Hilfsmittel in der Eheberatung. Ehe 5 (1968) 163 bis 175

Willi, J.: Der Gemeinsame Rorschach-Versuch, ein Mittel zum Studium von Partnerbeziehungen. Verh. 7. Int. Kongr. Psychotherapie, Wiesbaden 1967, Teil IV; Karger, Basel 1968 (S. 375–384)

Willi, J.: Joint Rorschach testing of partner relationships. Family Process 8 (1969) 64–78

Willi, J.: Der Gemeinsame Rorschach-Versuch – ein direkter Einblick in Struktur und Dynamik von Kleingruppen. Gruppenpsychotherap. Gruppendynamik 3 (1969) 11–30

Winkler, W. Th.: Tiefenpsychologie und moderne Kunst. Med. Welt 17 (1966) 987

Wittermans, A. W., B. Schulz: Genealogischer Beitrag zur Frage der geheilten Schizophrenien. Arch. Psychiat. Nervenkr. 185 (1950) 211–232

Wittman, P.: Diagnostic and prognostic significance of the shut-in personality type as a prodromal factor in schizophrenia. J. clin. Psychol. 4 (1948) 211

Wolf, Delia: Zur Frage der Beziehungen zwischen dyskrinem und schizophrenem Krankheitsgeschehen: Überprüfung der bisherigen Untersuchungen an größerem Untersuchungsgut. Arch. Klaus-Stift. Vererb.-Forsch. 21 (1946) 149

Wollenberg, R.: Über psychische Infektion. Arch. Psychiat. Nervenkr. 20 (1889) 62–88

Wynne, L. C.: Methodologic and conceptual issues in the study of schizophrenics and their families. In: The transmission of schizophrenia, hrsg. von D. Rosenthal, S. S. Kety, Pergamon Press, Oxford 1968 (S. 185–199)

Wynne, L. C., I. M. Ryckoff, J. Day, S. Hirsch: Pseudomutuality in the family relations of schizophrenics. Psychiatry 21 (1958) 205–220

Wynne, L. C., M. T. Singer: Thought disorder and family relations in schizophrenia. I–II. Arch. gen. Psychiat. 9 (1963) 191–206

Wyrsch, J.: Beitrag zur Kenntnis schizophrener Verläufe. Z. ges. Neurol. Psychiat. 172 (1941) 797

Wyrsch, J.: Die Person des Schizophrenen. Studien zur Klinik, Psychologie, Daseinsweise. Haupt, Bern 1949

Wyrsch, J.: Zur Geschichte und Deutung der endogenen Psychosen. Thieme, Stuttgart 1956

Wyrsch, J.: Klinik der Schizophrenie. In: Psychiatrie der Gegenwart – Forschung und Praxis, Bd. II, hrsg. von H. W. Gruhle, R. Jung, W. Mayer-Gross, M. Müller; Springer, Berlin 1960 (S. 1–26)

Yarden, P. E., B. F. Nevo: The differential effect of the schizophrenic mother's ages of illness on her children. Brit. J. Psychiat. 114 (1968) 1089–1096

Zablocka, Maria-Emma: Prognose bei der Dementia praecox. Diss. Zürich 1908; Reimer, Berlin

Zehnder, Margrit: Über Krankheitsbild und Krankheitsverlauf bei schizophrenen Geschwistern. Mschr. Psychiat. Neurol. 103 (1941) 231–277

Zerbin-Rüdin, Edith: Zur Erbpathologie der Schizophrenien. Mitteilungen der Max Planck-Gesellschaft 196 (1963) 87 bis 101

Zerbin-Rüdin, Edith: Endogene Psychosen. In: Humangenetik, Bd. V/2, hrsg. von P. Becker, Thieme, Stuttgart 1967 (S. 446–577)

Zocchi, A. F., T. T. Tourlentes, S. L. Pollack, D. Haim: Intermittent phenothiazine therapy with chronic patients. Arch. gen. Psychiat. 20 (1969) 726–728

Zolan, H., N. Bigelow: Family taint and response to treatment in functional disorder. Psychiat. Quart. 24 (1950) 672

Zurgilgen, B. A.: Untersuchungen über die konstitutionelle Verwandtschaft von Tuberkulose und Schizophrenie. Schweiz. med. Wschr. 79 (1949) 75

Zuring, J.: Kinder schizophrener Eltern. Z. Kinderpsychiat. 14 (1947/48) 165–174

Zurabashvili, A. D.: Problems of the psychology and pathopsychology of personality. Metsniereba Press, Tbilisi 1967

Papers Published from Our Clinic since 1942

Aall, Louise: Erfahrungen zum Thema in Tanganjika (Symposium über schizophrenieartige Psychosen und Aetiologie der Schizophrenie). Schweiz. Arch. Neurol. 94/2 (1964) 377 bis 379

Angst, J.: Begleiterscheinungen und Nebenwirkungen moderner Psychopharmaka. Praxis (Bern) 49 (1960) 506–511

Angst, J.: Psychopharmakologie und Familienforschung. Schweiz. Arch. Neurol. 91/1 (1963) 267–272

Angst, J.: Intoxikation mit Psychopharmaka. Therap. Umschau 22/4 (1965) 178–180

Angst, J.: Zur Aetiologie und Nosologie endogener depressiver Psychosen. Eine genetische, soziologische und klinische Studie. Monogr. a. d. Gesamtgeb. d. Neurol. u. Psychiat., H. 112. Springer, Berlin 1966

Angst, J.: Psychiatrische Pharmakogenetik. Klinische Psychopharmakologie. Mod. Probl. Pharmakopsychiatr., Vol. 1, S. 260–272. Karger, Basel 1968

Angst, J.: Neuere Entwicklungen der Pharmako-Psychiatrie. Praxis (Bern) 57/5 (1968) 143–148

Angst, J.: Die somatische Therapie der Schizophrenie. Sammlg. psychiatr. neurol. Einzeldarst., Thieme, Stuttgart 1969

Angst, J., C. Perris: Zur Nosologie endogener Depressionen. Arch. Psychiat. Nervenkr. 210 (1968) 373

Angst, J., W. Pöldinger: Klinische Erfahrungen mit dem Butyrophenonderivat Methylperidol (Luvatren). Vergleichender Beitrag zur Methodik pharmako-psychiatrischer Untersuchungen. Praxis (Bern) 52/44 (1963) 1348–1354

Angst, J., W. Pöldinger: Klinische Erfahrungen mit Protriptylin (Mk-240) (vorläufiger Bericht). Schweiz. Arch. Neurol. Psychiat. 94 (1964) 480–481

Angst, J., W. Pöldinger: Psychopharmaka. Therap. Umschau 22/5 (1965) 222–230

Avenarius, R.: Zur Wirkungsweise von Rauwolfiaalkaloiden und Phenothiazinderivaten bei Schizophrenen. Nervenarzt 27 (1956) 454–458

Baer, H.: Psychophysische Erregungszustände und ihre Behandlung durch neue Schlafmittelkombinationen. Schweiz. med. Wschr. 76 (1946) 582

Baer, H.: Psychotische Erregungszustände und ihre Bekämpfung durch Schlafmittel. Schweiz. Arch. Neurol. Psychiat. 60 (1947) 1–47

Barich, Doris: Zur Frage der Beziehungen zwischen dyskrinem und schizophrenem Krankheitsgeschehen: Infantil stigmatisierte Schizophrene und ihre Verwandten. Arch. Klaus. Stift. Vererb.-Forsch. 21 (1946) 1–36

Benedetti, G.: Psychotherapie der Schizophrenie. Nervenarzt 25 (1954) 197–201

Benedetti, G.: Psychotherapie einer Schizophrenen. Psyche (Heidelberg) 8 (1954) 1–16

Benedetti, G.: Die Welt des Schizophrenen und deren psychotherapeutische Zugänglichkeit. Schweiz. med. Wschr. 84 (1954) 1029

Benedetti, G.: Möglichkeiten und Grenzen der Psychotherapie Schizophrener. Bull. Schweiz. Akad. Med. Wissenschaft 11 (1955) 142–159

Benedetti, G.: Psychotherapie eines Schizophrenen. Psyche (Heidelberg) 9 (1955) 23–41

Benedetti, G.: A propos de l'accès psychothérapeutique au monde du schizophrène. Evol. Psychiat. 1955/1, 145–157

Benedetti, G.: Il problema della coscienza nelle allucinazioni degli schizofrenici. Arch. Psicol. Neurol. Psichiat. 16 (1955) 287–312

Benedetti, G.: Analisi dei processi di miglioramento e di guarigione nel corso della psicoterapia. Arch. Psicol. Neurol. Psichiat. 17 (1956) 971–988

Benedetti, G.: Terapia reserpinica in psichiatria. In: Symposium Nazionale sulla Reserpina e Cloropromazina in Neuropsichiatria. Soc. Edit. »Vita e Pensiero«, Milano, 1956, p. 183 (Suppl. zu Band 17, 1956, Arch. Psicol. Neurol. Psichiat.)

Benedetti, G.: Psychotherapie der Psychosen. In: *Hoff, H.:* Lehrbuch der Psychiatrie. Band X/XI der Bücherreihe »Psychohygiene – Wissenschaft und Praxis«, herausgegeben von Prof. Dr. H. Meng, Basel. Schwabe, Basel 1956

Benedetti, G.: Possibilità e limiti della terapia reserpinica in psichiatria. In: *S. Garattini, V. Ghetti:* Psychotropic Drugs. Elsevier, Amsterdam 1957, S. 527–533

Benedetti, G.: Klinische Psychotherapie. Huber, Bern 1964

Benedetti, G., H. Kind, F. Mielke: Forschungen zur Schizophrenielehre 1951–1955. Fortschr. Neurol. Psychiat. 25, 2/3 (1957) 101–179

Benedetti, G., H. Kind, A. S. Johansson (unter Mitarbeit von *P. F. Galli):* Forschungen zur Schizophrenielehre 1956–1961. Fortschr. Neurol. Psychiat. 30 (1962) 341–505

Benedetti, G., H. Kind, Verena Wenger: Forschungen zur Schizophrenielehre 1961–1965. Übersicht (Teil I). Fortschr. Neurol. Psychiat. 35/1 (1967) 1–34

Benedetti, G., H. Kind, Verena Wenger: Forschungen zur Schizophrenielehre 1961–1965. Übersicht (Teil II). Fortschr. Neurol. Psychiat. 35/2 (1967) 41–121

Bosia, G.: Zur Frage der Beziehungen zwischen dyskrinem und schizophrenem Krankheitsgeschehen. Eine maskuline schizophrene Frau und ihre Verwandtschaft. Arch. Klaus-Stift. Vererb.-Forsch. 25 (1950) 269

Von Brauchitsch, H. K.: Neuere Untersuchungen über die organische Natur der Schizophrenie. Diss. Zürich 1960

Von Brauchitsch, H. K.: The Influence of Thyroxine and Insulin on the Clinical Effects of Some Neuroplegic Drugs. In: *Rothlin, E.,* edit.: Neuro-Psychopharmacology, Vol. 2 (1961), S. 230–235, Elsevier, Amsterdam

Von Brauchitsch, H. K.: Endokrinologische Aspekte des Wirkungsmechanismus neuroplegischer Medikamente. Psychopharmacologia 2/1 (1961) 1–21

Von Brauchitsch, H. K.: Erfahrungen mit dem Methylaminbenzodiazepinderivat »Librium« in der psychiatrischen Poliklinik. Dtsch. med. Wschr. 86 (1961) 1669

Von Brauchitsch, H. K., A. Bukowczyk: Zur Frage der Verwendung des Chlorprothixem (»Taractan«) im psychiatrischen Hospital. Schweiz. Arch. Neurol. Psychiat. 90 (1962) 104–117

Brun, O.: Schwere schizophrene Verläufe. Diss. Zürich 1956

Von Brunn Ruth, W. L. von Brunn: Infantil stigmatisierte Schizophrene. Arch. Psychiat. Nervenkr. 189 (1952) 324 bis 340

Bukowczyk, A.: Weitere Infantile mit psychischen Erkrankungen und ihre Familien. Diss. Zürich 1962

Condrau, G.: Die präfrontale Leukotomie. Schweiz. med. Wschr. 80 (1950) 783

Corboz, R. J.: Reaktive Störungen bei Kindern schizophrener Eltern. Congress Report, IInd Internat. Congr. Psychiatr. Zürich 1957, Vol. III, 457–462. Orell Füssli, Zürich 1959

Corboz, R. J.: Les psychoses endogènes de l'adolscent. 6ième Congr. internat. Psychiatrie Infantile, Symp.: »Syndrômes psychiatriques spécifiques à l'adolescence«, 1966

Corboz, R. J.: Psychopharmaka im Kindesalter. Landarzt 44/19 (1968) 922–928

Corboz, R. J.: La psychopharmacothérapie de l'enfant et de l'adolescent. Expériences cliniques. In: Concilium Paedopsychiatricum, Verh. 3. Europ. Kongr. Pädopsychiat., Wiesbaden, 1967, S. 295–306. Karger, Basel 1968

Ernst, K.: Psychopathologische Wirkungen des Phenothiazinderivates »Largactil« (= Megaphen) im Selbstversuch und bei Kranken. Arch. Psychiatr. Nervenkr. 192 (1954) 573–590

Ernst, K.: »Geordnete Familienverhältnisse« späterer Schizophrener im Lichte einer Nachuntersuchung. Arch. Psychiatr. Nervenkr. 194 (1956) 355–367

Ernst, K.: Die Prognose der Neurosen. Monogr. a. d. Gesamtgebiet d. Neurol. u. Psychiat., Springer, Berlin 1959

Ernst, K.: Wann besteht Verdacht auf eine schizophrene Psychose? Schweiz. med. Wschr. 94 (1964) 776–780

Ernst, K.: Die psychiatrische Behandlung im Rückblick von Patient und Nachuntersucher. 20jährige Katamnesen von 70 hospitalisierten und 120 ambulanten Neurosekranken. Nervenarzt 35 (1964) 248–256

Ernst K., Cécile Ernst: 70 zwanzigjährige Katamnesen hospitalisierter neurotischer Patientinnen. Schweiz. Arch. Neurol. Neurochir. Psychiat. 95/2 (1965) 359–415

Ernst, K., (unter Mitarbeit von *Cécile Ernst):* Ergebnisse der Verlaufsforschung bei Neurosen. Eine vergleichende Literaturübersicht. In: *K. Ernst, H. Kind, Margrit Rotach-Fuchs:* Ergebnisse der Verlaufsforschung bei Neurosen. Monogr. a. d. Gesamtgebiet der Neurol. & Psychiat., H. 125, Springer, Berlin 1968, S. 1–106

Hicklin, A., J. Angst: Retrospektive und prospektive Studie über die klinische Wirkung von Clopenthixol (Sordinol) bei endogenen Psychosen. Schweiz. med. Wschr. 97/19 (1967) 615–621

Huber, H. U.: Statistische Untersuchungen über die Lebensverhältnisse späterer Schizophrener in ihrer Kindheit. Diss. Zürich 1954

Hurschler, H., H. Perrier: Schizophrenie und Tuberkulose. Schweiz. med. Wschr. 76 (1946) 95

Illberg, P.: Statistische Untersuchungen über die Lebensverhältnisse späterer Schizophrener in ihrer Kindheit. Diss. Zürich 1961

Kaufmann, J.: Zur Frage der Beziehungen zwischen dyskrinem und schizophrenem Krankheitsgeschehen: Maskulin stigmatisierte Frauen und ihre nächste Verwandtschaft. Arch. Klaus-Stift. Vererb.-Forsch. 18 (1943) 439

Kind, H.: Familienuntersuchung zur Frage des Zusammenhangs von Schilddrüsenfunktionsstörungen, Struma und Psychose. Schweiz. Arch. Neurol. Psychiat. 78 (1956) 138 bis 158

Kind, H.: Psychopharmaka in der täglichen Sprechstunde. Praxis (Bern) 53 (1964) 863–866

Kind, H.: Welche Fakten stützen heute eine psychogenetische Theorie der Schizophrenie? Psyche (Heidelberg) 19/3 (1965/ 1966) 188–218

Kind, H.: The Psychogenesis of Schizophrenia. Brit. J. Psychiat. 112/485 (1966) 333–349

Kind, H.: Prognosis. In: The Schizophrenic Syndrome. Grune & Stratton, New York 1969 (S. 714–734)

Kind, H., Margrit Rotach-Fuchs: Die Bedeutung der psychotherapeutischen und medikamentösen stationären Behandlung im langen Verlauf neurotischer Patienten. In: *K. Ernst, H. Kind, Margrit Rotach-Fuchs:* Ergebnisse der Verlaufsforschung bei Neurosen. Monogr. a. d. Gesamtgeb. d. Neurol. u. Psychiat., H. 125, Springer, Berlin 1968, S. 137 bis 164

Kirchgraber, D.: Klinik der Nebenerscheinungen eines »milden« und doch wirksamen neuroleptischen Mittels (Melleril). Schweiz. Arch. Neurol. Psychiat. 91/2 (1963) 412–445

Lutz, J.: Einige Bemerkungen zur Frage der kindlichen Schizophrenien. Z. Kinderpsychiat. 11, H. 6 (1945)

Lutz, J.: Über akute Begleitpsychosen körperlicher Erkrankungen und Schizophrenie im Kindesalter. Schweiz. med. Wschr. 80 (1950) 774

Meier, A. R.: Schizophrenie und Panik. Diss. Zürich 1958

Mielke, F. A.: Übersicht der klinischen Erfahrungen mit Serpasil am Burghölzli. In: Das zweite Serpasil-Symposium in der psychiatrischen Universitätsklinik Burghölzli, Zürich. Schweiz. med. Wschr. 85 (1955) 439–444

Mielke, F. A.: Über die medikamentöse und psychotherapeutische Führung der Serpasilkur. Schweiz. med. Wschr. 86 (1956) 162–165

Mielke, F. A.: Über das Rauwolfia-Alkaloid Reserpin (Serpasil) in der Psychiatrie. Arch. Psychiat. Nervenkr. 193 (1956) 263–288

Mielke, F. A.: Methods employed and results obtained in our psychiatric studies with new drugs acting on the brain stem. Amer. J. Psychiat. 114 (1957) 134–139

Mielke, F. A.: Anamnese und Katamnese Reserpin-behandelter Schizophrener. Nervenarzt 28 (1957) 111–119

Mittelholzer, K. W.: Konstitutionsanalytische Familienuntersuchung zur Frage der Korrelation von Struma und Psychose. Diss. Zürich 1957

Morf, Doris: Das Herkommen von psychiatrischen Exploranden. Diss. Zürich 1962

Müller, Chr.: Der Übergang von Zwangsneurose in Schizophrenie im Lichte der Katamnese. Schweiz. Arch. Neurol. Psychiat. 72 (1953) 218–225

Müller, Chr.: Die Pioniere der psychoanalytischen Behandlung Schizophrener. Nervenarzt 29 (1958) 456–462

Müller, Chr.: Psychotherapie der Psychosen. In: Die Psychotherapie der Gegenwart, herausgegeben von *E. Stern.* Rascher, Zürich 1958, S. 350–367

Müller, Chr.: Über das Senium der Schizophrenen. Bibl. Psychiat. Neurol., Fasc. 106. Karger, Basel 1959

Müller, Chr.: Die Psychotherapie der Psychosen. Fortschr. Neurol. 27 (1959) 363–391

Müller, Chr.: Die psychiatrische Klinik und die Psychotherapie der Schizophrenen. 2. int. Symp. Psychother. Schizophrenie, Zürich 1959, Bd. 2, S. 291–296. Karger, Basel 1960

Müller, Chr.: Die Psychotherapie Schizophrener an der Zürcher Klinik. Nervenarzt 32 (1961) 354–368

Müller, Jenny: Schizophrenes und endokrines Krankheitsgeschehen: Übersicht über die bisherigen Arbeiten. Arch. Klaus-Stift. Vererb.-Forsch. 19 (1944) 53–156

Müller, U. G.: Gesunde Familien Schizophrener im Rorschach-Versuch. Nervenarzt 21 (1950) 29

Ott-Schaub, Edith: Zur Frage der Beziehungen zwischen dyskrynem und schizophrenem Krankheitsgeschehen. Ein fettdysplastischer, kretinoider Schizophrener und seine Familie. Arch. Klaus-Stift. Vererb.-Forsch. 18 (1943) 411

Parin, P.: Über abnorme Ernährungszustände bei Schizophrenen. Schweiz. Arch. Neurol. Psychiat. 72 (1953) 231–243

Rattner, J.: Das Wesen der schizophrenen Reaktion. Diss. Zürich 1963

Rohr, K.: Beitrag zur Kenntnis der sogenannten schizophrenen Reaktion. Familienbild und Katamnesen. Arch. Psychiat. Nervenkr. 201 (1961) 626–647

Rohr, K.: Untersuchungen über die schizophrenen Reaktionen (Symposium über schizophrenieartige Psychosen und Aetiologie der Schizophrenie). Schweiz. Arch. Neurol. Psychiat. 94/2 (1964) 381–385

Rorschach, W. U.: Zürcher Erfahrungen an leukotomierten Schizophrenen. Schweiz. Arch. Neurol. Psychiat. 67 (1951) 355–364

Rotach, S.: Erfahrungen zum Thema im Kongo (Symposium über schizophrenieartige Psychosen und Aetiologie der Schizophrenie). Schweiz. Arch. Neurol. Psychiat. 94/2 (1964) 385

Rotach, S., A. Hicklin: Mitteilung über Broken-Home-Untersuchungen bei Stellungspflichtigen. Vjschr. Schweiz. San. Off. 42 (1965) 125–129

Rotach-Fuchs, Margrit: Hundert zehnjährige Katamnesen von stationär behandelten Neurosekranken. In: *K. Ernst, H. Kind, Margrit Rotach-Fuchs:* Ergebnisse der Verlaufsforschung bei Neurosen. Monogr. a. d. Gesamtgeb. d. Neurol.

u. Psychiat. H. 125. Springer, Berlin 1968, S. 107–136

Rubeli, Katharina S. D.: Untersuchung von Familienbild und Milieuverhältnissen bei 102 Schizophrenen unter spezieller Berücksichtigung des Einflusses dieser Faktoren auf den Verlauf der Psychose. Diss. Zürich 1959

Scharfetter, Chr.: Symbiontische Psychosen. Huber (Bern) 1970

Schollenberger, W.: Schizophrenie und Hypothyreose in ihrer Wechselbeziehung. Diss. Zürich 1966

Schweizer, Erica M.: Entwicklungsgeschichte eines frühverstorbenen schizophrenen Mädchens. Diss. Zürich 1954

Seiler, E.: Ein akromegaloider Schizophrener und seine Verwandtschaft. Diss. Zürich 1953

Staehelin, B.: Aus der Psychotherapie einer Schizophrenie. Acta psychotherap. 3 (1955) 341–360

Stockmann, Maria: Zur Frage der Beziehungen zwischen dyskrinem und schizophrenem Krankheitsgeschehen: Weitere maskulin stigmatisierte schizophrene Frauen und ihre Verwandten. Arch. Klaus-Stift. Vererb.-Forsch. 21 (1946) 171

Stoffel, A.: Zürcher Erfahrungen mit der präfrontalen Leukotomie. Diss. Zürich 1952

Stoll, W. A.: Leukotomie-Erfahrungen der Psychiatrischen Universitätsklinik Zürich. Nervenarzt 25 (1954) 195–197

Stoll, W. A.: »Conference on Reserpine in the Treatment of Neuropsychiatric Neurologica, and Related Clinical Problems«, New York, 3./4. Febr. 1955. Tagungsbericht am 2. Serpasil-Symposium der psychiatrischen Universitätsklinik Burghölzli, 4. März 1955. Schweiz. med. Wschr. 85 (1955) 439–440

Stoll, W. A.: Jodtraceruntersuchungen der Schilddrüse nach *Reiss* bei chronischer Schizophrenie. Schweiz. Arch. Neurol. Psychiat. 77 (1956) 310–329

Stoll, W. A.: Schizophreniebehandlung mit neuen Medikamenten. Neue Zürcher Zeitung, 1. Sept. 1957, Sonntagsausgabe

Stoll, W. A.: Die Pharmakotherapie und das psychiatrische Krankenhaus. Bull. Schweiz. Akad. Med. Wiss. 15/4–5 (1969) 278–285

Sulzer, H.: Zur Frage der Beziehungen zwischen dyskrinem und schizophrenem Krankheitsgeschehen: Ein akromegaloider Schizophrener und seine Familie. Arch. Klaus-Stift. Vererb.-Forsch. 18 (1943) 461

Tuor-Winkler, Lina: Zur Frage der Beeinflussung der Schizophrenie durch die praefrontale Leukotomie nach *Moniz.* Diss. Zürich 1948

Vogt, W.: Beitrag zum klinischen Vergleich der Wirkung von Largactil und Serpasil. Schweiz. Arch. Neurol. Psychiat. 77 (1956) 330–336

Voser, H.: Fettdysplastische Schizophrene und ihre Verwandtschaft. Diss. Zürich 1951

Voser, H.: Die Psychiatrie der Hirngeschwülste und die cerebralen Grundlagen psychischer Vorgänge. Acta neurochir., Suppl. II, Springer, Wien 1951

Walther-Büel, H.: Über Pharmakopsychiatrie. Schweiz. med. Wschr. 83 (1953) 483

Walther-Büel, H.: Drei Dezennien Narkotherapie. Mschr. Psychiat. (Basel) 125 (1953) 718–731

Walther-Büel, H.: Zur klinischen Therapie der endogenen Psychosen. Nervenarzt 25 (1954) 191–194

Wander-Voegelin, Margrit: Schizophrenes und endokrines Krankheitsgeschehen: Akromegaloide Schizophrene und ihre Familien. Arch. Klaus-Stift. Vererb.-Forsch. 20 H. 3/4 (1945)

Weber, E.: Ein Rauwolfiaalkaloid in der Psychiatrie: seine Wirkungsähnlichkeit mit Chlorpromazin. Schweiz. med. Wschr. 84 (1954) 968–970

Weber, H. J.: Beispiel einer konstitutionsanalytischen Untersuchung an einem Fall von schizophrenen und manischdepressiven Mischsymptomen, Struma, *Addie*schem Syndrom und orthostatischem Kollaps. Arch. Klaus-Stift. Vererb.-Forsch. 25 (1950) 243

Werner, A.: La schizophrénie (rappel de quelques notions). Rev. méd. Suisse rom. 64, No. 12 (1944)

Wilhelm, Elsa: Kinder schizophrener Mütter. Acta Paedopsychiat. 32/7–8 (1965) 203–222

Willi, J.: Die Schizophrenie in ihrer Auswirkung auf die Eltern. Schweiz. Arch. Neurol. Psychiat. 89 (1962) 426–463

Willi, J.: Untersuchungen über die Gemeinsamkeiten von Schizophrenen und ihren Angehörigen (Symposium über schizophrenieartige Psychosen und Aetiologie der Schizophrenie). Schweiz. Arch. Neurol. Psychiat. 94/2 (1964) 386–388

Wolf, Delia: Zur Frage der Beziehungen zwischen dyskrinem und schizophrenem Krankheitsgeschehen: Überprüfung der bisherigen Untersuchungen an größerem Untersuchungsgut. Arch. Klaus-Stift. Vererb.-Forsch. 21 (1946) 149

Zurgilgen, B. A.: Untersuchungen über die konstitutionelle Verwandtschaft von Tuberkulose und Schizophrenie. Schweiz. med. Wschr. 79 (1949) 75

My Earlier Papers Relevant to Topics Discussed in This Book

Vererbungsprobleme bei Schizophrenen. Z. ges. Neurol. Psychiat. 127 (1930) 321–388 und englische Übersetzung in: J. nerv. ment. Dis. 74 (1931)

Schizophrenia. Review of the work of Prof. Eugen Bleuler. Arch. Neurol. Psychiat. (Chicago) 26 (1931) 610–627

Psychotische Belastung von körperlich Kranken. Z. ges. Neurol Psychiat. 142 (1932) 780–810

Der Rorschach-Versuch als Unterscheidungsmittel von Konstitution und Prozeß. Z. ges. Neurol. Psychiat. 151 (1934) 571–578

Untersuchungen über die konstitutionelle Verwandtschaft von Tuberkulose und Geisteskrankheiten. Z. ges. Neurol. Psychiat. 153 (1935) 649–679 (zus. m. *L. Rapoport*)

Erblichkeit und Erbprognose: Durchschnittsbevölkerung, Schizophrenie, manisch-depressives Irresein, Epilepsie, 1933 bis 1936. Fortschr. Neurol. Psychiat. 9 (1937) 250–264

Erblichkeit und Erbprognose: Schizophrenie, manisch-depressives Irresein, Epilepsie, Durchschnittsbevölkerung. Fortschr. Neurol. Psychiat. 10 (1938) 392–403

Erblichkeit und Erbprognose: Schizophrenie, manisch-depressives Irresein, Epilepsie, Durchschnittsbevölkerung. Fortschr. Neurol. Psychiat. 11 (1939) 287–302

Erblichkeit und Erbprognose: Schizophrenie, manisch-depressives Irresein, Epilepsie, Durchschnittsbevölkerung (1939 bis 1940). Fortschr. Neurol. Psychiat. 13 (1941) 49–63

Krankheitsverlauf, Persönlichkeit und Verwandtschaft Schizophrener und ihre gegenseitigen Beziehungen. Thieme, Leipzig 1941

Das Wesen der Schizophrenieremission nach Schockbehandlung. Z. ges. Neurol. Psychiat. 173 (1941) 553–597

Die spätschizophrenen Krankheitsbilder. Fortschr. Neurol. Psychiat. 15 (1943) 259

Schizophrenes und endokrines Krankheitsgeschehen. Arch. Klaus-Stift. Vererb.-Forsch. 18 (1943) 403

Die Prognose der Psychosen, insbesondere der Schizophrenie. Periodische Mitteilungen der Schweiz. Lebensversicherungs-Ges. Druckerei Gebr. Leemann, Zürich. 11, 1946, 175–186

Forschungen zur Schizophreniefrage. Wien. Z. Nervenheilk. 1 (1948) 129–148

Untersuchungen aus dem Grenzgebiet zwischen Psychopathologie und Endokrinologie. Med. Psychiatr. Nervenkr. 180 (1948) 271–528 (mit Beiträgen von *H. Baer, G. Condrau, D. I. Jacobs, H. K. Knoepfel, W. Stoll, H. Wipf, Delia Wolf* und *W. Zubelin*)

Tuberkulose und Schizophrenie. Wien. med. Wschr. 99 (1949) 357 (zus. m. *B. A. Zurgilgen*)

Bedingte Einheitlichkeit im Erbgang – eine überwundene Schwierigkeit in der Konstitutionsforschung am Menschen. Arch. Klaus-Stift. Vererb.-Forsch. 2 (1949) 355–364

Endokrinologie in Beziehung zur Psychiatrie (Übersichtsreferat). Zbl. ges. Neurol. Psychiat. 110 (1950) 225

Forschungen und Begriffswandlungen in der Schizophrenielehre 1941–1950. Fortschr. Neurol. Psychiat. 19 (1951) 385 bis 452

Biologie und Entwicklungslehre der Persönlichkeit. Verh.

schweiz. naturforsch. Ges. Bern 1952, S. 26–43

Gedanken zur heutigen Schizophrenielehre – am Beispiel der Konstitutionspathologie erläutert. Wien. Z. Nervenheilk. 7 (1953) 255–270

Endokrinologische Psychiatrie. Thieme, Stuttgart 1954

Zur Psychotherapie der Schizophrenie. Dtsch. med. Wschr. 79 (1954) 841–842

Familial and Personal Background of Chronic Alcoholics. In: *Diethelm, O.*: Etiology of Chronic Alcoholism. Thomas, Springfield, Ill. 1955, S. 110–166

A Comparative Study of the Constitutions of Swiss and American Alcoholic Patients. In: *Diethelm, O.* (Hsg.): Etiology of Chronic Alcoholism. Thomas, Springfield, Ill. 1955, S. 167–178

Das Wesen der Serpasil-Behandlung an Schizophrenen. In: Das zweite Serpasil-Symposium in der psychiatrischen Universitätsklinik Burghölzli, Zürich. Schweiz. med. Wschr. 85 (1955) 439–444

Research and Changes in Concepts in the Study of Schizophrenia, 1941–1950. Bull. Isaac Ray Medical Library 3 (1955) 1–132

Clinical Use of Reserpine in Psychiatry: Comparison with Chlorpromazine. Ann. N. Y. Acad. Sci. 61, Art. 1 (1955) 167–173 (zus. mit *W. A. Stoll*)

Psychiatrische Irrtümer in der Serotoninforschung. Dtsch. med. Wschr. 81 (1956) 1078–1081

Comparaison entre les effets de la Chlorpromazine et de la Réserpine en psychiatrie. Encéphale 45 (1956) 334–338

Aspects secrets de la psychiatrie. Evolut. psychiat. 1956/I, 45–50

Eugen Bleuler. Die Begründung der Schizophrenielehre. In: Gestalter unserer Zeit. Bd. 4: Erforscher des Lebens. Stalling, Oldenburg 1955, S. 110–117.

Schizofrenia. Enciclopedia Medica Italiana, Ediz. scient. Sansoni, Firenze 1956 (S. 1476–1510) (zus. m. *G. Benedetti*)

Die Problematik der Schizophrenien als Arbeitsprogramm des II. Internationalen Kongresses für Psychiatrie. Nervenarzt 28 (1957) 529–533

Scopo e tema del nostro congresso. Pisani 71/3 (1957) 481 bis 491

Aims and Topic of our Congress. Hamdard, Medical Digest (Karachi) May 1958

International Cooperation in Research on Schizophrenia. Bull. Menninger Clinic 22 (1958) 43–49

Buts et thèmes de notre congrès. Congress Report, IInd Internat. Congr. Psychiatr., Zürich 1957, Bd. I, 37–43. Orell Füssli, Zürich 1959

Endokrinologische Behandlungsverfahren bei psychischen Störungen. In: Therapeutische Fortschritte in der Neurologie und Psychiatrie, hsg. v. *H. Hoff*, Urban und Schwarzenberg, Wien 1960, S. 294–305

In welchen Fällen wird heute noch eine Leukotomie ausgeführt? Dtsch. med. Wschr. 86/1 (1961) 51

Entwicklungslinien psychiatrischer Praxis und Forschung. Schweiz. med. Wschr. 91 (1961) 1549

Early Swiss Sources of *Adolf Meyers* Concepts. Amer. J. Psychiat. 119/3, (1962) 193–196

Probleme der Schizophrenie im Versicherungsrecht. Schweiz. Arch. Neurol. Neurochir. Psychiat. 89 (1962) 359–383 (zus. m. *M. Müller* und *G. Schneider*)

Schizophrenieartige Psychosen und Aetiologie der Schizophrenie. Schweiz. med. Wschr. 92 (1962) 1641–1647

Conception of Schizophrenia within the last fifty years and today. Proc. Roy. Soc. Med. 56 (1963) 945–952

Endokrinologische Psychiatrie. In: Psychiatrie der Gegenwart – Forschung und Praxis. Bd. I, 1b, Teil B, Springer, Berlin 1964, S. 161–252

Ursache und Wesen der schizophrenen Geistesstörungen. Dtsch. med. Wschr. 89 (1964) 40/41, 1865–1870 und 1947 bis 1952

Neue Therapiemöglichkeiten im Vergleich zu alten in der Psychiatrie. Dtsch. med. Wschr. 89 (1964) 501–505

Akute psychische Begleiterscheinungen körperlicher Krankheiten »Akuter exogener Reaktionstypus«, Übersicht und neue Forschungen. Thieme, Stuttgart 1966 (zus. m. *J. Willi* und

H. R. Buehler)
Significato della ricerca psicoterapeutica per la teoria sulla schizophrenia e per il paziente schizofrenico. Arch. Psicol. Neurol. Psichiat. 27/4–5 (1966) 353–368

Neue Entwicklung des Schizophrenieproblems. Praxis (Bern) 56/10 (1967) 326–331

A 23-year longitudinal study of 208 schizophrenics and impressions in regard to the nature of schizophrenia. In: The Transmission of Schizophrenia, edited by David Rosenthal & Seymor S. Kety, Pergamon Press, Oxford 1968, S. 3–12

The Genesis and Nature of Schizophrenia. Psychiatry Digest 30 1969/1, 17–26

Lehrbuch der Psychiatrie (von *Eugen Bleuler)*, Springer, Berlin. Bearbeitung der 7.–11. Aufl., 1943–1969, und Nachtrag zum Neudruck der 10. Aufl., 1966

Translator's Bibliography

Reference works

Arnold, Wilhelm; Eysenck, Hans Jürgen; and Meili, Richard. *Lexikon der Psychologie*. 3 vols. Freiburg: Herder, 1973.

de Vries, Louis. *German–English Medical Dictionary*. New York: McGraw–Hill, 1952.

Dietrich, Georg, and Walter, Hellmuth. *Grundbegriffe der psychologischen Fachsprache*. Munich: Franz Ehrenwirth, 1970.

Dorland's Illustrated Medical Dictionary. 24th ed., 1968. Philadelphia: W. B. Saunders, 1957.

Harrap's Standard French and English Dictionary. Pt. 1: French–English, edited by J. E. Mansion. London: George G. Harrap & Co., 1958.

New Cassell's German Dictionary. New York: Funk & Wagnalls, 1958.

Roget's International Thesaurus. 3rd. ed., 15th printing, 1967. New York: Crowell, 1962.

von Sury, Kurt. *Wörterbuch der Psychologie und ihrer Grenzgebiete*. 2nd ed., 1958. Basel: Benno Schwabe & Co., 1955.

Wahrig, Gerhard. *Das grosse deutsche Wörterbuch*. Gütersloh: C. Bertelsmann, 1966.

Webster's Seventh New Collegiate Dictionary. Springfield: Merriam, 1967.

Webster's New Dictionary of Synonyms. Springfield: Merriam, 1968.

Webster's Third New International Dictionary of the English Language. Unabridged. Springfield: Merriam, 1969.

Wildhagen, Karl, and Héraucourt, Will. *English–German German–English Dictionary in Two Volumes*. 14th ed., 1970. Wiesbaden: Brandstetter, 1953.

Scientific Literature Consulted

Bellak, Leopold. *Dementia Praecox. The Past Decade's Work and Present Status: A Review and Evaluation*. New York: Grune & Stratton, 1948.

Bleuler, Eugen. *Dementia Praecox or the Group of Schizophrenias*. Translated by Joseph Zinkin, 8th printing, 1968. New York: International Universities Press, 1950.

Harrison, Saul I., and Mc Dermott, John F., eds. *Childhood Psychopathology. An Anthology of Basic Readings*. New York: International Universities Press, 1972.

Hawkins, David, and Pauling, Linus, eds. *Orthomolecular Psychiatry: Treatment of Schizophrenia*. San Francisco: W. H. Freeman, 1973.

Romano, John. *The Origins of Schizophrenia*. Rochester: Excerpta Medica Foundation, 1967.

Rosenthal, David. *Genetics of Psychopathology*. New York: McGraw-Hill, 1971.

Rosenthal, David, and Kety, Seymour S., eds. *The Transmission of Schizophrenia*. Oxford: Pergamon, 1968.

Schizophrenia Bulletin. Rockville, Md., National Institute of Mental Health.

Index

DEMCO